# Int

# Literary Studies

# Introducing Literary Studies

Edited by
*Richard Bradford*

PRENTICE HALL
HARVESTER WHEATSHEAF

LONDON   NEW YORK   TORONTO   SYDNEY   TOKYO   SINGAPORE
MADRID   MEXICO CITY   MUNICH

First published 1996 by
Prentice Hall/Harvester Wheatsheaf
Campus 400, Maylands Avenue
Hemel Hempstead
Hertfordshire, HP2 7EZ
A division of
Simon & Schuster International Group

Typeset in 10/12 Times by
Mathematical Composition Setters Ltd, Salisbury, Wiltshire

Printed and bound in Great Britain by
T. J. Press (Padstow) Ltd

---

Library of Congress Cataloging-in-Publication Data

---

Introducing literary studies / edited by Richard Bradford.
    p. cm.
  Includes bibliographical references (p.    ) and index.
  ISBN 0-13-355223-3 (alk. paper)
  1. English literature–History and criticism–Outlines, syllabi,
etc.  I. Bradford, Richard, 1957–
PR87.I58  1996
820.9–dc20                        95-39361
                                  CIP

---

British Library Cataloguing in Publication Data

A catalogue record for this book is available from
the British Library

ISBN 0-13-355223-3 (pbk)

---

1 2 3 4 5  00 99 98 97 96

# Contents

# The contributors

**Richard Bradford** is a Lecturer in English at the University of Ulster at Coleraine.

**John Peck** is Senior Lecturer in English at the University of Wales, Cardiff.

**Michael Patterson** is Professor of Drama at De Montfort University, Leicester.

**Philip Tilling** is a Lecturer in English at the University of Ulster at Coleraine.

**Tony Bareham** is Professor of English at the University of Ulster at Coleraine.

**Amanda Piesse** is a Lecturer in English at Trinity College, Dublin.

**Eiléan Ní Chuilleanáin** is a Lecturer in English at Trinity College, Dublin.

**John McVeagh** is Senior Lecturer in English at the University of Ulster at Coleraine.

**Gail Baylis** teaches English at at the University of Ulster at Coleraine.

**Leon Litvack** is a Lecturer in English at the Queen's University of Belfast.

**Jan Jędrzejewski** is a Lecturer in English at the University of Ulster at Coleraine.

**Sophie Gilmartin** is a Lecturer in English at the University of Wales, Swansea.

**Elmer Andrews** is Senior Lecturer in English at the University of Ulster at Coleraine.

**David Pattie** is a Lecture in Drama at the University of Ulster at Coleraine.

**Randall Stevenson** is Senior Lecturer in English at the University of Edinburgh.

**R. A. York** is Professor of Modern Languages at the University of Ulster at Coleraine.

**Mark Currie** is a Lecturer in English at the University of Dundee.

**James Knowles** is a Lecturer in English at the University of Newcastle upon Tyne.

**Anne McCartney** is Research Associate and Tutor in Anglo Irish Literature at the University of Ulster at Coleraine.

**Liz McIntyre** is a Lecturer in English at the University of Ulster at Coleraine.

**Tamsin Spargo** is a Lecturer in English at Liverpool John Moores University.

**Robert Welch** is Professor of English at the University of Ulster at Coleraine.

**Mary Jones** is a Lecturer in English at the University of Ulster at Coleraine.

**Shirley Chew** is Professor of English at the University of Leeds.

**Geraldine Stoneham** is a Lecturer in English at De Montfort University, Bedford.

**Jill LeBihan** is a Lecturer in English at Sheffield Hallam University.

# INTRODUCTION

# How to use this book

To whom does this book introduce literary studies? In all probability you will be an undergraduate student, perhaps a sixth-former. You might be a lecturer wondering how best to direct your students' dwindling financial resources, or even a post-graduate student looking for an all-purpose guide to back up your specialized work. You will have one thing in common: an awareness of literary studies as an activity that is practically impossible to define.

A knowledge of literature is necessary; but someone who has read the complete works of Dickens, Thackeray and George Eliot might still be baffled by the essay questions, lecture titles and mission statements of the university courses in which these novelists feature. You might be baffled not so much by the intellectual rigours of the subject; more by the fact that there appear to be so many subjects, each demanding different intellectual registers and background reading. Dickens wrote novels, some with first-, some with third-person narrators. He wrote about a bewildering range of nineteenth-century experience: poverty, law, marriage, child-hood, morality, commerce, class. This we know, but the more we investigate these elements of his work the more we become aware of a vast intellectual industry of competing factions. Your growing interest in narrative technique will take you on tracks towards linguistics, formalism and structuralism, and raise further questions: Who had written first-person novels before Dickens? What does this technique tell us about the uneasy relation between telling stories and disclosing the truth? *Did* Dickens tell the truth about his time? Marxists, historians, feminists and deconstruc-tionists will all offer different approaches to these questions, and will involve you in new fields of received and evolving wisdom, different critical vocabularies and interpretive methods.

This book discusses each of these areas of study in individual units, and, for the first time in a single volume, builds bridges between them. The book is divided into four sections, on genre, literary history, critical theory and on different literary traditions within and beyond the British Isles. The book need not be read as a con-secutive, linear survey. You can consult it for a basic account of who the new historicists are and what they do (Section 3, Unit 21), and this unit will include worked examples of new historicist approaches to Shakespeare, particularly his history plays. As indicated by their name, the new historicists adopt a radical, unconventional approach to the relation between literature and its context, and you might wish to compare this approach with a more straightforward discussion of how the history plays fit into Shakespeare's broader programme of writing and how he and his contemporaries dealt with society and politics. Eventually you will need to reread the plays, but a reading of Units 5 and 6 on Shakespeare and Renaissance drama will help you form some preliminary ideas on the difference between conventional theories and their new historicist counterparts.

## Section 1   Genre

Section 1 will introduce you to the three literary genres: poetry, fiction and drama. These three units will equip you with a basic critical vocabulary and answer basic questions: what is free verse, a metaphor, a narrative structure, an absurdist play? They will show you how poems, novels and plays have changed their subjects and structures over the past five centuries and suggest reasons for these changes: social, political, cultural, capricious. You will be introduced also to how different critical schools deal with these questions of structure and history. The first three units are the foundations for the rest of the book. They will introduce concepts and ideas, and raise questions. Unit 1 uses extracts from the verse of, among others, John Donne, T.S. Eliot and Craig Raine. If these whet your appetite, Unit 7 will offer you a survey of Donne's context and the verse of his contemporaries, and Unit 17 will inform you of Eliot's role in the founding of modernism and Raine's as the initiator of the more recent and probably postmodern school of 'Martian' writing.

## Section 2   Literary history

Section 2 is a survey of literary history from the Renaissance to the present day. English literature did not begin in the sixteenth century and Unit 4 provides a confessedly brief survey of its medieval antecedents. Units 5–17 cover the Renaissance to the 1990s; their principal topics are British writing, with two units on American literature. Each unit will follow the same format. The Introduction will be a rudimentary guide to the literary schools and fashions of the period and to the historical, political and cultural factors that might, or might not, have affected them. The main part 'Texts, Authors, Contexts' will involve detailed readings of texts, discussions of why their authors did what they did and how they influenced or diverged from the work of their contemporaries. The exception to this regimented structure is Unit 5 on Shakespeare, a figure whose immense diversity, endurance and influence demands a more unsettled format.

   The Section 2 units are predominantly traditional in range and format, in the sense that traditionalists in literary studies advocate a particular canon of texts and authors, whose historical context is disclosed through the scholarly accumulation of fact and detail. But they will also show the reader how these facts can provoke critical debates that remain unsettled. Unit 10 investigates the familiar concerns of

Romanticism – individuality, radical culture, the mystery of the natural world – and it contrasts these with more recent perspectives: How did women feature in the Romantic world-view? What are the connections between Mary Shelley's *Franken-stein* and its poetic counterparts? Such questions feed into the much broader issue of feminist criticism and women writers. If you want to know more go to Units 23 and 24, in Section 3.

## Section 3 Critical theories and perspectives

Section 3 involves what is for most readers a familiar catalogue of isms and ologies. You will find a similar list in the contents page of many an introduction to literary theory. The difference in this book is that you will be provided with routes between the complex designs of Derrida, Foucault or Lacan and the broader literary landscape, and I shall explain how this network operates.

Section 3 reflects the pluralism of contemporary literary studies: new historicism and feminism are more recent than formalism and structuralism, but the latter are alive and well in the journals and lecture rooms of their advocates. The Section also however raises a more fundamental question. If Section 3 reflects the various affiliations and practices of contemporary theory, how do we categorize the methods of Sections 1 and 2?

In effect the relationship between Sections 1–2 and Section 3 will inevitably be antithetical, even antagonistic. Consult Unit 20 (Section 3) on reader-response criticism and you will encounter Stanley Fish who informs you that the formal structures of literature, upon which you base your evaluative judgements, are an illusion, constructs of an interpretive community, agreed protocols of reading through which we sustain the false ideal that literature has definitive and intrinsic characteristics. Now read Units 1–3, which will introduce you to the intrinsic characteristics of literature. It is up to you to decide whether the common-sense pragmatism of Units 1–3 invalidates the subtle observations of Fish, or vice versa. Similar tensions and similar decisions will be raised by practically all interrelations between Sections 1–2 and Section 3. If you advocate the principles of feminist criticism (Section 3, Unit 24), you will indeed be sceptical of the apparent impartiality of Sections 1 and 2. If you espouse the models of history, ideology and culture described in Unit 21 (Marxism and new historicism) you will question the character of the Section 2 units, which often celebrate the unpredictable, non-deterministic relation between literature and its context.

To advertise as an introduction to literary studies a volume which embodies tensions and antitheses might seem odd. On the contrary, it is realistic. Students reading English in higher education will encounter just the same tensions and antitheses. You will listen to academics who despise any kind of theoretical design that might cramp or disfigure the grandeur of literature (a dying breed, but it will be a while before the lights go out), and you will meet academics who contend, often with disarming literary style, that literature and the history of literary studies are an ideological confidence trick. From a more practical point of view you will find that, whatever your theoretical view of literary studies happens to be, it is a good idea first to imbibe a few old-fashioned details regarding literature. To appreciate the condition of the woman writer in relation to the patriarchal canon (Unit 23) you should know what this canon is (see Section 2). If you enrol for a course which will involve you in the deconstruction of literature you will need to understand the philosophical underpinnings of Derrida's project (see Unit 19); however, a clear perception of what a poem is (or at least what we think it is) must prefigure your attempt to deconstruct it (see Unit 1).

## Section 4   Literatures in English

The precondition that the old and established must be understood before we can appreciate the new and the subversive also informs Section 4 on 'Literatures in English'. All of the authors discussed in Section 4 write in English, but they do not necessarily respond to the stylistic, historical and social coordinates that enrich the Anglo-centric traditions of English and American writing. There are degrees of difference and the consecutive order of the units reflects this. The first three (25–7) involve a number of writers whose work features in Sections 1 to 3 (James Joyce in 25, Dylan Thomas in 26, Walter Scott in 27, and others). Swift, Yeats, Joyce and Beckett have all played important roles in the shaping and direction of English literary history. Unit 25 will inform you of the equally significant forces of Irish history and culture that have shaped their own work.

Units 28 to 30 could carry the subtitle of post-colonial literature. Each investigates traditions and modes of writing that are themselves often divided (native Australian and New Zealand writing involves a different stylistic and social agenda from its home-grown Anglo-centric counterpart), but each considers literary projects empowered and defined by political, topographical, ethnic and racial experiences that unite them in their difference from the literature of the British Isles.

Section 4 maintains the inter-unit fabric of the volume. Its units will define and specify literary independence, but they will also direct you back to points in Sections 1–3 where independence shades into mutual interdependence.

The volume is an introduction. It is more than a reference book or a glossary in that it combines definition, contextualization and critical interpretation. It will guide you through the puzzling landscape of literary studies and it will indicate where to go next and what to read. Full publication details of books and essays cited in the main text will be given in the unit's bibliography. The exception to this procedure is where a text is mentioned only once and full publication details are given on the spot.

Cross-references will often provide you with routes between related issues (e.g. 'For a feminist reading of this poem see Unit 24, pp. …'), but these cannot be comprehensive. If you need a different perspective on a particular text or idea, or another consideration of a critical term, consult the index.

RICHARD BRADFORD

# SECTION 1

# Genre

# UNIT 1

# Studying poetry

*Richard Bradford*

## What is poetry?

Poetry is unlimited in its range of subjects. The speaker of the poem can be old, young, male, female, mad, bad or mysteriously unidentifiable. The poem can be addressed to a fictive acquaintance, a friend, an enemy, a lover, a wife, a husband, God, or you, the reader. It can use all types of diction and idiom: local dialect, neo-Latinate syntax, formal or informal diction, grammatical, ungrammatical, hesitant or purposive modes of speech. Poetry can be, say or involve anything, but it will always be informed and influenced by another factor, the factor that identifies it as poetry.

John Donne's 'The Flea' (see Units 7 and 18) involves its male speaker in an attempt to persuade his female listener that sex with him will not be as disagreeable or shameful as she thinks. What is the difference between this and the kind of discourse that we might overhear in the pub? The intention, content and context of the public house seducer might be the same as those of Donne's speaker; they might even share a talent for elaborate and persuasive metaphor and a taste for informal, familiar idioms. It is unlikely, however, that the man in the pub will have marshalled his language into an iambic pattern and gathered his sentences into three identical and incredibly complex stanzas.

Metre and rhyme indicate a stylistic difference between poetry and other forms of language. Even those poets who reject rhyme and metre retain in free verse the unit that is the distinctive feature of poems: the poetic line. But the deployment and recognition of poetic form complicates rather than answers the question of why poetry is different. Surely the use of poetic form cannot fully explain the character of a genre as old as language, used in all languages and commanding, among many, a neo-religious respect?

Metre, rhyme and the use of the poetic line involve the organization of the material of language – sound, emphasis, rhythm – in a way that is impractical and arbitrary. In conversation rhyme is a peculiarity, even an embarrassment; when we write letters to the local council it is unlikely that we will divide up our language into free verse lines. The conventions and habits which prompt us to avoid such usages are based upon the precondition that ordinary language is concerned with the clear and efficient delivery of a message. Rhyme and the free verse line will interfere with the delivery of the message and draw attention to the medium through which it is delivered: language becomes self referential. Metre, rhyme and free verse are the most obvious cases of poetic self-reference. There are many others.

Craig Raine begins the final stanza of 'An Inquiry into Two Inches of Ivory' with,

> Day begins.
> The milkman delivers
> penguins with their chinking atonal fuss.

The visual and acoustic similarity between the white-bodied objects being gathered into a cosy group by the milkman and our memories, probably from television, of penguins huddling together and emitting random 'atonal' noises may not previously have occurred to us. Raine uses language to create an interface between prelinguistic images and ideas that have no logical or rational connection. The relations between the images and references of the poem effectively overrule our habitual modes of thinking. Such metaphoric uses are by no means forbidden in ordinary language. You could indeed point out to your neighbour that the milk bottles remind you of penguins, but, assuming that neither of you had recently consumed anything illegal, the conversation and your respective frames of reference would return to the prevailing context of the milk bottles as part of your familiar daily fabric of events and objects. Poems, rather than defer to the terms and conditions of the familiar world, tend to create their own worlds, in which connections and associations are formed in the mind of the poet. Raine begins his poem with the image of a vacuum cleaner which,

> grazes
> over the carpet, lowing,
> its udder a swollen wobble ...

Light switches become barn owls, light bulbs 'electric pears', wall phones wear spectacles and clothes 'queue up' in the wardrobe. The poem appropriates ordinary and familiar images and creates relationships between them that are disorderly, subversive of our conventional expectations of how language mediates the world.

Not all verse is as voraciously, self-consciously metaphorical as Raine's (see Unit 17, p. 516), but the creation of a world with its own internalized relations, which echo but do not replicate the world outside the text, is an endemic feature of poetry.

We have so far considered two characteristics of poetry: poetic form and metaphor. What they have in common is the ability to focus upon the nature and power of language itself rather than its practical, utilitarian function. Metre and sound pattern obstruct and complicate the production of meaning by foregrounding the material of language at the expense of transparency and clarity. Metaphor involves language in the appropriation and juxtaposition of ideas and objects that in the rational world language would classify, catalogue and distinguish. Poetry reverses the pragmatic, functional role of language. Language is generally used to refer to, specify, indicate, mediate or articulate things, feelings and ideas. Poetry draws words and their meanings into concentrated spheres where their expected distinctions and relationships will be variously unsettled, complicated or re-examined.

This definition of poetry can be tested against the two other literary genres which use language to create their own self-referring worlds: the novel (see Unit 2) and drama (see Unit 3). The best way to distinguish between poetry, the novel and drama is to compare a localized extract of the text with its entirety.

It is possible to locate sections of novels and plays which in their own right involve no obvious literary features. Sections of first- and third-person narrative could easily have come from a biography, an autobiography or a journal. Passages where narrative is integrated with dialogue or reported speech could belong to a magazine article on an evening in the local pub. Passages of dialogue from modern plays could have been recorded verbatim in a real front room, on a bus, in a courtroom.

The literariness of such passages, their difference from the real world, becomes apparent only when we recognize that their integration with the broader structural patterns of the text outweighs their correspondences with the world outside the text. As we read on we might find that the apparently objective third-person narrator has an exclusive and comprehensive knowledge of thoughts and activities of the main characters that in non-fiction would be implausible or impossible (see Unit 18, p. 534, on *Northanger Abbey*); or that the realistic dialogue between two characters actually functions as part of the patently unreal structure of a dramatic text which organizes, rather than reflects, the spatial and temporal actions of the characters.

Choose an extract from a poem and you will find that literariness, its patent and self-conscious difference from non-poetic discourse, will be far more localized and concentrated. The most obvious instance of this will be the interference of poetic form – from dense sound patterns to the line endings of free verse – in the routine production of meaning. Poems, such as Milton's *Paradise Lost* or Pope's *The Rape of the Lock*, can, like novels and plays, involve dialogue, extended narratives and narrators. But in poems each of these broader structural elements is informed by localized poetic devices. Milton's narrative account, the speeches and dialogic exchanges of God, Satan, Adam and Eve are pervaded by the metrical and syntactic conventions of blank verse. Pope's account, the narrative of the card game, Belinda's utterances, are organized by the tight symmetry of the heroic couplet. Shorter lyric poems such as Keats's odes, Shakespeare's sonnets or the two-line economies of the modern imagists might seem to have little in common with narrative verse, but all of these subgenres share a unifying characteristic: poetic language will constantly unsettle or intensify its familiar non-poetic function and form.

In what follows I will offer a more detailed account of the devices employed by poems to create their own networks of form and meaning.

## Prosody and poetic form

The most basic and enduring definition of poetry is that the poem, unlike any other assembly of words, supplements the use of grammar and syntax with another system of organization, the poetic line.

The poetic line draws upon the same linguistic raw material as the sentence but deploys and uses this in a different way. Our awareness of the grammatical rules which govern the way that words are formed into larger units of meaning is based upon our ability to recognize the difference between individual words. Words are made up of sound and stress, identified respectively by the phoneme and the syllable. The function of sound and stress in non-poetic language is practical and utilitarian: before we understand the operative relation between nouns, verbs, adjectives and connectives we need to be able to relate the sound and structure of a word to its meaning.

Traditional poetry uses stress and sound not only as markers and indicators of meaning but also as a way of measuring and foregrounding the principal structural characteristic of the poem, the line. In most poems written before the twentieth century the line is constructed from a combination of two or more of the following elements:

1.  A specified and predictable number of syllables. The most commonly used example of this is the ten-syllable line, the pentameter.
2.  A metrical pattern consisting of the relation between the stress or emphasis of adjacent syllables. The most frequently used metrical pattern in English involves the iambic foot, where an emphatic syllable follows a less emphatic one, with occasional variations, or 'stress reversals'.
3.  Rhyme. The repetition of the phonemic sound of a single syllable at the end of a line.
4.  Assonance and alliteration. The repetition of clusters of similar vowel or consonant-sounds within individual lines and across sequences of lines.

The persistent and predictable deployment of two or more of these features is what allows us to recognize the traditional line as an organizing feature of most pre-twentieth-century poems.


## Metre

The iambic pentameter, consisting of ten syllables with the even syllables stressed more emphatically than the odd, is the most frequently used line in English poetry. It is the governing principle of Shakespeare's blank verse; of non-dramatic blank verse poems, including Milton's *Paradise Lost* and Wordsworth's *The Prelude*; and of the heroic couplet, the structural centrepiece of most of the poems of Dryden and Pope. Examples of its shorter version, the octosyllabic line or tetrameter can be found in many of the couplet poems of Swift, in Matthew Arnold's 'Stanzas from the Grade Chartreuse', and in Tennyson's *In Memoriam*. The iambic pentameter consists of five iambic feet, its tetramer counterpart of four. The following are examples of these with ´ indicating the most emphatic and ¯ indicating the less emphatic syllables.

Iambic pentameter:

Sūch pléas | uῑe tóok | tʰe Sérp | eῑt tó | bēhóld
(from Milton's *Paradise Lost*).

Iambic tetrameter:

> Twō cóll | ege Sóphs | ōf Camb | rīdge grówth
> (from Swift's 'Cassinus and Peter').

These are examples of stress syllabic metre, in which a consistent balance is maintained between the number of syllables of a line and its stress pattern. Alternative stress-syllabic lines include seven-syllable tetrameters (see Blake's 'The Tyger'), which are comprised of three iambic feet and a single stressed syllable,

> Tý | gēr Tý | gēr, búr | nīng bríght.

Lines such as this, with an odd number of syllables, can also be scanned as trochaic

> ( ´-): Týgēr | Týgēr | búrnīng | bríght.

The trochaic foot more frequently features as a substitute or variation in a line of iambic feet. This occurs in the first foot of Shakespeare's line

> Nów is | thē wín | tēr óf | oūr dis | cōntént.

Stress syllabic lines consisting of three-syllable feet are generally associated with comic poetry and song. The three-syllable foot creates a rhythmic pattern that deviates from the modulation of ordinary speech far more than its two-syllable counterpart; as in Goldsmith's couplet, consisting of anapestic (-- ´) feet

> Hēre liés | Dāvīd Gár | rīck, dēscríbe | hīm whō cán
> Añ abrīdge | mēnt of all | thāt is pléas | ant iñ mán.

Some poems vary the syllabic length of a line, while maintaining the same number of emphatic or stressed syllables in each. This is called pure stress metre. An early example of pure stress metre is Coleridge's 'Christabel' and a more recent one occurs in T.S. Eliot's *Ash Wednesday*, in which the differing length of each line is anchored to a repeated pattern of two major stresses.

> Lády of sílences
>
> Cálm and distressed
>
> Tórn and most whóle
>
> Róse of mémory

The internal structure of the poetic line is only one element of its function as the organizing principle of poetry.

## Rhyme and the stanza

Rhyme binds lines together into larger structural units. The smallest of these is the couplet, rhyming aa bb cc (see the majority of poems by Dryden, Pope and Swift). More complex rhyme schemes enable the poet to create stanzas, the simplest of these being the quatrain, rhyming a b a b. (The octosyllabic quatrain is used by Donne in 'The Ecstasy' and its pentameter counterpart in Gray's 'Elegy Written in a Country Churchyard'.)

The stanza can play a number of roles in the broader structure of the poem. Narrative poems, which tell a story, often use the stanza as a way of emphasizing a particular event or observation while tying this into the broader narrative (see Spenser's *The Faerie Queene*, Keats's *The Eve of St. Agnes* and Byron's *Don Juan*). Tennyson in *In Memoriam* uses the so-called 'envelope stanza' (a b b a). This couplet within a couplet provides a formal counterpoint to the tragic or emotional focus of each stanza.

Shorter lyric poems, which focus upon a particular sensation, feeling or single event, often use the stanza as a counterpoint to improvisation and spontaneity. John Donne's 'The Relic' consists of three very complicated stanzas:

| | | |
|---|---|---|
| 8 syllables | When my grave is broke up again | a |
| | Some second guest to entertain, | a |
| | (For graves have learned that women-head | b |
| | To be to more than one a bed) | b |
| 6 syllables | {And he that digs it, spies | c |
| 10 syllables | {A bracelet of bright hair about the bone, | d |
| 7 syllables | {Will he not let us alone, | d |
| | And think that there a loving couple lies, | c |
| 10 syllables | Who thought that this device might be some way | e |
| | To make their souls, at the last busy day, | e |
| | Meet at this grave, and make a little stay? | e |

On the one hand the complex permutations of line length and rhyme scheme create the impression of flexibility and improvisation; as if the metrical structure of the poem is responding to and following the varied emphases of speech. But this stanzaic structure is repeated, with admirable precision, three times; and as we read the poem in its entirety we find that the flexibility of the syntax is matched by the insistent inflexibility of the stanza.

## The sonnet

The sonnet resembles the stanza in that it consists of an integrated unit of metre and rhyme: the Shakespearian sonnet consisting of three iambic pentameter quatrains followed by an iambic pentameter couplet, its Petrarchan counterpart rhyming abba abba cdc dcd. It differs from the stanza in that the sonnet is a complete poem. Most sonnets will emphasize a particular event or theme and tie this into the symmetries, repetitions and parallels of its metrical and rhyming structure (see Unit 7, pp. 154–6).

## The ode

The most flexible and variable stanzaic form will be found in the ode. Wordsworth's 'Ode on Intimations of Immortality' consists of eleven sections. Each of these involves a pattern of metre and rhyme just as complex and varied as Donne's stanza in 'The Relic', except that in the Immortality Ode the same pattern is never repeated. The open, flexible structure of the ode is well suited to its use, particularly by the Romantic poets, as a medium for personal reflection; it rarely tells a particular story, and it eschews logical and systematic argument in favour of an apparently random sequence of questions, hypotheses and comparisons. (See Unit 10, pp. 254–9, for a discussion of the structure and function of the Romantic Ode.)

## Blank verse

A form which offers a similar degree of freedom from formal regularity is blank verse, consisting of unrhymed iambic pentameters. Prior to Milton's *Paradise Lost* (1667) blank verse was regarded a mixture of poetry and prose. It was thought appropriate only for drama, in which language could be recognizably poetic (i.e. metrical) while maintaining realistic elements of dialogue and ordinary speech (without rhyme) (see Unit 5, pp. 105–6). *Paradise Lost* offered blank verse as an alternative to the use of the stanza or the couplet in longer narrative or descriptive poems.

Milton's blank verse creates a subtle tension between the iambic pattern of each line and the broader flow across lines of descriptive or impassioned speech (see below, p. 14, for an example). A similar balance between discursive or reflective language and the metrical undertow of the blank verse line will be found in the eighteenth-century tradition of landscape poems (see Thomson's *The Seasons* and Cowper's *The Task*) and in Wordsworth's 'Tintern Abbey' and *The Prelude*. The most flexible examples of blank verse, where it becomes difficult to distinguish between prose rhythm and metre, will be found in the poems of Browning, particularly *Ring and the Book*:

> So
> Did I stand question and make answer, still
> With the same result of smiling disbelief,
> Polite impossibility of faith.

## Free verse

Before the twentieth century poems which involved neither rhyme nor the metrical pattern of blank verse were rare. Smart's *Jubilate Agno* (1756) and Whitman's *Leaves of Grass* (1855) replaced traditional metre with patterns redolent of biblical phrasing and intonation, and Blake in his later visionary poems (1789–1815) devised a very individual form of free verse. It was not until this century that free verse became an established part of the formal repertoire of English poetry.

Free verse (from the French *vers libre*) is only free in the sense that it does not conform to traditional patterns of metre and rhyme (see T.S. Eliot's 1917 essay). The poetic line is maintained as a structural counterpoint to syntax, but is not definable in abstract metrical terms.

Free verse can be divided into three basic categories:

1. Poetry which continues and extends the least restrictive elements of traditional poetry, particularly those of the ode and blank verse. T.S. Eliot's 'The Love Song of J. Alfred Prufrock' is a monologue with an unpredictable rhyme scheme and a rhythmic structure that invokes traditional metre but refuses to maintain a regular beat or pattern (see Unit 17, pp. 501–2). A similar effect is achieved in Auden's 'Musée des Beaux Arts'. In *The Four Quartets* Eliot often uses an unrhymed form that resembles blank verse but which frequently deviates from a regular iambic pattern (see Part I of 'Little Gidding').
2. Poems in which the line structure reflects the apparent spontaneity of ordinary speech. Line divisions will often be used as an imitation of the process through which we transform thoughts, impressions and experiences into language. Easthope (1983) calls this form 'intonational metre'. A typical example of this is Lawrence's 'Snake'.

> A snake came to my water trough
> On a hot, hot day, and I in pyjamas for the heat,
> To drink there.

3. Poems in which the unmetrical line variously obstructs, deviates from or interferes with the movement of syntax. In Pound's 'In a Station of the Metro' the two lines function as an alternative to the continuities of grammar.

> The apparition of these faces in the crowd;
> Petals on a wet, black bough.

The space between the lines could be filled by a variety of imagined connecting phrases: 'are like', 'are unlike', 'remind me of', 'are as lonely as'. Individual lines offer specific images or impressions: the reader makes connections between them. (See Unit 17, p. 489, and *passim* for discussions of free verse.)

In William Carlos Williams's 'Spring and All' the line structure orchestrates the syntax and creates a complex network of hesitations and progressions (examples can be found in Bradford, 1994). The most extreme example of how the free verse line can appropriate and disrupt the structural functions of syntax will be found in the poems of e.e. cummings, where the linear movement of language is effectively broken down into visual units.

The best, brief guide to the mechanics of prosody and metre is G.S. Fraser's *Metre, Rhyme and Free Verse* (1970). Malof (1970) is more detailed, and Attridge (1982) combines metrical analysis with linguistics. Easthope (1983) offers a guide to the relation between verse form and modern literary theory.

Recognizing and naming the formal structures of poetry raises more complex questions. Most specifically: how do we account for the ways in which verse form variously creates and distorts meaning? We can note how an iambic pentameter organizes language, but how does it alter our understanding of it? Does the fact that words rhyme indicate some special relationship between their meanings? Pope begins his 'Epistle to Dr. Arbuthnot' with the couplet:

> Shut, shut the door good John, fatigued I said
> Tye up the knocker, say I'm sick I'm dead!

The semantic contrast between 'said' (living speech) and 'dead' (terminal silence) is itself underpinned by the metrical symmetry of the two lines. This is a case of poetic form supporting the wit and irony of its words. Less certain relationships between form and meaning occur in the dense sound patterns of Gerard Manley Hopkins's and Dylan Thomas's verse: to note and explain every interface between form and meaning in these would require a computer, not a human reader. We will consider examples of how to deal with poetic form in the section on 'Poetry and Criticism', but for the moment consider a conundrum. Criticizing poetry, either in an essay or in conversation, involves a form of translation. We discuss poems in the way that we discuss everything else. Our language is prosaic: we refer methodically to items, facts, devices, effects, apparent meanings. Criticism is normative; it reduces the oddities of poetic structure to the pragmatics of ordinary discourse. The conundrum: when we 'make sense' of a poem do we dispossess it of its principal intention – to oblige us to re-examine the means by which we make sense?

Some of the most subtle and sympathetic examples of how to make sense of poetic form will be found in Hollander (1975). A more methodical survey will be found in Bradford (1993). Brogan (1981) provides a comprehensive annotated bibliography of works on all types of metre and verse form.

## Metaphor

Metaphor is derived from the Greek verb 'to carry over'. When words are used metaphorically, one field of reference is carried over or transferred into another. Wordsworth (in 'Resolution and Independence') states that 'The sky rejoices in the morning's birth'. He carries over two very human attributes to the non-human phenomena of the sky and the morning: the ability to rejoice and to give birth. I.A. Richards (1936) devised a formula that enables us to specify the process of carrying over. The 'tenor' of the metaphor is its principal subject, the topic addressed: in Wordsworth's line the tenor is the speaker's perception of the sky and the morning. The 'vehicle' is the analogue carried over to the subject from a different frame of reference: in Wordsworth's line the activities of rejoicing and giving birth.

Metaphor is often referred to as a poetic device but it is not exclusive to poetry. Metaphors will be found in newspaper articles on economics; 'The war (vehicle) against inflation (tenor)'; in ordinary conversation, 'At yesterday's meeting (tenor) I broke the ice (vehicle)'; in novels, 'He cowered in the shadow (vehicle) of the thought (tenor)' (James Joyce's *A Portrait of the Artist as a Young Man*); in advertisements, 'This car is as good on paper (vehicle) as it is on the road (tenor)'.

The principal difference between Wordsworth's metaphor and its non-poetic counterparts is its integration with the iambic pentameter:

The sky | rējói | cēs iń | thē mórn | iñg's bírth.

We could retain the metaphor and lose the metre; turn it into the kind of unmetrical sentence that might open a short story or a novel:

I watched the sky rejoice in the birth of the morning.

One thing lost is the way in which the pentameter organizes and emphasizes the tenor and vehicle of the metaphor: 'sky | rējói | cēs' and 'mórn | niñg's bírth.' In order properly to consider differences between poetic and non-poetic uses of metaphor we should add a third element to tenor and vehicle: the ground of the metaphor (see Leech, 1969, p. 151). The ground is essentially the context and motivation of the metaphor. For the journalist the ground of the metaphor is the general topic of economics and inflation and the particular point that he/she is attempting to make about these issues. For the conversationalist the ground is the awareness, shared with the addressee, of yesterday's meeting and his/her role in it. For the advertiser the ground involves the rest of the advertisement, giving details of the make, price and performance of the car, and the general context in which cars are discussed and sold. In non-poetic uses of metaphor the ground or context stabilizes the relation between tenor and vehicle. The metaphor will involve a self-conscious departure from the orderly relation between the use of language and the prelinguistic world of facts and detail. It would be regarded as bizarre and mildly disturbing if the conversationalist were to allow the original metaphor to dominate the rest of his/her discourse: 'I sank through the broken ice into the cold water of the boardroom. There we all were: fishes swimming through a dark, hostile world ...'.

In poems, however, this relation between ground, tenor and vehicle is often reversed. It is the language of the poem, as much as the reader's a priori knowledge, which creates its perceived situation and context. It constructs its own ground, and metaphor becomes less a departure from contextual terms and conditions and more a device which appropriates and even establishes them. In John Donne's 'The Flea' the tenor is the insect itself and the bite it has inflicted upon the male speaker and the female listener. The speaker carries over this tenor into such an enormous diversity of vehicles that it becomes difficult to distinguish between the ground outside the words of the text and the ground which the text appropriates and continually transforms.

This flea is you and I and this
Our marriage bed, and marriage temple is.

We know that 'this flea' is the tenor, but the relation between tenor and ground becomes less certain with 'is you and I'. On the one hand it is literally part of them since it has sucked and mixed their blood. On the other the speaker has already incorporated this image of physical unity into a vehicle involving their emotional and sexual lives. He builds on this with the vehicle of the 'marriage bed' and extends it into an image of spiritual, eternal unity in the 'marriage temple'. Throughout the poem the flea and the bite become gradually detached from their actual context and threaded into a chain of speculative and fantastic associations. (See Unit 7, pp. 158–60, for detailed analysis of 'The Flea'.)

In ordinary language metaphor usually stands out from the rest of the discursive or factual nature of the statement. In poetry a particular use of metaphor will often underpin and influence the major themes of the entire text. Donne's 'The Ecstasy' begins with the stanza,

> Where, like a pillow on a bed,
> A pregnant bank swelled up, to rest
> The violet's reclining head,
> Sat we two, one another's best;

The tenor is the garden in which 'we two' are situated; the vehicle involves a combination of images denoting intimacy and sexuality: pillow, bed, pregnant, swelled up, the violet's (flower, denoting female) reclining head. This opening instance of the carrying over of rural horticultural images into the sphere of human sexuality becomes the predominant theme of the entire poem, underpinning more adventurous speculations on the nature of the soul. Again the dynamics of contrasting and associating verbal images has unsettled the stabilizing function of ground or context.

Donne is part of the metaphysical school of poetic writing (see Unit 7) whose taste for extended metaphor is a principal characteristic of their verse, but the practice of creating tensions and associations between the words and images of the poem at the expense of an external context transcends particular schools, fashions and historical groupings.

In Keats's 'Ode to a Nightingale' the image of the actual bird becomes a springboard for a complex sequence of associations and resonances: song, poetry, immortality, age, youth, death. The sense of there being a particular place and time in which Keats saw the bird and heard its song is gradually replaced by the dynamics of Keats's associative faculties: the relation between the vehicles unsettles the relation between vehicle, tenor and ground.

A classic case of vehicle undermining tenor occurs in T.S. Eliot's 'The Love Song of J. Alfred Prufrock' (lines 15–22). This begins with the tenor (the city fog) being carried over into the vehicle of an unspecified animal which 'rubs its back upon the window panes', 'rubs its nuzzle on the window panes' and 'licked its tongue into the corners of the evening'. By the end of the passage the actual vision of city streets which inspired the comparison has been overtaken by the physical presence of this strange beast, which 'seeing that it was a soft October night, Curled once about the house and fell asleep'.

Metaphor is the most economical, adventurous and concentrated example of the general principle of 'carrying over'. Samuel Johnson defined metaphor in his *Dictionary* as 'a simile compressed in a word'. Donne's metaphor (from 'The Relic'), 'a bracelet of bright hair about the bone', would, as a simile, be something like: 'the brightness of the hair about the bone reminds me of the difference between life and death'. Simile postulates the comparison: X is like Y. Metaphor synthesizes the comparison: X is Y. Metonymy is logical metaphor, in which the comparison is founded upon an actual, verifiable relation between objects or impressions: 'crown' is used instead of 'king', 'queen' or 'royalty' (see Unit 18, pp. 528–9). Allegory involves an extended parallel between a narrative and a subtext which the allegory variously reflects or exaggerates. Spenser's *The Faerie Queene* is a medieval fantasy with allegorical parallels in the actual world of the Elizabethan court.

Simile, metonymy and allegory establish a balanced relationship between the use of language and conventional perceptions of reality, and occur as frequently in non-poetic discourse as in poetry. Metaphor involves language in an unbalancing of perceptions of reality and is more closely allied to the experimental character of poetry.

Hawkes (1972) provides a brief, accessible guide to metaphor; Brooke-Rose (1958) and Black (1954) offer more detailed surveys.

## Syntax, diction and vocabulary

The terms poetic diction and poetic syntax should be treated with caution. Any word, clause, phrase, grammatical habit or locution used in non-poetic language can be used in poetry. But at the same time their presence within the poem will subtly alter their familiar non-poetic function.

In Donne's 'The Flea' the speaker reflects upon the likely objections to his proposal to the woman.

> Though parents grudge, and you, we are met,
> And cloistered in these living walls of jet.

We might explain the use of the phrase 'and you' as a result of hurried and improvised speech ('Though you and your parents grudge' would be a more correct form). But the fact that the placing of the phrase maintains the movement of the iambic metre and the symmetry between the two lines of the couplet shows us that the speech is anything but improvised.

The metrical structure of a poem can accommodate the apparent hesitations and spontaneities of ordinary speech, but at the same time fix them as parts of a carefully structured artefact. Consider what happens when syntax crosses the space between two poetic lines, an effect known as enjambment. A classic example of this opens Milton's *Paradise Lost*:

> Of Man's first disobedience, and the fruit
> Of that forbidden tree, whose mortal taste

The implied pause at the line ending might suggest, on Milton's part, a slight moment of indecision: is he thinking of the figurative 'fruit' (the result and consequences) of man's disobedience, or the literal fruit of the act of disobedience? He chooses the latter.

The placing of the word might also be interpreted as the complete opposite of fleeting indecision. The tension between the actuality of the fruit and the uncertain consequences of eating it is a fundamental theme of the poem, and Milton encodes this tension within the form of the poem even before its narrative begins.

In non-poetic language the progress of syntax can be influenced by a number of external factors: an act or verbal interruption by someone else, the uncertainty of the speaker or the fraught circumstances of the speech act. In poetry apparent hesitations or disturbances of syntax are a function of the carefully planned, integrated structure of the text.

The ability of poetry to absorb and recontextualize the devices and registers of non-poetic language is evident also in its use of diction, vocabulary and phrasing. The social or local associations of particular words or locutionary habits can be carried into a poem but their familiar context will be transformed by their new structural framework. In Tony Harrison's *V* (1985) the poet converses in a Leeds cemetery with an imagined skinhead whose hobbies include the spraying of graffiti onto gravestones.

> 'Listen cunt!' I said, 'Before you start your jeering
> The reason why I want this in a book
> 's to give ungrateful cunts like you a hearing!'
> *A book, yer stupid cunts not worth a fuck.*

The diction and idiom of both speakers is working-class and Northern, but this specific, locative resonance is itself contained within a separate language, with its own conventions: each regional idiomatic flourish is confidently, almost elegantly, reconciled to the demands of the iambic pentameter and the quatrain. The realistic crudity of the language is juxtaposed with the controlled irony of Harrison's formal design: the skinhead's real presence is appropriated to the unreal structure of the poem, involving the internal and external rhymes, 'book' and 'fuck'. In a broader context, the language of working-class Leeds is integrated with the same stanzaic structure used by Thomas Gray in his 'Elegy Written in a Country Churchyard' (1751), in which the poet similarly appropriates the voice of a 'hoary headed swain'. Gray's and Harrison's language and experience are centuries and worlds apart but they are brought into contact by the ahistorical forms and structures of poetry.

This tendency for poetry to represent and at the same time colonize the habits of non-poetic discourse is a paradox that has taxed poets and critics – most famously in Wordsworth's Preface to *Lyrical Ballads* (1798). Wordsworth rails against the stultifying poeticization of ordinary language, of how the conventions and style of eighteenth-century verse had dispossessed poetry of the 'real language of men'. But while he advocates a new kind of poetic writing he concedes that poetry must announce its difference in a way that will 'entirely separate the composition from the vulgarity and meanness of ordinary life'. In short, although poetry should be about 'ordinary life' it must by its very nature be separate from it.

D.H. Lawrence's poems in the Nottinghamshire dialect, Robert Burns's and Hugh MacDiarmid's (see Unit 27, pp. 689–90) use of Scots idiom, grammar and diction emphasize region and very often class, but no matter where the words come from or what social or political affiliations they carry, they are always appropriated and acted upon by the internal structures of poetry.

Wordsworth's desire to separate poetry from the 'vulgarity and meanness of ordinary life' sounds suspiciously elitist and exclusive, and there is evidence of this in the work of a number of our most celebrated poets. In Part II of *The Waste Land* Eliot represents the speech patterns and, so he assumes, the concerns of working-class women:

> Now Albert's coming back, make yourself a bit smart,
> He'll want to know what you done with that money he gave you
> To get yourself some teeth.

We will be expected to note the difference between this passage and the sophisticated command of metre and multi-cultural references of the poem's principal voice, Tiresias. With whom would we associate T.S. Eliot? Tiresias or the women?

The sense of poetry as carrying particular social and political allegiances (principally male, white, English, middle-class, educated) has prompted acts of stylistic revolution. William Carlos Williams in the free verse of *Spring and All* and *Paterson* effectively discards those conventions of rhyme and metre that restrict his use of ordinary American phrasing and vocabulary (see Unit 14, p. 370). Linton Kwesi Johnson makes the structure of his poems respond to the character of his language.

> But love is
> jus a word;
> give it MEANIN
> thru HACKSHAN.

MEANIN and HACKSHAN are words appropriated from 'standard' English by West Indians, and the fact that Johnson has used poetry to emphasize their ownership is significant (see Unit 28, p. 696). The unusual concentrations and foregroundings of poetry can unsettle just as much as they can underpin the allegiances and ideologies of diction and vocabulary.

Groom (1955) provides a survey of post-Renaissance poetic diction. Davie (1955) is good on the dynamics of poetic syntax. Jakobson (1960) offers the most complex linguistic survey of poetic syntax; see Bradford (1994) on this.

## Who's speaking?

Much of what we know of the speaker of a poem is provided by the poem itself. The information which enables us to construct a mental picture of the speaker is known as the poem's deictic features (from the Greek, 'pointing' or 'showing'). In Donne's 'The Flea' the deictic features tell us that the speaker is male, that his listener is female, that the speech act is in the present tense and improvised, and that their situation casts doubt upon seventeenth-century standards of health and cleanliness: the active presence of the flea does not seem particularly unusual or distressing. Renaissance lyric poetry is particularly prone to constructing such detailed dramatic contexts. The Romantic or the free verse lyric tends to tell us more about the effect of an experience or object upon the speaker than it does about his/her personal history, tastes or habits. A typical example is Wordsworth's sonnet 'Upon Westminster Bridge' where the words of the speaker construct an emotionally charged record of his vision of the city, but tell us little of who he is.

We can, of course, draw parallels between the speaker (the poetic persona), and what we know of the life, the historical, social, even psychological condition of the poet. This can be a speculative activity (did Coleridge's known habit of taking opium play a part in the bizarre, unstructured character of 'Kubla Khan'?); or it can be founded upon straightforward indications that it is the poet who is speaking: Tennyson's *In Memoriam* and Yeats's 'Easter 1916' are about real events experienced by each poet.

The shifting relation between our knowledge of the poem and the poet informs poetry criticism. The most extreme case of contextual-biographical interpretation is probably Lowes's *The Road to Xanadu* (1927) in which he traces every theme, image, virtually every word, of 'Kubla Khan' back to Coleridge's known reading and interests. The antithesis of this method is Jakobson's model of the poetic persona as a construction of the poem's own internalized system of images and stylistic devices (see Unit 18, pp. 530–1).

The relation between the persona, the perceived context of the poem and the actual context in which it was written is particularly important for feminist criticism (see Units 23 and 24). My own reference to the 'he' of Wordsworth's 'Westminster Bridge' is based only in part upon my knowledge that Wordsworth wrote it. An anonymous poem written in 1802 is far more likely to reflect the perceptions and experiences of a man than a woman, not simply because there have been more male than female poets, but, more importantly, because male habits, affiliations and roles are encoded in the apparently asexual conventions of traditional poetic writing. Consider a random selection of sixteenth- or seventeenth-century poems. Those which address or enact the issues of love or sexuality will be fashioned from the deictics of the male perspective, and those which are more concerned with God or philosophy will postulate an experience of scholarship, debate and a mastery of current learning that is incompatible with contemporary conventions of how women should think, act and speak. Anne Finch wrote in 1714,

> Alas! a woman that attempts the pen
> Such an intruder on the rights of men
> …
> To write, or read, or think, or to enquire
> Wou'd cloud our beauty, and exaust our time,
> And interrupt the Conquests of our prime;

There is a self-conscious tension in these lines between Finch's awareness of her perceived role and the fact that the conventions and stylistic features of her discourse (particularly the heroic couplet) are traditionally associated with the male voice.

It could be argued that the position of women in poetic writing is strengthened when habit and convention are overturned by revolutionary themes and techniques that have no established gender associations. Modernism proved to be a focal point for a variety of women poets whose creative energy was no longer frustrated by the monolith of male-dominated, traditional writing: Gertrude Stein, Amy Lowell, Harriet Monroe, Hilda Doolittle, Marianne Moore (see Miller (ed.), 1986, and Montefiore, 1987).

## Poetry and criticism

Poetry criticism is as old as poetry. Aristotle and Plato considered the value and function of poetry. They differed on this; Plato seeing it as a dangerous perversion of the correct relation between language and reality, Aristotle regarding its inventive, figurative character as a healthy contribution to the discipline of argument and debate. Criticism of English poetry began effectively in the sixteenth and seventeenth centuries and its practitioners inherited two principal concerns from their classical forebears. On the one hand writers such as Puttenham (*The Arte of English Poesie*, 1589) and Daniel (*A Defense of Rhyme*, 1603) were concerned with adapting the rules and conventions of classical rhetoric to the English language and to the new conditions of poetic writing (they were particularly interested in metre and rhyme). On the other the debate begun by Aristotle and Plato was continued: Philip Sidney's *The Defense of Poetry* (1595) involves itself with the status and influence of poetry within the turbulent contemporary discourses on politics and religion.

From the seventeenth to the end of the nineteenth century writings about poetry maintained the Renaissance emphasis upon its structure and function. Pope's *An Essay on Criticism* (1711) is a survey, in poetic form, of contemporary discussions of the classical origins of English poetry, of how poetry should treat the natural and political world and of the style, diction, metre and proper subjects of poetic writing. Johnson's *The Lives of the Poets* (1779–81) involves short studies of English poets since the Renaissance, in which Johnson comments on their stylistic qualities, influence and general relevance to cultural life. Johnson's sense of English poetry as indigenous tradition, responsive to its own historical conditions, would become a keynote of Romantic criticism. In his Preface to *Lyrical Ballads* (1798) Wordsworth engages with what he regards as the failure of the established English poetic tradition to offer new and challenging perspectives upon the condition of modern man; and the urge to revitalize poetry, to evolve original and provocative modes of writing, is a character- istic of the critical work of Coleridge, Shelley, Keats and Blake (see Unit 10).

Most pre-twentieth-century poetry criticism is involved with the activity of writing poetry and with the relation between poetry and its political, social and intellectual conditions. These concerns have been maintained through this century, particularly by poet/critics such as Pound, Eliot, Auden and Heaney, but they have been supplemented by the emergence of poetry criticism as an academic discipline. The theoretical principles and the potential social benefits of teaching and studying English poetry in schools and universities were first mooted by the Victorian writer Matthew Arnold (see Unit 18), but it was not until the 1920s and 30s that academic poetry criticism began to evolve the methodology and practices of an analytical discourse. Sidney, Pope and Wordsworth had discussed the respective qualities and styles of poets, the purpose, relevance and future of poetry. The new, educationally affiliated critics involved themselves in the activities of dissecting and reassembling existing poems; naming and analyzing their stylistic properties not for the purpose of writing verse but rather with the objective of showing how it works and contemplating its unique and perverse production of meaning.

The earliest and the most influential groups of academics were the New Critics and the Formalists (see Unit 18). Both begin with the premise that poetry by definition creates effects and levels of meaning that non-poetic discourse will deliberately avoid. In their book *Understanding Poetry* (1938) the new critics Cleanth Brooks and Robert Penn Warren discuss the procedures through which poetic writing is created:

> [The poet] cannot assemble them [an episode, a metaphor, a phrase, a metrical device] in a merely arbitrary fashion; they must bear some relation to each other. So he develops his sense of the whole, the anticipation of the finished poem, as he works with the poem, and moves from one part to another. Then as a sense of the whole develops, it modifies the process by which the poet selects and relates the parts, the words, images, rhythms, local ideas, events etc.... It is an infinitely complicated process of establishing interrelations. (pp. 526–7)

Brooks and Penn Warren present the poem as a separate linguistic and experiential universe. Their putative poet has not completely abandoned involvement with or reference to the world outside the text, but each of 'his' moves and strategies is governed principally by the interactive relation between the parts of the poem.

This model of how poems are created is reflected in the new critical procedures of analysis and interpretation. Brooks in *The Well Wrought Urn* (1947) is concerned with the use and effect of poetic paradox, but, as he explains, his objective is not simply to disclose a catalogue of oppositions, incompatible images and contradictions; rather, to treat paradox in poems as an element which permeates and unifies the broader fabric of the text. In his analysis of Donne's 'The Canonization' (Brooks takes his title from the poem's image of the urn, which seems variously to connote life, death, art and immortality) Brooks forages through the local stylistic effects of the poem and concludes that its metaphors, images and referential themes draw upon the all-embracing, paradoxical relation between transient pleasures of temporal love and the transcendent nature of the spirit. In Brooks's view the poem's reluctance to resolve or settle this grand paradox, but rather to build it into an all-inconclusive structural theme, is a testament to its quality: poem's enact and intensify the problems of the human condition; they do not solve them.

Brooks's general principle, that our ultimate critical objective is to show how the parts of the poem contribute to its complex entirety, underpins William Empson's *Seven Types of Ambiguity* (1930) and W.K. Wimsatt's essays on metre, diction and rhetoric in *The Verbal Icon* (1954). This critical activity is given the general title of close reading, and its archetypal Formalist version can be found in the much-discussed essay by Jakobson and Jones on Shakespeare's Sonnet 129 (see Bradford, 1994). Their method is analogous to the anatomist's or the pathologist's treatment of the human body. They list every semantic and syntactic operation of individual words and supplement this with an equally exhaustive survey of every feature of the text's deployment of metre, assonance, alliteration, rhyme and grammatical parallelism. Their objective is not to disclose a new dimension of the poem's meaning; rather, to show how forms such as the sonnet create a continuous, multidimensional interface between structure and effect and, as a consequence, resist paraphrase and summary. See Unit 18 for a study of Jakobson's methods.

Since the 1960s the New Critical and Formalist treatment of poetry has been subjected to a number of antagonistic, rejectionist rereadings.

The New Critics have been accused of detaching the study of poetry from the real experience of social, political and ideological division that informs our lives. Terry Eagleton (1983, pp. 48–9) argues that the new critics' emphasis upon the poem as 'a self-sufficient object' effectively 'disentangl[es] it from any social or historical context'; that their taste for showing how ' "tensions" "paradoxes" and "ambivalences" ' are 'resolved and integrated by its solid structure' was underpinned by their political ideal of a 'new organic society' redolent of fascism.

A more sustained assault upon the validity of New Critical practice has come from theorists who promote a reader-centred model of interpretation (see Unit 20). These theorists argue that the educational, cultural and social circumstances which influence our perceptions of poetry are principally responsible for what we claim to 'find' in it. Jonathan Culler (1975, ch. 8) re-examines the 'formal patterns' (metaphor, metre, poetic diction, genre, etc.) that provide critics with the methodology for their analysis of poems. He does not dispute the fact that these features exist as constituent parts of the text in question, but he claims that their apparent relation to each other and their resultant effect are due as much to the critic's own expectations of structure and signification as they are to the particular and unique operations of poems. To demonstrate his point he reprints a passage of philosophical prose by W.V. Quine as a free verse poem and claims to find in it a level of paradox comparable with Brooks's interpretation of Donne's 'The Canonization' (p. 163), and he analyzes a piece of Jakobson's prose and 'finds' the same symmetries of syntactic parallelism that Jakobson discloses as a special characteristic of a Shakespeare sonnet (pp. 62–3). Culler's point is that we should pay as much attention to the procedures that prompt us to 'recognize' poems as special, and which empower us to decode their meaning, as we do to the apparently separate and definitive features of poems themselves. For an amusing and more detailed version of Culler's exercise see Stanley Fish's 'How To Recognise a Poem When You See One' (1980, discussed in Unit 20) in which Fish convinces his undergraduate class that a random list of surnames on a blackboard is a Modernist religious lyric. Their interpretations are slick, sophisticated, informed and very depressing – depressing in the sense that robotic analysis has replaced evaluation.

The distinction between the ideas of Culler and those of the New Critics underpins a large number of recent critical debates. The New Critics base their work upon the precondition that poems are structurally and functionally different from other types of discourse and that consequently they create effects and meanings that do not occur in the non-poetic circulation of ideas and references. Culler and Fish shift our attention towards the context and circumstances in which the poem is understood and argue that poetic structure and function are variable elements, dependent upon such factors as the educational competence of the reader. This premise re-emerges in feminist criticism of poetry. The reading of poems which are primarily by men and which reflect the activities, concerns and desires of men (at least 80 per cent of all pre-twentieth-century verse) will inevitably be affected by the reader's own experience as either a man or a woman: whatever is apparently intrinsic to the poem (the New Critical emphasis) cannot remain immune from such a fundamental difference in the reader's sense of identity (see Units 23 and 24; Moi, 1985; and Todd, 1988).

Marxist literary theories have been concerned far more with fiction than poetry (see Unit 21). This, at least by implication, reinforces the new critical notion of poetic difference. Novels are more mimetic than poems; they draw more freely upon their own social and political contexts and consequently serve better the Marxist view that literature can only be properly understood within a larger framework of social reality. The patent oddities of poetic writing are frequently regarded by Marxists as a token of the privileges of middle-class or aristocratic culture: games played with language by those who dominate the social and political uses of language (see Caudwell, 1937). Christopher Hill's Marxist reading of *Paradise Lost* (1977) is concerned more with its relation to the social, religious and ideological conflicts of seventeenth-century England than with its effects and qualities as a poem *per se*.

Formalists and Structuralists (principally Jakobson, 1960; and Riffaterre, 1978) generally share with the New Critics the view of poetry as intrinsically different. However, they are far more involved with investigating poetry as one among many systems of organizing linguistic signs than they are with justifying or celebrating its aesthetic value (see Unit 18).

Freud (1900) compared the bizarre, surrealistic collages of the dream with its linguistic counterpart in 'a poetical phrase of the greatest beauty and significance'. Most psychoanalytic critics, including Jacques Lacan, regard poetry as variously subversive and symptomatic of the arbitrary relation between language and the unconscious. Perhaps our attraction for the unusual and sometimes disturbing effects of poetic language allows us a conscious glimpse of our rarely articulated desires, fears and fantasies. Norman Holland (1975 and 1980) supplements Culler's and Fish's notion of the reader's ability to impose coherence upon a poem with the belief that the unity we 'discover' is actually a reflection of our own desired psychological condition (see Unit 22).

Deconstruction (see Unit 19), like most recent theories of criticism, draws upon ideas and practices evolved outside literary studies. If deconstruction can be said to have a premise or founding principle it is that our perceptions of reality are sustained by our ability to postulate them in language. When we deconstruct a text we show how its apparent affirmation of order or truth is constantly unsettled by its necessary dependence upon the falsifications of language. This radical branch of philosophy found a welcoming home in the literary-critical academy of the late 1960s, particularly in the work of poetry critics who were tiring of the well-rehearsed practices of new criticism. The attraction was obvious: poetry deliberately and constantly unsettles the accepted relations between language and reality; it appropriates familiar images and ideas and (as the Formalists put it) defamiliarizes them. The problem that had taxed the New Critics was of how to return the perverse, irrational discourse of poetry to the world in which language is supposed to disclose truths and make sense. Deconstruction provided not so much a solution as an escape from the problem. Deconstructionists argue that our attempts to distil an unrefined and immutable truth from *any* kind of linguistic text is a contradiction in terms since language creates rather than mediates truth. Poems are self-deconstructive. Their use of ambiguity, irony, paradox, metaphors that are endless and self-sustaining involves a disclosure of the fact that language mediates nothing; rather it thickens and complicates levels of signification. Ergo: poetry critics should not concern themselves with resolving the paradoxes and contradictions of poetic discourse; they should follow, even celebrate, the limitless aporias (from the Greek – a track without end) of poetry. Culler (1983) performs a deconstructive reading of that New Critical classic 'The Canonization':

> [The] self referential element in Donne's poem does not produce or induce a closure in which the poem harmoniously is the thing it describes ... Self reference does not close it in upon itself but leads to a proliferation of representations, a series of invocations and urns, including Brooks's *The Well Wrought Urn* ... [which] are at once within the poem and outside it and can always be continued and has no end.   (pp. 204–5)

I cannot advise you of the 'best' way of studying poetry: your use of feminist or deconstructive method or your enthusiasm for Modernism over traditional poetry will be determined by your own inclinations and tastes – and this book offers you a closer look at the choices available.

*BIBLIOGRAPHY*

Attridge, Derek (1982) *The Rhythm of English Poetry*, Longman, London.
Black, M. (1954) *Models and Metaphors*, Cornell University Press, Ithaca.
Bradford, R. (1993) *A Linguistic History of English Poetry*, Routledge, London.
Bradford, R. (1994) *Roman Jakobson. Life, Language, Art*, Routledge, London.
Brogan, T.V.F. (ed.) (1981) *English Versification 1570–1980. A Reference Guide with a Global Appendix*, Johns Hopkins University Press, Baltimore.
Brooke-Rose, C. (1958) *A Grammar of Metaphor*, Secker and Warburg, London.
Brooks, C. and Warren, Robert Penn (1938) *Understanding Poetry*; references from 1960 edn, Holt, Rinehart & Winston, New York.
Brooks, C. (1947) *The Well Wrought Urn: Studies in the Structure of Poetry*; reprinted by Methuen, London, 1968.
Caudwell, Christopher (1937) *Illusion and Reality: A Study of the Sources of Poetry*; extract in D. Lodge (1972) *20th Century Literary Criticism. A Reader*, Longman, London.
Culler, Jonathan (1975) *Structuralist Poetics. Structuralism, Linguistics and the Language of Literature*, Routledge & Kegan Paul, London.
Culler, Jonathan (1983) *On Deconstruction. Theory and Criticism After Structuralism*, Routledge & Kegan Paul, London.
Davie, Donald (1955) *Articulate Energy: An Inquiry in the Syntax of English Poetry*, Routledge & Kegan Paul, London.
Eagleton, Terry (1983) *Literary Theory. An Introduction*, Blackwell, Oxford.
Easthope, Antony (1983) *Poetry as Discourse*, Routledge, London.
Eliot, T.S. (1917) 'Reflections on Vers Libre'; reprinted in *To Criticise the Critic* (1965), Faber, London.
Empson, William (1930) *Seven Types of Ambiguity*, Chatto & Windus, London.
Fish, Stanley (1980) 'How To Recognise a Poem When You See One', in *Is There a Text in this Class? The Authority of Interpretive Communities*, Harvard University Press, Cambridge, Mass.

Fraser, G.S. (1970) *Metre, Rhyme and Free Verse*, Methuen, London.

Freud, S. (1900) 'The Interpretation of Dreams', reprinted in *Standard Edition* (1953), Hogarth Press, London.

Groom, B. (1955) *The Diction of Poetry from Spenser to Bridges*, University of Toronto Press, Toronto.

Hawkes, Terence (1972) *Metaphor*, Methuen, London.

Hill, Christopher (1977) *Milton and the English Revolution*, Faber, London.

Holland, Norman (1975) *5 Readers Reading*, Yale University Press, New Haven.

Holland, Norman (1980) 'Unity, Identity, Self, Text', in *Reader Response Criticism from Formalism to Post-Structuralism*, ed. Jane P. Tompkins, Johns Hopkins University Press, Baltimore.

Hollander, John (1975) *Vision and Resonance. Two Senses of Poetic Form*, Oxford University Press, London.

Jakobson, Roman (1960) 'Closing Statement. Linguistics and Poetics', in *Style in Language*, ed. T. Sebeok, MIT Press, Cambridge, Mass. Reprinted in D. Lodge (1988) *Modern Criticism and Theory*, Longman, London.

Leech, G.N. (1969) *A Linguistic Guide to English Poetry*, Longman, London.

Lowes, J.L. (1927) *The Road to Xanadu*, Vintage Books, New York. Reprinted 1959.

Malof, J. (1970) *A Manual of English Metres*, Indiana University Press, Bloomington.

Miller, Nancy K. (ed.) (1986) *The Poetics of Gender*, Columbia University Press, New York.

Moi, Toril (1985) *Sexual/Textual Politics: Feminist Literary Theory*, Methuen, London.

Montefiore, Jan (1987) *Feminism and Poetry: Language Identity, Experience in Women's Writing*, Pandora, London.

Richards, I.A. (1936) *The Philosophy of Rhetoric*, Oxford University Press, London.

Riffaterre, Michael (1978) *Semiotics of Poetry*, Indiana University Press, Bloomington.

Todd, Janet (1988) *Feminist Literary History*, Polity Press, Oxford.

Wimsatt, W.K. (1954) *The Verbal Icon*, University of Kentucky Press, Lexington.

# UNIT 2

# Studying fiction and prose

*John Peck*

## What is a novel?

A novel is an extended work of fiction written in prose. The problem with this definition, of course, is that it merely states the obvious. It is difficult, however, to produce a more useful definition as individual novels vary so much; is there really any common ground between Jane Austen's *Pride and Prejudice* and James Joyce's *Finnegans Wake*, or between Herman Melville's *Moby-Dick* and Thomas Keneally's *Schindler's List*? There is the fact that each work, as with every novel, tells a story, but is there anything we can establish beyond that? Are there patterns, either thematic or structural, that appear in novel after novel; are there standard narrative conventions? If there are, an obvious point to make is that these patterns and conventions are less fixed than in poetry or drama. In both these genres, we can identify established forms – such as tragedy, epic, the sonnet – and recognize repeated features: in the case of poetry, metrical and stanza patterns; in the case of drama, a set sequence of exposition, complication and resolution. The novel has never had to accommodate itself within such received structures. Indeed, it can be argued that a large part of the drive behind the novel, why it began to establish itself in the eighteenth century, is because it was the genre that could best handle an idea of individual freedom, of breaking away from inherited structures. But it is the freedom of the novel, the fact that the genre is always genuinely 'novel', that makes it so difficult to define.

In order for criticism to function, however, there has to be a sense of the characteristics of a genre. Criticism cannot proceed on the basis of regarding each new work encountered as unique; to do so would deprive us of a framework of understanding. In other words, everyone studying a novel needs some sense of the rules that shape the genre in order to appreciate why the work under consideration is distinctive. To provide a simple example: most readers are aware that a lot of novels deal with individuals and the society in which they find themselves. Consequently, their enjoyment of a novel such as George Eliot's *The Mill on the Floss* will tend to focus on how well the author presents the experiences of her heroine, Maggie Tulliver. It could be argued that it is George Eliot who encourages us to focus on Maggie, but in fact the reader's interest in, and understanding of, Maggie's dilemma also stem from a well-developed grasp of the repeated concerns of novels.

The individual in conflict with society is one of the most common patterns in fiction; what the rest of this essay consists of is an elaboration of this and other thematic, structural and linguistic patterns critics have noted in the novel genre. As such, the essay represents a simple codification of basic assumptions which provide a shared vocabulary for discussing novels. For the student of literature, what follows, therefore, is the necessary descriptive language of novel criticism. At this point, however, it is necessary to introduce a note of caution. I started by suggesting how difficult it is to define a novel; if the genre is elusive, there is something suspect about too confident a labelling of its principal characteristics. We have to ask ourselves, are the features described in this essay inherent in novels or are they essentially the creation of critics? And, if critics describe novels in a certain way, is this at the expense of other, possibly more provocative, ways of describing the genre? What should become apparent is that, although a traditional sense of the devices and effects of fiction is not only useful but indispensable, these traditional definitions can limit our sense of the possibilities of the novel.

## The rise of the novel

The novel as most people think of it today appeared in England in the early eighteenth century. In 1719 Daniel Defoe wrote *Robinson Crusoe*. By the time Samuel Richardson's *Clarissa* (1748), Henry Fielding's *Tom Jones* (1749) and Laurence Sterne's *Tristram Shandy* (1760–7) had been published, the genre was not only well-established but its distinctive qualities were also apparent. The opening sentences of *Robinson Crusoe* illustrate a number of these central characteristics of novels:

> I was born in the year 1632, in the city of York, of a good family, tho' not of that country, my father being a foreigner of Bremen, who settled first at Hull. He got a good estate by merchandise, and leaving off his trade lived afterward at York, from whence he had married my mother, whose relations were named Robinson, a very good family in that country, and from whom I was called Robinson Kreutznaer; but by the usual corruption of words in England, we are now called, nay, call our selves and write our name, Crusoe, and so my companions always called me. (Defoe, [1719] 1965, p. 27)

The features in evidence here might not be typical of all novels, but can certainly be found in a great many.

For a start – and starting where any discussion of a novel should both begin and end, with the language of fiction – there is Defoe's plain prose style. Other novelists might adopt a different manner – Fielding, for example, exudes patrician authority – but the style of a novel always creates its content, and Defoe's businesslike style serves his purpose in conveying a world of commerce and middle-class life. This is significant: the novel, particularly in Europe, by and large reports upon the experiences of middle-class people who have to work for a living. Indeed, it can be argued that the novel emerged in the eighteenth century because a new kind of commercial society was taking shape at that time. The novel served as a mirror for this audience, a mirror in which they could see the dilemmas of their own lives reflected.

Such novels tended to be realistic (a surprisingly complex term, which I will return to) and secular. Up to and including the seventeenth century, people organized their lives principally in relation to God. Defoe remains a devout Christian, but if we consider the name Kreutznaer – it means 'the fool of the cross' – the way in which the religious echo in the name disappears as he becomes Crusoe suggests a move towards secular experience, towards assessing the world, as Defoe does here, in terms of class, social mobility, family and possessions. In just a few words, the opening paragraph of *Robinson Crusoe* tells us an immense amount about the complex cross-currents at work in society in the early eighteenth century.

## Critical approaches to the novel

How does an awareness of points such as these help us as students of the novel? Essentially, it is useful to have some idea what to expect, even if this is as basic as seeing that many novels deal with individuals making their way in, or finding themselves at odds with, the social world. A novel, as is the case with *Robinson Crusoe*, will often start by establishing a sense of the conventional order of society; it is this that the hero or heroine will have to contend with. A conflict will develop; we can guess here that Crusoe will reject the comfortable and seemingly secure world of his father.

It helps at the beginning of a novel, therefore, to try to get hold of the broad thematic pattern as quickly as possible: try to see what kind of world the novelist is establishing, and try to anticipate how characters might find themselves at odds with or stifled by this world. The vast majority of classic British, European and American novels – particularly those that are widely taught in schools – present the picture I am describing here of society and individuals. Typical examples are Jane Austen's *Emma*, which deals with Emma's social education; Charles Dickens's *Great Expectations*, in which Pip becomes a gentleman, but discovers that his new-found status is far from secure; Charlotte Brontë's *Jane Eyre*, in which a rebellious heroine learns to conform; and D.H. Lawrence's *Sons and Lovers*, in which the hero is at odds with both his father and society. A great part of the activity of novel criticism centres upon appreciating and describing how the novel under consideration presents this tension between society and the individual.

Having said that, however, it is necessary to start introducing qualifications. The pattern I have described is not inherent in the novel as a genre; novels do not have to present individuals at odds with society. That so many classic novels do is simply a historical fact, reflecting the post-1700 concerns of Western culture: the novel in England came into existence to dramatize the anxieties of the bourgeois hero or heroine, and, as a consequence, it is all too easy to think that this is the intrinsic subject matter of the genre. A critical approach that focuses on the life and trials of the central character is also likely to favour a certain kind of novel; the realistic novel is likely to receive the most attention, and there is bound to be praise for those novels that offer an intricate sense of the psychological development of the principal characters.

In this respect, it is worth thinking about the critical reputation of Henry James, a novelist so difficult that he might be expected to remain a minority taste, but who, over the years, has received far more critical attention than widely-read novelists such as Anthony Trollope or H.G. Wells. Henry James is one of the novelists that the critic F.R. Leavis included in his 'Great Tradition'; the others are Jane Austen, George Eliot and Joseph Conrad. That is, realistic society and the individual novelists, all noted for their subtle characterization (Leavis, 1948). A great deal of criticism from the 1950s and 1960s reveals a shared preference for this kind of novel, including Ian Watt's classic account of eighteenth-century fiction, *The Rise of the Novel*, in which realism is the central concept (Watt, 1957).

This traditional preference for realism led, it is interesting to note, to the neglect – and, until recently, exclusion from the syllabus – of whole categories of fiction, such as the gothic novel and the sensation novel. A work such as Wilkie Collins's *The Woman in White*, probably the best-known sensation novel, could be admired for its ingenious plotting and manipulation of suspense, but, to the critic bringing specific expectations to fiction, inevitably seemed shallow. The same could be said of responses to gothic novels, such as Horace Walpole's *The Castle of Otranto*. It is only recently, particularly with the development of feminist and psychoanalytic criticism, that critics have found non-dismissive ways of discussing the 'other' novels in the history of the novel. (See Unit 9 for a further discussion of the rise of the novel.)

## A broader sense of the novel

There is a further problem with focusing too much on society and the individual. It is this: if we read novels with certain expectations, there is a chance that we will miss other levels of meaning and significance in these works. This should become apparent if we return to the opening of *Robinson Crusoe* which, so far, I have discussed in terms of society and the individual. I commented on the fact that the passage seems to turn its back on religion, but possibly it is dealing with a worrying drift away from religion. Indeed, the passage might possess levels of meaning which, although not immediately apparent to the modern reader, are just as important as the fate of the individual. We could say, for example, on the basis of how Defoe focuses on names, that he even displays a radical scepticism about the whole notion of identity, of the self-named subject. Rather than offering a mirror to middle-class life, it could be argued that the passage, as it manipulates names, questions the very concept of self that the novel as a genre seems to value so highly.

We might also consider how Defoe plays with the notion of patriarchy. Crusoe shapes his life in the shadow of, and in relation to, his father. It is a power relationship in which the child will need to assert himself. But, given the references to religion in the passage, we could say that Defoe is more broadly, and indeed fundamentally, concerned with the patriarchal structure of experience. The point I am making is that if we come to a novel with different expectations, we are likely to construct a different sense of its central concerns. Traditionally criticism has focused on the fate of the individual in society, but if we adjust the angle of looking we might, as in the case of *Robinson Crusoe*, find levels of religious significance, or that a novel is posing different questions about the self, or that it is engaged in a more fundamental examination of the structure of power in society.

Just as it is possible to broaden our sense of what we are likely to encounter in a novel, we can, if we adopt a less restrictive definition, extend our sense of the history of the genre. It is simply the novel as we generally think of the form that started with *Robinson Crusoe*. We could, however, use the term to embrace any long narrative written in prose, such as Philip Sidney's prose romance *Arcadia* (*c.* 1580), or picaresque fiction, such as Cervantes' *Don Quixote* (1605–15). And there are numerous works from the seventeenth century, such as Aphra Behn's *Oroonoko* (1688) and John Bunyan's *The Pilgrim's Progress* (1678), which qualify if we employ a less prescriptive definition. In a sense, however, this merely takes us back to our point of departure: the difficulty of defining the novel. Novels are not just realistic fictions about the individual and society, but it is difficult to establish an alternative definition of the shared characteristics of the genre.

## Narratology

Criticism tends to concentrate on either the content or form of a literary work. Part of the problem in this discussion so far is that the emphasis has been on content, on the thematic concerns that surface in novel after novel. As we have seen, this provides a good foundation for the discussion of many novels, but constitutes too limited a sense of what is possible in novels in general, and possibly even too limited a sense of what is happening in a novel such as *Robinson Crusoe*. An alternative strategy is to turn away from content, and start with a sense of the formal structure of novels. The name for this kind of discussion is narratology, which means the study of how narratives work. In its purest form, narratology ignores content; the narratologist is interested exclusively in the systematic formal construction of a work, the structural elements that are present and how they combine, and the way in which the narrative gets told.

The most significant works in the history of narratology are Vladimir Propp's *Morphology of the Folktale* ([1928] 1968), A.J. Greimas's *Sémantique structurale* (1970), Gérard Genette's *Narrative Discourse* ([1972] 1980) and Seymour Chatman's *Story and Discourse* (1978). The attraction of narratology is obvious: if we are offered a sense of a standard narrative pattern, we are well placed to see how an individual work adapts and develops that pattern. But, almost inevitably, the issue is not as simple as that: it is possible to take issue with the impulse behind narratology, to argue that the patterns are imposed rather than intrinsic in fiction. And, even if the existence of the patterns is granted, it has to be recognized that the discovery of one pattern is likely to operate at the expense of other patterns that might be overlooked or simply missed (see Unit 18, pp. 532–8).

# The journey

As you can see, we return to the same problem that exists with a thematic approach: the novel is an elusive form, and any attempt to pin it down is unavoidably flawed. Criticism, however, would never get anywhere if we spent all our time questioning the validity of our approaches, and narratology, for all its shortcomings, does provide us with a solid foundation for studying individual texts. What follows here, though, is something far less complex than a comprehensive taxonomy of fiction. I simply want to draw attention to some of the recurrent structural features of novels. We can start by returning again to *Robinson Crusoe*: Crusoe, as everybody knows, goes on a sea journey, gets shipwrecked and lands on an island. In *Tom Jones*, Tom is expelled from the house of his protector, Mr Allworthy, and travels towards London with a schoolmaster, Partridge, experiencing a variety of adventures along the way. In Mark Twain's *Huckleberry Finn*, published in 1884, Huck, a schoolboy, and his friend Jim, an adult slave, travel down the Mississippi on a raft. On their journey they encounter rogues, mobs and even murderers. What links these three narratives is the structure of a journey, and this is, in fact, the most common narrative pattern in literature.

In each work there is also a breaking away from the father (in the case of *Tom Jones*, a father figure) at the outset, and this is also a familiar structure in fiction. Indeed, it has been said that the novel as a genre came into existence at that point in history when God the father ceased to be central in people's experience, and that all novels search for an order to take the place of the security of the original patriarchal order. The concept of the journey obviously exists before the novel came into existence; it is the narrative device at the heart of romance (for example, Edmund Spenser's epic poem *The Faerie Queene*), and the work that is sometimes regarded as the first novel, Cervantes' *Don Quixote*, parodies romance in a significant way. The Don, as with the heroes of romance, is on a quest, a symbolic journey through life, but it is the essence of picaresque fiction that the hero does not arrive at his goal, that he is endlessly waylaid. If we extend this idea, it could be argued that novels in general are always torn between the overall design of the onward progression of the journey/story, and local interruptions which impede progress. If we consider Bunyan's *The Pilgrim's Progress*, the most significant original prose work in English before *Robinson Crusoe*, it is a religious allegory of the Christian hero's journey through life, but what makes the work interesting – and what makes it resemble a novel – are the variety and complexity of the distractions that the hero encounters along the way, and the complex nature of his response to these temptations.

When we look at realistic fiction, the local distractions of life are overwhelming, and the structure of a journey is often obscured. In George Eliot's *Middlemarch*, for example, the Preface compares the heroine, Dorothea Brooke, to Saint Theresa on a spiritual journey, but in reading the work this informing structure is almost forgotten; what we notice are the demands of daily life. The heroine is, none the less, still caught between a sense of some larger meaning to her life and the mundane realities of ordinary life. It is a tension that is particularly prominent in Thomas Hardy's novels, where the overall structure is often that of tragedy – a literary form that imposes a significant structure upon life – but the page-by-page texture is that of realism. Eighteenth- and nineteenth-century novels by and large obscure the overall structure, often overwhelming us with the density of their social worlds, but late nineteenth-century and early twentieth-century novels frequently re-emphasize the idea of a symbolic journey: for example, Virginia Woolf's *To the Lighthouse*, D.H. Lawrence's *The Rainbow*, and the odyssey that runs through James Joyce's *Ulysses*. In American fiction, however, the sense of a symbolic journey has always been more prominent; indeed, it has been a feature of some criticism in the past to regard works such as *Huckleberry Finn* too exclusively as romances, and to overlook the extent to which such works were engaged in the political realities of nineteenth-century American life. The journey of Huck and Jim is not some kind of Walt Disney escapade, but a disturbing exploration of issues of race, class, gender, language and national identity.

## Plot

The simple sequence of events in a novel is a story, but the moment we start to take account of motivation and causation the story becomes a plot. The most famous definition of plot was given by E.M. Forster: '"The king died and then the queen died" is a story,' he explained, but '"The king died and then the queen died of grief" is a plot' (Forster, [1927] 1963, p. 93). Plot suggests all the decisions the novelist has had to make in terms of presenting the work in a certain order and duration; in a picaresque novel, like *Don Quixote*, the plot could be called loose and episodic, whereas, at the other extreme, a twentieth-century novel such as Joseph Conrad's *Nostromo* has a complex and intricate plot. Generally, however, we should be able to see the characters in the plot of a novel are caught up in a developing conflict which is normally resolved at the end.

The term 'plot' has to be included in this unit, as it has always been an important concept in literary criticism. Traditional novel criticism, for example, focused on theme, plot and character, with perhaps some discussion of the angle of narration and the language of a text. But the word 'plot' appears a lot less in criticism these days. The problem is that the concept of plot rather suggests a grand design, an overall unity and coherence within the text, as if everything slots together to make a grand statement. We can connect this with the impulse in traditional criticism to get at 'the meaning' of the text; such criticism is often referred to as expressive criticism, meaning that it contrives to get at the meaning the author is expressing. To offer an example: Charles Dickens's *David Copperfield* is the story of David's life, his relationship with his mother, his friendships, and his emotional attachments. The critic Gwendolyn B. Needham, in an essay that is typical of its time, suggests that at the heart of the novel is the idea of emotional growth, that David learns how to control his undisciplined heart (Needham, [1954] 1990). It is a plausible reading, but critics by and large no longer favour this kind of criticism that seeks to extrapolate a main point from the text. Criticism has swung towards an idea of the openness of texts. In the case of *David Copperfield*, critics are far more likely to stress the unresolved tensions at the heart of Victorian life, and to praise Dickens's ability to suggest the subtle and deep nature of these tensions, than to draw attention to any supposed solution Dickens might be said to have for the problems of his age. It is a novel's ability to suggest the complexity of issues, and not the quality of a novel's answers, that is central in criticism today.

## Closure

This change in critical direction is clearly illustrated in the emergence of the term closure and the large number of discussions of problems of closure. Quite simply, closure refers to the fact that novels end, and that the neatness of the closing pages is often at odds with the complexity of the work as a whole. At the end of *Tom Jones*, for example, Tom is revealed to be a relative of Mr Allworthy; Tom might have appeared a rogue, but we discover that he is really a gentleman. It is as if Fielding, a conservative thinker, reasserts the fundamental soundness of the social order, turning his back on the socially (and sexually) disturbing questions his novel has asked along the way. The issue of closure is discussed brilliantly in D.A. Miller's *Narrative and its Discontents: Problems of Closure in the Traditional Novel* (Miller, 1981). Concentrating on Jane Austen and George Eliot, he deals with the tension between suspense and closure in fiction; how there is a 'narratable disequilibrium' and set against this a state of 'non-narratable quiescence'. That is to say, a novel can only be interesting and continue when there is conflict and suspense; the moment social order is restored there is no story to narrate.

## Character

The thread that has run through this unit is that we undervalue the novel as a genre if we attempt to pin it down too much. Thematically, if we say that all novels are about the conflict between individuals and society, we are likely to overlook other, less manageable, levels of meaning in a work. Formally, if we stress unity of plot we reduce a novel to a simple pattern, and that tends to imply that the novel is making a simple statement. There are similar dangers involved in relying too much upon the concept of character. At first sight, character can appear to be the wild card in a text; if the structure of a plot is almost inevitably deterministic, character might seem to be the force that resists, that can pull against the tide. In practice, however, character is often latched on to as a glibly reassuring concept in a text.

I have already referred to a traditional critical view of *David Copperfield. David Copperfield* is a *Bildungsroman*, an education novel dealing with the growth to maturity of the central character; for a critic like Needham (referred to earlier), it is a novel about the growth of the liberal hero. But a critic less intent on extrapolating a positive overall meaning from the text might prefer to focus on the way in which David has acquired much of the hardness of his hated step-father, the ways in which David's conduct towards women is consistently suspect, and the ways in which there are numerous parallels between David and the two villains of the book, Steerforth and Uriah Heep.

The point is that traditional criticism usually accepted the overt pattern of the text: that the hero or heroine stood for individual integrity in a corrupt world. But the moment the critical impulse is reversed, the moment the critic focuses on the incoherence of the text, the frailty of the concept of the individual becomes apparent. David Copperfield is a self-constructed subject; more interesting than the equanimity he achieves at the end of the novel are the neuroses, confused desires, and worries about class and status that bedevil his life. We can apply a similar approach to *Jane Eyre*: traditional criticism focused on how Jane grows up, how she becomes a responsible person, leaving behind the instability of her younger years. More recent criticism, however, often focuses on the process rather than the product of the text, looking at Jane's instability, and even seeing something positive in it, specifically a protest against the male order that is dominant in society. The trend in criticism in recent years has, therefore, been not to abandon an interest in character, but, rather than seizing upon character as a reassuring presence, to see character as a precarious identity that is constructed in order to cope with the world. It is a split and disturbing interiority rather than a positive sense of the self that we could be said to encounter most commonly, particularly in the nineteenth-century novel.

## Realism

Many of the concerns of this unit are reflected in changing attitudes towards realistic fiction. As I have stated, traditional criticism favoured the realistic novel, but, starting in the 1960s, critical taste began, albeit temporarily, to turn against the realistic novel. For example, Colin MacCabe, in a book on James Joyce, mocked the 'classic realist text', specifically *Middlemarch*, as a kind of deception, a work which affects to offer us a comprehensive picture of experience, but one in which the narrator is, in fact, very much in control: controlling the plot, controlling the characters, and controlling the meanings available to the reader (MacCabe, 1978). This phase of dismissing George Eliot has now passed. The emphasis of a great deal of recent criticism is that *Middlemarch* is not the coherent and unified package that traditional critics seemed to want. It only appears like this if we impose concepts of theme, plot, character and the narrator's voice in too rigid a way. When we loosen that kind of critical control we can see that it is a work that is disturbingly open on questions of sexuality, gender, class, power, empire, marriage, society, the self – indeed, every vital aspect of Victorian life. In a similar way, when we start to relax our critical commitment to unity and coherence, we begin to acquire a critical vocabulary for appreciating the disturbing effects of, say, Dickens, and gothic novelists, and sensation novelists.

## Narration

D.H. Lawrence's *Sons and Lovers* deals with a young man with artistic leanings who is at odds with his family, particularly his father, and this young man's first sexual experiences. James Joyce's *A Portrait of the Artist as a Young Man* deals with a young man with artistic leanings who is at odds with his family, particularly his father, and this young man's first sexual experiences. There are, of course, all kinds of ways in which these works do not echo each other, but basic structures are repeated in novels as it is through a handful of situations – often involving sexual encounters – that people can be put to the test and gain a sense of who they are. The twists and turns of a novelist's plot, the characters he or she creates, and the physical setting in which the events of the novel take place all contribute to the distinctive feel of a novel, but what possibly more than anything else makes a novel distinctive is the manner of the narration. There is a voice narrating the events that are taking place, and this voice is invested with power and authority. As readers of a novel, we are not free to judge characters and actions as we might in real life: there is always a narrator directing our judgements.

Essentially, there are only two forms of narration, first-person narrative and third-person narrative. We can also refer to each of these as the point of view from which the events are narrated. In a first-person narrative, the narrator is a participant in the story, very often the central character. J.D. Salinger's *The Catcher in the Rye* is a first-person narrative. It begins:

> If you really want to hear about it, the first thing you'll probably want to know is where I was born, and what my lousy childhood was like, and how my parents were occupied and all before they had me, and all that David Copperfield kind of crap ... (Salinger, [1951] 1958, p. 5)

*David Copperfield* is, as you might realize from this, also a first-person narrative.

Third-person narrative relies upon a narrator who is outside the story proper. Nathaniel Hawthorne's *The Scarlet Letter* begins:

> A throng of bearded men, in sad-coloured garments and grey steeple-crowned hats, intermixed with women, some wearing hoods and others bareheaded, was assembled in front of a wooden edifice, the door of which was heavily timbered with oak and studded with iron spikes. (Hawthorne, [1850] 1992, p. 65)

This sentence provides a clear illustration of how a narrator is always shaping meanings and directing the reader. This is a group of people gathered at a prison door; we are unlikely to form the impression that they are liberal-minded citizens protesting at the punishment that is to be inflicted upon someone. On the contrary, we know they are unforgiving. The narrator does not, of course, state this directly; instead, he lets the references to their 'sad-coloured garments' and 'steeple-crowned hats' make the point. 'Steeple-crowned' associates their hardness with a religious hardness, just as the 'iron spikes' in the door tell us all we need to know about the prison regime. When we look at a narrative voice we are, before anything else, looking at ways such as this in which the narrator creates and controls the meanings of a work.

## Third-person narrative

The narrator who exercises the greatest degree of control over a novel is an omniscient narrator: this is a narrator who presumes to know everything, to be able to read every motive. In this example from *Middlemarch*, look at how we are told how the character feels: 'In his inmost soul Will was conscious of wishing to tell Dorothea what was new even in his own construction of things …' (George Eliot, [1871–2], 1994, p. 366). George Eliot does not just tell us what Will is thinking, but claims to convey his deepest thoughts, ideas that have barely formulated themselves even in his own mind. This kind of omniscience is most common in nineteenth-century realistic novels. The narrator seems to control the world and to have a discourse available for making sense of the whole of experience; as one might expect, it is a middle-class discourse. The world is being read from the perspective of those who possess political and economic power in society. The views offered by such a narrator strike us as sound and reasonable, but this is inevitable, for ideology serves the needs of the dominant class by encouraging everyone in society to believe that they share the same interests as this class.

There are two qualifications that should be entered here: one is that, if we simply generalize about George Eliot's narrator speaking in the dominant voice of society, we are likely to overlook the subtlety and complexity of that controlling voice. This is the qualification traditional critics would express. The other qualification, which I will expand upon later in this unit, is that George Eliot's narrative position is possibly not as confident as it might initially appear, that, if we shift our angle of evaluation, we might start to see the narrative voice as uncertain (one aspect of this is that George Eliot is a woman writing in the voice of a patriarchal society). At first sight, however, the narrative voice in *Middlemarch* seems confident, and particularly when we compare George Eliot with Thomas Hardy. Omniscience begins to break down towards the end of the nineteenth century. Look, for example, at this description of Henchard, the eponymous hero of *The Mayor of Casterbridge*: 'That laugh was not encouraging to strangers … . Many theories might have been built upon it. It fell in well with conjectures of a temperament which would have no pity for weakness …' (Hardy, [1886] 1974, p. 64).

The interesting thing about this is that Hardy has it both ways. He expresses a direct judgement on the character, but at the same time his comment is beset with qualifications: that all kinds of theories could be constructed about Henchard's laugh, that the view offered is conjecture. How do we explain this gradual retreat from omniscience? The answer would seem to lie in changes in society and thinking towards the end of the nineteenth century, a new sense that there is not one universal truth, only a series of relative perspectives. Hardy's method indicates that things can be interpreted in a variety of ways.

## First-person narration

This impression of a retreat from omniscience is confirmed if we look at the manner of narration in modernist fiction. Omniscience becomes less and less common, and more authors use dramatized, often fallible, narrators. Conrad in a number of his works, including *Heart of Darkness*, uses a character called Marlow as his narrator: this is one person, struggling to make sense of experience, and aware that life is more complex than his grasp of the world. It is quite often the case, as in F. Scott Fitzgerald's *The Great Gatsby*, that the dramatized narrator, in this instance Nick Carraway, is a middle-class character judging the world with certain values and a specific language; the events presented stretch beyond the comprehension of such a character. It is a way of indicating that we cannot read the world completely, that we can only offer relative perspectives.

When a novelist uses a dramatized narrator it is a form of first-person point of view, but as used by twentieth-century novelists it differs from the kind of autobiographical first-person mode that we encounter in novels such as *David Copperfield* and *Jane Eyre*. In both these Victorian novels, a mature narrator reflects upon his/her younger self; it is a fairly stable method of narration, the reader being encouraged to share the mature narrator's judgement on his/her youthful naivety. It could be said (although recent criticism might take issue with this view) that this form of first-person narration, just as much as omniscient narration, endorses a middle-class ideological reading of experience. By contrast, the use of a dramatized narrator in works such as those of Conrad and Fitzgerald indicates the limitations of a middle-class perspective. (See Unit 18, pp. 532–8, for a discussion of narrators and narrative method.)

## Stream of consciousness/interior monologue

Modernist fiction takes its experiments with narration furthest in the use of stream of consciousness and interior monologue, as encountered, for example, in the works of Virginia Woolf and James Joyce. Implicit in the presence of an omniscient narrator is the idea that there is a language and set of values that all reasonable people share. At the opposite extreme from this idea of a public and normative discourse is stream of consciousness, which purports to present the flow of a character's mental processes; sense perceptions mingle with conscious and half-conscious thoughts, with memories, and with random associations. The term is sometimes used interchangeably with interior monologue, but generally the distinction that is drawn is that stream of consciousness can include the intervention of a narrator whereas interior monologue presents the vagaries of the mental process far more directly, for example ignoring any requirement for grammatical sentences or a logical order.

## Experiments in narrative technique

Such experiments in narrative technique are, as in the works of Conrad, Woolf and William Faulkner (most successfully in *The Sound and the Fury*), often accompanied by disruption of the usual time sequence of a novel. Events might be narrated out of sequence, to the extent that we have to piece together the story rather than being guided through it. Such disruption again challenges the conventional structures that we rely upon to shape experience; a common-sense, ordered way of organising life is exposed as an arbitrary, but reassuring, way of making sense of the world.

All such effects are most brilliantly handled in Joyce's *Ulysses*. The story in *Ulysses* is simple: Stephen Dedalus meets up with a substitute father figure, Leopold Bloom. The manner of the narration, however, is extraordinary, for each chapter of the novel is narrated in a different style, or several different styles. It is an approach that alerts us to the way in which literature processes and orders experience through received or conventional discourses; by becoming self-conscious about style, Joyce challenges the notion of a univocal reading of experience, and draws attention to the different ways in which meaning can be imposed upon experience in a literary text.

The overall history of narrative control in the novel is, therefore, a move from omniscience towards rejection of the very idea of omniscience. At this point, however, as is so often the case in elaborating neat theories about the novel, we need to hesitate. Was the Victorian novel really as univocal as might appear to be the case? Or is it that, if we look for omniscience we are likely to be struck by omniscience, and, consequently, miss other things that are happening in a novel? I have already referred to the fact that a traditional critical vocabulary encourages us to view fiction in a certain way. That is again the case here. The traditional stress on point of view and omniscience promotes an expressive view of literature: attention is drawn to what the author says and his or her success in saying it. Even with modernist texts, where there seems to be a rejection of the narrator's conventional authority, the use of terms such as interior monologue in fact supports the idea that the author is very much in control of the possible meanings of the text. Criticism in recent years, however, has become much more interested in how a text challenges authorial control. (See Unit 16 for a detailed discussion of stream of consciousness and narrative experiment.)

## The polyphonic novel

One of the critics who has contributed most to new thinking about novels is Mikhail Bakhtin. We can see the impact of his work in changing views of *Middlemarch*. As I have suggested, traditional critics liked *Middlemarch*; they admired the subtlety of George Eliot's moral discriminations, and what they saw as the novel's timeless truthfulness to human experience. But when critical fashion turned, albeit briefly, against George Eliot her omniscience was dismissed as a narrowly middle-class view of life. The debate soon, however, moved on in a new direction: in an important article, David Lodge took a fresh look at *Middlemarch*, arguing that the narration is a good deal more complex than has often been assumed (Lodge, 1981). In formulating his case, Lodge calls upon the thinking of Bakhtin, in particular the proposition that, rather than there being one voice in a text, a novel is polyphonic. In *Middlemarch*, as soon as we begin to look at it in this light, we are no longer aware of just one omniscient voice but a host of different and competing voices representing different positions and perspectives. When we begin to consider an argument such as this, *Middlemarch* becomes a novel that fails to amount to a larger unity; there are always unresolvable differences, problems in the novel that the narrator cannot rhetorically control.

The broader significance of this change in critical thinking (it is, it must be pointed out, not just Bakhtin but the whole weight of poststructuralist theory that has changed our ideas) is that there is no longer the interest there used to be in looking for the large statement a text might be felt to be making. There is, on the contrary, an interest in the text as a site of struggle, articulating differences and divisions within the society of its day. One consequence of this change in critical thinking is a radical shift in the image of the author: the author is no longer regarded as a sage, offering words of wisdom to his or her contemporaries. On the contrary, the author is as confused as anyone else, articulating the problems of his or her day but not getting on top of them. In order for such a change in critical assumptions to take place, however, there had to be a move away from some of the central concepts of traditional criticism. If we talk about theme, plot, character and point of view, we build a coherent sense of what is going on in a novel and what the novel is trying to say. If, however, we focus more closely on the language of a text, we shift from a sense of broad controlling elements towards an awareness of local difficulties, of instabilities within each sentence. And the more we look at the language of a novel the more we are likely to notice the anxieties and strains in the discourse of a period.

## Discourse analysis

Bakhtin looks at the competing voices, the competing discourses within a novel. In any society, however, there will be a dominant discourse, the language of those in power. Feminist criticism has influenced general thinking here, for at the heart of much feminist writing is a dissection of how men have held on to power through controlling language. What a great deal of recent criticism is interested in is the nature of the dominant discourse in texts and also challenges to that discourse. *Jane Eyre* provides a clear example. Traditionally, *Jane Eyre* has been read as a text about a wayward heroine who needs to mature. This is, indeed, the overt thrust of the book: by the end of the novel Jane has acquired a new kind of balance. But recent criticism often reads against the grain of the overt pattern of the text, finding material at odds with the dominant pattern. Look, for example, at this brief extract from Jane's marriage ceremony:

> 'The marriage cannot go on: I declare the existence of an impediment.'
> The clergyman looked up and stood mute; the clerk did the same; Mr Rochester moved slightly, as if an earthquake had rolled under his feet ... (Brontë, [1847] 1994, p. 287)

There is a public language – formal, elaborate, legalistic – which is the language of the marriage service. It is a discourse that, combining religion and the law, declares where power resides in society.

Jane has to negotiate a position for herself, including a language for herself, within this order. Consequently, as against the public language, there is a private language from Jane that expresses her feelings; as in the reference to an earthquake, she makes use of metaphors from nature to express states of feeling which possibly have no existence in the conventional discourse of society. What is also significant here is that, the moment the usual order is challenged, the clergyman and the clerk lose the power of speech: they can only operate within the conventional order, and have no language available for handling a state of affairs outside that usual order. What we see in this scene is true throughout the novel, that Jane speaks for herself within a dominant discourse. What gives the book such force is that Jane's discourse is one of rage and anger, as she fights against the roles that are assigned to her. In order to get at this sense of the novel, however, we have to focus on its language.

There is, in fact, another level of complication in *Jane Eyre*: Charlotte Brontë is a member of the society of her day, and has absorbed its values and vocabulary in all kinds of ways. Consequently, in looking closely at the language of *Jane Eyre*, we are likely to find various ways in which Brontë, alongside her sympathy for Jane, reveals her commitment to the dominant ideological values of the period. There is, for example, Jane's pride in her middle-class status, her love of respectability and cleanliness, and, perhaps most interestingly, a colonialist vein of thinking: the novel consistently sets the civilized standards of Europe against the uncivilized standards of India and the West Indies. The fact is that Brontë is subversive in the society of her day, but also a member of that society; she challenges but also shares the assumptions that are built into its everyday speech. It might be felt that such a contradiction at the heart of a novel must be a shortcoming, but only if we expect a novel to make a coherent statement. If we abandon a desire for unity, and work outwards from the language of a novel – looking at how the novelist both relates to and dissents from a dominant discourse, and looking at how a novel contains meanings that the novelist is unconscious of – we are likely to arrive at a sense of how a novel expresses the deepest contradictions of the period of its production. It is not a pointless incoherence, but an incoherence that indicates the complexity of a novel's involvement with the political, cultural and social issues of its time. (Bakhtin's theories are dealt with in Unit 21.)

## The changing syllabus

Over the years an English Literature syllabus changes. Traditional criticism favoured steady novels expressing central truths about human experience. Recent criticism, as I have indicated, has been busily engaged in showing that these steady novels are not as coherent as might appear to be the case. At the same time, texts which for too long have been on the fringes of the syllabus have been given a more prominent role. This applies to the gothic novel, the sensation novel, a great many novels by women authors, and texts from Africa, Asia and the Caribbean.

*Frankenstein* provides a good example of a novel that has only recently found widespread acceptance on the English Literature syllabus. It tells the story of Victor Frankenstein who constructs a monster and endows it with life. The monster is benevolent, but is regarded with loathing and fear; consequently, its benevolence turns to hatred as it destroys its creator and his bride. Until recently, there was little criticism of *Frankenstein*. Such as there was focused more on the author, Mary Shelley, than the novel. It was sometimes discussed in relation to Romantic poetry, particularly in the context of the work of Mary's husband, Percy Shelley, and sometimes critics considered the story's hold upon the popular imagination. What is clear is that critics could not find a substantial or serious text to discuss in *Frankenstein*. Such a view begins to change, however, if we become less concerned with steady truths about human experience and redirect our attention to dissident and disturbing voices within a culture. In relation to *Frankenstein*, one possible approach is to argue that there are two realms in the novel: one, the public realm, is dominated by language and law, the other, the private realm, is secret, even incommunicable. This is the realm of Frankenstein and his monster. It is a world that exists outside society and language, containing only the monster and his creator. Victor has some connection with the public realm – his command of the discourse of society enables him to pursue his studies at a university – but the association with the monster points to an exploration of the dark places of his unconscious (see Unit 10, pp. 245–8).

A full elaboration of this line of argument would require consideration of the work of Jacques Lacan, in particular his idea of the Symbolic Order of society as opposed to the Imaginary Order of the pre-Oedipal stage; Victor has clearly not really adjusted to the Symbolic Order of society. Rather than pursue such an argument here, however, it is probably more useful to point out how this kind of reading of *Frankenstein*, and the same would be true of many current readings of this and other novels, focuses on language, and specifically interests itself in those who are excluded from or in a problematic relationship with the dominant discourse of a society. There is often a feminist dimension to such thinking: in the case of *Frankenstein*, for example, Mary Shelley's anxieties about her own role as someone creating and living by language, yet conscious that language, along with literary creation, is usually regarded as a masculine preserve.

## Non-fictional prose

The implication of much of what I have been saying is that if you alter the position from which criticism operates then you gain a different sense of what is involved in any particular text. A critical approach in which the key terms are theme, plot, character and point of view has little to say about *Frankenstein*, but a critical approach which places language at the centre of the discussion has a lot to say. This is true in relation to novels, but even more true in relation to the discussion of non-fictional prose. Non-fictional prose – works such as history books, works of philosophy, occasional essays, and even key scientific documents such as Charles Darwin's *The Origin of Species* – have always had a rather awkward role in a literature syllabus. It is clear that these works are important, but what to say about them has often been less clear. The tendency used to be to regard them as background texts, indicating the kind of cultural climate in which authors worked, and sometimes, as in the case of Thomas Carlyle, having a direct influence on the thinking of novelists. In so far as students read writers like Carlyle, they focused on their ideas; by and large, such texts were not subjected to the kind of critical analysis applied to novels, poems and plays.

There is, of course, nothing wrong with this; it might even be said that there is a great deal of sense in reading a philosophical or historical work for its content rather than from the point of view of form. In recent years, however, and again largely as a result of the current tendency to focus upon language, much more attention has been paid to non-fictional texts as works that respond well to critical discussion. One of the best examples of such critical analysis is Gillian Beer's *Darwin's Plots*, in which she looks at the evolutionary thought of Charles Darwin and its impact upon George Eliot and other nineteenth-century novelists. Darwin propounds a scientific theory, but Beer is alert to the problems Darwin faced in precipitating his theory as language:

> He was telling a new story, against the grain of the language available to tell it in. And as it was told, the story itself proved not to be single or simple. It was, rather, capable of being extended or reclaimed into a number of conflicting systems. (Beer, 1983, p. 5)

Can you see how Darwin's theory is treated as a narrative, a kind of story? Writing at a time of retreating religious faith, and, indeed, helping to accelerate that retreat, Darwin is involved in creating a new story to replace an old story. The difficulty and delicacy of the task is to a large extent reflected in the metaphoric language Darwin employs to achieve his ends. What Beer does, then, is read *The Origin of Species* as a literary text. The procedures she employs are now widely diffused in considerations of non-fictional prose: rather than just focusing on ideas, critics look at how the writer constructs a narrative, and how language functions in that narrative.

## The novel today

If we focus on the language of a text we tend to become absorbed with how an author confirms or challenges the discourse of his or her day. It is the problem every writer has to return to: not what to write, but how to write. Three brief examples from current fiction might make this clear. One of the most celebrated novels of recent years has been Graham Swift's *Waterland*. The title refers to the fens of East Anglia, where nothing is firm. The narrator of *Waterland* tries to build a structure on these unstable foundations; what he does is tell stories, specifically the story of his family and the story of his own life. Stories are, as we see in the novel, not just important but vital; we cannot live without the comfort and coherence of narratives. But what is also of note in *Waterland* is that it is narrated by a history teacher on the verge of retirement. He is declared redundant; the world has moved on and defies his understanding, but he continues to tell stories in his polite, educated, English voice. The proposition at the heart of *Waterland* seems to apply to a great deal of current British fiction: there is the world as it exists today, and the polite voice of the English author. How can such an author escape from the past, escape from the voice he has inherited, escape from set ways of thinking and speaking? We see novelists such as Martin Amis and Will Self trying to alter the accent of British fiction (although, perhaps we should say English fiction, for other voices can be heard in other parts of the United Kingdom), but it seems impossible for the English writer to break free from inherited ways of speaking.

At an opposite extreme is the work of Alice Walker, an African-American woman novelist. In *The Color Purple* we see her assuming, almost effortlessly, a voice that bears no resemblance to any of the traditional voices of literary culture. As such, Walker challenges the dominant discourse of her society. Or, at least, does so up to a point: there are critics who point out that, even though Walker's language breaks the mould, in other ways she accepts the ideological imperatives of white American society. For example, the heroine of *The Color Purple* achieves success as a self-employed businesswoman. Such a contradiction is, however, not a weakness in the text. The ways in which Walker's novel both resists and shows its commitment to the dominant values of US society indicate the confusing complexity of the issues at the heart of the novel. For a more extreme form of resistance we would have to consider the Kenyan novelist Ngugi wa Thiong'o, who, after completing *Petals of Blood* in 1977, stopped writing in English, arguing that while the bullet of the colonizer was the means of physical subjugation, language was the means of spiritual subjugation. The reality for every novelist, however, is an equally fraught and complicated engagement with language.

## BIBLIOGRAPHY

Beer, Gillian (1983) *Darwin's Plots: Evolutionary Narrative in Darwin, George Eliot and Nineteenth-Century Fiction*, Routledge & Kegan Paul, London.

Brontë, Charlotte (1994) *Jane Eyre*, Penguin, London [first published 1847].

Chatman, Seymour (1978) *Story and Discourse: Narrative Structure in Fiction and Film*, Cornell University Press, Ithaca.

Defoe, Daniel (1965) *Robinson Crusoe*, Penguin, Harmondsworth [first published 1719].

Eliot, George (1994) *Middlemarch*, Penguin, London [first published 1871–2].

Forster, E.M. (1963) *Aspects of the Novel*, Penguin, Harmondsworth [first published 1927].

Genette, Gérard (1980) *Narrative Discourse*, Cornell University Press, Ithaca [first published in French 1972].

Greimas, A.J. (1970) *Sémantique structurale*, Larousse, Paris.

Hardy, Thomas (1974) *The Mayor of Casterbridge*, Macmillan, London [first published 1886].

Hawthorne, Nathaniel (1992) *The Scarlet Letter*, Wordsworth, Ware [first published 1850].

Leavis, F.R. (1948) *The Great Tradition*, Chatto & Windus, London.

Lodge, David (1981) '*Middlemarch* and the Idea of the Classic Realist Text', in *The Nineteenth-Century Novel: Critical Essays and Documents*, rev. edn, ed. Arnold Kettle, Heinemann, London, pp. 218–38.

MacCabe, Colin (1978) *James Joyce and the Revolution of the Word*, Macmillan, London.

Miller, D.A. (1981) *Narrative and its Discontents: Problems of Closure in the Traditional Novel*, Princeton University Press, Princeton.

Needham, Gwendolyn B. (1990) 'The Undisciplined Heart of David Copperfield', in *David Copperfield*, ed. Jerome H. Buckley, Norton, New York and London, pp. 794–805 [first published 1954].

Propp, Vladimir (1968) *The Morphology of the Folktale*, University of Texas Press, Austin [first published 1928].

Salinger, J.D. (1958) *The Catcher in the Rye*, Penguin, Harmondsworth [first published 1951].

Watt, Ian (1957) *The Rise of the Novel: Studies in Defoe, Richardson and Fielding*, University of California Press, Berkeley.

# UNIT 3

# Studying drama

*Michael Patterson*

## What is a play?

One glance at the text of a play shows striking differences from poetry or narrative fiction. In the play text we find the following:

1. 'Stage-directions' with brief general descriptions of location and character (like a short-hand version of those found in a novel);
2. Dialogue introduced simply and formally by each character's name (again like a schematized version of dialogue passages from a novel);
3. 'Acts' and 'scenes' dividing the text into separate chunks of continuous time;
4. Above all a sense that what is being read is intended for performance by live actors in front of a live audience.

In fact, much drama that the student encounters may well not be mediated by the written word. It is possible to have read *Hamlet*, for example, as a piece of literature without ever having seen it performed. But when did you ever read the Christmas pantomime that you went to as a child or peruse the script of the television soap opera that you saw last week?

The origins of the word 'drama' reinforce this sense of a play being less a literary text than a blueprint for performance, for 'drama' derives from the Greek verb *dran*, meaning 'to do, act or perform' (and a common division for the sections of a play is the 'act'). As we shall see, what distinguishes drama from other genres is this overriding awareness that a play 'imitates an action'.

Other related words point in the same direction: the word 'theatre' derives from the Greek *theatron*, 'a place for viewing', which in turn comes from the Greek verb meaning 'to behold', *theasthai* (and we often talk about going to the theatre as 'seeing a *show*'). A particularly intriguing word is the noun the English language uses to describe a written text for the stage, 'play', and we may also recall that a now old-fashioned term for actors was 'players'.

We normally associate the word 'play' with children. It is what happens when youngsters get together to act out roles, 'Nurses and Doctors', 'Mothers and Fathers', or whatever. Children recreate in their imaginations situations they have encountered in 'real' life, and they may well dress up, perhaps paint their faces, adopt vocal and physical mannerisms observed from adults, and create a locale in which the action takes place, using a couch as an operating table or a corner of the room as an office or kitchen. This is the world of 'make-believe', and in this respect the play in the theatre is not dissimilar from the play of children. Here too the actors wear costume and greasepaint, perform roles observed from the external world and pretend to the audience that the action is taking place in a setting defined by scenery and lighting.

At a deeper level too, 'the play's the thing', as Hamlet says. It is true that for children play has some functional value, in that it prepares them for an adult existence and also helps them to cope with the pressures they encounter in real life (smacking a teddy-bear for being naughty may be just what is needed to become reconciled to the complexities of adult discipline). But it would be far-fetched to claim that children play only to serve some specific purpose. It seems a natural impulse, not confined to children alone, to pursue some activity that has no significant utilitarian function. As Schiller pointed out, there is a difference between actions that are purposeful and those which are purposive. A horse in a field suddenly breaking into a canter may be exercising its muscles, and yet there seems to be a playfulness about its behaviour which takes us beyond the mere serving of a physical purpose ('purposeful') and into a realm of free expression, that cannot be described merely in terms of its usefulness. And yet this free expression is not random; it will follow quite precise rules, pursuing its own purpose, whether it is the child who knows that the couch is an operating table and not an ambulance, the man who plays rugby according to carefully laid down laws which are being constantly adjudicated on by a referee, or a horse that will determine to cease its canter at one spot and no other. Such behaviour is definitely not random, but 'purposive'.

The same holds good for drama. More than most art forms, it has been called on to justify itself. There have been many attempts throughout the history of the theatre to prove its social usefulness, most recently by arguing that drama is a way of increasing political awareness. But we can recognize that these utilitarian justifications are not in themselves sufficient. In the theatrical play we encounter purposive play in its wider sense. What seeing a drama on stage offers, unless the performance fails totally, is the experience of transcendence. For as long as the play lasts, we transcend the limits of our own lives and involve ourselves with our imaginations in the lives of others, their milieu, their aspirations, their conflicts and their fates. This coming out of our selves may be socially useful, but it is something more than that. This willingness to 'play' at being someone else, whether as performer or spectator, is what determines our humanity, and throughout the ages the theatre has not only been the home of the 'play' but has also offered a safe but challenging opportunity for the human activity of 'play'.

## What distinguishes drama from poetry and narrative fiction?

Of course, the experience of transcendence is not confined to drama. The reader of poetry may join Wordsworth as he encounters a field full of daffodils, and the reader of the novel may be on Robinson Crusoe's island, struggling with him to find means of survival. But each of these is reported as though in the past: 'I wandered lonely as a cloud ...', 'I was born in the year 1632 ...'. Even where the present tense is adopted, as in some lyric poetry or even occasionally in the novel with the use of the historic present for especially vivid scenes, there is always the sense of distance, the sense that this is an emotion already experienced or an action that is now complete.

By contrast, drama communicates a sense of action in the present. Even if we know a play well, even if we are well aware that, for example, Hamlet – and many around him – will end up dead, we still enter into the game of suspense, and live through the tensions of the plot as it unfolds in front of us. Theatre persuades us much more than any other genre that we are experiencing events as they happen rather than looking back on the past. Drama is the genre of the present tense.

Another major distinguishing feature is the objectivity of drama. Most obviously lyric poetry expresses the individual and subjective emotions of the writer; but even the novel, except in some modernist cases, is written from the point of view either of a character or of a fixed narrator. What is different about drama is that, in the playwright Tom Stoppard's words, it gives the writer a wonderful opportunity to 'contradict himself in public'. The supremely skilled dramatist will so thoroughly submerge his or her identity in each of the characters, giving voice to each in turn, that it becomes difficult to establish what the writer's own opinions are. Our 'reading' of a play is dependent on our own experience of living through the events described and on drawing our own conclusions from them, for here there will be no poet pouring out his feelings nor generally any narrator reflecting on what has taken place.

Because the events described by a play are normally intended to be enacted in a theatre performance which will usually last for fewer than four hours, often for less than half that time, then there is a tendency for drama to pursue a concentration of time. At its extreme this may mean that stage time equals real time, so that what happens on stage lasts just as long as it would in reality. Quite often events are divided into several 'acts', which allow a passage of time to elapse before the next sequence of continuous action, even when sometimes as in the break between the third and fourth acts of Chekhov's *The Seagull*, many years may have passed.

In addition to concentration of time there is also compression of time: even where the events of a whole day pass before us on stage, we may be asked to believe that they are happening in a matter of minutes. So in the scene in Act II of *King Lear*, where Kent is put in the stocks, the action begins at dawn with Oswald unable to recognize Kent in the dim morning light and ends with an impending storm, as 'the night comes on'. Helped by a monologue by Edgar, which splits the scene, the audience accepts that time has passed so quickly that we have moved from sunrise to sunset within some twenty minutes.

By contrast, the novel will usually range over a period of years, and no attempt is made to relate reading time to actual time. Similarly, the novel can change location at will, free to move with the reader's imagination, unhindered by any consideration of establishing the setting other than with words. The stage play, even when played on the bare stage of the Elizabethan and Jacobean theatre, has to make sure that the audience understands where it is at any given moment and so is limited in the number of changes of location that it can effect. When the play is intended to be performed with a high level of realism, as, for example, in much of the work of George Bernard Shaw, then the need to define the location precisely and within feasible technical means, may compel the action of the play to remain in one location, e.g. in the single drawing-room settings beloved of many dramatists from the latter half of the nineteenth century onwards.

Finally, the major distinction between drama and poetry or narrative fiction is the one referred to above, namely that drama is written with the intention of being performed. It is true that poetry can be recited or sung, and this was the prevailing form of delivery for centuries until the growth of widespread literacy. The novel too can be read aloud, and spoken narrative fiction now forms part of the staple diet of BBC Radio. But, generally speaking, poetry and fiction are enjoyed by the reader alone, turning to this enjoyment according to individual choice. Plays can be read in the same way and enjoyed purely as literature. However, similar to the musical score that is only fully realized by being performed in a concert, drama achieves its full potential only when presented on stage.

Until very recently, such enactment of a dramatic text could take place at one's own home and at one's own convenience, only if one were rich or powerful enough to engage one's own theatre company. Now, with the invention of television and video recording, we may have royal command performances at will, merely by pressing a button or by sliding a cassette into its slot. Admittedly, this may not offer the same experience as a live performance, but we can gain access to superb performers and designers, costumes and sets at minimal cost to the spectator. With developments in the field of virtual reality, it is probably only a matter of time before it will be possible to have an experience that approximates very closely to a live performance.

However, for most of the history of drama, to see a play performed involved two things: a place, usually a building, set aside for the performance, and an agreement, usually announced by poster or other means, that performers and spectators would assemble at the same time for the performance to take place. Drama is intended to take place in a public situation. Indeed, with the exception of architecture, theatre is the most public of all the arts.

It is for this reason that the theatre has repeatedly been regarded as a threat to oppressive regimes and has been subjected to rigorous censorship, for the audience assembled in one place to witness a play poses a greater danger to the status quo than the same number of isolated individuals reading poems or novels, however subversive. The most recent case of the theatre acting as a focus for the aspirations of the community occurred in the former German Democratic Republic, where the theatres, together with churches, provided the buildings and the political fora for democratic debate that led directly to the collapse of the Communist regime.

Not only is drama typically experienced as a public rather than as a private event, but it is also a physical event, that is to say, while the study of poetry or the play requires no more than the printed word and the reader, drama to be fully experienced requires the physical presence of performers in a physical setting. The

Hamlet who dies in our presence may touch us more immediately and more deeply than one who speaks to us only from the page.

## Aristotle's theory of drama

We owe much of our thinking about drama, as well as the terms we use, to the Ancient Greeks. Apart from the models of the Greek tragedies, the earliest extant form of Western theatre, we look to a Greek philosopher, Aristotle, for the origins of dramatic theory. His *Poetics*, written about 330 BC, is not only the first discussion of drama, but it also dominated much European thinking about drama for around two millennia and is still a work of some relevance. It was he, who, in response to his philosophical mentor, Plato, who had condemned drama as not having any social use, made the first attempt to justify drama in terms of its 'purposefulness'. Let us dwell briefly on his theory of *catharsis*, even though we have already acknowledged that such utilitarian justification is undoubtedly misguided.

*Catharsis* was a medical term meaning purgation, a flushing out of the body, e.g. by taking a laxative. Aristotle argued that the experience of watching a tragedy gave the spectator catharsis of pity and fear, that is, rid us of these emotions by exercising them during the performance. The idea is that we become so involved in the fate of the tragic hero that we pity his downfall and fear for the outcome. By suffering in this way with the hero, we flush out these emotions and leave the theatre less pitying and less fearful. There are several objections to this idea. First, how can it be proved that these emotions are purged by experiencing them; might it not be argued that they could just as easily be reinforced? Secondly, it is clear that being less fearful might be socially useful, but why less pitying? For this one would have to enter into a debate into the differing values between our own society and that of Ancient Greece, where pity was less valued than in a Christian culture.

The debate about catharsis, which has consumed millions of words, is important in two respects: first, simply because it has preoccupied the minds of theorists throughout the ages; secondly, because it is the first and most famous example of the attempt to justify drama as being socially useful. In itself, however, it does not go very far in explaining how drama works.

Aristotle had more important things to say about the nature of drama, and here he is still useful. He defined tragedy, by which he meant serious drama as opposed to comedy, as 'the imitation of an action'. It is tempting to digress into a discussion about what is meant by 'imitation' (*mimesis*); obviously, it implies an attempt to reproduce reality on the stage, but equally clearly the theatre must observe so many conventions that an exact photographic reproduction of real life is out of the question (e.g. actors have to speak louder than in a normal conversational tone for the audience to know what is going on). But this is a question which all representational art is obliged to address, and our task here is to consider the special nature of drama.

Here the second keyword, 'action', is significant. Because play titles are often given in the form of a person's name, *King Oedipus*, *King Lear*, *Hamlet*, it is easy to assume that plays are about important individuals, that character lies at the centre of drama. But character is revealed and determined by the events of the play. Oedipus in himself is relatively unimportant, a moderately successful ruler of a small ancient city state; it is the fact that he has killed his father and married his mother that provides the possibility of his becoming a major tragic figure. Even in the richer psychological portrayals of post-Renaissance drama, character proceeds from action. Hamlet becomes Hamlet by virtue of events in Denmark, especially those associated with his father's death and his mother's remarriage.

Aristotle also usefully offered a list of the components of drama: Plot, Character, Dialogue, Meaning, Music and Performance. Less helpfully, Aristotle attempted to distinguish between drama and the epic (i.e. narrative fiction) by suggesting that the action of a play should be single, with no subplots, and that it normally takes place within twenty-four hours (whereas the epic, like the novel, thrives on subplots and may extend over a period of many years). We have seen that drama does indeed tend towards a greater concentration of both incident and time than in narrative forms. Unfortunately, however, and through no fault of Aristotle's, dramatic theorists of the seventeenth and eighteenth centuries seized on this part of the *Poetics* to establish the so-called Three Unities of Action, Time and Place. At its best, by the insistence on a unified plot which takes place within twenty-four hours and in one location, an intense and concentrated form of drama of immense power could be created, as in the finest tragedies of the French playwright, Racine. At its worst, the prescription could lead to lifeless or absurdly improbable dramas (even in one of the most popular tragedies in French, Corneille's *Le Cid* of 1637, the action is so packed with incidents in its twenty-four hour time-span that it has maliciously been called 'Le Cid's busy day'). Luckily for the English, the Unities made little impact on a nation poorly versed in neo-Aristotelian theory, and so Shakespeare has been able to exert his benign and powerful influence on world theatre, free from these prescriptive rules. Only in the seventeenth century were there some neo-classical experiments, as in the now rarely performed works of Dryden.

## The components of drama

### Plot

As we have seen, Aristotle emphasized the primacy of action and listed as the first of the elements of drama that of Plot. Plot (*mythos*) is quite different from mere story (*istoria*). The story is the raw material, which the playwright shapes into a plot. This is seen most easily in the use of historical subjects on stage, as in, for example, Shakespeare's exploitation of Holinshed's *Chronicles* for his history plays. The complexity of historical events needs to be simplified in order to become the stuff of a play. The Swiss playwright Friedrich Dürrenmatt once wondered whether Shakespeare could have written *Julius Caesar* had he known the detailed work of the Roman historian Mombert, because this scholarly account would surely have inhibited the boldness and clarity of Shakespeare's tragedy. A good dramatic plot is the carefully shaped version of a story.

To quote Aristotle again, 'a play must have a beginning, a middle and an end'. History, however, is all 'middle'. What is the beginning, for example, of the present conflict in Northern Ireland? The civil rights demands of the late 1960s? The partition of Ireland in the 1920s? Cromwell's expedition to Ireland in the seventeenth century? And so on. The playwright is obliged to choose a point at which to begin the play, and then inform the audience of what has preceded this by blending in an account of events leading up to this moment. This is called 'exposition'.

Exposition can be dealt with in quite unsubtle ways, as, for example, in the formal prologues one finds in Euripides – a short scene to establish the starting-point for the ensuing action, presented by one or two characters, who may then not reappear in the play itself. Even Shakespeare, as, for example, in *Cymbeline*, may resort to a quick recital of the background, as though eager to get on with the plot. In more modern plays, however, the tendency is to reveal the past gradually and naturalistically. A favourite device, as in Ibsen, is for one of the characters to reveal the situation to someone who is a partial stranger or who has been away for some time. Thus in Ibsen's *A Doll's House* Nora confesses her well-intentioned act of forgery to an old friend who has returned to the same town, and so allows the audience to know more than Nora's own husband.

Providing an end is also beset with difficulties, since, once again, history does not contain neat endings. Traditionally, one expects of a play that there will be a sense of completeness at the end – the finality of death in tragedy or the marriage of lovers in comedy. A tragic death offers a sense of finality and completeness to many serious dramas, even though there is often, as with Malcolm in *Macbeth* or Edgar in *King Lear*, a good character who points forward to a more hopeful future. Where a serious play ends without such a definite outcome, the piece may lack such a sense of completeness, leaving the audience wondering what will happen after the curtain has fallen: in *The Tempest* will Prospero be able to end his days in peace; in *Measure for Measure* can Isabella look forward to a happy marriage; in *A Doll's House* how long do we give Nora before she comes knocking on the door, wishing to return to her children and husband? In the case of more realistic drama, the sense of finality is even harder to achieve than in more poetic forms, because we know that in fact life does not yield a clear ending, as Aristotle demands. So when the actor hangs himself at the end of Gorky's *The Lower Depths* or Hedda shoots herself in the final moments of Ibsen's *Hedda Gabler*, we lack a sense that these deaths proceed inevitably from the situation of the play; they seem almost arbitrary. Perhaps it would have been a greater tragedy if these despairing individuals were obliged to live on in the miserable circumstances of their lives.

## Character

Much more so than in the novel, character in drama is revealed through action. In place of often lengthy description, used by the novelist when introducing a character, the way we get to know about the character of those on stage is primarily from what they do and what they say. Their appearance (whether based on stage-directions for the reader or on what the audience sees in performance) and what other people may say about them, will affect our view of them initially, but we eventually form our own judgements about them from their behaviour and their speech. Indeed, by having a negative or ridiculous character express opinions about a character before their appearance, an audience may be already persuaded to adopt the opposite attitude before the character has even entered (thus in the masterfully constructed play by Molière, *Le Tartuffe*, Orgon's absurdly solicitous questions about Tartuffe alert our suspicions as to the true nature of this classic hypocrite, before Tartuffe has even entered).

Because characters are determined by the situation of the drama in which they appear, they have little existence outside the drama. A rather silly critic once wrote a book on the childhood of Shakespeare's heroines – silly, because Lady Macbeth or Desdemona come into being only by virtue of being elements of the plot of the plays in which they appear. Beyond the five acts of *Macbeth* or *Othello* they cease to exist. The novel, by contrast, will either provide us with such background information or will allow us legitimately to speculate about characters' past lives.

The concept of character has evolved considerably in the history of drama. The first examples of 'character' were in the form of chorus leaders. Their function was to provide an individual voice, inviting responses from the chorus (apparently not dissimilar from the presumed origins of medieval drama in the *quem quaeritis?* liturgy). *The Danaids* of Aeschylus still essentially retains the form of these original dithyrambs, but in Aeschylus' other plays recognizable characters (e.g. Orestes, Clytemnestra) are portrayed for the first time in the history of Western drama. Sophocles took a further step by allowing three characters to appear on the stage at once, thus extending the possibilities of dramatic interaction. The notion of character is taken further still in Euripides, who portrays extreme types, for example, Medea, a woman driven to take the lives of her own children.

Despite these developments, throughout the drama of the Greek and medieval periods characters remained generalized figures with little psychological nuance. With a greater emphasis on realistic portrayal in the Renaissance, dramatic characters assumed a new level of psychological complexity. Thus *Hamlet* is not just the study of a young prince denied his inheritance and urged to revenge by the ghost of his dead father; it is also a subtle portrayal of a unique and complex individual. The figure of King Lear carries metaphysical resonances but he is real enough to shout for his dinner, to get soaking wet in a storm and to ask for a button to be undone at the most profound tragic moment.

It is this kind of character we are most familiar with today: what E.M. Forster in the novel called 'rounded characters'. So much so, that Brecht's experiments with 'flat characters', especially in his *Lehrstücke* (teaching plays) of the 1930s, seemed positively avant-garde.

Most dramatic characters on the stage today, and almost without exception those in film and television, are in the naturalistic mode, which became the dominant style in playwriting towards the end of the nineteenth century and is associated with writers like Ibsen, Strindberg, Shaw, Chekhov, Gorky and Hauptmann. In the case of such characters we are aware that they are not only determined by the dramatic situation but are also products of their heredity and environment. In this way such drama comes closer to the novel, and speculation about a character's existence outside the play is no longer such an absurdity as it is in enquiring after the childhood of Shakespeare's heroines.

Indeed, just at the time that naturalistic playwriting first began to flourish, perhaps the most decisive influence on modern theatre, the theatre director Konstantin Stanislavski, began his explorations of character, for example, in *An Actor Prepares* (1926). One of his methods was to seek out the 'given circumstances' of a character, so that an actor in approaching a role would be required, from clues in the text and from informed imagination, to provide a full biographical background for the character, right down to details about income, home life and, yes, childhood. This, allied with a conscious investigation of the psychological motivation of a character in Stanislavski's notions of 'objective' and 'super-objective', helped an actor to round out dramatic roles that might otherwise be flat. This is summed up in his oft-quoted dictum: 'There are no small parts, only small actors'.

This modern emphasis on psychological characterization has extended to the thinking of critics about the nature of drama. The Shakespearian scholar, A.C. Bradley, became notorious for discussing Shakespeare's protagonists in terms of fatal flaws in their characters: ambition in Macbeth, vacillation in Hamlet, etc. Such reductionist thinking also used to inform the silly examination questions, now fortunately rare, of the type: 'Give a character sketch of either Gertrude or Polonius or Laertes' – as though these figures have an existence as individuals divorced from the dramatic situation in which they find themselves.

As with Brecht, several modern playwrights have challenged what may be regarded as an outmoded concept of character. In particular, Samuel Beckett has created characters without a past or any of the 'given circumstances' one may legitimately establish with a naturalistic character. It would be especially pointless to attempt to trace the childhood of Vladimir and Estragon and would make little sense to propose where Pozzo and Lucky live. In a less abstract manner Harold Pinter has created characters who refuse to reveal their backgrounds, often to the annoyance of audiences. Who is Stanley in *The Birthday Party*, where has Davies in *The Caretaker* actually come from? As Pinter wrote: 'The desire for verification is understandable but cannot always be satisfied'.

The advantage of non-naturalistic characters like those of the Ancient Greeks or the tramps of Beckett is that, freed of the accidents of individuality, they can more easily become representative of the human condition. The advantage of realistic characters, as John Peter persuasively argues in his excellent book, *Vladimir's Carrot*, is that we can match their behaviour against our own. By contrast, the implications of a piece like *Waiting for Godot* form what Peter calls a 'perlocutionary act', that is, a statement not open to debate or challenge.

## Dialogue

Dialogue has undergone a similar transformation to character, crudely stated, from the poetic to the realistic. Until the eighteenth century almost all serious drama in

Western Europe was written in verse. Moreover, in classical and neo-classical drama the same linguistic register would be maintained in all the dialogue, so a messenger would speak like a king and a serving-woman like a queen. Once again, it is Shakespeare in which we encounter differentiated dialogue in his blank verse, often moving from poetry to prose to reflect status. More and more, stage dialogue has come to imitate everyday speech, from the prose dialogue of eighteenth-century middle-class tragedies to the seemingly authentic dialogue of Ibsen's plays.

In fact, of course, realistic dialogue only gives the impression of genuine speech. Conversations are set out as logically developed sequences, with each interlocutor normally waiting patiently for the other to finish before speaking. Attempts have subsequently been made to approach more closely to actual speech patterns, e.g. by Harold Pinter in his observation of the way people speak past each other without responding to each other's thoughts, or more recently in Caryl Churchill's device of organizing dialogue, so that one character begins speaking before another has finished.

However, even in these cases, dialogue in the theatre is a carefully contrived means of communication. Usually devoid of false starts, ellipses and non sequiturs, stage dialogue, even in its apparently most naturalistic manifestations, is as false as the scenery that surrounds it.

## Performance (theatrical elements)

As has been observed above, the written text is merely the basis or blueprint for performance. It has certain advantages over the performed play: it is usually more accessible (it is easier to walk down the road and buy *Hamlet* from the local bookshop than it is to find a production of it, convenient in time and place); one can stop and reread difficult or intriguing passages, whereas in performance you will hear the words spoken only once; it will represent best the author's intentions, since there can be no bizarre directorial intervention, no weak acting nor inappropriate costumes to mislead. But normally a play is written to be performed, and the student of drama should be literate in theatrical elements in order to understand fully what the written text contains.

The main areas to be considered are these: the physical setting (stage decor, lighting, sound); the appearance of the characters (costume, make-up, moves); and the manner in which the lines are delivered (intonation, pace, volume, etc.). The student should develop a sensitivity towards these elements almost as much as to the words on the page. Each element of performance contains theatrical 'signs', and the study of these signs is called 'semiotics'. Unlike the language of literary criticism, the language of semiotics is relatively recent and contains what seems on first acquaintance to be impenetrable jargon. It is all too easy to treat semiotic analysis as though in itself it unlocks an understanding of a play in performance. It won't, any more than a detailed metrical analysis of *Ode on a Grecian Urn* will explain what the special qualities of that poem are. Semiotics can act as a useful tool and offer a more scientific approach to performance than subjective and impressionistic responses will yield, but it remains a tool for analyzing performance, not an end in itself.

The opening stage directions, however sparse, will usually give an indication of where the action is set – for the whole play if there is no change of setting, for each scene if the action moves from place to place. The theatrical conditions of the day will affect the playwright's decision about setting. Shakespeare, writing for a bare stage, on which the location was established primarily through the dialogue, was free to roam across continents and to play scenes out of doors as often as indoors. By the end of the nineteenth century the theatre audience demanded authentic settings, and thus many plays were written for one location, usually an interior, in order to allow an elaborately authentic set to be constructed on stage. Where playwrights diverged from this, as, for example, Ibsen in his *Peer Gynt* (1867), the work was usually designated a 'dramatic poem' and was rarely performed and then only with massive cuts.

Even in quite realistic pieces, the setting, which will be created by stage scenery, by lighting and, to some extent, by sound effects, will make a statement about the play. This is where semiotic analysis may prove useful. The semiotician C.S. Peirce distinguished between the 'icon', the 'index' and the 'symbol'. Much of the time a theatrical sign will be all three. To take an example: when Ibsen's *A Doll's House* opens, we see a Christmas tree on stage. It is an icon, that is, in the first instance it is what it is, a Christmas tree (although admittedly placed there by the set designer or property manager and not by the family in the play, and possibly artificial, in order to stand up to the hot lights night after night of the play's run; therefore it is an 'icon' rather than the 'real thing'). It also has an 'indexical' function: it points to the fact that the play is set at or around Christmas. Finally, it has a 'symbolic' function: the tree represents family togetherness, domestic bliss and the renewal of life. Significantly, when Nora's domestic happiness is under threat, we see how the second act opens with the tree 'stripped of its ornaments and with burnt-down candle-ends on its dishevelled branches'.

Similarly, lighting may make statements about the action of the play. To cite another example from realistic drama, Ibsen's *The Wild Duck*, the fourth act opens with the room lit by afternoon sunshine. As the father of the family, Hjalmar Ekdal, learns the truth about his daughter's illegitimacy, night falls, and the final act with its tragic outcome is played out in 'a cold, grey morning light'. Sound, while usually only an intermittent element, may also provide a strong theatrical sign, perhaps most famously in the off-stage sound of the first cherry tree being cut down at the end of Chekhov's *The Cherry Orchard*, the icon of a tree being felled but also a significant comment on the destruction of the natural world to service the needs of the rich.

The appearance, gestures and moves of characters on stage also all have their meaning. Each costume, each hairstyle will tell us something about characters before they speak, and some playwrights are at great pains to describe them exactly on their first entrances. Once on stage, the way an actor gestures on a line or moves across the room may tell us more about what is going on than the lines that are being spoken. Equally, the way in which the lines are delivered may reveal the character's actual thoughts, what Stanislavski called the 'subtext', more powerfully than the actual dialogue. Most poetic drama is explicit, that is to say, what a character says will usually represent the actual opinion of that character. Where the character is deliberately deceitful, as with Iago, the audience is informed first by a soliloquy that the lines spoken will obscure the truth. When we come to the more realistic dialogue of nineteenth- and twentieth-century drama, soliloquies become impossible, because people do not talk to themselves much less to the audience. So before a line the playwright will often provide a gesture or move (e.g. 'placing his head in his hands', 'jumps up') or an adverb (e.g. 'animatedly') in order to define more precisely what the line contains. One might try the following experiment: take a line like 'I shall come and see you every day' and see how many different ways it may be spoken – from a declaration of love to a vicious threat, from joyful anticipation to the dread of an unpleasant chore. It will soon become clear how dependent the meaning especially of realistic plays may be on a sympathetic performance.

Using the word 'sympathetic' introduces another dimension, that of 'interpretation', whether by performer, set, costume or lighting designer, or by the person ultimately responsible for the overall impact of the performance, the director. Edward Gordon Craig, the great director, designer and theorist, prominent especially in the early years of this century, once declared that if one went to see Shakespeare performed, one would never see the play itself, only one company's version of it. This is possibly true: how can a single evening in the theatre embrace all that *King Lear* contains? A director and the cast will have to focus on that aspect of the play which to them is the most important to communicate to an audience. If they do not find a focus, then the result will inevitably be a dull affair, for as Peter Brook has rightly said, if one lets 'a play speak for itself', one may find that it has nothing to say. In the process of establishing this 'reading' of a play, certain distortions may occur, and the production may do a disservice to the original. In the case of Shakespeare, this may not be very important; there will be many other productions to act as a corrective to one individual aberration. With a lesser known playwright the theatregoer may be misled by an ill-conceived rendering of the piece into forming a false opinion of its worth. Thus, while the experience of performance is valuable, the student of drama should never rely wholly on a theatrical experience for a true understanding. (Performance and theatre practice in Shakespeare are dealt with in Unit 5, pp. 99–105.)

## Dramatic genres

### Tragedy

It is a curious fact, quite unlike narrative fiction and poetry, that most of the finest drama involves the experience of watching someone die, in the genre we call tragedy. It also appears to be a pastime peculiar to the Western world, for the dramas of other cultures may present heroic tales which involve death but they do not regard dying as the primary focus. Does this mean, as Rousseau suggested, that we merely take a sadistic delight in observing the misfortunes of others, or has our fascination with tragedy a more profound source?

To answer this, it helps to consider how we use the word tragedy in an everyday context (a proposal considered by Geoffrey Brereton in his book *Principles of Tragedy*, 1968). 'Airliner tragedy' as a newspaper headline has certain immediate connotations. First, it must involve death, probably the deaths of several individuals. 'Airliner tragedy: everyone survives' would be a nonsense; there can be no recovery from a tragedy. Secondly, the word 'tragedy' lends status to the event. 'Airliner tragedy' sounds much more meaningful than 'airliner disaster'.

At the root of Greek tragedy (for it was in Ancient Greece that tragedy was born) is the dual recognition that humankind suffers terribly but that the suffering is not without meaning. If we take the case of *King Oedipus* we encounter a man who unknowingly kills his father and marries his mother and is punished with guilt, self-blinding and banishment. It would be easy enough, as the Roman dramatist Seneca did in his later version, to regard Oedipus as the innocent victim of a particularly malicious fate. But this is not the Greek view. Sophocles is at pains to report Oedipus' uncertainty about his parentage and the clear warning that was given to him by the oracle. Despite this he killed a man old enough to be his father and married a woman old enough to be his mother, without either him or his fellow Thebans being able to contemplate the awful truth. He is not wicked, but he has been very neglectful – and he must pay terribly for his mistake (the *hamartia* or false step, of which Aristotle writes in his *Poetics*). It is as though, in Gilbert Murray's image, the tragic hero drinks water in a city where typhus is rife – it is not an evil act, but a very foolish one, and the consequences are out of all proportion to the cause. Oedipus had at least the privilege of being warned about his future; for the bulk of humanity we must simply tread carefully, aware that existence is a precarious business, knowing that overconfidence (hubris) will invariably be punished by downfall (nemesis). Is then the implication of classical tragedy that we should all become meek beings, humbly submitting to our fate, the kind of reading that made Brecht reject what he called 'Aristotelian theatre'?

This would be to overlook our admiration for the tragic hero. In retrospect Oedipus was not careful enough. But what would we want him to do on learning from the oracle that he was to kill his father and marry his mother? Go home to his supposed parents and sit around waiting for the prophecy to be fulfilled? On the contrary we admire his active moral sense in attempting to avert the oracle, his courage in going into voluntary exile in order not to incur this terrible guilt. The hideous, the 'tragic' irony is that it is this brave moral decision which puts him on the road to Thebes and so initiates the very crimes he is seeking to avoid.

What we have in tragedy, then, is the recognition that the world is an ordered place, that events are not governed by chance, that those who defy the order of this world will suffer terribly, but that their defiance is a magnificent gesture of the human spirit. To the Eastern mind such defiance against what is ordained is anything but admirable; it is a pathetic display of human egocentricity. Tragedy is a peculiarly Western and humanistic phenomenon.

Significantly, there was no tragedy in this sense to be found in the drama of the Middle Ages, a period in which profound religious faith urged total obedience to God's will. It was with the new humanism of the Renaissance and the rediscovery of classical models that tragedy once again was written for the European theatre. In Shakespeare we find all the major tragic elements: the sense of a great figure who refuses to conform, to take the easy way out, to accept his fate, and thus who plunges himself and others into tragic downfall. If only Hamlet could forget the nagging of the ghost of his dead father and become friends with Claudius; if only Othello didn't get so worried about the kind of flirtation that was no doubt common enough in Venice; if only Lear could forget what he feels he is owed by his daughters and settle down to an uncomplaining old age by the fire; if only Macbeth could laugh off the witches' prophecies and retire to quiet domesticity in Dunsinane; then all these figures would avoid their tragedies but they would lose our respect. Even the bloody and violent Macbeth gains our admiration for his energy and passion and allows us to suspend our moral judgement about the murders he commits. These are figures in whom we see our humanity writ large, and so their downfall does not leave us only with a sense of loss but also of triumph, a recognition that they have lived their lives to bursting point and must now pay the ultimate price for their vastness of spirit.

It is now a commonplace to speak of the 'death of tragedy', and indeed the phenomenon is eloquently discussed by George Steiner in his book of that name. Many reasons may be given for the demise of tragedy: the loss of religious faith, which means that we no longer believe that life conforms to a pattern; the loss of a sense of human individuality (as Dürrenmatt suggested, the modern version of *King Oedipus* would be: 'Creon's secretaries dispose of the case of Oedipus'); coupled with this, the loss of admiration for the great heroic figure, a not unreasonable democratically inspired view that no death is ultimately more significant than any other; perhaps above all, a superficial familiarity with death on a vast scale, fed by daily reports on television, radio and the press, of famine, atrocities and natural disasters, so that the demise of one individual cannot move us in the way it did our forebears, to whom death was more immediate and more special.

While it is certainly true that tragedies in the conventional sense are no longer being written, continuing attempts are made to re-present tragic insights on the modern stage. Already in the eighteenth century, with playwrights like George Lillo in England, Denis Diderot in France and Gotthold Ephraim Lessing in Germany, attempts were made to write 'bourgeois tragedies', and this search to introduce a sense of the tragic into middle-class and eventually into working-class situations has been a feature of much writing for the stage since. A recent example is that of Arthur Miller's *Death of a Salesman* (1949). (See also Unit 15, pp. 430–2.) As the title announces, we are to be shown one of the essential components of tragedy, the death of the central figure. The great difference from Ancient Greek or Shakespearian tragedy is that here the 'tragedy' focuses not on a larger-than-life heroic figure but on a very ordinary travelling salesman, whose very name, Willy Loman (=low man), is a reminder of his inferior status. Already the naturalist German playwright Gerhart Hauptmann had in his play *The Rats* of 1911 declared: 'In art as before the law all men are equal', and these sentiments are echoed by Mrs Loman:

> I don't say he's a great man. Willy Loman never made a lot of money. His name was never in the paper. He's not the finest character that ever lived. But he's a human being, and a terrible thing is happening to him. So attention must be paid. (*Death of a Salesman*, Act One)

Despite these assertions, such middle-class tragedies do not provide a sound basis for writing tragedy for the modern stage. The problem was summed up by the nineteenth-century German playwright Friedrich Hebbel as 'thirty taler moments', that is to say, that most of such tragedies could be averted by throwing a sizeable sum of money, 'thirty talers', onto the stage. If Willy Loman had won a sufficiently large amount of money, he could have given up his dismal job as an unsuccessful salesman, bought a ranch, and lived happily ever after. No gifts of thirty talers can save Oedipus, Lear or Hamlet. They still retain the freedom to incur guilt; their tragedy is absolute and not dependent on the conditionality of social situation. Only occasionally, as in the magnificent unfinished work *Woyzeck* by Georg Büchner, written in 1837 but seemingly much more contemporary, do we have a sense of the tragic associated with a poor and simple individual. A man, who is tormented by the infidelity of his mistress and who takes her and then (probably) his own life, would find no escape, even if offered thirty talers. But even here, as with more modern attempts to write tragedy, the play may generate pathos towards a victim; it does not create that mixed sense of admiration and horror, which we detected to be at the centre of classical tragedy.

## Comedy

Comedy, by contrast, thrives well on the modern stage. Comedy has always been a more populist form than tragedy. Perhaps we are fortunate that the writings of Aristotle on comedy were lost, so that there could be no neo-Aristotelian stranglehold on much subsequent European theatre as there was with the genre of tragedy. But comedy anyway usually finds its plot and characters in everyday figures from common life. Indeed, before *Woyzeck* any working-class figure, even in a serious work, was generally introduced only as a figure of fun.

Comedy, too, originated in Ancient Greece, deriving from fertility festivals: hence the common ending of most classical comedy in the marriage of young lovers ('just when their problems really begin', as a cynic once observed). The structure of traditional comedy is that of two lovers who find their path to happiness blocked by a figure with some power over them, often an older man, perhaps the father of the young woman. When this blocking figure is removed, or his attitude changed, the lovers can come together, and audience and lovers can celebrate a happy ending. Frequently the blocking figure is dominated by a particular vice; indeed, the titles of many of Molière's plays indicate this: *The Miser*, *The Hypochondriac*, *The Misanthrope*. Thus the audience receives the satisfaction of being strengthened in its sense of normality by being invited to mock the exaggerated behaviour of these comic figures. And here we run into difficulties, for, while we can laugh at excessive miserliness or obsession with health, the figure of Alceste, the 'misanthrope', seems to our modern way of thinking a quite sympathetic individual who is honestly rude to those he despises, but then we do not share the concern of Molière's age with social form. It is an indicator that comedy derives much more closely from the social context in which it is written and therefore seldom possesses the universal impact of tragedy.

A play with a comic structure may also occasionally develop such seriousness of theme that we no longer regard it as a comedy. If we take Shakespeare's *Measure for Measure*, for instance, then we find all the essential elements of comedy: two lovers whose happiness is threatened by a blocking character, Angelo, who through deception is led into his own downfall, and a 'happy ending' with the lovers brought together again and other marriages impending. However, these 'comic' elements are treated with such seriousness, with a death sentence hanging over the lovers, with Angelo a disturbingly manipulative hypocrite and not a figure of fun, with Isabella almost destroyed by the choice she is faced with, and finally with the ambiguity of the ending in which Isabella, who has been so determined to preserve her chastity, is now to be taken off to the Duke's wedding-bed. Critics, searching for a label to put on such work, have sometimes used the term, 'black comedy'.

'Black comedy' (or, in our more politically correct times, 'grotesque comedy') has become a popular form of comedy in the recent past, whether in the surreal images of Ionesco's 'Theatre of the Absurd' or the disturbing situations of Pinter's so-called 'Comedies of Menace'. If we examine, for example, the comedies of Joe Orton, we discover a reversal of classical comedy. In traditional comedy society was secure, and the laughter was generated by those individuals who stepped beyond social norms and attracted ridicule to them. In a writer like Joe Orton, and this is of course an especially modern way of looking at things, society itself is out of joint and laughable.

In conventional comedy the audience was reinforced in its social behaviour; in tragedy it was confirmed in its common humanity. Deprived of a strong sense of both social stability and religious faith, the modern theatre has had to go beyond traditional genres to find ways of addressing its audience.

## Tragi-comedy

Akin to 'black comedy' is the genre of tragi-comedy, in which the serious is blended with the comic. In his 'tragi-comedies' Sean O'Casey sometimes played on the tension between laughter and pain. So at the end of *Juno and the Paycock*, when Captain Boyle staggers on to the stage with his old friend Joxer and they reel around drunkenly in a room stripped of furniture and abandoned by Boyle's wife and daughter, the audience may laugh at their inebriated antics, but they will be unable to forget the desolation of Boyle's situation.

Such deliberate mixing of the genres has been brilliantly exploited by O'Casey's fellow countryman, Samuel Beckett. It was the German Romantic writer, Jean-Paul Richter, who distinguished between the satirist and the humourist. The former points at others and laughs at their follies, as Molière does in his comedies; the humourist includes himself and the follies of all humankind in his laughter. Life itself is perceived to be absurd, the biggest joke of all. So, in a play like *Waiting for Godot*, the unfulfilled waiting for someone who will never come offers us a view of humankind as abandoned in an existential void, but there is much laughter in this recognition, for as Nell says in Beckett's *Endgame*: 'There is nothing so funny as unhappiness.' So, as Vladimir and Estragon prepare to hang themselves, Estragon's trousers drop to the ground in one of the oldest gags in show-business.

In a writer like Beckett we can see how tragic recognition can be reinterpreted for the modern stage. At the end of *Godot* all may seem, in the words of *King Lear*, 'cheerless, dark and deadly', but as with *Lear* we have the comfort of our common humanity and the laughter we share to reinforce it. In this way tragi-comedy does not represent a dilution of the conventional genres but rather a mutual strengthening to meet the demands of our contemporary world.

## *BIBLIOGRAPHY*

Aristotle (1965) *The Poetics*, Heinemann, London [written *c*. 330 BC].

Banham, Martin (ed.) (1988) *The Cambridge Guide to World Theatre*, Cambridge University Press, Cambridge.

Barker, Harley Granville (1963) *Prefaces to Shakespeare*, 4 vols, Batsford, London.

Bentley, Eric (1968) *The Theory of the Modern Stage*, Penguin, Harmondsworth.

Brereton, Geoffrey (1968) *Principles of Tragedy*, Routledge & Kegan Paul, London.

Brown, John Russell (1969) *Shakespeare's Plays in Performance*, Penguin, Harmondsworth.

Brown, John Russell (ed.) (1995) *Oxford Illustrated History of Theatre*, Oxford University Press, Oxford.

Cole, Toby (ed.) (1961) *Playwrights on Playwriting*, Hill & Wang, New York.

Craig, Edward Gordon (1956) *On the Art of the Theatre*, Heinemann, London [first published 1914].

Dürrenmatt, Friedrich (1976) *Writings on Theatre and Drama*, Cape, London.

Elam, Keir (1980) *The Semiotics of Theatre and Drama*, Methuen, London.

Gascoigne, Bamber (1968) *World Theatre: An Illustrated History*, Ebury, London.

Hawkins-Dady, Mark (ed.) (1992, 1994) *International Directory of Theatre, 1: Plays, 2: Playwrights*, St. James Press, London.

Hilton, Julian (1987) *Performance*, Macmillan, Basingstoke.

Hirst, David L. (1984) *Tragicomedy*, Methuen, London.

Kitto, H.D.F. (1956) *Form and Meaning in Drama*, Methuen, London.

Kitto, H.D.F. (1961) *Greek Tragedy*, Methuen, London.

Nicoll, Allardyce (1923–59) *A History of English Drama 1660–1900*, 6 vols, Cambridge University Press, Cambridge.

Nicoll, Allardyce (1976) *World Drama*, 2nd edn, Harrap, London.

Peter, John (1987) *Vladimir's Carrot*, Deutsch, London.

Robertson, J.G. (1939) *Lessing's Dramatic Theory*, Cambridge University Press, Cambridge.

Salgado, Gamini (1980) *English Drama: A Critical Introduction*, Arnold, London.

Schiller, Friedrich (1993) *Essays*, ed. W. Hinderer, Continuum Publishing Co., New York.

Stanislavski, Konstantin (1980) *An Actor Prepares*, trans. E.R. Hapgood, Methuen, London [written 1926].

Steiner, George (1961) *The Death of Tragedy*, Faber, London.

Szondi, Peter (1987) *Theory of the Modern Drama*, ed. and trans. M. Hays, Polity Press, Cambridge.

Willett, John (ed.) (1964) *Brecht on Theatre*, Hill & Wang, New York.

Williams, Raymond (1968) *Drama in Performance*, Penguin, Harmondsworth.

Williams, Raymond (1969) *Drama from Ibsen to Brecht*, Oxford University Press, Oxford.

# SECTION 2

# Literary history

# UNIT 4

# The literature of pre-Renaissance England

*Philip Tilling*

Literature in English has, like the English people and language, undergone many transformations in its 1,400-year history. However, by the year 1500 or so (the traditional divide between the medieval and the modern), the basis of an English literary tradition had been clearly established. The major genres had been identified and there were clear ideas on form, style, language and the appropriate areas for literary exploration. Subsequent literary history is one of expansion, modification and experiment. The route towards this position is often tentative, irregular and confusing and is bound up with the history of the English people themselves. A reader who comes to the earliest literature in English unprepared will find it unfamiliar and difficult and in no obvious way English at all. The novels of Dickens, for example, hardly prepare us for the experience that is *Beowulf*.

## Old English literature

The earliest literature in English is essentially continental and Germanic and reflects the continental origins of the earliest English settlers (called Anglo-Saxons) who migrated to Britain from what is now northern Germany and southern Denmark in the late fourth and fifth centuries AD. These settlers brought with them their language (subsequently known by scholars as Old English) and a fully developed poetic style, through which they expressed their concerns and celebrated their heroes, both historical and legendary, in oral performance. Literature, as we may choose to call it, is at this stage entirely an oral art and the most enduring and effective form that this art took was poetry. Although there are signs of an Anglo-Saxon prose story-telling tradition (in parts of *The Anglo-Saxon Chronicle*, for instance), it has left little trace and creative, rather than purely functional, prose seems not to have emerged until the end of the Anglo-Saxon period.

Much of the Anglo-Saxon poetry that has survived is likely to have been created in oral performance and possibly reshaped and recreated through successive performances by the poet or *scop* who, in early Germanic society, was a learned man of high social status and was both poet and performer. Poems were only committed to writing late in the Anglo-Saxon period, when church and state together established the practice of written manuscript records. Consequently, there is often a wide disparity between the supposed date of a poem and the date of the manuscript in which it appears and we must also assume that what has survived represents only a fraction of what was at any time current. Although a few poets' names are known to us, most Anglo-Saxon poetry is anonymous, impersonal, thoroughly conventional and concerned with a limited number of reiterated themes.

Perhaps the most striking characteristic of Anglo-Saxon poetry is its conservatism. A single style prevails throughout the entire Anglo-Saxon period (from the sixth to the eleventh centuries), a style which fully reflects the oral origins of poetry, with its use of formulae, set-pieces and repetitions, all devised to assist a poet in the practice of his craft. Furthermore, the poet was required to express himself through an elaborate and exacting set of metrical rules, all of which derived from the nature of the spoken language. These rules depended on regular speech, yet they heightened and distilled it, both associating poetry with the spoken language yet, at the same time, distancing itself from it and marking itself out as special, as 'poetic' in fact. The tendency of Old English, in common with all the Germanic languages, to stress the root syllable of a word caused elaboration and ornamentation to be concentrated on the beginning of a word, in the form of alliteration or repetition of the same initial sound (only excepting vowels, which were allowed to alliterate together). Alliteration in Anglo-Saxon poetry was systematic and the poetic line is defined by the distribution of alliterating sounds between a fixed number of strongly stressed syllables (commonly four), arranged into two half-lines according to a limited number of patterns.

## Beowulf

Early Anglo-Saxon poetry is dominated by *Beowulf*, the only full-scale heroic epic to have survived from this period. Generalizations about the nature of the Anglo-Saxon epic based on *Beowulf* are likely to be risky, for the poem survives only in a single manuscript from the tenth century. The poem itself has been variously dated to the late seventh and early eighth centuries and is, on the face of it, deceptively simple. Beowulf, a warrior of the Geatish tribe in present-day southern Sweden, travels to Denmark to purge the Danish court of a marauding man-monster, called Grendel. Grendel is killed by Beowulf and so is his mother. Much later, back in Geatland, Beowulf, now an old king, kills a treasure-guarding dragon. Both Beowulf and the dragon are killed in the confrontation and Beowulf is succeeded as hero by his companion, the young Wiglaf. Much of *Beowulf* is pure folk tale and folk tale sources have indeed been established. The first surprise for a modern reader coming to *Beowulf* is that, language apart, there is nothing English about it. The setting is entirely Scandinavian and factual references within the poem are mostly to northern Germanic people and places. Grendel is clearly a Scandinavian troll. The Scandinavian link is reinforced by consideration of parallel tales (or analogues) of which there are several, notably the early fourteenth-century Icelandic prose saga *The Saga of Grettir the Strong* (*Grettissaga*). The most likely explanation is that both *Beowulf* and *Grettissaga* draw upon the same northern Germanic folk tale. Elsewhere, references to Scandinavian events and people of the sixth century AD may be explained by trading and cultural contacts between the East Anglians (with whom *Beowulf* is associated linguistically) and the Scandinavians or, perhaps, by the presence in the east of England of a tribe of Scandinavian settlers, whose presence may also be indicated by Swedish elements in the seventh-century ship-burial at Sutton Hoo, Suffolk.

Despite its apparent simplicity, *Beowulf* is artfully contrived and sophisticated in its structure. The three successive confrontations provide a basic tripartite structure and suggest that the tale was, in the first instance, told in three episodes. Cutting across this simple tripartite structure, however, is a further structure. Throughout the text, there are cryptic references to other personages and other deeds which, in contrast with the deeds of Beowulf and his non-human foes, are very much of the real, historical world. These references are among those which are sometimes, inappropriately, called 'digressions' and are carefully placed within the poem to contrast with, or comment on, events of the main narrative. Taken together, the events of this sub-plane concern the political and military affairs of Denmark and Sweden and become increasingly clear and coherent as the poem proceeds, binding the tripartite structure of the main narrative into a unified whole.

*Beowulf* presents the reader with a very clear picture of the Germanic warrior hero of the Dark Age period. He is, of course, of superlative strength, arrogant, self-confident, proud of his heroic deeds and of exceptional military ability, though, oddly, Beowulf is happier fighting monsters than men and his deeds in the world of men are dealt with rather summarily in the poem. The world of the hero is aristocratic and masculine and women play only a subservient role. A hero is driven by the desire to ensure a long-lasting reputation for himself and is loyally served by warriors who expect protection and reward for their service, in return for which they will fight to the death on behalf of their leader. Loyalty and disloyalty, through which such a society is threatened, are themes which are explored in both *Beowulf* and other Anglo-Saxon poems.

Whether we should regard *Beowulf* simply as a poetic narrative designed to entertain an early English audience interested in the deeds of strong men is a matter of continuing debate. Certainly, Beowulf acts as a deliverer of both the Danes and his own people and he finally meets his own death in the process. Through Beowulf, good undoubtedly triumphs despite obstacles both human and non-human. The issue is complicated by the Christian overtones within the poem which sometimes seem at odds with the generally pagan world of *Beowulf*, which would seem to be governed by a belief in fate (*wyrd*), though God is also often referred to. Furthermore, Grendel is unambiguously described as a descendant of the biblical Cain, the first murderer, in which case we might view Beowulf as a Christian avenger or even as a Christ-like figure who sacrifices himself in a Christian allegory. Given that the tenth-century manuscript was probably copied out in a monastic scriptorium (or writing room), there is also the possibility that the original text was tampered with, brought up to date, as it were, and given a Christian veneer.

Generally speaking, it seems reasonable to accept and judge *Beowulf* as we have it and to see it as a Christian poem, but a Christian poem about an age that was pagan. Hence the apparent mix of values. In any case, we should remember that Christianity was only gradually established in England throughout the seventh century and that a conscious attempt was made by the Christian missionaries to adapt to pagan practices and situations wherever possible. The nature of Anglo-Saxon Christianity was, in other words, quite different from that of the modern period and so was Anglo-Saxon Christian literature. This is plainly seen in those later Anglo-Saxon epic poems which are quite clearly Christian, such as *Judith* (the tale of the Old Testament Apocryphal heroine of the Jews who slew the Assyrian tyrant Holofernes) and *Elene* (which tells of St Helena, mother of the Christian Roman Emperor Constantine, and her search for the True Cross). In these poems, and others, the heroes, whether male or female, pursue their objectives with a ruthless determination that is worthy of any pagan hero. The only significant difference is that they fight in the name of God, rather than to establish a lasting reputation for themselves. The whole of the Anglo-Saxon period may, in fact, be seen as an age of transition from one set of values to another.

## Elegiac and meditational poetry

This spirit of transition is also encountered in *The Wanderer* and *The Seafarer*, the finest of a small group of poetic meditations on the theme of loss which are commonly known as 'elegies'. Both poems are usually dated later than *Beowulf* and are clearly Christian, but both, to a greater or lesser degree, seem to relate to an earlier age. Both are bedevilled by textual problems and both deal with the theme of isolation and the comfort that God can give to the lonely man. The narrator of *The Wanderer* is a lordless man, who has lost his protector in battle. His search for a new patron leads him to the realization that his best hope of security lies in God. There is a clear contrast in *The Wanderer* between the heroic world of the bulk of the poem and its Christian resolution.

*The Seafarer*, by way of contrast, is more thoroughly Christian and the narrator of the poem has chosen his exile. Whether he is simply a seaman or else a Christian exile from the world of men is a matter of debate. Again, the picture is one of man alone against a hostile nature, as the narrator conjures up, in this highly atmospheric poem, a vivid picture of ice-cold northern seas, with only the cries of sea birds as company. Mid-way through, the poem takes an allegorical turn, as exile is viewed as an escape from worldly pleasures, despite their temptations, to the more permanent pleasures of heaven. Life on earth is of value only if man has performed good deeds; the old heroic days, the narrator suggests, have gone. Humility and moderation better prepare man for the love of God.

Probably the best-known and the finest of all Anglo-Saxon Christian poems is *The Dream of the Rood*, a highly individual meditation on the crucifixion. Although, as expected, it is thoroughly conventional in language and metre, it has, nevertheless, an experimental feel. Again, although unambiguously Christian, it bears traces of an earlier, heroic cast of mind, as Christ is viewed in the poem as a young intrepid hero who willingly mounts the cross and embraces His crucifixion in His triumph over death. Uniquely, Christ's suffering is transferred to the cross itself which speaks of its suffering and torment. Unusually, we identify with the cross, rather than with Christ. This device of using the inanimate cross as narrator (*prosopopeia*) is infrequent in Anglo-Saxon literature, though inanimate objects in plenty do speak in the many surviving Anglo-Saxon *Riddles* and, perhaps, in the problematic elegy *The Husband's Message*. Also, too, *The Dream of the Rood* is cast as a dream poem, a very early example of a mode that was to become widely popular in the Middle Ages, in which the narrator dreams of the crucifixion and the cross, which then speaks. Following its description of the crucifixion and its aftermath, the cross describes its own burial, recovery and veneration and the value of the cross as a symbol of salvation. The dreamer wakes, inspired by the vision, and looks forward to the time when, through worship of the cross, he may join the ranks of the saved.

Although the complete text of *The Dream of the Rood* only occurs in a late tenth-century manuscript (in *The Vercelli Book*), fragments of an earlier version are carved in Northumbrian runes on the early eighth-century Ruthwell Cross in Dumfriesshire, an evocative setting for a cross that speaks. The poem itself, or at least some form of it, may be even earlier. Both poem and carved cross are likely to be part of the cult of the cross that was stimulated by the miraculous discovery of a fragment of the True Cross by Pope Sergius I in Rome in 701.

The majority of Anglo-Saxon poetry is, in fact, Christian in function and content and most surviving poems are semi-narrative pieces, with homiletic overtones, which describe the lives of saints or retell, very freely, certain books of the Bible (particularly the Old Testament). All adapt to the expectations of an Anglo-Saxon audience used to tales of heroes in action, though apart from *Beowulf* only fragments of these have survived.

## Later heroic poetry and the rise of prose

Two of the most obviously heroic poems in Old English, *The Battle of Brunanburh* and *The Battle of Maldon*, survive from the end of the Anglo-Saxon period, when we might suppose the heroic manner to have become outmoded. However, both revive the heroic style for what are clearly propagandist purposes. Both poems celebrate actual historical events; the one a triumph, the other a disaster. In both cases, events have been recast to show the heroes in the best possible light. *The Battle of Brunanburh*, which is found in some versions of *The Anglo-Saxon Chronicle* under the year 937, celebrates the victory of the English King Aethelstan and his brother Edmund against a combined force of Scandinavians, Norse-Irish and Scots. The poem is conceived in the manner of an Irish or Scandinavian praise poem, in being a succession of flattering statements. All is black and white; the heroes are Christian and fearless, their opponents are pagan, cowardly and flee from the battle humiliated. *The Battle of Brunanburh* is unashamedly partisan and by using the heroic style, both Aethelstan and Edmund are in consequence linked with the heroes of old.

At seventy-three lines, *The Battle of Brunanburh* is short. More substantial is *The Battle of Maldon*, with which it is often paired and contrasted. *The Battle of Maldon* also springs from an actual historical event which is reported in a few lines in *The Anglo-Saxon Chronicle* under the year 991. This was a minor skirmish, in which a party of Danes, attempting to make landfall from an islet off the coast of Essex, defeated the local 'ealdorman' and his troops. The picture that we get from *The Battle of Maldon*, however, is utterly different. The 'ealdorman' of Essex, called Byrhtnoth, has been transformed into an ancient, proud and determined warrior, served by men who are scarcely less heroic than he is. Unfortunately, treachery in his own camp and among the Danes, as well as his own pride, bring about Byrhtnoth's downfall and that of his men. The Danes are allowed to cross to the mainland for a fight to the death. Though outnumbered, Byrhtnoth fights heroically, even when mortally wounded, in a series of ferocious confrontations. Inevitably, he is killed and his fight is taken up by a succession of young warriors, who boast of their fitness for the fight, before one by one they are slaughtered. To a modern, cynical mind, *The Battle of Maldon* reads at times like a parody, as exaggerated boasts of heroic deeds to be performed lead only to death. Certainly, the poem seems written to a formula and has all the characteristics that we would expect of a heroic poem. Like *The Battle of Brunanburh*, it, too, is thoroughly partisan, with treacherous Danes destroying Christian heroes. Yet, the poem is inevitably of its age; a renewed attack by the Danes, such as occurred in 991, was a feared prospect, for memories of earlier Viking attacks were no doubt a live folk memory. *The Battle of Maldon* was written to boost morale; a defeat was not so much 'covered up' as transformed. The English might die, but there was nothing squalid about the way in which they met their deaths.

Anglo-Saxon prose 'literature' is, by way of contrast, largely functional in intent and arose during the course of the period to satisfy the needs of both Church and State. The earliest prose works are charters and legal documents which, though of linguistic and historical value, are of little, if any, literary interest. It was not until the reign of King Alfred of Wessex, who ruled from 871 to 899, that a prose literature developed that served, in large part, to instil a sense of national identity among Englishmen who were confronted by Danish occupation in the north and east. Chief of these 'government' prose works are the various versions of *The Anglo-Saxon Chronicle* (a series of annals which incorporated earlier materials and which continued to be compiled in various monastic centres throughout the rest of the Anglo-Saxon period) and the historical, educational and theological works which were translated or paraphrased under the auspices of King Alfred, if not, as was once thought, entirely by King Alfred himself. These include St Gregory's *Pastoral Care* (*Cura Pastoralis*), Paulus Orosius's *Histories against the Pagans* (*Historiae adversum Paganos*), Boethius's *Consolation of Philosophy* (*De Consolatione Philosophiae*) and St Augustine's *Soliloquies* (*Soliloquia*). What makes these particularly distinctive are the prefaces which precede each of them and in which we can discern the beginnings of an imaginative prose tradition in English. Perhaps the most interesting and popular, because of its subject matter, is the extended preface which precedes the paraphrase of Orosius's *Histories against the Pagans* and which includes the reports of two travellers to the north of Europe: that of Ohthere who travelled round the North Cape to the White Sea and that of Wulfstan who travelled along the coast of the Baltic. Both pieces are, strictly speaking, documentary prose and are the earliest examples of geographical writing in English.

The most mature and flamboyant prose in Old English is that which was designed for oral performance in service of the church, notably the contrasting collections of sermons associated with the names of Aelfric and Wulfstan, statesman and Bishop of London (996–1002) before becoming Bishop of Worcester and Archbishop of Canterbury. The sermons of Aelfric (of which there are 85) are learned expositions of themes or biblical texts appropriate to the major festivals of the Church calendar. Each is clearly argued and draws from an impressive array of theological and biblical sources and is presented in a prose which adapts the style and techniques of poetry in order to make it effective in performance. In contrast, the 21 surviving sermons of Wulfstan seem primarily designed for oral performance and use an abundance of classical rhetorical devices to underscore their argument. In fact, his most popular sermon, *The Sermon of the Wolf to the English* (*Sermo Lupi ad Anglos*) seems, at times, rather too self-consciously an exercise in rhetoric, with repetitions and parallel statements piled up in super-abundance, as Wulfstan attacks his English audience for its godlessness which has led to God's vengeance in allowing further Danish successes in late Anglo-Saxon England.

## The rise of Middle English

In many ways, the literary tradition that had been developing throughout the Anglo-Saxon period amounted to little, for political and cultural affairs were to be utterly transformed by the events that followed the Norman Conquest of 1066. From the late eleventh century until the accession of King John in 1204, England became effectively an extension of northern France. A new Norman-French speaking elite was transplanted into England where it had control of government (both secular and religious) and cultural life. The English language, both as a spoken tongue and as the language of literature, was marginalized and, consequently, nothing of literary substance survives in English from this new 'dark age' until the end of the twelfth century.

The Norman Conquest of England conventionally marks the beginning of the medieval period in English history and life, and the English that began to emerge as a literary language at the end of the twelfth century has been labelled Middle English by scholars, in recognition of the very clear differences between it and the preceding Old English and to identify its status as transitionary between the English of the Anglo-Saxon period and the new or modern English of the post-Renaissance period. Middle English is characterized, among other things, by large-scale lexical loans from French, the deletion of many words of Germanic origin, the development of a fixed word order and a simplification of the inflectional system that controlled nouns, adjectives and verbs.

The political and cultural forces that transformed Old English into Middle English are also responsible for the new kinds of literature that emerge during the medieval period in England, as increased familiarity with literature in Latin and French gave English writers access to new models, which provided new ideas and new forms. Thus, the Old English epic was transformed into the romance, by which hero tales became more fabulous, less earth-bound and more imaginative. Heroes, now commonly knights, were ruled by elaborate codes of conduct to do with chivalry and courtesy which governed the behaviour of knight towards knight and, importantly, knight towards lady. The romance was largely an aristocratic genre aimed at an elite who required as literary entertainment an idealized view of itself and its aspirations. Love between well-born men and ladies made a substantial appearance in medieval literature and was ritualized into *fin amour* or courtly love, whereby the precise behaviour of both parties was codified and prescribed into a refined and courtly game. Conversely, comic tales, called *fabliaux*, gave an alternative, often bawdy, view of sexual relations, usually among the bourgeoisie or low-born, where woman as descendant of Eve was preferred to woman as a derivative of the Virgin Mary.

These new narrative genres were composed in a variety of imported metres, syllabic and usually rhymed, and embellished with rhetorical devices derived ultimately from classical tradition. In the Middle Ages the domain of English poetry was extended to embrace a range of new forms: lyrical, dramatic, comic, romance, devotional. Yet, the earlier Old English poetic tradition did leave its mark, particularly in the western fringes of England and Scotland, where the alliterative tradition seems to have continued. In consequence, there was a degree of transition between the old and the new and the important *Brut*, by the Worcestershire priest Layamon, illustrates this, with its Germanic alliteration and rhyme (essentially a characteristic of romance poetry). Written towards the end of the twelfth century, the *Brut* (named after Brutus, the supposed grandson of Aeneas and founder of Britain) is a lengthy narrative poem chronicling the early history of Britain and is now chiefly read and remembered for those passages which concern the history of King Arthur, who here owes much to preceding notions of the Germanic hero. In fact, as the earliest example of Arthurian literature in English it is of crucial importance to the development of King Arthur as a prominent figure of romance tales in both verse and prose in English. Although Layamon invented and expanded certain details of his narrative, his work is essentially a retelling of existing materials. His immediate source is a lengthy verse chronicle in Norman French by the Jerseyman Wace called *Roman de Brut* (*c*.1155), which itself is a retelling of the lengthy and influential Latin prose history *The History of the Kings of Britain* (*Historia Regum Britanniae*) by Geoffrey of Monmouth who, it is generally agreed, completed his work some time during the 1130s.

## Early Middle English literature

With the rise of English as a literary language from the late twelfth century onwards, certain types of poetry and prose that would previously have been associated with Latin and French began to make their appearance in English, in a style and format that was largely new and unfamiliar to an English audience. An example is the late twelfth-century debate poem *The Owl and the Nightingale*, an astonishingly sophisticated and assured piece, whose maturity can only be explained if we see it as part of a long-established tradition, but a tradition that was Latin and French, rather than English. Yet, despite its non-English roots, *The Owl and the Nightingale* emerges as a thoroughly English piece, as a very human owl and nightingale debate the merits of their opposing lifestyles.

Although on the surface it is a light-hearted piece, *The Owl and the Nightingale* is clearly intended to be taken seriously. Whether we are to interpret the argument in general terms, as simply contrasting a life of pleasure with a life of sobriety, or as something more specific, contrasting a secular with a monastic life, for instance, is a matter of debate.

Although much of the prose of the medieval period is still largely functional, rather than imaginative, some of the religious prose does display an assurance and fluency which would seem to continue the tradition established by Aelfric and Wulfstan. Most important of the early medieval Christian prose works is the devotional handbook *Ancrene Riwle* of the late twelfth or early thirteenth centuries, which was later revised as the *Ancrene Wisse*. This lengthy, anonymous work was, apparently, written at the request of three noble ladies who had withdrawn from the world to live as Christian recluses or anchoresses and who required guidance on spiritual conduct. The *Riwle* begins and ends with a discussion of 'outer' matters, to do with religious observance and everyday behaviour, but, for the most part, it is concerned with the 'inner' or spiritual life, with moral values that are absolute. Much is made of worldly temptation and the special dangers to women, as the example of Eve is frequently contrasted with that of the Virgin Mary. Inevitably, there is much in the *Riwle* on sin and, almost inevitably, it is the depiction of sin and sinners that provides some of the liveliest and most graphic passages, as in its discussion of the Seven Deadly Sins. It is a learned work, yet a work that carries its learning lightly, mixing anecdote, scriptural exegesis and quotations from the Church Fathers. That this West Midlands work was influential is clear from the fact that it was revised for a wider audience and, unusually for an English work of this period, was translated into both Latin and French.

## Middle English literature: the 'golden age'

For much of the early medieval period, the status of English as a literary language remained uncertain and a writer was as likely to compose in Latin or French as in English. Even in the fourteenth century, the 'golden age' of medieval English literature, there was still a choice for, it should be remembered, English was only permitted for use in law courts in 1362 and it was not until 1385 (according to Trevisa) that English, rather than French, was generally adopted as the medium of instruction in schools. Thus it was that John Gower (*c*.1327/30–1408), the author of three substantial pieces, chose French as the language of his first major poem,

*Speculum Meditantis* (*The Mirror of One Meditating*), and Latin for his second, *Vox Clamantis* (*The Voice of One Crying*). It was only with his final collection of poetic tales, *Confessio Amantis* (*The Lover's Confession*), of which the first version dates to 1390, that he turned to English, his native tongue. However, the establishment of English as the prime vehicle for literature written in England was given a powerful boost by Geoffrey Chaucer (*c.*1337–1400), the most influential writer of the English Middle Ages who chose to write exclusively in English. Despite this, Chaucer was very much a European and his reworking of Italian and French texts elevated both his work and the English literary language to European rank. His prodigious output reflects both his learning and his social position. Although always close to the court, he was also a man of the world.

As a writer, Chaucer is largely associated with long narrative poems, compiled in a range of continental metres and stylistically in tune with European, rather than native English, traditions. Yet he also wrote lyric poetry, ballads and roundels and prose pieces, notably a translation of Boethius's *De Consolatione Philosophiae*.

Chaucer's work is conventionally divided into three periods, reflecting the degree to which he was dependent on external influences. To his first, French, period (before 1372) belongs his translation (of which only a part survives) of the allegorical *Roman de la Rose* (*Romance of the Rose*), by Guillaume de Lorris and Jean de Meun, a poem which was to exert an influence over much of Chaucer's later writing. From it Chaucer borrowed the device of the dream vision and the seasonal setting which he commonly used to introduce romantic and allegorical narratives, as in *The Book of the Duchess*, the major poem of his first period, which is said to have been written for John of Gaunt following the death of his first wife Blanche in 1369.

## Chaucer's *Troilus and Criseyde*

The major work of Chaucer's second, or Italian, period (1373–84) is the long philosophical romance *Troilus and Criseyde*, one of the twin peaks of his literary career. Prior to this are the two dream vision poems *The House of Fame* (*c.*1379), a sprawling, incomplete and unsatisfactory narrative, yet one that includes much that is typical of Chaucer's mature work and several passages of great invention, and the lively *The Parlement of Foulys* (*The Parliament of Birds*), 1382–83, a light-hearted debate piece, written for St Valentine's Day, which uses birds to contrast natural and courtly love.

However, Chaucer's most substantial examination of the theme of courtly love is his massive *Troilus and Criseyde* (1379–83), which, because of its panoramic sweep, its delineation of character and its exploration of moral issues, is sometimes regarded as a verse precursor of the novel. Chaucer has taken his story from Boccaccio's *Il Filostrato* and much of his thinking from Boethius's *De Consolatione Philosophiae*, yet he has convincingly made the borrowed material his own. As narrator, Chaucer is, as so often, a presence in the poem as he both reports and comments on his narrative. As the title suggests, central to the tale are Troilus and

Criseyde and the poem is the history of their tragic love; as Fate, politics, personality and the intervention of others all conspire against them. The aristocratic world that they inhabit is an unreal mix of courtly formality and realistic behaviour, just as the pagan Trojan and Greek background is, in the medieval manner, anachronistically reinterpreted into a medieval present, with life governed by both Fate or Fortune and the Christian God. Initially, both Troilus and Criseyde are reluctant lovers. Troilus, who is more in love with warfare than with women, is disdainful of love, until he sees Criseyde. Criseyde is a widow and, as such, is sexually aware, though love is for her a matter of the past. However, the intervention of Pandarus, Criseyde's uncle, as go-between, brings them together. Troilus is converted into the conventional lovesick knight of courtly romance, totally obsessed with an idealized view of the object of his veneration. Criseyde, though, always retains a degree of independence and is, surely, Chaucer's most complex and compelling character, one of the great women of fiction. To some extent, she acts freely and knowingly, yet, at the same time, she is the victim of circumstances beyond her control. She allows herself to fall in love with Troilus, but, like Guinevere in Arthurian story, at no time is she the idealized woman of Troilus's imagination. Called to the Grecian camp against her will, by her traitor-father, she is forced to abandon Troilus and, despite her promise to remain faithful to him, she allows herself to be seduced by the worldly-wise Grecian hero Diomede. Unlike Troilus, Diomede is an opportunist, practical and realistic, and through him and Troilus we have Chaucer's view of the inadequacies of the courtly love ethic when confronted by the values of the real world. Courtly love may work in the world of literary romance, but is ineffective elsewhere. Inevitably, Troilus is killed in action at the end of the poem and with him die his ideals, as both Diomede and Criseyde live on. For Troilus, at least, Boethius's Wheel of Fortune has turned full circle, driven by forces that Troilus has always felt powerless to resist. Yet the poem ends optimistically, as the final stanzas emphasize the value of Christian, rather than worldly, love and, in three stanzas that were absent from the first version of the poem, the soul of Troilus, the good pagan, flies to Heaven from where, enlightened, it views the foolishness of mankind.

Despite its serious theme, there is much to delight in *Troilus and Criseyde*. Its style is a fluent mix of the formal and the colloquial and passages of realism alternate with abstract speculation, all conveyed through a sequence of rhyme-royal stanzas over five books, which together mirror the rise and fall of Troilus and Criseyde's love. Characterization throughout is sharply delineated as four utterly different personalities (Troilus, Criseyde, Pandarus and Diomede) are brought into conflict. Not the least interesting is Pandarus, here essentially Chaucer's own creation, who provides a welcome light relief and a note of comic realism, as he uses any means, whether dishonest or not, to bring Troilus and Criseyde together.

## The Canterbury Tales

The masterpiece of Chaucer's third and final period, which is marked by a greater degree of originality, is *The Canterbury Tales* (begun *c*.1386), a compendium of tales told by pilgrims en route to the shrine of St Thomas à Becket in Canterbury. Chaucer's intention, as announced in his *Prologue*, was to give each of the thirty-one pilgrims four tales, two for the outward journey and two for the return, with conversational links and prologues to bridge the intervals between the stories and give unity to an otherwise diverse work. In the event *The Canterbury Tales* was never finished. Only twenty-two pilgrims tell complete stories and not all are linked, rendering the exact ordering of the tales problematic at times.

Although incomplete, *The Canterbury Tales* shows a significant advance in Chaucer's narrative art, as he is here obliged to create stories, most of them borrowed, through a variety of voices. The whole design is set in motion by a magnificent *Prologue* which sets the scene and introduces the pilgrims, including Chaucer and the congenial Host of the Tabard Inn at Southwark who takes charge of them. The pilgrims are drawn from a wide social spectrum and through them Chaucer creates an impression of a complete society; a society which is seen in terms of its classes or 'estates', as defined by both social position and occupation (see Mann, 1973). The pilgrimage, as one of the few places where the classes would mix, provides Chaucer with the ideal framework and, in this respect, *The Canterbury Tales* is much more effective than other such collections of tales that may have influenced him, such as Ovid's *Metamorphoses*, Boccaccio's *Decameron*, John Gower's *Confessio Amantis* and his own (unfinished) *Legend of Good Women* (1385–6).

Chaucer, in *The Prologue*, is both observer and omniscient narrator, as he describes what he sees and what he knows of the background of each of the pilgrims. An important theme of *The Prologue* is the clash between personality and the expectations of a profession as, for example, is made clear in the contrasting portraits of ecclesiastics. Only the Poor Parson, significantly, lives up to the ideals of the Church. Necessarily, Chaucer's attitude to the pilgrims varies, as some are regarded with respect, some are savagely satirized and others are exposed through gentle irony. The result, however, is a gallery of vivid, live and thoroughly believable characters, few of them without flaws.

The tales themselves are, inevitably, something of a patchwork. Some relate naturally to the tellers, such as the two very different kinds of Romance tale told by both Knight and Squire and the story of a Christian child murdered by Jews, which is told by the Prioress. Others arise dramatically from the context of the poem. Thus, the Miller tells a bawdy tale about a gullible carpenter and the Reeve, who is also a carpenter, retaliates with an equally bawdy piece about a corrupt miller who gets his come-uppance. Similarly, the Summoner's tale shows the hood-winking of a foolish and corrupt friar, which is the Summoner's response to the Friar who, in his tale, told of a lecherous and greedy summoner who is dragged off to Hell.

Several of the finest tales in the collection, however, appear to have no obvious relevance to their narrator. The Nun's Priest, who is scarcely mentioned in *The Prologue*, delivers one of the highlights of the whole *Canterbury Tales*, a delicious rendering of 'Chantecleer and the Fox', a well-known animal fable warning against pride, here reported as mock epic. Other highlights are the unattractive Pardoner's allegorical tale on the price of greed (highly ironic in view of the Pardoner's own character), the Franklin's moral tale on the problems of conflicting honour (to one's husband on the one hand and to one's word on the other) and the Merchant's witty reinterpretation of the stock *fabliau* plot of a jealous old husband who is outwitted by his young wife and her lover. Among the disappointments are the *Wife of Bath's Tale*, a quest piece, in which a young knight, under sentence of death, saves his skin and gains a beautiful wife by discovering what it is that women most desire. This comes as a massive anti-climax after the superlative Prologue that precedes it, in which the Wife of Bath gives a frank and bawdy autobiographical account of her succession of marriages.

Love and marriage, in fact, are dominant themes in *The Canterbury Tales* and are explored from a variety of perspectives; from the romantic and idealistic to the mercenary, realistic and often comic. As Chaucer had earlier shown in *The Parlement of Foulys*, courtly love or *fin amour* is the preserve of the knights and ladies of romance, whereas natural, realistic and, often bawdy, lustful 'love' is associated with the bourgeoisie. Style and topic in *The Canterbury Tales* are also perfectly matched. Where appropriate, colloquial speech and realism contrast with formal speech and an elevated, stately language, all usually conveyed through fluent heroic couplets. Learned references and all the devices of the classical rhetorical tradition amplify and underline his theme, whether Chaucer's intention is straightforward or ironic. Although Chaucer is, rightly, regarded as an original and innovative writer, his originality, like Shakespeare's, depends on his ability to recreate existing materials to suit his own style and purpose. Few of his tales, in other words, are his own invention, most are borrowed from Classical, Italian and French literary sources.

## The alliterative revival

Like all medieval writers, Chaucer wrote in a literary form of his own regional speech, that of the south-east midlands. Inevitably, given that this was the speech of London and the universities of Oxford and Cambridge, this was the dialect that ultimately became established as the literary norm, the basis of modern Standard Literary English. Hence, Chaucer's work is reasonably accessible to the modern reader. Less accessible, perhaps, are the important works associated with the west of England which, in the fourteenth century, saw a revival of an alliterative poetry which combined native English alliterative metres with Romance themes and ideas. William Langland's *Piers Plowman*, for instance, uses dream visions and allegory, but is otherwise an entirely English piece, alliterative and unrhymed. Written during the second half of the fourteenth century, it operates as a sequence of Christian moralities, in which the path to salvation is explored against a vivid background of vice and corruption throughout the whole of society. It is strongly didactic in tone, though often untidy and poorly structured. It survives in three versions (A, B and C), which suggests that it was subject to constant change and revision, and was clearly popular, as is indicated by the large number of surviving manuscripts.

The greatest achievements of the alliterative revival, however, are the works of the anonymous 'Gawain poet' who, on stylistic grounds, is thought to have written three lengthy religious poems *Pearl*, *Patience* and *Purity* and, most notably, the narrative romance which has given rise to his 'name', *Sir Gawain and the Green Knight* (late fourteenth century).

The alliterative *Sir Gawain and the Green Knight*, in fact, stands comparison with anything that Chaucer wrote, but its north-west midland dialect does cause difficulties. Its Arthurian theme may reflect north-western English Celtic associations and, significantly, certain elements of its story are paralleled in early Irish literature. Like so many Arthurian narratives, the poem is both quest and trial, in which the hero Gawain (and, by implication, Arthur and his court) is tested for his moral courage, in a manner which, unusually, highlights his vulnerability as a man, rather than knight.

## Medieval dramatic literature

The fourteenth century also sees the development of a tradition of English drama. Although secular plays are known to have been performed, virtually nothing has survived and medieval English drama commonly means religious drama, notably the cycles of Mystery plays that were often performed in urban and ecclesiastical centres on church festivals (particularly the Feast of Corpus Christi).

The Mystery plays, which are likely to have had their origins in quasi-dramatic expansions to the church liturgy at Christmas and Easter, were performed out-of-doors and often processionally on movable wagons (called pageants). They have as their purpose the Christian message of redemption through Christ, illustrated through a sequence (or cycle) of biblical plays that range from the Creation of the World and the Fall of Man to the Nativity, Passion, Resurrection and Last Judgement. Also included were Old Testament Plays on subjects believed to prefigure Christ. Each of the plays was mounted by Craft or Trade guilds (or mystéres), which gave their name to the genre.

Four more or less complete cycles have survived from the many that are known to have once existed; one, the so-called N-town Cycle, is variously associated by scholars with East Anglia or Lincoln, the others with Chester, York and Wakefield. All are in verse and all the plays are necessarily short, since the cycles were performed in the course of a single day (as with York and Wakefield) or over two days (Chester). All dramatize virtually the same biblical episodes, though their treatment is often strikingly different and each contains apocryphal, folk and invented materials to a greater or lesser degree. Anachronisms abound and biblical events are commonly set in a medieval present, establishing their message as true for all time. The Chester Cycle (usually dated to about 1375) is uniform in character and relatively straightforward, whereas the later York Cycle is mixed in character and clearly contains the work of several hands over several periods. The brevity of some of the York plays occasionally reduces their dramatic effectiveness and reflects the number of participating guilds in prosperous York. Among the best of the plays are those attributed to the so-called York Metrist and York Realist, notably the York Realist's play of *The Crucifixion*. The Wakefield Cycle (also called the Towneley Cycle, from the Lancashire family that once owned the sole manuscript) is clearly based in part on the York plays, which the authorities at Wakefield are thought to have borrowed. At some point in the first half of the fifteenth century, six plays (it is commonly thought) were replaced by those of a playwright conventionally known as the Wakefield Master and with these plays the Mystery play genre reaches its highest achievement. Despite the limitations imposed by the biblical sources and the confined playing area, the Master's plays give the impression of absolute freedom. Vigorous action and colloquial speech combine with apocryphal and folk material and frequent references to social ills. Yet the biblical source at the core of each play is left intact and the theological message is unimpaired. Clearly, though, what was perceived as an increasing secularization of the Mystery plays contributed to their being banned by the church authorities at the time of the Reformation. Most daring and adventurous of the Master's plays is his *Second Shepherds' Play* (*Secunda Pastorum*). At first sight, the adoration of the shepherds (the subject of the play) would seem to be marginalized, with the first two-thirds of this long play being given over to a 'pseudo-Nativity', in which a sinister sheep-thief, Mak, steals a sheep from the shepherds which is concealed by his wife in 'swaddling bands' and passed off as her own new-born child. Exposure follows a mock adoration by the shepherds, who then proceed to the actual nativity, which is marked by a tone of absolute reverence at odds with the rest of the play. Although the 'pseudo-Nativity' is undoubtedly comic and possibly distracting, its intention is certainly serious, with the stolen sheep, perhaps, to be seen as a 'false Christ' and 'his Father', Mak, as agent of the devil. In this play, and all the Master's plays (with the exception of *Cain and Abel*), he uses an intricate nine-line stanza, characterized by both internal and end-of-line rhyme which, astonishingly, never disrupts the dialogue, whether naturalistic or formal.

The N-Town Cycle, the latest of the Mystery cycles, is less obviously dramatic and differs in many ways from the other extant cycles. Its name derives from the preliminaries in the cycle's single manuscript; N (latin *nomen*) indicates where the name of the town in which the plays were to be performed was to be entered. The likelihood, therefore, is that the plays were performed in no one town only, nor are they thought to have been performed processionally. The cycle uniquely contains a sequence of episodes on the life of the Virgin Mary and this has given rise to the suggestion that we have here a composite cycle made up of separate cycles and plays.

Another kind of medieval religious play, the morality, arose alongside the Mystery plays and was to continue, in modified form, throughout the Tudor and Elizabethan periods, culminating in Marlowe's *Dr. Faustus*. The morality plays take as their theme the drama of human life, as mankind is continuously forced to choose between the forces of good and evil. An early example, *The Castle of Perseverance* (*c.*1420) takes the whole of man's life, from the cradle to the grave, as its subject. Later plays confine themselves to a single phase, as in the earthily humorous *Mankind* and the deeply serious *Everyman*, in which man, at the point of death, is forced to confront his lack of good deeds on earth and learns of the importance of contrition and confession.

## Printing and its aftermath

A key event in both the history of the English language and English literature was the establishment by William Caxton in 1476 of a printing press in the precincts of Westminster Abbey. Previously, literary texts had to be laboriously written by hand, but now multiple copies became more or less easily available. A degree of standardization of language and spelling became obviously necessary, marking an advance in the development of a Standard Literary English and heralding the decline of regional English as a medium of literature. The spread of texts also encouraged the practice of silent reading, where previously a text might have been 'performed' aloud.

Caxton approached his work as printer creatively, editing where necessary and often adding prologues and epilogues of his own composition. His chosen texts were essentially medieval favourites, including Chaucer's *Canterbury Tales* and French works which Caxton translated himself. Among the most important of Caxton's texts is Sir Thomas Malory's *Le Morte D'Arthur* (written in 1469 or 1470), which established prose, rather than poetry, as a suitable vehicle for Romance. Previously, apart from devotional works, prose in the English Middle Ages was essentially functional, rather than creative.

*Le Morte D'Arthur* is a massive and often frustrating work, by an author of whom virtually nothing is known. Before 1934, it was assumed that Caxton's edition represented Malory's intentions, but the discovery in Winchester in that year of a manuscript of *Le Morte D'Arthur* suggested that Malory had envisaged eight tales, which he arranged chronologically to illustrate the rise and fall of Arthur's court. Caxton, it seems, had regarded the whole collection as a single tale and had redivided it into twenty-one books. However we regard it, Malory established the basic Arthurian narrative for all time, bringing together, rearranging, translating and adapting key Arthurian texts from England and France in the manner of an historian. The result is a history of Arthur and his knights, imbued with the ideals of literary romance; a glamorized picture of a medieval past that never was and written in prison, as the author tells us, during the turbulence of the Wars of the Roses, which were to bring the medieval period to a close.

At the core of *Le Morte D'Arthur* is the rivalry between Arthur and his incestuously born son Mordred, conceived through a sinful act (though committed in innocence) that left Arthur forever doomed. Superimposed on this is the romance theme of illicit love, between Lancelot, favourite of King Arthur, and Arthur's queen, Guinevere, which provokes further division in Arthur's court and is the major cause of its downfall. In fact, the affair between Lancelot and Guinevere dominates much of *Le Morte D'Arthur*, for both Lancelot and Guinevere are more fully depicted than Arthur. Lancelot, the noble lover and superlative knight, is not without deceit, though he argues his innocence, and Guinevere is strong-minded in her disloyalty. Yet, in its attempt to be comprehensive, *Le Morte D'Arthur* contains too much; too much matter that seems only vaguely Arthurian, too many events that seem only loosely connected with its central theme, too much detail and too much repetition.

Despite the achievements of pre-Renaissance English writers, early English literature is, for most present-day English students, synonymous with the works of Chaucer. Yet, though Chaucer dominates his age, he wrote within a context of other writers, both English and European, whose work he used and recreated, and he, in turn, inspired others (notably the 'Scottish Chaucerian' poets of the fifteenth and sixteenth centuries). A study of Chaucer's context and his work can only extend our understanding of all that followed.

## *BIBLIOGRAPHY*

Most of the texts referred to in this unit are included (wholly or in part) in:

Alexander, Michael and Riddy, Felicity (eds) (1989) *The Middle Ages, Vol. One.* Macmillan Anthologies of English Literature, Macmillan, London.

For a modern edition of the works of Chaucer, the reader is referred to:

Benson, Larry D. (1988) *The Riverside Chaucer*, Oxford University Press, Oxford. This edition is based on F.N. Robinson, *The Works of Geoffrey Chaucer*.

The following series books provide useful critical essays and bibliographies:

Alexander, Michael (1983) *Old English Literature*, Macmillan History of Literature, Macmillan, London.
Brewer, Derek (1983) *English Gothic Literature*, Macmillan History of Literature, Macmillan, London.
Beadle, Richard (ed.) (1994) *The Cambridge Companion to Medieval English Theatre*, Cambridge University Press, Cambridge.
Boitani, Pietro and Mann, Jill (eds) (1986) *The Cambridge Chaucer Companion*, Cambridge University Press, Cambridge.
Godden, Malcolm and Lapidge, Michael (eds) (1991) *The Cambridge Companion to Old English Literature*, Cambridge University Press, Cambridge.
Mann, Jill (1973) *Chaucer and Medieval Estates Satire*, Cambridge University Press, Cambridge.

# UNIT 5

# Shakespeare

*Tony Bareham*

This unit will not follow the 'Introduction' plus 'Texts, Authors, Contexts' format of Units 6–17. The entry begins, instead, with Shakespeare's life (pp. 78–80) followed by the chronology and the generic subdivisions of his writing. Dates offered are conjectural dates of composition, which sometimes vary significantly from dates of first publication, or known date of first performance. All quotations are from the 'Alexander' text (Alexander (1951)). For the general reader this remains the most accessible of the reliable complete texts of Shakespeare.

The 'History Plays' occupy pages 80–2, the 'Comedies' pages 82–5, the 'Roman Plays' pages 85–6, the 'Tragedies' pages 86–90, and the 'Problem Plays' and the 'Last Plays' pages 90–2. Pages 92–5 approach the way in which performers, directors and interpreters have been influenced by changing theatre design and custom since the seventeenth century; and pages 95–9 consider the work of recent and contemporary literary criticism. The section on 'Shakespeare's theatre' (pp. 99–102) considers the conditions in which the playwright and his actors practised their art, and the following section (pp. 102–5) is concerned with the ways in which Shakespeare adapted his creative skills to these conditions. The concluding section concentrates on Shakespeare the dramatic poet (pp. 105–9).

Documentary evidence of Shakespeare's private life is partial and patchy. Much comes from parish records, from legal documents and equally terse origins.

William Shakespeare was christened at Holy Trinity Church, Stratford-upon-Avon in Warwickshire on 26 April 1564. Infant mortality in the sixteenth century prompted immediate baptism of the newly born. Thus we choose 23 April as Shakespeare's birthday, perhaps having in mind, conveniently for the iconographers, that it is also the national saint's day.

The playwright's father, John (1530–1601), was a master glover and wool-dealer, who held various municipal offices such as Mayor and Justice of the Peace. John Shakespeare was more than once fined for non-attendance at church. Does one construe from this a bias towards Roman Catholicism? The state religion changed three times during John Shakespeare's lifetime. What was one moment treason became, next moment, compulsory dogma. A great playwright born into this situation must surely react to such tensions? In fact we know *nothing* of Shakespeare's private convictions. Brilliant as are his portraits of the inner workings of men's minds, the author's own mind is entirely held in abeyance.

As with his religion, so Shakespeare's education is a matter of conjecture; John Shakespeare's civic status would entitle his son to a free place at the local grammar school, but no actual record proves he went there. Ben Jonson mentions Shakespeare's 'small Latine and less Greeke' in his verses 'To the Memory of ... Mr William Shakespeare ...' in the First Folio (1623). But we need to weigh this evaluation in the context of Jonson's own massive scholarship. In those heady days when the Renaissance had finally permeated every level of English cultural life, 'small' Latin and 'less' Greek would still formidably outmeasure the amount of classical learning acquired by most university students reading Shakespeare today.

The early years of Shakespeare's life are obscure. *Was* he tutor to a Catholic family in the north-west of England, in the period prior to that in which we can first trace him for certain as a 'prentice London playwright in about 1590? The Victorian version was that he poached deer from the park of a local magnate, and had to fly the coop. Pitching up in London, he held the heads of horses outside the playhouse until, miraculously, he was 'discovered'. Not a shred of hard evidence attaches to this charming version of the Whittington myth.

It *is* recorded in the parish register that William Shakespeare was married to Anne Hathaway in 1582 – a local girl, a full eight years his senior. The baptism of their eldest daughter, Susanna, is recorded a mere six months later. The nature of Tudor marriage contracts is too complex for us to construe the worst. Yet all too often it is asserted that the marriage was unsuccessful, and the playwright was driven up to London. Once there, goes the story, he neglected wife and children, grew embittered with womankind and, in his plays, vented his spleen on the opposite sex. Such speculation is pure fantasy.

At some date between the mid-1580s and the early 1590s Shakespeare certainly did move to London. The theatre impresario Philip Henslowe (d.1616) kept a diary in which he recorded the box-office success of *Henry VI* at the Rose theatre in 1592. Shakespeare was part-author or reviser of this work. Later in the same year the contentious pamphleteer Robert Greene (1560?–92) jibed at the young Shakespeare's enviable success with this work in which Greene himself probably had an original hand: 'an upstart crow, beautified with our feathers' ... 'the only Shake-scene in a country' (Greene: *A Groates Worth of Wit Bought with a Million of Repentance* (cit. Grosart, 1881–6)).

A period when the London theatres were closed because of the plague (1592–4), was probably the breathing space in which Shakespeare wrote his two long non-dramatic poems *Venus and Adonis* (published 1593), and *The Rape of Lucrece* (published 1594). Both of these highly coloured Ovidian poems are dedicated to the Earl of Southampton, but the precise relationship of poet to patron and his circle is cloudy, as is so much else in Shakespeare's biography.

The *Sonnets* were also probably commenced at about this time, though not published until 1609. Critics wring and torture the poetry to find covert biographical 'evidence' of Shakespeare's love-life, his homosexual inclinations, and his dark night of the soul. Magnificent as they are, Shakespeare's sonnets in fact encompass many themes conventional and common enough in sonnet sequences of this period, and the reader enters the field of biographical extrapolation at his or her peril.

Shakespeare's writing career spans twenty-five years. He had probably begun writing in earnest by 1585; *The Tempest* was his last complete play, written in 1611. During a time-span of that duration any good artist will develop, and his art will evolve as his life view changes. The philosophical, political and moral concerns which form the centres of interest for both author and audience will alter. Thus the extraction of themes and ideas for purposes of adducing biography – a process so beloved of Victorian critics – is fraught with dangers.

For instance, the Victorian scholar Edward Dowden (1843–1913) divides Shakespeare's drama into phases for which he invents a spurious biographical *raison d'être* (Dowden, 1875). The playwright is conjectured to have experienced an emotional crisis at about the turn of the century and to have turned from a benign view of the world (embodied in his comedy), towards a dark and misogynistic vision, which culminates in near breakdown in *King Lear* and *Timon of Athens* (*c*.1607). From this crisis he recovered to compose 'The Romances' – *Pericles* (?1608–9), *The Winter's Tale* (1609–10), *Cymbeline* (?1610), *The Tempest* (1611) – before retiring to enjoy the fruits of his life's work in Stratford-upon-Avon.

This account invents a pattern without taking any cognizance of the changing world in which Shakespeare lived. The accession of King James I, the new spirit of scientific rationalism, the creation of a new order of aristocracy, the pressures of pan-European politics, and many other factors, would explain shifts in Shakespeare's interests and in the temper of his writing, without recourse to romanticizing guesswork. A consideration of the plays, group by group, offers a more logical approach. For the best study of the Shakespeare biography industry, from his death to the 1970s, see Schoenbaum (1970), and for an accessible modern biography Schoenbaum (1976).

## The History Plays

In the first phase of his work Shakespeare shows great interest in the processes of history. The chronicle play was an established and popular genre during these years (*c*.1585–99). English national destiny was at stake; there was increasing anxiety about the problems of who would succeed the childless Elizabeth; state authority obtruded into all aspects of life – all Shakespeare's plays were subject to official censorship. But the nation prospered under the later Tudors. The defeat of the Spanish Armada in 1588 fostered a belief in national superiority – and then quite probably a post-war reaction.

In the standard chronicle play hero-kings like Edward III, or moral examples of bad monarchy like Edward II, offer statements about national character, identity and probity. Shakespeare's sceptical mind builds and extends upon these monolithic types. He develops the history play into a highly successful and idiosyncratic vehicle. By the usually accepted chronology, virtually half the plays Shakespeare wrote before 1600 are Histories.

He clearly feared and hated civil war – as did virtually all his contemporaries. Though the Wars of the Roses ended in 1485, the threat of civil insurrection was present right through the Tudor dynasty, and the horrors of internecine strife were preached from the pulpit each Sunday. Shakespeare's first history cycle comprises *Henry VI Parts 1, 2 & 3* (?1585–7), and *Richard III* (?1588–92). It was followed by *Richard II*, *Henry IV Parts I and II*, and *Henry V* (?1594–8). These plays give an account of periods of national dissension, greedy and self-interested rulers, and central authority factionalized and subverted. They show how exploitive are demagogues and dictators at all levels of communal life, and they assert man's constant and illogical greed for power.

The History plays yearn for a stable and prosperous nation living at peace with itself and thus accruing a strength which holds at bay the threat of foreign interference. But never for a moment does Shakespeare actually show that state of peace. Though the second cycle of Histories, ending with *Henry V*, purports to bring us to the moment where national destiny is fulfilled, where the reformed scapegrace becomes the perfect warrior-knight, the play's closing words evoke the imminent tumble into domestic chaos and international disgrace which accompanied the reign of Henry VI:

> Small time, but, in that small, most greatly lived
> This star of England. Fortune made his sword;
> With which the world's best garden he achieved,
> And of it left his son imperial lord. . . .
> Whose state so many had the managing
> That they lost France and made his England bleed;
> Which oft our stage hath shown; . . .
>
> *(Henry V: V, final chorus)*

The message is clear and simple:

> This England never did, nor never shall,
> Lie at the proud foot of a conqueror,
> But when it first did help to wound itself. . . .
> Come the three corners of the world in arms,
> And we shall shock them. Nought shall make us rue,
> If England to itself do rest but true.
>
> *(King John: V, vii, 112–18, passim)*

But this happy state never exists; England, through the greed of her nobility and the various disabilities of her rulers, never is true to itself.

Shakespeare is deeply suspicious of power itself, and of the human greed for it. Men who want sway are customarily usurpers, those outside the direct line of succession. Conversely, those in whom power naturally inheres often despise and abuse it, or are too feeble to make it work. Thus, in *Richard II* a feckless king rules irresponsibly. Henry Bolingbroke, his cousin, covets the throne and shows every sign of being a more likely ruler than the legitimate incumbent. Bolingbroke's rebellion leads to the deposition and murder of Richard, and brings the usurper the power he has desired.

Shakespeare imposes upon this sequence of 'real' historical events a pattern as inexorable and as timeless as the forces which underpin Greek tragedy. Bolingbroke proves no more effective as ruler than the man he has supplanted. The kingdom slides into anarchy and civil war. The usurper himself sickens and ages before our very eyes. Power dehumanizes men, the greed for it inevitably corrupts them.

In order to underline this pattern-making Shakespeare willingly subverts or conflates his sources, and invents details of his own. It matters not a jot whether Shakespeare's Richard is an accurate picture of the real monarch who reigned from 1377–99, nor even whether the characters who surround him are a mixture of the real and the invented. People are often hoisted anachronistically into contexts they could not actually have occupied. Yet each is a genuine suffering individual; each has his problems and virtues; each speaks, moreover, in a manner and in image patterns unique to himself. Shakespeare perceives the universal awe and majesty of kings, yet always gives it a unique savour of the flesh and blood common to us all.

The richest of these Histories are probably the two parts of *Henry IV*. The fairy-tale story of the scapegrace Prince Hal in his struggle against the power of attractive vice in the person of Falstaff is brilliantly humanized and counterpointed against the theme of national destiny. In Prince Hal we witness the tragedy of a young man who sells his humanity and his character in order to achieve power. That power he believes to be his right, always capable of forgetting that it is an illegal and blood-tainted inheritance for which his father committed murder.

The outcome, in *Henry V*, is a searching study of national myth-making. Henry arranges a war of aggression in France, to distract attention from the weakness of his position at home. He fulfils the national need for a warrior-hero. His campaign is 'blessed' by the famous victory at Agincourt and by his triumphant marriage to the daughter of the defeated King of France. The story conspires to laud Henry – as popular English history has always done.

Yet Shakespeare shows us that the personal cost is enormous, and, ironically, the physical success momentary. The Henry V story offers the kind of tension between perceived stereotypes and imaginative individuality which is precisely the hallmark of Shakespeare's questing and sceptical mind.

Shakespearian history offers no answers to the problems it poses. In that precisely lies its genius.

For further reading on the history plays see Tillyard (1943, 1944), Campbell (1947), Kantorowicz (1957) and Boswell-Stone (1907).

## The Comedies

Virtually all Shakespeare's comedies were written in the first third of his career, alongside the histories. After about 1602 comedy is sporadic and tends to act as counterpoint to serious matter: the gravediggers in *Hamlet*, or the Porter in *Macbeth*, for example.

Shakespeare began by experimenting with established forms of comedy. In *The Comedy of Errors* (1589–90) he produced a brilliantly tight and fluid farce of mistaken identity, based on the Roman comic writer Plautus. In *The Taming of the Shrew* (?1590), he turns deliberately to a different kind of farce, and makes play with the age-old device of the bringing-to-heel of a refractory female. The play is marked by its pace and energy, and by the comic inventiveness of Petruchio, the shrew-tamer. Taken seriously it might represent pretty routine Renaissance nastiness aimed at women who try to assert their own integrity. But to read a sixteenth-century text through twentieth-century eyes is merely self-destructive. Shakespeare never again struck this note in his comedy. Most of his comedies demonstrate the bravery and wit of young women in a male-dominated world.

*Love's Labours Lost* (?1594) shows Shakespeare exploring intellectual pretence. The callow King of Navarre and his cronies decide to establish 'a little academe', to devote their lives entirely to study and self-improvement, and to abjure the company of women. This daft notion is immediately set on its ears by the arrival of the Princess of France on state business, which Navarre cannot ignore. The women-folk have all the wit, all the energy, all the common sense. Were an apology needed for the assertion of male dominance in *The Taming of the Shrew* that apology is certainly present here.

Other early experiments with comic kinds are discernible in *The Two Gentlemen of Verona* (?1587–8). This play sets the pattern which several Shakespearian comedies will follow in the years up to the turn of the century. Young lovers are separated by fortune and/or parental interference. The forsaken female, disguised in male attire, goes questing for her loved one. The device of cross-dressing recurs in *As You Like It* (1599), in *The Merchant of Venice* (1596), in *Twelfth Night* (1600–1) and in *All's Well That Ends Well* (?1602, ?3, ?4). In this group of plays the young disguised female is always infinitely superior to the male she loves in terms of both honesty and wit. In each case, through the girl's endeavour, love apparently triumphs in the end.

Given the common device of disguise it is amazing how atmospherically different from each other these plays are – by which one may well mean how brilliantly individuated are the heroines themselves. In at least one case, furthermore, the real world obtrudes most painfully onto the idyllic setting. *The Merchant of Venice* enforces very worldly concerns upon the idealized fabric of the disguise-plot. As *The Taming of the Shrew* had asked us to scrutinize Shakespeare's attitude to the opposite sex, so *The Merchant of Venice* involves itself with anti-Semitism, and we are left to guess whether Shakespeare approves of the Jew-baiting which the play apparently indulges.

Antonio – the Merchant of the play's title – is asked for a huge loan by his fortune-hunting friend Bassanio to finance a trip to Belmont, where lives Portia, a lady 'richly left', but by the will of her dead father bound to accept as husband only he who guesses aright which of three caskets contains her portrait. Because his own resources are strained by his merchant ventures Antonio raises the money as a loan from Shylock, a Jewish money lender. Shylock, contrary to his usual practice, refuses to take interest but proposes a 'merry bond', whereby forfeiture of the bond will invoke the penalty of a pound of Antonio's flesh. Antonio defaults and the bond becomes due. With the entire Venetian male world at sixes and sevens, Portia disguises herself as a young lawyer and so expounds Antonio's contract with the Jew that Shylock is utterly defeated, stripped of his fortune, and forced to turn Christian.

The bare bones of the fairy-tale-like plot give no hint of the human passions, the deeply disturbing moral and ethnic issues and the ruthless analysis of middle-class values which the play provokes. It is open to fundamentally opposite interpretations.

*A Midsummer Night's Dream* (?1595–6) is amazingly different in tone and ambience from the comedies of disguise. The wedding of Duke Theseus of Athens to Hippolyta, the Queen of the Amazons, is imminent, but wedding preparations are interrupted by the emotional troubles of four of Theseus' young attendants. Hermia is intended by her autocratic father to marry Demetrius but has a reciprocated passion for Lysander. The heavy-handed judgement of Theseus is that she must either marry the man of her father's choice, die, or go to a nunnery.

Hermia and Lysander conspire to run away, making their trysting place the woods outside the city. They confide the secret to Helena, who is herself in love with Demetrius, who formerly paid court to her. Helena resolves to tell Demetrius of the intended elopement, hoping he will pursue the lovers, and be grateful to Helena if she also then runs after him.

Meanwhile a group of Athenian working men are rehearsing a play which they hope will be chosen for performance at Theseus' wedding festivities. Peter Quince the carpenter is attempting to lick into shape an enactment of 'Pyramus and Thisbe', despite the best endeavours of Bottom the Weaver, ineffably assured of his thespian excellence, and despite the wonderful incompetence of the rest of his cast. Shakespeare's picture of amateur actors at work is timelessly apt. Inevitably their best tragic endeavours are heading towards complete farce.

Elsewhere in the forest and with a breathtaking shift of mode, Oberon and Titania, King and Queen of Faerie, are at domestic odds. Their quarrel has dire repercussions upon the mortal world, and we suddenly see all the Athenians diminished in scale by the poetry, magic and potential destructiveness of the fairy world. The result is pure theatrical magic. We are spellbound into believing the reality of these fairy creatures. They are far more tangible and credible than the shadowy and petty mortals of Theseus' train.

In an attempt to humiliate his Queen Oberon resolves to anoint her eyes with a magic juice which will cause her to fall in love with the first thing she sees on awakening. His mischievous attendant, Puck, is commanded to take some of the same potion and use it on the young Athenian whom Oberon has overheard rejecting his female suitor. Puck of course mistakes Lysander for Demetrius and makes confusion worse confounded. As they all sleep, exhausted after losing their way, he puts the potion on Lysander's eyes. He, waking, by mischance sees not Hermia but Helena, and is immediately besotted by her.

Puck has meanwhile interfered with the rehearsal of 'Pyramus and Thisbe', and placed a magic ass's head on Bottom, to the terror of his colleagues who run away and leave him. Titania, under the influence of Oberon's spell, awakes and falls in love with the 'transformed' Bottom. The gross spectacle of the Queen of Faerie with a humanoid ass in her lap is leavened by the ineffable innocence of Bottom's responses. The lovely confidence with which he enjoys the fairy world is both moving and comic. Eventually all the emotional tangles are unwound, and the last act of the play is graced by the play-within-a-play – the enactment of 'Pyramus and Thisbe'.

The play convinces us of the reality and potency of magic, of the need for something beyond the authority of mortality. The grace with which it judges human kind, finds it sadly wanting, and offers forgiveness, manifests the mind of a truly unique creative artist. There are few more accessibly actable plays, and few more welcome to audiences.

Shakespeare made one foray into bourgeois domestic comedy in *The Merry Wives of Windsor* (?1600–1). The only kinds of comedy he did not practise extensively were City Comedy and Courtly Satire. Shakespeare's vision of the comic seems to have been romantic as opposed to satirical, gentle rather than savage. Yet it is never mawkish or sentimental. When Puck in *A Midsummer Night's Dream* exclaims 'Lord, what fools these mortals be' (III, ii, 115), he speaks for his creator. But in Shakespeare's eyes folly is itself humanizing and forgivable. Gary Waller's *Shakespeare's Comedies* (1991) is a collection of modern theoretical approaches to the genre. See also Bradbury and Palmer (1972), Leggatt (1974) and Kriegar (1979).

## The Roman Plays

The political thinking implicit in Shakespeare's Histories is furthered and continued in the Roman plays. We need to recall that the English Renaissance was founded on the values and myths of Rome not of Athens. Englishmen perceived Rome as the high point of the world's achievement in both art and empire – a civilization to be emulated.

Shakespeare's quiet but fundamental scepticism never accepted this premise. His Romans are greedy, shallow, frantically self-seeking. In *Julius Caesar* (*c*.1599) he presents ineffectual and mutually destructive political alternatives. Caesar himself is uxorious, maniacally vain, so consumed by the idea of being Caesar that he is entirely dehumanized. As with so many demagogues he has become lost in the myth of his own publicity. Opposing him are the extremes of intellectual idealism in Brutus and cynical pragmatism in Cassius. Their conspiracy to rid the State of the threat Caesar poses is without stable political foundation. They have no coherent programme of reform, no viable alternative to what they are destroying. Nor do they have any cohesive unity of intent. Inevitably their faction fragments. Caesar's chief ally, the sybaritic roué, Mark Antony, is unprincipled and self-indulgent. His loyalty to Caesar is entirely emotional but that emotion is of a power sufficient to sway the mob against Brutus' abstract appeals.

Behind all these confused and unheroic Romans lurks Octavius Caesar – the man of destiny, earmarked by history to become Augustus, founder of the Roman empire, patron of the arts, and exemplar of classical civilization at its peak. As a man he is cold, calculating, manipulative. The conundrum is that only such a man, apparently, can be successful. Yet his nature is such that the very value of success is put in question.

*Antony and Cleopatra* (1606–7) takes this theme further. Antony's hankering for the fleshpots has led him to renege upon his Roman responsibilities, and to live a life of self-indulgence in Cleopatra's decadent but gloriously human Egypt. Again the fish-cold passionless world of Octavius triumphs. But every fibre of our humanity has been wrung against him. If this is the price of 'success' the price is too high. The play sweeps from Egypt to Rome as focal points in the vastness of Empire. Its crowning glory is the character of Cleopatra, an unsurpassable study in sexuality, cunning, wit and manipulative charisma.

*Coriolanus* (1608) returns us to Rome – this time pre-Imperial Rome – where internal strife is counterpointed by utterly motiveless aggression against the neighbouring Volsces. Caius Martius, the principal Roman militarist, is the exemplar of all an Elizabethan schoolboy would have been taught to admire. He soon acquires the title 'Coriolanus' for his exploits in battle at the Volscian town of Corioli. Coriolanus is experienced in battle since his early teens, many times wounded, utterly without fear, an awesome machine of destruction. Yet significantly, even his fellow patricians never make him their principal war-leader. And as a candidate for civic power he is grotesquely incompetent. Rome is split by factions. Populists and aristocrats are entrenched in convulsive class war. There is little to choose between them, and if the good of the State lies in the welfare of its ordinary citizens then there is no good in Rome. The common people are used and exploited by both senators and tribunes of the plebs to serve their respective ends.

Coriolanus – arch exponent of Roman militarism – is manipulated by a mixture of his own intransigence and plebeian demagoguery into betraying Rome and joining the Volsces. All the while we are aware that this man among men, this embodiment of virile values is actually the product of his mother's psychopathic imbalance. The notion of Roman 'virtus' which Volumnia inculcates is sterile and destructive. Her son is emotionally dead and it is entirely her fault. In an uncanny manner Shakespeare here predicts the murderous matriarchy which underlies apparently male-dominated societies; our own century has furnished poignant examples. No play in the canon is more 'modern', more relevant to our times. Not surprisingly, it is the least poetic of all Shakespeare's works. Not one single memorable passage has come into popular currency from *Coriolanus*. The bleakness of the play is thus emphasized; but that emphasis also points to its power.

For further reading on the Roman plays see Stampfer (1968), Simmons (1974) and Spencer (1964).

## The Tragedies

Shakespearian tragedy is difficult to define and codify. The author seems to have had little interest in the theory of classic 'kinds' or genres. The early years of his career, as we have seen, were spent preoccupied with comedy and with history. The histories furnish a logical preparation for the writing of tragedy; Shakespeare's concept of national destiny, his insight as a psychologist and his sense of the cyclic nature of historical events prepared the way. However sceptical of literary theory he may have been, he was sufficiently a man of his times not to leap unprepared into the writing of tragedy. The Renaissance held that of all dramatic kinds tragedy was the supreme – just as it held that epic was the most important kind of non-dramatic poetry. A writer prepared himself for the highest form of drama, much as an athlete might prepare for running the marathon.

This adequately explains the relative absence of tragedy from the first third of Shakespeare's writing career. By the time the Globe playhouse was available in 1599, certainly by the time the old Queen's reign was ending in 1603, by the time he had achieved mastery of the forms of dramatic comedy and history, Shakespeare would have felt himself ready to tackle the high peak of tragedy.

There are two early assays at tragedy. *Titus Andronicus* (*c.* 1588) belongs among the earliest of Shakespeare's playscripts. It is very much of its time, full of Senecan goriness, thunderous, ornate but static verse, and relatively predictable characters. But the contempt with which it has been dismissed by some critics is misguided. The play belongs to the spirit of the times, to the revenge drama popularized by Thomas Kyd, and it positively revels in the high rhetoric popularized by Marlowe.

The play investigates the nature of power and integrity, and it offers a radical critique of the militarism and unimaginative inflexibility of Rome. In Titus it offers us the first of a series of protagonists who are well-intentioned, but whose stubborn pride, whose deeply personalized view of integrity verges on a monomania which blinds them to common-sense pragmatism. For all his military prowess, Titus is a fool in political terms. Strains of his character will later be found in Lear, in Coriolanus, in Julius Caesar.

The other early tragedy is *Romeo and Juliet* (*c.*1595). Patchy and inexperienced as it is, the play has moments of great tenderness in the relationship between the 'star-crossed lovers'; in Mercutio we are given a manic individualist exploding towards inevitable doom, and in Juliet's nurse Shakespeare creates a memorable and original character study. The play's plot is extremely un-Aristotelian. Its centre is not a man of power and destiny, who has one fatal flaw in his character, and who is brought down by overweening pride and a trick of fortune. Here the joint protagonists are teenaged youngsters, entirely without civic or state authority, and entirely innocent of pride or misjudgement. Their intentions never threaten the destinies of other groups; they never aspire to challenge or usurp political authority. Neither one of them is in any real sense responsible for the events which bring about their deaths.

In each of these respects the play deviates from what will be the normal conditions inherent in Shakespearian tragedy after the turn of the century.

Shakespeare's concentration upon tragedy begins in about 1599–1600, and runs for about nine years. The differences between these plays are more striking than enforced similarities. Bradley (1904) exemplifies the desire to perceive common ground within the group. Bradley tries to read Shakespeare as a latter-day Greek dramatist. He seeks for Aristotelian elements which might offer structural and ideological similarities. Careful and illuminating as Bradley's exegeses may be, they are heading in a wrong direction. No such homogenesis informs the stream of plays which mark this phase of Shakespeare's creative life. Drakakis (1992) replaces homogeneity with bewildering diversity, offering semiotic, feminist, new historicist, Marxist and poststructurist readings of the genre.

Aristotle suggested that tragedy elicits fear and pity in order to expose us to a purging or cleansing. The measure in which this effect is sought, and the balance between fear and pity varies hugely from play to play with Shakespeare. Fear may accompany contempt rather than pity at one end of the scale, as is the case with Timon of Athens or with Coriolanus. Pity may signally outweigh fear, as it does in *Hamlet* (1599–1600). The fundamentals of Aristotelian thinking on the nature of tragedy are called in question. Shakespeare even ventures into that territory where Aristotle suggested the tragic dramatist could not go, in creating the protagonist who is villain rather than hero – as in the case of Macbeth. He may call us to be covertly admiring of what we recognize to be the hero's faults, as in the case of Mark Antony.

The emotional state to which the ending of the play is leading us varies widely from play to play. In *Macbeth* (*c.* 1606) we are glad that the protagonist is dead, that the reign of terror is over. Yet we feel the littleness of the world which is left behind. Whilst *Hamlet* leaves us feeling merely glad that the hero has escaped this vale of tears, the ending of *Othello* (1604) elicits no such intimate sympathy. *Othello* is Shakespeare's only mature domestic tragedy, and it plays upon a set of emotional responses vastly different from those involved in *Coriolanus* or in *King Lear* (*c.* 1606). Indeed, *King Lear*, the most awesome and mysterious of all the tragedies, defies description of the intention of its ending. What *is* the meaning of those final words: 'The oldest hath borne most; we that are young / Shall never see so much nor live so long' (V, iii, 325–6)?

Nevertheless, for all his formal divergences from Greek tragedy, there are moments when one feels the spirit of the Greeks breathes again in Shakespeare the poet and thinker: 'Three masters, pain, Time, and royalty in the blood have taught me patience', cries Oedipus, in Sophocles' *Oedipus at Colonus*. Any reading of *King Lear* is enriched by this epigraph. Or by this, from Aeschylus' *Agamemnon*:

> Zeus setting us on the road,
> Made this a valid law,
> That men must learn by suffering.
> Drop by drop in sleep upon the heart
> Falls the laborious memory of pain.
> Against one's will comes wisdom.
> The grace of the Gods is forced upon us,
> Throned inviolably.

Structurally the great tragedies differ significantly from each other. *Hamlet* never lets us escape from the claustrophobia of the Danish court at Elsinore. It is the only one of these plays to preserve this unity of place. *Antony and Cleopatra*, conversely, sweeps from Rome to Athens, to Egypt, and into the far eastern reaches of the Roman empire. Its geographical spread is cosmic and insistent.

The death of the hero is customarily held back until the very end of the play; yet the death of Antony comes in Act IV, leaving Cleopatra alone to face the wiles of

Octavius Caesar. The very fact of having joint protagonists sets this play apart from the other mature tragedies.

These differences of structure are worth stressing since they offer clear warning against attempts to generalize about Shakespearian tragedy. It is more difficult to actually prove differences of 'feeling' or of ethos. But the compassion for the hero which informs *Hamlet* is awesomely absent in *Coriolanus*, for instance.

All the tragedies pose questions about power. Lear has absolute autocratic authority from which he tries to abdicate; Antony refuses to accept the responsibility which his public role demands of him; Macbeth is greedy for kingship which the natural line of succession denies him; Coriolanus is unable to reconcile his private contempt for the populace with the need to make public acknowledgement of his responsibility to the masses if he wishes to be consul. Hamlet, on the other hand, is the victim of his uncle Claudius's greed for power. Hamlet is also the only Shakespearian hero who is described as popular with the common people.

The ideas in the English and Roman history plays impinge upon the tragedies. They all examine Renaissance man, caught at a key moment in history, a moment which finds the conservative certainties of the passing medieval world challenged by an uncertain future into which the age of science was precipitating Europe. All the major creative artists of this era perceived the political, ethical, social and intellectual convulsions upon whose threshold they stood. Machiavelli (1469–1527) and Hobbes (1588–1679) articulated views of man which clashed with the traditional teaching of the Church. Such views became the more tenable as scientific advances – such as the optical telescope – revealed the possibility of man as a self-seeking animal in a jungle somewhere on the outer periphery of a godless universe. An instinctual malaise permeated the more intelligent minds of the period. Danby (1949) is particularly good on this subject.

*King Lear* gives expression to these feelings. On one level Lear himself represents the hitherto unchallenged autocracies which characterized medievalism. But now in his extreme old age, he seeks to adjust to the changing times. His progeny are approaching their prime, still unfulfilled, and greedy for their own chance to wield power. The 80-year-old King resolves to abdicate, and to divide his realm 'That future strife/May be prevented now' (I, i, 43–4). Feudalism is attempting to compromise with modernity. The heart of the tragedy is the impossibility of men making such accommodations for themselves. On the face of it Lear's scheme is admirable, rational and just.

But 'something' in the nature of things will not permit such adjustments. Even kings are bound by immutable laws which take no cognizance of compromise or common sense. And Fate, Destiny, the Gods – call it what you will – curses Lear with blighting self-will. His scheme to prevent strife is confused by his urge to hang on to the trappings of power, by his pathetic attempt to make the abdication depend upon protestations of particular love from his daughters, and by a hideous misjudgement of the nature of the elder two, Goneril and Regan. Machiavellian and Hobbesian modern man, in the shape of the illegitimate but wonderfully witty Edmund, also interposes in Lear's hierarchical schemes.

The play's poetry helps build this family and dynastic misfortune into a paradigm of the world's chaos. Tortured animalistic imagery reiterates the universal destructiveness; storm and darkness sanction the atmosphere of doom. Sexuality, procreation, justice, love are all turned to a surrealist nightmare.

Although set in the pre-Christian realm of Albion the play intentionally urges comparison with Shakespeare's own times and those he sees immediately following him. It is a despairing vision; the new generation will be no wiser and no better, and it will lack the heroic dimension of what it has superseded.

For further reading on Shakespearian tragedy see Brooke (1968), Muir (1972), Danby (1949), Honigmann (1976) and Bayley (1981).


## The Problem Plays and the Last Plays

As well as comedies, histories and tragedies, many accounts of Shakespeare's work make further genre divisions. *Troilus and Cressida* (*c.* 1602), *All's Well That Ends Well* (*c.* 1603), *Measure For Measure* (*c.* 1604), *The Merchant of Venice* and *Hamlet* are sometimes grouped as the 'Problem Plays'. These works enforce particular moral and social problems with vehement emphasis. *Measure For Measure*, for instance, shows an ineffectual Duke who has allowed moral standards in Vienna to decline for many years, and who is now unable to face the problem of putting things to rights. He appoints Angelo as his Deputy and then goes into hiding to watch the results of his action.

Angelo is quick to have arrested Claudio, who has made pregnant his fiancée, Juliet. The pair have been privately contracted to each other, and only await the chance to make a public declaration of their troth until Juliet's family is reconciled to the marriage and will thus pay her a due dowry. In other words it is an extreme technical point of law upon which Claudio is now arrested for immorality, and finds himself under threat of execution.

Claudio's sister, Isabella, is about to become a nun, but is persuaded to plead for her brother's life to Angelo. The hitherto cold-blooded Deputy is stricken with passion for her, and offers to release her brother if Isabella will sleep with him. The complications which follow are made more ironic by the disguised Duke's interference in the affairs from which he has abdicated, and by the substitution in Angelo's bed of his pre-contracted fiancée, Mariana, for Isabella.

The final act of the play struggles to find resolutions to these moral and ethical conundrums. The ending of *Measure For Measure* is curiously arbitrary. The Duke claims Isabella as his bride without any apparent regard for her feelings, or her prior intention of becoming a nun.

The play is given passionate intensity by the quality of its poetry. Anguished, tortured, guilt-ridden, its characters articulate with great vehemence the nature of their thinking and suffering. *Measure For Measure* gives tangible embodiment to virtually all the generalities which preoccupied Shakespeare in his middle period – Justice, Equity, Forgiveness, Integrity, Love, Duty, Government, Virtue – the list is daunting. Questions are posed with singular power; answers there are none.

The 'Problem Plays' may embody Shakespeare's response to the new vogue for tragi-comedy at the beginning of the seventeenth century. Given his sensitivity towards dramatic form elsewhere, it would be no surprise to know that there is a conscious element of experimentation in the way these plays are shaped and presented.

The last plays, or the Romances, are equally aware of new and changing fashion. The quasi-dramatic form of courtly masque had grown in popularity under the reign of James I. The plays of Shakespeare's last years respond by including masque-like elements. These plays – *Cymbeline* (*c.* 1610), *Pericles* (*c.* 1608), *The Winter's Tale* (1609) and *The Tempest* (*c.* 1610–11) – all create an initial atmosphere akin to that of the tragedies, but rather than enforcing a descent into the maelstrom of destruction which ends the works in the earlier group, the Romances describe the redemption of human error by acts of self-recognition and forgiveness.

So, in *The Winter's Tale* King Leontes of Sicilia is struck, in a sudden mad fit of jealousy, with the notion that his friend King Polixenes of Bohemia, has seduced and made pregnant his wife, Hermione. Despite warnings and portents Leontes wilfully pursues the punishment of Hermione, and decrees that her new-born child shall be abandoned in the wilderness abroad. Hermione falls senseless and is thought dead. A dreadful trail of destruction ensues when Leontes ignores the warning of the oracle that Hermione is innocent. His son Mamillius dies, the loyal courtier Antigonus is killed by a bear whilst disposing of Leontes' child on the sea-coast of Bohemia and, too late, Leontes sees the error of his judgement.

There now ensues a fourteen-year gap. The play's second phase takes us to Bohemia where the abandoned princess, Perdita, has grown to young womanhood, having been fostered by the shepherds who found her. Florizel, son of the King of Bohemia, falls in love with her. Polixenes violently opposes his son's choice, but all is eventually resolved, even to the reappearance of Hermione, who was not dead but in hiding, pending the adequate repentance of Leontes.

Yet, despite the forgiveness manifest at the last, we are painfully aware of the price which has been paid. The promise of youth is weighed against the painful experience of middle age.

The plays of this group all concern themselves with humanity's potential for redeeming itself from its gross errors, but they do not shirk a description of the cost to be paid. Victorian critics argued that Shakespeare emphasizes the redemptive power of youth. An unsentimental reading of the text elicits a far more tempered and saddened response.

In *The Tempest* Prospero, Duke of Milan, has been usurped by his brother Antonio, mainly as a result of his own selfish desire to be scholar rather than duke. Prospero is cast away on a desert island for fourteen years accompanied only by his daughter, Miranda. Prospero's magic powers eventually cast his enemies into his power, and he learns to forgive them. But the cost of this lesson is the voluntary loss of his magic powers, and a return to Milan as a prematurely aged man.

Many critics see the play as symbolic – Prospero is Shakespeare, yielding up the power of poetry as he prepares to go into retirement from his life in art. If it is so, then much sadness inheres in the play. 'Abdication', 'retirement' spells the end of creativity, and spells inevitable decline: 'Thence retire me to my Milan, where Every third thought shall be my grave...' (_The Tempest_: V, i, 310–11).

For further reading on the Problem Plays and the Last Plays see Lawrence (1931), Muir and Wells (1982), Tillyard (1938), Traversi (1953) and Yates (1975).


## Shakespeare since Shakespeare: later interpretations

'He was not of an age but for all time', wrote Ben Jonson ('To the Memory of ... Mr William Shakespeare ...'), in the commendatory verses at the beginning of the First Folio. Whilst the core of Shakespeare's integrity remains rooted in the English Renaissance, and he cannot be understood without some knowledge of the reigns of Elizabeth and James I, he speaks to succeeding ages as a still-living voice.

An eighteenth-century version of a Shakespeare play would be seeking a 'message' differing from that of a nineteenth- or a twentieth-century production. The play would look different, it would sound different, and would be received by an audience with its own differences. And none of these versions would concur with the spirit or 'feel' of performances of The King's Men at the Globe or the Blackfriars theatre during Shakespeare's lifetime. We may restore the bricks and mortar of the Globe; its spirit can never be recalled.

It follows, of course, that the major critics across the centuries will have reacted to Shakespeare in very different ways. There are no immutable constants in trying to assess our national bard. Attitudes to the very text itself have differed and acting versions reflect the times which bring them forth. Desire for classical symmetry in the late seventeenth century, for instance, wrote into _The Tempest_ a brother for Miranda, and sister for Ferdinand. In _King Lear_ neo-classical decorum was offended by the Fool and bewildered by the lack of apparent justice in the play's ending. Thus the text was adulterated to leave Lear alive, to marry Cordelia to Edgar and to cut out the Fool completely. Furthermore, it was this travesty of Shakespeare's text which held the English stage until well into the nineteenth century.

In 1642 the Puritan government interdicted the public performance of professional theatre. By 1660 when King Charles returned from exile at the French court bringing with him so many new social, political and cultural assumptions, every one of the old 'pre-closures' playhouses had vanished. The nature of 'Shakespearian' drama – open, fluid, schematized, making its impact through words before effects – was at odds with the new manners and style.

Women appeared on the professional English stage for the first time; the theatres themselves changed. The old Elizabethan apron stage disappeared. The proscenium arch now separated actors from audience, whilst upstage elaborate painted scenery became more and more of a fixture.

The plays themselves changed in style and content to meet royal and courtly demand. Tragedy was based on the neo-classical style of the French dramatist Jean Racine (1639–99): close, intense, vehemently rhetorical and bound by the so-called Aristotelian unities of Time, Place and Action. Tragedy melded into 'Heroic' drama.

Language became more and more inflated and bombastic, and the quest for poetic justice precluded the metaphysical uncertainties which deliberately cloud the ending of Shakespearian tragedy. Sexual licence was rife at Charles's court, and this permissiveness is reflected on stage in Restoration comedy. The licentious comedy of the Restoration had plots utterly unlike Shakespeare; it is not surprising that many of his plays were either abandoned or adapted. Most Restoration and eighteenth-century critics talk of Shakespeare as the giant of a more powerful but less well-formed age than their own. 'Improvement' of this rough genius proceeded apace. The more 'barbarous' of Shakespeare's language was cut or altered.

The evolution of the actor-manager, usually the star who chose the works which his own company would perform, further subverted the integrity of Shakespeare's text and meaning. Plays like *Richard III*, *Macbeth* and *The Merchant of Venice* which have one charismatic and dominant role became the staple of the Shakespearian repertoire, since they showed off the talents of the actor-manager himself.

The architecture of the playhouses built from the Restoration through to the early twentieth century further conspires to remove us from Shakespeare. The characteristic auditorium shape of the period is a horseshoe, where the audience are looking at each other as much as at the stage. The stage itself is segregated from the audience by either an orchestra pit and/or footlights. Every vestige of the intimate contact between players and audience, presupposed by the Elizabethan thrust stage, has now disappeared.

Plays whose message might be deemed iconoclastic, pessimistic, unpatriotic, failed to appeal. Shakespeare's political scepticism was not appreciated. Thus plays like *Coriolanus* were very seldom performed. Others like *Titus Andronicus* were misunderstood, their richness of Senecan conceit deemed merely 'barbarous'. This was far from quelling the tendency to create a cult which asserted the absolute primacy of Shakespeare among our dramatists. Bardolatry – the Shakespeare industry – owes its origins to the eighteenth-century actor David Garrick (1717–79), who inaugurated commemorative bicentennial festivities at Stratford-upon-Avon in 1764, with souvenir shops, sight-seeing, free hot dinners for the 'Great and Good', and the commencement of much myth-making.

Among Garrick's friends and more temperate admirers was the great eighteenth-century critic, Samuel Johnson, whose Shakespeare criticism has stood the test of time better than that of any of his contemporaries. Johnson dismissed the fashionable notion of Shakespeare's 'incorrectness', and his supposed ignorance of the neo-classical unities. With massive common sense characteristic of all his literary criticism, he asserts the value and necessity of yielding to the experience unfolding on stage, whilst we continue to realize fully that we are in a theatre and are witnessing an imaginary action, not a slice of life. A spectator knows perfectly well he is sitting on a padded seat in an artificially lit room, watching surrogate enactments. To constrain these enactments within the straitjacket of the neo-classical unities, Johnson argued, is mere folly. He pre-empts arguments later given more elaborate articulation by Coleridge (1772–1834) with his demand for the 'willing suspension of disbelief'.

Awareness of the relationship between the times, the style of production they elicit, and the resultant strictures of the critics, is of cardinal importance to the understanding of the history of Shakespeare criticism. Some of the most acute and receptive commentators have been consigned to watching the plays at particularly unfortunate times in the course of the history of Shakespeare production. It is not surprising that the Romantic critics, for instance, declared *King Lear* to be a marvellous dramatic poem, but an unactable live drama.

Victorian Shakespeare sustained the star system, and the primacy of the actor-manager. The emphasis is on the personality of the actor. The play becomes merely a vehicle to exhibit his talents. Thus, a typical nineteenth-century performance might well present the famous speech 'Hath not a Jew eyes ...' (III, i, 52 seq.) as the moment in *The Merchant of Venice* when Shylock apparently pleads for the common humanity of his persecuted ethnic group. But the context of the speech within the play was almost invariably suppressed or subverted by playing this speech entirely for sympathy. It is, in context, a lead-in to Shylock's justification of Old Testament revenge. And once this falsely attractive Jew is played alongside a sugar-sweet Portia (as most of the Victorian actresses played her), the exquisitely fraught nature of the problems in the play is lost.

The star actress helped to pull plays out of shape just as the actor-manager did. Sarah Siddons (1755–1831), for instance, was noted pre-eminently for her Lady Macbeth. Report suggests that her powerful performance dominated the play. For Shakespeare and the King's Men, the role was enacted by a boy-player, who could not possibly have dominated Burbage as Macbeth. Of course Lady Macbeth is the key agent in subverting the vacillating mind of her husband, but her part, in terms of the number of lines she speaks, is carefully and calculatedly kept very small – about 240 lines in all. The famous sleep-walking scene, so often the subject of pictures of nineteenth-century Lady Macbeths in full flight, is 77 lines in total, of which Lady Macbeth herself speaks 22.

The sentimentalization of Shakespeare's heroines warps the play's meaning. Rosalind, in *As You Like It*, is brave, witty and attractive. But she is also wonderfully bold, and her mind encompasses the comedy of sexuality as part of its rounded healthiness. No Victorian actress would have dared to make this boldness plain.

These monumental performances took place against increasingly heavy 'realistic' scenery. By mid-nineteenth century major landscape painters were being commissioned to create backdrops for plays which, when originally performed by the King's Men, had no scenery save the neutral backdrop of the playhouse itself. Apart from other meretricious implications for interpreting the plays, such scenic clutter hampered the pace of production, which in turn led to texts being cut to ribbons in order to accommodate the time required by the scene-shifters!

Gary Taylor's *Reinventing Shakespeare* (1990) is an excellent survey of the way in which different periods shape Shakespeare in their own image; Graham Holderness's *The Shakespeare Myth* (1988) is equally informative on our vision of Shakespeare as an accumulation of post-Shakespearian images and preconceptions.

Vickers's *Shakespeare The Critical Heritage* (1974–81) is a collection of reviews and criticism from the sixteenth to the twentieth century. Price (1973), Donoghue (1975) and Odell (1920) are historical surveys of theatrical performance.

## Modern responses to Shakespeare

In the nineteenth century criticism of the text itself drifted away from playhouse exigencies and into realms of academic speculation. Interpretation slid further and further away from the concept of a living, working, Renaissance dramatist operating with a great repertory troupe and performing for a demanding and changing audience.

The emergence of European theatre into a new era which was led by Ibsen (1828–1906), particularly in his social problem plays from 1875, encouraged George Bernard Shaw (1856–1950) to articulate a much more practical kind of Shakespeare criticism. Pungent intelligence and healthy wit help Shaw to cut away the nonsense from cluttered and sentimentalized performance. Shaw could be cantankerous, but his own practical experience of theatre helped him look for totality of meaning in the play rather than for brilliant patches of virtuoso performance or for esoteric and occult meanings.

Harley Granville Barker (1877–1946), actor, author, director, typifies the willingness to return and listen to Shakespeare himself, which Shaw fostered. Granville Barker's *Prefaces to Shakespeare* (1927–48) presents a version of the briefing he gave to casts who were about to perform under his direction. The plays begin to operate again as company works rather than as vehicles for a solo star.

The tide began to turn in favour of exploring and restoring something like the conditions under which Shakespeare had actually staged his plays. Representative of attempts to reconstruct the geography and the ambience of actual performance in Shakespeare's day are: Hodges, *The Globe Restored* (1968), Adams, *The Globe Playhouse* (1961) and Gurr, *The Shakespearian Stage 1572–1642* (1970).

It is probably true to say that late twentieth-century audiences now have a better chance of seeing Shakespeare enacted in conditions akin to those for which he wrote than at any time since 1660. Debate centres on how far such reconstructionism should go. The imitation Globe now nearing completion close to the site of the original, on Bankside in London, is the extreme of reconstructionist aspiration.

The best twentieth-century criticism of Shakespeare has responded positively to the challenge of making ideas and practicality meet. There is a perception that the texts exist not merely to preach statements but to entertain a paying audience. Critics like Kott (1967) have been able to bring to the text their personal experience of totalitarianism and to show Shakespeare's understanding of the terror implicit in power. Kott's Hamlet is a man beset by the secret police, by the threat of central dictatorship.

This and similar studies allow the twentieth century access to its own interpretation of Shakespeare. One of the principal benefits is that it has encouraged a fresh look at plays which were earlier seldom performed, like *Coriolanus*, or *Troilus and Cressida*.

Yet during the 1930s some academic criticism began to drift away from the notions of 'historical' Shakespeare, or 'Shakespeare in Performance' that underpin the work of Bradley or Granville Barker (q.v.). This trend took its cue from the New Critical emphasis upon the literary text as a holistic entirety of image patterns and stylistic habits: Shakespeare's plays were treated like lyric poems, coherent artefacts whose 'meaning' had as much to do with their own internal structure as with their dramatic or historical contexts.

Knight ([1930] 1949) and Clemen (1951) are typical of this method. The new mood is summed up in Knights ([1933] 1946) – *How Many Children Had Lady Macbeth?* – the implied answer being 'Who cares? Lady Macbeth is an emotive-aesthetic device, not a real person.' That archetype of New Critical analysis, Cleanth Brooks's *The Well Wrought Urn* (1947) contains an essay on imagery in Macbeth, and William Empson in *Seven Types of Ambiguity* (1930) ferrets out Shakespeare's bifurcated meanings.

Since the 1960s New Criticism and traditional, exegetical scholarship have been challenged by structuralism and poststructuralism. Structuralism can be divided into two principal schools: the linguists, who explain and demystify literary texts in terms of the broader configurations of the language system; and the semioticians who extend this analytical framework to the all-inclusive universe of signs – linguistic and non-linguistic – that shape our condition. The best known example of the former in Shakespeare criticism is Jakobson and Jones's (1970, reprinted in Pomorska and Rudy, 1987) analysis of Sonnet 129; this essay shows us how the linguistic density of Shakespeare's dramatic language is reflected in his non-dramatic verse. Shakespeare has remained largely immune from the attentions of the latter, but for a structuralist-semiotic reading of *Measure For Measure* see Unit 18, pp. 539–42, and see also Moretti (1983) which includes a chapter on the semiotics of Renaissance tragedy.

Shakespeare's fate in the hands of the poststructuralists (an umbrella term involving the activities of feminism, deconstruction, psychoanalysis and new historicism) is a more complex issue.

The new historicists are currently the most active and fashionable theorists of Renaissance literature; an example of their work on Shakespeare will be found in Unit 21. New historicism involves a confluence of Marxist ideas and the more complex cultural theories of Michel Foucault (again, see Unit 21). While the New Critics treated the literary text as a unique, self-determined entity, the new historicists regard literary writing as one element of the broad network of discourses which embody the cultural and ideological character of society. This approach differs also from conventional literary history in its shift from a perception of history as real events occurring outside literature to a notion of literature as one of the political and ideological codes through which a society shapes an image of itself. For example, we find in Greenblatt's (1988) seminal new historicist text that Prince Hal circulates and embodies the ideological motives of Machiavelli and of the colonists of Virginia. In Dollimore and Sinfield (1985) *Measure For Measure* is read as an enactment of the political tensions which gripped England at the accession of James I – the lower orders of the play are seen as a reflection of a potential for unaffiliated, decentralized chaos, and the disguised Duke as an emblem of the strategies by which a hierarchy reshapes and inculcates its authority. In short, the play's apparent subjects of justice, virtue and truth are less significant than its engagement in an ongoing and unsettled dialogue involving immediate problems of political instability.

The main problem with feminist readings of Shakespeare involves a telescoping of perceptions and contexts. Shakespeare, like most male writers within the pre-twentieth-century canon and like many since, reflects the gender roles and expectations of his context. These have since been exposed as repressive of the creative, social, professional and intellectual ambitions of women, but the question remains as to whether Shakespeare consistently endorses, or transcends and perhaps occasionally subverts, them. Two interesting and closely related test cases can be found in the situations of Portia in *The Merchant of Venice* and Isabella in *Measure For Measure*. Isabella enters the male-dominated discourse of justice in her plea to Angelo on her brother's behalf. The play itself quickly ensures that her intellectual presence is displaced by her role as a device in the various designs of men: Angelo transforms the subject of her discourse into an instrument for his own lustful ambitions, and the Duke uses her as both bait and trap in his secret machinations. Portia faces a similar situation in her desire to free Antonio from Shylock's contract. In order to operate outside her almost unreal habitation of Belmont and engage in the real-world contingencies of Venice, she has to disguise herself as a man.

In neither instance does Shakespeare present the woman as intellectually inferior to her male counterparts, but he does show that in reality a woman's intellectual condition is effectively determined by male-dominated social and cultural conventions.

Unit 24 offers a feminist reading of *As You Like It*. Dusinberre (1975) offers a broader feminist view in *Shakespeare and the Nature of Woman*. In *Shakespeare's Division of Experience* French (1982) acknowledges an essential difference between male and female identity and examines Shakespeare's presentation of the masculine and the feminine 'principles'. Belsey's *The Subject of Tragedy* (1985) considers Renaissance tragedy as a genre which explores and reformulates relations between masculine and feminine identity. See also Jardine (1983) and essays collected in Lenz, Greene and Neely (1980).

The psychocritics focus inevitably upon the Oedipal conundrum of *Hamlet*. For a discussion of this see Unit 22. Andrè Green extends Freud's classic reading of neurosis and psychosis to *Othello* (in *The Tragic Effect: The Oedipus Complex in Tragedy*, 1979). One of the prominent and most irritating assumptions of psychoanalytical literary criticism is that the author (and often the reader) is, like the patient, not entirely in control of the complex network of desire and dependency that underpins the work. Conversely, one might argue that the complex artistry of *Hamlet* and *Othello* reflects on Shakespeare's part a knowledge of the unconscious just as informed as Freud's or Lacan's.

Finally, to the blasted heath of deconstruction for readings hell-bent upon finding uncertainty or indeterminacy in a text, and drawing from this the absolute conclusion that nothing can be said about anything: this topic is elaborated in Unit 19. Read Atkins's and Bergeron's *Shakespeare and Deconstruction* (1988) and it will become evident that Shakespeare was probably the first deconstructionist. Nietzsche proposed and Derrida shows that beyond language there is nothing. Shakespeare at least offered us language that we can enjoy and understand. Evans's *Signifying Nothing* (1988) is the liveliest and most intriguing example of deconstructing Shakespeare: at one point he shows how the intrinsic 'meaning' of a single line from *As You Like It* disappears into 168 equally valid interpretative acts (pp. 147–64).

Terence Hawkes's *That Shakespeherian Rag* (1986) is poststructuralism in an engaging and reasonably accessible form. Particularly intriguing is his discussion of Shakespeare critic A.C. Bradley (pp. 27–50). Bradley is regarded as an archetypal traditionalist but Hawkes shows that the conflicts generated by his work early this century pre-empted the current mood of theoretical controversy. Conclusion: Shakespeare criticism tells us more about the perversities of literary analysis than it does about Shakespeare. Drakakis's *Alternative Shakespeares* (1985) is also a stimulating and thought-provoking collection.

Vickers's *Shakespeare. The Critical Heritage* (1974–81) offers a comprehensive selection of Shakespeare criticism from the sixteenth through to the twentieth century. The best way to measure your own preferences against the vast range of contemporary ideas and methods is to dip into two books: Vickers (1993) and Parker and Hartman (1985). The latter will give a slightly dated but symptomatic flavour of modern theoretical trends. The former is a compelling, polemical, learned attack upon the modes and assumptions of modern theory. Make your own decisions, but Vickers is without doubt the most accessible writer.

Before leaving the complex topic of Shakespeare and modern literary theory a worked example would be useful. The following is from Eagleton (1986), in which every element of the vast network of contemporary theory is brought to bear upon Shakespeare's work. Eagleton summarises his own reading of *Macbeth* thus:

> *Macbeth* fears this feminine fluidity as political anarchy, viewing diffusion as disruption. One of its more creditable reasons for doing so ... is that it is worried by the closeness of this fruitful interchangeability of signs, roles and bodies to a certain destructive tendency in bourgeois thought which levels all differences to the same dead level, in the anarchy and arbitrariness of the market place.
>
> (p. 8)

Let us decode this. In Eagleton's reading 'feminine fluidity' refers to the anarchic, deliberately puzzling language of the witches. These chaotic predictions prefigure the substance of the play, which continually unsettles any stable relationship between 'signs' (desire, justice, allegiance etc.), 'roles' (who exactly is the proper inheritor of the kingdom?) and 'bodies' (mortal existence is, throughout the play, a temporary, unreliable condition). All of this, according to Eagleton, involves an enactment of the destructive tensions of 'bourgeois thought' present within the broader fabric of Renaissance England; a society undergoing rapid change from feudalism to the 'anarchy', the 'market place', of modern capitalism.

We can identify at least two interpretative theories at work: feminism, in Eagleton's identification of the witches' discourse as the diffuse and disruptive utterances of a repressed gender (he has earlier referred to Lady Macbeth as a 'bourgeois feminist' striving to outdo the male system which subordinates her); and Marxism, in his perception of the play as a reflection of the uncertainties and tensions of the post-feudal transformation to the market economy.

There is a third theory at work in Eagleton's refusal to identify Shakespeare as the creator or originator of this network of meanings: '*Macbeth* [not the character but the play] fears this feminine fluidity ... *it* is worried ...'. The impression that the play has taken on a life of its own, irrespective of its author's intention, reflects Eagleton's acceptance of the keynote of modern theory, the death of the author: language creates and organizes meaning, not the person who uses it.

These critical theories are discussed more fully in Section 3. For the moment it might be questioned whether Eagleton's opaque collection of perspectives assists our appreciation of a brilliantly poetic dramatization of ambition, murder and retribution.

## Shakespeare's theatre

The first permanent building in England custom-built for drama was the Theatre (alternatively spelt 'Theater'), built by James Burbage (d. 1597) in Shoreditch, London in 1576. At that time William Shakespeare was 12 years old. Had Burbage built his theatre ten years earlier or ten years later things might have been very different. The dramatist (who probably arrived in London somewhere in the late 1580s) was at the ideal age to respond to the stimulus and challenge of literary life in the metropolis. He found professional drama established, settled, but still fresh and exciting.

England, London in particular, was increasingly assertive of its literary character. Not only the theatres but the Inns of Court (virtually the London University of the day), and the Queen's own royal court were full of young 'bloods' eager to thrust out their literary elbows, to invent or pursue new styles, daring experiments with form and language. Alongside them were the professional writers – the pamphleteers, gossip-mongers and hacks, whose trade often came into rivalry with the more aristocratic circles. The theatre was by no means the most prestigious organ for which to write, but its attraction was irresistible.

A sense of national pride informed this activity. England had discovered the Renaissance manifestly later than most of continental Europe. Earlier literature in English had been imitative of Italian, Spanish or French authors, or had followed the classics through translation. But under the Tudors, the vernacular flourished.

English was still a language in a fluid and experimental form. Its very unformedness offered special challenges. Grammar and syntax were not codified. New words could be coined at will. Shakespeare, born ten years earlier, would have found this language, as his theatre, not yet ready for the daring with which he treated it; ten years later it would have been much more set in its ways.

The same is true of the literary avant-garde with which he associated. At one and the same time he encountered the astonishing intellectual daring and verbal pyrotechnics of the metaphysical verse of John Donne (q.v.), the classical acerbity of Ben Jonson, and the courtly elegance of Edmund Spenser. 'Bliss was it in that time to be alive, But to be young was very heaven.' Never elsewhere in the history of English literary culture has there been quite such an eruption of talent. Whatever Shakespeare's 'genius' may comprise, he was manifestly very lucky to arrive in London when both theatres and literature were at this stage of development.

Audiences were drawn from a wider social range than ever before or again. The buildings themselves were still subject to improvement. And by the date of Shakespeare's retirement – certainly by the date of his death – the situation had changed again. The heyday of the outdoor, democratic auditoria was over. His own company, The King's Men, now performed most of their prestige work indoors at the Blackfriars, where admission prices and, consequently, audience expectation, deterred the 'groundlings' who had attended the Globe or the Theatre. But when Shakespeare arrived in London – let us guess at a date in the mid–late 1580s – the situation was absolutely fluid.

The origins of the 'Elizabethan theatre' (actually a term about as helpful as 'the twentieth-century football ground') are twofold. The guild plays of medieval times – the 'mystery' cycles of York, Chester, etc. (q.v.) – had been performed on specially prepared carts which were dragged round fixed stations in the town. Action flowed from cart to street, and thus schematized acting areas evolved, and acquired symbolic meaning. Under the cart would be hell, into which devils and sinners would fall to the accompaniment of vigorous stage effects representing hell fire. The cart itself is earth, and heaven can be readily built up from it as a superstructure. This symbolic undertow is still present in many of Shakespeare's dramatic conceptions.

The guild plays were amateur. But the number of professional troupes increased. Their *ad hoc* venue was often a handy inn yard. Many Tudor inns were built around a square, with galleries running around the inside of the structure to give access to the rooms. The building was entered by a main gate – which could easily be controlled during performances. A few planks placed across barrels at the back of the square, provided a ready stage. This arrangement offered several alternative entrances and exits for the actors, and favourable vantage points for spectators. The bull and bear baiting arenas on the south bank of the Thames may also have influenced the shape of the first theatres.

Burbage's was not the only playhouse in town. Inn yards continued to be used, and other custom-built theatres quickly followed Burbage's. The Curtain (1577), the Rose (1587), the Swan (1595) and the Hope (1613) were among the most prestigious. During much of Shakespeare's career he had competition from at least four or five alternative theatres. Latterly, there were indoor venues for more up-market audiences, and frequently the adult acting companies faced serious rivalry from the boy-actors trained in the schools. Hamlet discusses them with the Player Leader (*Hamlet*: II, ii, 333 seq.).

Because theatre-going was restricted to certain sections of the community, London's population of, say, 180,000 in 1595, could only support a high level of theatrical activity by the constant turnover of material. Popular plays were revived, but long runs of any particular work were virtually unknown. Thus playwrights had to work under intense pressure, often collaborating, frequently pillaging old story books. Many of them – like Shakespeare himself – were also acting in their own and other writers' plays, and taking a share in the administration and/or artistic direction of the company.

The best of the acting companies responded to the substantial prejudice against plays and players by acquiring a noble patron. They thus assured themselves of a barrier against the interference of magistrates, Puritan pressure groups and outraged neighbours. Liberal noblemen were willing to foster the new art form with their protection. Until the death of Elizabeth I (1603) Shakespeare's company was The Lord Chamberlain's Men. With the accession of James I they became supreme as The King's Men.

In 1599 the various pressures to move from Shoreditch came to a head. Trouble over the lease of the land on which the Theatre stood motivated Burbage to dismantle the building, beam by beam, and to move it across London to the south bank. Here, outside the jurisdiction of the City magistrates, stood many of the city's places of public entertainment, from bearpit to brothels. Presumably the rebuilding permitted a refurbishment. Eyewitness accounts of the Globe – as the re-erected building was now called – speak of its sumptuous appointments, its spaciousness, and the skill of its repertory company.

The company was owned by a limited number of shareholders who were usually active participants as writers and actors. These shareholders hired journeyman actors on a weekly basis to fill up their complement. Female roles were enacted by boys. Most senior members of the company had their own apprentices whom they trained to a level where they could credibly perform parts like Cleopatra, and Lady Macbeth.

By 1599 when the Globe opened Shakespeare had already written nineteen of the thirty-seven plays with which, wholly or in part, he is usually credited. Not all these plays had been performed at the Theatre. Yet despite this, and despite the fact that several of the last plays were put on at the Blackfriars, not the Globe, we still customarily look to the Globe as the model 'Shakespearian theatre'.

The wooden building was either circular or octagonal. It rose through three tiers of galleries. From the property stage structure an 'apron' stage projected into a central yard which provided standing space for the one-penny spectators, and the galleries housed the more expensive seats. We can glean some evidence of overall dimensions from builders' contracts which have survived. One such demanded a building 80 ft in exterior dimension, and 55 ft across inside. The stage itself was something like 43 ft broad, and was 27 ft deep. An overhanging roof, supported by pillars onto the stage itself, offered some protection against bad weather, and probably acted as a sounding-board which helped the acoustics of the building.

A trapdoor in the floor of the apron stage probably gave access to and from the 'cellarage' below. The ghost of Hamlet's father cries up from this below-stage area, and ghostly music is heard from the same area in *Antony and Cleopatra*. We may also assume a trapdoor in the roof of the overhanging canopy. A stage direction in *Cymbeline* says '*Jupiter descends in thunder and lightening, sitting upon an eagle*' and after Jupiter's ascension back to the heavens Sicilius remarks: 'The marble pavement closes, he is enter'd / His radiant roof.' (V, iv, 92 & 120). 'The heavens' – the technical name for the underside of this canopy – were painted with the signs of the zodiac, offering a clear schematic setting of cellarage = hell, stage = earth, canopy = heavens, very reminiscent of the old pageant cart symbolism.

The Globe probably housed about 2,000 spectators. Some estimates offer a significantly higher figure. What we don't know, of course, is what percentage capacity they customarily played to.

When we try to reconstruct the practical and artistic implications of acting in such a space we again enter the realm of speculation. It was a big stage. This readily permitted of pageantry and spectacle; plays of the period frequently exploit this. *Antony and Cleopatra* calls for extensive marching and counter-marching, and presupposes a cast of over twenty-five, even allowing for heavy doubling. Most of the Histories and the Tragedies assume a large playing area for their ceremonial groupings.

The precise nature of the stage buildings at the rear of the apron stage causes disagreement among reconstructionist experts. Certain points are clear, however. Stage directions like: *Enter one citizen at one door, and another at the other*, from *Richard III* (II, iii, 1) and, *Enter Richard Aloft..* (III, vii, 93) are authorial, as opposed to being stuck in by later editors. They are strong indicators of the flexibility of the Elizabethan playhouse. 'Aloft' certainly indicates a balcony and/or window available to the actors.

For further reading on Elizabethan theatres see Orrell (1983), Thomson (1983), Beckerman (1962) and Gurr (1970).

## Shakespeare's practical skills

Elizabethan acting was a stylized not a naturalistic art. We might well find it an overemphatic and physically vigorous style. Gestures and language were stylized partly because they had to be recognizable to an open-air audience, but partly, too, because the ritualistic element was important in its own right.

One can overemphasize the difficulties of acting on such a stage. Because of the shape of the auditorium no spectator was further than 40 ft from the centre of the stage (a more favourable distance than obtains in many modern theatres for a punter in the back row of 'the gods', for instance). It must also be remembered that Tudor and Jacobean spectators had no rival visual spectacles to adulterate their imaginations. When Prospero commands the spirit Ariel:

> Go make thyself like a nymph o' the sea; be subject
> To no sight but thine and mine, invisible
> To every eyeball else...

> (*The Tempest*: I, iii, 301–3)

the audience had no problem in accepting either the weird costumes, nor the fact that some characters on stage will see Ariel in this guise and others will see nothing.

Nor must we think of Elizabethan actors as bellowing hams. When the Player Troupe arrives at Elsinore, Hamlet reminds them of the decorum of their trade:

> Speak the speech, I pray you, as I pronounced it to you, trippingly on the tongue ... Nor do not saw the air too much with your hand... but use all gently; for in the very torrent,

tempest and, as I may say, whirlwind of your passion, you must acquire and beget a temperance that may give it smoothness...

(III, ii, 1–9)

Entrances and exits are often delayed or pre-emptive. 'Look, where sadly the poor wretch comes reading...' (*Hamlet*: II, ii, 167), draws attention to the entry of the Prince, several lines before he is going to speak or be involved in the action. Such pre-emptive indications of an entrance help an actor to cover the long distance he must travel from upstage to join a downstage group. Also, eavesdropping is convincing on the Elizabethan stage, because of the size of the platform.

Shakespearian stage action is often still tinged with elements of ritual. A very clear example is in the early *Henry VI, Part 3*. Act II scene v has King Henry enter aloft and alone. He laments the horrors of civil war and wishes he could abdicate his share of the blame. Then '*Enter a Son that hath killed his Father at one door; and a Father that hath killed his Son, at another door.*' These are clearly the two upstage entrances, below and to the sides of Henry's central position aloft. The two soldiers then bring their victims to the respective downstage corners of the apron, and we have a visual representation of the triangle of the medieval estates of England with the King at its apex and his common subjects at its bases.

Verbal activity emphasizes the pattern created. After Henry's choric lament, the Son utters some eighteen lines, first of self-congratulation then, when he discovers the identity of his victim, of horror and revulsion. The King, aloft, has a brief solo interposition, then the Father speaks. Exactly the same pattern is followed – about twenty lines of self-congratulation, turning to dismay, and another interposition from the King. There follows a 'trio' section in which the grief passes from speaker to speaker. This kind of drama is much closer to grand opera than to naturalistic theatre. We should not forget, of course, that Shakespeare always worked within a structure of five acts, around which he threaded the narrative and language of the play. The best guide to the history of the five-act form and Shakespeare's use of it is Baldwin (1947).

Recreate for a moment the open turbulent arena of the Elizabethan stage. There are no house lights to dim, no curtain to open, no overture to end. At a given moment a group of very flesh-and-blood thespians appear on that platform, quell the hubbub, attract the attention, lay the foundations for a story line, and arouse expectation for the appearance of the 'big guns' (Shakespeare almost never begins the show by exposing the principal actors to this preliminary flourish). You can probably say that the openers have about two minutes to achieve their task or the whole show may well be lost. Anecdotal evidence suggests that Elizabethan audiences were ruthless with plays in which they lost interest.

Getting the show under way is one of the challenges to which Shakespeare responds with particular gusto. His openings are exemplary. Take *Hamlet*: Midnight bell; jumpy sentries; talk of ghosts; scepticism of the rationalist scholar – 'T'will not appear...' Oh yes it will! A bare thirty lines of dialogue, and there it is, the spectre of the dead King, marching awesomely by them in full armour. What an opening!

It was the contention of Samuel Johnson that, brilliant as are his openings, the endings of many of Shakespeare's plays are a relative falling-off. Both *Macbeth* and *Measure For Measure* might seem cases in point. In *Macbeth* the problem is that whilst the moral part of the spectator wants this violent psychopath to arrive at his destined sticky end, another part is so besotted by the blinding power of Macbeth's poetry that we don't want to hear the last of him. When Macbeth collapses into contemptible hysteria, when he finally admits his utter reliance upon the tricksy predictions of the witches, a moral vacuum is created. But this carefully contrived vacuum is not a failing of Shakespeare's art. The desultory structure of Act V further emphasizes this world-in-flux: the perfunctory marching and counter-marching; the array of insipid characters; the failure of Malcolm to exert an active role in his own destiny.

Art which has withered into inconsequence may be the only logical sequel to the utterly negative events which carry the play itself. Macbeth doesn't only destroy Scotland and its nobility, he destroys the very play in which he takes part.

Intellectual pretension marked the deportment of many of the courtiers and men-about-town whom Shakespeare would have encountered around the London theatre scene. Our greatest wordsmith hated wordiness for its own sake. Pistol (*Henry IV Parts 1 & 2*), Parolles (*All's Well That Ends Well*), the melancholy Jaques (*As You Like It*), Don Armado (*Love's Labours Lost*), Osric (*Hamlet*) – the plays are full of wordy bores and snobs. The way in which men treat words often denotes the way in which they will treat other men. Yet the miracle, of course, is that in context these crass verbalists are hugely entertaining to us as outside spectators.

For all that the plays are full of tyrants, and men greedy for illegitimate power, Shakespeare himself can never be discerned as either 'liberal' or 'conservative'. His contempt for Coriolanus is only matched by his vehement distaste for Brutus and Sicinius the archetypal trade-union hacks who oppose him. If he seems anti-aristocratic, yet he is equally scathing of demagoguery, and without much sympathy for the gullible masses who are manipulated by popular agitators.

The very early *Henry VI, Part 2* shows these ideas already fully developed. Here is Jack Cade, populist loudmouth, rousing a brutal and venal mob with simplistic election promises:

> *Cade*: There shall be in England seven halfpenny loaves sold for a penny: the three hooped pot shall have ten hoops ... And when I am King, as King I will be –
> *All*: God save your Majesty ...

> (*Henry VI, Part 2*: IV, ii, 67–8)

A few lines later Cade's mob discovers an unfortunate clerk, and hales him off to be hanged for the mob-worthy reason that he can write. This is the very stuff of populist chaos. It is superbly managed – some of the most memorable drama in the first part of Shakespeare's career.

Ideas develop with Shakespeare, they do not disappear. In *Coriolanus*, where the theme is that of the monomaniacal irresponsibility of patrician power, the First Citizen (never honoured with a more specific name than that) speaks more articulately, more sensibly and more to the point than any other person in the play. Complaining that the people are starving whilst the patrician-controlled granaries are full, the First Citizen declares:

> What Authority surfeits on would relieve us; if they would yield us but the superfluity while it were wholesome, we might guess they relieved us humanely; but they think we are too dear. The leanness that afflicts us ... is an inventory to particularise their abundance.
>
> (*Coriolanus*: I, i, 15–22)

The voice of the timeless downtrodden common man rings in the First Citizen's rhetoric, a curiously articulate and elegant rhetoric, down to the last subjunctive. Only minutes later, Menenius, that good exemplar of middle management in its deliberately jocose and fraternizing mode manages, by his affable but clumsy chop-logic, to subvert the course of popular discontent. And thus wags the world.

An excellent, detailed study of Shakespeare's theatre practice can be found in Weimann's *Shakespeare and the Popular Tradition in the Theatre* (1978). Weimann makes use of the concept of *Figerenposition* ('the actor's position on the stage, and the speech, action and stylization associated with that position') and shows how the use of such devices as the 'aside', where an aristocratic character might speak direct to the audience, would have had immense socio-cultural significance. A more conventional survey is Coghill's *Shakespeare's Professional Skills* (1964); see also Hattaway (1982) and Bentley (1971, 1984).

## Shakespeare the dramatic poet

Consider the following passage from Act I, scene ii, of *Measure For Measure*.

> *Lucio*: Why, how now, Claudio, whence comes this restraint?

> *Claudio*: From too much liberty, my Lucio, liberty;
> As surfeit is the father of much fast,
> So every scope by the immoderate use
> Turns to restraint. Our natures do pursue,
> Like rats that ravin down their proper bane,
> A thirsty evil; and when we drink we die.

> *Lucio*: If I could speak so wisely under an arrest, I would send for certain of my creditors; and yet, to say the truth, I had as lief have the foppery of freedom as the morality of imprisonment.
>
> (ll. 118–29)

In this brief extract can be glimpsed the immense complexity of Shakespeare's stylistic and structural art. The two characters use two very different genres. Claudio, as minor aristocrat, describes his condition in the high-art form of blank verse. His answer to Lucio is almost a poem in its own right. Its apparent subject (his arrest and detention) is virtually swamped by a catalogue of metaphors and similes. Its status as an unplanned response to a question is further compromised by the enclosure of the syntactic flow within six decasyllabic, iambic lines.

As members of the audience, our sense of the unreal complexity of his language is checked by our knowledge that we are watching a play, a medium in which the contingencies of ordinary language are reshaped as art. However, Lucio too seems to be surprised by the manner in which Claudio is able to speak 'under an arrest'. Perhaps Lucio's sardonic reference to the 'foppery of freedom' versus 'the morality of imprisonment' involves an amused double meaning: the 'freedom' of unhindered prose, which as a low-life is his own medium, versus the 'imprisonment' of language in the aristocratic structures of poetry.

We should not dismiss this moment simply as an instance of Shakespeare making his style the subject as well as the medium of his work. In all of his plays we will encounter a tension between the two stylistic modes of blank verse and prose. Frequently their respective classifications as art and ordinary language are mirrored in the social status of their users and the profundity of their subjects: Prince Hamlet's soliloquy on the nature of existence (blank verse) would sound wrong if delivered in the less formal mode of Falstaff's bar-room ruminations (prose). Frequently, but not predictably: Caliban, that sub-human creation of his superhuman master, has an impressive command of verse style. The Duke in *Measure For Measure* switches between prose and blank verse as easily and convincingly as he assumes his disguise.

What should be remembered is that in the sixteenth and seventeenth centuries poetry was the only purely *literary* genre. The novel did not exist, and blank (unrhymed) verse provided drama with a stylistic bridge to the high art of non-dramatic poetry. Shakespeare's skill as a writer becomes increasingly evident the more we pay close attention to his blending of these two stylistic registers. We can paraphrase the plot or narrative of his plays but what will be lost is Shakespeare's subtle tilting of his language back and forth between the naturalistic, improvisational mode of ordinary speech and the self-conscious intricacies of verse. Such dovetailing of the familiar with the self-evidently aesthetic is the keynote of all great literature.

The most interesting approach to the socio-political significance of Shakespeare's style derives from the work of the Marxian critic Mikhail Bakhtin. In *Rabelais and His World* (1968) Bakhtin introduces the concept of the 'carnival' as a register of the social tensions in literary writing. It is evident from *Measure For Measure* that the disruptive 'carnival' aspect of society manifests itself in the freedom of prose, while authority, control, power and restriction are more closely associated with poetry (see Unit 21 for a discussion of Bakhtin and Marxism).

Another element of Shakespeare's dramatic style is a palpable tension between language and situation. On the one hand the words themselves create magnificent poetic effects that could exist independently of the play; on the other we are continually relating these effects to their use by a particular character with his/her own life within the play. 'His tears run down his beard like winter's drops from eaves of reeds' is the description given by Ariel of the good Gonzalo grieving over the frenzy of his spell-bound master (*The Tempest*: V, i, 16–17). Ariel's simile is at once totally original yet totally familiar. Anyone who has watched rain drip from the eaves of a thatched roof after a summer storm suddenly apprehends the completeness of Shakespeare's image, as the tears run from the old courtier's grizzled beard.

From the palpable to the unobservable ranges this extraordinary power of verbalized imagination. You may have seen dripping thatch, but this ...?

> Ye elves of hills, brooks, standing lakes and groves;
> And ye that on the sand with printless foot
> Do chase the ebbing Neptune, and do fly him
> When he comes back; you demi-puppets that
> By moonshine do the green sour ringlets make,
> Whereof the ewe not bites; and you whose pastime
> Is to make midnight mushrooms ...
>
> (*The Tempest*: V, i, 33–9)

Shakespeare here describes what no man has ever seen, but the scene is imagined with brilliant clarity. Fairy rings in a meadow *are* green, sour, untouched by the sheep. The observable fuses with the purely imagined and creates its own symbiotic conviction.

This power over words asserts itself over a vast range of styles and methodologies, transforming literary sources as well as observed experience. In *Antony and Cleopatra* (II, ii, 195, seq.) is a very famous passage where Enobarbus describes the first sight which he and Antony had of Cleopatra: 'The barge she sat in ...'.

Nearly every word of this is lifted from North's translation of the Roman historian Plutarch, who describes this incident in his *Lives of the Noble Romans*. Most of Shakespeare's original audience would sense that they had encountered this description somewhere before. The genius lies in attributing this familiarly literary and articulate stuff to such a hardened old pragmatist as Enobarbus. By golly, if Cleopatra made *him* feel like that, she surely is something to behold!

If you read the passage in North and then in Shakespeare you will apprehend the super-addition which Shakespeare's sense of rhythm brings to the description. The final impact transcends by light years anything in the original; it perfectly exemplifies the assuredness and the inevitability of Shakespeare's art:

> Age cannot wither her, nor custom stale
> Her infinite variety ...

Thus far the tone has been heroic. But Cleopatra is as sexually comfortable as a well-oiled seaboot. Caesar had her, Pompey enjoyed her. Her fascination is utterly confusing and compromised. She plays silly games, hops panting through the streets: earth-mother, Diana Spencer and Marilyn Monroe in one booby-trapped package. 'Holy priests bless her when she is riggish' concludes Enobarbus. 'Riggish' – randy, oozing sex, vampish. The word occurs nowhere else in Shakespeare. Change it and see how total is the damage you do.

The same play demonstrates Shakespeare's daring in wedding his poetry to his characterization. At times Cleopatra is a strident old tart. She can be bitchy, ruthless, selfish, childish, catty, irresponsible. But when it falls to her lot to play the Queen for the last time, she is utterly moving:

> Give me my robe, put on my crown; I have
> Immortal longings in me ...
> > Methinks I hear
> Antony call. I see him rouse himself
> To praise my noble act. I hear him mock
> The luck of Caesar, which the gods give men
> To excuse their after wrath. Husband, I come.
> Now to that name my courage prove my title.
> I am fire and air; my other elements
> I give to baser life.
>
> > > (V, ii, 278–87)

If that doesn't grip you in the guts, you are, no doubt, fit for macramé or economics, but leave Shakespeare alone.

Nor have we yet finished with the daring of the writing in this passage, the ferocious mixture of emotional temperatures conveyed. Just after this symphonic stuff Iras, Cleopatra's maidservant, falls dead. While Cleopatra has been playing the dying queen, Iras has performed the deed. Cleopatra deplores her own tardiness:

> > This proves me base.
> If she [Iras] first meet the curled Antony,
> He'll make demand of her, and spend that kiss
> Which is my heaven to have.
>
> > > (V, ii, 298–301)

In other words 'If I don't get on and kill myself quickly, I will find when I arrive in the next world that Antony couldn't wait, and he's making love to my maidservant.'

Very little in the dramatic art of any European nation compares with the daring of this deliberate mixture and confusion of contexts and genres. It breaches every concept of artistic decorum. How do you set bounds to the art of a man who screws you up and down like a fiddle peg, as this passage does? Nor is Shakespeare yet done with us. After that genuinely shocking notion of the brave Antony having a celestial hump while he waits for Cleopatra to kill herself with the asp, the register shifts again:

> > > ... Come thou mortal wretch
>
> *[To an asp, which she applies to her breast]*
>
> With thy sharp teeth this knot intrinsicate
> Of life at once untie. Poor venomous fool,
> Be angry and despatch ...
> > > Peace, peace,
> Dost thou not see my baby at my breast
> That sucks the nurse asleep.
>
> > > (*Antony and Cleopatra*: V, i, 301–7, *passim*)

The genius of this passage, its Shakespearian signature, exist in its ability at once to concentrate and expand its frame of reference. It involves the compact linguistic intensity of a lyric poem while at the same time each stylistic nuance carries a reference to a broader theme of the play. Grasp that image of the asp biting Cleopatra and thus poisoning her: the sudden maternal recollection of giving suck. The domestic peacefulness of the life-giving implied in the nursing image. Hold onto all that as you recall the vixenish tart who has betrayed Antony and been responsible for his entirely bathetic death. Then go back to that notion of the knot intrinsicate (i.e. intricate, tangled), being undone by the asp's tooth. There as Cleopatra speaks is the finality of death, the welcomeness of the long sleep, the repulsiveness of the cold-blooded reptile at that opulent breast. All overlaid with contrary currents of utter tragedy and clownish farce.

The most accessible studies of Shakespeare's style are Hussey's *The Literary Language of Shakespeare* (1982) and Hawkes's *Shakespeare's Talking Animals* (1972).

Two very useful general guides to contemporary and past criticism on Shakespeare are Wells's *The Cambridge Companion to Shakespeare Studies* (1985) and *Shakespeare. A Bibliographical Guide to Shakespeare Studies* (1990).

## BIBLIOGRAPHY

Adams, J.C. (1961) *The Globe Playhouse*, Barnes & Noble, New York.

Alexander, P. (ed.) (1951) *William Shakespeare. The Complete Works*, Collins, London and Glasgow.

Atkins, G.D. and Bergeron, D.M. (eds) (1988) *Shakespeare and Deconstruction*, New York University Press, New York.

Bakhtin, M. (1968) *Rabelais and His World*, MIT Press, Cambridge, Mass.

Baldwin, T.W. (1947) *Shakespeare's Five Act Structure*, University of Illinois Press, Illinois.

Bayley, J. (1981) *Shakespeare and Tragedy*, Routledge, London.

Beckerman, B. (1962) *Shakespeare at the Globe 1599–1609*, Macmillan, New York.

Belsey, C. (1985) *The Subject of Tragedy*, Routledge, London.

Bentley, G. (1971) *The Profession of Dramatist in Shakespeare's Time 1590–1642*, Princeton University Press, Princeton.

Bentley, G. (1984) *The Profession of Player in Shakespeare's Time 1590–1642*, Princeton University Press, Princeton.

Boswell-Stone, G.W. (1907) *Shakespeare's Holinshed*, Chatto & Windus, London.

Bradbury, C.M. and Palmer, D. (eds) (1972) *Shakespearean Comedy*, Stratford-Upon-Avon Studies, 14, Edward Arnold, London.

Bradley, A.C. (1904) *Shakespearean Tragedy*, Macmillan, London.

Brooke, N. (1968) *Shakespeare's Early Tragedies*, Methuen, London.

Brooks, C. (1947) *The Well Wrought Urn*, Dobson, London (rev. edn 1968).

Campbell, L. (1947) *Shakespeare's Histories. Mirrors of Elizabethan Policy*, Huntington Library, San Marino.

Clemen, W.H. (1951) *The Development of Shakespeare's Imagery*, Methuen, London.

Coghill, N. (1964) *Shakespeare's Professional Skills*, Cambridge University Press, Cambridge.

Danby, J. (1949) *Shakespeare's Doctrine of Nature*, Faber & Faber, London.

Dollimore, J. and Sinfield, A. (1985) *Political Shakespeare. New Essays in Cultural Materialism*, Manchester University Press, Manchester.

Donoghue, S. (1975) *Theatre in the Age of Kean*, Blackwell, Oxford.

Dowden, E. (1875) *Shakespeare: A Critical Study of His Mind and Art*, Kegan Paul, London.

Drakakis, J. (ed.) (1985) *Alternative Shakespeares*, Routledge, London.

Drakakis, J. (ed.) (1992) *Shakespearean Tragedy*, Longman, London.

Dusinberre, J. (1975) *Shakespeare and the Nature of Woman*, Macmillan, London.

Eagleton, T. (1986) *William Shakespeare*, 'Re-reading Literature', Blackwell, Oxford.

Empson, W. (1930) *Seven Types of Ambiguity*, Chatto & Windus, London.

Evans, M. (1988) *Signifying Nothing*, Harvester Wheatsheaf, Hemel Hempstead.

French, M. (1982) *Shakespeare's Division of Experience*, Cape, London.

Granville-Barker, H. (1927–48) *Prefaces to Shakespeare*, Sidgwick & Jackson, London.

Greenblatt, S. (1988) *Shakespearean Negotiations*, Oxford University Press, Oxford.

Green, A. (1979) *The Tragic Effect: The Oedipus Complex in Tragedy*, Cambridge University Press, Cambridge.

Grosart, A. (1881–6) *The Life and Complete Works of Robert Greene*, Kegan Paul, London.

Gurr, A. (1970) *The Shakespearean Stage. 1572–1642*, Cambridge University Press, Cambridge.

Hattaway, M. (1982) *Elizabethan Popular Theatre: Plays in Performance*, Routledge, London.

Hawkes, T. (1972) *Shakespeare's Talking Animals*, Edward Arnold, London.

Hawkes, T. (1986) *That Shakespeherian Rag*, Routledge, London.

Hodges, C.W. (1968) *The Globe Restored*, Oxford University Press, Oxford.

Holderness, G. (1988) *The Shakespeare Myth*, Manchester University Press, Manchester.

Honigmann, E.A.J. (1976) *Shakespeare: Seven Tragedies*, Macmillan, London.

Hussey, S.S. (1982) *The Literary Language of Shakespeare*, Longman, London.

Jakobson, R. (1987) *Language in Literature*, Harvard University Press, Cambridge, Mass.

Jardine, L. (1983) *Still Harping on Daughters*, Harvester Wheatsheaf, Hemel Hempstead.

Kantorowicz, E.F. (1957) *The King's Two Bodies*, Princeton University Press, Princeton.

Knight, G.W. (1949) *The Wheel of Fire*, Methuen, London [first published 1930].

Knights, L.C. (1946) *Explorations*, Chatto & Windus, London [first published 1933 as *How Many Children had Lady Macbeth?*].

Kott, J. (1967) *Shakespeare Our Contemporary*, Methuen, London.

Kriegar, E. (1979) *A Marxist Study of Shakespeare's Comedies*, Macmillan, London.

Lenz, C., Greene, G. and Neely, C. (1980) *The Women's Part. Feminist Criticism of Shakespeare*, University of Illinois Press, Urbana.

Lawrence, W.E. (1931) *Shakespeare's Problem Comedies*, Frederick Ungar, New York (rev. edn 1960).

Leggatt, A. (1974) *Shakespeare's Comedy of Love*, Methuen, London.

Moretti, F. (1983) *Signs Taken for Wonders*, Verso, London.

Muir, K. (1972) *Shakespeare's Tragic Sequence*, Hutchinson, London.

Muir, K. and Wells, S. (eds) (1982) *Aspects of Shakespeare's Problem Plays*, Cambridge University Press, Cambridge.

Odell, G.C.D. (1920) *Shakespeare from Betterton to Irving*, Charles Scribner, New York.

Orrell, J. (1983) *The Quest for Shakespeare's Globe*, Cambridge University Press, Cambridge.

Parker, P. and Hartman, G. (eds) (1985) *Shakespeare and The Question of Theory*, Methuen, London.

Pomorska, K. and Rudy, S. (1987) *Language in Literature*, Harvard University Press, Cambridge, Mass.

Price, C. (1973) *Theatre in the Age of Garrick*, Blackwell, Oxford.

Schoenbaum, S. (1970) *Shakespeare's Lives*, Oxford University Press, Oxford.

Schoenbaum, S. (1976) *William Shakespeare. A Compact Documentary Life*, Oxford University Press, Oxford.

Simmons, J.L. (1974) *Shakespeare's Pagan World: The Roman Tragedies*, Harvester Wheatsheaf, Hemel Hempstead.

Spencer, T.B. (ed.) (1964) *Shakespeare's Plutarch*, Peregrine, Harmondsworth.

Spurgeon, C. (1935) *Shakespeare's Imagery and What It Tells Us*, Cambridge University Press, Cambridge.

Stampfer, J. (1968) *The Tragic Engagement. A Study of Shakespeare's Classical Tragedies*, Funk & Wagnalls, New York.

Taylor, G. (1990) *Reinventing Shakespeare: A Cultural History from the Restoration to the Present*, Hogarth, London.

Thomson, P. (1983) *Shakespeare's Theatre*, Routledge, London.

Tillyard, E.M.W. (1938) *Shakespeare's Last Plays*, Chatto & Windus, London.

Tillyard, E.M.W. (1943) *The Elizabethan World Picture*, Chatto & Windus, London.

Tillyard, E.M.W. (1944) *Shakespeare's History Plays*, Chatto & Windus, London.

Traversi, D. (1953) *Shakespeare. The Last Phase*, Hollis & Carter, London.

Vickers, B. (ed.) (1974–81) *Shakespeare. The Critical Heritage*, 6 vols, Routledge, London.

Vickers, B. (1993) *Appropriating Shakespeare*, Yale University Press, New Haven.

Waller, G. (ed.) (1991) *Shakespeare's Comedies*, Longman, London.

Weimann, R. (1978) *Shakespeare and the Popular Tradition in the Theatre*, Johns Hopkins University Press, Baltimore.

Wells, S. (ed.) (1985) *The Cambridge Companion to Shakespeare Studies*, Cambridge University Press, Cambridge.

Wells, S. (ed.) (1990) *Shakespeare. A Bibliographical Guide to Shakespeare Studies*, Oxford University Press, Oxford.

Yates, E.A. (1975) *Shakespeare's Last Plays: A New Approach*, Routledge, London.

# UNIT 6

# Renaissance and seventeenth-century drama

*Amanda Piesse*

## Introduction

> *We are all framed of flaps and patches and of so shaplesse and*
> *diverse a contexture, that every piece and every moment playeth his*
> *part. And there is as much difference between us and ourselves, as*
> *there is between ourselves and others.* (Montaigne, *Essais*)

This unit deals with English Renaissance drama, covering the period 1485–1625. It introduces the reader to readily accessible plays which are representative of their period and their genre. In broadly generic terms, the unit examines tragedy, as represented in its Senecan form by Kyd's *Spanish Tragedy* ([1587] 1970), in its revenge form by Middleton's *Revenger's Tragedy* ([1606] 1967), in its partly medieval, partly classical form in Marlowe's *Faustus* ([1592] 1969) and in its individualized, high English Renaissance form in Webster's *The White Devil* ([1612] 1972) and *The Duchess of Malfi* ([1614] 1972). Comedy is represented in an early form by the unattributed *Gammer Gurton's Needle* ([1553], Whitworth, 1984) and Peele's *The Old Wives' Tale* ([1590] 1984), both of which draw on the classical norms of pastoral idyll in order to invert it and in the form of city comedy by Middleton and Dekker's *The Roaring Girl* ([1608] 1987) and Jonson's *The Alchemist* ([1610] 1979).

Whilst the term 'tragedy' probably needs no definition here, the general understanding in this unit is of a form broadly correspondent to that laid out in Aristotle's *Poetics*, which suggests the response of a central protagonist to a situation arising from her or his tragic or fatal 'error of judgement', or *hamartia* (sometimes translated as 'fatal flaw').

Senecan tragedy was written to be recited rather than acted, and the English assimilation of its complex plot and five-act structure sometimes combine with its formalized dialogue to put a highly stylized and often lamentably static drama on the stage. Sackville and Norton's *Gorboduc* ([1562] 1992) is one example of this type of writing. Writing Senecan tragedy into the form of revenge tragedy, however, gave rise to a greater flexibility as the requisite content – 'revenge, murder, ghosts, mutilation and carnage' (Abrams, 1981, p. 203) – dominates the structure, and dramatic effect vies for attention with elaborate dialogue. Kyd's *Spanish Tragedy* ([1587] 1970) was fundamental in establishing this kind of drama as a popular genre.

Much of the tragedy which flowered at the later end of the Renaissance period takes its strength from the degree to which it deviates from the classical norm, and there are types we will not address here. Domestic tragedy for example might be said to begin with the anonymous *Arden of Faversham* ([1591], White, 1982) which centres on the difficulties experienced within a bourgeois relationship. Reasons for critical neglect of such genres, and our subsequent inability to focus on them in the space provided here, are offered in the paragraph on canonicity at the end of this Introduction, where you will also find suggestions for further critical reading on the subject.

Comedy is less easy to define, not least because of its many forms. The classical notion of pastoral properly belongs to poetry but is evident as a strong influence in Renaissance comedy. The 'green world' which is regularly posited as the alternative to the constrictions of courtly or constructed behaviour is not always a place of classical rustic release and uncomplicated pastoral merrymaking. It can also be seen simply as an alternative place, and often a dangerous and uncertain place, where the quotidien world is turned upside down and the generally accepted hierarchical order brought under threat from subversion.

City or citizen comedy is a self-explanatory term: it describes comedy which deals with the nature of citizenship, with the mercantile, bourgeois class of Elizabethan society, especially in the city of London. Leggatt's *Citizen Comedy in the Age of Shakespeare* (1973) is a good initial guide to the genre, which he defines as 'comedy set in a predominantly middle-class social milieu', as being '*about* the middle class [while] not necessarily written *for* them' (pp. 3, 4), and as being directly descended from morality and chronicle plays, adapting these matters to the new social milieu. Gibbons's *Jacobean City Comedy* (1968) addresses the Plautine and Terentian traditions of intrigue comedy, and emphasizes the innate contradictions between the traditions, where 'high-minded theory confronts low-life experience of the city' (pp. 4–5). He draws attention to the interplay between the development of the generic form in the drama and the development of the real-life character of the mercantile classes, suggesting an important interaction. The growth of this form of drama especially towards the end of the sixteenth century reflects the degree to which political power and cultural activity were increasingly centred in the capital city. Beaumont and Fletcher's *The Knight of the Burning Pestle* ([1607] 1986) and Dekker's *The Shoemaker's Holiday* ([1599] 1986) belong to this genre. It is a distinct Englishing of a genre whose classical forms have little resonance with English life.

Thematically the unit seeks to address recurrent Renaissance issues. Some of these are academic, such as the development of a form of English verse and prose fit to import classical genres into the English canon, or the ability of rhetorical constructions to obscure and destroy meaning as well as to construct it. Neil Rhodes (1992) is an extremely readable and generally useful guide to these issues, which are self-consciously present in plays as diverse as Bale's *King Johan* ([1538] 1979),

*Gammer Gurton's Needle* ([1553] 1984), Marlowe's *Massacre at Paris* ([1593] 1969) and Jonson's *Bartholomew Fair* ([1614] 1979). Other Renaissance preoccupations are social rather than academic, such as the examination of the nature of class status in relation to nobility in the presence of an increasingly powerful mercantile class, or the preoccupation with gender and identity, most regularly expressed through anxiety over cross-dressing or the propriety or impropriety of certain types of speech in women. Tennenhouse (1986) and Altman (1978) give thorough examinations of the first, which finds its expression in academic plays like Medwall's *Fulgens and Lucres* ([1497] 1976), or repeatedly in the genre of citizen comedy, in plays like Beaumont and Fletcher's *The Knight of the Burning Pestle* ([1607] 1986) or Shakespeare's *Twelfth Night* (1604) or *The Merry Wives of Windsor* (1599). Anxiety about gender and identity is widely addressed in recent feminist criticism, among others by Dusinberre (1975), Jardine (1983), Drakakis (1985), Traub (1992), Howard (1994) and Levine (1994). It is one of the main subjects in Middleton and Dekker's *The Roaring Girl* ([1608] 1987), Jonson's *Epicoene* ([1609] 1979) and a repeated motif in Shakespeare's comedies, perhaps most obviously in *As You Like It, Twelfth Night* and *The Taming of the Shrew*. In an effort to point up such similarities and disparities of theme both within and across genre, the unit proceeds primarily generically and then chronologically within the generic pattern.

The influx of cultural influence from the continental Renaissance encouraged a reassessment and rewriting of English drama which transformed the traditions of mystery and miracle plays. The writing of the first fully secular plays towards the end of the fifteenth century and the shaping of the new form of the moral interlude in the early sixteenth demonstrate the extent to which the newer forms of English drama might be described as 'all framed of flaps and patches', a garment put together of different texts and contexts but nevertheless new and original in its final wholeness. Where the English morality tradition has operated on a huge scale and been mostly preoccupied with religious or allegorical representation of good or evil (*The Castle of Perseverance*, [1425] Happé, 1979, Skelton's *Magnyfycence*, [1515] Happé, 1979), the Tudor moral interlude operates on a smaller and more individualistic scale, and further matches the mood of humanism (i.e. going back to the sources of our literary civilization) by adapting classical tales, such as *Horestes* ([1567] Pickering, 1982) and *Thersites* ([1537] Udalls 1982) to the more secularized moral dilemmas – those of revenge, of justice, of proper human behaviour across social divides – which come to dominate a post-reformation England.

The influence of humanist education came to England chiefly through the writings and the visits of the Dutch humanist Erasmus (1466?–1536). Martindale (1985) gives an excellent introduction to extracts from key texts in the movement. In the eyes of the humanist, writers must return *ad fontes* and *ad res*, to the source and to reality: that is, must take into account both the teachings of literature of the ancients and the experiential education offered by the world in general (Martindale, 1985, pp. 18–21). Erasmus' attendance at the lectures of John Colet in Oxford gave rise to an academic relationship which saw Erasmus' writings informing the principles upon which Colet founded St Paul's School and also contributing to the textbooks, such as a manual for composition and the standard school grammar, which would influence the writing first of the educated English nobility, and later of the grammar school boy, right across the Renaissance period and beyond. (Martindale, pp. 23–8). Another irresistible influence is the increasingly intense politicization of the theatre in the middle and later years.

The twin influences of literary and linguistic development and social context in this period bifurcate our attention regularly between content in the first instance and context in the latter. Where a humanist reading invites us to concentrate on a source-based, scholarly reading, a new historicist reading invites us to read through the focus of political and historical context, accepting that the theatre fashions the society in which it operates just as much as the society fashions the theatre. Richard Wilson and Richard Dutton explain and exemplify this view of Renaissance cultural politics in their useful collection of essays, *New Historicism and Renaissance Drama* (1992). Since the study of literature involves both content and context, and since the English Renaissance is so inescapably motivated by 'the difference between us and ourselves' (the recognition of the possibility of seeing different versions of self through different frames of reference), it is entirely appropriate to present simultaneously the theoretical base from which the Renaissance academic views the drama of the period and the theoretical base most commonly invoked in current academic practice.

In *The Revels History of Drama in English* (Sanders *et al.*, 1980), the English Renaissance is approached emphatically not as a period in time but rather as 'one intellectual activity that Englishmen were involved in at this period; namely, the recovery of Greek and the refining of Mediaeval Latin in the light of the classical usage of that language' (II, p. 4). This, lest we underestimate the solemnity of such activity, is 'a very complex business' (II, p. 4).

In the early days of the early modern period the actions of recovery and refining led to a period of reassessment and reworking, not only of ancient literatures but also of the then current literatures of the nation and especially of the language in which they were written. It is important to understand that imitation and assimilation of classical form or even content is, as Emrys Jones puts it, 'something quite different from either repro-duction or translation' (Jones, 1977, p. 19). The typically reworked play is 'in no sense a copy of the old but rather a larger, denser ... transformation of it' (ibid., p. 20).

In rediscovering Quintilian on the art of rhetoric through Erasmus, for example, English Renaissance writers were to recognize and address the point that while 'rhetoric is most commonly defined as the art of persuasion ... its origins lie in the recognition of the power of the spoken word' (Rhodes, 1992, p. 8). It is this power of the spoken word which differentiates the drama from other literary forms.

In the process of humanist education, boys were trained in rhetoric by the assimilation of classical characters, invited to take on the role of, say, Brutus or Cassius and to present the character in appropriate language. A new language was to be learnt by imitation, assimilation and amplification (Jones, 1977, pp. 16–17). The process was almost theatrical, and the notion of instruction through the dramatic process easily established. The power of rhetoric both to move and to instruct was clearly understood:

> I have often seen actors, both in tragedy and comedy, leave the theatre still drowned in tears after concluding the performance of some moving role. But if the mere delivery of words written by another has the power to set our souls on fire with fictitious emotions, what will the orator do whose duty it is to picture to himself the facts and who has it in his power to feel the same emotion as the client whose interests are at stake? (Quintilian, *Institutio Oratoria*, VI. ii. 35, cit. Jones, 1977, p. 22.)

Some commentators, John Donne, Ben Jonson, Francis Bacon among them, found themselves moved to write against a rhetoric which they felt obfuscated rather than elucidated the matter it set forth, against assimilation of classical languages which marginalized the accessibility of classic-based texts and dramas to those who were able to avail themselves of a university education. (You can find a useful exploration of the ongoing debates in Rhodes, 1992.)

It is this objection that Webster will make Vittoria Corombona raise at her trial, in Act III of *The White Devil*. The recognition and articulation of the power of rhetoric makes theatre a recognized political force in a period which begins as an essentially oral cultural milieu and only gradually allows the ascendancy of the printed text as the century progresses. While Skelton's *Magnyfycence* ([1515] 1979), establishes drama as a powerful medium for social comment, Bale's *King Johan* ([1538] 1979) explicitly addresses the political power of rhetoric (see Kendall, 1986). In a culture where law is disseminated by proclamation from the pulpit, or in the market-place on a platform by a crier, the man who stands on stage and speaks carries a great deal of authority. For this reason as much as any, restrictive legislation surrounds the player, and there is great public discredit of those who engage in the profession from its earliest days.

Whilst Henrician legislation in 1543 advocated restraint for ostensibly religious reasons, allowing 'songs, plays and interludes ... for the rebuking and reproaching of vices and the setting forth of virtue' it warned that such plays were allowable only when they were not 'interpreting scripture' (Sanders *et al.*, 1980, p. 10). Edwardian legislation against the drama had a rather less pious base. In August 1549 all public drama was banned for two months; according to the chronicler Holinshed, a rebellion by one Robert Kett of Norwich in the same year had taken its impetus from the 16,000 troops Kett had mobilized from the audience at a play.

Edward legislated in 1549 against any drama 'anye thinge in derogacion depravinge or dyspisinge' of the Book of Common Prayer. Mary was more concerned with the suppression of anti-Papist interludes; but it was the accession of Elizabeth (1558) which saw the onset of seriously restrictive legislation for the City of London. As early as 1559, an Act of Parliament decreed that all playing was forbidden unless it was previously licensed and that patrons were responsible for good conduct of playwrights, players and audiences. The Act of Common Council of 1574 set up a series of censoring principles whereby plays and venues were to be 'perused and allowed' by the Lord Mayor of London and his aldermen. Plays were not to contain unchaste or seditious material, nor must they be put on on holy days, during mass or at times of plague. Owners of suitable venues were to pay a deposit in case of disturbances. Because of such restrictions, theatres began to appear outside the jurisdiction of the city authorities, either physically out of reach, beyond the liberties, or under the protection of private ownership.

Since public theatres could hold up to three thousand and were generally open to the elements, and private theatres took up to seven hundred and were more likely to be within walls, it is interesting to find out whether the play you are reading was written for or originally performed on a stage inside or out, before an intimate and hushed audience or over the roar of the rabble. Consider the difference in the power of the spoken word, or the visual image (especially light and dark, the representation of day and night), in the different venues. Secondary texts dealing with such practicalities as these (Gurr, 1987, for example) are as important in your secondary reading as accounts of the cultural politics of this period, such as Howard (1994) and Shepherd (1986) which raise similar questions about contemporary patrons and audiences, questions of both a practical and a political nature.

The early Tudor stage inherits, then, a preoccupation with the purpose and also with the power of rhetoric. The Elizabethan and Jacobean stages reveal an equal preoccupation with the power of the visual image, with the ability of the dramatist to show as well as to tell. Both Elizabeth and James made great use of the civic procession to demonstrate their power and to associate themselves, usually for political expediency, with classical personae. Elizabeth was able to present herself as Cynthia, virgin huntress, inconstant goddess of the moon, ruler of the oceans; as Gloriana; as Wisdom; as the normally male Phoenix, mystically self-reproducing, consort to the eternally faithful turtle dove; as Astraea, or Justice. She recognized the very real political potential of display and also saw how it could work against her on the occasion of the Earl of Essex's attempts to fuel rebellion by staging *Richard II* in 1601. The preoccupation of Elizabethan drama with identity, and often with identity through gender, is, therefore, scarcely surprising.

James, in writing instructively for his son, makes great use of the image of the King as father at the head of the nation-family, a rhetoric designed to lay to rest the gender confusions brought about by the long and genealogically fruitless reign of Elizabeth. He cleverly assimilates to himself several of the classical personae Elizabeth chose for herself, thus tapping into the system of rhetoric by which she already binds the people to her projected personae. One example, in his opening speech before Parliament in 1603, is specifically pointed: 'How much greater reason haue wee to expect a happie issue of this greater Vnion [that of England and Scotland] which is only fastened and bound up by the wedding ring of Astraea?' (McIlwain, 1918, p. 273) and the same rhetorical figure is assimilated for him as a visual image by Dekker and Jonson when, designing the King's entertainment in 1604, they show James directly descended from Brutus, ushering in a united time of peace, the figure of Astraea standing on the summit of two arches which illustrate the fortunate isles of Great Britain and, more importantly, the cedar, which signifies fertility. The King assimilates those parts of Elizabeth's iconography which are useful to him, conjoining them with his own to suggest that his rule is some kind of successful completion of a long-expected union.

The notion of seeking the other half of self, whether it is the spiritual dimension or the gendered dimension, is a motif which occurs and recurs in the analyses which form the second part of this unit. It is in part an extension of the Platonic androgyne myth, but it is also one of the consequences of a reformed religion which puts the impetus on the individual self to discover and take responsibility for the spiritual self. The important thing here, though, is to recognize that role-playing and the conscious search for identity through role-playing is an integral part of Elizabethan public and literary culture. The notion of the voyage of self-discovery might go some way, for example, to providing a *raison d'être* for the much maligned whistle-stop tour of Europe undertaken by Marlowe's Faustus in Act IV of the play.

This dislocation between 'us and ourselves' was expressed quite clearly in the rediscovery of Platonic theory, mostly through Ficino. The notion of a divided existence, this one on earth being merely an acting out of a perfected existence in a coexistent ideal state somewhere beyond our defective imagination, fuelled the neo-classical ability to perceive actuality and perfectibility simultaneously. The Platonic androgyne myth presents unequivocally the spirit of the search for the reunified self which is quite clearly present in pieces as diverse as Udall's *Jake Jugeler* ([1530–55] 1982), Spenser's *Faerie Queene* (1596) and Shakespeare's *Twelfth Night* (1604). Having explained how the gods became jealous of humankind's contented hermaphroditic existence and decided to split each happy little eight-limbed creature in two, Plato's Aristophanes goes on to tell how

> when the work of bisection was complete, it left each half with a desperate yearning for the other, and they ran together and flung their arms around each others' necks and asked for nothing better than to be rolled into one ... the fact is, that both their souls are longing for a something else – a something to which they can neither of them put another name, and which they can only give an inkling of in cryptic sayings and prophetic riddles. (Plato, 1951, pp. 61–2)

The search for completion is not merely physical, but also metaphorical. It may also be expressed as a literary partial understanding, the search for truth through linguistic formulae.

On the one hand, then, the period we are examining offers an essentially humanist agenda. For the individual this involves experiment, release, self-discovery and creativity, allowable by a creed which emphasizes the potential of the individual human being. Textually, it is characterized by a sophisticated sense of scenic development, or creativity at full flower as manifested in an increasingly assured English poetic line and idiom. However, it can also be characterized by restraint through legislation, through the anxiety of self-awareness, through awareness of the political power of the stage and through the legacy of classical theme and variation.

It is vital, finally, to remember that the assessment of a dramatic work for whatever reason is not an act simply of reading. The interrogation of the drama is specifically to do with the ability, on the part of the reader or audience, to exist in two states at once. It is to do with the ability to see two things at once, to suspend disbelief and to accept the dramatic world. We see the shapes and hear the sounds, and we ask whether they complement or contradict, like form and content in poetry. We ask whether the form fits the content, and, if it doesn't, whether it is bad writing or satire, or writing which is drawing attention to its own refusal to conform to expectation, for whatever reason. We apply a system of values through which we make a value judgement and we need to be sure where those values are coming from. We look for analogy through form and through content, and for instruction through visual form, through light and shade and movement and stasis and verbosity and silence, and for indications of hierarchy or ascendancy through physical position on stage.

This unit offers an overview of English Renaissance drama which takes as its starting point Kyd's *The Spanish Tragedy* ([1587] 1970) and as its endpoint Webster's plays, *The White Devil* ([1612] 1972) and *The Duchess of Malfi* ([1614] 1972). It will however be evident from the plays mentioned in passing in this Introduction and during the course of the unit that the canon, the corpus of works we accept as the literary output of the period, is not and never has been fixed; that the texts we acknowledge as accepted and static elements of the canon are often one option among many; that the privileging of some elements of the canon and some forms of text due to the ascendancy of particular modes of criticism at particular times in the history of the literary academy are continually being challenged, and properly so.

Hugely influential critical texts can, in series, foreground or diminish the stature of any particular text at any particular time. One thinks of Bradley (1904), Tillyard (1943), Kott (1965), Greenblatt (1980), Dollimore (1984) and Belsey (1985), each critical text in its turn offering an alternative methodology to what had gone before and bringing to the fore, as an alternative site of exploration, genre, historicity, the issue of class intervention in the writing of history, the interrelationship between theatre and history, the focus on male character as subject at the expense or even to the exclusion of female subjects. As each critical text champions a different approach to reading, so the plays which can most fruitfully provide material for the particular methodology being proposed come to the fore.

Bearing this possibility of shift in focus in mind, one might easily have constructed a discussion of the same issues around ten completely different texts: for example, Medwall's *Fulgens and Lucres* ([1497] 1976) for its preoccupation with identity and its experimentation with plot and subplot; Sackville and Norton's *Gorboduc* ([1562] 1992) for its dealing with the notion of the King's two bodies, the division of the kingdom and for its interest as a highly stylized, static Senecan drama, and as some kind of predecessor for *Lear*; the anonymous *Arden of Faversham* ([1591] White, 1982) for its examination of gender type-casting; Dekker's *The Shoemaker's Holiday* ([1599] 1986) for its overt dealing with citizen comedy and the social politics around soldiers returning from the Elizabethan wars; a Jonsonian masque for the relation of language to spectacle; the list could be made and remade indefinitely.

There is also the mundane but very practical issue of availability of texts. There is, for example, no cheap accessible edition of the moral interludes, which makes it impractical to place them at the centre of an undergraduate course. So while this unit presents itself as an overview of Renaissance drama, it should be borne in mind that it is in many ways a very partial view.

## Texts, authors, contexts

### Gammer Gurton's Needle

*Gammer Gurton's Needle* is a domestic comedy written either at the end of Edward's reign or in the early years of Elizabeth's. The generally accepted date is around 1553. The play is both a comedy of manners and a comedy of errors, and its plot is ostensibly based on a heated argument about the misplacing of a needle. In so far as it is a domestic comedy in a rustic setting, it might seem inappropriate at first that the classical Terentian five-act structure be used for it. But whether or not the play deserves the dignity of the classical form depends to a large degree on the way in which the apparently trivial action is interpreted.

The first speech in the play proper, and much of the externalized comment on the action throughout, is given to Diccon, introduced as 'a bedlam'. As Charles Whitworth (1984) has pointed out, Diccon

> exhibits the variety of influences and dramatic traditions which converge in the play ... in the farcical context of this play's world, Diccon is mischievous, no worse, but he owes as much to the vices of the English moralities and interludes and the cheeky servants of the mystery cycles ... as to the duplicitous, mocking pages, valets and messengers of Roman comedy. (p. xxx)

So right from the start the audience is aware that the filter through which the play is to be viewed is one of misrule, where irregular behaviour is the order of the day, and also one which valorizes the English tradition just as much as, if not more than, the continental. The domestic setting of the play on the other hand is shored up by the use of a vernacular dialect, indicating that the medium within which the characters in Gammer Gurton's household operate is a localized one with its own concerns, preoccupations and priorities. Incidences like Hodge's terror when he momentarily believes that the cat is the Devil come down the chimney help establish the setting as one of superstition and parochialism. Within that context, the enormous importance attached to the loss of the needle becomes less ridiculous. So the author sets up a situation whereby the context is simultaneously one of misrule, where ludicrous and unpreventable accidents are bound to take place, but also a world bound by its own smallness, where proportion and regulation are relative. The rustic idyll is split by strife and the notion of the pastoral comedy mocked into farce.

The rivalry between the two main female characters, in such a situation, becomes farcical very quickly. Diccon it is who blows up the disappearance of a cock and a needle into an incident requiring outright domestic warfare, and the spectacle of two fighting women epitomizes the way in which what might be large classical themes are ridiculed when brought down to a quotidien domestic level. The fight is of the order seen in the moral interludes (in Medwall's *Fulgens and Lucres* ([1497] 1976) for example, where the two servants are armed with brooms and kitchen armour, or in *Thersites* ([1537] Udall, 1982), where the intractable 'hero' runs in terror from a snail to hide under his mother's skirts), utterly serious for the protagonists and utterly ludicrous for the observers. Hodge stands safely in the doorway urging the two women on as they scream insults and beat each other with various bits of culinary equipment, disappearing swiftly inside as soon as they get too close or there is any suggestion he might be called on to get involved. The verbal slapstick and the basic knockabout tumbledown comedy of the first two acts transforms into real physical violence here, and one is tempted, with the editor of the New Mermaids edition, to envisage the fight as being between two pantomime dames, big men barely disguised as women, stressing the hyperbolic nature of the situation with falsetto exclamations and elaborate adjustments of dress (Whitworth, 1984, p. xxxi).

The play does indicate, too, through its basic preoccupation, that audience recognition of the 'female' protagonists as men is all part of the comedy. The stress on the loss of the needle, while comic in its obsessiveness, is reinforced by repeated descriptions of where it was when it was lost, what its function is and what it looks like. The obvious coarse laugh elicited when Dame Chat repeatedly demands her cock is well in keeping with the basic earthiness of the humour in this play, which bases itself, at one level, fairly simply on rude words and foul-smelling emissions. But Gammer's despair at the loss of her needle is only a little more subtle. It is Hodge's description and Diccon's deliberately delayed recognition in Act II, i which leaves the audience in no doubt as to the *double entendre* which is intended:

*Hodge*: Tush, tush, her nee'le, her nee'le, her nee'le, man – 'tis neither flesh nor fish!
A little thing, with a hole in the end, as bright as any silver,
Small, long, sharp at the point, and straight as any pillar ...

*Diccon*: I know not what a devil thou meanst! Thou bringst me more in doubt.

(II. i. 41–5)

Suddenly Hodge's despair at being unable to find a needle in his trousers is loaded too. Both Dame Chat and Gammer Gurton are men in women's clothes bewailing their temporary emasculation. Their readiness to get physically violent and the coarseness of their language keep their maleness apparent from behind the costumes, and the spectacle of each grieving the loss of a cock and a slender long sharp pointy thing without which (s)he can do nothing becomes, in the trivial bawdy atmosphere of the play, repeatedly hilarious. Once that interpretation is set on the search for the needle and the fight to get the cock back, other permutations become even more outrageous. At one level, it was quite appropriate for the dame's needle to be in the hole of the manservant's trousers, but once the metaphor of sexual inversion becomes the predominant vehicle of the inversion brought about by the motif of misrule, the whole episode becomes virtually obscene.

The playwright here encourages the audience to view something simplistic as something potentially hugely complicated. Is the play about a domestic feud, or is it about sexual politics? In order to keep Hodge in order, and Tib under control, and assert her comparability with Dame Chat, does Gammer Gurton really need a needle? When misrule is the order of the day, the trivial things become the most important things. The author of *Gammer Gurton's Needle* is right to invest domestic uproar simultaneously with a classical five-act structure and to articulate it with the most basic of rustic dialects. The dignity given to quotidien existence is regularly totally misplaced given the triviality of our preoccupations. This utterly irreverent account of gender politics affirms that high seriousness or utter trivia are only what they are because of the world-view we allow to predominate at any one time. It is interesting, too, to observe that it is a pre-Elizabethan play which allows this playing with gender misattribution to go ahead without the slightest hint of anxiety.

Peele's *The Old Wives' Tale* centres around a female character, too, but the whole notion of central character and the whole notion of comedy is very different from that of *Gammer Gurton*. Peele investigates the notion of comedy by using a dream motif with an externalized framing device so that he can use the drama as both exposition and commentary. The old wife at the centre of the play begins to tell a tale whilst her onstage audience, the boys who have lost themselves in the forest (a perfect occasion for an idyllic but mysterious fantasy tale), observe the characters take on a life of their own and enact the narrative she has begun. Within the play there is occasion for several different kinds of comedy. There is the main story of the grateful dead, the ghost who acts as guide in order to expiate his own sins and go to his rest at the end. There is the comedy of transformation and restitution in the case of the old man and Venelia, and of the rescue of a beautiful woman by the breaking of a wicked spell, in the matter of the two brothers, Delia and Sacrapant the conjuror. The Sacrapant episodes also allow for fantastic and comic entertainment through visual illusion. There is the slapstick comedy provided by the braggart Huanebango, whose boasting and fantastic manipulation of a double broadsword provides visual and verbal pyrotechnics to set off the gentler comedic resolutions of the other tales. There is the Green Man myth present in the oracular head which rises from the well to give bounty to the woman who shows it kindness. There is the ironic comedy of the ugly woman being borne off triumphantly by a blind man, and of the shrewish woman equally enrapturing the miraculously deaf Huanebango, and a similar sort of comedy in the aggressive exchanges between the churchwarden, the sexton and Wiggen.

By using the dream motif Peele allows the play to focus on different kinds of comedy all within the same framework. By siting an audience internal to the play on stage he invites the audience to acknowledge that they too are observers of an illusion. But it is Madge's comment at the end which really dislocates the suspension of disbelief which has allowed the play to chart its patchwork course. As the boys accuse her of having slept through the play (which metaphorically is what the audience has done if it has embraced the notion of the dream vision throughout) and Frolic asks 'Then have you made an end of your tale, Gammer?', they get the cheerful reply, 'Yes, faith. When this was done, I took a piece of bread and cheese and came my way, and so shall you have too before you go, to your breakfast' (ll. 903–5).

Madge responds as if the narrative she initiated was actual, something experiential in her past. The reality of the present moment is dislocated still further as her casual closure suggests that the alternative realities posited by the dream motif are rooted in experience. But if we accept Madge as simultaneously originator of and audience for the piece, the final speech is entirely appropriate. If she has participated in its conception and in the enjoyment of it, why not in the exposition of it also? Peele in the presentation of the play valorizes no one part of it. No genre and no one level of the play-within-the-narrative-within-the-play can be said to dominate. Comic resolution comes about because characters and narrators and observers alike are rediscovered and allowed to return to their appropriate forms, whether that means shedding a bearskin or simply dropping the suspension of disbelief and leaving the theatre. The real comedic experience here is entirely metatheatrical.

### The Alchemist

As the title of the play suggests, Jonson's *The Alchemist* ([1610] 1979) is about mutability, the conversion of a physical being from one state to another.

*The Alchemist*, like *Volpone* (Jonson, [1606] 1979) is a play of shape shifting and personal mutation. In the earlier play, Volpone's own deceptions and deliberate deformations are parodied in the permanent deformity of the freaks and the play draws attention to its own dramatic art, itself mutating into deformed dumbshow and mountebank charlatanism. It locates itself in a single centre, providing a stable central locus from which the instability of the characterization and also the undermining of the dramatic form can depart. One might further read *Bartholomew Fair* (Jonson, [1614] 1979) as a play of social and linguistic transformation, an arena where all types are possible and self-defining in the huge mass of humanity unified only by place.

In *The Alchemist*, Jonson's use of language and character is alchemical. He has a Baconian sense of the reducibility of language to a gold standard of pure meaning. It is an English tradition going back to the morality plays. In *Mankind*, for example, there is much made of Mercy's obfuscatory use of Latin, and the vice figures, Mischief especially, regularly parody the Latinate diction of authority. Jonson asserts in *Discoveries* that 'the chief virtue of a style is perspicuity ...' and if the language of the play is to be transparent, or deliberately otherwise in order to suggest parody or criticism of the character who uses it, the significance of the characters is to be equally apparent. To make plain the satirical element of his writing, the dislocation between what is said and what is signified (which is the basis of satire), Jonson uses allegorical naming and emblematic device, where the explicit symbol must be interpreted in order to achieve meaning. From 1598 onwards, Jonson tends to 'frame' his work with a prologue and an epilogue, and this – the alignment of the audience with the playwright through the use of an apparently objective direct address at the beginning of the play – is part of the successful working of satire, placing playwright and audience in a position superior to the characters within the play.

Jonson's prologue and mnemonic verse at the beginning of *The Alchemist* suggest subtly that the meaning of the play is self-explanatory, that one need only look at the patterning of its construction to spell out its meaning. The prologue establishes it as an English play and a city play, raising expectations immediately of social conflicts between commerce and the desire for nobility among the rising merchant classes. A cross-section of society resorts to Lovewit's house, in search of wealth through the process of alchemy, at a time when the master is absent and a period of misrule is evident. Where alchemy is the mythical refining process by which all base metals can be returned to a pure gold, Jonson uses the notion of transmutation from one state to another as a central motif to demonstrate debasement rather than refinement. Face is harangued:

> Thou vermin, have I ta'en thee out of dung,
> So poor, so wretched, when no living thing
> Would keep thee company, but a spider, or worse?
> Raised thee from brooms, and dust, and watering-pots,
> Sublimed thee, and exalted thee, and fixed thee
> In the third region, called our state of grace?
> Wrought thee to spirit, to quintessence, with pains
> Would twice have won me the philosopher's work?
> Put thee in words and fashion, made thee fit
> For more than ordinary fellowships?
>
> (I. i. 64–73)

At one level Face's condition has been improved, transmuted from when he walked 'piteously costive' taking only a 'meal of steam in, from cooks' stalls' (I. i. 28, 26); but from Jonson's point of view the slide into deception is hardly a process of refinement. Where the characters within the play are concerned with deceitful transmutation, appearing to change base metal to gold, Jonson is concerned with the degree to which we debase ourselves.

The language of alchemy deceives the characters: the language of comedy exposes that deception to the audience. It is the deception of the characters through the alchemical language and the physical disguise of the three alchemists that exposes the deceptive nature of language and the hypnotic deceptiveness of repeated familiar process to the audience.

Each time the long alchemical experiments are repeated, described, exhibited, the process becomes more familiar and more ludicrous, but almost believable within the paradigm of the play. Once each of the supplicants is part of the system within which he is to be deceived, he is more and more willing to suspend disbelief and go along with whatever antics are apparently necessary to achieve his desires. The suspension of disbelief, the inability to see a rhetorical and metaphorical process for what it is, is at the hub of Jonson's satire here.

Naming is an ongoing motif in the play. The mock heraldic projection of Drugger's name is a parody of the explicit nature of Jonson's naming of his characters as a dramatic tool. Subtle muses, loading the arbitrary act with mysticism,

> He shall have a *bell*, that's *Abel*;
> And by it standing one whose name is *Dee*,
> In a *rug* gown, there's D and *Rug*, that's *drug*;
> And right anenst him a dog snarling *Er*;
> There's *Drugger*, Abel Drugger. That's his sign.
> And here's now mystery and hieroglyphic!
>
> (II. vi. 19–24)

The forced onomatopoeic nature of what is in fact a rebus and not a mystical, alchemical hieroglyph at all, nevertheless apparently confers a certain degree of mystical status on Drugger. But the episode is significant in more than just its literal meaning.

The Argument at the beginning of the play could be seen to suggest that the meaning of what is seen can be spelt out from its name, since the plot is described from the mnemonic provided by the title to the play. Within the play, pretence at an altered state requires an altered image, and the altered image a name and so Jeremy the manservant becomes Face, just a face, a facade, a disguise. Subtle is precisely that, subtle, no less and no more: and Dol is always and ever Dol, whether she be, like Drugger, promoted in terms of heraldry as Dol Common, Dol Proper, Dol Singular or Dol Particular (one wonders why not rampant or couchant) or consciously acting out the roles of Queen of Faerie or mad gentlewoman.

The differentiation between the deceiver and the deceived is especially apparent through the naming in the play since the deceivers are named according to who they are and what they do, and if they want to do otherwise change their names and characters accordingly. They are in control of their own transmogrification. This is most obvious perhaps in the slanging match which takes place in the first scene and ends simply with the hurling of names (106–7). Not only is argument reduced to its absolute essence, the shouting of single-word epithets, but Jonson makes it plain that these three know exactly who they are and what they are about. The characters who are deceived, however, are firmly named by Jonson and remain so, and their names, semi-allegorical, demonstrate their functions in the play, in a way which suggests that Jonsonian satirical comedy is a type of morality play for the seventeenth century, dealing simultaneously in individuals and universals.

## The Roaring Girl

The Roaring Girl was a real person. She was Mary or Moll Frith, who, before the London Consistory Court on 27 January 1612,

> voluntarily confessed that she had long frequented all or most of the disorderly & licentious places in this Cittee as namely she hath visually in the habite of a man resorted to alehowses Tavernes Tobacco shops & also to play howses ... (Mulholland in Middleton and Dekker, [1608] 1987, p. 262)

While she admits to lascivious language and drunken behaviour and several types of blasphemy, she,

> being pressed to declare whether she had not byn dishonest of her body & hath not also drawne other women to lewdnes by her perswasions & by carrying her self lyke a bawde, she absolutely denied that she was chargeable with eyther of these imputacions ... (p. 263)

The epilogue to Middleton and Dekker's play states its business quite explicitly.

> A painter, having drawn with curious art
> The picture of a woman – every part
> Limned to the life – hung out the piece to sell.
> People who passed along, viewing it well,
> Gave several verdicts on it: some dispraised
> The hair, some said the brows too high were raised,
> Some hit her o'er the lips, misliked their colour,
> Some wished her nose were shorter, some the eyes fuller;
> Others said roses on her cheeks should grow,
> Swearing they looked too pale, others cried no.
>
> (Epilogue, 1–10)

There is obviously no problem here with exposing woman to the public view, because what is exposed is a representation, not a reality. What takes place above is not a discussion of the real attributes of womankind, but rather a discussion of means and kinds of representation. *The Roaring Girl* at once represents gendered identity and investigates its own means of doing so.

The prologue informs the playgoers that they will be shown, not told, what a roaring girl really is, and that Moll will be allowed to speak for herself:

> ... Thus her character lies –
> Yet what need characters, when to give a guess
> Is better than the person to express?
>
> (Prologue, 26–8)

The invitation to the audience to involve itself actively in the process of discovery is one which recurs throughout the play. The point of the play is to provide a platform for observation and interrogation. The dialogue begins with one of the main female characters the reluctant object of formulaic flattery (a form of disguised language), and an undisguised retort from the character addressed:

> *Neatfoot*: ... it is into his ears, sweet damsel, emblem of fragility, you desire to have a message transported or to be transcendent?
> *Mary*: A private word or two, sir, nothing else.
>
> (I. i. 2–5)

As Mary exposes manipulative language, so Moll repeatedly identifies, makes explicit and problematizes female stereotyping. Her behaviour contradicts typical female behaviour; her stage-presence as boy playing a cross-dressed woman blurs the distinctions between male and female behaviour; her outspoken challenges to men in the play who attempt to represent her behaviour according to their preconceptions counter the very real Renaissance notion that a good woman is a silent woman, since chastity and silence are inextricably entangled.

She challenges Laxton, and when he expresses surprise that she should expect him to draw his sword against her, explains,

> Thou'rt one of those
> That thinks each woman thy fond flexible whore:
> If she but cast a liberal eye upon thee,
> Turn back her head, she's thine; or, amongst company,
> By chance drink first to thee, then she's quite gone
> There's no means to help her ...
> How many of our sex by such as thou
> Have their good thoughts paid with a blasted name
> That never deserved loosely or did trip
> In path of whoredom betwixt cup and lip? ...
>     ... What durst move you, sir,
> To think me whorish? ....
> In thee I defy all men, their worst hates
> And their best flatteries, all their golden witchcrafts
> With which they entangle the poor spirits of fools ...
>
> (III. i. 72–7, 81–4, 88–9, 92–3)

Moll casts Laxton in a male stereotype similar to the female one he has provided for her. Although she is repeatedly referred to as 'unnatural' (I.ii.160), 'strange in quality' (I.i.100), 'a monster' (I.i.135), a 'mermaid' who has 'tolled my son to shipwreck' (I.ii.214–15) her behaviour through the play is, by an unprejudiced light, less monstrous than that say of Mistress Gallipot, who procures money by deception for her lover.

Dekker and Middleton encourage the audience to imagine the opposite to what is expected, and while they do this comically and with passion through Moll's slapstick, rhetoric and deadly wit, they also do it by putting the conventions of stage characterization under close scrutiny. The most important moment of revelation where the nature of gender is concerned comes when Sebastian and Mary Fitzallard arrange to meet in order to confound the former's father, who is opposed to their marriage. Mary, in order to be able to attend Sebastian, is dressed as a page. The moment on stage is doubly convoluted for the audience since the actor dressed as Mary dressed as a page is of course male in the first place. As Sebastian kisses Mary, Moll remarks thoughtfully, 'How strange this shows, one man to kiss another' (IV. i. 45), to which Sebastian replies,

> I'd kiss such men to choose, Moll;
> Methinks a woman's lip tastes well in a doublet.
>
> (IV. i. 45–6)

Within the fiction of the drama, Sebastian causes no anxiety by desiring Mary because it is plain to everyone that she is not a boy but a woman dressed as a boy, and the significance of the kiss is after all between the two characters, not between the two male actors. The irony of the situation resides in the fact that Moll has been continually reviled and sexually threatened when she is to all intents and purposes exactly the same, at this instant, as Mary, a female dressed as a male. Both Mary and Moll have to disguise themselves as male in order to achieve what they desire – one might even say, they must disguise themselves in order to be themselves. The difference, Middleton and Dekker make us see very clearly by this explicit juxtaposition, is that Mary Fitzallard wears this disguise as a temporary, holiday means to an end, just as she dressed as a maid at the beginning of the play. She dresses as a boy to disguise her real identity, whilst the anxiety caused by Moll is that she dresses as a man not to disguise but to express her true identity. This moment is breathtaking in the way it confronts the audience with the issue at the very hub of the play.

The important motif throughout this play is recognition. Moll recognizes the censure she attracts, and articulates it before it can be articulated against her. The audience recognizes the difference between Moll's disguise and Mary's, but is made also to recognize its own assessment of each set of disguising.

### The Spanish Tragedy

Kyd's *Spanish Tragedy* ([1587] 1970) opens with a framing device. The ghost Andrea and the abstract form of Revenge prompt the audience to consider the play as the intellectual and dramatic working out of the conflicts between justice and revenge. The audience sees and understands the distortion of classical propriety when, rather than being given a Virgil to lead him through the intellectual maze of the underworld to a finer understanding of self, Andrea is given Revenge to lead him back to the physical world. Kyd immediately presents conflict both in the content of the play and among the forms in which it will manifest itself.

Where Senecan tradition is one of intellectual and verbal working out, Kyd's play is one where language and action meet, and the notion of dramaturgy is moved forward by Kyd's inexorable meshing of language, action and Renaissance questioning of motivation. The impotence of empty language and hyperbole are continually addressed in the play. Lorenzo urges Pedringano to 'service of import/ and not to spend the time in trifling words' (II. i. 43–4), and promises practical recompense, 'not with fair words but store of golden coin' (II. i. 52), becoming irate when Pedringano begins to stall with questions in an attempt to qualify acceptance of his mission: 'What, villain, ifs and ands?' (II. i. 77) and threatening to end the talk with action (SD *offers to kill him*). The impetus of language into action becomes apparent when the sending of letters by Bel-Imperia to Horatio becomes the final motivation for the murder Lorenzo commissions (II. i. 84), and the swearing of an oath on the handle of a sword ('Swear on this cross...', II. i. 87) becomes the speech act which will become murderous action should Pedringano's information prove unreliable ('This very sword whereon thou took'st thine oath/ Shall be the worker of thy tragedy' (II. i. 92)), Lorenzo finally enunciating 'Where words prevail not, violence prevails' (II. i. 108). Immediately after this interaction, Balthazar, who woos Bel-Imperia for status rather than for love, is ridiculed by the conspicuously empty rhetoric he uses:

> it makes me glad and sad:
> Glad, that I know the hinderer of my love,
> Sad, that I fear she hates me whom I love.
> Glad, that I know on whom to be revenged,
> Sad, that she'll fly me if I take revenge.
>
> (II. i. 111–14)

It is the chiming of 'glad' with 'sad' and the unsubtle repetition which betrays Balthazar as a less than accomplished rhetorician, a betrayal amplified as the speech goes on and the repetition gets clumsier.

Bel-Imperia, who has already established that Balthazar's troping is transparent ('Alas my lord, these are but words of course,/ And but device to drive me from this place', I.iv.98–9), acerbically replies that unlike Balthazar's imagined perception her version of reality is consonant with her appearance:

> My looks, my lord are fitting for my love,
> Which new begun, can show no brighter yet.
>
> (III. xiv. 102–3)

and escapes by remarking on the entrance of her father, switching emphasis from fancy to reality. The audience remembers too that one of her last conversations with the man she does love, Horatio, remarks on his propensity to consider silently the action he sees unfolding before him (II.ii.25) (whilst Balthazar, in a parody of the true informing presence of Revenge and Andrea on the margin of the playing area, is an irritating stichomythic presence above the main dialogue) and that her own ability to describe the delights of love, while based in traditional tropes, suggests that she is capable of transforming the commonplace into something exceptional and personal. Her rhetoric acknowledges the predominance of conflict between love and war in their situation and aligns her to a certain extent with the controlling influence of the playwright:

> Let dangers go, thy war shall be with me,
> But such a war as breaks no bond of peace ...
> Give me a kiss, I'll countercheck thy kiss:
> Be this our warring peace, or peaceful war.
>
> (II. ii. 32–3, 37–8)

The arrangement to meet in the bower, the traditional site of pastoral innocence and amorous dalliance, is inevitably fraught with danger in a play where the classical norm is continually disrupted and dislocated. The gentle jesting around the interaction of love and war ('Then be thy father's pleasant bower the field', where 'field' means site of conflict (II.ii.42)) comes horrifically to fruition in the scene which inaugurates the final tragic motivation in the play. As Hieronimo rushes towards the bower in the middle of the night, seeking a temporal verbal reassurance for the cries that call him from his bed, fearing rightly that the horror before him is real and no dream, he reiterates, 'This place was made for pleasure, not for death'

(II.v.11). The murder which requires revenge has now moved from the hinterland of the dream-world to centre stage, and it has done this by the explicit misappropriation of the place of love for the place of murder. The classical style in which Hieronimo expresses his grief marries with the transmutation of speech into action (Hieronimo describes what he does as he does it) to inaugurate a new coherence of speech, action and form in the play.

This demonstrates a shift in the dramatic pattern of the play. Where rhetoric has predominated, where the telling of the various versions of Andrea's death (at I. i. 15 by Andrea, I. ii. 65 by the General, I. iii. 59 by Viluppo and I. iv. 9 by Horatio) has confused the actuality, at this moment the action of revenge begins to predominate. Hieronimo swiftly loses faith in words after he goes to plead with the King (III. xii) and, exhausting the word 'justice' in his pleading (III. xii. 63, 65), begins his next scene with a cry instead for vengeance, a cry which moves swiftly on from the Christian *vindicta mihi*, where God is implored to intervene, to a raw invocation of classical – in fact specifically Senecan – notions of wild justice (III. xiii).

The movement from language to action is completed as the dumb show at II. xv reveals what will happen when Revenge finally awakes to Andrea's appeal. In the closing stages of the play proper, there is an insistence that the play put on by Hieronimo should be both unscripted (IV. i. 100–7) and performed in sundry different languages (172–8). Kyd insists that the play within a play, which utterly inverts the nature of the dramatic illusion by the illusion of mass slaughter in fact being the truth, has been authored by Hieronimo only in terms of action and not in terms of specific language. Such linguistic elements as exist are both peripheral and unintelligible. This pessimistic view of the dislocation between deep emotion and its expression through language stands alongside Hieronimo's action in biting out his tongue in negating the effectiveness or trustworthiness of language as a self-reliant medium for truth. Isabella's destruction of the arbour in a brief moment between the rehearsal for the play and the play itself demonstrates the extent to which Kyd insists on the arbitrariness of literary signs.

Whilst Kyd's play exhibits many of the elements of Senecan tragedy, his assimilation of the form involves questioning at a fundamental level both the function of the dramatic illusion and also the privileging of language as the primary means of communication both within and outside of the theatre.

## The Revenger's Tragedy

Until recently Middleton's *Revenger's Tragedy* ([1606] 1967) was generally accepted to have been written by Tourneur, and most readily available editions still bear his name. So although I shall refer to the play throughout as Middleton's, the edition I refer to bears Tourneur's name.

The most obvious difference between the two revenge plays is the stylized diction and characterization in *The Revenger's Tragedy*. The tension between speech and action in Middleton's play resides in the form of the words themselves.

Sententiae and aphorisms, brief unexpanded quotations or moral sayings, appear throughout the play as if the characters are struggling to find a moral language which might contain the physical horrors which are overtaking them as the murders proliferate. Vindice's opening account of the duke is vindicated by the quotation, 'Age as in gold, in lust is covetous' (I. i. 38), his suspicions about his mother by 'Wives are made but to go to bed and feed' (I. ii. 131). It is as if a language authorized by time will stabilize a present which is being annihilated by vengeance. The notion of history itself being written falsely is another matter for concern. In I. ii the Duke complains that his stepson's rape has

> Thrown ink upon the forehead of our state
> Which envious spirits will dip their pens into
> After our deaths, and blot us in our tombs.
> For that which will seem treason in our lives
> Is laughter when we're dead.

> (I. ii. 4–8)

This notion of history being a literature written in blood which is unanswerable from beyond the grave is an early instance in the play of the interaction or dislocation between what is seen to happen and what is reported to be happening. Written history seems as evanescent as the deeds which it records, a sense reiterated by the judge whom the Duke addresses,

> ... for what is it to have
> A flattering false insculption on a tomb
> And in men's hearts reproach?

> (I. ii. 12–14)

Theatrical history is a further concern within this play. Where Kyd refers through form and diction to the classical play, Middleton's diction and characterization frequently resonates with the English tradition of the morality play. Spurio's evocative description of adultery, for example, only just stops short of representing Spurio, whose name in any case suggests he is in part the epitome of bastardy, as adultery personified:

> Adultery is my nature:
> Faith if the truth were known I was begot
> After some gluttonous dinner-some stirring dish
> Was my first father; when deep healths went round
> And ladies' cheeks were painted red with wine,
> Their tongues as short and nimble as their heels
> Uttering words sweet and thick; and when they rose
> Were merrily disposed to fall again.
> In such a whispering and withdrawing hour,
> When base male bawds kept sentinel at stair-head
> Was I stol'n softly-oh damnation met
> The sin of feasts, drunken adultery.
> I feel it swell me ...

> (I. ii. 177–89)

The heavy sweetness of the party is evident in the cluttering and clustering of sibilants and palatals, 'uttering words sweet and thick', evoking the whispers behind hands and the rustling of skirts, returned to again at the ambiguous 'withdrawing hour' where monosyllables strike sternly against the yielding sibilance of the description of the act of conception 'When base male bawds kept sentinel at stair-head/Was I stol'n softly'. The piece is hugely evocative of smells, sounds, tastes in itself, closely aligning the deadly sins of gluttony and lust, but it is also evocative of the morality tradition in its formula, and stands close comparison to, for example, the seven deadly sins' descriptions of themselves in *The Castle of Perseverance* (I. 885–1013) and to their introductions in Act II of Marlowe's *Faustus*.

Later in the play Castiza is put under pressure and to spark her to her own defence Vindice remarks dismissively, as though speaking of the abstract, 'All thrives but Chastity, she lies a-cold', where the simultaneity of the abstract and the particular figure acts together with the antiquated form 'a-cold' to invoke a former type of morality now seen to be fading fast.

But naming here is only semi-allegorical. This is essentially a play about a particular group of people which has universal resonance; it is not an allegorical universal which might be applied in the particular. While characters' names are allusive, they are not restrictive. No one character is the direct personification of the attribute their name glances towards; all are more complex and more capable of interrogation and development than that. Middleton is writing into a much more self-consciously turbulent, sophisticated arena than Bale or Skelton. Where Revenge is a helpless observer in Kyd's play, in Middleton's allegory and action, the spiritual and the physical selves are utterly consonant and strenuously at work in the physical world of the play. Similarly, the dumb show and mass killing at the end of *The Revenger's Tragedy* relies not on a clever metatheatrical device but on the simple fact of utter physical carnage. Middleton's is much more a play of the flesh, and this is borne out, paradoxically, in its iconography.

Visual and then verbal expositions of a situation can directly reflect the conflicting or consonant physical and moral situations experienced by people in this play. There are moments of visual iconography which are a parallel to the sententiae mentioned earlier, where the audience has its attention drawn to a visual set piece with a fixed meaning. Most effective is the description of Antonio's dead wife at I. iv. 13:

> *Antonio*
>               I marked not this before:
> A prayer book the pillow to her cheek;
> This was her rich confection, and another
> Placed in her right hand with a leaf tucked up,
> Pointing to these words:
> Melius virtute mori, quam per dedecus vivere.
> True and effectual it is indeed.
>
>                         (I. iv. 13–19)

Elsewhere in the play, there is a suppressed hysteria lurking just beneath the surface of the repeated plots, arguments and murders, a grim humour which just makes the carnage bearable. In parallel episodes in Acts III and V, grim asides verbalize the tricks being played as the dead bodies are initially presented as living. Vindice, about to expose the Duke as lecher and murderer, tells him the woman he is about to meet 'has somewhat/A grave look with her' (III. v. 135–6); as Lussurio recoils in absolute horror from the corpse of his father, Vindice leers calmly into the audience, 'That's a jest'.Vindice and Hippolito seem almost relieved to be arraigned and put to death at the end of the play; Revenge has exhausted itself.

## Dr. Faustus

Marlowe's *Faustus* ([1592] 1969) is at pains to demonstrate precisely the extent to which the nature of Renaissance tragedy is embedded in both English and classical cultural history, but more importantly is present in the individual internalized struggle for supremacy between the instinctive, embedded past and the intellectual-ized, assimilated present. In prefacing his play with a prologue full of classical reference, Marlowe points out that although this is not a play of the proportions of *Tamburlaine*, brimming with mighty deeds on a mighty scale, the matter, microcos-mically contained within the space of one human being, is of equally universal stature. The play opens with the eponymous tragic hero sitting in, or perhaps pacing, his study. Marlowe presents an immediate restlessness, as a glance at the opening soliloquy will show. Faustus moves swiftly through a number of classical academic texts and disciplines, claiming to have exhausted the potential for knowledge at the core of each. His egocentricity – the desperate accumulation of knowledge as if man's intellect could contain universal understanding – shows a Renaissance space with man very firmly at its centre. Moving on to scripture, Faustus's view is pessimistic:

> *Stipendium peccati mors est.* Ha! *Stipendium* etc.,
> 'The reward of sin is death.' That's hard.
> *Si pecasse negamus, fallimur, et nulla est in nobis veritas.*
> 'If we say that we have no sin
> We deceive ourselves, and there is no truth in us.'
> Why then, belike, we must sin,
> And so consequently die.
>
> (I. i. 39–45)

But Faustus's view here is partial. It is surely no accident that the passages he quotes are curtailed, and that the second part of each, as a compulsorily church-going, aurally-trained Renaissance audience would probably know, offers the hope that Faustus denies. The reward of sin *is* death, but, in the verse following the one that Faustus quotes, the gift of God is eternal life through Jesus Christ our Lord.

When Faustus conjures spirits, and the good and bad angels precede them to tempt him equally from right and left, the extreme bias of his intellectual activity becomes plain. Just as Mephistopholis refuses to acknowledge who made the world, so Faustus wilfully displaces a moralistic view of the world with an academic view which denies any spiritual insight. One might say he knows everything but understands nothing. Whenever he is tempted to turn back to good, it is through fear. The tension between Renaissance intellectualism, with self, intellect and the knowledge of good and evil at the centre of the universe, and the medieval morality tradition is made so plain in this play as to be almost parody. Lucifer and Mephistopholis arrange a pageant of the Seven Deadly Sins which, being thoroughly allegorical in a play which operates well beyond the allegorical paradigm, takes on much of the nature of pantomime as the characters introduce themselves. In performance, though, the moment can be used to remind the audience just how powerful gut-wrenching inarticulate fear can be, if the creatures are brought on in a frenzy of drumming and capering, especially from within the space separating the audience from the main action on stage. While Marlowe demonstrates the epic struggle between good and evil, between instinct and intellect, between superstition and reason in the microcosmic person of Faustus, he uses dramatic techniques and the dramatic, epic power of his 'mighty line' to make sure the audience undergoes some of the same experience. Thus the moment of intellectual activity at the beginning of the play is given as soliloquy, where the solipsistic academic appeals directly to the intellect of the audience with no interference from any other character or any kind of dramatic effect. As Mephistopholis is invoked, however, there is incantation, darkness, costume, wizardry, conjuring in an unfamiliar tongue, and it is our instinctive fear of the unknown and the unknowable which dominates.

   The audience is made to share the moment in solitude with Faustus as he hovers in spiritual suspense for the desperate, symbolic hour before midnight:

> Ah, Faustus,
> Now hast thou but one bare hour to live,
> And then thou must be damned perpetually.
> Stand still, you ever-moving spheres of heaven,
> That time may cease and midnight never come.
> Fair nature's eye, rise, rise again, and make
> Perpetual day, or let this hour be but
> A year, a month, a week, a natural day,
> That Faustus may repent and save his soul.
> *O lente, lente, currite nocte equi.*
> The stars move still, time runs, the clock will strike,
> The devil will come, and Faustus must be damned.
> Oh, I'll leap up to my God: who pulls me down?
> See, see, where Christ's blood streams in the firmament.
> One drop would save my soul, half a drop. Ah, my Christ!
> Ah, rend not my heart for naming of my Christ!
> Yet will I call on him. Oh, spare me, Lucifer!
> Where is it now? 'Tis gone:
> And see where God stretcheth out his arm,
> And bends his ireful brows,
> Mountains and hills, come, come, and fall on me,
> And hide me from the heavy wrath of God...

(V. ii. 143–64)

It works because Faustus, in soliloquy, pleads with the audience to see what he sees, to affirm his vision of grace, but the two modes of seeing and being have been so diametrically opposed that all the audience sees is a man struggling to see a vision. The playwright does not provide the vision for us too. Faustus is literally torn between the lyrical vision of Christian redemption ('See, see, where Christ's blood streams in the firmament'), fear of Old Testament wrath ('Mountains and hills, come, come, and fall on me/ And hide me from the heavy wrath of God') and the inexorable ticking away of modern time as the hours are told by the clock. He finally has to acknowledge that what he conjures (in lines 46–7) will not materialise (153–4). In the absence of the power of his conjuring rhetoric, Faustus turns to the invocation of religious rhetoric, but time has run out.

## The White Devil

T.S. Eliot is chillingly direct about Webster's preoccupations.

> Webster was much possessed by death
> And saw the skull beneath the skin;
> And breastless creatures underground
> Leaned backwards with a lipless grin.
>
> (from 'Whispers of Immortality')

Eliot's acute observation sees that the motivating forces in Webster's plays lie beneath the superficiality of words, and that the observer must look past the dialogues and through the soliloquies down to the bare bones of the ideas and almost inarticulate passions which hold them together. *The White Devil* is entirely preoccupied with what lurks beneath the surface; with simulation and dissimulation, with text and subtext. The *sotto voce* asides amidst full-pitch conversations which take place early in the play (I. ii. 119–94), and the silent representations and enactments of the more brutal acts of dispatch (the two dumbshows at II. ii and the speechless ghosts which maintain silent accusatory presences) repeatedly urge both the characters in the plays and the watchful audience to see into the heart of things rather than observe what is going on at face value, and to acknowledge the brutality and finality of the actions which belie the fluidity of the superficial courtly language which creates a world in which such actions are apparently unspeakable. The impossibility of a language brutal enough for such a time is a subject broached by both Isabella and Francisco, the former as she articulates the nature of her desired revenge on her husband's paramour (discussed below) and more succinctly and hopelessly by Francisco at V. i. 100–1: ''Tis a ridiculous thing for a man to be his own chronicle'. The continual rehearsal of *sententiae* in the play is a different version of the same motif. Where the moral framework of a courtly structure begins to crumble, the set phrases and formulae of the language which holds such a system together become themselves unstable and unreliable.

Cornelia points this out inadvertently by coupling such a dictum with a comment on the times,

> The lives of princes should like dials move
> Whose regular example is so strong
> They make the times by them go right and wrong.

(I. ii. 285–7)

The notion of dissimulation, especially dissimulation by women, is regularly rudely challenged, to begin with in what seem relatively trivial circumstances. Flamineo dismisses Vittoria's coyness as a feigned one, implying she is quite willing to act out something she would be reluctant to articulate: 'yet why should ladies blush to hear that named, which they do not fear to handle?' (I. ii. 20–2), but as the play progresses, it becomes absolutely apparent why women should dissimulate. Flamineo trivializes what will become an important motif in the play, the impossibility of articulating the reality and consequence of political action. Words will not describe what is really taking place, but will provide a version of events which is tolerable by the mores of the society in which they operate. When Brachiano casts Isabella aside, his dismissal of her is sudden and brutal, but he articulates it by an ironic reference to their wedding ceremony, giving his action some kind of perverted authority through such reference:

> This is the latest ceremony of my love,
> Henceforth I'll never lie with thee, by this,
> This wedding ring: I'll ne'er more lie with thee
> And this divorce shall be as truly kept,
> As if the judge had doomed it: fare you well,
> Our sleeps are sever'd.

(II. i. 193–8)

The exchange is private, between the two of them only, and Isabella is offered no explanation, expected by Brachiano to accept his word as absolute. When in full public view she uses almost exactly the same words to distance herself from him, she prefaces them with the language of revenge, thus showing the full horror of the separation from her own point of view:

> O that I were a man, or that I had power
> To execute my apprehended wishes, ...
> To dig the strumpet's eyes out, let her lie
> Some twenty months a-dying, to cut off
> Her nose and lips, pull out her rotten teeth,
> Preserve her flesh like mummia, for trophies
> Of my just anger...
> Henceforth I'll never lie with you, by this,
> This wedding ring...
> And this divorce shall be as truly kept,
> As if in thronged court, a thousand ears
> Had heard it, and a thousand lawyers' hands
> Seal'd to the separation.

(II. i. 242–3, 245–9, 253–4, 255–8)

Isabella articulates the physical manifestation of the situation as she perceives it. Moral decay has led to her husband's betrayal, and physical death and decay will be its ultimate result. Instead of speaking in riddles, she paints a graphic picture of physical revenge. The same language in a differently gendered mouth brought to a different level of articulation and in a different situation takes on an entirely different meaning. Meaning generally in the play is attached to context and to subtext. To the audience Isabella's speech is bitterly ironic; to the spectators within the play, it has no subtext and no embedded meaning and is thus utterly inexplicable. The relationship between Isabella and Brachiano is coded between them, and holds a variety of meanings: one for them, one for the onlookers within the play, and yet another for the audience.

It is precisely in order to dodge this kind of gendered coding that Vittoria refuses to be arraigned in a privileged language which allows only partial under-standing for the majority of onlookers. Even within that framework she must resist the imposition of meaning on her perceived behaviour, reacting indignantly when termed a whore by the cardinal. When he in turn deliberately misunderstands her indignation and goes into a long exposition of the term (III. ii. 79–101), she haughtily replies 'This character 'scapes me' and, as he sentences her, draws attention to the fact that it is interpretation of behaviour, the application of meaning yet again, which has given rise to the construction of her character within this particular framework. She draws attention to the double standards of the law, different behaviour being expected of different genders:

> Grant I was tempted,
> Temptation to lust proves not the act,
> *Casta est quam nemo rogavit,*
> You read his hot love to me, but you want
> My frosty answer.
>
> (III. ii. 197–201)

and insisting that the faults of which she stands accused are simply slanderous inferences from what has been an essentially innocent situation:

> Sum up my faults I pray, and you shall find,
> That beauty and gay clothes, a merry heart,
> And a good stomach to a feast, are all,
> All the poor crimes that you can charge me with:
> In faith my lord you might go pistol flies,
> The sport would be more noble.
>
> (III. ii. 206–11)

Ultimately her insistence that justice is subjective and gendered is expressed in terms of sexual molestation, as she calls 'A rape, a rape', making the male imposition of a certain kind of character on a woman the equivalent of social rape. Having drawn the court's attention to the power of symbolic rather than genuine reputation, she suggests that the cardinal's red garb makes him a scarlet whore as he, in her view, prostitutes the truth. But justice in this play concentrates on the rotten flesh of the nation, on the outward and visible sign, and not on the bare bones of metaphoric meaning. In the same way as during Isabella's outburst, it is suggested that to cry out such a version of the truth indicates madness, and Vittoria is defined by, as well as confined by, the house of convertites to which she is sent. Her reputation, and effectively her public life, are stifled at this moment.

In this play, then, truth is continually struggling against repression, suffocation, elusive redefinition. Madness and the suppressed bestiality of human nature lurk just beneath the surface, and frequently emerge at moments of crisis. The continual recourse to the motif of the howling wolf suggests the mad inarticulacy of grief which is so tightly sealed beneath the veneer of courtly control. The only motif of hope is in youth. Prince Giovanni repeatedly makes straightforward observations and recalls specific moments of physical tenderness between himself and his mother, suggesting an alternative world-view to that which has been allowed to dominate in the play. His presence dominates the closing moments. Curiously Webster figures a dead and decaying world which is somehow giving birth to something less corrupted than itself.

## The Duchess of Malfi

*The Duchess of Malfi* (Webster, [1614] 1972) ends less optimistically. While the final scene in the play also posits the next generation as a more hopeful emblem (the son of the slaughtered Antonio is displayed as the hope for the future as all the main protagonists lie dead), the presence of death in this play is even more marked. The duchess's declaration to Antonio at I. ii. 359 establishes clearly the related motifs that dominate the play. The first is that public office represses and eventually stifles the private person; the second, that death is essentially and inescapably present in every affirmation of life.

> You do tremble:
> Make not your heart so dead a piece of flesh
> To fear, more than to love me. Sir, be confident,
> What is't distracts you? This is flesh and blood, sir,
> 'Tis not the figure cut in alabaster
> Kneels at my husband's tomb. Awake, awake, man,
> I'd here put off all vain ceremony,
> And do appear to you, a young widow
> That claims you for her husband, and like a widow,
> I use but half a blush in't.
>
> (I. ii. 369–78)

The duchess asserts her identity. Who she is is not bound up in her dead husband's identity. Nor is she a mere piece of statuary, a representational woman with no pulse or impulse or imagination. Just as Vittoria resists a superficially imposed definition from the Cardinal, and resists conforming to any of the female types offered by Isabella, Cornelia or Zanche, so the Duchess refuses to be defined or confined by convention. She asserts her right to definition by criteria other than those which a crumbling hierarchy seeks to impose on her. The positive nature of her decision to choose Antonio (who, as rapidly becomes apparent, does right to tremble before her proposition, and not just with passion) is borne out by the tenderness evoked through their dialogue and gentle teasing in the only wholly domestic scene in the play at III. ii. But the tenuous clinging to life which characterizes the play rapidly becomes more apparent as this early assertion of life and love through a metaphor of death swiftly becomes one of the more positive images on offer. As the Duchess and Antonio part for the last time at Ancona, tricked into an ambush by the seemingly sympathetic Bosola, the denial of the supremacy of political and physical death present at the moment of her initial declaration of love and the tender love scene in Act III are brought tragically together in their last exchange:

> *Antonio*:
> > Do not weep:
> > Heaven fashion'd us of nothing; and we strive
> > To bring ourselves to nothing. Farewell Cariola,
> > And thy sweet armful. [To the Duchess] If I do never see thee more
> > Be a good mother to your little ones,
> > And save them from the tiger: fare you well.
>
> *Duchess*:
> > Let me look upon you once more: for that speech
> > Came from a dying father: your kiss is colder
> > Than I have seen a holy anchorite
> > Give to a dead man's skull.
>
> > (III. v. 78–87)

More common than these moments of desperate domestic tenderness is the less literal assertion of the skull beneath the skin, of the impossibility of meaningful utterance through a language which is repeatedly and increasingly characterized as an animalistic howling. Both notions are synthesized in the finally lycanthropic behaviour of Ferdinand, whose prurient fury at the imagined vision of his sister 'in the shameful act of sin' (II. v. 41) tips him into a verbal frenzy to the extent where the cardinal must restrain him with the warning,

> > ... there is not in nature
> A thing that makes a man so deform'd, so beastly
> As doth intemperate anger.
>
> > (II. v. 57–9)

Later, Ferdinand confronts his sister and Antonio with the notion that animalistic inarticulacy is the only language suited to the description of their (in his view) unnatural behaviour ('The howling of a wolf/ Is music to thee, screech-owl'). But the cardinal's distaste at his brother's slide into subhuman ranting and the obvious misapplication of the metaphor to his sister leaves the audience in no doubt as to where Webster considers the subhuman behaviour in this play to reside.

As the play draws dismally to the conclusion voiced earlier by Antonio, that 'heaven fashion'd us of nothing; and we strive/ To bring ourselves to nothing', the voice which reverberates from the graves among which Antonio paces serves to suggest that any attempt at reason will be mocked simply by the unintelligent and unintelligible reverberations of death.

## BIBLIOGRAPHY

PRIMARY TEXTS

Anon. (1425) *The Castle of Perseverance*, in *Four Morality Plays*, ed. P. Happé (1979, repr. 1987), Penguin, Harmondsworth.

Anon. (1553) *Gammer Gurton's Needle*, in *Three Sixteenth-Century Comedies*, ed. C.W. Whitworth, Jr (1984), Ernest Benn, London.

Anon. (1591) *Arden of Faversham*, ed. M. White (1982), New Mermaids, Ernest Benn, London, and W.W. Norton, New York.

Bale, J. (1979) *King Johan*, in *Four Morality Plays*, ed. P. Happe, Penguin, Harmondsworth, (reprinted 1987) [first published 1538].

Beaumont, C. and Fletcher, J. (1986) *The Knight of the Burning Pestle*, ed. M. Hattaway, New Mermaids, A. & C. Black, London [first published 1607].

Dekker, T. (1986) *The Shoemaker's Holiday*, ed. D.J. Palmer, New Mermaids, A. & C. Black, London; W.W. Norton, New York [first published 1599].

Happé, P. (ed.) (1979) *The Castle of Perseverance*, in *Four Morality Plays*, Penguin, Harmondsworth (reprinted 1987) [first published 1425].

Jonson, B. (1979) *Epicoene*, in *Ben Jonson's Plays and Masques*, ed. R.M. Adams, A Norton Critical Edition, W.W. Norton, London and New York [first published 1609].

Jonson, B. (1979) *The Alchemist*, in *Ben Jonson's Plays and Masques*, ed. R.M. Adams, A Norton Critical Edition, W.W. Norton, London and New York [first published 1610].

Jonson, B. (1979) *Volpone*, in *Ben Jonson's Plays and Masques*, ed. R.M. Adams, A Norton Critical Edition, W.W. Norton, London and New York [first published 1606].

Jonson, B. (1979) *Bartholomew Fair*, in *Ben Jonson's Plays and Masques*, ed. R.M. Adams, A Norton Critical Edition, W.W. Norton, London and New York [first published 1614].

Kyd, T. (1970) *The Spanish Tragedy*, ed. J.R. Mulryne, New Mermaids, A. & C. Black, London (reprinted 1984) [first published 1587].

Marlowe, C. (1969) *Dr. Faustus*, in *The Complete Plays*, ed. J.B. Steane, Penguin, Harmondsworth (reprinted 1985) [first published 1592].

Marlowe, C. (1969) *The Massacre at Paris*, in *The Complete Plays*, ed. J.B. Steane, Penguin, Harmondsworth (reprinted 1985) [first published 1593].

Medwall, H. (1976) *Fulgens and Lucres*, in *English Moral Interludes*, ed. G. Wickham, Dent, London [first published 1497].

Middleton, T. (1967) *The Revenger's Tragedy*, see under Tourneur.

Middleton, T. and Dekker, T. (1987) *The Roaring Girl*, ed. P. Mulholland, The Revels Plays, Manchester University Press, Manchester (reprinted 1992) [first published 1608].

Montaigne, M. (1958) *Essays*, trans. J.M. Cohen, Penguin, Harmondsworth [first published 1580].

Peele, G. (1984) *The Old Wives' Tale*, in *Three Sixteenth-century Comedies*, ed. C.W. Whitworth, Jr, New Mermaids, Ernest Benn, London [first published 1590].

Pickering, J. (1982) *Horestes*, in *Three Tudor Classical Interludes*, ed. M. Axton, D.S. Brewer, Cambridge [first published 1567].

Plato (1951) *The Symposium*, trans. W. Hamilton, Penguin, Harmondsworth.

Quintilian (1920–1) *Institutio Oratoria*, ed. and trans. H.E. Butler, Loeb edn, vols 124–7, Harvard University Press, Cambridge, Mass.

Sackville, T. and Norton, T. (1992) *Gorboduc*, in *Two Tudor Tragedies*, ed. W. Tydeman, Penguin, Harmondsworth [first published 1562].

Shakespeare, W. (1594) *The Comedy of Errors*, in *William Shakespeare. The Complete Works*, ed. P. Alexander (1951), Collins, London and Glasgow.

Shakespeare, W. (1599) *The Merry Wives of Windsor*, in *William Shakespeare. The Complete Works*, ed. P. Alexander (1951), Collins, London and Glasgow.

Shakespeare, W. (1599) *As You Like It*, in *William Shakespeare. The Complete Works*, ed. P. Alexander (1951), Collins, London and Glasgow.

Shakespeare, W. (1594) *The Taming of the Shrew*, in *William Shakespeare. The Complete Works*, ed. P. Alexander (1951), Collins, London and Glasgow.

Shakespeare, W. (1594) *Twelfth Night*, in *William Shakespeare. The Complete Works*, ed. P. Alexander (1951), Collins, London and Glasgow.

Shakespeare, W. (1599) *A Midsummer Night's Dream*, in *William Shakespeare. The Complete Works*, ed. P. Alexander (1951), Collins, London and Glasgow.

Shakespeare, W. (1604) *King Lear*, in *William Shakespeare. The Complete Works*, ed. P. Alexander (1951), Collins, London and Glasgow.

Skelton, J. (1979) *Magnyfycence*, in *Four Morality Plays*, ed. P. Happé, Penguin, Harmondsworth (reprinted 1987) [first published 1515].

?Tourneur, C. (1967) *The Revenger's Tragedy*, ed. B. Gibbons, New Mermaids, Ernest Benn, London [first published 1606].

Udall, N. (1982) *Jake Jugeler*, in *Three Tudor Classical Interludes*, ed. M. Axton, D.S. Brewer, Cambridge [first published 1530–55].

Udall, N. (1982) *Thersites*, in *Three Classical Interludes*, ed. M Axton, D.S. Brewer, Cambridge [first published 1537].

Webster, J. (1972) *The White Devil*, in *Three Plays*, ed. D.C. Gunby, Penguin, Harmondsworth (reprinted 1986) [first published 1612].

Webster, J. (1972) *The Duchess of Malfi*, in *Three Plays*, ed. D.C. Gunby, Penguin, Harmondsworth (reprinted 1986) [first published 1614].

White, M. (ed.) (1982) *Arden of Faversham*, New Mermaids, Ernest Benn, London; W.W. Norton, New York [first published 1591].

Whitworth, Jr, C.W. (ed.) (1984) *Gammer Gurton's Needle*, in *Three Sixteenth-century Comedies*, New Mermaids, Ernest Benn, London [first published 1553].


SECONDARY TEXTS

Altman, J.B. (1978) *The Tudor Play of Mind*, University of California Press, Berkeley and London.

Belsey, C. (1985) *The Subject of Tragedy*, Methuen, London.

Bradley, A.C. (1904) *Shakespearean Tragedy*, Macmillan, London.

Callaghan, D. (1989) *Woman and Gender in Renaissance Tragedy. A Study of King Lear, Othello, The Duchess of Malfi and The White Devil*, Harvester Wheatsheaf, Hemel Hempstead.

Cave, R.A. (1988) *The White Devil and The Duchess of Malfi*. Text and performance. Macmillan Education, London.

Dollimore, J. (1984) *Radical Tragedy*, Harvester Wheatsheaf, Hemel Hempstead.

Drakakis, J. (1985) *Alternative Shakespeares*, Methuen, London and New York.

Dusinberre, J. (1975) *Shakespeare and the Nature of Women*, Macmillan, London.

Gibbons, B. (1968) *Jacobean City Comedy*, Harvard University Press, Cambridge, Mass.

Greenblatt, S. (1980) *Renaissance Self-fashioning*, University of Chicago Press, Chicago.

Gurr, A. (1987) *Playgoing in Shakespeare's London*, Cambridge University Press, Cambridge.

Howard, J.E. (1994) *The Stage and Social Struggle in Early Modern England*, Routledge, London.

Jardine, L. (1983) *Still Harping on Daughters: Women and Drama in the Age of Shakespeare*, Harvester Wheatsheaf, Hemel Hempstead.

Jones, E. (1977) *The Origins of Shakespeare*, Clarendon Press, Oxford.

Kendall, R. (1986) *The Drama of Dissent*, University of North Carolina Press, Chapel Hill and London.
Kott, J. (1965) *Shakespeare Our Contemporary*, Methuen, London.
Leggatt, A. (1973) *Citizen Comedy in the Age of Shakespeare*, Toronto University Press, Toronto.
Leggatt, A. (1981) *Ben Jonson: His Vision and His Art*, Methuen, London.
Levine, L. (1994) *Men in Women's Clothing: Antitheatricality and Effeminization 1579–1642*, Cambridge University Press, Cambridge.
Martindale, J. (1985) *English Humanism: Wyatt to Cowley*, Croom Helm, London.
McIlwain, C.H. (1918) *The Political Works of James I*, Harvard University Press, Cambridge, Mass.
Rhodes, N. (1992) *The Power of Eloquence and English Renaissance Literature*, Harvester Wheatsheaf, Hemel Hempstead.
Shepherd, S. (1986) *Marlowe and the Politics of Elizabethan Theatre*, Harvester Wheatsheaf, Hemel Hempstead.
Tennenhouse, L. (1986) *Power on Display: The Politics of Shakespeare's Genres*, Methuen, London.
Tillyard, E.M.W. (1943) *The Elizabethan World Picture*, Chatto & Windus, London.
Traub, V. (1992) *Desire and Anxiety: Circulations of Sexuality in Shakespearean Drama*, Routledge, London.
Wilson, R. and Dutton, R. (1992) *New Historicism and Renaissance Drama*, Longman, London.

REFERENCE WORKS

Abrams, M.H. (1981) *A Glossary of Literary Terms*, Holt, Rinehart & Winston, New York.
Sanders, N. *et al.* (eds) (1980) *The Revels History of Drama in English Vol. 2 1500–1576*, Methuen, London and New York.

# UNIT 7

# Renaissance and seventeenth-century poetry

*Eiléan Ní Chuilleanáin*

## Introduction

This unit is concerned with the poetry of the English Renaissance. The term itself is a hard one to define: it describes an international event, since the Renaissance is a European phenomenon, a tendency which spread through a far-flung community of scholars, writers and artists but which spread at an unequal rate of progress across the map. So while the Italian Renaissance is generally thought of as belonging to the fifteenth century, an English poet like Skelton (1460?–1529), who wrote at the court of Henry VIII, is often categorized as a late medieval writer.

Our discussion starts with the verse of another courtier, Thomas Wyatt (1503–42) and his younger contemporary Henry Howard, Earl of Surrey (1517–47). English poetry is often spoken of as having been given a fresh start by these two writers by their translations from Italian and their importation of Italian forms, especially the sonnet. Translation and metrical innovation will be among our themes; to understand the English Renaissance we will also have to consider the impact of the Protestant Reformation, the nature of courtly culture and the influence of classical models on poetry written in the vernacular.

The Renaissance has been variously defined, as a rediscovery of ancient Greek and Latin texts and of the linguistic competence needed to understand them, and as a rebirth of the human spirit to a joy in the things of this world as opposed to a penitential preparation for the joys of Heaven. It is a mistake to ignore the deeply religious character of much Renaissance writing, including that which insists most on the wholesomeness of human affections, of sex and the body. What distinguishes the writers of the Renaissance is the high claims they make for their art, the seriousness with which they regard language and the study of literature, whether sacred or secular, as a means of bettering the human condition whether this is seen in political or religious terms. And the two are interconnected: royal courts and noble patrons are involved in bringing about changes in both Church and State, and the writers are, as we shall see, committed to aiding or impeding the same process. Enthusiastic servants of Queen Elizabeth like Sidney and Spenser, harsh satirists like the young Donne, Ben Jonson writing about the country house of a patron, devotional poets like Herbert and (in some moods) Marvell, are all alive to the

political import of what they say, to the clashes of their divided society. Protestantism, Puritanism, the politics of Queen Elizabeth's wars in Ireland and the disputes
between King and Parliament which led to the execution of Charles I and the
Protectorship of Oliver Cromwell – all these are not merely 'background' to the
poetry of our period: they are its subject and determine its tone and direction.

This survey ends with a brief look at John Milton (1608–74) whose *Paradise
Lost* was published in 1667. By then many new movements had begun in literature,
science and politics. Charles II had been restored to the throne of England, the
Anglican Church re-established, the Royal Society, that great centre for scientific
research, had been founded, and the Renaissance was firmly in the past. The faith in
the arts of language which had made rhetorical and poetical elaboration popular with
readers as well as writers was disappearing, and being replaced with a cultivated
plainness. Though Milton was a profoundly original thinker, in many ways a much
more 'modern' mind than the majority of his contemporaries, his verse shows the
persistence of the delight in just that elaboration which was becoming obsolete.

The most famous account of an apparent 'revival' of poetry at the court of
Henry VIII is George Puttenham's in his *Arte of English Poesie* (1589 but composed
earlier). He looks back over the sixteenth century to the beginnings of the English
Renaissance when a 'new company of courtly makers ... greatly polished our rude
and homely manner of vulgar Poesie' and claims that they are the direct ancestors of
'an other crew of courtly Makers Noble men and Gentlemen of her Majesties own
servants' of whom he names Sir Walter Ralegh, Sir Philip Sidney, Fulke Greville
and George Gascoigne (Smith, 1959, ii, pp. 62–4).

The court of a European monarch was during the sixteenth century the centre
not only of power but of much of a country's intellectual and aesthetic life. It was
the forum where the great religious change of the Protestant Reformation and the
contemporary shifts in European politics were discussed, the centre to which
travellers, diplomats and scholars returned with the results of their labours, as well
as the scene of dangerous intrigues in love and politics, and the showcase for beauty
and fashion. *The Book of the Courtier* (1976) – written in Italian by Baldessare
Castiglione (1528), widely read and much praised in the English translation by Sir
Thomas Hoby (1561) – emphasized the ideal courtier's grace and nonchalance, his
talents for music, dress and athletics as well as poetry, but also his philosophical and
moral seriousness.

Since the courtier poet was essentially an amateur, whose chief interests lay
outside literature, courtly poetry is frequently plain in style. Yvor Winters in an
influential essay, first published in 1939, praised the 'directness of diction and ...
rich but matter-of-fact humanity' of a line of plain-style lyricists from Wyatt to
Ralegh, Jonson and Donne which he defines as 'the major tradition of the century'
(Alpers, 1967, pp. 102, 123). C.S. Lewis's very useful if idiosyncratic and
conservative *English Literature in the Sixteenth Century* (1954), labels the plain
verse of the mid-sixteenth-century 'Drab' as opposed to 'Golden' – the term he
applies to the much more decorative poems of the late Elizabethan period, by
Sidney, Spenser, Daniel, Marlowe and others – and then argues that the 'Drab' need
not be understood as a pejorative term. Such critical positions as his and Winters's

are linked to other opinions, for example of the function of poetry as the vehicle for making uncomplicated, direct statements, or by contrast for liberating the reader into a world of fiction, fantasy and ornament. Stephen Greenblatt's *Renaissance Self-Fashioning* (1980) (one of the central texts of the movement known as new historicism) treats the courtly world, its individualism and ambition and the ways in which the image of the courtier could be created and manipulated in relation to the literature and the political structures of the sixteenth century. By contrast with historicist criticism the assumption behind the approach of both Winters and Lewis is that poetry demands to be considered in itself rather as it interacts with other systems of representation in a wider political world.

The courtly milieu was both public – closely linked with the parliamentary, ceremonial and religious life of the nation – and secret, bound together by personal ties between kings, queens and their servants, between patrons and clients. Women were both influential and highly vulnerable members of this society, as the fates of Henry VIII's queens show; their role in relation to poetry was deeply ambiguous. Their education was usually more limited than men's, though a number of women (Queen Elizabeth and her sister Queen Mary, Anne Bacon, Mary Sidney) were distinguished as translators.

In the courtly milieu poetry circulated between intimates, in manuscript – Walter Ralegh wrote 'A Poem put into my Lady Laiton's Pocket' – and through performance accompanied by music. However, there was also a book-buying public interested in the poems, and the appearance in 1557 of the collection of *Songes and Sonettes* known to posterity as Tottel's *Miscellany* was only the first of many similar enterprises which made courtly poetry more widely known.

The mainstay of Tottel's collection was its inclusion of the poems of Sir Thomas Wyatt and of Henry Howard, Earl of Surrey. They had been dead since, respectively, 1542 and 1547: posthumous publication was to be the frequent fate of the major poets of the English Renaissance who, with the notable exceptions of Spenser, Shakespeare, Jonson and Milton, tended to be amateurs. But poems circulating in manuscripts could lay claim still in that era to public fame; Surrey's resounding epitaph for Wyatt declared that he had 'A hand that taught what might be sayd in ryme/ That reft Chaucer the glory of his wit.'

Like Spenser later, Surrey felt the need both to claim, on Wyatt's behalf, descent from Chaucer and to displace him as a model; he is 'a mark the which, unparfited for time,/ Some may approche, but never none shall hit' (*Poems*, 1963, p. 27).

The poetry of Wyatt indeed shows a debt to medieval models. There is (as there was to continue to be in the work of Sidney, of Donne and Herbert, and the stage songs of Shakespeare and Jonson) a variety of lyrical forms, which show the continuity of the medieval court-music tradition linking poetry with song. The Chaucerian rhyme royal (see Wyatt's poem below, p. 152) is prominent among them.

Much critical emphasis has been laid on Wyatt and Surrey's translation and adaptation of Petrarch (Forster, 1969, remains the best account of Petrarchism as an international phenomenon). Wyatt however translated not only Petrarchan sonnets but a satire by Alamanni and psalms from the Old Testament. The satires describe a corrupt and dangerous life at a court which is clearly that of Henry VIII, however much they take their inspiration from the Italian original.

Another example of originality in translation is the work of the makers of the English Bible from the first illegal fragments of 1526 which found their way into the court of Henry VIII, to the great official version authorized by King James in 1611. As well as a revisiting of a primal source, and a discovering of one's own inner experience via a text from a remote time, in a strange original language (and the whole of the Protestant Reformation was based on the assumption that this was the duty of the Bible reader), such translating marks a great shift towards popularization, a reaching out to a wide audience in which printing was to be crucial, and which was soon to involve the work of the poet.

The Elizabethans were to continue the work of translation and the revival of classical kinds of poetry: satires, epistles, elegies – all genres practised by the young Donne – erotic narrative as written by Marlowe, Chapman and Shakespeare and parodied by Ben Jonson on stage, epic and epithalamion with Spenser. They were also to develop the interest in biblical poetry which was to flourish from Southwell to Vaughan and find majestic expression in Milton. The publication in 1573 of George Gascoigne's *A Hundred Sundry Flowers* and in 1579 of Edmund Spenser's *The Shepherd's Calendar* represented a new departure: young poets offering their work to the public directly, and setting off in quest of literary fame via the printing press. In Spenser's case the first collection is also a prospectus, in which he promises a work of heroic gravity in praise of Elizabeth and her courtiers: the first mention of the English epic *The Faerie Queene* (1590–6).

The rule of courtier poets keeping their verse private continued however; none of the works of Philip Sidney, whose mixed prose and verse *Arcadia* (1580, revised 1584–6) and sonnet-sequence *Astrophil and Stella* (1581–2) were the most admired fiction and poetry of the 1580s, saw print in his lifetime, although both *Arcadia* and the sonnets were well enough known to start fashions in their kinds. Sidney's *Apology for Poetry* (1581; also known as *Defence of Poetry*) seems to have originated as a response to a (not entirely serious) attack on the stage and on poetry by Stephen Gosson (*The Schoole of Abuse*, 1579). While Sidney does not think much of the drama of his contemporaries, and is sharply critical of much of their verse, he offers an enthusiastic picture of the potential of the poetic imagination, gives a skilful and witty account of the relationship between poetry, fiction and the moral and philosophical concerns of his age, and registers in the discussion of the poets of his time the development of an increasingly public programme, a sense of what poetry ought to be produced in a culture which aspired to equal prestige with the ancients and the outstanding modern literatures, especially Italian. The argument of the *Apology* makes poetry valuable because it can arouse readers to an enthusiasm capable of finding expression in an active, political life, a central concern for a Protestant gentleman like Sidney. Protestantism was a distinguishing mark of the culture he envisaged (see Weiner, 1978).

An extract from *The Faerie Queene* is discussed below. With his pastoral *Colin Clout's Come Home Again*, his sonnet sequence *Amoretti*, his *Epithalamion* (all published in 1595) and some now less admired works, it made Spenser the dominant poet of a decade in which however much else was happening. The sonnet-writing movement begun by Sidney continued to be developed by poets like Daniel and Drayton who were firmly committed to the printing-press, while Shakespeare's ambiguous contribution to the genre remained in private circulation. Daniel, Drayton, Marlowe and Shakespeare all developed a narrative poetry which differed from Spenser's: in some cases by being more straightforward as historical narrative, as with Daniel's *Civil Wars* (1595–1601) and Drayton's *Barons' Wars* (1603), in others such as Marlowe's *Hero and Leander* (1593, published 1598) and Shakespeare's *Venus and Adonis* (1593) and *The Rape of Lucrece* (1594), by being more unrestrainedly erotic, with a different kind of classical tinge.

Spenser combined a fertile talent for fiction – his long poem has an immensely complex plot, full of adventures, magic, strange, romantic turns of events and allegorical tableaux – with a political and religious seriousness and a personal voice which combines autobiography with self-effacement by means of the fictional identity of the shepherd Colin Clout. The same seriousness, the same use of his own identity as part of the poetic strategy, was to appear a half-century later in the work of Spenser's admirer Milton, who was however far from self-effacing and associates himself with fierce Old Testament prophets rather than humble shepherds.

Spenser aimed to write a national epic which would glorify Queen Elizabeth (the name he gives her is *Gloriana*), her championship of the Protestant cause in Europe and her courtiers' claiming of new American territories, and reasserting English rule in Ireland, all in her name. The colonizing impulse is most clearly visible in the treatment of Ireland, where Spenser himself profited from the Elizabethan reconquest and expropriation. An introduction to Spenser's political dimension is Simon Shepard's *Spenser* (1989); closely related are his religious views which are treated by Hume (1984), while his writing on Ireland is handled from various points of view in Coughlan (1989). An older view of Spenser, concentrating on his debt to medieval and classical literature and philosophy, is C.S. Lewis's *Spenser's Images of Life* (1967), while *The Spenser Encyclopedia* (Hamilton, 1990), is a valuable reference guide to the complexities of reading Spenser.

The court as centre of power is shown radiating outward to the margins of the political world in Spenser's unfinished poem. One of his heroes is thought to be based on his friend, fellow-poet and fellow-colonist, Sir Walter Ralegh. With Ralegh's poetry we are back at the centre, and are reminded that the perilous systems of service and dependency which darkened Wyatt's satires still existed at Elizabeth's court. Another of the fragmentary poems of the age, Ralegh's *The Ocean to Cynthia* (1592?) celebrated the Queen's beauty but also her changeableness, in a despair which reflected the reality not the fiction of her power: 'Shee is gonn, Shee is lost! Shee is found, shee is ever faire!' In 'The Passionate Mans Pilgrimage' he turned away from the earthly Court to a heavenly one: 'Where no corrupted voyces brall,/ No Conscience molten into gold,/ Nor forg'd accusers bought and sold ...'

Ralegh was to end on the scaffold in the reign of James I. His younger contemporary, the Jesuit Robert Southwell, had met the same death over twenty years earlier, in 1595. Southwell's verse was very popular, being printed in two collections in the year of his execution in spite of his notorious death. He owed – as

Crashaw was to do – something to the by now flourishing movement of religious writing in Catholic Europe which he had met at first hand during his education in the Low Countries, Paris and Rome. He showed more restraint than Crashaw; like Ralegh he drew on the native lyric tradition with its tendency to directness, but like Ralegh he can reach, in plain words, a tone of visionary clarity in poems like 'The Burning Babe', and there is a warmth of passion in his poems on Mary Magdalene which allow a feminine voice to be heard in a religious context.

Religious poetry was to develop in the seventeenth century in the Anglican church, but its roots in the Elizabethan period and especially, I suggest, the discovery of an audience which was avid for such poetry, were closely connected with the suppressed but still widespread Catholic culture. The half-mad clergyman William Alabaster, who changed his religion over and over, was the author, in a Catholic phase, of some very fine religious sonnets of the 1590s; and John Donne, whose religious poetry is now with Herbert's the best known of the period, was born and carefully educated within the Catholic tradition.

Donne's devotional poetry comes mainly from the middle period of his life, the years of anxiety that followed his marriage and preceded his ordination as a minister of the Anglican Church. John Carey (1981) has argued that Donne was haunted all his life by guilt for his abandonment of his childhood Catholicism. The 'Holy Sonnets' are indeed focused on ideas of sin, death and the after-life. All Christians, not just Catholics, were urged to keep these ideas before them and meditate on them frequently (Louis Martz's *The Poetry of Meditation* (1962) is an excellent treatment of the meditative tradition, concentrating on Catholic sources but arguing convincingly that these are relevant not only to Donne but to later Anglican poets such as Herbert and Vaughan.)

In Donne's witty satires and love-poems (such as 'The Flea', discussed below), some of which, at least, belong to a period when he had no particular religious affiliation, we find theological notions along with ideas and terms drawn from law, medicine, alchemy, mathematics and many other disciplines, twisted together like bits of scrap metal to make a new, angular and surprising artefact which has been named by critics – until this century in disparagement – the 'metaphysical' poem. The term was not invented by Samuel Johnson, but it was he in the 'Life of Cowley' (1946, i, p. 11) who gave it its most famous definition: 'The most heterogeneous ideas are yoked by violence together; nature and art are ransacked for illustrations, comparisons, and allusions.' Johnson found their energy and ingenuity insufficient to please readers because it lacked pathos and sublimity. It was T.S. Eliot, in an influential essay on 'The Metaphysical Poets', who swept aside the traditional apologies for the 'imperfections' of Donne's love-poetry and inaugurated a new critical orthodoxy which installed him once again, as in Thomas Carew's funeral poem, as 'the monarch of wit' and a prime focus for academic studies in the new and expanding University schools of English. Eliot announced that a group headed by Donne and including Crashaw, Vaughan, Herbert, Marvell, King and others was 'in the direct current of English poetry' – still a fairly modest claim. In the same essay, his most frequently quoted statement about Donne, that 'A thought to Donne was an experience; it modified his sensibility', followed one even more frequently

misquoted about the major Victorian poets who did not 'feel their thought as immediately as the odour of a rose' (Eliot, 1972, pp. 287–90). Donne, it was implied, did
so. Readers turned to his works for this legendary intensity and suddenly stopped
being put off by the technical language about hemispheres and canonizations.

The technical terms remain there, in the poems: the ingenuity and the allusions
to such abstruse notions as the trepidation of the spheres in 'A Valediction,
Forbidding Mourning'. Yet there can be plain and elegant language too as in the
conclusion to the same poem, where 'Thy firmnes makes my circle just/ And makes
me end, where I begunne.'

The intimacy of bodily feeling is one of Donne's special qualities, often in the
context of love, but also in such religious poems as 'Hymne to God, My God, in my
Sicknesse' where the prostrate body becomes a 'flat map' of the world. Space is
explored by means of the body and its wardrobe of metaphors, for example in the
'Anniversaries', where the death of a young girl prompts him to apply images of
decay to the whole world.

Though Donne's successors may have emulated his wit and compression, they
seem to have taken to heart Ben Jonson's warning that Donne 'for not being
understood, would perish' ('Conversations with Drummond of Hawthornden' in the
Oxford Authors *Ben Jonson*, 1985, p. 599). Modern critics write about a 'school of
Donne', but in the first half of the seventeenth century poets applied to be admitted
to the 'Tribe of Ben' Jonson. Jonson's combination of clarity and seriousness marks
in different ways the work of poets as diverse as Herbert, Herrick, Carew, Marvell
and Vaughan, beside whom Donne's fantastic hyperboles seem to look back to the
flourishes of the Elizabethans, though the sensibility his love-poems and satires
express is so new.

Within that tradition of plain and compact style, a pair of poets whose work is
marked by religious simplicity are Herbert and his imitator Vaughan. For them
(though they wrote with wit and originality) the very idea of originality caused
problems since the truths they were writing about were all already known, to be
found in the Bible. Their relation to the Bible text and to each other shows how
closely poets may follow their sources and yet remain themselves – another art they
probably learned from Jonson.

Thomas Carew may be Donne's closest successor in the sexually outspoken
mode, until we come to the libertine poetry of Rochester under the Restoration. But
another poet, much more florid and abundant, whose best poetry was almost all
religious, showed a taste for hyperbole and an adventurous use of sexual ideas
which do recall Donne's juxtaposing of erotic and sacred themes. Richard Crashaw's
poems on Mary Magdalene and Saint Teresa of Avila in part developed Herbert's
emphasis on divine love as the supreme poetic theme, but they entirely lacked, and
made a virtue of lacking, the older poet's restraint. His depiction of ecstatic states,
all centred on women, have a boldness in their approach to the body which is
unparalleled in religious poetry; perhaps as a result of this freedom he is able in one
of his finest poems to celebrate, as a quasi-sexual experience, the condition of being
a male reader of a woman's (Teresa's) account of her quasi-sexual vision of being
pierced by a burning dart in the hand of an angel. It is a poem which manages to be

equally eloquent about the arbitrariness of sexual stereotypes and the implications of writing and reading as 'active' and 'passive' processes.

While Andrew Marvell took the opposite side to Vaughan and Herrick in the English Civil War, he and Herrick, as they commented on the social relations of their time, were working within a shared tradition, one which made it possible to mingle public modes of address to a patron or a monarch with the informal, intimate manners of a friend writing to another on serious subjects. Jonson's 'Inviting a Friend to Supper' (published in 1616) had set the tone, combining the promise of good food and company with the chance of speaking freely on religion and philosophy. Marvell's 'Upon Appleton House', written in the early 1650s, praised the pleasures of the country against the tragic backcloth of the Civil War, as Herrick's 'Corinna's Going a-Maying' had in the 1630s joined rural folk-festivity with party politics: to salute and encourage the Mayday frolics was to align oneself with the King and court faction against the Puritans who disapproved of such traditional pastimes.

Milton, the Puritan par excellence, can also write sonnets in the vein of social relaxation, and in *Paradise Lost* especially celebrates the happiness of Adam and Eve and the pleasure they take in entertaining (to a gourmet vegetarian repast) the angel Raphael who drops in on them to warn them against the wiles of Satan and to tell them the tale of Satan's rebellion and the creation of the world. The central part of Milton's epic of demonic struggle and harsh human fate is thus given up to a leisurely dialogue mixed with narration. The poet is postponing his tragic conclusion but also making space for an important theme, the praise of a golden age of harmony and of sexual pleasure that had been denied by the ascetic tradition of Christianity. The dialogue between Adam and the angel includes Adam's account, in Book VIII, of his own self-discovery at the time of his creation, his urgent need for a mate and his first meeting with the newly created Eve. Her autobiography has already been given in Book IV, and it too is a romance of their first meeting and first love.

Adam's delight in the Creation-story reflects Milton's criticism of a tradition of epic poetry which had glorified war, destruction rather than creativity, rather than the love which reaches its most intense expression on marriage. The figure of Satan, however impressive in the early part of the poem, is in the end less interesting than the innocent, then sinful, then repentant figures of Adam and Eve, and their love. Milton had planned a major poem, probably on a biblical theme, since his youth; early works such as the sonnet on arriving at the age of 23 (1631) and 'Lycidas' (1637) expressed the urgency with which he felt his vocation, while *Comus* (1634), an aristocratic entertainment for a powerful Puritan family, proclaimed his religious and moral values. The events of the Civil War period led him to give up much of his time and creative energy to the writing of prose tracts on political issues and to the service of Cromwell's government; he probably did not begin *Paradise Lost* until the late 1650s, by which time he was blind and the English Republic was about to revert to a monarchy. It was published in 1667, after the Restoration of Charles II.

James G. Turner's *One Flesh* (1987) treats the connections between Milton's ideas of women and sexuality and his religious thinking; Christopher Hill's *Milton and the English Revolution* (1977) connects these themes with his politics and the history of the period 1640–60, when Milton was at the centre of the greatest convulsion that has ever affected English politics. Kester Svendsen's *Milton and Science* (1969) is illuminating on the relationship between the scientific knowledge of Milton's day – and Milton was a contemporary of both Galileo and Newton – and his narratives of the Creation and of Satan's epic voyage through the cosmos. Stanley Fish's *Surprised by Sin* (1971) examines the experience of the reader who has never known the innocence of Adam's and Eve's world and whose response is therefore in need of constant correction. William Empson's *Milton's God* (1981) famously challenges the Christian assumptions of the epic.

It is in the seventeenth century that women poets begin to appear with any frequency in English literature. At first they belonged mainly to the highest social groups; there is evidence too of high-born women such as Donne's friend Lucy Countess of Bedford writing verse which has not survived, perhaps because of the aristocratic prejudice against publication. But when Emilia Lanier, in 1611, published verse in praise of her lady patrons, when Anne Bradstreet moved after 1650 from large biblical themes to domestic and family subject-matter, they were inaugurating two traditions that were not to be broken: that of the female professional writing to live, and the home-based introspective one which women were to explore and dominate from Bradstreet to her fellow-Americans and poetic descendants, Emily Dickinson and Sylvia Plath. The work of the women poets of this age has recently begun to be republished, though much still remains to be done; among the best collections are Greer *et al.* (1988), and Gilbert and Gubar (1985). The poems of Lanier and Bradstreet have been edited by Rowse (1978), and Piercy (1978), respectively, and the complete works of the earliest English woman poet to receive critical recognition (after her death in 1664 at the age of 32), Katherine Philips, the 'matchless Orinda' have been published in 1993 by Stump Cross Books. (See Unit 23, pp. 609–12, for a survey of women writers of the period.)

Perhaps the recognition given to Katherine Philips, as later to Anne Killigrew for whom Dryden wrote a famous commemorative poem, is connected with a change in the tone of poetry after the Restoration. Poetry becomes less strenuous, more social, and a higher critical value is accorded to qualities such as ease, plainness of style, lightness of touch and, especially in the eighteenth century, strength of feeling. Mock-epic, parody, satire, poems on urban life, were to flourish, as later were the poetry of introspective meditation and natural description. A poem like Anne Finch's 'Nocturnal Reverie' (1713) shows the ability to reflect on landscape in a way that is new in its calm sensibility and quiet tone. The combination of deep seriousness with brilliant wit is no longer admired, though Dryden, Pope and Swift all show just that combination. T.S. Eliot lamented its disappearance, and castigated the post-Renaissance period in English poetry for what he called 'dissociation of sensibility', a relegation of feeling to a different mode of expression from thought. Even a committed lover of English Renaissance poetry may be allowed to take his or her leave of the period without any such dire diagnosis. Society changed, attitudes to language, rhetoric and psychology changed, and poetry changed too.

## Texts, authors, contexts

Thomas Wyatt

The first stanza of Wyatt's most famous poem runs:

> They flee from me, that sometime did me seek
> With naked foot stalking in my chamber,
> I have seen them gentle, tame, and meek
> That now are wild, and do not remember
> That sometime they put themself in danger
> To take bread at my hand; and now they range,
> Busily seeking with a continual change.

(Wyatt, 1975, xxxvii)

What is the effect of the poem's beginning with the pronoun 'they' instead of 'she'? Does this generalize the poet's complaint rather than confining it to the behaviour of – as we later are introduced to her – a particular woman?

If he is talking of faithlessness in general, does that direct our attention to a corrupt milieu instead of an individual emotional catastrophe? May a poem combine both elements, of social satire and personal lament? On the other hand, does the wide focus of 'they' just make way for the moment when the other party in the poem is defined as 'she' and caught in an exact moment of past time? Notice how the second line prepares for this with its sharp focus on a physical detail. Verbs such as 'seek', 'stalk', 'range' are appropriate to a description of hunting animals; what do you think is the meaning of the phrase 'to take bread at my hand'? Greenblatt in *Renaissance Self-Fashioning* (1980, pp. 14–8 and 150–4) discusses this poem and another one which uses imagery of wild animals in relation to women and suggests that 'wild' expresses an anxiety about 'the tenuousness and artificiality of society's elaborate codes'. Consider the representation of the lady in the second stanza of the poem: 'In thin array after a pleasant guise/When her loose gown from her shoulders did fall,/And she me caught in her arms long and small.' Why do you think the poet goes on to say 'It was no dream'? Have you read any of Chaucer's descriptions of women of which it might be said they have the quality of a dream or a vision? (See the description of Emelye in *The Knight's Tale*, 1048–55, or that of May in *The Merchant's Tale* who was so beautiful that 'Hire to beholde it semed fayerye', 1743.)

A plausible case has been made for Wyatt having been a lover of Anne Boleyn. If the lady in this poem were certainly Anne, would our reading of the poem gain anything? It is possible to see her as just one of a series of anonymous 'beauties' who like fairy visions appear and fade away in late medieval poetry and may perhaps be thought about as having no existence in the literal world. R.T. Davies's collection of *Middle English Lyrics* (1963), Nos. 143 and 173 are examples. But is this then just another male-centred rehearsal of sexual demands (including the demand for fidelity) where the woman exists only marginally, in memory, dream and fantasy, and the man's words crowd out any reply she might have to make?

The version of the poem quoted above is taken from an early sixteenth-century manuscript which may have belonged to the poet himself, the Egerton MS in the British Museum. When it was printed by Tottel in 1557 an editor made the rhythm more regular, so that the second line, for example, ran 'With naked foot stalking *within* my chamber'. What do you think of the rhythm of the line as it stands in the older version, or of the final couplet just quoted? Do they reflect the rhythms of the speaking voice? Does the rhythm of the poem's last lines suggest anger in the emphasis on the pronouns 'I' and 'she' or perhaps some other emotion?

To whom do you think the poet is speaking? Do you think he expects an answer to his final question? If it comes from a male reader of his own epoch and class, we would expect him to answer that the lady deserves to be punished. But has Wyatt deliberately left the question open at the end for readers, male and female, to give their verdicts? A contemporary Italian writer who visited the court of Henry VIII comments on the injustice of men's imposition of moral strictness on women:

> because we ourselves, as men, have made it a rule that a dissolute way of life is not to be thought evil or blameworthy or disgraceful, whereas in a woman it always leads to such complete opprobrium and shame that once a woman has been spoken ill of, whether the accusation is true or false, she is utterly disgraced for ever. (Castiglione, 1976, p. 195)

As in later love-poems by Sidney and Donne (see below) is there an opening in that last question for another voice and perhaps a contradictory one to answer Wyatt's challenge? Davies's *Lyrics* has some examples of the medieval 'Quarrel about women' which might be suggestive in this regard (1963, pp. 123, 125, 134–5, 174).

The space which Wyatt creates for contradictory opinions, the marked introspection of the mood of this poem and of some others (see for example 'My Lute Awake', *Collected Poems*, 1975, LXVI), where the poet speaks to himself, to his lute, to a possible reader rather than to the lady, may suggest that in his writing we find the beginnings of a tendency to make love poetry a pretext for writing on wider intellectual questions while keeping the immediacy of the erotic context – a tendency illustrated in the work of Sidney, Shakespeare and Donne. Greenblatt and others have connected Wyatt's introspective mood with the Protestant emphasis on personal salvation and private judgement. The same urgent sense of the individual's destiny and responsibility may lie behind the bitterness of Wyatt's *Satires* (*Collected Poems*, 1975, cv, cvii).

The uneven line which I have referred to above was to give way in the work of Surrey to a more regular iambic beat which was to characterize the poetry of the mid-sixteenth century and later, such as George Gascoigne. The iambic pentameter became a 'standard' line in lyric poetry, in such forms as the sonnet and the rhyme royal stanza – of which the Spenserian stanza is an expansion – and it established itself in the drama. In the sonnets of Sidney, Spenser and Shakespeare especially, a line developed which was more sure-footed than Wyatt's, less plodding than Tottel's revision of Wyatt, distinguished in Sidney's case by emphatic pauses, in Shakespeare and Spenser's by a flowing, supple movement which perhaps lacks Wyatt's eloquent hesitations.

In the sonnet by Sidney which lies at the centre of the next section, we will see another side of what is meant by the term 'court poetry' and of the love poetry of the sixteenth century.

## Philip Sidney

> I never drank of *Aganippe* well,
> Nor ever did in shade of *Tempe* sit:
> And Muses scorne with vulgar braines to dwell,
> Poore Layman I, for sacred rites unfit.
> Some do I heare of Poets' furie tell,
> But (God wot) wot not what they meane by it:
> And this I sweare by blackest brooke of hell,
> I am no pick-purse of another's wit.
>    How falles it then, that with so smooth an ease
> My thoughts I speake, and what I speake doth flow
> In verse, and that my verse best wits doth please?
> Guesse we the cause: 'What, is it thus?' Fie no:
>    'Or so?' Much lesse: 'How then?' Sure thus it is:
> My lips are sweet, inspired with Stella's kisse.

*(Astrophil and Stella*, Sonnet 74)

The first three lines of this sonnet by Philip Sidney are consciously allusive and mythological. They direct our attention to remote places and times: to a fountain and a valley in Greece associated with ancient poetry and to the belief that poets were inspired by the nine daughters of the god Apollo. If a modern reader feels excluded by such allusions the poet declares that he does too – he is a layman, an outsider. His inspiration and his poetic success come from the fact that he has at last kissed Stella.

The sonnets in *Astrophil and Stella* do not tell a story but there is a narrative succession of changing moods and situations – the kiss creates one of these. It is celebrated by a song, the Second Song in the sequence; the poet does not confine himself to the sonnet form. He had already written in the *Arcadia* a work which mixed prose narration with a wide variety of verse forms; *Astrophil and Stella* is restrained by comparison. But the variety of forms admits also a variety of moods. Spenser in *Amoretti* follows the stages of a courtship which has its ups and downs but ends in marriage, and by the way brings in themes of time, eternity, poetic fame and Christian redemption. Shakespeare moves from celebration of a young man's beauty, to meditation on time, on his own age and fame, to reproachful sonnets, to witty and then savage play with the theme of a woman's sexuality. If you look at Shakespeare's Sonnet 59 you will find a consideration of the theme of poetic originality which makes an interesting comparison with Sidney's sonnet, but also a marked difference of mood, of metaphor and of language.

We need to ask ourselves whether we are meant to believe Sidney's assertion of his lack of learning. He is after all writing verse of a quite complex type. He isn't using his own name or that of the woman he loves (she was Penelope, the wife of Lord Rich) but he lets their identities be known by puns and other references in the poems themselves. His claim to have no part in deliberate poetic art is, in this context, suspect.

The opening sonnet of the sequence had claimed that his poems came directly from his own experience: 'Foole' said my Muse to me, 'looke in thy heart and write.' C.S. Lewis commented that 'when a poet looks in his heart he finds many things there besides the actual' (1954, p. 328). Fiction can be closely related to real life and yet demand to be read as fiction. Sidney's claim to be an inspired idiot in poetry is countered by his adroit use of parody – the 'blackest brook of hell' is the kind of bombastic alliterative phrase that had been in fashion among an older generation of poets – by the virtuosity of lines 9–11 where the lines do indeed flow smoothly and easily and by the crowded interrogative phrases and brusque answers of lines 12–13. On the other hand what are we to make of the concluding line? According to one scale of values it is here that the poem touches the erotic sublime by referring to the kiss which he took from the sleeping Stella two poems earlier in the sequence. As well as celebrating the poet's achievement of even a moment of sexual bliss the conclusion gives a witty answer to the questions the poem has posed and simultaneously displays the totality of his obsession.

But are we meant to take seriously the standard which ranks such satisfaction, taken against the woman's will, so highly? Many other sonnets in the sequence emphasize Sidney's high visibility as an Elizabethan courtier, as the promising son of a distinguished family. He had an international reputation in his twenties, distinguished Continental writers corresponded with him. In Sonnet 30 twelve lines are taken up with queries addressed to the poet about European politics: What is happening in Turkey? In Russia, Poland, France, Germany, Holland, Ireland, Scotland? As there were no newspapers in 1582 only those – like Sidney – who had connections abroad would know the answers, and so he is pestered by news-hungry questioners: 'I, cumbred with good maners, answer do, /But know not how, for still I thinke of you.'

Sidney's contemporaries might then regard his obsession with Stella as causing dereliction of duty and leading to the collapse of his reasoning powers. Or they might recognize that social custom permitted courtiers, especially the young, to select a lady and address poetry to her as a kind of game – you might compare Sidney and Wyatt as users of this convention. Modern readers, not only feminists, may be shocked by his intrusion on a sleeping woman – the last line of the song where he celebrates his action exclaims 'Foole, more foole, for no more taking' – as indeed might Sidney's moral and religious mentors, and the Protestant theologians discussed in Alan Sinfield, *Literature in Protestant England* (1983). Again, the fact that the violation is a comparatively minor one, a stolen kiss not a rape, may lead to our classifying the sonnets as less than earnest, deliberately avoiding more serious subjects.

Sidney's contemporaries called him the 'English Petrarke' recognizing that he belonged to a tradition of sonnet-writing that stretched back to the great Italian poet. However, his claim to originality 'I am no pick-purse of another's wit' is a fair one. He uses motifs – such as the celebration of the kiss – which had been used before, and mythological allusions which had passed through many languages. His sharp, lively manner, his use of the court background – quite different from Wyatt's paranoid setting but still shot through with anxiety and guilt – his variety of tone from melancholy introspection to witty protestation, are all markedly individual. He makes the sonnet form work for him, often as in the example given using twelve or thirteen lines to build up a scene or an argument which is then cancelled or dispatched by a brief conclusion. He can be mellifluous but also write lines like the twelfth and thirteenth of the poem above, so packed with meaning that they refuse to flow, and demand to be spoken dramatically, with strong pauses. You might compare the poems by Donne and Herbert discussed in this section, and watch the ways in which they too admit dialogue into their poetry – and the ways in which as poets they retain control and ensure that the poet's own dominant voice gets the last word.

## Edmund Spenser

It is impossible to choose a representative sample for a book like this from Spenser's *The Faerie Queene*. We will be facing the same difficulty with Milton's *Paradise Lost*. Yet to present a brief snippet from the poem's unfinished bulk (six books of twelve cantos each, plus two detached cantos which may have belonged to a seventh book – out of an original project for two epics of twelve books each) may suggest the special kind of poetic energy which was generated by such an exhaustive project.

*The Faerie Queene* is an allegory. Its story on the surface is about knights, ladies, dragons, hermits – but the true subject is the battle between good and evil, between virtue and vice and between the True English Church, the Protestant Church, and the false Church of Rome. As its religious theme is also a historical one, figures who stand for historical personages such as Queen Elizabeth (Gloriana – the Fairy Queen) and Mary, Queen of Scots (Duessa) appear alongside personifications of Pride or Holiness. Each book has a main hero, while the hero of the whole poem is Prince Arthur – who, like the other Arthur of medieval romance, presides over a succession of minor heroes and their adventures. And each book celebrates a moral virtue while the totality shows the conflict between good and evil. All the heroes, all the tales, are linked together.

In Canto xi of Book I, the Red Cross Knight, St George, achieves the object of his quest and slays the Dragon. It is a climax but not a conclusion. The knight's story does not end here, and the reader never gets to meet the Fairy Queen towards whom or from whose ideal Court all the heroes of the poem are journeying. If you read more of the epic you may find yourself asking whether Spenser ever intended to finish it – modern critics have found especial interest in its incomplete form and you may like to look at Jonathan Goldberg's *Endlesse Worke: Spenser and the Structures of Discourse* (1981), which discusses the reader's experience of *The Faerie Queene*.

To return to Spenser's dragon:

> By this the dreadful Beast drew nigh to hand,
> Halfe flying, and halfe footing in his haste,
> That with his largenesse measured much land
> And made wide shadow under his huge wast;
> As mountaine doth the valley overcast.

> Approaching nigh, he reared high afore
> His body monstrous, horrible, and vast,
> Which to increase his wondrous greatnesse more,
> Was swolne with wrath, and poyson, and with bloudy gore.
>
> (stanza 8)

Spenser's stanza form is one he designed on the basis of rhyme royal (see Introduction, p. 145) with two extra lines, and an extra two syllables in the last one. Consider the effects of this expanded verse unit. A sense of leisurely progress (as we shall see) can change to rapidly flowing action; the repetition of rhyme sounds can involve duplication of meaning, e.g. 'huge wast', 'horrible and vast'. But 'wast' means both 'waist' and 'waste' so that Spenser can combine fullness of atmospheric description with suggestive economy.

The dragon described here in such insistently physical terms is also a spiritual enemy; he is the 'Old Dragon', Satan himself. He is thus the worst possible monster, but it is typical of Spenser's style of story-telling that he is not the only one in Book I. The Knight has already, at the very start of his adventure, defeated a creature called Error who like this Dragon was of huge size and spewed up poison just as the dragon 'belches' fire and 'filthy smoke/That all the land with stench, and heaven with horror choke' (stanza 44). And a seven-headed beast 'bred in filthy fen' featured in Canto vii of the Book. Parker (1979) usefully discusses the nature of this repetitive, episodic style, especially at pp. 64–77.

Spenser associates the Red Cross Knight with the classical hero Hercules at stanza 27, but it is in terms of the human weakness which they share. After wounding the dragon the Knight is scorched by his fiery breath and suffers as Hercules did when he was tricked into wearing a poisoned shirt. His enemy aims to finish him off with a sweep of his tail, but is foiled. Watch how Spenser handles this turning-point, moving from repetitive insistence on the knight's sufferings to brisk action by the dragon, to a total change of tone as he introduces an unexpected element of good and a glance back at a happier past:

> Faint, wearie, sore, emboyled, grieved, brent
> With heat, toyle, wounds, armes, smart, and inward fire
> That never man such mischiefes did torment;
> Death better were, death did he oft desire,
> But death will never come, when needes require.
> Whom so dismayd when that his foe beheld,
> He cast to suffer him no more respire,
> But gan his sturdie sterne about to weld,
> And him so strongly stroke, that to the ground him feld.
>
> It fortuned (as faire it then befell)
> Behind his backe unweeting, where he stood,
> Of auncient time there was a springing well,
> From which fast trickled forth a silver flood,
> Full of great vertues, and for med'cine good.
> Whylome, before that cursed Dragon got
> That happie land, and all with innocent blood
> Defyld those sacred waues, it rightly hot
> *The well of life*, ne yet his vertues had forgot.

Two kinds of fortune are at work here, Divine Providence and the power of the poet himself to shape his narrative. Spenser insists that in the kind of story he is writing strange and providential events do happen. Elsewhere in *The Faerie Queene* the working of chance may produce effects that are mysterious or ludicrous or simply send the protagonists off on a wild career of misunderstanding. Like episodic style, such interventions of fortune or providence are characteristic of romance. Spenser probably learned the technique from the Italian romance poet Ariosto whom he announced his intention of 'overgoing' when he was first discussing the plan of his poem. Here the sudden reversal of fortune, where the emphasis is first on the Knight's sufferings and then on the unexpected source of his help, is artfully set up. See Frye (1976) for suggestions about the way chance and wish-fulfilment work in romance.

The 'Well of Life' is magical; do we know at once that it will cure the Knight's wounds and enable him to fight better on the next day? The terms in which the name is ascribed are strongly ambiguous: the well was *once* truly called by that name, and it still has virtues – are we to understand *some* or *all* of those that it possessed long ago? The past and the moment of the narration overlap each other strangely here, and the effect is to give the past a special aura, to emphasize its quality as a paradisal Golden Age. In Jonson, Marvell and Milton we will be encountering other versions of the paradise myth, but none that places it so irrevocably in the past.

As well as its fairy-tale quality and its connection with antiquity, the well has a sacramental meaning, suggesting the water of baptism (the question of Spenser's allegorical symbolism is a very large one and interpretations of passages such as this differ widely. See Tuve (1974) and Fowler (1964).)

A last question. Is Spenser aiming in this encounter to mobilize certain responses of the reader, such as the taste for suspense, for monsters and magic, which are childish rather than sophisticated? Is he reviving older forms or exploring anew the sources of our delight in fiction?

## John Donne

Among many striking love poems by John Donne, 'The Flea' is a good one to focus on. Even the title is arresting and the poem has attracted much attention because of its energetic argument and dramatic setting. The opening plunges us into the centre of an erotic situation:

> Marke but this flea, and marke in this,
> How little that which thou deny'st me is;
> Mee it suck'd first, and now sucks thee,
> And in this flea, our two bloods mingled bee ...

It is an opening that instantly gives us the physical proximity of two people, and the impatient desire of the man to cancel the small distance between them, within which the woman is still manoeuvring, playing for time and demanding to be heard. The man's voice is both imperative and imperious, insisting on monopolizing her attention, with the repetition of 'marke'. To 'mark' the flea she must watch intently while her ears are pounded with Donne's argument, his dismissal of her fears of losing her virginity as anxiety over a fleabite.

Poems about fleas are not uncommon in the Renaissance; in 1582 a collection of over fifty of them in five languages was published in France to commemorate the sighting of one on a young lady's bosom (see Gardner's note to this poem in her edition of Donne's *Elegies and The Songs and Sonnets* (1970), p. 174). Does our awareness of the existence of such a fashion affect our reading of Donne's poem? Does the fact of such a massive and learned response to such a trivial event suggest a difference between our idea of suitable subjects for poetry and the ideas of Donne's age? Do we think of the subject as particularly witty? Do ideas of wit change from one period to another, and how do we feel about the appropriateness of this kind of wit to a love-poem? We have already (in the treatment of poems by Wyatt and Sidney) been looking at certain traditions of 'love poetry' and asking what kind of attitude to relations between men and women they involve.

Donne's poems are celebrated for their explosive opening lines, often expressing egotistic dominance, refusal to listen to differing viewpoints, violently interrupting another speaker with 'For Godsake hold your tongue' ('The Canoniz-ation') even exclaiming against the sun for intruding into the bedroom he shares with his beloved ('The Sunne Rising'). In 'The Flea' as in 'The Sunne Rising', 'The Canonisation', 'The Relique', an apparently casual, extempore argument is developed inside a complex stanza form, whose contrasting line-lengths and varied rhyme-scheme owes something to the sophisticated musical modes of the period; Donne like Wyatt and later, in a religious mode, George Herbert, can convey impatience and the wish to break through formal constraints in a highly formalized verse, and the poetry of all three shows a connection with a tradition of musical performance.

Would we describe the tone of 'The Flea' as witty or as aggressive? Is there some common ground between the two? Donne starts by taking the flea as an example of 'littleness' but as the poem develops it acquires other meanings. It 'enjoyes before it wooe' – it does not have to go through the process of courtship at all but achieves its desires as a predator. Is this Donne's image of the masculine ideal condition, one in which wooing and thus his love poetry would be redundant?

Some modern critics (e.g. Docherty, 1986) have emphasized the elements of aggression in Donne's love-poetry; feminist writers have questioned the good faith of most love-poetry written by men to women. In this poem, as in some other Renaissance love-poetry, the woman has a limited right of reply. Unlike some medieval writers about women who use the form of a debate and give women speakers equal time with men (Chaucer's 'Wife of Bath's Prologue' would be the best known example) poets like Sidney, Spenser and Donne allow the woman only oblique, limited or indirectly reported expression. You might consider, in this connection, those poems of Donne's which use male and female roles in a religious context. In 'Batter my Heart' he begs to be enslaved and ravished; in 'Show me Dear Christ' and 'What if this Present were the Worlds Last Night?' he courts and flatters.

As the poem progresses, what do you think of the way the flea's significance changes? Is the poet making entirely arbitrary use of the flea to signify anything he declares it to signify? Does the incorporation of religious terms – 'marriage', 'temple', 'cloysterd' and 'sacrilege' – imply a shift away from the 'libertine' attitude of the opening lines?

Donne's demand that the woman spare the flea's life makes use of the traditional idiom of love-poetry in which the woman is declared to be the aggressor – she is, he says, used to murder already, 'apt to kill mee', and when she does the deed he accuses her:

> Cruell and sodaine, hast thou since
> Purpled thy naile, in blood of innocence?

The flea's blood makes her a Herod-figure, who 'triumphs' in slaughter. The disproportionate accusation, the tininess of the bloodstain, may be parodying the tradition of calling women 'cruel', 'tyrannical'. Blood runs through this poem and we are reminded that blood has many metaphorical meanings. A woman may bleed when she loses her virginity and this is seen as the equivalent of the man's loss of semen. In pregnancy she may, with the flea, 'swell with one blood made of two'. If she is not married (and Donne has told us at line 14 that he is not acceptable to her parents) she may be compromising the honour of her family, her 'blood'. The role of the flea as a bloodsucking insect is thus a way of making the reader consider the connections between the body as it belongs to the animal domain, and as it involves cultural constructions such as marriage, courtship, a woman's honour and the honour of the patriarchal family she belongs to.

The minuscule drop of blood which has been made to bear so many meanings is an example of the Renaissance 'conceit', the device by which the love-poet avoided merely saying again what had been said so often. A conceit can be mythological, as in some of Sidney's sonnets (*Astrophil and Stella* 8, for example), or based on actual experience and contemporary custom (like Donne's 'The Will'); it can also be used in other contexts, as in Donne's religious poetry. In 'A Valediction: of Weeping' a tear (like the drop of blood, a bodily fluid) becomes a globe, a foetus, a coin, a mirror. Much time is spent on an analysis of Donne's imagery: the point less often stressed is the way the succession of unexpected meanings has the effect of enhancing his control over the poem, ensuring that the end is unpredictable.

'The Flea' like much of Donne's work refers to quite abstruse theoretical notions (such as the debate about where in the body the human soul was located, in the blood or elsewhere) and terms of church law like sacrilege and cloister. Elsewhere in his love-poetry (for example in 'Love's Alchemy', the 'Anniversaries', 'A Valediction Forbidding Mourning') Donne uses even more philosophical concepts and technical language than he does here; it is for this reason that he was called a 'metaphysical' poet. How important do you think such material is in 'The Flea'? Is it extraneous to the main argument? Are we as readers intended to ponder the mysteries of the soul, of human identity, and the connection between sexuality and the transmission of life – or merely to enjoy the comic inappropriateness of such grand ideas invoked in a joking exchange between a lover and his lady, all about a flea? (See Unit 18, pp. 528–32, for a Formalist analysis of 'The Flea'.)

## Ben Jonson

Unlike Donne's, Ben Jonson's poems privilege plain and public statement. While Donne was uneasy and apologetic about those poems which were published in his lifetime, Jonson oversaw the publication of his works himself. He installed himself firmly in the role of moral commentator with a responsibility to tell, if not literal truths then 'those truths which we expect for happy men' ('To the Immortal Memory and Friendship of that Noble Pair, Sir Lucius Cary and Sir H. Morison'). In that poem he praises virtue and lashes vice in a Pindaric Ode; 'Penshurst', which we will examine here, owes a debt to less exalted forms such as satire and epistle, but equally emphasizes the poet's right to be heard on matters affecting the welfare of communities and of the state:

> Thou art not, PENSHURST, built to envious show
> Of touch, or marble . . .

Why should a poet start a poem with a negative, an insistence on which materials were *not* used in its construction, which motives did *not* enter into its builders' minds? The description of Penshurst Place which follows is extremely brief, it just 'stands an ancient pile' and we hear no details of the house's appearance. Instead, in Jonson's poem, it functions as a focal point for various kinds of social interactions: we experience being there as guests, its hospitable board and lodging.

Penshurst's interest, the poet declares, lies in the way it performs its social function as centre of an estate and a district, its antiquity, its association with the family of the poet Philip Sidney who had died about twenty-five years earlier – and his poet brother Robert for whom the poem was written – and the beauty of its natural setting. The brief plain statement is a feature of Jonson's art of epigrammatic conciseness, but it is set off against quite luxuriant and detailed description of other features of the subject.

In reading the following account of the countryside, ask yourself what kind of landscape is being described:

> The lower land, that to the river bends,
> Thy sheepe, thy bullocks, kine, and calves doe feed:
> The middle grounds thy mares, and horses breed.
> Each banke doth yeels thee coneyes; and the topps
> Fertile of wood, ASHORE, and SIDNEY's copp's
> To crowne thy open table, doth provide
> The purple pheasant, with the speckled side:
> The painted partrich lyes in every field,
> And, for thy messe, is willing to be kill'd.

We see a scene in which not 'unspoiled' natural beauty but fertility is celebrated, where birds and animals throng the fields and crowd towards the house where they will furnish the plentiful tables of the Great Hall. The poem's assertion that the game-birds are 'willing to be killed' provokes the question, 'what kind of poem is this?' The obligation to praise Penshurst and its owners has clearly overridden any obligation to stick to the literal truth. Are we being warned that this is a fictional depiction of plenty and that the poet's compliments involve some exaggeration?

Again, the poet declares that although the walls of the house are built of local stone 'They are reared with no mans ruine, no mans grone'. He is referring to the fact that noble landlords often had the right to demand that their tenants perform compulsory labour on the estate and that this was a contemporary source of grievance. Again the Sidneys are praised for *not* being like other landlords. Their tenants visit them with presents;

> Some bring a capon, some a rurall cake
> Some nuts, some apples; some that thinke they make
> The better cheese bring 'hem; or else send
> By their ripe daughters, whom they would commend
> This way to husbands; and whose baskets beare
> An embleme of themselves, in plum, or peare.

Jonson treats these gifts as purely an expression of love, skimming over the fact that the tenants must pay rent, whether in cash or in produce. A recent critic, Don E. Wayne (1984) comments on Jonson's negatives – the tenants come, 'no one empty-handed' – that 'The introduction of negative constructions precisely at points involving social and economic relations suggests that it is in this domain that something is lacking' (p. 42).

Against the garden walls grow unfamiliar fruits, 'The blushing apricot, and woolly peach'. Read Marvell's poems 'Thoughts in a Garden' and 'Bermudas' (the latter is discussed below) and consider whether their use of fruits that do not grow easily in England, such as melons, pomegranates, and nectarines, has a similar effect to Jonson's.

If Penshurst is the home of plenty, is there a connection between this and the rejection of envy at the opening? Later Jonson says that the larder is so well stocked that the servant waiting at table needn't feel envy of a guest, even of one as gluttonous as the poet himself. If the poet has been a guest at the Sidneys' table is his praise for them devalued by the possibility that he is not being sincere?

A poem like this raises many questions about that unknowable quantity, the reality of feelings in a vanished age, as it does (perhaps more usefully) about the relationship between poets and their patrons in an age when the role of patron was extremely important. Donne for example wrote two long poems lamenting the death of a girl he had never met, who was the daughter of his patron Sir Robert Drury. Robert Sidney, Viscount De l'Isle, was a poet himself, a hardworking administrator for the King of England and an affectionate husband and father. Does our knowledge of his character influence our response to Ben Jonson's praise of him and his wife? In reading a poem about an obsolete way of life should we endeavour to read it as much as possible from a seventeenth-century perspective or bring to it our own ideas and values? For example, towards its close the poem compliments the lady of the manor as 'noble, fruitful, chaste'. It is clear that the poet considers these appropriate terms for praising a woman; are we, as modern readers, at ease with his assumption?

After commemorating his own entertainment at Penshurst Jonson celebrates a visit by King James. Observe the gradual progression through the lower orders – tenants, servants – to a guest, and finally to the King himself, and consider what view of society is implicit here.

## George Herbert

Like 'The Flea', George Herbert's 'Love' is a poem whose impact begins with its title. It does so subtly, all the more so because the collection in which it appears contains two earlier poems with the same name. Erotic love is the subject of the majority of short poems in the English Renaissance, so to the anthology reader it is likely to be a mild surprise that this one is about divine rather than human love. In reading the first six lines you might ask yourself just at what point you become aware of the religious meaning:

> Love bade me welcome: yet my soul drew back,
> > Guiltie of dust and sinne.
> But quick-ey'd Love, observing me grow slack
> > From my first entrance in,
> Drew nearer to me, sweetly questioning,
> > If I lack'd anything.

Is it the word 'soul' that sends the signal, or the next line's use of concepts of guilt and sin? Or the repeated word 'Love' which immediately becomes a person (rather than a personification) whom we gradually recognize as Jesus? How does the realization that we are expected to read for a special kind of meaning affect us as modern readers? Do we respond to the poet's assumption that the guilt he speaks of is a part of the human condition? Are we reading as 'Everyreader', are we welcomed more inclusively to this poem than we might be as the assumed male 'common reader' of secular poetry?

'Love' occupies a special position in Herbert's book of poems, *The Temple*. There are three sections in *The Temple*, of which the first and last consist of single long poems about morality and church history respectively. The central section, called 'The Church', is a collection of brief lyrics expressing intense emotion on religious subjects. 'Love' concludes this sequence, except for a brief quotation from the Bible. While many of the earlier pieces are witty and formally complex or experimental (poems shaped like wings or altars, a poem – 'Prayer' – with no main verb, another – 'The Collar' – where form is disrupted by the poet's rebellious passion) this poem is quiet and simple. What do this simplicity, this positioning of the poem suggest? Has the whole book been directed towards a redefining of love, as supreme poetic subject, so that its 'true' meaning, even its obvious meaning, is the love of God?

The poem's opening statement is about hospitality, Love as a host attempting to make a guest feel at ease. The guest's resistance is based on social shame about not appearing in the proper formal, cleaned-up style, but the equation asserted in line 2 between dust and sin makes it clear that the whole transaction is on a symbolic level. Consider whether this is the only way a poet can approach such subject-matter? Does Herbert use this method because he is writing in a tradition, one which begins with the interpretation of the Bible as a symbolic text in which the image of a banquet often recurs?

The host, 'sweetly questioning', begins a dialogue which continues until the last line of the poem. Observe the way questions and answers dovetail in the next stanza:

> A guest, I answer'd, worthy to be here:
>     Love said, You shall be he.
> I the unkinde, ungratefull?

Is this a self-questioning by the narrator in the poem? What does the 'shall' in Love's answer stand for: the polite insistence of a host or the assertion of God's absolute power to make us worthy if he chooses? The questions, as Stanley Fish has pointed out (1978), are a combination of catechizing – the standard way of instructing children in religious belief – and the Socratic method in philosophy, in which, by questioning, the teacher makes the pupil aware of what he/she knows already. The questions with which Love's argument develops are of this kind, 'Who made the eyes but I?' 'And know you not, sayes Love, who bore the blame?'.

The poem ends with the guest's resistance collapsing: 'So I did sit and eat.' Let us look again at the place of this action in the plan of Herbert's book. The central section is not merely called 'The Church', it contains poems with titles such as 'Superliminare' ('Above the Threshold'), 'The Church-floore', 'Church-lock and key', 'The Altar', 'The Windows'. The poem we are considering is the climax of the whole sequence. As well as completing the revelation of love as the perfect subject for poetry, as the perfect definition of the God revealed in the New Testament, it also defines the structure of the church as the house of God, where God invites Christians to the banquet of the Eucharist. 'You must sit down, sayes Love, and taste my meat' means not only 'be my guest' but also 'eat my body, drink my blood'.

The catechizing method already referred to is designed to instruct children, and the parables of Jesus were addressed to an audience of ordinary people. In this tradition Herbert's plain style is intended to reach unlearned readers. Do you find the language of 'Love' is adequately described by calling it plain or simple? How does it compare with the language of Marvell's 'Bermudas'? The poem refers to complex ideas like Eucharistic symbolism or the theology of sin and redemption: does it succeed in simplifying these ideas or merely in denying their inherent complexity? Rosemond Tuve (1952) is helpful on the symbolism; Helen Vendler (1975) remains the outstanding modern treatment of Herbert's language and techniques.

## Andrew Marvell

> Where the remote Bermudas ride
> In the ocean's bosom unespied,
> From a small boat, that rowed along,
> The listening winds received this song.

The opening lines of Andrew Marvell's 'Bermudas' contain adjectives which denote a place entirely cut off from a centre: 'remote', 'unspied'. The 'listening winds' suggest the absence of any other listener, and the 'small boat' is a speck in the midst of the ocean, while the islands 'ride' like ships at anchor. We as readers are about to hear the 'song' of the rowers but first of all they are being placed at this deliberate remove from any experience that might be thought of as 'normal'. How does this affect the reader's attitude to what follows? Is it being labelled as exotic and thus of limited interest? Are the readers supposed themselves to belong to some centre of culture by whose standards other places, at the margins, are to be judged? Is this centre England? As the poem progresses we should learn more about what elements in English culture Marvell might regard as setting a standard.

The 'song' at once defines itself as a hymn of praise to God who has led the travellers safely to an island 'so long unknown/And yet far kinder than our own'. Though whales are stranded and wrecked on the coast, the singers are safe:

> He lands us on a grassy stage,
> Safe from the storms, and prelate's rage.

They are religious refugees then, escaping from the intolerance of their own country, in particular of the bishops. Many Protestants in seventeenth-century England thought that there should be no bishops in a reformed church. King Charles I in the 1630s appointed bishops who stressed the importance of ritual and hierarchy in the Church of England and thus made it seem less Protestant than Marvell, Milton and the group known as Puritans could accept. A number of Puritans emigrated – some temporarily – to the New World and among them was a clergyman called John Oxenbridge whom Marvell was to know well in the 1650s. By then Charles I had been executed and England was governed by Oliver Cromwell on whom Marvell wrote five poems of praise.

How does our knowledge of these historical facts touch our experience of this poem? Marvell calls Bermuda 'an isle ... far kinder than our own' – what meanings cluster in that syllable 'kind'? It can refer to the beauty of the Bermudan climate, to the freedom from persecution that the emigrants sought. 'Kind' also means 'natural', and the natural world in this poem is both nurturing and strange, both perilous and presided over by a benevolent deity. The 'small boat' is a version of Noah's ark, emblem of the Christian church.

This then is a religious poem of a different kind from Herbert's 'Love', above. 'Bermudas' describes itself as a 'song', a 'holy and a cheerful note'; what difference do you find from Herbert's 'holiness' in verse? Is it less didactic than 'Love' or didactic in a different way? Is the message addressed only to a 'small group' who would agree for example with Marvell's slash at the bishops?

Donne, Herbert and Marvell were all interested in the idea of British colonists spreading the Gospel abroad, in particular in America. When the poem refers to 'a land so long unknown' do we forget that there may have been previous inhabitants? And Marvell's colonists are not just missionaries: they are spreaders of empire to the ends of the known world. The poem's last lines are ambiguous in their tone:

> And all the way, to guide their chime,
> With falling oars they kept the time.

'Chime', 'falling', 'keeping time' are all musical terms; they do not denote bodily effort. But the reader probably knows that rowing a boat in the open sea is strenuous and dangerous and may have heard that the Bermuda area was even then known for shipwrecks. As in his praises of Cromwell, Marvell is eulogizing the life of action and adventure, of conquest too, even if some of the imagery of 'Bermudas' reminds us of the sensuous delights of his poems in praise of gardens and retirement. Read 'Thoughts in a Garden' and 'The Mower against Gardens'; these different examples of Marvell's art show him drawn, as his friend Milton was, to the idea of a natural paradisal state. In 'The Mower' however the garden is the scene of unnatural cultivation, a forced manipulation of what was originally free. In 'Thoughts in a Garden' and 'Upon Appleton House' there is a Fall, though in the first it is a harmless one, whereas the garden of Appleton House makes the poet see all England as *politically* fallen:

> What luckless apple did we taste
> To make us mortal, and thee waste.

Such explorations of the ideas of innocence and guilt give a particular edge to Marvell's strange love-poem 'To His Coy Mistress' where, though the poet presses his mistress to grant sexual consummation, he looks back almost wistfully to a love-poetry which emphasized frustration and delay as for example Sidney's does. He *would* love her 'ten years before the flood' and she 'deserves' such praise.

Marvell is then a poet of contraries and paradox, of oppositions between action and leisure, nature and art, time and eternity; is this a facet of his wit? Do you think it shows the influence of Donne's style? How does the treatment of nature's plenty here compare with Jonson's in 'Penshurst' above? Finally, we must notice that with Marvell we are coming to the end of an era during which critics have suggested that the short lyric poem flourished with a peculiar complexity, brilliance and seriousness, in a culture where there was room for talents as various as the ones we have been studying. If you go on to read the short poems of Rochester, Swift, Anne Finch, you may like to consider the reasons underlying the division of literature into 'periods' and how this affects the way we read poems.


## John Milton

By contrast with the Marvellian plain, brief lyric, below is a piece of intensely formal verse which aims both at the highest kind of literary effectiveness, the *sublime*, and at the arousal of the reader's sympathies for the poet's own misfortune. Sublime style produces wonder; it is both convincing and astonishing and is the appropriate mode for dealing with the grandest subjects: God, the cosmos, the height of heroic effort.

In Milton's *Paradise Lost*, Satan has just emerged from the murky underworld to which he has been condemned for his sin of rebellious pride, and at the end of Book II he begins to see light. Book III opens with an invocation of light itself. It is the oldest of created things, also a symbol of God, of human intellect and it is actually what Milton, who went blind about six years before he wrote this, had lost:

> Hail, holy Light, offspring of heaven first-born
> Or of the eternal co-eternal beam
> May I express thee unblamed? since God is light,
> And never but in unapproached light
> Dwelt from eternity, dwelt then in thee,
> Bright effluence of bright essence increate.

Reading these opening lines we notice the use of repetition, alliteration, inversion of the normal word order to create an effect – would we call it rhetorical? Musical? How are we to take Milton's question in line 3? Is it only a rhetorical question, i.e. one introduced to give the point more emphasis without expecting any answer? Or does it seriously query the possibility of meaningfully talking about light at all?

The word 'express' suggests finding a verbal form for what has no form and cannot be drawn or described. This makes light analogous with God, and many of the phrases Milton uses are applicable to the very business of talking about God, telling stories about him or defining him. For example, most of the adjectives are negative, which is proper when talking about God who is so mysterious that we can't say what he is, only what he is not. But if it is impossible to speak directly about God, then what is Milton doing writing *Paradise Lost*, in which God appears, speaks, makes decisions, even enters into dialogue with human beings?

The style of the passage we have been looking at may in its exalted manner, its repeated use of ideas like eternity, holiness, brightness, be considered as setting the right kind of tone for such a heroically conceived story. Milton relates the first creation of light:

> Before the sun,
> Before the heavens thou wert, and at the voice
> Of God, as with a mantle didst invest
> The rising world of waters dark and deep ...

These are vast primal scenes of confrontation between light and darkness. Do they prepare the reader for a conflict of good and evil to come? Milton's readers would be expected to know the story of Adam and Eve and the serpent told in the Bible (Genesis 2) already, as well as the tradition that the serpent was the evil angel Satan in disguise. Does the fact that we first see the faint beginnings of light through Satan's eyes mean that we can never forget the power of lurking darkness? Or is Milton's 'Hail' a fresh beginning, a refusal to see light on darkness's terms?

He goes on to talk about himself in his role as poet, directly taught by the 'Heavenly Muse' whom he had already addressed in the opening of *Paradise Lost*. He sings 'with other notes than to the Orphean lyre' but like Orpheus in Greek myth he has, in his poem, visited the underworld and returned 'safe'.

Milton's claim of high stature and status for the poet is one of the most resounding in English literature, and he makes it plain that he is talking about himself. But he is also a suffering, ageing man whose political aims have all been defeated, who has fallen 'on evil days ... and evil tongues' (*Paradise Lost*, VII, 26).

He laments what he has lost:

> ... Thus with the year
> Seasons return, but not to me returns
> Day, or the sweet approach of even or morn,
> Or sight of vernal bloom, or summer's rose,
> Or flocks, or herds, or human face divine ...

Milton's style has been the subject of debate since *Paradise Lost* first became accepted as one of the great poems in the language. Eighteenth-century critics declared that 'Our language sunk under him' and that 'he formed his style by a perverse and pedantic principle. He was desirous to use English words with a foreign idiom.' [Johnson, 1946 quoting Addison and then giving his own opinion, i, 111–12] Do you find his idiom less appropriate to English than, say, that of Jonson or Marvell? In the 1930s T.S. Eliot and F.R. Leavis attacked Milton's style; it was effectively defended by Christopher Ricks (1963), ushering in a new age of Milton studies.

Eliot and Leavis were not merely discussing style but calling attention to the role of Milton as a major influence on later poets and thus a central figure in the 'canon' of English literature. A book like this one is organized around a traditional canon of the authors most studied in English courses in universities and colleges. It is a useful way to organize a book, but it would be wrong to suggest that the position of even a deeply interesting author like Milton in the canon has not been questioned.

Milton's major works are written in a 'grand' style and in large traditional forms like epic and tragedy. These choices express aristocratic assumptions which are also assumptions about society. The poems themselves contain ideas about religion, race and politics and about the relationship of man to woman which are now to say the least unpopular. Milton makes Eve say to Adam

> 'O thou for whom
> And from whom I was formed, flesh of thy flesh,
> And without whom am to no end, my guide
> And head ...' (IV, 440–3)

Adam discusses astronomy with an angel while Eve prefers to learn at second hand from her husband; the Fall of Man happens because he is 'fondly overcome with female charm' (IX, 999). And yet Milton tries to be fair to Eve; she is 'capable ... Of what was high' (VIII, 49–50); she behaves better than Adam after the Fall and saves him from despair by loyal love. And Milton was in his own time a revolutionary and a deeply original writer, insisting on the importance of personal and political liberty beyond what even most of the party who made the English revolution would accept (in particular in his views on divorce and censorship), and still remains a provocative one. For a reading of *Paradise Lost* which contextualizes Milton's work within the politics of the Restoration, go to Unit 8, pp. 174–7.

Does all this mean Milton should be removed from his prominent position in traditional English courses? If you are a woman or a non-English reader, would his opinions make it harder for you to stomach Milton? You cannot answer these questions without reading more than the bare snippet I have provided. But if you go on to read him you may find that (helped by the feminist reading of *Paradise Lost* provided in Unit 24, pp. 639–42, and by modern critics such as James Turner and Christopher Hill) that a reading of Milton has cast light on your own position, as a reader not merely of seventeenth-century but of literature in general, from sources that you might not have expected to be so rich or so revealing. For a brief, accessible guide to *Paradise Lost* and modern criticism, go to Bradford (1992).

## BIBLIOGRAPHY

Alpers, P. (ed.) (1967) *Elizabethan Poetry*, Oxford University Press, Oxford.

Bradford, Richard (1992) *Paradise Lost. An Open Guide*, Open University Press, Milton Keynes.

Bradstreet, A. (1978) *The Tenth Muse*, ed. J. Piercy, Scholars' Facsimiles and Reprints, Delmar, NY.

Castiglione, B. (1976) *The Book of the Courtier*, trans. G. Bull, Penguin, Harmondsworth.

Carey, J. (1981) *John Donne: Life, Mind and Art*, Faber, London.

Coughlan, P. (1989) *Spenser and Ireland: An Interdisciplinary Perspective*, Cork University Press, Cork.

Crashaw, R. (1957) *Poetical Works*, ed. L.C. Martin, Clarendon Press, Oxford.

Davies, R.T. (ed.) (1963) *Middle English Lyrics*, Faber, London.

Docherty, T. (1986) *John Donne, Undone*, Methuen, London.

Donne, J. (1970) *The Elegies and The Songs and Sonnets*, ed. H. Gardner, Clarendon Press, Oxford.

Donne, J. (1978) *The Divine Poems*, ed. H. Gardner, Clarendon Press, Oxford.

Eliot, T.S. (1972) 'The Metaphysical Poets' (1921), in *Selected Essays*, Faber, London.

Empson, W. (1981) *Milton's God*, Cambridge University Press, Cambridge.

Fish, S. (1971) *Surprised by Sin*, University of California Press, Berkeley.

Fish, S. (1978) *The Living Temple*, University of California Press, Berkeley.

Forster, L. (1969) *The Icy Fire*, Cambridge University Press, Cambridge.

Fowler, A. (1964) *Spenser and the Numbers of Time*, Routledge, London.

Frye, N. (1976) *The Secular Scripture*, Harvard University Press, Cambridge, Mass.

Gilbert, S. and Gubar, S. (1985) *The Norton Anthology of Literature by Women*, Norton, London.

Goldberg, J. (1981) *Endlesse Worke: Spenser and the Structures of Discourse*, Johns Hopkins University Press, Baltimore.

Greenblatt, S.(1980) *Renaissance Self-Fashioning*, University of Chicago Press, Chicago.

Greer, G., Hastings, S., Medoff, J. and Sansone, M. (1988) *Kissing the Rod*, Virago, London.

Hamilton, A.C. (ed.) (1990) *The Spenser Encyclopedia*, University of Toronto Press, Toronto.

Herbert, G. (1978) *Works*, ed. F.E. Hutchinson, Clarendon Press, Oxford.

Herrick, R. (1968) *Poetical Works*, ed. L.C. Martin, Clarendon Press, Oxford.

Hill, C. (1977) *Milton and the English Revolution*, Faber, London.

Howard, H. Earl of Surrey (1963) *Poems*, ed. Emrys Jones, Oxford University Press, London.

Hume, A. (1984) *Edmund Spenser, Protestant Poet*, Cambridge University Press, Cambridge.

Johnson, S. (1946) *Lives of the English Poets*, Everyman edn, 2 vols, Dent, London.

Jonson, B. (1985) *Poems* in *Ben Jonson* (Oxford Authors), ed. I. Donaldson, Oxford University Press, Oxford.

Lanier, E. (1978) *The Poems of Shakespeare's Dark Lady*, ed. A.L. Rowse, Cape, London.

Lewis, C.S. (1954) *English Literature in the Sixteenth Century*, Oxford University Press, Oxford.

Lewis, C.S. (1967) *Spenser's Images of Life*, Cambridge University Press, Cambridge.

Martz, L. (1962) *The Poetry of Meditation*, Yale University Press, New Haven.

Marvell, A. (1974) *Complete Poems*, ed. E.S. Donno, Penguin, Harmondsworth.

Milton, J. (1971) *Paradise Lost*, ed. A. Fowler, Longman, London.

Milton, J. (1971) *Complete Shorter Poems*, ed. J. Carey, Longman, London.

Parker, P. (1979) *Inescapable Romance*, Princeton University Press, Princeton.

Philips, K. (1990–3) *Collected Works*, 3 vols, ed. G. Greer, R. Little and P. Thomas, Stump Cross Books, Stump Cross.

Ralegh, W. (1986) *Selected Writings*, Penguin, Harmondsworth.

Ricks, C. (1963) *Milton's Grand Style*, Oxford University Press, Oxford.

Shepard, S. (1989) *Spenser*, Harvester Wheatsheaf, Hemel Hempstead.

Shakespeare, W. (1987) *Sonnets*, ed. S. Wells, Oxford University Press, Oxford.

Sidney, P. (1962) *Poems*, ed. W.A. Ringler, Clarendon Press, Oxford.

Sinfield, A. (1983) *Literature in Protestant England*, Harvester Wheatsheaf, Hemel Hempstead.

Smith, G.G. (1959) *Elizabethan Critical Essays*, Oxford University Press, Oxford.

Southwell, R. (1967) *Poems*, ed. J.H. McDonald and N. Brown, Clarendon Press, Oxford.

Spenser, E. (1970) *Poems*, ed. J.C. Smith and E. de Selincourt, Oxford University Press, Oxford.

Svendsen, K. (1969) *Milton and Science*, Cambridge University Press, Cambridge.

Tottel, R. (ed.) (1966) *Miscellany* (1557), facsimile edition, Scolar Press, Menston.

Turner, J.G. (1987) *One Flesh*, Oxford University Press, Oxford.

Tuve, R. (1952) *A Reading of George Herbert*, Faber, London.

Tuve, R. (1974) *Allegorical Imagery*, Princeton University Press, Princeton.

Vaughan, H. (1976) *Complete Poems*, ed. A. Rudrum, Penguin, Harmondsworth.

Vendler, H. (1975) *The Poetry of George Herbert*, Harvard University Press, Cambridge, Mass.

Wayne, D.E. (1984) *Penshurst: The Semiotics of Place and the Poetics of History*, Methuen, London.

Weiner, A. (1978) *Sir Philip Sidney and the Poetics of Protestantism*, University of Minnesota Press, Minneapolis.

Winters, Y. 'The 16th Century Lyric in England', *Poetry* LIII 258–72, 320–35; LIV 35–51. Reprinted in Alpers, 1967.

Wyatt, T. (1975) *Collected Poems*, ed. J. Daalder, Oxford University Press, Oxford.

# UNIT 8

# Poetry and drama 1660–1780

*John McVeagh*

## Introduction

The present unit describes the main political and cultural developments of the period between the Restoration of the monarchy (1660) and the revolutionary changes that brought the eighteenth century to a close, laying emphasis on the ways in which public events influenced creative writing. At the same time it offers a critical survey of the literature of the period. Attention focuses, in poetry, on the transition from epic to satiric poetry, as seen in Milton, Dryden and Pope, and on the slightly later development of descriptive and topographical poetry, in Thomson, Gray and Goldsmith; and on the increasing concern with emotional states in the poetry of some writers later in the eighteenth century. In drama, the development of the new comedy after 1660 is illustrated in the work of Wycherley, Dryden and Congreve. Later changes, including sentimentalism and moralism, are discussed as they affect the work of Farquhar, Lillo and Sheridan.

In 1660 Charles Stuart, eldest son of the executed Charles I, returned to England from French exile to be crowned King Charles II. In restoring its monarchy, England formally returned to the political system which had been disrupted by two decades of war and republican rule. As a modern historian has phrased it, somewhat tendentiously, in the 1660 settlement the natural rulers of England returned to power.

Yet the monarchy was never to be the same again. The person of the king may have been restored, but the old kingly (or aristocratic) ideal was unrestorable. Few people saw the charming but imperfect Charles II (1660–85) as a ruler vested with divine authority, and fewer still those of his distinctly uncharming successors James II (1685–8), William III (1689–1702), Queen Anne (1702–14), and the first four Hanoverian Georges (1714–27; 1727–60; 1760–1820; 1820–30). The traditional perception of the king as God's representative on earth had carried with it an absolutist but also an idealistic view of political authority. Both had been destroyed with the execution of Charles I. The actual monarchs who reigned after him could never recover that charisma. It has been suggested that in the person of Robert Walpole, who ruled as prime minister from 1721 to 1742 by a mixture of skill and patronage (that is, skill and bribery), a 'new, invisible monarch' came to replace the old one, with an unofficial control over public life no less complete than that available to regal power before. We may link these changes in society with new directions in drama and poetry between 1615 and 1715, and especially after 1660. Different as they are from one another, Restoration dramatists like George Etherege (1634?–91?), William Wycherley (1640–1716), William Congreve (1670–1729) and George Farquhar (1678–1707) share a prime interest in social interaction, habits and behaviour. They are less excited by themes like kingship, authority, social and political responsibility and moral justice – the obsessive concerns of their Jacobean predecessors. Poetry became more public, commercial and argumentative; less metaphysical.

After the accession of Charles II in 1660 monarchy increasingly came to resemble a negotiated settlement, not a divinely authorized fact. Charles II kept himself on the throne for a quarter of a century by a series of stratagems, at which he proved to be very clever. One of these was to attract to his side the most brilliant writer of the day, John Dryden, who dealt some devastating blows at the Whig opposition in a series of poetic satires in the 1670s and 1680s. Charles's brother James, by contrast, who proved less adept at political dealing, lasted a mere four years on the throne (1685–8). What English men and women made of the sudden termination of James's kingship depended on their political attitudes. He was either forced off his throne by a usurping son-in-law (the Jacobite view), or he voluntarily gave it up and William III nobly stepped into the breach (the Williamite interpretation). At any event most of the English ruling class had lost patience with James's combination of Catholic inclinations and authoritarian style. In 1688–9 William III was offered the English throne, partly because he had some claim to it, being married to James's daughter Mary, but more important because he was a Protestant.

William accepted the offer, came over from Holland, summarily defeated James in a few battles, and ruled for a dozen years (1690–1702). His arrival signalled a fall from favour for John Dryden (1631–1700), but in Dryden's place as poetic champion of the court appeared other writers, this time Whiggish rather than Tory. They included Daniel Defoe (1660?–1731), who early in his writing life cherished pretensions to poetry. Defoe sprang to the side of the Dutch Protestant monarch against xenophobic English mockery in *The True-Born Englishman* (1701), a poem of enormous influence in its day, but since dead. Literature, in this period, by involving itself with political in-fighting so much, can be described as a distinctly public art form. (Compare earlier, especially pre-Civil War writers, with their cult of privacy and seclusion.) In 1702 the Stuart line returned briefly, when Queen Anne succeeded William. But Anne was a staunch Church of England woman, not a Catholic. After her death in 1714 the throne was again offered to a foreigner, this time George, the Elector of Hanover, who, it has been said, was only fifty-seventh in line of succession: as with King William, the point was that George was Protestant.

The Hanoverian dynasty, in short, was established in power by a manipulative politics designed to keep England out of the hands of Catholic Europe. Writers continued and intensified a tradition of public discussion. Journalism appeared on the scene, and soon expanded massively under Richard Steele (1672–1729) and Joseph Addison (1672–1719), Daniel Defoe and Jonathan Swift (1667–1745), and many others. Alexander Pope (1688–1744), Dryden's great successor, and, like the late Dryden, a Catholic outsider to a Protestant court, conducted a lifelong campaign against the Hanoverians, victorious Whiggery and modern manners in general. What we see happening here is more than the concern of some individual writers with the public topics of their day. Public issues and literary endeavour were inter-involved. Literature was more political than before. The writers fought out the sociopolitical and cultural issues of the day. Pat Rogers discusses this development in more detail in his book *The Augustan Vision* (1974), to which the reader is referred (see especially Chapters 1 and 2).

The Hanoverian line lasted from 1715 until's the first quarter of the next century. This takes us well beyond the present unit's period.

The dynastic compromises described above achieved their end. True, there were Jacobite rebellions in 1715 and 1745. But England did not return to Catholic or Stuart rule. Nevertheless the compromises also tarnished the kingly ideal. When powerful Whigs and Tories combined, for example, to ensure that William III successfully assumed power the contention might have been ideologically trouble-free, so to speak, for the Whigs; but not for all the Tories. For some of them, to invite William to replace James meant putting aside their belief that the origin of the king's authority lay with God. Arguably, the Tory party never recovered from this self-inflicted damage. In terms of raw power, the subsequent century belonged to the Whigs and Tories were largely consigned to opposition. Perhaps as a consequence, much of the greatest satire in the period was written by Tories out of power, or by Opposition writers. Pope's *To Augustus* (1737) lambasts the Hanoverian monarch George II; contrast it with Dryden's handling of the theme of monarchy. In his play *The Beggar's Opera* (1728) John Gay (1685–1732) satirizes Robert Walpole, the Whig prime minister, for a mode of government relying on systematic bribery and corruption. Gay got away with his attack because of his engaging tone. Not so Henry Fielding (1707–54). His anti-government plays of the 1730s provoked an irate Walpole to close down his and many other London theatres in 1737. Samuel Johnson (1709–84), in his first published poem *London* (1738), also attacks Walpole, this time for failing to stand up for British interests against Spain. On the inter-involvement of politics and literature during the first half of the eighteenth century, with good detail on anti-Walpolian satire, see Downie (1994).

Johnson's poem incidentally exemplifies the way in which eighteenth-century writers often preferred to make their point by innuendo rather than direct attack. *London* can seem innocuous until you realize that it is an updated imitation of Juvenal's third satire, turning the Roman poet's references with stinging effect onto the contemporary scene. Juvenal, for English writers, typified the angry satirist, but he was not the only model available. Pope preferred adapting the sly poems of the other chief Roman model in satire, Horace, which gave him a double effect: apparent friendliness, wounding power. The writers' willingness to hark back to earlier ages was a character mark of the age. They chose their models chiefly from the early days of imperial Rome, when Augustus was emperor (27 BC to AD 14), and Virgil and Horace were among his poets. The period of Dryden, Pope and Johnson has come to be known as the 'Augustan' age in English literature.

Two other decisive influences on English literature after 1660, and particularly after 1690, were the rise of a scientific, moneyed and commercial interest in the national life; and secondly, the expansion of London's power as the economic and cultural centre of society. The Royal Society was founded in the 1670s. The Bank of England was founded in the 1690s, as were the original Lloyd's of London and other insurance offices and commercial companies. Economic growth, an expanding commerce and money market, in the shires an agrarian revolution and continuous agricultural improvement, overseas an increasing British presence, and sense of power, characterized the national life throughout the eighteenth century, at least until the 1770s and the loss of America. This awareness of increasing business, and of the spread of business ideas, was noted and described by many writers, praised by many, lamented by some. In drama from Congreve to Goldsmith a shift took place from the concerns of aristocratic to those of middle class. The shift is obvious in plays of mercantile propaganda like Steele's *The Conscious Lovers* (1722) and *The London Merchant* (1731) by George Lillo (1693–1739); less obvious ones in the interest shown by dramatists from Farquhar to Goldsmith (1730–74) in exploring the life of provincial town and country. In poetry? Pope laments the growth of business and business attitudes in *The Dunciad* (I–III, 1728; IV, 1742) and elsewhere – a theme later developed and intensified in some of Goldsmith's poems. One of the aims of James Thomson (1700–48) in writing *The Seasons* (1726–30) was to fuse the imaginative with the scientific way of looking at the world, to see science and poetry as one. Such writings illustrate the public aspect of early and middle-period Augustan literature – the outcome of a culture highly antagonistic, perhaps, but sharing certain values. Later in the century, as the consensus dwindles, poetry becomes more diverse as well as more inward. We can see this tendency in Goldsmith, compared with Pope; in William Cowper (1731–1800), compared with Thomson.

London nearly doubled in size during the eighteenth century to 900,000 inhabitants, partly because of natural population growth, partly because of a continued influx into the capital city of men and women from the regions. It expanded physically, but its cultural and artistic influence grew even more. Before Sir Walter Scott (1771–1832), before the Romantics, cultural activity was centripetal. Augustan life and letters focused on the capital. Writers and artists gravitated towards the metropolis from the provinces, Scotland, or Ireland. Many of the greatest literary figures in the Augustan period were provincials who had made London their home: James Thomson, Johnson and James Boswell (1740–95), Tobias Smollett (1721–71), Richard Brinsley Sheridan (1751–1816) and Oliver Goldsmith are examples. Counter-tendencies, praising the rural life, for example, cultivating retreat or philosophical withdrawal, only emphasize the predominating fashion.

## Texts, authors, contexts: poetry 1660–1780

When the English monarchy was restored in 1660, terminating nearly two decades of commonwealth government, political reprisals were immediately put in place against the leaders of the revolutionary party. Some were executed. Others fled. The mood swung between the nastily vengeful, and the compassionate. Although Cromwell had already been dead two years, his body was dug up and hanged in chains in a public place. John Milton (1608–74), however, Cromwell's one-time secretary, had his name taken off the wanted list, it was said, by the influence of a member of the triumphant royalists who happened to have read and liked his early poems. (This discussion of Milton will site him within the political context of the post-Civil War period. For a treatment of his relationship with his Renaissance predecessors, and peers, go to Unit 7, pp. 166–9.)

The basic fact of a deep political fracture in English life needs to be kept in mind while the poetry and drama of the Restoration are being read, for it explains much about them. Milton, for instance, had been a busy public figure at one time – effectively, foreign minister to Oliver Cromwell. Now he would spend the remainder of his life writing poetry. He finished his epic poems *Paradise Lost* (begun before the Restoration, but laid aside) in 1667 and *Paradise Regained* in 1671. As a companion piece to the latter poem, and appearing in the same volume, Milton also published the sacred drama *Samson Agonistes*. All three works owe something to the defeat of Milton's cause. They are theological works trying to make sense of the revolutionaries' failure to recast the world in the image of their God.

This is to call them Puritan poems; but they have a wider significance. In Milton's articulation of loss is expressed a general feeling in English life during the century following the 1660 Restoration. Royalists, no less than anti-royalists, understood and shared this feeling. For though the monarchy was restored institutionally the kingly ideal (after Charles I's execution) could never be recaptured.

That both sides had reason to feel that they had lost out in the national conflict and its aftermath may be a contributory cause of the satirical mood which invades nearly all creative writing for the next hundred years after the Restoration. It is true that *Paradise Lost*, the greatest poem of the age, is not satire. But it was to be the last great poem before *The Prelude* of William Wordsworth (1770–1850) not written in a satiric vein or framework. And even if the satirical tone is lacking, Milton's epic can be said to express in its opening lines the new awareness of imperfection.

> Of man's first disobedience, and the fruit
> Of that forbidden tree, whose mortal taste
> Brought death into the world, and all our woe,
> With loss of Eden, till one greater man
> Restore us, and regain the blissful seat,
> Sing, heavenly Muse, that on the secret top
> Of Oreb, or of Sinai, didst inspire
> That shepherd, who first taught the chosen seed,
> In the beginning how the heavens and earth
> Rose out of chaos: or if Sion hill
> Delight thee more, and Siloa's brook that flowed
> Fast by the oracle of God; I thence
> Invoke thy aid to my adventurous song,
> That with no middle flight intends to soar
> Above the Aonian mount, while it pursues
> Things unattempted yet in prose or rhyme.
>
> (*Paradise Lost*, 1667, 1, 1–16)

There is no space here to extend the quotation further, but the reader may recollect that a few lines further on Milton claims that he is writing in order to 'assert eternal Providence' and 'justify the ways of God to men'. The opening paragraph is written in the shadow of the defeat of the revolution in which the poet had invested so much energy. He will (like the defeated revolutionaries) tackle 'things unattempted', seeks heavenly aid and looks forward (in line five) to a new and different restoration.

The crash of his political hopes may also explain why Milton loads the opening of a poem purporting to offer spiritual consolation with such heavy imagery of loss. 'Disobedience', 'forbidden', 'mortal', 'death', 'woe', 'loss' make up a string of negatives which precede the mention of hope. In them he sounds the keynote of his poem.

To suggest that *Paradise Lost* hovers between affirmation and negation – in this, perhaps, a unique text among epic poems – is not to define a problem with Milton's writing. Rather, it is a way of underlining how truly Milton articulates the experience of the age. Whatever their politics, whatever side they took in the Civil War, the men and women of Milton's generation had to assimilate for the first time in English history the breakdown of a political system. For royalists, failure came in 1649; for revolutionaries, in 1660. After the latter date kingship would seem to many a soiled compromise. All this, Milton responds to in *Paradise Lost* by casting the loss of happiness as the story of God's triumph: a paradox. Perhaps it was inevitable that in such an inverted narrative, as Blake was to point out, the devil came to occupy centre stage. Alastair Fowler (1968) and Helen Gardner (1948) have drawn attention to the dark strain in the poem's texture. Fowler traces it to Milton's original plan to write a tragic drama, which produced 'a tragical epic rather than a pure epic' (Fowler, pp. 5–6). Given Milton's subject, he says, an epic on it cannot but be tragic. A socio-political aspect of this pessimistic strain may be read in the events of book two of the poem. Here Milton deals with the devils' debate on what policy they should adopt after being cast out from Heaven. Factious argumentation, not logical reasoning, is most in evidence. The discussions may reflect parliamentary infighting, as Milton recalled it from the Commonwealth. They also look forward to Whig and Tory dog-fights in the Commons after 1688.

Beside the poem's opening passage, let us set the lines which close it. For in them also a current of melancholy perception troubles the surface of the verse. Adam and Eve, history's first refugees, are *guided* – Milton's word – out of Eden by providence.

> Some natural tears they dropped, but wiped them soon;
> The world was all before them, where to choose
> Their place of rest, and providence their guide;
> They hand in hand, with wandering steps and slow,
> Through Eden took their solitary way.

(12, 645–9)

The first humans are solitary, but hand in hand. Under providence, they wander homeless. They are travellers with no destination. It is a perception of division, of contraries characteristic of the neo-classical period.

Notice too the equality of Adam and Eve in this final picture. After much poetic insistence throughout the poem on authority (especially male authority) and on the hierarchies of creation Milton rounds it off with male and female side by side, neither leading the other, neither following, both vulnerable, both silent in the world. The feminist critic Stevie Davies (1993) remarks that in *Paradise Lost* 'sexuality violates autonomy'. She goes on to argue that Milton both 'identified with and disowned something female which was experienced as part of the self'.

The botched and broken seventeenth century, therefore, made available for Milton only enough material to construct an epic of rejection. It might be suggested that the poem's high heroic point is Abdiel's refusal to join the rebel army in Book five. This brand of heroism is non-achieving; the hero defines himself by saying no. Milton alters his source here. In the Bible Abdiel had been one name on a list. Milton plucks him from obscurity and makes of him a heroic denier. Abdiel is the ultimate protestant. He forms a community of one. In the poem's inverted value structure this makes him a hero. Perhaps Milton wrote the short, emphatic, unforgiving *Paradise Regained* as a cold-blooded assertion of what had eluded him in *Paradise Lost*.

As suggested above, Milton's coloration of the epic with a sombre tone, his mixture of affirmation and denial, was no private idiosyncrasy. Rather it was characteristic of Restoration poetry and drama. From his epic, let us move to the next greatest poem of the late seventeenth century, Dryden's mock-epic *Mac Flecknoe*, written just over a dozen years later (first published in 1682). Moving from Milton to Dryden is a significant progression; from the heroic to the post-heroic world view. Dryden's poetic focus is the writer Richard Flecknoe (d. 1678?) of the preceding generation, and Thomas Shadwell (1642?–92) – in Dryden's satiric handling, Flecknoe's successor. But Dryden mythologizes his material. He transforms Flecknoe into a poet so inept as to stand for all bad artists, and all bad art.

This is to say that Dryden's strategy is the opposite of Milton's, who had aspired to an elusive epic affirmation. Dryden first creates an epic effect, then undercuts it by deliberate bathos. It is as if he gives himself the best of both worlds.

> All human things are subject to decay,
> And when fate summons, monarchs must obey.
> This Flecknoe found, who, like Augustus, young
> Was called to empire, and had governed long;
> In prose and verse was owned, without dispute,
> Through all the realms of Nonsense, absolute.
> This aged prince, now flourishing in peace,
> And blest with issue of a large increase,
> Worn out with business, did at length debate
> To settle the succession of the State:
> And, pondering which of all his sons was fit
> To reign, and wage immortal war with wit,
> Cried, 'Tis resolved; for nature pleads that he
> Should only rule, who most resembles me.
>
> (*Mac Flecknoe* (1682), 1–13)

On their own the first two lines sound completely serious; they could be called 'Miltonic'. But what do we make of line three? Dryden first creates a sublime effect,

then shatters it by the bathetic 'This Flecknoe found'. Who, the reader wonders –
especially the modern reader – is Flecknoe? Few would know. The result is a new,
complex poetry whose special quality comes from the equal presence of epic
affirmation and bathetic ridicule. The complexity is the main thing. Mock-heroic as
such is not new: see, for example, the short poem *On the Famous Voyage* (1616) by
Ben Jonson (1572–1637). But Dryden, unlike Jonson, preserves a dignified tone
throughout. He never descends to using 'groan' rhymes, which undercut the poem as
much as the poem's victim; his mock-epic sounds epic even when it is mocking. This
cannot be said of Jonson's *Famous Voyage*, nor of the celebrated *Hudibras*
(1663–78) (which is discussed later) by Dryden's poetic contemporary Samuel
Butler (1612–80).

In this shift from Milton to Dryden we see more than just a difference between
individual writers. Short as the period is when measured in years – from 1660 to
1680 – to move from Milton to Dryden is to move from one poetic age to another.
First there is a formal change. Rejecting blank verse, whose open-ended line is
adaptable to indefinite narrative extension, Dryden champions the heroic couplet,
whose form implants in the reader, every two lines, an expectation of syntactical
completion because the rhyme sounds as if it should finish the sentence off, even
when it does not do so. This expectation, admittedly, Dryden often overrides (see the
last four lines above). The heroic couplet tends towards epigram. Blank verse, by
contrast, accommodates the discursive, reflective mood of the epic. Dryden opts for
the couplet effect so as to constrain the epic, though he can still create an epic effect.
Miniaturization is a feature of Augustan poetry.

Dryden both shares and does not share Milton's attitude to epic poetry. Like
Milton, he was ambitious to write one. He tried a contemporary, unmythological
epic in *Annus Mirabilis* (1667). In his old age he translated Virgil's *Aeneid* into
English verse (1697). But in *Mac Flecknoe* and *Absalom and Achitophel* (1681),
we meet an inverted, ironical treatment of the material. He debunks and satirizes
rather than celebrates, and furthermore Dryden's satire is only partly directed
against Flecknoe or Shadwell. He belittles kingly installation, which in the society
Dryden has seen emerging does not invite epic treatment. (They were on opposite
sides in politics; but Milton might have shared this view.) Here is the crowning of
Shadwell.

> The hoary prince in majesty appeared,
> High on a throne of his own labours reared.
> At his right hand our young Ascanius sate,
> Rome's other hope, and pillar of the State.
> His brows thick fogs, instead of glories, grace,
> And lambent dullness played around his face.
> As Hannibal did to the altars come,
> Sworn by his sire a mortal foe to Rome;
> So Sh– swore, nor should his vow be vain,
> That he till death true dullness would maintain;
> And in his father's right, and realm's defence,
> Ne'er to have peace with wit, nor truce with sense.

(*Mac Flecknoe* (1782), 106–18)

Pretenders play out a mockery of kingliness, stupidity and disorder turn rampant in lines of faultless poetry – the tone nonchalant, the rhythm assured. The poet, historically in retreat, reconquers the rebels by his wit. Fifty years later, when Pope reran this scenario in *The Dunciad* he placed monarchy itself among the dunces.

Dryden defines this priority – irony is better than abuse – in the *Discourse Concerning ... Satire* (1693) (Conaghan, 1978, pp. 575–606, quotes the relevant bits) with the famous praise of a stroke fine enough to separate the head from the body and leave it standing in its place. In another example, he quotes the boast made by Mrs Jack Ketch, wife of the public hangman, that her husband could execute a man so neatly that even the victim found it pleasing. But rough or angry satire also exerted an appeal. For an example, see *Satyr Against Mankind* (1675) by the Earl of Rochester (1648–80). Here Rochester adopts a highly personalized and passionate voice in place of Dryden's catlike detachment. There is, in fact, a satiric line extending backwards from Rochester in this mood to the cult of abusive satire by the Jacobean poets John Marston (1575?–1634), Richard Middleton (of whose life nothing seems to be known), and others. And the line also extends forwards from Rochester to Pope. For some writers and readers, hard cudgel play was preferred to cool fencing; energetic statement was what mattered; the dignity of art could go hang. Dryden, in cherishing poetic dignity, kept in being a simulacrum – an aesthetic image – of the traditional authority he was defending. David Nokes, in *Raillery and Rage* (1987), discusses the variety of forms and strategies in eighteenth-century satire, with special emphasis on Pope, Gay and Swift.

Equally unimpressed by dignity was Samuel Butler, whose *Hudibras* (1663–78), now little read, but marvelled over in its time, arose from the mixed influences of foreign satirists like Cervantes and English Jacobean originals like Ben Jonson. Of Butler's technique, the following lines will serve as an example. He is describing his anti-hero Sir Hudibras, a Presbyterian fool, and in him the cross-grained spirit of Presbyterianism itself. The Presbyterians, Butler writes, were a sect

> whose chief Devotion lies
> In odd perverse Antipathies;
> In falling out with that or this,
> And finding somewhat still amiss:
> More peevish, cross, and spleenatick,
> Than Dog distract, or Monky sick.
> That with more care keep Holy-day
> The wrong, than others the right way:
> Compound for Sins, they are inclin'd to,
> By damning those they have no mind to;
> Still so perverse and opposite,
> As if they worshipp'd God for spight,
> The self-same thing they will abhor
> One way, and long another for.
> Free-will they one way disavow,
> Another, nothing else allow.
> All Piety consists therein
> In them, in other Men all Sin.

(*Hudibras*, First Part, Canto 1, 205–22)

Butler's hostility, unlike Dryden's, is uncloaked. Instead this kind of satire scoffs directly. Rhymes look and sound inept ('spleenatick ... Monky sick'); and Butler rejects the heroic couplet for a line of eight syllables which feels cramped and not dignified. Dignity is Butler's target.

Butler and Dryden differ in tone, but both are obsessed with antithesis. When Butler writes of the Presbyterians that 'All Piety consists therein / In them, in other Men all Sin', referring to their habit of taking their own way yet damning others for taking theirs, he constructs the statement so as to heighten to the utmost the sense of opposition it describes. 'All Sin' at the end balances 'All Piety' at the beginning; in the middle 'in them' is opposed by 'in other Men'. Each phrase and clause counterweighs its opposite. Like architects of the period, poets placed a premium on symmetry, on the balance drawn from equal forces opposing each other, on the tension produced by energies held in check.

Pope followed Dryden in championing irony in heroic couplets against Butler's octosyllabic ridicule and the influence of Dryden and Pope prevailed. But Butler was not buried out of sight. Swift preferred the Butlerian mixture, as in his scabrous *The Lady's Dressing Room* (1732). (Compare with Belinda at the dressing table in Pope's *The Rape of the Lock* (1714).) Roger Lonsdale has pointed out (1984, p. xxxiii) that the 'unpoetic' poetry which Swift deliberately writes, with its short lines and rapid rhymes undercutting readerly expectations about literature, was a strategy that not just poets, but writers generally in the English Augustan period, were fond of using. An interesting example of the varied ways in which a Miltonic-epic inheritance fed into the growing interest in satiric statement is the burlesque poem *The Splendid Shilling* (1705) of John Philips (1676–1709). Here, Miltonic learning and grand language are comically deployed in a description of the needy, joyless life of the poverty-stricken poet.

Recalling Dryden's satire against debased kingship, we may consider two passages from Pope. First, in *The Dunciad* (1742), half a century after Dryden, he deepens that poet's mockery of false authority.

> She ceased. Then swells the Chapel-royal throat:
> 'God save King Cibber!' mounts in ev'ry note.
> Familiar White's, 'God save King Colley!' cries;
> 'God save King Colley!' Drury-lane replies:
> To Needham's quick the voice triumphal rode,
> But pious Needham dropt the name of God;
> Back to the Devil the last echoes roll,
> And 'Coll!' each Butcher roars at Hockley-hole.
>    So, when Jove's block descended from on high
> (As sings thy great forefather Ogilby)
> Loud thunder to its bottom shook the bog,
> And the hoarse nation croak'd, 'God save King Log!'

(1, 319–30)

The issues may not have changed but they have become cruder and starker. And Pope's epistle to King George II – contemptuously called 'Augustus' (1737) – illustrates how, for the later poet, the moral blight has spread further outwards and upwards. We now have, not a poet mocking at the dunces who want to be literary kings, but a poet praising George II, himself a dunce, as the monarch of dunces, and too kingly to care about poetry and art.

> Oh! could I mount on the Maeonian wing,
> Your Arms, your Actions, your repose to sing!
> What seas you travers'd, and what fields you fought!
> Your Country's Peace, how oft, how dearly bought!
> How barb'rous rage subsided at your word,
> And Nations wonder'd while they dropp'd the sword!
> How, when you nodded, o'er the land and deep,
> Peace stole her wing, and wrapt the world in sleep;
> 'Till earth's extremes your mediation own,
> And Asia's Tyrants tremble at your Throne –
> But Verse, alas! your Majesty disdains;
> And I'm not used to Panegyric strains;
> The Zeal of fools offends at any time,
> But most of all, the Zeal of Fools in rhyme.
> Besides, a fate attends on all I write,
> That when I aim at praise, they say I bite.

(394–409)

These lines convey Pope's view that George II has turned the kingship into something cowardly and stupid. In Pope, Dryden's contrast between kingly values threatened by mob rule has given place to the perception of a single blight embracing king, court and society as a whole. This sense of a wider social context, and of a sharper cultural decline, is one of the differences between Pope and Dryden. (On this, see Howard Erskine-Hill's imaginative study (1975) of Pope's immersion, as satirist, in the social relationships of his time.) On satiric technique, Pope, one might say, prefers accumulative irony; each couplet adds a new element of false grandeur to the one before. There is a delayed reaction before the final explosion. Dryden prefers smaller and more local effects. Sometimes Pope's comments are so cunningly barbed that they could be read, so to speak, straight rather than satirically: line four above, for example, or line six. In fact a reader might get through the whole passage quoted without realizing that it was satire, at least until the phrase, 'when I aim at praise, they say I bite'. Pope goes in for satiric amplification, for an enlargement of the ironic effect. New is Pope's dramatic method, as seen, for example, in his dialogic format – one of his favourite devices. (Dryden never used it.) The technique allows the poet to exploit question-and-answer interplay, to multiply mood opposition, to vary the point of view. As readers, we are kept on our toes. Does Pope's friend here speak for us? Or is the friend a foolish listener, misinterpreting Pope? Pope's diversification of the satirist's role forms a significant part of his poetic development.

It is noteworthy that, as poet, Pope, like Milton, makes a great deal of personal feeling, contrasting with Dryden's assumed nonchalance (or sneering indifference) towards other people's opinions. Yet Pope formed one of a tightly-knit band of poets, novelists and playwrights who in 1713 grouped themselves together as the

Scriblerus Club, first as a Tory opposition group to the Whig Kit-Cat Club (which included Congreve, Addison and Steele) and then more widely as a self-styled centre of literary excellence in an age given over, as they saw it, to the praise of mediocrity. The Scriblerus Club included Swift, John Arbuthnot (1667–1735), John Gay and Thomas Parnell (1679–1718). Some account of Gay's most important work, *The Beggar's Opera*, is given elsewhere in this unit. Arbuthnot was an active contributor to the Scriblerian literature, chiefly, however, in prose rather than in poetry. Parnell's poetic interests spanned both satiric and religious writing, of which the latter is perhaps the more interesting. His meditative-descriptive *A Night-Piece on Death* (1722) foreshadows some later eighteenth-century poetry in its assimilation of the poet's emotional mood changes and delineation of the outer scene into the same creative utterance. In Samuel Johnson's view, it was a defect of Swift and Pope that their writings were unnecessarily obsessed with indecencies. But as poetic subject matter, filth and dirt appealed to many Augustan (and pre-Augustan) poets. They form an aspect of the satiric vision – the obverse side of panegyric. Examples are the descriptions of urban and personal squalor in Gay's *Trivia* (1716), Johnson's *London* (1738), Swift's *The Lady's Dressing Room* (1732), and other pieces.

As the eighteenth century proceeded, other satiric styles than Pope's were tried, and found favour. Meditative melancholy lightened by occasional humour characterizes Johnson's *The Vanity of Human Wishes* (1749). Johnson deliberately cultivates the rhetorical grandeur and heavy moralism of Juvenal's style (as interpreted by the eighteenth century), in contrast to the livelier interplay of Pope. A good example is found in the opening four lines:

> Let Observation with extensive view
> Survey mankind from China to Peru;
> Remark each anxious toil, each eager strife,
> And watch the busy scenes of crowded life;

Coleridge read this, unsympathetically, as meaning: 'Let observation, with extensive observation, observe extensively'. But 'observe', 'survey', 'remark', and 'watch' carry different nuances, and Johnson is a writer interested in fine distinctions. Compare with these distinctive styles the uncertain voice of Charles Churchill (1731–64), whose *Rosciad* (1761) betrays a great desire to be satirical, little perception of what to say, or how. Verse satire after the death of Pope hardens rhythmically in Churchill's couplets, turns grand but abstract with Johnson, or softens into the emotional rhetoric of Goldsmith.

But the couplet can be adapted to other modes equally well. Pope shows this in the reasoned argument of *An Essay on Man* (1732–4), the tragicomic narratives of the third and fourth books of *The Dunciad*, and, from his early years, the nature description of *Windsor Forest* (1704–13). Often though, in descriptive poetry of the eighteenth century, blank verse might be preferred over the couplet to reinvoke the sublime Miltonic mode. James Thomson, for instance, in *The Seasons* (1726–30), seems to wish to combine elements from descriptive and epic poetry in order to celebrate British landscape, climate and political culture all together. In

'Autumn', for instance,

> Attempered suns arise
> Sweet-beamed, and shedding oft through lucid clouds
> A pleasing calm; while broad and brown, below,
> Extensive harvests hang the heavy head.
> Rich, silent, deep they stand; for not a gale
> Rolls its light billows o'er the bending plain;
> A calm of plenty! till the ruffled air
> Falls from its poise, and gives the breeze to blow.
> Rent is the fleecy mantle of the sky;
> The clouds fly different; and the sudden sun
> By fits effulgent gilds the illumined field,
> And black by fits the shadows sweep along –
> A gaily chequered, heart-expanding view,
> Far as the circling eye can shoot around
> Unbounded tossing in a flood of corn.
>
> These are thy blessings, Industry, rough power!
> Whom labour still attends, and sweat, and pain;
> Yet the kind source of every gentle art
> And all the soft civility of life:

(28–46)

Thomson's adjectives in 'Attempered suns', that is suns made temperate or toned down from scorching midsummer, and 'lucid' or pearly white clouds suggest one source of the pleasing nature of his diction: its etymological precision. This can have the shock effect of a new coinage. Clouds, for instance, here 'lucid' or a source of light, are usually thought of as darkeners. This Latinate exactness recalls Milton's style, and an aim of Thomson was to recreate the Miltonic sublime in the context of natural, later national description. Though *The Seasons* continually addresses the deity, he seeks to bring the sublime down from the heavens and locate it on earth.

But Thomson was a poet of the eighteenth century, not a mere imitator of Milton. For example his phrase 'fleecy mantle of the sky' (line 9 above) – which means clouds again – illustrates Thomson's willing adoption of another eighteenth-century poetic technique, the generalizing epithet. This device, usually referred to as 'poetic diction', Wordsworth was to scoff at as poetic impoverishment but Thomson uses it to enrich his verse by making it verbally more dense. Connotations drawn from other contexts are assimilated into the poem by the unexpected – and at first sight the unspecific – figures used. Thus, to call the cloud layer a mantle is to irradiate the greyness overhead with warmer, reassuring associations; it is seen as a prophetic cloak ('mantle'), hence as the reminder of biblical covenants, of providence, and of protection. To call the clouds 'fleecy' reminds us of sheep, suggesting in a half-conceit that flocks of clouds, like sheep in an English field, are at pasture in the sky. Thomson evokes for his reader a picture of the autumn sky as intimately bound up with the familiar English countryside, even mirroring its appearance, and so as an element in its agriculture, out of which arises the woollen industry, and, out of that, English prosperity and power. The clouds have become benign objects, and Thomson's ideological aim of describing the universe as a friendly place receives a boost. Thomson and Pope prefer to use a different formal idiom, but in the work of both (in Pope's case, the early work, such as *Windsor Forest* (1713)) we see a description of England which is also a harmonious disposition of its society into an image of peace.

The reason for the chief formal difference between Thomson and Pope – Thomson's preference for blank verse, Pope's for the couplet – becomes obvious if we glance at Thomson's paragraphing; here, once again, a Miltonic influence might be in evidence. Thomson plays off against each other the base rhythm running through the reader's head and the actual rhythm of the lines as written. By the base rhythm is meant the normal metre of the iambic pentameter: ten syllables to each line, the syllables stressed alternately, as in the line 'And black by fits the shadows sweep along'. (Even here 'shadows' upsets things, dislodging absolute metrical regularity.) Above this metrical pattern, and sometimes against it, like a melody playing off the beat in music, Thomson sets an alternative rhythm in motion, that of the sentence structure itself. And this, as may be seen from the passage quoted above, runs across formal divisions like line breaks without a pause, or inserts an important division where the metre does not (as in the case of full stops in the middle of a line), or a mixture of the two.

Why does the poet manipulate the rhythms in this way? One of the functions of *The Seasons* is to refresh the reader's perceptions of the English scene, indeed of the material creation at large (for *The Seasons*, despite its title, constantly ranges beyond the temperate zone). It seeks to re-evoke wonder. Thomson's opening out of the verse form, coupled with his elevated style and the scientific precision of his diction, noticed earlier, all combine to keep the reader guessing, to evoke wonder, to make familiar things vivid and eye-catching, to render the known new. They signalize that the Miltonic sublime is being sought in a descriptive account of the English scene.

This mixture, in Thomson's verse, of wonder at the beauties of nature with an insistence on cosmic providentiality and pride in the English scene could, in less imaginative hands, degenerate into nationalistic boasting. In the passage quoted Thomson ends on a characteristic appreciation of 'Industry's' benefits. 'Industry' here means productive effort, not mechanized labour; but the word was soon to change its meaning. Industry, Thomson says, supports the cheerful scene which he witnesses. Industry gladdens his heart. Evident in this praise of toil is the expectation that the happy arrangement should continue, that toilers will keep at it, and that poets may continue to give thanks for it. How easily the theme could sink into imperial boasting, 'Rule, Britannia!' (1740) may illustrate. Thomson wrote six stanzas; here are the final three:

> Thee haughty tyrants ne'er shall tame;
>> All their attempts to bend thee down
> Will but arouse thy generous flame,
>> But work their woe and thy renown.
> 'Rule, Britannia, rule the waves;
> Britons never will be slaves.'

To thee belongs the rural reign;
    Thy cities shall with commerce shine;
All thine shall be the subject main,
    And every shore it circles thine.
'Rule, Britannia, rule the waves;
Britons never will be slaves.'

The Muses, still with freedom found,
    Shall to thy happy coast repair:
Blest isle! with matchless beauty crowned,
    And manly hearts to guard the fair.
'Rule, Britannia, rule the waves;
Britons never will be slaves.'

Kingsley Amis once pointed out that this is not a boast but a call to duty, a hymn. True; but the dividing line between praying and boasting is getting thin. Glancing away from Thomson, one could recognize as a subgenre of Augustan poetry, with a surprisingly strong following among readers and writers, a type of blank-verse celebratory description of nature, existing social arrangements and healthy spirits in *Pleasures of the Imagination* (1744) by Mark Akenside (1721–70), *The Art of Preserving Health* (1744) by John Armstrong (1709–79), *The Fleece* (1757) by John Dyer (1699–1758), and others.

Pope and Thomson share the same attitude to the poetic craft, the same strategy. Poetry is seen as a public utterance, and though Pope may lash the negative side of his age and Thomson celebrate its positive one both of them handle general characteristics and general truths. To an extent the same might be said of the following passage taken from *Elegy in a Country Churchyard* (1751) by Thomas Gray (1716–71), in which the poet laments the anonymous passing away of labouring rustics; notice particularly its reliance on personification and moral commonplace. But there is a difference.

For them no more the blazing hearth shall burn,
Or busy housewife ply her evening care:
No children run to lisp their sire's return,
Or climb his knees the envied kiss to share.

Oft did the harvest to their sickle yield,
Their furrow oft the stubborn glebe has broke;
How jocund did they drive their team afield!
How bowed the woods beneath their sturdy stroke!

Let not Ambition mock their useful toil,
Their homely joys and destiny obscure;
Nor Grandeur hear, with a disdainful smile,
The short and simple annals of the poor.

The boast of heraldry, the pomp of pow'r,
And all that beauty, all that wealth e'er gave,
Awaits alike the inevitable hour.
The paths of glory lead but to the grave.

(21–36)

How, we might ask, does the speaker of these lines compare with the Pope of satiric attack, the Thomson of public celebration? What relationship does he negotiate with the reader? What is his tone? Despite the explicitness of the moral he wants to enforce Gray adopts a disengaged position. He stands back. He addresses, not the reader, but a series of abstract concepts – 'Ambition', or 'Grandeur'. Matching the disengaged stance is his brooding, watchful attitude. As Goldsmith noted, Gray partly achieves this slow, dragging, melancholy tone by lengthening out the eight-syllable line to ten syllables with an interpolated 'non-essential' epithet such as the adjectives 'blazing', 'busy', 'envied', or the verb 'run to' in the opening stanza quoted above:

> For them no more the *blazing* hearth shall burn,
> Or *busy* housewife ply her evening care:
> No children *run to* lisp their sire's return,
> Or climb his knees the *envied* kiss to share.

How can a hearth burn but by blazing, a housewife ply her evening care but by being busy, a kiss be struggled for but by being envied? Are the italicized words then unnecessary? Not exactly. To leave them out would result in a different kind of poem – flatter and more banal (they are words of energy). What Gray draws on here is the poetic resources of personal emotion, moody feelings in the poet disengaged from active involvement with men and women, sombre and philosophical meditation. It has been suggested by Weinfeld (quoted in *The Year's Work in English Studies* 72, p. 259) that in this poem the pastoral form is symbolically dissolved; in its unexpected close Gray takes a step away from Augustan towards Romantic poetics.

Such verse, certainly, like nearly all eighteenth-century poetry, is generalized writing with a clear social dimension. But the direction of its gaze is mainly inward, giving it the appeal of private poetry, tuned in most of all to the individual's feelings, curious about mood. It is one of the characteristics of English poetry after the death of Pope in the 1740s. For example, William Collins (1721–59) wrote poems to feelings, as in his *Ode to Fear* (1747). Gray himself, in *The Bard* (1757), in which an ancient Welsh prophet-poet curses the conquering Edward I, strikes an eerie, intense note of foreboding and doom. Goldsmith gives us another example of this emotional intensification of mid-eighteenth-century poetry, or in his case, possibly, emotional softening. Consider these lines from *The Deserted Village* (1770):

> Yes! let the rich deride, the proud disdain,
> These simple blessings of the lowly train;
> To me more dear, congenial to my heart,
> One native charm than all the gloss of art;
> Spontaneous joys, where nature has its play,
> The soul adopts and owns their firstborn sway;
> Lightly they frolic o'er the vacant mind,
> Unenvied, unmolested, unconfined:

(251–8)

And in a glance at Thomsonian patriotism, Goldsmith adds:

> Ye friends to truth, ye statesmen, who survey
> The rich man's joys increase, the poor's decay,
> 'Tis yours to judge how wide the limits stand
> Between a splendid and an happy land.
> Proud swells the tide with loads of freighted ore,
> And shouting Folly hails them from her shore;

(265–70)

This ability to view Whiggish England from a less assured standpoint than that of James Thomson (though the Scottish-born Thomson was himself an outsider in Augustan London) may owe something to Goldsmith's upbringing in a different culture and country.

Goldsmith in 1770 though, in the last analysis, sustains in his own emotionally loaded idiom that critical analysis of public life begun by Andrew Marvell (1621–78) and continued by Dryden and Pope, with vigorous insistence, to the end of their lives. One might rather see some of the other poets of the middle years of the eighteenth century – Collins, Thomas Warton (1728–90), Christopher Smart (1722–71) – as turning away from an engagement with the life of their times into a world of pastoral fancy, or fantasy, or private meditation. Placing these later eighteenth-century poets in clear relation to 'Augustan' literature is not always an easy task. There is something to be said for resurrecting the older critical concept of 'pre-Romantic' writing, for example, for such a figure as Goldsmith, who carries onward the public poem but also anticipates the unease regarding some social developments (like urbanization, enclosures, spreading commerce) which were to surface in Blake and Wordsworth. In Collins's odes, or in Smart's songs, something of the subjective Romantic poem is also anticipated. In this connection, William Cowper (1731–1800) might be seen as a genuinely transitional figure. His *The Task* (1784), a poem in six books, begins as a mock-Miltonic address to the sofa (reminding us of the burlesque satire of John Philip's *The Splendid Shilling*, published eighty years earlier) but soon turns into an exploration of the poet's own feelings coupled with a description of natural sights, scenes and activities in a peaceful domestic setting in the English countryside.

Yet this emphasis on the inward-directed gaze, on privacy, and on poetic evasion in some middle and later eighteenth-century poetry could itself be overstated. In a recent anthology, part of whose appeal, to a modern reader, will lie in its author's willingness to trawl through the original sources of publication, Roger Lonsdale offers plenty of evidence of poets writing 'graphically if naively' (1984, p. xxxvii) throughout the period here covered about the utterly normal stuff of life: cricket and other sports, marriage and its problems, life in the various professions, travel and tours, visits and holidays, jobs or unemployment, war, suffering and poverty. Margaret Ann Doody (1985) also stresses the strangeness of eighteenth-century poetry, its experimentation, its concern with new forms and new subjects.

## Texts, authors, contexts: drama 1660–1780

Although Restoration drama and Restoration poetry share common concerns they differ in that poetry remained (as always) a private and continuous activity. But drama, necessarily, was public. Banned during the Commonwealth, drama reappeared as a vigorous expression of triumphant royalism in 1660. For years thereafter its associations remained with its patrons, the royalist and courtly party. Hence, in addition to its obsessive interest in modern issues, and modern material – it bristles with the here and now – Restoration drama adopted a strong political and ideological coloration.

Their involvement with new courtly values marks off Restoration dramatists from their Jacobean predecessors. But the disconnection can be overstressed. Public performances were banned during the period of godly rule, but drama did not die out. Plays could be and were staged in private, and they were also staged in the form of opera, as in *The Siege of Rhodes* (1656) by William Davenant (1606–68). The latter device had much influence on later writing. Nevertheless, 1660 saw as clean a new start in dramatic writing as can be found in the whole English tradition.

Two contrasting styles swiftly emerged on the London stage: ranting tragedy and comic, often bawdy, satire. Something was taken from Racine and Molière, whose plays had influenced the court in exile, though the Molière influence can be exaggerated. Norman Suckling suggests (1965, pp. 93ff., 107) that English writers had fewer illusions than Molière as to what should be, hence Restoration comedy leaves less room for 'the assumptions of romance'. This is well said, and might be lengthily illustrated if there were room here (which there is not) by considering the full significance of what Wycherley does to Molière in *The Country Wife* (1675): takes from him the Pinchwife story, adds to it from Terence, the Roman dramatist, the pretended-eunuch story, and makes out of the combination an intensely funny yet also disturbing study of the destructive nature of unchecked appetite.

Besides their knowledge of French drama, playwrights in 1660 were also influenced (unsurprisingly) by Jacobean dramatic satire and by Elizabethan tragedy and romance. They were conscious of this connection, and cherished it. Thus when Dryden in 1667 updated Shakespeare's fifty-odd year old play *The Tempest* – note the Restoration obsession with modernity – he used the prologue as a means of holding hands, metaphorically, with his great predecessor. He dwells on the image of a tree cut to the ground yet continuing to send out buds and shoots of later growth. It is typical of Dryden that the imagery in these lines – a felled tree, new branches – also carries a contemporary political reference which his audience could not have missed:

> As, when a tree's cut down, the secret root
> Lives under ground, and thence new branches shoot;
> So, from old Shakespeare's honoured dust, this day
> Springs up and buds a new reviving play:
>
> (Prologue, *The Tempest* (1667), 1–4)

But admitting French influence, and influence from Roman drama, and from earlier English drama, what Restoration dramatists produced was new. The concern with newness, including new critical attitudes to drama as well as new dramatic techniques, informs Dryden's prose essay *Of Dramatic Poesie* (1668), in which he compares old and new forms, and defends the use of rhyme in dramatic writing. The primary interest of Restoration dramatists in general lay in their own society, by which they meant chiefly, but not exclusively, its upper ranks. These the writers reflected and reflected on in blistering satire or elevated tragedy depending on whether they or their audiences happened to be in a mood of comic destruction or – equally likely – of romantic identification with the daredevil passions of kings and military leaders. Here, then, in its divided drama, is another instance of that schizophrenic strain in the literary personality of the Restoration period.

The most obvious character mark of Restoration comedy is its concern with sex. To understand this, it is worth keeping in mind, as a recent study makes clear (Hunt, 1965, pp. 179ff.) that the patents granted to Thomas Killigrew (1612–83) and William Davenant in 1660 stipulated that actresses should act women's parts, ostensibly in order that the plays could become 'useful and instructive representations of human life'. This was not a historically original development, as it happened; before the Commonwealth, French actresses had appeared on the London stage. But the actresses had been hooted off. After 1660 their presence on stage became the norm. Not unconnectedly, female dramatists appeared on the scene. Never as numerous as their male counterparts, they made their influence felt nevertheless. Though ignored by critics for a long time their work has recently begun to attract a growing interest in scholarly circles. The theatre critics Schofield and Macheski, for example, in a recent book (1991), have surveyed this twentieth-century rediscovery of the body of dramatic writing produced by female writers of the Restoration.

Such a development changed the drama by lifting the constraints imposed, for instance, on Shakespeare's representation of sex by having to use boys to play women's parts: a constraint, needless to argue, which Shakespeare turned to advantage. When actresses took over female roles Restoration dramatists found the realistic depiction of sexuality possible, indeed unavoidable. How this affected dramatic writing may be seen from a famous scene in Wycherley's *The Country Wife* (1675). Horner, the libertine-hero, pretends to the town that he is impotent. As a result of this women can visit him with impunity, indeed husbands encourage their wives to do so, and also come along themselves to mock at his supposed affliction. But what they don't realize is that Horner is cuckolding them in the back bedroom while they are laughing at him in the parlour. The joke backfires on Horner when several women come looking for their host's attentions at the same time.

> *Mrs. Squeamish.* Oh, are you here, grandmother? [to Old Lady Squeamish] I followed, you must know, my Lady Fidget hither; 'tis the prettiest lodging, and I have been staring on the prettiest pictures –
> [*Re-enter Lady Fidget with a piece of china in her hand, and Horner following.*]
> *L. Fid.* And I have been toiling and moiling for the prettiest piece of china, my dear.
> *Horn.* Nay, she has been too hard for me, do what I could.

*Mrs. Squeam.* Oh, lord, I'll have some china too. Good Mr. Horner, don't think to give other people china, and me none; come in with me too.

*Horn.* Upon my honour, I have none left now.

*Mrs. Squeam.* Nay, nay, I have known you deny your china before now, but you shan't put me off so. Come.

*Horn.* This lady had the last there.

*L. Fid.* Yes indeed, madam, to my certain knowledge, he has no more left.

*Mrs. Squeam.* O, but it may be he may have some you could not find.

*L. Fid.* What, d'ye think if he had had any left, I would not have had it too? for we women of quality never think we have china enough.

*Horn.* Do not take it ill, I cannot make china for you all, but I will have a roll-waggon for you too, another time.

*Mrs. Squeam.* Thank you, dear toad.

*L. Fid.* What do you mean by that promise?

(4, iii)

At a glance the scene appears more flauntingly sexual, the dialogue more suggestive, than anything in English drama before, but, looking again, we find nothing unchaste is required of the actors and actresses. Wycherley keeps the scene decorous throughout. It's all (to quote a cliché) in the mind. Yet he is portraying sexual desire on the stage with unprecedented freedom.

We have seen this strategy of combining opposites – here, euphemistic language with indelicate meaning – in the poetry of the period. The reader may observe a similar use of innuendo in Pope's poem *The Rape of the Lock*. (Pope as a young writer knew Wycherley well.) Drama gains from the indefiniteness of application of Wycherley's metaphor. What exactly does he mean by 'china'? Does he mean fucking, as in Mrs Squeamish's 'Oh, lord, I'll have some china too'? Does he mean semen, as in Horner's 'This lady had the last there'? Does he mean sexual gratification, as in Lady Fidget's 'toiling and moiling for the prettiest piece of china'? Does fragile china stand for female reputation, as when Lady Fidget carries hers in? Or is china, a receiving vessel, an image of female longing? In a sense you know exactly what the scene is about; in another Wycherley, by keeping it unspecific, generalizes his moral point.

Side by side with this satirical reduction of sexual relationships to physical intercourse (a comic theme here satirized by Wycherley) we might set the following speech from Dryden's *All For Love* (1678). This play was a reworking of Shakespeare's *Antony and Cleopatra* (1606–7) into the heroic tragedy form beloved of the early Dryden. In seeking to build up the character of Antony, as the genre required, into a charismatic superman, Dryden writes for him a style so intensely dignified that Antony can naturally assert to Cleopatra, in the following extract, that if the two of them were actually caught in the act of love-making, their heroic authority would silence laughter and quell all lookers-on into submission.

> Suppose me come from the Phleagraean plains,
> Where gasping giants lay, cleft by my sword,
> And mountain-tops pared off each other blow,
> To bury those I slew. Receive me, goddess!

Let Caesar spread his subtle nets; like Vulcan,
In thy embraces I would be beheld
By heav'n and earth at once
And make them envy what they meant their sport.
Let those who took us blush; I would love on
With awful state, regardless of their frowns,
As their superior god.

(III, i)

Restoration dramatists were themselves well aware of this double view of human nature which they were advancing: cynical in the comedies, idealistic in the tragedies. Indeed they exploited the tension between them. The same writer might turn out satirical comedy and heroic tragedy for the same audiences, sometimes in the same play. They appeal on both levels at the same time. In such writing the modes are not being confused; they are being mixed on purpose, like shot silk.

*Marriage à la Mode* (1672) can be used to exemplify this. In this piece Dryden knits together a satirical comedy and a heroic drama and lets them run their separate courses side by side. The scenes of witty intrigue between Rhodophil and Doralice (married), and Palamede and Melantha (soon to be married) constitute a typical satire of the period about lustful desire provoking adulterous chaos before being brought under control. That forms one strand of the plot. But in the other strand (which is not comic) king Leonidas struggles to the death against the usurper Polydamas.

Dryden mixes the comic and heroic stories in such a way as to make them one story. He invites his audience, that is, to respond to the characters both on a comic level and on a heroic level at the same time. Rhodophil's shaky marriage provides much satirical entertainment, yet Rhodophil, being captain of the guards, is liable to be executed if Polydamas beats Leonidas in the political struggle. The other characters also have this double function – heroic and comic side by side. Dryden has written in the same work a serious drama and a burlesque on serious drama. Of the resulting mixture it would be hard to say which is the main plot and which the minor plot. His point may be to highlight the arbitrary nature of dramatic typecasting and literary conventions, or, less pompously, to get some fun out of them.

Consider the following exchange between three of the four lovers in Act five. Rhodophil has just found Palamede, his friend, making advances to Doralice (Rhodophil's wife), so he challenges Palamede to a duel. Palamede, for his part, has previously suspected Rhodophil of tampering with Melantha (Palamede's mistress). So he accepts the challenge. Rhodophil has already admitted that he no longer loves Doralice. And Palamede, likewise, has admitted to himself that he has become tired of Melantha. So the duel, as far as romantic feelings go, could be dispensed with. But the men feel they are duty bound to fight. (Now read on.)

*Rhodophil.* Further arguments are needless; draw off; I shall speak to you now by the way of bilbo. [*Claps his hands to his sword*].
*Palamede.* And I shall answer you by the way of Dangerfield. [*Claps his hands on his*].
*Doralice.* Hold, hold; are not you two a couple of mad fighting fools, to cut one another's throats for nothing?

*Palamede*. How for nothing? He courts the woman I must marry.

*Rhodophil*. And he courts you whom I have married.

*Doralice*. But you can neither of you be jealous of what you love not.

*Rhodophil*. Faith, I am jealous, and that makes me partly suspect that I love you better than I thought.

*Doralice*. Pish! A mere jealousy of honour.

*Rhodophil*. Gad, I am afraid there's something else in't; for Palamede has wit, and, if he loves you, there's something more in ye than I have found: some rich mine, for aught I know, that I have not yet discovered.

*Palamede*. 'S life, what's this? Here's an argument for me to love Melantha; for he has loved her, and he has wit too, and, for aught I know, there may be a mine; but if there be, I am resolved I'll dig for 't.

*Doralice* [*to Rhodophil*]. Then I have found my account in raising your jealousy. O! 'tis the most delicate sharp sauce to a cloyed stomach; it will give you a new edge, Rhodophil.

*Rhodophil*. And a new point too, Doralice, if I could be sure thou art honest.

*Doralice*. If you are wise believe me for your own sake, etc.

(V, i)

Dryden has created a scene of honour struggling with affection, a scene so common to heroic drama as to be almost a cliché. Then he gives it the comic treatment. The result is an ironic mixture. The serious leads into the satirical, and the satirical leads back into the serious, posing a question for the audience. Is the play's tragic tendency the important action here? Or is the recoil from tragedy into comedy more important?

Restoration and eighteenth-century audiences liked this sophisticated recipe. Although not a sensational triumph, *Marriage à la Mode* was sufficiently popular to earn itself half a dozen revivals between 1672 and 1700, the year of Dryden's death.

On the subject of dramatic language, we can make a connection between this Dryden play about orgiastic sex with Wycherley's euphemistic dialogue, noted above. Dryden too, it will be noted, avoids any coarse expression while audaciously hinting at the most intimate of actions. (Consider what Palamede and Rhodophil are actually saying in the passage quoted above.)

Of the two modes here married in Dryden's play, tragedy soon faded from popularity, whereas satirical comedy remained longer in vogue. It was tragedy's extreme stylization which shortened its appeal. To later audiences the poetry of Thomas Otway (1652–85) and Nathaniel Lee (1653?–92) came to sound like bombast – rather unfairly; even Dryden fell out of love with the ranting style of his early years. A sympathetic formulation might be that heroic drama emigrated from literary into musical expression, first English dramatic opera, then after 1710, when George Frederic Handel (1685–1759) arrived in London, into Italian opera. Handel vigorously championed the latter form for twenty years after which Handelian opera had itself become a target for satire, as in John Gay's *The Beggar's Opera* (1728). From the 1730s onwards dramatic opera in England came under increasing challenge from dramatic oratorio. But that story would take another book.

Comedy was also changing. For example, in Congreve's *The Way of the World* (1700) plot and attitudes seem cut out of the familiar stuff of the comedy of manners – cosmopolitanism, witty rivalry, sex obsession, pleasure seeking. But Congreve redeploys the material. The dark Hobbesian psychology which may underlie the libertine heroes of Wycherley, Etherege and the young Dryden has been replaced by a gentler ideal. Take the following exchange, in which Mirabell and Millamant, who are about to marry, stipulate what they will and will not put up with after marriage. Congreve can be seen as maintaining the genre's satire on marriage. Marriage, however, remains the lovers' goal.

> *Mirabell.* Have you any more conditions to offer? Hitherto your demands are pretty reasonable.
>
> *Millamant.* Trifles. – As liberty to pay and receive visits to and from whom I please; to write and receive letters, without interrogatories or wry faces on your part. To wear what I please, and choose conversation with regard only to my own taste; to have no obligation upon me to converse with wits that I don't like, or to be intimate with fools because they may be your relations. Come to dinner when I please, dine in my dressing-room when I'm out of humour, without giving a reason. To have my closet inviolate; to be sole empress of my tea-table, which you must never presume to approach without first asking leave. And lastly, wherever I am, you shall always knock at the door before you come in. These articles subscribed, if I continue to endure you a little longer, I may by degrees dwindle into a wife.
>
> (4, i)

Mirabell requires Millamant to banish sworn confidants, make-up, tight lacing and strong waters. Congreve prioritizes honest feeling, always valued in the comedy of wit, but here incorporated within marriage.

Noteworthy too is Millamant's plainness. She speaks a simple prose. Congreve's preference for a vivid, witty, straightforward style is another sign of the new priorities of Restoration literature. All comic drama after 1660 is written in prose though tragedy remained poetic. The preference is part of a general literary shift towards simpler speech and plainness in the arts.

John Palmer and Bonamy Dobrée, among modern critics of Restoration drama, have extended and deepened the appreciation of Congreve's comedy. L.C. Knights, in a 1937 essay reprinted in 1964 (pp. 139–57) put the contrary view. Knight's disparagement of the drama, based on both moral and stylistic grounds, has tended to provide the starting-point for later critics' efforts to rescue its reputation. Against Knights, for example, Kenneth Muir discusses (1965, pp. 231–5) *The Way of the World*'s 'beautifully varied' style. He summarizes: 'No dramatist has equalled Congreve in the creation of character by diction and rhythm.' And challenging the assertion that Restoration comedy is narrow, he comments that Congreve's true subject is not manners but false relationships and false ideas – perennial targets of comic writing.

In a half dozen plays overlapping with those of Congreve, George Farquhar popularized an open, inclusive comedy with the emphasis on action rather than wit. This, in the opinion of some, sounded the death knell of the Restoration style, but Farquhar's influence helped to establish comedy as the dominant eighteenth-century mode.

Farquhar made another significant change. He took the style as far as it could go towards explicit morality without sacrificing entertainment. Beside Wycherley's china scene or Congreve's proviso scene, both discussed above, place the following exchange between Aimwell and Dorinda from Act five of *The Beaux' Stratagem*, Farquhar's last play of 1707. For four acts Aimwell has wooed Dorinda for her £10,000, and is now about to gain her hand in marriage. But she warns him against marrying for the wrong reasons and offers him a chance to pull out of the engagement. This suddenly overwhelms Aimwell with remorse. He had entered the scene as a representative of the old-style libertine, or rake, but he exits from it as a man of feeling:

> *Aimwell [aside]* Such goodness who could injure; I find myself unequal to the task of villain; she has gained my soul, and made it honest like her own; – I cannot, cannot hurt her. [To Foigard] Doctor, retire. [Exit Foigard] Madam, behold your lover and your proselyte, and judge of my passion by my conversion. – I'm all a lie, nor dare I give fiction to your arms; I'm all counterfeit except my passion.
>
> *Dorinda.* Forbid it heaven! A counterfeit!
>
> *Aimwell.* I am no lord, but a poor needy man, come with a mean, a scandalous design to prey upon your fortune: – but the beauties of your mind and person have so won me from myself, that like a trusty servant, I prefer the interest of my mistress to my own.
>
> (4)

Farquhar turns on its head what the comedy of manners had always taken for granted about human motivation: namely, that relationships were ego-driven. *The Country Wife* shows us the overloaded Horner, the lustful women and their smug husbands learning the difference between selfish fantasy and reality. A kind of self-interest, even Mirabell and Millamant seek to protect in their famous contract. However, in Aimwell's change of heart in *The Beaux' Stratagem*, selfish appetite melts before the warmth of generous feeling. More accurately, perhaps, spiritual self-interest has replaced material gratification.

While Farquhar brings the comedy of manners, in this way, nearer to ordinary experience – for did Horner, the pure rake, ever exist? – he takes care not to let the moral note sound too loud. He limits Aimwell's reformation to a few lines. He keeps much of the old comic material. If Aimwell has reformed, Archer has not, and havoc results when he finds out what sentiment has done to his financial scheming. But Archer belongs in the past, and Aimwell signals the drama of the century ahead.

Drama historians tend to interpret this ideological change as evidence that seventeenth-century comic categories no longer fitted eighteenth-century audiences. The business-minded, middle-class and moralistic theatre patrons of Georgian London demanded a more middle-class drama. (For a more detailed discussion, see Loftis's two books on early Georgian drama.) But we know little about the make-up of eighteenth-century audiences beyond the fact that they were a minute fraction of the population: 1.7 per cent of Londoners, it has been calculated, attended theatre performances. (See Pedicord's painstaking account of the make-up of eighteenth-century audiences (1954).)

Whatever the reasons may have been, drama in the eighteenth century began calling upon its audiences to be virtuously respectable, not wittily interesting. As Pope put it in his preface to Addison's *Cato* (1713):

> Britons, attend; be worth like this approved,
> And show you have the virtue to be moved.

(37–8)

John Palmer suggests that in Farquhar's writing we may see the manners tradition of comedy going into decline. But this is to pronounce judgement with hindsight. Farquhar himself was looking ahead, not back; more than anything else he was looking around him, and pushing comic drama closer to real life. His *Essay on Comedy* (1702) points out that people are mixed creatures, not monsters of vice or virtue, and also that theatre audiences, being diverse, would find a variety of entertainment more satisfying than one single dramatic offering. To this it could be replied that the new comedy of sentiment, not the old comedy of wit, would produce the real moral monsters.

After 1700 English drama tended towards ever greater generic variety, ever greater experiment. This lasted until 1737, when stage censorship was reintroduced. Editing a recent anthology of eighteenth-century drama, David W. Lindsay comments (1993, p. xxi) that he has included 'a neo-classical tragedy, a sentimental comedy, a ballad-opera, a dramatic burlesque, a bourgeois tragedy, a laughing comedy and a satirical comedy'. The references are to Addison's *Cato* (1713), Steele's *The Conscious Lovers* (1722), Gay's *The Beggar's Opera*, Fielding's *The Tragedy of Tragedies, or Tom Thumb* (1730), Lillo's *The London Merchant* (1731), Goldsmith's *She Stoops to Conquer* (1773) and Sheridan's *The School for Scandal* (1777). This list is varied enough, but even this leaves out Handelian opera sung in Italian, which after 1710 carried all before it for twenty years, and was replaced in popularity by its musical successor the oratorio, a form of still-life opera which Handel invented in the 1730s when public desire for the Italian variety was on the wane. Most popular of all, in the view of the audiences (though not of the critics), was the English pantomime devised in the 1720s by John Rich, theatre manager of Lincoln's Inn Fields. Rich was an extraordinary mime artist in his own right, and in his new entertainment mime and dance-drama were placed at the centre of attention, song and scenic display each supplied an essential element and dialogue found no place. His new miscellaneous comic-operatic form continued to attract crowded houses throughout the eighteenth century and into the nineteenth. English pantomime, in fact, was the despised money spinner of the eighteenth-century stage. Its profits paid for bigger theatres. It helped to finance the productions of legitimate drama, new and revived. It made possible the reinterpretations of Shakespeare for which Macklin, Garrick and Kean received such acclaim. Theatre historians, however, have ignored it as a worthless form.

By Farquhar's death in 1707 Richard Steele was already drafting *The Conscious Lovers* (1722), which became the new model for sentimental-reforming comedy. It is hard to know whether the notorious 1698 attack on libertine drama by Jeremy Collier (1650–1726), or a sea change in British life under Queen Anne, or evolutionary pressures within drama, or a mixture of all three, was responsible for this emphasis on sentimental morality. But there can be no mistaking the new tone. Steele's first audience in 1722, listening to the prologue written by Leonard Welsted (1688–1747), were encouraged to give their backing to the new cult of bourgeois decency and to discard the old rakish style.

> 'Tis yours, with Breeding to refine the Age,
> To Chasten Wit, and Moralize the Stage.
> Ye Modest, Wise and Good, ye Fair, ye Brave,

> To-night the Champion of your Virtues save,
> Redeem from long Contempt the comic Name,
> And Judge Politely for your Country's Name.
>
> (Prologue, *The Conscious Lovers*, 27–32)

Welsted's first auditors would know perfectly well what he meant by refining the age, chastening wit and moralizing the stage. He meant two things. He meant no longer sympathizing with the charismatic libertines Dorimant, Horner and Palamede. Secondly, he meant admiring Bevil Junior, Steele's new hero, a paragon of cheerfulness, sensitivity and stiff speech.

Welsted's prologue extends this moral point into a patriotic one by suggesting that the audience, by reconsidering these values, would uphold British honour. This political emphasis, too, Steele would have agreed with. He writes into the play the positive figure Mr Sealand, an international trader, whom it is not an exaggeration to see as a new British hero for the times. In the society depicted in the old comedy, Sealand might have been a fool or miser. Now, he is society's ruler.

> *Mr Sealand*. Sir, as much a cit as you take me for – I know the town, and the world – and give me leave to say, that we merchants are a species of gentry, that have grown into the world this last century, and are as honourable, and almost as useful, as you landed folks, that have always thought your selves so much above us. (*The Conscious Lovers*, 4, ii)

Against this moralizing tendency in English drama (and against much besides), John Gay in 1728 directed the scattershot satire of *The Beggar's Opera*. In Gay's play it would be difficult to say who or what is not being ridiculed. Even Polly, the heroine, reveals wretched judgement in doting on Macheath. The cult of sentiment was certainly in Gay's sights, as when the Peachums' reduction of all motivation to self-interest mocks the prudential morality encouraged by Richard Steele. Italian opera was a major target. Others were pantomime, realistic drama, criminal biography and ballad romance. Gay could include almost anything in *The Beggar's Opera* because, during his lifetime, drama itself was generically fluid. Yet his unified tone, easy manner and light touch on the page, or the stage, give the play its unique appeal, and these are less easy to explain. Consider the graceful way in which he rounds things off. The player and beggar watch Macheath being led to execution:

> *Player*. But, honest friend, I hope you don't intend that Macheath shall be really executed.
> *Beggar*. Most certainly, sir. To make the piece perfect, I was for doing strict poetical justice. Macheath is to be hanged; and for the other personages of the drama, the audience must have supposed they were all either hanged or transported.
> *Player*. Why then, friend, this is a downright deep tragedy. The catastrophe is manifestly wrong, for an opera must end happily.
> *Beggar*. Your objection, sir, is very just; and is easily removed. For you must allow that, in this kind of drama, 'tis no matter how absurdly things are brought about – so – you rabble there – run and cry a reprieve – let the prisoner be brought back to his wives in triumph.
>
> (3, xvi)

Gay here offers his audience entertainment on two levels: there is the plot, and secondly there is the plot stood on its head. Such fooling with convention was a habit of Gay's – his first play was a generic medley called *The What D'Ye Call It?* (1715). But it is also a form of self-referencing which can be described as peculiarly characteristic of eighteenth-century literature in general. Gay is writing a play about writing plays. Elsewhere, Pope writes poems about poetry. Swift's *Gulliver's Travels* (1726) uses, and mocks, the conventions of travel writing. Later in the century Henry Fielding, partly drawing on Scriblerian influences, shows the same self-referencing tendency as dramatist in his 1730s plays. (See, for example, *Tom Thumb the Great* (1730).)

Gay's light entertainment raises the questions: what governs literature; and how should it relate to life? In a recent study John Donaldson has pointed out that his ability to be at once 'ironical and sentimental, risible and grave' challenges neo-classical ideas on the division of kinds (1970, p. 161). (Farquhar's 1702 prose essay on dramatic comedy also threw out the rules.) A little later Donaldson writes (p. 163) that 'heroic tragedy, Italian opera, pastoral, popular ballads and sentimental comedy merge bizarrely together'. But, as has been suggested, Augustan theatrical experiment is even more varied than this implies.

Though some new tendencies in contemporary theatre come together in Gay's writing, the priority he gives to wit might be judged a throwback to an earlier style. More characteristic of the dramatic writing of the 1720s is Mr Sealand's declamatory speech in Steele's *The Conscious Lovers*: assertive rather than urbane. A decade later in *The London Merchant* (1731) George Lillo brought the same sententious style out of comedy into tragedy, in fact into bourgeois melodrama. In place of the neo-classical tragic restraint, of which Addison's *Cato* (1713) is a good example, *The London Merchant* offers melodramatic excess. This we may see in the lurid language given to Barnwell, the bad apprentice, when he addresses his seducer as he meets her on his way to the gallows:

> O turn your eyes from earth, and me, to Heaven, where virtue, like yours, is ever heard. Pray for the peace of my departing soul! Early my race of wickedness began, and soon has reached the summit. Ere Nature has finished her work, and stamped one man – just at the time that others begin to stray – my course is finished. Though short my span of life, and few my days, yet, count my crimes for years, and I have lived whole ages. Justice and mercy are in Heaven the same: its utmost severity is mercy to the whole, thereby to cure man's folly and presumption, which else would render even infinite mercy vain and ineffectual. Thus justice, in compassion to mankind, cuts off a wretch like me, by one such example to secure thousands from future ruin. (*The London Merchant*, 5, ii)

This scene (though not its language) may recall the close of Marlowe's *Dr. Faustus*, in which the devil demands Faustus's soul. Lillo's hero is indeed a bourgeois Faustus.

In *The London Merchant* raw feeling and ranting morality combine to produce that sensationalism which is the soft underbelly of Augustan suavity. The blank verse lines buried within Barnewell's speech (knowingly or not, who can tell?) gesture towards rhythmic elevation, and hint at poetry within the prose: 'O turn your eyes from earth, and me, to Heaven'; 'Though short my span of life, and few my days' – or, perhaps, in the latter case, 'and few my days, yet count my crimes for years'. It may go too far to suggest, with Norman Holland, that sentimental drama can already be seen in the writings of Congreve. But the popularity of Steele and Lillo with theatre audiences tells us that melodrama was alive and flourishing long before the nineteenth century.

Sheridan and Goldsmith in the 1760s launched a counter-attack against the lachrymose morality of these depictions. Their handful of witty pieces, harking back to an earlier period, were termed by Goldsmith 'laughing comedies' in an attempt to rescue the vivacity throttled by sentiment. There are differences between the two: Sheridan brings Congreve and Vanbrugh to mind, Goldsmith may be thought closer to Farquhar. Sheridan's *The School for Scandal* (1777) attacks the 'serious comedy' school by depicting a man of sentiment, in Joseph Surface, indistinguishable from the hypocrite. Goldsmith in *She Stoops to Conquer* (1773) had earlier championed honest feeling against pretentiousness of any kind. Both writers, however, invoke rather than reinvent the Restoration style. They echo it, but theirs is a tamed and toned-down version. Contrast, for example, with the depths of depravity explored by Wycherley in *The Country Wife* the superficiality of the evil dealt with by Sheridan in the following characteristic scene from *The School for Scandal*.

> *Mrs Candour.* Now, I'll die, but you are so scandalous, I'll forswear your society.
> *Lady Teazle.* What's the matter, Mrs Candour?
> *Mrs Candour.* They'll not allow our friend Miss Vermillion to be handsome.
> *Lady Sneerwell.* Oh, surely she's a pretty woman.
> *Crabtree.* I am very glad you think so, madam.
> *Mrs Candour.* She has a charming fresh colour.
> *Lady Teazle.* Yes, when it is fresh put on.
> *Mrs Candour.* Oh, fie! I'll swear her colour is natural: I have seen it come and go!
> *Lady Teazle.* I dare swear you have, ma'am: it goes off at night, and comes again in the morning.
> *Sir Benjamin.* True, ma'am, it not only comes and goes, but, what's more – egad, her maid can fetch and carry it!
> *Mrs Candour.* Ha! ha! ha! how I hate to hear you talk so!

(2, ii)

Evil – raw vice – would hardly be the term for the activity depicted here: it is mild bad manners. To place Wycherley's world of destructive appetite beside such chit chat is to register how the comic vision has thinned in a hundred years. Sheridan aims for wit, but in restricting himself to a cast of shallow gossips – a dramatized *Rape of the Lock* – he also keeps within safe boundaries, and falls in with his age.

By Sheridan's time Shaftesburian psychology, stressing innate virtue, had replaced the pessimistic theories of Hobbes. (For a more expansive discussion of the thought and literary influence of these two philosophers, see Basil Willey's two volumes listed in the bibliography.) We may phrase the difference in the following way. For Wycherley, to give way to instinct, as Horner does, is to take the first step on the road to chaos; for Sheridan, to give way to instinct, as Charles Surface does, is to move towards generous fellowship. Such is the reappraisal that English drama makes about human nature between 1660 and 1760. None of this is intended to underrate Sheridan or Goldsmith. One could argue that they are the more serious writers. Backbiting might do more damage than lust.

That Goldsmith felt the need to reinvent 'laughing comedy' in this fashion underlines his conviction that drama at mid-century had taken a wrong turn. But critics may differ over his analysis. To some it may seem that Goldsmith and Sheridan register an effective protest against the sentimental drama of Cumberland and Kelly. Against this one could argue that even in Sheridan benevolence has left its mark; despite his barbed style he does not revolt against the priorities of his age.

Let us end on Goldsmith. Although in his plays and poems sympathy is extended to the lowly, heart-wisdom is preferred over the wisdom of the head, and sentiment reigns, what makes him most interesting in the present context is his tension. Neo-classical restraint and the pressure of feeling counter-balance each other in his work. Such balance is a rare achievement. Meanwhile, around Goldsmith, sentimentalizing and democratizing tendencies growing ever stronger imply for creative writing a wholly different future direction. To begin discussing this would be out of place in the present unit.

## BIBLIOGRAPHY

Conaghan, John (ed.) (1978) *Dryden. A Selection*, Methuen, London.

Davies, Stevie (1993) *Milton*, Harvester Wheatsheaf, Hemel Hempstead.

Dobrée, Bonamy (1924) *Restoration Comedy 1660–1720*, Clarendon Press, Oxford.

Donaldson, John (1970) *The World Upside Down*, Clarendon Press, Oxford.

Doody, Margaret Ann (1985) *The Daring Muse: Augustan Poetry Reconsidered*, Cambridge University Press, Cambridge.

Downie, James Alan (1994) *To Settle the Succession of the State: Literature and Politics, 1678–1750*, Macmillan, Basingstoke.

Erskine-Hill, Howard (1975) *The Social Milieu of Alexander Pope. Lives, Examples and the Poetic Response*, Yale University Press, New Haven and London.

Fowler, Alastair (ed.) (1968) *John Milton. Paradise Lost*, Longman, London.

Gardner, Helen (1948) *Milton and the Tragedies of Damnation*, English Association.

Hunt, Hugh (1965) 'Restoration Acting', *Stratford-upon-Avon Studies 5. Restoration Theatre*, Edward Arnold, London.

Knights, L.C. (1964) *Explorations. Essays in Criticism Mainly of the Literature of the Seventeenth Century*, Penguin (in association with Chatto & Windus), Harmondsworth.

Lindsay, David W. (ed.) (1993) *The Beggar's Opera and Other Eighteenth-Century Plays*, J.M. Dent, London.

Loftis, John (1963) *The Politics of Drama in Augustan England*, Clarendon Press, Oxford.

Loftis, John (1979) *Comedy and Society from Congreve to Fielding*, Stanford University Press, Stanford, Calif.

Lonsdale, Roger (ed.) (1984) *The New Oxford Book of Eighteenth Century Verse*, Oxford University Press, Oxford.

Muir, Kenneth (1965) 'The Comedies of William Congreve', in *Stratford-upon-Avon Studies 5. Restoration Theatre*, Edward Arnold, London.

Nokes, David (1987) *Raillery and Rage. A Study of Eighteenth Century Satire*, Harvester Wheatsheaf, Hemel Hempstead.

Palmer, John (1913) *The Comedy of Manners*, Russell & Russell, New York.

Pedicord, Harry (1954) *The Theatrical Public in the Time of Garrick*, Southern Illinois University Press, Carbondale and Edwardsville.

Rogers, Pat (1974) *The Augustan Vision*, Methuen, London.

Schofield, Mary Anne and Macheski, Cecilia (1991) *Curtain Calls: British and American Women and the Theater 1670–1820*, Ohio University Press, Athens, Ohio.

Suckling, Norman (1965) 'Molière and English Restoration Comedy', *Stratford-upon-Avon Studies 5. Restoration Theatre*, Edward Arnold, London.

Weinfeld, Henry (1991) *The Poet without a Name: Gray's 'Elegy' and the Problems of History*, Southern Illinois University Press, Carbondale.

Willey, Basil (1934) *The Seventeenth Century Background. Studies in the Thought of the Age in Relation to Poetry and Religion*, Chatto & Windus, London.

Willey, Basil (1940) *The Eighteenth Century Background. Studies on the Idea of 'Nature' and the Thought of the Period*, Chatto & Windus, London.

# UNIT 9

# Prose and the novel 1573–1830

*Gail Baylis*

## Introduction

The emergence of the English novel in the eighteenth century involves a bewildering multiplicity of themes, methods and influences, and to introduce you to these phenomena I shall offer different perspectives on the event: the literary origins of the form in the picaresque, in romance, in prose forms (fictional and non-fictional) of the Renaissance; its debt to the concept of narrative in literature *per se* – including the classical epic, dramatic forms and periodical styles; the relationship with the cultural, political and social elements of the period of its rise. I will then deal with the following authors: Defoe, Swift, Richardson, Fielding, Burney and Austen.

### The rise of the novel and the context of literary production

The novel, more than drama or the poem, feeds upon a variety of non-literary registers and usage: dialogue, reported speech, reflection, letters, journals. Hence its birth in the eighteenth century might be explained in relation to the vast and complex multiplicity of these linguistic registers that went with modern urban society. The birth of the novel corresponds to trends that we are now familiar with as being modern. For example, during the eighteenth century we witness the triumph of bourgeois individualism and the desire of this group to legitimize materialist ideology (I use the word 'ideology' in its loosest sense as a dominant set of beliefs) with a literary analogue – Defoe's novels are often read in these terms. The novel was both a prime example and benefactor of the commercialization of leisure promoted by increased levels of literacy and an expanded readership drawn largely from this bourgeois group, especially among women. The demise of the patronage system and new methods of publication (subscription, cheap part-editions of novels, magazine publication and circulating libraries) which treated the production and reproduction of texts as a business venture corresponded to changes in the financial world and money system which in themselves fed into a climate that made the Industrial Revolution and radical changes in modes of work and living possible (by the end of the 1840s England was the first predominantly urban society in history). All these changes have their roots in the eighteenth century and the novel reflects how society was changing.

## The novel as a bourgeois form?

By now it should be clear that the novel has emerged from a variety of cultural and literary roots. Ian Watt defines the characteristic features of the novel as realism and an emphasis on individualism, qualities that Watt directly attributes to Puritan roots which later find a reflection in the orientation of bourgeois culture towards the independence of each individual (Watt, 1957, 1963). While Watt offers a persuasive argument for viewing the novel as a social project, his position has not gone unchallenged and needs some qualification. First, it is impossible to speak of early novelists as representing a homogeneous group and thus claim that the novel reflects a dominant bourgeois experience (see Rogers, 1974). Secondly, novels, far from reflecting unconditionally the triumph of a bourgeois world-view, for most of the eighteenth century are sites of competing discursive practices (see McKeown, 1988). Such flash-points occur with *Robinson Crusoe* and Swift's satiric version of the plain-speaking hero in *Gulliver's Travels*. At issue in Swift's reaction is an unmasking of what he considers to be the falsity of pseudo-objective representation underlying the mercantile vision. Later, essentially the same debate re-emerges with Richardson's *Pamela* and Fielding's parodic *Shamela* where Fielding's satiric intention is to reveal the commercial basis of the heroine's 'virtue' and thus call into question the moral intention of Richardson's text.

Swift's and Fielding's anti-novels form part of the eighteenth-century debate about the form and context that the novel should represent. The novel does not signal the abandonment of earlier prose forms like romance and satire, rather it incorporates these structures which in turn modify realistic intentions. Thirdly, the claim that the novel reflects the ordinary and therefore can be claimed to be a realistic form is qualified by the fact that most early heroes and heroines are exceptional rather than representative figures. Such characters exist on the margins of the society in which novels were produced and consumed: for example, Robinson Crusoe, whose adventures prove to be uncommon, or Eliza Haywood's pre-1720s heroines who hold only a marginal relationship to femininity as a code of social acceptability.

While the rise of the novel could not have come about without an enlarged reading public, it is difficult to ascertain with certainty the composition of this new constituency. Certainly it was enhanced by an increased mercantile class who had disposable income, privacy, literacy, and leisure (prerequisites for novel reading). Circulating libraries which began in the early eighteenth century reflect and promote an increased market for novels and the proliferation of pirated editions point to a potentially wider reading market. Watt's theory that the novel promoted and reflected an essentially bourgeois representation of experience, made possible by an expanded reading public drawn from this group, has not gone unchallenged by later critics (such as Bull, 1988) who propose a much broader network of social tastes and influences. However, while the early novel does exploit populist themes and involve characters from all social classes, it maintains a reluctance to advocate values and moral concerns that are not recognizably middle class. This is as true for Fielding and Smollett as it is for Defoe and Richardson – while the former do not necessarily endorse bourgeois sentiments, they are aware of the readership's expectations and often exploit irony as one method of recording their ambivalent relationship with the public.

What characterizes the early novel more than anything else is that it is an experimental form. Criticism of the novel (which was widespread) was social as much as literary, stemming from the perception that the form was challenging traditional notions of the writer's role and relationship with the public. The novel, then, is both a promoter and product of such changes. The early eighteenth-century novel held an improvisory status: whilst the genre often reflects bourgeois values, it also points to the places where those values break down (see Defoe's *Robinson Crusoe*, Richardson's *Pamela* and Fielding's *Shamela*).

## Status of the genre

The novel begins as a 'low' form where classical knowledge was not a prerequisite for literary competence (compare with poetry of the period: for example Gray's *Trivia*, 1719, Thomson's *The Seasons*, 1726–30). Early novelists often turn to prose fiction from other employment or literary avenues (Aphra Behn, Delarivier Manley, Eliza Haywood, Daniel Defoe). During the eighteenth century the main inducement for writing novels was financial. The history of the eighteenth-century novel reflects a genre that starts as a hybrid form, having neither fixed generic form or structure. The novel's close links with other prose forms is indicated by the confusion between fact and fiction in descriptive tags like 'history', 'memoir', 'romance', 'true life' and 'story'. The full titles of novels often reveal this indeterminate status of the genre as a separate prose form for much of the century. The word 'novel' itself indicates the newness with which the genre was regarded by critics, public and novelists. Early novelists reveal a confidence to experiment freely with an incipient form. By the close of the century the novel has gained status and a level of authority as a separate genre with a wide readership and with attendant structural and thematic rules. It is upon these achievements that Scott and later nineteenth-century novelists expand.

The combination of the novel's early status as 'illegitimate' art, and the possibility of pursuing novel writing within the domestic environment, encouraged many women during the century to write fiction. In fact, the majority of novelists during the eighteenth century were women and the genre can be seen as a female form. Restoration writers like Aphra Behn and Delarivier Manley did much to challenge the double standards of sexual morality and claim a voice for fictionalizing women's concerns. But they served as contradictory models for later women novelists because they took as their themes exceptional women: adventurers, seductresses and seduced women. The autobiographical reading of women's texts (reinforced by Manley's works where she self-dramatizes herself as a heroine) tended to conflate the personal lives of women with their works. The history of women's fiction for the eighteenth and much of the nineteenth century was in direct reaction to the achievements of the major Restoration women writers like Behn and Manley.

In contrast to the radical message of the Restoration woman writer, eighteenth-

and nineteenth-century fiction by women tended to emphasize the didactic and point to the costs of slippage for women. This change in orientation – from radicalism, to surface endorsement of the social order, though often revealing doubleness and subtexts, to renewed radicalism at the close of the century – is exemplified by the career of Eliza Haywood (1693?–1756). Haywood's career charts a movement from protest in women's fiction (many of her novels of the 1720s are scandal novels), where an emphasis on sexual relationships and the seduction theme reveal the double standards of society's morality, to an assertion of woman's innate moral superiority to those social laws while portraying heroines who still have to function within those standards. (For a full account of the roots of women's fiction, see Spencer, 1986, and Unit 23, pp. 614–18, of this volume).

## Terms of acceptance

Experimentation and innovation continued throughout the century. Testing the boundaries of what fiction could constitute probably reaches its fullest expression with Laurence Sterne's *Tristram Shandy* (1759–65). Sterne's hero Shandy tells his story through continuous digressions, shifts of perspective, by mixing up his 'story' with immediate concerns like a faulty parlour door (vol. III, ch. xxi). The uneasy relation between fiction and actuality in *Tristram Shandy* often earns it the status of an early Modernist text, pre-empting as it does the techniques of Joyce and Woolf (see Unit 16). The relationship between fiction and actuality which Sterne's playfulness constantly tests is in fact a typical concern of the eighteenth-century novel. *Tristram Shandy* is a self-conscious, extended version of the experiments conducted by Defoe, Fielding and eighteenth-century novelists in general who worked with an incipient form without given rules or structures (compare with the nineteenth-century novel where concepts of realism and story telling become fixed).

However, there is also a discernible desire by novelists to gain authority and legitimacy for the new form as a species of moral art. Attempts to structure the novel are reflected in greater attention being given to plotting and characterization. Characters become less 'type' figures standing exclusively for virtues and vices, and more individualized – more like people that the reader might know but whose lives are more exciting or problematic. Peripheral characters still often maintain type status (Allworthy as the ideal country squire in *Tom Jones* or Lovelace as the seducing aristocrat in *Clarissa*). Novels also grow in length reflecting greater attention being placed on both plot and characterization.

No longer are an isolated number of adventures drawn together loosely; attempts are made to suggest a sequential progression and interconnectedness. These developments do not follow a uniform plan; rather the novel develops by two main routes: (a) Fielding and the development of the picaresque tradition and (b) Richardson and the refinement of the epistolary form. Novelists do not necessarily follow either/or of these precedents, but often utilize aspects from both authors. For example Fanny Burney, who we can class as the heir of Fielding's social-satiric vision, emphasizes her heroines' misreading of social codes, but also stresses their refinement of virtue thus aligning her works with Richardsonian didacticism (*Evelina* and *Cecilia*).

Richardson, rather than creating anything radically new, capitalizes on the successes of earlier women novelists who developed the letter-novel into a form that could express emotional responses to situation. The Richardsonian novel is closely associated with the aesthetics of sensibility in which feminine style and finer feelings are given privileged status. (For an account of the novel of sensibility see Todd, 1986.) The ethos of sensibility (*c*.1740–70, also known as the Age of Sensibility) exemplifies a period when women's fiction was positively encouraged because the feminine 'voice' was considered to be more spontaneous and natural – Richardson's first two novels both reproduce feminine narrative speakers. The outcome of this valorization of things feminine in fiction and culture at large in the latter half of the eighteenth century becomes the codified ideal of the Angel in the House of the Victorian novel. The reaction against sensibility in Romanticism takes the form of an attack on its tearful self-indulgence which becomes associated with female weakness. However, it would be wrong to view sensibility as a totalizing system in the latter half of the eighteenth century – it was by no means inclusive or definitive. Not all writers adhered to a code of tender tearfulness and there remained a vein of social satire in novels and a tendency to ridicule sentimental excess. Fanny Burney and Oliver Goldsmith are equivocal about sensibility (refer to *Cecilia*, 1782, and *The Vicar of Wakefield*, 1766), Jane Austen is openly hostile to its excesses (*Sense and Sensibility*, 1811), and Mary Wollstonecraft argued that it was detrimental to women's education and rational faculties (*A Vindication of the Rights of Woman*, 1792).

## Radicalism and consolidation

1780–1830 marks a period of revolutionary upheaval followed by reactionary consolidation. Romanticism (*c.* 1770–1840) witnesses a reaction against the novel of sensibility and the re-emergence of poetry as the dominant form. For an insightful account of the relationship between literature, politics and culture during this period refer to Butler (1982). Prose and the novel of the period reflect the radical atmosphere: for example, Godwin's political novel *Caleb Williams* (1794), Wollstonecraft's *A Vindication of the Rights of Woman* (1792) and her radical gothic *Maria: or the Wrongs of Woman* (1798), and Mary Shelley's *Frankenstein* (1818). However, the main trend of the novel is towards realism. Praise of the novel increasingly stresses its verisimilitude, while rejecting eighteenth-century forms like the gothic and novel of sensibility which are seen as being fantastic, unrealistic and escapist. While the popular forms of the late eighteenth century fall out of vogue in the nineteenth century, their subversive potential is not fully rejected, as is illustrated by the strong vein of female Gothic and romance that runs through the nineteenth and twentieth centuries.

Walter Scott's phenomenal success was no doubt in part the result of his development of the novel as a vehicle for social cohesiveness. The novelty of

Scott's works (*Waverley* (1814) is often termed the first historical novel) was that they offered a historical and social perspective whilst maintaining a romance appeal. Where Scott's focus differs from Defoe's, who offers a retrospective narrative in *Robinson Crusoe* which can be read as a historicizing of capitalism, is in his placement of his hero off-centre: the emphasis is no longer on the individual *per se* but the individual within a social context (see Bull, 1988).

Like Scott, Jane Austen (1775–1817) in her fiction represents a consolidatory message. Austen is often viewed as a conservative thinker and as a novelist of 'manners' whose skill lies in representing the minutiae of domestic life and in rendering an ironic commentary on nuances and misinterpretations of language. All Austen's heroines are intelligent (if at times misleading) women whose 'education' takes the form of a realization of the limited options open to them. It is, therefore, possible to read Austen's fiction across the grain and see strategies of subversion competing with her overtly endorsing codes.

Horace Walpole's *The Castle of Otranto* (1764) is generally accepted to be the first true gothic novel. The word 'gothic' originally implied 'medieval' but the form soon became associated with romance as in Ann Radcliffe's *The Mysteries of Udolpho* (1794) and *The Italians* (1797), both of which are subtitled a 'romance'. Austen's *Northanger Abbey* (1818) satirizes this immensely popular form by ridiculing the conventions and mechanics by which Gothic horror operates: haunted castles, ruins, wild picturesque and the lone threatened heroine. Gothics hold a complex and contradictory appeal, both as expressions of fantasies of female power (Radcliffe's novels can be read in this way) and as subtexts for female anxieties regarding woman's place in society. In *Maria: Or the Wrongs of Woman* (1798), Wollstonecraft revises her position of *The Vindication* by radicalizing the gothic form. In Wollstonecraft's novel, the fantasies and anxieties of the heroine become, not an index of Gothic excess, but a reflection of woman's position in society where the home, the nexus of feminine identity, becomes a prison. Wollstonecraft expands the Gothic to offer a feminist protest against the imprisoning of women within codified roles which disallow autonomy or growth. Mary Shelley's *Frankenstein* (1818) yokes a social critique of industrial and scientific thought to the gothic formula through her rewriting of the birth myth. While the main trend from the eighteenth- to nineteenth-century novel is realism, subgenres of fantasy continue to modify and cast doubt on realistic intentions. For example, in *Jane Eyre* and *Wuthering Heights*, gothic structures cast ambiguity upon the socially cohesive closure of the texts.

## Prose forms and the novel

There was no single prose source for the novel. Early fiction drew upon an immense variety of styles, registers and sub-genres. To name but a few we might include: letter-novels, the diary and journal format, Puritan spiritual autobiographies, popular rogue and scandal tales, travellers' narratives, allegories and fables, conduct literature, satirical commentaries, confessional memoirs, chapbooks, jest-bio-graphies, 'cony-catching' pamphlets, character sketches, *novellas*, spiritual tracts, picaresque tales and romance structures. Before the eighteenth century no distinction was made between 'novel' as fictional representation and as news gossip or topical opinion.

Elizabethan and Carolean prose narratives exhibit many features which we can claim as being precursive to the novel. 'Historical' realism is one strategy adopted by the Elizabethan prose writer to negotiate the arbitrary relationship between author and print. Fictional works often appeared as translations or histories in order to facilitate the creation of a narrative relationship with the text as something already given: the narrator's role then becomes independent (or seemingly) of the text and that of commentator.

Prose fiction of the sixteenth and seventeenth centuries reflects a range of styles, themes and precedents. These can be divided into two main categories: (a) romances, such as Gomberville's *Polexandre*, which first appeared in English translation in 1674, Sidney's *Arcadia* (1590), which set precedents for pastoral romances, and the many translations of French sentimental, religious and anti-romances, which include a translation of Jean de Cartigny's *Voyage of the Wandering Knight* (1581), which set a precedent for Bunyan's *The Pilgrim's Progress* (1678), and (b) popular tales, in the form of tales of burgher life in Deloney's *Jack of Newberie* (1597?) and *Thomas of Reading* (1600?), jest books and 'cony-catching' pamphlets (the anonymous *The Tinker of Turvey*, 1630), jest biographies (*The Life of Long Meg of Westminster*, 1620) and criminal literature such as Deloney's *A Notable Discovery of Cozenage* (1591), which set a precedent for Defoe's criminal biographies and novels.

However, while it may be useful to categorize the various forms of Elizabethan and Carolean prose, it must also be acknowledged that a characteristic of prose fiction of this period is a mixture of elements (Nashe uses the term 'medley' to describe his intention in *The Unfortunate Traveller*). Greene, Nashe and Deloney all mix elements of serious and comic in their works and draw on elements from romance, popular tales, satires and jest-books. In this they set an important precedent for the eighteenth-century novel in which experimentation and improvisation remains a key element.

What distinguishes the Elizabethan writer from the eighteenth-century novelist most clearly is a public orientation – the allegorical framework is intended to serve as a point of mediation between public and private. Of course, allegorical intentions do not disappear in the eighteenth-century novel (consider *The Pilgrim's Progress* and *Robinson Crusoe*) but experience is placed less exclusively in the social perspective. One reason why the novel does not gain impetus until the eighteenth century may be to do with demography. The rise of city living (particularly London) created the anonymity necessary to make private experience of interest. In Elizabethan England while bourgeois values were being established there was not the scale of urban living necessary to make other ordinary people's experience (except in a symbolic mode) distinct and therefore potentially interesting. By the eighteenth century these conditions were present (see Margolies, 1985).

In Nashe's *The Unfortunate Traveller* the hero (Jack Witton) is also the narrator and this dual function proves problematic. While the loose structure of the work is nominally held together by the presence of the hero, his role as narrator and foil for Nashe's invective make his comments far from individual, a trait which is further reinforced by the hero's lack of any inner thoughts or consistency of outlook. Nashe sees no need to give his character plausible motives or a definite personality. This quality of the public function of the hero and action is reinforced through word-play and punning which are intended to draw attention to the author's virtuosity rather than to a delineation of character.

## Periodicals

The rise of the periodical and the novel occur in tandem. Episodic accounts in periodicals form an important stage in the development of the novel. What we might class as the characteristic narrative tone of the early novel (intimacy) bears a close resemblance to the friendly chattiness of Addison's and Steele's periodical narrator, Mr Spectator. The conversational style, the sense of familiarity between narrator and reader, the circumstantial approach that characterize *The Spectator* (1711–12) and prose journalism generally of the period also informs the novel. Compare Addison's direct, personalized method of narration in *The Spectator* (No. 171) with Fielding's similar method in *Tom Jones* of specifying time and place. Many novelists also wrote prose journalism (Defoe, Haywood, Swift, Fielding, Johnson, Goldsmith – to name but a few). Gender representation in journalism establishes a slightly different type of relationship between narrator and reader – a difference that would, as we shall see, be further complicated in the novel. *The Female Spectator* (edited for a period by Eliza Haywood) takes its lead from conduct literature which taught women that upon marriage it was their role to accept a diminution of power. Novels, while often endorsing a code of modesty for women, contradict the logic of conduct books by placing the heroine centre stage and thus making her the focus of interest.

## The picaresque tradition

The roots of the picaresque lie in sixteenth-century Spanish fictional narratives: particularly the anonymous *Lazarillo de Tormes* (1553), Metes Aleman's *Guzman de Alfarache* (1599–1640) and Francisco Quevedo's *La vida del Buscon* (1626). The picarèsque story involves the adventures of a rogue-hero, a trickster figure whose experiences offer the opportunity for comic action and satiric comment on the mores of society from the vantage point of the outsider. Picaresque offers the opportunity for rapid narrative pace and packed adventures whilst demanding only the loosest structural coherence. Picaresques can be satiric (Nashe's *The Unfortunate Traveller*, 1594, generally regarded as the first picaresque in English), discursive (Fielding's *Tom Jones*, 1749), or involve comic buffoonery (Smollett's *The Adventures of Roderick Random*, 1748). Smollett's picaroon's surname points to the organizing principle of medley and random experience drawn together nominally through the hero's presence. The appeal of picaresque for novelists lies in the range of subject matter it facilitates and styles of address that it accommodates. It formed an important source for eighteenth-century novelists (most notably Defoe, Fielding, Smollett) and is an acknowledged influence on early Dickens (see *The Pickwick Papers*).

However, the opportunity for freedom of invention and the discursive possibilities that picaresque facilitated were not open to women novelists for a number of stylistic and cultural reasons. The narrative position created for eighteenth-century women novelists meant that it was impossible for them to create the adventurous heroine without radically challenging their status as gentlewomen writers. This was a position that few genteel women were willing to assume because it would place them in open conflict with their society and, at best, open their text to the criticism of exaggeration and implausibility. Such adventures as roaming about the countryside and having encounters often of a sexual kind (see *Tom Jones*) were considered to be outside the remit of a polite lady's experience and at worst could cast serious moral aspersions upon the character of the author since women's writings were read primarily in a confessional context (see Figes, 1982). In contrast to the picaresque, the main trend in women's fiction was the domestic novel. One form of subversion developed by women novelists at the close of the eighteenth century was the female gothic in which the heroine does have roaming adventures, but she remains blameless because her actions are motivated by the need to escape the designs of an unscrupulous male. The gothic novel held an added attraction for the woman writer in that it allowed her to operate in a fictional context detached from the expectations and conventions of the real world.

## Romance structures

The novel is often considered to be the product of a rejection of earlier romance structures which come to be seen as representing an essentially aristocratic vision of experience; for example, seventeenth-century French romances such as Madeleine de Scudéry's *Clelia* (translated into English in 1656). Heroic romances proved popular in England during the seventeenth century (Gomberville's *Polexandre* and d'Urfé's *L'Astrée*). The theme of these works was the love of a great hero for his lady and the trials and tribulations that he underwent to win her favour. Italian and Spanish *novellas* were also popular: Cervantes' *Exemplary Novels* (first translated by Mappe in 1640 and thereafter reprinted in the seventeenth and early eighteenth centuries) set a model for the theme of divided lovers trying to unite in the face of parental disapproval. Key elements in romances are (a) the quest, (b) rise and progress (often during a period of exile either physically or from 'true' identity when commonly the hero or heroine starts life in a lowly station), (c) discovery and restoration (of true identity which is invariably accompanied by an elevation in social position), (d) resolution (the 'happy ending' in which the good are rewarded and the bad punished). Realistic intentions are often in tension with romance elements in the novel rather than dominating them. Romance elements occur frequently in novels and not solely in those that deal with love and marriage. Often romance elements are masked under the guise of authorial omnipotence when the good are rewarded and the bad punished at the closure of novels.

Romance plot structures, especially in the resolution of eighteenth-century novels, often point to the fictionality of fiction and reflect an ironic relationship between writer and text. When used in this manner the writer is often highlighting to the reader that what is being offered is representation and not reality. All the resolutions of Fielding's novels (*Joseph Andrews* (1742), *Tom Jones* (1749) and *Amelia* (1751)) reveal a doubleness of intention: whilst the author exploits romance structures to create happy endings, implicit in the texts is satire on the unreality and false expectations that such codes promote. Romantic resolutions can also serve as a critique of reality in which it becomes fictionally impossible to portray a 'realistic' representation of culture in which the good are rewarded and the bad punished. The romantic ending of *Amelia* (1751) strains plausibility because the foregoing grim analysis of contemporary society has stressed that goodness is a virtue of fidelity for the heroine, but also a trait that can offer her little protection in society. Like satire, romance elements are incorporated with story lines rather than being dominated by them: the accommodation is not always a balanced one. Certainly the ending of *Amelia* promotes doubleness which denies closure, offering instead variable readings of the novel as a structural failure or as a sustained satire reinforced by the romance structure.

Tobias Smollett (1721–71), like Richardson and Fielding, felt free to improvise on the form of the novel. In the Preface to *Roderick Random* he declares his distrust and rejection of romance structure which he claims 'no doubt, owes its origin to ignorance, vanity and superstition'. However, contrary to avowed intentions, romance structures inform Smollett's texts to such a level that they invite other readings. Consider how resolution is brought about in *Roderick Random* (1748) and *Peregrine Pickle* (1751, rev. edn 1758), or the artificiality of the multiple marriages at the close of *Humphry Clinker* (1771). The conventions of romance form part of Smollett's satiric intention – a deliberate arbitrariness denies readings of satisfactory realistic meaning, inviting instead marvel at the plot's audacity and artifice and pointing to the dysfunction of society (see Michael Rosenblum's 'Smollett and the Old Convention' reprinted in Damrosch, 1988). Like nearly every other eighteenth-century novelist, Smollett neither manages to free himself from or fully reject romance structures: exile, recognition, restoration, the staples of romance plotting are deeply embedded in his texts.

Romance elements have been most thoroughly associated with a woman's tradition of writing. However, women writers were often critical of the pernicious influence of romantic fiction on impressionable young females. In *The Cry*, Sarah Fielding and Jane Collier offer a criticism of romantic illusion while in *The Female Quixote* (1752), Charlotte Lennox presents an anti-romance through the medium of satire. The message of romantic plots – the virtuous heroine is rewarded with marriage, social position and, usually, economic security – undoubtedly reinforces certain ideological imperatives. But romance offers a complex response to women's experience which, far from offering single readings, in fact promotes doubleness and reflexivity. While romance elements reinforce the social formulation (by emphasizing love and marriage as woman's lot), forming arguably a dangerous form of escapism based on false expectations, they also serve as a critique of culture prompting the question: why should women want to escape their social role? In other words, romance offers a vehicle for oblique criticism of woman's lot. These two imperatives for instruction and escapism do not neatly divide. Consider the Cinderella structure and didactic intent of Fanny Burney's *Evelina* (1778) and particularly, how the text cannot fully justify the limits of the solutions it endorses (discussed below, pp. 220–3).

## Texts, authors, contexts

### Defoe

Daniel Defoe (1660–1731) wrote *Robinson Crusoe*, his first novel and generally considered to be the first English novel, in 1719. When Defoe turned to novel writing he was nearly 60 years old and the main inducement for his adoption of the form was financial. Within the space of five years Defoe wrote all his major novels: a second volume of *Robinson Crusoe* (*Farther Adventures*) appeared a few months later, *The Adventures of Captain Singleton* in 1720, *Moll Flanders*, *Colonel Jack*, and *A Journal of the Plague Year* (a fictionalized account of the Great Plague) all in 1722, *Memoirs of a Cavalier* and *Roxana* in 1724. Behind him was a prolific literary career and wealth of experience. In all Defoe wrote over 500 separate works including pamphlets, journals, poetry, satires, pseudo-biographies, ghost stories, historicized accounts, travel books, essays on projects and economics, history, crime, urban affairs and politics. Apart from this Defoe also held many occupations as a merchant, business man and government spy, to name but a few. The failure of many of his business ventures (including bankruptcy) did nothing to abate his championship of the business ethic which was closely linked to his Dissenting religious background: see Defoe's *Review* (1704–13), *The Complete English Tradesman* (1726) and the *Tour through the Whole Island of Great Britain* (1724–6).

    *Robinson Crusoe* did not emerge in isolation. Defoe as a popularist writer was astute enough to draw upon established forms and a ready-made readership for prose accounts, such as travelogues, Puritan spiritual autobiographies, popular rogue tales and criminal autobiographies. *Robinson Crusoe* represents a story that is both representative and exceptional, where the hero is both the exponent of mercantile values and a marginal figure who has very slight connection with the experiences of the average eighteenth-century reader. This is no back-to-nature book; rather it is a novel about 'home', about eighteenth-century commercial culture. What makes Crusoe believable is a balance between representative significance (a re-enactment of the ubiquitous theme of quest and survival that is the source of epic) and his apparent individuality (created through a narrative that records the minutiae of everyday existence). Turn to the opening paragraphs of the text and note how Defoe through the personal pronoun 'I' and the piling on of details and information creates the impression that because we learn so much about him the speaker must be 'real'. This plethora of circumstantial detail is a characteristic of all Defoe's fiction. Now turn to any passage of description of the exotic (for example, Crusoe's island or Roxana's oriental dance) and note how unreal and fantastic Defoe's writing can become.

Realism in a Defoe novel is invoked through the consciousness of the speaker.

> and I went through into Bartholomew Close, and then turned round to another passage that goes into Long Lane, so away from Charterhouse Yard and out into St. John Street, then, crossing into Smithfield, went down Chick Lane and into Field Lane to Holborn Bridge, when mixing with the crowd of people usually passing there, it was not possible to have been found out; and thus I enterprised my second sally into the world. (Defoe, *Moll Flanders*, [1722] 1978, p. 191)

This is an account of Moll's second crime. The stylistic method is essentially the same as the description of her first theft. While the reader responds to Moll as a tangibly 'real' narrator, she/he also finds it hard to believe how the heroine can remember events so precisely with such a vast amount of factual detail. Unlike Crusoe, Moll does not keep a journal. Defoe does not find it necessary to explain the implausibility of such a photographic memory which manages with apparent ease to stretch over such a vast period of time. This is fictional 'realism' in its infancy: while Moll's story is offered as retrospective narrative, the sheer amount of information and detail that inform events (what we could term Defoe's 'realism') suggest immediacy and the here and now. Moll seems to be able to close the gap between the distant past and the reported present in a manner that the reader often finds implausible. Later first-person narrators (for example, Pip in *Great Expectations*) supplement fact and detail with the stylistics of reflection and a self-conscious dressing up of memories as events.

All Defoe's novels offer retrospective accounts. Retrospective narrative re-creates a representation of how imagination works. In creating their stories, characters are attempting to place order on disparate experience and, in the process, make sense of it – in other words, create a story. In the gaps and fissures between act and recollection, Defoe's narratives enact a facsimile of how memory works. Defoe is a far more sophisticated writer than is often first perceived and his relationship with his characters is often ironic. Structurally Defoe's narratives are far from realistic; present is an element of wish-fulfilment deeply embedded in romance plots which the adherence to mercantile methodology works against. What a Defoe novel offers is not a 'mirror' of reality, but realism in the manner in which characters perceive significance.

It should be clear by now that the speaking 'I' of a Defoe novel is not the voice of the author speaking directly to the reader. In fact, Defoe's relation to his narrator is at times ironic and subversive. This is most obvious with his woman narrators whom he sees both as exponents of a capitalist economy and as victims of that ideology (see *Moll Flanders* and *Roxana*). Why, then, does Defoe take such pains to represent his fictions as truth and his narratives as the words of his heroes or heroines? Refer to any 'Preface' of a Defoe novel and you will become aware that the author is at pains to claim factuality for his narratives: words like 'true life', 'history', 'adventures of' are intended to encourage the reader to see the world through the narrator's eyes. This attempt at realism, which has been claimed by Ian Watt to be the hallmark of the genre, has also a more specific cultural context. Realism in fiction during the eighteenth century stems, in no small part, from attempts to legitimize the genre as a distinctive literary form. Until the mid-eighteenth century, no clear distinction between prose as factual or imaginative emerges. The novel's development parallels the emergence of two discourses whereby prose becomes categorized as either journalistic or fictional. What has recently been termed 'faction' (a hybrid form of novelistic reportage) was a distinction that would not have been clear, or seemed necessary, in the early eighteenth century.

Defoe's *Robinson Crusoe* takes as its imaginative starting-point Alexander Selkirk's experiences as a castaway and his *Journal of the Plague Year* offers a mixing of historical prose sources and a fictionalization of historical occurrences. Defoe's style of pseudo-autobiography reflects a prevalent tendency of the early novel to disguise prurience as moral instruction: note the popularity of French romances, particularly *histoire scandaleuse* which as the name suggests offered accounts of real or fictitious historical figures with an emphasis on what was scandalous in their lives (Defoe's *Roxana* is indebted to this form). By presenting stories as 'real life', Defoe imbues his texts with connotations of usefulness and moral soundness (thus developing the format of Puritan spiritual autobiographies). The deliberate masking of fiction as fact is one strategy employed by the author to counterbalance the novel's early reputation as immoral, fantastic, salacious, time-wasting, and escapist. Now, turn to Swift's *Gulliver's Travels* and consider how Swift satirizes the basic presumption of verisimilitude associated with the novel as a reading experience.

## Swift

Jonathan Swift (1667–1745) wrote as well as *Gulliver's Travels* (1726) political pamphlets, journalism (he edited and wrote for *The Examiner* 1710–11), satire and burlesques (*The Battle of the Books*, 1704, and *A Tale of a Tub*, 1704), a journal (*Journal to Stella*, 1710–13), letters and poetry. In the 1720s and 1730s he became increasingly involved in Irish affairs and central as a political writer on the Irish scene: *The Drapier's Letters* appearing in 1724 and *A Modest Proposal* in 1729.

*Gulliver's Travels* is Swift's only novel (or more correctly we should term it an anti-novel) and like all early fiction it is experimental and unplanned in structure and characterization. Indeed, Swift shows little or no interest in giving Gulliver an inner life and his character's lack of growth and inconsistencies are motivated by an overriding satiric imperative which dominates the narrative. What we might on first reading regard as 'realistic' features of the novel – for example, Gulliver's unadorned prose style and the amount of circumstantial detail – are present for parodic purposes: in these instances satire on the travelogue format and the values it implied. *Gulliver's Travels* offers many layers of reading: as a satire on contemporary politics and culture, as a traveller's tale, as a Christian apology, and as a Utopian fantasy. Swift is well aware of the metaphoric potential of the travel theme – in *Gulliver's Travels* he takes the idea of the voyage to its limits and over the edge. What Swift's representation of somewhere else does is to point obliquely to the real fictional element in most eighteenth-century travel literature (including *Robinson Crusoe*) which insists on the validity of empirical investigation and purports to be factual reportage.

Refer now to the opening paragraph of *Gulliver's Travels*. On first reading, our narrator Gulliver is offering the reader details of his history which are intended to support his claim that his adventures are fact. This is the procedure that Defoe follows in the opening of *Robinson Crusoe*. Swift exploits this realistic intention through Gulliver's detailed and precise account of his early education and familial relationships. Now, read on to the end of Chapter 1 and note the preciseness of Gulliver's recollections and the emphasis he places on fortune as an explanation for what might otherwise be considered to be implausible connections. Swift is offering a parody of the plain-speaking narrator of travel literature. The opening passages of *Gulliver's Travels* establish the tone of the novel with its mockery of the way eighteenth-century travel stories operate through a mass of circumstantial information to give the appearance of verisimilitude. Swift's parody closely follows the format of travel literature, right down to the inclusion of empirical methodology suggested by references to maps and nautical positions.

Throughout the novel, Swift uses Gulliver as a foil. Gulliver is not simply the voice of Swift; often the intention is ironic. Sometimes Gulliver reflects what Swift believes as, for example, when he attempts to bring about peace between Lilliput and Blefuscu; but more often Swift's irony is directed at his hero in order to reflect Gulliver's blindness of vision. Wearing spectacles carries metaphoric implications in this novel (see Rogers, 1985).

Consider now this extract from Gulliver's conversation with the King of Brobdingnag on the uses of gunpowder:

> I told him of an invention discovered between three and four hundred years ago, to make a certain power, into a heap of which the smallest spark of fire falling, would kindle the whole in a moment, although it were as big as a mountain, and make it all fly up in the air together, with a noise and agitation greater than thunder .... The King was struck with horror at the description I had given of those terrible engines, and the proposal I had made. He was amazed how so impotent and grovelling an insect as I (these were his expressions) could entertain such inhuman ideas, and in so familiar a manner as to appear wholly unmoved at all the scenes of blood and desolation .... A strange effect of *narrow principles* and *short views*! (Swift, *Gulliver's Travels*, [1726] 1986, pp. 174–5)

What is the tone? Does Swift endorse Gulliver's eulogization of the potential of gunpowder or is the author's satire directed at his hero's sense of self-importance, jingoism and short-sightedness? How close is the relationship between author and character at this point? Can we claim that Swift identifies with his hero, or is the intention to let him damn himself with his own words? There is a surplus meaning to

Gulliver's words and Swift's irony points to an opposing meaning to his hero's reading of significance. The overall effect is bathetic comedy. Note that Gulliver's motive for imparting the secrets of gunpowder to the King is to bolster his own self-importance (bear in mind the ratio of scale) and also how our hero is dumbfounded when his offer is refused. Surely the '*narrow principles*' and '*short views!*' that Gulliver accuses the King of holding are in fact his own? Gulliver reveals what we would now call a Eurocentric perspective: an inability to view difference in any terms except his European norms. Here the speaker is the butt of Swift's satire and a foil to promote a counter-argument to the one that Gulliver voices. Now read Chapters 6 and 7 (Part II) fully and consider where Swift is endorsing the norms of European politics and culture and where he is satirizing them.

The reader is also under attack in *Gulliver's Travels* – references to the 'gentle reader' are more than a polite address (see Rawson, 1983). Swift mocks the reader's expectation of seeking a story that will be anything but gentle. He also satirizes the expected relationship established in novels of intimacy between the adventurer hero and the reader. Structurally the novel subverts the symbolic potential of the journey as a metaphor for life and progress. The repeated pattern of outward movement and return to the same locale established by the four-part structure suggests circularity rather than linear progression. By the end of Part 4, Gulliver believes that he has gained spiritual enlightenment but his utopian projections induced by his experiences with the Huoyhnhnms are of questionable practical application and even absurd. The reader is justified in querying the validity of the hero's vision and the possibility of insanity in Gulliver's conclusions. At the close of the novel, Swift's satire suggests yet another example of where author and character are considerably distanced in meaning, interpretation and intention.

Writers like Swift and Pope supported an Augustan value system (*c.* 1660–1740). Broadly speaking, Augustan literature reflects the values of order, moderation, balance, harmony and decorum, and its dominant idiom is satire. Because Augustan writers valued the concept of order in both form and content they were also obsessed by its absence – hence the emphasis on the themes of madness and chaos. For a writer like Swift the individualism that the novel championed smacks of the impolite. The communal and cohesive intentions that underpin Augustan art seemed in the early eighteenth century to be challenged by this new breed of hybrid prose which sought to justify as 'realism' a personal and, in the view of Swift, highly dubious (because subjectivity is always open to distortion) interpretation of reality. In terms of early eighteenth-century cultural and literary values, *Robinson Crusoe* and *Gulliver's Travels* form part of a debate about the value and status of literature which is both generic and culturally inscribed.

## Richardson

Samuel Richardson (1689–1761) embodied the Puritan virtues of self-help, self-reliance and worldly success. His achievements offer an equivalent 'real-life' version of Defoe's *The Complete English Tradesman*. Richardson was a self-made man who received little formal education but was proud of his bourgeois credentials. His novels are noticeable in comparison to Fielding's for their lack of classical allusions and negative portraits of aristocratic figures such as Mr B— and Lovelace. Richardson entered novel writing after a successful career as a publisher and printer. Novels, in Richardson's case, start as the product of his business interests as a publisher: *The Apprentice Vade Mecum* (1733), a book of advice on morals and conduct was written to cater for a popular audience and *Letters ... to and for Particular Friends* (1741) which forms the germ for *Pamela* to fill a niche in the market. *Pamela* was published 1740–1 when Richardson was 51 and thereafter followed *Clarissa* (8 vols, 1747–9) and *Sir Charles Grandison* (7 vols, 1753–4). It is hardly surprising given Richardson's business acumen that his novels take the form of epistolary fiction. Women novelists had already established a ready-made market for letter novels. Where Richardson develops the letter novel form is in his emphasis on characterization, representation of psychological drama and strong moral emphasis. Prior to Richardson letter novels often under the guise of real-life accounts in the form of *histoire scandaleuse* comprised of salacious material and erotic fantasies: for example, Eliza Haywood's *A Spy upon the Conjurer* (1725) and *The Invisible Spy* (1754).

Richardsonian realism derives from the basic premise of confession in the letter form. Epistolary fiction exploits the private nature of letter-writing to promote a relationship of intimacy and revelation between reader and text. Note the length of a Richardsonian novel, promoted by minuteness of observation from the central correspondent. Such detail gives verisimilitude to the central consciousness of the narrator, but realism is based on a premise of suspended disbelief on the part of the reader. The sheer amount of information that we are offered, the reportage of the speech of others, and the actual amount of time that Pamela (the heroine of Richardson's first novel) would have had to spend writing letters would, in reality, deny the time for any action to occur. Pamela writes six letters on her wedding day, which if viewed realistically would have entailed her spending most of her wedding day writing.

Pamela's status as an exemplary heroine is based upon the premise that she is a dutiful daughter. Here is a fairly representative extract from the text.

> What business had he to send *me one way*, to his wicked house, and vile woman, *when I hoped to go another, to you*, my dear, worthy parents! *The very first fellow*! I scorn his reflection! He is mistaken in your Pamela. You know what I writ about Mr Williams; and if you, and my mother, and my own heart acquit me, what care I? – I had almost said. But these are after reflections. At the reading of his letter, I was quite broken-hearted.
>
> Alas for me! said I to myself, what a fate is mine, to be thus thought artful, and forward, and ungrateful! when all I intended was to preserve my innocence; and when all the poor little shifts, which his superior and wicked wit and cunning have rendered ineffectual, were forced upon me in my own necessary defence! (Richardson, *Pamela*, [1740–1] 1980, p. 204)

Drama is represented by the retelling of events through Pamela's consciousness: note the representation of movement and contesting directions when ostensibly the heroine's position is static. There is an element of self-interrogation in Pamela's monologic justification which is reinforced by the colloquialism of language, questions, rhetorical flourishes, exclamation marks and varying typographical styles; all intended to reinforce a sense of immediacy and conflict when structurally the heroine is retelling past events. However, the impression is not clearly one of retrospective narrative. The drama recreated through Pamela's projections of herself is one of active participation. By including commentary on retrospective events by comments such as 'I had almost said' and 'these are after reflections', Richardson promotes Pamela as an active commentator on her own virtue and as a passive spectator providing commentary on what she wished to have said. By these means, Richardson attempts to represent Pamela as an exemplar of passive femininity, whose role as an active proponent of these virtues is at once undercut by her writerly silence. Femininity as an ideal provided novelists with a number of problems, the most obvious of which being how to represent passivity as a virtue while needing a heroine who does things in order to provide a story line. Pamela's letter-writing style, with its immediacy and often inelegant drawing attention to her own fictionalizing on past events, is the way Richardson attempts to promote feminine passivity as an active virtue.

Whilst Richardson's epistolary method brought a new level of psychological realism to the novel it also proved problematic with regards to plausibility. Contrast Richardson's approach with Smollett's in *The Expedition of Humphry Clinker* (1771), where the epistolary form is expanded in order to shed an ironic light on the act of interpretation. The basic difficulty contesting Richardson's realistic imperative is that everything has to come from Pamela's letters. For example, consider the characterization of Mr B— and Mrs Jewkes – on one level these are psychologically realistic (given Pamela's mental state) but neither is realistic as a three-dimensional character. Following the logic of the text the reader becomes unclear about these characters; if Mr B— is as bad as Pamela depicts him then why does she marry him, and if we accept her reasons then we are forced to question whether such a radical reformation of character is possible? While the reader has to conclude that there may be other valid points of view (which counteract Pamela's reading), these are never given full voice. Also the situation that Pamela finds herself in and the outcome of her trials is highly unrealistic: the basic premise of a young innocent woman imprisoned by an evil tempter and his cohort predicts the structures of gothic fantasy and draws upon a tradition of fairy-tale and romance in a highly improbable restoration of the heroine through marriage.

Letters xxxi–xxxii reveal most glaringly where Richardson's realism is still finding its feet. Pamela asserts her full awareness of her dangerous situation and need to escape ('I'm in an evident hurry!', p. 121) and then goes on to write 'VERSES *on my going away*'. Obviously here Richardson's desire to underline his moral message works against plausibility. By page 123 (same letter) the epistolary medium breaks down completely.

> It is also to be observed, that the messenger of her letters to her father, who so often pretended business that way, was an implement in his master's hands, and employed by him for that purpose; and always gave her letters first to him, and his master used to open

and read them, and then send them on; by which means, as he hints to her [as she observes in one of her letters, p116], he was no stranger to what she wrote. Thus every way was the poor virgin beset. (*Pamela*, p. 123)

At this point the novelist is forced to interject and give the reader additional information necessary to understand the plot.

By the 1740s there is a discernible change in the current of feeling reflected in a concern for literature to be a conduit whereby the reader's relationship with the text becomes one of empathy and moral improvement. Richardson does not instigate such changes; rather he reflects broader cultural trends and develops on the achievements of women novelists who use romance to subvert the peripheral subject position of women within public discourse. With Richardson the novel becomes respectable. However, these changes do not go unchallenged: for example, Fielding's novels and Johnson's *Rasselas* (1759) maintain an adherence to Augustan principles and reveal a mistrust of the subjectivity inherent in sentimental fiction in general.

Much of the mid-century debate regarding the form and purpose of the novel revolved around discussion of the respective merits and shortcomings of Richardson's and Fielding's fiction. Both writers were viewed as establishing divergent paths for the novel to develop upon. Dr Johnson famously phrased the moral debate regarding the contesting merits of Richardsonian and Fieldingesque fiction as being 'between a man who knew how a watch was made, and a man who tells the hour by looking at the dial-pate' (Boswell's *Life of Johnson*, ed. R.W. Chapman, corr. J.D. Fleeman, Oxford University Press, London, p. 389). Elsewhere, Johnson voices widespread anxieties regarding novel-reading and the role models provided by mid-century fiction (see *The Rambler*, 31 March 1750). In its broadest terms the division between Richardson and Fielding is represented by insider and outsider perspectives, but such distinctions are also at times undermined by narrative patterns which subvert avowed moral intentions. Now, turn to Fielding and assess his different approach to novel writing and its claim to moral instruction.

## Fielding

Henry Fielding (1707–54) was a professional writer who combined a literary career with a legal profession as a Bow Street magistrate, Justice of the Peace for Westminster and Middlesex (from 1748 and 1749) and magistrate for the Western Assizes. Fielding's literary career reflects the developing role of the writer in the eighteenth century and the situation by mid-century when the writer now claimed professional status and recognition as such (see Dr Johnson's famous letter to the Earl of Chesterfield on the insufficiency of patrons which voiced the demise of the patronage system of literary production). Fielding started his literary career as a poet and dramatist. The strong vein of political satire to be found in his plays *The Grub Street Opera* (1731), *The Historical Register* (1737) and *Eurydice Hissed* (1737) did much to incur government displeasure and inaugurate the Licencing Act (1737).

Thereafter Fielding turned to journalism, satires, social pamphlets and novel-writing, producing *Shamela*, an anti-novel, in 1741, *Joseph Andrews* (1742), *Tom Jones* (1749) and *Amelia* (1751). In his novels Fielding attempts to create an amalgam which could combine satire and comedy in order to create a new language that he could call his own and a mode that would reflect contemporary life while retaining the force and wit produced by the Scriblerians and prominent in his own plays. Indeed, dramatic structures are deeply embedded in Fielding's novels.

*Tom Jones* does not offer the hero of the title as the narrative centre. Consider some of the reasons why this should be? The eclectic and ambitious plotting formula (including picaresque, romance, epic, and journey formats) might at first lead the reader to consider whether Fielding is sure of exactly what he wants to do in this novel. It is through the narrator–reader relationship that Fielding converts what might otherwise have been a disparate conglomeration of stylistic strands into a social reading experience. And, in this stress on art as a sociable exercise, Fielding reflects his debt to Augustan values. This is a very different reading experience from the ones we encounter in a Richardson or Defoe novel.

The most important character in *Tom Jones* is the narrator. It is through the omniscient third-person narrator that the reader gains knowledge or is denied information.

> THE reader will be pleased to remember, that, at the beginning of the second book of this history, we gave him a hint of our intention to pass over several large periods of time, in which nothing happened worth of being recorded in a chronicle of this kind.
>
> In so doing, we do not only consult our own dignity and ease but the good and advantage of the reader... (Fielding, *Tom Jones*, [1749] 1966, Book III, Chapter 1, p. 121)

With Fielding's *Tom Jones* we often get the impression of the narrator treading a fine line between actuality and fiction. The narrator directs the reader in the ways to react and interpret. In Book x, Chapter 8 the reader is asked to 'be pleased to remember' and 'to look a little back'. Here life as fiction and life as actuality (outside the covers of the novel) are mixed. Is the reader to look back in 'real times' or back through the pages of the book? The ambivalence here suggests an attempt at patterning wherein life and fiction corroborate while still acknowledging the essentially artificial basis of fiction. Note the narrator's varied use of tenses in Book x, Chapter 8 as he describes events which have led up to this point but treats the immediate events as though they were happening before his eyes. Possibly here we have an example of where Fielding's dramatic training transposes his fiction – the overall impression is one of fictional descriptions as an ongoing performance.

Now, read on and consider other passages of narrative commentary in the novel. Note the tone of playfulness established between narrator and reader. The digressive tendency of the narrator seems to draw away from development of plot line or character analysis. This is deliberate. What is being offered is an essentially external view of character: Tom Jones represents mankind, essentially well intentioned but flawed and apt to fail. The narrative relationship forces the reader to adopt an overview rather than any subjective relationship between character and reader. The narrator functions to promote a deliberate comic distancing (consider the significance of the stage-life analogy in Book VII, Chapter 1) and ensure that the reader never gets close to the drama being enacted on the page.

Now, turn to the chapter headings and note how the author is directing our responses. We are encouraged to be variably 'surprised', 'puzzled', 'brought into danger', offered 'five pages of paper', or 'little or nothing', withheld information from, allowed to confirm our suspicions, congratulate ourselves on our correct reading and, finally, bid farewell. Why should the author draw such attention to his own ingenuity, show us his literary cleverness so blatantly, and disrupt the story-line by offering tangential readings? One function of these devices is to make clear to the reader that it is not the author's intention to immerse us wholly in his fictional world. Another function is to promote a comic relationship between text and reader. These strategies are intended to establish a reader relationship with the text that is public and humorous rather than private and confessional.

Fielding's intention to 'classicize' the novel is reflected in his drawing upon epic themes and the framework of epic to offer comment on his own times. *Tom Jones* (1749) offers a vision that is panoramic – the novel takes the reader on a romp around the countryside and in the process enacts a latter-day Odyssey with the intention of offering an expansive view of the contemporary culture. In this novel Fielding exploits the epic convention of the journey as a metaphor for discovery. Mock heroic scenes (see Partridge's battle with his wife, the feast at Upton) are primarily intended to be comic; what is being mocked is not the values of classical literature, but the heroic diminishment of latter-day life. In *Tom Jones* we are offered a commentary on England of 1745, the love story of Tom Jones and Sophie Western, and a fairy-tale unravelling of disguised paternity.

Fielding's classicizing on the picaresque tradition is part of a programme to give the novel status, to bring the genre within the remit of 'polite' literature. His novels (rather than offering anything radically new which rejects the literature of the past) reflect a desire to make the novel a continuation of established forms and proven achievements in literature. Fielding is often termed a conservative-innovator. Whilst inheriting Swift's and Pope's literary values, Fielding was forced to acknowledge that times had changed since they wrote. In his fiction Fielding is attempting to make the novel a medium suitable to transmit classical values and represent the contemporary world.

## Burney

Fanny Burney (1752–1840) is best known as a novelist but she was also a prolific letter-writer, diary and journal-keeper. Her *Early Diary 1768–1778* (1889) reveals the pressures combatant upon a woman with literary aspirations in the late eighteenth century and offers a lively portrait of the social and literary world of the day; and the later *Diary and Letters...1778–1840* (1842–6) recounts Burney's experiences as a court official and offers a first-hand account of the Napoleonic era.

All of Burney's novels take as their theme the important marriage choice of the heroine but there is also a noticeable enlargement of scale, extended geographical range, and accentuated analysis of social convention from *Evelina* (1778), *Cecilia* (1782) and *Camilla* (1796) to *The Wanderer: or Female Difficulties* (1814). Burney's importance as one of the first 'respectable' professional woman novelists is reflected by the income she gained from her works (*Evelina* sold for 20 guineas, *Cecilia* for £250, the copyright of *Camilla* earned her £1,000, whilst her last novel *The Wanderer* earned her £1,500). Burney offered a model for later women novelists (cf. Jane Austen, Charlotte Brontë, Elizabeth Gaskell) of a 'respectable' writer who established literature as a viable profession for the genteel woman and one whose success did much to counteract the risqué reputation associated with women writers of the Restoration and early eighteenth century (cf. Aphra Behn, Delivierie Manely, Eliza Haywood). In many respects (in both subject matter and status) Fanny Burney predicts the position of the nineteenth-century woman novelist.

*Evelina* (1778) was published anonymously and was an immediate popular success. The theme of Fanny Burney's first novel is that of a young lady's entry into society. *Evelina* in theme and context reveals a debt to Eliza Haywood's *The History of Miss Betsy Thoughtless* (1751) with the emphasis on romantic love and the choices open to marriageable young women. The plot of *Evelina* is quite simple. As the full title reveals, it is the story of 'The History of a Young Lady's Entrance into the World'. What Burney offers is a contemporary version of the Cinderella story. The irony unmasked in *Evelina* is the duplicity in eighteenth-century sexual politics. While the reward for the heroine remaining pure is a happy marriage, Burney's analysis of social life reveals that it is this very trait that leaves women vulnerable. Whilst Burney's novels represent strong females who function in their own right as centres of interest, they are also shown as having to seek masculine approval and protection in order to maintain their purity. Purity becomes an ambivalent fictional and social ideal. Burney's own immersion in the ideology of romantic love is reflected in her maintenance of purity as an ideal in her fiction. But this is tempered by a developing awareness of the limitations and restrictions that society places on the value of innocence. Her last novel, subtitled 'or Female Difficulties', emphasizes this theme of vulnerability. (See Unit 23, pp. 615–16, for a further discussion of *Evelina*.)

Cecilia, the heroine of Burney's second novel, enters the world of fashionable life, in the phrase of Margaret Anne Doody, as a parodic man (Introduction to the World's Classic series, p. xvi). Like Evelina, her forerunner, she is also an orphan, but Cecilia is economically independent. The father figures in the form of her guardians all prove to be ineffectual, if not openly threatening. Like *Evelina* the world of *Cecilia* (1782) is one in which women are vulnerable due to their innocence, but equally a world in which purity is the mark of their worth. The masquerade scene (a trope in eighteenth-century fiction used to offer carnivalesque inversions of the social order) reveals the true position of Cecilia in her society.

Her expectations of entertainment were not only fulfilled but surpassed; the variety of dresses, the medley of characters, the quick succession of figures, and the ludicrous mixture of groupes, kept her attention unwearied: while the conceited efforts at wit, the total thoughtlessness of consistency, and the ridiculous incongruity of the language with the appearance, were incitements to surprise and diversions without end. Even the local cant of, *Do you know me? Who are you?* and *I know you*; with the sly pointing of the finger, the arch nod of the head, and the pert squeak of the voice, though wearisome to those who frequent such assemblies, were, to her unhackneyed observation, additional subjects of amusement. (Burney, *Cecilia*, [1782] 1990, p. 106)

The assembly displays an array of costumes revealing characters' true natures (the devil and chimney-sweep for example) and masks which suspend social decorum and incite licence through the taking on of other identities. What the masquerade reveals is that there is no one way of interpreting – identities are fluctuating and unstable. Naming (initially introduced through the theme of the codicil to the will) should provide a means for definition. At the masquerade the arbitrariness of naming is uncovered, and for the heroine an experience of the fluctuating nature of female identity highlights how femininity proves to be a precarious defence.

   The masquerade scene is thematically important and forms a base in the novel for variant readings of appearance and reality. Cecilia is the only person present at the masquerade who is not in costume. On a psychological level the scene gives expression to the heroine's vulnerable position within society and the paradoxes of purity and knowledge which culminate in the mad scene (Vol. V, Book X, Chapter VII). Thematically this scene is the outcome of Delvine's misinterpretation of Cecilia's motives and meanings. The masquerade scene is given full significance in Cecilia's flight into gothic escape when female identity and non-identity take on roaming expression. Whilst the logic of the plot makes this scene the outcome of Cecilia's fear of violence being done in her name, the text reveals alternative readings expressing real female fears regarding woman's non-identity in social terms.

To understand the work of eighteenth-century women novelists, it is essential to have some awareness of the context in which they lived and wrote, and the restrictions placed upon them as writers. As the century progressed literature by women attained a degree of authority by conforming to established ideas regarding what female style, subject matter and message should be. The term 'familiar style' or 'feminine style', an idea popularized by Richardson, was a highly codified term expressing cultural assumptions regarding women in general. It was assumed that women's fictional style naturally expressed feelings artlessly and simply. In other words, women's fiction was considered confessional and not the production of studied application. However, women's experience could not be neatly pocketed within such stylistic and cultural generalities. Burney's novels, in their rendering of how a young heroine should behave, reveal the subject's essential powerlessness and offer a subtle expression of the unfairness of this situation. The reward for the heroine in Burney's fiction is marriage, but the texts reveal the diminishment that women have to undergo to achieve this status.

   Burney writes in a period of revolutionary change and this context informs her fiction. She married an impoverished French émigré in 1793 (Alexandre d'Arblay) and experienced first-hand the ferment of continental unrest. Burney's response to the radical ideas and protest engendered by the social upheavals of the closing decades of the century was one of conservative feminism (see the portrait of Elinor Jorrdorel in *The Wanderer*). All of Burney's novels end by supporting marriage as the best alternative for the lone woman, but they also chart a darkening vision of the perils and snares that threaten the single woman in a hostile world.

An important theme in Burney's fiction is a young woman's entry into society. Her fiction can be read as novels of passage which reveal subtexts of anxieties and fear regarding the cost of conformity. The solution that the novelist proposes is marriage. How should we read such a conclusion? On one level, Burney reflects a widespread eighteenth-century tendency to incorporate romance structures within realistic narrative, a tendency that was assumed to be particularly prevalent in women novelists due to their saturation in the ideology of romantic love. Thus, it could be argued that Burney's fiction is a conservative endorsement of patriarchal culture, but she is also being realistic in her appraisal of the limited options and the vulnerable position of the single woman in eighteenth-century society.

Burney's texts, with their realistic imperatives and romantic solutions, pull in two directions. Their realistic assessment of a woman's position follows a strong didactic emphasis in eighteenth-century women's fiction which is itself supported by conduct literature of the period, while their vein of wish-fulfilment and the solutions proposed suggest attempts to escape such experience in their advocacy of romance structures. There is a double edge to Burney's fiction (and eighteenth-century women's fiction in general) of both endorsement and protest. The contradictions inherent in the texts offer the reader a means to analyze the inscription of the woman writer in the construction of gender roles and their ideological imperatives during the eighteeth century.


## Austen

Jane Austen (1775–1817) by comparison with Fanny Burney appears to have led an uneventful life: she was born, the sixth of seven children, in Steventon, Hampshire (1775) where her father was the incumbent rector. In 1801 the family moved to Bath and later, after her father's death, to Southampton (1806); from there she moved to Chawton, seat of her brother's estate in 1809 (and where *Mansfield Park*, *Emma* and *Persuasion* were written), and in 1817 died of Addison's disease. The period when Austen wrote her major fiction was a time of revolutionary political upheavals, rapid industrialization, a transitional phase in literature and currents of thought (from the social orientation of the eighteenth-century novel to Romanticism with its stress on the isolated and alienated individual), and a period of renewed radical feminism in the 1790s with the works of Mary Wollstonecraft. Modern criticism has rewritten the popular nineteenth-century seamless image of the novelist as an endorser of the status quo but there is still debate regarding how far Austen ingested the radical ideas of her times. For example, Marilyn Butler (1975) sees Austen as a conservative thinker writing in reaction to the radicalism of novels in the 1790s and as one who is in reaction to the traditions she inherits. Another view is offered by Meenakshi Mukherjee

(1991) who suggests that her heroines' attitudes and actions accord with Mary Wollstonecraft's views on female education: for Mukherjee, Austen's novels are 'particularly striking for their refusal to eroticise female inanition and to promote the cult of vulnerability' (p. 10).

Walter Scott in the nineteenth century praises Austen's novels for their 'exquisite touch which renders ordinary commonplace things and characters interesting'. Scott is reflecting a commonplace belief that Austen's fiction instigates a new type of novel in the nineteenth century. What Austen's emphasis on manners creates is certain changes of focus in the novel, while at the same time drawing upon a tradition of eighteenth-century women's writing. The plots of all of Austen's novels are based on making the correct marriage; within terms of a conservative gentry ideology this theme becomes a social rather than merely a personal decision. In an Austen novel, words and modes of discourse take on a new significance as indications of how characters will act. Often Austen makes her characters expose themselves through their own words; a moral evaluation is implicit in modes of expression rather than through direct authorial or narrational comment (compare with the omniscient Fielding narrator). While both Austen and Fielding adopt a comic and ironic mode, Austen's ironic emphasis places significance upon the localities of language and situation rather than on narrative overview.

In all of Austen's fiction the established vantage point is that of the heroine, but there is a considerable distance between author and heroine. Austen does not identify herself with any of her heroines; instead her relationship with them is ironic. In *Emma* (1816), the heroine consistently misreads the significance of actions and intentions and her education takes the form of a gradual enlightenment whereby Emma faces her own shortcomings, which ultimately result in a re-evaluation and clarification of moral values.

> EMMA WOODHOUSE, handsome, clever, and rich, with a comfortable home and happy disposition, seemed to unite some of the best blessings of existence; and had lived nearly twenty-one years in the world with very little to distress or vex her. (Austen, *Emma*, [1816] 1966, p. 37)

This is the opening of *Emma* where Austen introduces the reader to the heroine. Ostensibly the narrative suggests praise, but the language is quantitative: 'seemed', 'some', 'nearly' all imply faint praise, a measured, reserved appraisal of the heroine's qualities.

> The real evils indeed of Emma's situation were the power of having rather too much her own way, and a disposition to think a little too well of herself; these were the disadvantages which threatened allay to her many enjoyments. The danger, however, was at present so unperceived, that they did not by any means rank as misfortunes with her. (*Emma*, p. 37)

The opening paragraphs involve terms of diminution to ironically reveal the aggrandizing self-image of the heroine. The comedy of the situation derives from the reader being made aware and encouraged not to identify with the heroine but align herself/himself with the authorial ironic reading. Austen's conservative values are represented through her notion of conduct which insists that the possession of property (the traditional basis of gentry status) exists in the same broad moral plane as good manners and transparent speech. Austen's irony points to the fact that Emma Woodhouse is not fulfilling these duties.

All of Austen's heroines are championed or ironically depreciated on a scale of their discriminatory powers. Fanny Price in *Mansfield Park* (1814) holds an ambiguous position within the social hierarchy of the house. However, in the pivotal play scene it is Fanny who assesses correctly the value of others. The title of this novel indicates that Austen's focus is on the country house as a symbol of values which the traditional holders of property prove to be sadly insufficient in maintaining. Austen is an apologist for the gentry class but also its critic when she deems that the values traditionally associated with their status are not being adhered to.

The term most often used to describe Austen's works is the novel of 'manners'. The cultural context of the turn-of-the-century novel suggests a much broader focus than the term 'manners' first implies. In hierarchical and highly formalized societies manners denote moral positions and therefore carry social implications. Manners, then, in Austen's fiction involves a moral code. While the world of her fiction is the country house and one or two gentry families and their interactions, the significance of their behaviour is intended to imply a microcosmic critique of the public world. The problem that an Austen novel investigates is how a scheme of values can be articulated when traditional authority has been undermined. Such changes were not new: at the beginning of the century Defoe notes with pride in his *Tour* the infiltration of gentry status by bourgeois wealth, and at mid-century Richardson's *Clarissa* investigates the significance of gentry status upon bourgeois morality. While Defoe and Richardson both write from the position of bourgeois spokesmen, Austen's focus is that of a gentry apologist realizing the full effects of these changes.

Austen's fiction is often viewed in terms of an exemplary model of woman's didactic fiction which emphasizes personal relationships in the private context of the house. Such an emphasis has in the past received unfavourable critical responses, and her texts have been denigrated for their limited range and contrasted unfavourably with the panoramic focus of the Fieldingesque and Dickensian novel. However, Austen's subject matter is a result of choice rather than a reflection of her status as a woman of limited experience and knowledge. Her own family would have provided ample source material for the inclusion of public themes of the day in her fiction if she so chose: for example she had brothers who were involved in the public affairs of the day and relatives who experienced the French Revolution first hand. That Austen chose instead to focus on woman's marriage choices from a specific class vantage point suggests that she saw personal relationships as the foundation of cultural attitudes and actions. A feminist criticism would argue that the personal is political (a view arguably underscored by Austen's fiction), and also claim that the male valuation of domestic experience has led to the marginalization of woman's texts from the critical canon. Austen's fiction builds upon a very orthodox perception of what women should be and do, but her status as a writer should be judged against her ability to use these conditions as the focus for much broader notions of truth and morality.

## BIBLIOGRAPHY

The bibliography includes recommended reading for all the above themes and authors; not all of the recommended texts have been previously mentioned.

INTRODUCTION

Aers, D., Cooke, J. and Punter, D. (1981) *Romanticism and Ideology: Studies in English Writing 1765–1830*, Routledge & Kegan Paul, London.

Altman, J.G. (1984) *Epistolarity: Approaches to a Form*, Columbia University Press, Ohio.

Ballaster, R. (1992) 'Romancing the Novel: Gender and Genre in early theories of Narrative' in *Living by the Pen: Early British Women Writers*, ed. D. Spender, Teachers College Press, New York.

Booth, W.C. (1961) *The Rhetoric of Fiction*, University of Chicago Press, Chicago.

Brophy, E. Bergen (1991) *Women's Lives and the Eighteenth-century English Novel*, University of South Florida Press, Tampa.

Bull, J.A. (1988) *The Framework of Fiction: Socio-Cultural Approaches to the Novel*, Macmillan, London.

Butler, M. (1982) *Romantics, Rebels and Reactionaries: English Literature and its Background, 1760–1830*, Oxford University Press, Oxford.

Castle, T. (1986) *Masquerade and Civilization: The Carnivalesque in Eighteenth-Century English Culture and Fiction*, Methuen, London.

Conant, M.P. (1966) *The Oriental Tale in England in the Eighteenth-Century*, Octagon Books, New York.

Damrosch Jr, Leopold (ed.) (1988) *Modern Essays on Eighteenth-century Literature*, Oxford University Press, Oxford.

Davis, L.J. (1983) *Factual Fictions*, Columbia University Press, Ohio.

Downie, J.A. (1994) *To Settle the Succession of the State: Literature and Politics, 1678–1750*, Macmillan, London.

Figes, E. (1982) *Sex and Subterfuge: Women Novelists to 1850*, Macmillan, London.

Fleishman, A. (1971) *The English Historical Novel: Walter Scott to Virginia Woolf*, Johns Hopkins University Press, Baltimore and London.

Howard, J. (1994) *Reading Gothic Fiction: A Bakhtinian Approach*, Clarendon Press, Oxford.

Humphreys, A.R. (1954) *The Augustan World: Life and Letters in Eighteenth-Century England*, Methuen, London.

Kelly, C. (1976) *The English Jacobin Novel*, Clarendon Press, Oxford.

Lukács, G. (1955, Eng. transl. 1969) *The Historical Novel*, Penguin, Harmondsworth.

Macdermott, K. (1986) 'Literature and the Grub Street myth', in *Popular Fictions: Essays in Literature and History*, ed. P. Humm et al., Methuen, London and New York.

McKeown, M. (1988) 'Generic Transformation and Social Change: Rethinking the Rise of the Novel', in *Modern Essays on Eighteenth-Century Literature*, ed. L. Damrosch, Jr, Oxford University Press, Oxford and New York.

Margolies, D. (1985) *The Novel and Society in Elizabethan England*, Croom Helm, Beckenham.

Miller, N.K. (1980) *The Heroine's Text: Readings in the French and English Novel 1722–1782*, Columbia University Press, New York.

Patey, D.L. and T. Keegan (eds) (1985) *Augustan Studies: Essays in honour of Irvin Ehrenpreis*, University of Delaware Press, Newark.

Paulson, R. (1967) *Satire and the Novel in Eighteenth-Century England*, Yale University Press, New Haven and London.

Perry, R. (1980) *Women, Letters and the Novel*, A.M.S. Press, New York.

Porter, R. (1982) *English Society in the Eighteenth Century*, Penguin, Harmondsworth.

Price, M. (1964, 1970) *To the Palace of Wisdom: Studies in Order and Energy from Dryden to Blake*, Southern Illinois University Press, Illinois.

Richetti, J.J. (1969) *Popular Fiction before Richardson: Narrative Patterns 1700–39*, Clarendon Press, Oxford.

Rogers, P. (1974) *The Augustan Vision*, Weidenfeld & Nicolson, London.

Rogers, P. (1985) *Eighteenth-Century Encounters: Studies in Literature and Society in the Age of Walpole*, Harvester Wheatsheaf, Hemel Hempstead.

Smith, G. (1984) *The Novel and Society: Defoe to George Eliot*, Batsford, London.

Spacks, P.M. (1976) *Imagining a Self: Autobiography and Novel in Eighteenth-Century England*, Harvard University Press, Cambridge, Mass.

Speck, W.A. (1977) *Stability and Strife: England 1714–1760*, Edward Arnold, London.

Spencer, J. (1986) *The Rise of the Woman Novelist: From Aphra Behn to Jane Austen*, Basil Blackwell, Oxford.

Tampkins, J.M.S. (1932, 1961) *The Popular Novel in England 1770–1800*, Methuen, London.

Todd, J. (1986) *Sensibility: An Introduction*, Methuen, London.

Todd, J. (1989) *The Sign of Angelica: Women, Writing and Fiction 1660–1800*, Virago, London.

Watt, I. (1957, 1963) *The Rise of the Novel: Studies in Defoe, Richardson and Fielding*, Penguin, Harmondsworth.

Williams, I. (ed.) (1970) *Novel and Romance 1700–1800: A Documentary Record*, Routledge & Kegan Paul, London.

Würzbach, N. (ed.) (1969) *The Novel in Letters: Epistolary Fiction in the Early English Novel, 1678–1740*, Routledge & Kegan Paul, London.


DEFOE

Bell, I.A. (1985) *Defoe's Fiction*, Croom Helm, London and Sydney.

Curtis, L.A. (1984) *The Elusive Daniel Defoe*, Visions and Barnes & Noble, London.

Defoe, Daniel (1978) *Moll Flanders*, ed. J. Mitchell, Penguin, Harmondsworth [first published 1722].

Elliott, R.C. (ed.) (1970) *Twentieth-Century Interpretations of Moll Flanders*, Prentice Hall, Englewood Cliffs.

Furbank, P.N. and W.R. Owens (1988) *The Canonization of Daniel Defoe*, Yale University Press, New Haven and London.

Hunter, J.P. (1966) *The Reluctant Pilgrim: Defoe's Emblematic Method and Quest for Form in Robinson Crusoe*, Johns Hopkins University Press, Baltimore.

Moore, J.R. (1958) *Daniel Defoe: Citizen of the Modern World*, University of Chicago Press, Chicago.

Novak, M.E. (1963) *Defoe and the Nature of Man*, Oxford University Press, Oxford.

Richetti, J.R. (1987) *Defoe's Narratives: Situation and Structures*, Clarendon Press, Oxford.

Sill, G.M. (1983) *Defoe and the Idea of Fiction, 1713–1719*, University of Delaware Press, Newark.

Starr, G.A. (1971) *Defoe and Casuistry*, Princeton University Press, Princeton.

Sutherland, J. (1968) 'The Relation of Defoe's Fiction to his Non-Fictional Writing', in *Imagined Worlds: Some English Novels and Novelists in Honour of John Butt*, ed. M. Mack and I. Gregor, Methuen, London.


SWIFT

Brady, F. (1978) 'Vexation and Diversions: Three Problems in *Gulliver's Travels*', *Modern Philology* 75.

Castle, T. (1980) 'Why the Honyhnhnms Don't Write', *Essays in Literature* 7.

Davis, J.C. (1981) *Utopia and the Ideal Society*, Cambridge University Press, Cambridge.

Donoghue, D. (1969) *Jonathan Swift: A Critical Introduction*, Cambridge University Press, Cambridge.

Downie, J.A. (1984) *Jonathan Swift: Political Writer*, Routledge & Kegan Paul, London.

Ehrenpreis, I. (1962–83) *Swift: The Man, his Works and the Age*, 3 vols, Methuen, London.

Fabricant, C. (1982) *Swift's Landscapes*, Johns Hopkins University Press, Baltimore.

Hammond, B. (1988) *Gulliver's Travels*, Open University Press, Milton Keynes and Philadelphia.

Nicolson, Marjorie (reprinted 1967) 'The Scientific Background of Swift's *Voyage to Laputa*', in *Fair Liberty Was All His Cry: A Tercentenary Tribute to Jonathan Swift*, Macmillan, London.

Nokes, D. (1985) *Jonathan Swift: A Hypocrite Reversed*, Oxford University Press, Oxford.

Probyn, C.J. (1978) *The Art of Jonathan Swift*, Vision Press, London.

Rawson, C.J. (1973) *Gulliver and the Gentle Reader: Studies in Swift and our Times*, Routledge & Kegan Paul, London.

Rawson, C.J. (ed.) (1983) *The Character of Swift's Satire: A Revised Focus*, Associated University Press, London.

Rogers, P. (1985) *Eighteenth-Century Encounters: Studies in Literature and Society in the Age of Walpole*, Harvester Wheatsheaf, Hemel Hempstead.

Swift, Jonathan (1986) *Gulliver's Travels*, ed. P. Dixon and J. Chalker, Penguin, Harmondsworth [first published 1726].

Williams, K. (1958) *Jonathan Swift and the Age of Compromise*, University of Kansas Press, Kansas.

RICHARDSON

Brissenden, R.F. (1974) *Virtue and Distress: Studies in the Novels of Sentiment from Richardson to Sade*, Macmillan, London.

Carroll, J. (ed.) (1964) *Selected Letters of Samuel Richardson*, Oxford University Press, Oxford.

Carroll, J. (ed.) (1967) *Samuel Richardson: A Collection of Critical Essays*, Prentice Hall, Englewood Cliffs.

Doody, M.A. (1974) *A Natural Passion: A Study of the Novels of Samuel Richardson*, Clarendon Press, Oxford.

Eagleton, T. (1982) *The Rape of Clarissa: Writing, Sexuality and Class Struggles in Samuel Richardson*, Blackwell, Oxford.

Hill, C. (1958) 'Clarissa Harlowe and her Times', in *Puritanism and Revolution: Studies in Interpretation of the English Revolution of the 17th Century*, Secker & Warburg, London.

Kinkead-Weeks, M. (1973) *Samuel Richardson: Dramatic Novelist*, Methuen, London.

Richardson, S. (1980) *Pamela: Or Virtue Rewarded*, ed. M.A. Doody, Penguin, Harmondsworth [first published 1740–1].

Robinson Taylor, A. (1981) 'An Odd Grotesque Figure: Samuel Richardson, and *Clarissa*', in *Male Novelists and Their Female Voices: Literary Masquerades*, Whitson Publishing Co., Troy.

Straves, S. (1985) 'Fatal Marriages? Restoration Plays Embedded in Eighteenth-Century Novels', in *Augustan Studies: Essays in Honor of Irvin Ehrenpreis*, ed. D. Lane Patey and T. Keegan, University of Delaware Press, Newark.

Todd, J. (1983) 'Pamela or the Bliss of Servitude', *British Journal of Eighteenth-Century Studies*, vol. 6, part 2, pp. 135–48.

Traugott, J. (1977) 'Clarissa's Richardson: An essay to find the Reader', in *English Literature in the Age of Disguise*, ed. M.E. Novak, University of California Press, Berkeley.

Utter, R.P. and Needham, C.B. (1936) *Pamela's Daughters*, Macmillan, New York.

FIELDING

Battestin, M.C. and Battestin, R.C. (1989) *Henry Fielding: A Life*, Routledge, London and New York.

Compton, N. (ed.) (1970) *Tom Jones: A Casebook*, Macmillan, London.

Fielding, H. (1966) *The History of Tom Jones*, ed. R.P.C. Mutter, Penguin, Harmondsworth [first published 1749].

Hatfield, G.W. (1968) *Henry Fielding and the Language of Irony*, Chicago University Press, Chicago.

Hunter, J.P. (1975) *Occasional Form: Henry Fielding and the Chains of Circumstance*, Johns Hopkins University Press, Baltimore and London.

Miller, H.K. (1976) *Henry Fielding's Tom Jones and the Romance Tradition*, University of Victoria, Victoria.

Miller, H.K. (1966) 'Some Function of Rhetoric in *Tom Jones*', *PQ* 45, pp. 209–35.

Paulson, R. (1967) *Satire and the Novel in Eighteenth-Century England*, Yale University Press, New Haven.

Paulson, R. (1978) 'Fielding in *Tom Jones*: The Historian, the Poet, and the Mythologist', in *Augustan Worlds: Essays in Honour of A.R. Humphrys*, ed. J.C. Hillson et al., Leicester University Press, Bristol.

Paulson, R. (1979) *Popular and Polite Art in the Age of Hogarth and Fielding*, Notre Dame, Indiana.

Rawson, C.J. (1972) *Henry Fielding and the Augustan Ideal Under Stress*, Routledge & Kegan Paul, London.

Wright, A. (1965) *Henry Fielding: Mask and Feast*, University of California Press, Berkeley.


BURNEY

Bloom, L.D. and E.A. (1979) 'Fanny Burney's Novels: The Retreat from Wonder', *Novel: A Forum on Fiction* 12, pp. 215–35.

Braun, M.G. (1986) 'Fanny Burney's "Feminism: Gender or Genre"', in *Fetter'd or Free: British Women Novelists, 1670–1815*, eds Mary Anne Schofield and Cecilia Mackeski, University of Georgia Press, pp. 29–39.

Burney, F. (1990) *Cecilia: A Memoir of an Heiress*, ed. P. Sabor and M.A. Doody, Oxford University Press, Oxford [first published 1782].

Devlin, D.D. (1987) *The Novels and Journals of Fanny Burney*, Macmillan, London.

Epstein, J.L. (1986) 'Fanny Burney's Epistolary Voices', *The Eighteenth Century: Theory and Interpretation* 22, pp. 162–79.

Erickson, J.P. (1964) '*Evelina* and *Betsy Thoughtless*', *Texas Studies in Literature and Language* 6, pp. 96–103.

Hemlow, J. (1950) 'Fanny Burney and the Courtesy Books', *PMLA* 65, pp. 732–61.

Lowder Newtown, J. (1976) '*Evelina*: Or the History of a Young Lady's Entrance into the Marriage Market', *Modern Language Studies* 6, pp. 48–56.

Lowder Newtown, J. (1981) *Women, Power and Subversion: Social Strategies in British Fiction, 1778–1860*, University of Georgia Press, Athens, Georgia.

Rogers, K.H. (1984) 'Fanny Burney: the Private Self and the Public Self', *International Journal of Woman's Studies*, pp. 110–17.

Simons, Judy (1987) *Fanny Burney*, Macmillan, London.

Spacks, P. Meyer (1976) 'Dynamics of Fear: Fanny Burney', in *Imagining a Self: Autobiography and Novel in Eighteenth-Century England*, Harvard University Press, Cambridge, Mass.

Straub, Kristina (1987) *Divided Fictions: Fanny Burney and Feminine Strategy*, University Press of Kentucky, Lexington.

AUSTEN

Austen, J. (1966) *Emma*, ed. R. Blythe, Penguin, Harmondsworth [first published 1816].

Bradbrook, F.W. (1968) *Jane Austen and her Predecessors*, Cambridge University Press, Cambridge.

Brown, J.P. (1979) *Jane Austen's Novels: Social Change and Literary Form*, Harvard University Press, Cambridge, Mass.

Butler, M. (1975) *Jane Austen and the War of Ideas*, Oxford University Press, London.

Fergus, J. (1983) *Jane Austen and the Didactic Novel*, Barnes & Noble, New York.

Hardy, B. (1975) *A Reading of Jane Austen*, Peter Owen, London.

Lacelles, M. (1983) *Jane Austen and her Art*, Oxford University Press, Oxford.

Moles, K. (1963) *Jane Austen's Art of Allusion*, University of Nebraska Press, Lincoln, Nebraska.

Monaghan, D. (1980) *Jane Austen: Structure and Social Vision*, Macmillan, London.

Mudrick, M. (1952) *Jane Austen: Irony as Defence and Discovery*, Princeton University Press, Princeton.

Mukherjee, M. (1991) *Jane Austen*, Macmillan, Basingstoke.

Poovey, M. (1984) *The Proper Lady and the Woman Writer: Ideology as Style in the Works of Mary Wollstonecraft, Mary Shelley and Jane Austen*, University of Chicago Press, Chicago.

Tanner, T. (1986) *Jane Austen*, Macmillan, London.

Todd, J. (1983) *Jane Austen: New Perspectives*, Holmes & Heier, New York.

# Romanticism 1780–1830

*Leon Litvack*

## Introduction

This unit engages in a thematic treatment of Romantic literature in Britain, during the period 1780–1830. It begins with a survey of the unsettling effects produced by the various 'Revolutions' at the end of the eighteenth century, and emphasizes that the reactions of writers to these events were by no means unanimous or unequivocal. These events sparked an astonishing change of sensibility, irrevocably altering established ideas about the nature of the individual in society, the role of art and the artist, and affecting the very modes of expression available for literary production. In exploring these monumental questions the unit will investigate Romantic assumptions about genre, language, and the sources of literary inspiration; it will also show how Romanticism is difficult to identify because of its eclectic nature. Throughout the unit will emphasize the energy, freshness and excitement engendered by the texts and their subjects; it will simultaneously point to uniqueness and continuity, as writers engage with the great debates initiated by their changing circumstances.

Most studies of Romantic literature concentrate on six canonical writers: Blake, Wordsworth, Coleridge, Byron, Shelley, and Keats. In attempting to communicate a legitimate understanding of the period, the contribution of these figures must be acknowledged; however, the interpretation offered benefits from an engagement with recent critical discourses including new historicism, intertextuality, psychoanalysis, deconstruction and gender studies, thus providing a useful re-examination of established texts. To them this unit adds other voices: Mary Shelley, to introduce the contribution of women to writing of the period, and Thomas De Quincey, the essayist and opium-eater, to indicate the radical departures from the established norms which distinguish the age of Romanticism.

The Romantic period has certain characteristics that set it apart from its predecessor, the age of Sensibility, and its successor, the Victorian era. It is clearly distinguished by a turbulent social and political history, which profoundly affected the lives of people across the European continent and beyond. The age was one of revolutions – not only the emancipatory turmoils in America and France, but also the massive expansion of the industrial base in Britain, which changed the whole pattern of labour and social structure.

The French and American Revolutions represented the culminations of an eighteenth-century process of agitation for social and political change. French reformatory rhetoric was inspired by Jean-Jacques Rousseau (1712–78), whose work was concerned with the love of freedom, the state of human being in society, an interest in the self, and the admiration of nature. His idea of the sovereignty of citizens as the only form of legitimate government assisted in creating a climate conducive to popular insurrection. America too contributed to the oratory of change: the increasing dissatisfaction of the colonists, and their successful resistance of British tyranny, resulted in the development of a vocabulary of liberty which appealed to radical sensibilities. After the Declaration of Independence in 1776 the American states not only created a new political system, but also drafted a Constitution and Bill of Rights which served as markers for the country's citizens' rising to their full stature and entitlement as free human beings.

While events in France and America contributed to the discourse of change, the Industrial Revolution played a more significant role in transforming the lives of the British people. Since the development of the steam engine by James Watt in 1765–9, the small-scale production of cottage industries was rapidly replaced by collective manufacturing processes, bringing many workpeople to concentrated centres of production, and actuating a revolution in both ergonomics and economics for the country. The increase in manufacturing on a large scale led to a rise in demand for labour, and thus initiated a steady flow of population towards urban centres. The conditions of employment for workers varied tremendously: some employers provided humane conditions of employment and good housing, while others provided poor accommodation and inadequate sanitation. In general the physical conditions were poor, and the situation was exacerbated by a widespread sense of dehumanization brought on by the experience of living in cities and the repetitive processes of industrial production.

Libertarian writers in Britain were sensitive to the potential impact of each of these revolutions on its citizens, though the character of their responses was by no means unanimous. The independent republican Thomas Paine (1737–1809) supported both the American and French Revolutions, making friends abroad and enemies at home through the publication of his *Common Sense* (1776) and *The Rights of Man* (1791, 1792), which advocated constitutionally defined rights and liberties. The rationalist and republican William Godwin (1756–1836), who wrote the *Enquiry Concerning Political Justice* (1793), advocated human happiness and social well-being as the sole purpose of existence, and rejected Paine's idea of inherent natural rights. Godwin's wife Mary Wollstonecraft (1759–97) was an active member of a radical circle, and in 1790 published *Vindication of the Rights of Men*, a treatise which defended the French Revolution by attacking the system of aristocratic values which kept the greater portion of humankind in subservience. This was followed in 1792 by her *Vindication of the Rights of Woman*, which adapted and extended French revolutionary rhetoric to embody the universal needs of women. Writers also emerged who fundamentally questioned the aims of revolution. Edmund Burke, who in 1790 published *Reflections on the Revolution in France*, recognized the increasingly uneasy state of political affairs on both sides of the English Channel; he attempted to temper the optimism which greeted the French 'Declaration of the Rights of Man' in 1789. While understanding the excitement which some Britons felt had been growing since the time of Rousseau, Burke wished to restrain and condition the emerging libertarian optimism by an appeal to tradition and the status quo in order to maintain political balance.

This range of reactions among prose writers points to a fundamental character-istic of Romantic expression – whether enunciated by essayists, politicians, or imaginative writers: individuality. Such a statement, however, must take account of several contributing factors. First of all, the individuals concerned were bound together by the same range of social and political conditions to which they responded. Also, many were powerfully conscious of their agreement or disagree-ment with others. Some, such as William Wordsworth (1770–1850) and Samuel Taylor Coleridge (1772–1834), read each other's work, and occasionally collabor-ated in composition and publication. Consistent patterns of practice are, however, difficult to discern, and thus raise fundamental questions about the use of a term such as 'Romantic' to describe a corporate identity for writers of the period.

The novelty and experimentation apparent in Romantic writing was affected by the new political initiatives noted above, thus pointing to the strong affinity between the 'new' literature and the attempts to refashion society. In certain cases the two spheres intersected: Wordsworth, for example, spent some time in the years 1790–2 in France; and showed great enthusiasm for the Revolution (though this waned after the Terror); Coleridge and his friend Robert Southey (1774–1843) planned a utopian scheme of emigration to America called 'Pantisocracy'. In most instances the expressions were imaginative rather than experiential, and produced a variety of poems reflecting popular feeling. One anonymous lyric celebrating both the French and American Revolutions, 'The Trumpet of Liberty', included a chorus which began 'Fall Tyrants! fall! fall! fall!'. Another by John Wolcot ('Peter Pindar') entitled 'Hymn to the Guillotine' even welcomed this instrument of death, personified as the 'Daughter of Liberty', to England, where she would have much work to perform. The Industrial Revolution was also addressed, most famously by William Blake (1757–1827) in collections such as *Songs of Innocence* (1789) and *Songs of Experience* (1794), which point to the vulnerability of humankind, and outline the consequences of exploitation in such poems as 'Holy Thursday' from *Experience*, which identifies Britain as a 'land of poverty', and 'London', which points to the psychological degradation of the industrial classes, fettered in 'mind-forg'd manacles'.

In order for reformist sentiments to be disseminated, Romantic writers wished to give the impression of dispensing with class distinction, and to imbue their writings with a universal appeal and identification. Robert Burns (1759–96), the son of an Ayrshire tenant farmer, effected this association through his poems in Scots vernacular and his self-conscious attention to an ideal of human community. Wordsworth, who came from the Lake District, used his understanding of rural communal relationships to elevate the country dweller as an object for poetic contemplation. For his *Lyrical Ballads* (1798) he chose to describe and sentimentalize 'humble and rustic life', because in that condition 'the essential passions of the heart find a better soil in which they can attain their maturity'; he claimed in his celebrated preface to the collection that the types depicted 'speak a plainer and more emphatic language'. Unlike Burns Wordsworth did not use dialect; instead he emphasized passions and values which he believed bore little resemblance to those formulated in sophisticated or urban spheres. The novelty of his presentation lay not in poetic form (many of the poems derive from traditional genres such as ballad), but rather in the attempt to divert attention away from the eighteenth-century appeal to gentility and artificiality.

In many cases Romantic poets wished to consider expected or established responses to the peasantry before departing from convention to present an original view. In Burns's 'The Cotter's Saturday Night' of 1786 (a poem which enters into a dialogue with Thomas Gray's 'Elegy Written in a Country Churchyard'), the poet uses the cottage dweller to represent the poor, who are not responsible for either disasters or achievements; yet he simultaneously employs this figure to represent the noble, religious, and familial Scottish sensibility. Thus these verses go far beyond mere adulation of the peasantry to evoke a desire for Scottish political autonomy. Wordsworth also overturns conventional assumptions. In such poems as 'We are Seven' and 'The Idiot Boy' (both 1798) expectations are raised concerning conventional responses of rural inhabitants; these remain unfulfilled, owing to the inability of the 'sophisticated' narrators to understand the alternative wisdom communicated by the rustic poor.

Such poetic expression leads to the conclusion that some writers believed they could offer a deeper insight into recognizable situations, and speak with an authentic, authoritative voice. Poets such as Wordsworth, Coleridge, Percy Bysshe Shelley (1792–1822) and John Keats (1795–1821) were keenly aware of their roles and responsibilities, and used their writings as opportunities for self-expression at the deepest level. Wordsworth, for example, expended great effort in his preface to *Lyrical Ballads* in answering the question 'What then does the Poet?' His answer focused on an individual with acutely tuned powers of observation, regarding the external world, and celebrating particular moments of existence. The poet 'rejoices more than other men', he claimed, 'in the spirit of life that is in him'. Coleridge, in the *Biographia Literaria* (1817), claimed that the poet employs the 'magical power' of the imagination to produce his work. Shelley, in *A Defence of Poetry* (1821), ascribed to poets a set of extraordinary qualities which made them 'the unacknowledged legislators of the world'. Keats wrote about the role of poets and poetry in his letters, and identified the work of Wordsworth as embodying the quality of the 'egotistical sublime'. He also carefully considered his own role: he made a conscious decision to give up an honourable career as a surgeon's dresser to devote his life to poetry. His goal was to be 'among the English Poets' – thus indicating not only his ambition but also his faith in himself. Like Wordsworth, Keats was sure that he possessed 'Abilities greater than most Men'.

This self-consciousness about the processes of poetic production gave rise to evocations in which the individual played a prominent – even supreme – role. In part this preoccupation can be explained by the changing nature of the response of poets to crucial events. While Wordsworth, in *The Prelude*, proclaimed of the early 1790s, 'Bliss was it in that dawn to be alive', his support for the Revolution dissipated as the initial anticipation of reform gave way to the Terror of 1793. This event led to a moral crisis: the expectations of revolutionary reform were transformed into hopes for improvement by means of education and reason; for Wordsworth (and Coleridge) in particular, this led to a quest for revolution within the 'mind of man'.

The emphasis on the individual 'I' had significant implications: in addition to being highly selective, the concept was gendered. The answer to the question 'Who am I?' was affected by psychological, anthropological and political considerations. Since the time of John Locke's *An Essay concerning Human Understanding* (1690) it was believed that the intellectual, moral and spiritual senses were developed by associating sensations with ideas. In addressing the problem of 'What makes a human being?' scientific studies used essentialist arguments to discuss children, as well as so-called 'noble savages': that is, representatives of human beings in their pristine states, unaffected by adverse effects of socialization. Politics, through the writings of Rousseau, provided an answer to the question 'Who is fit to rule?' by advocating that democracy, regulated by rational 'man', was preferable to despotism.

Such considerations gave the 'I' visionary power to transcend the terrestrial limits of human existence for prophetic, momentary glimpses of a better world beyond. In order to sustain this appeal to the poet's mind, feelings, and ideas, an intuitive appeal to nature was seen as fundamental. Its treatment went beyond mere loco-description or appeal to the picturesque, to encompass the relationship between the perceiving mind and the object of perception; such contemplation could, in certain circumstances, be elevated to a state of consciousness which transcended the beautiful, and encompassed the 'sublime'. This is the process which is at work in Wordsworth's poem 'Lines Written a Few Miles above Tintern Abbey' (1798); the perceived intensity of the transcendent experience in the poem assists in explaining the long-cherished perception that Romantic poetry was primarily concerned with 'Nature' (usually capitalized).

The rhetorical strategy employed by many Romantic subjects implies that their objects occupy positions of silence, separateness, and otherness. This separation is true not only of the poet–nature duality, but also of the writer in relation to the silent auditors and addressees of Romantic literature, from Wordsworth's 'Tintern Abbey', where his sister Dorothy is the listener, to Coleridge's 'conversation poems' such as 'The Eolian Harp' (1795) and 'Frost at Midnight' (1798), which turn out to be blank verse monologues. While such works claim that a stable relationship exists between subject and object, the absence of opportunity for the listener to answer back problematizes the alliance.

The cases where the subject–object duality is questioned are revealing. Many of those which challenged the relationship directly were by women, and include Amelia Opie's 'The Maniac' (1808) and Mary Shelley's *Frankenstein* (1818). In Opie's poem the gap between the speaker and the listener/object is openly acknowledged, while in Shelley's novel the object (Frankenstein's creature) gains a voice, and offers a powerful critique of Romantic patriarchal egotism. Interestingly, it goes beyond this simple opposition: each of the major characters – Walton, Frankenstein, and the creature – serves as both narrator and listener, in an effort to seek out points of identification to relieve keenly felt anxieties. This duality was inherited and variously transformed by the Victorians, as you will find in the discussion of subjective–objective tensions in Unit 12.

Recent gender studies have forced a re-examination of canonical Romantic texts in ways noted above; the new critical climate has also allowed for the unearthing of a significant number of previously silenced women Romantic writers, including Felicia Hemans (1793–1835) and Laetitia Landon (1802–38), whose agendas are strikingly different from their male counterparts. There are, however, other means of revealing perceived fallacies in traditional assessments of Romantic literature. The assumption that Romantic writers expressed unabashed confidence in the supremacy of individual consciousness through the 'I' may be challenged by examining what Coleridge, in the *Biographia Literaria*, calls the 'anxiety of authorship'. Many Romantic texts become actively involved in the processes of reading by providing prefaces (as in the cases of Wordsworth's *Lyrical Ballads*, and *Poems* of 1815, as well as Coleridge's 'Kubla Khan' of 1816) or marginal notes (such as those for Byron's *The Giaour*, 1813, and Coleridge's 'Rime of the Ancient Mariner', added to the poem in 1817); such authorial commentary implies that writers were anxious to educate their readers in 'correct' ways of reading. In each case the prefatory material or marginalia prepares the reader for unfamiliar texts, providing a 'key' to understanding.

It would seem that writers such as Wordsworth, Coleridge, and Byron, in their roles as cultural arbiters or prophets, were apprehensive about whether or not their audiences were actually there. It should also be remembered that Coleridge published part of the *Biographia Literaria* for the same reason as Wordsworth had published his preface to *Lyrical Ballads*: to refute adverse criticism. The self-consciousness of writers extended to their questioning the nature of their addressees: while in many cases the listeners were denied speaking positions, in other instances the addressees were other writers: Coleridge, for example, addressed 'This Lime-Tree Bower my Prison' (1800) to Charles Lamb; Shelley addressed his elegy 'Adonais' (1821) to the dead Keats; Wordsworth's monumental poem *The Prelude* (1798, 1805, 1850) was addressed to his 'beloved Friend' Coleridge. This pattern indicates that writing to and about friends creates an ideal audience, which supposedly understands and sympathizes with the aims of the writer, and does not need to answer back. Yet fears do remain, and are most clearly enunciated by George Crabbe (1754–1832) in his verse tale 'The Patron' (1812), which presents the horror of the breakdown between writer and audience; the poet is seen as a kind of pet, who receives 'siren-flattery' from the aristocratic audience he is amusing. The narrative ends with his untimely death and descent into eternal silence.

The anxieties described represent another facet of the Romantic preoccupation with selfhood. When the individual personality is minutely examined in texts, writers often reveal a preoccupation with psychological struggle or conflict. The working out of a problem is directed inwardly, examining errors, guilt, division of allegiance, and a splitting of the ego-image. The Romantic art of confession is often depicted as a struggle within the character of the narrator or protagonist, and occasionally involves the internalization and reworking of biblical or classical texts. Such is the case in Wordsworth's 'Nutting' (1800), which engages with Genesis 2 and 3 and Milton's *Paradise Lost* to trace a four-stage process through transgression, recognition of error, admonishment and recovery. Another internalized study of motivation is Byron's *Cain* (1821), which examines the Fall and the first murder; here the struggle is seen as a battle of wills between the 'hero' Cain and the anti-heroic Lucifer. Byron (1788–1824) uses the Fall as the occasion for providing humankind with the 'gift' of reason, and generating the potential for inner conflict. Extended examinations of troubled states of mind are also provided by James Hogg (1770–1835) in his novel *The Private Memoirs and Confessions of a Justified Sinner* (1824) and Thomas De Quincey (1785–1859) in his autobiographical account of drug addiction, *Confessions of an English Opium-Eater* (1821).

Division within the self also inspires contemplation of ideal objects on which to rest hopes and aspirations; such is the case in Keats's 'Ode to a Nightingale' (1819), and Coleridge's 'Constancy to an Ideal Object' (1828). In each case the object of contemplation is an ideal, which does not exist in the material world. Keats represents himself as a figure of pain and melancholy, and the poem is an opportunity to consider whether or not the nightingale can serve as a vehicle for achieving spiritual and mental health. Coleridge's object is an elusive 'Thought', seen initially as 'The only constant in a world of change'. In each case the object departs, leaving the poet in a state of ambiguity, self-doubt and solitude. Another interesting example of Romantic struggle is Keats's 'Ode on a Grecian Urn' (1820), in which an imaginary object is contemplated, but with the added complication of the urn's enigmatic reply – 'Beauty is truth, truth beauty'.

As well as revealing anxiety and an occupation with inner struggle, Romantic treatments of psychological states could incorporate more sinister – even terrifying – impressions. Such is the character of gothic literature, a genre emerging as a response to the revolutions of the period, and characterized by a shift from the earlier eighteenth-century reliance on the enlightened rationality of humanity, to the questioning of the self and acknowledgement of the unconscious and darker side of the human psyche. It is firmly rooted in the psychology of the self, especially as manifested in altered or irrational modes of consciousness, such as sleeping, dreaming, and drug-induced states of mind. The works arising out of this interest represent a reaction against comfort, security and intellectual stability; above all, they resist the confining fetters of the reasonable, rational faculties.

Romantic texts containing features of the Gothic included ballads, such as William Taylor's 'Ellenore', Matthew Gregory Lewis's 'The Erl-King' (both 1795) and Coleridge's 'Rime of the Ancient Mariner' (1798); there were also real or imagined fragments, such as Coleridge's 'Christabel' and 'Kubla Khan' (both 1816). However, the genre which became the clearest embodiment of gothic elements was the novel, whose range was extended far beyond the eighteenth-century concern with sensibility to allow for extended treatment of deeply disturbing subjects. Some novels, such as Horace Walpole's *Castle of Otranto* (1764), William Beckford's *Vathek* (1786) and Lewis's *The Monk* (1796) offered limited psychological insight, and catered amply to the popular taste for the sensational and supernatural; others, including Shelley's *Frankenstein* and Hogg's *Justified Sinner*, went beyond merely satisfying the literary consumer to investigate the psychological motivations of the protagonist, and to probe the construction of moral responsibility. A discussion of the gothic novel in the eighteenth century will be found in Unit 9.

While the gothic exposed fallacies in the construction of a unified conception of selfhood, an alternative process was at work to sustain a synthesized image of both the human person and the national consciousness in the Romantic period. The ideology of Orientalism served as a public discourse which distinguished between a technologically advanced, morally validated, and comfortably domesticated West, and its opposite – the supposedly backward, silenced, and exotic East. While Egypt, India, Syria, Palestine and China interested travellers and scholars in the early nineteenth century, the nature of the published reports about the 'mystic' Orient disclosed a Eurocentricity which produced an unequal relationship, in which the 'Other' is silenced, spoken about authoritatively and has no opportunity to answer back. This statement applies to literary, political and architectural expressions: in each case interest was focused not on exact reproductions but rather on Western constructions of Eastern subjects.

The artificial nature of Orientalism can be seen in the work of William Jones (1746–94), a translator of Sanskrit and high court judge in Calcutta, who was avidly read by Byron and other Romantic poets; his poems, such as the 'Hymn to Na'ra'yena' (1785), represent a European appropriation of the Orient. For him the study of Eastern culture and languages strengthened the commercial relationship between Britain and colonies like India. In the process he domesticated what was perceived as foreign by pointing to affinities between the Indian tradition of epic and myth, and that of Europe, represented by the work of Hesiod and Milton.

Other writers paid more attention to the 'Otherness' of Eastern texts. Coleridge, for example, recognized the problems of interpretation posed by the perplexing visions in 'Kubla Khan'. Southey accentuated the foreignness of Oriental subject matter by using an unusual metre for *Thalaba, the Destroyer* (1801), and describing it as 'the Arabesque ornament of an Arabian tale'; so too did Walter Savage Landor (1775–1864) in *Gebir* (1798). These writers recognized that an unusual form was demanded to represent unfamiliar subject matter. At the same time, however, these texts served as opportunities to make political statements. *Gebir*, for example, condemns British foreign policy, while supporting Napoleon's invasion of Egypt. Byron (who advised his friend Thomas Moore to 'stick to the East' because 'the North, South, and West, have all been exhausted') published *The Giaour* to raise questions about the certainty of the British imperial project; in the process he revealed absences and frailties in Western constructions of identity, thereby offering a vision of a society in crisis.

Instead of offering an impression of synthesized literary response to social, political, and cultural developments in the years 1780–1830, this assessment of Romanticism has demonstrated that this relatively brief period was one of turmoil and disquiet, punctuated by feelings of restlessness, anxiety, and uncertainty. The responses were more individually motivated than corporate, dissonant rather than consonant. Canonical literary history has attempted to collectivize these views into recognizable and abiding patterns; more recent studies have, however, tended to discount such approaches. Nevertheless the period stands out as one of great energy, freshness and excitement, in which writers engaged with the great questions raised by the self and the world.

The best recent general studies of Romanticism are by Butler (1981), Everest (1990) and Chase (1993); Watson (1985; 2nd ed. 1992) on Romantic poetry is also highly recommended. The European context is ably surveyed by Furst (1976, 1979). The French Revolution and other political events are covered by Butler (1984), Roe (1988) and Everest (1991). Major themes are considered in collections by Aers (1981) and Curran (1993). On Romantic aesthetics, Abrams (1971) and Weiskel (1976) are useful. A detailed account of the problematic relationship between Romantic poets and genre can be found in Curran (1986). Canonical assumptions about the period are interrogated in McGann (1983) and Johnston et al. (1990). Studies which encourage rereadings based on recent critical discourses also abound: these include Levinson et al. (1989) on new historicism, Punter (1989) on psychoanalysis, Leask (1992) on Orientalism, and Mellor (1993) on gender. The collection by Wu (1995) contains a number of useful reassessments of individual authors. Two recent alphabetically arranged compendia by Dabundo (1992) and Raimond and Watson (1992) provide excellent and concise coverage of the major figures and issues of the period.

## Texts, authors, contexts

### Blake, Wordsworth and the novelty of Romantic expression

> O Rose thou art sick.
> (Blake, 'The Sick Rose', 1794)

> 'How many are you then,' said I,
> 'If they are two in heaven?'
> The little Maiden did reply,
> 'O Master! we are seven!'

> 'But they are dead; those two are dead!
> Their spirits are in heaven!'
> 'Twas throwing words away; for still
> The little Maid would have her will,
> And said, 'Nay, we are seven!'
> (Wordsworth, 'We Are Seven', 1798)

These two passages are characteristic of the ways in which Romantic poets reshaped ostensibly familiar subject matter for new purposes. Both Blake and Wordsworth wished to communicate an inadequate fit between real and apparent in the turbulent 1790s, by using the established and popular genres of ballad and song to examine contradiction and ambiguity in constructions which were supposedly secure.

'The Sick Rose' was part of a collection entitled *Songs of Experience* (1794) which, when joined to the earlier *Songs of Innocence* (1789), represented for Blake, as he noted in his subtitle, 'Two Contrary States of the Human Soul'. The poems are lyrics, or short, non-narrative verses presenting a single speaker expressing a state of mind. There is ample intertextual influence from the Bible, Milton and Dante, and moralizing children's poetry and hymnody; yet despite the apparent simplicity of subject matter and rhythm, Blake's poems contain complex religious and mythological associations which form an elaborate infrastructure for the collection. The *Songs* do not reflect merely oppositions, but a series of shifting perceptions pointing to a dialectic between Edenic innocence and worldly experience, in which an awareness of the shifting tensions of both states is essential.

Some poems in the collection are paired, and even display the same title (for example 'Holy Thursday' or 'The Chimney Sweeper') in order to examine a situation from different perspectives. Contrasts are rendered even more striking in the coloured plates which Blake (an engraver by profession) designed to accompany the text. 'The Blossom' from *Innocence* is the companion to 'The Sick Rose', and whereas long rhythmic lines of 'The Blossom' advocate the acceptance of happiness and sorrow unreservedly, the short, staccato effect produced by 'The Sick Rose' suggests destruction.

On a literal level, the discovery of meaning in the poem is problematic. While Blake's diction is easily understood, he is not engaging in simple botanical depiction which can be related to everyday experience. His frame of reference has shifted from non-verbal experience to literature, and it is only by considering other manifestations of literary roses that this poem can be understood. He assumes that his literate readers bring to their reading experience an intertextual awareness of a myriad of meanings for the word 'Rose'. The strong convention of the rose in literature has endowed it with standard, supposedly secure connotations of love, order and beauty. The reader thinks of the *Romance of the Rose*, Dante's Rose of Heaven, and Burns's poem 'O my Luve's like a red, red rose', to name but a few instances where the rose accords with expectations. Blake turns the conventional world of the rose upside down by identifying it as 'sick'; he challenges an established literary symbol by making it the opposite of what it should be.

In the context of the Romantic age 'The Sick Rose' can be seen to offer a critique of the adverse effects of the 'age of revolution' on a previously innocent, untainted agrarian population. The 'howling storm' in which the 'invisible worm' (another multivalent image) advances serves as an indication of the effect which the advancing forces of industrialism and materialism had on Britain's citizens. The poem can also be interpreted as an examination of the troubles engendered by sexual relationships, in which the 'dark secret love' of the worm finds the 'bed/Of crimson joy', and annihilates the Rose. While the message is rendered acceptable or more palatable by the use of the lyric mode, the subject matter is presented in a novel fashion, through the concept of a 'sick' rose. In this way Blake overturns the expectations of his readers and, through his extraordinary sensitivity to the conventional associations of words, provides a novel response to his changing times.

Wordsworth was also interested in the overturning of convention in his *Lyrical Ballads* (1798). In his preface to the collection he claimed that his aim was to choose incidents and situations from 'humble and rustic life', and present 'ordinary things' in an 'unusual aspect'. For this he was well qualified, owing to his intimate understanding of the rural community into which he was born. Like Blake he employed a familiar genre – the ballad – and embellished it with what he called the 'language really used by men' in order to celebrate a system of values which he believed was waning in his increasingly industrialized country. 'We Are Seven' is a characteristic example of the working out of Wordsworth's project. It presents an unimaginative, unfeeling narrator (who should not be identified with the poet), confronted with the intuitive vision and imaginative instinct of a rustic child, who insists that there are seven in her family; the rational narrator, obsessed by mathematical accuracy, counters with the assertion that two of them are dead, and there are therefore five. By the end of the poem there is a deadlock: neither character is willing to modify what was originally asserted. The situation is ostensibly simple, yet communicates knowledge which overturns conventional expectations.

Wordsworth was well aware of the eighteenth-century tradition of adulation of the peasant, and the idealization of this figure as the representative of a common humanity. Writers such as James Thomson and Thomas Gray observed rustic life from a sophisticated, elevated perspective, which provided a false impression of the subjects under observation. Wordsworth wished to break with the artificialities of this inherited tradition, and allow the rural inhabitants to speak for themselves in his poems. 'We Are Seven' departs from established tradition by depicting a confrontation between the educated, sophisticated adult narrator, who appears with long-cherished conventional expectations about rural life, and the child, whose power and wisdom stems from feelings and beliefs to which the adult has no access. The narrator's conventional view is marked by his unobservant description of the girl: 'She had a rustic, woodland air'; he also believes that the child's assertion of 'we are seven!' is nonsense, because her brother and sister lie buried in the churchyard. The questions he asks are typical and patronizing, and he does not like the answers he receives.

The poem depicts the narrator in the role of tourist, who hopes to appreciate something of nature and rural life which conforms to an established – and false – pattern. His disappointment serves to indicate the distance between himself and the child, who is Wordsworth's authentic image of a rural inhabitant, and who has developed an intimate relationship with the land, which is not disturbed by such considerations as death, seen here as a natural extension of life. For the girl the graves are incorporated into her domestic environment, and she goes there to knit stockings and hem kerchiefs. Her idea of community contrasts markedly with the isolation occasioned by life in the city, a place where, as Wordsworth was later to remark in *The Prelude*, next-door neighbours are strangers, and do not know each other's names. Rural environments, on the other hand, provide a location where community and family allegiances are strong; if the representative urbanized interlocutor (whom Wordsworth means his readers to recognize) divests himself of the exigencies of taste and accepts the rural inhabitant's pronouncements, he will recognize the meaningful, unconventional wisdom which such expression embodies.

The two poems examined are not radical because they embody revolutionary thought, or because they evoke sentiments of the underprivileged in society. Instead they operate by shifting their perspective away from gentility and false sophistication in order to force a self-conscious examination of the process of poetic production, as well as the situations described. Both Blake and Wordsworth were aware that in order to attune their audiences to what they saw as the pressing difficulties of their time, they had to move cautiously in order to overcome the pressing weight of tradition. Both employed established genres for new purposes, and in the process diverted attention away from canonical assumptions in order to force a re-examination of both the form and subject matter of poetry.

The best studies of Blake are by Frye (1967), Gleckner (1959) and Raine (1970). There are inexpensive editions, with coloured plates, of the *Songs of Innocence* (1971) and *Experience* (1984). Hilton (1986) has edited an essential collection of articles. Wordsworth's *Lyrical Ballads* are thoroughly examined by Jacobus (1976), Parrish (1973) and Sheats (1973). The 'humanity' in his poetry is explored by Beer (1978). A detailed study which contextualizes both Blake's *Songs* and Wordsworth's *Lyrical Ballads* is by Glen (1983).

## Wordsworth and the construction of the Romantic subject

> And I have felt
> A presence that disturbs me with the joy
> Of elevated thoughts; a sense sublime
> Of something far more deeply interfused,
> Whose dwelling is the light of setting suns,
> And the round ocean and the living air,
> And the blue sky, and in the mind of man:
> A motion and a spirit, that impels
> All thinking things, all objects of all thought,
> And rolls through all things.
>
> (Wordsworth, 'Lines Written a few miles above Tintern Abbey', 1798)

'Tintern Abbey' is a poem which embodies many of the features commonly associated with Romantic poetry: egotism, prophecy, the Sublime, Nature and transcendence. It was composed by Wordsworth during a ramble with his sister Dorothy in the Wye Valley, and first appeared at the end of the 1798 edition of *Lyrical Ballads*. Its full title, 'Lines written a few miles above Tintern Abbey, on revisiting the banks of the Wye during a tour, July 13 1798', excites expectations of picturesque description; however, as in 'We Are Seven', conventionality is abandoned in favour of something more fundamental: the poet, writing in autobiographical mode, wishes to explore the effects of memory, time and landscape upon the imagination. It is also unlike many of the other ballads in that it is written in blank verse paragraphs, and intended, according to Wordsworth's note, to recall the manner of the ode.

The poem contains several movements, emphasizing what the poet called 'the impassioned music of versification'. It opens traditionally, and lines 1–22 present the verdant landscape, composed of 'pastoral farms' and 'plots of cottage-ground', first visited five years before, in 1793. There then follows an exposition of the restorative powers of memory which, when recollected in tranquillity ('that serene and blessed mood'), produces an extraordinary power of joyful and harmonious vision to 'see into the life of things' (ll. 23–49). In an attempt to substantiate the source of this power, lines 50–112 reassert the conviction that it stems from a recollection of the Wye, which has evolved over time, from childhood (when nature was 'all in all') to adulthood, when he can perceive 'The still, sad music of humanity'; this feeling is not communicated entirely through the senses, but rather through an awareness of transcendence, that visionary intensity which allows the individual who has been burdened by the mechanism and empiricism, of terrestrial existence, to go beyond these limits to catch a momentary glimpse of a better world beyond. In the final paragraph (ll. 113–60) the poet addresses his 'dear Friend', his sister Dorothy, who has not reached the same level of development as he has, and so serves as the 'anchor' or touchstone from which he can depart for the sublime region of transcendence.

The pattern to which this poem adheres allows Wordsworth to subvert convention by transforming an eighteenth-century loco-descriptive poem into complex, revolutionary testimony to self-discovery. In the process he exhibits characteristics common to many Romantic poets, who wish to emphasize the position of authority occupied by the Romantic subject. Blake, for example, endorsed the idea of poet as prophet, or bard of imaginative and spiritual visions; Coleridge sanctioned the impression of the poet as imaginative seer, and as sufferer of dark visions of remorse; Shelley cast the poet as political visionary and spirit of radical change. While individual poems may express doubt or depict a troubled soul, in almost every case the authority of the individual – and the inability of the addressee to answer back – are confirmed. In 'Tintern Abbey' Wordsworth uses sensations of remembered natural scenery to contribute to an expression of joy at being able to apprehend the sublime sense of a living presence in the active universe. There is an awareness, however, that such perception is selective, and he is one of the chosen few.

'Tintern Abbey' has long been admired for its appeal to Nature (the capitalization is Wordsworth's). While Wordsworth was deeply absorbed by the revolutionary atmosphere and rhetoric in the 1780s and early 1790s, in these verses (which may be seen as an early poetic manifesto), the intensity of his love of nature precludes other concerns, such as class division, the effects of industrialization, or indeed the social enquiries prompted by the age of revolution. Here 'emotion recollected in tranquillity', as he notes in the preface to *Lyrical Ballads*, is singularly stimulated by Nature, then released in joyous confidence, and variously applied or illustrated by moral and social incident. The poem marks a subordination of social concerns in favour of an essentialism grounded in nature, which was in Wordsworth's day still largely untainted by human mismanagement, and therefore reliable as a touchstone for human experience.

Wordsworth's rhetorical strategy illustrates the common tendency in masculine Romanticism to delineate carefully between subject and object. In this poem both nature and Dorothy are objectified and silenced, thus having no presence or vitality of their own: they only exist in so far as they are of use to the poet. Feminized nature paradoxically serves as both mother and lover, with the power to create as well as arouse: she nurtures and cares for the masculine subject, relieving him of his 'heavy and weary weight', and providing the 'power/Of harmony' for his contemplation; she is also an object of desire, who helps him to achieve a climax which fills him with a 'sense sublime'. Dorothy, the addressee, is also objectified: she does not appear until the last paragraph, and serves as a mirror of what the poet once was – a steadfast point of reference. She is subordinated both physically and intellectually, left behind while her brother experiences 'elevated thoughts'. Like nature, she too is the archetypal victim of Romantic egotism.

The narrator seems to believe that the relationship between listener and addressee is stable; but there are hints of anxiety, elicited in the frequent use of 'if', as well as in the strong exhortations to Dorothy to remember his discourse with 'tender joy'. Such clues point to an uneasiness about the potential acceptance of the poet's statements by his audience. Although he yearns for responsive listeners, there is an innate awareness that the fragile relationship between speaker and listener might break down.

A greater degree of instability, anxiety and even self-pity is apparent in Coleridge's poem 'Dejection: An Ode'. It was the last of the 'conversation poems', and written in April 1802, when Wordsworth was composing his 'Immortality Ode'. 'Dejection' represents a stark contrast to 'Tintern Abbey', in its exploration of an 'affliction': the poet's failure to respond to the stimuli of natural phenomena, and the decay of his 'shaping spirit of Imagination'. The poem is a particularly interesting example of the insecure relationship between the speaker and listener, because in its several versions the identity of the addressee changes: when first drafted in April 1802 it was addressed to 'Sara' Hutchinson; by July 1802 it was directed to 'William' Wordsworth; in October 1802, when published in the *Morning Post* on Wordsworth's wedding-day, it was addressed to 'Edmund' (a pseudonym for Wordsworth); finally in 1817, when issued as part of *Sibylline Leaves*, attention reverts to Sara, who is called 'Lady'. Such indecision about the listener's identity points to Coleridge's fundamental inability to find an adequate repository for his particular vision. It would seem that the poet is effectively addressing the only stable consciousness in this desperate situation – himself, for only he can appreciate and respond to the correlatives he identifies in the poem: grief and joy, darkness and light, death and life, sterility and creativity – as he examines his own shifting, anxious condition.

Wordsworth's 'Tintern Abbey' is a far more confident poem than Coleridge's 'Dejection', and also a pivotal one: coming at the end of the *Lyrical Ballads*, it celebrates the distinctiveness of the watching and receiving heart. Like Coleridge's 'Frost at Midnight' (to which Wordsworth's poem responded) it contains assessments of past, present and future. It looks back five years to the poet's former self, as well as to the eighteenth-century loco-descriptive tradition from which it departs (for a discussion of the landscape poetry of Thomson, Akenside and Dyer, see Unit 8, pp. 183–7); it also addresses the way in which memories recalled in the present rescue experience from the ravages of time; finally it looks forward to a time when the poet can confidently incorporate the physical and psychological disturbances of his earlier years into a pattern of ultimate good.

The fulfilment forecast in 'Tintern Abbey' is finally achieved in *The Prelude*. Addressed to Coleridge, this long autobiographical poem in blank verse, first drafted in 1799, expanded in 1805, revised at intervals until 1839, and finally published posthumously in 1850, records the 'growth of a poet's mind', and shapes a set of momentous incidents in a poet's life into an ideal pattern of self-representation. It differs from 'Tintern Abbey' both in scope and in point of termination. In both cases there is celebration and elevation of the 'I' figure, but it is only in *The Prelude* that Wordsworth's mature thinking can be understood. Hope and vision are mingled with sorrow and disappointment; public appears alongside private. The self-declared theme is 'no other than the very heart of man', and in the course of the poem he considers nature, time, memory, and the building of the self. When he, 'foremost of the Band', reaches the top of Mount Snowdon in the climactic passage in book XIV (1850; XIII in 1805), climbing out of the mist into the moonlight to view the illuminating and symbolic chasm, he declares triumphantly: 'it appeared to me/The perfect image of a mighty mind'. It is here that Wordsworth experiences the profundity and sublimity of the poetic imagination, and stands as the epitome of the Romantic subject: authoritative, confident, and transcendent.

Of particular note is the essay by Hartman (1966) on *Lyrical Ballads* as well as the study by Gill (1991) on *The Prelude*. Also useful is the work by Hartman (1964) on the self and the external world in Wordsworth. Coleridge's 'Dejection: An Ode' is carefully considered by Dekker (1978). Identity and self-expression are considered by Ball (1968), and the question of authority is examined by Simpson (1979); the Romantic imagination is thoroughly interrogated in the casebook edited by Hill (1977). Gender issues in Wordsworth are given careful consideration by Mellor (1993); Dorothy in particular is examined by Barrell (1988).

## *Frankenstein* and the interrogation of Romantic individualism

When I reflected on the work I had completed, no less a one than the creation of a sensitive and rational animal, I could not rank myself with the herd of common projectors. But this thought, which supported me in the commencement of my career, now serves only to plunge me lower in the dust. All my speculations and hopes are as nothing, and like the archangel who aspired to omnipotence, I am chained in an eternal hell. My imagination was vivid, yet my powers of analysis and application were intense; by the union of these qualities I conceived the idea and executed the creation of a man. ... I trod heaven in my thoughts, now exulting in my powers, now burning with the idea of their effects. From my infancy I was imbued with high hopes and lofty ambition; but how I am sunk! Oh! My friend, if you had known me as I once was, you would not recognize me in this state of degradation. Despondency rarely visited my heart; a high destiny seemed to bear me on, until I fell, never, never again to rise. (Mary Shelley, *Frankenstein or, the Modern Prometheus*, [1818] 1985, p. 254)

An examination of Wordsworth's poetry demonstrates the extent to which masculine Romantic ideology was imbued with patriarchal rhetoric, radical politics, and the unquestioned authority of the subject. Feminine Romantic discourse, on the other hand, offered an alternative mode of expression based on the family politic, and promoted the idea that reform evolved gradually and rationally under the mutual guidance and nurturing of parents. Felicia Hemans, for example, demonstrated her support for domestic, social and spiritual pieties in poems such as 'The Graves of the Household' and 'The Homes of England' (both 1828). Laetitia Landon expressed a similar attitude in such sentimental lyrics as 'The Enchanted Island' (1825). Such themes may also be found in women novelists of the period, including Maria Edgeworth (1767–1849) and Jane Austen (1775–1817). Mary Shelley too was concerned with questioning many canonical assumptions about the value of individual ambition and endeavour, and the appropriate mechanisms for change; she extended her argument beyond those of her contemporaries, to challenge prevailing ideas concerning science, procreation and the constitution of selfhood.

Mary was the daughter of Mary Wollstonecraft (who died shortly after the child's birth) and William Godwin; she grew up in a household imbued with the principles of liberty and human rights. In 1814 she eloped with Percy Shelley (who was then still married), bore a daughter in 1815 (who died shortly after birth) and a son in early 1816; then, after the suicide of Shelley's wife Harriet, Mary and Percy married. *Frankenstein* was conceived in Switzerland during the summer of 1816, while in the company of her husband, Byron, and a Dr Polidori, and at a time when the works of Milton and Coleridge formed the staple of her reading programme. As she notes in her introduction to the novel, the narrative grew out of conversations on philosophy, nature, the myth of Prometheus, science, electricity, galvanism and 'the principle of life'. What emerged as her novel is a complex amalgam of these ideas, interwoven into a text of great psychological and moral insight.

The novel is narrated from three points of view, thus separating several levels of experience, and allowing for a delineation between the safe, domestic, familiar locations, and those which contain elements of the sublime and the gothic. The first narrator is Robert Walton, who dispatches matter-of-fact letters to his sister in England; he describes his journey towards the North Pole and his meeting with Victor Frankenstein (who is in search of the monster he has created, and now wishes to destroy). His function is to enclose the various narratives within a frame of realism, in order to decipher the occurrences for the domestic sensibilities of his sister, and to signal that such values must be left behind when men embark on their quests for adventure, passion and individual achievement.

The second narrative voice is that of Frankenstein, a Genevese student of natural science, disappointed by the unresponsiveness of social institutions to individual needs, and motivated by extravagant selfhood; he embarks on a confessional concerning his retreat from society and his creation of the monster, a Promethean accomplishment motivated by the elation he feels after discovering the secret of imparting life to matter (Shelley's response to the contemporary interest in galvanism and in the work of Erasmus Darwin). Horrified by the grotesque appearance of the creature (who serves as Victor's alter ego), he abandons it. The unnamed monster, who discovers impediments to his forming successful human relationships, then turns to murder and revenge, killing Frankenstein's friend Clerval, his brother, and his bride Elizabeth. This series of events represents a challenge to Victor's authority by his creation, who exclaims, 'You are my creator, but I am your master'.

The innermost narrative is that of the creature (identified by Frankenstein as a 'monster' and an 'abortion') who tells of his own misery at being continually rejected by society; he laments: 'Everywhere I see bliss, from which I alone am irrevocably excluded. I was benevolent and good; misery made me a fiend.' Although initially he is the epitome of the essential human being in the manner envisioned by Locke and Rousseau, untainted by the negative effects of social conditioning, he quickly realizes that those around him perceive him as representing a threat to their existence; indeed even virtuous and enlightened individuals like Frankenstein and Felix De Lacey fail to perceive his inner worth because of his outward appearance. This individual, like Frankenstein and Walton, is a victim of anxieties engendered by a society which cannot accept this individual it has helped to create. Shelley also draws intertextual parallels between the creature and Adam, whose creator gives him Eve as a companion on account of his lonely wretchedness. There are also echoes of Milton's Satan from *Paradise Lost*, who embarks on a course of jealous destruction in order to vindicate his dissociated existence. The connection is confirmed by the creature who, after reading Victor's journal, and thus confirming his real identity, exclaims: 'Accursed creator! Why form a monster so hideous that even you turned from me in disgust? ... Satan had his companions, fellow-devils, to admire and encourage him, but I am solitary and abhorred.'

The narrative structure resembles a set of three Chinese boxes, each contained in the other, and each with a similar moral: passion – that motivation of social progress envisioned by the Enlightenment, and that inward imperative and sign of authentic selfhood in Romantic fiction – serves to isolate the individual from society; it destroys the domestic affections, and brings the individual to the edge of self-obliteration. *Frankenstein* illustrates negatively what Percy Shelley identified as the work's chief concern: 'the exhibition of the amiableness of domestic affection, and the excellence of universal virtue'.

For nature and womanhood – the objectified, silenced receptors of masculine Romantic expression – the novel has special resonances. Frankenstein is imbued with scientific ambition and machismo; he is determined to 'penetrate into the recesses of nature and see how she works in her hiding-places'. He may be seen as wishing to dominate in a power relationship with nature, seeking (like Wordsworth) to achieve transcendental knowledge. Yet the 'unnatural' character of the experiment emphasizes the disparity between the ideal and the real, or the ambition and the accomplishment. Frankenstein's enterprise is misdirected: his attempt to achieve control over natural processes, to create a 'new species', goes horribly wrong. Not only is the monster (who should have served as the object of masculine Romantic ambition) given an identity, he is also permitted to speak and act independently, in a manner never envisioned by his creator. This usurpation of the position of the Romantic subject is used by Shelley to demonstrate the dangers inherent in the excesses of individualism.

The patriarchal structures of families and institutions are everywhere evident in the text, and there is a distinct lack of female presence; those who do appear, such as Justine Moritz and Elizabeth Lavenza, are weak, passive, and eventually killed. The case of Elizabeth (who is raised as Victor's sister) is particularly significant: she dies at the hands of the creature, on the night when her marriage to Victor should have been consummated. By not allowing Victor to experience a sexual union Shelley reinforces the degree to which he has removed himself from human companionship and sexual means of procreation. His becoming sole progenitor, thus usurping the one special power given to women, serves as an emblem of his complete dissociation from human community.

Useful studies of Shelley's life and work are those by Spark (1988) and Mellor (1988). Kiely (1972) and Kelly (1989) consider her fiction in the wider context of the Romantic novel in England; the collection by Knoepflmacher and Levine (1979) considers the enduring popularity of the work. Feminist approaches include those by Poovey (1984), Jacobus (1984) and Winnett (1990). The monster in particular is examined by Musselwhite (1987) and Baldick (1987), and the narrative structure is examined by Newman (1986).

## Coleridge and the Gothic

> 'God save thee, ancient Mariner!
> From the fiends, that plague thee thus!–
> Why look'st thou so?' – With my cross-bow
> I shot the albatross.
> > (Coleridge, 'The Rime of the Ancient Mariner', 1798)

> Then drawing in her breath aloud,
> Like one that shuddered, she unbound
> The cincture from beneath her breast:
> Her silken robe, and inner vest,
> Dropt to her feet, and in full view,
> Behold! her bosom, and half her side–
> A sight to dream of, not to tell!
> > (Coleridge, 'Christabel', 1816)

*Frankenstein* analyzes the complex constitution of personality by considering the inadequate fit between real and apparent. Certain experiences or situations in the novel, such as the search for hidden knowledge, cannot be linguistically validated through rational discourse, and must therefore be represented alternatively through an investigation of the darker aspects of human existence. The literary genre which evokes such altered states of consciousness has come to be known as the gothic.

'Gothic' was a term used originally to deride anything barbaric or uncouth. It is now applied to a particular form of literature and art which arose during the late eighteenth century, a time of revolution and changing intellectual attitudes, involving a shift from a reliance on the enlightened rationality of humanity, to the questioning of the self and acknowledgement of the darker side of the human psyche. The gothic is firmly rooted in the psychology of the self, especially the unconscious, and it is important to note the large number of writers working in the gothic mode (including Coleridge and Mary Shelley) who attribute their inspiration to dreams.

'The Rime of the Ancient Mariner' represents an attempt to depict the rhythms, forms and images of the dream world as part of a quest for new frontiers of consciousness. It uses the traditional ballad form to narrate a strange sequence of events: the mariner stops a man who is on the way to a wedding, and then relates a literal and figurative voyage of discovery, during which he arbitrarily shoots an albatross, then experiences guilt and immeasurable psychological suffering. The poem permits access to the unconscious mind, that pathway to a deeper exploration and realization of individual personality. The secrets of this mode of being are repressed during the rational, waking state, and can only escape in the world of sleep and dreams, where the psyche is unfettered from the restrictive demands of rationality and ordered social interaction. The literary dream text thus tends to free itself from all logical structure, and presents itself as a sequence of strange, anxiety-generating events (Coleridge's 'Christabel' and 'Rime of the Ancient Mariner') or as a sheer flow of intense images (Coleridge's 'Kubla Khan') .

The 'Rime' originally appeared as part of *Lyrical Ballads*, which Wordsworth and Coleridge published jointly. Coleridge defines the character of the poem in his *Biographia Literaria*, where he classes it with others whose 'incidents and agents were to be, in part at least, supernatural'. The seascape in which the events take place is free of identifiable landmarks, and so becomes the setting for a psychodrama which is difficult to relate to worldly experience. In this environment the troubled mind of the mariner conceives of burning seas, ghost ships, spectres playing dice, and water snakes. The wedding guest can only respond to these other-worldly experiences with alarm, exclaiming 'I fear thee, ancient Mariner!' He cannot, however, deny the substance or power of things which he clearly fails to understand; his experience, ruled by the social dictates of a communal ethos, is diametrically opposed to that of the mariner, who bemoans his solitude: 'Alone, alone, all all alone/Alone on the wide wide sea'. In this respect the poem bears some resemblance to *Frankenstein*: it describes a man no longer at peace with himself, and no longer an integrated member of a community, who attempts to expiate his guilt through the confessional mode, revealing in the process deep-seated suffering, perplexity, loneliness, longing, horror, and fear. The strange sequence of events brings the mariner to the fringes of madness and death; tranquillity and domesticity have given way to guilty and nomadic restlessness.

The mariner's experience is perplexing, and the reason for his suffering is elusive. To call the shooting of the albatross a crime is an over-simplification; for Coleridge it was an appropriate bird: rare, of exceptional size, haunting a limited, strange and evocative zone, harmless and by tradition beneficent. The mariner's crime was wanton and unintentional; the consequences are only realized when it is too late. Ultimately the search for meaning proves inconclusive; this enigma is in keeping with the spirit of the poem, which recognizes that the Mariner should not be judged by the ordinary standards of social life (represented by the wedding guest) for the breach of ordinary, rational obligations. Here the worldly order is transcended in order to explore feelings of guilt, loneliness and pathological misery, which are out of all proportion to any conventional human action.

There are other poems which evoke aspects of Coleridge's interest in the gothic. 'Christabel' is an enigmatic work, which was intended for the second edition of *Lyrical Ballads*, but was excluded, partly because of Wordsworth's dissatisfaction, and also because Coleridge left it as a fragment. It serves as an interesting complement to the 'Ancient Mariner' on account of its adherence to the ballad tradition and its linking of Christabel's experience to that of the mariner in its treatment of several levels of experience.

The precise nature of the action and relationship between Christabel and the beautiful Geraldine is difficult to discern. The other-worldly nature of the experience is enhanced by the poem's setting, which is suggestive of a mindscape or region of the dream world. Christabel, the daughter of Sir Leoline, who first appears at night in the wood, praying for her betrothed lover, is a solitary, lonely, vulnerable figure. With a mother dead, father in weak health, and lover far away, she has no defences against the machinations of Geraldine, who appears to embody sinister qualities (confirmed when the mastiff bitch moans and the light flickers as she passes by), and who seems to be completely in control of Christabel. The strongly sexual nature of the imagery is confirmed at various points; Geraldine is described as 'beautiful exceedingly', and when she undresses the narrator exclaims, 'Behold! her bosom and half her side –/A sight to dream of, not to tell!'

The entrance of Geraldine engenders a complexity of consciousness in the ballad, and suggests (as in the case of the 'Ancient Mariner') a state of calm threatened, a paradise about to be lost; yet her precise disposition and motivation remain a mystery. Her presence is made more effective by its ambiguity, as well as by the undescribed and unspecified occurrence in Christabel's bedroom. Critics have been divided over the nature of the incident: it is either something mystical/magical, or something physical/sexual. Geraldine might embody both benevolence and malevolence, thus displaying an awareness on Coleridge's part that good without evil (or, in the terminology of Blake, innocence without experience) is not desirable. The complexities are infinite, and allow the poem to balance two contrasting motivations and aspects of human nature.

There are useful general introductions to the gothic by Punter (1980) and Miles (1993). Wheeler (1981) provides an excellent introduction to Coleridge's work. The 'Rime' is the subject of scrutiny in Harding (1941) and Bostetter (1962). Beres (1951) provides an interesting psychoanalytic interpretation of the poem; the reasons for shooting the albatross are explored by Whalley (1946–7). 'Christabel' has received extensive critical examination, most notably by Edwards and Emslie

(1971), Emslie and Edwards (1970) and Swann (1984, 1985). The Romantic fragment poem is ably considered by McFarland (1981) and Levinson (1987).

## De Quincey, opium, and the exploration of altered states

> I took it:– and in an hour, oh! Heavens! what a revulsion! what an upheaving, from its lowest depths, of the inner spirit! what an apocalypse of the world within me!
> (Thomas De Quincey, *Confessions of an English Opium-Eater, being an Extract from the Life of a Scholar*, [1821] 1985)

While Shelley and Coleridge attempted to examine the divided self and the troubled consciousness of the individual by representing the struggles of fictional gothic heroes, De Quincey claimed to offer something more authentic by producing an autobiographical piece of 'impassioned prose', and claiming an undeniable affinity with his 'decent' English readers.

In an attempt to reproduce accurately the atmosphere and emotions associated with the unconscious, some Romantics attempted to induce such altered states experimentally. For example the painter John Henry Fuesli (1741–1825) was reported to have eaten raw beef or pork chops in order to produce imaginative reveries, which formed the basis of such evocative paintings as *The Nightmare* (1782–91). Southey's inducement of wild raptures through the agency of laughing gas found its way into the *Curse of Kehama* (1810). Coleridge and Crabbe engaged in imaginative exploration through ingesting opium in both liquid and solid form. The liquid form, known as laudanum, consisted of opium mixed with alcohol, and it was under the effects of this drug that De Quincey experienced the dreams which form the basis of the *Confessions*.

De Quincey was born in Manchester, and after attending school in Bath and elsewhere, he went on a walking tour of north Wales. He then ran away to London, where he occupied poor lodgings and lived by borrowing on the security of his father's will from ruthless money-lenders. During his five months in the capital he made friends with outcast women and prostitutes, and gained some of the most vivid and profound experiences of his early life. He was rescued by friends, and in 1803 went to Worcester College, Oxford, which he left in 1808 without taking a degree. It was during this period, on a visit to London (probably in 1804), that he first had recourse to opium, which was initially used as a cure for a dental abscess; soon he began to take the drug regularly. By 1807, when he met Coleridge (who also took opium) he was addicted, and the acquaintance only served to enhance De Quincey's interest in the effects of the drug. While Coleridge allowed himself only rare mentions of opium in his published work, and tried repeatedly to rid himself of the habit, De Quincey's fascination – and addiction – persisted, particularly during his association with Wordsworth and his residence at Grasmere. In 1819 he went to Edinburgh to write for *Blackwood's Magazine*, and in 1820 returned to London, where he finished his *Confessions*, which appeared in the *London Magazine* in October and November 1821, and in book form in 1822.

The work is a remarkable study of the effects of an obsession, which goes far beyond the gothic mode of examining imaginatively the darker aspects of human identity; it provides personal insight into the nature of the gulf between outward and inward existence. The title is misleading: it raises expectations of an avowal of culpability, of the type found in the work of Byron, Coleridge, or Hogg; yet De Quincey is at pains to point out that the book 'does not amount to a confession of guilt'. It is, rather, a 'report' by a 'scholar', who provides a documentary account of what he has lived through himself; what is clear is that the dream-visions it contains are memorable for their faithful rendering of the circularity, repetition and unexpected emphasis characteristic of the dream experience.

The work defies generic definition and structural analysis. It is a work which speaks about opium addiction openly, and studies its effects with almost clinical detachment. It is both instruction manual and personal history; documentary reportage is intermingled with narrative. Images of pain are juxtaposed with those of pleasure; dreaming is coupled with wakening, guilt with innocence, self-conquest with self-indulgence. The problem is exacerbated by De Quincey's statement that 'Not the opium-eater, but the opium, is the true hero of the tale'. Such oppositions point to a fundamental ambivalence concerning the author's subject, and serve to illustrate the paradoxical nature of opium dreams. De Quincey insists that the effects of the drug differ from those of alcohol. He observes that wine 'robs a man of his self-posses-sion', blurring identity, distorting loves and hates and encouraging a weak, maudlin disposition. Its pleasures are transient, and promote cycles of crisis and decline. Opium, by contrast, induces an intensification of the faculties – especially memory and dreaming – furnishing the user with the apparatus to understand the self. Through its engendering of 'serenity and equipoise' De Quincey learns 'consolations of the spirit', thus lessening his estrangement from the rest of humankind.

The narcotic state also enables him to step outside the confines of chronological time. It is this dispensing with linearity which makes the dream sequences – those symphonic, multivalent displays of imaginative power – so important to De Quincey's study. Through them, and through his vivid recollections from childhood, he develops a higher order of meaning which is imperceptible in the literal unfolding of events in time. The version of experience he presents employs an elliptical syntax capable of formulating the visionary worlds revealed to him by opium; in giving a careful account of them, he believes he is transcending the merely personal, to reveal a truth concerning the growth and structure of the human personality in general. In this sense the *Confessions* represent a prose equivalent to a work which De Quincey had the privilege of seeing in manuscript – Wordsworth's *Prelude*: both texts are intensely personal in the events they recall, yet objective in their mode of observation; through the exploration of autobiographical material, both works hope to offer an analysis of fundamental aspects of the human constitution.

The events recounted in the first part of the *Confessions* follow the events of De Quincey's early life: his flight from school, the itinerant journey through Wales, and the crucial months in London, where he endures hardship, and meets Ann, the 16-year-old prostitute who makes a significant impression on his psyche. There then follows a brief glimpse of his early days at Grasmere with the Wordsworths, and his expression of grief at the death of Wordsworth's 3-year-old daughter Kate. Each of these events is recalled in order to confirm the formative effect of memory on the human personality. He then embarks on a consideration of the 'pains of opium', of which the worst symptoms are an uncontrollable stream of fearful dreams which affected both his sleeping and waking lives. Yet he recognizes that they provide a 'master key' for unlocking the significant events of his life, providing 'the most exquisite order, legislation, and harmony'.

The pageant which unfolds includes an Easter Sunday dream; architectural dreams suggesting Giambattista Piranesi's *Carceri d'invenzione* (*Imaginary Prisons*); visionary scenes of the 'pomp of cities and palaces'; water dreams, with their 'tyranny of the human face'; Oriental dreams revealing guilty terrors; and a meditation on 'death and the wintry sterility of the grave'. Each of these visions is related to anxieties in his waking life, and by working through them De Quincey is better able to understand that incidents seemingly forgotten reside in the inner self, in 'chasms and sunless abysses'; by recalling to conscious memory that which was lost in the unconscious, he is able to confront inner anxiety, and overcome deep-seated fears. Opium helps him to recall his lapses as a young man: for example, as a reason for his vision of the 'tormenting' power of the human face, he proffers the missed appointment with the prostitute: 'Perhaps some part of my London life [the search for Ann among the fluctuating crowds] might be answerable for this.' He imagines her seated beneath Judean palms, 'with unusual solemnity of expression', and crying on account of his abandonment of her. On another occasion, when a Malay visitor appears at his cottage, De Quincey gives him a quantity of opium ('enough to kill three dragoons and their horses') which the guest immediately consumes; the anxiety resulting from this negligence is revisited upon him in a dream in which he is 'buried, for a thousand years, in stone coffins with mummies and sphinxes', and 'kissed, with cancerous kisses, by crocodiles'. In both these cases the dreamer learns that he has not fulfilled his obligations to his fellow human beings, and he is punished accordingly. The scenes generate shocks of recognition, in which De Quincey encounters his hitherto unrecognized self, and realizes that he is his own tormentor. Such a revelation is, according to De Quincey, only possible under the influence of opium, that paradoxical substance which intensifies both pleasure and pain, reveals what lies hidden in the depths of the human psyche.

The best studies of De Quincey are by Miller (1963), Davies (1964) and Maniquis (1976). The structure of the *Confessions* is discussed by Ramsey (1978), and its autobiographical aspects are examined by Holstein (1979). Abrams (1934) and Hayter (1968) provide excellent assessments of the effects of opium on the Romantic imagination.

## Coleridge and Romantic Orientalism

> In Xanadu did Kubla Khan
> A stately pleasure-dome decree:
> Where Alph, the sacred river, ran
> Through caverns measureless to man
> Down to a sunless sea.
>
> . . . . . . . . . . . . .

> But oh! that deep romantic chasm which slanted
> Down the green hill athwart a cedarn cover!
> A savage place! as holy and enchanted
> As e'er beneath a waning moon was haunted
> By woman wailing for her demon lover!
>
> (Coleridge, 'Kubla Khan, Or, A Vision in a Dream. A Fragment', 1816)

'Kubla Khan' bears some striking resemblances to De Quincey's *Confessions*, in both the circumstances of its composition and its subject matter. As Coleridge explains in a prefatory note, he had been taking opium during a bout of dysentery, and had experienced a 'sleep of the external senses' while reading a sentence from a travel book, *Purchas his Pilgrimage* (1617), concerning Kubla Khan's palace and its walled garden; in a dream this image formed itself into 'two or three hundred lines' of poetry. He roused himself from this reverie, and immediately began transcribing what he remembered of the dream, but was interrupted by the intrusion of 'a person on business from Porlock'; when he later returned to his writing, 'all the rest had passed away like images on the surface of a stream'. It is a fragmentary work, filled with exotic imagery, and lacking a rational structure; its rhythms suggest a mind vacillating between conscious and unconscious modes of being, representing what Coleridge called a 'psychological curiosity'.

Like the *Confessions*, 'Kubla Khan' is filled with contrasts. It opens with a carefully constructed image of a walled garden, containing 'incense-bearing' trees, and forests enclosing 'sunny spots of greenery'. The domesticated orderliness of the scene is reflected in the metre of the lines:

$$\bar{\text{In}} \mid \acute{\text{X}}\text{anād}\bar{\text{u}} \mid \text{d}\bar{\text{i}}\text{d K}\acute{\text{u}} \mid \text{b}\bar{\text{l}}\text{a K}\acute{\text{h}}\text{an}$$

$$\bar{\text{A}} \mid \acute{\text{s}}\text{tate}\bar{\text{l}}\text{y} \mid \text{pléas}\bar{\text{u}}\text{re dom}\overline{\text{e}} \mid \text{d}\bar{\text{e}}\text{crée}$$

Metrical scansion reveals that the words 'Xanadu' and 'Pleasure dome' are both stressed as dactyls ( ´ ˘ ˘ ), thereby instilling a serene, pastoral, even paradisal spirit into Kubla's realm. The strongly stressed, 'masculine' endings of the lines help to underline Khan's authority in the place he has created. His world is 'girdled round' and protected from undesirable or unharmonious influences. This scene stands in stark contrast with the opening of the second stanza:

$$\bar{\text{B}}\bar{\text{u}}\text{t óh} \mid \text{thāt déep} \mid \text{rōmán} \mid \text{t}\bar{\text{i}}\text{c chá} \mid \text{s}\overline{\text{m}} \text{ wh}\acute{\text{i}}\text{ch} \mid \text{slántēd}$$

$$\text{Dówn th}\overline{\text{e}} \mid \text{gréen h}\bar{\text{i}}\text{ll} \mid \bar{\text{a}} \text{thẃart} \mid \bar{\text{a}} \text{cé} \mid \text{dārn ćov} \mid \bar{\text{e}}\text{r!}$$

Here the atmosphere is different: the rational order of the garden has been replaced by a scene outside the walls which is 'savage', 'holy', and 'enchanted'. The dactyls have given way to a series of advancing iambs ( ˘ ´ ) and trochees ( ´ ˘ ), quickening the pace, and instilling in the lines a sense of urgency. The fusion of these two moods into the same poem indicates that there are opposite processes at work, with seemingly disconnected fragments coming together in an unexpected fashion, as they might in dreams. Also, the fountain which emerges from the chasm, 'As if this earth in thick fast pants were breathing', gives the impression of an involuntary effusion of images characteristic of the dream world. If the individual images are analyzed, it is possible to develop a pattern of associations linking the conscious and unconscious realms in a way entirely consistent with the investigative methods of psychoanalysis.

There is, however, another level on which the poem operates. While 'Kubla Khan' was composed in 1797, it was only published in 1816, on the advice of Byron, who was then publishing a series of *Eastern Tales*, which transformed him into the most popular poet in Britain. Coleridge's poem shares with *The Giaour* (1813), *The Corsair* (1814), *The Siege of Corinth* (1816) and other poems an interest in the Orient: those Asiatic cultures in which Britain had developed a cultural, political and economic interest, and which were becoming important components of the great imperial project of the nineteenth century. Literary interest in the East was stimulated by the translation into English of the *Arabian Nights Entertainment* in the early eighteenth century, which provided attractive settings, full of colour, excitement, magic and mystery for such writers as Samuel Johnson, who produced *Rasselas* in 1759, and William Beckford, who published *Vathek* in 1782. By the early nineteenth century the fashion for Oriental settings and themes had penetrated into the work of many prominent writers, including Wordsworth, Southey, Percy Shelley, Thomas Moore, Walter Savage Landor, De Quincey, and Mary Shelley.

The Orient took on particular characteristics in literary representation. Its distance from the first-hand experience of most of its proponents contributed to its 'exotic' feel, and confirmed the separation between the familiar 'Us' of the European West, and the strange 'Other' of the East. Its geography and inhabitants could be presented to British readers in such a way as to accentuate the separation of the two worlds in terms of culture, language, religion, and morality. This segregation allowed for a process of translation and subjugation of the Orient by the West, in which the 'Other' was objectified and spoken about by a confident, authoritative European sensibility, interested not in authentic representation, but in sublimation. The practice of subordinating the Orient to an Occidental 'centre' played a crucial role in the transformation of Asiatic cultures into European colonies. Coleridge, who had an avid interest in the affairs of state, was well aware of the powerful political and economic effects of this discourse, and a poem like 'Kubla Khan' can be seen as an articulation of anxieties about increasing European intervention in the East, and exploration of the dislocating effect of such incursions on British culture.

In 'Kubla Khan' the Orient is presented as a feminized object of desire, which (from reading travel books like *Purchas his Pilgrimage*) is known to exist, but only accessible to the poet-bard through the world of imagination and dreaming. The setting of the second stanza provides an attractive background for spectacular action, conveyed by means of the strongly sexual image of the rising fountain, accompanied by bursting, dancing, and flying through the air. This passionate upheaval is a profoundly shaking experience, and contrasts strongly with Kubla's pleasure-dome and its garden. The energy of the Orient is here readily apparent; so too is its danger.

The surrealistic passage describing the 'sunny pleasure-dome with caves of ice' attempts a synthesis of the savage chasm and pleasure garden. The opposites are momentarily reconciled: Orient and Occident are brought together in 'mingled measure'. This fusion demonstrates the instability of the relationship between East and West: the exhilaration felt by the 'centre' because of its interaction with the invigorating Oriental Other becomes confused with its dependence upon (and hence inseparability from) this same subjugated Other. Such blurring of definitions engenders anxiety for the colonizer, who wishes to remain separate from the colonized, but finds that precise delineation is no longer possible.

The poet suddenly remembers the vision of a damsel with a dulcimer, 'Singing of Mount Abora', the mountain compared to Eden by Milton in *Paradise Lost*. The lyrical moment which is celebrated is of such force and beauty that it is too powerful – and dangerous – to contemplate. On seeing the image the poet acquires 'flashing eyes' and 'floating hair', and his observers, filled with 'holy dread', cry 'Beware! Beware!' Like the Ancient Mariner, this solitary figure is isolated from the rest of society, and is marked out as fearful and dangerous because of his unique power of vision, which transcends ordinary, canonical definitions of the Occidental and Oriental, to embody a perspective which synthesizes the two in an exotic, attractive, terrifying fashion.

By integrating elements of East and West into a single vision Coleridge has pointed to a fundamental ambivalence in Romantic Orientalism: appropriation of the Orient for Western consumption – whether political, economic, or literary – carries with it the risk of obscuring the points of identification of the two spheres. While the East might provide exotic and attractive poetic locations, and more spectacular opportunities for action, the longing for something unfamiliar might necessitate a synthesis of conflicting elements, by what Coleridge describes in the *Biographia Literaria* as the 'magical power' of the 'imagination'. In such an imaginative poem as 'Kubla Khan' this transformation confirms not only the duality of the Oriental image, but also the attendant anxiety over the definition of self.

The seminal text for any study of Orientalism is Said (1985); Romantic Orientalism in particular is considered by Kabbani (1986) and Leask (1992). Raine (1964) relates 'Kubla Khan' to the world of dream and symbol. The poem's fragmentary nature is discussed and contextualized by Levinson (1987).

## The ode as embodiment of Romantic ideology: assertions and challenges

> When old age shall this generation waste,
>     Thou shalt remain, in midst of other woe
> Than ours, a friend to man, to whom thou say'st,
>     'Beauty is truth, truth beauty, – that is all
>         Ye know on earth, and all ye need to know.'
>                                     (Keats, 'Ode on a Grecian Urn', 1820)

Scatter, as from an unextinguished hearth
Ashes and sparks, my words among mankind!
Be through my lips to unawakened Earth
The trumpet of a prophecy! O, Wind,
If Winter comes, can Spring be far behind?

(P.B. Shelley, 'Ode to the West Wind', 1820)

Romantic writers developed a variety of strategies to embody disparate elements within the same text; in 'Kubla Khan' this problem was evoked by carefully balancing a rational narrative mode with an imagistic lyric discourse in a poem which Coleridge deliberately left as a 'fragment' in order to illustrate the irresolvable nature of the problem. For others the reconciliation of opposites was not as problematic, though it did demand a degree of innovation, and experimentation with poetic form. Keats invented a new and influential mode of symbolic lyric poetry, in which the deep-seated desires are submitted to the scrutiny of the sceptical mind. In 'Ode on a Grecian Urn', the most teasing and problematic work of his 'annus mirabilis' (1818–19), the progress and resolution of the poem is determined by the central symbol's inability to sustain the meanings that the poet would wish it to bear.

Keats was extremely well read and acutely self-critical. His letters record a series of impressions made by a variety of authors, but above all Shakespeare, to whom he constantly refers in expressing his insight into the nature of poetic creation, notably in 1817, when he coined the term 'Negative Capability'. For him it was the capacity to resist the urge to systematize, to have a freedom to contemplate reality without trying to reconcile its contradictory aspects, and without 'any irritable reaching after fact and reason', thereby engendering an invigorating openness of mind. He embodied this in the very fabric of the 'Ode on a Grecian Urn' through his creation of a unique stanzaic form, combining what he believed were the best features of the two traditional sonnet constructions. Each stanza begins with four lines rhyming ABAB, as in a Shakespearian sonnet, which gives a good regular beginning and then allows the reader to pause; this is followed by an adaptation of the Petrarchan sestet, sometimes embodying the regular rhyming pattern of CDECDE (stanzas 3 and 4), but freely adapting it into different combinations, including CDEDCE (stanzas 1 and 5) and CDECED (stanza 2). By uniting the Shakespearian quatrain and Petrarchan sestet, Keats showed that he could work within canonical poetic tradition, yet mould the material to his own advantage. In this way, as he noted in a letter of 1818, he was able to claim that what shocks the virtuous philosopher 'delights the chameleon poet'.

Keats was not the only Romantic poet to turn the traditional exigencies of the ode to his own purposes. Wordsworth and Coleridge were also aware of the creative potential of this verse form, and used it to great effect in such poems as 'Ode: Intimations of Immortality from Recollections of Early Childhood' (1807) and 'Dejection: An Ode'. By identifying each of these poems as 'Ode' in the title, there is an attempt to situate the verses within a tradition stretching back to classical times, in order to accommodate those shifts in subject and mood which have become identifying features of Romantic expression. Whereas earlier English odes, such as those by Dryden or Thomas Gray, were generally written to praise abstract concepts or impersonal subjects, Romantic odes (which were Pindaric rather than Horatian in spirit) were filled with individual insight and passionate meditation; they were inspired by external circumstances, but turned poignantly inward to explore both personally affecting situations and generally human ones. The flexibility embodied in irregular stanzaic structure, variable line length and changeable rhythm and metre, contributed to the impression of immediacy and uncertainty which Romantic poets wished to evoke.

Despite the contradictions and oppositions which Keats was able to represent in his 'Ode on a Grecian Urn', its structure is far more regular and traditional than the odes of many of his contemporaries. The urn which Keats addresses in the reverential, lyrical language of the ode, is a fine work of art, embodying ideas of perfection and permanence. The images depicted of the courtship dance (stanza 1), the bucolic lovers (stanzas 2–3) and the pagan sacrifice (stanza 4) are frozen and silent, suspended in time, and rendered eternal only through the intervention of art. The bold lover can never kiss his beloved, 'Though winning near the goal'; as a consolation for not having his 'bliss' he is offered her eternal youth and love by being fixed in time. By comparison to the urn, which evokes the eternal 'beauty' and 'truth', these human beings seem imperfect and transitory; and yet, for all its ideal perfection, the urn is only art. Its paradoxical nature is revealed by demonstrating that its advantages are simultaneously disadvantages: the urn's limiting deficiency is that it never changes, and its human characters never partake of the vicissitudes of earthly existence – joy and suffering, life and death.

It is in this sense that the urn forms the ideal symbol of Romantic struggle and yearning: its inhuman perfection is a source of tension. It embodies contrary suggestions of music and silence, movement and stasis, and as an *objet d'art* it cannot approach human realization. This distance is confirmed in the exclamation 'O Attic shape! fair attitude' of the last stanza, which dissociates the urn from the scenes depicted, and raises it to its proper sphere as aesthetic object. Yet the poem does not end there, but returns for a final confrontation to the time 'When old age shall this generation waste', in a quest for the meaning of reality, which is embodied in an ambiguous statement about the reconciliation of truth and beauty. What emerges is embodied in two conflicting apprehensions concerning the wonder of art, and its simultaneous limitations. Its 'still' and permanent beauty is refreshing to contemplate; yet there is an awareness that such beauty embodies a falsehood which disregards genuine human joy and despair. Examined in this way, Keats's ode demonstrates the elusiveness and complexity of symbols, as well as the tension which exists within them. It also demonstrates the perfect operation of Negative Capability, in which the apparently contradictory realms of imagination and reality can creatively coexist.

Shelley's 'Ode to the West Wind' is another lyrical address to an ideal object, inspired by a creative struggle within the self. It is a more confident and socially aware poem than that of Keats, and provides a more optimistic conception of the power and function of art, particularly poetry, as a vehicle for liberation. Many attributes ascribed to the poet in the ode later appeared in his *Defence of Poetry* (written in 1821, published posthumously in 1840), where he argued, like

Wordsworth, that the poet occupied the role of priest or prophet; but he went beyond Wordsworth in claiming for the poet the position of 'unacknowledged legislator', liberator, and explorer for a future society, which would recognize the appeal of the power of the imagination over a merely utilitarian view of art.

Like Keats's 'Grecian Urn', Shelley's ode embodies both associations with and departures from the tradition of the sonnet. It is written in five fourteen-line sections of *terza rima*, and struggles to idealize and unify contradictory aspects of existence by examining a natural phenomenon (the autumn wind), and simultaneously pointing to a reality transcending the physical. In his lyrics of nature Shelley uses such emblems as clouds, wind and skylarks to celebrate the joining of material and spiritual elements and reflect what he believes is a duality embodied in the poet – the exceptional individual who inhabits the corporeal, but is able to look prophetically beyond the veil of earthly existence.

The wind is the ideal vehicle for spiritual vision because of its freedom and power to blow where it wishes – an attribute which the poet recognizes in characterizing his addressee as 'tameless, and swift, and proud' and honouring it with the epithet 'O uncontrollable!' He prays that this autonomous liberator will lift him from his earthly prison – a place from which he is forced to exclaim 'I fall upon the thorns of life! I bleed!' Yet this same natural phenomenon is a 'Wild spirit', which appears as a destroyer in autumn, carrying away dead leaves and announcing the impending arrival of cruel, relentless winter. It is precisely this annihilating power which the poet wishes to embody: 'Be thou, Spirit fierce,/My spirit! Be thou me, impetuous one!' It is here that Shelley moves beyond the position of Keats, and claims for himself the role of prophet and social reformer, who can engender a new awakening through the 'incantation' of his verse. The process of rebirth is infused with Shelley's views on politics and religion: the destruction of the old, unregenerate world will allow for the construction of a new order, just as the destruction of winter gives way to the renewal of spring. The questioning conclusion to the poem serves as an encapsulation of some of the key features of Romantic discourse: through an investigation of the self and its surroundings the poet explores the possibility of finding a better world and a new life to replace the old systems and assumptions.

While it may be possible to identify a pervasive spirit within Romantic discourse, it is more difficult to discover a single object or mode of literary expression which captures the essence of this period. Nevertheless, given what has been said about the ode in its various manifestations, it might be attractive to identify this genre as the keystone of Romanticism. Many Romantic odes are epiphanic lyric meditations on a serious subject, presenting a determinate speaker in a particularized setting. This persona, who often embodies a privileged visionary capacity, is overheard carrying on a sustained interlocution, sometimes with himself or with an external object, but more frequently with a silent auditor, in the course of which there is an achievement of an altered mood, or a deeper insight into the contemplated object. Despite claims to the contrary, such self-intoxicating bardic *hauteur* encouraged the use of elaborate diction which was far removed from what Wordsworth called the 'language really used by men'; also, the exclusivity of the experience described endowed the odes with powerful alienating pretensions which could only be understood and shared by a privileged few.

The archetypal embodiment of such self-conscious identity and visionary experience is Wordsworth's 'Immortality Ode'. It contains moments of vision as well as a series of powerful sensations, exciting feelings of rapturous 'joy' (a word often repeated), and confidence in his own powers. The poem's adherence to the tradition of the Pindaric ode, with its circular structure and irregular stanzaic pattern, allows for the exploration of a wide spectrum of dualities, including life and death, childhood and maturity, physicality and spirituality. In the process the powerful, self-confident poet rejoices in his precise powers of recollection, and in the epiphanic nature of his priestly character.

Such is the view from the dizzy heights to which Wordsworth, a Romantic originator, had raised himself; yet even from this pinnacle of achievement, pangs of anxiety emerge. Although the rapturously self-assured image of the poet as gifted figure of authority has been a dominant one in traditional assessments of Romanticism, this impression has been open to question – not only by modern critics wishing to challenge canonical assumptions, but even by some Romantic writers considered in this unit. The most vociferous, articulate and celebrated of Wordsworth's pessimistic contemporaries was Byron, who achieved instant and enduring fame in 1812 with the issuing of the first two cantos of *Childe Harold's Pilgrimage*. The effects of this publication were immediate and far-reaching: he supplanted Walter Scott as the most popular poet in Britain, and captured the spirit of the age through his depiction of frenetic energy combined with satiric evocation of public discontent. Unlike Wordsworth, Byron did not rely on the contemplation of nature for the substance of his poetry; instead his work was informed by such elements as British politics and the turbulent European nationalistic struggles which emerged in the wake of the French Revolution. He readily assumed the role of commentator on his times, and relished the opportunities afforded him of denigrating the reputations and achievements of his Romantic contemporaries. As early as 1809, in *English Bards and Scotch Reviewers*, a verse satire after the manner of Pope, he referred to Coleridge as 'turgid' and Wordsworth as 'simple'; in later years, after extensive periods abroad, where he was able to reflect on what he saw as the insularity of poetic attitudes in Britain, he engaged in more sustained and energetic attacks, the most memorable of which was his anarchic, chaotic and comic *Don Juan* (1819–24), a work which overturned many contemporary expectations about the nature and purpose of poetic expression. His most memorable attack on the poets of his day appeared in the Dedication, where he noted:

> You – Gentlemen! by dint of long seclusion
>     From better company, have kept your own
> At Keswick, and, through still continued fusion
>     Of one another's minds, at last have grown
> To deem as a most logical conclusion,
>     That Poesy has wreaths for you alone:
> There is a narrowness in such a notion,
> Which makes me wish you'd change your lakes for ocean.

Such irreverence assisted in casting Byron in the role of outsider, vexed and amused by the anomalies of his age, and keen to redefine the criteria by which poetic production was assessed. He had no interest in the innovations proposed by Coleridge and Wordsworth, but preferred traditional language and style, especially the couplet and the Spenserian stanza; also he did not subscribe to the doctrine of the poet as prophet. He wished to supplant Romantic imagination by Romantic indignation, and it was his ridiculing of certain solemnly cherished ideas that placed him at odds with the guardians of canonical tradition. His ostracism was confirmed after his death in 1824, when the Dean of Westminster refused him a tomb in Poet's Corner – that emblematic resting place for a narrowly and somewhat arbitrarily defined 'Who's Who' of English letters. The omission was not rectified until 1969, when a memorial to Byron was installed in the Abbey.

The gauntlet thrown down by Byron to his contemporaries – and to us – is challenging and significant. Although his questioning of established norms was energetic and outspoken, the campaign mounted by those who valued the jurisdiction of Wordsworth and others resulted in a resounding victory for established authority. The enduring legacy of a restricted definition of Romantic aims and standards has been a change in the direction and perception of English poetry, causing it to be proscriptively distinguished as etherial, precious and intellectual. Continued support for this view – whether active or passive – jeopardizes the recovery of a position where poetry is capable of sustaining a variety of outlooks or opinions, some of which might lie outside the narrow confines of the socially or politically acceptable. The alternative reasoning of Byron points to the exciting opportunity offered by an unhindered embrace of tensions and anxieties, incongruities and oppositions, in developing a new definition of Romanticism.

The best introduction to Keats's poetry is by Barnard (1987); Vendler (1983) provides a good general assessment of the odes. Austin (1986) contains a useful survey of the various interpretations of the 'Ode on a Grecian Urn' and its enigmatic final lines. Informative introductions to the poetry of Shelley are those by Raine (1973) and Pirie (1988). Chernaik (1972) discusses Shelley's lyric poetry; Bloom (1959) and Webb (1977) provide fine analyses of 'Ode to the West Wind'. Abrams (1965), Dekker (1978) and Fry (1980) describe the more salient features of the Romantic ode. There is a useful guide to Byron's poetry by Rutherford (1961).

## BIBLIOGRAPHY

Abrams, M.H. (1934) *The Milk of Paradise: The Effect of Opium Visions on the Works of De Quincey, Crabbe, Francis Thompson and Coleridge*, Harvard University Press, Cambridge, Mass.

Abrams, M.H. (1965) 'Structure and Style in the Greater Romantic Lyric', in *From Sensibility to Romanticism*, ed. F.W. Hilles and H. Bloom, Oxford University Press, London, pp. 527–60.

Abrams, M.H. (1971) *Natural Supernaturalism*, Oxford University Press, London.

Aers, D. (1981) *Romanticism and Ideology: Essays in English Writing 1765–1830*, Routledge, London.

Austin, A.C. (1986) 'Toward Resolving Keats's Grecian Urn Ode', *Neophilologus*, vol. 70, pp. 615–29.

Baldick, C. (1987) *In Frankenstein's Shadow: Myth, Monstrosity and Nineteenth-Century Writing*, Clarendon Press, Oxford.

Ball, P. (1968) *The Central Self: A Study in Romantic and Victorian Imagination*, Athlone Press, London.

Barnard, J. (1987) *John Keats*, Cambridge University Press, Cambridge.

Barrell, J. (1988) 'The Uses of Dorothy', in *Poetry, Language and Politics*, Manchester University Press, Manchester, pp. 137–67.

Beer, J. B. (1978) *Wordsworth and the Human Heart*, Macmillan, London.

Beres, D. (1951), 'A Dream, a Vision, and a Poem: A Psychoanalytic Study of the Origins of *The Rime of the Ancient Mariner*', *International Journal of Psychoanalysis*, vol. 32, pp. 97–116.

Blake, W. (1971) *Songs of Innocence*, Dover, New York.

Blake, W. (1984) *Songs of Experience*, Dover, New York.

Bloom, H. (1959) *Shelley's Mythmaking*, Yale University Press, New Haven.

Bostetter, E.E. (1962) 'The Nightmare World of the Ancient Mariner', *Studies in Romanticism*, vol. 1, pp. 241–54.

Butler, M. (1981) *Romantics, Rebels and Reactionaries: English Literature and its Background 1760–1830*, Oxford University Press, London.

Butler, M. (ed.) (1984) *Burke, Paine, Godwin and the Revolution Controversy*, Cambridge University Press, Cambridge.

Chase, C. (ed.) (1993) *Romanticism*, Longman, Harlow.

Chernaik, J. (1972) *The Lyrics of Shelley*, Case Western Reserve University Press, Cleveland.

Curran, S. (1986) *Poetic Form and British Romanticism*, Oxford University Press, Oxford.

Curran, S. (ed.) (1993) *The Cambridge Companion to British Romanticism*, Cambridge University Press, Cambridge.

Dabundo, L. (ed.) (1992) *Encyclopedia of Romanticism: Culture in Britain, 1780s–1830s*, Routledge, London.

Davies, H. S. (1964) *Thomas De Quincey*, Longmans, Green, London.

De Quincey, T. (1985) *Confessions of an English Opium-Eater and Other Writings*, ed. G. Lindop, Oxford University Press, Oxford [first published 1822].

Dekker, G. (1978) *Coleridge and the Literature of Sensibility*, Vision Press, London.

Edwards, P. and Emslie, M. (1971) '"Thoughts so All unlike Each Other": the Paradoxical in "Christabel"', *English Studies*, vol, 52, pp. 236–46.

Emslie, M. and Edwards, P. (1970) 'The Limitations of Langdale: A Reading of "Christabel"', *Essays in Criticism*, vol. 20, pp. 57–70.

Everest, K. (1990) *English Romantic Poetry: An Introduction to the Historical Context and Literary Scene*, Open University Press, Milton Keynes.

Everest, K. (ed.) (1991) *Revolution in Writing: British Literary Responses to the French Revolution*, Open University Press, Milton Keynes.

Fry, P.H. (1980) *The Poet's Calling in the English Ode*, Yale University Press, New Haven.

Frye, N. (1967) *Fearful Symmetry: A Study of William Blake*, Princeton University Press, Princeton.

Furst, L.R. (1976) *Romanticism*, Methuen, London.

Furst, L.R. (1979) *Romanticism in Perspective: A Comparative Study of Aspects of the Romantic Movement in England, France and Germany*, Macmillan, London.

Gill, S. (1991) *Wordsworth: The Prelude*, Cambridge University Press, Cambridge.

Gleckner, R.F. (1959) *The Piper & the Bard: A Study of William Blake*, Wayne State University Press, Detroit.

Glen, H. (1983) *Vision and Disenchantment: Blake's Songs and Wordsworth's Lyrical Ballads*, Cambridge University Press, Cambridge.

Harding, D.W. (1941) 'The Theme of "The Ancient Mariner"', *Scrutiny*, vol. 9 no. 3, pp. 334–42.

Hartman, G.H. (1964) *Wordsworth's Poetry, 1787–1814*, Yale University Press, New Haven.

Hartman, G.H. (1966) 'Wordsworth', *The Unmediated Vision: An Interpretation of Wordsworth, Hopkins, Rilke and Valéry*, Harcourt, Brace & World, New York, pp. 1–45.

Hayter, A. (1968) *Opium and the Romantic Imagination*, University of California Press, Berkeley and Los Angeles.

Hill, J.S. (ed.) (1977) *The Romantic Imagination: A Casebook*, Macmillan, London.

Hilton, N. (ed.) (1986) *Essential Articles for the Study of Blake*, Archon Books, Hamden, Conn.

Hogg, J. (1990) *The Private Memoirs and Confessions of a Justified Sinner*, ed. J. Carey, Oxford University Press, Oxford [first published 1824].

Holstein, M. E. (1979) '"An Apocalypse of the World within": Autobiographical Exegesis in De Quincey's *Confessions of an English Opium-Eater*, 1822', *Prose Studies*, vol. 2, pp. 88–102.

Jacobus, M. (1976) *Tradition and Experiment in Wordsworth's Lyrical Ballads (1978)*, Oxford University Press, Oxford.

Jacobus, M. (1984) 'Is There a Woman in This Text?', *New Literary History*, vol. 14, no. 1, pp. 117–54.

Johnston, K. et al (eds) (1990) *Romantic Revolutions: Criticism and Theory*, Indiana University Press, Bloomington.

Kabbani, R. (1986) *Imperial Fictions: Europe's Myths of the Orient*, Macmillan, London.

Kelly, G. (1989) *English Fiction of the Romantic Period*, Longman, Harlow.

Kiely, R. (1972) *The Romantic Novel in England*, Harvard University Press, Cambridge, Mass.

Knoepflmacher, U.C. and Levine, G. (eds) (1979) *The Endurance of Frankenstein: Essays on Mary Shelley's Novel*, University of California Press, Berkeley.

Leask, N. (1992) *British Romantic Writers and the East: Anxieties of Empire*, Cambridge University Press, Cambridge.

Lefebure, M. (1974) *Samuel Taylor Coleridge: A Bondage of Opium*, Gollancz, London.

Levinson, M. (1987) *The Romantic Fragment Poem: A Critique of a Form*, University of North Carolina Press, Chapel Hill.

Levinson, M. et al. (1989) *Rethinking Historicism: Critical Readings in Romantic History*, Blackwell, Oxford.

Maniquis, R.M. (1976) 'Lonely Empires: Personal and Public Visions of Thomas De Quincey', *Literary Monographs* 8, ed. E. Rothstein and J.A. Wittreich, Jr, University of Wisconsin Press, Madison, pp. 49–127.

McFarland, T. (1981) *Romanticism and the Forms of Ruin: Wordsworth, Coleridge, and the Modalities of Fragmentation*, Princeton University Press, Princeton.

McGann, J.J. (1983) *The Romantic Ideology: A Critical Investigation*, University of Chicago Press, Chicago.

McGann, J.J. (ed.) (1993) *The New Oxford Book of Romantic Period Verse*, Oxford University Press, Oxford.

Mellor, A.K. (1988) *Mary Shelley: Her Life, Her Fiction, Her Monsters*, Methuen, London.

Mellor, A.K. (1993) *Romanticism and Gender*, Routledge, London.

Miles, R. (1993) *Gothic Writing 1750–1820*, Routledge, London.

Miller, J.H. (1963) 'Thomas De Quincey', *The Disappearance of God: Five Nineteenth-Century Writers*, Harvard University Press, Cambridge, Mass., pp. 17–80.

Musselwhite, D. (1987) *Partings Welded Together: Politics and Desire in the Nineteenth-Century Novel*, Methuen, London.

Newman, B. (1986) 'Narratives of Seduction and the Seductions of Narrative: The Frame Structure of *Frankenstein*', *English Literary History*, vol. 53, no. 1, pp. 141–63.

Parrish, S.M. (1973) *The Art of the Lyrical Ballads*, Harvard University Press, Cambridge, Mass.

Perkins, D. (ed.) (1967) *English Romantic Writers*, Harcourt Brace Jovanovich, New York.

Pirie, D. (1988) *Shelley*, Open University Press, Milton Keynes.

Poovey, M. (1984) 'My Hideous Progeny: The Lady and the Monster', *The Proper Lady and the Woman Writer: Ideology as Style in the Works of Mary Wollstonecraft, Mary Shelley and Jane Austen*, pp. 114–42, Chicago University Press, Chicago.

Punter, D. (1980) *The Literature of Terror*, Longman, London.

Punter, D. (1989) *The Romantic Unconscious: A Study in Narcissism and Patriarchy*, Harvester Wheatsheaf, Hemel Hempstead.

Raimond, J. and Watson, J.R. (eds) (1992) *A Handbook to English Romanticism*, Macmillan, Houndmills.

Raine, K. (1964) 'Traditional Symbolism in Kubla Khan', *Sewanee Review*, vol. 72, pp. 626–42.

Raine, K. (1970) *William Blake*, Thames & Hudson, London.

Raine, K. (1973) *Shelley*, Penguin, Harmondsworth.

Ramsey, R. (1978) 'The Structure of De Quincey's *Confessions of an English Opium-Eater*', *Prose Studies*, vol. 1, pp. 21–9.

Roe, N. (1988) *Wordsworth and Coleridge: The Radical Years*, Clarendon Press, Oxford.

Rutherford, A. (1961) *Byron: A Critical Study*, Oliver & Boyd, Edinburgh.

Said, E.W. (1985) *Orientalism*, Penguin Books, Harmondsworth.

Sheats, P.D. (1973) *The Making of Wordsworth's Poetry 1785–1798*, Harvard University Press, Cambridge, Mass.

Shelley, M. (1985) *Frankenstein, or, the Modern Prometheus*, ed. M. Hindle, Penguin, Harmondsworth [first published 1818].

Simpson, D. (1979) *Irony and Authority in Romantic Poetry*, Macmillan, London.

Spark, M. (1988) *Mary Shelley*, Constable, London.

Swann, K. (1984) '"Christabel": The Wandering Mother and the Enigma of Form', *Studies in Romanticism*, vol. 23, pp. 533–53.

Swann, K. (1985) 'Literary Gentlemen and Lovely Ladies: The Debate on the Character of "Christabel"', *English Literary History*, vol. 52, pp. 397–418.

Vendler, H. (1983) *The Odes of John Keats*, Harvard University Press, Cambridge, Mass.

Watson, J.R. (1985; 2nd edn 1992) *English Poetry of the Romantic Period, 1789–1830*, Longman, Harlow.

Webb, T. (1977) *Shelley: A Voice not Understood*, Manchester University Press, Manchester.

Weiskel, T. (1976) *The Romantic Sublime*, Johns Hopkins University Press, Baltimore.

Whalley, G. (1946–7) 'The Mariner and the Albatross', *University of Toronto Quarterly*, vol. 16, pp. 381–98.

Wheeler, K. (1981) *The Creative Mind in Coleridge's Poetry*, Heinemann, London.

Winnett, S. (1990) 'Coming Unstrung: Women, Men, Narrative, and Principles of Pleasure', *PMLA*, vol. 105, no. 3, pp. 505–18.

Wu, D. (ed.) (1994) *Romanticism: An Anthology*, Blackwell, Oxford.

Wu, D. (ed.) (1995) *Romanticism: A Critical Reader*, Blackwell, Oxford.

# UNIT 11

# The Victorian novel 1830–1900

*Jan Jędrzejewski*

## Introduction

As rich and diverse as Renaissance drama, but less distant in time and therefore more likely to appeal directly to the modern reader, Victorian fiction remains to this day the most widely read body of classic literature in English and as such arguably occupies the most central place in the literary consciousness of the English-speaking world. Taught widely in schools and universities, popularized through stage, film and television adaptations, and available in countless editions, popular as well as scholarly, in bookshops all over the world, Victorian novels still define not only the popular perception of what constitutes English literature, but also what might be described as the ultimate image of Britishness, a vision of social reality which, though deeply rooted in the nineteenth century and therefore long gone, is still explicitly or implicitly present both in much of modern Britain's perception of itself and in the image the country in many ways continues to impress on the outside world. This sense of unity and interdependence of literature and life is in Victorian fiction so pronounced that in order to appreciate the achievement of the genre it is necessary, first, to consider the context of the most important developments that shaped the social, political and cultural life of nineteenth-century Britain (pp. 265–8), and, secondly, to analyze the ways in which the novel as a literary form responded to these changes in terms of its themes and attitudes, its conventions and techniques (pp. 268–72). It is only when studied against the background of their epoch that the best and most representative works of the leading Victorian novelists can be seen in at least some of their variety and complexity (pp. 272–93).

Defining the boundaries of literary periods and movements is a notoriously difficult thing to do; the closer to our own time, with its increasing variety of ideas and forms of expression and its dominant spirit of movement and change, the more complex the task becomes. One of the traditional approaches is to relate developments in literature to those in social and political history; more often than not, however, the resulting picture still requires significant adjustments and alterations.

This is by and large not the case with the Victorian novel. The 1830s and 1840s witnessed the emergence of an entire generation of young writers, a great majority of them born in the second decade of the century, who were to transform the entire character of modern fiction. The suddenness of this transformation was of course related to the fact that Britain's literary scene, so vibrant in the first quarter of the century, was at the time markedly losing its impetus, the creative powers of those few of the leading Romantics who still survived, like Wordsworth, showing visible signs of strain and fatigue. This state of affairs extended to the novel as well, the gradual eclipse of the career of Sir Walter Scott epitomizing the general direction in which British fiction was moving before the triumphant arrival of the generation of Dickens and Thackeray. At the other end of the Victorian period, the border area is, admittedly, much more fuzzy; nevertheless, a comparison of the basically traditionalist story-telling mode of Hardy with the highly self-conscious, sophisticated literariness of his Anglo-American near-contemporary Henry James underlines the essence of the difference between the literary spirits of the nineteenth and the twentieth centuries. However, once the distinctiveness of Victorian fiction is recognized, it immediately proves very elusive – an era that produced *The Pickwick Papers* (1836–7) as well as *Daniel Deronda* (1876), and *Wuthering Heights* (1847) as well as *Jude the Obscure* (1894–5), must indeed have been a period of diversity as well as unity – a paradox not untypical of the Victorian period as a whole.

The key to the understanding of the Victorians is to realize that, more than any other period of British history, the Victorian era was an age of transition. The Britain of 1830 (the year of revolutions in Europe and of the accession of William IV, as good or bad an arbitrary historical threshold as the alternatives, 1832, the year of the death of Scott, or 1837, that of the accession of Victoria) was in many ways a country immersed in the past, its traditional pre-modern moral and social order still just about remaining in place; although economically well on the way to becoming 'the workshop of the world', Britain had not yet managed, despite the growing pressure for change, to transform its social, political and cultural structures to respond to the demands of the emerging new reality of modern industrial society. On the other hand, the Britain of the turn of the century, of 1900 or of 1901, the year of Victoria's death, would appear even to late-twentieth-century observers as a remarkably familiar country, modern in many of its fundamental structures and institutions even if not always so in matters of mentality or, most perceptibly, technology. It is another Victorian paradox that this transformation of the past into the present occurred over what was, in domestic terms at least, by any account a period of unprecedented stability; although the changes that took place during the period were nothing short of revolutionary, the Victorian era was not an age of revolution – it was an age of reform.

Perhaps the most basic aspects of the Victorian transformation were the changes in Britain's demography and economy. The total population of England, Wales and Scotland grew from 16.3 million in 1831 to 37 million in 1901 (the figures for Ireland show a reverse trend, due to mass emigration and to the consequences of the mid-century famine). This rapid increase in population was accompanied by major changes in its geographical distribution, with millions of people moving, in search of employment, from overpopulated rural areas to towns, and from the agricultural regions such as southern and south-western England to the industrial North. This growing phenomenon of social mobility, helped by radical improvements in transport and communications, was certainly a fundamental condition of the development of modern British economy and thus a key to achieving, in a longer term, widespread prosperity; on the other hand, however, it also led to a disintegration of traditional local communities and to a disturbing sense of uprootedness among the new urban working class. The resulting widening of the material, social and psychological distance between the rich and the poor led to a perception of the British society as consisting of 'two nations', inevitably generating potential and actual tensions and conflicts.

The socio-economic changes were reflected in the political life of the country as well. The largely Whig – or Liberal – middle classes dominant in the world of Victorian industry, finance, and professions faced the opposition of predominantly Tory – or Conservative – landed aristocracy, which at the beginning of the period was still in firm control of Parliament and government, largely through the antiquated and corrupt electoral system, dating back virtually to the Middle Ages. The ever-growing middle and, later, working-class pressure for political reform, resulting in the Reform Bills of 1832, 1867 and 1884, and in the introduction of voting by ballot in 1872, produced a fundamental democratization of British public life, helped the formation of modern political parties, and prepared the ground for the legal recognition, in the Parliament Act of 1911, of the shifting of effective power from the Lords to the Commons; on the local level, the same trends led to the creation of elected local councils.

The same progressive and democratic spirit expressed itself in other spheres of life as well. The Victorian era saw the beginnings of modern employment and public health legislation, designed to remedy the most drastic consequences of *laissez-faire* capitalism. The creation of new universities and changes in the structure and regulations of the old ones facilitated access to higher education for the middle classes, non-Anglicans and women, while the 1870 Education Act provided the framework for universal primary education, which became compulsory ten years later. There was a substantial improvement in the legal, economic and social position of women; though the women's movement did not yet manage to achieve its fundamental goal of equality of franchise, it clearly paved the way for the successful adoption of its principles in the aftermath of the First World War.

However successful the Victorian era was as a period of reform, it was not free from contradictions: it could not be, because the overall stability of the period naturally meant the coexistence, within the British society, of traditional and modern ideas, beliefs, and attitudes. Nowhere was this more pronounced than in the sphere of religion – indeed, matters of faith and doubt constituted perhaps the most vigorously discussed of all subjects of public debate in the Victorian era. On the one hand, the reign of Queen Victoria witnessed the reawakening of religious piety and seriousness, taking forms ranging from radical Protestant Evangelicalism both within and outside the Established Churches to the Oxford Movement and Roman Catholicism; on the other hand, the period saw, largely as a result of developments in the natural sciences, history, philosophy and biblical criticism, the emergence of a powerful tradition of freethinking and agnosticism. As a result, the relative simplicity of the broadly Christian philosophical and theological standpoint, accepted or rejected but rarely explored in the eighteenth and the early nineteenth centuries, had by 1900 been replaced by a plethora of world-views, leaving the people of the new post-Victorian era having to find their own way through the metaphysical maze their Victorian predecessors had left behind.

Related to the changes in Victorian spirituality and equally characteristic in its apparent paradoxicality is the fact that the process of the modernization of Victorian society coexisted with the growing acceptance, across the social spectrum, of the essentially middle-class idea of respectability and of the often restrictive moral code, to this day perceived as a fundamental element of the Victorian heritage. Rather similarly, the belief in the idea of progress was paralleled by the omnipresent concern with the past, perceived not only as crucial to the understanding of mechanisms shaping the present, but also as a repository of values; the often unquestioning acceptance of tradition reinforced the sense of the continuity and organic evolution of history, so typical of the specifically Victorian spirit of conservatism. At the same time, however, the acceptance of society and of the obligations it imposed upon its members coexisted among the Victorians with the belief in the Romantic ideal of freedom and with the appreciation of individuality. It was indeed this very diversity and apparent incongruity of ideas and viewpoints that constituted the essence of Victorianism; its spirit survived until the fundamental optimistic belief in society typical of the early phase of the period was eventually replaced, towards the end of the century, by the individualistic disillusionment with society, thus finally marking the demise of Victorianism and the birth of the new epoch – the age of modernism.

All these changes in Victorian society and its attitudes were more or less directly reflected in the novel of the period – it is rather characteristic that students of no other epoch in British history are as ready as Victorianists to use literature as a source of valid socio-historical evidence in their discussions of issues ranging from patterns of domestic life to mechanisms of party politics and directions in religious thought. This is due to the fact that the triumph of the novel as the dominant literary genre of the Victorian era was directly related to the economic, social, and political triumph of the middle classes – the social environment within which the modern novel grew and developed.

The association of the novel with the emerging middle classes dates back, of course, to the early eighteenth century; it was not, however, until a century later that the relationship reached its peak. Early and, in particular, mid-nineteenth-century novelists were not only creative artists, but also, and in many ways primarily, purveyors of reading matter, responding to the demands of their growing readership by producing works that reflected the tastes, concerns and interests of their readers, and being rewarded, often very generously, for doing so. It is quite characteristic that it was the Victorian era that saw the recognition of novel-writing not only as a profession, but also as a way of achieving public acclaim and respect; the stories of the artistic, commercial and public successes of Dickens, George Eliot and Hardy stand in characteristic contrast to the mixed fortunes that characterized the dramatically complex career of their great predecessor, Sir Walter Scott.

The fact that Victorian novelists wrote for a very specific audience resulted of course in certain particular tendencies in the selection of their themes and approaches. Because of the predominance among Victorian readers of respectable middle-class women, enjoying ample leisure thanks to the availability and cheapness of domestic service, as well as to the prevalence of the tradition of family reading, novelists had to adhere to a strict code of propriety, banning, in the first place, any direct discussions of matters of sex and physiology (or indeed any references to anything that could be seen as 'dirty'), and forcing specific moral judgements, such as unconditional condemnation of sexual irregularity and obligatory punishment of 'fallen women', however compassionately presented (*Ruth* (1853), *Far from the Madding Crowd* (1874)). As a result, the leading novelists of the period adopted a practice of self-imposed censorship or devised covert ways of conveying their meaning through elaborate systems of symbolic codes and allusions. The need for this kind of manipulation was related to the fact that the Victorian literary market was dominated, due to relatively high prices of books, not so much by writers and readers, but by middlemen: publishers of monthly-part novels, editors of literary magazines, and owners of circulating libraries, able to offer thousands of readers cheap access to current best sellers, but also powerful enough to dictate to authors the conditions that had to be fulfilled before their works could be deemed safe for consumption by those paragons of Victorian innocence, unmarried daughters of country vicars. It was not until the educational reforms of the 1870s and 1880s led to a significant growth of the potential novel-reading market that the situation began to change; the consequences of this process included, on the one hand, a proliferation of lowbrow sentimental or sensational novels and, on the other hand, an increased commercial feasibility of cheap one-volume editions, which replaced the standard three-volume novel (the 'three-decker'), thus spelling the end of the mid-century-style modes of novel circulation and freeing the authors from the restrictions they imposed.

The influence of the forces of the Victorian literary market on the development of the novel was not, however, always restrictive: thus, for instance, serial publication not only allowed novelists to alter and develop their original schemes as the work progressed, as was the case, most notably, with *The Pickwick Papers* and *Martin Chuzzlewit* (1843–4), but also invited such literary techniques as the creation of sharply delineated and thus easily remembered characters and the manipulation of plots to maintain episode-to-episode suspense. In some novels, such as *Jane Eyre* (1847), it is possible to detect a tripartite structure of the plot reflective of the original structure of the three-decker; towards the end of the period, the adoption of the one-volume format produced novels that were both shorter and rather more concentrated and focused in terms of theme, plot and characterization.

To attribute the changes in both the content and the form of the Victorian novel exclusively to the impact of the developments in the world of commercial publishing would, however, be a gross misrepresentation – though undoubtedly influenced by the more practical aspects of the cultural environment in which they operated, the leading Victorian novelists nevertheless managed to develop, within the limits of their genre, a most impressive variety of approaches, resulting in the creation of a body of work which, in its sheer volume, diversity and level of artistic achievement, may indeed compare with the imaginative richness of Elizabethan and Jacobean drama. Among the *c*.40,000 novels published in Britain between 1830 and 1900, there were novels of manners and novels of adventure, sentimental love stories and novels of ideas, novels set in London and tales of regional and provincial life, historical romances and semi-documentary accounts of the life of modern industrial society. Most of the best novels of the period could not of course be easily categorized, their very success consisting largely in the dynamism of theme, plot and character that allowed them to transcend the limits of individual sub-genres; it is, however, important for a full appreciation of the achievement of the best of Victorian novelists to remember that much of what is now seen, in comparative terms, as second-rate work is indeed by its own standards fully satisfactory as literature. The imaginative power of Dickens's *Bleak House* (1852–3) or *Little Dorrit* (1855–7) stands out even more clearly when juxtaposed with the presentation of the world of nineteenth-century politics in the novels from Trollope's Palliser series (1864–80) – witty, acutely perceptive, eminently readable, and yet lacking the passion, the commitment, and the inexhaustible energy of Dickens's creative genius.

The diversity of Victorian fiction was also related to the impact of the heritage of the literary tradition within which Victorian novelists operated and which they so successfully developed. The influences were manifold: the broadly realistic tradition of the modern epic in prose represented by Fielding; the picaresque stories of Smollett; the domestic novel of manners in the style of Fanny Burney and, in particular, Jane Austen; the Gothic romances of Walpole and Mrs Radcliffe; finally, and perhaps most importantly, the historical novels of Scott (see Unit 9). Partly because of this very diversity of literary antecedents, and partly as a result of the imaginative and formal freedom afforded by the genre, still perceived, due to its basic story-telling, non-classical origin, as popular rather than serious, and in consequence largely free from prescriptive rules and theories, the novel in the Victorian period, particularly in its earlier years, became an all-inclusive and therefore sometimes rather amorphous literary form; created very much as an attempt to offer a comprehensive reflection of life and addressed to a readership that was, for its time, remarkably heterogeneous, it did not at first develop a tradition of aesthetic self-consciousness that would turn it into a fully-established form of literary art. The beginnings of this process of artistic maturation, related to the impact of the aesthetic theories and the literary practice of such continental novelists as Flaubert and Turgenev, began to penetrate British fiction around the middle of the century, mainly through the influence of George Eliot and George Meredith; when the highbrow literary novel of the kind represented by Henry James and Joseph Conrad finally secured for itself, around the turn of the century, a safe place in the literary tradition of the English language, the Victorian novel finally had to give way – the shifting of the focus of fiction from the story itself to the actual process of story-telling marks the transition from Victorianism to modernism.

A rather similar process of development can be observed in the sphere of the values and attitudes implied in the works of leading Victorian novelists. Like most of their contemporaries, the writers who dominated the literary market in the second quarter of the nineteenth century basically accepted the moral and philosophical principles of their age; if they were at odds with the world around them, it was because they disagreed with those individual elements of it which they thought contravened the natural, positive order of things and needed to be rectified – this is, for instance, what Dickens implies in the social criticism of his early novels, such as *Oliver Twist* (1837–8) or *Nicholas Nickleby* (1838–9). However, from the 1850s onwards this optimistic belief in the essential goodness of man and in the possibility of individual and social progress began to erode; although novels like *Bleak House*, Trollope's Barsetshire series (1855–67), or *Middlemarch* (1871–2) represent the quintessence of Victorianism, the philosophical and social tensions they suggest were indeed the first signs of the process of the disintegration of the Victorian world – neither the standard metaphysical assumptions about God, man, and the universe nor the optimistic belief in the regenerative potential of the human society could any longer be taken for granted. A consequence of this process was of course the shifting of focus from the society to the individual; if the novelists of the early Victorian period, like their eighteenth- and early-nineteenth-century predecessors, tended to find solutions in the integration of their protagonists into their respective social environments, the later Victorians tended to stress the isolation of their characters and the indifference, or indeed hostility, of the world they lived in to their struggles and sufferings – thus, again, preparing the way for the individualistic visions of Joseph Conrad and his modernist successors.

The way in which the Victorian novel reflected the epoch's changing systems of values is indeed an aspect of the most characteristic feature of the genre: its inclusiveness, its intense topicality and its direct responsiveness to the problems of the society in which, and for which, it was created. The novels of the period were not only sources of entertainment, but also vehicles for ideas – social, political, religious, moral, philosophical – that shaped the life of the Victorians. The main sources of dramatic tension in the novel of the period are therefore precisely the same as those that stimulated the development of Victorian Britain; the dichotomies of matter and spirit, individual and society, tradition and change, town and country were the same in the novel as they were in real life. In consequence, the development of British fiction between 1830 and 1900 reflects the phases in the development of the society that created it: the novels of the Brontës and the early works of Dickens, with their tension between realism and romance, parallel, in a way, the dynamism of the social and economic processes that characterized the emergence of the Victorian system in the 1830s and 1840s; the great mid-century novels of Dickens, Elizabeth Gaskell and George Eliot are literary equivalents, or indeed literary fulfilments, of the mid-Victorian era of equipoise; the slow but relentless disintegration of the Victorian world produces the works of Hardy and Butler.

This sense of organic connection between the changes in the character of Victorian fiction and the broader socio-economic, philosophical, and cultural developments in the life of Victorian society becomes even more pronounced if perceived in the context of the processes shaping many of those trends in nineteenth-century European thought that were to find their most direct literary echoes in the new, modernist climate of the first years of the twentieth century. The ideas of Marx, Darwin, Nietzsche and Freud (cf. Units 16, 17, and 21) derived from realities, dilemmas and concerns of nineteenth-century Europe that were in broad terms the same as those reflected, in the specifically British context, in the novels of the great Victorians; as a result, analogies and parallels, not surprisingly, abounded. Dickens felt and represented the condition of the urban poor just as intensely as Marx and Engels; Hardy's *Tess of the d'Urbervilles* (1891) carries just as stark a vision of a world governed by chance and by merciless fate as is implied in Darwin's version of the theory of evolution; Butler's balance between scepticism and nihilism is as fine as Nietzsche's and at least as dramatic; finally, the Victorian fascination with the dark, hidden aspects of the human psyche, with the obsessive and the irrational, signalled in the works of Dickens and Emily Brontë and later developed by Robert Louis Stevenson and Henry James, reflects the central concerns of the work of Sigmund Freud.

For general studies of the social and cultural background of Victorian literature, see Lerner (1978) and Gilmour (1993; useful up-to-date bibliography); see also Houghton (1957) and Altick (1974). Broader socio-historical perspectives are offered, for instance, by Briggs (1959) and Royle (1987).

The best recent general studies of Victorian fiction include Wheeler (1985), Gilmour (1986), and Horsman (1990), all offering useful bibliographies; see also the relevant sections of Van Ghent (1953), Allen (1954), Pollard (1969; 2nd edn 1987), and Williams (1970). There are countless studies of specific issues, themes, motifs, subgenres, etc.; some of them include Leavis (1948) on the moralistic tradition, Tillotson (1954) on the novels of the 1840s, Buckley (1974) on the *Bildungsroman*, Sutherland (1976) on the literary market, Wolff (1977) on the religious novel, Showalter (1977) and Gilbert and Gubar (1979) on women's writing, Sanders (1978) on the historical novel, Beer (1983) on the impact of Darwinism, Wright (1986) on the influence of Positivism, Orel (1986) on the short story, etc.

## Texts, authors, contexts

### Charles Dickens: *The Pickwick Papers* (1836–7)

> 'Ah! you should keep dogs – fine animals – sagacious creatures – dog of my own once – Pointer – surprising instinct – out shooting one day – entering enclosure – whistled – dog stopped – whistled again – Ponto – no go; stock still – called him – Ponto, Ponto – wouldn't move – dog transfixed – staring at a board – looked up, saw an inscription – "Gamekeeper has orders to shoot all dogs found in this enclosure" – wouldn't pass it – wonderful dog – valuable dog that – very.'
>
> 'Singular circumstance that,' said Mr Pickwick. 'Will you allow me to make a note of it?' (Ch. 2, pp. 79–81)

Accompanied by appropriate drawings, such as in this instance one of 'a sagacious dog', snapshots like this gave rise to a story that was to become one of the greatest literary best sellers of all time. Although the original conception was that of a loose collection of sketches of travel and sporting life, not unlike Robert Smith Surtees's *Jorrocks's Jaunts and Jollities* (1831–4), the book soon gathered momentum of its own: the introduction into the story of the streetwise if thoroughly honest Sam Weller provided a dramatically stimulating counterpoint to the characters of the four eccentric and thoroughly naive Pickwickians, while complications in the lives of the protagonists, most notably those resulting from Mr Pickwick's ill-fated conversation with his landlady Mrs Bardell, produced important elements of continuity and suspense. This was particularly important in the context of the fact that *The Pickwick Papers* was published as a monthly serial, a format until then not normally used for new fiction. The need to ensure the commercial viability of the enterprise and later on to maintain its success led Dickens, in an effort to stimulate sales, to adopt technical devices ranging from playing on readers' curiosity by withholding from them, until the subsequent instalment, vital information to aiding their memory through the association of individual characters with idiosyncrasies of speech, behaviour or physique. Chapman and Hall's gamble paid off; the eventual triumph of the novel was complete as its circulation grew from the initial 400 to around 40,000 copies a month, establishing Dickens as the leading writer of the day and transforming the country's entire literary scene in the process.

Although more complex in structure than its original semi-journalistic conception assumed, *The Pickwick Papers* remains fundamentally a picaresque novel of the open road, very much in the tradition of Fielding and Smollett (see Unit 9), both of whom Dickens knew and admired from the early years of his childhood. The backbone of the book is the story of the journeys around southern England that the four members of the Pickwick Club undertake in quest of adventure and 'observations of character and manners' (Ch. 1, p. 68); although in the course of the story some of the episodes, such as those related to the pursuit of Mr Jingle or to the Bardell v. Pickwick suit, begin to form more complex lines of plot, the dominant movement remains that of simple progression through time and space, with the characters themselves rather than the logic of their actions providing the organizing principle of the novel and with the individual episodes, stories, and jokes carrying most of its imaginative power. Similarly conventional is the cast of characters, most of them based on stock figures of eighteenth-century comedy; the sharp definition and grotesque exaggeration of their physical appearances and of the oddities of their behaviour, underlined by the allusiveness of their very names (Mrs Leo Hunter), are in many ways reminiscent of Smollett. Mr Pickwick himself, with his gentle and well-meaning if often misguided and gullible innocence (as in his response to the story of Ponto), is a close cousin of Fielding's Parson Adams and Goldsmith's Dr Primrose, while his master–servant (or indeed almost father–son) relationship with Sam is a modified version of the traditional pattern of Cervantes's Don Quixote and Sancho Pansa or Fielding's Tom Jones and Partridge. There is, in fact, a great deal of eighteenth-century feeling about the whole atmosphere of the novel: its world of stage-coaches and country inns, pretentious spinsters and officious lawyers, chance encounters and convivial feasts is indeed little different from those of *Tom Jones* and *Humphry Clinker*.

For all its links to its antecedents, *The Pickwick Papers* is, however, at the same time unmistakably Dickens. There is here, in the first place, the characteristic Dickensian mingling of realism and fantasy, producing the comic effects of the consistent (if mostly tongue-in-cheek) seriousness of the narrative voice when contrasted with the pure nonsense and absurdity of the events narrated; there is also, nowhere so clear as in the staccato monologues of Mr Jingle, Dickens's unsurpassed ear for speech and its individual aberrations. The richness of Dickens's imagination and the inventiveness of his sense of comedy, verbal as well as dramatic, result in the novel's intense theatricality; some of the scenes are in fact ready-made dramatic études which Dickens himself used, in his later years, for his public readings. There is in *The Pickwick Papers*, in more serious terms, an awareness of the social and political situation of nineteenth-century England: ignorant as they originally are of the realities of life, the Pickwickians gradually learn about the abuses of the electoral system, the selfishness of lawyers, the drama of imprisonment. There are also, and perhaps most depressingly, echoes of the moral evils of egoism, jealousy, greed and hatred, and of the horrors of poverty, insanity, illness and death; these themes feature most prominently in the novel's nine interpolated stories, which in this way turn out to foreshadow some of the darker sides of the complex vision of the world that Dickens was to develop in the later stages of his career. All this is there – and yet Mr Pickwick emerges, after his traumatic experience of imprisonment in the Fleet, a wiser perhaps, but by no means a sadder man, presiding over a finale which is in effect a fairy-tale-like affirmation of life and love that is fuller, warmer and more unconditional than anything else in the house of Victorian fiction.

The classic biography, with insightful critical commentaries, is by Johnson (1953); a more recent life is by Ackroyd (1990). Useful critical introductions include Fielding (1965), and a study of the early novels by Marcus (1965); other important studies are by Daleski (1970), Carey (1973) and Slater (1983).

## Emily Brontë: *Wuthering Heights* (1847)

'May she wake in torment!' he cried, with frightful vehemence, stamping his foot, and groaning in a sudden paroxysm of ungovernable passion. 'Why, she's a liar to the end! Where is she? Not *there* – not in heaven – not perished – where? Oh! you said you cared nothing for my sufferings! And I pray one prayer – I repeat it till my tongue stiffens – Catherine Earnshaw, may you not rest, as long as I am living! You said I killed you – haunt me then! The murdered *do* haunt their murderers. I believe – I know that ghosts *have* wandered on earth. Be with me always – take any form – drive me mad! only *do* not leave me in this abyss, where I cannot find you! Oh God! it is unutterable! I *cannot* live without my life! I *cannot* live without my soul!' (Ch. 16, p. 204)

This passionate outcry of Heathcliff's desperation and suffering constitutes one of the focal points of *Wuthering Heights*. It is exactly here, in this peculiar outburst of love and anger, of tenderness and resentment, of bitterness and fury, that Emily Brontë comes closest to verbalizing the central concern of the novel: the fundamental questions of the relation between matter and spirit and of the nature of life and death. Emily Brontë was not, however, a philosophical writer; implied in Heathcliff's rejection of standard perceptions of and conventional assumptions about the world, the novel's central vision of the essential spiritual unity of existence and of the irrelevance of the temporal notion of mortality is never argued but asserted through the very power and intensity of the experience presented. *Wuthering Heights* is therefore much more than an account of the turbulent history of the Earnshaws, the Lintons and Heathcliff; the most unusual of Victorian novels, it becomes in its unique way a statement of mystical insight into the nature of the universe.

This visionary, mystical dimension of *Wuthering Heights* is reflected in many features of the internal structure of the novel as well: most prominently in its insistence on the duality of forces operating within the spiritual universe, on the clash between the principles of peace and violence, restraint and freedom, stasis and dynamism, calm and storm. The most direct illustration of this dichotomy is offered in the contrasting presentation of the novel's two locales, Thrushcross Grange and Wuthering Heights, but it extends much further as well: into the personal character-istics of the Lintons on the one hand and the Earnshaws and Heathcliff on the other, their respective attitudes, ways of life, even physical features. Importantly, too, Emily Brontë does not pass any moral judgements: her world is one without ethical alternatives, her characters operating, throughout the novel, almost as personifications of primeval, elemental forces or principles.

The essence of Emily Brontë's artistic achievement lies, however, not so much in the uniqueness of her metaphysical vision as in the fact that her novel succeeds in conveying this vision through the apparently non-congenial medium of fiction. However poetic, mystical, profoundly antirealistic, and thus essentially non-novelistic the spirit that it derives from, *Wuthering Heights* remains first and foremost a novel, its characters, settings, and situations retaining their fictional validity even if and when they stretch the boundaries of conventional realism and probability. The story is, unexpected as it might be given the almost cosmic nature of its thematic concerns, most firmly grounded in the rustic world of late-eighteenth- and early-nineteenth-century Yorkshire, with its landscapes and weather, with details of its social structures and its patterns of domestic life, and with most precise timetabling. There is a similarly paradoxical quality about the novel's lyrical intensity too (cf. the section on Lawrence, Unit 16, pp. 457–9) – the consistency of its emotional tone and atmosphere and the assurance with which it forces the reader to accept its own terms of reference prevent it from turning into grotesque or melodrama: Heathcliff's mourning cry, verging on incoherence and sentimentality as it is when read out of context, acquires in the light of the whole novel a complex metaphorical significance and a special kind of poetic truth.

This blending of realism and mysticism, of fictional cohesion and lyrical power is achieved by means of a highly sophisticated and strikingly proto-modernist narrative technique (cf. the section on Conrad, Unit 16, pp. 447–50). The story is told by several narrators, whose accounts of the events they witnessed, enveloped within one another in a multi-layered structure of telling and retelling, produce the effect of distancing required, perhaps, by a Victorian woman novelist struggling with the supposedly 'unwomanly' material of the story (cf. the section on *Wuthering Heights* in Unit 23, pp. 621–2), and in any case needed to give the novel its essential framework of fictional credibility. Furthermore, the two main narrators, the outsider Mr Lockwood and his housekeeper Nelly Dean, although not involved in the central family drama and reliable enough as long as they merely report on past events, are by no means always fully trustworthy when it comes to their opinions and interpretations of what they see or experience; the reader's task is therefore not just to accept their stories at face value but to read them critically enough not to be misguided by the sympathies and prejudices of Nelly or by the views and reactions of the conventional, emotionally repressed Lockwood. This is where, ultimately, lies the modernity of Emily Brontë's novel – however archetypal and timeless its subject, however firmly rooted, historically, geographically and sociologically, its central story, however Romantic its literary provenance from the Gothic, Byron and Scott (see Units 9 and 10), *Wuthering Heights* is in many ways the most disturbingly modern work of Victorian fiction, open-ended in theme if not in plot, full of imaginative tension, posing questions rather than offering answers. Not easily interpreted or categorized, it remains monumental but solitary, something of a paradox in the world of Victorian fiction – but a paradox confirming the adaptability and inclusiveness of the genre as a whole.

For Emily Brontë's life, see Gérin (1971) and Barker (1994); for critical discussion of *Wuthering Heights*, see Craik (1968) and Gilbert and Gubar (1979). There is a Casebook by Allott (1970; 2nd edn 1992), and a New Casebook by Stoneman (1993), as well as monographs by Goodridge (1964), Holderness (1985) and Knoepflmacher (1989).

## Charlotte Brontë: *Jane Eyre* (1847)

> It was not without a certain wild pleasure I ran before the wind, delivering my trouble of mind to the measureless air-torrent thundering through space. Descending the laurel walk, I faced the wreck of the chestnut-tree; it stood up, black and riven: the trunk, split down the centre, gasped ghastly. The cloven halves were not broken from each other, for the firm base and strong roots kept them unsundered below; though community of vitality was destroyed – the sap could flow no more: their great boughs on each side were dead, and next winter's tempests would be sure to fell one or both to earth: as yet, however, they might be said to form one tree – a ruin, but an entire ruin.
> (Ch. 25, p. 304)

The intensely personal tone of narration, the passionate directness of expression, the nervous movement of thought, the use of dramatic and heavily symbolic imagery – all these could of course hardly be considered trademarks of Victorian literary style and imagination. The world of *Jane Eyre* is indeed in many ways one of traditional romance, in which the lonely, orphaned heroine struggles through life, determined to preserve her integrity against the dangers of poverty, human hostility, dishonesty, deception and hypocrisy, to be finally rewarded by a happy marriage, motherhood and material prosperity. Many of the novel's settings, characters and situations derive rather directly from the conventions of the genre and the epoch: the improbable and highly patterned plot, the fearful atmosphere of the red room at Gateshead, the aura of mystery and horror that envelops Thornfield, the grotesque characters of Mr Brocklehurst and Grace Poole, the madness of Bertha Mason, and the use of strongly contrasted imagery (ice and fire, light and darkness), all have an unmistakably Gothic flavour, while the Byronic ancestry of the dark, secretive, passionate Mr Rochester and the extensive, sometimes obsessively symbolic use of nature suggest the influence of mainstream Romantic poetry. This is all true – and yet Charlotte Brontë's best-known novel is much more than just another sentimental love story; not only a long-established Victorian classic and a popular favourite, it is also the fullest expression of the spirit of Romanticism in Victorian fiction. A complete contradiction?

Not quite – the greatness of *Jane Eyre* lies in the very paradoxicality of its blending of Romanticism and Victorianism, in the demonstration that for all the appearances to the contrary the Victorians were at heart latter-day Romantics, adapting, modifying and rationalizing the world they inherited from their fathers, but nevertheless remaining faithful to their fundamental ideals and principles. The key issue in this respect was the recognition and appreciation of human individuality and subjectivity, nowhere pronounced more exactly than in *Jane Eyre*, a novel more completely than any other work of Victorian fiction identifiable with its heroine, intelligent, sensitive, but first and foremost independent, prepared to stand up and defend her principles even at the cost of sacrificing not only her passion, but also her hard-won basic domestic stability and security. The impression of the novel's total immersion in Jane's sensibility is achieved through Charlotte Brontë's careful manipulation of her first-person narrative voice, the viewpoint shifting almost imperceptibly between the mature Jane, telling the story of her childhood and youth from the perspective finally revealed as that of her ten-year marriage to Rochester, and the young Jane remembered as she was actually experiencing the events described. This complex technique on the one hand preserves the sense of emotional directness, immediacy and intensity of feeling while on the other hand retaining a unity of tone, offering a sense of assured if vague and undefined existential stability, and safeguarding the novel against excessive sensationalism and sentimentality.

The crucial thing about Jane is, though, that the values she believes in and so single-mindedly defends are in fact Victorian as much as Romantic: her independence and assertiveness may be revolutionary, but only in the sense that they are directed against the restrictions that prevent her from freely choosing to accept the fundamental values of honesty, charity, selflessness and commitment that are for her the essence of humanity and the only possible basis on which to build a meaningful existence. The spirit of *Jane Eyre* is thus profoundly Christian; it is, in fact, very much a story of Bunyan-style quest for spiritual truth, with Gateshead, Lowood, Thornfield, Moor House and Ferndean representing the symbolic stages in Jane's moral and spiritual growth, the poetic unity of her pilgrimage justifying the novel's departures from the standards of traditional realism.

There is, however, another side to the problem as well. However symbolic its essence, the story of the Thornfield governess is still set in a recognizably nineteenth-century world, in which Jane's attempts to maintain her independence are conditioned by the social and economic circumstances in which she finds herself and against which she has to define her identity. *Jane Eyre* is thus also an early example of Victorian *Bildungsroman* (*David Copperfield* (1849–50), *The Mill on the Floss* (1860), *Great Expectations* (1860–1), *The Way of All Flesh* (1903)), and a very specific one at that – Jane's assertion of individuality is also an expression of her identity as a woman, her struggle for independence being at the same time a protest, in the name of equality, against male domination in the world in which the Brocklehursts, the Rochesters and the St John Riverses wield the power and define the rules. Jane thus becomes a personification of a new, modern type of woman-hood, a prototype for the heroines of Elizabeth Gaskell and George Eliot, and indeed a feminist icon (cf. the relevant section of Unit 24, pp. 642–6). Unlike even the strongest of her eighteenth- and early-nineteenth-century predecessors, all of them ultimately prepared, like Jane Austen's Emma (cf. Unit 9, p. 224), to accept, for all their independent-mindedness and intelligence, the established rules and conditions which will effectively have pre-defined their lives for them, she insists on spelling out her own agenda – not necessarily very radical, admittedly, but emphatically hers, and negotiable only on terms of full freedom and equality. In this way, *Jane Eyre* becomes an expression of the spirit of progress and democracy – perhaps the most essential aspect of the Romantic heritage of the Victorian era.

The best modern biography is by Gérin (1967); more recent studies are by Fraser (1988) and Barker (1994). Critical books include Craik (1968), and the feminist studies by Showalter (1977) and Gilbert and Gubar (1979). There is a Casebook on *Jane Eyre* by Allott (1973) and a monograph by King (1986).

### William Makepeace Thackeray: *Vanity Fair* (1847–8)

> And, as we bring our characters forward, I will ask leave, as a man and a brother, not only to introduce them, but occasionally to step down from the platform, and talk about them: if they are good and kindly, to love them and shake them by the hand: if they are silly, to laugh at them confidentially in the reader's sleeve: if they are wicked and heartless, to abuse them in the strongest terms which politeness admits of. (Ch. 8, p. 117)

It is exactly to the constant presence, throughout the novel, of this narratorial voice – urbane, witty, eloquent, talking to the reader rather than hiding himself from view, treating his characters at best as somewhat unruly children and at worst as puppets whom he can, as the Manager of the Performance, call to life, manipulate and dispose of as he thinks fit – that *Vanity Fair* owes its unique place among the leading achievements of Victorian fiction. Unlike most of his contemporaries, whose works in most cases aim to create complete, credible illusions of reality, Thackeray does not try to deny the fictionality of his story – the most powerful presence in the novel, his narrator plays with the conventions of the genre, constantly undermining the status of his characters as supposedly genuine living people while at the same time making every attempt to present them to the reader with all the precision and realism of social, psychological, and physical detail. The technique is, admittedly, not always used very consistently: thus, for instance, towards the end of the novel, when the narrator claims to have actually met the Sedley family party during their stay at Pumpernickel, the border between the world of the narrator and that of his story becomes rather blurred; on the whole, however, narration in *Vanity Fair* appears in some ways very modern, even prophetic of some of the twentieth-century disputes about the nature of fiction in general. At the same time, though, Thackeray's narrative method also looks back to the tradition of the eighteenth century, of the enthusiastic story-telling of the garrulous Tristram Shandy and, principally, of the omniscience and virtual omnipotence of the narrator of *Tom Jones* (cf. Unit 9, pp. 219–20).

The parallel with Fielding is by no means accidental – though not the only one of major nineteenth-century novels to be set at a time several decades prior to the time of writing and thus to take a long historical perspective (*Waverley* (1814), *Adam Bede* (1859)) *Vanity Fair* has about it a curiously old-fashioned, almost eighteenth-century air. Not only is it the case that the partly aristocratic, partly upper-middle-class milieu that the novel presents is thoroughly immersed in the conservative, pre-industrial atmosphere of its Regency background; much more importantly, the imaginative spirit of the novel and its implied system of values seem to bear no evidence whatsoever of any influence of Romanticism. *Vanity Fair* is a quintessential novel of manners; its concern is with the ethics of personal and public life, with social stratification and mobility, with snobbery, hypocrisy and the power of money: a broad range of themes that is perfectly compatible with Thackeray's dispassionately realistic, detached, satirical picture of modern society, but which appears, in comparison with the visions of the world offered by Dickens or the Brontës, curiously one-dimensional, dry and conservative. There is indeed, appropriately for a novel taking its title from Bunyan, something allegorical about the world of the Crawleys and the Sedleys, of Becky and Dobbin; it is perhaps something of a modern version of the visions of William Langland, with the narrator concentrating, while drawing a picture of modern society, on the direct satirical exposition of its faults and shortcomings. This is of course not to deny *Vanity Fair* its vitality, humour and dynamism of character and plot; the novel, however, does lack the sense of personal intensity and direct emotional immediacy, as well as the spirit of individualism, questioning and perhaps even rebelliousness, so central, in their various manifestations, to the Romantic and post-Romantic tradition of the nineteenth century.

All this said, *Vanity Fair* is not quite just an old-fashioned novel either: thus, for example, it is very modern in rejecting the conventional machinery of mystery plot; there are no mistaken identities, no hidden wills or unexpected legacies, no imprisoned innocents, no Gothic villains. The events develop naturally, gathering impetus from the tensions between distinctively depicted and sharply contrasted characters, many of whom, the splendidly drawn, ambitious, intelligent and energetic Becky Sharp in the first place, are among the most memorable characters in Victorian fiction. Thackeray's confidence in his control of the plot goes indeed so far that he can afford to have one of his central characters, George Osborne, killed, half-way through the story, on the battlefield of Waterloo – a death that goes against the conventional standards of plot design and yet manages to be perfectly true to the spirit of the novel, functioning simply as an element of the natural order of life and death to which everybody is subject. As much as the plot develops organically in accordance with the logic of situation and character, so do the characters, some of them at least, display, as the novel unfolds, new aspects of their personalities; in the case of one or two of them, most notably Rawdon Crawley and old Mrs Sedley, the portraits are indeed subtle character studies foreshadowing the development of psychological realism in the works of Elizabeth Gaskell, George Eliot and the modernists. The panoramic vision of *Vanity Fair* makes it the Victorian period's closest equivalent, before *Middlemarch*, of the works of Balzac and Tolstoy. Once made, however, the comparison demonstrates the limitations of Thackeray's perspective, its predominantly satirical intent implied in the dominant role of the didactically oriented narrator denying it the breadth of vision, understanding and compassion that would have turned it from a brilliantly executed piece of moral and social criticism into a universal masterpiece of literary art.

By far the best biography, with important critical commentary, is by Ray (1955–8); for critical discussion, see Tillotson (1954), Carey (1977), and Peters (1987). Pollard (1978b) is a useful Casebook on *Vanity Fair*; there is a monograph by Gilmour (1982).

### Elizabeth Gaskell: *North and South* (1854–5)

> 'Where do you live? I think we must be neighbours, we meet so often on this road.'
> 'We put up at nine Frances Street, second turn to th' left at after yo've past th' Goulden Dragon.'
> 'And your name? I must not forget that.'
> 'I'm none ashamed o' my name. It's Nicholas Higgins. Hoo's called Bessy Higgins. Whatten yo' asking for?'
> Margaret was surprised at this last question, for at Helstone it would have been an understood thing, after the inquiries she had made, that she intended to come and call upon any poor neighbour whose name and habitation she had asked for. (Ch. 8, pp. 112–13)

One of the most characteristic qualities of the novels of Elizabeth Gaskell is the ease and authenticity with which she dramatizes the central social and moral problems she addresses in her works. This is very much the case in *North and South*: the scene of Margaret Hale's first conversation with Nicholas Higgins and his daughter, introduced in a perfectly natural way as part of the account of the Hales' first weeks in Milton-Northern, evokes at the same time the novel's fundamental concern with the divisions splitting the British society of its day – on the one hand, the existence of the 'two nations' of the rich and the poor, and on the other hand, the contrast between the traditional rural South and the rapidly growing modern industrial North. Mrs Gaskell was of course by no means the first major novelist to approach the 'condition-of-England' question (Disraeli, *Sybil, or The Two Nations* (1845)), nor indeed to attempt a presentation of the provincial industrial scene: unlike her predecessors like Charlotte Brontë (in *Shirley*) or Dickens (in *Hard Times*), however, she viewed the new urban communities of the North of England from the inside, her position as a Manchester clergyman's wife offering her a chance to observe life around her from a viewpoint which was both close and at the same time detached enough not to be identified with that of either side of the industrial conflict, and which therefore permitted both realism of description and objectivity of judgement. As a result, *North and South* never descends into mere social, economic or political propaganda; its message, not untypical of the tradition of Christian socialism (Kingsley, *Alton Locke* (1850)), is, if not necessarily that of full reconciliation, then at least one of the need for compromise, with both employers and employees advised to learn to understand and negotiate their mutual positions in the same way as the people of the South and the North have to learn to recognize the strengths and weaknesses of their respective attitudes and ways of life.

This fundamental stress on the need to shed preconceptions is nowhere so clear as in the story of Margaret Hale. The whole novel is in many ways an account of her moral and social education, the point of which is exactly her gradual recognition of the limitations of her earlier vision of the world and of the necessity to accept not only the existence, but also the validity of other standpoints; the essence of her romance with John Thornton lies, as a result, in their mutual adaptation to the changing personal, social and cultural context of their lives, with all its moral and psychological consequences. The pattern is thus in many respects the same as, for instance, in *Pride and Prejudice*; the difference between Mrs Gaskell and Jane Austen lies, however, in the modernity of Margaret Hale's world, permitting her a far greater degree of personal and social independence. As a result, in a manner reminiscent of Jane Eyre rather than Elizabeth Bennett, Margaret insists on defining her place as a person and as a woman not only in the domestic and personal sphere, but also in the broader social world. An elder sister of Dorothea Brooke, not only does she fully accept her responsibilities within the family circle, but she also determines to play a part in the broader life of the community: her defence of John Thornton during the strike in his factory is the most direct expression of this spirit of liberty and assertiveness, while her eventual receipt of Mr Bell's legacy, somewhat contrived as it might appear in terms of the novel's plot, does nevertheless place her in a position of economic power symbolic of her moral and psychological strength.

The impression of modernity conveyed by *North and South* is not only, however, the question of the modernity of the settings, problems and attitudes presented; much of it depends also on the overall tone of the narration, simple, direct, unobtrusive, for the most part associated with the viewpoint of Margaret, but sometimes imperceptibly shifting towards some of the other characters as well.

Unlike Dickens and the Brontës, Mrs Gaskell is not a poetic novelist; her world is a simple one of realistically rendered everyday life, developing organically in accordance with the nature of her characters, the broader processes of social life and the requirements of common-sense logic and probability. She may lack the dynamism and intensity of some of her contemporaries, and she does not always manage, in her attempts to draw a broad realistic panorama of society, to control the material of her stories carefully enough to make it correspond with the thematic and formal structure of her novels – thus, for instance, *North and South* fails to explore further the typically Victorian problem of faith and doubt implied in Mr Hale's decision to resign from the Church, and the final chapters are obviously hurried and thus not fully satisfactory. All this granted, the courage of Mrs Gaskell's social vision, the subtlety of her moral and psychological insight, her gift for dramatization and dialogue and the subtlety of her presentation of provincial background place her firmly among the major novelists of the Victorian era, a worthy successor to the tradition of Jane Austen and an equally worthy predecessor of authors so diverse as George Eliot, Hardy, Bennett and Lawrence.

The best biographies are by Gérin (1976) and Uglow (1993); introductory critical studies include Pollard (1965), Craik (1975) and Easson (1979).

### Charles Dickens: *Little Dorrit* (1855–7)

> Mr Merdle's complaint. Society and he had so much to do with one another in all things else, that it is hard to imagine his complaint, if he had one, being solely his own affair. Had he that deep-seated recondite complaint, and did any doctor find it out? Patience. In the meantime, the shadow of the Marshalsea wall was a real darkening influence, and could be seen on the Dorrit Family at any stage of the sun's course. (Book I, Ch. 21, p. 300)

It is indeed not only over the lives of William Dorrit and his family that the Marshalsea casts a dark shadow – its sinister presence is in fact the dominant motif of the whole novel, reflecting the central themes of physical, social, moral and psychological imprisonment and paralysis pervading the entire world of the Clennams and the Meagleses, the Plornishes and the Barnacles. Just like Mr Dorrit, not only deprived of freedom in the physical sense, but also, and more importantly, unable to free himself from the psychological and social constraints resulting from his confused understanding of his own and his family's circumstances, so is Mrs Clennam a prisoner, literally, of her dark and gloomy house and of her physical condition, and metaphorically, of her distorted and uncharitable perception of right and wrong, of guilt and expiation. Similarly, Mr Merdle can never free himself from the consequences of his frauds just as Miss Wade remains a prisoner of her neurosis. The same motif governs Dickens's presentation of the current social and political problems of his time, particularly in the aftermath of the crisis of the Crimean War (the novel, ostensibly set in the 1820s, frequently alludes to events of the 1850s): thus, the people of Bleeding Heart Yard are imprisoned by their poverty just as much as the government of the whole country is paralysed by Circumlocution Office's principle of 'how not to do it'. The only hope for freedom rests with those who are capable of genuine honesty, selflessness and generosity – even their efforts are, however, like Daniel Doyce's, likely to be frustrated: the most they can expect is that their voice, representing the true spirit of Christianity (as opposed to Mrs Clennam's dour Calvinism), will be too weak to be heard, as was Amy Dorrit's when in 'the roaring streets (...) the noisy and the eager, and the arrogant and the froward and the vain, fretted and chafed, and made their usual uproar' (Book II, Ch. 34, p. 895).

Dickens's vision of life in *Little Dorrit* is thus completely different not only from that implied in *The Pickwick Papers*, but also from that shared, to a greater or lesser degree, by most of his contemporaries: he can no longer accept either the optimistic Victorian belief in the self-regenerative powers of society or the interpretation of the moral and social evils he saw around him as minor aberrations in its otherwise successful progress towards universal prosperity and happiness. Related to this is the change in Dickens's perception of the actual nature of society itself: the fragmentary and generally rather superficial sociological sketches of *The Pickwick Papers* are replaced by an all-inclusive picture of society as an integrated structure, almost a living organism whose constituent elements are linked by a complex network of visible and invisible connections. In consequence, corruption and evil, whether in the form of the Barnacle-style (mis)handling of power or that of Mr Merdle's complaint – 'simply Forgery and Robbery' (Book II, Ch. 25, p. 777) – can infect and eventually destroy the entire fabric of modern society.

The complexity of Dickens's moral vision and the bitterness of his social and political satire find a direct equivalent in the form of the novel. Although it starts off as a series of apparently unrelated scenes set in places ranging from a Marseilles prison to a London coffee-house and introducing characters as different as Mrs Clennam's old servant Affery Flintwinch and the powerful politician Tite Barnacle, *Little Dorrit* gradually emerges as a highly unified fictional structure, in which numerous lines of plot are all finally integrated into one complex and all-encompassing mechanism. The formal mystery plot, itself symbolic, through its associations with deception and hatred, of the novel's central concern with moral corruption, is indeed more than a mere technical device; to a degree much greater than in the works of Fielding, the Gothic novelists, or Charlotte Brontë, its influence actually penetrates into the very texture of Dickens's writing, generating as a result a unique atmosphere of uncertainty and powerlessness experienced by the individual in the face of an incomprehensible world. This impression is strengthened by Dickens's manipulation of the narrative voice: constantly shifting, sometimes clearly representing the point of view of a particular character, elsewhere detached and ironical, it never turns into a stable point of reference comparable to those offered by the narrator of *Tom Jones* or by the narrator-heroine of *Jane Eyre*.

However dark and gloomy its overall tone, *Little Dorrit* does not, however, lose its characteristic Dickensian flavour of imaginative richness and emotional intensity: it is here, for instance, that Dickens produces some of his most important studies in psychopathology, and it is also here that he achieves a rare success in the blending together, in the satirical scenes of high society dinner-parties, of acute perception of modern detail and almost medieval-style full-scale allegory. The usual qualities of Dickens's imagination, such as the taste for the bizarre and the eccentric, for theatricality and for sentiment, are all here as well; so is even, despite the novel's depressing subject matter, Dickens's humour, subdued, often bitter, sometimes melancholy, but nonetheless distinctly his. Most importantly, however, *Little Dorrit*'s claim to recognition as one of Dickens's best works rests on the success with which it integrates and balances standard ingredients of Victorian fiction, such as a basically realistic framework and social and moral didacticism, with the poetic quality of symbolism; as a result, it transcends the limitations of topicality and becomes one of the epoch's leading statements about the nature of human society.

For general studies of Dickens, see section on *The Pickwick Papers*. The later fiction is discussed by Leavis and Leavis (1970). There is a monograph on *Little Dorrit* by Reid (1967) and a Casebook by Shelston (1985).

### Anthony Trollope: *Barchester Towers* (1857)

> 'The work of a bishop of the Church of England,' said Dr Proudie, with considerable dignity, 'is not easy. The responsibility which he has to bear is very great indeed.'
> 'Is it?' said Bertie, opening wide his wonderful blue eyes. 'Well; I never was afraid of responsibility. I once had thoughts of being a bishop, myself.'
> 'Had thoughts of being a bishop!' said Dr Proudie, much amazed.
> 'That is, a parson – a parson first, you know, and a bishop afterwards. If I had once begun, I'd have stuck to it. But, on the whole, I like the Church of Rome the best.'
> The bishop could not discuss the point, so he remained silent. (Ch. 11, pp. 83–4)

No more characterization is needed – even when taken out of context, this brief scene of the Bishop of Barchester's conversation with Bertie Stanhope is fully sufficient to offer the reader direct insight into the two men's attitudes, temperaments and ways of thinking. Both Dr Proudie and Bertie are engaged in what is, on one level, perfectly natural small talk; at the same time, however, they give themselves away in every word they utter, every change of the tone of voice and every reaction each of them displays in the course of their encounter. The dramatic effect of the scene is made even more pronounced by the discreetly ironical comments suggested (rather than explicitly made) by the narrator; apparently detached and concerned merely with factual detail, he is nevertheless a master of understatement, exposing the real nature of his characters through the acuteness of his observation and the sharpness of the occasional, seemingly innocent and yet deeply significant, detail or comment.

It is exactly Trollope's masterful characterization and his ability to create simple and realistic, but highly dramatically effective dialogue that lie at the heart of his reputation as the most easy-going and natural of Victorian story-tellers. The word 'story-teller' does indeed describe Trollope rather more accurately than 'novelist' – to a degree greater than any other of his contemporaries, he manages to create a world that gives the impression of existing not only within, but also in a sense outside his texts, an independent, alternative reality as complex as the real world itself and therefore as impossible to describe in terms of the structurally closed form of the tightly plotted novel typical of the mid-Victorian period. Instead, Trollope presents the reader with an experience of life; his concern is with ordinary situations involving ordinary people, with events which do not form dramatically structured patterns, but develop as part of the natural fabric of day-to-day existence, with celebrating the everyday and the usual – it is characteristic how ordinary and unglamorous are, in *Barchester Towers*, the protagonists of the novel's romantic subplot, the naive widow Eleanor Bold and the rather bland if worthy ex-Oxford cleric Mr Arabin. The result is that Trollope's fiction may seem somewhat amorphous, with the same characters, settings and problems reappearing in several novels (*Barchester Towers*, the second of the six books constituting the Barsetshire cycle, is itself very much a continuation of its predecessor, *The Warden* (1855)) and thus turning the stories into sample illustrations of a pre-existing Trollopean world rather than independent works of art establishing autonomous imaginative worlds of their own.

It is exactly this all-inclusiveness of Trollope's domestic realism that makes his world essentially Victorian: in fact, the work of none of his contemporaries justifies more closely than his Henry James's famous description of the novels of the period as 'loose, baggy monsters'. The centrality of Trollope to the tradition of nineteenth-century fiction goes, indeed, far beyond the formal aspects of his novels into the world of values, beliefs, and thematic concerns. Rather like Jane Austen and Thackeray before him, he fully accepts the traditional moral and social standards of his age, satirizing those who through snobbery and pretentiousness or through greed and ambition attempt to subvert the stable, humane, organic and thus essentially happy order of things inherited from the past. However direct and unsentimental he may be in his criticism, though, he never fails to perceive and respect the individual, personal dimension of his characters, as a result of which even the most strongly caricatured of them, like Mrs Proudie or Mr Slope, retain their essential humanity and never become mere flat grotesques. Trollope's defence of good old conservative values, personified in the character of his kind-hearted and benevolent hero Mr Harding, extends to virtually all spheres of life, individual as well as public – once again characteristically Victorian in its topicality, *Barchester Towers* echoes the political and, most importantly, religious upheavals of the day, including the internal tensions within the Church of England between its Tractarian and Evangelical wings as well as the impact on the religious life of mid-nineteenth-century England of the growing significance of Roman Catholicism. The public concerns merge almost imperceptibly with simple, informal treatment of the domestic affairs of Barchester clergy and their families; the Grantlys and the Proudies, the Stanhopes and the Quiverfuls are presented without flattery and sentimentalization, but at the same time with a spirit of tolerance and understanding that underlines in human shortcomings and failings their humorous rather than dramatic and possibly destructive potential. The overall message of the novel is thus fundamentally mid-Victorian – one of the affirmation of life and tradition and of the significance of the principle of peaceful adaptability as a way of handling the demands of the modern world and responding to the spirit of progress. As a result, though by no means the best novel of its epoch, lacking the imaginative richness and the poetry of the works of Dickens and the Brontës and the intellectual rigour of the novels of George Eliot, *Barchester Towers* becomes one of the most direct expressions of the spirit of the age of equipoise and thus one of the most central achievements of Victorian fiction, the book that comes closest perhaps to being 'the ultimate Victorian novel'.

There are several recent biographies, among them Hall (1991) and Glendinning (1992); for critical discussion, see Kincaid (1977), Pollard (1978a) and Wall (1988). There is a Casebook on the Barsetshire novels by Bareham (1983).

### George Eliot: *Middlemarch* (1871–2)

> 'Yes, indeed,' said Dorothea, brightening. 'I shall be quite grateful to you if you will tell me how I can help to make things a little better. Everything of that sort has slipped away from me since I have been married. I mean,' she said, after a moment's hesitation, 'that the people in our village are tolerably comfortable, and my mind has been too much taken up for me to inquire further. But here – in such a place as Middlemarch – there must be a great deal to be done.' (Ch. 44, p. 477)

The scene of Dorothea's conversation with Lydgate about the needs of the New Hospital in Middlemarch provides a most characteristic example of the way in which George Eliot develops the fictional world of her novel through creating a web of relationships, personal, social, professional and financial, involving, in a network of complex interdependencies, virtually all the people of *Middlemarch* and in consequence not only defining their respective places in society, but also, through constant comparison and contrastive analysis, reflecting their perceptions, opinions and attitudes. Thus, Dorothea's anxiety to 'help to make things a little better' is completely different, and much more significant, than the conventional interest in charity work expected of a Victorian clergyman's wife. For the ambitious, intelligent and profoundly earnest, but at the same time deeply frustrated woman that she has become as Mrs Casaubon, a possibility of helping in a venture that by its very nature represents social and moral progress is in fact a chance to find an alternative answer to her fundamental problem – that of defining her place in life in a way that would allow her to fulfil her intellectual, moral and spiritual potential. Dorothea's search for a meaningful identity is indeed an aspect of one of the central themes of the whole novel: the theme of vocation and aspiration, of the moral and social dimensions of work, duty, and responsibility. Almost all the characters of the novel, Fred Vincy the young man looking for career opportunities and Mr Brooke the aspiring politician alike, are indeed in various ways and at various times in their lives involved in defining their professional, public, or family roles; as a result,

*Middlemarch* becomes something of a multi-strand *Bildungsroman*, in which everybody is constantly learning and relearning new truths about themselves and the world, and restructuring their lives and attitudes accordingly.

This typically Victorian stress on the significance of moral and social education is linked, in *Middlemarch*, with other concerns characteristic of the epoch. It is by no means irrelevant that Dorothea's discussion with Lydgate should focus, ultimately, on the question of promoting social progress. Although set around 1830, technically just before the beginning of the Victorian era, the novel addresses numerous issues that remained central elements of British political, social and cultural life throughout the century. The progress of science, the question of political reform, the consequences of religious diversity and change, the social and economic situation of women – all those fundamental issues of the mid-Victorian era are reflected in the world of *Middlemarch*, making the book one of the most comprehensive statements the Victorian novel made about the nature of contemporary society.

The achievement of *Middlemarch* lies, however, not so much just in its analysis of the social reality of nineteenth-century provincial life as in the way in which this analysis is integrated with the novel's ethical and psychological vision. However prominently George Eliot's characters function in their public, social and professional capacities, they are first of all brilliantly characterized individuals, having to face the various complexities of their personal as well as social lives, experiencing joys and frustrations, reflecting on the past and contemplating the future, facing moral dilemmas and trying to resolve them. The subtlety of George Eliot's understanding of character transpires from the very way in which she relates her story – as in Dorothea's response to Lydgate's appeal on behalf of the hospital, a small change of the tone of voice, a brief pause, or a mere facial expression can often be enough to convey a moral attitude or a state of feeling. As a result, George Eliot becomes an analyst as much as a story-teller: by far the most intellectual of Victorian novelists, she penetrates the inner workings of the human mind with an imaginative sympathy and a firmness of vision and judgement that make her at the same time the language's first fully successful modern psychological novelist and a great moralist, on both counts the direct predecessor of the two turn-of-the-century giants, Henry James and Joseph Conrad.

However important it is as a point of departure for the development of pre-modernist and modernist fiction, *Middlemarch* still remains in virtually all its aspects an unmistakable product of the mid-Victorian era, in many ways the culmination of the first four decades of the development of the Victorian novel. It combines the Dickensian scope and power of vision with the minuteness of the domestic realism of Mrs Gaskell and the relaxed story-telling of Trollope; its plot, fully realistic and growing organically from character as in *Vanity Fair*, is in its way as strongly and consistently symbolic as the plots of the novels of the Brontës; its narrative style, based on the seemingly straightforward third-person narrative voice, manages to combine objective analysis with metaphorical intensity and unobtrusive but significant commentary with subtle dramatization. Written at the time when Victorianism was at its very peak, *Middlemarch*, in the words of Henry James, 'sets a limit ... to the development of the old-fashioned English novel'. The most complete, the most serious, the most artistically self-conscious of Victorian novels, it is perhaps the best single achievement of nineteenth-century English literature and one of the greatest works in the literary tradition of the English language.

The standard biography is by Haight (1968); the best introductory critical studies are by Hardy (1959), Allen (1965), and Ashton (1983). On *Middlemarch* there is a Casebook by Swinden (1972), and a New Casebook by Peck (1992), as well as monographs by Daiches (1963), McSweeney (1984) and Chase (1991).

## George Meredith: *The Egoist* (1879)

> 'You have seen Vernon?'
> 'It was your wish.'
> 'You had a talk?'
> 'We conversed.'
> 'A long one?'
> 'We walked some distance.'
> 'Clara, I tried to make the best arrangement I could.'
> 'Your intention was generous.'
> 'He took no advantage of it?'
> 'It could not be treated seriously.'
> 'It was meant seriously.'
> 'There I see the generosity.'
> Willoughby thought this encomium, and her consent to speak on the subject, and her scarcely embarrassed air and richness of tone in speaking, very strange: and strange was her taking him quite in earnest. Apparently she had no feminine sensation of the unwontedness and the absurdity of the matter! (Ch. 47, p. 568)

Even the most cursory reading of this scene, and indeed of virtually any passage from *The Egoist*, conveys a clear impression of a radical distinctiveness and unconventionality of George Meredith's artistic method. The most conspicuous aspect of it is certainly his prose style – very elaborate and formal, at its best epigrammatically condensed and achieving a rare degree of the concentration of pointed wit and unexpected metaphor, but at its least controlled coming dangerously close to unwarranted artificiality and mannerism. This is true about the sections of the novel originating directly from the third-person narrator as much as about the dialogue – as Clara's description to Sir Willoughby of her earlier meeting with Vernon Whitford suggests, everybody at Patterne Hall converses rather than talks, and does so very much on a level of linguistic and conceptual sophistication far away from the more straightforward realism characteristic of the novels of most of Meredith's predecessors and contemporaries. The atmosphere of *The Egoist* is, in fact, reminiscent not so much of that of other Victorian novels as of the mood of Restoration comedy: the novel's subtitle defines it, in fact, as 'a comedy in narrative', its world is self-confessedly dominated by 'a coy attachment to the Court of [the Martyr Charles's] Merrie Son' (Ch. 2, p. 44), and some of the exchanges between Clara and Sir Willoughby are indeed almost direct echoes of the verbal battles between Congreve's Millamant and Mirabell. With its limited cast of aristocratic and upper-middle-class characters, its strict observance of the unities of time, place and action, and its exclusive focus on character and relationships, *The Egoist* indeed reads rather like a modern version of *The Way of the World*, admittedly much more reserved and circumspect in its treatment of the theme of sexuality, but equally concerned with issues of truth and falsehood, honesty and hypocrisy, altruism and selfishness, and the nature of love and marriage.

In themselves, Meredith's themes are not of course much different from those addressed by some of the other Victorian novelists – one could, for instance, mention a degree of indebtedness that *The Egoist* owes to the moralistic quality of Thackeray's satirical didacticism in *Vanity Fair*. The fundamental difference lies elsewhere – in Meredith's wholesale rejection of the conventional understanding of fiction as deriving, fundamentally, from straightforward story-telling and thus attempting to be a reflection of life, in favour of a highly metaphorical poetic structure in which characters and their actions function primarily as exponents of the author's intellectual conceptions rather than as fully developed personalities whose stories might matter as stories in their own right rather than as means of conveying the author's preconceived theories and ideas. As a result, the characters of *The Egoist* in a way never fully materialize; they may not be quite flat in the traditional sense, but they are devoid of palpable realistic authenticity, appearing to the reader as semi-abstract shadows rather than as real living people. Rather similarly, the novel's rare references to the external world, for instance to the navy career of Lieutenant Crossjay Patterne or to Clara's intended flight to London, serve as little more than symbolic illustrations of particular stages in the moral and psychological development of the central characters. In consequence, the setting of the novel remains very vague and undefined, which gives it a rather peculiar feeling of timelessness, placelessness and therefore abstraction. On its own terms, the conception operates most successfully: *The Egoist* maintains its carefully paced tempo and atmosphere in a smooth and tightly controlled way, the plot, though very simple, is nevertheless powerful enough to expose in most of the novel's characters a variety of forms of egoism, while passages analyzing the dilemmas and doubts of the inner lives of Sir Willoughby and, most importantly, Clara, from whose point of view most of the story is told, are not without considerable psychological interest. Within its limits, *The Egoist* is unquestionably a major artistic achievement – and yet it was not a great popular success in its time and it still remains, for all its high critical standing, probably one of the least read of the major novels of the period. Another Victorian paradox?

The reason is that *The Egoist* is one of the first novels written consciously and consistently against the prevalent spirit of the aesthetic expectations of the second half of the nineteenth century. Unlike the other writers dominating the British literary scene in the 1870s, notably George Eliot, Hardy and the newly-emerging American Henry James, Meredith did not choose to integrate his dramatic conception into the conventional framework of broad social and psychological realism – at the same time, however, he did not develop it into a pure fantasy along the lines of Samuel Butler's *Erewhon* (1872). The result is a book that begins to break the boundaries of Victorian fiction; although rather isolated in its unconventionality among the novels of the period and not immediately influential, it is nevertheless one of the earliest examples of the aesthetic self-consciousness of the last quarter of the nineteenth century, the trend that was to develop, through the turn-of-the-century works of James and Conrad, into the modernist spirit of Virginia Woolf, James Joyce and D.H. Lawrence (see Unit 16).

For Meredith's life, see Lindsay (1956) and Williams (1977); criticism includes works by Beer (1971) and Wilt (1975).

## Thomas Hardy: *Tess of the d'Urbervilles* (1891)

> Though the sky was dense with cloud a diffused light from some fragment of a moon had hitherto helped them a little. But the moon had now sunk, the clouds seemed to settle almost on their heads, and the night grew as dark as a cave. However, they found their way along, keeping as much on the turf as possible that their tread might not resound, which it was easy to do, there being no hedge or fence of any kind. All around was open loneliness and black solitude, over which a stiff breeze blew. (Ch. 58, p. 483)

The image of the lonely figures of Tess and Angel Clare on their journey through the emptiness, darkness and desolation of the great plain of Mid-Wessex towards the sacrificial altar at Stonehenge is in many ways emblematic of the central themes not only of *Tess of the d'Urbervilles*, but also of most of Hardy's fiction in general: the themes of the insignificance of man against the universe, of the directness of the link between man and nature, or indeed, as Hardy himself put it, between character and environment, and finally of the crucial importance in human life of love, loyalty and compassion. The melancholy vision of the Wessex landscape, at the same time both actively hostile to Tess and Angel in its gloom and chilliness, as suggested by the image of the sinking moon, and yet offering them, through its very stillness and darkness, a form of shelter and protection, represents the typical Hardyan paradox. A child of nature, Tess depends on it for the inner strength she needs before she can face the ultimate challenge of society's revenge against her for her desperate attempt to break away from the vicious circle of fate in which she finds herself because of the inflexibility of the harsh rules which that very society imposes. At the same time, however, it is precisely the power of the forces of nature that underlines her psychological and spiritual isolation and her vulnerability and powerlessness against the forces of fate governing the universe.

Hardy's stress on the essential loneliness of the individual human existence, perceived against rather than within its social context, represents a fundamental shift of focus that characterized late-Victorian mentality. The early and mid-Victorian vision of society as essentially sound, improvable even if and when occasionally imperfect, and thus offering individuals a chance of achieving a basic sense of existential, social and personal certainty, is in *Tess of the d'Urbervilles* replaced by a far more pessimistic, indeed tragic, conception of humanity as ultimately helpless, dependent for its future largely on coincidence, chance and fate. Tess is alone in her suffering because the social world in which she lives is itself disintegrating: the story of the Marlott dairymaid is set against the background of an environment in which centuries-old traditions, ways of life, and patterns of thinking are gradually being displaced by the influence of destructive external forces representing the aggression, ruthlessness and selfishness of modern life; the almost timeless, archetypal rural communities of Wessex are doomed just like Tess's own fate is sealed when she is raped/seduced by Alec Stoke-d'Urberville. Other certainties are gone as well: family links can often be, due to human weakness and folly, as catastrophic in their consequences as the influences of the society at large; no alternative either can be found in religion, which proves to be little more than an institutionalized form of social and moral convention restricting human liberty and preventing spontaneous expression of natural human values. Socially, economically and spiritually uprooted, Hardy's characters retain only one hope, a belief in the individual capacity for love and compassion; even these, however, can secure for them only a temporary reprieve from the ultimately tragic destiny of loneliness, suffering and death.

The darkness of Hardy's simple but powerful vision of the inescapability of fate and the imaginative intensity of his creation of character make his novels the closest equivalents Victorian fiction offers of ancient Greek tragedy. A mere peasant girl from Dorset, Tess rises in the course of the novel to the stature of a full-scale tragic heroine, 'a pure woman' destroyed by the cruel indifference of the world around her. The development of the character of Tess is indeed a mark of what is perhaps the central achievement of Hardy's art – the merging of his broad metaphysical vision with the realism, sometimes even naturalism, of his presentation of the rural scene of Wessex, his version of nineteenth-century south-west England centred around his native Dorset. An heir to the tradition of the regional novel represented by Maria Edgeworth (cf. Unit 25, p. 661) and Sir Walter Scott (cf. Unit 27, pp. 687–8), Hardy is very much a traditional old folkstory-teller, whose tales of frustrated love, jealousy, pride, ambition and hatred, told by the conventional third-person narrator, are among the most direct, straightforward and easily accessible works of Victorian fiction (cf., however, the section on *Tess* in Unit 24, pp. 646–9). At the same time, though, he remains in many ways a poet and an iconoclast, modifying the mainstream tradition of Victorian fiction by interpreting the world of Wessex in symbolic as well as purely realistic terms and by refusing to accept (at least for purposes of book rather than magazine publication) those of the conventions of the fiction of his time, such as the taboo on matters of sex and the principle of poetic justice, that clashed with his deeply felt aesthetic, ethical and existential convictions. It is exactly the dynamism between the conservative and radical elements of Hardy's perception of the world and of his creative genius that places him at the turning point in the development of the modern British novel. Beginning firmly within the conventions of his period, he develops a fictional world that radically subverts the very foundations of Victorianism; telling apparently simple, realistic, sometimes drab stories of rural life, he creates almost impressionistic poems in prose, whose lyrical power foreshadows the achievements of much of twentieth-century poetic fiction, including in the first place the works of D.H. Lawrence.

By far the best biography is by Millgate (1982); good introductory studies include Howe (1967) and Page (1977), while Millgate (1971) is the fullest analysis of the novels. There are essays on *Tess of the d'Urbervilles* in a Casebook by Draper (1975; 2nd edn 1991), and in a New Casebook by Widdowson (1993); monographs include Hugman (1970) and Kramer (1991).

## Samuel Butler: *The Way of All Flesh* (1903)

> Before Ernest could well crawl he was taught to kneel; before he could well speak he was taught to lisp the Lord's prayer, and the general confession. How was it possible that these things could be taught too early? If his attention flagged or his memory failed him, here was an ill weed which would grow apace, unless it were plucked out immediately, and the only way to pluck it out was to whip him, or shut him up in a cupboard, or dock him of some of the small pleasures of childhood. Before he was three years old he could read and, after a fashion, write. Before he was four he was learning Latin, and could do rule of three sums. (Ch. 20, p. 117)

Is this passage really taken from a Victorian novel, one might ask? The subject of education, religious and moral as well as academic, is admittedly in many ways very typical of the period; at the same time, however, Butler's picture of the childhood of Ernest Pontifex displays nothing of the characteristic Victorian softness, tenderness and sentimentality – on the contrary, it is harsh, oppressive, brutal and yet curiously cool and detached in its manner, offering as a result no clear suggestion (in any direct sense at least) of immediate sympathy or compassion for the victimized child. Butler's vision of the world, though rather similar to Dickens's in its use of caricature and grotesque – the idea of a 3-year-old Ernest beginning to learn Latin is a perfect example of his precarious balancing of realism and fantasy, verging on the borders of pure nonsense and yet managing to preserve, by the narrowest of margins, the impression of fictional acceptability – is not, however, remotely Dickensian in spirit. Instead, the novel brings to mind, in the savagery of its satire and in the peculiar atmosphere of misanthropy that pervades its every page, the bitter denunciation of humankind that characterized the works of Jonathan Swift.

It is exactly the Swiftian disgust with the generally accepted religious, moral, social and educational standards of his day that made Butler's novel perhaps the most direct expression, in fiction, of the turn-of-the-century revolt against the traditional values of the Victorian era. Begun in the 1870s and revised over a long period, *The Way of All Flesh* remained unpublished, primarily because of the radicalism and outspokenness of its treatment of the largely autobiographical subject-matter of the story, until after the author's death; as a result, it became in more senses than one a posthumous work, a fictional statement of the ultimate disintegration of most of the central assumptions that constituted the fundaments of the Victorian moral and social ideal. Among the important concerns of *The Way of All Flesh* are the issues of faith and doubt, of religious controversy and of the nature of social and moral progress; the central place in Butler's analysis of the values of his era belongs, however, to the question of the nature and significance of the family. Unanimously accepted by the Victorians as a haven of emotional security and the ultimate focus of personal life, the middle-class Christian family is for Butler little more than another oppressive social institution, at best a place of misguided if well-intentioned application of false moral and educational principles and a source of personal alienation, and at worst a direct source and cause of deceit, depravity and abuse. The life of Ernest Pontifex is nearly destroyed – as are, in the moral sense, those of his father, brother and sister – through the combined influences of the dogmatism of narrowly understood Christian ethics, of the relentlessness of the economic and social conditions of modern society, and of individual naivety, stupidity, and selfishness. Rescued from abject poverty by the almost *deus-ex-machina* assistance of his godparents, he finally develops an attitude of disillusioned, reserved and sceptical detachment, isolating himself into the kind of comfortable retired bachelorhood which, for all the limitations and selfishness that it can be associated with by the late-twentieth-century reader, offers him, as it did in real life to Butler himself, opportunities for creative work and for some form of intellectual fulfilment.

The Way of All Flesh is thus, in a very untypical way, a Victorian *Bildungsroman* turned upside-down; in the same way as it undermines the basic beliefs and assumptions of the Victorian era, it also subverts some of the fundamental patterns of its own genre. The differences lie, for instance, in the rather un-Victorian austerity in the novel's use of background detail and in its somewhat unconventional adoption of the narrative viewpoint of a minor character, Ernest's godfather Edward Overton, as a first-person external observer. The main focus remains, however, on the changing relationship between the central character and his social environment. The predecessors of Ernest Pontifex, like Jane Eyre or David Copperfield, may have had to work against obstacles put in their way by unfortunate circumstances, individual human selfishness and envy, or the particular injustices of modern society; the eventual outcome of their struggle was, however, invariably that of resolving their differences with society and finding ways of accommodating their visions of life into the broader reality of Victorian Britain, whose values and ideals they fundamentally shared. For Ernest the situation is different: in order to achieve creative freedom he has to reject the limitations not only of religion and family, but also of social life itself; in his splendid isolation, he becomes the first modernist artist of British fiction, an elder brother of Lawrence's Paul Morel and Joyce's Stephen Dedalus (cf. Unit 16, pp. 454–7).

The best modern biography is by Raby (1991); critical studies include Holt (1964) and Knoepflmacher (1965).

## BIBLIOGRAPHY

*Note: All quotations and page references in this unit are taken from Penguin Classics editions.*

Ackroyd, P. (1990) *Dickens*, Sinclair-Stevenson, London.

Allen, W. (1954) *The English Novel*, Dent, London.

Allen, W. (1965) *George Eliot*, Weidenfeld & Nicolson, London.

Allott, M. (ed.) (1970; 2nd edn 1992) *Emily Brontë: 'Wuthering Heights': A Casebook*, Macmillan, London.

Allott, M. (ed.) (1973) *Charlotte Brontë: 'Jane Eyre' and 'Villette': A Casebook*, Macmillan, London.

Altick, R.D. (1974) *Victorian People and Ideas*, Dent, London.

Ashton, R. (1983) *George Eliot*, Oxford University Press, Oxford.

Bareham, T. (ed.) (1983) *Trollope: The Barsetshire Novels: A Casebook*, Macmillan, London.

Barker, J. (1994) *The Brontës*, Weidenfeld & Nicolson, London.

Beer, G. (1971) *Meredith: A Change of Masks*, Athlone Press, London.

Beer, G. (1983) *Darwin's Plots: Evolutionary Narrative in Darwin, George Eliot and Nineteenth-Century Fiction*, Routledge & Kegan Paul, London.

Briggs, A. (1959) *The Age of Improvement 1783–1867*, Longman, London.

Buckley, J.H. (1974) *Season of Youth: The Bildungsroman from Dickens to Golding*, Harvard University Press, Cambridge, Mass.

Carey, J. (1973) *The Violent Effigy: A Study of Dickens' Imagination*, Faber, London.

Carey, J. (1977) *Thackeray: Prodigal Genius*, Faber, London.

Chase, K. (1991) *George Eliot: 'Middlemarch'*, Landmarks of World Literature, Cambridge University Press, Cambridge.

Craik, W.A. (1968) *The Brontë Novels*, Methuen, London.

Craik, W.A. (1975) *Elizabeth Gaskell and the English Provincial Novel*, Methuen, London.

Daiches, D. (1963) *George Eliot: 'Middlemarch'*, Studies in English Literature, Edward Arnold, London.

Daleski, H.M. (1970) *Dickens and the Art of Analogy*, Faber, London.

Draper, R.P. (ed.) (1975; 2nd edn 1991) *Hardy: The Tragic Novels: A Casebook*, Macmillan, London.

Easson, A. (1979) *Elizabeth Gaskell*, Routledge & Kegan Paul, London.

Fielding, K.J. (1965) *Charles Dickens: A Critical Introduction*, Longman, London.

Fraser, R. (1988) *Charlotte Brontë*, Methuen, London.

Gérin, W. (1967) *Charlotte Brontë: The Evolution of Genius*, Oxford University Press, Oxford.

Gérin, W. (1971) *Emily Brontë: A Biography*, Oxford University Press, Oxford.

Gérin, W. (1976) *Elizabeth Gaskell*, Oxford University Press, Oxford.

Gilbert, S.M. and Gubar, S. (1979) *The Madwoman in the Attic: The Woman Writer and the Nineteenth-Century Literary Imagination*, Yale University Press, New Haven.

Gilmour, R. (1982) *Thackeray: 'Vanity Fair'*, Studies in English Literature, Edward Arnold, London.

Gilmour, R. (1986) *The Novel in the Victorian Age: A Modern Introduction*, Edward Arnold, London.

Gilmour, R. (1993) *The Victorian Period: The Intellectual and Cultural Context of English Literature 1830–1890*, Longman, London.

Glendinning, V. (1992) *Trollope*, Hutchinson, London.

Goodridge, F. (1964) *Emily Brontë: 'Wuthering Heights'*, Studies in English Literature, Edward Arnold, London.

Haight, G. (1968) *George Eliot: A Biography*, Oxford University Press, Oxford.

Hall, N.J. (1991) *Trollope: A Biography*, Oxford University Press, Oxford.

Hardy, B. (1959) *The Novels of George Eliot*, Athlone Press, London.

Holderness, G. (1985) *'Wuthering Heights'*, Open Guides to Literature, Open University Press, Milton Keynes.

Holt, L.E. (1964) *Samuel Butler*, Twayne, New York.

Horsman, A. (1990) *The Victorian Novel, Oxford History of English Literature* (vol. XIII), Oxford University Press, Oxford.

Houghton, W.E. (1957) *The Victorian Frame of Mind 1830–1870*, Oxford University Press, Oxford.

Howe, I. (1967) *Thomas Hardy*, Macmillan, London.

Hugman, B. (1970) *Hardy: 'Tess of the d'Urbervilles'*, Studies in English Literature, Edward Arnold, London.

Johnson, E. (1953) *Charles Dickens: His Tragedy and Triumph*, Gollancz, London.

Kincaid, J. (1977) *The Novels of Anthony Trollope*, Oxford University Press, Oxford.

King, J. (1986) *'Jane Eyre'*, Open Guides to Literature, Open University Press, Milton Keynes.

Knoepflmacher, U.C. (1965) *Religious Humanism and the Victorian Novel: George Eliot, Walter Pater and Samuel Butler*, Princeton University Press, Princeton.

Knoepflmacher, U.C. (1989) *Emily Brontë: 'Wuthering Heights'*, Landmarks of World Literature, Cambridge University Press, Cambridge.

Kramer, D. (1991) *Thomas Hardy: 'Tess of the d'Urbervilles'*, Landmarks of World Literature, Cambridge University Press, Cambridge.

Leavis, F.R. (1948) *The Great Tradition*, Chatto & Windus, London.

Leavis, F.R. and Leavis, Q.D. (1970) *Dickens the Novelist*, Chatto & Windus, London.

Lerner, L. (ed.) (1978) *The Victorians*, Methuen, London.

Lindsay, J. (1956) *George Meredith: His Life and Work*, Bodley Head, London.

Marcus, S. (1965) *Dickens: From Pickwick to Dombey*, Chatto & Windus, London.

McSweeney, K. (1984) *'Middlemarch'*, Allen & Unwin, London.

Millgate, M. (1971) *Thomas Hardy: His Career as a Novelist*, Bodley Head, London.

Millgate, M. (1982) *Thomas Hardy: A Biography*, Oxford University Press, Oxford.

Orel, H. (1986) *The Victorian Short Story: Development and Triumph of a Literary Genre*, Cambridge University Press, Cambridge.

Page, N. (1977) *Thomas Hardy*, Routledge & Kegan Paul, London.

Peck, J. (ed.) (1992) *'Middlemarch'*, New Casebooks, Macmillan, Basingstoke.

Peters, C. (1987) *Thackeray's Universe: Shifting Worlds of Imagination and Reality*, Faber, London.

Pollard, A. (1965) *Mrs Gaskell: Novelist and Biographer*, Manchester University Press, Manchester.

Pollard, A. (1969; 2nd edn 1987) *The Victorians, Sphere History of Literature* (vol. VI), Sphere Books, London (republished in *Penguin History of English Literature*, vol. VI).

Pollard, A. (1978a) *Anthony Trollope*, Routledge & Kegan Paul, London.

Pollard, A. (1978b) *'Vanity Fair': A Casebook*, Macmillan, London.

Raby, P. (1991) *Samuel Butler: A Biography*, Chatto & Windus, London.

Ray, G. (1955–8) *Thackeray: I. The Uses of Adversity 1811–46; II. The Age of Wisdom 1847–63*, Oxford University Press, Oxford.

Reid, J.C. (1967) *Dickens: 'Little Dorrit'*, Studies in English Literature, Edward Arnold, London.

Royle, E. (1987) *Modern Britain: A Social History 1750–1985*, Edward Arnold, London.

Sanders, A. (1978) *The Victorian Historical Novel 1840–1880*, Macmillan, London.

Shelston, A. (ed.) (1985) *Dickens: 'Dombey and Son' and 'Little Dorrit': A Casebook*, Macmillan, Basingstoke.

Showalter, E. (1977) *A Literature of Their Own: British Women Novelists from Brontë to Lessing*, Princeton University Press, Princeton.

Slater, M. (1983) *Dickens and Women*, Dent, London.

Stoneman, P. (ed.) (1993) *'Wuthering Heights'*, New Casebooks, Macmillan, Basingstoke.

Sutherland, J.A. (1976) *Victorian Novelists and Publishers*, Athlone Press, London.

Swinden, P. (ed.) (1972) *George Eliot: 'Middlemarch': A Casebook*, Macmillan, London.

Tillotson, G. (1954) *Thackeray the Novelist*, Cambridge University Press, Cambridge.

Tillotson, K. (1954) *Novels of the Eighteen-Forties*, Oxford University Press, Oxford.

Uglow, J. (1993) *Elizabeth Gaskell: A Habit of Stories*, Faber, London.

Van Ghent, D. (1953) *The English Novel: Form and Function*, Rinehart, New York.

Wall, S. (1988) *Trollope and Character*, Faber, London.

Wheeler, M. (1985) *English Fiction of the Victorian Period 1830–1890*, Longman, London.

Widdowson, P. (ed.) (1993) *'Tess of the d'Urbervilles'*, New Casebooks, Macmillan, Basingstoke.

Williams, D. (1977) *George Meredith: His Life and Lost Love*, Hamish Hamilton, London.

Williams, R. (1970) *The English Novel: From Dickens to Lawrence*, Chatto & Windus, London.

Wilt, J. (1975) *The Readable People of George Meredith*, Princeton University Press, Princeton.

Wolff, R.L. (1977) *Gains and Losses: Novels of Faith and Doubt in Victorian England*, Garland, New York.

Wright, T. (1986) *The Religion of Humanity: The Impact of Comtean Positivism on Victorian Britain*, Cambridge University Press, Cambridge.

# UNIT 12

# Victorian poetry

*Sophie Gilmartin*

## Introduction

This survey of Victorian poetry deals with a period in Britain which was viewed by some who lived in it as a 'pewter age' (Elizabeth Barrett Browning, *Aurora Leigh*), an age which had degenerated from a 'Golden Age' which had existed at some misty point in the past, and by others as a Golden Age where gods of industry and heroes of empire-building walked the English earth. The Victorian period is rife with such contradictions and self-consciousness, and this is reflected in its poetry. My Introduction places the poetry in the context of its time, with a look at the major social, political and religious developments of the nineteenth century. The inheritance of the past and the need for the Victorians to place their own age in relation to past ages is introduced and will be a theme running through this unit. The influences of John Ruskin, Thomas Carlyle, Charles Darwin, Charles Lyell and John Henry Newman are also outlined. Turning to the poetry, my discussion of Tennyson and Browning introduces the debate over subjective and objective poetry, the post-Romantic elements in Victorian poetry, and the distrust of Romantic subjectivity. The tension between subjective and objective poetry is most emphatically played out in the dramatic monologues of Tennyson and Browning, and also in the tension between the private and public aspects of Tennyson's *In Memoriam*. Debates over the role of literature, and particularly of poetry in society, are foregrounded with reference to the divergent philosophies and the very different poetries of Matthew Arnold and Arthur Hugh Clough at mid-century. Of the Pre-Raphaelite poets, the main discussion is centred around the poems of Dante Gabriel Rossetti, Christina Rossetti, William Morris, George Meredith, and Algernon Charles Swinburne. Again, the dialectic between subjective and objective poetry is important here, and is linked to a particular perception in Pre-Raphaelite painting, as well as to questions of power, and, especially in Christina Rossetti's poetry, to questions of gender. Swinburne and Gerard Manley Hopkins are both transitional figures between Victorianism and modernism. Both poets experiment with old metrical forms and with the sound of poetry, but Swinburne's use of the symbol looks forward to the work of the French Symbolists who were to be an important influence upon modernism, while Hopkins's poetry was appropriated for modernism by the early modernists because of its metrical experimentation which allowed a greater freedom in the poetic line. I will begin this unit, then, with extracts from two poems that exist, respectively, at the centre and beyond the edge of the Victorian period:

> Wandering between two worlds, one dead,
> The other powerless to be born...
> (Matthew Arnold, *Stanzas from the Grande Chartreuse*, 1850–5)

> Surely some revelation is at hand;
> Surely the Second Coming is at hand.

> ---

> And what rough beast, its hour come round at last,
> Slouches towards Bethlehem to be born?
> (Yeats, *The Second Coming*, 1920)

Both Arnold in the 1850s and Yeats in 1920 saw themselves as living in an age of anticipation, an age which was still waiting to be born. Matthew Arnold belongs most decidedly to the Victorian age, a period which his poetry and prose so often attempted to define and to come to terms with, and the period which is to be the focus of this unit. But what 'age' did Yeats consider himself to be a part of? He wrote 'The Second Coming', partially quoted above, after the First World War, in an age which was aggressively defining itself as 'modernist', especially in reaction to the Victorian age. Nevertheless, Yeats did live and write within the Victorian period; his early poetry was written through the 1890s and he is included in Quiller-Couch's 1912 collection of *The Oxford Book of Victorian Verse*.

Yeats's case is an example of just how blurred the dividing lines between historical or literary 'ages' can become. In our own case today we partly live with the legacy of the early modernists, who in their enthusiasm for the birth of a new century, and perhaps also for the death of an old monarch, wished to slough off the Victorian age like a dead skin. Joyce's sneering nickname for the the poet Tennyson, 'Lawn-Tennyson, gentleman poet', gives some indication of the modernist reaction to the Victorian period. It is a reaction which we are still influenced by today, and the twentieth-century perspective on the previous century is still that it was 'repressed', 'moralistic', 'heavy' and as suffocating as the popular image of a Victorian parlour full of bear rugs, bric-à-brac, and overstuffed horsehair sofas. At the end of the twentieth century, however, this view of the previous century is under revision. An exploration of some of the major poetry of the period may serve to question some of the labels the age has been given, and also serve to explore the most popular label which the Victorians gave to their own time, 'the age of transition'.

The Victorians were acutely self-conscious about what they often termed the 'Spirit of the Age'. This term was first used by Hazlitt to name a group of essays published in 1825, before our period. But the term was used later by John Stuart Mill, the essayist and utilitarian social reformer. Mill's essay, 'The Spirit of the Age' was first published in a radical newspaper in 1831, the year before the Great Reform Bill, the first of three reform bills in the nineteenth century which were to greatly extend the franchise, first to the middle classes, and eventually to the working classes. Mill described the age as in a 'crisis of transition', and by this he was referring principally to what he and many others saw as the crucial necessity of Britain's transformation of its government from one controlled by men of landed wealth to one which more equally represented the British manufacturing classes and the population in general. But the 'age of transition' could refer to many of the complex and changing features of culture, politics and society in the nineteenth century which include: expansion of the empire; revolutionary advances in science; internal and external challenges to the Established Church; expansion of industry and the corresponding movement from the country to the city.

As Britain extended her empire over foreign nations and races which were now to become part of a British 'family', questions of assimilation versus difference, and of national and racial definition came to the fore. How was England to define herself as nationally and racially different from other nations and people over which she ruled? One way was through language, and in the nineteenth century linguists and philologists searched for evidence of a 'pure English', a language unadulterated by the Latin and French words and phrases which are so imbedded in the English language. Many linguists found this 'pure English' in Anglo-Saxon, and some poets of the period also turned to the use of earlier poetic forms found in medieval alliterative poetry or Anglo-Saxon verse in their own poetry (notably William Barnes, Hopkins and, occasionally, Hardy and Swinburne).

Victorian Britain also sought self-definition by attempting to place its own age within history. In a time of political, social and religious uncertainty it became important to 'stabilize' the past, to fix former historical eras so that those living in the nineteenth century could look to a known past to see where they had 'progressed' from (and the idea of 'progress' was crucial to the Victorian world-view) and so gain a clear understanding of where their transitional age was proceeding to. The particular age that an artist chose to evoke in Victorian painting, novels and poetry often varied according to his or her political or religious bias. Generally, however, historical periods which most often found their way into artistic representation at this time were: the biblical (Old and New Testament); the classical of ancient Greece and Rome and, of particular importance in the poetry, the medieval (for instance in the poetry of Tennyson and the Pre-Raphaelites) and the Renaissance (as in Robert Browning's poetry, and later, Walter Pater's writings).

John Ruskin (1819–1900) wrote prolifically and influentially on numerous subjects in art, culture and society. The historical period which he held up as a positive example to the Victorians was the medieval because it represented in his view a pre-capitalist era of feudal and Christian values. Ruskin vilified the utilitarianism, self-interest and competition of his own time. The so-called Gothic Revival which had begun in the late eighteenth century in reaction to the classicism of that century, was a movement in art and architecture which imitated medieval, pre-Renaissance art. The medievalism which Ruskin and the Gothic Revival helped to popularize in the nineteenth century was an important influence upon the poetry of the time.

The Victorian concentration upon uncovering the 'truth' of past historical events was particularly intense because the truth of the past, especially as told in written documents, was being disturbingly shaken in the nineteenth century. The primary written document which was not only supposed to hold the truth, but in fact to *be* the essence of Truth and The Word itself was the Bible. In the 1830s biblical 'Higher Criticism' from Germany was beginning to take intellectual hold in England. This criticism questioned the authority of the Gospels, and through scholarly research, questioned the *historical* truth of the Bible. If the validity of the Bible was under attack from historical scholarship on the one hand and from the recent advances in geology and evolutionary theory on the other, then it is understandable that the Victorians became anxious about how to locate and then fix the truth of the past, whether that past was told through religious or secular history. If the Bible was no longer a written document that could be trusted to speak truth, then what written document or historical account *could* be trusted?

The historian and social critic Thomas Carlyle (1795–1881) gave six lectures in 1840 on 'Heroes, Hero-Worship and the Heroic in History'. The immense popularity of these lectures (they were published the following year) reveals much about the yearning to find a stable perspective on the past, to find the true facts and meaning of history. Carlyle opened his first lecture with the statement that, 'Universal History, the history of what man has accomplished in this world, is at bottom the History of Great Men' (Carlyle, [1841] 1993, p. 3). In other words, we can find truth in history by searching for the inner nature of particular men. This view of history which concentrated upon the subjectivity of an individual was to influence Robert Browning's dramatic monologues, as discussed below. But Browning's wife, Elizabeth Barrett, an enormously popular poet in the nineteenth century, had her own views on her age's fascination with the past:

> Ay, but every age
> Appears to souls who live in it (ask Carlyle)
> Most unheroic. Ours, for instance, ours:
> The thinkers scout it, and the poets abound
> Who scorn to touch it with a finger-tip:
> A pewter age – mixed metal, silver-washed;
> An age of scum, spooned off the richer past,
> An age of patches for old gaberdines,
> An age of mere transition, meaning nought
> Except that what succeeds must shame it quite
> If God please. That's wrong thinking, to my mind,
> And wrong thoughts make poor poems.
>
> (*Aurora Leigh*, Book V, ll. 156–66)

She saw those around her as wrong in viewing their age as one made up of an unheroic hodge-podge of different periods, uncertain of its own definition. But a dissatisfaction with the time, a searching for past periods for models, and uncertainty, almost inevitably accompany a period of transition; if Elizabeth Barrett felt that these were 'wrong thoughts' which would make 'poor poems' they are nevertheless thoughts which are at the base of many of the major Victorian poems to be discussed in this unit. (For a discussion of Elizabeth Barrett Browning within the broader context of women's writing see Unit 23, pp. 622–4.)

An important factor contributing to the general uncertainty of the period was spiritual doubt, partly effected by the new advances in science. In his *Principles of Geology* (1830–3) the geologist Charles Lyell put forward his theory of uniformitarianism, a theory of the earth's development which gave geological evidence that the earth was far older than previously believed. This evidence flew in the face of scripture and especially the story of creation in Genesis. The naturalist Charles Darwin published his *On the Origin of Species* in 1859. His account of natural selection and the 'struggle for existence' not only discounted the story of creation in Genesis, but also disturbingly undermined a Romantic view of a natural world in harmony with man: this new natural world, as popularly conceived by the many readers of Darwin, was alien, indifferent to man, and those who lived in it were involved in a cruel struggle for survival. Darwin's theory, and the popular conceptions (and frequently, misconceptions) of his work had a profound impact upon the intellectual and religious climate of the day, an effect which is certainly evident in the poetry.

Under attack externally, through scientific evidence, the Church was also experiencing radical, internal changes. Dissenters and Nonconformists had broken away from the Established Church, and the evangelical movement gained great strength in the Victorian period. But there were controversial and divisive trends within the Established Church itself. The most important of these, the 'Oxford Movement' (also known as 'Tractarianism') was a movement within the Church of England which endeavoured to ensure that the Church remained a divine institution and did not become subordinate to the State. Followers of Tractarianism wished to revive High Anglican rituals and practice, rituals which were derived from those of the Roman Catholic Church. A number of followers of the Oxford Movement did convert to Roman Catholicism, the most famous of these being John Henry Newman (1801–90) who had been the leader of the movement until his conversion in 1845. Twenty years later he was greatly to influence the undergraduate poet, Gerard Manley Hopkins.

In the midst, then, of this 'age of transition' it was crucial for the Victorian British to find a stable self-definition both as an age and as a nation. An internal or domestic definition of the nation and of national stability was founded upon the central importance of the family unit, and particularly of the middle-class family and middle-class morality. A more global definition of the nation, of the place of the British Isles in the world, was founded upon the nation's view of itself as of central importance and power on the globe (or at least as central in the British empire which at this time could be found in most parts of the globe). These two aspects of national definition, the domestic/internal and global/external, come together in this sentimental poem by the minor nineteenth-century poet, Charles Tennyson Turner (elder brother of Alfred Tennyson). The poem is entitled 'Letty's Globe'.

> When Letty had scarce pass'd her third glad year,
>   And her young artless words began to flow,
> One day we gave the child a colour'd sphere
> Of the wide earth, that she might mark and know,

> By tint and outline, all its sea and land.
>> She patted all the world; old empires peep'd
> Between her baby fingers; her soft hand
>> Was welcome at all frontiers. How she leap'd
>> And laugh'd and prattled in her world-wide bliss;
> But when we turn'd her sweet unlearned eye
> On our own isle, she raised a joyous cry –
> 'Oh! yes, I see it, Letty's home is there!'
>> And while she hid all England with a kiss,
> Bright over Europe fell her golden hair.

'Our own isle' pointed out by a baby's finger on the globe domesticates the image of England as powerful centre of the expanding empire ('her soft hand / Was welcome at all frontiers') and presents the isle of England as 'Letty's home'. Home and empire, domestic and global, sentimentally define the nation here. In addition to national definition, the poem offers a reduced and manageable image of the earth: it has been made into a 'colour'd sphere', a child's plaything. At a time when geology was disturbing previous beliefs about the age and creation of the earth, and increased travel, imperial expansion and the new science of anthropology were expanding British understanding of the complexity of the nations and peoples on earth, this move to reduce the earth to the simplicity of a child's toy is perhaps understandable.

Romantic poetry, and especially that of Wordsworth, assumed that man could and should live in harmony with nature. But the increasing alienation from nature through the growth of cities, industry and science meant that the Victorians began to lose the sense that there could be an emotional or psychological correspondence between their minds or internal selves and nature. In Wordsworth's poem *The Prelude*, for example, the poet describes the River Derwent that ran near his childhood home as 'the fairest of all rivers' which 'loved / To blend his murmurs with my nurse's song' and which 'sent a voice / That flowed along my dreams...' (*The Prelude*, Book 1, ll. 271–4). The Romantic poet's early childhood is nurtured by the river, and the harmony between his psyche and the river is so complete that it can even enter his unconscious self, flowing along his dreams. A radically different description of a river occurs in Thomas Hood's poem, 'The Bridge of Sighs' (1843). The poem describes raising the body of a prostitute who has drowned herself in the Thames. The river is 'black, flowing' and 'rough', a polluted river of 'muddy impurity' flowing through a city in which social problems of poverty, homelessness and prostitution are rife... 'O, it was pitiful! / Near a whole city full, / Home she had none'. This river, far from harmonizing with man, must be repellent to him because it is polluted not only by the effluence of London, but also by the suicides and murders which are a sign of the city's moral ills. The poet challenges the reader to drink and wash in the river, thinking of the dead woman: 'Dissolute Man! / Lave in it, drink of it, / Then, if you can!'. Thomas Hood (1799–1845) wrote a number of popular poems on themes of social problems which plagued nineteenth-century Britain, the most famous being 'The Song of the Shirt' (1843) which draws attention to the sufferings of overworked and underpaid seamstresses.

The above comparison of rivers in a Romantic and a Victorian poem draws an extreme contrast. Of course there is a great deal of Victorian poetry which describes the beauty and peace found in nature. Even so, these descriptions of nature do not see the same harmony and commensurability between man's inner self and the outside world; rather, the poems often evoke either a yearning to find a harmony with the world outside the self, or a disturbing alienation from that world. The often anguished relationship between the internal or 'subjective' perspective and the external or 'objective' will be a central and recurring theme in the following discussion of Victorian poetry. Subjective versus objective poetry was a contention within Victorian poetics, particularly in reaction to Romantic poetry (which was seen as subjective). The development of these two perspectives in the poetry of the day is an important gauge of the changes in the relationship of self and society, man and earth, man and God, nation and empire.

For further discussion of themes addressed in this introductory section see Williams (1973), Cosslett (1982), Culler (1985), Jay (1983) and Armstrong (1993).

## Texts, authors, contexts

### 'The Web Floats Wide': Tennyson and Browning

In 1850 Tennyson published his long poem *In Memoriam*, his great elegy to his friend Arthur Hallam who had died in 1833, at the age of 22. The poem had been seventeen years in the making, and it was to ensure that Tennyson received the Poet Laureateship the following year in succession to Wordsworth. Also in 1850 Wordsworth published the long poem which he had been working on for many years, *The Prelude*. The coincidental publication of these two poems at mid-century, one by a poet regarded as quintessentially Victorian, and the other by a poet regarded as quintessentially Romantic, together with the passing of the Laureateship from the one to the other, serves as a reminder of the difficulty of fixing a date to when 'Romanticism' in poetry stopped and 'Victorianism' began.

Alfred Tennyson (1809–92) and Robert Browning (1812–89) are two Victorian poets, close contemporaries, whose poetic careers both span and poetically evoke the nineteenth century. For these two poets, who lived through a greater part of the century than any of the other poets discussed here, the legacy of the Romantic poets was both an influence and a poetic inheritance against which they defined themselves.

From the medieval scholastic philosophers to the present day, the terms 'subjective' and 'objective' have been used and debated in a variety of discourses. In the Victorian period these terms had become popular catchwords in discussions of art and literature. Because these terms are particularly important to nineteenth-century poetry I will clarify them by giving the dictionary definitions which come closest to their Victorian usage. Subjective is defined as 'Relating to the thinking subject, proceeding from or taking place within the subject: having its source in the mind' (*OED*, 'subjective', def. 3); also, 'Expressing ... the individuality of the artist or author' (*OED*, 4.b.). Sometimes in this period 'subjective' carried the negative connotations of 'given to brooding over one's mental states' (*OED*, 4.c.), and this connotation will be apparent in Matthew Arnold's assessment of the subjective, discussed below. The definition of 'objective' for our purposes is more straightforward; 'Dealing with ... that which is external to the mind; treating of outward things or events, rather than inward thoughts or feelings' (*OED*, 'objective', def. 3.a.).

Much Victorian ink had been spilt over the terms 'subjective' and 'objective' poetry by the time Browning wrote his 'Essay on Shelley' in 1851. In this essay, Browning both eulogizes the Romantic poet who had so influenced him, and also marks out and defines how he differs in his own poetic project. Shelley, according to Browning, was a subjective poet, that is, a poet who writes from the perspective of the inner self, and whose concerns transcend the objective, material world. In this essay it becomes clear that Browning wishes to identify himself as an objective poet. Far from rejecting the agenda of the subjective poet, however, Browning writes in the 'Essay on Shelley' that the human mind's needs in poetry alternate between the subjective and objective perspective. But he feels that at the time he writes, the 'general eye' has had a surfeit of the 'loftier visions' and abstractions of the subjective poet (Jack *et al.*, 1991, p. 428). The danger of a subjective poetry which is never relieved by objectivity is that man may begin to live in a shadowland of visions, a mirage of ideals, in which, as Browning writes, 'the world is found to be subsisting wholly on the shadow of a reality, on sentiments diluted from passions, on the tradition of a fact, the convention of a moral, the straw of last year's harvest' (Jack *et al.*, 1991, p. 428). Browning clearly sees this situation as signalling his moment for poetic action; the moment of the objective poet who presents the world from a slightly distanced objective perspective, but through whom the world, its phenomena and men and women will be seen directly and not through a haze of abstraction. He writes that there will be in objective poetry a supply of 'new substance', and many 'objects for men's outer and not inner sight, shaping for their uses a new and different creation from the last...' (Jack *et al.*, 1991, p. 428).

In the 1830s when Tennyson and Browning were beginning to publish their poetry, there was an awareness that the subjective poetry of the Romantic school had lost much of its impetus, and little seemed to be happening to fill the gap left by the death of Shelley, Keats, Byron and the old age of Coleridge and Wordsworth. If Tennyson and Browning are, as we term them today, 'Victorian' poets, does this mean that their poetry was caught up in a great swing of the pendulum, such that all subjective concerns in poetry were to be discarded so that the day of the objective poet could have its turn? Or did these poets, and others who began writing later in the century, forge something new and distinctively Victorian by attempting to bring together the subjective and objective view? The poet Elizabeth Barrett certainly thought the latter the case in the poetry of her future husband, Robert Browning. She wrote in her second letter to Browning

(January, 1845; a letter written before she had ever met him, and before their famous elopement):

> You have in your vision two worlds – or to use the language of the schools of the day, you are both subjective and objective in the habits of your mind. You can deal both with abstract thought and with human passion in the most passionate sense. (Kintner, 1969, 1, p. 9)

Employed by Tennyson and Browning, among others, the dramatic monologue is one poetic strategy which allows for a vision in two worlds of the subjective and objective: the poet writes a monologue in the voice of a character, allowing the *character* to be completely subjective, but allowing the distanced poet and reader to remain objective. Often these *dramatis personae* (the title of Browning's 1864 book of poetry) are historical figures, or at least characters who could have existed according to nineteenth-century versions of history.

## Tennyson

'The Lady of Shalott' (1832, rev. 1842) is one of the most famous of Tennyson's poetic *dramatis personae*. The poem is not a dramatic monologue, so we do not see into the Lady's subjective self with the same immediacy as we do in some other of his poems such as 'Maud' or 'St. Simeon Stylites'. The Lady does speak in the poem, but the true insight into her subjectivity is gained by witnessing the moment in the poem in which she moves from a stagnant subjective world to an alien, objective world. The shock of this transferral kills her. The Lady of Shallot lives in a castle tower on an isle, completely isolated from the world and human contact.

> Four gray walls and four gray towers
> Overlook a space of flowers,
> And the silent isle embowers
> The Lady of Shalott.
>
> (ll. 15–18)

The Lady of Shalott weaves a tapestry in her castle tower. She is under a curse which dictates that she may not look at the world outside her window directly, but only at its reflection in the mirror before her. Into the tapestry she weaves scenes from the outside world that she has seen reflected in her mirror: a reflection of a reflection.

> And moving thro' a mirror clear
> That hangs before her all the year,
> Shadows of the world appear.
>
> (ll. 46–8)

Many critics have interpreted the lady weaving as a figure for the artist or poet, and the tapestry as a figure for art or, specifically, for poetry. If she is a figure for the poet, then the poem seems to interpret the poet's world as one of 'shadows' or reflections of reflections of reality (the mirror and the tapestry being doubly-removed from the outside world), rather than a direct representation of life.

According to this interpretation, the poet may not 'stay / To look down on Camelot', at the objective world, just as the Lady may not look out the window. If the poet does so, the curse of the poem would seem to declare that he or she (as artist) and the poem will be destroyed.

Some critics have argued that even though the tapestry, the artistic creation, may not engage directly with the real world, it is a thing so beautiful that the embowerment and isolation of the artist from the world is worth it. According to this interpretation the lady should have stayed in her tower away from exposure to the curse and death. But Tennyson's poem is more complex in its imagery than this interpretation allows for.

In line 70 the lady sees reflected in her mirror, 'two young lovers lately wed' and this leads her to admit, 'I am half sick of shadows'. The desire for communion – represented by the wish for love and sexual union – with the outside world, and the erotic symbolism in the ensuing stanzas when she watches the reflection of Sir Lancelot in the mirror is a clear indication of her need for direct connection with the world below her tower. The quiet solitude of her 'silent isle' is only broken in the first eight stanzas (before she sees Lancelot) by her singing, which 'Only reapers, reaping early' hear the echo of. The silence, solitude and the fairy song heard by few are abruptly interrupted by the noisy arrival of Sir Lancelot. It is the sight of Lancelot in her mirror which tempts her to move away from the world of reflection and shadow and to take a direct look at life.

In the crisis stanza of the poem she discards the solitude, stillness and silence of her turret room and tapestry or 'web', and moves energetically towards the outside world;

> She left the web, she left the loom,
> She made three paces thro' the room,
> She saw the water-lily bloom,
> She saw the helmet and the plume,
>     She look'd down to Camelot.
> Out flew the web and floated wide;
> The mirror crack'd from side to side;
> 'The curse is come upon me,' cried
>     The Lady of Shalott.

(ll. 109–17)

In turning from her loom, from her art to join the everyday world outside her tower and (as she hopes) Lancelot, the lady seems to abandon her artistic expression (her tapestry, her song) for the rather dubious quality of Lancelot's 'artistic expression' revealed in ll. 107–8: '"Tirra lirra", by the river / Sang Sir Lancelot.' Lancelot may be handsome, 'bold' and 'brazen', but he is no poet.

Can this poem, then, be seen to represent the dilemma of the poet? If the Lady and her tapestry represent the poet and his poetry, then is the move to join the objective world (the journey to Camelot) an inevitable abandonment of the poetic art? A number of critics have interpreted the poem in this way, and have seen it as foreshadowing Tennyson's anxiety over accepting the Poet Laureateship in 1850. Naturally the Poet Laureateship is officially the most public role a poet may have.

Apparently, Tennyson vacillated over accepting it, even writing 'two letters, one accepting and one declining, and threw them on the table, and settled to decide which I would send after my dinner and bottle of port' (quoted in Ricks, 1972, p. 232). Again he said, 'but I wish more and more that somebody else had it (the Poet Laureateship). I have no passion for courts but a great love of privacy' (Ricks, p. 232). The Lady of Shalott, however, has a 'passion for courts'; specifically to find passion and life, rather than a world of shadows, in the court of Camelot.

In John Stuart Mill's review (1835) of this very popular poem he castigated those who seek to know 'the precise nature of the enchantment' which is on the Lady of Shalott (Jump, 1967, p. 88). Like many of Tennyson's poems, the meaning of 'The Lady of Shalott' relies partly upon accepting the 'mystery' of her curse and allowing the poem to remain ambiguous. An interpretation which allows for this uncertain quality in the poem is one in which the Lady's abandonment of her loom is not a discarding of her art, but an abandonment of a wholly subjective poetry. In this light the embowered desolate isle and the tapestry she weaves there is equivalent to a subjective, internalized or even solipsistic art. This subjectivity needs to be abandoned for some experience of the direct gaze, and communion with outside phenomena or the 'objective'. Indeed in his 'Essay on Shelley' Browning sees a wholly subjective poetry as in danger of resulting in a 'world' which is 'found to be subsisting wholly on the shadow of a reality', and as the Lady of Shalott says of the reflections in her mirror and tapestry, 'I am half sick of shadows'.

When 'She made three paces thro' the room' the lady exhibits a more surprising energy and violence than anything that Lancelot, the man of 'bold' and 'brazen' action exhibits below the castle towers. The mirror is cracked and 'Out flew the web and floated wide'. Rather than this entailing a destruction of her tapestry (art, poetry), the web or tapestry floats 'wide' out the window for everyone in the outside world to view. It is no longer kept hidden in the tower.

As for the Lady's 'fairy song' which previously had been heard only by the reapers, it is now heard by all the countryside as she is carried by the boat on the river current into Camelot: 'Singing in her song she died / The Lady of Shalott' (ll. 152–3). The Lady, as a figure of the artist/poet, dies on her journey towards the world, not of shadowy representations, but of objective reality. According to this interpretation there is much anxiety over the move from subjectivity (the silent enclosed spaces of isle and turret room) to objective reality (the court, the riverside world of commerce). This journey may lead to death, but in the Lady's death there is a type of immortality: the 'web floats wide', her song is heard, and she is no longer virtually anonymous because before her journey on the boat, 'round about the prow she wrote / *The Lady of Shalott*' (ll. 125–6).

The Lady of Shalott's poetry and name are known, but she dies as a result of a direct gaze upon the world. The poem is ambiguous and open-ended over the wisdom of the Lady of Shalott's choice. Subjective and objective hang in a precarious balance in this important poem, which after its publication in 1832 was much revised for republication in 1842. The choice between these two types of vision (and the possibility of having both) are also evident in the poem 'Ulysses' (1842) of the same period. 'Ulysses' is a dramatic monologue, spoken entirely in the voice of the Greek hero of

Homer's epic, after he has returned to Ithaca from his adventures. Tennyson takes up the hero *after* his final moment in Homer's *Odyssey*. Ulysses' voice is no longer that of the epic hero trying to get home; he has reached the goal of Homer's epic but now is restless, dissatisfied with the domestic life and yearns to return to sea travels. The dramatic monologue catches Ulysses in a moment of transition between the domestic 'still hearth' of Ithaca and the epic adventures on the seas. The poem opens:

> It little profits that an idle king,
> By this still hearth, among these barren crags,
> Match'd with an aged wife, I mete and dole
> Unequal laws unto a savage race,
> That hoard, and sleep, and feed, and know not me.
> I cannot rest from travel: I will drink
> Life to the lees...

Ulysses plans to leave Ithaca again, passing on 'the sceptre and the isle' to his son Telemachus who is characterized by a 'slow prudence'. Telemachus is 'centered in the sphere of common duties' and of him his father says, 'He works his work, I mine'. The *centrality* of Telemachus is crucial here; if he is 'centered' in the round of Ithaca's administration and rule, he is also centred in an embowered isle, similar in some ways to the Lady of Shalott. Although, unlike her, he is not completely isolated from human company, the 'still hearth' of Ithaca still seems to be separated from the outside world and an active life of adventure. Telemachus is 'centered' and Ulysses wishes to move as far from the centre as he can go, to the margins of the world: '... for my purpose holds / To sail beyond the sunset, and the baths / Of all the western stars, until I die' (ll. 60–1). Ulysses defines himself by what he has seen and known in that objective world: 'I am a part of all that I have met'. Centre versus the margin; the domestic in contrast with the life of the world; the balance between the subjective and the objective; the role of England within an expanding empire: these are a few of the oppositions and dilemmas within Victorian poetry and culture which are represented by Ithaca versus the 'margins of the world'.

Ulysses' yearning is, as expressed in the final line of the poem, 'To strive, to seek, to find, and not to yield'. The poem ends with a powerful dedication to the active life and to a search for the objective world outside the self. However just as the conflicting images in *The Lady of Shalott* lead to an ambiguity over the consequences of subjective versus objective at the end of that poem, so *Ulysses* contains a similar dilemma, and part of this ambiguity comes from the powerful epic which lies behind the poem.

Ulysses' wife, Penelope, is referred to in the second and third lines of the poem; she is the 'aged wife' who has her proper place by the 'still hearth' within the domestic sphere. In Homer's *Odyssey*, Penelope waits for Ulysses through the many years of his wanderings as he tries to reach home. She ensures that there will be a home for him upon his return by refusing the many suitors who try to gain her hand and the kingship of Ithaca. This she ensures by bargaining with them that as soon as she has finished the tapestry that she is weaving, she will choose a man for husband and king. But every night she unravels the tapestry she has woven in the day, as a delaying tactic. Like the Lady of Shalott, Penelope weaves a tapestry on her island.

Penelope's 'art' (both her weaving and her wiles) ensure that she can remain chaste and Ulysses' wife, so that if he does return, there will be a place for him to return *to*. Since Homer's epic is the story of a journey home, it would not exist without Penelope's weaving. And since Tennyson's poem is derived from Homer's, neither would the Victorian poem exist without the 'aged wife' and her tapestry in the background. In a poem which so powerfully points to the active, objective life of the world, Penelope's 'web' which represents internalized, subjective art may not be discarded or forgotten. As in *The Lady of Shalott* 'the web floats wide': both poems represent a product of the subjective (the tapestry, the poem) without which the objective (the journey out to the world) would never be known, or would not exist.

In a review in *Fraser's Magazine* in 1850, the novelist and proponent of 'muscular Christianity', Charles Kingsley, hailed Tennyson's *In Memoriam* as 'the noblest English Christian poem which several centuries have seen' (Jump, 1967, p. 183). Kingsley, who was a clergyman, saw the poem as an affirmation of faith in an age of religious doubt. The poem was immensely popular, going through three editions by the end of 1850, and eighteen editions by 1866. Kingsley was clearly not the only Victorian who saw in this elegy a powerful affirmation of immortality and of spiritual belief; Queen Victoria herself told Tennyson that she had found great solace in the poem after the death of her husband Albert in 1861.

The poem, made up of 132 sections of varying numbers of stanzas, was written in memory of Arthur Henry Hallam, Tennyson's closest friend whom he met while they were Cambridge undergraduates. The stanzas are composed of four octosyllabic lines, rhyming abba, and although the elegy was composed over seventeen years, the poetic time is three years which are marked particularly by three stanzas taking place at Christmas (poems XXVIII, LXXVIII, CIV). In the elegy Tennyson confronts his grief over Hallam's death and this confrontation brings to the fore many of the central anxieties and debates of the Victorian period: religious doubt; evolution; questions of memory and the fading of grief; of the subjective versus objective view. The many aspects of the poet's mind are presented not as a coherent whole, but as a fragmentary narrative of alternating vacillation, indecision, hope, despair and struggle towards faith.

Because the poem is an expression of loss and of mourning for a beloved friend it is naturally subjective, representing inner thoughts and emotions. In section CVIII Tennyson recognizes the danger of a subjectivity so intense that it could become solipsistic and removed from mankind. Tennyson addresses his dead friend in stanzas 1 and 4, respectively:

> I will not shut me from my kind,
> And, lest I stiffen into stone,
> I will not eat my heart alone,
> Nor feed with sighs a passing wind:
>
> . . .
>
> What find I in the highest place,
> But mine own phantom chanting hymns?
> And on the depths of death there swims
> The reflex of a human face.

When the poet's mind raises itself to the 'highest sphere' to search for Hallam's spirit, he finds only his own 'phantom', and when he descends to the 'depths of death' he sees 'the reflex of a human face', and that face, again, is his own, not Hallam's. At this point the poem becomes a nightmarish vision of self-reflection and subjectivity. The poet cannot escape himself, and therefore the firm determination of the first line of the section, 'I will not shut me from my kind' becomes crucial. Carol T. Christ has written about the anxiety which is implicit in Tennyson's and Browning's move away from what they saw as the subjectivity of the Romantic poets; she writes that they saw it as 'a disabling focus upon the self' and that the two poets 'often associate the imagination's inner voice with madness' (Christ, 1984, pp. 5–6). Certainly in many of Browning's dramatic monologues the intense subjectivity of some of his characters could be viewed as madness (or at least extreme idiosyncracy), and in Tennyson's dramatic monologue 'Maud: A Monodrama' (1855) we see the isolation and solipsism of the narrator's fragmented self approach madness and paranoia.

Although Tennyson's elegy is deeply personal, and therefore subjective to a degree, it does not 'shut' him from his 'kind' because it addresses many of the concerns of his Victorian contemporaries. Through a personal vision he writes often in the poem of an objective world, as, for example, in Sections LIV–LVI in which he deals with the troubles of religious doubt brought about by the advances in science. In Section LIV, st. 3, the poet attempts to trust in God that all the arbitrariness and cruelty that he sees around him in nature is part of a divine plan. He struggles to have faith,

> That not a worm is cloven in vain;
> 　That not a moth with vain desire
> 　Is shrivell'd in a fruitless fire,
> Or but subserves another's gain.

Rocking the poet's spiritual faith is an objective study of geological evidence, inspired, most probably, by Lyell's *Principles of Geology* (1830–3, see Introduction). The evidence of geology indicates to the poet that nature is both 'careless of the single life' and also of the 'type':

> 'So careful of the type?' but no.
> From scarped cliff and quarried stone
> She cries, 'A thousand types are gone:
> I care for nothing, all shall go'.

In this moment of doubt, the immensity of the geological timescale, exhibited in the fossils of the 'scarped cliff', diminishes humanity: humankind, rather than being God's chosen, receiving his special care, is simply a 'passing type' which will die out as have other types that leave their remains in the rock.

Another great Victorian elegist, Thomas Hardy (1840–1928) was born at the time when Tennyson was composing his elegy to Hallam. His group of elegiac poems in memory of his first wife Emma, the 'Poems of 1912–1913', falls outside the period which we may officially term 'Victorian' (Victoria died in 1901).

Nevertheless Hardy wrote both his poems and novels (see Unit 11) throughout the Victorian period and was considered in the early twentieth century, as he is today, one of the 'late, great' Victorians. Hardy's poem 'At Castle Boterel', one of the 'Poems of 1912–1913' also takes up the theme of geological time versus human time. In the poem Hardy has returned to the scene of his courtship after many years, and looking at a scarp of cliff that faces a road, remembers when he walked that road with Emma in their youth:

> Primaeval rocks form the road's steep border,
> And much have they faced there, first and last,
> Of the transitory in Earth's long order;
> But what they record in colour and cast
> Is – that we two passed.

(st. 5)

While Tennyson doubts and almost despairs when faced with the geological record, Hardy challenges its potential obliteration of the importance of the single human life; of his walk with Emma, he writes, 'But was there ever / A time of such quality, since or before / in that hill's story?'. He challenges nature's indifference to human life by locating the most important moment that the cliff has witnessed, not in the millions of years' change over the geological epochs, but in a single moment of two human lives. Hardy, essentially an atheist, cannot believe like Tennyson that there is an afterlife, but through elegy he can attempt to 'immortalize' in verse a single moment in the human time-span.

Tormented by doubt in Section LVI of *In Memoriam*, Tennyson asks, 'What hope of answer, or redress?' and answers himself in the next line 'Behind the veil, behind the veil'. The answers to all the spiritual questions which disturb him as he looks upon a 'Nature, red in tooth and claw' (Section LVI) will, he trusts, be granted when he passes behind the veil which separates life and death. The elegy ends with an epithalamion (a poem celebrating a wedding) for his sister Cecilia. Hope for mankind in this ending to the poem is both figuratively and literally 'behind the veil': behind the veil of the afterlife, but also behind the veil of the bride, as in her union she will give birth to children, a hope for the future. Tennyson sees these children as part of an evolutionary process in God's plan towards the gradual improvement of the human race. His dead friend Hallam was a superior man, 'Appearing ere the times were ripe' ('Epilogue', st. 35). The poet's hope and faith is that men and women are gradually improving: 'No longer half-akin to brute', they may one day attain the distinction and superiority of a man like Hallam. Tennyson's trust in the evolutionary process that this may be accomplished is evident in the epithalamion and also in the fact that he named his own son Hallam. These hopeful gestures, both in the poem's ending and in the naming of his son, are somewhat tempered when we hear Tennyson's own verdict upon *In Memoriam* as told to James Knowles in 1893:

> It begins with a funeral and ends with a marriage – begins with death and ends in promise of a new life – a sort of Divine Comedy, cheerful at the close. It is a very impersonal poem as well as personal ... It's too hopeful, this poem, more than I am myself'. (Jump, 1967, p. 172)

A poem which goes a long way to defining the central concerns of the Victorian period, it is both objective and subjective ('impersonal' and 'personal') and subject to the uncertainties of an 'age of transition'.

Suggested further reading on Tennyson: Ricks (1972), Culler (1977), Sinfield (1971) and Colley (1983).

## Browning

Thomas Hardy made an entry in his notebooks in December 1865 which plays with the subject's understanding of the timescale he (or in this case, it) occupies: 'To insects the twelvemonth has been an epoch, to leaves a life, to tweeting birds a generation, to man a year' (Millgate (1984), p. 56). In Hardy's poem 'At Castle Boterel' discussed above, a single moment in the human timescale was juxtaposed with the daunting geological and evolutionary timescale. In the quotation above Hardy again juxtaposes timescales as seen by insects, leaves, birds and finally, man. As with these various living organisms, so with man it is the case that an understanding of one's 'time', of one's particular historical 'moment', is highly subjective.

As mentioned in the Introduction, Thomas Carlyle's lectures in 1840 on 'Heroes, Hero-Worship, and the Heroic in History' presented a way into the historical past through the 'History of...Great Men'. In a sense, history becomes subjective because Carlyle's biographical approach concentrates on the personal life stories of these men rather than upon factual documents recounting battles, treaties, sieges – a more traditional definition of history. Like Carlyle, Browning finds a way into the past through a subjective approach; through the dramatic monologue he presents a character from the past in a particular moment. However, Browning's historical characters are not the 'Great Men' of whom Carlyle spoke: they are, on the contrary, usually minor or secondary players in history. Too busy concentrating upon themselves and their everyday needs, they are often ignorant or indifferent to their role in history (which would be far less likely in a 'great man' of Carlyle's definition). The gaps in the understanding of these minor figures enable us to distance ourselves from the character, to note the lacunae in the character's knowledge of his own context, and fill them in for ourselves.

One such minor historical character is the Duke Alfonso of Ferrara, the speaker of Browning's dramatic monologue, 'My Last Duchess' (1842). Browning chose not only a minor character but a minor moment in history, which nevertheless lies shrouded in a certain degree of conjecture and mystery: in 1564 Duke Alfonso II of Ferrara was negotiating for the hand in marriage of the niece of the Count of Tyrol. His first wife had died three years before at the age of 17 and it is thought that she had been poisoned. The poem's moment is one of transition: the former wife is dead and the contract for the new wife has not yet been signed. Browning is fond of depicting both personal and historical moments of transition: they reveal much about a person or an era, because they are times which are less defined and may therefore more easily disclose essential qualities and anxieties. Perhaps these 'moments of transition' are also interesting to the poet because they reflect in some ways his own era's sense of being in that state.

The dramatic monologue 'My Last Duchess' takes the form of a speech that the Duke makes to one of the envoys from the Count of Tyrol, sent to negotiate the new marriage contract. He has taken the envoy upstairs to view his art collection, and draws the curtain which reveals the painting of his 'last duchess'. The poem opens:

> That's my last Duchess painted on the wall,
> Looking as if she were alive. I call
> That piece a wonder, now: Fra Pandolf's hands
> Worked busily a day, and there she stands.
> Will't please you sit and look at her? –

At the opening of the poem we realize that we, as well as the envoy, are being asked to look at the painting. Unlike the envoy, we cannot see the painting directly, but only through the description given us by the Duke's lecture. The painting, framed in itself, is also framed by the poem and in order to interpret the poem we must 'read' in a double act of interpretation both the Duke's words and the painting.

In fact the poem is partly about 'reading' and the tricky act of interpretation; the Duke goes on to explain

> – I said
> 'Fra Pandolf' by design, for never *read*
> Strangers like you that pictured countenance,
> The depth and passion of its earnest glance,
> But to myself they turned (since none puts by
> The curtain I have drawn for you, but I)
> And seemed as they would ask me, if they durst,
> How such a glance came there; so not the first
> Are you to turn and ask thus.
>
> (my italics, ll. 5–13)

But did the envoy 'turn and ask' about the Duchess's expression? It seems, on the contrary, that the Duke is interpreting the viewer of the painting, and it becomes clear as the poem continues that this Duke is capable of dangerous *over*-interpretation. His pride, jealousy and perhaps paranoia lead him both to read conjecture into the envoy's expression (conjecture as to who the Duchess is smiling and blushing *for*) and to misinterpret the flush and 'spot of joy' which lies on the Duchess's cheek in the painting. The Duke ominously explains that her 'earnest glance' and blush were brought to her face not by 'her husband's presence only'; the Duchess experienced equal joy by the painter-friar's mild compliments and by a number of small things such as the sunset, cherries, a ride on her horse. In her love of so many things around her she did not make the Duke feel sufficiently appreciated. He would not 'stoop' to correcting her behaviour, but simply states, 'I gave commands; Then all smiles stopped together' (ll. 45–6). Her smiles upon him and upon others are erased by his 'commands'. How is the envoy, and how are we to interpret this? Did she become melancholy because he gave her severe orders? Or did his 'commands' order her poisoning, erasing her smile through death? Browning leaves the historical facts still in mystery, but the tone of the poem is certainly ominous.

Just as the Duke of Ferrara wishes to control the thoughts and behaviour of his 'last Duchess', so he wishes to control the envoy's (and, by extension, our) interpretation of the painting. He alone may reveal the painting ('since none puts by / The curtain I have drawn for you, but I'). But the Duke is doomed to failure in his desire to control thought or interpretation, for once the painting is revealed, once the poem is there to be read, the 'web floats wide' – the work of art (the painting and its 'frame', the poem) is open to interpretation. This is not to say, however, that Browning is claiming that it will be easy or even possible to find one, true interpretation of this historical moment. Indeed the poem makes us aware that the Duke's interpretation is only one of many possible, but that the other 'readings' of this history which we may wish to know are not available to us because they have been silenced. Browning has silenced the envoy, because his poem is a dramatic monologue (although it would be a brave soul who would interrupt the Duke, anyway); the last Duchess is of course most emphatically silenced with poison and paint; and it does not appear that the new Duchess-to-be will have much of a chance to voice her opinion with all the counts, dukes and envoys speaking for her.

The duchess-to-be is alluded to in the last lines of the poem:

> The Count your master's known munificence
> Is ample warrant that no just pretence
> Of mine for dowry will be disallowed;
> Though his fair daughter's self, as I avowed
> At starting, is my object. Nay, we'll go
> Together down, sir. Notice Neptune, though,
> Taming a sea-horse, thought a rarity,
> Which Claus of Innsbruck cast in bronze for me!

The Count's daughter is 'objectified' in that she is defined in terms of money (the dowry), but in addition the Duke unconsciously reveals that he has the same plans for her as he had for his last Duchess, who is now part of his art collection. He says that 'the daughter's self ... is my object' and then immediately goes on to draw the envoy's attention to another object in his collection, the bronze statue. As feminist critics would point out, women who have been 'objectified' have as little voice, as little chance of expressing desires, will, or opinion as would a bronze ornament or a painting. Their silence in literature and history compared with the voices of men is part of their 'objectification' within a patriarchal power structure which denies a voice to their subjectivity. Again, and this time from the perspective of gender, 'subjective versus objective' is at issue. But of course it is not only the women who are silenced in this poem. The intense and idiosyncratic subjectivity of the Duke of Ferrara has probably inspired him to 'silence' many men and women, through death, fear and the wielding of his power and name.

Browning's 'My Last Duchess' makes us aware of the silences, the lacunae in history to which we do not have access, and makes us aware that it is very difficult to hear the 'whole story' because it is made up of many versions, some of which are silenced. The poem draws attention to the fact that there are subjectivities which are closed to us, not only in history, but in the everyday lives of those around us in the present day.

The Duke finds his last Duchess's pleasure in momentary, transitory things insulting because she seems to gain as much gratification from things of the moment as from his ancient lineage. As in Hardy's and Tennyson's poetry discussed earlier, there is again in Browning's poem a juxtaposition of timescales: the momentary pleasures of the Duchess, and the Duke's 900 years of the House of Este. Browning's dramatic monologues also juxtapose the moment with the centuries, by giving a few moments from centuries ago a present-tense immediacy.

Browning's choice of the Renaissance as the historical setting for many of his poems is a reaction against the medievalism so popular in the Victorian period, and as such an expression of his religious and political views. Medievalism was often associated with the Anglo-Catholicism of the Oxford Movement, because both looked back to the early Christian period of art, faith and ritual. Browning was brought up in a Dissenting family and he was highly suspicious of both Roman- and Anglo-Catholicism. As a result he peoples his dramatic monologues with a number of unsavoury and unholy representatives of the Catholic Church: a materialistic bishop giving orders for the decoration of his tomb to his illegitimate sons as he lies on his deathbed ('The Bishop Orders His Tomb at Saint Praxed's Church'); a furiously vitriolic (and very funny) monk in 'Soliloquy of the Spanish Cloister'; and the friar-painter Fra Lippo Lippi who, in the poem named after him, is caught having just returned from the 'red light district' of fifteenth-century Florence. Browning's agenda in these poems was partly to dispel what he saw as a wrong-headed nostalgia for the rituals of the Catholic Church, but the Renaissance setting is also attractive to him because it is a time of great artistic energy and change.

Both his anti-Catholicism and his admiration for the Renaissance are evident in the poem 'Fra Lippo Lippi' (1855). Lippo Lippi was a fifteenth-century Florentine painter and Carmelite monk, known for his naturalistic, realistic style, the latter seen particularly in his painting of sweet, young Madonnas (he was notorious for having affairs with his female models).

Browning saw Lippo Lippi's work as embodying the transition from a medieval style of painting to the more naturalistic style of the High Renaissance. The monks are shocked at Lippo Lippi's realistic portrayal of the human body. They see it as 'a devil's game' because in their eyes the function of religious painting is to make people forget the material world of flesh and blood, to 'lift them over it' to the spiritual. Lippo Lippi thinks differently, and in his defence of his art, he voices also Browning's poetic manifesto: art which looks at the world objectively, which attempts to represent things as they really are, is itself a path to the transcendent or the spiritual:

> – we're made so that we love
> First when we see them painted, things we have passed
> Perhaps a hundred times nor cared to see;
> And so they are better, painted – better to us
> Which is the same thing. Art was given for that;
> God uses us to help each other so,
> Lending our minds out.

(ll. 300–6)

The relation between Lippo Lippi's view of his artistic role and Browning's becomes clearer if we remember Browning's 'Essay on Shelley' discussed earlier. In that essay it is evident that Browning wishes to be an 'objective' poet, a poet who *sees* and records 'objects for men's outer and not inner sight'. In the last quotation from 'Fra Lippo Lippi' above, Browning refines this goal: the artist who can record the outer objects of men's sight will, if he represents them truly and objectively, cause those outer objects to enter the inner sight of man. An artist must see, so that he can help others to see, and sight in this case is not simply visual, but visionary. The poet approaches the elevated role of 'prophet' that he occupied in Shelley's 'Defence of Poetry' (1821), when the Romantic poet described poets as 'the unacknowledged legislators of the world'. But, unlike Shelley, Browning sees this goal as being attained not by writing subjective poetry dealing with abstractions, but by writing objective poetry which deals with the material world.

Suggested further reading on Browning: Bristow (1991), Flowers (1976), Armstrong (1974), Bloom and Munich (1979) and Day (1991).

## Arnold and Clough

Like Tennyson and Browning, Matthew Arnold (1822–88) and Arthur Hugh Clough (1819–61) were born within three years of each other. They were at school together at Rugby, were undergraduates together at Balliol College, Oxford, and had both taken fellowships at Oriel College, Oxford. They both wrote poetry. Alike in many ways, they differed over the latter. Their friendly criticisms of each other's poetry produced a dialogue which reveals much about what was thought of as poetry's role in culture and society, and its developments at mid-century.

In his seminal critical statement, the 'Preface' to his 1853 volume of *Poems*, Matthew Arnold began to formulate what was to become one of the major literary-critical voices of his time. The 'Preface' begins with Arnold's explanation why he decided to omit the poem 'Empedocles on Etna' from the 1853 volume. Arnold felt that this poem was of an overly subjective, even morbid nature, and goes on to explain why he believes both his own poetry and indeed all new poetry should move away from subjectivity:

> What then are the situations, from the representations of which, though accurate, no poetical enjoyment can be derived? They are those in which the suffering finds no vent in action; in which a continuous state of mental distress is prolonged, unrelieved by incident, hope, or resistance; in which there is everything to be endured, nothing to be done. (Allott and Allott, 1979, p. 656)

Clearly this unhappy situation must be avoided, and Arnold then gives his famous formula for the best poetry; an excellent poem must be based upon 'an excellent action':

> and what actions are the most excellent? Those, certainly, which most powerfully appeal to the great primary human affections: to those elementary feelings which subsist permanently in the race, and which are independent of time. (Allott and Allott, 1979, p. 657)

Arnold however is rather paradoxical when he advises that the contemporary poet seek these 'excellent actions', these 'elementary feelings' in the *past* – and particularly within classical literature. If these 'feelings ... subsist permanently in the race', why cannot the poet write about them as they appear in his own time?

This is a question which Clough may have asked of his friend. Clough's poetry, with its contemporary settings, and colloquial, even slangy language is itself a challenge to Arnold's demands and definition of excellent poetry. We can hear Clough's poetic differences with Arnold in his periodical review of Arnold's poetry in July, 1853. He says of Arnold's poems:

> Not by turning and twisting his eyes, in the hope of seeing things as Homer, Sophocles, Virgil, or Milton saw them; but by accepting them as he sees them, and faithfully depicting accordingly, will he attain the object he desires. (Dawson, 1973, pp. 75–6)

## Arnold

Matthew Arnold looked to past ages and literature for the 'excellent action', because, like many Victorians, he seems to have felt that his own time was unheroic. The tone he seems to give to his own time in his poem 'Stanzas from the Grande Chartreuse' (1855) is 'autumnal': 'The autumnal evening darkens round, / The wind is up, and drives the rain' (st. 2, ll. 1–2). The age is, like the subject of the poem, in a state of disturbing and uncertain transition:

> Wandering between two worlds, one dead,
> The other powerless to be born,
> With nowhere yet to rest my head,
> Like these, on earth I wait forlorn.

(ll. 85–8)

This language, expressing the confusion and doubt of the times, is echoed in the following passage from the 'Preface' of 1853. Here he is referring specifically to literature, but as will become clear, for Arnold the relationship between literature and life is very close indeed:

> The confusion of the present times is great, the multitude of voices counselling different things bewildering, the number of existing works capable of attracting a young writer's attention and of becoming his models, immense. What he wants is a hand to guide him through the confusion, a voice to prescribe to him the aim which he should keep in view ... (Allott and Allott, 1979, p. 663)

Although he states that 'Such a guide the English writer at the present day will nowhere find', Arnold wrote and worked for most of his life to become that guide. His many essays, his thirty-five years of work as a School Inspector, and his Professorship of Poetry at Oxford did much to guide and to change the way in which English literature was taught and valued in Britain.

It is somewhat ironic that Arnold himself only rarely took up his own poetic challenge made in the 'Preface' of 1853. He wrote little new poetry after this time, and devoted himself to the prose writings for which he is so famous. A number of his poems do look back to classical literature, however: the subject of 'The Strayed Reveller'

(1849) is Homer's Ulysses on Circe's island; 'Philomela' (1853) takes up a story from Greek myth, and his 1867 poem 'Palladium' takes place during the Trojan War. Nevertheless many of Arnold's best-known poems are not those of great or 'excellent actions' from the past, but contemplative, subjective poems which deal with the poet's present state of mind, and often, with his personal response to the age in which he lives. These are poems such as 'Dover Beach' (1867), 'The Buried Life' (1852), 'To a Gypsy Child By the Sea-shore' (1849) and 'To Marguerite – Continued' (1852).

The latter poem, essentially a poem of parted lovers, also deals with the isolation of man:

> Yes! in the sea of life enisled,
> With echoing straits between us thrown,
> Dotting the shoreless watery wild,
> We mortal millions live *alone*.
>
> (ll. 1–4)

Arnold frequently uses sea imagery to symbolize human beings as isolated islands, shut out from reading each other's inner lives. (He describes that inner life, or the unconscious self as 'the buried life' in his poem of that name.) As he writes in the last line of 'To Marguerite – Continued', the lovers (and, by extension, all humankind) are separated by 'The unplumbed, salt, estranging sea'.

'Dover Beach' is thought to have been written when Arnold was at Dover at the beginning of his honeymoon. Appropriately perhaps, the sea imagery which begins this poem is *not* 'estranging' to the lovers:

> The sea is calm tonight.
> The tide is full, the moon lies fair
> Upon the straits...
>
> (ll. 1–3)

He calls to his wife: 'Come to the window, sweet is the night air!'.

> Only, from the long line of spray
> Where the sea meets the moon-blanched land,
> Listen! you hear the grating roar
> Of pebbles which the waves draw back, and fling,
> At their return, up the high strand,
> Begin, and cease, and then again begin,
> With tremulous cadence slow, and bring
> The eternal note of sadness in.
>
> (ll. 7–14)

Even the most intimate moment with the beloved is disturbed by the 'grating' of pebbles and sea, and by 'an eternal note of sadness'. In the third stanza of the poem the sea becomes the 'Sea of Faith' which in an age of spiritual doubt is now receding from the world. The cry in the last verse, 'Ah, love, let us be true / To one another' is a cry for some trust or faith in a world which has been left 'drear', 'confused' and vulnerable ('the naked shingles of the world') through loss of faith.

But in much of Arnold's poetry, the chance that two souls will be able to find communion and reveal their 'buried lives' to each other is uncertain. 'Dover Beach' ends on a confused and melancholy note. Will the poet find a haven from the 'darkling plain' of the world with his lover? Because Arnold places so much faith in literature, and especially in literature of the classical period, it could be argued that his connection with the soul of the Greek tragic dramatist, Sophocles, is more likely than a spiritual connection with the beloved woman at the window in the poem. Listening to the retreat of the sea on the pebbly strand, Arnold notes:

> Sophocles long ago
> Heard it on the Aegean, and it brought
> Into his mind the turbid ebb and flow
> Of human misery...

(ll. 15–18)

Arnold so often writes that we are essentially alone, 'enisled' by our subjectivity or 'buried lives'. Yet he also writes in the 1853 'Preface' that there are 'great primary human affections', 'elementary feelings' which we all share. How may we gain access to those shared feelings so that we are no longer so isolated from one another? For Arnold, an emotional and intellectual connection with the great writers of the past opens a way to communion with those around us in our own time. In an age when the 'Sea of Faith' is receding, this secular–humanist project takes on for Arnold almost religious overtones. The truths of the Bible may have been questioned, but one may still 'believe' in the plays of Sophocles.

Suggested further reading on Arnold: ApRoberts (1983), Honan (1981) and Carroll (1982).

## Clough

Thomas Carlyle saw history through the lives of 'Great Men', and Browning more frequently through the lives of minor figures. Arnold thought poetry should base itself on great or 'excellent actions', Clough on minor actions. Arnold wrote in the 1853 'Preface' that 'a great human action of a thousand years ago is more interesting to it [i.e. the elementary part of our nature] than a smaller human action of to-day' (Allott and Allott, 1979, p. 657). Arthur Hugh Clough's two long narrative poems, 'The Bothie of Tober-na-Vuolich' (1848), and 'Amours de Voyage' (1858), together stand against and do much to refute Arnold's judgement. Rather than heroic actions, 'The Bothie' relates the summer vacation dalliances of a group of Oxford undergraduates on holiday in Scotland, and 'Amours de Voyage' humorously relates in epistolary form an abortive romance between two English tourists in Rome.

Although Clough did not turn to classical literature for thematic inspiration, he did employ the hexameter, traditionally a Greek metre, for both 'The Bothie' and 'Amours de Voyage'. Clough had translated a number of the classical poets, and at the time he was composing 'The Bothie' he was considering translating Homer's *Iliad* into English hexameters (a project which he never finished before his early death). Clough chose the hexameter, rarely used in English verse, primarily because it gave him more freedom with the poetic line, enabling him to use colloquial and often slangy language. This is particularly evident in 'The Bothie' in which the undergraduates' jargon is mixed with epigraphs to each Canto of the poem taken from the classical authors. Clearly Clough's look back to the classical period is not in accordance with Arnold's quest for the heroic, but is mock-heroic.

'Amours de Voyage' is a verse novella in epistolary form (again in hexameter) which is set at the time of the French siege of Rome in 1848. This siege brought down the Roman Republic which had been established the year before. Clough had been in Rome at the time of the siege, and had witnessed the political and military strife at first hand. One might expect, then, that this setting would offer more scope to satisfy Arnold's call for great actions in poetry: 1848 may be far removed from the classical period, but it was certainly a year of 'action', indeed of revolution, in much of Europe. However, Clough ignores the opportunity for heroics that the Roman siege might have given him. Claude, an intellectual Englishman visiting Rome and Clough's central character, is for the entirety of the poem in two minds – whether or not to commit himself politically and take an active part in the events around him, whether or not to commit himself romantically and declare his love for Mary Trevelyan, one of an English family also visiting Rome. Claude never makes up his mind, and the poem peters out with all his possible intentions. We hear of the dramatic political events and characters through the letters of various characters, but as in the following example, these events hardly take a central place in the poem or in the minds of the characters. A minor character (Mary's sister Georgina) writes to a friend in England: 'George has just seen Garibaldi, dressed up in a long white cloak, on / Horseback, riding by, with his mounted negro behind him' (Canto II, ll. 218–19) and a few lines later she reveals her true concerns:

> Mary allows she was wrong about Mr. Claude *being selfish*;
> He was *most* useful and kind on the terrible thirtieth of April.
> Do not write here any more; we are starting directly for Florence:
> We should be off to-morrow, if only Papa could get horses;
> All have been seized everywhere for the use of this dreadful Mazzini.
>
> (Canto II, ll. 226–30)

In spite of the revolutionary events occurring around her, Georgina is really far more interested in what is happening between her sister and Claude. When she does mention the political events in this passage she is concerned with details such as what Garibaldi was wearing, and whether the leader Mazzini will prove an inconvenience by making it difficult to find horses for their journey. It is a highly trivialized and subjective account of major historical events.

The poem is written in the early days of Thomas Cook's travel agency, which greatly contributed to the phenomenon of the British middle-class tourist by providing inexpensive and pre-arranged travel packages to Europe. Catering to the middle-class traveller were the famous guide books of the era, Baedeker's from Germany and Murray's from Britain. Before Cook, Murray and Baedeker, a first-hand knowledge of European art, architecture and customs had been the privilege of the aristocratic or upper class, and especially of the wealthy youth on his 'Grand Tour'. Now the middle-class tourist could experience Europe and even further afield for himself, rather than relying upon the writings of Ruskin or the numerous travel writers of the day.

The tourists in 'Amours de Voyage' are, however, peculiarly oblivious both to the great historical events happening about them, and to the backdrop of immense and powerful 'pastness' in Italian art and architecture. Claude finds his surroundings in Rome 'rubbishy' and 'disappointing':

> What do I find in the Forum? An archway and two or three pillars.
> Well, but Saint Peter's? Alas, Bernini has filled it with sculpture!
>
> (Canto I, ll. 43–4)

Certainly this assessment of Rome would not agree with the Baedeker or Murray's guide-books of the day. Murray's, for example, adopts a stately, rather awed tone at the opening of its introduction to Saint Peter's:

> We shall therefore commence our description of the churches with this most magnificent of Christian temples, which our great historian of the Decline and Fall of the Roman Empire designates as 'the most glorious structure that ever has been applied to the use of religion'. (Blewitt, 1843, p. 381)

Like the more adventurous middle-class tourists in E.M. Forster's novel *A Room With A View* (1908), Claude travels without his Baedeker or Murray's Guide, but, unlike them, does not allow Italy to 'enter his soul'; he trivializes the vast history of the city and feels the momentous political events of 1848 as anticlimactic because that is the state of his own mind. The subjective view wins over the objective in this poem, but it is a Pyrrhic victory because Claude's mind is incapable of progress or decision (just as Claude's travel progress through Europe seems to have no goal). This indecision or ambivalence is a feature of a number of Clough's poems, and the title of his well-known poem 'Dipsychus' (first published posthumously in 1865) is the Greek for 'double-mindedness' or ambivalence. Like Tennyson, Clough writes convincingly about doubt and uncertainty, but while Tennyson struggles in his poetry towards certainty and faith, Clough rarely does so. Fluidity, flux, the divided mind, are what Arnold referred to as 'the confusion of the present times' which it was necessary to attack by concentration upon great actions. Clough hears Arnold's call to action, but is more wary. As Claude rather limply says towards the conclusion of 'Amours de Voyage':

> *Action will furnish belief,* – but will that belief be the true one?
> This is the point, you know. However, it doesn't much matter.
>
> (Canto V, ll. 21–1)

Suggested further reading on Clough: Biswas (1972) and Greenberger (1970).

## The Pre-Raphaelites

The 'Pre-Raphaelite Brotherhood' came together in September 1848, and of its seven original members only one, Dante Gabriel Rossetti, directly concerns us in the sphere of poetry. The other members were primarily painters, and formed the

Brotherhood in reaction to what they saw as the limited, stale strictures on painting style and theme at the Royal Academy, which was the main exhibition space and school of art in Britain.

The 'PRB', as they styled themselves, had various and diverse interests, and as they matured their work developed in different and separate ways. In a discussion of poetry, the term Pre-Raphaelite is almost meaningless in itself, as it refers more to the members' aims in painting. They had been inspired by Ruskin's many-volumed work *Modern Painters* to look at early Italian art preceding the work of the Italian painter Raphael (1483–1520). Nevertheless, in spite of the looseness of association and varying styles of the members of the Brotherhood, and in spite of the vagueness of the term 'Pre-Raphaelite' with regard to poetry, there are themes common to the Brotherhood which shift and change in emphasis from the middle to the end of the nineteenth century. These themes or interests include, in both the painting and the poetry: medievalism; a preoccupation with colour, light, the meticulous detail of objects, and often an endowing of these objects with symbolic value; depiction of scenes of intense moral crisis; use of themes from literary sources. A well-known example of the latter is Holman Hunt's painting, *The Lady of Shalott*, which was inspired by Tennyson's poem.

The interests of the Pre-Raphaelite movement are too diverse and interwoven to fully unravel here (William Morris (1834–96), for example, was poet, painter, early socialist, and designed and made furniture, tapestry, wallpapers, stained glass, etc.). But an exploration of some of their poems serves as a guide to the century's poetic progress. Their response to the debate over subjective and objective poetry is also a helpful guide to the composition and reception of poetry in the later Victorian period.

The poets Dante Gabriel Rossetti (1828–82) and Christina Rossetti (1830–94) were the children of an Italian émigré who had been forced into exile because of his political activities promoting Italian liberty. Their mother, who was three-quarters Italian, was a devout Anglo-Catholic. The influence of Anglo-Catholicism and the Oxford Movement ran deep in the family: Christina's and Dante's sister became an Anglican nun; much of Christina Rossetti's poetry is devotional, and religious (specifically, Catholic) imagery and symbolism is common in Dante Gabriel Rossetti's painting and poetry.

Their father was a Dante scholar and named his son after the Italian poet (1265–1321). Dante Gabriel took his name very seriously indeed, and the Italian poet was an enormous influence upon his poetry and painting. The Pre-Raphaelite Dante addresses his father in a poem entitled 'Dantis Tenebrae':

> And did'st thou know indeed, when at the font
>   Together with thy name thou gav'st me his,
>   That also on thy son must Beatrice
> Decline her eyes according to her wont...

(ll. 1–4)

'Beatrice' was Dante Alighieri's poetic and spiritual muse. He had loved her, he writes in his *Vita Nuova*, since she was a 9-year-old girl and when she died in

1290, Dante in a sense beatified her as his spiritual guide. In his great work, the *Divine Comedy*, it is Beatrice as well as God who is the goal of the spiritual journey. This mixture of sensuous and divine love for a beatified woman/poetic muse was taken up by Dante Gabriel Rossetti and became an intense focus for many of his paintings and poems. The combination of sexuality and spirituality may be seen in his poem 'The Blessed Damozel' (first published 1850), in which the beloved woman waits in heaven for her lover to die and so join her in bliss. It is a bliss which is 'fleshly' as well as ethereal, for, as 'The blessed damozel leaned out / From the gold bar of heaven', by stanza 8 her leaning has become as tangible as the warmth of skin:

> And still she bowed herself and stooped
> Out of her circling charm;
> Until her bosom must have made
> The bar she leaned on warm...

> (st. 8)

William Morris exhibits the same delight in the erotic-ethereal in his poem 'Praise of My Lady' (1858). The poem's twenty-two stanzas are devoted in turn to a catalogue of his lady's nose, forehead, hair, lashes, brows, eyes, underlid, lips, neck, hands and the 'slim tree' of her body. Each of the three-line stanzas repeats the refrain 'Beata mea Domina!', becoming in its repetition like an eroticized series of 'Hail Marys', reminiscent of the Roman Catholic prayers which make up the Rosary.

Algernon Charles Swinburne's (1837–1909) poem 'Dolores', from his 1866 *Poems and Ballads*, is reminiscent of the above formula, with its refrain to a beatified (or, in this case, demonized) lady. This poet's lifelong fascination with sadism, and the symbolic association of sex, death and the spiritual in his work ensured that this notorious poem and a number of others in the collection were either ridiculed or vilified:

> Cold eyes that hide like a jewel
> Hard eyes that grow soft for an hour;
> The heavy white limbs, and the cruel
> Red mouth like a venomous flower;
> When these are gone by with their glories,
> What shall rest of thee then, what remain,
> O mystic and sombre Dolores,
> Our Lady of Pain.

> (ll. 1–8)

This playing with the dividing line between flesh and spirit, erotic and religious, is simply one of a number of themes in the poetry of Rossetti, Morris and Swinburne. Nevertheless it was prevalent enough in their work to gain them the title in 1871 of 'The Fleshly School of Poetry' in a vitriolic article by George Buchanan by the same title in the *Contemporary Review*.

Christina Rossetti (see Unit 23, p. 622) provides her own comments on the traditional role of the beloved lady in early Italian poetry. In the foreword to her sonnet sequence *Monna Innominata* (undated, possibly circa 1866) she notes that there may be a price or penalty to pay for becoming a beatified lady in poetry. This price entails an idealization which renders the woman 'scant of attractiveness' because she is unreal, and lacks individuality and her own poetic voice. Rossetti conjectures that some of these ladies may have had 'poetic aptitude' themselves, and wonders what the result would have been if the lady had 'spoken for herself'. These voiceless and unnamed women ('innominate') are perhaps just as common in her brother Dante Gabriel's or in other Pre-Raphaelite poetry as they are in traditional early Italian poetry. As a sister to the Brotherhood, and an ambitious poet in her own right, it is little wonder that she conjectures what the poetry would reveal if the beloved lady were to find her voice. In many Pre-Raphaelite poems the lady never speaks. Some important and powerful exceptions to this are William Morris's Arthurian poems 'The Defence of Guenevere' and 'King Arthur's Tomb' (1858), and, to a lesser degree, George Meredith's sonnet sequence, *Modern Love* (1862).

Meredith's poem *Modern Love* lives up to its name in many ways: its sexual politics are more 'modern' than Victorian in that it chronicles sexual infidelity and the break-up of a marriage with surprising openness. The wife's loneliness, alienation and pain which both lead to and result from her sexual infidelity are hinted at, although it would be too much to claim for Meredith that he allows the woman to speak for herself. In fact it is only very rarely that she is heard in the poem, and when she is, it is because the powerful voice of the male persona is quoting her. It is in Meredith's novels, such as *The Egoist* and *Diana of the Crossways*, rather than in his poetry, that he most effectively presents the woman's point of view. This may be accounted for by the very nature of nineteenth-century poetry as opposed to the novel: at this period poetry has not yet developed the multivocal range of the most ambitious nineteenth-century novels; it is far more subjective and univocal. *Modern Love* tells of a man's feelings of exposure, jealousy and thwarted love in his own voice. The husband's affair, subsequent to that of his wife, adds to the complexity of the sexual and power relations between men and women in 'modern love'. (For a discussion of Meredith's novel *The Egoist*, see Unit 11, pp. 288–90.)

Christina Rossetti's poetic voice is primarily subjective and private – so private in fact as to become at times coy and secretive, as in her poem 'Winter: My Secret' which opens:

> I tell my secret? No indeed, not I:
> Perhaps some day, who knows?
> But not today; it froze, and blows, and snows
> And you're too curious: fie!
> You want to hear it? well:
> Only, my secret's mine, and I won't tell.

(ll. 1–6)

The colon after 'well' in the penultimate line gives the reader a pause to hold his or her breath. 'Well' seems to indicate that the speaker will give in and tell, only the rhyme of 'well' and 'tell' in the last two lines of the stanza endow a note of finality, a 'snapping shut' of the stanza and the speaker's mouth as it is about to disclose the secret. The following stanza also ends with a rhyming of the last two lines, to similar effect. The final stanza, however, ends abruptly with:

> Perhaps my secret I may say,
> Or you may guess.

Hope that the secret may be revealed is raised once more, only to be dashed by this sudden and jarring conclusion, the final and shortest line of the poem. It is a tantalizing, humorous poem and plays with the delight of having secrets, and the desire to tell them. A secret is by definition a very private matter; it is internalized, held within the subjective self. But a secret is defined not only by its private quality, but also by the possibility that it may become shared or public. In a poet whose work is often melancholy, deeply religious and internalized, 'secrets' are an important symbol of the constant play and ambivalence over the public and the private life, or between the objective and the subjective.

The cold 'nipping' day in 'Winter: My Secret' convinces the speaker of the poem to keep the chilly draughts from the outside world away, and to curl into herself and the privacy of her secret. In Rossetti's poem 'Love from the North' the lover enters like a chill blast of northern air, putting a stop to her wedding to a lover from a 'soft south land'. The speaker cannot keep the cold out this time because the northern lover will not take no for an answer; he abducts her from her wedding, 'But never ask'd me yea or nay' (st. 7). This lover is completely alien to her, arriving from a climate quite opposed to her 'soft south land'. Her former lover concurred in all her moods and desires:

> He saddened if my cheer was sad,
> But gay he grew if I was gay;
> We never differed on a hair,
> My yes his yes, my nay his nay.

This eventually rejected lover is a complete reflection of herself. The structure of the stanza above reproduces the reflective or mirroring effect of her first lover: saddened/sad; gay/gay; nay/nay. Finally the speaker wishes to stay with the northern lover; the air may be cold, but it is different and bracing. Could the difference, the otherness of the northern lover be in some way Christina's comment upon the love poetry of her brother and other members of the Brotherhood? After all, a convenient aspect of the 'blessed damozel' type of muse in many of their poems is that she cannot say 'yea' or 'nay' because she cannot say anything at all. Without a voice in the poem, she can be a perfect reflection of the poet's desires, and often that is a reflection of himself – either in the lady's eyes (a common figure in early Italian poetry) or, as in Dante Gabriel's lines from *The House of Life*, in a reflection in water. He writes, 'Our mirrored eyes met silently / In the low wave' and

> Then the dark ripples spread to waving hair,
> And as I stooped, her own lips rising there
> Bubbled with brimming kisses at my mouth.
> (*The House of Life*, 'Willowwood', Section 1, ll. 6–7 and 12–14)

In Christina Rossetti's poem 'Love from the North' the desire is finally for a lover who is not simply a reflection of oneself. The 'mirrored eyes' and the lover's absolute concurrence in desire belong to a love poetry which she rejects: its mirroring imagery is a vision of complete self-reflection or subjectivity. Christina Rossetti resists this subjective or even solipsistic vision, reaching for the outer, objective world of the northern lover.

Pre-Raphaelite painting is marked by its intensity of colour and acute detail. As we have seen in, for instance, William Morris's poem, 'Praise to My Lady', the poetry sometimes mixes abstract, intangible qualities of the spirit with a plethora of very tangible, fleshly detail. In a number of Pre-Raphaelite poems the concentration upon physical detail is so intense under the gaze of the poetic subject (whether he be the poet or not) that the object appears both to the viewer's inner and outer vision, or to his subjective and objective gaze. This simultaneous vision often marks the poetry of Rossetti, Morris and Swinburne.

Two comparable moments of vision in Rossetti's 'The Woodspurge', and Morris's 'Sir Galahad' bear this out. In Rossetti's poem a man sits in deep despair and gazes at the ground as he bends over his knees. The last two stanzas are as follows:

> My eyes, wide open, had the run
> Of some ten weeds to fix upon;
> Among those few, out of the sun,
> The woodspurge flowered, three cups in one.

> From perfect grief there need not be
> Wisdom or even memory:
> One thing then learnt remains to me, –
> The woodspurge has a cup of three.

This posture of numb and 'perfect grief' as the figure sits with his head between his knees contemplating the ground, is found also in Morris's poem 'Sir Galahad'. In both poems the gaze upon the ground limits the sphere of vision, and allows for an intense concentration upon the insignificant objects which lie before the poem's subject. In Morris's poem, Sir Galahad is 'wearied and forlorn' and sits down near the chapel at night. He looks down on the floor between his feet:

> I saw the melted snow that hung in beads
> Upon my steel shoes, less and less I saw
> Between the tiles the bunches of small weeds:
> Heartless and stupid, with no touch of awe
> Upon me...

> (ll. 12–16)

In 'The Woodspurge' grief has left the speaker blank and numb, so much so that all he can remember ('wisdom or even memory') is an image of weeds and a flower. But this image of nature is not one that he can wax poetical about in the conventional sense. He does not extol the beauty of the woodspurge, but keeps to facts, and begins to sound faintly like an amateur botanist rather than a poet as he counts that there are *ten* weeds, and repeats that 'the woodspurge has a cup of three'. This is all he can ascertain or remember from that moment of 'perfect grief'. Similarly, as Sir Galahad is numbed into a half-sleep through weariness and despair, all *he* knows as he stares between his feet is that there are beads of melting snow on his armoured boots, and, as in 'The Woodspurge', bunches of small weeds.

This is not to argue, of course, that the poetic symbol was completely dead in the latter half of the century. In much Pre-Raphaelite poetry, the object of attention (a flower, flesh, blood, breath, etc.) fluctuates between functioning as a symbol (transcending itself) and simply being the object that it is, in all its 'fleshliness' or materiality.

Nowhere is this more apparent, or taken further, than in the poetry of Swinburne. Isobel Armstrong has written of Swinburne that he 'bring[s] together ... spirit and matter in the symbol' (Armstrong, 1993, p. 404). Words, which are in themselves symbols – linguistic signifiers which 'stand for' a signified meaning – in Swinburne's poetry 'yearn after an unreachable or unknown beyond which transcends their limits ... Words have to transgress their limits and move beyond the boundaries constituted for them' (p. 405).

One way in which Swinburne forces his words to 'transgress their limits' is by 'taking them in vain', or blaspheming. The poem, 'Dolores', for example, is sub-titled, 'Notre Dame des Sept Douleurs' invoking a title usually reserved for the Virgin Mary. But Swinburne's 'Our Lady' is intoned and 'prayed to' as 'Our Lady of Pain' in highly charged sexual and sadomasochistic imagery. This inversion of Christian prayer and symbolism is common in Swinburne, and is one of the tropes which he employs to bring flesh and spirit together in a Christian symbolism which he twists around, transgresses and blasphemes against.

Suggested further reading on the Pre-Raphaelite poets and poets associated with them: Rees (1981), Battiscombe (1981), Mayberry (1989), Pater (1889), Stansky (1983), Lindsay (1975), McGann (1972), McSweeney (1980), Henderson (1974) and Beer and Harris (eds) (1983).

## Gerard Manley Hopkins

In terms of the *reception* of his poetry, Gerard Manley Hopkins (1844–89) could be termed a modernist rather than a Victorian. Very few of his poems were published until his friend, the poet Robert Bridges, brought out a first edition in 1918. In *The Oxford Book of Victorian Verse* (1912) only one poem by Hopkins appears, while in the *Faber Book of Modern Verse* (1936) Hopkins is the first poet in the volume and nineteen pages are dedicated to his verse. His readership, then, began with a generation of modernists, many of whom wanted to leave behind Victorianism.

Modernists appropriated Hopkins as a precursor to their linguistic innovative-ness: they hailed his experiments with metre, rhythm, diction and imagery as un-Victorian, and they viewed his innovativeness as part of a literary project which they would continue to push against the limits of, as is evident in their experiments with free verse or in the writings of James Joyce.

But this modernist perspective, in its decided rejection of the Victorian period, has somewhat skewed our understanding of Hopkins's poetry. Hopkins was in fact very much a late Victorian, influenced, especially while an undergraduate at Oxford, by Tractarianism, by Matthew Arnold's lectures, and by Walter Pater's teaching of what has come to be known as Aestheticism, a late-nineteenth-century movement concerned with the study of beauty, and 'art for art's sake'.

In 1864, the year after Hopkins came to Oxford to study classics, John Henry Newman published his famous spiritual autobiography, *Apologia pro Vita Sua*. Newman had been the leader of the Oxford Movement (also known as 'Tractarianism': see Introduction) until he converted to Roman Catholicism in 1845. Newman's eloquent defence of his faith won the respect of many Victorians. Hopkins was already disposed through his upbringing to High Anglicanism and the Oxford Movement, and moved gradually closer to Roman Catholicism. In 1866 he was received into the Roman Catholic Church under Newman's sponsorship. Two years later he began his course of study and preparation to become a Jesuit priest.

After his decision to enter the priesthood he wrote little poetry until 1876, when he composed 'The Wreck of the Deutschland' while studying in a seminary in North Wales. Later on in his short life, Hopkins was to refer to his time in North Wales as his 'salad days', partly perhaps because it was here that he began to write again, and here that he developed his own language of poetics. The latter included his development of what he termed 'sprung rhythm', 'inscape' and 'instress'.

'Sprung rhythm' was Hopkins's name for his particular use of metre. Modernists have responded to sprung rhythm as if it were a precursor of free verse, and certainly its metrical system did give Hopkins great freedom with the poetic line. But at the same time that Hopkins's metrical system was looking forward, in a sense, to modernist freedom and innovation, it was also looking back to very old forms of English and Welsh poetry. Sprung rhythm is founded upon the number of strong stresses in a line, rather than the number of syllables, and disregards the number of unstressed syllables. Hopkins was inspired to use this accentual verse through a study of medieval alliterative poetry, Anglo-Saxon poetry and nursery rhymes. As discussed in the Introduction, Victorian philologists turned to Anglo-Saxon in their search for a 'pure' form of English, untainted by Latin and French. Hopkins was interested and influenced by their work, although his exploration of early forms of English does not exhibit their nationalist, Anglo-Saxonist agenda. Anglo-Saxonists often regarded the Celtic languages as belonging to a conquered and inferior people. Hopkins, however, brought no such prejudice to his study of British languages, and this is evident in the enthusiasm with which he studied the Welsh language, Welsh metre (*cynghanedd*), and in the fact that he wrote a number of poems in Welsh. The freedom which the Anglo-Saxon and Welsh metres allowed him was as much a product of the philological studies of the Victorian period, as it was a precursor to the modernist.

Hopkins thought of 'inscape' as the essential and individual pattern or quality of each thing in Nature: 'inscape' makes the thing unique and means that it can never recur. 'Instress' is the divine power which upholds the inscape of every thing, and also the divine force which makes it possible for inscape to be impressed upon the mind of the observer. For Hopkins, an important part of the poet's role is to make inscape apparent to others; through poetry, then, the essential pattern of each thing (inscape) may be impressed upon the minds of others (instress). A theological influence upon Hopkins's poetic thinking was the Scottish Franciscan theologian Duns Scotus (*c.*1266 or 1270–1308) who developed his theory that while God was inherent in everything in the universe, each thing had its own individuality or 'thisness' (*haecceitas*). This theory of individuality clearly appealed to Hopkins's sense of the uniqueness of each thing in nature within the divine plan or hierarchy.

Hopkins saw an analogy between medieval or feudal hierarchy and God's divine hierarchy, as becomes clear in his poem 'The Windhover'. The poem's heady, almost ecstatic alliteration and stress imitate the flight of a kestrel. It is an example of Hopkins's linguistic innovation in which the language itself aspires to become meaning, rather than our usual expectation that meaning will determine the language chosen:

> I caught this morning morning's minion, king-
> dom of daylight's dauphin, dapple-dawn-drawn Falcon, in his riding
> Of the rolling level underneath him steady air, and striding
> High there, how he rung upon the rein of wimpling wing
> In his ecstasy!

> (ll. 1–5)

The words 'minion', 'kingdom', 'dauphin', 'wimpling' and the poem's theme of falconry hearken back to the court hierarchy of the medieval period, and in the second stanza, again, the same language hails 'O my chevalier!'. But the 'chevalier' who is owed knightly service is clearly 'Christ Our Lord' to whom Hopkins dedicates his poem. Hopkins saw medieval or feudal hierarchy as an order in which the individual's place was fixed and ordained, but paradoxically, also as an order which allowed for individual expression. As Carol T. Christ has noted, for Hopkins, 'The fecundity and variety of the gothic appeared to express the virility of the will to individuation in a unified culture...' (Christ, 1984, p. 438).

Hopkins's poetic project is devotional, attempting to make apparent to his readers the 'inscape' or particular pattern of all nature in God's hierarchy. He wants others to *see* the essential qualities and patterns around them, which without poetry they may overlook. (Compare this with Browning's poetic manifesto as spoken in 'Fra Lippo Lippi', discussed earlier.) To Hopkins's thinking the hierarchy of the medieval period allowed for individual artistic expression as opposed to nineteenth-century industrial methods of production. If this hierarchical structure enabled artistic expression, then in Hopkins's theology, the hierarchy of God's universe allows for each individual's particular and unique transcendence. If Tennyson's most powerful poetry could be said to issue from his religious doubt and anxiety, much of Hopkins's could be said to arise from his religious certainty and his faith in a fixed and (literally) ordained place in God's hierarchy.

In his intense concentration upon the things in the world about him, whether 'thrush's eggs' or 'finches wings', Hopkins gazed hard and long at the material objects of the objective world. Through 'instress' he brought those objects to man's inner attention, into the reader's subjective world. In his own treatment of the subjective and objective view, in his religious influences, in his elegaic nostalgia for the past, Hopkins was very much a Victorian. Hopkins's response to Nature was conservationist; as he writes in his poem 'Inversnaid', 'Long live the weeds and wilderness yet'. In this and in many other ways he speaks to our own time, as he spoke to the early modernist period with the energy and freedom which he gave to poetic language.

In 'Binsey Poplars' Hopkins regrets that his 'aspens dear' have been cut down, and that the 'growing green' of the countryside is being 'delved', 'hewed', 'hacked' and 'racked' to make way for the growing cities, their industry and residential suburbs – those same suburbs of the nineteenth century which he called 'the base and brickish skirt' dividing the city from nature in his poem 'Dun Scotus's Oxford'. The elegy of 'Binsey Poplars' to the 'rural scene' could also be an elegy to a type of poetry which was coming to an end at the close of the nineteenth century. The Introduction to this unit discussed the differences between the representation of nature in Romantic poetry and later nineteenth-century or Victorian poetry, arguing that in much Victorian poetry there was a growing disillusionment with the idea that nature was in harmony with humankind. Nevertheless, Victorian poetry was most often still faithful to the Romantic tradition of using nature as a fund of poetic settings, themes and imagery.

The 'base and brickish skirt' of the suburbs encroaches upon the natural world and upon poetic themes increasingly in the later nineteenth century. A poet of the 1890s, John Davidson, writes rather differently of the suburbs than did Hopkins. His satirical dramatic monologue is spoken by a city clerk who is struggling to raise a family on 'thirty bob a week' (also the poem's title). The clerk says nothing about the countryside or the solace of nature – he is too busy trying to survive by making the journey every day from the suburban to the urban, as he explains in the third stanza:

> For like a mole I journey in the dark,
> A-travelling along the underground
> From my Pillar'd Halls and broad Suburbean Park,
> To come the daily dull official round;
> And home again at night with my pipe all alight,
> A-scheming how to count ten bob a pound.

The suburban is a transitional place, lying in between the country and the city. In this light, the journey of Davidson's speaker in this dramatic monologue from his 'Suburbean' home to work in the city mirrors the transition of poetry at the end of the nineteenth century from the rural or natural concerns of much Romantic and Victorian poetry, to the modernist preoccupation with the urban environment. Indeed, T.S. Eliot admired Davidson's poetry, and particularly 'Thirty Bob A Week' for its grim urban imagery. While many nineteenth-century novels had already turned to the city for its setting and theme (the novels of Dickens, Gaskell and Kingsley are especially relevant here) poetry was slower to do so, perhaps because urban themes and imagery imply a fragmentation and a multiplicity of individual voices which are ill-suited to the subjectivity of the lyric poem, or to the single persona of the dramatic monologue. John Davidson's poem makes the transition from the suburban to the urban, and although it is a dramatic monologue, it is also a precursor to the fragmented, alienated voices which, in the poetry of T.S. Eliot, Ezra Pound and many other writers, was to become a defining characteristic of modernism.

Suggested further reading on Hopkins: Storey (1984), Robinson (1978), North and Moore (eds) (1984) and Ong (1986).

## BIBLIOGRAPHY

Allott, K. and Allott, M. (eds) (1979) *The Poems of Matthew Arnold*, 2nd edn, Longman, London.

ApRoberts, R. (1983) *Arnold and God*, University of California Press, Berkeley.

Armstrong, I. (1972) *Victorian Scrutinies: Reviews of Poetry 1830–1870*, The Athlone Press of the University of London, London.

Armstrong, I. (1993) *Victorian Poetry: Poetry, Poetics and Politics*, Routledge, London.

Armstrong, I. (ed.) (1974) *Robert Browning*, Writers and their Background, G. Bell & Sons, London.

Battiscombe, G. (1981) *Christina Rossetti: A Divided Life*, Constable, London.

Beer, G. and Harris, M. (eds) (1983) *The Notebooks of George Meredith*, Institut für Anglistik und Americanistik, Universität Salzburg, Salzburg.

Biswas, R.K. (1972) *Arthur Hugh Clough: Towards a Reconsideration*, Clarendon Press, Oxford.

Blewitt, O. (1843) *Murray's Guide to Central Italy, Rome and Florence*, John Murray, London.

Bloom, H. and Munich, I. (eds) (1979) *Robert Browning: A Collection of Critical Essays*, Prentice Hall, Englewood Cliffs.

Bristow, J. (1991) *Robert Browning*, Harvester Wheatsheaf, Hemel Hempstead.

Bristow, J. (ed.) (1987) *The Victorian Poet: Poetics and Persona*, Croom Helm, London.

Browning, E.B. (1993) *Aurora Leigh* (ed. with an Introduction and Notes by K. McSweeney), Oxford University Press, Oxford [first published 1857].

Buchanan, G. ('Thomas Maitland') (1871) 'The Fleshly School of Poetry: Mr. D.G. Rossetti', *Contemporary Review*, vol. XVIII, pp. 334–50, Strahan, London.

Carlyle, T. (1840–1; 1993) (Notes and Introduction by Michael K. Goldberg) *On Heroes, Hero-Worship, and the Heroic in History*, University of California Press, Berkeley.

Carroll, J. (1982) *The Cultural Theory of Matthew Arnold*, University of California Press, Berkeley and London.

Christ, C.T. (1984) *Victorian and Modernist Poetics*, University of Chicago Press, Chicago.

Colley, A.C. (1983) *Tennyson and Madness*, University of Georgia Press, Athens, Georgia.

Cosslett, T. (1982) *The 'Scientific Movement' and Victorian Literature*, Harvester Wheatsheaf, Hemel Hempstead.

Culler, A.D. (1977) *The Poetry of Tennyson*, Yale University Press, New Haven.

Culler, A.D. (1985) *The Victorian Mirror of History*, Yale University Press, New Haven.

Dawson, C. (1973) *Matthew Arnold: the Poetry (The Critical Heritage)*, Routledge & Kegan Paul, London.

Day, A. (1991) 'Introduction', *Robert Browning: Selected Poetry and Prose*, Routledge, London.

Edmond, R. (1988) *Affairs of the Hearth: Victorian Poetry and Domestic Narrative*, Routledge, London.

Faulkner, P. (ed.) (1973) *William Morris (The Critical Heritage)*, Routledge & Kegan Paul, London.

Flowers, B.S. (1976) *Browning and the Modern Tradition*, Macmillan, London.

Fraser, H. (1992) *The Victorians and Renaissance Italy*, Blackwell, Oxford.

Gardner, W.H. (1953) 'Introduction', *Gerard Manley Hopkins: Poems and Prose*, Penguin Books, Harmondsworth.

Greenberger, E.B. (1970) *Arthur Hugh Clough: The Growth of a Poet's Mind*, Harvard University Press, Cambridge, Mass.

Harrison, A.H. (1990) *Victorian Poets and Romantic Poems: Intertextuality and Ideology*, University Press of Virginia, Charlottesville.

Henderson, P. (1974) *Swinburne: The Portrait of a Poet*, Routledge & Kegan Paul, London.

Honan, P. (1981) *Matthew Arnold: A Life*, Weidenfeld & Nicolson, London.

Hyder, C.K. (ed.) (1970) *Swinburne (The Critical Heritage)*, Routledge & Kegan Paul, London.

Jack, I., Fowler, Rowena, and Smith, Margaret (eds) (1991) *The Poetical Works of Robert Browning*, vols i–iv (Browning's 'Essay on Shelley' appears in vol. iv, Appendix A, pp. 421–42), Clarendon Press, Oxford.

Jay, E. (ed.) (1983) *The Evangelical and Oxford Movements*, Cambridge University Press, Cambridge.

Jump, J.D. (ed.) (1967) *Tennyson (The Critical Heritage)*, Routledge & Kegan Paul, London.

Kelvin, N. (1961) *A Troubled Eden: Nature and Society in the Works of George Meredith*, Oliver & Boyd, Edinburgh.

Kintner, E. (ed.) (1969) *The Letters of Robert Browning and Elizabeth Barrett Browning*, vols 1 and 2, The Belknap Press of Harvard University Press, Cambridge, Mass.

Knowles, J. (January 1893) 'Aspects of Tennyson, II', *Nineteenth Century*, London.

Lindsay, J. (1975) *William Morris: His Life and Work*, Constable, London.

Mackenzie, N.H. (ed.) (1990) *The Poetical Works of Gerard Manley Hopkins*, Clarendon Press, Oxford.

Mayberry, K.J. (1989) *Christina Rossetti and the Poetry of Discovery*, Louisiana State University Press, Baton Rouge and London.

Mayhew, H. (1849–61; 1985) *London Labour and the London Poor*, Penguin, London.

McGann, J.J. (1972) *Swinburne: An Experiment in Criticism*, University of Chicago Press, Chicago.

McSweeney, K. (1980) *Tennyson and Swinburne as Romantic Naturalists*, University of Toronto Press, Toronto.

Miligate, M. (ed.) (1984) *The Life and Work of Thomas Hardy by Thomas Hardy*, Macmillan, London.

Mulhauser, F.L. (ed.) (1974) *The Poems of Arthur Hugh Clough*, (2nd edn), Clarendon, Oxford.

Newman, J.H. (1864; 1994) *Apologia pro Vita Sua*, Penguin, London.

North, J.S. and Moore, M.D. (eds) (1984) *Vital Candle: Victorian and Modern Bearings in Gerard Manley Hopkins*, University of Waterloo Press, Waterloo, Ontario.

Ong, W.J. (1986) *Hopkins, the Self, and God*, University of Toronto Press, Toronto and London.

Pater, W. (1889) *'Dante Gabriel Rossetti'*, *Appreciations with an Essay on Style*, Macmillan, London.

Phillips, C. (1991) *Gerard Manley Hopkins: Selected Letters*, Oxford University Press, Oxford.

Rees, J. (1981) *The Poetry of Dante Gabriel Rossetti: Modes of Self-expression*, Cambridge University Press, Cambridge.

Ricks, C. (1972) *Tennyson*, Macmillan, New York.

Ricks, C. (ed.) (1987) *The Poems of Tennyson*, 3 vols, 2nd edn, Longman, Harlow.

Robinson, J.G. (1978) *In Extremity: A Study of Gerard Manley Hopkins*, Cambridge University Press, Cambridge.

Sinfield, A. (1971) *The Language of Tennyson's 'In Memoriam'*, Blackwell, Oxford.

Stansky, P. (1983) *William Morris*, Oxford University Press, Oxford.

Storey, G. (1984) *Gerard Manley Hopkins*, Writers and Their Works, Profile Books, Windsor.

Thomas, D. (ed.) (1990) *The Post-Romantics*, Routledge, London.

Wheeler, M. (1990) *Death and the Future Life in Victorian Literature and Theology*, Cambridge University Press, Cambridge.

Williams, R. (1973) *The Country and the City*, Oxford University Press, Oxford.

# UNIT 13

# American literature to 1900

*Elmer Andrews*

This unit, in considering the development of a distinctively American literature, introduces such topics as the myth of America, New England Puritanism, American Transcendentalism and Pragmatism, the Frontier, the evolution of a myth of the South, and the discovery of an American vernacular voice. The characteristic tensions in the American tradition between history and myth, realism and romance, pessimistic despair and transcendent hope, the desire for freedom and recognition of the need for order are highlighted. The second section examines some of the major nineteenth-century texts, relating them to their social, cultural and historical contexts.

## Introduction

Inventing America

From the beginning, America was seen as unique and different by European navigators, travellers, historians and philosophers. The very idea of a 'New Founde Land' excited the mythopoeic imagination. Columbus not only thought he had discovered a group of Asiatic islands (which he called 'the Indies', their inhabitants 'Indians') in 1492, but saw himself as having fulfilled biblical prophecy in finding the Garden of Eden, the 'Terrestrial Paradise'. In 1524, the Florentine explorer, Giovanni da Verrazzano described the idyllic landscape of Virginia as 'Arcadia'. The myth of Utopia (Sir Thomas More's *Utopia* was first printed in 1516) informed much Renaissance thinking and writing about America. One of the first to engage in the great cultural project of writing America was Captain John Smith (1580–1631), founder of the first permanent settlement in Jamestown, Virginia, in 1607. Smith referred to the 'incredible abundance' of the New World: 'heaven and earth never agreed better to frame a place for man's habitation'. Prefiguring the emphasis which Benjamin Franklin (1706–90) placed on self-improvement, Smith helped frame the myth of America as the open society, the land of opportunity to those with the self-discipline and industry to take advantage of its infinite resources. The early explorers' and settlers' narratives thus set the pattern for an American literature that would find the New World a kind of wonderland, inexhaustibly new and fascinating.

American literature, like American society, speaks of new beginnings, a second chance for mankind, the opportunity for the realization of dreams without traditional hindrances. Man need not think of himself as inevitably condemned to oppression and victimization, but could recreate himself. The characteristic American themes and images derive from this sense of fresh starts, from a revived faith in the Enlightenment values of progress and possibility. In *Walden* (1854), Henry David Thoreau expresses in miniature the impulse which lay behind the whole American adventure:

> I went to the woods because I wished to live deliberately, to front only the essential facts of life, and see if I could not learn what it had to teach, and not, when I came to die, discover that I had not lived.

This move was more than a backing off from civilization and a return to nature: it was a spiritual quest, a pilgrimage of renewal.

One of the first major statements of the promise of America was that of the Frenchman, J. Hector St John de Crevecoeur (1735–1813) in his *Letters from an American Farmer* (1782). De Crevecoeur articulated the excitement and wonder of the new, the sense of freedom from European corruption and constraint, a vision of harmonious relationship between the natural and the civilized, a Whitmanesque delight in the infinite variety of the world. He particularly admired the sturdy independence of the frontier mentality. The absence of traditional hierarchies, far from posing a difficulty to the organization of an ordered life, held out the promise of equality for all. He particularly commended the American democratic ideal, rejoicing in its racial pluralism, its capacity to assimilate all races and cultures to produce 'a new race of men'. In contrast to Puritan America, de Crevecoeur represented a secular, Enlightenment view. His 'new man' was the settled farmer and artisan, Jeffersonian man, rather than one of the Puritan 'elect'. For de Crevecoeur, America seemed to promise, as it did for Gatsby two centuries later, the opportunity for man to become anything he wants. In America a man could 'embark on schemes he never would have thought of in his own country'. Concentrating on future possibility rather than present actuality, de Crevecoeur articulated a simple optimism, a faith in man's perfectability and the inevitable march of progress that epitomized the American Dream:

> The American is a new man, who acts upon new principles; he must therefore entertain new ideas, and form new opinions. From involuntary idleness, servile dependence, penury, and useless labour, he has passed to toils of a very different nature, rewarded by ample subsistence – This is an American.

Growing out of the idea of the 'new man' in the new Eden was the figure of the American Adam, which R.W.B. Lewis defines in his book, *The American Adam* (1955) as follows:

> a radically new personality, the hero of the new adventure: an individual emancipated from history, happily bereft of ancestry, untouched and undefiled by the usual inheritances of family and race; an individual standing alone, self-reliant and self-propelling, ready to confront whatever awaited him with the aid of his own unique and

inherent resources ... The world and history lay all before him. And he was the type of creator, the poet par excellence, creating language itself by naming the elements of the scene about him.

Philip Freneau (1752–1832), poet and propagandist of the American Revolution, gave free rein to this kind of utopianism in his poem, 'The Rising Glory of America':

> Paradise anew
> Shall flourish, by no second Adam lost,
> No dangerous tree with deadly fruit shall grow
> No tempting serpent to allure the soul
> from native innocence.

The American Adam is incarnated in the figure of Natty Bumppo, the creation of James Fenimore Cooper (1789–1851), and in Emerson (1803–82) and Thoreau (1817–62) who together were the first great spokesmen of brave new beginnings, of discovery, openness, of all that was hopeful in America. He appears in the form of Benjamin Franklin, Walt Whitman (1819–92) who presented himself 'As Adam, early in the morning' (the title of one of his poems), Melville's Billy Budd (in the novella of that name) who 'might have posed for a statue of some Adam before the fall', and Twain's boy-hero in *The Adventures of Huckleberry Finn* (1885) struggling to preserve his integrity in a corrupt world. Henry James (1843–1916) indicates the Adamic innocence of his Americans by calling them Christopher Newman and Adam Verver, and describing Isabel Archer (in *A Portrait of a Lady*) as a young lady with 'a fixed determination to regard the world as a place of brightness, of free expansion, of incontestable action'. In the twentieth century, the American Adam makes notable appearances as F. Scott Fitzgerald's Jay Gatsby (*The Great Gatsby*), Saul Bellow's Augie Marsh (*The Adventures of Augie Marsh*), J.D. Salinger's Holden Caulfield (*Catcher in the Rye*) and, of course, Ernest Heming-way's Nick Adams (*In Our Time*).

Lewis writes out of a confident sense of the Adamic individual's capacity for self-realization. But the individual may not find himself at all 'happily' bereft of ancestry, and Adamic innocence may not at all be the defining characteristic of man. There is no guarantee that the individual thrown back on his or her own resources will be able to deal with chaos. American literature is the story of lost, drifting orphans (Huck Finn) as well as powerful liberated adventurers (Ahab), and neither the career of Huck Finn nor Captain Ahab is a 'happy' one. In Melville (1819–91), the 'individual standing alone' is an image of rampant, self-destructive egotism (Ahab) or helpless victim in an ironic world (Billy Budd); in Hawthorne (1804–64), she is a wanderer 'without rule or guidance, in a moral wilderness' (Hester Prynne in *The Scarlet Letter*).

The pessimism of American literature, it has been suggested, lies in the individual's inability to find fulfilment in conforming to social values, and the awareness that escape from them is an illusion. In *Huckleberry Finn*, escape from civilization is an adolescent fantasy. Thoreau eventually discovers his need of society and returns to civilization at the end of *Walden*. To be neither inside nor outside society, it would seem, is to be in the great American tradition. Enforcing a dichotomy between individual integrity and social corruption, the American writer nevertheless affirms the ideal of a limited kind of comradeship – Ishmael and the cannibal Queequeg (*Moby-Dick*), Leatherstocking and the Indian Chingachgook (*The Pathfinder*), Huck Finn and Nigger Jim. As Leslie Fiedler observes in *Love and Death in the American Novel* (1967), these homoerotic, interracial unions are a version of universal brotherhood on the model of Defoe's *Robinson Crusoe*, only in democratic America there is more of a marriage of equals.

The awareness of a tragic discrepancy between the vision of Adamic innocence and actual social conditions has persisted throughout the history of America. Yet however much the curse of slavery, the genocidal process of Indian dispossession, Civil War, Depression, Hiroshima, Korea, Vietnam, Watergate, inner-city violence may have damaged the American Dream, it continues to be a powerful motivating force in the American imagination. Fitzgerald ends *The Great Gatsby* with a moving expression of the classic American attitude:

> Gatsby believed in the green light, the orgiastic future that year by year recedes before us. It eluded us then (the time of the early settlers), but that's no matter – tomorrow we will run faster, stretch out our arms farther ... And one fine morning .... (pp. 171–2)

## Puritan New England

Where the navigation and exploration literature relating to America is in many languages (Spanish, Portuguese, French, Dutch, English), the literature of the early settlers was almost exclusively in English (in the early eighteenth century over 90 per cent of colonists were English). It was also predominantly the literature of New England. It was also predominantly a literature serving a religious purpose, an instructional and propagandistic literature explaining and justifying the Puritan way of life. Though essentially a utilitarian rather than a belle lettristic writing, it was both varied and, perhaps surprisingly in light of the famous Puritan distrust of art and imagination, both imaginatively powerful and often rhetorically extravagant.

There were historical accounts, such as William Bradford's *Of Plymouth Plantation*, written between 1630 and 1647. On 16 September 1620, the 'Mayflower' set sail with 102 Plymouth Pilgrims on board, fleeing James I's repression of their Calvinistic beliefs. Their first impressions of the New World, as recorded by Bradford (1590–1657), were not those of a New Eden but of a 'hideous and desolate wilderness, full of wild beasts and wild men'. Bradford articulates one of the first recorded instances of the disappointment of the American Dream, but also affirms the unquenchable American spirit which keeps the dream alive no matter how gravely actuality throws it into doubt. *Of Plymouth Plantation* is prophetic in its combination of alienation and a tenacious, future-oriented optimism.

There were journals, such as that penned by John Winthrop (1588–1649), the Massachusetts Puritan Governor, who sought to establish the ideal 'city upon a hill'. Puritan millenarianism was an important strand in the weaving of the American Dream. In his magisterial *Magnalia Christi Americana* (1702) and *Theopolis*

*Americana* (1710), the great Puritan divine, Cotton Mather (1663–1728), with a prodigious display of learning, framed his epic Puritan vision of a distinctive American experience: 'Put on thy beautiful garments, O America the Holy City!'

Sermons, of course, figure prominently in the literature of New England. Jonathan Edwards (1703–58) authored the famous 'Sinners in the Hands of an Angry God' which helped to make him one of the leading lights in the evangelical revival known as 'The Great Awakening' that swept America in the 1740s and posed a powerful challenge to traditional church authority. Edwards sought to reverse the rationalist and liberalizing tendencies in Puritanism, asserting that the individual's feelings or 'affections', not his works, were the only guarantee of his spiritual state. His sermon is a nightmarish fantasy of eternal suffering and damnation in which Edwards thrills to the *mysterium tremenduum* of God's overwhelming omnipotence.

The major poets of the colonial period were Ann Broadstreet (1612–72), notable for her poems about family life in New England, and Michael Wigglesworth (1631–1705), who wrote the most popular literary work of Puritan New England, 'Day of Doom' (1662), a version of God's Judgement Day, expressive of the Puritan apocalyptic temper. Two black voices of the period were those of Jupiter Hammon (1720–c.1800) and Phyllis Wheatley (1754–84). Hammon was a mainly religious poet who spoke for slavery as the means whereby blacks could be brought to Christianity. Likewise, Wheatley declared in her poem, 'On Being Brought from Africa to America': ''Twas mercy brought me from my pagan land,/ Taught my benighted souls to understand/ That there's a God, that there's a Saviour, too.'

The colonial literature included autobiography. Mary Rowlandson's *A Narrative of the Captivity and Restoration of Mrs Mary Rowlandson* (1682) was a best-seller in its day. In her account of Indian attack, captivity and escape, Rowlandson (c.1637–c.1710) turns her story into a demonstration of exemplary Puritan steadfastness in the face of grievous 'trials and afflictions', and an affirmation of 'the strange providence of God' which eventually assured her release. Rowlandson's narrative not only set the agenda for the demonization of the Indian, but initiated a long tradition of popular wild west frontier fiction.

The most celebrated autobiographer of the time was Benjamin Franklin (1706–90). His unfinished, rags-to-riches *Autobiography*, written between 1771 and his death in 1790, is modelled on the English Augustan style of Addison and Steele, and influenced by the rationalist philosophy of Locke and Newton. It is a major exposition of what Max Weber called the 'Puritan work ethic'. While continuing the Puritan tradition of self-consciousness and self-examination, Franklin opposed the traditional Puritan emphasis on miraculous regeneration through the operation of God's Grace, stressing instead personal responsibility and self-improvement. Espousing the Enlightenment philosophy of Deism that saw God, not through the Bible or divine revelation, but in the orderly workings of the physical world, he urged individuals to organize their lives in imitation of this rational model.

The Puritan world was composed out of a series of stark binary oppositions – good and evil, light and dark, heaven and hell, the elect and the damned, faith and works. The visible world was but the sign and symbol of God, and had to be interpreted accordingly. The Calvinistic doctrine of Original Sin taught that all mankind is born in sin and doomed to eternal damnation unless, by God's grace, they are saved. The 'elect' or the 'saints' were those chosen by God for eternal life, and it was they who constituted both the spiritual and the civil authority in the Puritan townships. Confronted with a vast, untamed wilderness, hostile Indians and the incursions of the English and the French, the colonists saw the paramount need for consensus and conformity in the interests of both social stability and religious confidence. From the beginning, American Puritanism was bedevilled by the conflict between conformism and private conscience. Ironically, the New England community, born out of a quest for freedom and tolerance, distinguished itself by its harsh and punitive treatment of the 'other'. Slavery was legalized, Indian lands ruthlessly seized and all internal dissent quelled in the name of God. Quakers were tortured and expelled on pain of death from the Massachusetts Bay Colony. Witchcraft and heresy, products of theocratic repression, were hunted down zealously.

The influence of Puritanism continued strongly into the nineteenth century, and even today is an important strain in the psychology of American culture. Writing in 1846, Melville opined of Hawthorne: 'Certain it is ... that this great power of blackness in him derives its force from its appeals to that Calvinistic sense of Innate Depravity and Original Sin, from whose visitations ... no deeply thinking mind is always and wholly free.' Where Emerson's is an essentially idyllic world in which the 'other' can be humanized and thereby brought under control by the power of mind, Melville sees the world as irreducibly alien: Emerson's garden pastoral contrasts with Melville's (ocean) wilderness, Emerson's God within is replaced by Melville's demonic Parsee who erupts from the hold of Ahab's ship. For Melville, experience is always ambiguous, and cannot be contained within either Puritan or transcendentalist frameworks. Hawthorne's own attitude to his Puritan heritage is also highly ambivalent and one of his central thematic preoccupations. Both he and Melville develop the emblematic discourse of Puritanism in important new directions. Where the Puritan mind was essentially allegorical, Melville and Hawthorne exchanged allegory for symbolism. Allegory expresses a stable world, a fixed ideology in a system of one-to-one correspondences: Melville and Hawthorne found the less securely defining, more suggestive significations of symbolism better suited to their questing, sceptical mind.

## The frontier

The frontier is one of the central themes of American literature, and has remained a potent image in the national consciousness. Frontiers, walls, fences and other images of boundary, actual or metaphorical, pervade the American imagination and its literature. The actual frontier marked the push, mostly westward, whereby the wilderness was gradually incorporated into the dominant culture centred in the East, a process which continued up to 1890 when the Census of that year declared the frontier officially closed. Frontier life offered a return to primal nature, an escape from civilization and a recovery of the lost Eden. It promoted the virtues of hardy individualism, the sense of freedom and self-sufficiency. It bred a new American hero, the frontiersman: Leatherstocking, Daniel Boone, Davy Crockett, Buffalo Bill.

And it generated its own distinctive literature: guides and manuals for frontier living, Indian narratives, stories of the legendary exploits of frontier heroes, the tall tale, 'local colour' fiction. The myth of the frontier survives in the American response to the intellectual, physical and moral challenge of contemporary life. Modern versions of the old narratives of excursion into the wilderness and into Indian territory would be stories of the flight into outer space (*Star Trek*'s 'final frontier') and into the inner space of hallucinogenic experience (as in the work of William Burroughs). These versions of crossing the frontier are all analogues for what has traditionally been figured as a Journey or Quest or Pilgrimage towards a transcendental goal, a moment of vision.

William Byrd (1674–1744) lived on his Virginia tobacco plantation like a learned London aristocrat; but his *History of the Dividing Line* (1729) makes it clear that he was aware of the closeness of the wilderness which continually fascinated him. Since the frontier has always been associated with lawlessness as well as freedom, hardship as well as opportunity, danger as well as democracy, it has naturally always aroused ambivalent feelings. William Bradford's Puritan wilderness was a place of bestial evil, chaos and old night. For Cooper and Thoreau, however, it was the source of renewal. The frontiersman is Whitman's hero, and in 'Song of the Broad-Ax' (1856) he celebrates 'the beauty of independence, departure, actions that rely on themselves/ The American contempt for statutes and ceremonies, the boundless impatience of restraint'. In *The Adventures of Huckleberry Finn*, the only way Huck can preserve his innocence is 'to light out for the territory' away from the Widow Douglas's efforts to 'sivilize' him. Throughout the novel, Huck moves back and forth between the river where he feels 'easy and satisfied' and the social world which he is continually forced to flee or turns away from in disgust. One thinks of Hester Prynne who lives in the 'neutral territory' between the town and the forest, committed to neither. Or Cooper's Natty Bumppo who combines innocence and experience, continually fleeing the civilization of the settlements yet is 'the foremost of that band of pioneers who are opening the way for the march of the nation across the continent' (*The Pioneers*).

In some works, the pioneer world exists as a powerful memory. It haunts Sherwood Anderson's *Winesburg, Ohio* (1919) and Willy Loman's dreams in Arthur Miller's *Death of a Salesman* (1949). John Steinbeck's Joad family in *The Grapes of Wrath* (1939) re-enact the early pioneers' long trek to find, not the promised land, but vicious exploitation and bitter disappointment. Fitzgerald in *The Great Gatsby* reverses the movement from East to West and has his characters converge in the cities of the East in pursuit of their dreams. Hemingway's heroes, having fought the Old World's wars, make their 'separate peace' with a violent world and return to a simple, natural life of hunting and fishing.

### America's declaration of intellectual independence

*The Declaration of Independence*, largely the work of Thomas Jefferson (1743–1826), was issued in 1776, declaring every American's 'inalienable right' to 'life, liberty and the pursuit of happiness'. However, political independence did not mean cultural independence. In the years after the Revolutionary war many Americans were concerned by the question of the American national identity and the need to evolve distinctive American cultural forms, namely an American language and an American literature. The early writers who sought to celebrate the American landscape and people tended to do so in the neo-classical forms and measures of European literature. 'The Prairies' (1833) by William Cullen Bryant (1794–1878) who along with Freneau was the major poet of the New Republic, can stand for any number of examples:

> These are the gardens of the Desert, these
> The unshorn fields, boundless and beautiful,
> For which the speech of England has no name –
> The Prairies.

Bryant's lines epitomize the way the newness and distinctiveness of American life were contained within the structures of established order. The deeply rooted tension in the American tradition between rebelliousness and conservatism was especially acute in the post-revolutionary period when the impulse towards what Thoreau called 'extra-vagance' was checked by a concern for restraint and decorum as the guarantee against any tendency towards excess and anarchy.

Being an American, according to Henry James, was 'a complex fate' that entailed 'fighting against a superstitious valuation of Europe'. Noah Webster (1758–1843), seeking to define a distinctively American language, produced his *American Dictionary of the English Language* in 1828, a project motivated by patriotism and a strong desire for national unity. Emerson, in 'The American Scholar' (1837), called for a distinctively American literature founded on American experience and grounded in a new respect for the commonplace:

> This perception of the worth of the vulgar is fruitful in discoveries ... The world is nothing, the man is all; in yourself is the law of all nature ... in yourself slumbers the whole of Reason; it is for you to know all; it is for you to dare all ... this confidence in the unsearched might of man belongs to the American Scholar. We have listened too long to the courtly muses of Europe.

That last statement was described by a fellow countryman, Oliver Wendell Holmes (1809–94), as 'America's Declaration of Intellectual Independence'. Emerson represents a move from culture to nature, a return to first principles, to the sources of creativity. He stresses the ultimate value of direct, childlike engagement with the natural world unmediated by reason or language.

Where the social and historical conditions in England promoted the novel of manners and morals, those conditions did not exist in America for the American writer merely to continue the English tradition. James Fenimore Cooper (1789–1851), along with Brockden Brown (1771–1810), Hawthorne and James complained about the 'poverty of materials' in America. In *Notions of the Americans: Picked up by a Travelling Bachelor* (1828), Cooper opined:

> There is scarcely an ore which contributes to the wealth of the author, that is found here, in veins as rich as in Europe. There are no annals for the historian; no follies (beyond the

most vulgar and commonplace) for the satirist; no manners for the dramatist; no obscure fictions for the writer of romance; no gross and hardy offences against decorum for the moralist; nor any of the rich artificial auxiliaries of poetry.

Though influenced by Scott, Cooper saw himself in a public and national role, as one concerned with the development of a distinctively American writing – a 'pathfinder' of American literature. Claiming that America's 'mental independence is my object', he established the centrality of the frontier in American life and consciousness, and opened up the sea (in *The Pilot*, 1823) as well as the dark forests as important American themes. Departing from a strict realism, he experimented with a Romantic delineation of mythic landscape and legendary embodiment of the frontier virtues of individualism and independence in the person of Natty Bumppo. Crucially, Cooper embodies some of the dilemmas at the very heart of American culture, chief of which is the tension between anarchism and conservatism, between traditional communal values and those of the lone individual haunting the margins of society. This tension, which can be traced through Melville and Twain to Faulkner, Cooper seeks to resolve in the figure of Natty Bumppo who represents his ideal balance between nature and civilization.

Cooper explored not only native themes, settings and characters that later writers would constantly return to in seeking to define the American cultural identity, but inaugurated a characteristic American form of the novel which Hawthorne insisted we should call the 'romance'. In the English and European novel, the individual is grounded in a particular, carefully delineated social and moral order, a given network of relations with other people, with the past, with the environment, and with God. In literary terms, this means that the writer is inscribed in a tradition which provides an agreed sense of the nature of reality and of social values. The American writer, on the other hand, has always felt that he must imagine his destiny rather than simply inherit one as his European counterpart could do. The American has to make his world, invent a fiction, not merely reflect a commonly agreed reality. This sense of freedom from the past, from class and community, from any given patterning of reality gives the American character a large and luminous generality. He assumes a mythic dimension. Think of Cooper's Natty Bumppo, Hawthorne's Hester Prynne, Melville's Captain Ahab, Twain's Huck Finn. American writing has characteristically tended towards the allegorical, the symbolic and the romantic, towards a principle of imaginative autonomy rather than mimesis and direct historical engagement. Romance was a freer, 'wilder' form of fiction than that which we associate with the English tradition. The romancer, Hawthorne writes in the Preface to *The House of the Seven Gables* (1851), 'wishes to claim a certain latitude' beyond that to which he would be entitled 'had he professed to be writing a Novel'. Romance occupies that 'neutral territory' to which he referred in 'The Custom-House' section of *The Scarlet Letter* – 'somewhere between the real world and fairyland, where the Actual and the Imaginary may meet, and each imbue itself with the nature of the other'. As the examples of Brown, Poe (1809–49), Hawthorne, Melville and Twain would suggest, the American Romance contains strong gothic elements. Gothic is a form of anti-realism, expressive of the terrorized imagination.

It concerns itself with hidden evil, nightmarish horror, melodramatic psychology, with ghosts, omens, signs and portents, with the diabolic and the mysterious. The central action often involves a Faustian bargain with the devil: Hester and Dimmesdale's sinful union, Ahab's blasphemous pact with Fedallah, Huck Finn's resolve to go to Hell rather than give up a runaway slave.

## Texts, authors, contexts

### Ralph Waldo Emerson: *Selected Essays* ((1836–62) Ziff, 1982)

The first major expression of Emerson's ideas was his essay 'Nature' (1836) in which he elaborates his central precept that man should 'enjoy an original relation to the universe' that is direct and personal and not dependent on tradition. In a famous passage, he attempts to communicate directly the experience of transcendence, a rare example of this kind of thing in Emerson. Usually he is the theorist and it is to Thoreau we go for a more performative style. Emerson is on Boston Common, alone, under the stars:

> Standing on the bare ground, – my head bathed by the blithe air, and uplifted into infinite space, – all mean egotism vanishes. I become a transparent eyeball; I am nothing; I see all; the currents of the Universal Being circulate through me; I am part or parcel of God. (p. 39)

Compare Emerson's experience with Wordsworth's intuitions of the 'Sentiment of Being spread/ O'er all' in *The Prelude* (Book I, 418–20). Wordsworth's 'wise passiveness' has its counterpart in Emerson's suspension of active will and conscious thought while he submits to nature's supernatural power. Caught up in forces beyond his conscious control, he is 'uplifted' from the world of matter to the flowing world of spirit. Transcending the life of the body and the senses, he ascends towards mystical union with Spirit, God, the One, the Over-Soul – all of these terms interchangeable for what Emerson understood as an all-encompassing, eternal, moral, benign mind or spirit. The broken syntax and intoxicated rhythms signify the struggle to express an almost unbearable lightness of being. As the image of the 'transparent eyeball' suggests, the crucial transformation Emerson calls for is a new kind of seeing.

Emerson's belief in the essential divinity of man was the basis for a wonderfully optimistic cultural programme. Where the Puritans started with a concept of Original Sin, Emerson emphasized the basic goodness of man. For Emerson, salvation was available to all, not just the Puritan 'elect' – an idea which happily coincided with the broad contemporary belief in the potential perfectability of man and the general sense of optimism and faith in progress which characterized American thought and life at this time. Through the exercise of Reason man could escape Determinism and open up new worlds, new possibilities for himself.

In 'Nature' Emerson delivers the ringing exhortation 'Build therefore your own world'. Leaving aside the question of what a slave might have made of this exhortation (if he could have read it), compare the emphasis on the active construction of truth with the posture of passive waiting affirmed in the description of the Boston Common experience. Does power come from within or without? Which comes first, mind or universe? In the early essays he seeks to resolve division by affirming a reconciliation or identification or what he called 'consanguinity' between inner and outer, subject and object, mind and universe, the human and the divine. However, by the time we come to 'Experience', one of the essays in the Second Series (1844), he is less confident of this kind of harmonious relationship, which now tends to express itself as desire rather than reality. The pressure of his own experience (especially the death of his 5-year-old son) forced him to revise his early optimism and to recognize the limits of human existence as well as its enormous potential. On the 'sliding scale' between subjective and objective, the Ideal and the Real, is the 'temperate zone', the middle region which is the desired one for the 'well-mixed' life.

Poetic language, as Emerson emphasizes in 'The Poet' (1844), has a special capacity to 'flux' the 'wall' (pp. 386–7) of fact and dogma, to break down conventional perception and the monoliths of ideology. But this sense of the fluid, freeing activity of the poet's language coexists with a profound scepticism about language. Language, like action (see the essay on Napoleon) can confine the transcendental mind: 'every thought is also a prison, every heaven is also a prison. Therefore we love the poet, the inventor, who ... has yielded us a new thought' (p. 278). These are ideas which are strongly echoed by other American writers, from Sherwood Anderson to Wallace Stevens and William Carlos Williams. For Emerson, the ultimate project of language is to assist in its own annihilation by creating the conditions for a direct, unmediated encounter with the Godhead.

Thus, Emerson in his own writing resists definition, finality and closure, accepts contradiction ('a foolish consistency is the hobgoblin of little minds') and affirms provisionality. 'I am too young yet by some ages to compile a code' (p. 309), he says. For all his sermonizing, he is anxious not to become merely another traditional metaphysician or essentialist myth-maker. 'Let me remind the reader', he writes, 'that I am only an experimenter. Do not set the least value on what I do ... I unsettle all things. No facts are to me sacred; none are profane; I simply experiment, an endless seeker with no Past at my back' (p. 236). The notion of a pure origin is replaced by a concept of self continually in process, repeatedly, endlessly, creating its own arbitrary 'beginnings': 'Every ultimate fact is only the first of a new series ... There is no outside, no inclosing wall, no circumference to us', he writes in 'Circles' (p. 227). Evading the issue of truth, he disclaims any foundationalist metaphysical status for his philosophy. The style of his essays – fluid, associative, fragmentary, aphoristic, contradictory, cumulative rather than following a strictly logical procedure – is quite different from conventional philosophical discourse and more akin to the provisional, experimental approach to knowledge associated with the antifoundationalist, antiphilosophical tradition of American Pragmatism. His writing evades normal rational procedure and, unable to resolve its internal tensions, tends to unfold in a repeated pattern of confident assertion followed by sceptical withdrawal or qualification. This tidal, cyclical movement, expressive of what

Emerson called the 'principle of Undulation' (p. 300), naturally unsettles any metaphysical consistency or stability.

For Emerson, as for many others, Transcendentalism was a revolt against Unitarian conservatism. Unitarianism, which was originally an eighteenth-century reaction against the emotionalism of Jonathan Edwards (1703–58) and 'The Awakening' of the 1740s, grew out of Deism, a body of religious thought that emphasized human reason and saw God directly in the workings of the ordered physical world. Emerson, who came from a long line of New England ministers, was himself a Unitarian minister, but after six years as pastor of Boston's Second Church he resigned in 1826. Chafing under the yoke of church dogma and ritual, and longing for a more direct access to God, he believed Unitarianism had become too formalized and rational.

The great challenge facing Emerson was to reconcile the idealist and materialist positions. In attempting to do so, he opened up the problems which have preoccupied many succeeding American writers: how independent and autonomous is the self from its culture and society? How can it survive in the world without being taken over either by environment or by its own desires? For to the extent that either of these conditions prevails, man is a prisoner.

There is the Enlightenment Emerson who believes in the possibility of reconstructing Eden, who sees the earth as man's home, and who puts his faith in a divine order amenable to human reason. But there is also what we might call the postmodern Emerson brought to us by Richard Rorty, Cornel West and Richard Poirier, the Emerson who takes his place at the head of a line of thinkers including Marx, Nietzsche, Freud, Saussure, Wittgenstein, Heidegger, Derrida and Foucault who have challenged the basis of traditional philosophical inquiry since Plato, undermining its 'grand narratives' and denying its truth-claims. This neo-pragmatic philosophy emphasizes, in Emerson's words, 'man thinking' (that is, the culturally conditioned *process* of thought) rather than thought itself (that is, the system or theory which is its product).

Nietzsche, an ardent admirer and kindred spirit, described Emerson as 'one who instinctively nourishes himself on ambrosia leaving behind what is indigestible in things'. To Emerson, evil is certainly much less real than goodness. Many of his contemporaries regarded transcendentalism as out of touch with the pressing realities and unprecedented social change of the aggressively materialistic Gilded Age (1870–90), when the Transcendentalist view of nature was replaced by that of the entrepreneur and the industrialist. Emerson's ideas of self-reliance, instead of being the means to spiritual freedom and self-realization, were turned into the rationale for a rugged, exploitative individualism. If Emerson led 'the party of hope' in American intellectual life, the critics of Transcendentalist optimism, the representatives of the so-called 'party of despair', such as Melville and Hawthorne, emphasized in their fiction the demonic potential of the individual. In doing so, they were more in tune with the sceptical modern temperament, which was usually more convinced of man's capacity for evil and destruction than of his basic goodness.

## Henry David Thoreau: *Walden* ((1854)1962)

Towards the end of *Walden* Thoreau issues the following ringing exhortation to his readers:

> Be a Columbus to whole new continents and worlds within you, opening new channels, not of trade, but of thought. Every man is the lord of a realm beside which the earthly empire of the Czar is but a petty state, a hummock left by the ice. (Ch. 18, p. 227)

*Walden* is an account of the narrator's own pioneering adventures, both physical and spiritual, which he offers as an example to his readers. *Walden* is not simply about withdrawing from society and returning to nature, but it is about a journey of self-discovery in which there can never be any final destination, only the endless process of the quest. This quest is for the transcendental, the divine spirit in the common world of nature. Thoreau knows that he is chasing the unattainable, as the enigmatic fable of the hound, the bay horse and the turtle-dove which he tells in the 'Economy' chapter (p. 24) would imply. Nevertheless, the book has a fundamentally optimistic tone: 'if one advances confidently in the direction of his dreams ... he will meet with a success unexpected in common hours. He will put some things behind, will pass an invisible boundary.' To cross this 'invisible boundary' and pass from the world of nature into the realm of spirit, the narrator emphasizes the need to relax our hold on reason: 'Not till we are lost, in other words not till we have lost the world, do we begin to find ourselves, and realize where we are and the infinite extent of our relations' (p. 228).

In the search for transcendence, Thoreau never denies the sensuous life. His writing is always appreciative of the intense and varied experience of all the senses. He wants to 'live deep and suck out all the marrow of life'; he reminds us that 'heaven is under our feet as well as over our heads'.

> I found in myself, and still find, an instinct toward a higher, or, as it is named, spiritual life, as do most men, and another toward a primitive rank and savage one, and I reverence them both. I love the wild not less than the good. (Ch. 11, p. 154)

The book is not just a loose series of anecdotes and meditations, but a coherent, developing narrative which dramatizes an intense dialectical movement towards an integrated life. The 'I' is a fictional construct, Thoreau's ideal self, involved in the struggle to reconcile the higher and lower laws of his nature, civilization and nature, society and self, the modern technological world and his pastoral ideal. Complex systems of related images and motifs amplify the central theme, giving the book its richly textured fabric, its intricate symbolic structure and organic unity. Consider, for example, the way the narrator's development is related to natural process, the seasonal and diurnal cycles, to ideas of rebirth, renewal, building, purifying, metamorphosis. Simple, practical activities such as housebuilding, baking, fishing, walking in the snow, are described realistically, but with a poetic intensity that captures the magic of the ordinary. Realism continually presses towards Romance, towards the poetic, the numinous and the legendary.

When the narrator moves back to society he is a different person. The distance he has travelled may be measured by comparing an early passage about the narrator's life in Concord with some later passages describing life by Walden Pond. In the first chapter the style of writing is in keeping with the narrator's state of mind. It is staccato and bombastic, a language of dogmatic pronouncement, self-righteous zeal and comprehensive criticism of the people of Concord: 'Who made them serfs of the soil?'; 'It is very evident what mean and sneaking lives many of you live' (pp. 16–18). There is no feeling for or understanding of other people. The narrator is the angry young man embittered with a society which he feels has not fully appreciated his talents. Turn now to the account of an early episode in his life by Walden Pond:

> I sat in my sunny doorway from sunrise till noon, rapt in a revery, amidst the pines and hickories and sumachs, in undisturbed solitude and stillness, while the birds sang around or flitted noiseless through the house, until by the sun falling in at my west window, or the noise of some travelers' wagon on the distant highway, I was reminded of the lapse of time. I grew in those seasons like corn in the night ... (Ch. 4, p. 88)

Here, the style is quiet and serene. The language does not draw attention to itself. The controlling structure is coordinate rather than subordinate, a listing of things as they occur to the eye or the mind. A subordinate structure would have suggested a more active play of mind, but here the movement is leisurely, receptive, open, relaxed. One long trailing sentence covers the events of the whole day. The narrator, having freed himself from routine responsibilities, drifts into a world outside time and sense. He merges with nature's processes. The boundary between subject and object dissolves.

The central image of the fusion of the natural and the spiritual is the pond, which is 'the earth's eye' and a symbol of the unconscious self in which man sees the divine within him.

> In such a day, in September or October, Walden is a perfect forest mirror, set round with stones as precious to my eye as if fewer or rarer. Nothing so fair, so pure, and at the same time so large, as a lake, perchance, lies on the surface of the earth. Sky water. It needs no fence. (Ch. 9, p. 140)

Starting from a specific point in place and time, Thoreau pushes toward an unbounded revelation of perfect happiness. The poetic language, with its repetitions, alliterations and singing rhythms reflects heaven not life. The pond is an image of both freedom ('it needs no fence') and containment ('set round with stones'). Normal sentence structure is replaced by a direct imagistic expression which loosens the conventional grammatical rules and logical controls: the writing emphasizes fluidity – sky merges with water, the natural with the divine. The expression 'sky water' might put one in mind of an Indian name, and aptly so for Thoreau is describing a kind of primitive nature magic. This magic of reflection, this breaking down of the usual categories of experience, signifies a kind of visionary, even hallucinatory, intensity, an order of perception rooted in but going beyond normal seeing. The ordinary conceptual structure of the world is deranged and different orders of being flow in on one another. The liquefaction of set limits engenders a Wordsworthian sense of the mysterious unity of Being.

Thoreau wants a kind of writing that is substantial, physical, muscular, urgent, rooted in the earth, capable of confronting 'the essential facts'. But he also wants to give facts a halo of suggestion. He is interested, not in offering a mere autobiographical or naturalistic account of what happened at Walden Pond, but in giving us the experience of transcendence. Look closely at the 'Conclusion', where he describes the kind of language he wants: 'The words which express our faith and piety are not definite, yet they are significant and fragrant like frankincense to superior natures'. The biblical language indicates his fundamentally religious purpose. His ideal language is a language of adoration. Like the fragrance of the frankincense it will combine a strong sensuous appeal with an infinite subtlety and suggestiveness. He fears lest his expression may not be '*extra-vagant*' enough, may not sufficiently exceed the usual bounds. His language may not be as extravagant as that of Whitman's rhapsodies or William Burroughs's hallucinations, but, as Thoreau says, 'it depends how you are yarded. The migrating buffalo which seeks new pastures in another latitude, is not extravagant like the cow which kicks over the pail, leaps the cowyard fence, and runs after her calf, in milking time'. The activity in the farmyard may be just as extravagant as that in the wilderness. Thoreau wants to escape from a utilitarian language to a 'volatile' one.

Thoreau's theme of self-renewal through withdrawal from society to sacred nature contrasts sharply with Melville and Hawthorne's emphasis on the dangers of a rebellious and uncompromising individualism. It also contrasts with Huck Finn's lighting out for the wilderness, in that Huck's is an act of moral self-preservation to escape the corrupting pressures of civilization, while Thoreau aspires to a transcendent unification and fulfilment of the self. The recovery of a revitalized and unified self (which is not available to the radically dissociated Huck Finn) allows Thoreau to return to society (albeit as 'sojourner') at the end of the book.

*Walden* bears clear evidence of Thoreau's close association with Transcendentalist thinking. In 1841 he went to live with the Emerson family, working for them as a handyman and helping to edit the Transcendentalist journal *The Dial* (1841–3). It was on Emerson's land that he built his hut by Walden Pond in 1845. Like Emerson, he affirms the limitless possibilities and worth of the self, and seeks communion with the soul or spirit that circulates through nature and all creation. Like Emerson, he urges recognition of the mythologic and fabulous character of the world, and recommends the adoption of an innocent childlike view of things that is to be found in the work of many succeeding American writers from Whitman and Twain to Hemingway and Salinger. But while sharing Emerson's belief in man's ability to realize his divine potential, Thoreau is much more firmly grounded in the sensuous world. *Walden* represents a kind of applied Emersonianism in which Thoreau not only translates Emerson's ideas into the practical life of the frontiersman but evolves a new, distinctively Transcendental language (a project taken much further by Whitman) to *enact* the kind of experience which Emerson tends to treat in a more intellectual and theoretical fashion. It is arguable that the author of *Walden* is a poet before he is a naturalist, teacher, economist, social philosopher, autobiographer or anarchist.

Nathanial Hawthorne: *The Scarlet Letter* ((1850) 1970)

Here is the first picture Hawthorne gives us of his heroine, Hester Prynne, the scarlet woman:

> The door of the jail being flung open from within, there appeared, in the first place, like a black shadow emerging into the sunshine, the grim and grisly presence of the town-beadle, with a sword by his side and his staff of office in his hand. This personage prefigured and represented in his aspect the whole dismal severity of the Puritanic code of law, which it was his business to administer in its final and closest application to the offender. Stretching forth the official staff in his left hand, he laid his right upon the shoulder of a young woman, whom he thus drew forward; until, on the threshhold of the prison-door, she repelled him, by an action marked by natural dignity and force of character, and stepped into the open air, as if by her own free will. She bore in her arms a child ... she took the baby on her arm, and, with a burning blush and yet a haughty smile, and a glance that would not be abashed, looked around at her townspeople and neighbours. On the breast of her gown, in fine red cloth, surrounded with an elaborate embroidery and fantastic flourishes of gold thread, appeared the letter A. (Ch. 2, p. 80)

You will notice the contrast between the 'dismal severity' of Puritan patriarchal authority and the 'natural dignity' of Hester. The town-beadle, with his phallic sword and staff of office, is an oppressive figure, associated with claustration and darkness; Hester, with her baby in her arms, later reminds the narrator of the madonna and child, and is associated with light and the open air. The two figures of town-beadle and adulterous woman represent the opposition of civil law and natural law (allied with divine law). Hester's first action of 'repelling' the town-beadle is an act of defiant independence. Refusing to be 'abashed' about her sin, she flaunts baby and scarlet letter in front of the Puritan fathers. Her embroidery, we are told, was 'so artistically done, and with so much fertility and gorgeous luxuriance of fancy' that it went 'greatly beyond what was allowed'. Proclaiming her femininity and her artistic nature which the Puritans would try to suppress, she transcends the expectations of the onlookers. They expect her to be 'obscured by a disastrous cloud' and are astonished 'to perceive how her beauty shone out, and made a halo of the misfortune and ignominy in which she was enveloped'. She is a figure of the artist, capable of redefining the 'A', the simple, single identity of Adulterer which the Puritan patriarchy has fixed upon her.

Now turn to Chapter 5, 'Hester at Her Needle', where we read this:

> It might be, too, – doubtless it was so, although she hid the secret from herself, and grew pale whenever it struggled out of her heart, like a serpent from its hole, – it might be that another feeling kept her within the scene and pathway that had been so fatal. There dwelt, there trod the feet of one with whom she deemed herself connected in a union, that, unrecognized on earth, would bring them together before the bar of final judgement, and make that their marriage-altar, for a joint futurity of endless retribution. (Ch. 5, p. 105)

The important thing about this passage is that it explicitly takes the form of interpretation and conjecture rather than definitive statement. The narrator refuses a traditional omniscient role. In trying to account for Hester's remaining among a community which has dealt so severely with her, he raises the spectre of demonic possession, speculating fearfully that at some deep level of her being she entertains the shocking, blasphemous hope that she will be reunited with her lover forever in hell. However, in the very same paragraph, he considers other reasons – more acceptable to both society and Hester's own conscious mind, reasons which imply Christian penitence and redemption:

> Here, she said to herself, had been the scene of her guilt, and here should be the scene of her earthly punishment; and so, perchance, the torture of her daily shame would at length purge her soul, and work out another purity than that which she had lost; more saint-like, because the result of martyrdom.

Hawthorne portrays Hester as a profoundly ambiguous character, torn between unconscious desire and conscious rationalization.

Chapter 13, 'Another View of Hester' (the title emphasizing the multifaceted-ness of her character), gives us a view of her dangerous intellectual independence and rebelliousness:

> The same dark question often rose in her mind, with reference to the whole race of womanhood. Was existence worth accepting? ... As a first step, the whole system of society is to be torn down, and built up anew ... before woman can be allowed to assume what seems a fair and suitable position. (Ch. 13, p. 184)

This is the Hester who has been embraced by feminists. If the scarlet letter pinned on her by the Puritan fathers was intended to make her subservient, it 'had not done its office'. Hawthorne is capable of great sympathy with the feminine but he refuses to push Hester into becoming an outright rebel. He immediately undercuts the value of her revolutionary thinking: 'A woman never overcomes these problems by any exercise of thought.' Her heart, we are told, 'had lost its regular and healthy throb, wandered without a clew in the dark labyrinth of mind'. Forced to suppress her femininity and sexuality, and retreating from the role of 'prophetess' of 'a new truth', she is returned at the end to an unthreatening posture of nurturing Mother and community worker, content with her isolation and marginal status.

Hawthorne emphasizes the complexity of motive, the fundamental mystery of human nature. Pearl is an even greater enigma than her mother, and defies all the attempts of the Puritans to find out her identity. Of her ultimate destiny we are told 'None knew – nor ever learned, with the fullness of perfect certainty' (p. 273). Dimmesdale, the holy sinner, is another paradoxical figure. Even Chillingworth, the arch-fiend, is in the end Pearl's most generous benefactor, the one who prompts the narrator to wonder 'whether hatred and love be not the same thing at bottom'. Resisting simple moral categorization, Hawthorne refuses to reduce complex reality into a convenient opposition between absolute terms of good and evil. He follows the Puritans in seeing 'some deep meaning behind the phenomenon of the physical world', but what that 'deep meaning' might be is intensely problematical. Eschewing the Godlike role, he exchanges the fixed one-to-one correspondences of allegory for the constantly shifting significations of symbolism. Take the book's central symbol, the scarlet letter. Hawthorne evokes possible meanings for it but never imposes any single meaning upon it. The letter constantly changes its appearance and signification. A is for 'Adulterer', but the townspeople come to wonder if it should not be for 'Angel' or 'Able' so impressed are they with Hester's strength and kindness. We might also think of A for 'America' and Hawthorne's narrative as the story of the creation of an American national identity. Or we might think of A for 'Alpha' and *The Scarlet Letter* as an epistemological quest novel exploring the source and grounds of meaning. Similarly, the narrator offers a whole range of possible interpretations of the meteor which may or may not have formed 'a great red letter in the sky' on the night of Governor Winthrop's death (Chapter 12, 'The Minister's Vigil'), and of the 'scarlet letter' which may or may not have been imprinted on the dying Dimmesdale's breast (Chapter 24, 'Conclusion'), but no authoritative account of these things is given. Meaning is disconcertingly destabilized and we are forced to decide for ourselves what to believe. The forest is the place where nature, in sympathy with the lovers, releases them from guilt and shame and, in a flood of sunshine, gives them its blessing: but it is nevertheless 'the untamed forest', associated with lawless libidinal energy, the place where Indians roam and the witch, Mistress Hibbins, meets the Black Man. Hawthorne deals in ambiguous symbols rather than straightforward statements, and preserves to the end a moral disinterestedness, a detachment from the life he writes about, a kind of complex seeing.

Refusing to assert meaning in an authoritarian, dogmatic or final manner, Hawthorne challenges both Puritan and Transcendentalist certainties. For all his criticisms of Puritanism he still inserts his heroine safely and uncomplainingly within the Puritan community at the end and enforces Dimmesdale's conformity by having him repent. Equally, he qualifies Transcendentalist notions of self-reliance in emphasizing the dangers as well as the virtues of Hester's individualism, contradicts the Wordsworthian and Emersonian idolization of the child of nature in his characterization of Pearl as 'demon offspring', and questions the transcendentalists' optimistic construction of human nature in his presentation of Chillingworth. The opening 'Customs-House' chapter establishes a narrator who, very much a product of his Puritan heritage, acknowledges that his Puritan forefathers would never have approved of his artistic pursuits. As if to allay his own guilt and anxiety about engaging in storytelling, he stresses the factual basis of his story ('the main facts ... are authorized and authenticated by the document of Mr. Surveyor Pue', p. 63). But, simultaneously, he is driven by an irresistible urge to embellish and interpret the bare facts ('I have allowed myself ... nearly or altogether as much license as if the facts had been entirely of my own invention', p. 63). His guilt about his transgressive activity may be seen to be projected into the characterization of the guilt-ridden Dimmesdale who also has broken the Puritan code and has as much difficulty admitting that Pearl is his child as the narrator has admitting that the narrative is his invention. Equally, the narrator's defiant artistic side may be seen to be projected into the characterization of Hester, for just as the narrator sets about 'dressing up the tale' (p. 63) he has found, so Hester takes the scarlet letter and makes of it a gorgeous embroidery. The 'Customs-House' section may thus be seen as an organic part of the novel as a whole, introducing the central tensions between the Actual and the Imaginary, Puritan authority and free imagination, realism and romance which inform the main narrative.

New historicist approaches to *The Scarlet Letter* provide enlightening insights into the novel as a product of the dominant ideology of nineteenth-century America. Both the period in which the novel is set (1642–9), and the period during which Hawthorne actually wrote it (1848–52) were periods of intense social upheaval. The former spans the years of the English Civil War in England, the second the time leading up to the Civil War in America. Though set 250 years earlier than the time of writing, the novel reflects many of Hawthorne's present fears – about the dangers of abolitionist agitation, the rise of feminism and Communism, and the spread of revolutionary activity from Europe. 1848 was the 'Year of the Red Scare', Chartist unrest in England, the first Paris Commune and the publication of *The Communist Manifesto*. Hawthorne makes frequent reference to revolutionary Europe. There are allusions to scaffold and guillotine. 1848 also saw the defeat of the Whigs by the Democrats in America, a political upheaval which impinged directly on Hawthorne's own career in that it brought to an end his tenure as surveyor in the Salem customs-house. In 'The Customs-House' he links the Whig victory and his own loss of office with the revolutionary terror in France. 'My own head,' he says, 'was the first that fell'. His fear of revolutionary upheaval finds expression in the novel's deeply conservative subtext.

## Herman Melville: *Moby-Dick* ((1851) 1972)

*Moby-Dick* is the story of an old sea captain, maddened by the loss of his leg, chasing a white whale around the world to wreak his revenge on it. Stated like that, Ahab's obsession sounds absurd. In effect, the language that is used turns Captain Ahab into a larger-than-life figure, and his quest into a metaphysical desire, a rage to know, to surpass the normal human bounds:

> If man will strike, strike through the mask! How can the prisoner reach outside except by thrusting through the wall? To me, the white whale is that wall, shoved near to me. Sometimes I think there's naught beyond. But 'tis enough. He tasks me; he heaps me; I see in him outrageous strength, with an inscrutable malice showing it. That inscrutable thing is chiefly what I hate; and be the white whale agent, or be the white whale principal, I will wreak that hate upon him. Talk not to me of blasphemy, man; I'd strike the sun if it insulted me. (Ch. 36, p. 262)

The style of Ahab's speech immediately forces us to abandon realistic expectations for those of tragedy or epic. We are reminded of Shakespeare's tragic heroes, particularly Lear on the heath. There are echoes of Perseus the heroic slayer of the Gorgon, of Milton's Satan, of Faust and of Prometheus the fire-stealer. The violence of Ahab's language reveals a monstrous egoism driving him to destroy the world and swallow it up in self. Nothing will distract him from his quest. He exerts an 'irresistible dictatorship' over the crew. He claims he is fated to the pursuit ('I am the Fate's lieutenant'), though Melville insists that he has alternative courses of action. Others attempt to persuade him to desist from the chase, but Ahab cannot recognize the 'other'. His is a story of the unregenerate will, and the wages of his colossal pride is death. He suffers, but unlike Hester Prynne, he is not purified by suffering. He is never delivered from the evil forces that control him. Where Emerson and Thoreau stressed the virtue of self-reliance, Melville offers a tragic image of the alienation that results from self-dependence in its extreme forms. Melville's themes are solipsism, imprisonment within the self, the terrifying consequences of an individual's separation from his fellow beings. Ahab exemplifies a ruinous individualism.

For Melville, as for Emerson and indeed the early Puritans in general, the world was a text in which God's will and purpose could be read. 'Particular natural facts', Emerson wrote in his essay 'Nature', 'are symbols of particular spiritual facts' (Ziff, 1982, p. 48), an idea that is echoed in Ahab's cry: 'O Nature, and O soul of man! how far beyond all utterance are your linked analogies!' (p.418). However, Ahab differs from the Transcendentalists in interpreting the idea or spirit circulating in and through the natural world as evil. He identifies the whale not only with his bodily woes but also with all his 'intellectual and spiritual exasperations' (p. 283). Ahab's sin is to think that the white whale means one thing only, and that he can harpoon the whale, pin down its elusive mystery. But the white whale, like the painting in the Spouter Inn (Chapter 3), or the doubloon (Chapter 99) means different things to different people: 'There's another rendering now; but still one text. All kinds of men in one kind of world, you see' (p. 545). Moby-Dick is a book about seeing and interpreting. In contrast to Ahab, the narrator, Ishmael, represents another kind of seeing, another set of values, a more healthy and balanced attitude to life. Right from the start, Ishmael nails his colours to the mast and tells us there is no point in looking for absolute meanings in life. The image that continually swims before us, he says, 'is the image of the ungraspable phantom of life'. He acknowledges the inscrutable otherness of nature. Chapter 52, 'The Albatross', for example, ends with his recognition of human limits: 'But in pursuit of those far mysteries we dream of, or in tormented chase of that demon phantom that, some time or other, swims before all human hearts; while chasing such over this round globe, they either lead us on in barren mazes or mid-way leave us whelmed' (p. 340). He says he has both doubts and intuitions: 'Doubts of all things earthly, and intuitions of some things heavenly; this combination makes neither believer nor infidel, but makes a man who regards them both with equal eye' (p. 482). The difference between the monomaniac captain and the speculative harpooner is that Ishmael can live with doubt. The man is doomed who cannot do so.

Ahab pays the price for his hubris in thinking that he can possess a totality of meaning. Melville formally refutes such a Promethean impulse by having the narrator disclaim finality or completion for his story. The whole book, Ishmael says, 'is but a draught – nay, but the draught of a draught' (p. 241). For Ishmael, life is 'ungraspable'; he promises 'nothing complete because any human thing supposed to be complete, must for that very reason infallibly be faulty'; the whale 'lives not complete in any literature ... his is an unwritten life' (p. 229). The novel resists absolute meanings. The book opens with a chapter on 'Etymology', suggesting that whatever the whale may mean depends on the words we use. The next section,

'Extracts', reviews popular 'knowledge' and myth about the whale, but the speaker (we cannot be sure if it is Melville or Ishmael) warns us against taking these extracts 'for veritable gospel cetology. Far from it'. The whole book evinces an extreme self-consciousness about its linguistic and formal procedures. Melville absorbs all previous literatures on whaling, he approaches his subject from a great many different angles, on many different levels, using a wide variety of styles, including epic, drama, journalistic reportage, naturalistic narrative, technical manual, sermon. This stylistic restlessness is symptomatic of the struggle to define what continually eludes the net of language. 'There is no quality in this world', says the narrator, 'that is not what it is merely by contrast. Nothing exists in itself' (p. 148). Not surprisingly pun and paradox are dominant compositional principles. The white whale is both beautiful and terrible, infernal and heavenly, benign and malevolent. Its whiteness is a 'colorless all-color' (p. 296), signifying death and corruption, but also 'divine spotlessness'. Similarly, a coffin is a canoe, a sea chest, an art object and ultimately a lifebuoy. Queequeg's tomahawk is both vicious weapon and peace-pipe. Queequeg sells human heads but is the one who teaches Ishmael love and contentment. Melville asks us continually to respond to the contradictoriness of things. He refuses omniscience: what we have is merely Ishmael's point of view. Melville even breaks his own rules: there are times in any story when third-person narration would be useful, and Melville is soon experimenting with ways to let voices other than Ishmael's be heard – including that of the omniscient author, but also that of Father Mapple in Chapter 9, 'The Sermon' and later that of Captain Ahab. In Chapter 34, 'The Cabin-Table', the third person takes over, giving information that Ishmael could not have heard. Chapter 44, 'The Chart', begins: 'Had you followed Captain Ahab into his cabin ... you would have seen ...'. But no one did. How does Ishmael know what is going on? He doesn't; he assumes the persona of the third-person narrator.The title of the chapter, 'Surmises' candidly proclaims its status as conjecture. But in other places there is not even lip-service paid to the notion of an intelligent guess, as when we are given Ahab's reaction in 'The Dying Whale': 'that strange spectacle ... to Ahab conveyed a wondrousness unknown before' (p. 606). In a daring move, Melville several times does away with the narrator altogether, presenting certain chapters as stage scripts, complete with directions: see Chapters 121 and 122. The narrative preoccupations of the book also leap about wildly. Much of the first part of the book is concerned with the newly blossoming friendship between Ishmael and Queequeg; later on, Queequeg has only a little more narrative time spent on him than the other two savages. In Chapter 3, the character of Bulkington is introduced in a way that hints he will become important later in the book. But Melville unexpectedly buries him in a 'six-inch' grave in Chapter 23.

*Moby-Dick* is a novel with a double focus. It expresses Melville's admiration of Ahab's nobility of spirit, his tragic grandeur, his enormous vitality and romantic charisma. In a typical paradox, Ahab is that 'grand, ungodly, god-like man': his strength of mind and will exalts him above common mortals. But if his quest is heroic, it is also demonic for Ahab's *idée fixe* carries him and his crew to their doom. Melville recognizes the dangers of Ahab's single-minded purpose and acknowledges the force of Ishmael's complex seeing. In a hectic passage he attempts to give

Ishmael's hymn of praise to Emersonian man and the democratic ideal a suitably elevated expression to match Ahab's spiritual glamour:

> But this august dignity I treat of, is not the dignity of kings and robes, but that abounding dignity which has no robed investiture. Thou shalt see it shining in the arm that wields a pick or drives a spike; that democratic dignity which, on all hands, radiates without end from God; Himself! The great God Absolute! The centre and circumference of all democracy! His omnipresence, our divine equality! (Ch. 26, p. 212)

In contrast to Ahab's commanding presence, Ishmael is on the whole an insignificant figure, longing for brotherhood (see Chapter 94, 'A Squeeze of the Hand') and given to pantheistic reverie (see Chapter 35, 'The Mast-Head') as an escape from isolation. His voice is continually under threat of being suppressed or marginalized or taken over; he finds it difficult to sustain his faith in 'our divine equality' ('take mankind in the mass', he says, 'and for the most part, they seem a mob of unnecessary duplicates'). Neither Ahab, with his insane pride and limitless self-assertion, nor Ishmael, the lost lonely orphan, is a complete man. Perhaps that is Bulkington, but he cannot survive in the real world. The novel takes its life from this central tension between romantic individualism and democratic conformism that is characteristic of so much American literature.

*Moby-Dick* was written at a time of unprecedented expansion of American land, wealth and power. Melville offers a maritime version of the popular pioneering tale in a work that also responds to the contemporary Transcendentalist call to 'be a Columbus to whole new continents and worlds within you' (Thoreau, 1962, p. 227). His novel reflects his faith in the literary potential of a distinctively American experience in which the writer could find his theme in nature if not in culture, as his European counterparts had done. It shows the influence of his readings not only in Shakespeare, Emerson, Shelley's 'Prometheus Unbound' and Carlyle's *Sartor Resartus*, but also in mariners' narratives of shipwreck and distant voyagings, and in works of natural history. But like most of Melville's fiction, the germ of *Moby-Dick* lay in personal experience, specifically his sea-adventures aboard the whaler 'Acushnet' (1841–2).

In the 1850s he turned to story-writing for magazines (selected in 1856 as *Piazza Tales*) in which he continues to present us with puzzles (in *Moby-Dick* it was the white whale, in 'Benito Cereno' it is the eerie slave-ship, in 'Bartleby, the Scrivener' the enigma of the white-faced copyist), and to disrupt a complacent American optimism (represented by the lawyer in 'Bartleby', by Captain Delano in 'Benito Cereno') with disturbingly complex, darkly ironic situations. In *The Confidence-Man* (1857) he satirizes Emerson and Thoreau, and in the unfinished, posthumously published *Billy Budd* ponders the inextricable connection of good and evil. With his emphasis on point of view and the relativity and fictionality of truth, his suggestion of life's absurdity in a godless universe (the 'naught beyond'), his dispensing with plot and rational procedure, his disruptions of naturalism and his general stylistic restlessness, Melville is an important precursor of the twentieth-century modernist experiment.

## Walt Whitman: *Poems* ((1855–91) Hall, 1968)

Whitman's central achievement was *Leaves of Grass* which began in 1855 as a small, anonymous collection of twelve poems including 'Song of Myself' and was subsequently expanded and revised throughout his life. Altogether, there were nine editions produced, culminating in the famous 'death-bed' edition of 1891–2. For Whitman life was continual process, and poetry should enact process. Hence, the notable open-endedness of his work, its refusal of completion and closure.

Look at Section V of his long poem 'Song of Myself'. You are probably first struck by the rhapsodic style and bold sensuousness of these lines. This is something different from the controlled, subtly wrought lyricism prized by the New Critics. Whitman himself spoke of his 'barbaric yawp' (p. 62). Eschewing the confinements of traditional structure, he sought a new freedom and fluidity of expression. In the free, rolling rhythms of the verse, he calls for a 'loafing' and a 'loosing', a relaxing or freeing of the self from routine responsibilities, from rationality and from language itself, as a prelude to experiencing a mystic oneness. The sound he wants is not that of the articulate individual but the primitive, 'valved voice', the undifferentiated 'lull' and 'hum' of the pre-literate, aboriginal pulse of life. Reacting against the Puritan repression of the body, he sings the union of body and soul and all creation. The addressee in the first two lines is 'my soul', but this flows into the figure of a remembered lover, enacting the fusion of the spiritual and the physical. Kissing merges with sexual penetration which merges with a spiritual ravishment which merges with a general physical embrace. Sex is sacred. It is the revelation of God, inducing the biblical 'peace that passeth all understanding'. There are other mergings:

> And I know that the hand of God is the promise of my own,
> And I know that the spirit of God is the brother of my own,
> And that all the men ever born are also my brothers, and the women my sisters and lovers,
> And that a kelson of the creation is love,
> And limitless are leaves stiff or drooping in the fields,
> And brown ants in the little wells beneath them,
> And mossy scabs of the worm fence, heap'd stones, elder, mullein and poke-weed.
>
> (pp. 26–7)

Those lines all beginning with 'And' start out as a list of things the poet 'knows'. However, the 'I know' construction is dropped after the first two lines, the controlling 'I' of the main clause loses force, and the objects of the poet's knowing take on a primary actuality of their own. Perceiver merges in perceived, subject in object, the poet in his world. The list itself has no hierarchical structure and so also enacts a mergence of 'high' and 'low', human and natural.

The poetry is a sustained attempt to break down conventional categories of experience, to transcend the anxieties and divisions of the time. He sets up a dialectical relationship between self and world, identifying the 'I' with the 'en-masse' and asserting that only through mergence of self and other can personal fulfilment be found. There is no conflict between the two. Celebrating the transcendent unity of all creation, he abolishes the gap between poet and reader, and erases the distinctions between past, present and future. The sacred and the profane flow into each other, male into female, to produce a poetic persona that is an image of the unified man, multiple, open, androgynous, optimistic. This is the prelapsarian Whitman, an American Adam, spokesman of the American Dream. He assumes both a ready intimacy with the reader and the wisdom and authority of the seer. He shares Emerson's notion of the transcendental self, but for Whitman selfhood is firmly rooted in the social and material world, which is an emphatically American world. Where Emerson and Thoreau retreated from society to experience the full potential of the self, Whitman eagerly identifies with hounded slave, lonely woman, bridegroom, trapper, bereaved wife, 'cotton-field drudge', 'cleaner of privies', mutineer, convict, 'mash'd fireman', 'old artillerist'. He is both 'old and young', 'wise and foolish', cheerfully accepting contradiction as Emerson had done. Whitman's is therefore a shifting, elusive, restless self, often affirming highly incongruous, wittily far-fetched identifications. Continually putting on different masks, he is, as he says, 'both in and out of the game and watching and wondering at it' (p. 26).

'Song of Myself' exemplifies an unquestioning faith in the power of the creative imagination to bring about a new world. Whitman seeks to bring us into his poem to share his enthusiasms and visions. To do this he develops an idiosyncratic form of 'free verse' that follows no strict rational procedure. With his rhapsodic, celebratory and declamatory style, he seeks to conjure unity out of tension and division. The poem expresses struggle, the attempt to affirm harmonious relationship. As Donald Hall observes, 'the seen world hardly exists for him, because he spiritualizes everything. He is the ultimate poet of dream' (p. 7). Insisting that its purpose is to help us to re-invent our own lives, Whitman echoes Emerson's and Thoreau's concern that we should see the poem, not as completed art-object, but as the spur to our own creativity: 'You shall no longer take things at second or third hand .../ You shall not look through my eye either, nor take things from me,/ You shall listen to all sides and filter them for yourself' (p. 24).

The dream is not always easy to keep alive, and Whitman often finds it hard to sustain the celebratory or prophetic role. Thus, in 'Years of the Modern' he admits confusion and doubt about the future; in 'I Sit and Look Out' he finds himself reduced to silence by the sorrows of the world; while in 'A Lonely Patient Spider' he confronts a lonely vastness which he must somehow try to bridge. His best poems – 'When Lilacs Last Round the Dooryard Bloom'd' (an elegy on the death of President Lincoln, Whitman's ideal democratic man) or 'Out of the Cradle Endlessly Rocking' – are produced at that juncture where the ideal and the real, love and death, song and suffering are held in close and creative relationship. Whitman's verse is a direct response to Emerson's call for a great American epic that would celebrate the distinctive qualities of American life and culture, and help give Americans a clearer sense of their identity. He may thus be seen to continue the preoccupation with the meaning of being an American which has been a central theme of the American literary tradition from the days of the early Puritans (see, for example, Cotton Mather's *Magnalia Christi Americana* (1702), the first major

American epic). Where the traditional epic celebrated the legends and memories of the past and the feats of ancient heroes – Achilles, Ulysses, Aeneas, Roland, El Cid – Whitman focuses on the ordinary democratic man, the poet himself who creates himself in the writing of the poem and who identifies with the nation, with all mankind, and ultimately with God himself. In celebrating the democratic life, Whitman embraces all aspects of his world. Even the material and technological advances of his time were compatible with the spiritual life. In 'Passage to India', the building of the transcontinental railroad and Suez Canal and the laying of the Atlantic Cable are considered as the material expression of a spiritual quest for transcendental union. The poem is, we might say, Whitman's statement of faith in man's ability to emulate the wondrous bridge-work of the noiseless, patient spider. But he also warned against regarding 'wealth, science, materialism – even the democracy of which we make so much' as ends in themselves.

'I was simmering, simmering, simmering; Emerson brought me to a boil' (Trowbridge, 1903, p. 367), Whitman said. Like Emerson, and in very similar language, Whitman urges passionate acceptance of the miracle of the ordinary, a renewal of our capacity for wonder. Emerson's democratic listings, his non-hierarchical syntax, the apparent withdrawal of the mediating consciousness – these are also staple features of Whitman's verse, which eminently fulfils Emerson's call for a poetic that would be open-ended, provisional, multiform and celebratory. Asserting an Emersonian self-reliance, Whitman demonstrates in practical form Emerson's view that 'it is not metres, but a metre-making argument, that makes a poem' (Ziff, 1982, pp. 263–4). The great poet, Whitman declared in his 1855 Preface to *Leaves of Grass*, spoke with an utterly individual and distinctive voice, unconstrained by 'custom or precedent or authority'. He thought of poetry as music or oratory or 'song', and often structured his verse operatically, adapting such features as aria and recitative. Going beyond mere realism, he sought an expression that would be 'transcendent and new' (McQuade *et al.*, 1987, p. 2438). He was the precursor of the great modernist experimentalists, the line of American poets coming down through William Carlos Williams, the Objectivists, Charles Olson, Alan Ginsberg and the Beats.

## Emily Dickinson: *Poems* (1858–84; Reeves, 1959)

A poem such as 'It Might Be Lonelier' gives us a strong impression of the distinctive qualities of Emily Dickinson's poetic world. It is a world of loneliness, it is devoid of 'hope', a world of 'suffering' and failure. Paradoxically, however, these qualities are all invested with positive value. The speaker argues that they are her very reason for living and are much preferable to any conventional kind of 'peace' or 'delight'. Words such as 'sacrament', 'blaspheme' and 'ordained' give loneliness a religious force. The ecclesiastical language may perhaps be intended to relate particularly to the Reverend Charles Wadsworth who, it has been suggested, was the one great passion of Dickinson's life, and whose move from Philadelphia to San Francisco in 1832 left her feeling lonely and depressed.

Commonly, Dickinson treats the idea that to lose is somehow to gain, that desire is more intense than satisfaction, that renouncing something or failing to achieve it is to possess it the more: 'Success is counted sweetest/ By those who ne'er succeed' (p. 1). Suffering is empowering: 'A wounded deer leaps highest' (p. 10). Pain is the guarantor of authenticity: 'I like a look of agony/ Because I know it's true' (p. 18). It is in the presence of loss or death that life acquires new vividness and meaning. Death has a kind of estranging effect, promoting new seeing:

> The last night that she lived
> It was a common night
> Except the dying – this to us
> Made nature different.
>
> We noticed smallest things,
> Things overlooked before,
> By this great light upon our minds
> Italicised, as 'twere. (p. 84)

Despite her interest in death and suffering, Dickinson exhibits a lively responsiveness to the world around her. Read 'A Bird Came down the Walk', one of her best-known nature poems.

This poem gives a detailed, vivid picture of the bird. The first four stanzas, composed of short, sharp statements and simple, compact words, jump from one thing to another, reflecting the erratic movements of the bird. Each stanza runs into the next, giving the impression of the bird's continuous movement, never finishing anything it starts. The first two stanzas rhyme ('grass'/'pass', 'saw'/'raw') which helps create the image of a playful, cocky little creature and a cheerful, confident mood. The bird arouses contradictory ideas and feelings: the speaker's identification with the natural world (the bird is 'he', the worm a 'fellow') is checked by the distaste with which she views the bird's savage treatment of the worm. However, she goes on to emphasize the bird's delicacy in the way it drinks from 'a convenient grass' (an idealized image), and its courteousness and friendliness in letting the beetle pass. In the third stanza, we note the rhyme is dropped. The bird's playfulness and confidence give way to panic, for it is a creature both wild and timid, a representative of untamed nature. The fourth stanza, broken by commas, emphasizes the bird's jumpiness. In the fifth stanza, however, when it soars into the air, it is transformed into an image of gracefulness, serenity and majestic beauty. The bird was not in its natural element on earth as we sense in the disjointed, heavily stressed first fourteen lines, but once in flight a much more romantic vocabulary is employed. The repetition of 'And' in lines 16–17 ('And he unrolled his feathers/ And rowed him softer home') suggests relaxed, expansive movement, while the long open vowels work especially well as a foil to the narrow, jerky sounds in the first three stanzas. 'Rowed' describes the smooth, balanced, rhythmic motion of the bird's wings which, like oars, seem to cut the sky, but unlike oars leave no ripple or trace of their movement. The assonance in 'rowed' and 'home' emphasizes softness, placidity, an almost hypnotic movement. Setting up a complex equivalence of air and ocean, bird and butterfly and boat, the movement of the bird's wing and the movement of an oar, the poet suggests a profound oneness. Through these strange mergings of diverse elements we are given a sense of the unity of the created world, an intuition of 'seamlessness', in contrast to the earth-bound disjointedness described earlier. However, the speaker remains outside this mystic union. The personification of the bird suggests an attempt at identification between animal and human, but the poem ultimately acknowledges difference. The bird flies away on the approach of the human, who figures only as fascinated observer struggling for a language, especially in those strange last four lines, to describe the bird which proves increasingly elusive and alien. In the end it moves into another more ethereal dimension altogether, out of sight, out of consciousness, out of the poem, leaving the speaker earth-bound and wondering.

Compare 'A bird came down the walk' with another equally well-known Dickinson nature poem, 'A narrow fellow in the grass'. This poem is usually taken to be about a snake in the grass. There is, however, no explicit reference to a snake. The 'narrow fellow' appears for a moment, then as suddenly disappears, without ever being clearly identified. The poem is about an elusive something that is never named, that remains hidden, submerged, that never attains full presence, that paradoxically registers its presence as a disquieting absence.

But, first, consider the progression of the speaker's feelings with regard to this 'something' in the grass. The phrase, 'A narrow fellow', establishes a casual friend-liness, the use of the word 'narrow' alerting us to the speaker's highly individualistic way of seeing things. The atmosphere of relaxed chattiness is maintained in the direct address of line 3 ('You may have seen him – did you not?'), but the hard-sounding, heavily disrupted formulation of line 4 ('His notice sudden is') suggests the shocked stoppage of the normal flow of speech when the speaker catches his first glimpse of the snake. The second stanza relaxes again, the lines expanding and contracting like the movement of the snake in the grass. The speaker further attempts to detach himself from present anxiety by shifting to the past, but his recollection is one of vulnerability ('when a boy and barefoot'), of uncertainty and violence ('Have passed, I thought, a whiplash'), and of frustration ('When, stooping to secure it,/ It wrinkled and was gone'). Abruptly returning to the present, the penultimate stanza has a jaunty air. The speaker affirms an enthusiastically 'cordial' relationship with the natural world, which he attempts to humanize. However, the sense of harmony cannot be sustained. In the last stanza the 'narrow fellow' becomes the utterly and terrifyingly alien. From 'cordiality' we move to a climactic primeval sensation of horror, from jauntiness to 'lighter breathing/ And zero at the bone'.

The poem, then, may be interpreted as an exploration of the relation between the human and the natural, in which optimistic transcendentalist notions of harmony and divinity are complicated by the recognition that nature's beauty and attractiveness coexist with the demonic. Nature is both life-force and *memento mori*. The traditional biblical implications of the serpent in the garden are unavoidable, Dickinson's version of the Edenic myth pressing irresistibly towards acknowledge-ment of the reality of loss and death.

The sexual interpretation is equally unavoidable with the images of riding, opening and closing, going 'barefoot', 'whiplash', 'wrinkling', 'transport' and 'tighter breathing'. The snake is both attractive and frightening. The poem betrays a deep ambivalence about masculinity and patriarchal convention. Curiously, Dickinson adopts a male persona. A psychoanalytic reading might see this as a kind of female psychic defence mechanism against a sense of overwhelming threat posed by the phallic snake. Such a reading might then relate the experience of loss and absence which the poem describes to the female discovery of sexual difference, and see the poem as the expression of a Freudian 'castration complex' (Atkins and Morrow, 1989, pp. 158–80).

Finally, the poem might be interpreted as being about a metaphysical loss and absence. The 'narrow fellow' is continually disappearing, 'unbraiding in the sun' and leaves the speaker with a feeling of 'zero at the bone'. The poem, we might say, refuses a logocentre or, more specifically, a phallogocentre. It dramatizes a condition where one is left without firm focus or coherent system of meaning, whether that supplied by conventional Calvinism or Transcendentalism. The disorienting experience of finding oneself isolated, without faith or bearings or emotional or ideological support of any kind, is a recurrent theme in Dickinson's work. Compare, for example, 'There's a certain slant of light', which ends with a similar intuition of horror and despair. As in 'A narrow fellow', this poem powerfully expresses a sense of the inscrutable 'otherness' of nature. Emily shares Emerson's interest in experience unamenable to rational structure, the same sense of awe and wonderment. But where in Emerson the ordinary world dissolves into spirituality and the experience is one of flying, lightness and transparency, Dickinson dissolves into madness, nightmare, the dark night of the soul, 'zero at the bone'. Emerson's intuitions are pre-eminently those of potency and possibility, Dickinson's of death and cosmic emptiness. Emily refuses to idealize the self as the Transcendentalists did: she knows blankness and despair as well as 'transport' and joy. For her, the meaning of experience is always problematical.

Dickinson's poetry is notable for its intensity of focus and feeling, and for the integrity and originality of her perception and expression. The poetry often seems to be written out of crisis, its intensities contained in a controlled, elliptical, tense, almost breathless expression. Typically, her poems are compressed, oracular messages written in a kind of poetic telegraphese. They display a remarkable playfulness and riskiness, a love of ambiguity, extravagant metaphorical flourishes, disorienting synaesthetic effects, strained associations, Metaphysical wit. She is particularly noted for her unconventional punctuation and syntax, the use of dashes and capitalized abstractions which produces a highly disrupted, estranging effect, inhibiting any complacent sense of predictable, fixed or reliable meaning and relation. Moving back and forth between abstractions and sensual images, she attempts a reconciliation of two worlds, the seen and the unseen, body and soul, time and eternity.

Emily's life was lived largely within the confines of her traditional, Calvinistic, middle-class home in Amherst, and it is one of the great mysteries of American literature how so reclusive and sheltered an individual could write with such understanding and passion of love and death. We really do not have enough biographical information to know how far her love poems were inspired by a particular man, and how far they represent purely imaginary relationships. She gave a voice to secret passion, and to buried fears and desires. She found release within confinement, within brief, suggestive poems as within the narrow compass of her room and garden where her imagination could roam free. Though she said she saw 'New Englandly', her truth did not lie within the limited Puritanical nineteenth-century consciousness of New England. 'The soul selects her own society,/ Then shuts the door' (p. 25) she wrote, in a proud, arrogant declaration of independence from traditional values and beliefs. She rejects experience in favour of the inner drama of the self, but ends the poem with a grim recognition of the dangers of solipsism: 'I've known her from an ample nation/ Choose one,/ Then close the valves of her attention/ Like stone'.

In contrast to the public bardic voice ('A call in the midst of the crowd,/ My own voice, orotund, sweeping and final', Hall, p. 69) and the Emersonian role of the poet as prophet and 'liberating god' (Ziff, 1982, p. 277) which were available to Whitman, Dickinson's is a quiet, highly personal, brief, gnomic poetry, expressive of unorthodox, subversive, female sensibility. Both she and Whitman, the two main poetic voices in nineteenth-century America, were pioneering spirits, but where Whitman's is a poetry turned outwards, joyously embracing all of life, Dickinson's is turned inwards, to the soul's own society, neurotically convinced of the perplexing 'otherness' of the world outside. The self she explores is commonly under threat of annihilation or breakdown (see 'I Started Early – Took my Dog' or 'I Felt a Funeral in my Brain') and expresses itself haltingly, incompletely, provisionally, as her use of dashes, half rhymes and distorted syntax emphasizes. Her Beckettian intuition of limitation and impotence is the other side of Whitman's confident sense of infinite possibility and triumphant self-realization.

## Mark Twain: *The Adventures of Huckleberry Finn* ((1884) 1978)

*Huckleberry Finn* is a novel about the eponymous hero's effort to preserve individual freedom and integrity by withdrawing from civilization, society, authority, knowledge, rationality. The echoes of Thoreau's *Walden* (1854) are unmistakable. Twain is reworking a classic American theme – the tension between personal freedom and authoritarian control.

Everything depends on the voice and attitude Twain creates for his narrator. Read the first chapter carefully, paying particular attention to how swiftly, vividly and subtly Twain brings his hero before us. Note how Huck, a kind of orphan who has been taken in hand by the Widow Douglas, views the forces of civilization: 'When you got to the table you couldn't go right to eating, but you had to wait for the Widow to tuck down her head and grumble a little over the victuals' (Ch. 1, p. 49). The Widow 'tucks down her head' rather than 'bows her head', and she 'grumbles' rather than 'prays' or 'says grace'. Our enjoyment of Huck's humour depends on the fact that he has absolutely no sense of humour. He reports directly and factually what he sees and hears, without judging, in a language that is unaffected by conventional social valuation or coloration. His perceptions are of defamiliarizing conventional behaviour. His naivety and literal-mindedness force us to see with the eyes of a child, as if for the first time.

Huck's values are pragmatic. He objects to the Widow's forbidding him to smoke when she has never tried it herself (though he notes her hypocrisy in that she takes snuff). He rejects Miss Watson's fundamentalist heaven: 'She said all a body would have to do there was go around all day long with a harp and sing, forever and ever. So I didn't think much of it' (p. 51). His only criterion to judge the fitness of an action is what practical benefit it would have. His is the primitive morality later espoused by Hemingway's characters wherein the 'good' is what makes you *feel* good. Huck has no language to allow him to make moral and intellectual discriminations. Rejecting the women's religion of incomprehensible concepts and practices, boring Bible-reading, and pointless prohibitions and restrictions, he is drawn towards the magic and superstition of the Negro's oral-based natural religion.

Huck's limited, but wholly authentic language contrasts with the conventionalized languages of a whole range of impostors and fantasists who surround him. It undercuts Tom Sawyer's ridiculous artificiality and the romantic charade of the Grangerfords' feud of honour. The genuine, wordless anguish he feels at the death of his friend Buck Grangerford contrasts with the hilariously sentimental excess of Emeline Grangerford's tribute to Stephen Dowling Botts. Huck can consciously reject Tom's romancing, the Grangerfords' feuding, the 'flapdoodle' of the protean king and duke, even Miss Watson's and the Widow's Christianity, but the one thing he cannot denounce is slavery. On the raft, temporarily free of the prevailing social pressures, he and Nigger Jim relate to each other as equals and friends. Actual experience becomes the basis of their relationship rather than the reigning ideology. To some extent the raft experience is an idyll outside time and history, but it is no easy romantic escape. Rather it is the very site and catalyst of Huck's moral crisis.

Turn to Chapter 31, where Huck's dilemma comes to a head as he debates with himself whether or not he should continue to help Jim to freedom. First, we note how Huck's speech is permeated with the evangelical rhetoric of Miss Watson and the Widow: 'people that acts as I'd been acting about that nigger goes to everlasting fire ... So I kneeled down. But the words wouldn't come ... my heart warn't right ... I warn't square ... was letting on to give up sin' (p. 282). He thinks of helping Jim to freedom as 'stealing a poor old woman's nigger that hadn't ever done me no harm'. Having decided on writing to Miss Watson to tell her of Jim's whereabouts, 'it was astonishing the way I felt as light as a feather, right straight off, and my troubles all gone'. But once the note is written Huck's thoughts return to happy times with Jim on the raft: memories of Jim's affection, loyalty and unselfishness flood Huck's mind. Tearing up the note to Miss Watson, Huck makes the momentous decision, "'All right, then, I'll go to hell'" (p. 283).

Thus, Twain dramatizes the way, as he put it, 'a sound heart and a deformed conscience came into collision and conscience suffers a defeat' (quoted by Coveney, 1978, p. 31). Huck is a split subject who speaks two irreconcilable languages, the language of the racist South and the intimate language of the heart's affections. He defies his society's values but in a language which is substantially shaped by those values. He is unable to reject the dominant moral and religious ideology, even when values. He is unable to reject the dominant moral and religious ideology, even when he decides to act against it, and even when such rejection would seem to be the inevitable consequence of the experiences he has had. To him, helping a slave to freedom is still both criminal and sinful. Huck is never more than a *potentially* subversive force.

What comes after Chapter 31 is generally regarded as an anticlimax – the Wilks' episode with its mechanical plotting and hollow characterization of the Wilks' girls; and the move away from the river to Phelps's Farm where Twain seems to give an inordinate amount of attention to Tom's tomfoolery which is more tedious than amusing. In this last section, there is a shameless reliance on the most far-fetched coincidence. Note, too, how Twain's own authorial voice increasingly usurps the function of Huck's vernacular. Why, one asks, did Twain decide to reduce Jim from the noble figure he had become to a minstrel clown? Why did he displace the intense moral concern that was brought to a climax in Chapter 31 with the triviality of Tom's schemes for freeing Jim? These questions have exercised the critics, and one must weigh Lionel Trilling's affirmation of a 'certain formal aptness' in the 'return to the tone of the first section' (quoted by Coveney, 1978, p. 37) against Peter Coveney's view that 'with this episode at Phelps' Farm, one sees how very clearly Twain's uneven talent ran towards failure much of the time' (p. 37).

In returning to the domestic, matriarchal world of St Petersburg at the end, the novel acquires a cyclical structure. There is no clear direction or fulfilled objective in the story of the voyage down the river. No purpose has been served by it, for, as it turns out, Jim has been free all along, and Huck, as we have seen, learns nothing from his experience. The novel has the flowing rhythm of the river itself, the story's loose associative progress mirroring the movement of Huck's own unstructured subjectivity. At the end, our hero, in flight once again from society, opts for perpetual motion rather than stasis and fixity (compare the many American narratives about being 'on the road'), and decides to 'light out' for the wilderness.

Opting out of society may be a central theme in American literature but its origins lie in the social philosophy of European Romanticism, in the writings of Rousseau and in the poetry of Blake and Wordsworth. The Romantics enforced an opposition between 'innocence' and 'experience', the natural and the civilized, the individual and society. The child was idolized as the representative of innocence, nature and uncorrupted, spontaneous perception. American writers have often adopted the child's eye view, from Emerson and Twain down to Hemingway in *In Our Time*, J.D. Salinger in *Catcher in the Rye* and Saul Bellow in *The Adventures of Augie Marsh*. James's Isabel Archer in *The Portrait of a Lady* may not be a child but she is an innocent.

Huck of course is not just a product of European and American Romanticism, but of Twain's own childhood. The St Petersburg of *Tom Sawyer* and *Huckleberry Finn* is a version of Hannibal, a small river-town in Missouri where Twain grew up. Though written between 1876 and 1883, *Huckleberry Finn* is set during the 1840s, some twenty years before the Civil War (1861–5), when Missouri was still a slave state. But while there is a strong streak of nostalgia in *Huckleberry Finn*, as in the idyll of the raft in Chapter 19, the novel registers Twain's fierce indignation at the corruption of the South, its tawdriness, venality and brutality, its pernicious romanticism and 'medievalism' (epitomized by Tom Sawyer and the Grangerfords) which he saw as emanating principally from the influence of Sir Walter Scott.

Another context for *Huckleberry Finn* is Twain's wide experience as a popular journalist. As such, he specialized in humorous sketches, anecdotes and travel stories, exploiting the comic and expressive potential of various regional dialects with which he was familiar from boyhood. As his 'Explanatory' note on the variety of dialects in *Huckleberry Finn* shows, he knew he was doing something new with serious novelistic prose style. He was, in fact, adapting to his own purposes the southern populist vernacular tradition as practised by humorists such as George Washington Harris (1814–69), author of the popular Sut Lovingood yarns; Artemus Ward, pseudonym for Charles Farrar Browne (1834–67); and T.B. Thorpe (1815–78), whose 'The Big Bear of Arkansas' was one of the most famous of all frontier tales.

Regionalist writing was one way of declaring both an American literary independence of English tradition, and a regional independence of the patrician orthodoxy of New England. Going against the genteel conventions governing nineteenth-century literary composition in America, Twain gave his narrative over to the vernacular or 'folk' voice of an ill-educated child. The author's subversive intentions are further evidenced in the way he later turns the great canon of English literature into a source of humour when the duke and the king rehearse their Shakespeare. Twain challenges the notion of a fixed, stable canon, producing an open-ended narrative that resists closure and is composed out of a wide range of voices, including that of the Negro as well as the child. The novel's generic eclecticism has been well documented by Harold Beaver and Peter Messent, who have pointed out Twain's use of elements of the picaresque, the epistolary, the autobiography, the adventure story and the fugitive slave narrative. Drawing on a multiplicity of styles and genres, *Huckleberry Finn*, like *Moby-Dick*, enacts the struggle to express an infinitely diverse and seemingly uncontrollable reality which constantly eludes any established form. With his use of the vernacular and distinctively American experience, Twain, as T.S. Eliot said, 'discovered a new way of writing' (quoted by Coveney, 1978, p. 39). In dealing with the tensions between individual freedom and social conformity, we may also say he had taken up a quintessentially American literary theme.

## BIBLIOGRAPHY

INTRODUCTION
Bercovitch, S. (1975) *The Puritan Origins of the American Self*, Yale University Press, New Haven.
Bradbury, M. and T. Howard (1990) *Introduction to American Studies*, Longman, London.
Chase, R. (1957) *The American Novel and Its Tradition*, Bell, London.
Cunliffe, M. (ed.) (1975) *American Literature to 1900*, Sphere Books, London.
Fiedler, L. (1967) *Love and Death in the American Novel*, Paladin, London.
Gidley, M. (1993) *Modern American Culture*, Longman, London.

House, K.S. (ed.) (1966) *Reality and Myth in American Literature*, Fawcett, Greenwich, Conn.

Lewis, R.W.B. (1955) *The American Adam*, Chicago University Press, London.

Marx, L. (1964) *The Machine in the Garden: Technology and the Pastoral Ideal in America*, Oxford University Press, New York.

McQuade, D. *et al.* (eds) (1994) *The Harper American Literature*, 2 vols, Harper, New York.

Meserole, H.T. (ed.) (1972) *Seventeenth-Century American Poetry*, Norton, New York.

Miller, P. and H.J. Thomas (eds) (1963) *The Puritans: A Sourcebook of Their Writings*, Harper Torchbooks, New York.

Ziff, L. (ed.) (1982) *Ralph Waldo Emerson: Selected Essays*, Penguin, Harmondsworth.

EMERSON

Poirier, R. (1985) *A World Elsewhere*, Wisconsin University Press, Madison.

Poirier, R. (1992) *Poetry and Pragmatism*, Faber, London.

Rorty, R. (1982) *Consequences of Pragmatism: Essays, 1972–1980*, Harvester Wheatsheaf, Hemel Hempstead.

Tanner, T. (1965) *The Reign of Wonder*, Cambridge University Press, Cambridge.

West, C. (1989) *The American Evasion of Philosophy: A Genealogy of Pragmatism*, Macmillan, Basingstoke.

Whicher, S.E. (1953) *Freedom and Fate: An Inner Life of Ralph Waldo Emerson*, Philadelphia University Press, Philadelphia.

Ziff, L. (ed.) (1982) *Ralph Waldo Emerson: Selected Essays*, Penguin, Harmondsworth.

THOREAU

Bloom, H. (1971) *The Ringers in the Tower: Studies in the Romantic Tradition*, Chicago University Press, Chicago.

Cavell, S. (1992) *The Senses of Walden: An Expanded Edition*, Chicago University Press, Chicago.

Thoreau, H.D. (1962) *Walden*, Macmillan Collier Books, New York [first published 1854].

HAWTHORNE

Bercovitch, S. and Jehlen, M. (eds) (1986) *Ideology and Classic American Literature*, Harvard University Press, Cambridge, Mass.

Colacurio, M. (ed.) (1985) *New Essays on The Scarlet Letter*, Cambridge University Press, Cambridge.

Hawthorne, N. (1970) '*The Scarlet Letter*, Penguin, Harmondsworth [first published 1850].

James, H. (1967) *Hawthorne*, Macmillan, London.

Reynolds, L.J. (1985) *The Scarlet Letter* and Revolutions Abroad', *American Literature* 57, pp. 44–67.

MELVILLE

Melville, H. (1972) *Moby-Dick*, Penguin, Harmondsworth [first published 1851].

Thoreau, H.D. (1962) *Walden*, Macmillan, New York.

Ziff, L. (ed.) (1982) *Ralph Waldo Emerson: Selected Essays*, Penguin, Harmondsworth.

WHITMAN

Hall, D. (ed.) (1968) *A Choice of Whitman's Verse*, Faber, London.

McQuade, D. *et al.* (eds) (1987) *The Harper American Literature*, vol. 1, HarperCollins, New York (contains Preface to 1855 edn of *Leaves of Grass*).

Trowbridge, J.T. (1903) *My Own Story*, Houghton, Mifflin, Boston, Mass.

Ziff, L. (ed.) (1982) *Ralph Waldo Emerson: Selected Essays*, Penguin, Harmondsworth.

DICKINSON

Anderson, C. (1960) *Emily Dickinson's Poetry: Stairways of Surprise*, Holt, Rinehart & Winston, New York.

Atkins, G.D. and Morrow, L. (eds) (1989) *Contemporary Literary Theory*, Macmillan, London.

Barker, W. (1987) *Lunacy of Light: Emily Dickinson and the Experience of Metaphor*, Southern Illinois University Press, Carbondale.

Johnson, T.H. (1960) *The Complete Poems of Emily Dickinson*, Little, Brown, Boston, Mass.

Reeves, J. (ed.) (1959) *Selected Poems of Emily Dickinson*, Heinemann, Oxford.

Willbern, D. (1989) 'Reading After Freud', in *Contemporary Literary Theory*, ed. G.D. Atkins and L. Morrow, Macmillan, London.

Ziff, L. (ed.) (1982) *Ralph Waldo Emerson: Selected Essays*, Penguin, Harmondsworth.


TWAIN

Beaver, H. (1987) *Huckleberry Finn*, Allen & Unwin, London.

Eliot, T.S. (1950) *Introduction to 'The Adventures of Huckleberry Finn'*, Crescent Press, London.

Messent, P. (1990) *New Readings of the American Novel*, Macmillan, London.

Twain, M. (1978) *The Adventures of Huckleberry Finn*, ed. P. Coveney, Penguin, Harmondsworth [first published 1884].

Trilling, L. (1951) *The Liberal Imagination*, Secker & Warburg, London.

# UNIT 14

# Modern American literature

*Elmer Andrews*

The first section of this unit is generically subdivided into 'Poetry', 'Fiction' and 'Drama', with a concluding section on Black American writing. The Poetry section aims to give some sense of the variety and richness of modern American poetry, starting with traditionalists such as Robert Frost and Edwin Arlington Robinson, and then moving to the great American modernists, Ezra Pound, T.S. Eliot, William Carlos Williams, Wallace Stevens and Hart Crane; the New York School of Marianne Moore and e.e. cummings; the Chicago School of 'Prairie Poets'; the Southern School of John Crowe Ransom and Allen Tate; the Confessionals; the Beats; the Black Mountain poets; and the contemporary New York School headed by John Ashbery. The Fiction section outlines the differences between the American and European novelistic traditions, and goes on to discuss the naturalistic tradition of John Steinbeck and Richard Wright, the modernism of Sherwood Anderson, F. Scott Fitzgerald and Ernest Hemingway, the fiction of the Southern Renaissance, Jewish fiction, American postmodernism, contemporary realism, and the New Journalism of Norman Mailer and Tom Wolfe. The Drama section traces the search for a distinctively American theatre language and outlines the influence of European naturalism, expressionism, epic theatre and Theatre of the Absurd. The last section traces the development of black literary expression in America from the assimilationist writers at the beginning of the century through the racial discovery and assertiveness of W.E.B. DuBois and the Harlem Renaissance in the 1920s, to the cultural nationalism of the Black Arts Movement of the 1960s, and the complex investigations of Afro-American identity that have been undertaken by Ralph Ellison, James Baldwin, Toni Morrison and Alice Walker. The second part of the unit offers a close analysis of key texts by major modern American writers in the period.

## Introduction

### Poetry

The new American poetry of the early twentieth century, represented by Robert Frost (1874–1963) and Edwin Arlington Robinson (1869–1935), was written in conscious reaction against Victorian conventionalism and gentility, and was notable for its concreteness, directness of expression, concentration of effect, its use of a live, contemporary speech and its variety of subject matter. Where Robinson's is an urban, intellectual, alienated voice, Frost wrote with a deceptive simplicity on rural themes. Nevertheless, Frost had his own dark side that coincided with Robinson's pessimism. The older poet was in fact an important model for Frost, demonstrating as he did the poetic possibilities of the tragic drama of the personal life.

While Robinson and Frost, using traditional forms and reflecting traditional humanist values, developed a distinctively American poetic voice, the great modernist experiment was being shaped by the American expatriates T.S. Eliot (1888–1965) and Ezra Pound (1885–1972), who were engaged in a process of internationalizing and intellectualizing the American aesthetic. At the beginning of the century two cultural events in America had an important influence in helping the new poetry into existence. In 1912 Harriet Monroe founded *Poetry: A Magazine of Verse*, in Chicago. This was the first of many experimental 'little magazines' offering an alternative to the poetic and cultural conservatism of the East Coast. Poets such as Pound, Eliot, Stevens, Williams, Vachel Lindsay, Amy Lowell, Carl Sandburg, Edgar Lee Masters and Marianne Moore were all published in *Poetry*. Then, in 1913, the Armory Show visited New York, introducing Americans to the new developments in the visual arts in Europe – Fauvism, Cubism, expressionism, Pointillism, and to artists such as Van Gogh, Cézanne, Picasso and Duchamp. For poets such as Williams, the Armory Show had an enormously freeing effect, demonstrating the possibilities of radically new concepts of art.

Of greatest importance to the development of the new American poetry was the movement of Imagism, originating among the expatriates Pound, Amy Lowell (1874–1925) and Hilda Doolittle (1886–1961) who came together in London in 1913. In reaction against the conventional moralizing and outworn forms of earlier verse, the Imagists advocated the use of the language of common speech, experimentation with new rhythms and new moods, an absolute freedom in the choice of subject matter, the need to present an image with hard-edged clarity and accuracy of description, and a notion of concentration as the very essence of poetry. (See Unit 17, pp. 481–9, 495–505, for a discussion of Imagism, Pound and Eliot.)

Imagism reflected the pragmatic American concern with the concrete that we find so conspicuously in poets as different as Frost, Williams and Stevens. It expressed a typically American concern with the miracle of the commonplace, such as distinguishes the classic American poetic of Emerson, Thoreau, Whitman and Dickinson. Likewise, the Imagist advice to compose 'in sequence of the musical phrase not in sequence of the metronome' (F.S. Flint) may be seen to continue the American experiment in freeing poetry from traditional forms initiated by Emerson, Whitman, Poe and Dickinson. It is perhaps no coincidence that the four leading lights of the Modernist Movement – Eliot, Pound, Stevens and Williams – were all American. By 1914 Pound had moved on from Imagism to Vorticism, a movement promoting a more dynamic concept of the image based on the example of Cubist abstract art. A later development of Imagism was Louis Zukofsky's, George Oppen's and William Carlos Williams's concept of Objectivism in the 1930s which

emphasized the formal and musical elements in the realization of the image/object/
poem.

In pursuing a cult of impersonality and objectivity, Pound and Eliot developed a
poetry of self-dramatization through the use of personae and dramatic monologue.
Seeking to relate the past to the present, they specialized in a poetry of pastiche and
imitation of earlier verse. Eliot was influenced by the Indian Upanishads, by
Baudelaire, Laforgue and the French Symbolists, by Renaissance art, and by the
Metaphysicals and the Jacobeans. His portrait of the neurotic and impotent Prufrock
in 'The Love Song of Alfred J. Prufrock' (1917) prefigures the poet's concern with
a cultural and spiritual breakdown and crisis of confidence in *The Waste Land*
(1922) and 'The Hollow Men' (1925). His poetry is a search for formal order,
continuity and authority, which he eventually discovered in Christianity. Pound, in
seeking to understand and renew the present, looked to past civilizations – to
fourteenth-century Italian poets such as Guido Cavalcanti, to Latin, ancient Chinese
and Anglo-Saxon poetry. Both his and Eliot's monologues are modelled on
Browning. Other modernists similarly reflected diverse cultural influences. Wallace
Stevens and Archibald MacLeish (1892–1982) were indebted to the French
Symbolists, cummings to the linguistic playfulness of Guillaume Appollinaire and
Mallarmé, the French Surrealists and Dadaists, and the Italian Futurists.

William Carlos Williams (1883–1963) and Hart Crane (1899–1932), representing a divergent strain in the American Modernist Movement, strenuously opposed
Eliot's and Pound's internationalism and intellectualism. '*The Waste Land*', Williams
declared in his *Autobiography*, 'wiped out our world ... Eliot returned us to the
classroom' (1951, p. 146). Objecting to Eliot's and Pound's return to the past and to
European culture to seek out significance, Williams championed a radically new
indigenous poetry to give a voice to the impoverished, forgotten life of contemporary
America. He wanted to create a democratic art 'in the American grain'. Yet, though he
certainly took his language and subject matter from the world around him, his
aesthetic owed more to modern European art, especially the work of Duchamp, than
he might have cared to admit. In attempting to record a direct encounter with reality,
Williams broke with conventional poetic structures and routinized forms of
perception. Dispensing with the normal measured line and stanza, he experimented
with a free verse composed out of the language and rhythms of natural American
speech. Form, he believed, should be dictated by subject matter. The result is a poetry
which often seems quite arbitrarily divided into lines and stanzas. No explanatory or
abstracting comment is allowed to intrude upon direct objective presentation. The
impression is of energy and flux, of an intransigent reality that refuses to conform
willingly to the artist's efforts at control. (See Unit 20, p. 564, for a discussion of
Williams's 'This Is Just to Say', and Unit 17, pp. 496–7, for a discussion of 'So Much
Depends'.) Where the Pound or Eliot poem expresses the need for system and control,
in Williams's poetry 'so much depends' on the thing itself and the relationships that
may be discovered between things. 'No ideas but in things' was his famous motto
(Williams, *Paterson*, 1963, Book I, section i), indicative of a characteristic American
anti-intellectualism.

Williams's poetry is nothing if not controversial. The charge is sometimes
levelled against him that his poetry is inconsequential and unsatisfying, that his

extreme objectivism, his concentration on the thing itself, his refusal of symbolism or 'meaning' results in a poetry that is too lacking in coherence, depth or vitality. However, at its best, his poetry has the effect of blazing revelation, satisfying an ideal of both poetic order and expressive freedom.

Wallace Stevens (1879–1955), like Williams and Whitman, rejects all received myths and beliefs, and insists on the need for each individual to make his own world. Where Eliot ultimately grounds his poetic in Christianity and Pound in a concept of tradition, Stevens repudiates all objective authority and proclaims the fictionality of all truth. For Eliot, art is an attempt to express the transcendent: for Stevens there is no objective or absolute reality beyond individual consciousness. Imagination is all there is to redeem reality: 'After one has abandoned a belief in God poetry is that essence which takes its place as life's redemption' ('Adagia', *Opus Posthumous*, 1957, p. 177). Unlike Pound and Eliot, Stevens was not absorbed by society or history, and unlike Williams or Frost he had no poetic interest in the lives of actual people. There is, in fact, little of the ordinary everyday world in Stevens's poetry. Though he may continually stress the 'interdependence of the imagination and reality as equals' ('The Noble Rider and the Sound of Words', in *The Necessary Angel*, 1951, p. 27), his poetry proclaims his powers of fictionalizing the thing rather than any naturalistic fidelity to the thing itself. Stevens's language, like Whitman's, is grandly extravagant, but where Whitman represented a crude energy, Stevens, whose influences include Shakespeare, Keats and the French Symbolists and Imagists, is 'the great dandy' of American literature. Paradoxically, of course, the more extravagant Whitman's and Stevens's poetry becomes, the more apparent their desperate and frustrated longing for the silence of full presence.

Stevens's notion of the self as centre and creator of the world is at the very heart of the American tradition. When Thoreau declared in Chapter 2 of *Walden*: 'Wherever I sat, there might I live, and the landscape radiated from me accordingly', he is inverting the traditional view of man's relation to the world by suggesting that man makes his own world rather than simply occupying an appointed place in a world order fixed by authority and tradition and preordained by God. Similarly, Emerson writes of man at the centre of the universe animating a barren wilderness through his powers of thought and language:

> He (man) is placed in the centre of beings, and a ray of relation passes from every other being to him. And neither can man be understood without these objects, nor these objects without man. All the facts in natural history taken by themselves have no value but are barren like a single sex. But marry it to Human history and it is full of life. (Ziff, 1982, p. 21)

For Stevens, as for Emerson and Thoreau, reality *is* consciousness, though Stevens did not enjoy the Transcendentalists' optimistic belief in a benevolent Oversoul, of which the individual consciousness partook. What he shares with them, along with Whitman, Pound and Williams (but not Eliot the Anglo-Catholic), is a view of the poet as pioneer facing an unmade wilderness, relying on nothing else but his own personal resources to produce his own meanings and transform the wilderness into a new Eden. There is no firm ground of faith except what the human individual can produce himself. This is a source of scepticism but also promotes an exhilarated sense of freedom, the opportunity for personal and linguistic experimentation, for rejuvenating the self and the culture, and reinvigorating what in American life is sustaining and defining.

Hart Crane is best known for his last great poem *The Bridge* (1930), which he offered as an alternative to the 'pessimism' of Eliot's *The Waste Land*. *The Bridge*, like Whitman's *Leaves of Grass*, Eliot's *The Waste Land*, Pound's *Cantos*, Archibald MacLeish's *Conquistador* (1932), Williams's *Paterson* (1946–58), and Zukofsky's *A* (1940–78), attests to the American poet's interest in producing an epic for the modern world which, in the case of Whitman, Williams and Crane, was an emphatically American world. Where Eliot looked to Europe, Crane turned westward to the American frontier, to New England, to the Spanish conquistadores and to native Indian dance in an attempt at a Whitmanesque synthesis of American culture, an affirmation of unity in diversity, a vision that seeks to transcend a commercialized barbarous modernity. Both Williams's and Crane's democratic temper and obvious sympathy for the proletariat contrast with Eliot's Anglo-Catholic royalism, Pound's fascism and Stevens's conservative Republicanism. *Paterson* and *The Bridge*, though American in theme, were modernist in form, extensions of Eliot's and Pound's experiment with the discontinuous epic, employing a wide variety of styles and juxtaposing ideas, images, characters and events in collage or kaleidoscopic fashion. The contortions and eccentricities of his diction, image and syntax recall Dickinson or cummings, while his swift, evocative, associational technique looks forward to later poets such as Allan Ginsberg who also specialized in a poetry of swarming, dazzling impressions.

Other poets associated with the Modern Movement in America were Archibald MacLeish (1892–1982) and e.e. cummings (1894–1962). MacLeish made himself famous with his pronouncement in his poem 'Ars Poetica' that 'a poem should not mean/But be'. e.e. cummings was the great champion of individualism, the most boldly eccentric of American poets, playful, passionate, obscene and tenderly lyrical by turns. In his poetry he opposed regimentation and abstraction, and enacted his ideal of personal freedom in the verbal and typographical eccentricities of his poems. The idea was that poetry should be like music, and his syntactical convolutions and use of capital letters, elisions and parentheses were designed to help us see and hear anew. Like Emerson and Whitman he wanted to emulate a child's freshness and immediacy of perception and lively spontaneity of expression.

Cummings, Williams and Stevens were associated with the magazine *Others* published in New York. The New York School of poets, as they were sometimes called, included Marianne Moore (1887–1972) whose remark that 'we must have the courage of our peculiarities' suggests her affinity with cummings's highly individualistic approach to poetry. Her very closeness and precision of description worked to open the imagination, providing 'piercing glances into the life of things'. Poets, she said, should be 'literalists of the imagination' and 'present imaginary gardens with real toads in them' ('Poetry').

As well as the New York School there was the Chicago School associated with Harriet Monroe's *Poetry* magazine, and including the 'Prairie Poets' Vachel Lindsay (1879–1931), Edgar Lee Masters (1868–1950) and Carl Sandburg (1878–1967). Lindsay, who was much influenced by Poe, Whitman and oral tradition, sought to contribute to the construction of an optimistic, celebratory, heroic, folk-based myth of America. Masters is remembered for one volume, his *Spoon River Anthology* (1915–16), offering sharp vignettes of the inhabitants of Spoon River in epitaph form. These pictures of small-town Midwestern life written in a free verse form and a plain style represent a continuation of Whitman's democratic celebration of American life in *Leaves of Grass* and are comparable to both Edwin Arlington Robinson's 'Tilbury Town' poems and Sherwood Anderson's exploration of the secret, repressed life of the grotesques in *Winesburg, Ohio* (1919). Sandburg's poetics, also drawn from Whitman and the folk tradition, extended the American revolt against the conventional 'genteel' tradition.

A Southern School, associated with Vanderbilt University in Nashville, Tennessee, and dating from 1915, produced John Crowe Ransom (1888–1974), Allen Tate (1899–1979) and Robert Penn Warren (1905–). This group, which became known as the Fugitives, after their magazine *The Fugitive* (1923–5), opposed both the dehumanizing contemporary trends which accompanied the industrialization of the Old South and a decadent Southern romanticism. In contrast to the iconoclasm and internationalism of the Imagists, the Fugitives emphasized traditional, regional, classical values, emphasized form over freedom, and specialized in a poetry of wit, irony and ambiguity. Many Fugitives were associated with the Southern Agrarian Movement of the 1930s and contributed to its manifesto *I'll Take My Stand* (1930) which opposed the modernization of the South, and the rationalistic, scientific world-view on which it was based. As a theorist, Ransom wanted critical attention to focus on the poem itself rather than on its historical or philosophical context and advocated a New Criticism of scientific rigour. He is chiefly known for his seminal work *The New Criticism* (1941) (see Unit 18, p. 523).

Post-war American poetry took shape against a background of unprecedented prosperity and complacent affluence. By the end of the war America was a world superpower. The literature of social protest which had characterized the depressed years of the 1930s was no longer in vogue. Many poets of the 1940s and 1950s, as Richard Gray has noted, 'withdrew from active involvement in issues of public concern or ideology into formalism, abstraction, or mythmaking' (1990, p. 215). These new directions were evident in the work of the 'war poets' Randall Jarrell (1914–65) and W.S. Merwin (1927–), and most interestingly in the poetry of Richard Wilbur (1921–) and Elizabeth Bishop (1913–79). Wilbur confronted the chaos of the modern world and sought to contain it within elaborate formal structures that recall George Herbert. Refusing to give up on either community or conventional religious values or traditional forms, Wilbur's is a poetry of penetrating observation, of wit, irony, ambiguity and linguistic ingenuity. Elizabeth Bishop specializes in careful descriptions of the ordinary world, allowing objects to dilate in the imagination and take on a magical, dream-like quality. Hers is an estranged, sceptical, ironical perspective reminiscent of Emily Dickinson. The work, in its elegance and formality, is modelled on George Herbert and the hymn-book and is enlivened by natural speech rhythms. Along with Wilbur, Bishop continues the line of older formalists like Frost, Stevens and Moore.

One of the most notable developments of post-war American poetry was the emergence of a 'confessional poetry' grounded in autobiography and giving direct expression to the poet's personal life which was no longer hidden behind masks and personae. Poetry was once again, as it had been for Whitman, a song of the self, addressing the reader directly, often intimately, delving into the unconscious feelings, dreams and intuitions. In offering candid accounts of extreme experiences of alienation, frustration and isolation that result in mental breakdown and madness, as Robert Lowell (1911–77), Sylvia Plath (1932–63), John Berryman (1914–72), Theodore Roethke (1908–63), Anne Sexton (1928–74) and Allan Ginsberg (1926–) have done, these poets opened up new, hitherto taboo subjects for poetic treatment. In their concern with the dark side of the personal life, they reflected a prevailing social fear and unease, for this was the age of the Bomb and the 'Cold War' and the paranoia that produced Senator Joseph McCarthy's House of Representatives Un-American Activities Committee. In exploring the intimate details of sexual and domestic life they reflected a new personal and sexual freedom that was to manifest itself most sensationally among American youth of the 1950s and 1960s.

The greatest of the 'confessional poets', Robert Lowell (1911–77), links his own spiritual breakdown to an historical degeneracy, juxtaposing present and past, the personal and the historical. Like Fitzgerald's story of Jay Gatsby, Lowell's life also becomes the story of America, representative of a culture. In *Life Studies* (1959) he wrote about his life and family, looking for a self-identity, a sense of stability and order in the process of his own remembering and the exercise of his (re)creative powers. In comparison with his earlier work, his language becomes less contorted and feverish, more serene and controlled, formal but flexible, subtle and ironic. In his last books, *Notebook* (1969), *History* (1973) and *The Dolphin* (1973), collections of irregular sonnets, he continued the process of self-creation. It was Lowell's poems in *Life Studies* about his experiences in a mental hospital that helped Sylvia Plath to find her own poetic voice and subject. Hers is a poetry of despair and personal suffering. Like Poe, Dickinson and Hemingway, she was preoccupied with death. Dedicated though she was to the craft of poetry as a means of asserting order and meaning in the face of emptiness, art in the end could not protect her from the desire for oblivion and the absolute freedom of suicide.

Another strand of the confessional tradition was that represented by the 'deep image poets' – Robert Bly (1926–), Robert Kelly (1935–), Galway Kinnell (1927–), James Wright (1927–80), W.S. Merwin (1927–). Using free verse forms and loose associative structures, dream images, incantatory language, they register the deep rhythms of personality, probing the dark, mystical forces of the unconscious, excavating the self to the primal sources of being. Using more conventional forms and maintaining closer contact with the public world, Louis Simpson (1923–), like Lowell, expresses a representatively American self. Anne Sexton (1928–74) and Adrienne Rich (1929–) have helped develop a distinctively female American poetry.

The 'Swinging Sixties', presided over by the youthful John F. Kennedy who was inaugurated as President in 1961, were a time of buoyant confidence, material abundance and cultural and personal experimentation. In the arts the avant-garde flourished. In poetry the formalists and confessionals were joined by the Beats – Allan Ginsberg (1926–), Lawrence Ferlinghetti, (1919–), Gary Snyder (1930–),

Gregory Corso (1930– ), Robert Duncan (1919–88); the Black Mountain poets – Charles Olson (1910–70), Robert Creeley (1926– ), Robert Duncan, Denise Levertov (1923– ); and the New York School – John Ashbery (1927– ), Frank O'Hara (1926–66), Kenneth Koch (1925– ).

Many of the Beat poets came originally from New York, but gravitated towards the West Coast to constitute what is sometimes referred to as the San Francisco Renaissance. The term 'beat' suggests a number of things: the influence of jazz music; the point of view of the 'beaten', the outcast, the victim, the alienated, the rebellious hipster; the notion of beatitude that relates to the religious, rhapsodic and mystical nature of the poetry. Beat poetry represented a radical, anti-establishment consciousness, a concern with personal and spiritual rather than political freedom. Ginsberg was chief guru, and established himself as a major poet with his first collection *Howl* (1956), which was seized by the San Francisco police on grounds of obscenity. He was influenced by Blake's mysticism and by Whitman's messianic purpose. Like Whitman he dramatizes himself as an American Everyman. He also learnt from Whitman's long rhapsodic line and natural speech rhythms, while Williams confirmed for him the expressive possibilities of a breath-conditioned poetry. *Howl* illustrates Ginsberg's improvisatory approach, a poetry based on violent juxtapositions and surreal imagery designed to disrupt routinized, rational perception. The poem criticizes the materialism of the modern world which has stifled the visionary impulses.

The Black Mountain poets were associated with Black Mountain College in North Carolina where Charles Olson taught and acted as mentor to other poets such as Denise Levertov (1923– ), Paul Blackburn (1926–71), John Wieners (1934– ), Robert Creeley (1926– ), Ed Dorn (1929– ) and Robert Duncan (1919–88). These poets published in *Origin* and then *Black Mountain Review*. Olson's programmatic 1950 essay, 'Projective Verse' (in *The New American Poetry 1945–1960*, ed. Donald Hall), reasserted the Imagist and Objectivist emphasis on the concrete specific, on the notion of poetry as re-enactment, and on open forms. Opposing 'closed', formalist verse, Olson advocated an 'open' poetry in which 'form is never more than an extension of content'. His emphasis on the syllable and the rhythm of breathing as the basis of composition echoes Pound and Williams. 'Field Composition', as he called the writing of a poem, seeks to 'enact' rather than merely 'describe'. Freeing itself from both referentiality and intellectuality, the poem is composed as a physical performance regulated by the breath. His major work is the *Maximus Poems* (1983) in which the eponymous speaker is an 'Isolated person in Gloucester, Massachusetts' where the poet grew up. Like Whitman's *Leaves of Grass* or Williams's *Paterson*, the *Maximus Poems* is another American epic, and in it Olson pursues his mythological, archaeological and anthropological interests.

The poets of the New York School – Ashbery, O'Hara and Koch – were associated with the Abstract Expressionist painters, and specialized in a colloquial poetry of the personal life. Ashbery is generally regarded as the best of the New York School. He shares O'Hara's devotion to the particular, but has a more epistemological bent. His poetry, which is startlingly inventive and suggestive, allusive, surreal, conversational, shows the influence of Picasso, Klee, Matisse and the Dadaists. He reworks traditional forms – the sonnet, sestina, ode, elegy – while proclaiming a daring freedom from convention. Like Stevens, he believes that poetry creates rather than merely reflects the world, and like Stevens he emphasizes a postmodern provisionality, deferring any ultimate meaning, refusing any possibility of totality or closure or organic integration. His poetry refuses any paraphrasable meaning. It reflects indeterminacy and irresolution.


## Fiction

Malcolm Bradbury (1992), Bernard Bergonzi (1970) and Richard Chase (1957) offer provocative discussions of the differences between the American and English or European novel. The American novel is characteristically an individual writer's world, the assertion of a personal vision rather than the recreation of a shared world. In contrast, the English tradition may seem unexciting, genteel – but safe and substantial, offering a carefully detailed social world, close psychological investigation, traditional attitudes. In the English and European novel, the individual tends to be seen in his or her social context, which provides the norms whereby individual behaviour can be judged. There is an agreed reality, shared by both writer and readers. At the heart of the founding myths of America was the promise of freedom from cultural constraint, oppressive convention and social formality. Rather than merely accept a given reality, the American writer feels the need to make his world, to impose his own sense of order on the chaos of experience – in Wallace Stevens's words, he invents a fiction. Where in the European novel the individual is inscribed in a traditional network of hierarchical relations with family, community and God, the American character is basically alone, living in adversarial relation with society, anxious to preserve his personal integrity, his freedom and innocence.

The American emphasis on self-reliance, on taking charge of one's own destiny, may be seen to translate, in literary terms, into the writer's taking responsibility for the creation of his own world, his own code of conduct, his own values, as the early pioneers had sought to do in taming the wilderness and developing the land. The American writer resists the given (European or English) patterns of structuring reality and seeks to devise his own. The great challenge, as Tony Tanner points out in *City of Words* (1976), is to find a stylistic freedom which is not simply a meaningless incoherence; to find a form which will not trap the writer inside existing definitions. The whole American adventure – cultural and ideological – has always been a tension between received Old World forms and the improvization of new forms, between culture and anarchy, civilization and nature. One aspect of this tension is linguistic, and there is in American writing a pervasive awareness of the problematic relationship between language and reality, a self-consciousness about language which stems from the corrosive feeling that it can never adequately express a vast, mysterious, infinitely varied and ultimately unknowable world. Consequently, American writing invariably draws attention to its provisionality and artificiality. The artist's fictive world is the 'world elsewhere', a phrase which Richard Poirier has taken as title for his study of American literature. This 'world elsewhere' – the world of words – is also the subject of Tony Tanner's magisterial book on the twentieth-century American novel, *City of Words*.

As the work of Theodore Dreiser, John Dos Passos, John Steinbeck, James T. Farrell and Richard Wright would attest, there were of course realistic and naturalistic novels, but these tended to be marginalized by a critical orthodoxy emanating from the New Critics and the New York intellectuals affiliated with *The Partisan Review*, which privileged the symbolic, mythic mode of the Romance. The emerging literary canon was largely the construction of such influential criticism as that of D.H. Lawrence's *Studies in Classic American Literature* ([1924] 1971), F.O. Matthiessen's *American Renaissance* (1941), R.W.B. Lewis's *The American Adam* (1955), Richard Chase's *The American Novel and its Tradition* (1957) and Leslie Fiedler's *Love and Death in the American Novel* (1960). It was the growth of ethnic writing and women's writing that broke up this orthodoxy and forced social concerns back onto the literary agenda. The postmodern novel of Vladimir Nabokov (1899–1977), William Burroughs (1914–), Kurt Vonnegut (1922–), William Gaddis (1922–), William Gass (1924–), John Hawkes (1925–), Joseph Heller, Thomas Pynchon (1937–), John Barth (1930–) and Philip Roth (1933–) expresses a characteristically American emphasis on freedom from fixed forms and, as Tony Hilfer (1992) suggests, may be seen to continue the nineteenth-century Romance tradition. The postmodern novelist disrupts traditional narrative structures and problematizes the reliability of the narrative voice. He sees the self as fluid and constructed rather than socially or historically determined. In constructing his own world in a self-contained verbal universe, he stresses the fantastic, the fabulous and the allegorical.

The 1920s was the great decade of American fiction. It began with Sherwood Anderson's *Winesburg, Ohio* (1919) in which the author, using a loose, flowing method of story-telling, seeks to reveal the significance of ordinary, apparently insignificant, lives. The book is dedicated to Anderson's mother who, he says, 'first awoke in me the hunger to see beneath the surface of lives'. The twenty-two stories trace the development of George Willard, a thinly veiled portrait of the artist as a young man, in his difficult effort to assume the role of artist rather than becoming yet another Winesburg grotesque. The fiction of the 1920s also included the central achievements of Hemingway, Fitzgerald, Faulkner, Dreiser, Sinclair Lewis and Willa Cather.

Written in the aftermath of the First World War, these stories and novels belong to the 'Roaring Twenties', a time of affluence, abundance and moral decadence. But they also register the deep psychic wounds left by the war, especially on those expatriates who had experienced the war in Europe. This was the age of what Gertrude Stein called 'the lost generation'. The frantic revelry concealed disillusionment and spiritual crisis. In 1929 the carnival suddenly came to an end when the American Stock Market crashed and the Great Depression began. The most celebrated chronicler of the decade was F.S. Fitzgerald whose own life and career seemed to follow uncannily the larger historical trajectory from boom to bust. The 1930s, beginning in Depression and ending in world war, saw a revival of naturalistic social protest literature, the outstanding examples of which were Dos

Passos's *USA* (1938), Steinbeck's *The Grapes of Wrath* (1939), Farrell's Studs
Lonigan trilogy (1932, 1933, 1934) and Wright's *Native Son* (1940), though even
these never entirely avoided the tendency of the 'proletarian novel' to subordinate
art to polemics.

From the mid-1930s radical politics in America declined markedly. This was the
time of the 'Red Scare', the beginning of the Cold War and the emergence of the
Southern Agrarian Movement, committed to the values of the Old (pre-Civil War)
South, which was taken to represent an ideal, unified culture. The Southern
Renaissance was characterized by a turn from politics, for only by suppressing the
facts of history, especially slavery, could the Southern pastoral be maintained. These
writers, while experimenting with modernist techniques, embodied traditional moral
and religious values. The literature was validated by a formalist, university-based
critical theory and practice – the New Criticism – which represented an alternative to
radical political perspectives. The New Critics championed the idea of the
autonomous work of art free from political or ideological contamination. Literature,
they believed, should deal with universal values above and beyond any merely social
or historical concern. As well as Faulkner other contributors to the Southern
Renaissance were Erskine Caldwell (1903–87), Katherine Anne Porter
(1890–1980), Thomas Wolfe, Robert Penn Warren (1905–), Allen Tate
(1899–1979), Tennessee Williams (1911–83), William Styron (1925–), Carson
McCullers (1917–67), Flannery O'Connor (1925–64) and Truman Capote
(1924–84). As a consequence partly of the influence of the New Critical orthodoxy,
partly of a post-war disillusionment with politics, whether left or right, social protest
fiction was gradually marginalized during the 1930s and 1940s. Interest shifted from
the social to the personal, the psychological, the mythic and universal.

The 1950s has been called 'the Jewish decade' (Hilfer, 1992, p. 76), and
brought to the fore writers such as Saul Bellow (1915–), Bernard Malamud
(1914–86) and Philip Roth (1933–). The Jewish experience was proposed as a
paradigm of the alienated, outcast existential condition of modern man.
'Personally', Malamud has said, 'I handle the Jew as a symbol of the tragic
experience of man existentially. I try to see the Jew as universal man. Every man's a
Jew though he may not know it' (Field and Field, 1975). Both Malamud's and
Bellow's work may be seen as a pursuit of the grounds of affirmation: 'We love
apocalypses too much, and crisis ethics and florid extremism with its thrilling
language. Excuse me, no. I've had all the monstrosity I want', says Bellow's
eponymous hero in *Herzog*. Herzog is the epitome of modern alienated man. Like
Augie Marsh, he resists the efforts of others to define him, whether those directly
involved in his life or, rather more remotely, the framers of the modern intellectual
world – Hegel, Heidegger, Nietzsche, Kierkegaard. Herzog is engaged in a
Thorovian process of self-discovery, and like Thoreau he has removed himself from
the social world, isolating himself among the Berkshire Mountains to ponder
alternatives to the contemporary embracement of despair and nihilism. The ending is
problematic. Is Herzog's final stasis the sign of exhaustion, or a blissful Thorovian
peace?

The postmodern novel which has developed since the end of the Second World
War is expressive of the kind of apocalyptic and absurdist vision that Bellow

complains about. It is a literature which reflects the breakdown of the 'grand narratives' of the past, whether of progress or rationality or of God. The idea of the essential, integral self is dismantled: the self becomes protean, performative. The text similarly resists coherence, totalization and closure, and relies on parody and pastiche. Postmodern fiction is written against the centripetal tendencies in the culture – the homogenizing, bureaucratic, routinizing, rationalizing forces in economic and social life, conspicuously evident in the influence of the mass media and advertising, and the emphasis placed on scientific and technological efficiency. All these developments have resulted in an unmagicking or demystifying or despiritualizing of the world and a decentring of the individual. Thus, Yossarian in Heller's *Catch-22* rebels against a regimented, systematized world that has been rationalized into absurdity and paranoia. Though set during the Second World War, the novel spoke powerfully to the generation of the 1960s, acquiring the status of a cult novel among the critics of America's involvement in Vietnam.

Much postmodern fiction is concerned with questions of 'reality' and fictionality, as in Barth's *The Sot-Weed Factor* (1960), Nabokov's *Pale Fire* (1962), Pynchon's *V* (1963), Barthelme's *Come Back, Dr Caligari* (1964). The best postmodern writing continues to reflect a dialectical tension between fiction and reality. It still engages the real world and is not concerned merely to elaborate an individually conceived, self-contained verbal universe. The less successful examples of postmodernist fiction, though they may be ingenious and virtuoso linguistic displays, tend to lose touch with ordinary human life in their elaborations of alternative realities.

Alongside the postmodernist extravaganza there continues to exist a healthy strand of realistic fiction, represented by the work of John Cheever (1912–82), E.L. Doctorow (1931–), John Updike (1932–), Raymond Carver (1933–88), and by women writers such as Mary McCarthy (1912–89), Joyce Carol Oates (1938–), Katherine Anne Porter (1890–1980), Eudora Welty (1909–), Flannery O'Connor (1925–64), Toni Morrison (1931–) and Alice Walker (1944–). Realism, as Tony Hilfer notes, lends itself to the woman writer's concern with the personal, domestic and emotional life, the concentration on character rather than action.

The 1960s saw the emergence of yet another kind of writing that combined the fictional, the autobiographical and the documentary, and is largely associated with the work of Norman Mailer, especially his book *The Armies of the Night* (1968). This work, which is based on Mailer's experience of the 1967 march on the Pentagon in protest against the Vietnam war, presents 'History as a Novel/The Novel as History'. Tom Wolfe's account of the experiments of Ken Kesey and the Pranksters in *The Electric Kool-Aid Acid Test* (1968) and of the duplicitous world of journalism, politics and the law in *The Bonfire of the Vanities* (1987) are developments of what has become known as the 'New Journalism'.

## Drama

At the beginning of the century, American theatre was a parochial, exclusively commercial theatre, driven by market forces and dominated by sentimental Victorian values, a superficial realism, which was brought to new heights of technical brilliance by the director David Belasco (1859–1931). The introduction of the naturalistic drama of Ibsen, Strindberg, Shaw and Chekhov helped to transform American theatre. At about the same time as Stanislavsky and the Moscow Arts Theatre visited New York in 1922–3 with productions of Chekhov, the American Laboratory Theatre was founded to teach the Stanislavsky method of realistic acting. A number of new theatre groups emerged, responsive to the experiment in naturalism and expressionism that was reaching America from Europe, and offering an avant-garde alternative to the commercial Broadway theatre.

American drama began on 28 July 1916 with the Provincetown Players' production of Eugene O'Neill's first play, *Bound East for Cardiff*, which brought a shocking new realism to the American stage in terms of subject matter and language. The play also proved that the new realism could be commercially popular, for *Bound East for Cardiff* moved to Broadway in 1918. Though O'Neill (1888–1953) dominated American theatre during the 1920s and 1930s, a number of other lesser but still interesting talents emerged: Elmer Rice (1892–1967) Clifford Odets (1906–63), William Saroyan (1908–81), Lillian Hellman (1905– ), and Thornton Wilder (1897–1975). Rice's first major success was *The Adding Machine* (1923), a boldly expressionistic play that may have been influenced by O'Neill's *The Emperor Jones* (1920) and *The Hairy Ape* (1922). Rice satirizes a dehumanized, mechanical, commercialized society in which Mr Zero, the protagonist, is a mere adding machine.

Odets wrote his best-known plays during the depressed 1930s. *Waiting for Lefty* (1935) is an 'agitprop' play combining episodic expressionism with realistic scenes presenting individual portraits of a group of striking taxi-men, and ends with a rousing exhortation to strike. *Awake and Sing!* (1935) is a tragi-comic dramatization of the life of a Jewish family in the Bronx during the Depression. *Golden Boy* (1937) is a psychological study of the brutalization of the individual in a competitive, capitalistic world.

Saroyan's sprawling dramas, *My Heart's in the Highlands* (1939) and *The Time of Your Life* (1939), exhibit a Whitmanesque optimism, energy and joyousness, a faith in human possibility that was out of tune with the prevailing mood of the times. Hellman combined well-made melodrama and the Ibsenite or Shavian play of ideas in *Children's Hour* (1934), *The Little Foxes* (1939) and *Toys in the Attic* (1960). Wilder was an immensely popular playwright, an accessible, affectionate celebrant of the wonder of the commonplace. In *Our Town* (1938), which has been called 'the most popular of all American expressionistic plays' (Styan, 1983, vol. 3, p. 116), he presents an image of democratic, traditional, pre-First World War America. Using simple character types, a ritualistic structure and imaginary props, Wilder aims to create an archetypal situation and, while acknowledging loss and death, affirms traditional humanistic values.

The major dramatists following O'Neill were Tennessee Williams (1911–83), Arthur Miller (1915– ) and Edward Albee (1928– ). All three have combined realism and expressionism. Williams specializes in a kind of psychological and poetic melodrama that is influenced by O'Neill and Strindberg, while Miller is associated with an Ibsenite social drama with an unashamedly moral purpose. Albee's name has been linked with the European Absurdists – Beckett, Ionesco, Genet and Pinter. But while adopting many of the techniques of the European writers, Albee's drama continues to reflect a traditional American pragmatism and optimism. There is a redemptive aspect to his drama that is foreign to the anti-humanist strand of the Theatre of the Absurd. Unlike Beckett, Albee does not see man as the victim of an indifferent universe, but self-created victim of his own illusions. Man is still in charge of his destiny. For Albee, it is through the exercise of choice and through confronting reality that the individual can end isolation and unmeaning, and attain dignity. Albee attacks not life itself but inauthentic responses to it. He is more concerned with the world than Beckett or Pinter. Where Beckett or Pinter merely present their worlds, Albee, continuing the moralistic tradition of American drama, wants his world reformed. His is thus a drama of moral protest and movement towards enlightenment or change, discernible in characters such as Peter in *The Zoo Story* (1963), George and Martha in *Who's Afraid of Virginia Woolf?* (1965), Julian in *Tiny Alice* (1965) and Tobias in *A Delicate Balance* (1966). Like Beckett and Pinter, Albee is concerned with the breakdown of communication, but, unlike Beckett or Pinter, never consistently differentiates between his characters and what they say. His people are always created through what they say, not what they don't say. This results either in caricature (*The American Dream*, *The Sandbox*) or in a drama that believes that people finally can communicate (*Who's Afraid of Virginia Woolf?*, *A Delicate Balance*).

The two most exciting new playwrights are David Mamet (1947– ) and Sam Shepard (1943– ). Mamet's *Sexual Perversity in Chicago* (1974) charts the sexual exploits of two young men in a rapid series of thirty-one sketches. Using a similar fragmented style, *Edmund* (1982) deals with the protagonist's frantic search for identity by leaving his middle-class family for the violent New York underworld. *American Buffalo* (1975), *Glengarry Glen Ross* (1984) and *The Vermont Sketches* (1986) offer an ironic contemporary picture of Emersonian self-reliance in their depiction of the debased and vulgar values of the representatives of small-time, entrepreneurial America. Shepard, in plays such as *La Turista* (1967), *The Tooth of Crime* (1972), *Buried Child* (1978), *Curse of the Starving Class* (1978), *True West* (1980) and *Fool for Love* (1982), writes a highly theatrical drama that has a magical, ritualistic, surreal quality, explores the demonic forces in American life and landscape, and probes the interaction between myth and reality.

## Black writing

Though slavery officially ended with the Civil War, by 1880, with the end of Reconstruction and the spread of the Ku Klux Klan, African Americans felt vulnerable, insecure and culturally alienated. Charles W. Chestnutt (1858–1932), from North Carolina, is generally regarded as the father of African American fiction. James Weldon Johnson's controversial *Autobiography of an Ex-Colored Man* (1912), about interracial marriage and a light-coloured black man's 'passing' in white society, was published anonymously. The major poet of the early twentieth century was Paul Laurence Dunbar (1872–1906). Dunbar's dialect verse, which exploited the stereotype of the happy plantation slave, was popular, but white America was less enthusiastic about the more authentic utterance of his non-dialect verse. Black success stories were as popular as white ones: Booker T. Washington (1865–1915) told of his rise to become President of Tuskegee Institute, Alabama, in *Up From Slavery* (1901). Washington was an accommodationist who campaigned for the black man's economic rehabilitation and development within the American system. Patience, self-reliance and hard work were his watchwords. The most important black intellectual leader of the early twentieth century was the prolific W.E.B. DuBois (1868–1963), who provided the classic formulation of the black man's dilemma in *The Souls of Black Folk* (1903):

> The Negro is a sort of seventh son, born with a veil, and gifted with second-sight in this American world – a world which yields him no true self-consciousness, but only lets him see himself through the revelation of the other world. It is a peculiar sensation this double-consciousness, this sense of looking at one's self through the eyes of others, of measuring one's soul by the tape of a world that looks on in amused contempt and pity. One ever feels his twoness – an American and a Negro; two souls, two thoughts, two unreconciled strivings; two warring ideals in one dark body, whose dogged strength alone keeps it from being torn asunder.

DuBois helped to set the scene for the 'Harlem Renaissance' of the 1920s, which reflected a growing sense of racial identity and solidarity amongst African Americans. Blackness was equated with the virtues of spontaneity, vitality and sensuality, in contrast to western rationalism and materialism. This was the age of the 'New Negro' (see Locke, 1925), who rejected the assimilationist ideal and asserted a distinctive, separate African heritage and identity.

Black literary and cultural activity during the 1920s centred on Harlem, though two of the most important black writers of the 'Harlem Renaissance' – Claude McKay (1889–1948) and Langston Hughes (1902–67) – lived elsewhere. McKay, originally from Jamaica, is best known for the poetry collected in *Harlem Shadows* (1922). Hughes, 'the most influential African American writer in the history of American literature' (McQuade, 1994, p. 1164), under the influence of Carl Sandburg's oral-based, populist poetic voice, exploited the resources of the black experience represented by the blues, work-songs, jazz, spirituals, sermons and everyday speech. Seeking to express 'racial rhythms', he experimented with poetry written for jazz, blues or gospel performance. Succeeding poets such as Allan Ginsberg and LeRoi Jones owe much to Hughes's performative poetry. As well as ten volumes of poetry, he wrote five volumes of Simple stories. These were immensely popular, humorous, sharply observed stories of a street-wise black Everyman, Jesse B. Simple.

Two other important artists of the 'Harlem Renaissance' were Jean Toomer (1894–1967), author of *Cane* (1923), a collection of sketches, stories and poems offering a powerful, lyrical evocation of black life, notable for its musical quality, and Countee Cullen (1903–46), who explores the African American dilemma of the 'double consciousness' in his poetry, *Color* (1925), *Copper Sun* (1927), *The Ballad of the Brown Girl* (1928) and *The Black Christ* (1929).

The 'Harlem Renaissance' collapsed with the Great Depression, in which blacks suffered more than whites. Where African American writing of the 1920s embodied a spirit of black pride and racial affirmation, the writing of the 1930s and 1940s tended towards radical racial protest. The outstanding writer of this period was Richard Wright (1908–60), author of *Uncle Tom's Children* (1938), a collection of four stories concerned with racial violence in the South, *Native Son* (1940) and *Black Boy* (1945), an autobiographical account of Wright's experience of the Deep South. Another notable work of this period was Zora Neale Hurston's (1903–60) *Their Eyes Were Watching God* (1937), a novel set in Florida offering a sensitive account of the personal life of black women.

In 1955, in Montgomery, Alabama, Rosa Parks was arrested for refusing to give up her seat on a bus to a white person, and Dr Martin Luther King came to prominence as a black Civil Rights leader determined to overthrow segregation. Another equally charismatic leader of the time was Malcolm X, who preached Black Power and militant separatism, a programme with more appeal to many rebellious, disadvantaged urban blacks in the 1960s than King's non-violent protest and implicit integrationist agenda. In the late 1960s, racial unrest erupted in big-city riots across America. The Black Power activists emphasized the need for black people to see the world in their own terms: the apologists of the Black Arts Movement made the same point in the context of aesthetics. The Black Arts Movement advocated cultural separatism, a black literature written exclusively for black consumption. Instead of using their energy to prevent being 'torn asunder' by the 'double consciousness', African Americans were urged to reject the American, white side and concentrate on developing the black African side of their identity. The new black literature was to be functional, committed and collective. It was to root itself in black folk culture, black music, black religion, black street speech, black 'soul'.

Nevertheless, much of the drama of the Black Arts Movement is remarkably conventional. While rejecting the white avant-garde as decadent, many of these dramatists accepted white Odets as a literary model. LeRoi Jones (1934– ), who later changed his name to Imamu Amiri Baraka on his conversion to Islam, was the most exciting and boldly experimental in style and technique. Starting out as a Greenwich Village Beat, his early plays – *The Toilet, The Baptism, Dutchman* and *The Slave* – are neither ideologically nor aesthetically truly revolutionary. His primary dramatic interest lies in the consciousness of the individual rather than in racial solidarity or political activism. However, while these early plays have most of the characteristics of conventional socially oriented drama, the drama after 1965 – *Experimental Death Unit 1, Slave Ship, A Black Mass, Great Goodness of Life, Home on the Range, The Death of Malcolm X* and *Bloodrites* – are more schematic, composed of violent and symbolic gesture, readily employing highly stylized characterization and subordinating conventional dramatic dialectic to the polemics of the revolution. Blackness is the source of all heroism, integrity and spirituality; whiteness of all horror, stupidity and cruelty. In pulling away from the conventions of naturalism, Jones/Baraka devises new forms. But as he uses these forms, they are also, in the widest sense, traditional. Some of them still originate in the conventions of absurd drama; others are powerful stylizations of modes indigenous to African American culture, yet even they (participation, song, ritual, triumphant celebration) have antecedents in earlier or contemporary white drama.

The poetry of the Black Arts Movement is similarly intended to serve the cause of Black Power. To Jones/Baraka and his followers – Don Lee, Nikki Giovanni, Sonia Sanchez, Etheridge Knight, A.B. Spellman – poems are 'Assassin poems ... that wrestle cops into alleys/ and take their guns leaving them dead'. Despite their explicit cultural separatist emphasis, these poets are also indebted to contemporary developments in the American poetic in general. Not only in his early poetry in *The Dead Lecturer* (1964), but in later work in *Black Magic* (1969), Jones/Baraka shows the influence of William Carlos Williams and the Beats who were themselves influenced by jazz and who deliberately set out to scandalize the bourgeois establishment. Like Olson and the Projective Verse poets, the black revolutionary poets sought to capture the tone and phrasing of the speaking voice, and experimented with a poetry to be declaimed rather than read. Typographical layout was often intended to suggest various vocal and musical effects in the manner of cummings's poetry.

Other African American writers of the 1960s such as Ralph Ellison (1914–), James Baldwin (1924–87) and Lorraine Hansberry (1930–65) were more interested in the drama of the individual self than in racial separatism or political revolution. Thus, Ellison in his masterpiece, *Invisible Man*, refuses ready-made identities and superficial political programmes, interrogating the dominant stereotypes of his day – the exotic African of the 1920s, the Communist Brother of the 1930s, the post-*Native Son* rebel of the 1940s and the black revolutionary of the 1960s.

Confronted by the agonies of the 'double consciousness' it is no surprise that the black writer has sought to avoid such conflicts by retreating to Europe, as Wright and Baldwin did. Baldwin, in fact, embodies the conflicts particularly strikingly. In 1948 he moved to Paris, where he spent the next nine years ('I wanted to prevent myself from becoming merely a Negro, or even, merely a Negro writer!'), returning to his own country when the Civil Rights movement began to gain momentum in the 1950s. In 1949 he published 'Everybody's Protest Novel', an assault on what he took to be Wright's naturalistic reduction of complex Negro experience. Criticizing Wright's 'unrewarding rage', Baldwin declared that 'the first problem is how to control that rage so that it won't destroy you' (Charney, 1963). 'That artist is strangled', he wrote in another essay, 'Many Thousands Gone', 'who is forced to deal with human beings solely in social terms' (in *Nobody Knows My Name*). His early work is concerned with the quest for personal identity. His best later work is his essays – *Notes of a Native Son* (1955), *Nobody Knows My Name* (1961), *The Fire Next Time* (1963) and *The Price of the Ticket* (1985) in which, ironically, protest becomes his theme and he assumes the prophetic role.

The 1970s and 1980s have seen the emergence of two important female writers, Toni Morrison (1931–) and Alice Walker (1944–), both of whom have presented uncompromising pictures of black sexual relations and family life in basically realistic modes. Both have been concerned with sexism as well as racism. Morrison's first novel, *The Bluest Eye* (1970), includes the rape of a young girl by her drunken father, while in Walker's *The Color Purple* (1982) the tender Celie is abused first by

Pa and then passed by Pa to Mr. Both writers also offer examples of strong black womanhood – Morrison's Sula (*Sula*, 1973), and Walker's Celie, whose slow progress toward self-realization and reunion with her sister Nettie formed the substance of *The Color Purple*.

## Texts, authors, contexts

### Robert Frost: *Selected Poems* ((1913–62) Hamilton, 1973)

In the poem, 'Birches', the speaker is thinking of how the birch trees have become bent:

> But I was going to say when Truth broke in
> With all her matter of fact about the ice storm,
> I should prefer to have some boy bend them
>
> ........
>
> He learned all there was
> To learn about not launching out too soon
> And so not carrying the tree away
> Clear to the ground. He always kept his poise
> To the top branches, climbing carefully
> With the same pains you use to fill a cup
> Up to the brim, and even above the brim.
> Then he flung outward, feet first, with a swish,
> Kicking his way down through the air to the ground.
> So was I once a swinger of birches.
>
> (p. 81)

Frost's famous description of the birch-swinger is an image of great power and poise. The writing is precise, rooted in careful observation and direct experience yet resonant with symbolic implications. Frost is concerned with how far one may sensibly go out on a limb before swinging back to earth again. How 'extra-vagant' may one risk being before falling into chaos? The poem elaborates a tension between the impulse to transcend our given world and the need to keep our feet on the ground. Frost does not just discuss this tension between the ideal and the real, he enacts it. His own writing is a balancing act between respect for the empirical facts and the free play of mind. Registering his impatience with the resistant drag of the actual upon the autonomous imagination ('But I was going to say when Truth broke in ...' ), the speaker self-consciously offers his picture of the boy swinging on the birches as fantasy rather than fact: he knows the birches were bent by the weight of the ice, but prefers 'to have some boy bend them'.

The tension between Truth and Imagination is present from the very beginning of the poem: 'I like to think some boy's been swinging them', the narrator says in line 3, and then admits: 'But swinging doesn't bend them down to stay/ As ice storms do'. Yet, even while accepting the factual explanation, his rendering of it quickly presses towards a playfully imaginative extravagance: 'You'd think the inner dome of heaven had fallen', he says describing the 'crystal shells' that fall from the birches. Always, he is careful to distinguish between his imaginings and the actual facts. But if he declares his interest in getting away from earth awhile, he does not want to escape for good, 'not to return': 'Earth's the right place for love:/ I don't know where it's likely to go better'. The poem holds the real against the ideal, imagination against actuality, rootedness against transcendence, love of life against dissatisfaction with it.

Relishing the ambivalences and paradoxes of everyday life, Frost acknowledges uncertainty and rejects the temptation to embrace any absolute or transcendent truth (see the poem 'For Once, Then, Something'). Truth is never simple nor single: 'all truth is dialogue' (Lathem, 1966, p. 169). In poems such as 'The Tuft of Flowers', 'Neither Out Far Nor in Deep', 'The Strong are Saying Nothing', 'The Middleness of the Road', 'Two Tramps in Mud-Time' he balances opposing viewpoints or sides of his own personality. Sometimes he adopts different personae, as in his dramatic monologues ('Mending Wall', 'The Mountain') and eclogues ('Home Burial', 'Death of the Hired Man', 'A Hundred Collars'). Truth is embedded in particular experience and cannot be abstracted from it.

Here is the beginning of 'Mending Wall':

> Something there is that doesn't love a wall,
> That sends the frozen ground-swell under it
> And spills the upper boulders in the sun,
> And makes gaps even two can pass abreast.
> I have come after them and made repair
> Where they have left not one stone on a stone,
> But they would have the rabbit out of hiding,
> To please the yelping dogs. The gaps I mean,
> No one has seen them made or heard them made.
> But at spring mending-time we find them there.

(p. 43)

The title itself is a little strange, the omission of the article giving the poem an emblematic force and alerting us to the larger implications of the theme. We are also struck from the very first line by the strongly idiomatic, circuitous, almost rambling language in which the poem is written. Frost is concerned to give us the living word of a real person in a real situation, vividly bringing before us a particular individual – a Yankee farmer with time to talk and a curiously mixed-up attitude. In the first three lines the speaker advances the idea that nature itself (with which the poet is playfully identified in the connection between Frost and 'frozen') is opposed to man-made walls and keeps undermining them. But then, in line 5, when the speaker turns to consider the wanton depradations of the hunters and the value of the wall as a sanctuary to the hunted rabbit, it is he – the one who mocks his neighbour's wish to see the wall maintained – who repairs the damage done by the hunters. His sympathy with the weak and the vulnerable leads him to act in ways which contradict his conscious attitude. Significantly, a little further on, it is again he who initiates the annual ritual of wall building: 'I let my neighbour know ...'. There is a 'gap' between consciously held opinion and unconscious drives.

A more obvious tension is that between speaker and neighbour. The speaker is established as a garrulous, playful individual: he tells of using a 'spell' to make the boulders sit; he regards the project as 'just another kind of outdoor game'; he whimsically thinks of 'elves' being responsible for damaging the wall; he entertains the extravagant image of his neighbour as 'an old stone savage armed'. The speaker's playful, inquisitive, disruptive manner contrasts with the picture he gives us of the dour and plodding neighbour who refuses to 'go behind his father's saying'. The last line of the poem – 'He says again, "Good fences make good neighbours"' – reiterates the neighbour's firmly held, unshakeable traditionalism, and it contrasts with the poem's first line which immediately establishes the speaker's vague, roundabout, speculative manner.

But Frost does not simply reject the neighbour's point of view. We should be careful not to identify the speaker too closely with the poet. The poem in its formal entirety is the poet's statement, not what the speaker says. Frost works by balancing two antithetical viewpoints. Against the speaker's scornful dismissal of his neighbour's point of view, we might note that the wall is what brings these two people together as well as keeps them apart, that the speaker himself admits *some* walls are necessary, that he feels compelled to check his own 'extra-vagance' (see p. 348) in line 9 in the interests of coherence and good order, and, most significant of all, that the poem itself is a firm structure, so constructed as to accommodate the vagaries of natural speech within the regular, pre-established iambic pentameter. The poem, that is, enacts the interplay of discipline and 'extravagance', direction and indirection, free play and responsible fencing. These oppositions are organized in the exquisite formal balance of the poem's 'design' (see the poem 'Design', which contemplates the dark possibility that there may be no design in life, or, if there is, that it is malevolent, but does so within the strict design of the sonnet form).

Frost's entire manoeuvre may be seen to move out from traditional Georgian pastoral into a modernist sense of alienation while consistently preserving detached control and classical decorum. Though Frost himself cultivated an avuncular self-image of 'lovable, plain-dealing New England farmer-poet' (Hamilton, 1973), there was a darker side to his poetic personality that receives memorable expression in poems such as 'After Apple-Picking', 'Out, Out', 'The Witch of Coös', 'Home-Burial', 'A Servant to Servants', 'The Subverted Flower' and 'Storm Fear'. Complicating Emerson's Transcendentalism, he emphasizes ambivalence, irresolution and uncertainty. But while opening his poetry to darkness, wildness, madness, loneliness and violence, he never loses faith in human nature or in an ultimately benign creative force. Concerned though he is with walls, conflicts, limitations and failures, he is also capable of registering wonder and delight in the natural world. For Frost, life holds the potential of both beauty and terror.

Although he was born in San Francisco (in 1874) and spent most of the first eleven years of his life in California, it was New England, to which the Frost family moved in 1885 and where Robert spent most of the rest of his life, that was the inspiration of his poetry. From earlier poets such as Longfellow, Whittier and

Bryant he learned the possibilities of New England regionalism. The title of his first volume, *A Boy's Will*, was taken from Longfellow. Frost's poetry combined the American colloquial tradition with the mainstream English tradition of pastoral realism from Wordsworth to Hardy. Compare Frost's monologues and eclogues with the Wordsworthian pastoral narrative of the poor, the forgotten and the insane, in poems such as 'The Idiot Boy', 'The Thorn', 'The Complaint of a Forsaken Indian Woman' and 'The Old Cumberland Beggar', written in 'the language that men do use'. Also, compare the dramatic quality of Frost's poetry with the manner of Browning's depth-charged dramatic monologues. Frost is no more a simple folksy farmer-poet than Browning is a comfortable Victorian moralist. The dramatic quality of his poetry also owes a good deal to Virgil's *Bucolics* and *Georgics*, a version of pastoral which took the form of an exchange between two or more characters in a rural setting. Philosophically, Frost's opposition to theory and abstraction, his rejection of absolutes and refusal to commit himself derives from the sceptical and pragmatic ideas of William James and George Santayana whom he read during his two years at Harvard (1897–9).

Though Frost ultimately became a kind of national institution, the epitome of patriotic conservatism, famously reciting 'The Gift Outright' at J.F. Kennedy's inauguration, he first found success, not in America, but in England. As a young poet he was greatly encouraged by Edward Thomas and by Ezra Pound who admired his vernacular American voice. Frost, however, represents a very different strand in the American poetic tradition from the modernism of Pound and Eliot. Where Pound and Eliot reflect a disintegrated culture and looked to Europe, Frost celebrates an indigenous rural ethos, continuing a vein of vernacular humour associated with Twain. Where Pound and Eliot parade an encyclopaedic learning, Frost wears his lightly. The voice in Eliot's poetry is querulous and insubstantial, constantly seeking the grounds of authority: Frost's is more coherent and assertive. Despite their classical impersonality and concern with tradition, Eliot's and Pound's is a much more disrupted poetic than Frost's. Where the former specialized in free verse, Frost thought free verse was like 'playing tennis with the net down'. He refuses to give up on traditional resources, seeking freedom within formal authority.

## Ernest Hemingway: 'Big Two-Hearted River' ((1925) 1988)

The story tells of Nick who has just disembarked from a train, entering the burned and blackened countryside around the town of Seney, to go on a fishing trip. Think about what the burned town might signify? The destruction of civilized values? What connections are to be made between Hemingway's scorched countryside and Eliot's Waste Land and Fitzgerald's Valley of Ashes? The grasshoppers around Seney, Nick notices, have adapted to their environment by turning black to match it. The detail suggests Nick's subconscious recognition that he too must adapt to a changed world. Leaving the social world, he strikes out on his own across the devastation, heading for the river, a traditional symbol of life and the permanence of nature. Compare the 'perfect pastoral' of Thoreau's Walden with Hemingway's description of the river. Hemingway's landscape resonates with tension and danger:

'Nick's heart tightened as the trout moved. He felt all the old feeling. He turned and looked down into the stream. It stretched away, pebbly-bottomed with shallows and big boulders and a deep pool as it curved away...' (1988, p. 341). The river, with its treacherous races and deep pools, comes to symbolize Nick's stream of consciousness, his secret fears and threatening memories. The story is not just about a fishing trip but about Nick's efforts to come to terms with his own traumatized psyche. Like the trout 'keeping themselves steady' in the water, Nick struggles to maintain a psychic equilibrium.

The account of his pitching camp is described in the minutest detail, with scientific accuracy. Nick acts mechanically, mindlessly, his actions constituting a kind of ritualized escape from nightmare.

> Inside the tent the light came through the brown canvas. Already there was something mysterious and homelike. Nick was happy as he crawled inside the tent. He had not been happy all day. This was different though. Now things were done. There had been this to do. Now it was done. It had been a hard trip. He was very tired. That was done. He had made his camp. He was settled. Nothing could touch him. It was a good place to camp. He was there, in the good place. He was in his home where he had made it. (p. 345)

The short, simple sentences enact on a stylistic level the small area over which Nick feels he has control. Having turned his back on civilization, Nick establishes his own 'good place', his own 'home' where he can feel safe and secure.

Fishing is Nick's main form of therapy. He prepares his rod with ceremonial exactness, and the fishing has an almost magical power to absorb and focus his dishevelled mind. But the fishing is also symbolic of Nick's struggle for self-control. He starts fishing in the shallows, confronting the less dangerous memories first:

> He stepped into the water. It was a shock. His trousers clung to his legs. His shoes felt the gravel. The water was a rising cold shock.
> Rushing, the current sucked against his legs. Where he stepped in, the water was over his knees. He waded with the current. The gravel slid under his shoes. He looked down at the swirl of water ... (p. 351)

The writing is repetitive, tightly controlled, almost breathless with tension. It registers Nick's fear of annihilation, the repetition of 'he' expressive of his desire to assert identity in the face of the 'swirl' which threatens to carry him away completely.

When he hooks a fish in deeper water he experiences serious difficulty:

> Nick struck and the rod came alive and dangerous, bent double, the line tightening, coming out of water, tightening, all in a heavy, dangerous, steady pull. Nick felt the moment when the leader would break if the strain increased and let the line go.
> The reel ratcheted into a mechanical shriek as the line went out in a rush. Too fast. Nick could not check it, the line rushing out, the reel note rising as the line ran out.
> With the core of the reel showing, his heart feeling stopped with the excitement, leaning back against the current that mounted icily his thighs. Nick thumbed the reel hard with his left hand. It was awkward getting his thumb inside the fly reel frame.
> As he put on pressure the line tightened into sudden hardness ... (p. 353)

The struggle to control the fish symbolizes Nick's struggle to control himself and, as the pun on 'line' would suggest, Hemingway's struggle to control his materials. The heavy, irregular stresses at the beginning of the passage, the repetition of 'tightening' and then the slow, regular stresses on 'heavy, dangerous, steady pull' reflect the mounting threat to Nick's control. His personal anguish is encoded in the 'shriek' of the reel. Under the strain, normal sentence structure collapses, and we have the impression of the writing itself 'rushing out' towards breakdown and chaos. 'With the core of the reel showing' further suggests a dangerous vulnerability, the imagery in the rest of the paragraph giving Nick's hysteria an unmistakably sexual inflection. After the intense excitement, the sentences lengthen and become more flowing. The detumescent Nick has lost the trout. He is dry-mouthed, 'his heart down', his 'hand was shaky'. He feels 'a little sick'.

But after this climax, he regains control and starts fishing again. This time he has more success, enacted in the easy, flowing rhythms of the writing style. But Nick also knows that the big fish – his most painful and threatening memories – are in the treacherous swampy places of his mind: 'in the fast deep water, in the half light, the fishing would be tragic. ... He didn't want to go down the stream any further today. ... There were plenty of days coming when he could fish the swamp.'

The story communicates largely through its style. The style is intense, terse, colloquial, unliterary. Hemingway favours short words, simple sentence structure, an absolute economy of means, intense objectivity. Events tend to be presented directly as they occur, as if unmediated by rational mind. Authorial comment is kept to a minimum. Nick's strenuous concentration on details is a 'trick' to keep from thinking, and Hemingway's narration forces us to share Nick's neurotic strain. The story is important for what it does not say, for all the things Nick does not allow himself to recall. The real action is subterranean and symbolic. Hemingway's style reflects and embodies the control and self-discipline of the famous 'Hemingway Code'. His refusal to comment, elaborate or abstract is an expression of the need to concentrate on the little area that can be confidently mastered, the small space that isn't an emotional swamp or moral quagmire where he can feel safe. Hemingway's world is thus a very limited one, very largely a world of things and sense impressions. It is a world of violence, crisis, trauma, continually under the shadow of death, often quite literally a world at war. In such a world pleasure is the pleasure of the senses – eating, drinking, fishing, hunting, bull-fighting. Morality is a pragmatic matter of what you feel good after, and involves the qualities which Nick in the story strives to demonstrate: stoical endurance, practical competence, 'grace under pressure' (the phrase is from Hemingway's first novel, *The Sun Also Rises*, first published in the United Kindom as *Fiesta* in 1927).

'Big Two-Hearted River' is the last story in Hemingway's first collection, *In Our Time* (1925), the title an ironic allusion to the Book of Common Prayer: 'Give peace in our time, O Lord' – ironic because there is no peace in Hemingway's world. All of Hemingway's stories deal with horrific violence, from the spectacle of the Indian who has cut his head nearly off with a razor witnessed by the young Nick in the first story in *In Our Time* ('Indian Camp') to the derangement Nick experiences as a result of his war experiences in 'A Way You'll Never Be' and 'Now I Lay Me' in the later collection, *Winner Take Nothing* (1933). One of the sketches in *In Our Time* is a vivid description of Nick's wounding by machine-gun fire, the origins of which lie in Hemingway's own experiences in the First World War when, serving as a Red Cross ambulance driver on the Italian front, he was badly injured in the knee. In both his life and his art he was preoccupied with the proofs of manhood, and the great challenge of confronting danger and death bravely. Formally, the mode of composition of *In Our Time*, intercutting the stories with fragments of autobiographical reminiscence – brief images of bull-fighting, war, shootings, an execution – enforces our sense of violent disruption and unease.

The Nick Adams of 'Big Two-Hearted River' is like Hemingway returning from the European war to America in 1919, lighting out for a solitary sojourn in the Michigan woods to recuperate. Nick is the prototype of the Hemingway 'wounded hero'. Jake Barnes, the hero of *The Sun Also Rises*, suffers from an emasculating wounding and, like Nick in 'Now I Lay Me', cannot sleep or bear the darkness. *A Farewell to Arms* (1927) returns to the Italian front where Hemingway was wounded and describes Frederick Henry's leg-wounding, his 'separate peace', and further wounding when Catherine dies in child-birth. Harry Morgan in *To Have and Have Not* (1937) has lost his arm. Robert Jordan in *For Whom the Bell Tolls* (1940) seeks to compensate for a psychological wounding, the knowledge of his father's suicide. *Across the River and Into the Trees* (1950) has the battle-scarred Colonel Cantwell (and his creator) revisit 'the exact place where ... he had been wounded thirty years before'. The action of *The Old Man and the Sea* (1952) is figured as a crucifixion of Santiago.

Hemingway's main fictional preoccupation is how to live with the symbolic wounding, which is the sign of the individual's endurance and knowledge. In Nick Adams we have the beginnings of the 'Hemingway Hero': the wounded man who has rejected the traditional values and high-sounding abstractions of conventional morality ('I was always embarrassed by the words sacred, glorious, and sacrifice and the expression in vain', says Frederick Henry), and who aspires to an ideal of personal honour, tight-lipped endurance and courage, a cool ironic nonchalance in the face of a bleak and hostile world. The 'Hemingway Code' is most triumphantly demonstrated by such heroes as the bullfighter Romero in *Fiesta*, Santiago in *The Old Man and the Sea* who is destroyed but refuses to accept defeat, and Wilson, the British hunting guide in 'The Short Happy Life of Francis Macomber'.

The Hemingway world reflects not only a personal, psychological condition, but also an historical reality of post-war disillusionment with traditional values. The figure of Nick Adams implies the infiltration of original New World Adamic innocence by 'old Nick'. Through the Nick Adams stories, Hemingway portrays an image of innocence wounded, young life scarred, the dream betrayed. Compare Nick Adams with Huck Finn: both boys are disoriented by the violence they encounter and are afflicted by nightmares; both are fugitive figures, cut off from the supports of family and society; both undergo a painful rite of passage.

The international dimensions of Hemingway's fiction suggest the universality of the exacerbated conditions which he describes. His preoccupation with the need to withstand violence and chaos, and his assertion of an aesthetic response of concrete precision, irony and impersonality place him alongside the Moderns such as Eliot, Pound, William Carlos Williams and Joyce. Though often regarded as a spokesman of what Gertrude Stein famously called the 'Lost Generation', Hemingway himself rejected the term, asserting instead the positive values of the Code and a residual pastoral and Transcendental idealism, 'with the earth abiding for ever as hero' (quoted in Baker, 1969, p. 81).

### John Steinbeck: *The Grapes of Wrath* ((1939) 1951)

Steinbeck's novel had strong topical appeal. It deals with one of the great natural disasters in American history – the Dust Bowl in Oklahoma and the consequent migration of thousands of poor farmers westwards to California. *The Grapes of Wrath* is one of the great protest novels in American literature. Steinbeck protests against the impersonal economic forces in the form of the banks and the big conglomerates which destroy the poor and the vulnerable. He protests against the obsolescence of the individual small farmer in a world caught up in the inexorable march of technological and economic progress. The modernizing forces are responsible for producing a traumatic alienation epitomized by the figure of Muley Graves (his name suggestive of both his stubbornness and the living death to which he has been condemned) who has been dispossessed and left to wander helplessly around the countryside. Steinbeck further protests against a pervasive greed and exploitativeness which, his migrant family of Joads encounter at the hands of sharkish predators, ranging from second-hand car salesmen to the land syndicates in California who let the fruit rot on the ground to keep up prices rather than use it to feed the destitute. Steinbeck castigates the short-sighted ignorance of such a policy which he believes will ultimately lead to revolt. Because of their ill-treatment, a resentment grows among the oppressed that, Steinbeck angrily warns, will ultimately bring about the overthrow of the capitalist system: 'and in the eyes of the people there is the failure; and in the eyes of the hungry there is a growing wrath. In the souls of the people the grapes of wrath are filling and growing heavy, growing heavy for the vintage' (1951, p. 320).

Steinbeck is no pessimist. His criticisms of the corrupt society are matched by a faith in man's elemental instinct to survive. Addressing the capitalists, he writes:

> If you could separate causes from results, if you could know that Paine, Marx, Jefferson, Lenin were results, not causes, you might survive. But that you cannot know. For the quality of owning freezes you forever into 'I', and cuts you off for ever from the 'we'. (p. 139)

He is more interested in underlying conditions than in ideological programmes. The development of a revolutionary proletariat, he insists, derives not from a political perspective but from an essential desire for survival. Rather than propounding or recommending any particular dogma, he offers a parable of how fear converts to wrath, which in turn becomes the dynamic force for change. His faith lies in a concept of inevitable natural progression, symbolized by the heroic struggle of the turtle in Chapters 3 and 4, and explicitly proclaimed in statements such as this: 'man reaches, stumbles forward, painfully, mistakenly sometimes. Having stepped forward, he may slip back, but only half a step, never the full step back' (p. 138). New social conditions, Steinbeck shows, produce new social forms. Thus, the people who are initially organized in families, Steinbeck's basic image of hierarchical order, interdependence and cooperation, see the advantages of inter-family solidarity. Then they form themselves into the still larger social groupings of the camps. Weedpatch Camp, recalling various Transcendentalist ventures in communal living in the nineteenth century, represents the triumph of democracy and confirms the greater power of the group over the individual. Ultimately, the people organize themselves into labour unions to confront the depradations of capitalist exploitation.

Steinbeck reinforces his message through the development of exemplary individuals. The crudely idealized Ma Joad, who was originally concerned only with her family, realizes towards the end that people must help everyone. Jim Casy, the preacher and Christ-figure of the book, sacrifices himself for others, but his message is carried on by his disciple, Tom, who, along with Ma and Rosasharn, moves towards acceptance of the whole world as his family. In the final episode, Rosasharn gives the dying man her milk. This is the book's culminating image of Christian sacrifice and selfless action. Sentimental though it may be, it affirms the continuity of life and Steinbeck's belief in the need for union and solidarity in order to survive.

Steinbeck's is a basically Christian and humanitarian outlook on the world rather than political. Like Fitzgerald in *The Great Gatsby*, he is concerned to give his story the largest possible mythical and archetypal resonance. In the first chapter, following the example of Thomas Hardy, he emphasizes the epic character of his narrative by first establishing nature's massive, timeless processes, represented by the dust storm, and then gradually introducing his human figures into this awe-inspiring scene:

> And the women came out of the houses to stand beside their men – to feel whether this time the men would break. The women studied the men's faces secretly, for the corn could go, as long as something else remained .... But it was all right. The women knew it was all right, and the watching children knew it was all right. Women and children knew in themselves that no misfortune was too great to bear if their men were whole. The women went into the houses to their work, and the children began to play, but cautiously at first. As the day went forward the sun became less red. It flared down on the dust-blanketed land. The men sat in the doorways of their houses; their hands were busy with sticks and little rocks. The men sat still – thinking – figuring. (Ch. 1, p. 7)

The writing has the simplicity of parable, stripping humanity to the bare essentials, presenting 'unaccommodated man' at a pre-individualized, pre-literate stage of his development. The 'something else' in line 3 of my quotation is what the rest of the novel sets out to define and demonstrate: what is clear is that the people's faith has nothing to do with any particular ideology, but all to do with man's elemental spirit of fight and survival. By the end of the passage the men have confirmed their enduring will in the face of the worst life has to bring. The language of this passage is picked up again towards the end of the book after the flood, when man's instinctive will to live is reflected and symbolized in nature itself:

> The rain stopped. On the fields the water stood, reflecting the grey sky, and the land whispered with moving water .... The women watched the men, watched to see whether

the break had come at last .... And the women sighed with relief, for they knew it was all right – the break had not come; and the break would never come as long as fear could turn to wrath. Tiny points of grass came through the earth, and in a few days the hills were pale green with the beginning year. (Ch. 29, p. 398)

Through the simplicity of the language and the imagery of the flood, Steinbeck recalls the biblical story. Similarly, the trek westward is related to the biblical journey to the Promised Land. The migration is also presented in primitive, biological terms. The humans migrating along Route 66 are driven by the same basic instincts as those of the simplest organisms: 'In the daylight they scuttled like bugs to the westward; and as the dark caught them, they clustered like bugs near to shelter and to water.'

Steinbeck is concerned to give events a representative character. Thus, in Chapter 5, the confrontation between 'tenant men' and the 'owner men' who have come to take the tenant farmers' land is presented in broad allegorical outline as a kind of parable between good and evil in which the enemy is a ravenous, vicious 'monster' that is out of control and devours the poor.

> We're sorry. It's not us. It's the monster. The bank isn't like a man.
> Yes, but the bank is only made of men.
> No, you're wrong there – quite wrong there. The bank is something else than men. It happens that every man in a bank hates what the bank does, and yet the bank does it. The bank is something more than men, I tell you. It's the monster. Men made it, but they can't control it. (Ch. 5, p. 32)

Since the 'tenant men' are being dispossessed by an unseen, nameless force, their plight is all the worse, for they don't know how they can fight it. Through the biblical simplicity of his style Steinbeck turns the specific incident into representative image.

Steinbeck's central theme being the evolutionary processes of life itself, the great artistic challenge facing him was how to represent these natural and social forces. Using the 'inter-calary' chapters, he intercut the realistic story of the Joad family with chapters of a more general nature which keep us aware of the representative nature of the Joads' experience, and place their adventures in the context of the larger social and historical forces at work. By combining naturalistic story-telling with symbol and parable he was able to reach beyond the immediate circumstances and present a story of an elemental human struggle which has proved to have a wide and long-lasting appeal.

Throughout his career Steinbeck sought to speak for the inarticulate, the poor, the forgotten and the dispossessed. While deliberately generalizing his themes so that he could offer an image of the universal human condition, his starting-point was actual experience. *The Grapes of Wrath* is based on his first-hand observations of the plight of the migrants. He travelled with them from Oklahoma to California and saw for himself the conditions in the camps. He wrote about these experiences in a series of newspaper articles and in the pamphlet *Their Blood is Strong* (1938). A novel, *In Dubious Battle* (1936), took a fairly sympathetic view of a Communist-inspired strike of migrant workers in California. Steinbeck thus has affinities with that tradition of American documentary fiction which culminates in the writings of Norman Mailer and Thomas Wolfe.

*The Grapes of Wrath*, when it first appeared, was read as a social document, and even as a Communistic political tract, rather than as a work of art. It was criticized for its depiction of the Okies and for its view of Californian big business. Since then it has been more properly judged as a powerful social critique which at the same time promotes human values rather than political ideals. Nevertheless, Steinbeck is not always able to find artistic embodiment for his ideas and strong feelings, and as a result the book does not entirely escape being sentimental or melodramatic or propagandistic or overtly rhetorical.

His views of the human condition were shaped and informed by his interest in zoology and marine biology. *The Sea of Cortez* (1941) is an account of the marine organisms that Steinbeck and his friend, Ed Ricketts, owner of the Pacific Biological Laboratories in Monterey, collected during an expedition to the Gulf of California (the Sea of Cortez). Characteristically, Steinbeck describes human life in animal terms. His philosophy also owes a good deal to Emerson as well as to Darwin. Casy discovers that the individual soul is part of 'one big soul ever'body's a part of', an idea picked up later by Tom in a passage where Steinbeck blatantly manipulates his character for the sake of his own moral purpose. The result is embarrassingly sentimental:

> Well, maybe like Casy says, a fella ain't got a soul of his own, but on'y a piece of a big one – an' then – Then it don't matter. Then I'll be aroun' in the dark. I'll be ever'where – wherever you look. Wherever they's a fight so hungry people can eat, I'll be there.
> (Ch. 28, p. 385)

This idea of the 'en-masse' comes straight from Emerson's notion of the Oversoul and Whitman's sense of the ultimate unity and holiness of a wonderfully diverse world. One of Steinbeck's central concerns is with the twin and often contradictory claims of the individual and the group. In the form he devised for *The Grapes of Wrath* he sought to reconcile these claims by asserting that individual fulfilment could only be attained through democratic identification with the 'en-masse'.

Finally, *The Grapes of Wrath* has to be read in the context of the perennial 'American Dream'. The migration west is a manifestation of the pioneering spirit which reaches out towards new experience and new possibility. Steinbeck emphasizes disappointment and frustration, but also insists that since the obstacles in the way of fulfilment are man-made they may be removed or overcome by man. The dream of romantic possibility vested in the special individual (Gatsby, for example) is replaced by a minimal idealism, by a rather more modest faith in mankind's elemental instinct to survive.


## Richard Wright: *Native Son* ((1940) 1972)

*Native Son* is divided into three books. Book One, 'Fear', describes a day in the life of the black boy Bigger Thomas, who longs for a 'bigger' life than the one to which white society has condemned him. Bigger's day begins with the killing of a rat in the cramped apartment he shares with mother, sister and brother, and ends with the killing of the white girl Mary Dalton. Book Two, 'Flight', presents Bigger's discovery of a new sense of freedom, potency and exhilaration that murder has given him. Wright is at his best describing, in a taut and economical prose, the chase and final capture of Bigger on a tenement rooftop. Book Three, 'Fate', breaks with the naturalistic method of the first two books and attempts to offer analysis and interpretation of Bigger's actions, thoughts and feelings in a series of contrived quasi-symbolic episodes.

In Book Three, the representatives of the forces and influences that have figured in Bigger's life are brought together, each eager to explain the black boy. There is Buckley, the official representative of 'the State', who thinks it is simply in the nature of the 'Nigger' to kill. Buckley condemns Bigger with biblical zeal: 'Every decent white man in America ought to swoon with joy for the opportunity to crush with his heel the woolly head of this black lizard' (1972, p. 441). Buckley's rhetoric is repeated in the language of the newspaper reporters: 'But the brutish Negro seemed indifferent to his fate ... He acted like an earlier missing link in the human species. He seemed out of place in a white man's civilization' (p. 318). More insidious is the language of white middle-class liberalism. Mr Dalton's tokenistic capitalism is really a cover-up for guilt, and Max, Bigger's Jewish lawyer, criticizes the white philanthropist for thinking his gift of ping-pong tables will solve the problem of disaffected inner-city black youth: 'My God, man! Will ping-pong keep men from murdering? ... Don't you grant as much life-feeling to other men as you have?' (p. 332). Equally unsatisfactory is the Christian interpretation of Bigger's life represented by the preacher and by Bigger's mother: 'It was the old voice of his mother telling of suffering, of hope, of love beyond this world. And he [Bigger] loathed it because it made him feel as condemned and guilty as those who hated him' (p. 320).

However, the bulk of Book Three is devoted to Mr Max's long courtroom defence of Bigger in which the Jewish lawyer attempts to provide an explanation of the psychological and social factors which gave rise to the black boy's murderous actions. Max insists that Bigger is a product of his environment and that only through his wild act of violence was he able to break the stranglehold of the white world on his life:

> He murdered Mary Dalton accidentally, without thinking, without plan, without conscious motive. But, after he murdered, he accepted the crime. And that's the important thing. It was the first full act of his life; it was the most meaningful, exciting, and stirring thing that had ever happened to him. He accepted it because it made him free, gave him the possibility of choice, of action, the opportunity to act and to feel that his actions carried weight.... Multiply Bigger Thomas twelve million times, allowing for environmental and temperamental variations, and for those Negroes who are completely under the influence of the church, and you have the psychology of the Negro people. (pp. 430–1)

Max wants the white world to understand that Bigger's horrific act of violence was not an act of retaliation or revenge against a specific individual, but a symbolic gesture against what Bigger took to be 'the natural structure of the universe', a metaphysical revolt against the very conditions of his existence. In accepting responsibility for murder, Max explains, Bigger felt that 'he was free for the first time in his life', that he had transcended the condition of invisibility and nameless-ness (the central concepts of Ellison's and Baldwin's racial analysis as reflected in the title of Ellison's novel *Invisible Man* and Baldwin's collection of essays *No Name in the Street*). Murder, says Max, gave Bigger's life new meaning, new purpose and new potency.

Max's speechifying, in its eloquence, passion and sheer length, clearly voices a good deal of Wright's own thinking. Unashamedly, Wright allows art to be subordinated to the polemics of Communist ideology. But in the end, he shows that Max's attempt to explain the black psyche is also inadequate. The passage illustrates the kind of historical, socio-economic language that Max uses to define Bigger's inchoate turmoil, and Bigger ultimately rejects it. Max cannot appreciate that terrorism might mean more to Bigger than constructive social revolution, that a perverse and self-destructive individualism may take precedence over a Commu-nistic idealism. Communist determinism is displaced by a concept of demonic existentialism.

Only Bigger himself can point to the real reason for his actions – his urge to create his own identity as a human being: 'What I killed for, I *am*' (p. 461). He murdered to carve out an identity for himself through violence. Wright does not sentimentalize or excuse Bigger: he insists on the awfulness of his deeds and refuses to use Max simply to move responsibility for the black man's murderous actions from the (black) individual to (white) society. Although it is not a first-person narration from Bigger's point of view, it is very close to it: we tend to see from Bigger's perspective. Thus, we feel the panic and undefined unease that Bigger feels when chauffeuring Mary and Jan, and we feel Bigger's guilt and fear when he returns to the furnace to see if Mary's body has been completely consumed. We are never allowed into the minds of the other characters and we know as little, or nearly as little, as Bigger does. Bigger's language has a raw power in its broken expression of his frustration, but it is still extremely limited. Bigger, disqualified by his surliness, inarticulacy and limited consciousness, is unable to speak for himself.

Ultimately, it would seem, there is no language to express Bigger. He is excluded from the dominant discourses. He is isolated both from his own people, his family and friends and other black people, and also from the modes of communi-cation, the images and symbols and language of the white 'centre'. Defined as marginal, he is denied access to power or fulfilment of desire. Everybody tries to explain him, speak his story. But Bigger is the Other that cannot be spoken in any language, neither the languages of Marxism or Christianity, nor the official languages of the media or the State. Not even the narrator's clinical naturalism can express Bigger. There is no master discourse to give him reliable identity and enable the novel to achieve completion and closure. Bigger remains to the end the unassimilable Other, an embodiment of the dark demons in human nature that elude definition and refuse to be incorporated within the rational ideal of socialist realism. He cannot be defined or explained because the dominant discourse has no place for him. He is Other, marginal, invisible, available only as a stereotype of crime and horror. His presence is an absence, a blank, a gap, a silence in the midst of the central discourse.

Wright as a black writer cannot approach the American Dream in any other way than to twist it, deconstruct it, disturb it through inserting an unspeakable Other in its midst. The only way for an African American to achieve the self-creation that is the goal of the American Dream is to break the law, become an outcast, a criminal, a devil. Bigger represents a demonization of the American Dream, a perversion of the Emersonian ideal of self-reliance and belief in the self's unlimited possibility. All his life Bigger has been both inside and outside American society: he dreams its dreams but feels excluded from any possibility of realizing them by the accepted means. Bigger shares Gatsby's Nietzschean powers of self-transformation but, a much more radically alienated figure than Gatsby, it is through murder that he 'created a new life for himself'. His actions alienate him as completely from the black as from the white community. Committed to a purely personal quest for authenticity, Bigger proudly accepts his position as 'outsider', unlike Carson McCullers's characters who, though similarly condemned to frustrating isolation in a cruel and ironic world, are lonely hunters longing for love and striving for community. Bigger is a voluntary *isolato*, a figure of the wolfish being Ishmael might have become had not it been for the healing influence of the social bond with Queequeg. Bigger is, rather, a son of Ahab, the exponent of a ruinous and diabolic self-assertion, though in Bigger's case, his rejection of community and the claims of the 'other' is rooted in a powerful social critique. Following Nietzsche, Heidegger and Sartre, Bigger rejects the old myths and values and accepts the existential burden of freedom. Like Camus's Caligula, he becomes his own god, the creator of his own world, and in the process turns himself into a monster, for only a murderous nihilism makes him feel alive.

Where Eugene O'Neill and Tennessee Williams responded to the sense of determinism with a compassionate understanding of illusion, Wright does so with the assertion of an apocalyptic violence, a dream of revenge. He pursues this dream at the expense of the black character, which he reduces to a simple image of brutality. In redirecting self-hatred towards whites, Bigger exchanges the role of passive, servile black man for that of a depraved and dangerous black beast. James Baldwin objects, saying that the real tragedy of Bigger Thomas

> is not that he is cold or black or hungry, nor even that he is an American black, but that he has accepted a theology that denies him life, that he admits the possibility of his being subhuman and feels constrained, therefore, to battle for his humanity according to those brutal criteria bequeathed him at his birth. (Baldwin, 1961, p. 23)

Baldwin criticizes Wright for doing what the white man had so often done – reducing complex Negro experience to a simple stereotype. Such reductiveness, Baldwin insists, is the inevitable limitation of social protest literature. Wright, however, believed that the figure of the isolated, deracinated, alienated, monstrous Bigger Thomas was the archetypal image of modern man. 'The Negro', he declared, 'is America's metaphor' (Gross and Hardy, 1966, p. vii).

*Native Son*, like Steinbeck's *Grapes of Wrath* or Theodore Dreiser's *An American Tragedy*, is based on actual events. The style is influenced by the naturalism of Hemingway and Dreiser, and by Zola and the European realists. In his concern with the dark underside of consciousness, the experience of nightmare, monstrous evil and wide-eyed terror, Wright also continues the tradition of American gothic coming down from Charles Brockden Brown, Poe, Hawthorne and Melville. The substance of the book is drawn from Wright's own boyhood experiences of racism in Mississippi where he was born and grew up, and from his later experiences of urban life in Chicago to which he moved at the age of 19. The book is shaped by the rigours of the 1930s, for with the Depression came social tension, race riots and aggressive protest. This was the time of the founding of the Black Muslims, protests against the trial of the Scottsboro boys charged with rape in Alabama, the continued migration from rural America to the urban centres, the racial protest of the National Association for the Advancement of Colored People (NAACP). The novel also bears the imprint of Wright's Communist involvement, which lasted from 1933, when he joined the American Communist Party, to his break with the party in 1944. In his essay, 'I Tried to be a Communist' (1944), Wright registers his rejection of a narrowly ideological response to life, an attitude that also makes itself apparent in *Native Son*. For conflicting with the Marxian ideal of a militant collectivism is an existentialist emphasis on individual freedom and responsibility. Wright's later novel, *The Outsider* (1953) is more explicitly a product of the existentialist imagination with its self-consciously intellectual protagonist, Cross Damon, who can articulate his position more fully than Bigger Thomas.

The displacement of Marxism by an emergent existentialism in *Native Son* signals a turn from politics that is continued in novels such as McCullers's *The Heart is a Lonely Hunter* (1940), Robert Penn Warren's *All the King's Men* (1946), Norman Mailer's *The Naked and the Dead* (1948), Ellison's *The Invisible Man* (1952) and Baldwin's *Go Tell It on the Mountain* (1953). After *Native Son*, naturalistic social protest fiction in the 1940s was gradually modified, partly in response to the marginalizing tendency of the rising formalist orthodoxy of the 'New Criticism' which called for the separation of art and politics. Thus, the social emphasis which characterized the literature of the 1930s was replaced by an interest in the personal, the psychological and the question of identity. Fraught with existential anxiety, the American novel continued to deal with the universal quest for love and redemption, or collapsed into solipsism and absurdism in the absence of community and communication.

## Carson McCullers: *The Ballad of the Sad Cafe* ((1951) 1963)

McCullers's title should immediately alert us to the inappropriateness of applying the criteria of a strict realism in assessing the novella. She has set out to adapt the conventions of the ballad world to her own narrative purposes. M.H. Abrams in *A Glossary of Literary Terms* (1981) offers the following definition: 'Typically, the popular ballad is dramatic and impersonal: the narrator ... tells the story tersely by means of action and dialogue ... and tells it without expressing his personal attitudes or feelings.' *The Oxford Dictionary* adds to the definition by describing the ballad as 'a simple song; sentimental song ... narrating popular story'. Originally a form of oral folk culture, the ballad was usually addressed directly to the listener and featured a short, simple, repetitive narrative that could be easily memorized. Hence, it also tended to be symmetrical, made use of repeated motifs and refrains, and often exhibited a circular structure. To keep the listener interested, all sorts of rhetorical devices were employed to create mystery and arouse curiosity and suspense.

The opening section of *The Ballad of the Sad Cafe* immediately establishes the distinctive tone and atmosphere of the narrative:

> The town itself is dreary; not much is there except the cotton-mill, the two-room houses where the workers live, a few peach trees, a church with two coloured windows, and a miserable main street only a hundred yards long. On Saturdays the tenants from the near-by farms come in for a day of talk and trade. Otherwise the town is lonesome, sad, and like a place that is far off and estranged from all other places in the world.... If you walk along the main street on an August afternoon there is nothing whatsoever to do... sometimes in the late afternoon when the heat is at its worst a hand will slowly open the shutter and a face will look down on the town. It is a face like the terrible dim faces known in dreams – sexless and white, with two grey crossed eyes which are turned inward so sharply that they seem to be exchanging with each other one long gaze of grief... here in this town there was once a cafe .... The owner of the place was Miss Amelia Evans. But the person most responsible for the success and gaiety of the place was a hunchback called Cousin Lymon. One other person had a part in the story of this cafe – he was the former husband of Miss Amelia, a terrible character who returned to the town after a long term in the penitentiary, caused ruin, and went on his way again. The cafe has long since been closed, but it is still remembered. (1963, pp. 7–8)

The writing gives us the feel of legend, myth, fairytale, dream. McCullers creates a timeless world, removed from society and its wider problems. The desolation, the portents of disaster, the freakish characters, all contribute to the air of mystery. An atmosphere is strongly evoked – an atmosphere of loneliness and decay which permeates the whole human condition in the novella. The setting serves as a metaphor of the spiritual isolation which is McCullers's main theme. There is just enough specificity to concretize the location in our imagination. McCullers is not interested in time, place (the town remains nameless) or other such details except where they relate directly to her story. Her concern is with the direct presentation of elemental thoughts and feelings, not with intellectualizing or rationalizing them. The story she has to tell is a universal one, and it is told with a childlike directness and simplicity.

The action, we see, is to be in the nostalgic mode, and takes the form of an extended flashback. We can see the influence of the oral tradition in the way McCullers seeks to engage the reader from the outset. The direct address in the present tense creates an intimacy between narrator and reader. Things are half-explained, hinted at. We are given the barest outline of what is to happen. Our curiosity is aroused: we want to know what *did* happen in this godforsaken place. What is the story of that strange ghostly face? What of those other freakish characters who are introduced so randomly and briefly? The characters are viewed objectively, at a distance: neither here nor elsewhere in the narrative are we offered close psychological insight into their inner lives. They all quickly acquire mythic resonances. Miss Amelia is a version of the mad woman in the attic or, perhaps, the white witch, in view of her strange healing powers and addiction to 'the magic of the number seven'. The 'terrible character' (as yet unnamed) is the beautiful devil, Marvin Macy, another mythical figure of demonic proportions: he 'never sweated, not even in August, and that surely is a sign worth pondering over' (p. 63). The third character introduced in the passage, Cousin Lymon, is comparable to an incubus in the way he quite literally clings to Miss Amelia's back, drawing the life-force from her. The pervading sense of mystery and evil turns the story into a version of southern Gothic, while the impersonality frees the narrative from all tendentiousness and adds to the universal quality. The narrator is never judgemental so that, although there is a moral to the tale – that all humans need to communicate and love in a more balanced way – it is not a moral that condemns people, rather it accepts and understands. There is simply a sad inevitability and matter-of-factness about the dreariness and lonesomeness which characterize the situation.

The language is notable for its simplicity and repetitiveness: 'there is nothing whatsoever to do' is echoed in 'there is absolutely nothing to do' on the next page. Words like 'lonesome' and 'sad' resonate through the whole story: 'he [Cousin Lymon] was so delighted that he wanted to glory with himself alone'; 'Marvin Macy took a quart bottle of whiskey and went with it alone into the swamp'; 'Her [Miss Amelia's] look that night, then, was the lonesome look of the lover'. McCullers elaborates a repetitive structure of action: Marvin Macy loves Miss Amelia, she loves Cousin Lymon and he loves Marvin Macy.

The climax of the story is the great fight between Marvin Macy and Miss Amelia:

> Just at the stroke of seven Miss Amelia showed herself at the head of the stairs. At the same instant Marvin Macy appeared in front of the cafe and the crowd made way for him silently. They walked towards each other with no haste, their fists already gripped, and their eyes like the eyes of dreamers.... And what took place has been a mystery ever since. (1963, pp. 78–80)

The fight is a legendary, apocalyptic confrontation between good and evil, a deadly ritualistic showdown, the preparations for which are described in detail. It brings to a head the magical, supernatural element, the pervading sense of foreboding. On the day of the battle 'a hawk with a bloody breast flew over the town and circled twice round the property of Miss Amelia' – an ominous portent, for at the moment when Miss Amelia gets the better of Marvin Macy, the hunchback sprang forward 'as though he had grown hawk wings'. One of Canada's most famous ballad-makers, Robert Service, in such ballads as 'Dangerous Dan McGrew' and 'The Man from God Knows Where' wrote of the larger-than-life fights between tough miners and frontiersmen. McCullers reworks the conventional fist-fight: the fight is between a man and a woman, but as with Service, it has mythic pretensions. Instead of at high noon, the fight begins 'just at the stroke of seven' (Miss Amelia's 'heavenly number'). Characteristically, McCullers deflates the myth by having the hunchback settle the issue by jumping onto Miss Amelia's back. The whole episode illustrates McCullers's brand of grotesque humour, a humour of action rather than words.

*The Ballad of the Sad Cafe* is a story of failure, of deviant, needless violence, after which Miss Amelia boards up her property and goes into seclusion. The characters have all failed themselves and each other. The town reverts to what it was. The conclusion of the novella replays the beginning. We are left despondent. But then the human voice is suddenly raised in song in the coda performance of the chain-gang. Despite the chains and shackles binding the body, the soul is free. Where freedom is denied, the 'Twelve Mortal Men' live in harmony and brother-hood. The call and response of the chain-gang has its origins in Negro Spiritual music which asserts human courage and resilience in the face of adversity. Song continues despite suffering. The convicts' song 'swells', as the cafe-life did earlier, but soon the crescendo 'sinks down' (p. 84) to a single voice in the wilderness, the last ineradicable affirmation of the human spirit. Like *The Great Gatsby*, McCullers's novella becomes an American fable, telling of promise, then of the distortion and loss of ideals, but finally affirming the imperishable human capacity to hope and dream.

The novella highlights McCullers's interest in enlarging the possibilities of conventional, realistic story-telling. Her first major novel, *The Heart Is a Lonely Hunter* ([1943] 1961), written when she was 23, exhibits a similar interest in the poetic, the fabulous and the mythic, though she is rather less successful in combining the literal and the symbolic in the earlier work. Her central theme – the quest for a god – is enacted at least four times over (in the stories of Mick Kelly, Jake Blount, Dr Copeland and Biff Brannon), with symmetrical punctiliousness, Singer the deaf-mute being the object of all four characters' mythologizing attentions, and all four quests ending in an equivalently depressing fashion. The proliferation of examples does not substantially extend, either intellectually or emotionally, our view of human illusion and spiritual isolation. Singer's four acolytes become representative figures (the adolescent girl, the itinerant radical, the Negro activist, the philosophical observer), and Singer is turned into a symbolic figure, not only by the four characters but by McCullers herself, as a consequence of which he loses some of his rich humanity.

With the arrival of Singer comes the promise of an end to loneliness and isolation, just as the opening of the cafe promised a new beginning in *The Ballad*. Despite loss and failure, both works emphasize enduring human will. The novel's title juxtaposes the will to search for communion with intimations of failure in the word 'lonely'. The idea of a 'hunt' carries a sense of violence or desperation where there is inevitably a victim. The tension in the title runs through the whole book, and through much of American literature. Although hopes are defeated or left unfulfilled, the quest goes on. This is Fitzgerald's message in his 'boats against the current' image with which *The Great Gatsby* ends. At the close of *The Heart Is a Lonely Hunter*, Biff's brief suspension between the 'radiance and darkness' (p. 312) is a Joycean epiphany, a confirmation of the human being's position in a spiritually paralyzed world. The action of McCullers's novel is pessimistic, but the tone conditions despair, and the insights into the characters that we are given emphasize human worth and nobility, the need to love and be loved. The novel is full of ironic comments on the futility of existence, and violence and disappointment are endemic. Life always beats humanity. Yet McCullers affirms faith, hope, the future. The book's closing image is of Biff composing himself 'to await the morning sun': whatever the quantum of existential pain, there is always the knowledge, which McCullers shares with Hemingway, that 'the sun also rises'.

McCullers's treatment of the theme of spiritual isolation in a southern, small-town setting is comparable to Sherwood Anderson's treatment of the same theme in the mid-western small-town setting of *Winesburg, Ohio* (1919). In 'The Book of the Grotesque', which prefaces *Winesburg, Ohio*, Anderson defines the 'grotesque' as that condition arising out of a character's obsession with a 'single truth' which closes him or her off from the 'Other' in experience. Hence, Anderson's interest in those individuals unable to find support, bearings, direction or stability from relationship with others and who fall prey to the dangers of solipsism, self-enclosure, fantasy and unchecked egotism. Like McCullers's 'freaks' (*The Heart Is a Lonely Hunter*, 1961, p. 23), Anderson's 'grotesques' suffer from a deadly imbalance. Both writers seek to give a voice to the secret life of their characters, to reveal the hidden passions and repressed energies. Both treated the victim and the outcast with great tenderness and sympathetic understanding, an attitude which in McCullers's case no doubt derived in some measure from her own situation as an artist and bisexual from Georgia in the heart of America's fundamentalist 'Bible Belt'. Where McCullers looked for an expression beyond the confines of realism, Anderson's style likewise demonstrates an experimental resistance to fixity, certainty and transitivity, a refusal to be locked into obsessive patterns or any notion of 'single truth'. Instead, he aimed for 'a new looseness'. 'Life', he said, 'is a loose, flowing thing. There are no plot stories in life' (quoted in Bradbury, 1992, p. 62).

## Tennessee Williams: *A Streetcar Named Desire* ((1947) 1962)

Williams's theme is the plight of the victim, the weak and oppressed, the injured one, the hypersensitive individual, the artistic spirit, the disoriented and the sick, in a harsh, uncaring world. He shows the life of flight, anguish and guilt-ridden struggle to survive. The central character in *Streetcar*, Blanche DuBois, like all the characters in *The Glass Menagerie* (1944), the members of the Wingfield family, leads a life of repressed desperation and neurotic dreaming, unable to deal with the coarse and cruel world around her. Williams dramatizes the continual failure of these characters in a broken world where gentility has been replaced by brutality. The only way sensitive individuals can survive is either to become brutalized themselves (as Stella in *Streetcar* does) and adapt to new conditions, or to retreat into illusion (as Blanche does).

Here Blanche outlines her desperate plight to her sister Stella:

> I never was hard or self-sufficient enough. When people are soft – soft people have got to court the favour of hard ones, Stella. Have got to be seductive – put on soft colours, the colours of butterfly wings, and glow – make a little – temporary magic just in order

to pay for – one night's shelter! That's why I've been – not so awf'ly good lately. I've run for protection, Stella, from under one leaky roof to another leaky roof – because it was storm – all storm, and I was – caught in the centre ... And so the soft people have got to – shimmer and glow – put a – paper lantern over the light ... But I'm scared now – awf'ly scared. I don't know how much longer I can turn the trick. It isn't enough to be soft. You've got to be soft and attractive. And I – I'm fading now! (1962, p. 169)

Blanche is the decadent paragon of the southern belle. Like Amanda in *The Glass Menagerie*, she is a distracted version of Scarlett O'Hara in *Gone with the Wind*, the ultimate image of southern beauty and femininity. She is an outsider to the brash, vibrantly coloured, loud, 'hard' world of the New Orleans backstreets. Her aristocratic name and manner, and the delicacy of her feelings, immediately mark her off from Stanley's working-class, animalistic, 'polack' world. She is one of the fugitive kind, immensely vulnerable, deracinated, anxious. All that is left her of the glorious past, of 'Belle Reve' her family home, is a trunkful of opulent clothes and accessories, sadly out of place in the cramped, diminished conditions of Stella's tenement home. Blanche is one of the 'soft' people, given to illusion, alcohol, dim lights and muted colours in the effort to make a harsh world bearable. She knows that softness only disqualifies her from success in this world. But she possesses a degree of self-awareness beyond that of any of the other characters, and quite beyond anything that that other dreamer, Willy Loman in Arthur Miller's *Death of a Salesman*, is capable of. Williams's dreamers retain a grasp of reality where Willy is totally immersed in illusion, actually living in his own created world, talking in a way that leaves those around him baffled. He cannot tell the difference between dream and reality, at one point carrying on a conversation with real Charlie and fantasy Ben. Blanche, on the other hand, simply lies in the world of actuality. Both Blanche and Willy feel inadequate: Willy is not the success his brother Ben was; Blanche caused her husband's suicide, which drove her to nymphomania in the hope of recapturing lost love and lost self-respect, while only intensifying her loneliness and self-loathing. To Blanche, desire is the negation of death, but she feels she must 'civilize' desire by hitching it to a dream of Southern *courteos*. She wears a genteel mask, knowing that society would disapprove of her. She is aware she cannot stand reality: 'I don't want realism, I want magic.' She knows she is one of the soft, moth-like people. She recognizes her faults and understands what she is doing: 'I didn't lie in my heart' (p. 205), she says. She is aware that she misleads people. Willy, on the other hand, appears to mislead himself more than anyone else. (See Unit 15, pp. 430–2, for a discussion of *Death of a Salesman* and modern American drama.)

For both Williams's and Miller's characters, illusions are essentially self-defence mechanisms to protect them from the world, but Willy is more blameable than Blanche. Miller sees the dreamer as a danger to himself and others, corrupting lives with false values. Willy prefers to die rather than be stripped of illusions that give him whatever dignity he has. But he has alternatives, as offered by Charlie and represented by Biff. He could have followed his natural instincts. His predicament is at least partly of his own creation. Because Willy contributes to his own downfall, Miller inevitably treats his dreaming more critically than Williams treats his dreamers. Where Miller sees dreamers like Willy as morally inept (though he still judges them in a pitying and understanding way), Williams depicts Blanche as a sacrificial victim of a materialistic, commercial world which has no time for the transcendental values of love or beauty or art. Williams's world is harder than Miller's. There is more justification for dream, illusion, escapism in Williams's jungle. Williams does not blame Tom Wingfield in *The Glass Menagerie* for dreaming or living his life through the movies when the reality of his life is work in a warehouse, giving his money towards the upkeep of the family, and an overwhelming sense of being trapped. Williams explores his characters' faults – Tom's restlessness, Blanche's inability to accept her husband's homosexuality, Laura's withdrawal from reality – but he seems to place the blame more heavily on society than upon the soft, artistic, tender individuals. With Blanche's removal to the asylum at the end of *Streetcar*, the harsh people have won.

Both Williams and Miller present the past as a period of Golden Opportunity, and the present as a bleak and terrifying place. Blanche's and Amanda's dreams represent an older, more gracious, prelapsarian form of life, which Williams sets against the grim, urban present. In contrast to Blanche or Amanda, Willy aspires to a contemporary dream, one of aggressive, cut-throat competition on which capitalist America is founded. Blanche, Amanda and Laura attain significance as victims of their society, rather than heroines, while Miller intends Willy's ultimate altruistic sacrifice to turn him into a tragic hero-dreamer quite absent from Williams's drama. Williams's victims are passive: Willy Loman actively tries to direct his life. Blanche is memorable for the exquisiteness of her suffering, Willy for the passion of his devotion to an ideal.

In *Streetcar* the forces of American materialism are represented by the macho, brutish Stanley, a potent symbol of the revitalizing energy needed for an industrial, world-competing country. Blanche recognizes Stanley's potential: 'he's what we need to mix with our blood now that we've lost Belle Reve' (p. 141). However, Stanley lacks a spiritual dimension and moral integrity. He has no appreciation of the higher consciousness.

> He acts like an animal, has an animal's habits! Eats like one, moves like one, talks like one! There's even something – sub-human – something not quite to the stage of humanity yet! Yes, something – ape-like about him, like one of those pictures I've seen in – anthropological studies .... Maybe we are a long way from being made in God's image, but Stella – my sister – there has been some progress since then! Such things as art – as poetry and music – such kinds of new light have come into the world since then! In some kinds of people some tenderer feelings have had some little beginning! That we have to make *grow*! And cling to, and hold as our flag! In this dark march toward whatever it is we're approaching .... *Don't don't hang back with the brutes!* (pp. 163–4)

This passage is typical of the way Stanley throughout the play is constructed in Blanche's image of him, a projection of everything she both desires and fears. Thus, she flirts with him because he represents an attractive sensual, Lawrentian vitality; and she shrinks from him because he is the brutal male torturer of the poetic spirit. The perspective of the sensitive individual determines the form of *Streetcar*, as it does the form of *The Glass Menagerie*. *Streetcar* tends towards melodramatic extremism and pessimism, and is constructed out of a stark conflict between the 'apes' and the 'moths' with no convincing middle ground. Since Williams works primarily with two such extreme characters as Blanche and Stanley, we cannot easily identify with either. Neither Mitch in *Streetcar* nor Jim in *The Glass Menagerie* is a strong enough character to represent a valid normative option. Williams dramatizes an essentially static, unchanging situation: at the end, the Kowalskis return to their old routine, the cycle of sex and violence simply continues.

When asked about the theme of *Streetcar*, Williams, alluding to the same notion of anthropological regression as Blanche, replied: 'Watch out or the apes will inherit the earth'. Williams is on the side of the 'soft' people. He sees animalism threatening to obliterate tenderness. He speaks for the sensitive souls revolted by savagery, forced into all kinds of ignominious strategies for survival, and all doomed to failure. Where Miller and Edward Albee insist upon the need to confront reality, Williams follows O'Neill in offering a compassionate view of desperate illusion as a way in which the artistic soul can sustain an artist's vision in a harshly materialistic world. Williams shows life, not like Miller with the suggestion that it should be better, but that it merely is what it is. Where O'Neill and Williams see the benefits of illusion, Miller and Albee see the dangers. But it would be wrong to conclude that the former wholly approve and the latter wholly disapprove. Williams does not portray Stella and Stanley's marriage as satisfactory and does not suggest that refuge in illusion should be anything other than a last resort. Similarly, Willy is not painted in wholly unsympathetic colours for otherwise Miller would not have gone to such pains to emphasize the complexity of his mind or the intensity with which he was capable of following a dream, 'wrong' though it might be. In *Streetcar* there is no sincerely happy alternative to Blanche's delusions of grandeur and impractical attitudes. Stanley's realistic acceptance of life expresses itself as brute force, animalistic ignorance, rape and violence, although at times admirably uncomplicated. Stella's rejection of Blanche at the end is not straightforward rejection of all Blanche represents because Stella too expresses regret about her situation, and she can only continue living with Stanley by deluding herself that he did not rape Blanche. Blanche's illusions are not to be lightly dismissed. If they were, the play would allow no pity or sympathy for Blanche at the end, and Blanche's madness would be farcical rather than 'tragic' (Williams's word to describe her countenance at the end). For both Blanche and Stella, as well as for Amanda and Laura in *The Glass Menagerie*, illusion allows life to continue.

*BIBLIOGRAPHY*

INTRODUCTION

Allen, Donald (ed.) (1960) *The New American Poetry*, Grove Press, New York.
Allen, Walter (1986) *Tradition and Dream: The English and American Novel from the Twenties to Our Time*, Hogarth Press, London.
Baldwin, J. (1961) *Nobody Knows My Name*, Corgi, London.
Baldwin, J. (1972) *Notes of a Native Son*, Corgi, London.
Bergonzi, B. (1970) *The Situation of the Novel*, Macmillan, London.

Bigsby, C.W.E. (1967) *Confrontation and Commitment: A Study of Contemporary American Drama 1959–1966*, McGibbon & Kee, London.

Bradbury, M. (1992) *The Modern American Novel*, Oxford University Press, Oxford.

Charney, M. (1963) 'James Baldwin's Quarrel with Richard Wright', *American Quarterly*, vol. XV, no. i.

Chase, R. (1957) *The American Novel and Its Tradition*, Bell, London.

Cookson, W. (1978) *Ezra Pound: Selected Prose 1909–1965*, Faber, London.

DuBois, W.E.B. (1903) *The Souls of Black Folk*, A.C. McClurg, Chicago.

Dukore, B.F. (1984) *American Dramatists 1918–1945*, Macmillan, London.

Fiedler, L. (1970) *Love and Death in the American Novel*, Paladin, London.

Field, L.A. and Field, J.W. (eds) (1975) *Bernard Malamud: A Collection of Critical Essays*, Prentice Hall, Englewood Cliffs.

Flint, F.S. (1913) 'Imagisme', *Poetry*, March, Chicago.

Gray, R. (1990) *American Poetry of the Twentieth Century*, Longman, London.

Gross, S.L. and Hardy, J.E. (eds) (1966) *Images of the Negro in American Literature*, Chicago University Press, Chicago.

Hall, D. (ed.) (1971) *Contemporary American Poetry*, Penguin, Harmondsworth.

Hilfer, T. (1992) *American Fiction since 1940*, Longman, London.

Lawrence, D.H. (1971) *Studies in Classic American Literature*, Penguin, Harmondsworth [first published 1924].

Lewis, R.W.B. (1955) *The American Adam: Innocence, Tradition and Tragedy in the Nineteenth Century*, Chicago University Press, London.

Locke, A. (1925) *The New Negro*, A. & C. Boni, New York.

McQuade, D. *et al.* (1994) *The Harper American Literature*, vol. 1, HarperCollins, London.

Matthiessen, F.O. (1941) *American Renaissance: Art and Expression in the Age of Emerson and Whitman*, Oxford University Press, New York.

Poirier, R. (1985) *A World Elsewhere*, Wisconsin University Press, Madison.

Stevens, W. (1951) *The Necessary Angel*, Vintage Books, New York.

Stevens, W. (1957) *Opus Posthumous: Poems, Plays and Prose*, ed. S.F. Morse, Faber, New York.

Styan, J.L. (1983) *Modern Drama in Theory and Practice*, 3 vols, Cambridge University Press, Cambridge.

Tanner, T. (1976) *City of Words*, Jonathan Cape, London.

Thoreau, H.D. (1962) *Walden*, Macmillan Collier Books, New York [first published 1854].

Williams, W.C. (1951) *Autobiography*, New Directions, New York.

Williams, W.C. (1963) *Paterson*, New Directions, New York.

Ziff, L. (ed.) (1982) *Ralph Waldo Emerson: Selected Essays*, Penguin, Harmondsworth.

FROST

Cox, H. and Lathem, E.C. (1966) *Selected Prose of Robert Frost*, Holt, Rinehart & Winston, New York.

Hamilton, I. (ed.) (1973) *Selected Poems*, Penguin, Harmondsworth.

Lathem, E.C. (1966) *Interviews with Robert Frost*, Holt, Rinehart & Winston, New York.

HEMINGWAY

Baker, C. (1963) *Ernest Hemingway: The Writer as Artist*, Princeton University Press, Princeton.

Hemingway, E. (1988) 'Big Two-Hearted River: I' and 'Big Two-Hearted River: II', in *The Essential Hemingway*, ed. M. Cowley, Collins, London, pp. 340–57 [first published 1925].

Young, P. (1966) *Ernest Hemingway*, Pennsylvania State University Press, Philadelphia.


STEINBECK

French, W. (1972) *A Companion to The Grapes of Wrath*, Viking Press, New York.

Lisca, P. (1958) *The Wide World of John Steinbeck*, Rutgers University Press, New Brunswick.

Steinbeck, J. (1951) *The Grapes of Wrath*, Penguin, Harmondsworth [first published 1939].


WRIGHT

Baldwin, J. (1972) *Notes of a Native Son*, Bantam, New York.

Bone, R. (1965) *The Negro Novel in America*, Yale University Press, New Haven.

French, W. (1969) 'The Lost Potential of Richard Wright', in *The Black American Writer*, ed. C.W.E. Bigsby, vol. 1, Penguin, Baltimore.

Margolies, E. (1969) *Richard Wright*, Southern Illinois University Press, Carbondale.

Seymour, G. and Hardy, J. (eds) (1966) *Images of the Negro in American Literature*, Chicago University Press, Chicago.

Wright, R. (1972) *Native Son*, Penguin, Harmondsworth [first published 1940].

Scott, N.A., Jr (1969) 'The Dark and Haunted Tower of Richard Wright' in *Black Expression*, ed. A. Gayle, Jr, Weybright & Talley, New York.


MCCULLERS

Abrams, M.H. (1981) *A Glossary of Literary Terms*, Holt, Rinehart & Winston, New York.

Anderson, S. (1988) *Winesburg: Ohio*, Picador, London.

Bradbury, M. (1992) *The Modern American Novel*, Oxford University Press, Oxford.

McCullers, C. (1961) *The Heart Is a Lonely Hunter*, Penguin, Harmondsworth [first published 1943].

McCullers, C. (1963) *The Ballad of the Sad Cafe*, Penguin, Harmondsworth [first published 1951].


WILLIAMS

Jackson, E.M. (1965) *The Broken World of Tennessee Williams*, Wisconsin University Press, Madison.

Miller, A. (1961) *Death of a Salesman*, Penguin, Harmondsworth.

Stanton, S.S. (ed.) (1983) *Tennessee Williams: A Collection of Critical Essays*, Prentice Hall, Englewood Cliffs.

Tischler, N. (1965) *Tennessee Williams: Rebelious Puritan*, Citadel Press, New York.

Williams, T. (1962) *Sweet Bird of Youth, A Streetcar Named Desire, The Glass Menagerie*, Penguin, Harmondsworth [first published 1947].

# UNIT 15

# Modern drama

*David Pattie*

This unit examines the development of modern drama from the rise of naturalism to the present. The first part of the Introduction deals with the various movements that influenced European theatre; the second and third parts cover the influence of those movements on British and American drama respectively. If the history of modern drama has an identifiable pattern, it is that developments originating in mainland Europe have an almost simultaneous impact on British and American drama; the first section gives an overview of these developments, while the second section analyzes them in more detail, using the following texts: *Ghosts* (Ibsen), *Man and Superman* (Shaw), *Mother Courage* (Brecht), *Waiting for Godot* (Beckett), *Death of a Salesman* (Miller), *The Caretaker* (Pinter) and *Top Girls* (Churchill).

## Introduction

Each winter, at the beginning of the new theatre season, I fall prey to the same thoughts. A hope springs up in me, and I tell myself that before the first warmth of summer empties the playhouses, a dramatist of genius will be discovered. Our theatre desperately needs a new man who will scour the debased boards and bring about a rebirth in an art degraded by its practitioners to the simple-minded requirements of the crowd. Yes, it would take a powerful personality, an innovator's mind, to overthrow the accepted conventions and firmly install the real human drama in place of the ridiculous untruths that are on stage today. I picture this creator scorning the tricks of the clever hack, smashing the imposed patterns, remaking the stage until it is continuous with the auditorium, giving a shiver of life to the painted trees, letting in through the backcloth the great, free air of reality. (Zola, 1877)

It is as difficult to give a precise date for the birth of modern drama as it is for any literary era, but Zola's impassioned plea for a new type of dramatist – one who would take as his subject the real lives of human beings, in a society portrayed as realistically as possible – provides as convenient a starting point as any. The style of theatre that Zola is calling for – a style that comes under the general description of Naturalism – is not only the first, recognizably modern dramatic style; it is also, arguably, the century's standard dramatic genre. It could be argued that the development of drama from the 1870s to the present has been that of a series of reactions to, developments of, and diversions from, this dominant style.

Naturalism, simply defined, is an attempt to put the real lives of real people in a realistic setting on stage. What distinguishes Naturalism from a simple representation of everyday life is its quasi-scientific attitude to humanity. For the naturalist, every human being could be analyzed and defined by a careful study of his or her heredity, social position and upbringing. This approach links naturalism to modernism – a wider artistic/cultural movement committed to celebrating and making use of the new (new technologies, new sciences, new social movements). Naturalist writers were often regarded as social prophets, a description which certainly applies to the first important naturalist playwright: Henrik Ibsen.

Ibsen came to naturalism rather late in his life. He had been moderately successful as the author of historical dramas and of two poetic epics – *Brand* and *Peer Gynt*. In the 1870s, however, Ibsen came under the influence of the critic Georg Brandes; and the sequence of plays that follow Ibsen's first truly naturalistic drama, *The Pillars of Society*, can be seen as a response to Brandes's call for a drama that concerned itself with the problems of realistic human beings in a realistic society. *The Pillars of Society* is itself a rather mechanical thesis-play, designed to demonstrate that social hypocrisy is ultimately self-defeating. *A Doll's House*, however, is both a partial vindication of Brandes's theories and an emphatic demonstration of theatre's ability to intervene in a wider social debate. The central character, Nora Helmer, comes to realize that her marriage is a sham, and that she has never at any time in her life been allowed to think for herself; the play ends with one of the most famous sound effects in modern theatre – a door slamming offstage, as Nora leaves her home, husband and children.

*A Doll's House* was greeted with an almost universal hostility; so much so that for the first German production, Ibsen had to rewrite the final scene (in the new ending, Nora cannot bring herself to leave her husband). The play was not performed unchanged until 1889. *Ghosts* received the same welcome, but to a greater, more virulent degree; the play, a study of the effects of heredity and social pressure on a family, was widely denounced as obscene. These two plays established Ibsen as a cultural *cause célèbre*. However, Ibsen was not the only dramatist whose work was to prove controversial. Gerhardt Hauptmann's *The Weavers* (1892), a brutally naturalistic play about a weavers' revolt in Silesia in 1884, had to wait eleven years for its first production. George Bernard Shaw's early play *Mrs Warren's Profession*, had to wait eight years; Mrs Warren's profession was prostitution – a plot detail that the Lord Chamberlain's office, who at that time had the power to censor or ban plays altogether, found rather hard to bear.

Ibsen's plays also provoked a reaction from two writers who, in their own ways, were to prove as influential as the Norwegian: August Strindberg and Anton Chekhov. Strindberg is an idiosyncratic writer whose copious output spans many different styles. Like Ibsen, he began as a historical playwright; he turned to naturalism in the 1880s, and his two greatest naturalistic plays – *The Father* (1887) and *Miss Julie* (1888) – were written partly in response to Ibsen, whose portrayal of women Strindberg found especially unnatural. The plays, though, are indisputably

Strindberg's. They portray a world riven by primal, archetypal, unresolvable conflicts: between the lower and upper classes, between those with power, and those who want to acquire power, and, most importantly for Strindberg, between men and women.

In contrast, the plays of Anton Chekhov seem to move in the opposite direction, towards an increasingly detailed representation of reality. *The Seagull* (1896), written in response to Ibsen's *The Wild Duck* (1893), ends on a note of muted melodrama: the writer Trepilov commits suicide offstage. His next three plays – *Uncle Vanya* (1899), *Three Sisters* (1901) and *The Cherry Orchard* (1904) – manage to do without even this small concession to the accepted way of creating a dramatic impact. Chekhov instead undertakes a detailed analysis of the Russian middle classes and their society, a society that he treats with a curious, but highly effective, blend of sympathy and satire. Chekhov's peculiar skill as a dramatist is to focus so closely on the small details of life that those details themselves begin to take on a symbolic or poetic meaning. For example, in the second act of *The Cherry Orchard* almost nothing happens. A landowning family, their friends and their servants take the air on their estate; when the light begins to fade, they go indoors. However, by the end of the act, the accumulation of small details – the listless dialogue, the inconclusive arguments – has built into a profoundly moving yet unsentimental portrait of a society in decline.

Strindberg and Chekhov, in their differing ways, helped to develop a more symbolic form of naturalism: this development is paralleled by that of Ibsen, whose later plays (from *Rosmersholm* onward) become increasingly poetic. His final play, *When We Dead Awake*, a meditation on the artist's responsibility to the life he portrays, breaks with naturalism altogether. The break, however, was not as final and as definite as that of Strindberg, whose later dramas – *To Damascus*, *Dream Play*, and *The Ghost Sonata* – draw on a growing preoccupation with mysticism (particularly Strindberg's idiosyncratic reading of Buddhism), and with the half-ordered, half-logical atmosphere of dreams.

This move away from what one might term pure naturalism parallels the development of theatre in general. From the 1890s to the late 1920s, a series of artistic and cultural movements responded to naturalism's scientific, rational approach in various ways. The first movement, Symbolism (which flourished in the 1890s), was concerned with man as an unchanging, archetypal essence, and symbolist drama was correspondingly poetic, elliptical and self-consciously mysterious. The advent of the First World War spawned a variety of movements: futurism (which all but canonized the machine); constructivism (a post-revolutionary version of futurism); Dadaism (a movement that regarded all human endeavour as meaningless – hence its nonsensical name); surrealism (which puts its faith in the obscure logic of dreams and the subconscious); and expressionism (which sought to respond to a society seen as authoritarian and stifling by elevating the poetic, spiritual individual). Some of these movements (Dadaism, surrealism, symbolism) spread across Europe; others stayed largely confined to one country (futurism to Italy, expressionism to Germany). Generally, though, each of these movements helped to contribute to a widespread atmosphere of experimentation and change.

In the theatre, this experimentation found expression in the work of a number of writers. Maurice Maeterlinck's poetic plays are the purest examples of symbolism in drama; Alfred Jarry's most famous creation, Pa Ubu (who first appeared in *Ubu Roi* (1896)) is a bizarre, grotesque figure who presides over a cruel, amoral world. Frank Wedekind, in *Spring Awakening* (1891), shows a group of realistically drawn young people whose innocence is destroyed by a group of adults as grotesque as anything in Jarry; his later plays, *Earth Spirit* and *Pandora's Box*, take a similarly sardonic look at society, and also blend realism with the grotesque. Ernst Toller's plays show idealized, youthful heroes in revolt against post-war German society; Vladimir Mayakovsky attacked post-revolutionary Russia in the satires *The Bedbug* and *The Bathhouse*. Luigi Pirandello's plays resemble nothing so much as elaborate intellectual games, in which the precise nature of reality is always in doubt. Finally, Federico Garcia Lorca mixed surrealism with Spanish folklore in plays such as *Blood Wedding* (1933) and *The House of Bernalda Alba* (1936).

Expressionism provided both a model and a target for the early work of one of the century's most famous playwrights, Bertolt Brecht (1898–1956). It is sometimes mistakenly assumed that Brecht began his career as an expressionist; in fact, his first plays (*Baal, Drums in The Night*) take the staples of expressionist drama (the misfit hero, on his own in an oppressive society) and subject them to a cynical revision. For example, the expressionist hero is frequently purer than pure; Brecht's heroes are earthy, with appetites that must be satisfied. The breezy cynicism of his early style finds its finest expression in the plays *Man is Man* and *The Threepenny Opera* (written in collaboration with Elizabeth Hauptmann, with a score composed by Kurt Weill). In the late 1920s, Brecht began to study Marxism, and became a committed Communist at the time when the National Socialist Party was preparing for power. This is not to say that Brecht's dramas are overtly didactic, or merely the dull working out of a set of theories. The great plays of Brecht's maturity, written at the time of his exile from Nazi Germany (*The Good Person Of Schezuan, Puntilla and Matti, Gallileo, Mother Courage and her Children*, and *The Caucasian Chalk Circle*) are written on the grand scale, with large casts, and teem with life; their arguments are always incarnated in characters who are intensely alive, and full of contradictions and inconsistencies. (Brecht's theories of theatre will be discussed in the second part of this unit.)

Brecht's influence on writers and directors alike spread through Europe in the 1950s, as his theatre company, the Berliner Ensemble, undertook a number of European tours. At the same time, a group of writers who drew their influence partly from Dadaism and surrealism began to write their first plays. The Theatre of the Absurd is the title generally given to the work of a number of writers – Samuel Beckett, Eugene Ionesco, Jean Genet, Arthur Adamov – whose work seemed at first to be a delayed reaction to the Second World War. The war had provided enough evidence to shake even the most determined modernist's faith in humanity; the absurdists seemed to answer this with a drama that seemed to cast man adrift in an ultimately meaningless universe. However, this blanket definition masks profound differences in the writers' philosophies and approaches; Adamov's later plays are sharply surreal social satires; Genet became increasingly concerned with the ways in which power manifests or hides itself. Both Adamov and Genet, in fact, are political playwrights; Genet went so far as to abandon the theatre for direct political action. Eugene Ionesco places his characters at the mercy of proliferating objects (eggs, rhinoceroses, suitcases, chairs), or traps them in repetition, while both their ability to communicate and their personalities disintegrate.

Samuel Beckett is, like Jarry, an entirely unique writer; his spare, minimal writing, with its emphasis as much on tone and rhythm as on dialogue, sometimes seems closer to music than to drama. His first major play, *Waiting for Godot*, has two tramps waiting, with all the resources of humour, compassion and endurance that they can muster, for Godot's infinitely delayed arrival. It has been variously interpreted: as a metaphor for meaninglessness, as a play about redemption through endurance, or as a vision of life as a cruel joke; the play can support each one of these interpretations. Indeed, Beckett's work generally has become something of an intellectual Rorschach test, in which academics find whatever shapes they wish to find. The play in performance, however, renders most, if not all, of these theories superfluous. It does not explain the tramps' predicament; it draws the audience into the tramps' experience of endless waiting. As it develops, Beckett's theatre becomes even more narrow and confined. *Endgame* traps its characters in a single room; and Winnie, the central character of *Happy Days*, finds herself gradually being swallowed by the earth. The tramps' hope that things might change when Godot arrives is replaced by either a desire for extinction or an alternately grim or furious resignation to the situation in which they find themselves. By the time Beckett writes his last plays (*Not I*, *Footfalls*, *What Where*) the characters are frozen into place, doomed either to search through their memories or to ask the same unanswerable questions while they gradually slide towards extinction.

The dramas of Brecht and of the absurdists were first performed in Britain in the 1950s; and they helped to revitalize a dramatic scene which had become increasingly moribund as the century wore on. This was not always the case: in the 1890s, the British stage, in common with the rest of Europe, began to turn to naturalism. But, although naturalism came to dominate the stage in the period that followed, it was not generally the naturalism of Chekhov or of Ibsen. Rather, it followed a peculiarly British direction – a concern with linguistic dexterity, and with the polished presentation of an argument or a social situation. The British stage, it is true to say, was a place where to succeed, you had to speak well.

Partly, this is a traditional concern of the British stage; but also it was a continuation of the well-made play tradition that naturalism was supposed to react against. The plays of A.W. Pinero, for example, might portray the downfall of the great and the good (or at least those with shady pasts), but they always included at least one figure whose purpose it seemed was to entertain the audience with a dazzling, perfectly expressed wit. This tendency reached its peak in the work of Oscar Wilde, whose early plays (*A Woman of No Importance*, *An Ideal Husband*, *Lady Windermere's Fan*) are textbook examples of the witty well-made drama. Wilde, however, had dabbled in other forms of drama (in symbolism, for example, in *Salome*); and something of the symbolic survives in his one undisputed masterpiece, *The Importance of Being Ernest*. The play is as consciously patterned as a minuet: apparently realistic characters are, as the play progresses, revealed as witty mannequins; and the great themes that one might expect would be the occasion for mystical poetry in a symbolist drama (life as struggle, the mystery of identity and of parentage) are incarnated in the smallest, most everyday objects – a handbag, a set of sugar tongs, cucumber sandwiches, and cake.

The British stage did produce work that was Ibsenite or Chekhovian; the plays of Harley Granville-Barker, for example, or the social dramas of John Galsworthy. But the dominant dramatist in Britain for much of the first half of the century was a man whose initial commitment to naturalism did not lead him to a minute study of reality. George Bernard Shaw was an enthusiastic supporter of Ibsen; he wrote one of the earliest and most influential books on the Norwegian (*The Quintessence of Ibsenism*). In this book Shaw creates an image of Ibsen that is, if partial, certainly very persuasive; Ibsen as a social crusader, as a political analyst of remarkable acuteness. Shaw initially modelled himself on this particular version of Ibsen; his early plays were exposés of various social hypocrisies – slum landlords (*Widowers' Houses*), marriage (*The Philanderer*) and, in good Ibsenite fashion, the question of women (*Mrs Warren's Profession*). Shaw, though, was always more of a rhetorician than a realist; in his later plays (*Man and Superman* being an excellent example) the characters often seem subordinate to the argument, as though they exist purely because Shaw needs them to present one point of view. This is not to say that Shaw is a dull dramatist; the arguments are always couched in perfectly crafted dialogue, and his characters, although sometimes drawn with the broadest of brushes, are generally dramatically very effective.

Shaw's skill and longevity was perhaps one of the reasons why the British reaction to naturalism took the shape that it did. The British stage tended to rely on words, rather than on images; whether the language was the language of debate (as it was with Shaw) or whether, as with the plays of Coward, it was an end in itself, it was dominant. Also typically, a British play would tend to concern itself with a relatively small section of society: generally the kind of comfortably middle-class people who would form the play's audience. This audience would either watch a reflection of itself (in the plays of Terence Rattigan); be reminded of its social duty (as in J.B. Priestley's *An Inspector Calls*); or sit appreciatively as society's more bohemian or louche aspects were lightly satirized (as in the plays of Coward, and, to an extent, of Somerset Maugham). The occasional experiment (Auden and Isherwood's *The Ascent of F.6*; Priestley's time plays; or the vogue for poetic drama after the Second World War) was simply that – occasional reactions against a dominant style.

It is not that the British stage suddenly became anti-naturalistic after 1956; but for the first time, those influences that had shaped the European stage for the past forty years began to shape the British stage as well. Ironically, though, the herald of the new British drama was itself a rigorously traditional naturalistic play. *Look Back In Anger*, by John Osborne, chronicles the life of Jimmy Porter, a young(ish) man who feels at odds with everything around him. What marks the play out is Jimmy's eloquence: the play is structured around a number of setpiece speeches in which Jimmy rails against every part of the British establishment. In retrospect, the play is not outstanding; the plot is weak and, aside from Jimmy, the characters are sketchily presented. Also, the play seems curiously negative: although Jimmy is undoubtedly angry, his rage is fundamentally impotent (the play could as easily be called *Sit Back and Whine*). At the time, however, Jimmy seemed to be a revolutionary; he proved a convincing spokesman for those disillusioned by what was still a rather staid, stifling society.

Osborne's early success focused attention on the theatre as a social barometer; and it also ushered in something of a golden age for British drama – a golden age influenced by the major figures in European theatre. Brecht was a profound influence on the work of John Arden, for example: *Serjeant Musgrave's Dance*, *The Workshop Donkey* and *Armstrong's Last Goodnight* take the wide social canvases of Brecht's great plays and combine them with elements drawn from folk traditions or from forms of popular entertainment, such as the music hall, to create a particularly rich and poetic form of political theatre.

Beckett was the strongest influence on the early work of Harold Pinter, whose voice was one of the most distinctive in the theatre of the 1950s and 1960s. The atmosphere of the early plays – *The Room*, *The Birthday Party* and *The Caretaker* – is sometimes rather vaguely termed menacing and ambiguous, and it is true that the characters do live in a world in which surreal violence coexists with the most mundane realities, and that their background, pasts, and sometimes even their names, are subject to alteration. However, Pinter's plays are dramatically effective because their central conflicts are always clearly defined; although the precise details might be obscure, at the heart of each one of the early plays there is a raw, tense power struggle fought out mainly in the dialogue. Pinter's characters do not so much use language to inform as to tease, wound and control the people around them. Linguistically, his writing is in the British tradition of carefully crafted stage speech; but the style's reliance on repetition, on ellipses and on the careful use of silence (the pause has become Pinter's trademark) creates a powerful sense of an always immanent threat from the simplest, most common words and phrases.

Osborne, Pinter, Arden and others (Arnold Wesker, Shelagh Delaney, Charles Wood, Robert Bolt, among others) formed the first wave of fresh dramatic writing in the 1950s and early 1960s; this impetus was maintained through the 1960s by writers such as Edward Bond and Joe Orton. Bond, in his own words, writes about violence as naturally as Jane Austen wrote about manners; but it is probably truer to say that he writes, not about violence, but about the social structures that either force or encourage people into violence. In an early play, *Saved*, a gang stones a baby to death in a South London park – not because they have been provoked into it, but simply because they are there, and there is nothing else to do. The scene, disturbing enough in itself, acts also as a condemnation of a society that dehumanizes its members, the gang as much as the child. In later plays, Bond explores the structure of society in greater detail, and his analysis becomes overtly Marxist; but his plays never lose their ability to move or to shock. Equally shocking, though in a completely different way, are the plays of Joe Orton. The three full-length plays he completed before his early death (*Entertaining Mr. Sloane*, *Loot*, *What the Butler Saw*) are ornately written, outrageous black farces, in which social taboos about sexuality, madness, illness and death are gleefully overturned. In *Loot*, for example, a young criminal hides the money from a robbery in his dead mother's coffin (he bundles her body, upside down, into a cupboard); the play ends with vice triumphant – the criminal, his accomplice and the nurse who murdered his mother share the proceeds with the investigating police officer, and the criminal's father, who threatens to expose them, is carried off to jail.

British dramatists before 1968 tended to learn their craft in London, where they wrote either for the commercial stage (like Orton) or, as was more common, for the venues that specifically encouraged new writing (the most famous of these being the Royal Court Theatre). In the late 1960s this changed, and a generation came to prominence by another route. The social upheavals of the late 1960s produced a large number of small theatre groups, mostly politically motivated, who provided fertile ground for new work. David Hare, Howard Brenton, Howard Barker, David Edgar, and Trevor Griffiths all either began their careers with these groups, or worked with them for a while. In retrospect, the period is notable for a number of remarkable state-of-the-nation plays: David Hare's *Knuckle* and *Plenty*, Howard Brenton's *Weapons of Happiness*, Brenton and Hare's *Brassneck* and *Pravda*, Edgar's *Destiny* and *Maydays*, Griffiths's *Comedians*. For the first time, too, women playwrights began to make an impact on the British stage. Before the 1970s, sheer prejudice had largely kept what women writers there were more or less invisible; the 1970s saw the formation of a number of specifically feminist theatre companies, and the development of a number of women playwrights: Pam Gems, Sara Daniels, and the most influential, Caryl Churchill. Churchill's plays combine verbal dexterity with an idiosyncratic approach to structure. *Cloud 9*'s first act is set in colonial Africa at the end of the nineteenth century; its second act, in London in the 1970s. The characters, however, have aged only twenty-five years. Churchill uses this double time-frame to examine the persistence of outmoded ideas on gender and sexuality; the characters face the 1970s with a set of values inherited from the 1870s – values that prove both unhelpful and very hard to replace.

American drama in the twentieth century followed a similar path. Prior to O'Neill, there were no important American dramatists; and as with Britain, a dramatic renaissance only began with the importing of models from European theatre.

Eugene O'Neill (1888–1953) first began to write for the theatre in the aftermath of the First World War; his early work, for a company called the Provincetown Players, is expressionistic (although O'Neill claimed not to have seen an expressionistic drama until the early 1920s). Whatever the truth of this claim, O'Neill and the expressionists did share a common ancestor in August Strindberg; and it was to Strindberg's use of heightened dialogue and blatantly unreal onstage elements that O'Neill turned. *The Hairy Ape* (1922), for example, uses those elements that had already become staples of the expressionistic stage: an everyman figure as central character; the use of distorted/unreal sets; and the idea of life as a conflict between archetypes – in this case a stoker and the rich of New York's Fifth Avenue.

O'Neill's later work shows a gradual shift away from overt expressionism: first to a wider use of radical techniques (his trilogy *Mourning Becomes Electra*, an attempt to update the *Oresteia* to the *ante bellum* South, grafted Freudian theory onto classical tragedy), and then at the end of his life to an abandonment of experimentation altogether. His later plays – *The Iceman Cometh* (1939), and *Long Day's Journey Into Night* (1941) – are long, detailed and realistic. *The Iceman* reworks Maxim Gorky's *The Lower Depths*, showing the gradual destruction of the dreams of a group of deadbeats by Hickey, an ambiguous intruder, half-cruel, half-kind. *Long Day's Journey* presents a thinly veiled portrait of O'Neill's own family: parsimonious ex-matinée idol father, drug-addicted mother, drunken, womanizing brother, and, in Edmund, O'Neill himself – a consumptive drifter.

O'Neill's voice, in its various manifestations, dominated the American stage in the 1920s and early 1930s. However, the political upheavals of the Depression ushered in a form of theatre new to America; a theatre that was socially committed, more or less overtly left-wing, and profoundly idealistic. This style of theatre found its most authentic voice in the early work of Clifford Odets (1906–63), most especially in his first three plays (*Waiting for Lefty*, *Awake and Sing*, and *Paradise Lost*). Odets's is a unique voice, highly-strung, sometimes absurdly inflated, but more frequently powerful and memorable. *Awake and Sing* and *Paradise Lost* are realistic depictions of life in the New York Jewish community in the 1930s. *Waiting for Lefty*, on the other hand, is an unashamedly propagandistic piece of political theatre: a group of striking taxi-drivers meet in a garage to wait for Lefty, a labour organizer; while they wait, they talk about (and, in a set of flashbacks, we see) the conditions under which they are forced to live. The news, at the end of the play, that Lefty's body has been discovered, riddled with bullets, moves them to call on the audience to join them in a chant of 'Strike!'. Odets's work falls off markedly from this high point: his later plays are more obviously contrived (*Golden Boy*'s (1937) central character gives up a promising future as a concert violinist to pursue a career as a boxer; his development is handled well, but the initial situation is simply unbelievable).

Arthur Miller's (1915–) early work also contained a streak of Odets's puritanical political outlook; but his first notable success, *All My Sons* (1947), is an Ibsenite social conscience play, much in the style of *The Pillars of Society*. Miller's next play (*Death of a Salesman* (1949)) is both a continuation of and an advance in American naturalism; it incorporates symbolism (the set design, the use of music) and expressionism (the archetypal central character, the episodic structure) within a naturalistic framework. Willy Loman, the central character, may be a put-upon everyman (the name Loman suggesting Low Man), but he is also unique – a liar, a dreamer, a man whose allegiance to a false idea of success has destroyed his family and eventually destroys him. Miller's next play, *The Crucible* (1953), is straightforward. It is in retrospect a rather schematic treatment of persecution, transposing the then current atmosphere of anti-Communist hysteria to the sixteenth-century Salem witch trials; it is dramatically effective, but rather unsurprising. A far more interesting play is Miller's next, *A View From The Bridge*, which touches on one of Miller's favourite themes – the need to live with some kind of honour – but incarnates the struggle in one character, the longshoreman Eddie Carbone, whose incestuous desire for his niece leads him to inform on two illegal immigrants hiding in his house, simply because one of the immigrants has fallen in love with her.

Where Miller is a moralist, committed to the idea of drama as a social forum,

Tennessee Williams (1914–83) is a writer whose approach is far more personal. It is probably too simplistic to think of Williams as Strindberg to Miller's Ibsen, but the contrast has some validity. Like Strindberg, Williams's writing gains much of its strength from a set of very private concerns – chief among them Williams's upbringing and his sexuality; and, like Strindberg, he creates characters that hover between reality and myth. In *A Streetcar Named Desire*, Williams describes the struggle between Blanche DuBois, a fading Southern belle, drowning the memory of her fading past in drink, and her brother-in-law Stanley Kowalski, a man who is simply alive – who has a few basic appetites that he must satisfy as soon as they arise. Blanche loses; at the end of the play she is taken to an asylum, after Stanley has raped her. Blanche is one of a number of Williams characters – Laura in *The Glass Menagerie*; Brick in *Cat On A Hot Tin Roof*; Alma in *Summer and Smoke* – who are simply too fragile for the world. Their particular kind of innocence is simply too weak to survive in a society where to succeed is to cheat and to lie. Williams's peculiar skill is to make these characters' defeat both pathetic and oddly heroic.

Williams is also capable of experimentation – in poetic dramas such as *The Rose Tattoo* and *Camino Real* – and the urge to try new forms and new ways of writing is not alien to Miller either: *After the Fall*, for example, a sprawling symbolic memory play that takes place inside its central character's mind. Both writers, however, stay roughly within the framework of naturalism – or at least with the real lives of real people.

This mixture is found also in Edward Albee (1928– ) whose early work shows signs of the influence of the Theatre of the Absurd. In Albee's most famous play, *Who's Afraid of Virginia Woolf?*, a college professor and his wife invite a younger colleague and his wife back to their house after a party; in the course of a drunken night, all four are forced to face up to the fact that their lives are largely built on illusion. The play acts both as a metaphor for America (the central characters are called George and Martha – the same first names as the country's symbolic parents, the Washingtons) and as a play about the need to make contact. However, the only way that the characters can communicate is in the aftermath of violence (here presented symbolically, as George kills off the imaginary son that he and Martha have used both as a source of comfort and as a weapon).

The characters in David Mamet's plays are compulsive communicators, at least on the surface. Mamet's use of dialogue is almost Pinterian, but whereas Pinter's characters use language to gain power over other people, Mamet's tend to use a language that bolsters their sense of themselves. *Glengarry Glen Ross* is only nominally a play about a group of real-estate salesmen; the first scenes pass before the audience has a clear idea of what these men actually do. This confusion is unimportant, however, because the real business of the play is to examine the brutality that a particular kind of speech encourages. The salesmen are not of the same breed as Willy Loman; there is no sense in the play of new frontiers waiting to be conquered, as there is in *Death of a Salesman*. Rather, Mamet takes us into the lives of the salesmen and, without presenting any moral judgements, shows a group of characters whose job allows them no loyalty, and whose language serves only to dehumanize both their clients and themselves.

## Texts, authors, contexts

*Ghosts* by Henrik Ibsen

(Oswald Alving, in a light overcoat, with his hat in his hand, smoking a large meerschaum pipe, comes in through the door on the left.)

*Oswald*: (Stopping in the doorway) Oh, I'm sorry – I thought you were in the study. (Coming in) Good morning, Pastor.

*Pastor Manders*: (staring) Extraordinary!

*Mrs Alving*: Well, what do you think of him, Mr Manders?

*Pastor Manders*: I – I – No, it really can't be!

*Oswald*: Yes, it's really the prodigal son, Pastor.

*Mrs Alving*: (Beaming with pleasure) I know someone who's kept both his soul and body unharmed. Just look at him, Pastor Manders.

*Oswald*: (Pacing across the room) All right, mother, all right!

*Pastor Manders*: Ah certainly – that's undeniable. And you've begun to make a name for yourself already. The papers have often mentioned you – most favourably, too. Though I must admit, I don't seem to have seen it so often recently.

*Oswald*: ... No, I haven't been painting so much recently.

*Mrs Alving*: Even an artist must have a rest now and then.

*Pastor Manders*: Yes, I can see that – so that he can collect his forces and prepare himself for something great.

*Oswald*: Yes – will lunch be ready soon, Mother?

*Mrs Alving*: In less than half an hour. He's got a good appetite, thank heaven.

*Oswald*: I found father's pipe in my room, so –

*Pastor Manders*: Ah, so that was it!

*Mrs Alving*: What?

*Pastor Manders*: When Oswald came in at the door with the pipe in his mouth, it was like seeing his father in the flesh.

*Oswald*: Oh, really?

*Mrs Alving*: No, you can't say that! Oswald takes after me.

*Pastor Manders*: Yes, but there's a look about the corners of his mouth – something about the lips – that definitely reminds me of Alving. Especially now he's smoking.

*Mrs Alving*: I don't agree. I think Oswald has more of a clergyman's mouth.

*Pastor Manders*: Yes – yes – several of my colleagues have said so.

*Mrs Alving*: But put your pipe away, my dear boy; I won't have smoking in here.

*Oswald*: (Putting the pipe down) Of course. I only wanted to try it – I smoked it once before, as a child.

*Mrs Alving*: You?

*Oswald*: Yes, it was when I was quite small; I remember I went up to Father's study one evening when he was in a particularly good mood...

*Mrs Alving*: Oh, you don't remember anything of those days.

*Oswald*: Yes, I remember it distinctly – he picked me up and put me on his knee and let me smoke his pipe. "Smoke it, boy," he said, "Go on, boy, smoke away!" And I smoked as hard as I could, till I felt myself turning pale, and great drops of sweat broke out on my forehead. Then he burst out laughing.

*Pastor Manders*: How extraordinary.

*Mrs Alving*: My dear pastor, it's only something Oswald must have dreamed!

> *Oswald*: No, I'm sure I didn't dream it, Mother. Because, don't you remember, you came in and carried me off to the nursery. Then I was sick, and I saw that you were crying. Did father often play tricks like that?
>
> *Pastor Manders*: When he was young, he was full of high spirits...
>
> *Oswald*: And yet he managed to achieve so much in the world, so much that was good and useful – although he died so young...

This is a section of dialogue from the first act of Henrik Ibsen's *Ghosts*. The play chronicles a period of forty-eight hours in the lives of the Alvings, a wealthy, apparently respectable Norwegian family. Oswald, the son of the late Captain Alving, has returned to the family home, ostensibly for the opening of an orphanage that will bear his father's name. However, the family has a number of secrets. Oswald's father was a libertine whose respectable image was maintained by his wife; Mrs Alving, early in her marriage, ran away from her husband and sought help from Parson Manders, with whom she was in love; Regina, the family maid, is in fact Oswald's half-sister, her mother having been seduced by Captain Alving. Oswald himself has his own secret; he has returned to die – he has been diagnosed as suffering from hereditary syphilis, and intends to commit suicide before the disease causes irreversible brain damage.

It is one of the characteristic features of naturalism that the characters' actions be explicable in terms of their social class and their heredity; put simply, for the naturalist you are what you are because your parents were what they were, and because your society is what it is. This means that, in naturalistic drama, a great deal of time is spent on background, on determining precisely what the influences on the characters are.

*Ghosts*, as the title might suggest, is a play obsessed with the past, and its ability to affect the present; the ghosts the title refers to are not only human, but are also the ghosts of outmoded social ideas and traditions. First, the human ghosts. At the beginning of the extract, Manders reflects on the uncanny similarity between Oswald and his father; this is quickly denied by his mother, who implies a very different parentage for her son ('Oswald takes after me', 'Oswald has much more of a clergyman's mouth'). It is of course not that Mrs Alving is suggesting that the Pastor is Oswald's real father; rather, Mrs Alving and the Pastor have their own reasons for claiming a different influence on Oswald's life. Pastor Manders, a conservative man, who is to dedicate the orphanage to Captain Alving's memory, has an unsurprisingly conventional idea of what constitutes a good family. He sees the generations succeeding each other smoothly, each one a credit to the family (he talks, near the end of the extract, about Oswald drawing inspiration from his father's name). It is notable that the Pastor cannot quite account for Oswald's memory of his father's cruelty; it is 'extraordinary', something to be dismissed as an early indiscretion ('When he was young, he was full of high spirits'). Mrs Alving, on the other hand, knows the truth; her husband was, if not cruel, then certainly unthinking and selfish. She is as interested as the Pastor in preserving the family name, but for a different reason. It is not only that she wants to protect her son's image of his father; it is that she wants simultaneously to deny the father's influence on the son. She tries to achieve this by simple denial. Pastor Manders's 'It was like seeing his father in the flesh', is countered immediately by her 'Oswald takes after me'. Oswald's memory of his father is something that he 'must have dreamed' because he 'doesn't remember anything of those days'. Oswald, unsurprisingly, is caught in the middle of these contradictory accounts: Manders's wholehearted approval/his mother's emphatic denials. At one moment, he is approving (his father 'achieved so much in the world'); immediately before, he recalls a memory that is both unpleasant and troubling. His father was cruel to him, and his father enjoyed being cruel to him; but his father was also a good man – everyone in his home town tells him so. This contradiction is even more troubling for Oswald, because his disease is inherited; his father must be responsible for the condition that will end his life, but his father *could not* be responsible, because his father was such a respectable man.

In this extract also, Ibsen is careful to show the effect that social pressure has on his characters. Manders is society's advocate. Painting, for him, is not really a respectable occupation, but Oswald has been reviewed in the papers that Manders reads, so Oswald is at least partly respectable. Oswald's memory of his father might give the Pastor pause, at least momentarily; but it too can be assigned to its proper, respectable place – youthful high spirits, before the onset of necessary respectability. Mrs Alving's knowledge of the workings of society is at least as great as that of the Pastor; but she is not so concerned about securing a good social position for herself as she is in protecting her son from society's disapproval. Elsewhere in the play she calls herself a coward for bowing to the pressure of a society she does not believe in. In this extract, her main concern is for her son ('I know someone who's kept both his soul and body untainted', she tells the Pastor). For her, it is important that her son escape not only the influence of his heredity, but the equally damaging influence of his society. After all, social pressure warped his father's character; she does not want the same thing to happen to her son. But at the same time, when Oswald's memories threaten to intrude too much on the image of the respectable Alvings that she maintains, she must deny them. Oswald himself has both to defend his current life to society's representative (the Pastor) and to defend his father – the incarnation of this society's virtues. At the end of the extract, he comes close to an outright comparison between his father's life and his own. Oswald is like his father, he is going to die young; but Oswald, unlike his father, is not an industrious and valued member of society. The outside world values solid achievement; Oswald isn't painting as much as he was – and he will die before his work matures. The name he leaves will, he believes, not be nearly as worthy as that of his father.

As noted in the Introduction to this unit, there is a strongly Darwinian streak to naturalistic drama. The writer works in much the same way as a Darwinist, assembling a series of cause-and-effect chains, and by drawing a conclusion that is the logical outcome of these chains. Therefore, the Alving family will be destroyed because the power of the past will prove too great to be denied, and because they are still far too much in thrall to a stifling, overly respectable society. Pastor Manders, on the other hand, will as a defender of that society be fooled over and over again, because to defend society as strongly as he does, he has to cultivate a kind of social blindness.

## *Man and Superman* by George Bernard Shaw

*Tanner*: ...But you, Tavy, are an artist; that is, you have a purpose as absorbing and as unscrupulous as a woman's purpose.

*Octavius*: Not unscrupulous.

*Tanner*: Quite unscrupulous. The true artist will let his wife starve, his children go barefoot, his mother drudge for his living at seventy, sooner than work at anything but his art. To women, he is half vivisector, half vampire. He gets into intimate relations with them to study them, to strip the mask of convention from them, to surprise their inmost secrets, knowing that they have the power to rouse his deepest creative energies, to rescue him from his cold reason, to make him see visions and dream dreams, to inspire him, as he calls it. He persuades women that they may do this for their own purpose whilst he really means to do it for his. He steals the mother's milk and blackens it to make printer's ink to scoff at her and glorify ideal women with. He pretends to spare her the pangs of child-bearing so that he may have for himself the tenderness and fostering that belong of right to her children. Since marriage began, the great artist has been known as a bad husband. But he is worse; he is a child-robber, a blood-sucker, a hypocrite, and a cheat. Perish the race and wither a thousand women if only the sacrifice of them enable him to act Hamlet better, to paint a finer picture, to write a deeper poem, a greater play, a profounder philosophy! For mark you, Tavy, the artist's work is to show us ourselves as we really are. Our minds are nothing but this knowledge of ourselves; and he who adds a jot to such knowledge creates new minds as surely as any woman creates new men. In the rage of that creation he is as ruthless as the woman, as dangerous to her as she is to him, and as horribly fascinating. Of all human struggles there is none so treacherous and remorseless as the struggle between the artist man and the mother woman. Which one shall use up the other? That is the issue between them. And it is all the deadlier because, in your romanticist cant, they love each other.

This speech is from the first act of George Bernard Shaw's *Man and Superman*. It is spoken by the hero, John Tanner, during the course of a conversation with his friend Octavius Robinson. They are discussing, although it may not be immediately apparent, Ann Whitfield (whom Octavius loves, but who will eventually marry Tanner).

Shaw is both typical and untypical of the generation of dramatists that emerged in England in the 1890s and 1900s. Typical, because he is a resolute follower of Ibsen, and a writer committed to the idea of the theatre as a social forum; untypical because although he was an early champion of Naturalism, his plays remain resolutely theatrical. His near contemporaries – Granville-Barker, Galsworthy – would be careful to script dialogue which reproduced as far as possible the sound and rhythm of real speech. Shaw, on the other hand, is a playwright whose dialogue is always witty and well-crafted; his characters are able either to provide a quick, intelligent reply to any enquiry, or to form an argument from whatever material is to hand.

This extract demonstrates the second of these abilities. Tanner, at this stage in the play, is rather wary of the idea of marriage at least for those who can see through the conventional idea of the institution to the real reason it exists, which, for

Tanner, is the continuation of the species by the most direct means available. It is a feature of Shaw's writing that Tanner proceeds to this general conclusion from the specific details of his own situation; Shaw's are plays of ideas – and the ideas are always lodged, sometimes securely, sometimes less so, in the framework of the plot.

It is not, however, that Shaw simply stops the action of his plays while the more articulate characters are allowed to have their say. Rather, the action in Shaw's work is contained within the language, because the work itself is structured as a debate. The arguments are presented in setpiece speeches, constructed and presented with a great deal of rhetorical force and skill; and the speeches, when they occur, will generally have been prepared for with a great deal of care.

This is the case here. This speech comes at the end of Octavius's and Tanner's short dialogue; immediately before, Tanner has been discoursing on the effects of what he terms elsewhere the life-force in women; the vital woman, according to Tanner, is caught up in a blind fury of creation, looking for nothing more from a marriage than access to a breeding partner. This speech sets up a male archetype, the artist, in partial opposition to the vital woman; this is the type, according to Tanner, to which his friend Octavius belongs. In each sentence of what is a rather lengthy speech the opposition between the artist and the vital woman is either explicitly or implicitly indicated.

Tanner employs a range of rhetorical tricks to drive the argument home. He uses the epigram ('To women, he [the artist] is half vivisector, half vampire'); the accumulation of detail and image ('The true artist will let his wife starve, his children go barefoot, his mother drudge for his living at seventy...'); and the balanced sentence. As an example of this last, consider the sentence beginning 'He gets into intimate relations with them...'. This sentence begins with a series of clauses describing the artist's relationship to women, and ends, after the words 'knowing that...', with a series of clauses describing precisely what the artist seeks to gain from this relationship. This technique – where the conclusion of the sentence simultaneously echoes and reverses the beginning of the sentence – is used again in the next three sentences (the first sentence hinging on the word whilst, the second on the word milk, and the third on the words 'so that').

But it is in the overall shape of the speech that we are most aware of Shaw's rhetoric at work. Tanner begins with an introductory sentence on the amoral obsessiveness of the true artist ('The true artist...' to 'sooner than work at anything but his art.'), then he devotes a long sequence to the relation between the true artist and women, starting with the epigram quoted above, and finishing on '...a greater play, a profounder philosophy'. In this section, Tanner builds up a cumulatively damning case against the true artist, using terms that become increasingly powerful and negative ('He is a child-robber, a bloodsucker, a hypocrite, and a cheat'). Having built up to the strongest possible condemnation, Tanner then reverses the case that he appears to have established; he justifies the artist by conferring upon him the same power that women have – the power to create ('Our minds are nothing but this knowledge of ourselves; and he who adds a jot to such knowledge creates new minds, as surely as woman creates new men'). He then moves to a conclusion that places his idea of a true artist firmly in the context of his view of marriage (which is, after all, the point with which the argument began). The essential amorality of both the artist and the vital woman is restated; the ferocity of their opposition is emphasized; and Tanner ends, not by reconciling the two, but by stating their opposition in the clearest possible terms ('Which shall use up the other?').

Shaw's intention in this speech is to use the characters' words not so much to define their motivation as to state the positions they hold. He will allow his characters to put forward ideas that are, for the time, shocking – all the more shocking for being put in such a rhetorically sophisticated way. This, of course, strains the concept of naturalism, as Shaw was the first to realize; he would, in rehearsal, ask his actors to pay as much if not more attention to the construction of their dialogue as to their characters. Even though at the time this may have seemed a regressive step, harking back to the overly theatrical speech-making that dominated so much of the drama of the nineteenth century, it has proved to be a recurring feature on British drama in the twentieth century. The setpiece speech, or the setpiece argument, features strongly in the work of, among others, John Osborne, Arnold Wesker, David Edgar, Trevor Griffiths and David Hare.

## *Mother Courage and Her Children* by Bertolt Brecht

12. BEFORE FIRST LIGHT. SOUND OF THE FIFES AND DRUMS OF TROOPS MOVING OFF INTO THE DISTANCE

In front of the cart Mother Courage is squatting by her daughter. The peasant family are standing near her.

*The Peasants*: (With hostility) You must go, missus. There's only one more regiment behind this one. You can't go on your own.
*Mother Courage*: I think she's going to sleep. (She sings)
          Lullaby baby
          What's that in the hay?
          Neighbours' kids grizzle
          But my kids are gay.
          Neighbours' are in tatters
          And you're dressed in lawn
          Cut down from the rainment an
          Angel has worn.
          Neighbours' kids go hungry
          And you shall eat cake
          Suppose it's too crumbly
          You've only to speak.
          Lullaby baby
          What's that in the hay?
          The one lies in Poland
          The other – who can say?

Better if you'd told her nowt about your brother-in-law's kids.

*The Peasant*: If you'd not gone to town to get your cut it might never of happened.

*Mother Courage*: Now she's asleep.

*The Peasant's Wife*: She ain't asleep. Can't you see she's passed over?

*The Peasant*: And it's high time you got away yourself. There are wolves around, and, what's worse, marauders.

*Mother Courage*: Aye. (She goes and gets a tarpaulin to cover the dead girl.)

*The Peasant's Wife*: Ain't you got nobody else? What you could go to?

*Mother Courage*: Aye, one left. Eilif.

*The Peasant*: (As Mother Courage covers the dead girl) Best look for him, then. We'll mind her, see she gets proper burial. Don't you worry about that.

*Mother Courage*: Here's money for expenses. (She counts coins into the peasant's hands. The peasant and his son shake hands with her and carry Kattrin away.)

*The Peasant's Wife*: (As she leaves) I'd hurry.

*Mother Courage*: (Harnessing herself to the cart) Hope I can pull cart all right by myself. Be all right, nowt much inside it. Got to get back in business again.

(Another regiment with its fifes and drums marches past in the background.)

*Mother Courage*: (Tugging the cart) Take me along!

(Singing is heard from offstage.)

> With all its luck and all its danger
> The war is dragging on a bit
> Another hundred years or longer
> The common man won't benefit.
> Filthy his food, no soap to shave him
> The regiment steals half his pay.
> But still a miracle might save him
> Tomorrow is another day!
>
> The New Year's come. The watchmen shout.
> The thaw sets in. The dead remain.
> Wherever life has not died out
> It struggles to its feet again.

This is the final scene from Bertolt Brecht's *Mother Courage and Her Children*. Anna Fierling, nicknamed Mother Courage, is a businesswoman who sells goods to both sides during the Thirty Years War. At the start of the play, she has three children and a wagonful of goods; at the play's end all her children are dead, and the wagon is empty, but she is still determined to continue trading by following the war. Brecht, however, does not simply tell Courage's story; rather, he follows his familiar technique of presenting a montage of events from Courage's life. Scene 12 is the only scene that follows on directly from its predecessor. Kattrin, Mother Courage's daughter (who is a mute), has just been killed while performing the play's only unambiguously heroic act. Climbing onto a farmhouse roof, she has alerted the inhabitants of the nearby town of Halle that they are about to be invaded by banging loudly on a drum until the townspeople take up the alarm. She has done so, not because she is allied with one side or the other, but because she wants to save the lives of the children in the town. Courage has gone into Halle to conduct some business; she returns to find her daughter dead.

Much has been made in both standard and specialized books of the influence of Brecht's theories on his drama. They are seen by some commentators as an imposition on Brecht's material; other commentators claim that Brecht is too good a dramatist to be judged by any set of theories, including his own. It is worth pointing out, however, that Brecht's theoretical work is not purely a matter of stage technique. The best place to start the discussion is with a working definition of the term which is always invoked when Brecht is under discussion – alienation.

Alienation, or the alienation effect, is a translation from a German term (*Verfremdungseffekt*) for which there is no English equivalent. Roughly, it means that what the audience accepts in real life must on the stage be made unfamiliar, and that the unfamiliar should in turn be made familiar. To achieve this, Brecht employed a number of stage techniques, designed as a constant reminder to an audience that it is in a theatre, and that what it is watching is something unreal; the idea being that an audience convinced of the unreality of the play's world would be more likely to take a critical attitude to the events presented.

Another cliché of Brechtian criticism is that emotion has no place in Brecht's theatre. This is untrue; rather, Brecht wanted to avoid the easy emotional involvement between actors and audience that, for him, characterized Western theatre. He wanted the audience to be involved with the drama intellectually as well as emotionally; to watch the characters react to their society, and from that, to form a judgement about that society for themselves.

With this in mind, consider the scene again. It is a conventional mourning scene; a mother who can't believe her child is dead, and who sings a lullaby over her body – a mother, moreover, who is herself the victim of a cruelly ironic delusion, that her son Eilif is still alive (he was killed, as the audience is aware, three years before). After arranging for her daughter's burial, she leaves the stage, dragging the dead weight of her cart behind her. On the surface, the scene seems unambiguously tragic; the audience's sympathies should be with Courage as she limps after the departing armies.

And, to an extent, it is. Given the visual impact of the scene, it is impossible not to sympathize with Courage at least to some extent. Brecht, however, carefully injects a sourer, more realistic note into the scene; he does so in three ways. First, in the dialogue between Courage and the peasants; secondly, in Courage's lullaby; and thirdly, in Courage's exit.

First, the dialogue. Kattrin has saved the town, and the peasants should be grateful; however, this is a war's front line, and anything that draws the attention of an army is a danger to the civilians. The peasants, therefore, are not sympathetic; they want Courage to leave as soon as possible, so that they can deny ever having met her. The first time a peasant speaks, it is 'with hostility'; and it is a command, not a request ('You must go'). Even the offer to bury Kattrin, seen in this light, is suspect; they do not want to reassure the mother – they want to get rid of the evidence. Only the peasant's wife voices some kind of concern, and even that is tentative ('Ain't you got nobody else? What you could go to?'). Courage alternates between incomprehension ('I think she's going to sleep') and the impulse to blame someone else ('Better if you'd told her nowt...'). It is only when the peasants offer to bury Kattrin that Courage recovers; and she recovers at least partly because she has some business to conduct. The audience by this stage need no reminding that it is Courage's desire to conduct business that has led, directly and indirectly, to the deaths of her children.

Secondly, the lullaby. Courage's is not a sad song. It is a song that describes happiness purely in terms of material possessions ('Neighbours' [kids] are in tatters/ and you're dressed in lawn/ cut down from the raiment / an angel has worn...'). Courage's best hope for her children has always been that they be wealthy – and that their fortune will be secured by their mother's ability to turn the war to profit. There are signs, at the end of the song, that Courage is at last beginning to realize that this aim has destroyed her family; the end of the lullaby is muted, and seems to conjure up the deaths and displacements that are part of any war ('The one lies in Poland/ the other – who can say?'). But any recognition is, at best, temporary; she stops singing, only to blame the peasants for her daughter's death.

Thirdly, the exit. Courage leaves, as Brecht noted, having learned nothing. She is as committed to the idea of war profiteering at the play's end as she was at its beginning; her last words, addressed to the armies, are 'Take me along'. She has learned nothing from the war because, as Brecht says, there is nothing to be learned from war itself; the only sensible course of action for anyone involved in conflict is to pack up, leave the battlefield, and to go home. It is hard to sympathize fully with someone who thinks that a war can be turned to advantage; even more so, when the person has seen the destruction of her family by the very war she follows. We as an audience may sympathize with her plight; but it is hard, in the circumstances, not to find ourselves condemning her actions.

## *Waiting for Godot* by Samuel Beckett

*Estragon*: What's wrong with you?
*Vladimir*: Nothing.
*Estragon*: I'm going.
*Vladimir*: So am I.
*Estragon*: Was I long asleep?
*Vladimir*: I don't know.
   Silence.
*Estragon*: Where shall we go?
*Vladimir*: Not far.
*Estragon*: Oh yes, let's go far away from here.
*Vladimir*: We can't.
*Estragon*: Why not?
*Vladimir*: We have to come back tomorrow.
*Estragon*: What for?
*Vladimir*: To wait for Godot.
*Estragon*: Ah! (Silence) He didn't come?
*Vladimir*: No.
*Estragon*: And now it's too late.
*Vladimir*: Yes, now it's night.
*Estragon*: And if we dropped him? (Pause) If we dropped him?

*Vladimir*: He'd punish us. (Silence. He looks at the tree.) Everything's dead but the tree.

*Estragon*: (Looking at the tree) What is it?

*Vladimir*: I don't know. A willow.

  Estragon draws Vladimir towards the tree. They stand motionless before it. Silence.

*Estragon*: Why don't we hang ourselves?

*Vladimir*: With what?

*Estragon*: You haven't got a bit of rope?

*Vladimir*: No.

*Estragon*: Then we can't.

  Silence.

*Vladimir*: Let's go.

*Estragon*: Wait, there's my belt.

*Vladimir*: It's too short.

*Estragon*: You could hang on to my legs.

*Vladimir*: And who'd hang on to mine?

*Estragon*: True.

*Vladimir*: Show all the same. (Estragon loosens the cord that holds up his trousers which, much too big for him, fall about his ankles. They look at the cord.) It might do at a pinch. But is it strong enough?

*Estragon*: We'll soon see. Here.

  They each take an end of the cord and pull. It breaks. They almost fall.

*Vladimir*: Not worth a curse.

  Silence.

*Estragon*: You say we have to come back tomorrow?

*Vladimir*: Yes.

*Estragon*: Then we can bring a good bit of rope?

*Vladimir*: Yes.

  Silence.

*Estragon*: Didi.

*Vladimir*: Yes.

*Estragon*: I can't go on like this.

*Vladimir*: That's what you think.

*Estragon*: If we parted? That might be better for us.

*Vladimir*: We'll hang ourselves tomorrow. (Pause) Unless Godot comes.

*Estragon*: And if he comes?

*Vladimir*: We'll be saved.

  Vladimir takes off his hat, peers inside it, feels about inside it, shakes it, knocks on the crown, puts it on again.

*Estragon*: Well? Shall we go?

*Vladimir*: Pull on your trousers.

*Estragon*: What?

*Vladimir*: Pull on your trousers.

*Estragon*: You want me to pull off my trousers?

*Vladimir*: Pull ON your trousers.

*Estragon*: (Realizing his trousers are down) True.

  He pulls up his trousers.

*Vladimir*: Well? Shall we go?

*Estragon*: Yes, let's go.

  They do not move.

This is a section of dialogue from the end of the second act of Samuel Beckett's *Waiting for Godot*. The play has a simple plot: at evening each day two tramps, Vladimir and Estragon, meet by a tree on a country road to wait for a Mr Godot, who does not arrive. Their vigil is interrupted in both acts by Pozzo and his servant Lucky. In the first act, Pozzo is taking Lucky to market to sell him; and in the second act, Pozzo, who is blind, and Lucky, who is mute, are still united; at the end of each act a small boy enters to tell the tramps that Godot will not come today, but that he will surely come tomorrow. The tramps decide to leave, but when the act ends they have not moved.

*Waiting for Godot* is generally accepted as one of the classic texts of the Theatre of the Absurd. As with other absurdist texts (Ionesco's *The Chairs*, Boris Vian's *The Empire Builders*, Jean Genet's *The Blacks* or *The Balcony*) its setting is determinedly non-naturalistic; it contains realistic elements – a country road, a tree – but they are presented without a defining context. The plot is circular; it does not build to the climax of action that we might expect in Ibsen, for example. The characters are, by any realistic standards, bizarre. The tramps are strangely eloquent and well read; Pozzo and Lucky are grotesques. The audience – and, again, this is a feature of absurdist theatre – are presented, not with a stage world that can be easily accepted, but with a stage world that constantly surprises, in this case, because nearly all of the conventional elements that shape a performance are missing.

This means that an audience, watching an absurdist play, will have to focus its attention on those parts of the performance that other dramatic styles would consider comparatively unimportant (the set; the stage picture that is created and recreated from moment to moment; and the rhythm and texture of the dialogue).

The set has already been described; it is, in contrast to other absurdist plays (which tend to take place on cluttered or complex stages), monastically stark. However, it does fulfil the genre's requirements, in that it suggests an atmosphere, rather than providing a meaning. The best absurdist sets are those that function poetically; that provide, by yoking together elements that would not generally exist together (Ionesco's *Amedee*, for example, with its giant corpse and glowing mushrooms in a stuffy Parisian flat), a powerful visual symbol for the play. *Godot*'s set works in the opposite direction; rather than yoking together elements not normally associated with each other, it removes those elements that you might expect to find – bushes, grass, a backdrop showing fields or a sky. As an image, it is hauntingly simple, and precisely because it is simple, it can be read in a variety of different ways: the tree is a cross, and this is the tramps' Golgotha; this is a wasteland, and the tramps are among the few humans that are left; or even that this is a blatantly artificial set, and that the tramps are performers, going through their routine each night. Each of these readings finds at least some support from the text, and each is suggested – strongly suggested – by the simple image that Beckett creates.

Secondly, the action. In absurdist theatre, physical action generally does not have much to do with the emotional life of the characters, because the characters do not have an emotional life: they are grotesque figures, whose actions have something of the mechanical nature of circus clowns. This is certainly the case in *Godot*. In this scene, Estragon's trousers fall down – a typically clownish image that undercuts the seriousness of the dialogue (the tramps are discussing suicide). Mechanical actions are also repetitive; Beckett's characters are generally doomed to repeat the same actions time and time again. At the end of the extract, Vladimir takes off his hat, feels around inside the brim, and puts the hat back on. He has done so periodically throughout the play; at first, the action seems significant (Vladimir is plagued by something that makes him uncomfortable, but that he can't remove). By the end of the play, this action has been dulled by repetition; it has been revealed as meaningless, as purely habitual, as simply something that Vladimir does to pass the time.

Thirdly, the dialogue. The dialogue of the Theatre of the Absurd is as much a matter of sound as sense. In Ionesco, for example, language seems constantly on the verge of breaking down; characters chop words up into individual syllables, stretch the vowel sounds of others, and turn commonplace words and phrases into chants or war cries. In Beckett, language is constantly at the point of exhaustion. The characters search for new words to describe their predicament, but they are almost always frustrated; the characters must always fall back on (as Clov says in *Endgame*) 'the words that remain'. In this extract, both Vladimir and Estragon are tired. They communicate in short sentences, and confine themselves to simple statements, questions and answers. The dialogue is constructed entirely of a series of repetitions or near-repetitions ('I'm going'; 'Let's go far away from here'; 'Let's go'; and the final exchange, 'Well, shall we go?' 'Yes, let's go'). Questions are framed and answered in the same way ('And if we dropped him?' 'He'd punish us'; 'And if he comes?' 'We'll be saved'). The dialogue also includes exchanges drawn from the rest of the play. The last exchange is repeated, word for word from the end of the first act; the sequence beginning 'Oh yes, let's go' to 'Ah! (Silence)' expands on the play's most common exchange ('Let's go' 'We can't' 'Why not?' 'We're waiting for Godot' 'Ah!'). Finally, the extract repeats, in a more concise form, the exchange at the end of the first act. This is in keeping with the general atmosphere of the second act; the characters have gone through the same sequence of events in both acts, but in the second act everything is rather more difficult – their conversations are halting, because the words seem to be slipping away from them. At the end of the play, the dialogue is almost completely exhausted; it is as though we are watching a pair of comics who have largely forgotten their act, and who are merely going through the motions, using only those few phrases that they can still remember.

## *Death of a Salesman* by Arthur Miller

A melody is heard, played upon a flute. It is small and fine, telling of grass and trees and the horizon.

Before us is the SALESMAN'S house. We are aware of towering, angular shapes behind it, surrounding it on all sides. Only the blue light of the sky falls on the house and forestage; the surrounding area shows an angry glow of orange. As more light appears, we see a solid vault of apartment houses around the small, fragile-seeming home. An air of the dream clings to the place, a dream rising out of reality. The kitchen at centre seems actual enough, for there is a kitchen table with three chairs, and a refrigerator. But no other fixtures are seen. At the back of the kitchen there is a draped entrance, which leads to the living-room. To the right of the kitchen, on a level raised two feet, a bedroom furnished only with a brass bedstead and a straight chair. On a shelf over the bed a silver athletic trophy stands. A window opens onto the apartment house at the side.

Behind the kitchen, on a level raised six and a half feet, is the boys' bedroom, at present barely visible. Two beds are dimly seen, and at the back of the room a dormer window (this bedroom is above the unseen living-room). At the left a stairway curves up to it from the kitchen.

The entire setting is wholly or, in some places, partially transparent. The roof-line of the house is one-dimensional; under and over it we see the apartment buildings. Before the house lies an apron, curving beyond the forestage to the orchestra. This forward area serves as the back yard as well as the locale of all Willy's imaginings and of his city scenes. Whenever the action is in the present the actors observe the imaginary wall-lines, entering the house only through the door at the left. But for the scenes of the past these boundaries are broken, and characters enter or leave a room by stepping 'through' a wall onto the forestage.

This is a description, written by the author, of the set for Arthur Miller's *Death of a Salesman*. Willy Loman, the salesman of the title, is a man who has difficulty in separating fantasy and reality, and the present from the past. He takes refuge in memories, to escape from the fact that he is slowly losing control of his life – he can no longer do his job, his relationship with his sons is deteriorating, and his marriage is tainted by the memory of infidelity. Willy and his sons are fervent believers in the American dream, in the idea that success will automatically come to those who are talented and personable, that there must always be something to look forward to, that any setbacks are temporary, and are usually the fault of someone else. To maintain that dream, the family have, over many years, constructed an elaborate fantasy life for themselves. The play shows this fantasy disintegrating. Willy, we learn, was never as good a salesman as he claimed; of his sons, one (Biff) is a dreamer who can't keep a job and who has spent time in jail, and the other (Happy) is a compulsive womanizer. At the play's end, Biff tries to bring Willy back to reality; but the knowledge that his son still loves him drives Willy to suicide, so that his son can benefit from the insurance.

Miller is one of the most important twentieth-century American dramatists; his work is generally ranked alongside that of O'Neill, Tennessee Williams, Edward Albee and David Mamet. As noted in the Introduction, the influence of European movements – the Absurd, Epic theatre – on the American stage was at most tangential; they exert an influence on the dominant style – naturalism – but they never usurp it. This is not to say that twentieth-century American drama is simply Ibsen plus additions; American dramatists have developed their own particular techniques and traditions. One of these – the most frequently noted – is the language; the American dramatist writes in a style which manages to be both poetic and demotic, that mixes slang with surprising eloquence. This aspect of American drama has been comprehensively covered. Also typically American, however, is the technique that Miller employs here: the symbolic set.

Miller's play begins almost cinematically. Before the set is revealed, we listen to some introductory music; and as the curtain rises the set does not so much appear as swim into focus. When the lights come up, we are shown, not a fully formed image, but one that seems half finished; something that looks, as Miller puts it, like 'a dream rising out of reality' – the salesman's fragile house, surrounded by high, oppressive tower blocks.

This set is both functional and symbolic. It is functional, because it allows swift transition from scenes set in the present to scenes set in the past. In the present, it is cramped, hemmed in by the apartment blocks that surround it. The actors treat the invisible walls as tangible barriers; they are confined, for most of the play's present-day scenes, to a relatively small area of the stage. When the play moves into the past, these barriers are removed; the lighting changes, blanking out the apartment buildings, and the green silhouettes of leaves are projected across the set. The action can become faster, more fluid, and the characters are freer; they are free, for example, to walk through the set's non-existent walls.

Secondly, the set's symbolic function: Miller's initial title for the play was *The Inside of His Head*, and the first idea for the set was, to say the least, rather impractical – when the curtain rose, the audience was to see a huge mask (the salesman's face) that would open to reveal the salesman's house. This idea was quickly abandoned; but something of it remains in the set Miller finally created. The house, we learn, has been extensively remodelled: Willy has taken a great deal of care over it (after his death, Biff says 'You know something .... There's more of him in that front stoop than in all the sales he ever made'). The house is therefore strongly identified with Willy; and Miller plays on this identification, creating an image of threatened fragility (the house surrounded by a 'vault' of tower blocks) that exactly mirrors Willy's state of mind at the play's opening. Willy's memories of the past are happier, freer and brighter than his experience of the present; and the set's design allows the expression of this freedom, as the characters move more easily across a lighter, more attractive stage. Similarly, the music (which Willy, as a stage direction informs us, 'hears but is not aware of') is linked to the salesman. Willy's father travelled the country selling handmade flutes; flute music, to Willy, symbolizes both the past and the freedom the past contained, and that he has now lost.

It could be said that this set, although definitely non-naturalistic, is still very much in the tradition established by Ibsen. It functions in much the same way as Captain Alving's pipe does in *Ghosts*. It provides a kind of visual shorthand, conveying information about the characters and the play's atmosphere, not in the allusive way that one might find in an absurdist play, but directly. The house *is* a symbol for Willy, as the pipe *is* a symbol for the Captain. It could be said that the whole set is symbolic in this naturalistic sense; all that has changed is the scope of the symbol. Instead of forming one element in an otherwise realistic stage, realistic props and furniture are now contained within a nakedly symbolic set.

## *The Caretaker* by Harold Pinter

> *Mick* is seated, *Davies* on the floor, half seated, crouched. Silence.
> *Mick*: Well?
> *Davies*: Nothing, nothing, nothing.
>   A drip sounds in the bucket overhead. They look up. *Mick* looks back to *Davies*.
> *Mick*: What's your name.
> *Davies*: I don't know you. I don't know who you are.
> Pause.
> *Mick*: Eh?
> *Davies*: Jenkins.
> *Mick*: Jenkins?
> *Davies*: Yes.
> *Mick*: Jen...kins. (Pause) You sleep here last night?
> *Davies*: Yes.
> *Mick*: Sleep well?
> *Davies*: Yes.
> *Mick*: I'm awfully glad. It's awfully nice to meet you. (Pause) What did you say your
>   name was?
> *Davies*: Jenkins.
> *Mick*: I beg your pardon?
> *Davies*: Jenkins! (Pause)
> *Mick*: Jen...kins. (A drip sounds in the bucket. *Davies* looks up.) You remind me of my
>   uncle's brother. He was always on the move, that man. Never without his passport. Had
>   an eye for the girls. Very much your build. Bit of an athlete. Long-jump specialist. He
>   had a habit of demonstrating different run-ups in the drawing-room about Christmas-
>   time. Had a penchant for nuts. That's what it was. Nothing else but a penchant. Couldn't
>   eat enough of them. Peanuts, walnuts, brazil nuts, monkey nuts, wouldn't touch a piece
>   of fruitcake. Had a marvellous stop-watch. Picked it up in Hong Kong. The day after
>   they chucked him out of the Salvation Army. Used to go in at number four for
>   Beckenham Reserves. That was where he got his Gold Medal. Had a funny habit of
>   carrying his fiddle on his back. Like a papoose. I think there was a bit of the Red Indian
>   in him. To be honest, I've never made out how he came to be my uncle's brother. I've
>   often thought that it was the other way around. I mean that my uncle was his brother and
>   he was my uncle. But I never called him uncle. As a matter of fact I called him Sid. My
>   mother called him Sid too. It was a funny business. Your spitting image he was. Married
>   a Chinaman and went to Jamaica. (Pause) I hope you slept well last night.
> *Davies*: Listen! I don't know who you are!
> *Mick*: What bed you sleep in?
> *Davies*: Now look here –
> *Mick*: Eh?
> *Davies*: That one.
> *Mick*: Not the other one?
> *Davies*: No.
> *Mick*: Choosy.

This extract is from the beginning of the second act of Harold Pinter's *The Caretaker*. The play is essentially a three-handed struggle for power: Ashton, an ex-mental patient, invites Davies, a tramp, back to the house that he is converting for his brother, Mick. Davies tries to play Mick off against Ashton, but is rejected by both.

Pinter rose to prominence in the late 1950s with a series of plays initially perceived as dense, elliptical and difficult. He was at first considered Britain's leading Absurd dramatist, and there are many points of similarity between his work and the work of Ionesco and Genet: the use of language as much for rhythm as for meaning; the sudden eruption of the unexpected into the world of the play; and an atmosphere of squalor and unease that underlies his work, even when the plays' locations begin to move upmarket.

However, the dramatist that Pinter most resembles is Beckett. The two were friends, and from the 1960s onward Pinter would send his manuscripts to Beckett for comment. From Beckett, Pinter takes the idea of a simple, confined setting (all of his early, and most of his late plays take place in a single room); the regular use of pauses and silences, and the ambiguities that litter Pinter's work – the shifting names, the contradictory versions of the past, and so on.

Pinter, though, is even at this stage in his career far from being a fully fledged absurdist. For one thing, his plays all have realistic settings: we always get the sense of a world existing outside the stage. The stage itself always remains strictly realistic (the walls are not demolished by giant feet; the stage does not fill up with luggage, chairs, or eggs). The language of the plays, although patterned, remains within the boundaries of everyday speech; indeed, Pinter's speech sometimes reads as though it is simply normal speech transcribed. Finally, although the precise status and identity of the characters might be ambiguous, the central conflicts within the plays are almost always clear.

Language for Pinter isn't a device to obscure meaning (as it is sometimes for Ionesco and Beckett); language for Pinter is most often a weapon. For example, this extract starts immediately after the abrupt climax of the first act (Davies has been rummaging around in the piles of rubbish strewn around the room; Mick enters silently and attacks Davies, forcing him to the floor; after silently checking through Davies's clothes and bedding, he sits, and asks the crouching tramp 'What's the game?'). At the beginning of Act 2, which takes place as Pinter informs us 'a few seconds later', we might expect Mick to interrogate Davies. This new character has obviously some connection with the property (the play begins with Mick standing silently in the middle of the room; he leaves before Ashton and Davies enter), and he is obviously threatening. We might expect him either to assault Davies, or at the least to bombard him with questions and demands.

This is not what happens. The previous act has finished at a moment of violent tension; the second act begins in silence, with the characters frozen into place. The dialogue proceeds slowly: a question and answer, then a pause, then a series of questions and answers, punctuated by pauses. The questions Mick asks are either neutral or ludicrously polite ('What's your name?...You sleep here last night?...Sleep well?...What did you say your name was?'). Then, instead of picking up the pace of the dialogue, Mick takes what seems to be a long digression into the past ('You remind me of my Uncle's brother...') before returning to his bland questions ('What bed did you sleep in?...Not the other one?'). Davies responds tensely, but does not allow himself to panic; his fear emerges as anger ('I don't know you. I don't know who you are...Listen! I don't know who you are!').

On the page, this exchange appears ambiguous. We know Davies tolerably well (we've had an act to get used to him) but we do not know Mick at all, and we learn little about him from the text. His dialogue – particularly the excursion into the past – seems designed to mislead the tramp. However, when performed, the dialogue becomes considerably clearer; clear enough, in fact, to bear out Pinter's assertion that *The Caretaker* is a relatively straightforward play.

The anticipated reaction to the scene is in fact correct; this is an interrogation. As so often in Pinter, language is used by one character to unsettle and to dominate another. It might have proved something of a relief to Davies if the interrogation proceeded conventionally, no matter how viciously it was conducted; the fact that it does not unsettles the tramp completely. The repetitive dialogue is not, as it might be in Beckett, a sign of futility or waste; it is itself a powerful source of tension – Mick hammers on a small number of banal questions with all the force of a policeman who doesn't believe the suspect's story. The contrast between the matter and the manner of Mick's interrogation is profoundly disturbing, for the tramp and for us.

The same is true of the speech. During it, Mick seems to totter on the verge of coherence; the speech is introduced as a piece of relevant information ('You remind me of my uncle's brother'). However, the life story that Mick tells becomes increasingly absurd: from the mundane ('He was always on the move, that man') to the apparently irrelevant ('Had a marvellous stopwatch. Picked it up in Hong Kong'), to the absolutely unbelievable ('Married a Chinaman and went to Jamaica'). The speech works, because it implicitly conjures up the kind of speech that Mick should, in normal circumstances, be making; even though the details become increasingly surreal, they follow the patterns of everyday discourse, with one thought triggering another of greater or lesser relevance.

As with the dialogue, Pinter takes the habitual rhythms of language, and renders them bizarre. However, this does not mean that language for Pinter is meaningless; on the contrary, he forces us to pay attention to the underlying impulses behind the words, because we cannot trust their surface (just because a detail is established doesn't mean that it can't be changed). We become, therefore, far more sensitive to the atmosphere that the words create, so sensitive that phrases that might otherwise seem meaningless or comic become troubling. For example, take the phrase 'You remind me of my Uncle's brother': is Mick saying that Davies resembles Mick's father? Nothing is made of the point, we never learn for sure whether or not this is the correct interpretation; the implication is left with us, and continues to unsettle us precisely because it is never resolved.

## Top Girls by Caryl Churchill

*Nijo*: Don't you like getting dressed? I adored my clothes./ When I was chosen to give sake to His Majesty's brother,

*Marlene*: You had prettier clothes than Isabella.

*Nijo*: the Emperor Kameyana, on his formal visit, I wore raw silk pleated trousers and a seven-layered gown in shades of red, and two outer garments,/ yellow lined with green and a light

*Marlene*: Yes, all that silk must have been very...

The *Waitress* starts to clear the first course.

*Joan*: I dressed as a boy when I left home*

*Nijo*: green jacket. Lady Betto had a five-layered gown in shades of green and purple.

*Isabella*: *You dressed as a boy.

*Joan*: It was easy. I was only twelve. Also women weren't/ allowed in the library. We wanted to study in Athens.

*Marlene*: You ran away alone?

*Joan*: No, not alone, I went with my friend./ He was sixteen.

*Nijo*: Ah, an elopement.

*Joan*: but I thought I knew more science than he did and almost as much philosophy.

*Isabella*: Well I always travelled as a lady and I repudiated strongly any suggestion in the press that I was other than feminine.

*Marlene*: I don't wear trousers in the office./ I could but I don't.

*Isabella*: There was no great danger to a woman of my age and appearance.

*Marlene*: And you got away with it, Joan?

*Joan*: I did then.

The *Waitress* starts to bring the main course.

*Marlene*: And nobody noticed anything?

*Joan*: They noticed I was a very clever boy./ And when I

*Marlene*: I couldn't have kept pretending for so long.

*Joan*: shared a bed with my friend, that was ordinary – two poor students in a lodging house. I think I forgot I was pretending.

*Isabella*: Rocky Mountain Jim, Mr Nugent, showed me no disrespect. He found it interesting, I think that I could make scones and also lasso cattle. Indeed he declared his love for me, which was most distressing.

*Nijo*: What did he say?/ We always sent poems first.

*Marlene*: What did you say?

*Isabella*: I urged him to give up whisky,/ but he said it was too late.

This is a scene from the first act of Caryl Churchill's *Top Girls*. The play's central character, Marlene, has just become managing director of the Top Girls employment agency, an agency which specializes in finding work for female executives. We learn, however, that in doing so she has abandoned her daughter (who is rather backward), and turned her back on her family and her upbringing. She is successful, but her success is compromised; she doesn't recognize that hers is part of a wider struggle.

However, in this scene, Churchill gives the audience almost none of this information. The story outlined above only starts at the beginning of the second act. In the first act, we learn that Marlene has been promoted; and, as one might expect, she is celebrating. The celebration, though, takes an unexpected form. The guests are women who have struggled, and who have managed to succeed, even if the success is partial, in a male-dominated world. These figures are historical (Isabella is Isabella Bird, a Victorian woman who travelled extensively; Lady Nijo was an Emperor's courtesan, before she became a Buddhist monk) or fictional (Dull Gret, who is present in the scene but who does not speak, is a figure taken from a Brueghel painting; she is shown leading an army of women through hell). The other character on stage, Pope Joan, is a woman whose existence has not been definitely established, but she is thought to have been Pope from 854 to 856.

It is hard to imagine a more unrealistic (or unnaturalistic) gathering; and at first glance it does seem a strange scene with which to introduce a realistic play. Churchill, however, does not explain the scene. The characters react to each other with no surprise; they seem to accept each other immediately. The scene's place in the play is never resolved (Is it a dream, or a fantasy of Marlene's? We are given no evidence to assume that it is). The scene is simply presented to the audience as if it were as real as anything else in the play.

This is a feature of much of the new theatre writing that followed in the wake of the Alternative theatre movement in the late 1960s. It became possible to take risks: risks with subject matter, risks with presentation, and risks with structure and characterization. This last is Churchill's particular territory; her plays take liberties with the conventional forms of drama, liberties even more extreme for being unexplained. And yet the risks work; they do so, because they are never taken arbitrarily. For example, here: to bring together a group of women who have fought the status quo throughout their lives is to make the point that the struggle has, up until this point, been marginalized or hidden. These women's stories are as extraordinary as those of Stanley, Livingstone, Confucius, or Dante; but their stories are nowhere near as well known. The male story becomes common currency; the female story is forgotten. Partly, what Churchill attempts in this scene is an act of historical reclamation; she digs up these hidden stories, and presents them as part of a difficult long-term conflict, between what is expected of women and what women are capable of achieving.

Secondly, Churchill's work plays with the conventional way in which playwrights tell their stories. Each one of the plays discussed so far has a linear structure: events are presented in sequence, either with a clearly established set of causal links (as with Ibsen, Shaw and Miller) or in temporal order (as with Brecht). Even Pinter, ambiguous as he might appear, never breaks the cause-and-effect chain (the closest he comes to this – in *Betrayal* – is to reverse the direction of time, and to tell the story from the end to the beginning). Churchill, however, will present scenes out of order: the last act of *Top Girls* takes place one year before the second act; in another play, *Cloud 9*, the interval between the two acts spans almost a century, but the characters only age twenty-five years. Paradoxically, though, Churchill's confused time sequences bring her work closer to the way in which we experience life; she manages to create the impression of time passing subjectively, for her characters and for us. We face the present with a world-view that has not advanced much beyond Victorian times; and the development of time in *Cloud 9* reflects this. We cannot escape the influence of past choices; the last act of *Top Girls* reminds us of this. And we are sometimes aware of the context of our lives, seeing them as part of a wider, more significant whole. *Top Girls'* first act is a demonstration of this: there is no reason why a character like Marlene (who is presented to us as an intelligent, realistic, contemporary woman) should not be aware of the existence of the historical and fictional figures with whom she dines; there is no reason to assume that she might not, at some point, imagine herself in their company. Churchill simply takes that subjective experience (whose status, whether as dream or fantasy, does not *have* to be defined) and stages it.

## BIBLIOGRAPHY

Bigsby, C.W.E. (1990) *Modern American Drama*, Cambridge University Press, Cambridge.

Bradby, D. and McCormick, J. (1978) *Peoples' Theatre*, Croom Helm, London.

Bull, J. (1984) *New British Political Dramatists*, Macmillan, London.

Esslin, M. (1980) *The Theatre of the Absurd*, Methuen, London.

Innes, C. (1992) *Modern British Drama*, Cambridge University Press, Cambridge.

Innes, C. (1993) *Avant-Garde Drama*, Routledge, London.

Macdonald, J. (1986) *The New Drama*, Macmillan, London.

Russell Taylor, J. (1970) *Anger and After*, Methuen, London.

Styan, J.L. (1981) *Modern Drama in Theory and Practice*, (3 vols), Cambridge University Press, Cambridge.

Williams, R. (1968) *Drama from Ibsen to Brecht*, Hogarth Press, London.

Zola, E. (1877) 'Naturalism in the Theatre', in *The Theory of the Modern Stage*, ed. E. Bentley, Penguin, Harmondsworth.

ON PLAYWRIGHTS

Most of the playwrights discussed in this unit are covered in depth in the Macmillan Modern Dramatists series. There are also three excellent essay collections in the Cambridge University Press Companions series: *The Cambridge Companion to Ibsen* (Cambridge, 1994, ed. J. Macfarlane); *The Cambridge Companion to Brecht* (Cambridge, 1992, ed. P. Thomson and G. Sachs); *The Cambridge Companion to Beckett* (Cambridge, 1994, ed. J. Pilling).

# UNIT 16

# The modern novel

*Randall Stevenson*

## Modernism and the novel, 1900–39

'They've changed everything now ... we used to think there was a beginning and a middle and an end', remarked Thomas Hardy, discussing contemporary fiction with Virginia Woolf in 1926 (Woolf, [1953] 1989, p. 97). As he suggests, by that date a revolution in writing had occurred which was radical enough to unsettle much of what people 'used to think' about the form and style of fiction. By the mid-1920s comparable innovations had appeared in other arts, such as painting and music, and are as clear in the poetry of the early twentieth century (see Unit 17) as in its fiction. They can be traced in the work of many writers outside Britain – William Faulkner, Ernest Hemingway or John Dos Passos in the United States, or Marcel Proust in France, or Thomas Mann in Germany – as well as in the fiction of Joseph Conrad, Henry James, Ford Madox Ford, James Joyce, Virginia Woolf, May Sinclair, Dorothy Richardson, D.H. Lawrence and Wyndham Lewis. Many of this latter group are considered in detail in the analyses which follow this introduction to the period. 'Modernist' is the term now usually applied to their work and the wider movement of which they formed a part – appropriately enough, since a motive many of them shared was to 'make it new', in Ezra Pound's phrase: to make a literature adjusted to the changing pressures of a modern age.

'Modern Fiction' was the title Virginia Woolf chose for an essay published in the 1920s in which she explains that 'the proper stuff of fiction' could no longer be created by following the example set by many of the novelists who were successful earlier in the century (Woolf, 1966, II, p. 106). In another essay, she dates precisely the origin of conditions she considered made their work obsolete, remarking that 'in or about December, 1910, human character changed' (Woolf, 1966, I, p. 320). As she suggests, the early years of the century are worth examining for the new conditions apparent in the life of the time, and for the way these were addressed by novelists whom the modernists nevertheless thought it necessary – with some important exceptions – to supersede. Yet Woolf's choice of date seems surprising in a number of ways, not least in passing over the First World War to locate profound change in an age often since considered the most placid in the twentieth century. Looking back on the time before the war (usually referred to as the Edwardian age, though Edward VII died in 1910), George Orwell describes it as 'a good time to be alive', one when 'it was summer all the year round' and people had 'a feeling of security ... of continuity'. Orwell also admits, however, that 'if you look back on any special period of time you tend to remember the pleasant bits' (Orwell, [1939] 1962, pp. 37, 102, 107, 106). In relation to later, still more disturbed periods the Edwardian years have come to seem serene. The year 1910, however, saw not only the death of a king, but continuing troubles in Ireland and violent reactions to the suffragettes on the streets of London, as well as threats by the reforming Liberal government to abolish the House of Lords. Such threats might have seemed serious enough, in challenging a basis of the class-divisions so engrained in British life, to account for Woolf's view that 'all human relations ... shifted' at this time (Woolf, 1966, I, p. 321).

The Edwardian period, however, was from its start a time of shifting values and vanishing certainties. Even before Queen Victoria died in 1901, the Boer war had shocked the British public into realizing the empire might be indefensible in moral as well as military terms. These doubts grew with the century, matched by comparable questions on the domestic scene. Acquisitiveness encouraged by plentiful raw materials and market monopolies overseas seemed reduplicated in expanding commercialization and industrialization within Britain. In an age of declining religious faith, this often seemed unchecked by altruism and shaped only by greed. These were issues often addressed by Edwardian writers. In *Lord Jim* (1900), for example, Joseph Conrad implicitly criticizes the kind of contemporary adventure story – made popular by authors such as Rider Haggard, Arthur Conan Doyle or John Buchan – which supported the values of honour and heroism on which the empire was ostensibly based. In Conrad's vision, these turn out to be thoroughly difficult or distracting to sustain in practice. Ford Madox Ford provides a similar picture of the hollowness of contemporary values in *The Good Soldier* (1915, see below). Conrad's criticism of empire is extended in *Heart of Darkness* (1902, see below), and in *Nostromo*, which examines the displacement of altruism in empire by materialism; by 'the religion of silver and iron' Conrad shows shaping the history of an imagined South American republic (Conrad, [1904] 1969, p. 71).

Materialism on the domestic scene similarly concerned Edwardian novelists such as H.G. Wells, John Galsworthy, E.M. Forster and Arnold Bennett. Wells was interested in a wider range of social issues, including the emancipation of women in *Ann Veronica* (1909), or the possibility of scientific or socialist progress towards a utopian future examined in his novel *In the Days of the Comet* (1906). But questions of commerce, class and wealth predominate in Edwardian social comedies such as *Kipps* (1905) and *The History of Mr Polly* (1910), and in *Tono-Bungay* (1909), whose narrator sums up much contemporary uneasiness when he complains that in 'the whole of this modern mercantile investing civilisation ... ultimate aims [are] vague and forgotten' (Wells, [1909] 1972, p. 186). Each of these novels follows a hero forced by some unexpected circumstance to abandon his usual station in life and experience a number of others: 'a succession of samples', as Wells calls them, chosen to reveal the broad construction of 'mercantile civilisation' and its effects within contemporary British life (Wells, [1909] 1972, p. 3). *The Forsyte Saga* (1906–29) has a similar aim. John Galsworthy suggests the family he portrays are

representative of their era as a whole, and shows their destruction of true values –
and often true love – through their obsession with property and convention.

E.M. Forster's Edwardian writing is more optimistic, finding in love and the
capacity to 'connect' ways of resisting class differences and social pressure. The
heroine of *A Room with a View* (1908) learns to reject Victorian constraints on
personal and social life in favour of art and passion. Even in *Howards End* (1910) –
concerned with a mercantile world of 'telegrams and anger' similar to that examined
in Wells's *Tono-Bungay* – the sensitive heroine's marriage to a businessman shows
some possibility of restoring wholeness to a fragmented society, and of resisting the
spreading 'rust' of industrialization which threatens the countryside. Forster's liberal
faith in social reintegration fades only in his writing after the First World War, when
examining the sharper antitheses of empire in *A Passage to India* (1924).

Optimism is largely absent from the work of Arnold Bennett, whose protagonists, sensitive or otherwise, can do little to escape conditions life imposes upon them
and the numbing effects of their environments. His novels are often set in a
landscape already overrun by mercantile civilization, leaving characters trapped in
factory towns 'mean and forbidding of aspect – sombre, hard-featured, uncouth'
(Bennett, [1902] 1976, p. 25). Whereas a lucky legacy allows Wells's hero in *Kipps*
to escape his dreary circumstances, even a substantial inheritance does not free
Bennett's heroine in *Anna of the Five Towns* (1902). Later novels such as *The Old
Wives Tale* (1908) likewise illustrate in minute detail the pressures of physical,
environmental factors on self and destiny.

Bennett, Wells and Galsworthy, the novelists Woolf considered the 'most
prominent and successful ... in the year 1910', are the ones her essays criticize most
fiercely (Woolf, 1966, I, p. 326). Yet as the above discussion suggests, neither they
nor other Edwardian writers could be justly accused of ignoring contemporary life or
pressures on the 'human character' Woolf saw changing in that year. Indeed, this is
not the basis of her criticism. Instead, it is on the issue of method that Woolf attacks
Bennett and his contemporaries – not for any failure of attention to contemporary
life, which she sees presented almost *too* attentively in their work. She attacks
Bennett, in particular, for his wish to 'describe ... describe ... describe': a
determination to communicate endless facts about the environment of his characters
which puts 'an enormous stress upon the fabric of things' and leaves too little time
to look truly 'at life ... at human nature' (Woolf, 1966, I, pp. 332, 330). In one way,
such criticism misses the point of Bennett's fiction, which follows the French
writers he admired in treating 'the fabric of things' not as separate from human
nature, but as the principal shaping force upon it. Yet in another way so much
detailed attention to the material circumstances of existence does allow a kind of
materialism to dominate Bennett's vision, and sometimes Wells's and Galsworthy's.
This makes their work inadvertently complicit with the very aspects of modern life
they sought to criticize, emphasizing the material world and marginalizing the inner
life or spirit of the individual much as contemporary social forces did in reality.
Woolf's criticisms of this kind of materialism were also supported by other authors.
D.H. Lawrence found Galsworthy's characters 'only materially and socially
conscious ... too much aware of objective reality' rather than 'the psychology of the

free human individual' (Lawrence, 1955, pp. 123, 120). Reaching the end of his career in the Edwardian period, Henry James criticized contemporaries such as Wells and Bennett for offering in their work a 'slice of life' too full of the 'quarried and gathered material' of reality to exist properly as art (James, 1914, pp. 268, 262).

Along with Joseph Conrad, Henry James is exempt from Woolf's criticism of the Edwardians. Each can be seen as an early exemplar or precursor of modernist fiction, free of the limitations its authors found in other Edwardians. James's techniques and ideas, in particular, offered Woolf herself – and Dorothy Richardson and other later writers – alternatives to the 'materialism' and preoccupation with 'objective reality' which seemed to limit other Edwardian novelists. Rather than carrying life over into fiction in raw slices, James considered it should be shaped into art by the use of a 'structural centre', a figure through whose perceptions the novel could be focused (James, 1934, p. 85). He praised Conrad for finding this kind of centre in the figure of Marlow, the talkative seaman who narrates the story in *Lord Jim* and *Heart of Darkness*, supposedly to a circle of more or less silent listeners. Marlow's idiosyncratic vision of the world directs attention upon the way he presents the story, and on the subjective reactions of the person telling it, and away from any securely defined 'objective reality'. These tactics and similar ones used by Ford Madox Ford are further discussed below.

James achieves much the same effect in his own fiction by what he calls 'placing advantageously, placing right in the middle of the light, the most polished of possible mirrors of the subject'. As an example of this kind of mirror, James points to his use in *The Ambassadors* (1903) of Strether, an 'intense perceiver' of complex relations encountered during a delicate mission to Paris (James, 1934, pp. 70, 71). Unlike the narrators used by Conrad and Ford, Strether does not tell the story in his own words, but the narrative nevertheless remains closely confined to his point of view. In the same way as Impressionism in painting, such tactics ensure that attention centres not only on Paris life and manners, but on the reflective medium in which it is represented: on Strether's perception and reactions; on his nature as 'mirror'. James's disposition to 'place the centre of the subject in ... consciousness' in this way anticipates one of the defining priorities of the modernist authors discussed below (James, 1934, p. 51). Woolf particularly approved of his determination to 'illumine the mind within rather than the world without', a strategy she extends in her own writing (see below) and stresses in 'Modern Fiction' (Woolf, 1966, II, p. 81). To find 'the proper stuff of fiction' and to avoid the concentration on 'the fabric of things' which she felt limited the work of Bennett and others, she considers that the novelist should

> Look within ... examine ... an ordinary mind on an ordinary day. The mind receives a myriad impressions ... Is it not the task of the novelist to convey this varying, this unknown and uncircumscribed spirit ... with as little mixture of the alien and external as possible? ... to reveal the flickerings of that innermost flame which flashes its messages through the brain. (Woolf, 1966, II, pp. 106–7)

By the time Woolf published her essay, several of the novelists considered below had evolved new means of presenting the inner flow of consciousness; for recording not, as Conrad or Ford did, the voice of a narrator addressing silent listeners, but of characters silently, inwardly, addressing themselves. One of these novelists is D.H. Lawrence, who in one way, in *The Rainbow* (1915) and *Women in Love* (1921), redirects the attention of fiction towards inner life simply by means of the volume of attention he accords it. Whole paragraphs describing inner thoughts appear in these novels between single lines of direct speech. Like James before him, however, Lawrence not only describes characters' thoughts but deploys to a new extent means (see below) of approximating to the form in which these thoughts supposedly occur within the mind.

Such approximation is taken a decisive step further by Dorothy Richardson in her use in *Pilgrimage* – a novel-sequence which began publication in 1915 – of a stream-of-consciousness form which seeks to present characters' thoughts with the immediacy of their actual occurrence (see below). While Richardson invented or reinvented this stream-of-consciousness form for writing in English, its most spectacular development appeared in the novel which Woolf had much in mind when she set out her priorities in 'Modern Fiction': James Joyce's *Ulysses* (1922). Much of the Dublin of *Ulysses* is seen only in so far as it is reflected in the mind of Joyce's protagonist Leopold Bloom as he wanders around the city. His mental life is presented through a full range of the devices developed by James, Lawrence, Richardson and others for recording 'the mind within', and so thoroughly and inventively that one critic has suggested that Joyce 'rewrote for the modern novel generally the definition of a man' (Friedman, 1972, p. 442). It is in the last section of *Ulysses*, however, that Joyce's stream-of-consciousness tactics are deployed most extensively, not in presenting a man, but rather the mingling thoughts and memories of Bloom's wife Molly as she hovers on the edge of sleep. Such writing ensures that – whether or not 'human character' itself had changed – by the early 1920s the way character could be represented in fiction *had* changed decisively (see Unit 18, pp. 533–4).

This new modernist concentration on the mind and inner life was accompanied by related changes in the structure of the novel, also retraceable to the example of Conrad and Ford. In *Lord Jim*, as in *Heart of Darkness*, Marlow tells his story in a single evening, relying for its construction on a fickle memory which does not always present events in chronological order. The result is what Conrad calls in his Preface to *Lord Jim* 'a free and wandering tale'. Later modernist writers are similarly innovative with their chronology and construction. Rather like Marlow's story, the narratives of *Ulysses* and Woolf's *Mrs Dalloway* (1925) are confined to a single day, though one which allows readers an acquaintance with characters' lives in some ways as full as any offered by Victorian fiction. What is new in modernist fiction is the way such acquaintance is made. As the novel increasingly reflects 'the mind within', so it comes to rely on what Woolf calls 'time in the mind' rather than 'time on the clock': on characters' memories and recollections, returning to and associating with the present moment events long distant from it in time, stitching past experience into present consciousness (Woolf, [1928] 1975, p. 69).

'Life is not a series ... symmetrically arranged' Woolf suggests in 'Modern Fiction', complaining in her diary about the 'appalling narrative business of the realist: getting on from lunch to dinner' (Woolf, 1966, II, p. 106; [1953] 1985, p. 138). Avoiding this business by relying on 'time in the mind' creates another of modernism's distinctive features – its rejection of the serial chronology conventional to Victorian or Edwardian fiction in favour of more fluid approaches to structure. For the Victorians, the onward flow of history and the life in time may have seemed sufficiently coherent to provide a valid structuring basis for the novel, and Orwell was probably right to see some such 'feeling of continuity' surviving into the Edwardian period. After the outbreak of the war, and as a result of other factors discussed below (see especially on Lawrence), the modernists found in the passage of time and history not coherence but the 'nightmare' Stephen Dedalus speaks of in *Ulysses*, and the old structures of the novel consequently in need of change (Joyce, [1922] 1992, p. 42).

No wonder, then, that it was the absence of a conventional beginning, middle and end in contemporary fiction which Hardy remarked on in 1926. He might, of course, have registered other new aspects of modernist fiction: not only its transcriptions of inner consciousness, but a new interest within the novel in art and writing, often focused through characters who are painters or writers. This is further discussed below in relation to Joyce and Woolf. And yet, despite the scale and variety of contemporary innovation, Hardy might have been more restrained than to assert that modernist fiction had changed *everything* by 1926. That year also saw the publication of Gerald Bullett's study *Modern English Fiction*, which emphasizes – despite its title – the survival of the conventional novel, and of esteem for it. Bullett assesses Bennett, Wells, Galsworthy and Forster as the most significant of living authors, while Joyce, Woolf, Lawrence and Dorothy Richardson receive attention only in a last chapter devoted to 'Eccentricities'. Later judgements have on the whole accepted this latter group as among the great writers of the twentieth century, though they have not always seen them as belonging to what Bullett calls the 'main road of English fiction' (Bullett, 1926, p. 121). Indeed, the modernist novel is almost by definition an alternative to this road, as it comes down through the Victorians and Edwardians, and the new styles and strategies it offers have been valued variously by the generations of authors who have followed since the 1920s. (See also the second part of this unit.)

Critics and readers have likewise never been unanimous in modernism's praise. Its innovations need to be seen as responses to the shifting, challenging forces of history in the early twentieth century (see below, especially on Lawrence). Yet modernist writing is sometimes so successful in distancing or effacing these forces that it risks the accusation of ignoring them altogether; so successful in avoiding the material world and social concerns which preoccupied Edwardian novelists, in favour of the inner life of the individual, that it has sometimes been considered escapist and irresponsible. Apparent evasion of the public world might seem to extend into a partial evasion of the public itself, complexity and unusualness of technique never allowing modernism the wide readership some Edwardian authors enjoyed. Criticisms of this kind are forcefully expressed by the Hungarian Marxist Georg Lukács, for example, who challenges modernism for what he sees as its 'rejection of narrative objectivity, the surrender to subjectivity ... disintegration of the outer world ... the reduction of reality to a nightmare ... the denial of history' (Lukács, [1955] 1972, pp. 479, 484, 486).

Some answers can be found to Lukács's criticisms. Some of Roland Barthes's ideas, for example, might be used to suggest that the complexity and unfamiliarity of modernist texts might not diminish but enhance their responsibility in political terms. Readers required to piece together a fictional world out of fractured chronologies and streams of consciousness are less likely to be passive recipients of the views and values of the author, as might be the case with more conventional fiction. In Barthes's terms, readers who are the 'producers' and 'no longer the consumers' of a text are more likely to engage critically with a world, and a way of envisaging it, which they have had to reconstruct to such an extent for themselves (Barthes, 1974, p. 4).

Debates about the values of modernism continue to occupy critics at the end of the twentieth century. Obviously, this was a matter of immediate concern in the 1930s, a time when several authors expressed the kind of criticism Lukács outlines, and sought an orientation for their novels which was quite different from modernist fiction in the previous decade. George Orwell complained of modernism that it showed 'no attention to the urgent problems of the moment, above all no politics in the narrower sense' (Orwell, 1970, p. 557). Orwell and others in the 1930s found they had many 'urgent problems' to confront, and less opportunity than the modernists to retreat from them into memories of a supposedly more secure age before the First World War. The Wall Street Crash late in 1929 set off a decade of mass unemployment, poverty and political unrest within Britain, and the economic crises it contributed to abroad hastened the rise to power of dictators – Hitler and Mussolini – whose belligerence made a second war seem inevitable. Franco's rebellion and the Civil War in Spain, sharply dividing opinion in Britain between right and left, sometimes seemed a dire rehearsal of what was to follow for Europe as a whole.

Consequences of this sense of crisis can be illustrated by the progress of Christopher Isherwood's early career. An acknowledged debt to Joyce, Woolf and other modernists appears in the interior monologues and time-shifts which shape his first two novels, *All the Conspirators* (1928) and *The Memorial* (1932). In *Mr Norris Changes Trains* (1935) and *Goodbye to Berlin* (1939), however, he gives up complexities of modernism in favour of a more documentary style, communicating directly the threat of fascist politics Isherwood had discovered for himself in 1930s Berlin. His narrator in *Goodbye to Berlin* emphasizes this style's immediacy when he describes himself as 'a camera with its shutter open, quite passive, recording, not thinking' (p. 11). Entirely passive recording is scarcely possible in prose, or perhaps in any other medium, but Isherwood's definition of his tactics at the end of the 1930s suggests a very different set of attitudes from the modernists': a rejection of their 'impressionism' and emphasis on inner consciousness in favour, once again, of documentary attention to outward reality and social being.

These attitudes sometimes disposed 1930s writers to return to the example of the Edwardians whom modernism had discarded, George Orwell recording particular admiration for H.G. Wells. Much of Orwell's 1930s writing is in the form of documentary: of factual accounts of poverty in Britain in *The Road to Wigan Pier* (1937), or of the war in Spain in *Homage to Catalonia* (1938). In novels such as *A Clergyman's Daughter* (1935) or *Coming up for Air* (1939) he adopts tactics very similar to Wells's, following a central figure whose changes in income and social sphere allow broad investigation of contemporary society.

Similar interests and similar straightforwardness appear in the early work of Graham Greene, who settled in the 1930s on the 'straight sentences, no involutions' which continue, throughout his fiction, to demonstrate an ambition to 'present the outside world economically and exactly' (Greene, 1980, p. 33). Like Orwell's, his 1930s (and some later) writing is marked by a broadly socialist outlook on contemporary poverty and injustice: this is especially apparent in novels such as *It's a Battlefield* (1934) and *England Made Me* (1935), before Greene enters with *Brighton Rock* (1938) and *The Power and the Glory* (1940) a phase also shaped by the Catholicism to which he had been converted a decade or so earlier. Conflicts between political and religious imperatives, as well as moral and emotional ones, continue to dominate Greene's writing throughout a career lasting until the 1990s (see the second part of this unit), also adding to the intensity he brings to the genres of thriller and spy fiction.

The Catholicism of another convert, Evelyn Waugh, remained covert until *Brideshead Revisited* (1945). 1930s fiction such as *Vile Bodies* (1930) and *A Handful of Dust* (1934) follows his first novel, *Decline and Fall* (1928), in satirizing the smart set of the times. The shifting patterns of behaviour and belief which encouraged the experiments of modernism made the years after the First World War also a strong age of satire. This shapes the work of authors Waugh draws upon, such as Ronald Firbank, as well as Aldous Huxley's anatomies of contemporary values in *Crome Yellow* (1921), *Antic Hay* (1923) and *Point Counter Point* (1928), and Wyndham Lewis's huge attacks on modernist style and the artistic pretensions of the 1920s in *The Childermass* (1928) and *The Apes of God* (1930). Though more or less opposite in politics to Greene and Orwell, in his 1930s satires Waugh does share their directness of style, and the pace and visual quality of his writing, like the work of Greene and Isherwood, shows the increasing influence of the cinema on narrative at this time.

Similarities of this kind in the styles of 1930s authors, and often in their politics, have allowed critics such as Samuel Hynes and Bernard Bergonzi to construct a view of the decade as one of shared, collective interests, sharply differentiated from those of modernism. While Thomas Hardy found 'everything changed' in 1926, he might well, in this view, have found much of it changed back a decade later – back to some of the conventions of Edwardian fiction, and to its concern with society and the material world. This is not an inaccurate picture of 1930s writing, but it is more convenient than it is complete. Modernism was not as universally rejected as it suggests, even by some of the authors usually supposed to do so. Orwell still uses the tactics of the Nighttown chapter (15) of *Ulysses* at one stage of *A Clergyman's Daughter*, and Greene a kind of stream of consciousness in *England Made Me*. Even Waugh's reliance on dialogue and implication probably owes something to Ernest Hemingway. There were also authors who adopted the methods of modernism much more extensively. Rosamond Lehmann and Elizabeth Bowen show some of its freedom with chronology and structure, and follow tactics similar to Virginia Woolf's in tracing what Bowen calls in *The House in Paris* 'the you inside you ... reflections ... memories' ([1935] 1983, p. 77). Other novelists such as Lewis Grassic Gibbon, considered below, found that modernist tactics did not necessarily obscure the political concerns of the age, but could be used to focus them; while Edward Upward and Rex Warner – perhaps under the influence of Franz Kafka, first translated into English in the 1930s – showed that political issues could be expressed as forcefully by means of fantasy and allegory as in realist styles. These were methods Orwell also came to use in his later fiction in *Animal Farm* (1945) and *Nineteen Eighty-Four* (1949).

The modernists themselves, of course, did not stop writing in the 1930s. Woolf extends her methods of interior monologue in *The Waves* (1931), and her experiments with the genre of fiction in *The Years* (1937) and *Between the Acts* (1941). The publication of *Finnegans Wake* (1939) completes the experimentation with language which Joyce began as 'Work in Progress' in the late 1920s. The 1930s also saw the emergence of a new generation of writers ready not only to adopt modernist tactics but to reshape them for purposes of their own. Like Lehmann and Bowen, Jean Rhys adapts to the communication of women's consciousness a range of modernist methods, fluently intermingling uncertain thoughts, memories and present experience. Malcolm Lowry's wordplay and streams of consciousness in *Ultramarine* (1933); Henry Green's idiosyncratic language; Lawrence Durrell's adoption of some of the interests and methods of D.H. Lawrence; and Samuel Beckett and Flann O'Brien's extension of the example of Joyce (see below) had all confirmed by the end of the 1930s that modernism did not perish during the decade, but continued as an influence for the future. Its effects, however, were partly postponed and redirected by the Second World War. The second part of this unit considers the legacies of this period in later writing, and the competition and coalescence of conventional and innovative styles in the latter half of the twentieth century.

## Texts, authors, contexts

### Joseph Conrad: *Heart of Darkness* (1902)

'Kurtz ... at the time I did not see – you understand. He was just a word for me. I did not see the man in the name any more than you do. Do you see him? Do you see the story? Do you see anything? It seems to me I am trying to tell you a dream – making a vain attempt, because no relation of a dream can convey the dream-sensation, that commingling of absurdity, surprise, and bewilderment in a tremor of struggling revolt, that notion of being captured by the incredible which is of the very essence of dreams....'

He was silent for a while.

'...No, it is impossible; it is impossible to convey the life-sensation of any given epoch of one's existence – that which makes its truth, its meaning – its subtle and penetrating essence. It is impossible. We live, as we dream – alone....'

He paused again, as if reflecting, then added –

'Of course in this you fellows see more than I could then. You see me, whom you know ...'

It had become so pitch dark that we listeners could hardly see one another. For a long time already he, sitting apart, had been no more to us than a voice. There was not a word from anybody. The others might have been asleep, but I was awake. I listened, I listened on the watch for the sentence, for the word, that would give me the clue to the faint uneasiness inspired by this narrative that seemed to shape itself without human lips in the heavy night-air of the river. ([1902] 1995, p. 50)

The passage's most repeated words are 'see' and 'dream', and the tension between what each implies about truth and perception – present throughout *Heart of Darkness* – is a shaping force in the evolution of modernism more generally. As recently as his Preface to *The Nigger of the 'Narcissus'* (1897) Conrad had claimed that his task as a novelist was 'before all, to make you *see*', but of the seven occurrences of the verb 'to see' in this passage, five are in interrogative sentences, or in ones expressing doubt or negation. Conrad's narrator Marlow repeatedly questions the possibility of making his audience – becalmed on a yacht in the Thames at nightfall – 'see the story' or its main character Kurtz in any straightforward way, concluding that the 'life-sensation' may be 'impossible to convey'. It fades instead towards an equally impalpable 'dream-sensation', and an equation of living and dreaming which suggests that each occurs alone, an ineluctable possession of individual experience and consciousness.

Such problems are typical of modernism's general scepticism of conventional realism – in particular, of the possibility of seeing or communicating any experience independent of its subjective construction by an individual observer. The early appearance of such scepticism in Conrad's fiction helps to locate it within an intellectual climate already established at the end of the nineteenth century. Epistemologic doubts about the validity of contact between mind and world had been extensively expressed, for example, in the philosophy of Friedrich Nietzsche, denying the existence of any 'absolute truths' or 'eternal facts' (Nietzsche, [1878] 1986, p. 13). Modernism's emphasis on the individual mind – on living and dreaming alone – results partly from uncertainty of any surely knowable world beyond it; any objective, factual reality. Marlow indicates a wider feeling underlying the development of modernism in the early twentieth century when he remarks earlier in *Heart of Darkness* 'For a time I would feel I belonged still to a world of straightforward facts; but the feeling would not last long' (p. 30).

The passage also speaks for later modernists, as well as the feelings of its own age, in the doubts it casts over words and language. Marlow's audience listens apparently in vain to his benighted voice, waiting 'for the sentence, for the word' that could communicate decisively his uneasy individual vision. Loss of faith in a knowable world also threw doubt upon the capacities of language used to represent it: Henry James's brother William was only one of several late-nineteenth-century philosophers to suggest that 'language works against our perception of the truth' (James, 1890, I, p. 241). Such doubts often appear in later modernist fiction, and are further discussed below in relation to Joyce and Flann O'Brien. Conrad was likely to encounter them on account of an experience shared by several other modernists – exile. As a Polish seaman who learned French before English, he was inevitably aware of the competing versions of reality different languages create, and the unlikeliness of establishing absolute truths in any of them.

*Heart of Darkness* may also be considered in the light of another contemporary thinker who challenged the capacities of language and conventional relations of self and world. Given the passage's stress on 'the essence of dreams', it is a significant coincidence that *Heart of Darkness* first appeared in serial form in 1899, the same year that Sigmund Freud published *The Interpretation of Dreams*. Virginia Woolf was later inclined to suggest that the change in 'human character' she locates in 1910 may have been owed partly to Freud, whose work was first translated into English the previous year. Though Freud's work may have encouraged the modernists to 'look within' and 'examine the mind' it also suggested limits to what could be seen or recorded there, since the unconscious Freud describes is at most partially accessible to intellect and language – an issue later to concern both D.H. Lawrence and James Joyce.

The nature and existence of a dark core of being, outside the intellect, is in other ways of obvious significance for *Heart of Darkness*. Conrad's novella relies strongly on the symbolic – an idiom figuring in the work of many later modernists, such as Lawrence, and perhaps also encouraged by the example of Freud. Travelling into the interior in quest of Kurtz – 'the chief of the Inner Station' (p. 47) who has been overtaken by madness and savagery – Marlow is also symbolically journeying into himself. Much of Conrad's fiction is concerned with conflicts of the rational and orderly with the irrational or unreliable: in this case, between Marlow, reliant on 'an honest concern for the right way of going to work', and Kurtz, 'a soul that knew no restraint, no faith' (pp. 65, 108). Many of Conrad's central characters, however, find themselves secret sharers of values they had thought antithetical to their own, and Marlow is disturbed and fascinated to find Kurtz not simply a figure of depravity, but one in whom intelligence and enlightenment have somehow ceased to exist independently of their opposites. This reveals a darkness from which Marlow cannot consider himself immune. The 'absurdity, surprise and bewilderment' of this discovery, and Marlow's 'tremor of struggling revolt', precipitate a near-fatal illness, further confirming his identification with Kurtz, who dies on the way down river.

While Marlow cannot distance himself from Kurtz, the context of his story-telling ensures that the 'civilized' world is likewise fully implicated in the darkness he discovers in Africa. His narrative opens with the judgement, while looking over the Thames at London – an area once itself subjugated by the Roman empire – that 'this also ... has been one of the dark places of the earth' (p. 18). The kind of diminished distinction between civilization and barbarism, reason and anarchy, which his remark implies later concerned modernism in various ways, especially after the First World War. It also has immediate political implications about the immorality of empire. Much of *Heart of Darkness* shows the impropriety of any European civilization believing in or trying to enforce upon its colonies the superiority of its ways, or assuming itself an 'emissary ... of science, and progress' (p. 47). Conrad has recently been criticized for an imperialism of his own – a facile and unexamined equation of 'niggers' and 'savages' with the darkness which concerns him – but in other ways *Heart of Darkness* is a sharp, early critique of empire.

Significantly, Marlow's only unreserved, affirmative use of the verb 'to see' occurs when he assures his audience they can see him and his part in the story more clearly than he could himself – even though, as darkness falls, he becomes invisible even as he speaks. As the presence of his immediate audience on the Thames emphasizes, an attempt must be made to see Marlow's role in his narrative, difficult though this may be. As he half-confesses in the passage above, his story concerns an encounter with a dark, unseen side of himself, and with what lies beyond his powers of interpretation and communication: it is part of 'the essence of dreams', after all, to be often opaque to the dreamer. Readers must therefore deduce what is at best implied in his narration, such as his identification with Kurtz. For example, when Marlow recounts seeing Kurtz seeming to stare at him out of the 'glassy panel' (p. 118) on his fiancée's door in Brussels, readers are left to deduce that he is actually seeing a reflection of himself.

Marlow's suggestion that his audience 'see more than I could then. You see me, whom you know' is echoed in contemporary fiction when in Henry James's *The Ambassadors* (1903) Strether remarks of his story 'You see more in it than I' and his companion replies 'Of course I see you in it' (James, [1903] 1973, p. 46). Like the fiancée's door, the texts of James and Conrad present a 'life-sensation' in which, regardless of the ostensible subject, the nature, motives and thoughts of central observers or narrators is always reflected. No longer uncomplicatedly showing the life-sensation of the external world, but drawing attention towards the dream-shaped depths of its inscription in the individual mind, both Conrad and James anticipate a major concern of modernism and a shaping imperative of its form. (See Unit 19, pp. 553–6, for a deconstructionist reading of *Heart of Darkness*.)

### Ford Madox Ford: *The Good Soldier* (1915)

It is very difficult to give an all-round impression of any man. I wonder how far I have succeeded with Edward Ashburnham. I dare say I haven't succeeded at all. It is even very difficult to see how such things matter. Was it the important point about poor Edward that he was very well built, carried himself well, was moderate at the table and led a regular life – that he had, in fact, all the virtues that are usually accounted English? ([1915] 1977, p. 140)

I have, I am aware, told this story in a very rambling way so that it may be difficult for anyone to find their path through what may be a sort of maze. I cannot help it. I have stuck to my idea of being in a country cottage with a silent listener, hearing between the gusts of the wind and amidst the noises of the distant sea, the story as it comes. And, when one discusses an affair – a long, sad affair – one goes back, one goes forward. One remembers points that one has forgotten and one explains them all the more minutely since one recognises that one has forgotten to mention them in their proper places and that one may have given, by omitting them, a false impression. I console myself with thinking that this is a real story and that, after all, real stories are probably told best in the way a person telling a story would tell them. They will then seem most real. (p. 167)

George Orwell suggests in *Coming up for Air* (1939) that the Edwardians believed that 'the old English order of life couldn't change', but that they actually 'lived at the end of an epoch, when everything was dissolving into a sort of ghastly flux' ([1939] 1962, pp. 108–9). Looking back on an earlier, apparently innocent and splendid life in those Edwardian years – spent travelling with his wife Florence and their friends the Ashburnhams – Ford Madox Ford's narrator John Dowell likewise comments 'Permanence? Stability? I can't believe it's gone ... that long, tranquil life, which was just stepping a minuet, vanished' (p. 13). Ford highlights a final cause of this era's loss of permanence and stability by locating his novel's crises on the date, 4 August, on which the First World War eventually broke out. But in the figure of Edward Ashburnham he also draws attention to the temper of an epoch which was 'dissolving' well before it finally collapsed in 1914. Like this era itself, Ashburnham is solid-seeming on the surface, yet actually dissolute: his 'well-built' appearance, suggestive of 'all the virtues' of the Englishman, belied by spectacular infidelities and a long-standing affair with Florence. Like Conrad's Lord Jim, another hero unable to live up to the virtues he seems to personify, Ashburnham is one of the 'hollow men' who often appear in literature at this time, his representativeness of the Edwardian age emphasized by his first name.

Ford collaborated with Conrad earlier in the century, and *The Good Soldier* shares some of the characteristics of Conrad's narrative, discussed above. Like *Heart of Darkness*, it is concerned with uncertainties which are perceptual rather than only personal; with the unreliability not only of Ashburnham himself, but with ways in which it is 'very difficult to see' him or to communicate any final truth about his character or anything else. Dowell does not claim to have attempted a true picture, but only an impression, doubts if he has achieved even this much with success, and warns that any impression he does manage to communicate may be false. His narrative and its contradictions confirm these doubts: Dowell denying, for example, that '[his] own psychology matters at all to this story', yet also mentioning a 'mysterious and unconscious self' and 'unconscious desires' (pp. 99, 100, 213). Deep involvement with the events he narrates impedes objectivity: even more fully than Marlow, he exemplifies the kind of unreliable narrator some critics consider characteristic of the modern novel. J. Hillis Miller suggests that 'Victorian novels were often relatively stabilised by the presence of an omniscient narrator ... a trustworthy point of view and also a safe vantage point' (Miller, 1970, p. 220). Such figures, however, belong to a less uncertain age – perhaps corresponding to faith in an omniscient, omnipotent God – whereas twentieth-century epistemologic uncertainty spreads to the teller as well as the tale. Like *Heart of Darkness*, *The Good Soldier* is in this way typical of the situation defined by the critic Gérard Genette when he considers the novel after the end of the nineteenth century 'caught between what it tells (the story) and what tells it (the narrating)', and moving increasingly towards 'domination by the latter (modern narrative)' (Genette, 1986, p. 156).

There are other aspects of his narrative about which Dowell is usefully conscious and explicit. Like *Heart of Darkness*, though this time in 'idea' only, *The Good Soldier* is supposedly an oral narrative, Dowell narrating events in the order he

happens to recall them – each 'as it comes'. His narrative therefore 'goes back ...
goes forward', exemplifying conclusions Ford recalls reaching when working with
Conrad, that:

> what was the matter with the Novel ... was that it went straight forward ... To get ... a
> man in fiction you could not begin at his beginning and work his life chronologically to
> the end. You must first get him in with a strong impression, and then work backwards
> and forwards over his past. (Ford, 1924, pp. 129–30)

Relying on 'time in the mind' through the fickle memories of narrators such as
Marlow or Dowell, the fiction of Conrad and Ford shows the beginnings of
modernism's movement away from conventional structure and 'life as a series'. Yet
Dowell is still ready to acknowledge another, 'proper' place for episodes in his story
– presumably in the conventional chronological order of their occurrence. He adds,
however, that 'what will seem most real' will not necessarily be created by following
this order. His comments indicate some of the tensions underlying the development
of modernism, suggesting a gap between 'proper' or established conventions of
fiction, and what is 'real': between the novel's traditional strategies for representing
the world, and a world that seems to have outgrown them. Modernism might be
considered to bridge this gap by a kind of extension of realism: a representation not
only of a fictional world, but also – in the novels of Joyce, Woolf and Richardson
– of minds that perceive it, or in Conrad and Ford's work, of 'what tells it', of the
devices of 'a person telling a story'. Modernism is less a complete break with
realism than a radical reshaping of its established conventions: including, in
particular, a foregrounding in the represented picture of the means of its perception
or creation.

### Dorothy Richardson: *Pilgrimage* (1915–67)

> She was surprised now at her familiarity with the detail of the room ... that idea of
> visiting places in dreams. It was something more than that ... all the real part of your life
> has a real dream in it; some of the real dream part of you coming true. You know in
> advance when you are really following your life. These things are familiar because
> reality is here. Coming events cast *light*. It is like dropping everything and walking
> backwards to something you know is there. However far you go out, you come back. ...
> I am back now where I was before I began trying to do things like other people. I left
> home to get here. None of these things can touch me here. (1979, II, p. 13)

> I *must* have been through there; it's the park. I don't remember. It isn't. It's waiting. One
> day I will go through. Les yeux gris, vont au paradis. Going along, along, the twilight
> hides your shabby clothes. They are not shabby. They are clothes you go along in, funny;
> jolly. Everything's here, any bit of anything, clear in your brain; you can look at it. What
> a terrific thing a person is; bigger than anything. How *funny* it is to be a person. (II,
> p. 256)

Richardson admired Henry James, following in the early volumes of *Pilgrimage*
what she describes in her Foreword as his tactics of 'keeping the reader incessantly

watching ... through the eye of a single observer' (I, p. 11). Her observer is Miriam Henderson, whose experience remains central throughout the thirteen-volume sequence of *Pilgrimage*. (The above extract comes from the fourth volume, *The Tunnel*, 1919.) Miriam, however, is described as 'something new – a kind of different world', as a 'new woman' (I, pp. 260, 436), and much of her experience is shaped by, and explores, new social possibilities and ways of thinking for women early in the twentieth century, including a sense of the inadequacy of literary conventions established by men. Miriam feels there are 'millions of books I can't read' because they are written with 'some mannish cleverness that was only half right. To write books, knowing all about style, would be to become like a man ... a clever trick, not worth doing' (I, p. 284; II, p. 131). In her Foreword Richardson discusses ways of avoiding these tricks of established style, suggesting the need for 'a feminine equivalent of the current masculine realism ... feminine prose ... moving from point to point without formal obstructions' (I, pp. 9, 12). She admired Joyce as a writer of this kind of prose, most in evidence in the unobstructed, unpunctuated flood of Molly Bloom's mind at the end of *Ulysses*.

The two passages above illustrate the progression of her own early writing – before the publication of *Ulysses* – towards a 'new realism' and new prose able to enter more fully into the 'new world' of feminine consciousness. Like Ford in *The Good Soldier*, or Conrad comparing 'life-sensation' and 'dream-sensation', the first passage makes the nature of realism and true perception almost explicitly an issue, repeating the terms 'real', 'really' and 'reality', often alongside 'dream', and suggesting that life is 'real' only when somehow in touch with 'the dreaming part of you'. The passage itself likewise moves between something close to conventional realism and a much more subjective, inward register of the 'dreaming part of you'. It begins objectively enough, the first sentence opening with an authorial report of Miriam's state of mind, using the third-person pronoun 'she' and the past tense. 'Now', however, suggests the time-frame of the character rather than the author, and the passage soon moves entirely into the present tense, with the more colloquial 'you' replacing 'she', also indicating a closer transcription of Miriam's inner voice. 'You' is used much in the sense of 'one', part of a gradual slippage from third person to first, from authorial report to character perception. This makes the final appearance of 'I' in the last lines seem quite natural, though it actually marks a final, decisive change from the objectivity of the opening in favour of a stream-of-consciousness form which records Miriam's thoughts in the way they supposedly occur to her. The second extract illustrates this form in fuller, uninterrupted operation. Richardson uses alternately the pronouns 'you' and 'I' to represent the first person, without the more external, objective 'she' or any distanced voice of authorial report. Instead, it follows the wandering, associative progress of Miriam's polyglot inner voice, demonstrating the new intimacy and immediacy with which stream of consciousness looks within the mind and reaches towards the core of 'what ... a person is'.

The first passage also helps to clarify ways Richardson's invention or reinvention of stream of consciousness may have derived from specifically female vision of 'what ... a person is'. Virginia Woolf talks in *A Room of One's Own* (1929) of the 'alien and critical' feelings women experienced for what they more and more recognized, in the early twentieth century, as a male-dominated society, and of the 'splitting off of consciousness' which was the result (Woolf, [1929] 1975, p. 96). Women, and women writers, may therefore have been particularly disposed to look within the mind, within a 'split off' consciousness, for a private space, the 'room of their own' otherwise denied them by contemporary society. Yet they could scarcely have ignored ways this society so often evaluated them, not in terms of their inner lives but of their appearance, even as objects. However subjectively they wished to see themselves, awareness of a contrary external perspective inevitably remained, creating not only a consciousness 'split off' from the world but one partly split by it. The resulting division between external and internal views of self may nevertheless have helped to create just the kind of fluidity between pronouns and subject positions the first passage illustrates: the movements between 'she' and 'I' which lead towards the stream-of-consciousness form. There may therefore be a particular logic in the first appearance of stream of consciousness in English in *Pilgrimage*, a new woman's vision of a new woman's mind. Its development in Richardson's writing supports the conclusion reached by Sandra M. Gilbert and Susan Gubar – that 'women writers are the major precursors of all 20th-century modernists, the *avant-garde* of the *avant-garde*' (Gilbert and Gubar, 1986, p. 1). As these and many other critics have recently shown, modernist writing and its innovations particularly require to be seen in the context of changing gender roles and assumptions in the society of their time. (See Unit 23 for a discussion of women writers and modernism.)

## James Joyce: *A Portrait of the Artist as a Young Man* (1916)

He drew forth a phrase from his treasure and spoke it softly to himself:
– A day of dappled seaborne clouds.

The phrase and the day and the scene harmonized in a chord. Words. Was it their colours? He allowed them to glow and fade, hue after hue: sunrise gold, the russet and green of apple orchards, azure of waves, the grey-fringed fleece of clouds. No, it was not their colours: it was the poise and balance of the period itself. Did he then love the rhythmic rise and fall of words better than their associations of legend and colour? Or was it that, being as weak of sight as he was shy of mind, he drew less pleasure from the reflection of the glowing sensible world through the prism of a language many-coloured and richly storied than from the contemplation of an inner world of individual emotions mirrored perfectly in a lucid supple periodic prose? ([1916] 1973, pp. 166–7)

In the passage from *Heart of Darkness* discussed earlier, Marlow becomes 'no more ... than a voice', his narrative eventually seeming to 'shape itself without human lips'. While Conrad shows language almost detaching itself from its speaker, the above extract suggests a language detaching itself from the world, its pleasures and possibilities existing for Stephen Dedalus almost independently of its conventional semantic, representational function. The passage extends in this way some of the epistemologic doubts about relations of mind, word and world identified in Conrad's work at the turn of the century: a mistrust of language continues to appear throughout twentieth-century writing, and was already a central concern for the modernists. Rather than transparently representing reality, for many modernist authors language came to seem as much a screen between mind and world, or the 'prism' Joyce mentions in the passage above, obscuring reality or warping its light into patterns and colours of its own. Dorothy Richardson's heroine Miriam sums up such feelings in *Pilgrimage* when she suggests that 'language is the only way of expressing anything and it dims everything' (1979, II, p. 99). As an Irishman growing up in Dublin, still under English rule, Joyce had particular reasons for sharing some of these feelings. In *Portrait*, while discussing words with an Englishman, his semi-autobiographical hero Stephen reflects that

> The language in which we are speaking is his before it is mine. ... His language, so familiar and so foreign, will always be for me an acquired speech. I have not made or accepted its words. My voice holds them at bay. My soul frets in the shadow of his language. (1973, p. 189)

Stephen's fretful sense of English as the language of a foreign power, slightly distanced from him and the Ireland he inhabits, helps explain some of the sense in the above extract of a gap between words and the world they supposedly serve (see Unit 25, p. 665).

The whole passage, however, sees this less as a problem than as a source of possibility, and it is significant that Stephen eventually discovers that his feelings of foreignness as well as familiarity for his language actually equip him to know and use it *more* fully than his English interlocutor. Joyce might likewise be thought to have found in his particular relation to words a sense of freedom from the bounds of convention and of opportunity for his writing – one which may also help to explain why so many modernist authors were exiles. A sense of English as a partly foreign and 'acquired' language – added to by a life abroad, in Trieste, where he worked as an English teacher, and later in Zurich and Paris – places Joyce close to the position of the exile defined by Julia Kristeva when she remarks that

> lacking the reins of the maternal tongue, the foreigner who learns a new language is capable of the most unforeseen audacities when using it ... since he belongs to nothing ... that weightlessness ... gives him the extravagant ease to innovate. (Kristeva, 1991, pp. 31–2)

Joyce's most audacious innovation is usually considered his use of stream of consciousness and other methods in *Ulysses* to reflect the inner lives of his characters. Looking with only 'weak ... sight' at the external world, and, instead, contemplating 'an inner world of individual emotions' may therefore seem the ideas in the above passage most significant for his later fiction. Nevertheless, its concern with the shape, rhythm, and balance of words – with the whole existence of language, rather than only what it represents – defines an equally important direction in this later writing. Joyce remarked of *Ulysses* that 'it is the material that conveys the image ... that interests you' (Budgen, 1934, p. 180), and this interest in the medium of fiction, language, is sustained throughout the novel, not as a matter of actual discussion as in the passage above, but largely by means of parody. Casting

Bloom as an unlikely modern equivalent of Odysseus, journeying through a single Dublin day, *Ulysses* is parodic throughout, but individual chapters also mock specific styles of literature, journalism, advertising or ordinary speech. Parody, stylistic variation and exaggeration make the nature of language impossible to ignore, ensuring that representation is as much a subject of interest throughout as what is represented – that *Ulysses* once again involves its readers as much, in Genette's terms, in 'what tells it' as in 'what it tells'. (A deconstructive perspective on *Ulysses* will be found in Unit 19, pp. 455–6.)

This is a balance which shifts in *Finnegans Wake* (1939), in which elements of character or story are harder to discern through Joyce's 'screens of language', as the critic Hugh Kenner calls them (Kenner, 1978, p. 41). In one way, Joyce's last work attempts a final extension of modernism's urge to look within the mind, creating a kind of stream of unconsciousness: 'waters of babbalong' moving towards areas hitherto beyond the reach of language (p. 103). Joyce's 'babbalong', however, constantly directs attention upon its components: upon the nature and relations of words; on linguistic issues such as phonetics, etymology, and the semantics of English and other languages. Such interests can be summed up by one of the novel's own phrases, 'say mangraphique, may say nay por daguerre!' ([1939] 1971, p. 339). Among its multilingual puns can be found the suggestion that Joyce's work is primarily 'graphique', not 'por daguerre': it is writing, writing for itself, not as daguerrotype or any other quasi-photographic attempt to represent reality. As a contemporary commentator on Joyce's work remarked,

> The epoch when the writer photographed the life about him with the mechanics of words redolent of the daguerrotype, is happily drawing to its close. The new artist of the word has recognised the autonomy of language. (Jolas, [1929] 1972, p. 79)

Recognized by Stephen Dedalus and developing throughout the modernist period, in Joyce's writing especially, this sense of autonomy – as both a problem and an opportunity for fiction – also reaches towards the postmodernism discussed below in relation to Flann O'Brien.

Other important developments in early twentieth-century fiction are illustrated by passages such as the above, and by *Portrait* as a whole. Along with novels such as Arnold Bennett's *Clayhanger* series (1910–18) or Compton Mackenzie's *Sinister Street* (1913–14), *Portrait* shows in one way the survival into the twentieth century of the *Bildungsroman* – the novel of personal education and growth towards maturity, such as *David Copperfield*, popular in Victorian times. Joyce's title, however, and the interest in language and aesthetics in many passages such as the above, suggest that *Portrait* is more of a *kunstlerroman* than a *bildungsroman*: more interested in the achievement of maturity as an artist rather than only as an individual. A comparable interest appears in many contemporary works of fiction: in D.H. Lawrence's *Sons and Lovers* (1913), Marcel Proust's *A la recherche du temps perdu* (1913–27), May Sinclair's *Mary Olivier* (1919) and Dorothy Richardson's *Pilgrimage*, as well as the novel serialized immediately after *Portrait* in *The Egoist* magazine – Wyndham Lewis's *Tarr* (1918), its title a near-anagram of 'art', and its hero, like Stephen, much concerned with discussion of aesthetic theories of interest to his author, and to the novel in which he appears. Sharing in a move from

*Bildungsroman* to *Kunstlerroman*, these novels also demonstrate a wider readiness among modernist writers to establish within the domain of language and art a 'harmony', 'pleasure', or 'poise' which could hardly be imagined continuing to exist in reality, especially after the First World War. This modernist concentration on art and vision rather than social reality is further considered below in relation to Virginia Woolf. (For a discussion of Joyce's and Flann O'Brien's work in their Irish context, see Unit 25, pp. 657–8, 665 and 666.)

## D.H. Lawrence: *Women in Love* (1921)

> The thought of the mechanical succession of day following day, day following day, *ad infinitum*, was one of the things that made her heart palpitate with a real approach of madness. The terrible bondage of this tick-tack of time, this twitching of the hands of the clock, this eternal repetition of hours and days – oh God, it was too awful to contemplate ...
>
> Oh, how she suffered, lying there alone, confronted by the terrible clock, with its eternal tick-tack. All life, all life, resolved itself into this: tick-tack, tick-tack, tick-tack; then the striking of the hour; then the tick-tack, tick-tack, and the twitching of the clock-fingers.
>
> Gerald could not save her from it. He, his body, his motion, his life – it was the same ticking, the same twitching across the dial, a horrible mechanical twitching forward over the face of the hours. What were his kisses, his embraces. She could hear their tick-tack, tick-tack ...
>
> Oh, why wasn't somebody kind to her? ...
>
> Gerald! Could he fold her in his arms and sheathe her in sleep? Ha! ...
>
> The Geralds of this world ... Let them turn into mechanisms, let them. Let them become instruments, pure machines, pure wills, that work like clockwork, in perpetual repetition ... perfect parts of a great machine ...
>
> Poor Gerald, such a lot of little wheels to his make-up! He was more intricate than a chronometer-watch. But oh heavens, what weariness! What weariness, God above!
> ([1921] 1971, pp. 523–5)

Readers of this passage – and many others like it throughout *The Rainbow* and *Women in Love* – might wonder who it is who says 'oh' and 'ha!' and invokes the deity. However passionate an author Lawrence is supposed, such interjections are unlikely to belong to his authorial voice. Instead, it is clear enough that the oh-ing and ha-ing, and much of the pattern and content of this passage besides, represent the thinking of a character; in this case, Gudrun's thoughts about her relationship with Gerald as it reaches its fatal climax at the end of *Women in Love*. Yet Gudrun's thinking is not conventionally represented in the text either as direct speech, in the first person and the present tense – in the form, for example, of "'Oh", she thought, "why isn't somebody kind to me?"' – or as indirect speech, in the third person and the past tense, such as 'she asked herself why somebody wasn't kind to her'. Instead, Gudrun's thoughts emerge in a form which preserves some of the features of both direct and indirect speech, and of the voice of both author and character. This form of combinatory discourse – following the work of Mikhail Bakhtin, recently of much interest to narrative theorists – is usually known as Free Indirect Style or Free Indirect Speech (see Unit 18, p. 356).

Frequently appearing in earlier fiction – in the work of Charles Dickens and Jane Austen, for example – this style is by no means Lawrence's invention. Nor is it his only means of communicating the consciousness of his characters: the first sentence in the passage above is typical of authorial reporting of thought which Lawrence often sustains at much greater length. Free Indirect Style, however, is used in Lawrence's novels more extensively and sometimes more subtly than by nineteenth-century writers, and it is similarly important for many other modernists. It is one of the devices Henry James uses to keep the reader 'incessantly watching ... through the eyes of a single observer', as Dorothy Richardson puts it, and Richardson herself employs it in much the same way to ensure concentration around Miriam Henderson's mind, especially in the early stages of *Pilgrimage*, when she uses stream of consciousness less often. Joyce also relied on Free Indirect Style to draw the draft material of *Stephen Hero*, begun about 1904, into the firmer focus around the thoughts of Stephen Dedalus which figures in *Portrait*: it shapes much of the passage from the novel discussed earlier, for example. For Joyce and the modernists more generally, it is a style which marks a kind of half-way stage – retaining the voice of the author but also engaging with the inner life of characters – in the progression from the fairly conventional realism of novels such as *Stephen Hero* toward the full entry to the mind offered by stream of consciousness in *Ulysses* and elsewhere.

The passage also suggests why the modernists found it necessary to move in this direction, and to restructure their novels in doing so. Gudrun's terror of 'the mechanical succession of day following day' is an extreme version of Virginia Woolf's suspicion of 'life as a series', and the passage's concentration on Gerald helps indicate an origin for such feelings, additional to modernism's wish, discussed earlier, to escape the 'nightmare' of history. Throughout *Women in Love*, Gerald is portrayed as 'The Industrial Magnate'. In the chapter of that name, Lawrence shows him forcing upon his mines 'the great reform', one which ensures that they are 'run on the most accurate and delicate scientific method' and that 'the miners were reduced to mere mechanical instruments ... they became more and more mechanised' (p. 259). These reforms correspond to the introduction of principles of Scientific Management in the United States and Britain after the turn of the century, principles which in several ways did ensure that 'all life resolved itself into tick-tack'. Following the introduction of 'clocking in' for factory work in the 1890s, and based on 'time and motion study', new management principles and industrial practices worked on the assumption that time is money; a dimension to be commodified by the clock and used to control and reward workers made virtually as mechanical in their labour as the machinery of the workplace. Ironically, Gerald becomes as much the victim as the instigator of the attempt described in 'The Industrial Magnate' at 'substitution of the mechanical principle for the organic' (p. 260) in running his industry. Gudrun sees him as a pure machine, personified in her vision as the very instrument, the chronometer, on which his capitalist industrialism has come to be based.

Modernism can be seen to react to these new conditions in twentieth-century life in a number of ways. Not only in this passage, but often elsewhere in modernist fiction, there is an explicit hostility to the clock. Virginia Woolf remarks in *Orlando* that it seems 'a great shock to the nervous system, hearing a clock strike' ([1928] 1975, p. 85), and there are a number of characters who strike back: in William Faulkner's *The Sound and the Fury* (1929), for example, Quentin Compson twists the hands off his watch at the start of his last day at Harvard. In another way, modernist authors, Faulkner included, 'strike back' themselves by devising structures for their novels which depart from chronological succession and 'time on the clock' in favour of memory and 'time in the mind', as discussed in the Introduction. Typically of modernism, the challenges of the contemporary world are incorporated and resisted not so much at the level of theme, argument or statement – as the Edwardians might have done – but through finding new forms and shapes through which life can be differently or more positively imagined.

Much the same is true of the strategies deployed by Lawrence and others to create what he calls 'a deeper sense than any we've been used to exercise' (Lawrence, 1962, I, p. 282) in order to sustain a coherent sense of self and individuality: to see if beneath the 'little wheels' there could still be discovered some organic principle to substitute for the mechanical aspects modern life had installed within the self; to find some way of continuing to establish, in Dorothy Richardson's phrase, 'what a terrific thing a person is'. Her heroine Miriam's idea that 'Everything's here, any bit of anything, clear in your brain; you can look at it' is therefore not just a personal discovery, but indicative of a possibility modernism required to establish for itself in general. By 1910, 'human character' was threatened as never before by industrialization, materialism and reification, and Virginia Woolf naturally insists on a literature which could find some domain of the mind aloof from such pressures. Threatened by a first phase of industrialism, the literature of the Romantics recreates a sense of integral individuality through contact with external, green nature. Challenged by an accelerating industrialized technology in the early twentieth century, modernism turns instead to the inner fields of the self.

### Virginia Woolf: *To the Lighthouse* (1927)

Everything seemed possible. Everything seemed right. Just now (but this cannot last, she thought, dissociating herself from the moment while they were all talking about boots) just now she had reached security; she hovered like a hawk suspended; like a flag floated in an element of joy which filled every nerve of her body fully and sweetly, not noisily, solemnly rather, for it arose, she thought, looking at them all eating there, from husband and children and friends; all of which rising in this profound stillness (she was helping William Bankes to one very small piece more and peered into the depths of the earthenware pot) seemed now for no special reason to stay there like a smoke, like a fume rising upward, holding them safe together. Nothing need be said; nothing could be said. There it was, all round them. It partook, she felt, carefully helping Mr Bankes to a specially tender piece, of eternity ... there is a coherence in things, a stability; something, she meant, is immune from change, and shines out ... in the face of the flowing, the fleeting, the spectral, like a ruby; so that again tonight she had the feeling she had had once today already, of peace, of rest. Of such moments, she thought, the thing is made that remains for ever after. This would remain. ([1927] 1973, pp. 120–1)

The second section of *To the Lighthouse*, 'Time Passes', emphasizes the need discussed above in relation to D.H. Lawrence to turn towards inner life rather than the external nature of the Romantics. Surrounding the Ramsays' Hebridean holiday home is a natural world which in the family's absence seems a lonely domain of stones, stars and things hostile or at best indifferent to humanity. Especially when near a sea stained by the destruction of the First World War, it is impossible to continue, as the Romantics had, 'to marvel how beauty outside mirrored beauty within'. Instead, 'contemplation was unendurable; the mirror was broken' and 'Time Passes' suggests that only 'those mirrors, the minds of men' offer an uncertain contact with surviving dreams of order and happiness (pp. 153, 150). The above passage illustrates the tactics Woolf uses in the other two parts of the novel to look within these minds and trace their reflections, following in this case Mrs Ramsay's thoughts at her triumphal dinner party, towards the end of the first section.

Woolf remarked of *To the Lighthouse* that 'it is all in oratio obliqua' (Woolf, 1953, p. 102). As she suggests, the use of the third person and the past tense in passages such as the above, along with frequent authorial cues such as 'she thought', 'she felt' or 'she meant', creates a form close to indirect speech – though here used, of course, to record unspoken thoughts. There are times, too, when this 'oratio obliqua' moves closer to Free Indirect Style of the kind described above in the work of D.H. Lawrence, or towards imitation of patterns of thinking even when not necessarily representing thoughts themselves. The complicated syntax of the long third sentence, for example, and the rhythms which result, suggest the gradually unfolding associations of Mrs Ramsay's thoughts, even if these are described as much as transcribed. Though less immediate in its recording of thoughts than stream of consciousness, this is a style which achieves as comprehensive an enclosure of narrative within the mind as appears in *Ulysses* or *Pilgrimage*. The inner life exists so richly in passages such as the above that nothing need – or can – be found to match it in actual speech, or to connect it with the everyday world. On the contrary, this banal world of conversations about boots is relegated to parentheses, emphasizing Mrs Ramsay's mental 'dissociation' from the moment: free to float like a hawk, flag, or fume.

However privately it may be enjoyed, the richness and security of Mrs Ramsay's inner life nevertheless depends upon the sense of community established by her dinner party. She knows herself that 'it arose ... from husband and children and friends'. The first part of *To the Lighthouse* ends with a further consummation of her sense of community: with two members of the Ramsays' holiday party engaging to marry, as Mrs Ramsay had wished; with her reassuring thoughts of her brilliant children, safely asleep upstairs; and of her own marriage, drawn into tranquil harmony once again. This note of social cohesion and apparent 'immunity from change' – of stability and continuity, emphasized by marriage – brings this first section to a conclusion like that of many Edwardian or Victorian novels. *To the Lighthouse*, of course, does not end there. Its short, painful second section, 'Time Passes', quickly shows the redundancy for modernist fiction of this kind of conclusion, along with the irony of Mrs Ramsay's sense that it represents a kind of 'remaining for ever'. 'Time Passes' emphasizes the hostility not only of the natural world, but of the modernists' old adversaries: time and history. Covering the years of the First World War, it shows decay and loss intruding upon the Ramsays' family home, upon the family itself, and on all its hopes for the future. Mrs Ramsay and her daughter Prue die, and her son Andrew is blown up in the trenches. When remnants of the family and its friends return to the Hebridean house in the third section of the novel, painful memories of those more placid Edwardian times, ten years before, are all that remains of Mrs Ramsay's coherence and 'eternity'.

One of these family friends is Lily Briscoe. Finding the post-war world 'changed completely', she is ready to move beyond what she sees as Mrs Ramsay's 'limited, old-fashioned ideas', such as her 'mania ... for marriage' (pp. 198, 199). For Lily, refuge from 'eternal passing and flowing' (p. 183) can be found not in stability achieved in the lived, social world, as Mrs Ramsay tried to, but in art. She reflects that '"you" and "I" and "she" pass and vanish; nothing stays; all changes; but not words, not paint' (p. 204). Just as Lily rejects Mrs Ramsay's old-fashioned ideas, so *To the Lighthouse* moves in its third section beyond the principles of order and closure conventional in Victorian or Edwardian fiction and towards a sense of coherence and conclusiveness achievable in art rather than in life. Lily's interest in art and in her own painting are in other ways correlative with Woolf's strategies throughout the novel. For example, a solution to one of Lily's problems, 'a line there, in the centre' (p. 237), is close to Woolf's use of the short middle section of the novel to separate the days of experience, ten years apart, recorded in the novel's first and third parts. Painting and fiction are also co-terminous, Lily's decision of her work that 'it is finished ... I have had my vision' (p. 237) also concluding the novel. In such ways, *To the Lighthouse* draws attention to its own techniques as part of its interest in art and vision – apparently the only alternatives to a social reality now too disrupted by the 'nightmare' of history to offer the stability on which Victorian or Edwardian fiction had relied. In this way – as well as in its reliance on memory, restructured chronology and inner consciousness – *To the Lighthouse* is paradigmatic of modernist fiction's changes of form, style and emphasis, and indicative of some of the aspects of contemporary history which helped bring these about. Its three-part structure, in particular, emphasizes how distant Edwardian life had come to seem in the 1920s; how, in the novelist Richard Aldington's terms, the war had left 'adult lives ... cut sharply into three sections – pre-war, war, and post-war' (Aldington, [1929] 1984, p. 199). (See Unit 23, pp. 625–30, for a feminist reading of *To the Lighthouse*.)

## Lewis Grassic Gibbon: *A Scots Quair* (1932–4)

Here she was now, watching the east grow pale in the dawn.

Pale and so pale: but now it was flushed, barred sudden with red and corona'd with red, as though they were there, the folk who had died, and the sun came washed from the sea of their blood, the million Christs who had died in France, as once she had heard Robert preach in a sermon. Then she shook her head and that whimsy passed, and she thought of Robert – his dream just a dream? Was there a new time coming to the earth, when nowhere a bairn would cry in the night, or a woman go bowed as her mother had done, or a man turn into a tormented beast, as her father, or into a bullet-torn corpse ...

> Suddenly, far down and beyond the toun there came a screech as the morning grew, a screech like an hungered beast in pain. The hooters were blowing in the Segget Mills. ([1933] 1978, *Cloud Howe*, p. 36)

> [Cronin] took to the reading of the daftest-like books, about Labour, Socialism and such-like stite. *Where would you be if it wasn't for Capital?* you'd ask old Cronin, and he'd say *On the street – where the capitalists themselves would be, you poor fool. It's the capitalists that we are out to abolish, and the capital that we intend to make ours.* And he'd organised a union for spinners and if ever you heard of a row at the mills you might bet your boots a Cronin was in it, trying to make out that the spinners had rights, and ought to be treated like gentry, b'God. (*Cloud Howe*, p. 68)

Virginia Woolf describes the 1930s as a time when young writers 'could not go on discussing aesthetic emotions and personal relations . . . they had to read the politicians. They read Marx. They became communists; they became anti-fascists' (Woolf, 1966, II, p. 172). In one way, the last lines of the first passage above might be read as exemplary of changes in literature Woolf and many other commentators suggest as typical of the 1930s, and of the fate of modernism within it. Modernism's complex styles and emphasis on inner consciousness are often supposed to have been superseded by attention to working life and the political issues of the time, much as the above passage shows Lewis Grassic Gibbon's heroine Chris Guthrie finding her reveries rudely interrupted by the harsh sounds of modern industry.

Chris's reverie, however, could hardly have less to do with 'aesthetic emotions and personal relations'. Instead, it is typical of hopes often expressed in the 1930s for social and political change – for 'a new time coming to the earth', to be created by the kind of socialist politics Cronin outlines in the second passage. The red dawn Chris witnesses is symbolic: even the landscape she watches it from adds to political implications emphasized throughout Gibbon's *Scots Quair* trilogy. It is dominated by Standing Stones, representative of an ancient time 'without gods and classes' ([1932–4] 1978, *Grey Granite*, p. 48) which characters believe socialist politics may re-establish in a new form for the future.

Typical in this way of much 1930s thinking, each passage nevertheless exemplifies the particularity of Gibbon's style. Chris's vision in the first passage incorporates a sense of the present, emphasized by the repeated 'now' in its first lines, within hopes for the future and a clear awareness of the past. Dawning dreams of new times are strongly coloured, in this case, by angry recollection of the slaughter of the First World War. This kind of historical thinking is emphasized by the trilogy's adroit structure throughout. Chapters are circular, beginning at a moment later than the events they go back to describe, ending with the story advanced again to the moment at which the chapter began. Much as the Standing Stones impose a broader perspective on the novel's physical landscape, this temporal pattern ensures immediate events are contained within wider vision of their significance. Showing a modernist freedom in its approach to chronology and structure, such patterning allows A *Scots Quair* to remain completely engaged with contemporary conflicts and injustices, while also indicating their historical origins and their implications for a future envisaged beyond them.

Gibbon is similarly flexible in representing the inner voice of his characters. The first passage sometimes employs the kind of Free Indirect Style, discussed earlier, to represent the thoughts of the heroine. The unusual, colloquial 'you' form illustrated in the second is also used on occasion to communicate the thinking of principal characters – Chris sometimes included – rather in the manner of the passage from *Pilgrimage* examined above. But this form transcribes the voices of a range of minor figures as well, and sometimes the collective thinking of whole groups. Showing ironically the prejudices Cronin's ideas encounter, the sceptical view of socialism in the passage above is not located with a particular character, but only as what 'folk said' – a voice almost of choric commentary. In moving so flexibly between individual and collective expression, Gibbon democratizes the vision of the novel as a whole, finding in the voice of his fiction, as in its structure, a formal reflex for some of the political ideals of the 1930s.

Gibbon's background – growing up among the class and community he came to write about – probably contributed to this achievement. By contrast, the fiction of many of the young writers of the 1930s Woolf mentions – novelists such as Orwell, Isherwood, Greene or Upward – can be seen as limited by the public school, Oxbridge education they shared. This kept them at a distance from the working life towards which their politics inclined them, making inevitable their role, discussed earlier, as distanced documentarists, camera-like observers. Gibbon was one of few novelists in the 1930s with a chance to represent contemporary political and working life with the inwardness and immediacy modernism had made available during the previous decade: his trilogy confirms the survival of a modernist idiom even in a decade, and in treating subject matter, usually thought unfavourable for it. This helps to make *A Scots Quair* one of the most powerful, sophisticated treatments of its times.

### Flann O'Brien: *At Swim-Two-Birds* (1939)

Having placed in my mouth sufficient bread for three minutes' chewing, I withdrew my powers of sensual perception and retired into the privacy of my mind, my eyes and face assuming a vacant and preoccupied expression. I reflected on the subject of my sparetime literary activities. One beginning and one ending for a book was a thing I did not agree with. ([1939] 1977, p. 9)

The novel was inferior to the play inasmuch as it lacked the outward accidents of illusion, frequently inducing the reader to be outwitted in a shabby fashion and caused to experience a real concern for the fortunes of illusory characters ... The novel, in the hands of an unscrupulous writer, could be despotic ... a satisfactory novel should be a self-evident sham to which the reader could regulate at will the degree of his credulity. (p. 25)

Flann O'Brien's narrator considers that the works of 'Mr Joyce' are 'indispensable to all who aspire to an appreciation of the nature of contemporary literature' (p. 11), and *At Swim-Two-Birds* extends in various ways, usually comic and parodic, directions established in the contemporary novel by modernism in general and James

Joyce in particular. The narrator is a kind of parodic extension of Stephen Dedalus, engaged not just in 'contemplation of an inner world', as Stephen is in Joyce's *Portrait*, but instead withdrawing completely his 'powers of sensual perception' in favour of privacy within the mind. Like a contemporary novel by another author impressed by Joyce, Samuel Beckett's *Murphy* (1938) – whose hero prefers to 'come alive in his mind' ([1938] 1973, p. 6) rather than in 'contact with outer reality' (p. 101) – *At Swim-Two-Birds* sometimes shows an extreme version of modernism's urge to 'look within ... with as little mixture of the alien and external as possible'.

As well as being aware of the streams of consciousness of modernism, however, both Beckett and Flann O'Brien witnessed the growing interest in language and writing evident in the late 1920s and 1930s in Joyce's 'Work in Progress' – finally published as *Finnegans Wake* in the same year as *At Swim-Two-Birds*, 1939. It is this later, self-referential phase of Joyce's writing which is probably most influential on their work. While Stephen Dedalus remains concerned with 'individual emotions' as well as 'perfect prose' within his 'inner world', the private mental space of the narrator of *At Swim-Two-Birds* is apparently occupied by reflection on 'literary activities' alone. Such reflections continue to appear throughout, sometimes in the form of half-ironic critical essays such as the second extract above. The narrator also includes discussions of his own narrative problems – including mislaying parts of his text – as well as extracts from literary works which happen to interest him.

The literary principles discussed in this way are also exemplified and enacted throughout *At Swim-Two-Birds*. Suggesting the insufficiency of 'one beginning for a book', the narrator goes on to provide three. One of these introduces the story of Dermot Trellis, who is an author himself: his characters, however, rebel against him, take over his narrative, and indulge story-telling ambitions of their own as revenge for his earlier 'despotic' treatment. Ostensibly the work of a range of these competing narrators, *At Swim-Two-Birds* becomes a story about writing a story about story-telling; a collage of narratives and commentaries on the nature of fiction. This is a pattern comparable to Samuel Beckett's in the trilogy (*Molloy, Malone Dies, The Unnamable*, 1950–2) which followed *Murphy*. Each author matches the 'autonomy of language' critics saw in *Finnegans Wake* by establishing a kind of autonomy of fiction – novels no longer principally reflecting a lived reality in plausible actions and characters, but concerned as much or more with examining their own medium and creative processes; the strategies through which the 'sham' of literary illusion is established and sustained.

The novel, in short, begins to look at itself rather than the world. This is a direction which can be seen as a logical extension of Woolf's interest in Lily Briscoe's painting, or Stephen's scrutiny of words and their pleasures in *Portrait*. Novels such as Beckett's and Flann O'Brien's, however, are obviously more explicit than their predecessors in dealing with questions of art and writing, and more directly self-referential in examining these issues in relation to their own practice. Following from modernism, yet entering in this way a new phase of imagination, such texts make appropriate the term 'postmodernist' now often applied to them and many others like them appearing since the war. The critic Brian McHale (1987) provides another comparable model for this transition from modernist to postmodernist literature. McHale sees the epistemologic concerns of modernism – discussed at several points above – giving way to a postmodernist writing defined by practices and interests which are principally ontologic: concerned, that is, not so much with how the mind encounters the world, but with its capacity to project imaginative domains – worlds – of its own. Thus in Joyce's *Portrait* Stephen Dedalus may be sensitive to the potential autonomy of language, but the epistemologic issue of its relation to 'the glowing sensible world' and its capacity to reflect it remains an important interest. On the other hand, Beckett's narrators – or Flann O'Brien's – are resigned to detachment from this world, and interested instead in the ontologic freedoms of language and imagination to create worlds of their own, separate from the real one.

Many critics see *Finnegans Wake* and other novels around the time of the Second World War marking a point of transition or terminus for modernism, and McHale's is one of several models of how modernist fiction relates to writing in recent decades. Elements of postmodernism are often seen as central to this period's thinking in general, though 'postmodern' is a term still very variously defined. Most commentators, however, would agree that the increasing examination of 'literary activities' within recent fiction can be seen as part of a wider postmodern challenge to all theories, explanations or versions of life: part of a widespread scepticism of any construction of reality. Such scepticism is appropriate to an era more than ever enthralled by its media; one in which language and image must be seen not as innocent means of representing a world, but as inevitably bound up with intentions to condition and control it.

## The novel in Britain since the Second World War

In 1940, George Orwell talked of 'the *impossibility* of any major literature until the world has shaken itself into its new shape' (Orwell, [1940] 1970, p. 578). Reviewing war fiction in 1941, Tom Harrisson indicates some of the problems for contemporary writers when he finds 'the reconstruction and rearrangement of life's events (literature) taken over, as it were, by the more powerful and less manageable pressures of gigantic war. It is difficult ... to work it into the familiar patterns' (Harrisson, 1941, pp. 435–6). The pressures of war – the bombing raids of the Blitz, for example, nightly reshaping the landscape of major cities – did often seem to 'take over' reality, outstripping anything fiction could conventionally contain. Yet such challenges to literature, such fracturings of the familiar, did encourage some writers to establish *new* shapes and patterns: rearrangements or reconstructions of fiction which make the war and immediately post-war years a distinct period in the history of the novel, and a more successful one than Orwell, Harrisson and most later commentators suggest.

James Hanley, for example, makes the war's fracturing unfamiliarity an aspect of style as well as subject in *No Directions* (1943). Confining the narrative within the consciousnesses of characters caught together in the Blitz, Hanley communicates unusually immediately the patternless disorientation the war forces upon them. P.H. Newby was to create a comparable immediacy in *The Retreat* (1953), presenting events during the evacuation of Dunkirk at the moment they impinge on the minds of his characters, before they can be fully understood or formulated in language. Newby's *Something to Answer For* (1968) later offered a similarly disorienting vision of the Suez conflict.

Henry Green's *Caught* (1943) also emphasizes the war's subversion of conventional language and pattern. Its hero admits of the Blitz that 'there's always something you can't describe' and his attempts to communicate his experience contrast sharply with actual recollection of it ([1943] 1978, pp. 179–80). Believing life 'oblique in its impact upon people' (Green, 1950, p. 506), Green is concerned throughout his fiction with the uncertainties of communicating or sharing any experience, often teasing readers with symbolic or other patterns of meaning eventually left inconclusive or incomplete. Set in a London fire-station before and during the Blitz, *Caught* exemplifies his location of such uncertainties among the tensions generated by a group of people 'caught' together in situations of work or leisure. *Living* (1929) concentrates on a similar group in a Midlands factory, also illustrating Green's interest in language, dialect and dialogue: his late novels *Nothing* (1950) and *Doting* (1952) are almost entirely in direct speech. One of the most accomplished and unusual of twentieth-century novelists, Green's demonstration of the uncertainties of language and of fiction's shaping of experience has affinities with the French *nouveau roman* of the 1950s (see below): it also coincided productively with challenges to conventional patterning around the Second World War, a time when he published more than at any other stage of his career.

Showing its hero escaping the Blitz when he returns to the countryside of his childhood, *Caught* also indicates a direction followed by novelists who avoided presenting directly the violent action of the war. P.H. Newby defines this direction when he remarks that

> experience could be divided into two halves: childhood and adolescence on the one hand and war on the other. Unless one wandered off into fantasy or allegory these were the inescapable themes and of the two childhood probably proved the more attractive. (Newby, 1951, p. 8)

As Newby suggests, writers often turned to fantasy in the war years and those that followed, though more often as a means of analyzing the violence of contemporary history rather than attempting only to escape it. C.S. Lewis's trilogy *Out of the Silent Planet* (1938), *Voyage to Venus* (1943) and *That Hideous Strength* (1945) transposes earthly politics, allegorically, into interplanetary settings. Tracing a dark struggle for power among a cast of grotesques, Mervyn Peake's trilogy *Titus Groan* (1946), *Gormenghast* (1950) and *Titus Alone* (1959) can likewise be seen as a nightmare projection of European history. Concerned with overcoming a malign power in the East, even J.R.R. Tolkien's trilogy *Lord of the Rings* (1954–5) has been connected with contemporary conflict. Such connections are clearer in Wyndham Lewis's late fantasies *Monstre Gai* (1955) and *Malign Fiesta* (1955), which refer clearly enough to fascism, Hitler, and the invention of nuclear weapons.

As Newby indicates, childhood and adolescence proved a stronger interest among writers around the time of the war, though one that offered still less chance than fantasy to escape its gigantic pressures. Such possibilities are denied by George Orwell's *Coming up for Air* (1939): seeking to escape the shadow of impending war by returning to the countryside of his Edwardian childhood, Orwell's hero finds it has ceased to exist except as a happy memory. The idyll of childhood turns out to be equally precarious in Rosamond Lehmann's *The Ballad and the Source* (1945), which traces the consequences of adultery on subsequent generations of a family, several of whose members narrate this complexly structured novel. L.P. Hartley's *Eustace and Hilda* trilogy (1944–7) follows more straightforwardly the results in later life of events in an Edwardian childhood – a theme concisely focused later, in Hartley's most popular novel, *The Go-Between* (1953). Its narrator retraces the emptiness of his life to disillusion he experiences with people he met on an idyllic holiday in 1900 and made into 'inheritors of the summer and of the coming glory of the twentieth century' ([1953] 1983, p. 264).

Such reflections in *The Go-Between*, and the tactics of some of the novels mentioned above, show authors seeking within individual experience some context in which to consider a wider sense of loss in the twentieth century itself. In *The Heat of the Day*, Elizabeth Bowen's heroine likewise comes to feel that 'the fateful course of her fatalistic century seemed more and more her own', and that she and her lover are 'creatures of history' ([1949] 1983, pp. 134, 194). The narrators in each part of Joyce Cary's brilliant wartime trilogy *Herself Surprised* (1941), *To be a Pilgrim* (1942) and *The Horse's Mouth* (1944) also function as 'creatures of history', though the connection of personal destiny with the fateful course of the century is of particular interest in *To Be a Pilgrim*. The pressing moral concerns which shape its narrator's search for a source of present evils nevertheless extend in various ways throughout the trilogy. They are emphasized by the highly individual styles and views – often of the same relationships and events – which appear in each of its parts, forcing readers to arbitrate between disparate yet self-consistent sets of moral priorities. Strong moral concerns of this kind feature not only throughout Cary's writing, but also in other fiction of this period, a result of a war often conceived as a struggle between good and the evil forces of fascism; or, at a deeper level, between light and dark, civilized and barbaric tendencies innate in the human condition. Such conflicts (further considered below) also appear in Somerset Maugham's *The Razor's Edge* (1944), in C.P. Snow's *The Light and the Dark* (1947), and in Evelyn Waugh's *Sword of Honour* trilogy (1952–61), which traces the doom of decency and idealism across a broad wartime landscape.

The novel Waugh completed during the war, *Brideshead Revisited* (1945), helps elucidate a pattern apparent in much of the fiction discussed above. *Brideshead Revisited* reflects troubled wartime experience in its first and third parts, while its idyllic second section, looking back at youth and country-house life before the war, is entitled 'Et in Arcadia Ego' ('I too was in Paradise'). The phrase reappears graven on the skull the narrator keeps as an eccentric decoration, and can be seen to sum up ways that fear of death and disaster forced contemporary novelists to look through contemporary history towards myth – towards stories of Eden and paradise lost which are sometimes referred to directly, sometimes just suggested by an idyllic, often rural past reconsidered not in order to escape from present darkness, but to try and discover its origins. Rosamond Lehmann's title, *The Ballad and the Source*, and her novel's investigation of 'what poisons from what far-back brews went on corroding' ([1944] 1982, p. 42) are likewise paradigmatic of this Edenic pattern in contemporary novels, one often confirmed by their unusual structures. It is only around the time of the war, or in writing about it, that Orwell, Waugh or Graham Greene (in *The End of the Affair* (1951), each of whose opening chapters seeks to 'turn back time' (p. 66), as the narrator puts it) much depart from the straightforward chronology which usually structures their fiction. Similar inclinations to 'turn back time' appear in *The Go-Between*, *The Ballad and the Source*, *To Be a Pilgrim* and *The Heat of the Day*. Edenic retrospection in these novels, and the structures that accentuate it, show fiction finding a particular pattern within which to contain the darkness and destruction which had fallen like a primal curse on contemporary life.

This distinctively wartime pattern also shapes the outstanding novel of the 1940s, Malcolm Lowry's *Under the Volcano* (1947). Typically, it opens after the outbreak of war, going back in later chapters to examine the dissolution of a 'creature of history' whose drunkenness and self-destruction symbolize the wider experience of his times. His tragedy and its brilliant Mexican background are refracted through a series of interior monologues and streams of consciousness: along with confinement of the narrative largely to a single day, these show a debt to James Joyce and the modernists unusual in writing at this time. They also create a 'whirling cerebral chaos' ([1947] 1983, p. 309) which disorients readers as thoroughly as the writing of Henry Green, James Hanley or P.H. Newby, forcefully communicating the crises of the world envisaged. These are further focused by reflections on 'the old legend of the Garden of Eden' (p. 137) and the hero's recollection of a notice which he translates to himself as 'You like this garden? Why is it yours? We evict those who destroy!'.

Lowry reproduces a final version of this warning on the last page of the novel, the use of atomic weapons at the end of the war further linking his protagonist's self-destructiveness with what he calls 'the ultimate fate of mankind' (Lowry, [1946] 1985, p. 66). Concern with the new nuclear threat appears in many other novels at this time and later. Aldous Huxley's *Ape and Essence* (1948), the popular novelist Nevil Shute's *On the Beach* (1957), John Bowen's *After the Rain* (1958) and L.P. Hartley's *Facial Justice* (1960) all anticipate the likely fate of mankind after nuclear war. Along with the Allied armies' discovery of the concentration camps and the beginnings of the Cold War, such anxieties contributed to an exhaustion and disillusion in the late 1940s and early 1950s in some ways deeper than any that existed between 1939 and 1945 – ensuring that, as P.H. Newby commented in 1951, 'the war seems, in spirit, to go on and on' (Newby, 1951, p. 14).

As a subject for fiction, it has certainly done so. The war accentuates stresses within the relationship Olivia Manning depicts throughout the adventure story she sets in Bucharest, later Athens, in *The Balkan Trilogy* (1960–5), moving to the arena of the desert war in Egypt in *The Levant Trilogy* (1977–80). Moral questioning which the war encouraged in contemporary fiction extended in the early sixties to novels examining the rise of Nazism from a German point of view. Set in Germany immediately after the First World War, Richard Hughes's *The Fox in the Attic* (1961) continues, in a more political context, an investigation of conflicts of innocence and experience begun in his celebrated first novel, *A High Wind in Jamaica* (1929). Gabriel Fielding's *The Birthday King* (1962) considers the problems and passions of the same period, along with the gradual connivances which led from them to the ultimate horror of the concentration camps. Even as the war has faded from immediate memory these horrors have continued to haunt later novels: Julian Mitchell's *The Undiscovered Country* (1968), for example; or D.M. Thomas's *The White Hotel* (1981).

The shadow of war and something of its patterning of writing also figure in long novel sequences begun around the time of its occurrence: the fifteen volumes of Henry Williamson's *Chronicles of Ancient Sunlight* (1951–69); the twelve in Anthony Powell's *A Dance to the Music of Time* (1951–75); and C.P. Snow's eleven-volume *Strangers and Brothers* (1940–70). Rather like Joyce Cary's trilogy, each can be seen as an attempt to locate within individual destiny some of the wider developments of what L.P. Hartley calls in *The Go-Between* 'the most changeful half a century in history' ([1953] 1983, p. 269). Only *A Chronicle of Ancient Sunlight*, however, much engages in the kind of Edenic retrospection discussed above, its early volumes presenting the nature and hopes of a new century during the Edwardian period, though also – in *A Fox Under my Cloak* (1955), *The Golden Virgin* (1957) and *Love and the Loveless* (1958), which reflect Williamson's own experience in the trenches – the destruction of what peace and harmony this period possessed. Snow's *Strangers and Brothers* traces disillusion in a slightly later period: the aftermath of the First World War in *George Passant* (1940); the drift towards the Second in *The Light and the Dark* and *The Masters* (1951), and the development of the atom bomb in *The New Men* (1954), for example. Throughout, Snow is principally concerned with public life and office and their relations with private morality, an interest summed up by the phrase his title *Corridors of Power* (1964) added to the language. Public life and history remain further in the background in Powell's work, private relationships among the shallow, moneyed upper classes taking up much of the attention of *A Dance to the Music of Time*. In particular, the determination to claw his way up the social ladder shown by the sequence's main eccentric – and counterpointed against the fastidiousness of the narrator – helps to delineate what the latter calls 'the general disintegration of society in its traditional form' (Powell, [1955] 1983, p. 128), Powell's chief interest throughout.

It was a central interest in many other novels in the 1950s: in William Plomer's *Museum Pieces* (1952), for example, another novel of Edenic retrospection whose characters lament the passing of a more genteel era. But there also appeared in the 1950s a new generation of writers apparently enthusiastic for the demise of social convention and gentility. By the mid-1950s, life in Britain had indeed shaken itself into a newish shape, the war's erosion of assumptions and traditions, the creation of the Welfare State just after it, and a wider spread of education and affluence contributing to what Malcolm Bradbury calls 'a quiet but still fundamental social revolution' (Bradbury, 1993, p. 275). This helped re-establish the kind of interest in class and social mobility exemplified in John Braine's *Room at the Top* (1957) and John Wain's *Hurry on Down* (1953). Moving respectively up and down the social scale, the adventures of the heroes in each – like those of H.G. Wells's protagonists (see the first part of this unit) – carefully reveal the nature of the social strata they cross. Like Kingsley Amis's pseudo-rebel in *Lucky Jim* (1954), each nevertheless ends in a secure job and an affluent marriage, showing the tendency of their authors, supposedly 'Angry Young Men', towards reconciliation with a society they were sometimes thought at the time to seek to reform.

Shallow or covertly conservative in its values, their fiction was equally conventional in style, drawing on the example of Wells or the sceptical, colloquial narrative tone of William Cooper's influential *Scenes from Provincial Life* (1950). Cooper's work also encouraged a movement towards provincial settings which appears in the treatment of the Northern working class in, for example, Alan Sillitoe's *Saturday Night and Sunday Morning* (1958) and Stan Barstow's *A Kind of Loving* (1960). Cooper spoke for several of these fifties novelists when suggesting – rather as some commentators had in the 1930s – that 'the Experimental Novel had got to be brushed out of the way' before contemporary fiction could properly tackle social issues (Rabinovitz, 1967, p. 6). C.P. Snow concurred in finding experiment and the example of modernism 'at best a cul-de-sac' (Snow, 1958, p. iii). Only Sillitoe gained anything from this example, following D.H. Lawrence's style of transcribing the inner thoughts of characters, creating a warmth and inwardness in the portrayal of working-class life which sets him apart from other writers at this time. Post-war exhaustion seems to have settled heavily on their work, allowing it to be reabsorbed, without much real challenge, by English fiction's perennial obsessions with class, society and manners – which too often exclude technical sophistication or depth of feeling or vision. No wonder so many comments about 'the death of the novel' were made at the time. On the evidence of the Angry Young Men, it is the mid-1950s, and not, as Orwell suggested, the 1940s, which look most bereft of worthwhile fiction.

The 1950s, however, also saw the beginning of several careers more promising than those of the Angry Young Men, though the novelists concerned were often, sometimes understandably, numbered among them at the time. The tough Northern setting of David Storey's first novel, *This Sporting Life* (1960) has affinities with the work of Alan Sillitoe or John Braine, but later fiction such as *Pasmore* (1972) confirms that Storey's concern with class and social change always reached towards deeper interests in identity and self – sometimes, as in *Radcliffe* (1963), in almost allegoric form. William Golding's fiction is likewise close to allegory or fable, abandoning the social issues of the 1950s in favour of deeper areas of moral and philosophic investigation. As Golding has often explained, his principal concerns were shaped earlier, arising from his dark experience of the Second World War. 'The end of innocence, the darkness of man's heart' as he calls it in *Lord of the Flies* ([1954] 1967, p. 223) is a main concern not only of this first novel, tracing the rapid descent to savagery of a group of 'civilized' children after a war. It also shapes his next, *The Inheritors* (1955), describing a kind of wider Fall for the entire human species, and much of the fiction that follows. It remains a central issue in his outstanding 'Sea Trilogy', *Rites of Passage* (1980), *Close Quarters* (1987) and *Fire Down Below* (1989), examined as always with exceptional vividness in describing the natural world and its forces, and a moral complexity which in this later fiction moves further from fable and the allegorical directness of his first novels.

Moral concerns reintroduced by the war remain apparent long afterwards not only in Golding's writing, but in the work of a number of other novelists whose careers began in the 1950s and continued successfully into the 1990s. Like Golding, Iris Murdoch finds 'two wars and the experience of Hitler' continuing shadows upon the life of the later twentieth century (Murdoch, [1961] 1977, p. 23): their effects are apparent in *A Fairly Honourable Defeat* (1970), showing an ex-inmate of Belsen insouciantly destroying his acquaintances. Murdoch's tactics, however, are in some ways almost opposite to Golding's reliance on fable or allegory. The moral vision she begins to develop from her first novel, *Under the Net* (1954), depends upon recognition of the 'unutterably particular' ([1954] 1983, p. 82) in every situation and individual, and this is matched by a densely realistic style which resists the abstraction of allegory and of over-exigent moral judgement of any kind. In her own way, Muriel Spark is similarly critical – in *The Prime of Miss Jean Brodie* (1961), for example – of figures who attempt to impose their will and judgement at the expense of the particular nature of other individuals. Comparable relations of good and evil, freedom and will, preoccupy Anthony Burgess throughout much of his work – examined in *A Clockwork Orange* (1962) in a threatening future world, and a form close to fable, but traced, in his outstanding novel, *Earthly Powers* (1980), through a long, detailed examination of twentieth-century history from before the First World War up to the time of writing.

This is also the area covered in Angus Wilson's *Anglo-Saxon Attitudes* (1956), one of several novels whose realist style and investigation of contemporary social strata place this phase of his writing closer than any of the authors just mentioned to the manner of the early 1950s and the Angry Young Men. Wilson's later fiction, however, shows a much greater technical range. While covering nearly the same historical period as *Anglo-Saxon Attitudes* – though eventually showing the emergence of a new 1960s generation, habitués of pot and the pill – *No Laughing Matter* (1967) engages in a series of parodies and employs many of the resources of modernism in presenting inner consciousness. In this way, *No Laughing Matter* is a good example of a readiness to experiment or depart from convention which appeared alongside a renewed liberalism in ideas and 1960s life in general. This created new possibilities and interests for fiction which in various ways – considered below – can be seen to have lasted more or less until the present day. In a decade which saw at last the uncensored publication of D.H. Lawrence's *Lady Chatterley's Lover* (1928), a particular liberation was in attitudes to sex: one result was a new questioning of gender roles, further encouraged by the appearance of an organized women's movement towards the end of the decade. New consciousness of women's outlook and social role helped open up new directions for women's writing, which has developed since the 1960s as strongly and even more diversely than in the modernist age.

The two periods are comparable, and sometimes directly connected. Sensitive registers for inner thought established by Virginia Woolf, May Sinclair and Dorothy Richardson, extended into the 1930s by Elizabeth Bowen, Rosamond Lehmann and Jean Rhys, were carried forward into the 1960s by Rhys's publication of *Wide Sargasso Sea* (1965), and the subsequent reissue of her earlier novels. Techniques they offer have continued to develop in the work of recent women writers such as Anita Brookner and Eva Figes – author of an influential feminist tract, *Patriarchal Attitudes* (1970) as well as novels such as *Waking* (1981), close to Woolf's *The Waves* (1931) in structure and style. In novels such as *Providence* (1982), which alternates between an objective, third-person narrative voice and first-person transcription of the heroine's inner thought, Brookner's writing also shows some of the divided vision discussed earlier in relation to women's fiction in the modernist period. Such divisions are apparent elsewhere in recent fiction: in Margaret Drabble's *The Waterfall* (1969) or Fay Weldon's *Down Among the Women* (1971), for example, each of which alternates between first- and third-person forms. Both authors, however, are often closer to a social realist tradition than to modernism, Drabble declaring admiration for Arnold Bennett and an interest in questions of 'justice, guilt and innocence' (Drabble, [1965] 1981, p. 84): issues also of concern to Fay Weldon, though focused more particularly by a feminist perspective upon them. Splittings of identity figure in more experimental form in the writing of Emma Tennant, investigating in *The Bad Sister* (1978) what she calls a 'double female self' ([1978] 1979, p. 101), highlighted by the narrative's own movement between a realistic account of women's roles and their extrapolation into dimensions of dream and hallucination. Novels such as Angela Carter's *The Passion of New Eve* (1977) and *Nights at the Circus* (1984) or Jeanette Winterson's *Sexing the Cherry* (1989) have recently used this latter domain of fantasy not just to escape a male-dominated reality, but to satirize its assumptions, and to engage, independently of them, in a free re-examination and exploration of gender roles and identities.

Fantasy, realism, split narratives, divided selves and investigations of gender roles not only appear at various points throughout the fiction of Doris Lessing, but are combined in a single novel, *The Golden Notebook* (1962). This contains both a short novel and the notebooks kept by its central character, reflecting the problematic nature of experience as 'free woman', socialist, private being, and, above all, as a writer. *The Golden Notebook* has a strong realist component, fulfilling Lessing's wish to 'give the ideological "feel" of our mid-century' (Lessing, [1962] 1972, p. 11), but it has more than enough reflection on the nature of fiction and fragmented examples of various sorts of text to ensure that language and representation are central subjects. (See Unit 23, pp. 625–30, for a detailed study of Lessing.)

This experimentation and self-consciousness about writing, along with such diversity in envisaging the contemporary world, make *The Golden Notebook* paradigmatic of distinct though related strands of development in women's writing since the 1960s. As the work of Drabble and Weldon helps suggest – along with the example of recent novelists such as Maureen Duffy, Rose Tremain, Penelope Mortimer, Beryl Bainbridge, Penelope Lively or Penelope Fitzgerald – this writing is particularly equipped to 'give the ideological "feel"' of contemporary society from a specific, often sceptical and satiric point of view. Yet as Dorothy Richardson pointed out, as part of their rejection of a conventionally allotted place in society, women writers need to reshape conventional modes of narrative. Evident in several of the writers discussed above, this reshaping is the particular concern of recent novelists such as Marina Warner, Maggie Gee, Zoe Fairbairn or A.S. Byatt, whose *Possession* (1990) offers a collage of narrative strategies as diverse and mutually illuminating as Doris Lessing's in *The Golden Notebook*.

Exemplary of recent developments in women's writing, *The Golden Notebook* also shares in a wider movement towards experiment – a turn towards postmodernism – which occurred in the late 1950s and the 1960s. Writers at this time can be seen to extend several aspects of the modernist experiment identified in the first part of this unit. Modernism's restructuring of the novel – its challenges to conventional chronology and concentration on single days of consciousness – extends into the more radical abbreviation practised by William Golding in *Pincher Martin* (1956), or the challenge to conventional order created by B.S. Johnson in his loose-leaf novel-in-a-box *The Unfortunates* (1969). Lawrence Durrell also creates his own radical 'challenge to the serial form of the conventional novel' (Durrell, [1962] 1974) in *The Alexandria Quartet* (1957–60), offering in each of the first three novels of the sequence a sharply differentiated perspective on the same set of events, before allowing time to flow forward again in the fourth.

Durrell is one of the new generation of novelists, ready to carry on the idiom of modernism, which had emerged by the end of the 1930s. The war and other factors, however, deferred much of their success and influence until the 1960s. Flann O'Brien's *At Swim-Two-Birds*, for example, was less well received when first published in 1939 than when reissued in 1960 – the year after the last section of Samuel Beckett's trilogy *Molloy, Malone Dies, The Unnamable* (1950–2) had been translated into English. Much bleaker than O'Brien's work, Beckett's narrative is equally self-reflexive: each carries forward towards the writing of the 1960s the 'autonomy' of language and fiction discussed earlier in this unit; each in this way adding to the major area in which writing at the time can be seen, in the critic Brian McHale's terms, as a 'logical and historical *consequence*' of modernism (McHale, 1987, p. 5). Like *The Golden Notebook*, *The Alexandria Quartet* shows a thoroughly self-reflexive – postmodernist – concern with art, literature and its own means of representation. Aesthetic discussion proves a surprisingly powerful distraction from the love and sexual relations which otherwise preoccupy Durrell's community of artists, writers and spies. Their analyses and demonstrations of aesthetic ideas – including many affecting the text in which they figure – justify Durrell's opinion that his novel 'is only half secretly about art, the great subject of modern artists' (Durrell, 1963, p. 231).

It is a subject which has shaped novels since the 1960s often enough to make the term 'postmodernist' quite widely applicable to recent writing, though perhaps less so in Britain than elsewhere. B.S. Johnson records James Joyce, Beckett, and Flann O'Brien as influences, and appears in *Christie Malry's Own Double Entry* (1973) to discuss the progress of the story with its hero, and in *Albert Angelo* (1964) to assure readers that, as a story-teller, he is merely lying. In his Epilogue to *Lanark* (1981) – which appears long before the end of this chronologically fragmented novel – Alasdair Gray also discusses his narrative with its hero, and provides a list of experimental and other authors he has supposedly imitated or plagiarized. Under the influence of the French *nouveau roman* – which both foregrounds and undermines its own language and means of meaning – in novels such as *Thru* (1972) Christine Brooke-Rose likewise enacts and discusses relations between fiction and reality, word and world. Such issues are raised in other ways by John Berger in *G.* (1972), emphasizing concerns with political liberty while highlighting conventional constraints of narrative and encouraging his readers to free themselves from them.

Something similar is attempted by John Fowles in *The French Lieutenant's Woman* (1969). Set in Victorian times, Fowles's story follows the education of a hero who frees himself from that age's assumptions about social and gender roles. This movement is paralleled by Fowles's attempt to free his readers from their conventional expectations of fiction: by his demand that they choose between alternative endings to the novel, and his insistence throughout on the constructed, artificial quality of the story. In this way, *The French Lieutenant's Woman* once again illustrates parallel departures, in the 1960s, from conventions in lifestyle and in literature. Recreating much of the atmosphere of the Victorian novel, yet framing this within postmodernist investigation of writing and literary artifice, Fowles's work is also typical of the general condition of contemporary fiction David Lodge analyzes in his essay 'The Novelist at the Crossroads' (1971). Like Gerald Bullett in 1926 (see above), Lodge sees the main road of English fiction to be 'the realistic novel ... coming down through the Victorians and Edwardians' (p. 18). This is a main road which runs on throughout the twentieth century, widening from time to time, especially in the 1930s and early 1950s. But ever since the modernist period, and in the light of postmodernist and other experimental directions following from it, there have been what Lodge calls 'formidable discouragements to continuing serenely along the road of fictional realism' (p. 22).

Something of this crossroads of possibilities appears in the careers of most of the distinguished post-war novelists discussed above. William Golding and Muriel Spark retain conventional-enough interests in issues of morality, yet each employs unusual narrative tactics in examining them. For example, Spark uses repeated prolepses in *The Prime of Miss Jean Brodie* to illustrate the consequences of her heroine's powerful influence on her pupils, while the self-referentiality of *The Comforters* (1957) or *The Driver's Seat* (1970) shows her proximity to the *nouveau roman*. In *The Black Prince* (1973) and *The Sea, the Sea* (1978), Iris Murdoch goes beyond the realism of much of her fiction to engage in postmodernist scrutinies of language and narrative. Though these are thoroughgoing interests of *The Golden Notebook*, Doris Lessing also expresses admiration for 'the work of the great realists' of the nineteenth century, and follows their example more exclusively elsewhere in her writing (Lessing, 1957, p. 14). Anthony Burgess has expressed a similarly divided determination to 'welcome experiment in the novel', yet without discarding all that fiction has 'learned throughout the slow centuries of its development' (Burgess, 1971, p. 192). His own fiction alternates between realistic reflection of his colonial experience in the Malayan trilogy *The Long Day Wanes*

(1956–9) and the innovative tactics of novels such as *A Clockwork Orange*, whose verbal inventiveness reflects his admiration for James Joyce. If the postmodern idiom which has followed from the example of writers such as Joyce is less widely or clearly discernible in Britain than elsewhere, it is partly because, in the work of many of the most successful of recent novelists, it has been sustained alongside or digested within more traditional interests.

Once again reviewing the progress of fiction in 1991, Lodge remarks that it is possible to see 'the novelist still at the crossroads' (Lodge, 1991). As he suggests, dual allegiances he identified in the early 1970s continue to shape the work of writers emerging since, his own and that of his academic colleague Malcolm Bradbury included. Each draws on the conventional example of Kingsley Amis's *Lucky Jim* as part of the comic campus background of much of their fiction. In Lodge's *Small World* (1984) or Bradbury's *Rates of Exchange* (1983), however, each also flirts with the experimental possibilities Bradbury has been equally ready to analyze at work in the contemporary novel. These also figure at various points in the careers of J.G. Ballard, moving between the realism of *Empire of the Sun* (1984) and the fantasy of *The Unlimited Dream Company* (1979); or of Brian Aldiss, alternating his regular science fiction with a *nouveau roman*, *Report on Probability A* (1968), and realistic novels such as *Ruins* (1987). Traditional tactics continue to appear juxtaposed or amalgamated with innovative ones even within single novels. Julian Barnes's *Flaubert's Parrot* (1984) combines realism with bestiary, pseudo-biography, a kind of dictionary, and various conversations with the reader. In *Hawksmoor* (1986), Peter Ackroyd alternates chapters set in contemporary and in eighteenth-century London, each written in the style of its period. Alasdair Gray's *Lanark* uses dystopian fantasy alongside – and as a commentary upon – a portrait of the artist as a young Glaswegian. Martin Amis outlines his own version of Lodge's crossroads in suggesting that his novels attempt to combine the 'staid satisfactions' of Jane Austen with the 'tricksy' manner of a principal author of the *nouveau roman*, Alain Robbe-Grillet (Amis, 1978, p. 18) – an intention apparently realized in novels such as *Other People* (1981) and *London Fields* (1989). Each provides an unusually constructed but sharp satire of unemployment, depression and the decay of inner cities under Tory government in the late twentieth century: a grim landscape also surveyed by other members of a new generation of novelists such as Ian McEwan and James Kelman.

Exemplifying a crossroads of innovative and conservative styles in late twentieth-century fiction, *The French Lieutenant's Woman* also points to origins of some of the alternatives to the main road of realism. The novel's opening shows its heroine looking longingly across the Channel at France: Fowles confirms this scene's figuration of some of his own interests when he acknowledges the influence of Alain Robbe-Grillet, Roland Barthes and other 'theoreticians of the *nouveau roman*' ([1969] 1977, p. 348). Like Fowles, authors in recent decades have regularly looked abroad, quite often to France and the *nouveau roman*, for alternatives to a social realism still a dominant influence at home. This is not a new situation, of course. Many of the alternatives to the main road of Victorian and Edwardian fiction earlier in the twentieth century, in the modernist period, came from across the Channel, or across the Atlantic. They also come from across the Irish Sea, and this and other alternatives to the metropolitan mainstream, within the British Isles, continue to be influential at the end of the century. Roddy Doyle, Benedict Kiely, and Bernard MacLaverty illustrate the continuing vitality and influence of twentieth-century Irish fiction. Within the United Kingdom – in recent decades, not always much united in culture or politics – Scottish fiction has lately been equally successful. Alongside Alasdair Gray's stylistically diverse portraitures of Glasgow life, in novels such as *A Disaffection* (1989) James Kelman enters desolate reaches of the mind as powerfully and comprehensively as Samuel Beckett to show the reflexes of urban deprivation deep within the self. Their work has encouraged and sometimes shaped the fiction of a promising new generation, including novelists such as Duncan McLean, Andrew Greig, Brian McCabe, Ron Butlin, A.L. Kennedy and Iain Banks.

Other aspects of innovation in recent fiction can be recognized as one of the many consequences of the British empire for late twentieth-century life and writing. Throughout the century empire has provided novelists such as Joseph Conrad, Somerset Maugham, E.M. Forster, Joyce Cary, Doris Lessing or Anthony Burgess with a variety of colourful contexts in which characters could be confronted with unfamiliar values or an exiled loneliness sharpening questions about their own identity. Moving beyond the domestic landscape of much of his 1930s writing (see above), Graham Greene has perhaps made especially good use of such contexts since the war. Novels such as *The Heart of the Matter* (1948), *The Quiet American* (1955) or *The Honorary Consul* (1973) use conflict in distant parts of the world to focus and amplify protagonists' individual crises and moral dilemmas: their preservation of an improbable grace even in a fallen, soiled modern life adds to the appeal which has made Greene one of the most popular, as well as critically admired, of twentieth-century novelists.

The context of empire has also been used successfully by Paul Scott in *The Raj Quartet* (1966–75); Ruth Prawer Jhabvala in *Heat and Dust* (1975), and J.G. Farrell in *The Siege of Krishnapur* (1973) and *The Singapore Grip* (1978). Recently, however, it has become clear that the empire's most significant literary legacy has not been only in providing a challenging set of contexts for fiction, but rather, as Anthony Burgess remarks, that 'British colonialism ... exported the English language, and a new kind of British novel has been the eventual flower of this transplanting' (Burgess, 1971, p. 165). This 'export' has led many writers of foreign origin to use English as their literary language: Timothy Mo, a resident of Hong Kong until the age of 10; Adam Zameenzad, brought up in Pakistan; the Indian Anita Desai, or the West Indian Caryl Phillips, a winner of the James Tait Black Prize in 1994. The Booker Prize – another annual indication of the best non-US fiction published in English – further confirms the strength of recent writing by authors with strong cultural roots outside Britain. The 1980s began with its award to Bombay-born Salman Rushdie for *Midnight's Children* (1981); the 1990s with the success of *The Famished Road* (1991) by the Nigerian novelist Ben Okri. Winners in the years between included the New Zealander Keri Hulme, the Australians Thomas Keneally and Peter Carey, and Kazuo Ishiguro, for *The Remains of the Day* (1989). While earlier novels such as *An Artist of the Floating World* (1986) reflect Ishiguro's Japanese background, the precise anatomy of English social life in *The*

*Remains of the Day* illustrates the objectivity and irony which exile can add to authors' observations of a society not wholly their own.

Social concerns, however, keep *The Remains of the Day* relatively conventional in style. The new kind of writing Burgess sees as a legacy of empire is more conspicuous in the work of Salman Rushdie and Timothy Mo. The latter's comprehensive examination of the rise of Hong Kong in *An Insular Possession* (1986) intersperses fictional narrative with newspaper reports and contemporary journals, while in *Midnight's Children* and later work Rushdie – like Okri – brings into writing in English the powerful intermingling of fantasy and the quotidien practised by South American 'magic realists' such as Gabriel García Márquez and Mario Vargas Llosa. Rushdie also confirms an almost inevitable disposition towards experiment among many of the writers mentioned above when he describes the sensibility of 'migrants' – people 'in whose deepest selves strange fusions occur' and who 'must, of necessity, make a new imaginative relationship with the world' (Rushdie, [1985] 1991, pp. 124–5). As he suggests, no author aware of two or more cultures can remain unquestioningly content with the conventions of one of them. Contact with other cultures and literatures helps create for writers a sense of the character and limitations of their own, encouraging pursuit of alternatives, of possibilities for innovation, of self-conscious interrogations and fusions of different styles. Critics have sometimes seen the postmodernist tendencies in writing since the 1960s therefore giving way to an age better considered postcolonial – or have considered the latter always subsuming the former; self-reflexive and innovative fiction in the later twentieth century (perhaps throughout) best understood as the result of frictions, fusions and mutual critiques of cultures in which colonialism has been a main agent.

However it may finally be named or understood, the contemporary situation of the novel seems productively complex: conventions surviving or being subordinated by innovative alternatives; foreign or marginal influences competing with or contributing to the mainstream. The main road of realist tradition running through the century will no doubt remain a strong direction at its end. Yet the range of alternatives – modernist or postmodernist – has grown sufficiently diverse to make David Lodge's crossroads seem an inadequate metaphor. The novel has moved beyond the crossroads to a kind of spaghetti junction, a formation whose complexity and faintly foreign flavour make it a more appropriate image for an era in which long-serving main roads may remain discernible, but increasingly overlaid with new directions, recombining and diversifying the old. This should lead to a fruitful period for English literature around the millennium, though it will in another way mark its end, 'the English novel' remaining English only in terms of linguistic rather than in any firm sense of national identity.

## BIBLIOGRAPHY

MODERNISM AND THE NOVEL [1900–39]

Aldington, R. (1984) *Death of a Hero*, Hogarth Press, London [first published 1929].
Bakhtin, M. (1981) *The Dialogic Imagination: Four Essays*, ed. M. Holquist, trans. M. Holquist and C. Emerson, University of Texas Press, Austin.

Barthes, R. (1974) *S/Z*, trans. R. Miller, Hill & Wang, New York.

Beckett, S. (1973) *Murphy*, Picador, London [first published 1938].

Bennett, A. (1976) *Anna of the Five Towns*, Penguin, Harmondsworth [first published 1902].

Bergonzi, B. (1978) *Reading the Thirties*, Macmillan, London.

Bowen, E. (1983) *The House in Paris*, Penguin, Harmondsworth [first published 1935].

Budgen, F. (1934) *James Joyce and the Making of Ulysses*, Grayson & Grayson, London.

Bullett, G. (1926) *Modern English Fiction: A Personal View*, Herbert Jenkins, London.

Conrad, J. (1969) *Nostromo*, Penguin, Harmondsworth [first published 1904].

Conrad, J. (1995) *Heart of Darkness*, Penguin, Harmondsworth [first published 1902].

Ford, F.M. (1924) *Joseph Conrad: A Personal Remembrance*, Duckworth, London.

Ford, F.M. (1977) *The Good Soldier*, Penguin, Harmondsworth [first published 1915].

Friedman, A. (1972) 'The Novel', *The Twentieth Century Mind*, ed. C.B. Cox and A.E. Dyson, Oxford University Press, London.

Genette, G. (1986) *Narrative Discourse*, trans. J.E. Lewin, Blackwell, Oxford.

Gibbon, L.G. (1978) *A Scots Quair (Sunset Song, Cloud Howe, Grey Granite)*, Pan, London [first published 1933].

Gilbert, S.M. and Gubar, S. (eds) (1986) *The Female Imagination and the Modernist Aesthetic*, Gordon & Breach, London.

Greene, G. (1980) 'God and Literature and So Forth', interview with Anthony Burgess, *The Observer*, 16 March.

Hynes, S. (1976) *The Auden Generation: Literature and Politics in England in the 1930s*, Bodley Head, London.

Isherwood, C. (1982) *Lions and Shadows: An Education in the Twenties*, Methuen, London [first published 1938].

Isherwood, C. (1983) *Goodbye to Berlin*, Granada, London [first published 1939].

James, H. (1914) *Notes on Novelists: With Some Other Notes*, J.M. Dent, London.

James, H. (1934) *The Art of the Novel: Critical Prefaces*, ed. R.P. Blackmur, Charles Scribner's Sons, London.

James, H. (1973) *The Ambassadors*, Penguin, Harmondsworth [first published 1903].

James, W. (1890) *The Principles of Psychology*, 2 vols, Macmillan, London.

Jolas, E. (1972) 'The Revolution of Language and James Joyce' in Samuel Beckett *et al.*, *Our Exagmination Round his Factification for Incamination of Work in Progress*, Faber & Faber, London [first published 1929].

Joyce, J. (1971) *Finnegans Wake*, Faber & Faber, London [first published 1939].

Joyce, J. (1973) *A Portrait of the Artist as a Young Man*, Penguin, Harmondsworth [first published 1916].

Joyce, J. (1992) *Ulysses*, Penguin, Harmondsworth [first published 1922].

Kenner, H. (1978) *Joyce's Voices*, Faber & Faber, London.

Kristeva, J. (1991) *Strangers to Ourselves*, trans. S. Roudiez, Harvester Wheatsheaf, Hemel Hempstead.

Lawrence, D.H. (1955) *Selected Literary Criticism*, ed. A. Beal, Heinemann, London.

Lawrence, D.H. (1962) *The Collected Letters of D.H. Lawrence*, ed. H.T. Moore, 2 vols, Heinemann, London.

Lawrence, D.H. (1971) *Women in Love*, Penguin, Harmondsworth [first published 1921].

Lukács, G. (1972) 'The Ideology of Modernism', in *20th Century Literary Criticism: A Reader*, ed. D. Lodge, Longman, London [first published 1955].

McHale, B. (1987) *Postmodernist Fiction*, Methuen, London.

Miller, J.H. (1970) 'The Interpretation of *Lord Jim*', in *The Interpretation of Narrative: Theory and Practice*, ed. M.W. Bloomfield, Harvard University Press, Cambridge, Mass.

Nietzsche, F. (1986) *Human, All too Human: A Book for Free Spirits*, trans. R.J. Hollingdale, Cambridge University Press, Cambridge [first published 1878].

O'Brien, F. (1977) *At Swim-Two-Birds*, Penguin, Harmondsworth [first published 1939].

Orwell, G. (1962) *Coming up for Air*, Penguin, Harmondsworth [first published 1939].

Orwell, G. (1970) 'Inside the Whale', in *The Collected Essays, Journalism and Letters of George Orwell*, ed. S. Orwell and I. Angus, vol. 1, Penguin, Harmondsworth [first published 1940].

Richardson, D. (1979) *Pilgrimage*, 4 vols, Virago, London [first published 1915–67].

Wells, H.G. (1972) *Tono-Bungay*, Pan, London [first published 1909].

Woolf, V. (1966) *Collected Essays*, 4 vols, Hogarth, London.

Woolf, V. (1973) *To the Lighthouse*, Penguin, Harmondsworth [first published 1927].

Woolf, V. (1975) *Orlando*, Penguin, Harmondsworth [first published 1928].

Woolf, V. (1975) *A Room of One's Own*, Penguin, Harmondsworth [first published 1929].

Woolf, V. (1985) *A Writer's Diary: Being Extracts from the Diary of Virginia Woolf*, ed. L. Woolf, Triad, London [first published 1953].

## FURTHER READING

Listed below are a number of accessible or introductory studies and critical surveys covering the fiction of the first decades of the century, addressing either the whole period or sections of it.

Batchelor, J. (1982) *The Edwardian Novelists*, Duckworth, London.

Bradbury, M. and McFarlane, J. (eds) (1976) *Modernism: 1890–1930*, Pelican, Harmondsworth.

Bradbury, M. (1993) *The Modern British Novel*, Secker & Warburg, London.

Friedman, A. (1966) *The Turn of the Novel*, Oxford University Press, New York.

Gindin, J. (1992) *British Fiction in the 1930s*, Macmillan, London.

Johnstone, R. (1982) *The Will to Believe: Novelists of the Nineteen-Thirties*, Oxford University Press, Oxford.

Scott, B.K. (ed.) (1990) *The Gender of Modernism: A Critical Anthology*, Indiana University Press, Bloomington.

Stevenson, R. (1993) *Modernist Fiction: An Introduction*, Harvester Wheatsheaf, Hemel Hempstead.

Stevenson, R. (1993) *A Reader's Guide to the Twentieth-Century Novel in Britain*, Harvester Wheatsheaf, Hemel Hempstead.

Trotter, D. (1993) *The English Novel in History 1895–1920*, Routledge, London.

## THE NOVEL IN BRITAIN SINCE THE SECOND WORLD WAR

Amis, M. (1978) 'The State of Fiction: A Symposium', *The New Review*, Summer.

Bowen, Elizabeth (1983) *The Heat of The Day*, Penguin, Harmondsworth [first published 1949].

Bradbury, M. (1993) *The Modern British Novel*, Secker & Warburg, London.

Burgess, A. (1971) *The Novel Now: A Student's Guide to Contemporary Fiction*, Faber, London.

Drabble, M. (1981) *The Millstone*, Penguin, Harmondsworth [first published 1965].

Durrell, L. (1963) interview in *Writers at Work: The 'Paris Review' Interviews*, ed. M. Cowley, second series, Secker & Warburg, London.

Durrell, L. (1974) 'Prefatory Note' to *The Alexandria Quartet* (1957–60), Faber, London, p. 9 [first published 1962].

Fowles, J. (1977) *The French Lieutenant's Woman*, Panther, London [first published 1969].

Golding, W. (1967) *Lord of the Flies*, Faber, London [first published 1954].

Green, H. (1950) 'A Novelist to his Readers – Communication without Speech', *The Listener*, 9 November.

Green, H. (1978) *Caught*, Hogarth Press, London [first published 1943].

Greene, G. (1976) *The End of the Affair*, Penguin, Harmondsworth [first published 1951].

Harrisson, T. (1941) 'War Books', *Horizon*, December.

Hartley, L.P. (1983) *The Go-Between*, Penguin, Harmondsworth [first published 1953].

Lehmann, R. (1982) *The Ballad and the Source*, Virago, London [first published 1944].

Lessing, D. (1957) 'The Small Personal Voice' in *Declaration*, ed. T. Maschler, MacGibbon & Kee, London.
Lessing, D. (1972) *The Golden Notebook*, Granada, London [first published 1962].
Lodge, D. (1971) *The Novelist at the Crossroads and Other Essays on Fiction and Criticism*, Routledge & Kegan Paul, London.
Lodge, D. (1991) 'The Novelist: Still at the Crossroads?', lecture to the British Council Cambridge Seminar, 'The Contemporary British Writer', Christ's College, Cambridge, July.
Lowry, M. (1985) Letter to Jonathan Cape, 2 January 1946, in *Selected Letters of Malcolm Lowry*, ed. H. Breit and M.B. Lowry, Penguin, Harmondsworth [first published 1946].
Lowry, M. (1983) *Under the Volcano*, Penguin, Harmondsworth [first published 1947].
McHale, B. (1987) *Postmodernist Fiction*, Methuen, London.
Murdoch, I. (1983) *Under the Net*, Granada, London [first published 1954].
Murdoch, I. (1977) 'Against Dryness' in *The Novel Today*, ed. M. Bradbury, Fontana, Glasgow [first published 1961].
Newby, P.H. (1951) *The Novel 1945–1950*, Longmans, Green, London.
Orwell, G. (1970) 'Inside the Whale', in *The Collected Essays, Journalism and Letters of George Orwell*, ed. S. Orwell and I. Angus, vol. 1, Penguin, Harmondsworth [first published 1940].
Powell, A. (1983) *The Acceptance World*, Fontana, London [first published 1955].
Rabinovitz, R. (1967) *The Reaction against Experiment in the English Novel, 1950–1960*, Columbia University Press, New York.
Rushdie, S. (1991) 'The Location of Brazil' in *Imaginary Homelands: Essays and Criticism 1981–1991*, Granada Books, London [first published 1985].
Snow, C.P. (1958) 'Challenge to the Intellect', *Times Literary Supplement*, 15 August.
Tennant, E. (1979) *The Bad Sister*, Picador, London [first published 1978].

FURTHER READING

Listed below are a number of studies which analyze fiction since the Second World War, or consider sections of this period.

Allen, W. (1964) *Tradition and Dream: The English and American Novel from the Twenties to Our Time*, Dent, London.
Bergonzi, B. (1979) *The Situation of the Novel*, Macmillan, London.
Bradbury, M. (1993) *The Modern British Novel*, Secker & Warburg, London.
Bradbury, M. and Palmer, D. (eds) (1979) *The Contemporary English Novel*, Arnold, London.
Burgess, A. (1971) *The Novel Now: A Student's Guide to Contemporary Fiction*, Faber, London.
Burgess, A. (1984) *Ninety-nine Novels: The Best in English since 1939*, Allison & Busby, London.
Gasiorek, A. (1995) *Post-War British Fiction: Realism and After*, Arnold, London.
Gindin, J. (1962) *Postwar British Fiction: New Accents and Attitudes*, University of California Press, Berkeley.
Karl, F.R. (1972) *A Reader's Guide to the Contemporary English Novel*, Thames & Hudson, London.
Lee, A. (1990) *Realism and Power: Postmodern British Fiction*, Routledge, London.
Rabinovitz, R. (1967) *The Reaction Against Experiment in the English Novel, 1950–1960*, Columbia University Press, New York.
Stevenson, R. (1986) *The British Novel since the Thirties*, Batsford, London.
Stevenson, R. (1993) *A Reader's Guide to the Twentieth-Century Novel in Britain*, Harvester Wheatsheaf, Hemel Hempstead.

# UNIT 17

# Modern poetry

*R.A. York*

## Modernism and poetry, 1900–39

This section will be concerned with what many readers consider one of the most exciting movements in English literature, the poetry of the twentieth century. This poetry belongs to the movement now known as 'modernism' which affected all the arts, in different ways, throughout Europe and North America. The movement can be approximately dated as starting at about the turn of the century; it cannot be said to have an end, for much writing being produced now, nearly a hundred years later, is still basically modernist in spirit. The movement does however develop, and it is fairly easy to recognize works from its earliest years, works which express the spirit of formal experiment, moral and social questioning and cultural openness which are most typical of it; works from a somewhat later period – the 1930s and 1940s – tend to integrate these qualities with a sense of tradition, restraint, social responsibility and concern for clear communication. The most distinctive starting-point of modern poetry is the school known as Imagism, of which the leading figure is the American poet and theorist Ezra Pound. This school distanced itself very consciously from the poetry which was still being written in a more or less Romantic tradition by rejecting regular verbal form and concentrating on the image, the sharply focused presentation of a single sense experience. This tends to reduce the apparent importance of feeling, reflection and abstract generalization in the poem: immediacy of experience displaces context and narrative development. Strongly influenced by this cult of the precise image was a friend of Pound's, T.S. Eliot. Eliot became very well known in the 1920s, especially for his long poem, *The Waste Land*, and his poetry startled many readers through the strangeness and seeming incoherence of his images. As time has gone on, however, and especially in the light of his more calm and traditional later poetry, it has become possible to see Eliot as making use of the new techniques and concerns of modernism within an ongoing tradition of English reflective poetry. Also much influenced by the new movement was W.B. Yeats, an Irish poet who had started his career in what some would consider a self-indulgently Romantic manner, but who matured to become one of the most powerful and imaginative writers of the century.

One should not too sharply distinguish modern poetry from the poetry of the nineteenth century. Modern poetry can be seen as arising from the Romantic and post-Romantic cult of the imagination, of the visionary and the sensual, and of a type of language which communicates through the suggestions of image and rhythm rather than through the presentation of ideas and emotions which allow themselves to be – at least approximately – paraphrased; so there are clear analogies between the work of, say, Blake and Yeats. Similarly the modernist concern for the individual speaking voice often produces echoes of Browning. But there does come – as with the other arts – a clearly marked shift in the normal style of poetry in the early years of the century. So in his pioneering study *New Bearings in English Poetry* (1932), F.R. Leavis saw his period as marking a 'decisive reordering of the tradition of English poetry', while a few years later Cleanth Brooks, in his important study *Modern Poetry and the Tradition* (1939), claimed that modern poetry implied a literary revolution comparable to the Romantic Revolt. More recent studies, such as C.K. Stead's *The New Poetic* (1975) have taken a more balanced approach; but the basic shift is incontrovertible. It is often traced in the contrast between the Georgian poets, whose work maintains the rural settings, coherent, moderate and explicit emotional stance and lucid organization typical of the nineteenth century, and the Imagists, whose work is characteristically modernist: discontinuous in style, sometimes obscure through the failure to specify links between sentences, uneven in rhythm, affecting the reader's sensibilities through concrete presentation of distinct and disparate experiences, elusive as to the personality of the speaker, sometimes referring to distinctively modern, mechanized and urban settings, sometimes referring to remote civilizations such as those of China or ancient Greece. A typical example is Richard Aldington's 'New Love' (1915):

> She has new leaves
> After her dead flowers,
> Like a little almond tree
> Which the frost hurt.

Poetry of this kind seems strange to the reader; it extends one's experience and challenges one to comprehend it.

The implication of such writing is that experience has to be faced in itself, as something fresh and difficult, without the guidance of religion, social morality or normal patterns of personal relationship and emotional responsiveness. There was indeed at that time a considerable questioning of the norms which society offers to the individual's feeling about other people, the established culture and the physical world. Christianity had lost some of its status among intellectuals as a result of a feeling that it was incompatible with science (and especially with Darwinian evolution), and non-Christian thinking was widespread among philosophers; Nietzsche had just rejected Christianity with particular vehemence. The political order was threatened by an awareness of the extreme social disparities of the modern city, and a realization was starting to grow of the dangers and injustices of colonialism. The relativity of different national cultures came to be more readily felt; it is revealing that of the four major figures to be considered in this unit two were American by birth and one Irish, while the fourth, W.H. Auden, spent a large part of his life outside England. The sense of the personality was undermined by such thinkers as Marx, who regarded individual consciousness as a product of social and economic forces, and by Freud who regarded the personality as a product of primitive drives of which the individual must be unconscious. Soon the value of Western civilization was to be very radically brought into question by the futile slaughter of the First World War. There is, then, a general atmosphere among writers at the beginning of the century of doubt and readiness for change; it is fuelled in part by the exploratory kinds of writing already undertaken abroad, notably in France by such writers as Mallarmé, Rimbaud, Laforgue and Corbière. In this atmosphere the major changes in poetry are marked by the appearance of the Imagist anthologies (1914–17), their manifesto (1915), the appearance of Eliot's early verse (*Prufrock and Other Observations*, 1917), and Yeats's discovery of a modernist style, after his post-Romantic Celtic beginnings, with *Responsibilities* (1914). The period after 1914 sees, thus, the establishment of a new kind of verse. This reaches maturity with Eliot's *The Waste Land* (1922), Pound's *Mauberley* (1920) and several volumes of Yeats, especially perhaps *The Tower* (1928). All three poets continued to write after the 1920s, and developed in divergent ways. Yeats develops from a Romantic standpoint to a modernist one, bringing with him a cult of myth and of mystical vision which he tempers with a harsh awareness of the bleakness of the modern world, with an acute lucidity about his own feelings and a masterful sense of rhythm and construction. A characteristic passage is the opening of his sonnet 'Leda and the Swan':

> A sudden blow: the great wings beating still
> Above the staggering girl, her thighs caressed
> By the dark webs, her nape caught in his bill,
> He holds her helpless breast upon his breast.

The violent sensuality of this, enhanced by the onward surge of the rhythm and the rich pattern of echoing sounds, may suggest Keats rather than the cold accuracy of the imagists such as Aldington; but the cultural complexities which will emerge later in the poem make it unmistakably modernist. Pound starts his career with short poems of epigrammatic wit and startlingly sharp observation, and goes on to produce in his *Cantos* (1925–) a series of long poems, in which he combines his accuracy of physical depiction with his immense learning to convey an extraordinarily ambitious vision of the movement of history. The first of the *Cantos*, for instance, starts with a long, skilful pastiche of Homeric epic, but after two pages this is interrupted by a sudden imperative and then by details of publication:

> Then Anticlea came.
> Lie quiet Divus. I mean, that is Andreas Divus,
> In officina Wechseli, 1538, out of Homer.

The canto ends in mid-sentence, with the words 'So that:' and Canto 2 starts with a disrespectful parody of a modern poet:

> Hang it all, Robert Browning,
>      there can be but the one 'Sordello'.

Eliot, starting with ironic and disturbing poems about the confusions and frustrations of urban life in the early twentieth century, later produces deeply meditative poems on the significance of Christian faith in a world of war, suffering and frustration, in which the poet's sensitivity to atmosphere and intellectual honesty acutely convey the experience of a mind searching for meaning.

A second generation of modernist poetry is usually associated especially with the decade of the 1930s, and in particular with the anthologies *New Signatures* (1932) and *New Country* (1933). The young poets of the 1930s clearly had learnt much from the generation of Eliot and Pound in economy, indirectness and unconventionality of expression; they are distinct from them in their close concern with the immediate contemporary world and especially with the acute political and economic problems of their time, and by greater use of a light, conversational, playful and ingenious style, by a sense of poetry as game and fantasy. The outstanding figure of this generation was immediately recognized to be W.H. Auden, who wrote brilliantly original, witty and fantastic poems on the wish for personal and political renovation characteristic of his generation. Auden was the centre of a group of writers including the poets Louis MacNeice, Stephen Spender and C. Day Lewis, who share his concern with the public themes of the state of England and the need for political and social change, his concern for sincere friendship, his fear of public pressures on private life and his search for a fresh poetic style which would correspond to the speed, sophistication, novelty and social variety of their age. There are also important individual poets such as William Empson, with his densely wrought, intensely intellectual and subtly ironic reflections on personal relationships, and there are literary movements which reflect similar preoccupations to those of the central modernist figures, but with a considerable difference of emphasis: such as the surrealist poets including David Gascoyne and Hugh Sykes Davies, inspired by the French surrealists in their cult of the startling images that demonstrate the free play of the irrational imagination and, later, the neo-Romantics such as Dylan Thomas.

There is, then, in twentieth-century poetry, a wide variation of subject matter, and of personal belief and character; what the poets have in common is the conviction that poetry is not simply an elegant statement of important views, but that it is a search for a new way of formulating meaning that will meet the challenge of a period in history when traditional beliefs and traditional relationships between writers and readers are being threatened.

Such a new form of expression is likely to be difficult. The difficulty of poetry is very lucidly discussed by T.S. Eliot, who places it in the context of a discussion of why poetry matters. Eliot comments that

> poets in our civilisation, as it exists at present, must be difficult. Our civilisation comprehends great variety and complexity and this variety and complexity, playing upon a refined sensibility, must produce varied and complex results. The poet must become more and more comprehensive, more allusive, more indirect, in order to force, to dislocate if necessary, language into his meaning. (Eliot, 1951, p. 289)

The passage is an important one. First, it shows that what Eliot looks for above all in a poet is a 'refined sensibility'; the idea of 'refinement' obviously does not refer to trivial grace of manner but to the subtlety with which poets grasp experience. Secondly, it shows that Eliot regards poetry as a product of society and a judgement of it; the combination of fine perception and lucid judgement implies an important task for poetry, which preserves human values threatened by 'our civilisation, as it now exists'. Thirdly, he lists very acutely the techniques of modern poetry which make it difficult to many readers, and presents these as a means of controlling language. In one of his poems he translates the phrase used by the French poet Mallarmé to define the task of the poet: 'To purify the language of the tribe'. Poetry, that is, is essentially an enterprise within language, and one that requires great discipline and consciousness. One might think that poetry is not about language but about such major concerns as death, love and nature. Eliot implies that we can only really think about such things if we have a reliable language. Elsewhere in this same essay he comments that 'the ordinary man's experience is chaotic, irregular, fragmentary'. The remark may annoy many people who reasonably think that it is precisely modern poetry which is 'chaotic, irregular and fragmentary'; Eliot implicitly defends these qualities of poetry by claiming that they are a genuine reproduction of a difficult world, and indeed that it is the poet who, ideally, brings order and cohesion into the world.

How exactly is poetry to do this? For one major answer we may turn to Ezra Pound, a friend and inspiration of Eliot, who called him, in the dedication of *The Waste Land, il miglior fabbro,* the better craftsman, and elsewhere claimed that he was 'more responsible for the twentieth-century revolution in poetry than any other individual'. For Pound's basic conception is that poetry is a craft which brings precision to language. Pound's influence was most strongly marked within the movement known as Imagism (or *imagisme*) in association with which he produced much of his early work, and his views were disseminated through the periodicals of that movement. But they also represent a major tendency in a great deal of the poetic theory of the twentieth century, and correspond to some important aspects of modern poetic creation. Pound's views are most approachably formulated in his 'A retrospect' ([1918] 1972, pp. 58–68), and particularly in the three principles which he presents as the essence of Imagism.

The first of these is 'direct treatment of the "thing" whether subjective or objective'. The centre of the poem is the 'thing', which may be objective or subjective. The interest of the poem, that is, lies in the reactions of the poet to a specific experience, and the experience should be conveyed as precisely as possible. To bring out the implications of this, one needs first to stress that the concern is with 'things' and not with ideas; the poem is aimed against abstraction, against language which intervenes between reader and experience, against what is often called rhetoric. The poem, in short, for the imagists, should be concrete. The point is reiterated by Eliot in an essay on Swinburne, often regarded by modern poets as the typical example of the faults they reject in the poetry of the nineteenth century, which Pound refers to as 'a blurry, messy sort of period': 'Language in a healthy state presents the object, is so close to the object that the two are identified' (Eliot, 1951, p. 327).

The point of this concreteness is partly to revive the language and sensibilities of the reader, to bring clarity and vigour to both. Pound approvingly quotes the older poet A.E. Housman as saying that 'good literature read for pleasure must ... do some good to the reader, quicken his perception ... sharpen discrimination ... mellow rawness of personal opinion' (Pound, 1985, p. 66). But there is more to it than that. The quickened perception is an answer to one of the traditional problems of Western culture, the distinction we usually make between mind and body or thought and emotion. In discussing one of his literary heroes, the Italian medieval poet Guido Cavalcanti, Pound comments that for such a poet 'the senses at first seem to project for a few yards beyond the body ... The conception of the body as perfect instrument of the increasing intelligence pervades' (Pound, 1985, p. 152). Heightened perception forms a bridge between the outer world and the mind; human life is consistent within itself and continuous with the outside world, and the feeling of not being in command of one's own experience vanishes. This too is the implication of Eliot's famous concept of the 'dissociation of sensibility'. According to him, the poets of the Metaphysical era were capable of 'a direct sensuous apprehension of thought' (Eliot, 1951, p. 286). Since that time, thought and the senses have been dissociated. One may well doubt whether this 'dissociation' is a real historical event. It is however important to recognize the poet's sense that in our time it is difficult to treat ideas as part of our general sensibility, and to see that the difficulty of much modern poetry arises from an attempt to do so, even though this goes against the grain of our usual way of speaking or thinking. The point may be approached through a line from Donne which Eliot quotes: when Donne speaks of 'A bracelet of bright hair about the bone', the contrast of the bright colour and narrow line of the hair with the dull and less clearly shaped bone helps us to focus on the implicit contrast of sensuality and mortality. Eliot perhaps aims at a similar contrast in his own memorable lines, from 'Little Gidding':

> Ash on an old man's sleeve
> Is all the ash burnt roses leave;

The triple contrast of ash, cloth and flower similarly – though perhaps less acutely and more oddly – points to a contrast of beauty and ageing.

This fascination with the object can also be seen as part of a broader tradition. This is the symbolist tradition, which was developed most consciously in nineteenth-century France and became known in England through the work of such authors as A.J.A. Symons in his book *The Symbolist Movement in Literature* ([1899] 1971). The word *symbol* may be misleading, because it frequently suggests that some word or picture 'stands for' an idea (so that the cross is the symbol of Christianity). This is not the sense of the word here. Its meaning is best conveyed by the French poet Baudelaire, who speaks of moments when 'the depth of life reveals itself' wholly in the sight, however ordinary it may be, that one has in front of one's eyes. The sight becomes the symbol of it.' The symbol, that is, is a significant concentration of experience; by extension the task of the poet or artist is to find or create moments in which the depth of life is similarly concentrated and expressed. So when a character in *The Waste Land* describes himself as 'Looking into the heart of light, the silence', what is conveyed is not just an intense sense-experience; it is also the potential of a purer and richer life and the limitations of our everyday life which prevent us from attaining it. The image that Pound cultivated is partly important because it is different from the perceiving mind; but it is also important because it focuses on some qualities of experience that do matter to the subjective observer.

A poet such as Yeats stresses much more the traditional symbolist view of the meaningfulness of objects in poetry: referring explicitly to Symons's book, he stresses the creative force of the symbol, which can produce new emotions or new ideas: the symbol lies in the combination of aspects of the thing depicted, and the combination names an emotion or an idea which has no existence before it is named. Naming is seen, by many modern poets in an almost mystic sense, as a way in which human beings can gain control over their experience. Auden, notably, says that poetry is concerned with the encounter of the imagination with what he calls 'sacred beings'; and that beauty arises when a ritual is constituted which gives expression to this encounter: 'In poetry the rite is verbal; it pays homage by naming' (Auden, 1975, p. 57). By 'sacred beings' here Auden does not necessarily refer to any supernatural existence, but to moments in which life seems specially significant. He approvingly quotes a passage from the novelist Charles Williams which strongly recalls Baudelaire's view of the symbolic moment: 'One is aware that a phenomenon, being wholly itself, is laden with universal meaning. A hand lighting a cigarette is the explanation of everything; a foot stepping from the train is the rock of all existence . . .' (Auden, 1975, p. 55). Auden, that is, wants to treat vision as a sort of revelation; and in this he speaks for a major tendency in modern poetry.

Eliot gives a somewhat different emphasis to the question of emotion in poetry. Emotions and feelings, he recognizes, have a part in the experience of which poetry is composed, but they are formed into a 'new compound' which 'is a concentration, and a new thing resulting from the concentration, of a very great number of experiences which to the practical and active person may not seem to be experiences at all' (Eliot, [1919] 1972, p. 76). This means that 'the emotion of art is impersonal' or that 'Poetry is not a turning loose of emotion, but an escape from emotion; it is not the expression of personality, but an escape from personality' (Eliot, [1919] 1972, p. 76). Pound placed his emphasis on the thing, subjective or objective; Eliot comes to emphasize a distillation of things, in which the poet is essentially a catalyst, and which transcends the distinction.

There is in all of this a centring of interest on the imagination. Yeats, at the very beginning of the century, called for a 'return to imagination, [an] understanding that the laws of art, which are the hidden laws of the world, can alone bind the imagination' (Yeats, [1900] 1972, p. 34). Auden, much later, in discussing the 'sacred beings', speaks of 'the sacred encounters of the imagination' and insists that 'Whatever its actual content and overt interest, every poem is rooted in imaginative awe' (Auden, 1975, p. 60). Yeats's view of the 'hidden laws of the world' relates to a mysticism which later poets might not have endorsed; what they might have accepted is Auden's view that imagination is a response of the whole mind, with its massive accumulation of memories, knowledge and feeling, to the challenge of exceptional experience. It is thus a unifying force in the incoherence of modern life.

It is also an irrational force; the imagination draws upon the whole range of associations of the words of a poem, emotional, formal, cultural, mythical, as well as the strict logic of meaning. Eliot, notoriously, commented that 'genuine poetry can communicate before it is understood'; in the immediate context he was thinking of the poetry of Dante which may be not understood because it is in a foreign language, but the principle might also validate poetry in English which is not understood because it contains unclear references or because it suppresses steps in argument.

Language, then, needs to be fully exploited. This is the theme of Pound's second principle. One should 'use absolutely no word that does not contribute to the presentation'; one should 'go in fear of abstractions'. Consistently with this view he defines great literature as 'language charged with meaning to the utmost degree'. And this meaning is to come from all aspects of the language: the images conveyed, but also the sound of language, its 'music' and its connotations. Elsewhere Pound implies that a vital criterion of good poetry is that it should contain 'an invention, a definite contribution to the art of verbal expression' (Pound, 1985, p. 17); creation in language is essential because it adds to the range of things that can be expressed, and so to our imaginative command of our experience and our own feelings. The urgency and difficulty of the task is recalled, anxiously, by Eliot in one of his major poems:

> And so each venture
> Is a new beginning, a raid on the inarticulate
> With shabby equipment always deteriorating
> In the general mess of imprecision of feeling,
> Undisciplined squads of emotion.
>
> 'East Coker', V, 7–11

Precise, disciplined articulation of feeling: this, for Eliot, is the essence of poetry.

If much modern poetry can be seen as a celebration of the imagination, one should not assume that the imagination is too simply endorsed. Poets are often conscious that the imaginary is the fictive, or at least close to it; and so as well as presenting the symbolic vision, they often challenge it, simultaneously or in rapid succession, by irony. So Eliot praises Marvell's 'wit' (in the seventeenth-century sense of the word) because it restricts the authority of the experiences the poet presents; there is in Marvell, he thinks, 'a recognition, implicit in the expression of every experience, of other kinds of experience which are possible' (Eliot, 1951, p. 303). A very obvious example in Eliot's own early work is 'Sweeney Erect'; the poem starts with grandiose classical speech:

> Paint me a cavernous waste shore
> Cast in the unstilled Cyclades,

but it proves to be about a woman in a modern brothel having an epileptic fit, and the final tone is very different as a character remarks that 'It does the house no sort of good'. Which tone is more appropriate? How can one decide?

Auden, himself a master of ironic and playful writing, comments in similar spirit that 'in poetry, all facts and all beliefs cease to be true and become interesting possibilities' (Auden, [1963] 1972, p. 640) and continues, with characteristic subtlety and complexity: 'In so far as poetry, or any other of the arts, can be said to have an ulterior purpose, it is, by telling the truth, to disenchant and disintoxicate' (p. 645). One may further here refer to Pound's (eccentrically named) concept of 'logopoeia', a kind of poetry in which words are used with a sense of their normal contexts and associations, and so exposed to 'ironical play'. This sort of writing Pound calls 'the dance of the intellect among words'; the phrase elegantly sums up one dimension of modern poetry. Poetry, for modern poets, is both celebration of vision and disenchantment of ideas. If they are right, poetry is a valuable hygiene in a world in which language is threatened by abstraction and cliché, and in which an imprecise language may impede our feeling for concrete experience.

The symbol must be given further life and placed in a context by formulation in a rhythmically ordered text. Yeats lays much emphasis on rhythm as a means of 'prolonging the moment of contemplation', which makes the reader especially receptive to the symbol, placing the reader in a state which he regards as akin to trance. Yeats's formulation may suggest a dreamy passivity which is more characteristic of late nineteenth-century writing than of much modernist literature; it is however important to note that Yeats is conscious of the double effect of rhythm which both lulls through 'alluring monotony' and stimulates by variety.

The balance of monotony and variety becomes a major aspect of twentieth-century verse, not least in the thinking of Pound and Eliot. Their aesthetic gives great weight to surprise, which one might expect to lead to a stress on variety. Traditionally, verse is distinguished from prose by its regularity; the stresses of words (in English) form regular patterns, these patterns form lines of regular length, the division of the lines is enhanced by rhyme; moreover there is much sameness in poetry, brought about by repetitions of sound or by repetitions of ideas or images. Etymologically speaking, prose is what goes straight on, verse is what turns back and – in some sense – does the same things again. It is easy to think that this consistency of style and content is not appropriate either to a kind of writing that claims to be new, or to a world which the poets regard as unpredictable and incoherent. And so it is not surprising that irregular verse, the so-called *vers libre*, becomes common in twentieth-century poetry. (Though more or less regular verse continues to be used also to great effect by many writers, and there is for instance little free verse by Yeats or Auden.)

The poets are then eager to define exactly what free verse consists of, and exactly how regular verse can continue to be used with freshness and pertinence. Pound especially, the better craftsman, devotes much attention to the form of verse, though the other poets are not far behind in their sense of the discipline of verse-writing. Pound's third principle of imagism is in fact a cautious justification of free verse; he recommends that poets should 'compose in the sequence of the musical phrase, not in sequence of a metronome'. He returns to the issue in his account of early music. He assembles many quotations from early musicians showing that they advised against over-strict following of metre, and recommended that one should 'imitate the irregularities of the beautiful voice' (Pound, 1985, p. 439). Natural speech is the point of reference of Pound's poetry; rhythm should heighten it and not distort it. An example is the beginning of 'Cino':

> Bah! I have sung women in three cities,
> But it is all the same;
> And I will sing of the sun.

If there is a regular rhythm here, it is in the suggestion of a recurring three-syllable metre; but this is far from overriding the speaker's shifts of feeling and energy. This spoken rhythm imposes on the poet the need for a subtle judgement (apparent, for instance, when Pound asks himself if he has not gone too far towards making his rhythms flexible and discreet): he has both to reproduce ordinary language and to transform it. The dilemma is one inherent in the whole project of modern poetry which both reproduces the discontinuities and incongruities of modern life and creates order and significance within it. There is a real tension here; and the honesty and lucidity with which modern poets have faced up to the tension is a sign of the importance of their work.

## Texts, authors, contexts

### W.B. Yeats

The first important poet of the modernist period in the British Isles is W.B. Yeats. Yeats did not however begin his career in a modernist style; his early work is largely a continuation of a Romantic tradition, with strong references to Irish folklore, sometimes in ballad form, making heavy use of conspicuous effects of lulling sound echoes and insistent rhythms and primarily expressing fairly simple emotions of nostalgia, longing, heroism and love: a typical example comes from 'The Song of Wandering Aengus':

> Though I am old with wandering
> Through hollow lands and hilly lands,
> I will find out where she has gone,
> And kiss her lips and take her hands.

But as his career develops, his style matures, growing less ornate, relying more on dense and uneven rhythms and focusing more on the concrete details of perception. With the important volume *Responsibilities* (1914) Yeats discovers an urgent public subject matter, in the cultural and political state of Ireland, at the same time that he begins to evolve an elaborate mythical scheme of history which tacitly underlies many of his works (see Unit 25, pp. 662–6). The combination of personal emotion, public commentary and eccentric vision makes him a challenging writer and many critics have sought to characterize his work; one may particularly recommend

Ellmann (1965) and Henn (1966). Yeats increasingly feels his poetic role to be that of the outsider who can criticize and judge the civilization from which he emerges. The poem 'A Coat' announces the new bareness of his style and its significance as a vehicle of opposition. His song, he says – thinking of his early Romantic work – was

> Covered with embroideries
> Out of old mythologies,

but he has been robbed of it. He accepts his loss:

> For there's more enterprise
> In walking naked.

The effect of this new bareness of writing on Yeats's view of one of the great myths is apparent in a poem from *Responsibilities*:

> THE MAGI
> Now as at all times I can see in the mind's eye,
> In their stiff, painted clothes, the pale unsatisfied ones
> Appear and disappear in the blue depth of the sky
> With all their ancient faces like rain-beaten stones,
> And all their helms of silver hovering side by side,
> And all their eyes still fixed, hoping to find once more,
> Being by Calvary's turbulence unsatisfied,
> The uncontrollable mystery on the bestial floor.

Yeats, it is apparent from this poem, is a master of transitions. The poem starts with the poet, apparently in rather dull chatty mood, recounting his own imaginations (the incidental 'at all times' and the cliché 'the mind's eye' do a lot to set a mood of vague curiosity); it ends with an intense and disturbing vision: the symmetrical form of the last line, paralleling 'uncontrollable' and 'bestial'; the extreme emotions conveyed by these words and especially the apparently misplaced clinging to respectable order implied in 'uncontrollable'; the imprecise suggestions of the horrifying sacrifices of the pagan mystery religions, together with the indirect treatment of the Christian story of the Incarnation which takes place in the animal (if not bestial) context of a stable, all of these things make a powerful conclusion to the poem. And Yeats passes from the prosy opening to the overwhelming end within a single sentence (of 153 words), in which we are forced constantly to vary our expectation as to the way the poem is going to develop, and in which the changes in attitude are delicately underlined by changes in the rate at which information is provided. So the first half of the poem teases the reader by appearing to complete the sentence structure, but then withholds the actual conclusion (so the first two lines seem to imply that the speaker sees the 'unsatisfied ones', but it then proves that he sees them appear and disappear). It seems rather as if there is here a gesture by the speaker of holding back the information which is either particularly fascinating or particularly frightening by filling up his utterance with, chiefly, visual detail: the colours, the stiffness, the stones; this detail stressing the remoteness, age, immobility of the people referred to – as if they were no more than figures in a painting, while the delayed climax stresses the personal urgency of dissatisfaction and hope. These variations in the flow of information are delicately underlined by changes in rhythm (a fine example is the pause in the middle of line 6) and by a subtle play of sound (the 'h' and 's' sounds in line 5, for instance, creating a sense of 'hovering'). The rhyme patterns add yet a further nuance to the difficult coherence of the poem, since line ending does not always coincide with syntactic grouping; the rhyme words are not always in fact pronounced alike, and the grouping of lines by rhyme does not correspond to grouping by verbal pattern. It is only towards the end of the poem that the rhymes seem really to articulate some major new step in the reader's knowledge; the fairly uninformative 'side by side' leads to the key term 'unsatisfied' and 'once more', apparently innocuous when it first appears, leads to the 'bestial floor' and a wholesale reviewing of the Nativity story; it is debased by being reduced from manger to floor and, most crucially of all, it becomes not unique, as it is for Christians, but something repeatable, something which can be seen 'once more'.

In addition to this there is a fluctuation in the reader's confidence in grasping the subject matter. Does it describe the Magi or a picture of them? Does it show respect or irony towards them? What moment of their life is depicted? We learn, little by little, that the poem is not the tribute to Christian story that the title might have led us to expect, but an appropriation of it. The Magi are dissatisfied not with the pre-Christian life that leads them to seek the redeemer, but with Calvary, the culminating sacrifice of the Christian religion, reduced to mere turbulence (perhaps more suggestive of the brawling on the Mount of Olives). Yeats approaches this new incarnation deviously, through the pale, stone-like fixity of the Magi, sign both of obsessiveness and of unimmediacy, and finds something too immediate. What reaction does the poem require the reader to show to the 'hope' of the Magi? On the one hand, the poem seems to agree that Calvary was indeed turbulent, and to set this against the almost ghostly inaction of the Magi; but the logic of the last line seems to be that Calvary was not turbulent enough and that what they want is more extreme, more beyond human control, more acutely focusing the difference between the divine and the animal. The paradox of the text then is that it uses a restrained, calm, discreet, perhaps delicately ironic tone to articulate the wish for an overwhelming transcendence.

Such paradoxes are not uncommon in modern poetry; nor is the fascination with the mythical and visionary, or the unorthodox use of myth. This concern with myth is in fact typical of the later Yeats: another powerful revision of the Christian story is 'The Second Coming', in which the poet, aghast at a century of 'mere anarchy', prophesies the coming of a 'rough beast', which 'Slouches towards Bethlehem to be born'. Non-Christian legend and history also become the material of a transfiguration, as with the two poems 'Sailing to Byzantium' and 'Byzantium', in which the changeless impersonal art of Byzantium becomes a temptation or a threat for the vulnerable and passionate speaker. Another case is 'Leda and the Swan', which counterpoints the brief violence of the rape of Leda with the tragic history which it inaugurated, and the brutal force of the god with the cultural knowledge which gives depth to the scene.

The past has intense immediacy for Yeats: the point is apparent in our second Yeats poem:

LONG-LEGGED FLY
That civilisation may not sink,
Its great battle lost,
Quiet the dog, tether the pony
To a distant post;
Our master Caesar is in the tent
Where the maps are spread,
His eyes fixed upon nothing,
A hand under his head.
*Like a long-legged fly upon the stream*
*His mind moves upon silence.*

That the topless towers be burnt
And men recall that face,
Move most gently if move you must
In this lonely place.
She thinks, part woman, three parts a child,
That nobody looks; her feet
Practice a tinker shuffle
Picked up on a street.
*Like a long-legged fly upon the stream*
*Her mind moves upon silence.*

That girls at puberty may find
The first Adam in their thought,
Shut the door of the Pope's chapel,
Keep these children out.
There on the scaffolding reclines
Michael Angelo.
With no more sound than the mice make
His hand moves to and fro.
*Like a long-legged fly upon the stream*
*His mind moves upon silence.*

The literary theorist Roman Jakobson believes that poetry is distinguished from prose by the fact that it is dominated by the 'principle of equivalence'; the words in a poem do not just complement each other to form meaningful sentences, but also resemble each other in sound and sense, so as to create a sense of consistency or sameness in the text (see Unit 18, pp. 528–32). This poem by Yeats clearly illustrates the principle: the three stanzas are very conspicuously composed to be equivalent to each other in content, grammatical form, the speaker's relationship to the hearer (or reader), the verse form and the rhythm, and the resemblance between them is strongly emphasized by the repeated refrain.

Each stanza recounts a moment of calm intimacy involving a major figure from history or legend, calls on the listener not to disturb the moment, and presents it as a preparation for some major event which is enshrined in our culture. But there are variations between victory and defeat, intellect and bodily motion, male and female, activity and passivity, power and sexuality, variations in the intelligibility of the preparation, in the dignity of the characters, in the explicitness of reference to them. These differences are reinforced by shifts within the basic rhythmic pattern. Yeats, it seems, is insisting that history and culture are constituted not only by acts – by such decisive and sometimes catastrophic acts as the victories of Caesar and the fall of Troy – but by a quality of preparedness, of anticipation, of potential; his three stanzas depict examples of such potential, which are also examples of awe-inspiring characters: the soldier, the beautiful and seductive woman, the creative artist. But the idea of potential – though of great importance to modern writers and especially modern poets – is itself a tenuous one which is manifest in various forms: mental and physical (and it seems the distinction corresponds to that of male and female), intended by the character or incidental, self-assured or involving social tension, creative or destructive.

What most unites these disparate images in the poem is the refrain. This, it is true, may at first seem to the reader actually to add another difficulty, since the fly on the stream has no obvious connection with the people depicted and the relation of fly to water is not obviously 'like' that of mind to silence. On reflection it proves that the 'likeness' is so complex and many-sided that the long-legged fly becomes a true symbol. The fly is light, free, elegant, vulnerable; the stream, by contrast, is deep – and so partially unknown – it is continuous and of a single consistency and it makes predictable progress. Now this relationship, of the free creature paradoxically drawing support from the dangerous and elusive depths, might most readily be applied to the great figures who appear memorably in what we sometimes call the stream of history, whom we understand in the context of a series of events but who retain their separate identity. But Yeats has transferred the symbol from this obvious sense – which readers are unlikely to forget completely – to relate it to the atmosphere of silence in which the characters are glimpsed. The moment of stillness, of isolation, is what allows the distinctive gesture – just as the gesture itself allows the creation and preservation of a continuing culture in which modern people think about Rome, Troy and Adam. The fly image is an image of separateness in continuity; and the great continuity of life is what forms the consistency of this poem.

The reader, moreover, is fictitiously involved in the poem, being put into the position of an observer – which readers, in one sense, necessarily are. But the scenes and people are familiar not from first-hand observation but from learning, and the text makes this very apparent, in the broad historical perspective of the 'sinking' of civilization, in the modified quotation of Marlowe's 'face that launch'd a thousand ships/ And burnt the topless towers of Ilium', in the theological implications of 'the first Adam' and the very modern explicitness about puberty and welcome for sexual alertness. In each stanza the text moves from a concern with the lasting values of civilization – conceived as dramatically precarious, or built on sacrifice or on an eternal sexuality – to an imaginative intrusion into a private scene, the stanza ending with humble physical detail, so that the legendary Helen becomes a hopping child. Readers are reminded both that they belong to history and possess a culture (and Yeats's culture here is somewhat broader than that of most of us and a good deal more elaborately thought out) and also that they are capable of moments of significant vision.

Yeats, in a sense, is putting his personal intensity of feeling and imagination to the test of an exterior culture and of a lucid and disciplined language. The same may be said of the many poems in which he comments on contemporary events, notably the Irish campaign for independence and the subsequent civil war, memorably contemplated in 'Easter 1916', 'A Meditation in Time of War', 'Meditations in Time of Civil War' and many other poems, or in which he pays tribute to people he knows, such as Eva Gore-Booth and Constance Markiewicz, Parnell or Lady Gregory, or to the way of life they incarnate, or which is implicit in certain places, such as the 'Ancestral Houses' or 'Coole Park'. Increasingly also, however, Yeats finds himself preoccupied with the extremities of irrational feeling, with 'the foul rag-and-bone shop of the heart', and the difficulty of reconciling passion with order, and seeks through the discovery of a series of personae to give dignity to the recognition of bodily need and decline: the 'Crazy Jane' poems are a fine example, but there are also times when the persona is very near the real Yeats, who complains, for instance, in 'The Tower' of

> this caricature,
> Decrepit age that has been tied to me
> As to a dog's tail.

A fine example of the balance of objective and subjective vision is 'Among School Children', in which the poet first sees himself from outside as 'a sixty-year-old smiling public man' but then goes on through a series of private memories, fantasies, cultural allusions, to meditate finally on the relation of beauty to suffering, of the work to the author, to end with the unifying vision of the dancer who is identical with her art: 'How can we know the dancer from the dance?' Art becomes self-justifying and self-sufficient, because art is corporeal; the balance of knowledge, sensation and imagination that characterizes Yeats's writing becomes an image of an ideal life.

## Ezra Pound

Ezra Pound is known not only for his poetry but, as we have seen, for his critical and theoretical writings and also for his dynamic effect in stimulating new thought about poetry through personal contact and through his role in the little magazines of the early years of the century. As a poet he is perhaps best known – even notorious – for a few poems which consist entirely of a sharply observed image. One quite extreme example is this:

> IN A STATION OF THE METRO
> The apparition of these faces in the crowd;
> Petals on a wet, black bough.

This is the whole of the poem: it almost blatantly refuses anything beyond the noting of an impression, an impression that depends on a comparison which the reader can recognize as incongruously apt. The startling economy of this text has achieved for it the status of a modernist icon and you will find a reading of it in Unit 1, p. 10.

Other poems, some not much longer, show the influence of Chinese verse and the *haiku* in that their effect depends on a delicate shift of reference in the final line. One instance is 'Liu Ch'e': the first four lines of the poem evoke an autumnal scene of dead leaves, and in the fifth the speaker regrets his beloved: 'And she the rejoicer of the heart is beneath them'; the sixth and last line, printed after a blank, turns to a new external detail which is presented without comment but nevertheless seems symbolically to unite inner and outer: 'A wet leaf that clings to the threshold'. This sort of poetry, in which the poetic effect appears to arise from the presentation of objects (though in fact verbal rhythm and the implied metaphorical structure also play a large part), is typical of Imagism. Several other poets of the movement produced works with a similar accuracy of vision and economy of phrasing: one may mention, for instance, T.E. Hulme with 'Autumn' (in which the speaker sees the stars 'With white faces like town children'), H.D. (Hilda Doolittle) with such works as 'Oread' (which presents the steep waves of the sea as pine-trees) or 'Hermes of the Ways' (which clearly demonstrates the verbal restraint of the movement:

> Apples on the small trees
> Are hard,
> Too small,
> Too late ripened
> By a desperate sun
> That struggles through sea-mist.)

or Amy Lowell (whose three-line poem 'Middle Age' compares the speaker's heart to

> black ice
> Scrolled over with unintelligible patterns by an ignorant skater.)

The movement had a great influence in America: a poet associated with it, William Carlos Williams, was to produce an important body of poetry based on the belief expressed in the slogan 'no ideas but in things', poetry which perhaps focused even more on the uninterpreted object than that of the Imagists proper, as in this poem which relies on a symmetry of rhythm – which one may feel to be artificially induced by the line breaks – and on the tension between the portentous 'depends' and the apparently humdrum naming of objects:

> So much depends
> upon
>
> a red wheel
> barrow
>
> glazed with rain
> water
>
> beside the white
> chickens.

And this manner was to have an important heritage in such poets as Zukofsky, Charles Olson and Robert Creeley – see Unit 14, pp. 374–5.

But one should not too exclusively stress the imagist side of Pound. It is complemented in his early work by a fascination with different cultures and ways of life: his first volumes of verse are called *Personae* because they show him adopting personalities drawn from ancient Greece and Rome or medieval France and Provence; later he was to add Anglo-Saxon England and China. The sense of a somewhat alien, artificial self-expression through role-playing is never quite absent from his work. It sometimes produces an elegant wit, sometimes a fairly broad humour, sometimes a grave pathos or a delicate sensuality: in all cases the reader is conscious of a distancing of the poet from the character, of his sense of the oddness and indirectness of life. A poem which combines an acute precision of image with complex ironies of cultural observation is this:

> THE GARDEN
> *En robe de parade.*
> > Samain
>
> Like a skein of loose silk blown against a wall
> She walks by the railing of a path in Kensington Gardens,
> And she is dying piece-meal
> > of a sort of emotional anaemia.
>
> And round about there is a rabble
> Of the filthy, sturdy, unkillable infants of the very poor.
> They shall inherit the earth.
>
> In her is the end of breeding.
> Her boredom is exquisite and excessive.
> She would like some one to speak to her,
> And is almost afraid that I
> > will commit that indiscretion.

This is a sort of epigram; it economically depicts a person and in a pithy final line implies an ironic judgement. The style of writing can be traced back to the poets of Greece and Rome, in whom Pound felt a strong interest, and is a sign of his fidelity to literary tradition as well of his liking for dry, precise, unsentimental writing; but there is a great deal in the poem in addition to these qualities, and it can well be described in Pound's phrase as a 'dance of the intellect among words'.

The poem is based on a glimpse of a person, seen in a well-known public place. Like *The Magi*, it is a poem of transitions: its interest lies in the way the speaker passes from a direct visual perception of the person to a presentation of her assumed attitude to himself, by way of an assessment of her general character and a characterization of the people around, the children playing in the Gardens. The subject may seem an extremely slight one (man sees woman). But it in fact presents complex attitudes: the speaker admires and criticizes the woman and the children, the woman, the last line hints, both wishes and fears contact with the speaker; more broadly the poem both accepts an 'aesthetic' detachment from life and regrets the 'end of breeding'. It would be easy to summarize this as a straightforward satire.

The woman suggests the aesthetes of the late nineteenth century, who were popularly thought of as concerned with dress, disdainful of the ordinary people, cultivating isolation and therefore boredom and appearing superior to the life of the body. The speaker, it appears, contrasts this over-refined sensibility with the healthy vigour of the poor, and mocks the inability of the aesthete to maintain whole-heartedly the solitude she has chosen. The speaker, on this account, is a strong personality, active enough to begin a healthy social contact perhaps inclining to flirtation.

But the various ambiguities and unclarities we have noted already show that things are not so simple. The final line is indeed ironic in its adoption of the woman's (presumed) point of view. But the beginning actually celebrates an aesthetic perspective. It presents the person in purely visual terms – so much so that the reader does not even know yet that there is a person there; it implies a knowledge of clothing ('skein' is a fairly technical term); it shows a fascination with movement ('blown') and with contrast of textures and character (the 'loose silk' and the solid wall). Moreover, although this is strictly a simile (the woman is *like* silk), there is every temptation to read this as verging on metonymy, if we assume the woman looks like silk because she is actually wearing silk. And the shift in the line from vision to movement is reinforced by a delicate set of sound echoes and a rhythmic shift at the word 'blown'. Complexity of linguistic effect corresponds to intensity of vision.

Two questions remain. Is this poetry? And is it modern? Some of the techniques of writing could, of course, appear in prose: the shifting distance from the subject, the changing point of view, the echoes of certain kinds of language (biblical or 'refined'). What transposes this into the poetic is the opening image, the effects of sound repetition, unobtrusively handled throughout, and most of all the effects of rhythm, the line expanding and contracting to match the speaker's fascination or brusque decisiveness. Is the poem modern? It is difficult to say that no such features could be found in, say, Browning; but the combination of brevity and apparent incompletion, allusiveness, ambiguity and instability at least points in the direction modern poetry was to follow.

If the early *The Garden* is not unmistakably modernist, Pound's *Cantos*, which form his largest poetic undertaking and occupied much of his later life, are modernism in its most extreme form. They too contain many vivid images; but they extend Pound's readiness to adopt personae derived from alien cultures to the point of creating a kind of writing so eclectic as to be extremely difficult for most readers to comprehend with any certainty. So much so, in fact, that Pound has had few followers in this style (unless one is to include Basil Bunting). A typical example is this:

> *from* CANTO LXXIV
> The enormous tragedy of the dream in the peasant's bent
>     shoulders
> Manes! Manes was tanned and stuffed,
> Thus Ben and Clara *a Milano*
>         by the heels at Milano

That maggots shd/ eat the dead bullock
DIGONOS, δίγονος, but the twice crucified
              where in history will you find it?
yet say this to the Possum: a bang, not a whimper,
    with a bang not a whimper,
To build the city of Dioce whose terraces are the colour of stars.
The suave eyes, quiet, not scornful,
              rain also is of the process.
What you depart from is not the way
and olive tree blown white in the wind
washed in the Kiang and Han
what whiteness will you add to this whiteness,
              what candor?

There is a great deal in a passage such as this to bewilder almost any reader; if modernism can be thought of as giving evidence of the difficulty of literary communication in the twentieth century brought about by the lack of a common culture between poet and reader and by the poet's persistent concern for his private feelings and associations of ideas, it is difficult to imagine any passage which is more obviously modernist. Indeed some readers may feel that this is not far from parody of modernism. So we have fragmentary sentences, ill-constructed sentences, sentences which succeed each other without obvious connection, rapid shifts in tone, apparent or actual quotations with no explanation of their source or their relevance, references to people and places the reader may not be able to identify, a word in Greek, repeated in Greek type, and a phrase in Italian, then partly translated. We have, too, trivial annoyances such as the eccentric abbreviation for 'should' and the apparently random use or avoidance of capitals at the beginning of lines of verse. At first sight, this is an outrageous infraction of the normal courtesy of writer to reader, which requires the writer to ensure as far as possible that there is no obstacle to comprehension. And it must be admitted that some degree of such discourtesy – if that is what it is – is not rare in modern verse.

Why then should we read such material? There are, I think, three reasons: Pound's mastery of tone, his complex thematic structure and his wide culture.

The two lines about Dioce and the 'suave eyes' show something of the mastery of poetic expression of which Pound is capable. The echoes of 'd', 's', 't', 'k' sounds link the key words so as to create a curiously indirect consistency of texture, reinforced by the slow and flexible rhythm of the two lines. The two figurative expressions complement each other in focusing on the process of seeing and transposing it to an atmosphere of calm pleasure; this is then characterized morally, 'quiet, not scornful' contrasting with the images of cruelty and distaste earlier in the poem, and then transposed to a new visual sensation, that of the rain. Poetry in these lines gives verbal form to the complex activity of seeing things carefully.

This acutely observed detail takes its place in a broad pattern of feeling. Up to this point the passage has been concerned with death, defeat, finality, though it has also contained the hint of a dream which might give some satisfaction to the hard-worn peasant; from the Dioce image on, the passage is concerned with a discovery of new meaningfulness and purity, with a 'way' from which one may not depart – or cannot depart – in nature and brightness, in 'candor', both personal honesty and, etymologically, the whiteness of the landscape. The poem is turning from a preoccupation with the ugliness of actual history to a hope for peace in nature and myth.

Thirdly, the reader is conscious of a mind turning with great rapidity to a number of domains of experience and to a number of ways of talking about them. Even totally uninformed, the reader may be impressed – if also disquieted – by the refusal to dissociate the poet's knowledge of the immediate scene, his acquaintances, and his cultural knowledge of Greece and China, or his familiarity with the rhythms of everyday conversation, elegiac lament, romantic verse, a specific modern poem, gnomic wisdom, his own earlier bare lyric. The attempt to combine these things, of course, lays bare their separateness in the minds of most of us, and so creates a fragmentary impression; but this fragmentation can be seen as an honest attempt to face up to the confusing multiplicity of modern culture.

In any case, most readers are not totally uninformed. It is not difficult to get the reference to the dictator Benito Mussolini and his mistress Clara Petacci, killed and hung upside down in a public square in Milan at the end of the war, and many readers may know of Pound's misguided admiration for Mussolini; for all readers then this is a reminder of the cruelty of war, and for those capable of feeling some sympathy with Pound it is also a sign of a sense of the end of a worthwhile epoch. Most people familiar with modern poetry will have little difficulty with Old Possum, and see in the reference a friendly nod to an ally in gloom.

There remain the unfortunate Manes, Digonos, Dioce, Kiang and Han. Some research will identify these. Woodward's *Ezra Pound and the Pisan Cantos* (1980) reveals that Manes is a prophet and *digonos* ('twice-born') a term referring to the god Dionysos, both of these references placing the death of the dictator in a context of myth and sacrifice, and that Dioce is the builder of a holy city in Herodotus. Flory's *Ezra Pound and the Cantos* (1980) identifies Kiang and Han (not surprisingly) as Chinese rivers, and (more importantly) traces the line about washing to a quotation from Mencius which also appears in Pound's *Confucius*.

As these cases may suggest, the encyclopaedic character of Pound's writing has given rise to a vast amount of commentary and explanation. A particularly comprehensive and pertinent example is Hugh Kenner's *The Pound Era* (1972). Research in such works, of course, may not produce the spontaneous emotional response that recognition does; in practice many readers are left in a state of half-comprehension (if they don't do the research) or half-response (if they do). They recognize in fact the limits of communication, when it is communication with a mind as varied and demanding as Pound's; and the effort to close in those limits can be a very rewarding one.

## T.S. Eliot

We turn next to T.S. Eliot, perhaps the most respected and influential modern poet in England. Eliot's first poems, published in 1917, are remarkable for their intensity and complexity of feeling, for their command of a rhythm which combines forceful progress with an elusive irregularity, for their apt and economical evocation of characteristic modern scenes, for their ironic account of characters and situations from modern sophisticated society (as with the Jamesian 'Portrait of a Lady'). The influence of the less well-known French poets of the late nineteenth century, with their hybrid style made up of lyricism, parody, realism and irony, is apparent in some works (very obviously in 'Conversation Galante'), but Eliot's tense richness of significance gives a very individual tone to such lines as these (from 'Preludes'):

> His soul stretched tight across the skies
> That fade behind a city block,
> Or trampled by insistent feet
> At four and five and six o clock.

The volume is named after its most striking poem, one which presents an elusive and complex character through a kaleidoscope of scenes and manners of speech, 'The Love Song of J. Alfred Prufrock'. These are the opening lines:

> Let us go then, you and I,
> When the evening is spread out against the sky
> Like a patient etherised upon a table;
> Let us go through certain half-deserted streets,
> The muttering retreats
> Of restless nights in one-night cheap hotels
> And sawdust restaurants with oyster-shells:
> Streets that follow like a tedious argument
> Of insidious intent
> To lead you to an overwhelming question...
> Oh, do not ask, 'What is it?'
> Let us go and make our visit.

This is a dramatic monologue, but very different from those of Browning, which seek to present to the reader the strong emotions of a forceful and self-confident personality – a technique discussed in Unit 12, pp. 312–16. The personality here is evasive, and his relationship with the reader is not at all clear or consistent. The speaker proposes a shared exploration of the city, but an exploration which he views with both wit and distaste. The invitation, pressing as it is, is not specially attractive: symbolically the atmosphere conveyed is that of suffering, helplessness, tedium and menace; realistically conveyed is a world of isolation, poverty and discomfort.

The urban setting is typically modern. It is presented both through sharp realistic detail (the oyster shells) and through phantastic imagery. The relationship of reader to speaker is unclear: is the reader to identify himself or herself with the person addressed (whoever this may be)? Moreover, the tone adopted towards the reader verges on the hectoring: the poem apparently starts in mid-conversation, takes for granted the relationship of 'you and I', insistently repeats phrases, and, in line 12, seems to casually brush off the listener's possible reluctance. The reader, like the listener, does not even know what the overwhelming question is: there are in fact a number of questions later in the poem, such as 'Do I dare/ Disturb the universe?' and, much repeated, 'How should I presume?' and one or more of these may, or may not, be the overwhelming question, delayed.

It is above all the two striking similes that give strong emotional significance to this apparently awkward communication. Both imply a crucial difficulty. In what sense is the evening 'spread out against the sky' and in what sense does it resemble the patient? There is no problem in seeing that the patient may be spread out, but it is difficult to apply this to the evening until we know what about the evening it is that is spread. (Could it be that the darkness, starting to cover the sky, can be seen stretching along the horizon of a lighter sky?) There is moreover a curious appropriacy in the ether, which is both an anaesthetic (in the simile) and the sky itself (in traditional poetic diction). Similarly, if less obscurely, the streets follow one from each other in the sense that one walks through one to get to the next – and in doing so, the poem implies, carries on a train of thought, 'just as' the conclusion of an argument follows from its premises. The second example is a brilliant coalescence of the narrated process of walking and thinking with the suggested process of deduction, but its brilliance is a sleight of hand: what the 'just as' really indicates is not much more than a pun.

The text then seems both to assert that the observed scene is continuous with the character's (or the characters') anxieties and to leave the reader unsettled about the nature of this continuity. The consistency of outer and inner world is strengthened by a mastery of free verse structure that has its own insidious intent, involving the reader in a curiosity that leaves him ready to ask the momentous question, or at least wishing to know more.

The rhyme scheme essentially consists of couplets. The rhymes themselves may seem banal. A certain banality is indeed one aspect of the text, which is colloquial, conversational, not obviously sophisticated (but really very sophisticated). But there are subtle variations in this simplicity of style. Two lines do not rhyme with anything. The first startling image, the table, shocks the reader into expecting some symmetrical phantastic vision; it does not come, and the poem goes into realistic listing. The 'question' arouses acute curiosity as to what it will be, but the line fades out in dots and there is no complement to the line. Some of the rhymes are awkward too: the final pair 'is it' – 'visit' verges on the comic, and the pair 'argument' – 'intent' works fully only if we give 'argument' a false stress. The rhythm of the poem is a masterly exploitation of the musical rhythm advocated by Pound. It hovers between a two-syllable and a three-syllable metric foot, between a solemn regularity and conversational spontaneity. If we give extra stress to the last syllable of 'argument' we get a very emphatic line of basically iambic character, in which the key terms 'streets', 'follow', 'tedious', 'argument' all receive heavy stress; if we maintain a normal stress, 'follow' is likely to be reduced to lower prominence, obscuring its key position in the texture of thought. This elusive flexibility of rhythm is further reinforced by a set of word echoes: here 'insidious' echoes the sound of 'tedious', while 'leads' appears to correspond in sense to 'follows', leaving us surprised that the streets can both lead and follow.

All this makes the poem ambiguous. Essentially, it presents the state of mind of the character as arising inevitably from the context; but this inevitability also appears to be a rhetorical fiction, the result of the speaker's attempts to entice the listener or reader into complicity with him.

The major poem of Eliot's youth, *The Waste Land*, is an extension of the concerns of 'Prufrock': it too shows a rootless and fragmented modern life through a variety of apparently incoherent voices, shifting rhythms, boldly suggestive images and an extraordinary – and at first obscure – range of cultural reference and citation. But it goes far beyond 'Prufrock' in its aspiration to spirituality, conveyed largely through references to the Arthurian myth of the Grail which gives new grace to a deathly land – a myth which, in accordance with the anthropological viewpoint of Sir James Frazer and Jessie Weston, is superimposed on the pattern of death and rebirth in the cycle of the seasons – and through its transcending the viewpoint of a single character to give a series of snapshots of disparate but equally bleak scenes typifying the desperation, discontinuity and emotional impoverishment that Eliot sees in modern life. Some of these scenes may seem distasteful, since the emotional impoverishment may in fact seem to be little more than Eliot's lack of sympathy for working-class and lower middle-class life (and other such passages were edited out as part of a general pruning undertaken by Pound at his friend's request); even so, the attempt to unify the multiple experience of the modern city within a mythic vision is an impressive undertaking. *The Waste Land* is too ambitious and complex a work to present thoroughly in a general study; but it must be recognized as one of the peaks of modern poetic creation.

This vein is further developed in a number of poems in which Eliot approaches ever closer to traditional Christian feeling and rejection of the secular world: 'The Hollow Men', 'Ash Wednesday', the 'Ariel Poems'. These are poems in which distinctive symbols come to bear more and more the weight of the poet's contemplation: the 'eyes I dare not meet in dreams' of 'The Hollow Men', the winding stair of 'Ash Wednesday'. At the same time the style acquires a solemn almost ritual repetitiousness, a certain generality and abstraction of vocabulary and a slow measured rhythm, sometimes counterpointed with a strong sense for the individuality of the speaking voice. The tender gravity to which the poet attains as he approaches Christian faith is especially finely conveyed in 'The Journey of the Magi' (from the 'Ariel Poems') through a style which is almost conversational but actually delicately suggestive in its rhythms and the precision of its vocabulary:

> A cold coming we had of it,
> Just the worst time of the year
> For a journey, and such a long journey
> The ways deep and the weather sharp,
> The very dead of winter.

There are other sides to Eliot's achievement. Notably there are the neatly patterned, erudite and amusingly ironic 'quatrain poems' of 1920, where the elegance can be at least disconcerting, as in 'Mr Eliot's Sunday Morning Service':

> Polyphiloprogenitive,
> Sapient sutlers of the Lord
> Drift across the window-panes.
> In the beginning was the Word.

There is, too, the bleak low-life drama of 'Sweeney Agonistes', with its banal conversations, perfunctory relationships and final music-hall song set against Sweeney's memories of the man who 'did a girl in' and his assertion:

> Birth, and copulation, and death.
> That's all the facts when you get down to brass tacks.

But Eliot's major poetic achievement comes in a further development of the meditation on spiritual need and cultural context adumbrated in 'Prufrock'; it is the series of poems, each named after a particular place, and conveying a strong sense of the character of places, called *Four Quartets* (1935–42). After this work, Eliot published no major new poems, but concentrated on drama and on critical writing. An extract will show how, in this mature poetry, the difficulty of communication central to 'Prufrock' and *The Waste Land* will, in important ways, have been transcended:

> *from* EAST COKER
> In my beginning is my end. Now the light falls
> Across the open fields, leaving the deep lane
> Shuttered with branches, dark in the afternoon,
> Where you lean against a bank while a van passes,
> And the deep lane insists on the direction
> Into the village, in the electric heat
> Hypnotised. In a warm haze the sultry light
> Is absorbed, not refracted, by grey stone.
> The dahlias sleep in empty silence.
> Wait for the early owl.

But there is still a great deal in 'East Coker' that recalls the strategy of 'Prufrock': this poem is again a reflection on place, a place not just 'half-deserted' but 'empty', in which the setting orients the attention of the person addressed, who again is not clearly identified, and who again is subject to peremptory instruction ('wait'). Again there is a confident assumption of a known kind of scene, which the van shows to be modern. Some differences are immediately apparent: the scene is rural, the time is afternoon (though evening is anticipated in the last line quoted), the atmosphere is primarily one of comfortable tranquillity, of rest and warmth. One thing that makes this a very fine piece of writing in fact is the way a calm fullness of attention is conveyed by the steady but varied pace of the lines, by the repeated consonants (notably the 'd's and 'l's), by the repetitions of words or ideas (notably of depth and heat), by the line-endings which echo without quite rhyming, and by the gradual evocation of a typical scene: field, lane, bank, village, grey stone. But there is more to the poem than this; there are elements which don't quite fit the calm harmony of the scene. There are the contrasts between open field and closed lane, darkness and light, leaning and mobility; the discreet hint of coercion in 'insists' and 'hypnotised'; the curious intellectual precision, almost pedantry, in the eighth line, bringing with it a shift of rhythm to the almost prosaic; and the sharp reorientation at the end of the passage, as line 9 suddenly focuses on a very specific flower and places it in a figurative context. The attention of the poet is partly sunk into the soporific warmth of the day; he is also aware of what could be different, of the potential for change in the scene and in his own sensibility.

The poem may seem to be a transcription of a picture. But the picture implies movement and so time. The passage ends – perhaps rather incongruously – by exhorting the hearer to wait. Immediately the hearer is to wait for evening, for the night bird appearing early. Later in the poem the theme of waiting for God and of the 'darkness of God' will become major ones; the English landscape anticipates a longing for the divine. And the passage has begun with a reflection on time, even more alien to the tone of the description itself. 'In my beginning is my end': the phrase is a repetition of the opening words of the whole poem, sixteen lines earlier (and, incidentally, a quotation from Mary Queen of Scots) and will be echoed in the last phrase of this section of the poem, thiry-eight lines later.

The poem has an elaborate construction in repeated motifs, like those in a string quartet; as contrasting themes in music intertwine and complement each other, so here the themes of time and space interact. The previous section has expressed fascination at the idea of change, of the sequence of birth and death. The musical repetition may seem to still this process of variation in time, and the moment of pause gives rise to a sudden concentration on the 'now' – implicit in which is the sense of futurity and of a possible disruption of time.

This then is a kind of philosophical poetry, concerned with the basic dimensions of human life, space and time. It considers them not through abstract argument but through detailed and sensitive attention to a scene. It is not difficult to see this as part of a tradition of meditative landscape poetry in which the greatest figure is probably Wordsworth. As the poem shows its allegiance to a literary tradition, so it shows its fidelity to a traditional view of a rural England (threatened at the time of writing by war). The modernist features are still there: the discontinuity, the impressionistic construction, the self-awareness tending towards irony, the sense of disquiet. But these things are now very restrained; the outsider's search for significance that made 'Prufrock' so provocative, eccentric and disquieting has been succeeded by a feeling of belonging, a loving acceptance of a familiar world, which has become the basis of a perhaps even more deeply questioning search for understanding.

## W.H. Auden and the poetry of the 1930s

The poets who came to prominence in the late 1920s and early 1930s – the best-known names are those of W.H. Auden, Louis MacNeice, Stephen Spender and C. Day Lewis – were viewed at the time as aggressively modernistic because of their insistent references to the contemporary world, with its technical and economic progress (pylons, subject of a poem by Spender, are often thought to be specially characteristic of the movement), with the rise of a popular culture of cinema and journalism, with that greater awareness of different social classes, with the rise of new and potentially subversive theories and styles of thought such as Freudian psychology and Marxism, and above all with the political and social insecurity brought about by economic catastrophe, high unemployment, the rise of extremist political movements, the spread of war in many countries and the fear of war involving Britain. A fine study of the whole movement is Hynes (1976). These poets are modern in the sense that they reflect in almost a journalistic spirit the world known to their readers. If we consider the essence of Eliot's modernism to be a weakening of the sense of the integrity of individual personality and a readiness to adopt a variety of – perhaps incompatible – personae, then the poets of the 1930s are much less clearly modernistic, and their use of a new poetic style, marked by surprising epithets, discontinuities of argument, similes which are compressed to the point of unclarity, learned or private allusions and sudden shifts in tone or in attitude to the reader, is less a matter of discontent with the potential of literary communication than of a rhetoric intended to heighten the novelty or immediacy of their experience. A case is W.H. Auden's *1929*:

> It was Easter as I walked in the public gardens,
> Hearing the frogs from the pond,
> Watching traffic of magnificent cloud
> Moving without anxiety on open sky –
> Season when lovers and writers find
> An altering speech for altering things,
> An emphasis on new names, on the arm
> A fresh hand with fresh power.
> But thinking so I came at once
> Where solitary man sat weeping on a bench,
> Hanging his head down, with his mouth distorted
> Helpless and ugly as an embryo chicken.

These opening lines take up the general setting of 'Prufrock', the stranger walking through the city and defining its character and atmosphere, but the tone is very new. The poem is presented as a reminiscence of the speaker rather than as a dialogue, and serves indirectly to characterize the speaker as lover or writer. The speaker is delighted with novelty; the spring season brings with it a feeling of openness, freedom, strength. Auden is conscious of belonging to a new generation, capable of new ways of life – personal and political – and new forms of expression. The passage ends with the individual who does not fit in to this new world, the weeping solitary, who leads the poet to reflect, in later parts of the poem, on the death and suffering that form an essential sacrifice as part of the Easter renewal. There is then a harsh contrast, strongly underlined by the sudden change in style, from the long complex first sentence, marked by continuous brilliance of effect, by surprise, incongruity and conspicuousness, with verbal parallels, sudden shifts of focus, elusive metaphor and rhetorical repetitions, to the second sentence, which verges on the lax or prosaic until the distasteful shock of the final simile. The first sentence manifests the speaker's pride in his *joie de vivre*; his delight in 'an altering speech' is apparent in the cunning illusions of language he has prepared for his readers. The second sentence shows a moment of reluctant observation, totally external to the speaker, illustrating the limits of human pride, and finally coming into horrible focus in the chicken image.

The image itself, though, is one more of Auden's illusions. It is difficult to see how a mouth can resemble a chicken, as the text appears to claim: it is much easier to think of the helpless form and especially the disproportionately thin neck of the chicken as representing the whole figure of the man with bent head. The image is neat: the spring chicken is a symbol of Easter; but this aborted embryo is a cruel parody of the new life of spring. But here we come to a crucial factor in Auden, and especially the early Auden. The reader of such material is very struck by the ingenuity, wit, inventiveness of the writing; we may even be struck by such small eccentricities as the omission of articles with some nouns ('traffic', 'cloud' and 'man' here). Such originality is extremely attractive; it is not clear that it is appropriate, either for the apparent pride in new life or for the disquiet at ugliness: the speaker seems to show more enjoyment in verbal creativity than we might expect. It also serves a dramatic purpose: the speaker is at first characterized as a *flaneur*, a light-hearted observer, and the encounter with suffering is his first step to the political and personal commitment that is expressed at the end of the whole poem. And yet what is always striking in Auden is the note of hyperbole, the readiness to fantasize and exaggerate – and a note of irony directed to such imaginary freedom.

The poet, that is, is both observer and fantasist, both objective and introspective. These complex tendencies are apparent in much of the writing of the 1930s. In Auden himself, for instance, we find such 'documentary' poems as 'Casino', 'Oxford', 'Dover' and many other poems describing places and characters; MacNeice as well as Auden wrote about Birmingham; in other poets we find such works as Spender's 'Landscape near an Aerodrome' or Bernard Spencer's 'Allotments: April'. Among current events the Spanish Civil War attracted a vast amount of poetic comment, notably from Auden, Spender and MacNeice, as well as John Cornford who was to die in that war; such issues as unemployment, mass holidays, urbanization and industrialization are reflected in a great many poems of the time. Especially deserving of mention is MacNeice's *Autumn Journal*, a long meditative poem reflecting on many aspects of urban life and public affairs in the late 1930s as well as on the poet's private emotional life. But as well as all this responsible public commentary there is a constant vein of dream, fantasy and purely personal feeling. One extreme is the surrealistic tendency seen in, for instance, much of David Gascoyne or in Philip O'Connor's 'Blue Bugs in Liquid Silk', which begins

> blue bugs in liquid silk
> talk with correlation particularly like
> two women in white bandages

But in Auden too the private note is very strongly struck: the outsider, the spy, the 'helmeted airman' of the early verse is not just the objective observer, but also the exile, the solitary; the world of the 1930s is threatened not just by poverty and war but by such menacing figures of imagination as in 'The Witnesses':

> the hooded woman, the hump-backed surgeons
> And the Scissor-Man.

Some of his most deeply felt verse, in fact, is concerned with the need to preserve a private life despite the pressure of the public: 'Lullaby' seeks to assert love despite its own instability and despite his awareness of 'the fashionable madmen' with 'their pedantic boring cry', and 'A bride in the 30s' rehearses the signs of the times: travel, steel and polished glass, tyranny and mass demonstrations, names Hitler, Mussolini, Churchill, Roosevelt, van der Lubbe, but ends with the voice of the heart asserting in characteristically elusive images and dense syntax, the centrality of moral choice:

> 'Yours the choice to whom the gods awarded
> The language of learning, the language of love,
> Crooked to move as a money-bug, as a cancer,
>     Or straight as a dove'.

Auden, like Eliot, was to mature, especially after his move to the United States in 1939, which coincided with his conversion to Christianity and a new subject matter for his poems, which display a less tense and spectacular kind of verse. An example is this:

> *from* MOUNTAINS
> To be sitting in privacy, like a cat
>     On the warm roof of a loft,
> Where the high-spirited son of some gloomy tarn
>     Comes sprinting down through a green croft,
> Bright with flowers laid out in exquisite splodges
> Like a Chinese poem, while, near enough, a real darling
> Is cooking a delicious lunch, would keep me happy for
>     What? five minutes? For an uncatlike
>         Creature who has gone wrong,
> Five minutes on even the nicest mountain
> Are awfully long.

This is the final stanza of a sort of landscape poem: it differs a great deal both from his own earlier picture of an observed scene in *1929* and from Eliot's depiction of place in 'East Coker'. Firstly, Auden here does not purport to re-enact a situation in which he participates directly; he discusses the feelings people have about mountains, and he speculates on a setting which *would* keep him happy. Moreover the incongruous details – the cat comparison, the eccentric vocabulary, the definite article in 'the high-spirited son', the 'splodges' – suggest that this is not a real mountain at all but some conventional image of a mountain. And finally the speaker turns away from the scene altogether to think about love and lunch. This looks like blatant frivolity. Wordsworth, discreetly evoked earlier in the poem, might have been outraged. The approach to the reader, moreover, largely maintains a tone of modest amusement which suggests an unpoetic – even a non-written – casualness, and it may seem very far from the high ambitions for poetry as a special kind of communication voiced and practised by many modern writers.

Except that things are really rather more complex. This complexity has three aspects. First, those casual and naive phrases do seem to go slightly wrong. Mountains, for instance, are not nice; the claim that they are is a blatant evasion of the tradition of awe and heroism they have acquired. Secondly, this is verse. It may be difficult to remember the fact, since the metre is so varied as to be barely recognizable at times and since there are only two rhyme pairs in these eleven lines. But in fact the lines do show the real distinguishing features of poetry: the sound and rhythm of the lines do affect the reader's response. And they do so rather strangely at times: lines 3–4, for instance, recount a rapid movement, but give an awkward conglomeration of stressed syllables, consonant groups, and obtrusive sound echoes. There is effort in this sprinting: or rather in the poet's imagination of it, in his exploitation of Romantic fairy-tale. Finally, there is a phrase which is not immediately intelligible, as good conversation should be: why is Auden (or why is humanity in general) 'an uncatlike/ Creature who has gone wrong'? The adjective, moreover, undermines the argument because it implies that the whole of the introductory section, in which Auden envies the cat, is irrelevant. How has mankind gone wrong? One obvious answer is through original sin, which, for Christians, is part of the crucial difference between people and animals. The complacent ease of communication, the enjoyment of familiar legends, of aesthetics, of domesticity: these are real values, charmingly communicated in much of the poem. But they are not the ultimate values, which the poem is too discreet to formulate exactly.

Modern poetry, as we have seen, is a challenging and vital exploration of what language can achieve; it may be called 'experimental' in the sense that poets have sought to establish how richly a sensibility can be conveyed in language, despite the widespread feeling that life is becoming more private, that the gap between the particular culture of the individual writer and the general culture of readers is widening, and that the language is being debased and oversimplified by such forms of mass communication as journalism, advertising, political and religious propaganda and sensational fiction. This experimentation is an enterprise that deserves our respect for its refusal to compromise. It is intriguing to notice that while Pound grew more experimental with age, Eliot and Auden grew less so, whether through personal maturing or through an increasing feeling that modern culture – at least a substantial minority culture – had developed to the point where ready communication has become possible. We shall see in the closing part of this unit that the tension between experimentation and community was to continue in later poetry.

## Poetry since 1945

The best-known poet in Britain in the post-war years was no doubt Dylan Thomas. Thomas had in fact been writing verse throughout the 1930s (his first mature poems date from 1930, when he was 16: hence his sarcastic reference to himself as 'the boy Rimbaud of Cwmdonkin Drive'). But his work was alien to the mainstream of 1930s poetry, as represented by Auden and his group, and his reputation is most firmly settled by such collections as *Deaths and Entrances* (1946) and the *Collected Poems* of 1952. His reputation was enhanced by a notoriously Bohemian lifestyle and by the exceptional success of his radio play *Under Milk Wood*, which owes its popularity to his astoundingly exuberant verbal inventiveness and his ironically good-natured view of the everyday excesses of Welsh village life. As a poet, he represents a culmination of a Romantic-symbolist tradition: his subject matter is predominantly the biological-spiritual domain of death, vitality, birth, childhood, ageing and God; the imagery is predominantly elemental: earth, air, water, the human body; the rhythms are dense and reinforced by a rich set of sound echoes. Most crucially of all, the metaphors are so numerous and so closely interwoven that almost no clue is given to the literal sense of some texts, a quality heightened by the poet's tendency apparently to start the poem in the midst of some unspecified situation. The result may be that readers at first let themselves be carried along by the poet's intoxicating love of words, the only landmarks being provided by some coherently linked keywords and by some strikingly compressed phrases: 'a grief ago', 'all the sun long', 'it was my thirtieth year to heaven'. The total effect is as of a Hopkins out of control (see Unit 12, pp. 327–30 for a discussion of Hopkins's verse and technique). But in fact Thomas is not, at best, out of control: a passage such as this shows a complex organization of tone, verbal play, sensuous apprehension, verse rhythm and syntax:

> Now as I was young and easy under the apple boughs
> About the lilting house and happy as the grass was green,
> > The night above the dingle starry,
> > Time let me hail and climb
> Golden in the heydays of his eyes...

('Fern Hill', ll. 1–5)

This aims at synthesis rather than precision: it appears to be both day and night, 'Time' appears to be a vague stand-in for some concept such as 'those people around me in my youth in whose eyes I was perceived'; but the sense of varied joy is acutely conveyed by the reader's awareness of a landscape dear to the poet but not quite accessible to his audience. And one should recall that this is not Thomas's only vein; among his most impressive work is the comparatively austere dignity of 'Do not go gentle into that good night' and the balance of symbolic punning and explicit apothegms in the 'Refusal to mourn the death, by fire, of a child in London'.

Dylan Thomas brought to an extreme the idea of poetry as a special language, in which fullness of meaning strains against the discipline and energy of syntax. This attitude may be found in other neo-Romantic poets of his generation: David Jones, Vernon Watkins, George Barker, John Heath-Stubbs. A harsher, less expansive view of poetry, which however still depends on the creation of a dense and startling language, is found in R.S. Thomas, with his sense of the limits and hardships of Welsh farming life:

> Too far for you to see
> The fluke and the foot-rot and the fat maggot
> Gnawing the skin from the small bones,
> The sheep are grazing at Bwlch-y-Fedwen...

('The Welsh Hill Country', ll. 1–4)

But the next major tendency in poetry in the post-war years was the creation of a range of styles in which poetic language was closely aligned to the everyday speech of educated people. This is the group of writers known as 'The Movement' (see Blake Morrison's study, 1980); its arrival in the public domain can most closely be located in the publication of Philip Larkin's volume *The Less Deceived* (1955) and of the anthology *New Lines* (1956). The tone of the Movement may also be seen in the popular novel *Lucky Jim* (1954) by one of the *New Lines* poets, Kingsley Amis: it is close to everyday experience (especially the experience of the middle- or lower-middle classes), suspicious of theory, abstractions and pretensions, cautious and self-restrained, sometimes self-mocking, often given to conspicuously rational argument and to systematic debate, witty, ironic and observant. 'The most glaring fault awaiting correction' in poetry before the Movement, according to *New Lines* editor, Robert Conquest, 'was the omission of the necessary intellectual component from poetry'; the most obvious example of the unintellectual or irrational – although he is not named – is Dylan Thomas.

The outstanding figure of the Movement was undoubtedly Philip Larkin; starting in his youth in a rather Yeatsian vein (*The North Ship*, 1945) he finds in the almost prosaic ordinariness of his chosen stance a discipline which allows him to engage discreetly and lucidly with major issues. A famous and typical example is 'Church Going'. The speaker in the poem, like most intellectuals of his generation, is not a Christian believer, and visits churches (by bicycle) out of a tourist's curiosity. The opening stresses his ignorance and indifference, in awkwardly colloquial tones:

> Once I am sure there's nothing going on
> I step inside, letting the door thud shut.
> Another church: matting, seats and stone,
> And little books.

The rhythm of 'thud shut' gives an acute sense of seclusion; the vagueness and flatness of the rest suggests tedium. But as the speaker departs, leaving an Irish sixpence as a crudely comic donation, he starts to reflect on what, if anything, churches still mean. And gradually the detached cynicism yields to a respect for 'this special shell', and the poet concludes by recognizing 'A hunger in himself to be more serious' and a pull towards

> this ground,
> Which, he once heard, was proper to grow wise in,
> If only that so many dead lie round.

This is a poem in which honesty and self-discipline seem almost as one, and in which they are conveyed by the neat verse form, the constant qualifications of the points made ('he once heard', 'if only'), the slow shift from the superficial to the solemn: wisdom, seriousness, specialness, the modern reader may feel, may be claimed all the more convincingly because they emerge from a sense of embarrassment and strangeness. Larkin remained throughout his creative life a keen observer of the surfaces of modern life (the city of Hull and its environs are captured with intimate knowledge and commitment, if not enjoyment); he extended his mimetic power in depicting different styles of speech and types of personality; and throughout his work there is the aspiration to celebrate the emptiness which he finds behind the busy world of commerce, leisure and work, or to tentatively endorse the social structures that seek to transcend it – a fine example is the rural 'Show Saturday', of which he reflects that it should be

> something people do
> Not noticing how time's rolling smithy-smoke
> Shadows much greater gestures;...

Larkin essentially is anti-modernist. He rejects the imprecise suggestiveness of much modern verse, and the sense of the poet as visionary and guide that sometimes goes with it. His conservatism (literary and political), his respect for clarity and for the actual appearances of things, can lead him back to an expression not far from the Georgian style, as in this delicately melancholy nature poem, 'Cut Grass':

> Cut grass lies frail:
> Brief is the breath
> Mown stalks exhale.
> Long, long the death
>
> It dies in the white hours ...

Of the other *New Lines* poets, one of the most prominent has been D.J. Enright, with his economic wit and irony, his sense of place, related to wide-ranging travels, his concern for political dilemmas, and his preference for a questioning, inconclusive, understated persona. Still better known has been Thom Gunn, whose early works show a complex metaphysical argumentativeness, allied to an acute self-awareness and an interest in motor cyclists, but whose later work under the influence of American models abandons the Movement decorum to investigate less formal models of verse (including syllabic verse) and a more direct, more literal depiction of personal relationships, and of the experiences of travel and place.

A new mood in poetry is indicated by the 1962 anthology *The New Poetry*. The editor, A. Alvarez, uses his introduction to argue against the principle of gentility, which he found all too normal in English life and writing – including the writing of the Movement – and to recommend 'a new seriousness', most exemplified by the American poets Robert Lowell and John Berryman (and especially by Lowell's latest, confessional volume *Life Studies*), in which poets would face 'the full range of [their] experience' – including their irrational fears and desires, including the extremes of experience. Alvarez illustrates his point by a comparison between two poems. Philip Larkin's 'At Grass' gives a gently melancholy picture of animal life; Alvarez characterizes it as 'elegant and unpretentious', as 'a nostalgic recreation of the Platonic (or *New Yorker*) idea of the English scene'; and he contrasts this with Ted Hughes's 'A Dream of Horses', an image of violent, intense animal life and of the challenge of controlling it, which Alvarez sees as grasping 'unfalsified and in the strongest imaginative terms possible, a powerful complex of emotions and sensations'.

Alvarez chose his example well: Hughes, already one of the most distinctive poets of his generation, was to become a major figure through his attunement of poetic rhythm to the sense of energy and resistance, his acute observation of concrete detail, his capacity for imaginative empathy, his knowledge of the harshness of natural life, his feeling for a stoical English past and his deployment of a grotesque and excessive mythology, largely concerned with creation and survival. The opening lines of a recent poem (1989) illustrate the fullness of his imaginative concern:

WOLFWATCHING
Woolly-bear white, the old wolf
Is listening to London. His eyes, withered in
Under the white wool, black peepers,
While he makes nudging, sniffing offers
At the horizon of noise, the blue-cold April
Invitation of airs.

The wolf is reduced, but fumblingly alert, limited by a horizon, displaced in a city, withered by age and yet persistent in his sense of invitation; and all this becomes incongruous in various ways: the wolf is like a woolly-bear, like a clandestine radio-listener, like a sheep, like a shady trader, his eyes reduced to peepers (as in the popular song 'Jeepers Creepers') – or perhaps, small, bright and round, they are reduced to black peppers. And the rhythm conveys the observer's fluctuations of surprise and curiosity, while the alliterations suggest effort and uneasy coherence of ideas. There is almost too much here for the reader to grasp in a coherent way; the sense is of the intensity of life perceived by the observer – who will go on to combine this intensity of need with the tedium of age and captivity, as the poem itself is realigned to hopeless emptiness. This is a poem of conflict, of will and loss, effective as a tribute to a futile vitality.

A poetry of intensity or excess does establish itself in the 1960s. One may mention Geoffrey Hill, with his densely wrought meditations on the immanence of a transforming supernatural, and Peter Redgrove, with his unremitting fascination with his own blood and body. The poet who, in the British domain, comes closest to the American confessional style is Sylvia Plath (herself American by birth) who expresses with astonishing directness an acute neurotic sensibility, painfully open to the force of visual sensation and unrelenting in judgement of herself and her family. This may produce something like a mystical vision, as with her sense that 'The high green meadows are glowing, as if lit from within' or (in the same poem, 'Blackberrying') the discovery of empty sea and sky from a rock 'That looks out on nothing, nothing but a great space/Of white and pewter lights'. Elsewhere it may produce a harshly abstracted and dramatized self-accusation, as in the treatment of suicide and survival through the myth of resurrection and through the disturbing echoes of the Holocaust in 'Lady Lazarus':

Dying
Is an art, like everything else.
I do it exceptionally well.

It may be helpful to see in this context of the flight from gentility one of the unmistakably major figures of the period, the Northern Irish poet Seamus Heaney.

His work, like that of Hughes, shows an ongoing engagement with the force of animal life, with the demands of simple farming and the contact of the elements, expressed in a language rich in sense reference and dense in sound, a language energetic and self-conscious. Three lines from 'Glanmore Sonnets' will show the interdependence of poet and natural world, and of senses and intellect:

> Old ploughsocks gorge the subsoil of each sense
> And I am quickened with a redolence
> Of the fundamental dark unblown rose.

Most distinctive in his work are perhaps his awareness of the troubles of Northern Ireland and his capacity for viewing them through myth and history (see Unit 25, pp. 668–9). The series of poems which confront death through the uncertain pathos of the 'bog people' (bodies, often of sacrificial victims, preserved in bogland) subtly correlate a directly physical response to the transformed body with a sense of cultural and moral relativities. In 'Punishment', for instance, he visualizes the victim as part of a natural cycle:

> her shaved head
> like a stubble of black corn,
> her blindfold a soiled bandage,
> her noose a ring
>
> to store
> the memories of love.

But the poet, 'the artful voyeur', also sees her as a contemporary victim of IRA retribution, and both feels 'civilised outrage' and also understands 'the exact/and tribal, intimate revenge'. Imagination, detachment, introspection interact in a compound which is rightly unstable, the gravity of the topic outweighing the observer's fascination. A particularly impressive work is the sequence 'Station Island', in which the tone and manner of Dante are applied to the rituals of Irish Catholicism to engender a grave and calm self-knowledge, in which various dimensions of memory and culture, various degrees of immixture in his native community, come to a mature equilibrium.

But this movement to expressionism, to physicality, extreme emotion and the word as effortful gesture, is not the only tendency in the poetry of the 1960s. As well as a number of poets who do write in this manner, Alvarez's anthology includes John Fuller, a poet of elegance and wit who owes much to the playful inventiveness of Auden. His erudition, wide culture, sense of fantasy, mastery of syntax and of the modest sophistication of educated conversation give a constant urbanity to his writing which creates a fascinating tension in association with his feeling for the vulnerability of middle-class life, the limitations of the body and the problematic nature of the personal relations and of people's images of themselves.

Another poet who works from within a very manifest high culture, in which art, music, poetry (including foreign poetry) play a conspicuous part, is Charles Tomlinson. Direct personal feeling is very muted in his work, which depends rather on the creation of apparently objective images, aesthetically perceived, with an acute sensitivity to light and colour, and especially to change of colour, and formulated in a discreet, evenly paced and meditative verse, in which surprise and emphasis are rare and the poetic effect lies rather in consistency of tone and delicacy of statement. A few lines from 'Tramontana at Lerici' (a title which itself seems a blow struck against the Movement's dislike of abroad) illustrate the approach:

> Leaf-dapples sharpen. Emboldened by this clarity
> The minds of artificers would turn prismatic,
> Running on lace perforated in crisp wafers
> That could cut like steel.

What is precisely captured is not the minds (which are purely hypothetical) but the leaves, which – by a sort of pun on 'sharpen' – become a threat and a model for art, permitting the mind to become geometrical.

A similar emptiness of landscape characterizes much of the work of another Northern Irish poet, Derek Mahon. Mahon is largely a poet of exile, who rejects what he sees as the alienating harshness of Northern Ireland without finding an alternative or breaking his attachment to the place of his origin. Art again plays a major part in his work, as with his poem on de Hooch's view of Delft, which becomes a way of viewing at a distance the meticulous domestic order of Protestant Belfast. Perhaps his best-known poem is 'A Disused Shed in Co. Wexford', in which some mushrooms left for years in darkness become – pathetically and absurdly – images of the abandoned dead from Treblinka to Pompeii; the insistence on the bodily decline and distaste, on solitude and stoical endurance, is qualified by a wide learning (discreetly displayed), by an almost parodistic enlivening of the topic (the mushrooms cry for 'elbow room') and by an occasional exuberance of verbal invention, as when, for instance, the light cast on them by visitors opening the door becomes a 'flash-bulb firing squad'.

A Northern Ireland poet of similar lucidity and orderliness is Michael Longley. Longley's is largely a poetry of witness as he records with affectionate gravity characters, landscapes and incidents typical of the various ways of life of Ireland, and especially those characteristic of an unsophisticated, unchanging rural and tribal Ireland and of the conflicts of the North. His vision is precise, his sense of space and texture is acute, his tone is measured and implies real sympathetic familiarity with the people and places he writes of.

One may briefly mention other poets from Northern Ireland who show similar qualities of concern, cultural and rural awareness, powers of observation, feeling for environment and control of form and tone: Tom Paulin, Frank Ormsby and Medbh McGuckian. One who has drawn special attention recently is Paul Muldoon. Although Muldoon is capable of this kind of poetry based on intimacy, familiarity, and modest efficiency in verbal form, he has also explored a more fantastic and innovative form of writing, as in his 'Immram', in which the voyage literature of the Irish classical tradition is transformed by the superimposition of a modern American Chandler-style adventure narrative, fast-moving, tough, worldly and cosmopolitan in its reference, open to politics, current affairs and dream, and displaying virtuoso skill in narrative transitions, in verse form and in the creation of comic and grotesque incident, while his more recent *Madoc* attempts an elusive philosophical debate on the basis of a complex imagined history of American exploration, told in brief, economical fragments, tending towards a certain abstraction and understatement.

There are now a large number of young poets writing in varied styles, and it is not possible to group them readily in any way (nor is it easy to select those most deserving of mention in a survey such as this). A good selection may be found in Blake Morrison and Andrew Motion's anthology, *The Penguin Book of Contemporary British Poetry* (1982). This is a far less programmatic work than *New Lines* or *The New Poetry*. Its editors claim to note a shift in poetic sensibility which calls for a reformation of poetic taste, but this shift is in fact very diverse; what they assert as a common purpose is 'to extend the imaginative franchise', or to 'reassert the primacy of the imagination in poetry'. Some readers might feel that this impulse had never been absent from twentieth-century poetry, even in the 'empirical' poetry, based on observation, which they associate with Philip Larkin. Indeed, their own selection shows that contemporary poets balance the cult of the imagination with social and political observation and commentary (notably in the cases of Douglas Dunn and Tony Harrison), so that if there is a shift it may be of degree rather than of kind.

The most widely publicized instance of this revival of imagination is the so-called 'Martian' school – which in fact appears to consist of only two people, Craig Raine and Christopher Reid (and Reid is perhaps doubtful). The movement takes its name from Raine's poem 'A Martian sends a postcard home'. Unfamiliar with the customs and objects of Earth, the Martian names them by what the terrestrial reader sees as a set of ingenious and surprising metaphors; so books (or 'Caxtons') are 'mechanical birds with many wings'. The reader enjoys the strangeness of this, as the ordinary is made new. There is obviously a risk of triviality in this style of writing, which may look like a chain of riddles (though riddles, one should recall, are an ancient poetic form); the risk, one may feel, is evaded here by the range of suggestiveness, hardly masked by the teasing of the riddle form: books are free as birds but also part of an elaborate socio-economic mechanism. To a large extent, these poets are concerned with the uneventful domestic life of the middle classes: what they show is that, with enough inventiveness, almost any detail can be made revealing (see Unit 1, p. 4, for a further discussion of Raine). So Reid's 'Disaffected Old Man' lights a cigarette from his wife's, which is already burning:

> Leaning, we kiss with cigarettes
> To make a tremulous bridge for love.

Distance and closeness are allied in the superficial intimacy of a long marriage. This kind of writing risks, in addition, producing poems which are a string of surprising ideas rather than coherent structures; the risk is often held at bay, perhaps more in Reid than in Raine's early work, and Raine's largely autobiographical collection *Rich* suggests an ambition to move on to more consistent exploration of theme (though his latest volume, the novel in verse *History: The Home Movie*, may cast some doubt on the depth of this ambition).

The immediate contemporary scene remains extremely varied. There is the lucid, sensitive and economical narrative writing of Andrew Motion, and the wry and witty autobiography of Hugo Williams and Michael Hofmann, there are Eavan Boland and Helen Dunsmore with their discreet and subtly varied reflections on domestic life and on landscape, U.A. Fanthorpe's neat ironies, Paul Durcan's energetic accumulation of experience formulated through a lively conversational narration. Perhaps the most recent discernible tendency is to a virtuoso playfulness, combining wit and a compressed verbal inventiveness with social observation, ironic introspection and parody of the personality-types offered by mass media, previous literature and social stereotypes: one may name Andrew Greig, Glyn Maxwell, Gerard Woodward and Simon Armitage. Two major figures from the Commonwealth offer a very different style of poetry: Les Murray and Derek Walcott both produce works which are mythical, even visionary, expansive, concrete in description and symbol, deeply conscious of the processes of nature and of humanity's relation to its environment, and eager to bear witness to the wish for personal fulfilment and enrichment of experience.

Poetry is in general in a healthy state. Some observers note that it no longer has mass appeal, and consider that it is kept alive primarily by its place in the educational system. It is obvious that it is a minority taste, compared with fiction notably, so that it may not be easy to find a good selection of contemporary verse in bookshops or libraries outside the major cities. Nevertheless, the considerable range of poetic creation in Britain and Ireland – as well as the continuing interest in American verse and the growing interest in verse translated from European languages – shows that poetry remains a vital concern for many people. In a world where language is often used vaguely or cynically, there is a special excitement in a kind of literature that explores the potentiality of our language in order to grasp new aspects of our personal and social lives.

## BIBLIOGRAPHY

Andrews, E. (1988) *The Poetry of Seamus Heaney*, Macmillan, Basingstoke.
Auden, W.H. (1972) 'Writing', in *Twentieth Century Literary Criticism*, ed. D. Lodge, Longman, London, 636–45 [first published 1963].
Auden, W.H. (1975) *The Dyer's Hand*, Faber, London.
Auden, W.H. (1976) *Collected Poems*, ed. E. Mendelson, Faber, London.
Bradbury, M. and McFarlane, J. (1978) *Modernism*, Harvester Wheatsheaf, Hemel Hempstead.
Brooks, C. (1939) *Modern Poetry and the Tradition*, University of North Carolina, Chapel Hill.
Butscher, E. (ed.) (1979) *Sylvia Plath, the Woman and the Work*, Peter Owen, London.
Corcoran, N. (1993) *English Poetry since 1940*, Longman, London.
Eliot, T.S. (1951) *Selected Essays*, Faber, London.
Eliot, T.S. (1962) *Collected Poems*, Faber, London.
Eliot, T.S. (1972) 'Tradition and the Individual Talent', in *Twentieth Century Literary Criticism*, ed. D. Lodge, 71–7 [first published 1919].
Ellmann, R. (1965) *Yeats, the Man and the Masks*, Faber, London.
Flory, W.S. (1980) *Ezra Pound and the Cantos*, Yale University Press, New Haven.

Furbank, P.N. and Kettle, A. (eds) (1975) *Modernism and Its Origins*, Open University Press, Milton Keynes.

Gardner, H. (1968) *The Art of T.S. Eliot*, Cresset, London.

Grubb, F. (1965) *A Vision of Reality*, Chatto & Windus, London.

Heaney, S. (1990) *New Selected Poems 1966–87*, Faber, London.

Henn, T.R. (1966) *The Lonely Tower*, 2nd edn, Methuen, London.

Hughes, T. (1995) *New Selected Poems*, Faber, London.

Hynes, S. (1976) *The Auden Generation*, Bodley Head, London.

Jeffares, A.N. (1962) *W.B. Yeats, Man and Poet*, Routledge & Kegan Paul, London.

Jones, P. (ed.) (1972) *Imagist Poetry*, Penguin, Harmondsworth.

Kenner, H. (1951) *The Poetry of Ezra Pound*, Kraus, New York.

Kenner, H. (1972) *The Pound Era*, Faber, London.

Larkin, P. (1988) *Collected Poems*, ed. A. Thwaite, Marvell, London.

Leavis, F.R. (1972) *New Bearings in English Poetry*, Penguin, Harmondsworth [first published 1932].

Mahon, D. (1979) *Poems 1962–78*, Oxford University Press, Oxford.

Moody, A.D. (1980) *Thomas Stearns Eliot, Poet*, Cambridge University Press, Cambridge.

Morrison, B. (1980) *The Movement, English Poetry and Fiction of the 1950s*, Oxford University Press, London.

Morrison, B. (1982) *Seamus Heaney*, Methuen, London.

Morrison, B. and Motion, A. (1982) *The Penguin Book of Contemporary British Poetry*, Penguin, Harmondsworth.

Pinto, V. da S. (1967) *The Crisis in English Poetry 1880–1940*, Hutchinson, London.

Plath, S. (1981) *Collected Poems*, Faber, London.

Pound, E. (1968) *Collected Shorter Poems*, Faber, London.

Pound, E. (1972) 'A Retrospect', in *Twentieth Century Literary Criticism*, ed. D. Lodge, 58–68 [first published 1918].

Pound, E. (1975) *The Cantos of Ezra Pound*, Faber, London.

Pound, E. (1985) *Literary Essays*, Faber, London.

Rosenthal, M.L. (1978) *Sailing into the Unknown, Yeats, Pound and Eliot*, Oxford University Press, New York.

Sagar, K. (ed.) (1983) *The Achievement of Ted Hughes*, Manchester University Press, Manchester.

Schmidt, M. (1972) *British Poetry since 1960, a Critical Survey*, Carcanet, Oxford.

Skelton, R. (ed.) (1964) *Poetry of the Thirties*, Penguin, Harmondsworth.

Skelton, R. (ed.) (1968) *Poetry of the Forties*, Penguin, Harmondsworth.

Stead, C.K. (1975) *The New Poetic, Yeats to Eliot*, Hutchinson, London.

Stead, C.K. (1986) *Pound, Yeats, Eliot and the Modernist Movement*, Macmillan, Basingstoke.

Symons, A.J.A. (1971) *The Symbolist Movement in Literature*, Haskell House, New York, [first published 1899].

Thomas, D. (1971) *Collected Poems*, Dent, London.

Tomlinson, C. (1985) *Collected Poems 1951–81*, Oxford University Press, Oxford.

Woodward, A. (1980) *Ezra Pound and the Pisan Cantos*, Routledge & Kegan Paul, London.

Yeats, W.B. (1972) 'The symbolism of poetry', in *Twentieth Century Literary Criticism*, ed. D. Lodge, 28–34 [first published 1900].

Yeats, W.B. (1977) *Collected Poems*, 2nd edn, Macmillan, London [first published 1957].

# SECTION 3

# Critical theories and perspectives

# New criticism, formalism and structuralism

*Richard Bradford*

## New Criticism

New Criticism is a twentieth-century phenomenon. It is the name given to the theories developed between the 1920s and 1950s by a group of American and British writers and academics. The activity of literary criticism – commenting upon and explaining the operation and significance of literature – has been going on since Plato and Aristotle, and the newness of the New Critics derives principally from their role as advocates and practitioners of literary criticism as an academic discipline.

The literature of classical Greece and Rome had been studied in the older universities since their formation. The study of modern (that is post-medieval) literature in English gained a foothold in higher education in the late nineteenth century, and New Criticism grew out of the determined and sometimes desperate attempts to establish it as a respectable university subject. The arguments against 'reading English' were powerful. Any literate person with a modicum of intelligence could 'study' English drama and poetry: they didn't need to go to university to do so. Indeed the formal study of literature was a contradiction in terms: modern literature was part of contemporary popular culture. Literature might involve religion, philosophy or morality, but it didn't engage seriously with these issues. It combined them with the less profound activities of story-telling and acting; the decorative style of poetry bespoke intelligence and artistry, but it did not make a significant contribution to the sum of knowledge.

In Britain the attempts to answer these charges of amateurism, dilettantism and irrelevance gained credence from a growing enthusiasm for English culture. Matthew Arnold, nineteenth-century poet and education theorist, is acknowledged as the originator of a number of precepts and maxims that sustained English Studies in its late-Victorian infancy and which survive in today's debates on the national curriculum and English in the universities. Arnold argued that the study of literature would inform and, mysteriously, harmonize the fragmented ideology and social disunity of modern British society. Literary studies would supplement, perhaps even replace, the Church as a touchstone for intellectual and social cohesion: it would cultivate or 'hellenize' the new and potentially philistine influence of the middle classes; for the working class it would promote sympathy and fellow feeling with those who might be better off but who shared with their lower brethren a deep admiration for the universality and classless beauty of literary writing (for a detailed account of these theories and their implementation, see Baldick, 1983 and Ch. 1 of Eagleton, 1983).

Arnold's ideas would be paralleled and extended by the New Critics, but the notion of literary studies as a civilizing force begged a more specific question. What is literature? If literary studies was to be a useful component of the education system its advocates must first be able to define its subject, and then show how the detailed consideration of these intrinsic qualities might procure intellectual, cultural, social, even moral benefits.

New Criticism incorporates a complex and diverse body of opinion and practical work and this is underpinned by these two objectives: define literature; justify its broader significance as an educational subject.

The poet T.S. Eliot claimed in his essay on 'The Metaphysical Poets' ([1921] 1972) that

> a poet is constantly amalgamating disparate experience; the ordinary man's experience is chaotic, irregular, fragmentary [falling in love, reading Spinoza, the noise of the typewriter, the smell of cooking]; in the mind of the poet these experiences are always forming new wholes. (p. 2024)

Eliot's definition of poetry would be preserved and elaborated by the New Critics. Arnold himself had pre-empted it. The 'grand power' of poetry, he claimed, was not in its 'explanation of the mystery of the universe' (activities devolved to philosophy and religion) but in its ability to 'awaken in us' a sense of being in contact with the 'essential nature' of ordinary, mundane events and objects 'to have their secret, and to be in Harmony with them' (Arnold, [1865] 1970, pp. 157–8).

Eliot and Arnold promoted poetry as a vehicle for harmony and unification; not as a practical solution to disagreements in theology or morality or as offering some insight into the problems of social and political disunity; rather as a kind of personal, intellectual palliative, a discourse which involved a retreat from the utilitarian paradoxes of the real world to a world created by the poet, the literary text, in which the 'chaotic, irregular, fragmentary' material of experience would be coerced into 'new wholes'.

I.A. Richards was the first British literary critic to attempt to implement these principles as an academic programme – based upon his own work in the Cambridge English Faculty. He argued in *Principles of Literary Criticism* (1924; references from 1966 edition) that although poetry engages with the same problems and material as referential language (objects, intellectual and philosophical questions, etc.) it does so by promoting their purely *emotive* effects: 'the question of belief or disbelief, in the intellectual sense, never arises' (1966, p. 277). In place of an engagement with the poet's philosophical credence or religious integrity, the reader and critic should pay attention to the experience that is unique and particular to the reading of the poem. The critic should not be involved in paraphrasing or historicizing the text but in recreating within himself what is assumed to be the mental condition of the poet, the 'relevant mental condition' (1966, p. 1) shared by poet and reader. This might sound like a rather vague pseudo-mystical enterprise, but Richards rooted his objective in instructive guides (in *Practical Criticism*, 1929 and *Principles of Literary Criticism*, 1924) to the stylistic features and characteristics of poems which implement and sustain the 'relevant mental condition' of reading them. An example of this will be found in Unit 1, p. 11, with his precise definition of how poetic metaphor transforms language from its ordinary, utilitarian function.

The common feature of these theories is the idea that poetry is both relevant to the modern condition, in its ability to absorb and telescope the diversities of life into particular poems, and perversely elevated from the puzzling and sordid actualities of that condition. This double assertion permeates new critical thinking and manifests itself in a number of ways.

American New Criticism gained much of its cohesion and unity from a group of academics working in Vanderbilt University, Tennessee during the 1920s: principally, John Crowe Ransom, Allen Tate and Robert Penn Warren. Ransom's essay 'Criticism Inc' ([1937] 1972) economically summarizes the concerns and objectives of the group (references from reprint in Lodge, 1972). Ransom lists those elements that contribute to but which should not dominate the critical enterprise; and the subtext of his list of exclusions is his desire to isolate literary studies from the encroachment of other academic disciplines – particularly history, philosophy, linguistics and the newly emergent social sciences. 'Personal registrations' (tears, humour, desire, excitement) can be procured by the chemist or the Broadway producer. 'Synopsis and paraphrase' is the stuff of 'high school classes and women's clubs'. 'Historical studies' tell us about the author and his circumstances but are of no necessary relevance to the particular effect of the poem. Similarly, 'Linguistic Studies' might assist with a 'perfectly logical' understanding of 'content', but not with a proper understanding of the poem – and with 'Moral Studies': 'moral content is not the *whole* content' (p. 236). Ransom claims that although the critic may inform himself of these materials 'as possessed by the artist' his real business is to 'discuss the literary assimilation of them' (p. 236). The poem is a 'desperate ontological and metaphysical manoeuvre' in which the normal registers of language, fact, logic and emotion are transformed by its 'living integrity' (p. 238).

Given that we accept that poetry is capable of uniquely refracting and transmuting the commonly perceived world the problem remains of what the critic should do with all of the (in Ransom's view) extraneous information that will affect his/her reading; very few people read poems by Donne without some prior knowledge of the religious, marital and professional aspects of his life. In 'The Intentional Fallacy' (1946) and 'The Affective Fallacy' (1949, reprinted in *The Verbal Icon*, 1954) W.K. Wimsatt and Monroe Beardsley set about tackling this problem. They asked: If we can clarify the 'intention' or the 'affective' (i.e. emotional) register of a non-poetic statement by enquiring into its context or motivation, why not do so with literary statements? Their answer, though more detailed and better illustrated, was the same as Ransom's: literature involves the material of non-poetic discourse, but cuts itself off from the cause-and-effect relations which govern that discourse.

There have been a number of attempts by new critics to explain and quantify the mysterious power of poetry to project itself into this other-worldly realm. The best known and most widely discussed are William Empson's *Seven Types of Ambiguity* (1930) and Cleanth Brooks's *The Well Wrought Urn* (1947). The respective themes of these studies are the linguistic effects of 'ambiguity' and 'paradox'. In non-poetic language these effects are generally the result and cause of uncertainty, misapprehension or indecision. In poetry, however, they purposively inform the text, and, rather than producing puzzlement, effectively disclose the deep-rooted tensions and unresolvable conflicts that underpin our reasonings and perceptions of the world.

Brooks, for example, analyzes the fruitful paradoxes of Wordsworth's sonnet 'Composed Upon Westminster Bridge',

> Dear God! the very houses seem asleep;
> And all that mighty heart is lying still.

> To say they are 'asleep' is to say they are alive, that they participate in the life of nature. ... It is only when the poet sees the city under the semblance of death [heart is lying still] that he can see it actually alive – quick with the only life that he can accept, the organic life of 'nature'. (Lodge, 1972, p. 294)

Brooks's critical method is firmly rooted in the idealistic tradition of Arnold and Eliot. He argues that Wordsworth telescopes broader universal themes (the city and nature; life and death) into localized and uniquely poetic tensions and paradoxes.

The New Critical programme of focusing upon how literature refracts and transmutes ordinary perceptions of the world is consistent with their earliest objectives of establishing literary studies in the university: as I have stated, we can reinterpret Ransom's catalogue of exclusions in terms of the potential threat to the integrity of literary criticism posed by other academic disciplines. Many critics, however, claim to find more disturbing motives.

The American new critics of Vanderbilt University published a journal called *The Fugitive* (earning themselves the collective title, 'The Fugitives') which, along with literary criticism, promoted the nostalgic and rather fantastic ideal of the coherence, harmony and unity of the rural society of the Old South – as opposed to the industrialized and decadent culture of the North. Terry Eagleton (1983, Ch. 1) discusses the relation between the methods of New Criticism and its ideological underpinnings.

> A typical New Critical account of a poem offers a stringent investigation of its various 'tensions', 'paradoxes' and 'ambivalences', showing how these are resolved and integrated by its solid structure ... poetry was to be the new organic society in itself, the final solution to science, materialism, and the decline of the 'aesthetic' slave owning South. (p. 49) (See also Unit 14, p. 378.)

To sum up the points that have arisen so far, we can say that the new critical enterprise involves two dimensions of literary interpretation: (a) attention to the constituent features and operations of the literary text – those which characterize it as different from non-literary texts; (b) the capacity of literature, particularly poetry, to give us rich and 'concrete' apprehensions of experience, while at the same time remaining immune from the determinate conditions of politics, society, philosophical and religious discourse.

Point (a) has since the 1960s been challenged by a variety of theorists who for the sake of convenience we can categorize as Reader-Response Critics and Poststructuralists (see Units 19 and 20). Much more damaging challenges have focused upon point (b), and these have come from Feminists, Marxists, New Historicists and a broad range of writers who advocate that the study of literature must involve a perception of literary texts as only one dimension of the broader cultural, social and political fabric (see Units 21, 23 and 24).

In order to reach your own judgement on the value and validity of New Criticism you will need to read the critical texts cited in these units. For the time being consider the arguments of F.R. Leavis. Leavis, based along with I.A. Richards at Cambridge, has had a formative influence upon English Studies in British universities. Like his contemporaries in the United States Leavis believed that literary criticism rests upon the engagement of intuitive and irreducible values (variously described by him as 'felt life', 'maturity', 'humanity', 'sensitivity' and 'profound seriousness') which are at once addressed and concretized in our encounters with literature and which also underpin our sense of social responsibility and commitment. He describes the activity of criticism as follows: 'The critics aim is, first, to realize as sensitively and completely as possible this or that which claims his attention; and a certain valuing is implicit in the realizing' (Lodge, 1972, p. 623). The 'this or that' can be anything, from the dominant theme of the text (the fall of Man in *Paradise Lost*, the concept of justice in Dickens's *Bleak House*) to the distribution of particular images or ideas in a poem (the city and nature, life and death in Wordsworth's 'Ode on Westminster Bridge').

> As he matures in experience of the new thing he asks, explicitly and implicitly: 'Where does this come? How does it stand in relation to ...? How relatively important does it seem?' and the organisation into which it settles as a constituent in becoming 'placed' is an organisation of similarly 'placed' things, things that have found their bearings with regard to one another, and not a theoretical system or a system determined by abstract considerations. (Lodge, 1972, p. 623)

The questions which Leavis cites for the putative critic are those which would be raised in practically all our encounters with statements on God, life, love, society, politics, philosophy – the 'this and that which claims [our] attention'. In literature, however, our response must be qualified by the realization that the organization (i.e. the textual structure) into which those issues 'settle' and are 'placed' obliges us to give attention as much to other elements of the same text ('things that have found their bearings with regard to one another') as we do to 'systems' outside the text.

You will recognize similarities between this argument, Ransom's exclusion of literary criticism from contextual matters and Eliot's notion of the 'new wholes' which constitute the fabric of poems. You might also recognize dissimilarities between it and your own experience of literature. If you are a woman you might find it difficult to completely dissociate Shakespeare's treatment of women characters from the 'systems' of gender role and displacement that have endured outside and beyond literary texts since the seventeenth century. The 'placing' of an issue in a literary text does not necessarily strip it of the polemical, oppressive or unjust associations that it carries in the real world.

In fact, Leavis's model of critical practice is a gross falsification of his own preferences and methods. His self-created *Great Tradition* (1948) of novelists (principally Austen, George Eliot, Henry James and D.H. Lawrence) reflects his own commitment to middle-class liberalism and the moral touchstones of English non-conformity. Leavis's 'mature' and 'serious' response to these novels, to their 'universal' themes, conceals his own 'system' of partial and particular allegiances. To have supported overtly the values embodied in these texts would have dragged them into the kind of moral and political argument that is anathema to the perception of literature as detached from the 'abstract' and 'theoretical' 'systems' of the real world. To state that 'I believe D.H. Lawrence is a great writer because he expresses a disdain for the shallow and decadent intellectual condition of early twentieth-century Britain' would provoke comparisons with the writings of politicians, psychologists and sociologists, and in turn raise questions regarding the proper purpose and objective of literary criticism.

The quotation from Leavis is part of his response (later published in *The Common Pursuit*, 1952) to a letter written to the journal *Scrutiny* by René Wellek. Wellek, while admiring Leavis's book *Revaluation* (1936), observed that Leavis had failed to state explicitly and defend systematically his implicit assumptions regarding the nature and value of poetry. Wellek asked Leavis to become 'conscious that large ethical, philosophical and ... ultimately aesthetic *choices* are involved' in poetry criticism. What Wellek was seeking was an abstract, theoretical model which would specify the form and function of poetry as distinct from other discourses, and which would enable us properly to distinguish between 'ethical and philosophical' choices of the real world and those that are transformed by the 'aesthetic' of literature.

This objective had, to an extent, been pursued by critics such as Richards, Empson and Brooks but it was more firmly rooted in the European tradition in which Wellek (born in Vienna, 1903) had developed as a critic. And it is to this tradition that we now turn.

Eagleton (1983) and Jefferson and Robey (1982) contain good introductions to New Criticism. For more detailed accounts see Stewart (1965) on the Fugitives, and Fekete (1977) and Lentricchia (1980) on the general objectives and ideology of the New Critics. Extracts from the work of the New Critics will be found in Lodge (1972).

## Formalism and structuralism

Formalism originated in Russia in 1915 with the founding of the Moscow Linguistic Circle and, in the following year, of its St Petersburg counterpart Opayaz. Its most influential founding members are Viktor Shklovsky, Vladimir Propp and Roman Jakobson. Translations of their work, along with material by their fellow theorists

Brik, Tomaskevsky, Eikhenbaum and Tynyanov will be found in Lemon and Reis (1965) and Bann and Bowlt (1973). It would be unjust and inaccurate to regard the Formalists as a united collective but few of them would have quarrelled with the following summary of their ideas.

Formalism involves the reversal of the traditional relation between form and content. In classical and in post-sixteenth-century European thought definitions of literature were drawn principally from the discipline of rhetoric. Rhetoric involves the classification of linguistic devices (metaphor, antithesis, metre, sound pattern, pun, repetition, etc.) which variously amplify and distort ideas and concepts. It is underpinned by the belief that pre-linguistic ideas and concepts (content) exist as immutable entities, and that language enables us to decorate, document, clarify or promote them (form). Literary language, principally poetry, is more prone to the use of formal devices than its practical, utilitarian counterpart. In short, literature is licensed to foreground form at the expense of content.

The Formalists challenged this assumption by arguing that language, be it literary or non-literary, is a formative rather than a reflective or transparent system of representation. All classical and post-classical modes of Western thought are founded upon the assumption that reality (involving tangible objects and events, empirical and speculative reasoning, and programmes of belief) exists before and outside its representation in words. Formalism proposes that the structure of reality is effectively determined and shaped by language: form predetermines content. (Ferdinand de Saussure's contribution to this idea will be discussed below, p. 538, and in Unit 19, pp. 547–55.)

The concept which underpins all Formalist work on literature is *ostranenie*, variously translated as making strange or defamiliarization. Donne's subtle metaphor, 'a bracelet of bright hair about the bone' makes strange familiar connotations of life (the wearing of a bracelet, having bright hair) and death (the fleshless bone) by compressing them into a single image. The Formalists did not regard *ostranenie* as a perverse distortion of reality: since reality is a construct of language, *ostranenie* foregrounds and exposes this interdependency.

Structuralism owes a considerable debt to this Formalist precept. Structuralists such as Claude Lévi-Strauss (see *Structural Anthropology*, 1972) and Umberto Eco (see *A Theory of Semiotics*, 1976) are as much concerned with culture and society as they are with literature. Their basic premise is that human activity and its products, including religion, social conventions, ritual, art and philosophy, are constructed and not natural. All of our actions, beliefs and habits – from our belief in God to our proper use of a knife and fork – are elements of a structure. They are meaningful, argues the structuralist, not because they reflect a transcendent reality, but because they are related to each other within a sign system which sustains our perception of reality. Structuralism contends that our perceptions of reality and the world are made possible by signs (visual, acoustic, tactile, behavioural, etc.) whose relation to one another overrides their relation to a transcendent, immutable truth. In short, life is like language.

As we shall see, this kind of anthropological Structuralism influenced the work of a number of literary Structuralists, such as Greimas and Todorov. Such work has earned the opprobrium of many Anglo-American critics – new, old and unaligned – for a number of reasons. It seems to them to have appropriated literature as yet another sign system, comparable with but not necessarily superior to film, rock music, or clothes (see Ransom's list of exclusions above, p. 523); and it seems to dispossess literature of the sense of neo-religious mystique from which it derives its creative power (see Leavis and Wellek above, pp. 525–6).

At the same time, however, many critics who are categorized as Formalist or Structuralist have sought to emphasize a clear distinction between literature and the non-literary sign systems which it variously reflects, redefines and unsettles. It is with this emphasis in mind that we shall consider the work of some of the major Formalists and Structuralists.

The first history in English of Formalism was by Erlich (1955); and Steiner (1984) offers a more recent exposition of their theories. The best, introductory accounts of the origins and methods of Structuralism are Hawkes (1977) and Robey (1973). Culler (1975) gives a detailed account of Structuralism's debt to linguistics and emphasizes the role of the reader in Structuralist interpretation. Lane (1970) and Lodge (1988) offer a collection of seminal Structuralist writings.

### Jakobson and poetry

Roman Jakobson (1896–1982) began his work on linguistics and poetry during the Formalist heyday of the 1900s to 1920s, but the Anglo-American branch of literary studies only became fully aware of his ideas with his 1960 paper called 'Closing Statement: Linguistics and Poetics'. Jakobson's most quoted and widely debated statement is his definition of the so-called projection principle. 'The poetic function projects the principle of equivalence from the axis of selection into the axis of combination' (1960, p. 39). These two axes can be represented as follows:

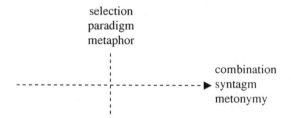

The axis of combination involves the system of rules and conventions (grammar and syntax) through which individual words are combined into larger units of meaning: the dominant, all-purpose unit of combination being the sentence, or in Jakobson's terms the syntagmatic chain. The axis of selection involves the choices made at each stage in the syntagm from the different words available for each grammatical class or type – in Jakobson's terms paradigmatic selection. For example, in order to describe the progress of a woman along the street we might use different verbs to describe the same activity:

the woman walks; the woman strolls; the woman moves; the woman strides. We can choose different verbs from the selective axis while maintaining the same syntagmatic-combinative formula (article–noun–verb).

The principle of equivalence involves the matching of the two axes; first, in terms of the rules of the syntagmatic chain ('Its woman is walk' is grammatically incorrect), and secondly, in terms of the agreed or 'equivalent' relation between the rules of the syntagm and the perceived relation between language and the prelinguistic world. If I stated that 'A tree walks' I would have satisfied the rules of the syntagm ('walks', like 'grows' or 'lives' is a verb used in its correct grammatical position), but I would have disrupted the perceived or equivalent relation between language and the prelinguistic world: trees as far as we know cannot and do not walk. This unusual and unexpected use of the selective axis is the basic principle of metaphor.

Jakobson claims that 'for poetry, metaphor – and for prose metonymy – is the line of least resistance and consequently the study of poetical tropes is directed chiefly toward metaphor' (Jakobson and Halle, 1956, pp. 95–6). This does not mean that all prosaic language is metonymic; rather that metonymy is more indicative of the logic of prose while metaphor embodies the fundamental illogic of poetry. Metonymy involves a comparison between two conditions or elements that have a pre-established connection in the empirical world. We frequently refer to elements of monarchial government in terms of 'the crown' (crown forces, crown lands, etc.); and we might refer to a person's car as 'her wheels'. Metonymy involves the substitution of one element of an object or condition for its entirety; and, as Jakobson argues, it embodies the governing principle of prosaic, non-poetic language; that language should reflect and articulate the perceived condition of the prelinguistic world. Metaphor, conversely, uses the selective axis to variously disrupt and refocus the perceived relation between language and reality. In John Donne's 'The Flea', the speaker effects a number of radical shifts from the logic of metonymy to the more adventurous illogic of metaphor:

> Mark but this flea, and mark in this,
> How little that which thou deny'st me is;
> Me it suck'd first, and now sucks thee,
> And in this flea, our two bloods mingled be;
> Confess it, this cannot be said
> A sin, or shame, or loss of maidenhead,
> > Yet this enjoys before it woo,
> > And pamper'd swells with one blood made of two,
> > And this, alas, is more than we would do.
>
> Oh stay, three lives in one flea spare,
> Where we almost, nay more than married are:
> This flea is you and I, and this
> Our marriage bed, and marriage temple is;
> Though parents grudge, and you, w'are met,
> And cloistered in these living walls of Jet.
> > Though use make thee apt to kill me,
> > Let not to this, self murder added be,
> > And sacrilege, three sins in killing three.

> Cruel and sudden, has thou since
> Purpled thy nail, in blood of innocence?
> In what could this flea guilty be,
> Except in that drop which it sucked from thee?
> Yet thou triumph'st and see'st that thou
> Find'st not thy self, nor me the weaker now;
>      'Tis true, then learn how false, fears be;
>      Just so much honour, when thou yield'st to me,
>      Will waste, as this flea's death took life from thee.

In the first stanza he combines verifiable fact (the flea has bitten both of them) with broader issues of sexual morality (a sinne, or shame, or losse of maidenhead); and in the second stanza the logic of metonymy is transformed into the persuasive anti-logic of metaphor. The literal combining of blood becomes the figurative, metaphoric image of 'three lives' and 'more than married'; the actual mixing of their physical presences (this flea is you and I) is transmuted into a compound metaphor involving their 'marriage' bed and temple, religious symbolism (*cloistered* in these living walls of jet), and the literal and figurative 'murder' of their relationship. This procedure involves a gradual shift from the axis of combination, in which words are combined according to the logical, factual meaning (the fleabite and the literal mixing of their blood) towards an extended metaphor in which the discourse is dominated by the selection of words which create new and unexpected levels of meaning.

The continuous and persistent use of metaphor in a text does not automatically define it as a poem. 'The principle of similarity underlies poetry; the metrical parallelism of lines or the phonic equivalence of rhyming words prompts the question of semantic similarity or contrast; there exist, for instance, grammatical and antigrammatical but never agrammatical rhymes' (Jakobson, 1987, p. 114). Along with their projection of the axis of selection into the axis of combination (metaphor) poems also create a continuous level of interference between poetic form (metre, rhyme, assonance and alliteration) and the practical, non-poetic registers of syntax and semantics. Consider the way in which the internal and external rhymes of 'The Flea' tend to fix our attention upon the tenor (the flea and fleabite) of the metaphor: 'this flea', 'in this', 'me is', 'Me', 'thee', 'be', 'this flea', 'and this', 'temple is', 'kill me', 'added be', 'killing three', 'guilty be', 'from thee', 'fears be', 'to me', 'from thee'. The principal themes of the speaker's argument are drawn into a network of semantic and phonetic associations – mainly 'this flea' 'is' 'thee' 'be' 'me' – that creates an almost subliminal counterpart to the metaphor. As Jakobson states, the logical meaning of the words of a poem are tied into a system of phonemic and rhythmic similarities and parallels: in this case the persuasive echoes of the rhyme scheme insinuate themselves into the rhetoric of the extended metaphor.

Jakobson describes the combined effect of metaphor and sound pattern upon the poetic function:

> Not only the message itself but also its addresser and addressee become ambiguous. ...
> The supremacy of the poetic function over the referential function does not obliterate the
> message but makes it ambiguous. The double sensed message finds correspondence in a
> split addresser, in a split addressee as well as in a split reference. (1960, p. 50)

Jakobson uses the term ambiguity differently from its application by William Empson (see above, p. 524). He does not refer only to instances of uncertain or paradoxical meaning, but rather to a more general 'split' between what happens in the poem (who is speaking to whom and with what intention or effect) and our expectation of how such transferences of meaning would be achieved in non-poetic language.

In 'The Flea' this split becomes apparent when we attempt to submit the poem to the circumstantial terms and conditions of non-poetic language. We know that it is a first-person, present tense discourse which draws upon immediate events and circumstances (the proximity of addresser and addressee and their shared experience of the fleabite) and which shows the ability of the speaker to adjust and improvise his argument according to ongoing events: he clearly responds to the woman's attempt and eventual success in crushing the flea. The split becomes evident when we recognize that the real-world conditions of spontaneity and improvisation are at odds with the baroque complexity of the text. No one could improvise a stanzaic structure which consists of three couplets, each involving an octosyllabic followed by a pentameter line, and which terminates with a triplet of one octosyllabic and two pentameter lines. Jakobson's point is that on the one hand we need to decode a poem in terms of its paraphrasible meaning (its 'referential' function – in this case a man responding verbally to a woman's silent rejections), while on the other we should recognize that its 'poetic' function is particular to the structure of the text in question and untranslatable into the terms and conditions of non-poetic discourse (in this case the addresser and addressee are effectively constructs of an unimprovised, self-consciously contrived system of metrical and rhyming patterns).

Jakobson's work incorporates the multidisciplinary strands of modern literary studies. He held that in order to understand the distinction between poetic and non-poetic discourses we must first conduct an exhaustive survey of the operations and the material constituents of language. His (and Jones's) analysis of Shakespeare's sonnet 129 (1970, reprinted in Pomorska and Rudy, 1987) reflects his consistent assertion that poems concentrate and crystallize the more diffuse, practical operations of non-poetic language: metaphor becomes the subject rather than the instrument of communication; metre, rhyme and sound pattern promote the phoneme and the syllable from the status of pragmatic bridges between sound and meaning to the means by which the sound of a poem organizes its meaning. On the one hand his working principle that literary studies needs the assistance of linguistics in order properly to understand literature goes against many of the New Critical doctrines of isolation (see above). On the other, many of the more recent Structuralist and Post-structuralist critics have condemned his work for advocating what they regard as the institutional elitism of literature as 'different' from ordinary discourse (see Culler, 1975, and Units 19 and 20).

Lévi-Strauss adapted Jakobson's work on phonology to his own studies of the habits and rituals of different tribes and cultures: just as the irreducible concept of the phoneme underpins our perceptions of the different meanings, and function of words in whatever language, so, argues Lévi-Strauss, there are similarly irreducible elements (eating, cooking, sexual intercourse) which underpin different codes of social behaviour (see Jakobson and Halle, 1956; and Lévi-Strauss, 1972).

Jacques Lacan, one of the leading post-Freudian theorists of language, literature and the unconscious has made use of Jakobson's distinction between the selective and combinative dimensions of language as a basis for his own explorations of language and the unconscious (see 'The Insistence of the Letter in the Unconscious', 1957 and Unit 22). David Lodge (1977) projects Jakobson's metonymy-metaphor model into the sphere of fictional and non-fictional prose.

For a complete survey of Jakobson's work and its relation to broader elements of literary and cultural theory see Bradford (1994).

## Formalism, Structuralism and the novel

The two Formalists who have made the most significant contributions to subsequent theories of fiction and narrative are Viktor Shklovsky and Vladimir Propp.

Shklovsky reduced fictional structures to two opposing and interactive dimensions, syuzhet and fabula. Fabula refers to the actuality and the chronological sequence of the events that make up the narrative; and syuzhet to the order, manner and style in which they are presented in the novel in question. The fabula of Dickens's *Great Expectations* involves the experiences, in and around London, from the early childhood to the adulthood of Pip. Its syuzhet involves the presentation of these events in terms of Pip's first-person account of their temporal, spatial and emotional registers.

In Dickens's novel the first-person manner of the syuzhet has the effect of personalizing the fabula; Pip's description of Miss Havisham and of his relationship with Estella is necessarily influenced by factors such as his own emotional affiliations, his stylistic habits and his singular perspective upon spatio-temporal sequences and conditions. If *Great Expectations* had an omniscient, third-person narrator we might learn more about the events that contributed to Miss Havisham's condition and we might be offered a more impartial two-dimensional perspective upon the relationship between Pip and Estella. In short, the syuzhet can effectively alter our perceptions of the fabula. Shklovsky showed a particular taste for novels which self-consciously foreground the interaction between these two elements, and his essay (1921) on Sterne's *Tristram Shandy* is frequently cited as an archetype of Formalist method. Throughout this novel the eponymous narrator maintains an interplay between his story (the fabula), the activity and conditions of telling it (syuzhet). There is a close relation between Jakobson's distinction between the poetic function (the operation and effect of poetic devices) and the referential function (what the poem is about) and Shklovsky's distinction between syuzhet (narrative devices) and fabula (the story; what the novel is about).

Shklovsky and Jakobson focus upon the ways in which poems and novels variously integrate and transform the non-literary registers of language and experience. Propp, in his *The Morphology of the Folktale* (1928), shifts our attention towards the ways in which social and behavioural structures influence and determine fictional narrative. Propp devised a grammar of the folk tale based on two concepts: the roles filled by the characters (the kidnapper as villain, the princess as the kidnapped person, the king as provider, etc.) and the functions that they perform in the plot. In a fairy-tale several characters might be involved in a single function (the king and kidnapper might be involved in villainous activities) or one character might perform a number of functions (the king might be both hero and villain). But Propp demonstrates that there is a predictable and finite number of permutations of the role–function relation. This scheme is comparable with Jakobson's division between the syntagmatic axis of language (villain, hero, helper, etc., create narrative sequences in the same way that noun, verb and adjective create syntactic units) and its paradigmatic axis (king and hero can be substituted in particular functional roles in the same way that the verbs walk, stroll or stride are substitutable in the same place in a sentence). Both models are constrained by the agreed relation between language/narrative and perceptions of the real world. The sentence 'the tree ate its dinner and then walked home' is grammatically correct, but its paraphrasible message is implausible and absurd. Similarly a folk tale in which the princess kidnaps her father, the king, in the hope of eliciting a ransom from the villain would be dismissed as absurd because it distorts the usual realm of possibilities within the social-familial network of roles and functions in the non-fictional world.

Propp's model of a predictable relation between narrative structures and the social and mythological structures of the world outside the novel became the prototype for later Structuralist analyses of fiction.

A.J. Greimas (1966 and 1970) regards narrative patterns as involving systems of consecutive ordering very similar to the syntagm, while at the same time arguing that fictional narratives reflect the deep-rooted 'grammars' of human society: *syntagmes contractuels*, formal contracts, family bonds, close relationships, institutional ties, etc.; *syntagmes performanciels*, trials, arguments, the performance of tasks, etc.; *syntagmes disjonctionnels*, physical movements, departures, arrivals, etc. Just as in the syntagmatic chain of a sentence each word and phrase is tied into an accumulative sequence which generates larger units of meaning so in a novel single incidents such as marriages, commitments to particular professions and journeys are combined to produce extended narrative structures. Tzvetan Todorov in his analysis of Boccaccio's *The Decameron* (1969) extends this parallel between syntax and narrative by reducing the latter to parts of speech (characters are nouns, their attributes adjectives and their actions verbs), propositions involving one or more of the characters (A has sex with B; D divorces Y) and sequences in which a string of propositions makes up the complete narrative structure.

Propp, Greimas and Todorov focus principally upon the fabula and less upon the syuzhet, and this raises a number of problems. In a novel such as James Joyce's *Ulysses* (1922) the activities of the characters and their socio-familial relationship with each other could, potentially, be related in the impartial third-person manner of George Eliot's *Middlemarch* (1872). The syntagmatic–narrative structures identifiable by Greimas and Todorov would remain the same, but what would be overlooked in this procedure is the effect upon the narrative of Joyce's novel of its bewilderingly diverse range of styles and techniques. The final chapter, which consists of Molly Bloom's extended interior monologue, could be analyzed in terms of her references to various contracts, tasks, trials, bonds and journeys; it could, in Greimas's terms, be reduced to a catalogue of *syntagmes contractuels, performanciels* and *disjonctionnels*. But such an approach would obscure the effect that the passage seeks to achieve. The following is Molly's account of a sexual liaison: 'the day I got him to propose to me yes first I gave him the bit of cheesecake out of my mouth and it was leapyear like now yet 16 years ago my God after that long kiss ...'. Our awareness of a paraphrasible, narrative structure is continually unsettled by the random, disorganized style of the discourse.

Joyce's novel is an extreme example of the way in which style, or syuzhet, can interfere with story, or fabula, but it reminds us that a constant emphasis upon the extended narrative as a catalogue of events and acts – an emphasis which underpins the work of Propp, Greimas and Todorov – should be balanced by our attention to more localized instances of the novel's style, an approach advocated by Shklovsky. (See Unit 11 for a discussion of Eliot's work and Unit 16 for Joyce.)

A more recent practitioner of the stylistics of fiction is Gérard Genette. In *Narrative Discourse* (1980, first published in French as *Figures III*, 1972) Genette evolves a theory of analysis known as focalization. In general terms focalization involves the specifying of a particular and consistent relationship between the presence which controls the discourse – in most novels the narrator – and the level of awareness offered to us, the readers. Open any novel at random, choose a passage, and you will become engaged in the process of focalization. Our basic linguistic competence will enable us to understand what the words mean, but when we focalize their meaning we create a mental image of the scene described: Who is speaking? How much are we being told about the events, the physical characteristics and mental operations of the characters? Is the narrator offering us an impartial, omniscient perspective upon the events? Is the narrator a participant in the narrative?

These questions cannot properly be answered in terms of such traditional distinctions as first- or third-person narrator. There can be very different types of what Genette calls the extradiagetic (third-person, apparently impartial, omniscient) narrator. Jane Austen's narrator in *Northanger Abbey* describes the principal character of the novel in its opening sentences. 'No one who had ever seen Catherine Morland in her infancy would have supposed her born to be a heroine. Her situation in life, the character of her father and mother, her own person and disposition, were all equally against her.' Throughout the novel the narrator never discloses any personal, social or familiar relation with the characters. But it is clear from this brief extract that the narrator has a knowledge of Catherine's life, experiences and mental condition that only Catherine herself or someone with whom she has had a close personal relationship would have. Throughout the novel the narrator maintains the peculiar position of someone who knows things that only Catherine herself could plausibly know yet who is able to offer us insights into the motivations and psychological make-up of other characters, of which Catherine is obviously unaware. At the beginning of Chapter IX we are offered a detailed survey of Catherine's mental condition, her movement from 'The Rooms' to Pulteney Street, her hunger, her longing for bed and the exact duration of her 'sound sleep' (9 hours). Within the next 100 words we are offered a detailed account of the habits and mental idiosyncrasies of one Mrs Allen, whom Catherine encounters next morning. The narrator is not entirely omniscient since the narrative never extends much beyond the activities and movements of Catherine; but at the same time the narrator is able to tell us things about Catherine's acquaintances (Mrs Allen for example) that Catherine could not know.

In Genette's schema, the narrator is the focalizer, in that he/she has ultimate control over what we know of each character's acts, movements and thoughts; while Catherine is the focalizing agent, in that her presence, physical and mental, operates as a centralizing focus for the focalizer's narrative design. This distinction offers us a much more accurate means of analyzing narrative than general designations such as first- and third-person narrative (see Unit 2 for discussion of these narrative positions).

At the beginning of Dickens's *Great Expectations* the first-person narrative of Pip is split between his own controlling perspective of adult, retrospective focalizer and the focusing agent of his remembered self, aged about 10. This is the account of the young Pip's experiences after having stolen the pork pie.

> The gates and dykes and banks come bursting at me through the mist, as if they cried as plainly as could be, 'A boy with Somebody else's pork pie! Stop him!'. The cattle came upon me with like suddenness staring out of their eyes and steaming out of their nostrils 'Holloa young thief!'. One black ox, with a white cravat on – who even had to my awakened conscience something of a clerical air – fixed me so obstinately with his eyes ...

It is likely that a child would have experienced a combination of guilt, fear and anxiety in these circumstances, but it is less likely that, at the time, he would have mentally transformed the non-human entities of gates and dykes into vengeful human presences or perceived the white collar on the cow as a correlative for that symbol of correctness and morality, the clergyman. The sophisticated focalizer, aged thirty-something, employs his acquired intellectual and linguistic skills to transform and organize his memories of childhood fear.

Compare this act of retrospective focalization with the opening of Joyce's third-person narrative, *A Portrait of the Artist as a Young Man* (1916):

> Once upon a time and a very good time it was there was a moocow coming down along the road and this moocow that was down along the road met a nicens little boy named baby tuckoo ...
>
> His father told him that story: his father looked at him through a glass: he had a hairy face.
>
> He was baby tuckoo. The moocow came down the road where Betty Byrne lived; she sold lemon platt.

The focalizer of this novel is an unidentified third-person narrator, but, as this passage shows, this focalizer attempts to integrate the disorganized mental and linguistic resources of the focalizing agent, the child, as the dominant feature of the narrative; whereas Dickens employs the mature intellect of the focalizer as the normative stylistic feature.

Focalization enables us to specify the relationship between the narrator and the constituent parts of the narrative. The use of dialogue and reported speech is the point at which narrational control is at its least secure or intrusive. Leech and Short

(1981) and McHale (1978) offer a typology of relations between narrative discourse, speech and conversation.

The two most frequently used methods of differentiating speech from narrative are direct and indirect speech (DS and IS).

> DS: She said, 'I'm going home'
> IS: She said she would go home.

Narrative reports of speech arts (NRSA) offer us the meaning of the character's speech while leaving us uncertain about whether the report is a verbatim account of the words used (IS) or the narrator's paraphrase of their message.

> NRSA: She spoke for five minutes. She wanted to go home.

Free direct speech is dialogue with the reporting clause ('she said') left out. Novels will sometimes include extended sequences of FDS, but these will always be enclosed by contextualizing narrative passages.

The most puzzling interaction between narrative and speech is free indirect speech (FIS) where the borders between narrative and reported speech become blurred. In *Northanger Abbey* the narrator describes Catherine's thoughts about the possible departure of Captain Tilney. 'But Captain Tilney had at present no intention of removing; he was not to be of the party to Northanger, he was to continue at Bath' (Ch. XIX). A more economical way of summing up Catherine's knowledge of the intentions of Captain Tilney would be to state that: Captain Tilney would not be going to Northanger; he would remain at Bath. The elaborate specification of his intention in the use of two subclauses following the semi-colon makes us suspect that the narrator's report of Catherine's thoughts involves in turn her memory of his particular verbal communication of those details.

This method of integrating speech acts with narrative (FIS) is taken to its most extreme in Molly Bloom's interior monologue: 'I near lost my breath yes he said I was a flower of the mountain yes so we are flowers all a womans body yes that was the one true thing he said in his life ...'. The conventions that enable us with *Northanger Abbey* to distinguish between the narrator's discourse, Catherine's thoughts and the remembered speech of Captain Tilney are here eroded. We will never be certain if this is a recollection of 'I near lost my breath. "Yes", he said'; or, 'Yes, he said I was "a flower of the mountain ..."'. Interior monologue or stream of consciousness (used also by Woolf and Faulkner – see Unit 16) can also involve free indirect thought (FIT). On the one hand, Molly's discourse is verbalized (it is in the novel, and it can be read aloud); on the other, it is a verbal facsimile of unspoken, 'interior' mental operations, where the distinctions between the remembered speech acts of other people, of the thinker herself, between immediate concerns and past incidents, coalesce as a fluid, ungrammatical sequence. (See Unit 16, p. 457, for an example of FIS in Lawrence's *Women in Love*.)

As we have seen the analysis of fiction can range from attempts to reduce the structure of complete texts to predictable and transferable 'grammars' (Propp, Greimas, and Todorov) to the decoding of localized interactions between focalizer, focalizing agent and reported speech (Genette, Leech and Short). Wayne Booth

(1961) and Seymour Chatman (1978) have devised a diagrammatic representation of how these general and local perspectives relate to each other.

$$\frac{\text{Actual}}{\text{Author}} - \frac{\text{Implied}}{\text{Author}} - \text{Narrator} - \text{Narratee} - \frac{\text{Implied}}{\text{Reader}} - \frac{\text{Actual}}{\text{Reader}}$$

Narrator and narratee are constructs of the text, fixed and determined by the conventions of the novel in question. When Jane Austen's narrator begins *Northanger Abbey* with a description of the life history, circumstances and mental condition of Catherine we as narratees begin to adapt our range of expectations to the level of interaction between focalizer and focalizing agent, teller and tale, that will be established and maintained throughout the novel. We respond to the text's own structural and stylistic conditions; to adapt Coleridge's dictum, we suspend disbelief and at the same time reassemble our world view according to the methods used to create the world of the novel.

The relationship between implied author and reader operates on a more impartial, analytical plane. Whereas narrator and narratee confine themselves to the terms and conditions of the fictional plane, implied author and reader take a step back to a point where comparisons are possible between the world constructed by the novel in question, the perceived non-fictional world at the time the novel was written and is read and other methods of relating fictional to non-fictional worlds.

Real author and reader are extended versions of their implied counterparts. You and me, as real readers of the 1990s, can supplement our experience as narratees (of the world created by novels), and as implied readers (of the structural mechanisms involved in their creation) with historical and biographical details that could have contributed to the real author's decisions in creating his or her fiction. For example, scholarly work has disclosed details regarding Emily Brontë's use of the asexual pseudonym Ellis Bell for her novel *Wuthering Heights* (see Unit 23, p. 621). The status and experience of a woman author in the mid-nineteenth century was, we know, very different from that of her male counterpart. The prospect of a woman writing about a relationship which appeared to transgress accepted levels of behaviour and decency might well have prompted Brontë both to disguise her own gender and to submerge the story of Catherine and Heathcliff in a complex multiplicity of narrators and narratees (see Units 23 and 24). The diagram's emphasis on the dynamic relation between the text and the real world reflects the influence of Structuralism upon earlier Anglo-American notions of literary autonomy (see Ransom above, p. 523).

Booth's and Chatman's six categories of interaction with the novel do not exist in isolation from each other but they do allow us to identify interpretive foci. Shklovsky and Genette are principally concerned with narrator and narratee, implied reader and implied author. Principally, but not exclusively, their work on narrative structure prompts questions as to why and how the Victorian novel and its Modernist counterpart differ so radically in terms of their respective uses of the syuzhet and methods of focalization. As Colin MacCabe (1978) and David Lodge (1981) demonstrate, the reluctance of a Victorian novelist such as George Eliot to problematize the relation between narrator and narratee and the enthusiasm of Joyce to foreground and investigate this relation can be explained properly only if we pay attention to the social, cultural and intellectual environment of each real author. Similarly Propp, Greimas and

Todorov seek to locate abstract formulae, based upon grammatical and syntactic rules, by which real authors translate their own experiences and perceptions into the fictional worlds controlled by their implied authors and disclosed by their narrators.

Culler (1975) offers a good introductory guide to Structuralism and the novel and Selden (1989) provides basic, worked examples. Toolan's *Narrative* (1989) is a useful guide to detailed linguistic analysis. Rimmon-Kenan (1983) provides an excellent guide to the style and form of narrative fiction.

## Binary oppositions

Peruse any introduction to structuralist criticism and you will find that Ferdinand de Saussure's *Course in General Linguistics* (1915) is cited as its founding moment. Saussure was a linguist and his theories provide a bridge between the study of language *per se* and the use of language as a methodological foundation for the analysis of the sign systems (linguistic and non-linguistic) that enable us to perceive and organize our social, cultural and intellectual life – the latter activity being variously known as Structuralism and Semiotics.

We have already seen how theorists such as Jakobson, Shklovsky, Propp, Greimas and Todorov made use of the systems and conventions of language to define literary writing and to indicate parallels and distinctions between literary meaning and the circulation of meaning in non-literary discourse. In what follows I shall examine what is arguably the simplest and most effective borrowing of literary Structuralism from Saussurian linguistics: binary oppositions.

Saussure's fundamental proposition is that languages are systems, constituted of signs that are arbitrary and differential: in language there are only differences without positive terms. There is no natural or necessary relationship between the sound of the word 'house' (the signifier) and the thing or idea that the word represents (the signified). The most radical and influential feature of Saussure's observation is that the system, language, which enables us to organize individual signs as larger units of meaning is, in part, a means of constructing and organizing the prelinguistic world. We use binary distinctions between signifiers to mark differences in an otherwise apparently random sequence of features and thus to give shape and cohesion to our experience of the world. The world as we know it consists partly of tangible objects and events, and our ability to perceive and articulate the relation between them is based upon fundamental oppositions between their signifiers: up/down; sky/earth; air/water; vertical/horizontal; inside/outside. These empirical, verifiable oppositions enable us to build bridges between the tangible world and its intellectual, emotional or spiritual counterpart. Mortality (which we experience) enables us to postulate its opposite, immortality (about which we can only speculate).

Binary oppositions are fundamental to the dependent relation between language and reality. Archetypal binary oppositions inform all of our perceptual and linguistic experiences: man/woman; good/bad; hot/cold; day/night; high/low; open/closed; happy/sad; old/young; rich/poor; black/white. Indeed it is the relations between different pairs of oppositions (known as homologous relations) that have sustained a number of enduring cultural and social beliefs. Feminists have successfully challenged the assumption that there is a natural or genetic relation between the following homologies:

| | |
|---|---|
| Man | Woman |
| Male | Female |
| Active | Passive |
| Intellect | Intuition |

Feminists have demonstrated that it is social custom and practice, sustained by linguistic habit, that perpetuates the false belief in these homologies as intrinsic or natural; and Saussure's formulation that systems of language can support and maintain systems of belief and perception is here clearly validated (see Unit 24).

Binary oppositions provide us with a tool for comparing the world created by the literary text with the world experienced and perceived outside the text.

The following is a diagrammatic representation of binary oppositions in Shakespeare's play *Measure for Measure*:

### A structuralist diagram for *Measure for Measure*

*Binary oppositions*

*Ideals*

| | |
|---|---|
| Order | Anarchy |
| Justice | Injustice |
| Honesty | Deceit |
| Marriage | Promiscuity |

*Rogue oppositions*

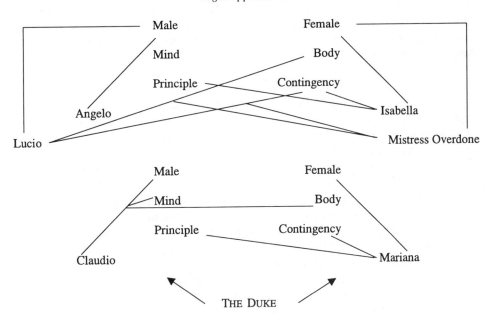

Induces conflict and mediates

The homology of 'Ideals' refers to the principles of governance, morality and social order which inform both the play and the English state of the early seventeenth century. Order, Justice and Honesty belong together and are respectively opposed to Anarchy, Injustice and Deceit. The association of Marriage with the left-hand column and Promiscuity with the right is the moral premise upon which *Measure for Measure* is based. The law, broken unwittingly by Claudio, is the thematic foundation of the play: it is argued that a slippage away from the ideals of Marriage and towards Promiscuity will promote broader shifts away from the moral and social ideals of Order, Justice and Honesty.

The homology of 'Rogue' oppositions relates to the activities of the characters in the play. The biological and social distinctions between Male and Female underpin the major events of the plot: the physical, intellectual and circumstantial relations between Isabella and Angelo, Angelo and Mariana, Lucio and Isabella, Claudio and Julia, Claudio and Isabella generate and intensify the language of the text. In each instance there is supplementary conflict between the mental and physical dimensions (Mind/Body) of the respective characters. Angelo is perceived as a man who is governed principally by strength of Mind, a figure whose intellectual and judicial character earns him the position of ruler in the absence of the Duke. However, when Isabella addresses his Mind regarding the judicial equity of her brother's death sentence, his motives and subsequent actions become governed by her physical presence and his physical desire.

Isabella is similarly presented as someone whose mental character lifts her above the state of unbridled physicality that the Duke and Angelo are attempting to control. With typical Shakespearian irony it is Lucio, the embodiment of hedonistic incaution, who persuades her to leave the nunnery and approach Angelo. And here the opposition between Principle and Contingency is drawn into the thickening homology of rogue oppositions. During Act II, scene ii, as Isabella and Angelo address the moral and judicial principles of Claudio's case, Lucio acts as a kind of theatrical prompter, almost certainly aware that her bodily demeanour will have as much effect upon Angelo as her intellect. This reduction of moral Principle to the Contingency of circumstance is maintained with the intervention of the Duke (the figure of Contingent secular authority temporarily disguised as the embodiment of religious Principle) who suggests the famous bed-trick to Isabella. The bed-trick, in which Mariana, Angelo's abandoned fiancée, pretends to be Isabella, is the archetype of Contingent practice. It may be designed to bring about a fair and equitable result, but it actually involves all of its participants in acts of deceit, falsification and disguise.

The social structure, which supposedly reflects the moral and intellectual superiority of the aristocracy over the ungoverned opportunism of the lower orders, is disrupted. Angelo and Isabella are drawn by a combination of desire and circumstances into positions which unsettle their presentation of and belief in their real identity. Angelo proves to be a far more cruel and far less efficient opportunist than Lucio and Isabella, like Mistress Overdone, is obliged, albeit symbolically and vicariously, to use her body as an instrument of trade.

Structuralist diagrams such as this are not designed to unlock a puzzle or enigma of the text. Rather, they operate as intermediaries between the text and the conditions and circumstances upon which it feeds.

The non-literary text with which the play invites comparison is the pamphlet *Basilicon Doron* (or 'Royal Gift') by James I, which offers a survey of how 'Lawes ... ordained as rules of vertuous and social living' should be interpreted and enforced. It is known also that the extreme Puritan faction in English social and religious life of that period was arguing for laws which would transform the sin of adultery into a crime punishable by death. Within such non-literary discourses the homologies of the diagram would be perceived as the immutable truths of statesmanship and religion: in Saussurean terms the configuration of the signifiers Male, Mind and Principle as opposed to Female, Body and Contingency would be regarded as an accurate representation of the natural order and its manifestation in social and intellectual life. Shakespeare's play is involved in a very different form of representation; throughout the text the words the characters use to maintain or promote beliefs, practices and ideals are continuously undermined by the disclosure, in language and action, of an almost limitless fabric of deceptions, hypocrisies and untruths. Literary texts such as *Measure for Measure* foreground the unsteady, unpredictable slide between language and actuality, signifier and signified; whereas it is the function and purpose of non-literary discourse to maintain that there is a secure unitary relationship between the perceived and idealized world and the system of signs through which we represent it. (For a consideration of New Historicist approaches to Renaissance drama, including *Measure for Measure*, see Unit 21.)

The most intriguing binary opposition of the play is also its most obvious and tangible: it is written partly in prose and partly in blank verse (see Unit 5, pp. 105–6). The latter is patently and self-consciously literary. As Jakobson has shown, verse at once releases and encloses the meaning of language: it discloses the intention and situation that prompted the words, but at the same time freezes them in a self-evidently unreal and contrived artefact. Its status bespeaks culture, refinement, taste, literacy; and, appropriately, the higher social classes of the play (and indeed of most Renaissance plays) converse and reflect primarily in blank verse. The lower orders, however, such as Lucio and Mistress Overdone, seem more comfortable with prose: where the stylistics and structure of each statement are governed more by exigency and circumstance. Note for example the amusing exchange between Claudio (aristocrat, blank verse) and Lucio (lower-class opportunist, prose) (Act I, scene ii, 133–205), in which Lucio seems rather puzzled by Claudio's habit of dressing the details of his dreadful situation in poetic language. However, just as the play disrupts the binary ideals of order and justice versus anarchy and corruption so it unsettles their linguistic distinction in verse and prose. In Act III, scene i, Claudio and Isabella debate – unhappily and inconclusively – their respective circumstances and the moral implications of Angelo's sexual bribe – in blank verse. Later in the same Act the Duke proposes to Isabella the only solution to the judicial problem, the pragmatic if morally questionable contingency of the bed-trick – in prose (see Bradford, 1993 for a survey of this passage). The tension between the two stylistic patterns of the play underpins its engagement with moral and judicial themes. Spoken prose is driven by contingency and pragmatism (both of which involve male desire and the female body) while verse tends towards the contemplation of the absolutes of principle. In the aesthetic and intellectual realms of the text the latter can claim superiority; in the realm of pragmatism and necessity, the former has seized control.

Jakobson and Halle consider the linguistic basis of binary oppositions in *Fundamentals of Language* (1956), Lévi-Strauss their use in the analysis of social and cultural structures (1972) and Culler (1975) contends that they enable us to impose order upon, rather than find it in, literary texts. Selden (1989) shows how they operate in Arthur Miller's *Death of a Salesman*.

## BIBLIOGRAPHY

Arnold, M. (1865) *Essays in Criticism*; references from reprint in *Selected Prose* (1970), Penguin, Harmondsworth.

Baldick, C. (1983) *The Social Mission of English Criticism, 1843–1932*, Clarendon Press, Oxford.

Bann, S. and Bowlt, J. (1973) *Russian Formalism*, Edinburgh University Press, Edinburgh.

Booth, W. (1961) *The Rhetoric of Fiction*, Chicago University Press, Chicago.

Bradford, R. (1993) *A Linguistic History of English Poetry*, Routledge, London.

Bradford, R. (1994) *Roman Jakobson. Life, Language, Art*, Routledge, London.

Brooks, C. (1972) *The Well Wrought Urn: Studies in the Structure of Poetry*, in *Twentieth Century Literary Criticism. A Reader*, ed. D. Lodge, Longman, London [first published 1947].

Chatman, S. (1978) *Story and Discourse*, Cornell University Press, Ithaca.

Culler, J. (1975) *Structuralist Poetics, Structuralism, Linguistics and the Study of Literature*, Routledge & Kegan Paul, London.

Eagleton, T. (1983) *Literary Theory. An Introduction*, Blackwell, Oxford.

Eco, U. (1976) *A Theory of Semiotics*, Indiana University Press, Bloomington.

Eliot, T.S. (1972) 'The Metaphysical Poets', in *Oxford Anthology of English Literature*, ed. F. Kermode, J. Hollander *et al.*, Oxford University Press, London [first published 1921].

Erlich, V. (1955) *Russian Formalism: History-Doctrine*, Mouton, The Hague.

Fekete, J. (1977) *The Critical Twilight: Explorations in the Ideology of Anglo-American Literary Theory from Eliot to McLuhan*, Routledge & Kegan Paul, London.

Genette, G. (1980) *Narrative Discourse*, Cornell University Press, Ithaca (first published in French as *Figures III* (1972), Seuil, Paris).

Greimas, A.J. (1966) *Sémantique Structurale*, Larousse, Paris.

Greimas, A.J. (1970) *Du Sens*, Seuil, Paris.

Hawkes, T. (1977) *Structuralism and Semiotics*, Methuen, London.

Jakobson, R. (1960) 'Closing Statement, Linguistics and Poetics', in *Style in Language*, ed. T. Sebeok, MIT Press, Cambridge, Mass. References from reprint in Lodge (1988).

Jakobson, R. (1987) *Language in Literature*, ed. K. Pomorska and S. Rudy, Harvard University Press, Cambridge, Mass.

Jakobson, R. and Halle, M. (1956) *Fundamentals of Language*, Mouton, The Hague.

Jefferson, A. and Robey, D. (eds) (1982) *Modern Literary Theory. A Comparative Introduction*, Batsford, London.

Lacan, J. (1988) 'The Insistence of the Letter in the Unconscious', in *Modern Criticism and Theory. A Reader*, ed. Lodge, Longman, London [first published 1957].

Lane, M. (1970) (ed.) *Structuralism: A Reader*, Cape, London.

Leavis, F.R. (1936) *Revaluation: Tradition and Development in English Poetry*, Chatto & Windus, London.

Leavis, F.R. (1948) *The Great Tradition*, Chatto & Windus, London.

Leavis, F.R. (1952) *The Common Pursuit*, Chatto & Windus, London. References from Lodge (1972, p. 623).

Leech, G. and Short, M. (1981) *Style in Fiction*, Longman, London.

Lemon, L. and Reis, M. (eds) (1965) *Russian Formalist Criticism: Four Essays*, University of Nebraska Press, Lincoln.

Lentricchia, F. (1980) *After the New Criticism*, Athlone Press, London.

Lévi-Strauss, C. (1972) *Structural Anthropology*, Penguin, London [*Anthropologie Structurale*, 1958, Plon, Paris].

Lodge, D. (ed.) (1972) *Twentieth Century Literary Criticism. A Reader*, Longman, London.

Lodge, D. (1977) *The Modes of Modern Writing: Metaphor, Metonymy and the Typology of Modern Literature*, Edward Arnold, London.

Lodge, D. (1981) *Working With Structuralism*, Routledge & Kegan Paul, London.

Lodge, D. (ed.) (1988) *Modern Criticism and Theory. A Reader*, Longman, London.

MacCabe, C. (1978) *James Joyce and the Revolution of the Word*, Routledge & Kegan Paul, London.

McHale, B. (1978) 'Free Indirect Discourse: A Survey of Recent Accounts', *Poetics and Theory of Literature*, no. 3, pp. 249–87.

Pomorska, K. and Rudy, S. (eds) (1987) *Language in Literature*, Harvard University Press, Cambridge, Mass.

Propp, V. (1968) *The Morphology of the Folktale*, English trans., University of Texas Press, Austin [first published 1928].

Ransom, J.C. (1937) 'Criticism Inc.', first published in *Virginia Quarterly Review*; reference from reprint in Lodge (1972).

Richards, I.A. (1924) *Principles of Literary Criticism*, Kegan Paul, London; references from 1966 edn.

Richards, I.A. (1929) *Practical Criticism*, Kegan Paul, London; references from 1964 edn.

Rimmon-Kenan, S. (1983) *Narrative Fiction: Contemporary Poetics*, Routledge, London.

Robey, D. (ed.) (1973) *Structuralism. An Introduction*, Oxford University Press, Oxford.

Saussure, F. de (1974) *Course in General Linguistics*, Fontana, London [*Cours de Linguistique Générale*, 1915].

Selden, R. (1989) *Practising Theory and Reading Literature. An Introduction*, Harvester Wheatsheaf, Hemel Hempstead.

Shklovsky, V. (1965) 'Sterne's *Tristram Shandy*: Stylistic Commentary' in *Russian Formalist Criticism: Four Essays*, ed. L. Lemon and M. Reis, University of Nebraska Press, Lincoln [first published 1921].

Steiner, P. (1984) *Russian Formalism. A Metapoetics*, Cornell University Press, Ithaca.

Stewart, J.L. (1965) *The Burden of Time: The Fugitives and the Agrarians*, Princeton University Press, Princeton.

Todorov, T. (1969) *Grammaire du Decameron*, Mouton, The Hague.

Toolan, M. (1989) *Narrative. A Critical Linguistic Introduction*, Routledge, London.

Wimsatt, W.K. (1954) *The Verbal Icon*, University of Kentucky Press, Lexington.

# UNIT 19

# Poststructuralism and deconstruction

*Mark Currie*

Poststructuralism and deconstruction transformed literary criticism in the 1970s and 1980s into something very different from the earlier practices of new criticism, formalism and structuralism. In these two decades literary criticism acquired a new complexity that many have seen in a negative light, an often jargonesque terminology, and an attitude of apparent self-importance at the expense of literature. Under the influence of poststructuralist ideas about language, literary texts were no longer seen as objects in their own right, with inherent form and content, but as things that could be constructed by other discourses in an almost infinite number of ways. Deconstructions were acts of criticism which did not really respect the idea of a text as something with objective properties, and seemed more interested in the method employed by a critical discourse to represent a literary text. The reading had become more important than the thing read.

Looking back this does not seem like a perverse or surprising change in emphasis. The ascending importance of readings and interpretations can be seen as part of a larger movement in criticism and literature: the decline of realism. There are two preliminary ways in which the ascent of reading can be linked to the decline of realism in literature. First, the non-realist literary text tends to produce much more ambiguous and multiple meanings than those that are rooted in the faithful representation of reality: they are open to and provocative of different interpretations and readings so that the burden of sense-making lies as much in the critic's construal of the text as in the literary text's construal of the world. Secondly, the decline of realism can be seen not so much as a turn away from realism by writers who favour non-realistic modes but as a process of questioning the viability of realism as a concept. Non-realist writing, new forms of realism and certain kinds of criticism have conspired to unsettle the concept of realistic literature by seeing it as a kind of reading – one among many. To view realistic literature as a kind of reading is to emphasize that reality is not prior to language and interpretation but a product of it, as well as to massively extend the scope of the term reading.

In the early twentieth century these two tendencies, of turning away from realistic modes and of unsettling the concept of realism, were gathering a momentum in literature and criticism, establishing the conditions and raising the questions that would result in the literary critical fashion for deconstruction in the

1970s and 1980s. This was a process of growing doubt about the ability of language to refer to a pre-existing reality. The modernist novel drew much of its experimental energy from the rejection of realistic conventions established in the eighteenth and nineteenth centuries and strongly endorsed the view of language as a condition rather than a reflection of experience. The Imagist and Vorticist poets of the modernist period developed a dense and opaque language that asserted the absolute inseparability of the form and content of a poetic text, thus rejecting the basis of realistic representation. One need only think of Joyce's collages of different styles and perspectives in *Ulysses* or the rigorous foregrounding of language itself in Pound's Cantos to glimpse the modernist origins of a poststructuralist sense of the importance of language in reading and constructing experience (see Units 16 and 17.

The decline of realism has been equally in evidence outside of literature, in Saussurean linguistics, and in various other formalist camps of literary criticism such as American new criticism and Russian formalism which doubted the validity of the representational model of language. Saussure aside, this doubt often began in relation to the problem of the realist novel and its apparent claim that language could evoke the outside world in a transparent and unproblematic way. New critics such as T.S. Eliot and the Russian formalist Viktor Shklovsky were followed by a wave of critics in the middle of the century, such as Northrop Frye, Tzvetan Todorov, A.H. Greimas, Gérard Genette, Roman Jakobson and Roland Barthes, who broadly contended that realism was just a complex and collective way of agreeing what reality was like – a consensual illusion. Realism came to be seen as a kind of sham, as a discourse in which language effaced itself and so disguised its role in projecting shape and form onto the world (see Unit 18).

This was also the claim of Saussure in his *Course in General Linguistics* (1972), where words are seen as capable of reference only because they project their system of differences onto the non-linguistic world. Like literary realism then, language in general is a shared system we use to make sense of the world, but which we assume to be a reliable and transparent index, or reflection, of a pre-existing world. This is one of the most influential propositions of the century: that our knowledge of the world is given its shape and structure by language which we then assume is the objective shape and structure of the world. Its influence on post-structuralist thought is profound. It places us all in what Frederic Jameson called a kind of prison-house of language (Jameson, 1972). It means that everything is like a linguistic text, even if we assume otherwise. Above all, it raises a problem which is distinctly poststructuralist: that if language doesn't so much refer to a pre-existing world as project its structure onto it, what about language which is used to refer to other language (metalanguage), like criticism? Reference to a literary text, after all, is not different from reference to anything else, so that critical language, like language in general, invents or constructs its objects (literary texts) even while it assumes that it is being objective.

This is a good way of defining the difference between structuralism and poststructuralism. Structuralism was a kind of science and like most sciences it assumed that it could tell the truth about its objects. It assumed that its own language was transparent and unproblematic, even when it was describing the way that language other than its own had an active role in constructing the things that it referred to and meant. Poststructuralism was really a way of turning structuralism's basic attitude to language back on itself, so that 'metalingual' discourses like linguistics and criticism are seen in the same light as discourses which claim to refer to the world: as dishonest claims to transparent objectivity.

Poststructuralist terminology for this problem is confusingly varied. As a philosophical issue, it is often expressed in terms of subject and object relations. The terminology of subject and object is a kind of dualism which sees knowledge, analysis and meaning as processes based on the opposition of a knowing subject and an object taken possession of in the act of knowing. Traditionally, language is perceived as a mediation in these processes. The poststructuralist claim, however, is that the role of language is much more fundamental than that of mere mediator: that the subject and object are in a sense simply facets of language, or that it is impossible to think about subject/object relations except as a problem thrown up by language. Poststructuralism sought to displace the dualism of subject and object with a monism in which a knowing mind and an object of knowledge were both inextricably determined by the structures of language.

The opposition of subject and object underlies much of the notorious jargon in poststructuralist writing. When critics and linguists talk about the *transparency* or *opacity* of language, the former term suggests the possibility that a subject can know an object by looking through language as one looks through a window, whereas the latter suggests either that the attention is arrested by language (as for example in poetry: see Unit 1, p, 3–5), or that we should realize that when we think we are looking through a window at objects we are in fact looking at language. Optical metaphors like this are particularly common in criticism, where poststructuralism is often seen as a tendency away from the *reflection* model of language and literature towards a *production* model: that a realistic novel, for example, does not reflect reality but produces a sense of transparency or faithful reflection by adhering to conventions of language use, degree of detail and linear sequence which are collectively deemed realistic. There is a sense here of language acting as a kind of shared subjectivity, where the *structure* of experience is seen not as objective properties of the real world but as an act of collective *construction*. The whole idea of seeing or reflecting a real world objectively is challenged by poststructuralist theory, which tends to favour the notions of opacity, production and construction.

There is a line of argument in poststructuralism that there is something unhealthy and dishonest in language use which assumes its own transparency, or effaces its own language. Paul de Man saw it as a kind of ideology based on the 'confusion of linguistic with natural reality, of reference with phenomenalism' (de Man, 1986, p. 11); Roland Barthes used the term 'the unhealthy signifier' for language which did not draw attention to itself and its role in constructing the object being represented. There are two strong strains of poststructuralism aimed against the unhealthy signifier. The first is an attempt in poststructuralist discourse itself to make its own language opaque, self-conscious, often playful and poetic so as to avoid the structuralist problem of assuming the transparency of one's own language when denying it to others. Much of the difficulty of reading poststructuralist philosophers and critics can be attributed to a strategy of trying to highlight language itself as the lens through which all objects are perceived and discussed. This strategy is often referred to as *reflexivity* or *self-consciousness*, and seen as a kind of self-subversion in the sense that any illusion of transparency to an object is quickly undermined. The strategy is often borrowed from literature, where a realistic illusion can be broken by a poetic quality in language or by some self-commentary which reveals the process of construction at work, or from philosophy – from Nietzsche's very literary way of expressing a philosophical idea, or from Heidegger's concept of *erasure*, in which a word is used and withdrawn in the same breath. The second strain is a critical preoccupation with those discourses seen as most unhealthy, where language is at its most self-effacing. Just as poststructuralism has tried to show that the realist novel is not as transparent to the world as it seems, so too it has turned its attention to non-literary discourses in which language tries to pass itself off as a transparent material, in areas such as history and science.

A confusing aspect of deconstruction is that it has devoted so much of its energy towards deconstructing metalingual discourses: texts which are about language itself rather than about some apparently extra-linguistic world. It is easy enough to accept the idea that objects are always constructed by language, but confusing when the object is language – that is, when language is an object which is itself constructed by language. One reason for the deconstructive obsession with metalingual discourses might be that they are, in a sense, the very model of the world that poststructuralists are advancing. Poststructuralism does not recognize the difference between a metalingual text and a realist one because, if everything is constructed by language, if everything is interpretation, any text will in a sense be a text about language. It is very common to read deconstructions which see even the most realist text as a metalingual text. A realist novel can often be difficult to recognize in a deconstructive reading because the novel is treated as if it were some kind of obscure linguistic tract on the nature of language. This is a common theme in deconstruction – the idea that a novel is somehow always about itself, that it narrates its own constitution, or is always self-referential even when it seems to be referring to something other than itself. This idea can be illustrated best by looking at deconstructions of manifestly metalingual texts in linguistics and literary criticism before looking at deconstructions of literary works themselves.

Perhaps the most common misunderstanding of deconstruction is that it is, at root, a theory of language. Deconstruction certainly engages with many issues in language theory and philosophy, but there is no systematic account of what language is or how it works. There are many observations made by structuralist linguists about the nature of language which poststructuralists seem to accept and modify, and it is worth exploring some of these as an approach to the question of poststructuralism's relation to structuralism, and to the role that language theory plays in deconstructive reading in general. The obvious place to start is in Saussure's concept of the sign. Saussure's basic insights about the nature of a linguistic sign were (a) that it is a two-sided entity which consists of a signifier (sound image) and a signified (a concept to which it refers), not a name and a thing; (b) that the relationship between the signifier and signified is arbitrary, 'united in the brain by an associative bond'; and (c) that the sign has no substantive content but generates meaning through the system in which it is differentiated from all other signs. Taken together, these insights underlie Saussure's two most cited statements about language: that 'language is a form and not a substance' and that 'in language there are only differences without positive terms'. This emphasis on the relational identity of the sign, the idea that it does not have any content other than its relationship with other signs in the language system, is wholly accepted by poststructuralists. Indeed the only real problem with this account of the sign is that it does not go far enough in pursuit of its own insight.

Derrida, for example, claims that we should not think of the sign as a two-sided entity at all (Derrida, 1976). The whole idea of the sign as a signifier and a signified is, according to Derrida, a supposition inherited from the old, dualist idea of representation which can separate the 'thing itself' from the way that it is represented. For Derrida these things cannot be separated in the way that the binary concept of the sign suggests. When we encounter language we encounter only the signifier. When we try to explain the meaning of the signifier we can do so only with reference to other signifiers. In short, there is no such thing as a signified. For Derrida, the binary concept of a sign is an excellent example of the way that analysis unwittingly projects massive philosophical assumptions onto the things that it analyzes. In his early work Derrida often referred to these philosophical assumptions as 'the metaphysics of presence' – a whole philosophical paradigm based on what he calls a 'desire for presence'. The desire for presence is usually also a desire to get back to the origin of something – that genetic turn of mind that guides so much historical explanation. In the case of the sign, Derrida sees the signified as a notional origin of the sign, where the signifier is a second-order representation of that signified. It is a desire for the presence of meaning in a sign, when in fact we can only ever encounter signifiers and their relations with each other. The signified is, in Derrida's terminology, endlessly deferred, in the sense that we cannot point to what it is, to its presence, except as part of a signifying structure or as part of the language system:

> There is no phenomenality reducing the sign or the representer so that the thing signified may be allowed to glow finally in the liminosity of its own presence. The thing itself is always already a representamen shielded from the simplicity of intuitive evidence. The representamen functions only by giving rise to an interpretant that itself becomes a sign and so on to infinity. The self-identity of the signified conceals itself unceasingly and is always on the move. The property of the representamen is to be itself and another, to be produced as a structure of reference, to be separated from itself. (Derrida, 1976, p. 49)

This qualification of Saussure's concept of the sign is characteristically poststructuralist in the sense that it insists on the fact that the signified, the 'thing itself' or the conceptual content of the sign, has no independent existence at all, so that the distinction between signifier and signified is meaningless. It is a distinction with an in-built dualism, or a vestige of traditional theories of representation, which poststructuralism would like to replace with a more thorough monism.

Just as Saussure's insights about the relational identity of the sign lead him to a theory of *difference* as the principle by which signs generate meaning, so too

Derrida's modified account of the sign leads him to a modified account of difference. In the last quotation, Derrida states that the signified is 'always on the move'. This idea comes out of an objection to Saussure's decision to make his study of language synchronic, or frozen in time. The synchronic approach is quite effective in pointing to one of the ways in which the signified is not present in language – in the sense that the only way to explain the meaning of a sign is to refer to other signs which it is not: the idea that the meaning of a word is not really within it, but is also absent or spread across the other words in the language system on which the meaning of a sign depends. Terry Eagleton illustrates this principle with the idea of a dictionary (Eagleton, 1983). The dictionary definition of a word is stated by other words, so that if we did not know the meanings of the words used by the definition, we would have to look them up in turn. In each case, the definitions we would find would themselves be constituted by words which we would have to look up, and so on. We would end up in a labyrinth of words all making references to each other by way of explanation. However far we explored, we would encounter only signifiers; the signified would never be present. But for Derrida, there are other ways in which the signified is never present which a synchronic account of language cannot accommodate.

The term 'presence', which is so crucial in Derrida's writing, has both a temporal and spatial sense. An object can be spatially present, as opposed to absent, in the way that a student is spatially present or absent in a classroom, but also temporally present or absent in the sense of currency: present as opposed to past or future. Derrida wants to modify the structuralist notion of *difference* to be able to account for the temporal dimension of a sign, or the idea that a sign might bear the trace of the past and the future. A sign must be repeatable to have its meaning: we must be able to repeat words in the knowledge that they will mean the same thing, or preserve their differential relations with other words. Similarly, a word is usually combined with other words in a sequence, or sentence, so that any explanation of the word's meaning will have to take into account its context in the sequence, where it is modified and specified by the other words which surround it. The sign therefore bears the trace of those other words which precede and follow it in a sentence, so that its meaning is not self-contained or present. The meaning of a word is always on the move because it is always somewhere else – several other places at once – and can never be made to stand still. Derrida names this motion, this deferral of the signified meaning of a word, *différance*. *Différance* clearly invokes Saussure's spatial principle of *difference* but adds a time dimension – *différance* being a pun in French which combines the meanings of differ and defer, or put off until later. Meaning is not present in a sign then, both in the Saussurean sense that it depends on other words in the language system, but also in the sense that it is always determined or structured by temporal absences like prior uses or other words in a sentence. This is what is meant when poststructuralists say that meaning is endlessly deferred from signifier to signifier.

The term *différance* carries one other important implication which defines Derrida's qualification of structuralist theory. *Différance* is a pun which, in French, and like many other puns, cannot be heard. Because the pronunciation of *différence* and *différance* are the same, it is only in writing that it can really be observed as a pun. The joke here is that this gives writing an extra power which speech does not have, and therefore implicitly rejects Saussure's decision in *Course in General Linguistics* to exclude writing from the study. The joke fits in with a constant theme in Derrida's work, argued at length in *Of Grammatology*, that speech enjoys a privileged status in relation to writing because it is perceived as being closer to the mind than writing. This is another kind of presence that Derrida's account of language rejects: the idea that language is under the control of the mind which produces it, or that it contains within it the presence of a signifying intention. The problem with writing in this respect is that it is seen as a way of allowing language to operate in the absence of the signifying intention – on sheets of paper, rather than coming out of the head which contains the mind which produced it. It may already be apparent that Derrida understands language and meaning as too complex and difficult to pin down to be understood as the successful communication of intended meanings to a listener. Against Saussure's focus on speech, Derrida often refers to language as 'writing' because it leaves out the supposition that the signifying intention is present in language. Writing, for Derrida, is the name of two absences: the absence of the referent and the absence of the signifying intention (Derrida, 1976). His account of language as writing therefore refuses to underpin meaning in either of these ways.

This elevation of the term *writing* in Derrida's work points to an important modification that poststructuralists have made to structuralist theory. Structuralist linguistics placed an enormous importance on the idea of the binary opposition as the basic meaning-generating unit in language: that a word often depends on its antonym, or opposite, as the basis of its intelligibility. Poststructuralists generally accept this, but claim that an opposition is not just an innocent structural feature of the language system. Instead, an opposition is usually a hierarchy, where one of the terms is primary and the other secondary, or one is seen as good and the other evil. One of the obsessions of deconstruction is with uncovering these hierarchies as they operate in arguments, analyzes and texts of all kinds. In this case, Derrida takes the opposition of speech and writing and shows that the privilege given to speech over writing, the idea that writing is a derivative and secondary form of language, is based on a metaphysical prejudice that speech is prior because of its proximity to the mind. Deconstruction is particularly interested in binary hierarchies of this kind because they are places where values are subtly projected onto an object of study while presenting themselves as neutral analytical distinctions. What Derrida does when he elevates the term writing to name all language is characteristically deconstructive. First, he challenges the distinction by arguing that speech is only distinguishable from writing on the basis of a presupposed privilege attributed to speech; secondly, he inverts the hierarchy between the two terms so that the secondary term is given priority, and in so doing, inverts the hidden value system that underlies the hierarchy. In this case, then, to deconstruct means to strip a text down to its most basic assumptions, to locate these assumptions in a hierarchical opposition, and to reverse this hierarchy as a strategic rejection of its inherited presuppositions.

Summaries like this one make deconstruction sound as if it is a theory of language, which it is not. It would not even be accurate to say that deconstruction is a way of reading which is based on linguistic premises. What Derrida does when he reads Saussure's text is an attempt to expose the ways that a text which is apparently transparent to its object – in this case language – actually construes its object on behalf of a philosophical paradigm. Thus, the oppositions which make Saussure's study of language possible, such as speech/writing, synchrony/diachrony and signifier/signified are far from innocent, and effectively determine and shape the object of study in advance: by excluding writing he implies the presence of a signifying intention, by excluding the temporal dimension of presence he reduces the complexity of language to a stable structure, and by distinguishing between signifier and signified he imports a dualistic concept of the relationship between a meaning and its representation.

But how did this kind of reading come to have an impact on literary studies? There are two basic approaches to this question. On one hand, there are consequences for literary studies that come out of the specific arguments about Saussure and structuralism which Derrida raises, mostly in *Of Grammatology*; and on the other, there are more general consequences which derive from the method of reading a text which is exemplified by Derrida's reading of Saussure. When Derrida published *De la grammatologie* in 1967, literary studies was very firmly, and particularly in France, under the influence of structuralist methods and Saussurean ideas. Derrida's writings represented a challenge to the authority of Saussurean linguistics, to the synchronic approach of literary structuralism, and to the idea of language and literature as static structures. Perhaps more importantly, Derrida's work was following through a line of thought that was emerging in literary structuralism which questioned the scientific authority of structuralism. The loss of confidence in science within structuralism would be complicated to chart. Perhaps it would suffice to point to Roman Jakobson's influential article 'Closing Statement', published in 1960, in which he calls for literary studies to be internalized within the field of general linguistics: 'Poetics deals primarily with problems of verbal structure.... Since linguistics is the global science of verbal structure, poetics may be regarded as an integral part of linguistics.' By the end of the decade, accounts of literary structuralism were no longer evangelizing criticism on behalf of a scientific authority: 'The unity of a science is not constituted by the uniqueness of its object.... It is hardly necessary to repeat that the method creates the object, that the object of a science is not given in nature but represents the result of an elaboration.' This reminder, written by Tzvetan Todorov in 1968, challenges Jakobson's call for a consensual science of literature with the more poststructuralist idea that different questions about an object will construct it in different ways. Derrida's work on Saussure, by exposing values that a scientific linguistics projects onto its object of study, by shaking the linguistic premises of structuralism, helped to break the authority of the scientific paradigm.

On a more general level, Derrida's way of reading suggested several new directions. The first is the idea of an immanent critique, a reading which sets a text against itself, or which seeks to show that a text undercuts its own positions. When

Derrida follows the 'tension of gesture and statement' in Saussure he suggests that the text somehow undermines its own claims about language, yet he also insists that this is not a weakness in the text, but a strength. The text is seen to have a kind of blind spot in which its most profound insights about language and its own attempts to systematize language are located. This is a very important principle for deconstruction because it values the ability of a text to yield meanings which are not intentional and which are often contradictions of the manifest purpose of the discourse. The deconstruction of literary texts is often a way of reading against the grain of the text, for contradictory meanings, gaps and exclusions which constitute the most profound insights that text has to offer. Reading against the grain like this can be seen as a perverse refusal to cooperate with the text, but deconstructionists would see this as a necessary perspective on its values. Deconstructionists argue that the critic is not just perversely seeking to subvert the text, but that the text is self-subverting, self-deconstructing. Criticism before deconstruction tends to look for textual qualities such as consistency, unity, development and coherence, ignoring evidence which disrupts the impression. In a sense deconstruction gets its own authority from the idea that qualities such as unity and coherence are critical structures of exclusion – that they exclude aspects of a text in order to construe it as a unity – and therefore that a deconstruction shows a greater respect for the complexity of a text without trying to smooth it over and present it as an unproblematic entity, or the vehicle of a single meaning. The idea of a self-deconstructing text is potentially misleading in that it seems to claim that a text is objectively contradictory and self-subverting, and that no intervention is required from a critic for deconstruction to occur. But this kind of objective authority is, as we have seen, unavailable to the poststructuralist critic. The idea of self-deconstruction has to be taken with a pinch of salt, but it does illustrate an important principle of many deconstructive readings: that the critic is a close reader who unravels the text from within, or that deconstruction is a process at work in literary texts, and in culture, whether we notice it or not.

One reason that the idea of self-deconstruction is unsatisfactory is that readings of this kind which locate blind spots and contradictions in a literary text very often do so in terms which are quite alien to the language of the text itself. Barbara Johnson and Paul de Man are critics who illustrate this point: both characteristically translate the binary hierarchies of literary texts into metalingual terms, so that moments of irresolvable doubt (*aporias*) and self-subversion are construed as insights into the nature of language rather than mere self-contradictions. Johnson's celebrated analysis of Melville's *Billy Budd* (Johnson, 1980), for example, involves seeing the contrasting characters of Billy and Claggart as representatives of different models of language and interpretation, literal and ironic. (Culler's discussion of this reading (Culler, 1983, pp. 235–42) offers an excellent account.) This translation of the story into metalingual terms allows Johnson to see the text as an elaborate allegory of its own possible readings, where these readings are seen as part of the text itself rather than anything that the critic has brought to it. Paul de Man's reading of Proust's *A la recherche du temps perdu* (de Man, 1979) is similar, translating a passage in which Marcel reflects upon the virtues of reading into a series of statements 'claiming the priority of metaphor in a binary system that opposes metaphor to metonymy', statements which are later subverted by aspects of Proust's text which disrupt the opposition of metaphor and metonymy. In the case of Proust there is clearly some self-analysis taking place in the text in Marcel's contemplation of the act of reading, though not enough to justify de Man's transformation of the text into such outright metalingual terms as self-deconstruction. In both cases there is a dynamic at work between the idea of self-deconstruction and the idea of critical intervention, the confusion of which seems to militate against seeing criticism as subject and literary text as object.

Because deconstruction operates under the conviction that a literary text has no identity of its own, that its identity is constructed by reading, interpretation and its representation by criticism, the search for presuppositions, hierarchical oppositions, contradiction and structures of exclusion has been largely conducted in relation to critical and theoretical texts rather than in literary texts themselves. There is no doubt that the impact of deconstruction in literary studies has been more profound in theoretical discussions on the nature of literature and criticism than it has been in its reading of literary texts. In this way it is like literary structuralism, which was always accused of being a fascinating theory of meaning while having very little of interest to say about individual works of literature. It is true that a deconstruction of a literary text often reads its text through some philosophical or critical question which it seems more interested in than the text itself. A definition of literary deconstruction then faces the initial problem that deconstruction does not really believe that literature exists at all in its own right. Another difficulty is that deconstruction is not an abstractable system in the way that structuralism was. Deconstruction is not a method, or a theory which can be applied to any text, or imposed on it like a system. A deconstruction in a sense always emerges from within the rhetoric of a specific text, and not something which is imposed from the outside, from a critical distance. Indeed the distinctions between literary and critical acts, or between the theory and practice of reading, are placed in question by deconstruction, or left behind along with the more general model of subject and object relations to which they belong. Thus although the term deconstruction is taken from his work, Derrida has had to campaign against the way the term has been used by other critics whenever it seems to refurbish the model of subject and object relations as the basis of a critical engagement with a literary text. One example of this campaign is that Derrida has regularly insisted on the plural form of the term – deconstructions – to preserve the specificity of each reading and avoid the implication of some common denominator between readings which would make deconstruction a unified or consensual project which can be methodically applied to texts.

With these cautions in mind, we can turn to the question of how a literary critic can employ Derrida's critique of Saussure and his more general reading strategies in the analysis of a literary text. A good example is J. Hillis Miller's analysis of Joseph Conrad's *Heart of Darkness* (Miller, 1989). Conrad's story is modelled· on a conventional 'grail quest', or a story in which the pursuit of a divine object gives the narrative its forward movement and its promise of some kind of ultimate revelation. In such a story, the quest for the grail becomes a quest for the meaning of the story, where the discovery of the grail is the event which gives the whole narrative its significance. In *Heart of Darkness*, the journey undertaken by Marlow towards Kurtz's inner station in the Congolese jungle is seen in just such terms, as the journey to some revelation and towards the meaning of the narrative. The starting-point of Miller's analysis is that this kind of journey to revelation is the structure of a parable, in which a reader reaches some obvious and detachable moral at the end of the narrative such as 'crime doesn't pay' or 'honesty is the best policy'. What then interests him is the description that Conrad's external narrator gives of Marlow's method of story-telling:

> The yarns of seamen have a direct simplicity, the whole meaning of which lies within the shell of a cracked nut. But Marlow was not typical (if his propensity to spin yarns be excepted), and to him the meaning of an episode was not inside like a kernel but outside, enveloping the tale which brought it out only as a glow brings out a haze, in the likeness of one of these misty halos that sometimes are made visible by the special illumination of moonshine. (Conrad, 1973, p. 8)

Miller finds in this commentary a theme closely related to Derrida's critique of the Saussurean sign, that the meaning of a sign is not really within it at all, but that it lies outside it in the structure to which it belongs. For Miller, a traditional parable, like the traditional yarns of seamen, advances a straightforward model of the relation of a tale to its meaning, where the story itself is 'the inedible shell which must be removed and discarded so the meaning of the story may be assimilated' (Miller, 1989, pp. 211–12). Marlow's story, however, does not see meaning in this way, on this model of the story as a shell within which its meaning is contained like a kernel. The darkness which lies at the heart of Conrad's tale is also something which envelops it, and which is metaphorically represented by the dark atmospheric conditions of Marlow's journey and by the dark clouds which hang above the Thames as Marlow narrates. The quest for meaning in Conrad's tale is a grailless quest in the sense that when we reach Kurtz all is not revealed – the meaning that we expect to discover at the heart of the narrative, the nature of the heart of darkness, the detachable moral towards which we think we are proceeding, remains obscure. At the climax of the novel, in Kurtz's dying words 'The horror! The horror!', the expectation of revelation is dashed and we are left looking only at words the meaning of which is, at best, left suspended, suggestively spread across the tale and its images of the darkness which envelop Marlow's quest.

The Derridean themes are clear in this reading. The grailless quest for meaning in *Heart of Darkness* is the quest for presence of meaning in a sign – a quest which never comes to rest, or which never finds its grail in some kernel content. For Derrida, the desire for presence is a desire to escape from language as pure exteriority and identify an inner meaning, to reach beyond the signifier to the signified, or to find in the container a contained meaning. Thus, Derrida saw writing, which is traditionally conceived as the exterior container of meaning, as the condition of all language, or as the prison house from which no escape is possible, and indeed Conrad's text seems to advance the same model. To illustrate this, Miller points to the failure of Marlow's narrative not only to reveal its meaning through

Kurtz, but also to support ideas of language which assume the presence of a signified content, such as the idea of communication or of reference to an outside world. Marlow's narrative regularly falters in moments of fear that the narrative cannot convey his experience, and at such moments both the referential and the communicative models of language are explicitly questioned:

> He was just a word for me. I did not see the man in the name any more than you do. Do you see him? Do you see the story? Do you see anything? It seems to me I am trying to tell you a dream – making a vain attempt because no relation of a dream can convey the dream sensation... No, it is impossible; it is impossible to convey the life-sensation of any given epoch of one's existence – that which makes its truth, its meaning – its subtle and penetrating essence. (Conrad, 1973, p. 39)

Both Marlow and the reader are stuck in the exteriority of language, and in the impossibility of expression. We cannot see Marlow, or experience Kurtz directly any more than Marlow can penetrate the meaning of Kurtz's final words, because ultimately our experience as readers is of written words and exterior signifiers. In this way, any assumptions of the transparency of language are undermined by such reminders of its inescapable opacity.

Even in this skeletal account of Miller's essay it is probably clear that *Heart of Darkness* is a particularly cooperative example of a narrative for a poststructuralist, in that it seems itself to have a deconstructive sensibility. (See Unit 16, pp. 447–50, for a more conventional reading of *Heart of Darkness*.) But what happens when a text does not indulge so explicitly in self-commentary, does not so obviously doubt the ability of language to communicate, or does not so conveniently thematize language and narrative in terms of its inside and outside? Much of Miller's own work on less cooperative novels of the nineteenth century (e.g. Miller, 1982) would serve as an answer to this question. Another interesting case is Paul de Man, whose readings often find these Derridean thematics in the most unlikely places. Whereas Miller finds a deconstructive logic in Conrad's narrative which upsets the traditional scheme of the inside and outside of language, there is a sense in which de Man brings this logic with him to the reading of a text. In the introduction to *Allegories of Reading*, for example, de Man begins from the same problem: 'The recurrent debate opposing intrinsic and extrinsic criticism stands under the aegis of an inside/outside metaphor which is never being seriously questioned' (de Man, 1979, p. 5). Intrinsic criticism is criticism which operates on the internal mechanisms of form and structure in a text, whereas extrinsic criticism brings external and contextual knowledge to bear on its text. As such, the distinction imposes a metaphor similar to Conrad's shell and kernel in that intrinsic criticism generally supposes the meaning of a text to be contained within it like a kernel where extrinsic supposes that its meaning is context-bound. Characteristically, de Man reads a text through the lens of this inside/outside metaphor in order to deconstruct it, or to show that the text does not cooperate with it. Such a reading usually proceeds by isolating fundamental hierarchical oppositions of a text and exploring the ways that these oppositions unwittingly prop up the inside/outside metaphor. De Man then deconstructs these oppositions in a manner akin to Derrida's deconstruction of Saussurean oppositions, by finding evidence in the text which contradicts this hierarchy. By inverting the hierarchy in an opposition, or conflating the terms of a distinction, de Man's readings pull away the prop he has established for the inside/outside metaphor in criticism, and therefore uses the reading to support metalingual propositions which radically reject this metaphor: 'the paradigmatic linguistic model is that of an entity which confronts itself'; or 'the trope is not a derived, marginal or aberrant form of language but the linguistic paradigm par excellence'; or 'the paradigm for all texts is that of a figure and its deconstruction'. De Man's deconstructions of hierarchical oppositions generally defy summary, and are usually organized to demonstrate that texts advance incompatible models of language which a reader cannot decide between. De Man can find in the structure of a single image an undecidable oscillation between literal and figurative meanings which render the image too complex to conform to the either/or choice of intrinsic and extrinsic approaches, as for example in his reading of the closing image of Yeats's poem 'Among School Children' (de Man, 1979, pp. 11–12). In fact the co-presence of different meanings in a single image, for de Man, is often used as the basis for an argument that language does not really refer to the outside world at all, because that referential meaning is in collision with some uncontrollable figurative meaning which cannot simply be banished by the critic for the sake of a coherent interpretation. A text, for de Man, is always in a sense an allegory of the impossibility of reading it in any single way. This means, first, that a text is always partly about itself, even when it does not indulge in self-commentary, and consequently there is no obligation to find cooperative texts to find concepts of the inside and outside of meaning at work.

De Man's phrase *allegory of reading* is deliberately ambiguous to this effect: does the allegory belong to the reading or is it an allegory about reading? This ambiguity is another kind of undecidability as to whether an allegorical meaning can be located in the object text or whether it is part of the reading. This can be seen as an example of the broad poststructuralist conviction that an object and its construction by an analytical discourse are categorically inseparable: in this case that a literary text and its reading are facets of the same process. There is always a kind of irony in de Man's readings, that he is capable of translating them into unrecognizable allegories about the ability of language to refer and communicate while claiming that he is not really doing anything to them at all. Deconstruction, de Man says, 'is not something we have added to the text but it constituted the text in the first place' (de Man, 1979, p. 17). The idea that a reading constitutes a text is a clear example of the way that deconstruction has tried to escape the metaphysics of presence which is inherent in any analysis which clearly separates the subject from the object.

The influence of this kind of thinking in literary studies has been profound. The introduction of a new and difficult linguistic terminology in criticism aside, the impact of this thought can be seen in terms of a departure from the inside/outside model in criticism. Derrida's own readings of literary texts have endlessly problematized the relation between a text and its reading. In 1984, when asked to address the Ninth International James Joyce Symposium in Frankfurt, Derrida produced a long and apparently rambling account of his own journeys round the world prior to the conference, making only comic and fragmented references to his text, *Ulysses*. On closer reading, Derrida's text is an elaborate parody of *Ulysses* which appears to digress into external irrelevancies in the act of locating itself ironically within Joyce's. The influence of this kind of parodic critical act has been to challenge the boundary between fiction and criticism, so that an act of criticism can be a literary creation no less than a fiction can have a critical function. Much of the fiction of the 1980s and 1990s can be seen as operating within a poststructuralist paradigm in the sense that it is fiction with a critical function, fiction which deconstructs other fiction through parody. Criticism-as-fiction of this kind is deconstructive in the sense that it is criticism which is neither outside nor inside literature, criticism which doubts the ability of criticism to stand outside of its object texts and refer to them transparently.

It is probably true to say that deconstruction as such gave way, in the middle of the 1980s, to new critical fashions such as new historicism and various forms of cultural criticism. The influence of deconstruction on these subsequent developments, which cannot be explored here, lies in the profound shift away from the idea that language and discourse are capable of transparently reflecting their objects towards the view that discourses actively construct our world. Critics who now focus on issues in the representation of history or cultural identities tend to do so from a textualist point of view, that is from the belief that history and culture are themselves discourses which interpret the world, and discourses which can be deconstructed. The legacy of deconstruction in literary studies has been above all to extend the scope of criticism beyond literature, and to extract criticism from an age-old opposition between formalist and historicist approaches to literature. When history and culture are seen as texts, as elaborate systems of representation, reading becomes elevated to a new status in which political, ideological and philosophical positions are defined. As in literary studies, so in culture, the reading has become more important than the thing read, the representation more important than the representamen, because, in Derrida's words, 'il n'y a pas dehors-texte'. Deconstruction then entails the entextualization of everything and the demonstration that texts are always too complex to be reduced by interpretation to unproblematic entities.

## BIBLIOGRAPHY

Conrad, J. (1973) *Heart of Darkness*, Penguin, Harmondsworth.
Culler, J. (1983) *On Deconstruction: Theory and Criticism after Structuralism*, Routledge, London.
de Man, P. (1973) *Blindness and Insight: Essays in the Rhetoric of Contemporary Criticism*, 2nd edn, Methuen, London.
de Man, P. (1979) *Allegories of Reading: Figural Language in Rousseau, Nietzsche, Rilke, and Proust*, Yale University Press, New Haven.
de Man, P. (1986) *The Resistance to Theory*, Manchester University Press, Manchester.
Derrida, J. (1976) *Of Grammatology*, trans. G. Spivak, Johns Hopkins University Press, Baltimore.
Derrida, J. (1982) *Margins of Philosophy*, trans. A. Bass, Harvester Wheatsheaf, Hemel Hempstead.

Eagleton, T. (1983) *Literary Theory: An Introduction*, Blackwell, Oxford.
Jakobson, R. (1960) 'Closing Statement: Linguistics and Poetics', in *Style in Language*, ed. T. Sebeok, MIT Press, Cambridge, Mass.
Jameson, F. (1972) *The Prison House of Language: A Critical Account of Structuralism and Russian Formalism*, Princeton University Press, Princeton.
Johnson, B. (1980) *The Critical Difference: Essays in the Contemporary Rhetoric of Reading*, Johns Hopkins University Press, Baltimore.
Miller, J.H. (1982) *Fiction and Repetition: Seven English Novels*, Blackwell, Oxford.
Miller, J.H. (1989) 'Heart of Darkness Revisited', in *Heart of Darkness: A Casestudy in Contemporary Criticism*, ed. R. Murfin, St Martin's Press, New York.
Saussure, F. (1972) *Course in General Linguistics*, trans. R. Harris, Duckworth, London.

## RECOMMENDED READING

Bloom, H. (ed.) (1979) *Deconstruction and Criticism*, Seabury, New York.
Culler, J. (1983) *On Deconstruction: Theory and Criticism after Structuralism*, Routledge, London.
Derrida, J. (1992) *Acts of Literature*, ed. D. Attridge, Routledge, New York and London.
Felperin, H. (1985) *Beyond Deconstruction: The Uses and Abuses of Literary Theory*, Clarendon Press, Oxford.
Leitch, V. (1983) *Deconstructive Criticism: An Advanced Introduction*, Hutchinson, London.
Lentricchia, F. (1980) *After the New Criticism*, Methuen, London.
Norris, C. (1982) *Deconstruction: Theory and Practice*, Methuen, London.
Norris, C. (1987) *Derrida*, Fontana Press, London.
Young, R. (ed.) (1981) *Untying the Text*, Routledge, London.

# UNIT 20

# Reader-response criticism

*James Knowles*

Reader-response criticism is not a unified theory; rather it encompasses a variety of approaches all of which emphasize the reader and the reading process in the critical project. This range can be illustrated through two of the German terms which are often used by adherents of reader-response criticism: *Rezeptionasthetik* and *Wirkungsasthetik* (Freund, 1987, p. 134). 'Reception aesthetics' concentrates upon the audience response, pursuing a more overtly historical thesis, concerned with the reception of works within their contemporary context and the (often dialectical) relationship between the moment of cultural production and consumption. This type of study is most associated with Hans Robert Jauss. In contrast, *wirkung* defines the 'effect and response' engendered by a text and the reading process. This method, developed by Roman Ingarden (Ingarden, 1931) and Wolfgang Iser, is closely associated with the University of Konstanz, where the study of reception aesthetics has been explored systematically, so that sometimes its proponents are referred to as the 'Konstanz School'. Ingarden, Iser, Jauss and their followers all evince a major shift away from the author as the determinant of meaning, consequently introducing a more subjective stance to critical practice, and they share a common, if variously received, intellectual heritage from the German philosophical tradition of phenomenology. Reader-response criticism cannot be grasped without some knowledge of phenomenology.

Phenomenology argued that perception and the role of the perceiver were essential in our comprehension of meaning and reality. Indeed, Husserl, the German philosopher who established and expounded this view, argued that things could only be understood by us through our consciousness, and that the patterns of our perception and consciousness were the proper objects of philosophical study (Eagleton, 1983, pp. 54–61). Phenomenology is named after the Greek word 'phenomena' (meaning 'things appearing'), and this approach emphasizes how we cannot be certain that objects exist, but only of their presence as things intended by consciousness. Consciousness is always of something and Husserl argues that things are intended by our consciousness, that is, the subject imagines and conceptualizes objects, which actually brings those objects into being. Realities are, in fact, phenomena, available only in our consciousness. This consciousness is not of a particular thing, but rather the essence of the thing (for example, colour in general rather than any particular colour).

Phenomenology had a major influence on criticism because its emphasis upon consciousness and the process of perception focused attention on the reader. For critics like George Poulet the book was an inert object which required realization by the consciousness of the reader in order to become a work and function. Poulet imagined reading as the invasion of one consciousness by another (accessed through the work): 'the extraordinary fact in the case of a book is the falling away of the barriers between you and it. You are inside it; it is inside you; there is no longer either inside or outside' (Poulet, 1980, p. 42). The reading consciousness will activate the text and so become aware of the author's consciousness and almost inhabit the *lebenswelt* (or lived/perceived world) of the author. Thus phenomenological criticism often highlights the process of perception of time, space, material worlds, and the sense of self, or self–other interaction.

A parallel but contrasting approach was assayed by the Polish critic Roman Ingarden (also influenced by Husserl), who argued that the reader did not surrender to the consciousness of another, but that he/she had to construct that consciousness from elements in the work. Whereas Poulet stressed the work as pure phenomenon and imagined the reader as a passive figure invaded by the consciousness of the work (Poulet, 1980, pp. 43 and 47), Ingarden argued that works were 'heteronomous', that is, they have some inherent properties and some which are attributed to them by the active perceiving consciousness of the reader. The literary work is neither simply ideal nor real; it is between the two, requiring an act of concretization. Ingarden argued that this was achieved through various schemata or points of indeterminacy which must be perceived and realized in the act of reading. In other words, the text is a kind of 'internalized probability system' (William Meyer, cited in Kermode, 1975), like a musical score. The notes provide a skeleton which guides the performer, but they are only fully realized in the performance.

Ingarden argues that the text and its schema, activated by the reader, are the source of meaning, while the most prolific advocate of *Wirkungsasthetik*, Iser, builds upon the notion of texts as a heteronomous formation, arguing that literary texts occupy a 'peculiar halfway position between the external world of objects and the reader's own world of experience' (Iser, 1989, p. 8). Rather than the invasion of the reader's consciousness by the work espoused by Poulet, Iser suggests that meaning comes from the interaction of text and reader. He posits a bi-polarity, of the author's 'artistic' object and the reader's 'aesthetic' object, and that the 'work' exists somewhere between these two possibilities (Iser, 1978, p. 21; 1980a, p. 106; 1989, p. 8). The job of the reader is to interact with the text, composing meaning as reading progresses, and the text aids this process through its structures, an idea Iser adapts from Ingarden's schemata (Iser, 1980a, pp. 111–12). Reading becomes a journey through the text as the reader is offered, and constructs, various perspectives which are then gradually assessed and organized into a coherent whole (Iser, 1989, p. 13).

On a practical level, Iser argues that the text consists of 'gaps', either 'blanks' or 'negations' which are structured into the text, and which the reader must resolve, giving the reader a 'chance to build ... bridges' (1989, p. 9) and offering various interpretive possibilities. If 'blanks are the unseen joints of the text', then negations 'invoke familiar and determinate elements of knowledge only to cancel them out' (1980a, p. 112). So the reader of a novel must work between the various perspectives offered (by narrator, characters, plot and the fictitious or implied reader), deciding at various points of indeterminacy, such as chapter breaks or changes of narrative, direction, how to interpret. As implied here, such an approach works particularly well with eighteenth- and nineteenth-century novels (Iser, 1980b, contains an exemplary discussion of Tom Jones; see also Selden, 1985, p. 113). It can also work well with drama, since it highlights the pauses and silences which are so significant in the form (Selden, 1989, section 17 on Pinter and Beckett).

For example, a novel like *Great Expectations* maps the concept of 'gentility', or being a gentleman, its various meanings, and how these relate to material wealth and the rapidly changing social structure of the nineteenth century. This is achieved through the metaphorical and literal journey of the central character, Pip, who encounters various figures representing ideas of gentility (Matthew Pocket, Bentley Drummel and Estella and her trainer Miss Havisham) as he learns how to behave as a gentleman. Each figure articulates a different aspect which Pip needs to balance, and these in turn are linked to the question of how money supports and relates to gentility (through Pumblechook, Miss Havisham, the always empty Pocketses, Jaggers and Magwitch). The reader must, with Pip, connect these possibilities together into a coherent pattern, which is complicated by the oscillation between the actions of the plot, apparently in the present but actually in the past, Pip's reactions, and the voice of the narrator, the older Pip (see Unit 18, p. 532). Immediate, or apparently immediate, responses are juxtaposed with the retrospective narration, and the reader again must read the gaps to determine what position – a combination of identification and distantiation – to adopt. These gaps or interpretive cruxes, which the reader must bridge, shape the text in other ways, since the novel is also based upon personal relationships between characters which are divided into kin and step relations, and as the novel progresses these categories become confused and new connections between figures emerge, so that Estella's parentage is revealed or the identity of Pip's mysterious benefactor is uncovered. In this way the text plays with the idea of 'expectations', since we expect certain relations, or are surprised by some, such as the emergence of Magwitch, or tantalized by others, for instance the role of Miss Havisham. Constantly we are made to expect, or asked what are our expectations. These gaps and indeterminacies become an enigma which we as readers continually seek to solve, such as why the plot has the lawyer at its centre, pointing towards the influence of early detective fiction, a device which frustrates and fascinates us. The structure of chapters, the instalments of the serial version, and the interweaving of plot strands, preventing our knowledge or discovery of key facts, add to the delay and dilation of the plot, which heighten our involvement. The idea articulated by Joe Gargery ('Pip, dear old chap, life is made up of ever so many partings welded together' (Dickens, 1994, p. 222)) embodies both the complex patterns of connection and non-connection in the novel, and the subtle coherences and incoherences which we are offered as readers. We are to weld together the partings of the text.

Not all reader-response criticism belongs to continental Europe. The other major exponent of reader-response criticism, the American theoretician Stanley Fish, develops some of the more radical possibilities of Ingarden's and Iser's work. While both Ingarden and Iser argue that the text structures its own indeterminacy, a structure of internalized probabilities, which cannot be realized by any one reader, Fish pursues an argument which places meaning within the reader rather than in the text or in the literary or linguistic system. His work falls into two broad phases, both showing the influence of phenomenology (and also J.L. Austin's linguistic theories), but the later stage is distinguished by a radical thrust absent in earlier essays. Most of Fish's early work focuses upon Renaissance literature (Fish, 1967 and 1972), showing how the texts generate a self-awareness in the reader of the reading process in order to provoke doubt about the reader's competence and interpretive skills: almost an internalized 'exegetical drama' (Freund, 1987, p. 94).

In *Surprised By Sin* (Fish, 1967) Fish explores Milton's *Paradise Lost* as an educative experience which faces the reader with the plight of fallen man through his inability to interpret and thus also to understand God or his actions. Essays such as 'Interpreting the *Variorum*' (Fish, 1976) explore the constant structuring and restructuring effected in the process of reading. In this case, the plural meanings offered in the *variorum* edition of Milton's shorter poems illustrate how the reader experiences a variety of possible meanings which must be considered, rejected, absorbed, reconsidered in the light of further reading. Fish concerns himself with the micro-levels of reading or

> descriptions of a succession of decisions made by readers about an author's intention; decisions that are not limited to the specifying of purpose but include the specifying of every aspect of successively intended worlds; decisions that are precisely the shape, because they are the content, of the reader's activities. (Fish, 1976, p. 476)

In practical terms this means the critic looks for the interpretive cruxes where such myriad decisions must be made. For instance in Marlowe's *Hero and Leander*:

> Buskins of shells all silvered used she,
> And branched with blushing coral to the knee,
> Where sparrows perched, of hollow pearl and gold,
> Such as the world would wonder to behold:
> Those with sweet water oft her handmaid fills,
> Which as she went would chirrup through the bills.
> (Marlowe, 1979, ll. 31–6)

The lines belong to the opening description of Hero, whose own beauty combined with the astonishing workmanship of her clothes amaze both men and nature, so that bees would seek honey from her breath and men would 'praise the sweet smell as she passed' (line 21), whilst her 'veil was artificial flowers and leaves,/ Whose workmanship both man and beast deceives' (lines 19–20). This description belongs to the well-known Renaissance topos of nature outdone by art, and begins a complex exploration of the power of art and artifice to entrance and so transport the reader into a literal and metaphorical Golden Age. For the poet, the act of rewriting the poem (Marlowe follows an earlier poem attributed to the mythical archetypal poet

Musaeus) itself demonstrates the imitation and surpassing of the earlier model, a tribute to his own brilliance and skilled workmanship. So these lines occur at a crucial moment and serve to embody for the reader how Hero's observers are deceived (and the nature/art boundary blurred), as initially we read the lines as if the buskins of shell are simply covered with branch-like coral. All of a sudden we are told that 'sparrows perched' (line 33) on these branches, throwing the reader's perceptions momentarily into confusion. Are they real sparrows, deceived like the bees? Doesn't this seem incredible, or suggest that Hero is immensely tall (which might be an image of a heroic age)? So how are we to interpret this, literally or metaphorically? These questions and the moment of indecision are then resolved as the passage develops and we are told that the birds are in fact hydraulic automata, themselves, obviously, marvels of workmanship. So the crux and the decisions we are faced with as readers force the realization of the techniques of art to deceive and go beyond nature. Not only is the reader thus alerted to the reading process, an important part of the meaning of the poem which is filled with coded narratives, but the passage equally allows the reader to experience the sensory confusion elicited by Hero's passage.

Fish uses such passages in two ways, making intellectual points about the poem (often working from an apparently insignificant textual detail to a major idea in Renaissance culture), and also showing how reading involves the reader. Indeed, he continues to argue that readers make the meaning of poems just as much as their formal elements and structures and that the reading process and the interpretive process actually constitute the meaning. This is the more radical potential of reader-response criticism, best seen in 'Literature in the Reader: Affective Stylistics' (1970), and in the two later essays 'Is There a Text in This Class?' and 'How To Recognise a Poem When You See One' (1980). 'Affective Stylistics' seeks a radical reorientation in critical practice, moving away from the spatial patterns of new criticism, towards a temporal understanding of the text: we should look at the text as an event, as it happens, and how we experience its occurrence (Fish, 1972, pp. 73 and 83). This is what is meant by 'affective'; not an emotional response, but the intellectual, analytical response triggered by the process of making sense of the text as we work through it (p. 74). Critics should stop asking 'What does it mean?', allowing them to ignore whole areas of texts, but rather ask 'What does it do?' (p. 72). Criticism should 'slow down the reading experience' (p. 74) to show how the uncertainties of the text are 'progressively decertainizing' (p. 71).

In 'Affective Stylistics' Fish appeals to the notions of linguistic and literary competence to limit the potential pluralism of meaning introduced by the affective approach, arguing that there are internalized rules within language and within literature which will allow only a certain latitude in interpretation, and will constrain wayward readers. Later essays such as 'Is There a Text in This Class?' abandon such claims and with great panache and glee argue that there are no determinate meanings, and that all meanings are constructed (Fish, 1980, p. 317) by readers. Meaning is irreducibly plural. So for Fish, 'Interpretation is not the act of construing, it is the act of constructing. Interpreters do not decode poems; they make them' (p. 327). This is the triumph of the reader.

Fish's essays provoke some difficult interpretive questions, especially his insistence that the reader actually constructs the poem. For example, take this simple note:

> This is just to say I have eaten the plums that were in the icebox and which you were probably saving for breakfast – forgive me, they were delicious, so sweet and so cold.

Can this be read as a poem? Fish would argue that it is not the formal or poetic qualities of the writing which make this a poem or not but the way we read it (Fish, 1980, pp. 326–7). As it stands we might read it as a casual note on a fridge with slightly wayward grammar suggestive of haste, and the more alert reader might notice the use of 'icebox' redolent of 1950s America. Yet, if we were to rearrange the words so that it looked like a poem, we would approach the matter in a totally different way, and so read it as if it were a poem, fulfilling Fish's argument that 'It is not that the presence of poetic qualities compels a certain kind of attention but that the paying of a certain kind of attention results in the emergence of poetic qualities' (Fish, 1980, p. 326). So, we can reorder the words thus (Williams, 1969, p. 55):

This Is Just To Say

I have eaten
the plums
that were in
the icebox

and which
you were probably
saving
for breakfast

Forgive me
they were delicious
so sweet
and so cold

Simply changing the physical arrangement means that we read this as a poem because we expect poems to be organized in this fashion, and so we now read in a particular way, looking for poetic features. For instance, we might emphasize the Christian connotations of 'saving' and 'Forgive me', especially since we would now place greater emphasis upon the phrase which opens a stanza. Fish, however, goes further, using the example of a nonsensical list of names on a classroom blackboard, which his students (who were expecting to talk about seventeenth-century religious poetry) obediently interpreted as if it were a religious lyric:

Jacobs – Rosenbaum
Levin
Thorne
Hayes
Ohman (?)

His point is to show that the different ways of reading encountered here (between what was actually a reading list and what the students read as a poem) are generated not by any inherent formal or linguistic properties, but by the way the readers approached the different texts, and that 'the mental operations we perform are limited by the institutions in which we are already embedded' (Fish, 1980, p. 331). He argues that all meaning is 'communal and conventional' and that it is the 'interpretive communities' (in this case of academia) who generate the protocols by which we read (p. 321). Fish's later writings explore the workings of such interpretive communities, especially in the creation of legal discourses, which have become a site of major intellectual and political debate in contemporary America (Fish, 1989, pp. 141–60).

Fish's theories of reading are highly contradictory in that they appear to posit the dominance of the reader in interpretation, yet his reader is a curious fish, apparently unable ever to learn to read a full sentence without falling into its traps or ambiguities; and as this reader becomes more active so he/she (paradoxically) becomes increasingly subject to the manipulations of the author (Culler, 1983, pp. 65–71). The most important issue, of control (that is, who organizes meaning), is not really addressed, while the appeal to the notion of a unified reading experience in the interpretive community discounts the variety possible within an interpretive community: must all women trained in academic reading approach texts in the same ways as men? Despite these problems the opportunities offered by reader-response criticism are immense, particularly since it highlights the ways different readers approach texts and so enfranchises the divergent readings of groups such as women, those from ethnic minorities or gay men (Culler, 1983, Ch. 1). Moreover, Fish's interest in the communal and conventional nature of interpretive protocols highlights the link between ideology and reading. If interpretation is a socially constructed process, then it is legitimate to ask by whom and for what ends and upon what basis are interpretations generated.

Perhaps the most exciting possibilities are offered by the gradual merging of two approaches (to the historical limits of reading and to the psychology of the process) in the work of the new historians of reading. Critics such as Tompkins (1980b) and Jauss have pointed the way forward using a historically oriented approach. Jauss explores how the 'horizons of expectation' of the audience contemporary to a work are transformed or fulfilled by contact with the work, and he sees reception theory as a bridge between historical and textual approaches (Jauss, 1982, pp. 24 and 18). For Jauss the 'history of literature is a process of aesthetic reception and production that takes place in the realization of literary texts on the part of the receptive reader' (Jauss, 1982, p. 21), so that

> Significance, which is unlocked through aesthetic experience, arises from the convergence of effect [*Wirkung*] and reception. It is no atemporal, basic element which is always already given; rather it is the never completed result of the process of progressive and enriching interpretation, which concretizes – in an ever new and different manner – the textually immanent potential for meaning in the change of historical life-worlds. (Jauss, 1979, p. 183)

Such approaches can be assimilated to the broad historical project of understanding how individual readers read (and still read) texts, and how we can construct a more complex history of reading (Darnton, 1986). Cultural historians such as Roger Chartier have used the interactions of readers and texts to consider how popular culture operated in the early modern era, reading each moment of cultural consumption as another moment of cultural production (Chartier, 1984), while the medievalist Brian Stock examines how texts spread through 'textual communities', where the interpretation and knowledge of particular texts shape the behaviour of religious groups and societies, inculcating group consciousness and solidarity (Stock, 1990, also 1983). Within literary studies, the lasting effect has been the liberation of criticism from the constraints of patriarchal conceptions of authorship (Culler, 1983, p. 60). The 'death' of the author, argues Barthes, is the 'birth of the reader' (Barthes, 1977). Reader-response criticism thus marks a major shift in perceptions and functions as the necessary precursor to many later critical approaches, placing a new emphasis upon the radical potential of reading and systems by which meanings are created. The shift to the reader prefigures feminism, post-colonialism, gay criticism in its focus upon the divergences between readers; the consideration of reading as a process and the generation of meaning underpins structuralist and poststructuralist approaches; and the interaction of these two emphases, upon how meaning is created, for whom and by whom, also underlies much recent Marxist discussion of the ideological production and function of the institution and discipline of criticism. Asking who reads, how, for what reasons and with what results are the fundamentals of any self-reflexive and self-critical interpretive practice and as such form the basis of modern literary criticism.

The best introductory collections of reader-response criticism are Tompkins (1980a) and Suleiman and Crosman (1980), both of which provide a range of essays including Iser's 'Interaction between Text and Reader' (Suleiman and Crosman) and Fish's 'Literature in the Reader' (Tompkins), along with stimulating and accessible introductions. Other student-friendly texts include Iser's 'Indeterminacy and the Reader's Response in Prose Fiction' (Miller, 1971, and Iser, 1989) and Fish's *Is There a Text in This Class?* (Fish, 1980). An excellent (advanced) exposition is given in Freund (1987), and interesting critiques can be found in Eagleton (1983) and Ray (1984).

## BIBLIOGRAPHY

Barthes, R, (1977) 'The Death of the Author', reprinted in D. Lodge (1988), *Modern Criticism and Theory. A Reader*, Longman, London.
Burke, P. (ed.) (1991) *New Perspectives in Historical Writing*, Polity Press, Cambridge.
Chartier, R. (1984) 'Culture as Appropriation: Popular Cultural Uses in Early Modern France', in *Understanding Popular Culture*, ed. S. Kaplan, Mouton, Berlin, 229–53.
Culler, J. (1983) *On Deconstruction. Theory and Criticism after Structuralism*, Cornell University Press, Ithaca.
Darnton, R. (1986) 'History of Reading', *Australian Journal of French Studies*, 23, 5–30 (reprinted in Burke, 1991).
Dickens, C. (1994) *Great Expectations*, ed. M. Cardwell, Oxford University Press, Oxford.
Eagleton, T. (1983) *Literary Theory: An Introduction*, Blackwell, Oxford.
Fish, S. (1967) *Surprised by Sin: The Reader in 'Paradise Lost'*, Macmillan, London.

Fish, S. (1970) 'Literature in the Reader: Affective Stylistics', *New Literary History*, 23, 123–62 (reprinted in Fish, 1972).

Fish, S. (1972) *Self-Consuming Artifacts: The Experience of Seventeenth-Century Literature*, University of California Press, Berkeley.

Fish, S. (1976) 'Interpreting the *Variorum*', *Critical Inquiry*, 2, 465–85 (reprinted in Tompkins, 1980a).

Fish, S. (1980) *Is There a Text in This Class? The Authority of Interpretive Communities*, Harvard University Press, Cambridge, Mass.

Fish, S. (1989) *Doing What Comes Naturally: Change, Rhetoric and the Practice of Theory in Literary and Legal Studies*, Oxford University Press, Oxford.

Freund, E. (1987) *The Return of the Reader: Reader-Response Criticism*, Methuen, London.

Ingarden, R. (1931) *The Literary Work of Art, an Investigation on the Borderlines of Ontology, Logic and Theory of Literature*, Northwestern University Press, Evanston, Ill. (originally published as *Das Literische Kuntswerk*).

Iser, W. (1974) *The Implied Reader: Patterns of Communication in Prose Fiction from Bunyan to Beckett*, Johns Hopkins University Press, Baltimore.

Iser, W. (1978) *The Act of Reading: A Theory of Aesthetic Response*, Johns Hopkins University Press, Baltimore.

Iser, W. (1980a) 'Interaction between Text and Reader', in *The Reader in the Text: Essays on Audience and Interpretation*, ed. S.R. Suleiman and I. Crosman, Princeton University Press, Princeton, 106–19.

Iser, W. (1980b) 'The Reading Process: A Phenomenological Approach', in *Reader-Response Criticism: From Formalism to Post-Structuralism*, ed. J.P. Tompkins, Johns Hopkins University Press, Baltimore, 50–69.

Iser, W. (1989) 'Indeterminacy and the Reader's Response in Prose Fiction', in *Prospecting: From Reader Response to Literary Anthropology*, Johns Hopkins University Press, Baltimore (originally published in Miller, 1971).

Jauss, H.R. (1979) 'The Alterity and Modernity of Medieval Literature', *New Literary History*, 10, 181–229.

Jauss, H.R. (1982) *Toward an Aesthetic of Reception*, trans. T. Bahti, Harvester Wheatsheaf, Hemel Hempstead.

Kermode, F. (1975) *The Classic*, Faber, London.

Marlowe, C. (1979) *The Complete Poems and Translations*, Penguin, Harmondsworth.

Miller, J.H. (ed.) (1971) *Aspects of Narrative*, Columbia University Press, New York.

Poulet, G. (1980) 'Criticism and the Experience of Interiority', in *Reader-Response Criticism: From Formalism to Post-Structuralism*, ed. J.P. Tompkins, Johns Hopkins University Press, Baltimore, 41–9.

Ray, W. (1984) *Literary Meaning: From Phenomenology to Deconstruction*, Blackwell, Oxford.

Selden, R. (1985) *A Reader's Guide to Contemporary Literary Theory*, Harvester Wheatsheaf, Hemel Hempstead.

Selden, R. (1989) *Practising Theory and Reading Literature*, Harvester Wheatsheaf, Hemel Hempstead.

Stock, B. (1983) *The Implications of Literacy: Written Languages and the Models of Interpretation in the Eleventh and Twelfth Centuries*, Princeton University Press, Princeton.

Stock, B. (1990) *Listening for the Text*, Johns Hopkins University Press, Baltimore.

Suleiman, S.R., and Crosman, I. (eds) (1980) *The Reader in the Text: Essays on Audience and Interpretation*, Princeton University Press, Princeton.

Tompkins, J.P. (ed.) (1980a) *Reader-Response Criticism: From Formalism to Post-Structuralism*, Johns Hopkins University Press, Baltimore.

Tompkins, J.P. (1980b) 'The Reader in History: The Changing Shape of Literary Response', in *Reader-Response Criticism: From Formalism to Post-Structuralism*, ed. J.P. Tompkins, Johns Hopkins University Press, Baltimore, 201–32.

Williams, W.C. (1969) *Selected Poems*, New Directions Books, New York.

# UNIT 21

# Marxism, new historicism and cultural materialism

*James Knowles*

## Marxism and literary criticism

Marxism has been the most powerful influence on criticism throughout the twentieth century. Either alone or in combination with other approaches such as psychoanalysis or feminism, the very pervasiveness and power of Marxism, compounded by its own internal variety, makes this impact difficult to describe adequately. Any survey of Marxist critical strategies must avoid the implication that a Marxist critical monolith exists and delineate the *plurality* of Marxisms and criticisms. Yet the core of these Marxisms is stable and simple: Marxism situates any cultural practice (literature, art, craft, film, whatever) in its historical contexts, and this history is specifically, but broadly, one of socio-economic development (Selden, 1989, p. 136). So, in general, Marxist critical practice eschews narrow conceptions of literary criticism and prefers *cultural* critique, asserting *historical* rather than formalist approaches to texts.

Marxism describes history as the history of the conflict between classes. The practical engagement of Marxism with politics fosters some of the bewildering variety within Marxism. In virtually every country different Marxisms, adapted to local history and traditions, have thrived in response to practical political conflict and struggle (McClellan, 1979). To Western readers, however, the most familiar Marxism remains that of the former Eastern bloc, more accurately described as Leninism or Stalinism which, despite its associations with tyranny, retained an intellectually vital and productive streak especially during the 1920s. Those who seek to diminish the significance of Marxism often highlight Eastern bloc Marxism (its emphasis upon socialist realism, the *proletkult*, notions of political commitment and reflectionism) to depict Marxism as vulgarly reductive. This ignores both the complexity of Marxist traditions outside the Soviet orbit and the many developments in Marxist theory over the last seventy years. In reality even the most demonized figures, such as Lenin and Trotsky, could produce intelligent and flexible cultural criticism (Eagleton, 1976, ch. 2), while the recent revival of interest in the work of Bakhtin/Volosinov rebukes such simplistic views of post-revolutionary Russian aesthetic thought. To simply caricature Marxism as reductive also elides the subtle interactions between Marxist critiques in economics, history, philosophy, politics and cultural studies, a series of encounters which provide much of the energy, power and sophistication of Marxist aesthetics.

To start we might ask a very simple question: what has literary criticism to do with a theory of political economy? Intellectually, both Marx and Engels were imbued with a deep interest in arts and literature while Marx, particularly, educated within the German classical and humanist tradition, wrote fiction and drama early in his career, and was highly influenced by aesthetic theory (Eagleton, 1976 and Singer, 1980). Recently it has even been argued that the central concept of the 'cash nexus' is derived from Marx's reading of *Timon of Athens* (White, 1993). Thus, though Engels's and Marx's actual remarks on literature are fragmented, its influence is pervasive, and where the issues are explicitly addressed (in discussions of Balzac and Sue, for example), their analyses are acute and undogmatic (Marx and Engels, 1976). This *historically* explains the conditions which produced Marxism, but it doesn't satisfy the basic question: what has art got to do with political economy? The answer really lies in *our* conceptions of 'politics', 'economics' and 'literature', which tend to be narrowly defined to facilitate a separation which requires reconsideration. 'Politics' (a term derived from the Greek *polis*, city or city-state) covers the science of human relations in the public sphere, just as 'ethics' are focused on human relations in the private sphere. Politics in the broadest sense are about the interactions of society and social organization. Similarly, 'economics' (another Greek term for the science of domestic management) should not be narrowly confined to material exchanges, but to the *social values* which are placed upon exchanges: what material exchanges *mean* in any given society.

These broader definitions illustrate how politics and economics cannot be simply separated off from the concerns of our lives or siphoned off into the narrow regimes of party politics and underpins the thrust of the Marxist thesis which argues that politics and economics form the substance of our existence and that our lives and histories are shaped by those forces. Marxism as a historical theory argues that politics and economics shape not only historical events but also human consciousness – the very ways in which we perceive and know who we are. This history has a particular form: it is the history of a struggle between different social classes and between varying modes of economic production.

These views are succinctly stated in Marx's Preface to *Critique of Political Economy*:

> In the social production of their life, men enter into definite relations that are indispensable and independent of their will, relations of production which correspond to a definite stage of development of their material productive forces. The sum total of these relations of production constitutes the economic structure of society, the real foundations, on which rises a legal and political superstructure and to which correspond definite forms of social consciousness. The mode of production of material life conditions the social, political, and intellectual life process in general. It is not the consciousness of men that determines their being, but, on the contrary their social being that determines their consciousness. (Marx, 1977, p. 389)

This passage introduces the key ideas of Marxism, particularly the insistence that human consciousness is determined by 'social being', and not vice versa as in most philosophies. This social being is in turn produced by the 'relations of production' within society.

The Preface also raises three topics which are crucial to understanding Marxist criticism. First, the primacy of economic forces in the formation of social structures, called here the 'relations of production'. Secondly, Marx introduces a structure, often simplistically described as bi-partite, with the 'real foundation' (called the 'base') and the 'superstructure', which underpins many arguments about and within Marxism. Thirdly, Marx links these to 'definite forms of social consciousness', also often called 'ideology', another essential element in Marxist criticism. It is important to understand each of these ideas not only because their meanings and interpretations provide the basics of Marxist criticism, but because their differing inflections will help distinguish between the kinds of Marxist criticism.

## The 'relations of production'

For Marx the factors which shape society are not simply the forces of production but the *relations* of production. So, for instance, in feudal society the forces of production might include the handmill, an important point, but most significant will be the relation of production: is the mill owned or hired by the miller? Ownership, rental, serfdom, employment are all different possible relations of production. These relations, called the *base*, will in turn generate certain types of social structure, or *superstructure*, and kinds of consciousness. Feudalism, a mode of production, requires certain relations of production which will determine the consciousness of individuals: a feudal subjectivity (sense of selfhood). In other words, Marxism is less concerned with the technical sense of economics than with the mode of production as a form of social organization.

Two additional points should be made about this formulation. First, we might ask how does change occur? For Marx change was primarily economic and even technological. The handmill or watermill are challenged by the invention of the steam mill which, to operate efficiently, requires the concentration of people in towns, a movement which causes the feudal relations of production to collapse and a new capitalistic mode of production to arise with a new set of relations of production: property rights, competitiveness, egoism and individualism. Secondly, we should note the complexity that this interaction between modes of production and relations of production introduces. Far from being based on economic determinism, as is often claimed, Marx insists it is not the mode of production which institutes change but rather the mediating relations of production, and that when change occurs it is not necessarily direct or simple in its operations.

This may seem very remote from literature, but at least one kind of Marxist criticism highlights how the modes, means and relations of production shape literary production. For example, the distribution of roles in the Shakespearian theatre might be considered, since it was based not on talent but on economic ownership. The companies were divided into three bands: sharers (who owned the company and sometimes the building), hired men and boys (apprentices attached to the sharers).

The best roles always went to the sharers. This might be extended if the broad economic position of theatre in the early modern era is considered, since this ownership structure is close to the guild system (the craft unions of late medieval urban culture). Yet at the same time many of the buildings were leased by entre- preneurs such as Philip Henslowe, who owned the Rose Theatre. This locates early modern theatre between the patronage system (a residual mode closely associated with aristocratic culture) and the newly emerging systems of the urban market. Some critics have argued that the economic position of theatre, between modes and relations of production (feudalism and capitalism, put crudely) explains the peculiar force and ideological complexity of sixteenth-century theatre (Cohen, 1985 and Kavanagh, 1985) (see Unit 5, pp. 99–102). Another, different, example might be the impact of the circulating libraries upon the form of the nineteenth-century novel which some critics posit. These subscription libraries (the most famous being Mudie's Circulating Library) required that the largest number of volumes be lent to the public to maximize profit, and so longer novels bound in separate volumes could be hired to more subscribers. Therefore, Mudie's preferred longer texts and so the 'triple-decker' or three-volume novel arose to satisfy economic demands.

## Base and superstructure

Marx's argument that economic forces ultimately determine social and individual consciousness is refined through his terms 'base' (called the 'real foundations' in the Preface) and 'superstructure'. The base, that is, productive forces, the modes of production and the relations of production, shape the superstructure, which is the legal, political, philosophical, religious or aesthetic formation which the base produces. Thus the feudal base, serfdom, will produce the feudal superstructure, usually seen as developing an authoritarian and hierarchical religion, a moral code based upon obedience, loyalty and the fulfilment of duties ordained by the individual's God-given status.

For Marxist criticism the most important arguments centre on the relations between base and superstructure, particularly to what extent and by what means the base determines the superstructure. Most contemporary Marxists emphasize how Marx never envisaged a simple, direct relation between base and superstructure, and certainly never envisaged it as a symmetrical relationship. Engels argued:

> According to the materialist conception of history, the *ultimately* determining element in history is the production and reproduction of real life. More than this neither Marx nor I have ever asserted. Hence if somebody twists this into saying that the economic element is the only one, he transforms that proposition into a meaningless, abstract, senseless phrase. The economic situation is the basis, but the various elements of the superstruc- ture – political forms of the class struggle ... juridical forms and even the reflexes of these struggles in the brains of the participants, political, juristic, philosophical theories, religious views... – also exercise their influence upon the course of historical struggles and in many cases preponderate in determining their *form*. There is an interaction of all these elements in which... amid all the endless host of accidents... the economic movement finally asserts itself as necessary. (Letter to Bloch, September 1890, cited in Hall, 1977, pp. 53–4).

Many Marxists, Eagleton among them, follow Engels and argue for a high degree of autonomy in the base–superstructure articulation and grant art particular independence from any simple determinism (on 'determinism' see Williams, 1983). In his own historical writings Marx argued 'Men make their own history', a position which implies autonomous agency although he goes on to argue 'but they do not make it just as they please'; instead they work within circumstances 'directly encountered, given, and transmitted from the past' (*Eighteenth Brumaire* in Marx, 1977, p. 300). Exactly *how* these encounters operate and how base shapes superstructure define many of the different Marxist critical approaches.

David Forgacs has usefully categorized the myriad responses to the base–superstructure problem into two broad types: the reflection model and the production model (Forgacs, 1986). Under the *reflection model* superstructure reflects the base so that literature reflects the economic conditions. Art is an image or imitation (mimesis) of society and critics who follow this approach tend to emphasize the realistic properties of writing, as in the work of the Hungarian critic Lukács. Lukács does not simply suggest art holds a mirror up to nature, or in this case social reality, instead he distinguishes between direct reflection which is not, in fact, true reflection or realism, but what he calls naturalism. He castigates Zola for exactly this failure. True reflection is a knowledge of the actual shape of social reality, which is what he calls a 'dialectical totality' or the contradictory and complex interaction between the changing forces of base and superstructure. This totality is a part of the form of the world, the shape that contributes to historical process, and it is that form which the forms of literature must reflect to be truly realist. In essence, Lukács requires literature to eschew concentration upon detail (naturalism) in favour of the selection of details and characters which typify a larger historical pattern. Bloom in *Ulysses* fails because while he embodies the traits of the married lower-class Jew, he is not represented as typical of the historical situation of his class or part of the dialectical process of history. Waverley in Scott's novel, on the other hand, focuses the extreme, opposed classes of the novel, bringing them together in conflict which represents the true dialectical history of the period, making *Waverley* a truly realistic novel.

Most current Marxist criticism would question the rigid separation of base and superstructure, and writers such as Williams (1977) and Wolff (1981, ch. 2) often stress how key institutions, such as the family, belong to both base and superstructure. The family is both economic (part of the mode of production) and ideological (part of the mode of superstructural reproduction). Other critics have argued for the asymmetry of base–superstructure relations, emphasizing the autonomy of the two parts, and even argued that superstructure can transform base. The most radical approach to this problem is associated with the work of the French philosopher Louis Althusser who rejected the idea that 'base–superstructure' should form the only determination of social reality, arguing instead for a structurally complex notion of social totality in which 'relatively autonomous' practices each with their own power entered into dynamic and overdetermined conjunctions and configurations in which economic determination only operated, in accordance with Engels's comment to Bloch, 'in the last instance'. This view has not been accepted uncritically (many Marxists argue that it denies the very point of historical materialism) but its power within cultural critique cannot be denied because it frees the critic from simply finding a reflection or refraction of class politics within the aesthetic object and allows for a dynamic interaction of economic, social and aesthetic factors both in the work and in its relation to, or representation and construction of, reality. Indeed, the thrust of Marxist criticism over the last twenty years has been towards the liberation of the superstructure and towards a recognition of its centrality and its complexities. Many Marxists now focus upon the 'definite forms of social consciousness', or *ideology*, which has become the central term in critical discourse.

## Ideology

The complexity of this term stems, in part, from its extensive and nuanced use during a long period by many different theorists. The term arises first in the eighteenth century in rationalist philosophy where it simply describes 'the philosophy of the mind' or 'the science of ideas' with an emphasis upon human ideas, rationality and the scientific mind. Raymond Williams (1977) distinguishes three broad senses of the term:

- a system of beliefs characteristic of a class or group;
- a system of illusory beliefs (often associated with false consciousness);
- the general process of the production of meanings and ideas.

In *The German Ideology* Marx outlines the nature and function of ideology as false consciousness, the manifestation of the material domination of a particular class and its interest ('the dominant material relationships grasped as ideas'):

> Consciousness can never be anything else than conscious existence, and the existence of men is their actual life processes. If in all ideology men and their circumstances appear upside down as in a *camera obscura*, this phenomenon arises just as much from their historical life-process as the inversion of objects on the retina does from their physical life-process. (Marx, 1977, p. 164)

These 'ruling ideas' are designed to justify the power of the dominant class and persuade the ruled that their condition is natural, even encouraging them to collude in their subordination and, as a 'false consciousness', to cloak the fact of subordination from its subjects. Ideology seeks to naturalize the current distribution of power and suggest it is permanent, unchangeable and even unthinkable to demur from the status quo. Hence in feudalism the feudal structure not only inculcates obedience, but teaches that disobedience is a sin because the social order is divinely ordained.

Ideology in Marxism is distinguished as a conceptual system propagated by a dominant class for its own ends, a theory which leaves the subordinate class (those at whom ideology is, in part, directed) as passive receptors, and it can seem simplistic and mechanistic. We might, for instance, ask *how* exactly the subordinate classes can be forced into this belief which is so obviously against their interest? To circumvent some of these problems Williams and the cultural materialists have appropriated another term, 'hegemony', derived from the writings of the Italian Marxist, Antonio Gramsci (Gramsci, 1971, pp. 57–60). Williams describes hegemony in the following terms:

> It is a whole body of practices and expectations, over the whole of living: our senses and assignments of energy, our shaping perceptions of ourselves and our world. It is a lived system of meanings and value – constitutive and constituting – which as they are experienced as practices appear as reciprocally confirming. (Williams, 1977, p. 110)

Hegemony is a more generalized world-view, based on political power, and it involves all classes actively in its creation, continuance and reception. For Williams, 'hegemony' asserts, in a flexible and complex manner, the importance of cultural formations in the shaping of society and consciousness, as distinct from the base–superstructure model, which ultimately relies upon economic or political factors to drive change. The adoption of hegemony is the logical extension of the third part of the definition of ideology given in *Marxism and Literature*, seeking to avoid the reductiveness which determinist Marxism might foster. In this sense it belongs to the post-Althusserian moment, which denies simple causality to economic factors and stresses the complexity of the social totality, and to the thrust in Marxist criticism which focuses upon the productive and material nature of the superstructure. Yet, equally, this use of hegemony has come under attack from some Marxists who argue that Williams misunderstands the nature of base–superstructure, which is a 'conceptual' tool rather than an ontological statement, and because the logical conclusion of this argument is to deny the determination which Marx saw at the heart of his theory: 'the key point crystallised in the base/superstructure doctrine, is that those determinations are not symmetrical, that in the production of human society some activities are more fundamentally determining than others' (Eagleton, 1989, p. 169).

The substitution of hegemony for ideology and the continued critical attention to cultural production have been very significant, notably in the work of the cultural materialists and new historicists, especially since such arguments mesh with those of Michel Foucault on the relations of power, language and selfhood. These emphases, however, depend upon another, perhaps the most important, revision of the theory of ideology found in Althusser's 'Ideological State Apparatuses', which links ideology with subject-formation. Althusser argues that ideology is a system of representations which forms individuals as social subjects who apparently freely adopt a particular framework of assumptions: an internal 'picture' of the social world and their place in it. Ideology, in this version, is a system of perceptions, representations and images that encourages people to regard their place in society as inevitable and natural as a result of the 'real' world, whereas it is no such thing but actually a 'false consciousness' or illusion designed to disguise the actual social conditions, the 'real' real. This complex process can be described as a 'web of determinations', shaped by 'sex, gender, religion, region, education, ethnicity ... [and] ... class' which allows us to imagine our society, our place in the social system, and our sense of selfhood and identity: it constitutes us (Kavanagh, 1990),

p. 311). The concept of 'subjection' or subject-formation, called 'interpellation' by Althusser, argues that the subordinate class are not simply oppressed, rather they are coerced to conform to norms desirable to the dominant classes whilst believing they are free, or at least determined by social conditions beyond their control.

A good example of this would be our response to advertising which obscures 'the real issues of society, those relating to work: to jobs and wages and who works for whom' substituting instead 'systems of social differentiation which are a veneer on the basic class structure of our society' (Williamson, 1983, p. 47). Adverts not only obscure the nature of society, they achieve this through persuading and constituting us (indeed, persuading us to constitute ourselves) as unique individuals and so obscure our community of oppressions and interests. They create images by which we understand ourselves and obscure the fundamental economic issues with glossy images, meanings and 'lifestyles'. So in the famous 1985 Levi Jeans commercial when Nick Kamen washed his jeans in a launderette stripped to his boxer shorts accompanied by a soundtrack of 'Grapevine', the point was to sell jeans as sexy and rebellious (Simpson, 1994, p. 98). There is, however, a complex interplay of viewpoints from which the advert can be viewed, positions into which the viewer is interpellated through the spectators in the launderette. The first shows a comic-reading boy who looks up at Kamen (the first shot shows his head at the level of the actor's jeans-clad crotch), and whose eyes follow the seductive figure as he walks to the washing machine until it is interrupted by his mother, giving Kamen a disapproving look and shooing the boy away. This first interpellation raises awkward sexual tensions (Simpson sees this as a 'mixture of envy, desire and disdain' symbolic of heterosexual distaste for the 'queer'). This second interpellation (disapproval) gives way to the giggling girls who treat Kamen as heterosexual, allowing the male viewer safely to enjoy the male striptease, imagining events through female eyes without undermining his masculinity. The key point of Simpson's analysis of 'Launderette' is precisely to see this suppressed homo-erotic quality and to question why patriarchy and capitalism currently flaunt and exploit the eroticized and fetishized male body. From our point of view the process of image creation through interpellation of the spectator (illicit desire/disapproval–licit desire) shows how advertising – like any other form of cultural production – can be used to create a sense of self. If we buy this product we will be sexy, transgressive and individualistic, even whilst purchasing a mass-produced item usually manufactured in Far Eastern sweatshops and worn by millions.

A more sophisticated extension of this approach considers the concept of realism, a central problem within Marxist criticism ever since Engels's famous description of realism as the 'truthful reproduction of typical characters under typical circumstances'. For many Marxist critics realism, and particularly social or socialist realism, was the most progressive form of art, promoting political change. This reached its acme in the *proletkult* (see above) and Soviet realism, even though Engels actually argues a more sophisticated stance without reliance on direct polemic and uses Balzac, a conservative novelist, as an example of a writer who revealed the tensions of bourgeois society in spite of his overt political allegiance (Marx and Engels, 1976, pp. 89–92). Lukács in *The Historical Novel and Studies in European*

*Realism* pursues these arguments as part of the reflection model and as part of his rejection of modernism as overly subjective: 'The question arises whether it is the unity of the external and internal worlds or the separation between them which is the social basis of the greatness of the novel...' (Lukács, [1950] 1972, p. 2). His espousal of reflectionist realism brought him into conflict with Brecht who saw the opportunities for social criticism through the montage and fragmentation, in part as an expression of the alienation of late capitalism, but also as distancing devices which shattered the illusion of theatre or novels in order to promote critical awareness in the audience (Arvon, 1973, ch. 7). These arguments have been revived, although with a different emphasis, in the distinction made by Colin MacCabe between the 'classic realist text' (the Victorian novel and specifically *Middlemarch*) and the modernist texts of Joyce. Whereas Lukács saw great power in the nineteenth-century novel, MacCabe prefers (in a perfectly reasonable fashion) the subjectiveness and linguistic experimentation of Joyce (MacCabe, 1978, ch. 2).

MacCabe's essay centres upon the idea that in the nineteenth-century novel the narrative voice acts as a 'metalanguage' which places the reader in a dominant position over the characters and their narratives. He further argues that the nineteenth-century novel promotes a hierarchy of discourses in which the mimetic elements (the parts spoken in another's voice, such as direct speech) are subordinated to the diegetic elements (the narrative voice which tells the reader how to read and think about the situations or characters). Moreover, the metalanguage seeks to deny its own status as writing, and simply pretends to be a transparent 'window' on the world, simply observing and reproducing the truth. In contrast, Joyce pursues a more mimetic form without the authoritarian voice of the narrator intervening to control and interpellate the reader into certain reading positions. This neatly reverses Lukács and aligns itself with Brecht, seeing the revolutionary potential of mimesis and through the alienation of readers from the fiction, making them aware of the fictive, constructed, nature of the view they are presented with, and thus creating a kind of critical realism. In this form, the reader revels in the plenitude of language and realizes the fragmentation and alienation, recognizing the constructed nature of the perspective being offered, or the conflict between discourses which prevents a simple, totalized view, and so escapes any simple interpellation as a reader. Reading becomes resistance if not a revolutionary act.

MacCabe's work is the logical extension of the Lukács/Brecht debate, but also highlights a politics of writing and reading, whereby for fiction to deny its artificiality is seen as a dangerous form of illusionism, likely to deceive and lead the reader into passive acceptance of the metalanguage and its readings of the characters and plots. This distinction lends a political relevance to the argument advanced in Barthes' *S/Z*, which distinguished between the 'lisible' (readerly) and 'scriptible' (writerly) text, the former transparent, the latter resistant to easy assimilation and interpretation (Barthes, 1970). It should be noted, however, that not everyone accepts this view of the nineteenth-century novel or modernism. Modernism has often been haunted by the fascist connections of many of its proponents (Eliot and Pound), while critics like David Lodge argue for a more sophisticated multi-vocality in the nineteenth-century novel (Lodge, 1991). Using the notion of 'free indirect speech' (see Unit 18, p. 536) Lodge questions the mimesis/diegesis dichotomy, showing how it travesties the complexity of the narrative 'zig zags' of *Middlemarch* (he has a particularly fine reading of Book 1, Chapters 1 and 15 (Eliot, 1986)), and replaces the MacCabe view of novelistic metalanguage with terms drawn from Bakhtin/Volosinov's reading of the Russian novelist Dostoevsky:

> One of the essential peculiarities of prose fiction is the possibility it allows of using different types of discourse, with their distinct expressiveness intact, on the plane of a single work, without reduction to a single common denominator. (Bakhtin, cited in Lodge, 1991, p. 176)

Lodge finds a much more flexible and fluid voice in the narrators of nineteenth-century novelists, while his application of Bakhtin reads the highly wrought and apparently controlled cadences as riven with suppressed contradictions and struggles. In fact, by summoning up the 'polyphony' of the nineteenth-century novel, Lodge reads these texts as much closer to modernism than either Lukács or MacCabe realizes.

These arguments also suggest how crucial interpellation and the politics of reading have become in contemporary Marxist criticism. Do realist texts simply foster passive readers, illusionism and, by implication, the false consciousness of an un-critical approach to texts and the text/world articulation? Do the fragmentations of modernism conservatively mimic the alienation of modern humanity and yearn for lost unity, or do montage, reflexive and self-conscious narrators and narratives promote an activated and thus radicalized reader? We might pose this question in terms of films. Some films promote a passive viewer their content through glossy surfaces and spectacular form: we simply sit and marvel. Musicals are good examples, from *Carousel* to *Grease*. Some films support family values or patriotism in crass terms, such as *Philadelphia* or *Top Gun*. But some directors offer more complex and disruptive fare, sometimes in their content (Tarkovsky's *Andrei Rublev* or Greg Araki's *The Living End*), while others undermine the pleasure effect of cinema. A good example would be Christine Edzard's *Little Dorrit* where some scenes are repeated, filmed from different angles, to convey the differing perceptions of the narrators, so complicating the cinematic interpellation of the spectator. Another would be Harold Pinter's screenplay for *The French Lieutenant's Woman*, where the two endings of the novel are turned into two intertwined plots of the love affairs between the characters of the story and the actors who are filming an adaptation of their story. Both Edzard and Reisz (the directors) use film to question illusionism, just as novels can in the nineteenth and twentieth centuries, fostering a multiplicity of voices and interpellations. This self-consciousness alerts us to the media in which works (be they films or books) are presented and how they interfere with, if not control, the nature of what we see or read. Such self-reflexive forms seek, by highlighting the nature of the medium and through our consequently awakened critical responses, to allow us to tease out the techniques and positions we are offered by cultural forms and so criticize and neutralize them.

Althusser's revision of ideology has another dimension. In the process of subject formation and interpellation Althusser argues that certain key institutions, what he calls 'Ideological State Apparatuses' (ISAs), inculcate '"know-how" but in forms which ensure *subjection to the ruling ideology* or mastery of its "practice"', (Althusser, 1971, pp. 6–7). So the necessary 'reproduction of labour power' depends not simply on the reproduction of skills but also upon

> a reproduction of its submission to the rules of the established order... a reproduction of submission to the ruling ideology for the workers, and a reproduction of the ability to manipulate the ruling ideology correctly for the agents of exploitation and repression....
> (Althusser, 1971, p. 7)

Thus Althusser opens a huge field of study to contemporary Marxist criticism in examining how the ISAs (church, army, schools, universities and so on) reproduce the dominant ideology. So both Williams and Eagleton have made particular studies of the role of 'English Literature' (as a concept) and academic and institutionalized criticism in the maintenance and propagation of the status quo. Such studies have fed into the broad-based movement within English studies which isolates and questions the ideological construction of the canon and 'literature' (Williams, for instance, prefers the less loaded term 'writing').

These post-Althusserian approaches have been particularly fruitful for socialist feminists and those interested in post-colonial critiques, facilitating a sophisticated exploration of the interconnections of class, gender and subjectivity. Cora Kaplan, a leading member of the Marxist-Feminist Literature Collective, presents a powerful case for the historicized study of subjectivity as part of a project connecting the 'unconscious structures that construct subjective identity' with the 'structures through which class is lived and understood' and 'through which political subjection and rebellion are organised' (Kaplan, 1985, pp. 165–6). Class, subjectivity and gender are all interlinked, so feminism needs to reject any simplistic privileging of gender difference for a more complex model which incorporates this interaction of which the novel is an especially rich repository. The aim is to reject both humanistic definitions of the subject and traditional socialism's collapsing of gender oppression into an index of class oppression, and instead engage with the interaction between new understandings of subjectivity from psychoanalysis, semiotics and post-Althusserian theory, along with a proper grasp of how class operates to shape the specific determinations of subjectivity.

The nineteenth-century novel emerges in this account of historical subjectivity as a key platform for the construction, representation and contestation of ideologies of self, especially those designed for or by women (Kaplan, 1985, p. 166). In particular, Kaplan takes issue with Virginia Woolf's attack on the 'flawed' nature of *Jane Eyre*, notably the 'bright visions' of Volume I, Chapter 12, after Jane has glimpsed the attic which contains Grace Poole (Kaplan, 1985, pp. 169–74). Jane comments:

> It is in vain to say that millions of human beings ought to be satisfied with tranquillity; they must have action; and they will make it if they cannot find it. Millions are condemned to a stiller doom than mine, and millions are in silent revolt against their lot. Nobody knows how many rebellions besides political rebellions ferment in the masses of

life which people earth. Women are supposed to be very calm generally; but women feel just as men feel; they need exercise for their faculties and a field for their efforts as much as their brothers do; they suffer from too rigid a restraint, too absolute a stagnation, precisely as men would suffer; and it is narrow minded in their more privileged fellow-creatures to say that they ought to confine themselves to making puddings and knitting stockings, to playing the piano and embroidering bags. It is thoughtless to condemn them, or laugh at them, if they seek to do more or learn more than custom has pronounced necessary for their sex. (Kaplan, 1985, p. 170)

Immediately after this polemic Jane again hears Grace Poole's demented laugh, and the juxtaposition of feminist anger with a distinct radical edge and the madwoman in the attic appears to suggest the dangers which face the disobedient woman. Kaplan finds in the very jerkiness which Woolf rejected as 'unaesthetic' the power of art to articulate the 'mixed incoherence of subjectivity spoken from subordinate and rebellious positions within culture' (Kaplan, 1985, p. 174). Moreover, the passage presents a momentary rupture in the explicit class politics of the text when 'the congruence between the subordination of women and the radical view of class' cannot be resisted: women 'are supposed to be very calm generally' but occasionally 'agitated...to pain' their 'silent revolt' must be articulated. Even though the madwoman in the attic can be momentarily stilled she still exists, and so the text images the darker side of romantic female subjectivity, the dangerous qualities which it would suppress. Symbolically, the madwoman must eventually die because her existence and the radical association between political and gender revolution threaten the more conciliatory approach of the novel (see Unit 24, pp. 642–6).

The approach of materialist feminism outlined here illustrates the fusion of semiosis, psychoanalysis and Marxist theory which has produced much of the most powerful feminist work of the last decade (see also Wayne, 1991). Kaplan's essay illustrates another trend in post-Althusserian approach to narrative, accentuating the contradictions within the narrative (here between the controlled rationalist discourse, the visionary moments, the fleeting suggestions of a discourse close to madness). This approach is particularly associated with the work of Pierre Macherey, and which is described by David Forgacs as belonging to the *production model* of Marxist theory (Forgacs, 1986). Production is used here in a double sense. First, it refers to the writer as producer, downplaying the post-Romantic mystification of creativity. The writer assembles the text, like a car worker, from pre-existing parts, in this case literary conventions and genres, discourses, ideology. This noting of production highlights the transformation which occurs in the act of creativity and also the constructedness of the text which gestures towards another of Macherey's key ideas, that texts are neither complete nor seamless. Secondly, the production envisaged is also the production of ideology. For Macherey ideology is a complete but illusory system of knowledge which, when it is incorporated into a text, is transformed or staged; that is, it gains shape and form and in so doing its limits are revealed. In other words the production of ideology serves to discover the conditions which allowed that ideology to operate, but which it had to repress or secrete in order to function. The best analogy is the Freudian one, whereby in order to live in certain ways (often regarded as 'normal') the subject must repress particular desires which do not actually disappear but which could be said, paradoxically, to be the precondition of 'normality'. It is the effect of writing, and more importantly the function of criticism, to articulate and recover ideology's repressed preconditions or unconsciousness: the things it cannot say in order to exist.

From this it will be clear that Macherey's conception of the text differs markedly from earlier theorizations. Texts such as novels by Verne and Balzac are seen as 'disparate' or 'faulty' precisely because they reveal the gaps and silences of the ideologies which are embedded within. The incompleteness of the text, the internal dissonances and contradictions which its production of ideology generate, are precisely the object of critical attention. Eagleton summarizes this especially well:

> The work does not 'reproduce' ideology, in a way which would make its own contradictions reflective of historical contradictions. On the contrary: the contradictions within the text are the product of an ideologically determined *absence* of such a reflection of real contradictions. It is the work's problematical *relationship* to ideology which produces its internal dissonances. Rather than 'reproducing' ideology, the text *produces* it, setting it in motion, endowing it with a form, and in so doing reveals in its own internal dislocations the gaps and limits which signify that ideology's contradictory relation to real history... in transforming rather than merely reproducing ideology, the text necessarily illuminates the 'not-said' which is the significant structure of the 'said'. (1986, pp. 15–16)

The critic must explore these silences and articulate the ideological preconditions which the work itself silences, not to finish off the work in some way but to bring out its internal contradictions and dissonances (Kavanagh and Lewis, 1982, p. 49). So, for example, in Hardy's fiction critics have discerned a tension in his style between the educated discourse of the narrator and the rustic discourse of his peasants which was also often seen as unrealistic. Indeed, Hardy's fiction was frequently depicted as clumsy and inelegant. A Machereyan approach would revel in these contradictions and in the 'ceaseless play and tension between these two modes' (Eagleton, 1986, p. 43) because it reveals the ideological determination of what good writing is claimed to be (itself an ideologically defined concept) but also because the conflict between discourses challenges the organicist beliefs often implicit in realist texts and the political structures which underpin realism.

Macherey's theories have three important consequences. First, his view of the relation between text, ideology and social and material reality allows Marxist criticism to escape some of the more naive forms of reflectionism implicit in the espousal of realism as the ultimate aesthetic mode. The emphasis upon the *transformation* of the raw materials of fiction (social reality, conventions, ideologies) permits a complex articulation between the textual and social domains, based upon multiple determinations (including generic and other formal systems), stressing their *re-presentation* rather than simple reflection. Both these senses return us to the early view of Engels (shared to some extent by Marx) that socialist fiction should 'break... down conventional illusions' through its dramatizations rather than direct polemic, and that realism consists not in the simple reproduction ('truth of detail') but typical characters in typical situations (Marx and Engels,

1976, pp. 89–92). Secondly, Macherey's criticism permits a role to issues of language and form. Specifically, fictional language and the devices and genres available within the literary mode bring about the transformation of the concealed conditions of ideology, laying bare its devices and limitations to the reader. Thirdly, Macherey assigns a peculiar power to the critic and suggests an entirely new way of reading, less based on the interpretation of features present in the text and more focused on the discovery of the ideological blind-spots of the text. Indeed, Macherey's critical strategies point the way forward for Marxist criticism positing a more flexible relation of texts, ideologies and social realities and accepting the impact of language and form in creating the differential nature of fictional writing. Although formalism and Marxism have often been radically opposed, both historically and conceptually (Bennett, 1979, ch. 2), Macherey's arguments lay the groundwork for a integration of the two approaches: what might be called the 'politics of form'.

The 'politics of form' in contemporary Marxist cultural critique brings together many of the issues which are at the centre of the debates traced throughout the history of Marxism, but especially the base–superstructure articulation, and the precise nature and degree of independence allowed to cultural formations within the social totality. On one level it focuses upon the ideological nature of language and language usage. Most post-Saussurean theories of language detach language from its social (referential) elements. Saussure famously posited the arbitrariness of the signifier/signified relation, and also the need to study language synchronically, in a move redolent of the ahistoricism of formalism. Marxist critics reject this formulation as in Volosinov's *Marxism and the Philosophy of Language* which echoes Marx's Preface to *The Critique of Political Economy*:

> Consciousness takes shapes and being in the material of signs created by an organised group in the process of its social intercourse. The individual consciousness is nurtured on signs; it derives its growth from them; it reflects their logic and laws. The logic of consciousness is the logic of ideological communication, of the semiotic interaction of a social group. (Volosinov, 1973, p. 13)

For Volosinov language is material ('the material of signs' generates consciousness) because language is a social and therefore an ideological and material process. The social dimension of the sign is an element emphasized by Williams in his own account of language and materialism, but he fundamentally alters Saussure's view of the binary sign by arguing that in its very inception the sign is imbricated in social and political practice. Thus, whereas Saussure regarded the signifier/signified relation as arbitrary, Williams saw it as 'conventional', with language as a continuing social process of contest, negotiation and transformation, historically shaped by political and material conditions of production (Williams, 1977, p. 37; 1979, p. 330). These observations offer a powerful tool to Marxism, especially when utilized in conjunction with modern discourse theories, such as those of Michel Pêcheux.

Pêcheux's work develops from Althusser's recognition that discourses exist in antagonistic relationships, not just between ISAs which, although generally aligned with the dominant ideology, may conflict at points of overlap, but also internally:

> the ideology locally dominant in an ISA comes from a position in struggle, it is pinned down where it acts as a weapon, and it is reshaped through struggles... an ideology, however dominant it may be in an ISA, does not exist without some opposing ideology and that opposing ideologies are shaped by each other... (Macdonell, 1986, p. 35)

Pecheux locates the site of this struggle in language, arguing that 'words, expressions, propositions... change their meaning according to the positions held by those who use them' (Macdonell, 1986, p. 25) and that

> Occasionally, the whole class struggle may be summed up in the struggle for one word against another word. Certain words struggle amongst themselves as enemies. Other words are the site of an *ambiguity*: the stake in a decisive but undecided battle. (Macdonell, 1986, p. 51, citing Pêcheux, 1982)

This presents the most attractive dimension of Pêcheux's work (which also questions Althusser's 'interpellation' with the idea of resistant subjectivities refusing dominant subject-positions through 'disidentification' (Macdonell, 1986, pp. 39–42)), giving a sense of culture as process (Williams, 1983, pp. 87–92) and, centrally, as contest.

Examples of these struggles abound, such as recent reappropriations by the English right wing of terms such as 'individualism', 'liberty' or 'rights' (which have shifted significantly from human rights to consumer rights) or, indeed, the ongoing introduction of business language and practice into the NHS or higher education. On a more complex level the 1995 debate over the nature of British identity and its propagation through the school curriculum suggests how the use of language also materially defines our sense of self. To be Scottish, Irish, Welsh (and perhaps even northern English) is to 'disidentify' with the dominant southern English paradigm and its discourses. This, of course, is the core of much of Raymond Williams's work, especially *Keywords*, which is an attempt to understand the struggle for the control of meaning through specific examples. (Compare the uses of 'popular' outlined in Schiach, 1989.) It also fuels the processive definition of culture espoused by Williams and the cultural materialists, seeing a continuous contest for hegemony through control of the ISAs and the discourses. Williams described a pattern of dominant, residual and emergent ideologies and forms in culture which others (Sinfield, 1994, pp. 66–7) have modified to argue that subcultures and individuals operate in either 'negotiated' or 'oppositional' relations to the dominant ideology and its apparatuses. Negotiation means that the disidentified groups adapt the dominant system and seek to accommodate it (the assimilationist arguments with women's, gay and black politics, such as Emily's List or Stonewall), whilst the oppositional or radical groups refuse the interpellations and discourses (niggers with attitude or queer politics seen in groups like Queer Nation or ACTUP).

A second important dimension to post-Machereyan Marxist theory is the role it assigns to the ideological production of forms which is, to some degree, an extension of the arguments rehearsed above about the ideological nature of language. A good example of can be seen in the use of 'convention' by Raymond Williams, a term traced back in *Keywords* to its other sense of a shared or agreed set of assumptions. This can be applied to literary conventions, depicting realism as an agreed manner of the representation of the social and material worlds. Such critical strategies also facilitate the introduction of the ideological determination of form through the institutions of the State, such as schools and universities. Forms, systems of writing (what constitutes good or bad style, suitable languages or decorum and so on) can all be placed within their ideological contexts (see Williams, 1981, chs 2, 3, 6 and 7). So the choice of tragedy can be explored as a marker of the class-status of the subject and through its associations with classical learning and Senecan or classical tragedy. This reveals the radical impact of dramas such as *Arden of Faversham*, which depict the lives of the middling sort within the tragic frame or, more broadly, the inherent radicalism in the substitution of vernacular for neo-Latin writing and the wholesale appropriation of classical devices for a wider audience seen in the plays of Kyd and Marlowe. This broadly is what Williams means when he speaks of locating texts within the conditions of production, the material and cultural matrices which shape a text, although he was also aware that this could lead to a naively sociological approach. In *Politics and Letters* he comments:

> We do not now read Shakespeare, we read editions of Shakespeare and this is not just in the technical sense of when the pages were printed, but in a very much more substantial sense of the reproduction of the text in a quite different culture... The conditions of production thus always include the conditions of making a text contemporary; to forget this would be to fall into a mere sociologism of the originating condition. All the forces which keep the text current are among its conditions of production. (1979, pp. 344–5).

This, of course, leads to another field of study: the performance history of the text in relation to the institutions of production. Adaptation, performance, teaching approaches, earlier criticism can all be absorbed in the construction of the changing history of the conditions of production, but Williams is centrally concerned with how modern theatrical and critical practices help reproduce the play and the uses those appropriations might foster. These suggestions are developed most thoroughly in the work of the British cultural materialists, with their interest in institutions such as the RSC and their role in the continuance of the dominant culture of England and Englishness.

Shakespeare's *Coriolanus* shows some of these approaches in operation. The play opens with the starving citizens of Rome demanding corn of the patricians only to be fobbed off with the fable of the body told by Menenius. The body acts as an image of the state (a political commonplace of the period) and is used by Menenius to justify the control of the aristocracy (described as the 'belly' or centre of the body) while the plebeians are the 'mutinous members' (Shakespeare, 1986: *Coriolanus*, I. i. 147). Although the plebeians eventually do submit and return to their homes their very presence on stage and the threatened riot illustrate how the corporeal image was being contested, as it was during the period when some political commentators argued that the body was an image of equality and cooperation in contrast to other more hierarchical interpretations. Indeed, the image belongs to a complex, contested political discourse in the period and even those who argued for the hierarchical body imagined a community based on mutual and reciprocal duties of care and obedience. Thus the patricians were supposed to be charitable and to respect the 'moral economy of the period' (Thompson, 1971), a point often emphasized by the city council in early modern London (Knowles, 1993), and of particular resonance in 1607, the year of the play's composition, due to enclosure riots in the Midlands.

The body politic of the play presents a good example of the class struggle encapsulated in images and words because the patricians have, according to the plebeians, failed in their duty and disrupted the moral economy by hoarding. Here, another conflict starts to appear between the moral economy model and the developing market-led economics which required the generation of shortages to raise prices and create profit. Moreover, against the emergent market the conservative body image is being redefined to exclude the duties of rank and simply to insist on obedience. Those disidentified with the system were also starting to fight back and construct the body image as one of democratic participation. So the use of the fable as a paradigm for a play crucially built round the individual/society conflict provides a highly charged image open to the ambiguities which Pêcheux envisaged as the markers of class struggle.

The form of *Coriolanus* is equally significant. As a Roman tragedy the play drew upon a widely used vocabulary in the period which compared either Roman republican or imperial history with the state of England (Smuts, 1994). The Roman imagery was highly charged because, abetted by Ben Jonson, James I had started to utilize Roman imperial imagery for his own monarchy, depicting himself as the new Augustus come to refound a nation through the union of the crowns and to restore true classical order. The choice of Roman setting in *Coriolanus* is doubly interesting. First, it brings an essentially erudite, literate, contested and controversial discourse out of the study and court and into the primarily oral and less socially exclusive arena of the public theatre. Secondly, the specific choice of a moment of crisis in the Roman republic registers strongly in the contemporary context. *Coriolanus* situates itself at a cusp between nascent tyranny and the continuance of the republic, and Shakespeare's choice of moment may have been influenced by the libertarian reading of Livy's Roman history found in Machiavelli's *Discourses* (Barton, 1985 and Patterson, 1989, ch. 6).

So the choice of period, style and even images and vocabulary within *Coriolanus* all point towards how the play engages with contemporary debates and struggles. Yet we might go further and consider the figure of *Coriolanus* in the light of Pêcheux's theory of 'disidentification'. Coriolanus occupies a contradictory position within the text. He is both hero and villain (if we can use such simplistic terms momentarily), a patrician to the hilt, yet his class's own worst enemy. He is the symbol of Roman masculinity, yet he takes his name from their defeated neighbours, the Corioles (itself a highly ambiguous nomination which locates him as victor and vanquished, patriot and foe), whilst his body seems to epitomize the political body which the play invokes. At times he seems more like a piece of monumental art than a human: 'He sits in his state as a thing made for Alexander' (V. iv. 21–2). So, even as Coriolanus epitomizes Roman martial virtue (marked in his association with the god of war, Mars), we are made aware of the contradictions of his position. Our awareness of these tensions is only increased by the plethora of views of Coriolanus we are offered, complicating any assessment of his personality and role.

These contradictions then emerge forcefully in the process of disidentification which the play dramatizes. Through his mother Volumnia and the account of his son's childhood (I. iii) we can imagine the kind of education and indoctrination Coriolanus was subjected to, and we see his actions in war and in peace, and how the virtues of the one are the handicaps of the other. Thus when he is expelled from Rome and must rebuild himself away from the very qualities that made him, we see dramatized the process of disidentification: the refusal of his Roman identity. Of course, it is Coriolanus's tragedy that he cannot escape that original interpellation, as his mother demonstrates, so destroying her son. This momentary return to childhood and to the patterns of his former allegiance leads directly to Aufidius's taunt: 'Name not the god of war, thou boy of tears' (V. vi. 102), confirming not only Coriolanus's infancy, but also suggesting how he ceased to be a real man (hence the 'tears' which contrast the solidity associated with male martial virtue to the soft, fluidity culturally attached to women). His final dismemberment is a terrifying visualization, not only of mob fury, but of the destruction of the political and natural body at the heart of this play. It is equally a moment of final complication in the audience's responses to Coriolanus and the dilemmas and situations embedded in the plot, for momentarily we can sympathize with the violence of the avenging families. In fact the audience undergoes a similar process of interpellation and disidentification as the play unfolds, our divided responses to Coriolanus, the Roman citizens, the tribunes and Aufidius and his compatriots, continuously frustrating any simple identification or sympathy. It is as if the play constantly offers to interpellate the spectator then simultaneously undoes that identification. No wonder Brecht found it a suitable play for rewriting.

It is perhaps fitting to close this unit with an East German writer since the fall of the East German regime precipitated the crisis within the whole of the Soviet bloc (which some erroneously refer to as the 'fall of communism'). The collapse of the Soviet empire does not mean the 'defeat' of communism or the irrelevance of Marxist theory in cultural studies. Rather, this is one of the great moments of opportunity for Marxism, the point when the revisionist elements within Marxism have been freed, finally, from association with an oppressive state. Within the academy Marxism flourishes, as an expression of the broadly accepted need to embed cultural forms in their historical context, and as part of the diversification of the subject. The basic principles of Marxism still speak loud in societies increasingly filled with forms of economic oppression and where human rights are constantly challenged in the name of efficiency, flexibility and competitiveness. In this world, Marxist theory provides the mechanism whereby as readers, writers, teachers and thinkers we can all contribute to a critique of our societies and their values.

The best introductions to Marxist theory remain T. Eagleton's *Marxism and Literary*

*Criticism* (1976) and D. Forgacs, 'Marxist Literary Theories' (1986). Williams in *Politics and Letters* (1979), particularly the section on 'Marxism and Literature', is very revealing about the major issues of Marxist criticism and his own attempts to negotiate them. 'Marxism and Literature', although rather abstract when read in conjunction with *Politics* and *Letters*, provides one of the most stimulating manifestos for a Marxist critical practice. A wider variety of critical approaches can be sampled in Mulhern (1992). An outstanding introduction to language and ideology can be found in Macdonell (1986).

## New historicism and cultural materialism

New historicism and its British counterpart, cultural materialism, have developed from Marxist criticism during the 1980s. Both approaches signalled a return to history along with a determination to understand texts in their culture, and to use texts to explore how cultures represent and reproduce themselves. Crucially, new historicism differs from old historical scholarship in its insistence upon the availability of the past only through its narratives, self-representations and texts, using the play between 'history' as past events, and 'history' as the narrative of past events; summarized by Louis Adrian Montrose as 'the Historicity of Texts and the Textuality of History' (Montrose, 1986b, p. 8).

Although new historicist and cultural materialist methods have considerable overlapping theoretical bases and fields of interest (embodied in the appearance of the leading new historicist Stephen Greenblatt's 'Invisible Bullets' in the flagship volume for cultural materialism, *Political Shakespeare*), the differences between their approaches have become more apparent recently and, indeed, within new historicism there are considerable internal fissures, between figures such as Greenblatt and others such as Louis Adrian Montrose (Montrose, 1981, 1986a and b, 1989). This is to say nothing of the vigorous critiques from outside, especially from historians concerned at the inaccuracies of historicism, from feminists disenchanted with the unconscious misogyny of much new historicism, or from critics concerned by doubts about the political orientation of the method, which can appear to be very conservative, or at least nihilistically affirmative of the power of the state to dominate its subjects.

The differences between new historicism and cultural materialism lie in their shared Marxist heritage and the divergent responses of American and British intellectuals to the post-Althusserian shift, to the crisis in Marxist thought brought about by the Cold War and the Paris (and other) uprisings of 1968, and to the different political circumstances introduced by the accession of Reagan and Thatcher to power in the 1980s (Dutton and Wilson, 1992, 'Introduction'). In Stephen Greenblatt's *Renaissance Self-Fashioning* (1980), the first major work of new historicism, the most cited theoretical influences are Althusser and Foucault, whereas in *Political Shakespeare* (edited by the cultural materialists Jonathan Dollimore and Alan Sinfield and published in 1985), although Althusser and Foucault have key roles, the influences of Gramsci, Brecht, and crucially the British Marxist tradition represented by

Christopher Hill (the historian) and Raymond Williams (the literary critic) can also be traced. These differences become even more marked in later work as the influence of Bordieu permeates Greenblatt's later work, drawing him further away from the avowedly materialist emphases of cultural materialism (Romany, 1989, pp. 273–4).

So what are the major tenets of new historicism and cultural materialism, and how do they treat texts? The quintessential new historicist essay remains Greenblatt's 'Invisible Bullets: Renaissance Authority and its Subversion, *Henry IV* and *Henry V*', which links the activities of Hal in Cheapside to the Elizabethan colonialist enterprise, and envisions the play as a kind of internal colonialism, as Hal explores in order to control all the better the underbelly of his kingdom. In a typical new historicist strategy Greenblatt starts with an anecdote about Thomas Harriot (a contact of Marlowe and purported atheist) who reported how the Indians believed that the Europeans were killing them with 'invisible bullets' (in fact smallpox). Faced with this belief the Europeans recognized both the arbitrary nature of faith but also its utility in coercing the natives into obedience; and, indeed their own faith is restored by this event, since the savages have been punished, showing the existence of divine providence. This incident and its reporting by Harriot in his *Brief and True Report of the New Found Land of Virginia* (1588) functions as an analogy for a process which Greenblatt sees as endemic in early modern society, whereby power continually defines itself through whatever threatens it. Indeed, he takes the argument a stage further to urge that 'subversiveness is the very product of ... power and furthers its ends. One may go further and suggest that... power... not only produces its own subversion but is actively built upon it...' (Greenblatt, 1985, p. 24). A moment of subversive doubt such as a sceptical impulse not to believe in providence thus becomes the tool to recognize that others may be oppressed by the arbitrary nature of faith (they may be coerced to believe), and that the potentially subversive moment becomes a way to reinforce order.

This realization is then used by Greenblatt as a model for the whole of *Henry IV*, where Hal is less the apprentice king learning about his nation's ways so that he may govern well, than a Machiavellian manipulator, surveying the potentially subversive elements so that he may know and contain them. Indeed, Hal provokes the very crimes that he will then condemn, as a reinforcement of his own power. The 'mock-trial' scene (II. v) (Shakespeare, 1986) illustrates this as Hal persuades Falstaff to play his father (Henry IV), and arraign his recalcitrant 'son' for the faults of his life. Unsatisfied with Falstaff's rule (a deeply symbolic moment itself), Hal insists that he will now play the King, and proceeds to show his knowledge of Falstaff and his faults (450–70), finally provoking Falstaff (now playing Hal) to argue that he should not banish Falstaff:

> FALSTAFF
> Banish not him thy Harry's company.
> Banish plump Jack, and banish all the world.
>
> PRINCE HAL
> I do; I will.
>
> (*1 Henry IV*, II. v. 483–6, in Shakespeare, 1986)

The chilling certainty of this moment which envisions and enacts the future (especially in the double sense of 'will') provides an exact model for the operation of power described by Greenblatt. Power (Hal) provokes subversion (Falstaff) and then uses that subversion to invoke the necessity of power to suppress its constitutive suppression. This grim picture is only strengthened by the sense of the pervasiveness of power figured in the disguised prince acting as an agent provocateur to entrap his own people.

This example provides one of the key patterns of new historicism, the movement from power to subversion to containment. Power creates subversion in order to create and justify itself. It is as if the whole of early modern society functions like a court masque, where the antimasque conjures up disorder which the vision of royal order and power in the masque will dissolve, although even as Greenblatt celebrates the theatricality of this power (all power is performance in new historicism) he admits the stark material world which underlies the image in his recitation of the tortures and violences done by this society. For Greenblatt, the marginal voices and pluralities of culture that he wishes to capture simply fuel the containments of power: 'There is subversion, no end of subversion, only not for us.'

It is in the different treatment of power-containment-subversion that divergences between new historicism and cultural materialism emerge. Cultural materialism concurs in the basic analysis of the operations of power. For example, the opening sentence of Dollimore's reading of *Measure for Measure* (Dollimore, 1985, p. 72) is a classic statement of subversion-containment. But cultural materialists place much greater emphasis upon conflict and contradiction within society and within ideology, and the power of marginalized voices, so that 'low-life transgression' in *Measure* is regarded as '*positively* anarchic, ludic [and] carnivalesque – a subversion from below of a repressive official ideology of order' (Dollimore, 1985, p. 73). The shift to 'transgression' registers a more mobile and flexible sense of the powers of those marginalized by 'the authoritarian demonising of the deviant' (p. 74) to swerve away from authority's grasp. Dollimore and Sinfield oppose the totalizing vision of culture implied by Greenblatt (see Greenblatt, 1990):

> Ideology has always been challenged, not least by the exploited themselves, who have resisted its oppressive construction of them and its mystification of their disadvantaged social position. One concern of a materialist criticism is with the history of such resistance, with the attempt to recover the voices and cultures of the repressed and marginalized in history and writing. (Dollimore and Sinfield, 1985b, p. 214)

This method owes much to the Machereyan notion of 'reading against the grain', but also deploys a more dynamic model of social and cultural structures, allowing for social change, and which derives ultimately from Williams's description of the residual, emergent and dominant parts of culture.

A cultural materialist reading would, then, place greater emphasis upon the subversive potentials of the marginal voices of a text, such as the prostitutes in *Measure* (Dollimore, 1985, pp. 85–6), giving greater weight to the presence of these oppressed and marginalized voices within the play to challenge authority (see also Wilson, 1987). Thus in *1 Henry IV* the Cheapside scenes allow marginal voices (women, prostitutes, tapsters) an independent presence which counters the colonialist impulse to record their dialect and idiom the better to control them. The 'mock-trial' and the Gad's Hill robbery (encouraged by Hal) become images of the institutionalized brutality and property-theft which underlie the state. Indeed, the assumption of the king's role by Falstaff (perhaps played by a clown, and certainly drawing upon the medieval Vice figure for his characteristics) serves as a demystification of power: king and clown are equated. Cultural materialism revels in exactly these juxtapositions which reveal the contradictions and conflicts within society, placing the 'deviant' and the authoritative against each other to show their similarity and interdependence.

The juxtaposition of new historicism and cultural materialism uncovers some of the problems in their method. First, the subversion/containment argument became both commonplace and sterile, with cultural materialists and new historicists trading subversions and containments like pantomime characters. Sometimes it can seem as if new historicism consists of nothing but subversion or containment, and the neat formulation also allows all sorts of radical moments to be detected in texts, without rigorous substantiation or demonstration of their presence or proper explanation of their effects. The second question about new historicism is related to this issue, because the way it describes culture generates much of the power of the subversion/containment paradox. Yet, as cultural materialism stresses, cultures are more complex, dynamic and plural, and if we accept the initial new historicist model, social change (and, indeed, change of any kind) becomes impossible. Greenblatt later shifted his ground on this point to allow for a more dynamic view of culture (Greenblatt, 1990, pp. 229 and 231), recognizing that it was a process more than a state. The term 'negotiation' starts to invest his work, replacing subversion/containment with a more flexible and dynamic process which implies greater balance between power and its subjects (Greenblatt, 1988; 1990, p. 229; see also Leinwand, 1990). The third question we might raise is the status of the anecdotes with which new historicism always prefaces its readings and which, in addition to providing the striking style and impact of much new historicist criticism (Veeser, 1994, p. 5), shapes the models through which it interprets culture. These anecdotes are highly problematic, because on one hand they seem to be *objets trouvés*, merely little examples which preface the main story, and which provide a neat, memorable encapsulation of the argument (think of Harriot and the invisible bullets). They are designed to show the illogicality of history and its discontinuity (part of the new historicist celebration of the plural, marginal and strange), and in this sense they are simply 'contingent', in that they have only a chance connection to the main argument. Yet these anecdotes are often then expanded as analogies, standing as interpretive models for whole cultures, which suggests that everything is connected to everything else, and that history is not illogical and discontinuous, but 'contingent' in another sense, that is causal (Veeser, 1994, p. 4). These analogies become crucially important to the whole new historicist project, and on their veracity much of the project stands or falls; but new historicists are notably reticent about tracing out the precise connections, the actual causality that underlies the apparent casuality of the fable, to such an extent that factual analysis becomes very difficult (Veeser, 1994, p. 4; Ross, 1990; Romany, 1989).

One of the most interesting aspects of both new historicism and cultural materialism has been the development of its interest in 'subjectivity', influenced by both Foucault and Althusser. Foreshadowed at the end of *Renaissance Self-Fashioning* (which examines how self and society mutually shape each other), 'Invisible Bullets' initiates an exploration of how the early modern state controlled its subjects, suggesting that rather than using physical force, hidden controls were introduced, using surveillance to persuade individuals that if they transgressed they would be caught and punished. (The agent provocateur prince of *1 Henry IV* and the disguised friar/duke of *Measure* embody exactly this process.) Moreover, ideological weapons were used to inculcate the individual into certain patterns of 'good' behaviour in the interest of the State, while 'bad' mores were rejected. The crucial locale of this education was the individual's sense of self: their subjectivity. This is an analysis developed from Foucault's thesis (expressed most succinctly in *Discipline and Punish* (Foucault, 1977)), that modern state formation was marked by a transformation in modes of power. The (early) modern state no longer sought to control through simple physical punishment, but rather through systems of belief and behaviour, or 'discipline', a term which suggests a code of practice about how to behave but which also retains overtones of coercion and punishment. The model is close to Althusser's notion of the reproduction of ISAs through the subject and his/her interpellation, that means one's sense of identity is embedded in and created by ideology, and that to be, to know consciousness, is to be ideologically determined. Greenblatt saw exactly these systems (what he termed 'coercive belief') in operation throughout the period.

From this starting-point a whole strand of new historicism and cultural materialism developed, designed to show how the 'process of *subjectification*' operated to shape 'individuals as loci of consciousness and initiators of action, to endow them with subjectivity', a process which simultaneously 'positions, motivates, and constrains them within – subjects them to – social networks and cultural codes that exceed their comprehension or control' (Montrose, 1986b, p. 9). In Britain this argument was pursued by Francis Barker and Catherine Belsey (among others, including Dollimore (1985) and Montrose (1986a and 1989)), to show how new senses of selfhood developed in the early modern period, related to emergent concepts of privacy, individuality and property (Barker, 1984; Belsey, 1985). For Belsey subjectivity becomes the subject of Renaissance drama (she calls her book *The Subject of Tragedy*) whilst Barker uses *Hamlet* to posit the development of the 'bourgeois subject' (which the play in a contradictory and inconsistent manner manifests) precisely so that we can, from the historical vantage point offered by the text, illumine the constructedness of our modern sense of self, and its basic hollowness. For both, to pursue the history of subjectivity is to question the whole structure of modern society and to interrogate the basis of the current political order. The scale of this project and the desire to produce a clear narrative history (even if it does include discontinuities and allow plurality) marks another divergence from the heavily poststructuralist suspicion of metahistories found in American new historicism, and it has also laid them and the whole approach open to fierce criticism (Aers, 1992; Mauss, 1991).

Both new historicism and cultural materialism have been immensely productive critical methods and have fuelled a revival of interest in the Renaissance which would have been hard to conceive at the start of the 1980s. Despite this, or perhaps because of this success and the stranglehold new historicism seemed to have on the academy, especially in America, the approach has also attracted great opprobrium, even as it has spread to compass the medieval period (Patterson, 1990), Romanticism (Hunt, 1989; Liu, 1989a; Simpson, 1991), the Victorian period (Gallagher, 1985; Miller, 1988), American literature (Berkovitch, 1986; Seltzer, 1984; Tompkins, 1994) and many more. In particular, criticism has focused on its dubious historical scholarship (Barroll, 1988; Cressy, 1991) and unwillingness to explore class or macroeconomics with any clarity or rigour (Abrams, cited in Veeser, 1994; Romany, 1989). The most strident rejection of new historicist readings of Shakespeare will be found in Brian Vickers's traditional, scholarly counter attack (1993). Others have noticed a persistent disregard of arguably the most important feature of early modern life: religion. Added to these are more theoretically oriented criticisms, particularly directed at the static view of culture in early new historicism, and at the anthropological models used. The uncritical acceptance of Geertz's 'thick description' and the totalizing view of culture it involves has raised further doubts about the method. Suitably, for a paradoxical method some of the paradoxical effects of new historicism have also placed questions against its results, especially the way in which, although the method ostensibly celebrates the marginal and the non-literary and the interconnection of high and low cultures, the main thrust of its criticism has focused on canonical texts. New historicism might start with an appeal to plurality but it closes with an affirmation of the centrality of the canon (Felperin, 1990; Holstun, 1989). Ironically, some of the most radical work has not stemmed directly from cultural materialism, even with its greater political commitment and interest in the ideological reproduction of the state and culture (Sinfield, 1985a and 1985b), but rather from the older English Marxist tradition of 'history from below' in Margot Heinemann's attempt to place canonical texts within the context of a radical tradition in English Renaissance drama (Heinemann, 1990).

Despite these criticisms the return to history in criticism has had some beneficial effects and produced some excellent and engaging criticism. Although there are questions about the attitude to women with new historicism, it has also helped fuel a revival of interest in early modern women writers. The powerfully political and subjective nature of the method (called by one critic 'narcissistic' (Liu, 1989b)) has also allowed the infiltration of minority voices into the heart of the academy. It is no accident that both Dollimore and Sinfield have moved into gay studies (Dollimore, 1991; Sinfield, 1994), and that the rise of a more historical criticism has opened the question of the position of all sorts of minorities and subcultures within early modern society. If this emphasis continues, engaging with the plurality of cultures (whatever the period), then new historicism and cultural materialism will have acted powerfully in the necessary diversification of criticism and the academy.

Four collections of essays provide a useful selection of new historicist and cultural materialist texts (Dollimore and Sinfield, 1985a; Dutton and Wilson, 1992;

Greenblatt, 1988; and Veeser, 1994). The introductions to Dollimore and Sinfield, Dutton and Wilson and Veeser provide good discussions, while a more complex critique is mounted in Veeser (1989). Leinwand (1990) provides an interesting discussion of some practical applications of Greenblatt's later work (and an illuminating discussion of the use of Foucault). Aers (1992) presents a salutary correction from a strongly Marxist position.

## BIBLIOGRAPHY

MARXISM AND LITERARY CRITICISM

Althusser, L. (1971) *Essays on Ideology*, Verso, London.
Arvon, H. (1973) *Marxist Esthetics*, trans. H.R. Lane, Cornell University Press, Ithaca.
Barthes, R. (1970) *S/Z*, Seuil, Paris.
Barton, A. (1985) 'Livy, Machiavelli and Shakespeare's *Coriolanus*', *Shakespeare Survey*, 38, 115–29.
Bennett, T. (1979) *Formalism and Marxism*, Methuen, London.
Bloomfield, J. (ed.) (1977) *Papers on Class, Hegemony, Party*, Lawrence & Wishart, London.
Cohen, W. (1985) *Drama of A Nation: Public Theater in Renaissance England and Spain*, Cornell University Press, Ithaca.
Drakakis, J. (ed.) (1985) *Alternative Shakespeares*, Methuen, London.
Eagleton, T. (1976) *Marxism and Literary Criticism*, Methuen, London.
Eagleton, T. (1983) *Literary Theory: An Introduction*, Blackwell, Oxford.
Eagleton, T. (1986) *Against the Grain: Selected Essays*, Verso, London.
Eagleton, T. (1989) 'Base and Superstructure in Raymond Williams', in *Raymond Williams: Critical Perspectives*, ed. T. Eagleton, Polity Press, Cambridge.
Eagleton, T. (ed.) (1994) *Ideology*, Longman, Harlow.
Eliot, G. (1986) *Middlemarch*, ed. D. Carroll, Oxford University Press, Oxford.
Forgacs, D. (1986) 'Marxist Literary Theories', in *Modern Literary Theory: A Comparative Introduction*, ed. A. Jefferson and D. Robey, Batsford, London, 166–203.
Frow, J. (1986) *Marxism and Literary History*, Blackwell, Oxford.
Gramsci, A. (1971) *Selections from the Prison Notebooks*, trans. Q. Hoare and G. Nowell Smith, Lawrence & Wishart, London.
Greene, G. and Kahn, C. (eds) (1985) *Making a Difference: Feminist Literary Criticism*, Methuen, London.
Hall, S. (1977) 'Re-thinking the "Base and Superstructure" Metaphor' in *Papers on Class, Hegemony, Party*, ed. J. Bloomfield, 43–72.
Hawthorn, J. (ed.) (1984) *Criticism and Cultural Theory*, Edward Arnold, London.
Jefferson, A. and Robey, D. (1986) *Modern Literary Theory: A Comparative Introduction*, 2nd edn, Batsford, London.
Kaplan, C. (1985) 'Pandora's Box: Subjectivity, Class and Sexuality in Socialist Feminist Criticism', in *Making a Difference: Feminist Literary Criticism*, ed. G. Greene and C. Kahn, Methuen, London, 146–76.
Kavanagh, J. (1985) 'Shakespeare in Ideology', in *Alternative Shakespeares*, ed. J. Drakakis, 144–65.
Kavanagh, J. (1990) 'Ideology', in *Critical Terms for Literary Study*, ed. F. Lentricchia and T. McLaughlin, University of Chicago Press, Chicago, 306–20.
Kavanagh, J. and Lewis, T.E. (1982) 'Interview with Etienne Balibar and P. Machery', *Diacritics* 12, 46–52.
Knowles, J.D. (1993) 'The Spectacle of the Realm: Civic Consciousness, Rhetoric and

Ritual', in *Theatre and Government in Early Stuart England*, ed. J.R. Mulryne and M. Shewring, Cambridge University Press, Cambridge, 157–89.

Lentricchia, F. and McLaughlin, T. (ed.) (1990) *Critical Terms for Literary Study*, University of Chicago Press, Chicago.

Lodge, D. (1991) '*Middlemarch* and the Idea of the Classic Realist Text', in *George Eliot: A Critical Reader*, ed. K.M. Newton, Longman, London (reprinted from A. Kettle (ed.), *The Nineteenth-Century Novel: Critical Essays and Documents* (1981)).

Lukács, G. (1972) *Studies in European Realism*, Merlin Press, London [first published Hillway Publishing, London, 1950].

MacCabe, C. (1978) *James Joyce and the Revolution of the World*, Macmillan, London.

McClellan, D. (1979) *Marxism After Marx*, Macmillan, London.

Macdonell, D. (1986) *Theories of Discourse: An Introduction*, Blackwell, Oxford.

Macherey, P. (1978) *A Theory of Literary Production*, trans. G. Wall, Routledge & Kegan Paul, London.

Marx, K. (1977) *Selected Writings*, ed. D. McClellan, Oxford University Press, Oxford.

Marx, K. and Engels, F. (1976) *On Literature and Art*, Progress Publishers, Moscow.

Mercer, C. (1984) 'Paris Match: Marxism, Structuralism and the Problem of Literature', in *Criticism and Cultural Theory*, ed. J. Hawthorn, Edward Arnold, London, 43–58.

Mulhern, F. (ed.) (1992) *Contemporary Marxist Criticism*, Longman, Harlow.

Mulryne, J.R. and Shewring, M. (eds) (1993) *Theatre and Government in Early Stuart England*, Cambridge University Press, Cambridge.

Patterson, A. (1989) *Shakespeare and the Popular Voice*, Blackwell, Oxford.

Pêcheux, M. (1982) *Language, Semantics and Ideology*, trans. H. Nagpal, Macmillan, London.

Schiach, M. (1989) *Discourse on Popular Culture: Class, Gender and History in Cultural Analysis, 1730 to the Present*, Polity Press, Cambridge.

Selden, R. (1985) *A Reader's Guide to Contemporary Literary Theory*, Harvester Wheatsheaf, Hemel Hempstead.

Selden, R. (1989) *Practising Theory and Reading Literature: An Introduction*, Harvester Wheatsheaf, Hemel Hempstead.

Shakespeare, W. (1986) *The Complete Works*, ed. G. Taylor and S. Wells, Oxford University Press, Oxford.

Sharpe, K. and Lake, P. (eds) (1994) *Culture and Politics in Early Stuart England*, Macmillan, London.

Simpson, M. (1994) *Male Impersonators: Men Performing Masculinity*, Cassell, London.

Sinfield, A. (1994) *Cultural Politics – Queer Reading*, Routledge, London.

Singer, P. (1980) *Marx*, Oxford University Press, Oxford.

Smuts, M. (1994) 'Court-Centred Politics and the Uses of Roman Historians, *c.*1590–1630', in *Culture and Politics in Early Stuart England*, ed. K. Sharpe and P. Lake, Macmillan, London, 21–44.

Thompson, E.P. (1971) 'The Moral Economy of the English Crowd', *Past and Present*, 50, 76–136.

Volosinov, V.N. (1973) *Marxism and the Philosophy of Language*, trans. L Matejka and I.R. Titunik, reprinted 1986, Harvard University Press, Cambridge, Mass.

Wayne, V. (ed.) (1991) *The Matter of Difference: Materialist Feminist Criticism of Shakespeare*, Harvester Wheatsheaf, Hemel Hempstead.

White, R.S. (1993) 'Marx and Shakespeare', *Shakespeare Survey* 45, 89–100.

Williams, R. (1977) *Marxism and Literature*, Oxford University Press, Oxford.

Williams, R. (1979) *Politics and Letters*, Verso, London.

Williams, R. (1980) *Problems in Materialism and Culture: Selected Essays*, Verso, London.

Williams, R. (1981) *Culture*, Fontana Paperbacks, London.

Williams, R. (1983) *Keywords: A Vocabulary of Culture and Society*, Fontana Paperbacks, London.

Williamson, J. (1983) *Decoding Advertisements: Ideology and Meaning in Advertising*, Marion Boyars, London, 4th impression [first published 1978].

Wolff, J. (1981) *The Social Production of Art*, Macmillan, London.

## NEW HISTORICISM AND CULTURAL MATERIALISM

Aers, D. (1992) 'A Whisper in the Ear of the Early Modernists; or Reflections on Literary Critics Writing the "History of the Subject"', in *Culture and History, 1350–1600*, ed. D. Aers, Harvester Wheatsheaf, Hemel Hempstead.

Barker, F. (1984) *The Tremulous Private Body: Essays in Subjection*, Methuen, London.

Barroll, J.L. (1988) 'A New History for Shakespeare and his Time', *Shakespeare Quarterly* 39, 441–64.

Belsey, C. (1985) *The Subject of Tragedy: Identity and Difference in Renaissance Drama*, Methuen, London.

Berkovitch, S. (1986) 'The Problem of Ideology in American Literary History', *Critical Inquiry* 12, 631–53.

Braunmuller, A.R. and Hattaway, M. (eds) (1990) *The Cambridge Companion to English Renaissance Drama*, Cambridge University Press, Cambridge.

Cressy, D. (1991) 'Foucault, Stone and Shakespeare', *English Literary Renaissance* 21, 121–33.

Dollimore, J. (1985) 'Transgression and Surveillance in *Measure for Measure*', in *Political Shakespeare: New Essays in Cultural Materialism*, ed. J. Dollimore and A. Sinfield, Manchester University Press, Manchester, 72–87.

Dollimore, J. (1991) *Sexual Dissidence: Augustine to Wilde, Freud to Foucault*, Oxford University Press, Oxford.

Dollimore, J. and Sinfield, A. (eds) (1985a) *Political Shakespeare: New Essays in Cultural Materialism*, Manchester University Press, Manchester.

Dollimore, J. and Sinfield, A. (1985b) 'History and Ideology: The Instance of Henry V', in *Alternative Shakespeares*, ed. J. Drakakis, Methuen, London, 206–27.

Drakakis, J. (ed.) (1985) *Alternative Shakespeares*, Methuen, London.

Dutton, R. and Wilson, R. (eds) (1992) *New Historicism and Renaissance Drama*, Longman, Harlow.

Felperin, H. (1990) *The Uses of the Canon: Elizabethan Literature and Contemporary Theory*, Oxford University Press, Oxford.

Foucault, M. (1977) *Discipline and Punish: The Birth of the Prison*, Penguin, Harmondsworth.

Gallagher, C. (1985) *The Industrial Reformation of English Fiction: Social Discourse and Narrative Form, 1790–1867*, Chicago University Press, Chicago.

Greenblatt, S. (1980) *Renaissance Self-Fashioning*, University of California Press, Berkeley.

Greenblatt, S. (1985) 'Invisible Bullets: Renaissance Authority and its Subversion, *Henry IV* and *Henry V*', in *Political Shakespeare: New Essays in Cultural Materialism*, ed. J. Dollimore and A. Sinfield, Methuen, London, 18–47.

Greenblatt, S. (ed.) (1988) *Representing the English Renaissance*, University of California Press, Berkeley.

Greenblatt, S. (1988a) *Shakespearean Negotiations: The Circulation of Social Energy in Renaissance England*, Clarendon Press, Oxford.

Greenblatt, S. (1990) 'Culture', in *Critical Terms for Literary Study*, ed. F. Lentricchia and T. McLaughlin, University of Chicago Press, Chicago, 225–32.

Heinemann, M. (1990) 'Political Drama', in *The Cambridge Companion to English Renaissance Drama*, ed. A.R. Braunmuller and M. Hattaway, Cambridge University Press, Cambridge, 161–205.

Holstun, J. (1989) 'Ranting at the New Historicism', *English Literary Renaissance* 19, 189–225.

Hunt, L. (ed.) (1989) *The New Cultural History*, University of California Press, Berkeley.

Leinwand, T.B. (1990) 'Negotiation and New Historicism', *Papers of the Modern Language Society of America* 105, 477–90.

Lentricchia, F. and McLaughlin, T. (1990) *Critical Terms for Literary Study*, University of Chicago Press, Chicago.

Liu, A. (1989a) *Wordsworth, the Sense of History*, Stanford University Press, Stanford.

Liu, A. (1989b) 'The Power of Formalism: the New Historicism', *English Literary History* 56, 721–71.

Mauss, K.E. (1991) 'Proof and Its Consequences: Inwardness and Its Exposure in the English Renaissance', *Representations* 34, 29–52.

Miller, D.A. (1988) *The Novel and the Police*, University of California Press, Berkeley.

Montrose, L.A. (1981) 'A Poetics of Renaissance Culture', *Criticism* 23, 349–59.

Montrose, L.A. (1986a) 'The Elizabethan Subject and the Spenserian Text', in *Literary Theory/Renaissance Texts*, ed. P. Parker and D. Quint, Johns Hopkins University Press, Baltimore, 303–40.

Montrose, L.A. (1986b) 'Renaissance Literary Studies and the Subject of History', *English Literary Renaissance* 16, 5–12.

Montrose, L.A. (1989) 'Professing the Renaissance: The Poetics and Politics of Culture', in *The New Historicism*, ed. H.A. Veeser, Routledge, London.

Parker, P. and Quint, D. (eds) (1986) *Literary Theory/Renaissance Texts*, Johns Hopkins University Press, Baltimore.

Patterson, L. (1990) *Literary Practice and Social Change, 1380–1530*, California University Press, Berkeley.

Romany, F. (1989) 'Shakespeare and the New Historicism', *Essays in Criticism* 39, 271–88.

Ross, M.B. (1990) 'Contingent Predilections: The Newest Historicisms and the Question of Method', *Centennial Review* 34, 485–538.

Selden, R. (1989) *Practising Theory and Reading Literature*, Harvester Wheatsheaf, Hemel Hempstead.

Seltzer, M. (1984) *Henry James and the Art of Power*, Cornell University Press, Ithaca.

Shakespeare, W. (1986) *Complete Works*, ed. S. Wells and G. Taylor, Oxford University Press, Oxford.

Simpson, D. (ed.) (1991) *Subject to History: Ideology, Gender, Class*, Cornell University Press, Ithaca.

Sinfield, A. (1985a) 'Introduction: Reproductions, Interventions', in *Political Shakespeare: New Essays in Cultural Materialism*, ed. J. Dollimore and A. Sinfield, Manchester University Press, Manchester, 130–3.

Sinfield, A. (1985b) 'Royal Shakespeare: Theatre and the Making of Ideology', in *Political Shakespeare: New Essays in Cultural Materialism*, ed. J. Dollimore and A. Sinfield, Manchester University Press, Manchester, 158–81.

Sinfield, A. (1994) *Cultural Politics – Queer Reading*, Routledge, London.

Tompkins, J. (1994) 'Sentimental Power: *Uncle Tom's Cabin* and the Politics of Literary History' in *The New Historicism Reader*, ed. H.A. Veeser, Routledge, London, 206–28 (reprint from *Sensational Designs: The Cultural Work of American Fiction, 1790–1860*, Oxford University Press, Oxford, 1985).

Veeser, H.A. (ed.) (1989) *The New Historicism*, Routledge, London.

Veeser, H.A. (ed.) (1994) *The New Historicism Reader*, Routledge, London.

Vickers, B. (1993) *Appropriating Shakespeare. Contemporary Critical Quarrels*, Yale University Press, New Haven and London.

Wilson, R. (1987) 'Shakespeare's Roman Carnival', *English Literary History* 54, 31–44.

# Psychoanalytic literary theory

*Anne McCartney*

> for one who'd lived among enemies so long:
> if often he was wrong and, at times, absurd,
> to us he is no more a person
> now but a whole climate of opinion
> under whom we conduct our different lives...
> (W.H. Auden, 'In Memory of Sigmund Freud', *Collected Poems*,
> Faber & Faber, London, 1991)

As Auden suggests, Freud's influence on modern thought has been a lasting one even though his theories have been a continual subject of controversy and a source of challenge. This is especially true in the field of psychoanalytic literary criticism where, despite constant revisions and refinements, new developments have tended to be assimilated into the old framework, with the effect that all psychoanalytic criticism has its origins in Freud's theories. Psychoanalysis aims to understand individuals by uncovering desires hidden deep within the mind and revealing their connections with the conscious surface, and it is this approach which psychoanalytic literary critics take to the text.

   For the critic undertaking a psychoanalytical reading, three interrelated Freudian categories are essential: the unconscious; the sexual origin of human motivation in repressed infantile incestuous desires; and the symbolic manifestation of unconscious wishes in dreams, jokes, errors and significantly in literary works. According to Freud, we each harbour an unconscious mind which operates by more primitive rules than those of consciousness. Our earliest childhood desires and fantasies, primarily sexual in origin, remain permanently lodged in our unconscious minds because they are so frightening and guilt-producing. This is linked to Freud's theory of human psychological development. For Freud, the myth of Oedipus as dramatized in Sophocles' play expressed a profound insight into an important stage of development in that it can be seen to be a tribal wish fulfilment of the taboos of patricide and incest (see Freud, 1953, Vol. VII). Freud saw this as a consequence of the child's close involvement with the mother's body throughout the pregnancy and feeding process. The child's love for the nurturing mother remains dominant throughout the formative years and eventually, according to Freud, the boy-child begins to see the father as a rival for this love, to the point where he fantasizes about killing him. What persuades the boy-child to abandon this incestuous desire is the father's unspoken threat of castration. By perceiving his mother's lack of a penis, the child begins to imagine that this is a punishment which might be used against him, and so represses any incestuous desire; he detaches himself from the mother and identifies with the father as a symbol of a power to which he can eventually aspire. The boy-child has therefore been introduced into the symbolic role of manhood. He has become a gendered subject but in doing so he has repressed his forbidden desires.

The most famous example of the Oedipus complex is, of course, *Hamlet*, and Freud himself was first to point this out in his footnote to *The Interpretation of Dreams* (Freud, 1900) in which he sees Hamlet's inability to kill Claudius as a projection of Shakespeare's own unresolved Oedipus complex. Certainly the character of Hamlet and the reasons for his delay in revenging his father's death are more easily understood in psychological terms. Freud speculated that at the beginning of the play, Hamlet, like all mature males, had gone through the Oedipal stage and repressed his desires so successfully that his prime emotion was one of admiration and love of his father. The murder of his father, however, since it is in effect the realization of his childhood wish, revives his Oedipal 'thoughts' of patricide and incest, and the inner conflict which this causes makes Hamlet hesitate. In *Hamlet and Oedipus* (1949) Ernest Jones develops Freud's theory by suggesting that although Hamlet's guilty feelings, as expressed by the ghost, cause him to plan revenge, he unconsciously identifies with Claudius since, by killing Old Hamlet and marrying Gertrude, Claudius has merely carried out what he, himself, unconsciously desired. Hamlet's hesitation to act stems from the fact that in killing Claudius he would be killing himself. The relationship between Hamlet's conflict and Shakespeare's own psyche, can be better understood in the light of Freud's observation that the play is not the dramatization of a wish fulfilment but is rather a representation of the inhibitions and repressive facets of the writer's mind. Freud believed that events in Shakespeare's life, the death of his father and son, fulfilled in part his unconscious Oedipal wish. However, the guilt and taboos associated with this demand inhibition and self-punishment, and it is this unconscious conflict which surfaces in his plays.

Later Freudian critics took his methods a stage further and saw *Hamlet* as neither a direct wish fulfilment nor a circuitous inhibited one but as a highly elaborate defence mechanism. Edmund Bergler (1979) points out that the then-underdeveloped nature of psychoanalysis prevented Freud from seeing the deeper defensive layers in Shakespeare's psyche. He argues that the overt Oedipal representation in Hamlet is made accessible by Shakespeare in order to screen a 'deeper, repressed guilt', that of his frustrated homosexual impulses.

> It seems to me that Hamlet's crime of Oedipal fantasies, so brilliantly elucidated by Freud, is but a camouflage obscuring a deeper conflict which antedates the Oedipal one.... That Shakespeare himself saw male homosexuality only in terms of femininity is one of the poet's rationalizations (for example, the queen in Hamlet compares her son with a 'female dove').

However, this 'deeper reading' is still tied to Freud's assumption that art transmits under repression the artist's taboo drives, wishes and impulses and that the work's form is both a disguise and a 'forepleasure' for the forbidden desires lurking in the unconscious layers of the psyche.

In *Creative Writers and Daydreaming* (1908), Freud argues that the artistic work is a vehicle for externalizing in a socially acceptable way, a combination of the role-play games of children and the daydreams and fantasies of adulthood. The artist masks his egocentric daydreams to transform primitive desires into culturally acceptable meanings and, in so doing, creates a surrogate neurosis in which the audience or reader can participate safely, its enjoyment being based on illusion. For Freud, aesthetic pleasure is derived from this release from repression. The therapeutic value of art, both for the artist creating it, and for the audience witnessing it, is that it allows emotional identification with its protagonist, while remaining remote enough for the ego not to be completely submerged by the fiction. It is worth noting here that the period in which Freud was evolving his theories (the beginning of the twentieth century) was also the time of the modernist revolution in literary writing. It was hardly a coincidence that the techniques of this style included stream of consciousness, disjointed time sequence, free verse, etc., all of which shifted linguistic expression closer to its mental (subconscious) origins (see Unit 16, p. 453, and Unit 17, p. 489).

The early psychoanalytic critics therefore adopted a variety of approaches to the text. They could begin with a study of the elements in a writer's biography that helped to shape and condition his imagination and apply this to the work. One example of this is Edmund Wilson's essay (*The Wound and the Bow*, 1941) in which he attempts to show how Dickens's works were influenced by the circumstances of his childhood: his father's imprisonment for debt, the humiliation of working in a blacking factory and the bitter indignation and resentment he felt towards his mother who tried to force him to continue working there. Wilson argues that Dickens's whole career was an attempt to digest these early shocks and hardships and to explain them to himself. The danger of the literary critic constructing a psychoanalytical diagnosis of the writer from the hearsay of external writings such as letters, diaries and autobiographies and using this to illuminate the works in this way is all too apparent.

A more common approach of psychoanalytic criticism is to use the work as the equivalent of the confession on the analyst's couch and proceed to draw conclusion about the writer from this, in other words to argue like Bergler (1949) from *Hamlet* about Shakespeare's life and state of mind. Another example is Mary Shelley's *Frankenstein* which, as already shown in Unit 10, is replete with repressed, subverted references to childbirth and procreation and expresses a fear of pregnancy and its connection with death, all of which lends itself to this form of psychoanalytic reading. Ellen Moers (1977) links the creation of Frankenstein's monster with its 'motif of revulsion against newborn life, and the drama of guilt, dread, and flight surrounding birth and its consequences' (p. 142) to fears about monstrous childbirth engendered by Shelley's mother's death in bearing her and by her stressful experience as an outcast's daughter, teenage mother and illegitimate wife. Critics of psychoanalytic literary criticism have tended to deride the reductivism of Freud's 'art out of neurosis theory' with its compulsion to uncover the secret obsessions of writers and characters and the reduction of Shakespeare's genius to a subliminal mastery of homosexual impulses and Swift's satire to anal sadism (see Norman O'Brown's essay on Swift in Lodge, 1972). But just as the discrediting of Freud's methodology and the questioning of the validity of his case studies have not halted advancements in clinical psychoanalysis, neither have the crudities of early Freudian literary criticism halted more subtle developments in that sphere.

Elizabeth Wright (1984) gives a comprehensive account of the changes which have occurred in this field. Wright explores the ego-psychology of Ernest Kris (*Psychoanalytic Explorations in Art*, 1964); the reader-response work of Norman Holland (*The Dynamics of Literary Response*, 1968; *Recovering 'The Purloined Letter'*, 1980) and the theories of Carl Gustav Jung (*Man and his Symbols*, 1978) who saw the unconsciousness as a common reservoir of highly charged symbols. This notion of the 'Great Memory' has been made familiar through the poetry of W.B. Yeats, while Doris Lessings in her novel *Memoirs of a Survivor* (Lessing, 1974) makes use of Jungian typology in the plot, the characterization and the metaphoric imagery. Lessing calls this novel an 'autobiography' because it is the story of every immature soul. The novel ends with a Jungian vision of the renewed primal family following the female 'Shining One' through the opened gates to the new era, trailed by an archetypal procession of children of all races and the Great Mother's lion mascot.

A further development in psychoanalytic theory occurred with the object-relation theories of Winnicott and Klein. As we have already seen, in the traditional psychoanalytical view human psychology is driven by the impulse to express instinctual drives and in order to do this, relationships with others are formed. In object-relation theory this is reversed with the assumption being that the ego is always striving to form relations with others. In Melanie Klein's view (*Envy and Gratitude and Other Works*, 1975) the newborn infant is imbued with the instincts of life and death as well as enough ego to experience anxiety and to employ certain defences against this anxiety. The infant defends itself by means of projection – expelling the bad, and introjection – absorbing the good. The primary object, the breast, is experienced as a 'good object' when it gratifies the child's hunger, and a 'bad object' when it is withheld. Human development, in Klein's account, involves the gradual increase in the complexity and strength of the ego so that both of these contradictions can be tolerated. When the child learns to see the mother as a separate person, it fears that it has caused the mother injury by its previous 'split' fantasy about her body, and wishes to make reparation. This desire to restore the mother is seen to play a crucial part in the creative process which strives after 'wholeness'. Klein's theories of infantile sexuality and primal terrors figure largely in modern horror films such as Ridley Scott's *Aliens* with its portrayal of Kleinian formulations such as nurturing figures, especially the mother, who become destructive; aggressive tendencies which punish internally and externally, and a place where self and world are not sharply delineated from each other. In this art form we can re-encounter our infantile anxieties and primal terrors in order to have another chance to resolve them and to make reparation.

> Reparation proper can hardly be considered a defence, since it is based on the recognition of psychic reality, the experience of the pain that this reality causes, and the taking of appropriate action to relieve it in phantasy and reality. (Segal, 1973, p. 95)

Klein's theory therefore emphasizes a dialectical process in which the contradictions of the external world and the internal world meet, intertwine and resolve.

D.H. Lawrence's short story *The Prussian Officer*, although written from a self-consciously Freudian perspective, in many ways anticipates these later object-relation theories. The story rather overtly makes the point that the officer's sadistic treatment of his orderly is an attempt to deny his homosexual attraction to him. Traditional Freudians could regard the officer's horror and fascination with the orderly's scarred thumb as a fear of retaliatory castration for these repressed wishes, and his overaction to the spilled wine as fear of arousal to ejaculation. This, of course, is part of the story, but it is also possible to see the relationship between the officer and the young orderly as a parody of the symbiosis between mother and child. What at first appears to be a denial of sexual attraction reveals itself, both for the officer and for the orderly, to be a denial of symbiotic fusion, which is shown by the way in which the two shadow each other and by their sensitivity to each other's eyes – the essential communication between mother and child during nursing. The killing of the officer and the semi-delirious wanderings of the orderly afterwards can be understood better in the light of this relationship.

In this early object-relation theory, as in Freudian and ego-psychology, the human subject is a battleground for conflicting instincts. However, under the influence of structuralism, critics such as Jacques Lacan challenged this notion of the human subject. For Lacan, there is nothing, not even the unconscious, that has pre-existent form as a germ of a 'self' or 'ego'. Instead the subject is constructed in and through language. As we have already seen in Unit 19, the work of Ferdinand de Saussure in the early part of the century emphasized the significance of the relationship between things over and above the things themselves. In his study of language he laid the foundations for a theory of the linguistic 'sign' that stresses the arbitrariness of the links between words and meanings (loosely, 'signifiers' and 'signified') and the way these links can be constructed as a series of differences, from other possible links. Psychoanalysis, with its concern with the interchangeability of symbols and the distorted significations that arise through the effect of the unconscious on mental life, invites a decoding of its underlying relationship structures, but Lacan goes further than employing the methods of structuralism to psychoanalysis: he makes psychoanalysis a branch of structuralism, specifically, cultural linguistics.

Lacan borrows Jakobson's two poles of verbal organization, metaphor and metonymy (see Unit 18, pp. 528–32) and equates these with Freud's characterizations of displacement and condensation. Condensation (*verdichtung*) corresponding to metaphor, i.e. an image or item linked to others by their apparent similarity in the mind of the subject (the paradigmatic axis) and metonymy corresponding to displacement (*verschiebung*), i.e. item being associated with item by being next to it in a chain (i.e. continuity or syntagmatic chain). Lacan's concern was not merely to align each linguistic term with a mode of unconscious mental functioning, the terms 'metaphor' and 'metonymy' play a signifying game of their own. Whereas Freud regarded subconscious images (e.g. dreams) as pre-existent and variously transformed by the structures of language (such as metaphor and metonymy), Lacan argues that these same linguistic terms form and determine relations between our conscious and subconscious states. This distinction has a counterpart in literary genres. Poetry tends to foreground metaphor (or condensation), i.e. any unitary relation between word and meaning is replaced by a surface relation between words and other words (perhaps as a substitute for repressed meaning). The novel on the other hand is more closely related to metonymy (or displacement) in that it relies upon a chain or sequence of events or items. In Lacan's theory narrative involves an endless chain of signifiers in pursuit of 'real' truth or satisfaction.

When Lacan states that the human subject is constructed in and through language, he is not implying that there is a pre-existent subjectivity which learns to express itself in the words made available to it by language, but rather that the initially 'absent' subject becomes concrete through its positioning in a meaning-system which pre-exists it and is greater than it. The infant is placed in a flux of a signifying system it does not possess and is created according to the possibilities offered to it by words.

> It is the world of words that created the world of things – the things originally confuse in the *hic et nunc* of the all in process of coming-into-being – by giving its concrete being to their essence, and its ubiquity to what has always been. (Lacan, 1953, p. 65)

The 'word' then dominates over the construction of psychic organization through the medium of pre-existent cultural categories, and the way in which our 'selfhood' is actually constructed is through a series of shifts, first from the mother, and then from the illusory identification of the self as a perfect unity, until the subject's place in the symbolic world is found and the unconscious produced.

According to Lacan, the child begins life as a primordial non-subject, an 'hommelette' whose desires spread in all directions, unfettered and unorganized, with no sense of the self or of the boundary between desire and gratification. The child lives in a 'symbiotic' relation with its mother's body which blurs any sharp boundary between the two. Lacan calls the first split from this uncoordinated stage 'the mirror-stage' since it is bound up with the child's perception of him/herself in the mirror or in the gaze or responses of the other with whom the child interacts. Finding this reflection of itself, the child mistakenly imagines a unified image of itself, for the image reflected back to the child both is and is not itself, there is still a blurring of subject and object. The child's perception thus produces a fiction, the fiction that he/she is whole and has a clearly ascertainable identity, when what is really happening is that the child is identifying with a vision that comes from elsewhere. What the mirror phase achieves is an alteration of the infantile psyche from the immersion in fragmentary drives to the experience of integration which at least allows for the possibility of an individual self being recognized, but it is only when this narcissistic relationship is interrupted that a fully social human subject is formed. Wordsworth's 'We are Seven' provides a useful example of the 'hommelette' stage since the child in the poem seems to be unable to distinguish between life and death. The poem therefore would appear to be an exploration (metaphorically) of Wordsworth's intuitive sense of the arbitrary relation between language, reality and identity. In this way, the adult properties of 'life' and 'death' can be seen to be functions of our command of their linguistic distinctions (see Unit 10, pp. 241–2).

The second developmental split comes with the child's entry into the language system. The symbolic order of language – what Lacan calls the Name-of-the-Father, emphasizing its patriarchal nature – conveys the values of the social system which it reflects, supports and encompasses. In order to produce meaning and communicate with others the child must adopt its functioning system. Language therefore moulds the child into a speaking subject and shapes its perceptual world. In this way language confers individuality on the child as it positions the subject as a separate, speaking entity engaging in a dialogue with others, but it also confirms its alienation from those others: 'What I seek in speech is the response of the other. ... I identify myself in language, but only by losing myself in it like an object' (Lacan, 1953, p. 86). One of the lessons the child learns unconsciously from language is its place within the pre-given social and sexual relationships which form the underlying structure of society. Like Freud and Lévi-Strauss, Lacan believes that the symbolic structuring of kinship patterns takes the form of the Oedipal complex. In this case it is the symbolic order of language, what Lacan calls the Law of the Father, which threatens castration. The child is defined by *exclusion* (the incest taboo), and by *absence*, since it must give up its earlier bond with the mother's body, and in so doing it negotiated its passage through the Oedipus complex. However, as in Freud's theory, a residual unconscious desire for the symbiotic union with the mother remains. Symbolically, language stands in lieu of the absent mother and is equivalent to her death: 'the symbol manifests itself first of all as the murder of the thing, and this death constitutes in the subject the eternalization of his desire' (Lacan, 1977, p. 104). The language system therefore creates a sense of lack in the separation from the mother and the desire to fill that lack through language. Although language implies that it 'stands in' for objects beyond the words, it is merely an endless chain of signifiers, there is no transcendental meaning or object to ground this continual yearning. Lacan therefore sees the unconscious as a 'sliding of the signified beneath the signifier', a constant sliding and hiding of meaning that will never yield up its secret to interpretation. The unconscious mind makes itself manifest only in distorted forms of language in puns and word-play. In his interpretation of *Hamlet* therefore Lacan moves away from analyzing the character or the writer and focuses instead on the text:

> One of Hamlet's functions is to engage in constant punning, word play, double ententre – to play on ambiguity. Note that Shakespeare gives an essential role in his plays to those characters that are called fools, court jesters whose position allows them to uncover the most hidden motives, the character traits that cannot be discussed frankly without violating the norms of proper conduct. It's not a matter of mere impudence and insults. What they say proceeds basically by way of ambiguity, of metaphor, puns, conceits, mannered speech – those substitutions of signifiers whose essential function I have been

stressing. Those substitutions lend Shakespeare's theatre a style, a color, that is the basis of its psychological dimension. Well, Hamlet, in a certain sense must be considered one of those clowns. (Lacan, 1977, pp. 11–52)

It is only by means of Hamlet's word-play that the underlying trauma of the Oedipus complex is revealed. It is in the 'play' of literature with its multiplicity of meanings and shifting signifiers that we can, time and time again, re-experience unconscious desires. (For a full Lacanian reading see his *Seminar on 'The Purloined Letter'*, 1972, discussed in Wright, 1984, pp. 114–22 or Terry Eagleton's reading of D.H. Lawrence's *Sons and Lovers* in *Literary Theory*, 1983.)

As we have seen, although the perspective of psychoanalytical interpretation has shifted through the years, the constant feature of the theories has been the Oedipal complex. The phallocentric nature of this concept is obvious and it is hardly surprising therefore that, in recent years, feminist literary critics have focused on psychoanalytic theories of sexual identity. Freud creates a development theory for woman as little-man-minus. In his view, in the genital stage the little girl recognizes the inferiority of her sexual organ, her lack of a penis, and feels a sense of her own inferiority and her distance from power. This engenders a hatred for her mother for having created her in her own image, and a passionate envy of the penis possessed by father and brother alike. The girl thus shifts from mother love to father love.

> No phallus, no power – except those winning ways of getting one. ... The girl's entry into her feminine 'destiny' is characterised by hostility to the mother for her failure to make her a boy; it is an entry marked by penis-envy, that in its turn must be repressed or transformed. (Mitchell, 1974, p. 96)

The recognition of herself as already castrated pushes the girl into the Oedipal situation in which her desire is to displace the mother in order to get a share of the father's power. Finally the desire for the penis must be renounced and replaced by the desire for a baby, and Freud suggests that the mother's happiness 'is great if later on this wish for a baby finds fulfilment in reality and quite especially so if the baby is a little boy who brings the longed-for penis with him' (Freud, 1953, Vol. XXII, p. 167).

Lacan, too, gives an account of women which makes them marginal outsiders. The little girl is a 'little man' with no existence in her own right. For Lacan a child's sense of identity comes through its introduction to language, the symbolic order, which the child enters only as a result of culturally enforced separation from the mother and his – though not her – identification with the Father, the male in-family representative of culture. Thus Lacanian theory reserves the positive symbol of gender for men. Women, because they lack the phallus, the symbol of authority around which language is organized, occupy a negative position in language. Moreover, because masculine desire dominates language and presents woman as an idealized fantasy fulfilment for the emotional lack caused by the separation from the mother, woman in Lacanian theory is merely a gap or a silence, the invisible and unheard 'other'.

Milton's *Paradise Lost* has already been discussed in Unit 8 and, from a feminist perspective, in Unit 24, but the following extract from Book IV, in which

Eve looks into the lake, provides an interesting illustration of Lacan's view of women:

> A shape within the watery gloom appeared
> Bending to look on me; I started back,
> It started back, but pleased I soon returned,
> Pleased it returned as soon with answering looks
> Of sympathy and love; there I had fixed
> Mine eyes till now, and pined with vain desire
> Had not a voice thus warned me, what thou see'st
> What there thou see'st fair creature is thyself,
> With thee it comes and goes: but follow me
> And I will bring thee where no shadow stay
> Thy coming.
>
> (ll. 461–72)

This passage gives rise to many questions about psychoanalysis and gender. Eve at this point is like the child at the 'mirror stage' in Lacan's theory – she desires an image of herself. A voice (God/man) advises her that her desire is vanity and tells her that 'He' will bring her to a correct realization of what she really is and how her mind should respond to instinct and desire. It is significant that Eve has to hear 'a voice' and that her image of herself 'comes and goes' since this demonstrates Lacan's contention that woman's identity is 'fixed' by her entry into the phallocentric system of language. If, as this would suggest, woman's image of herself is shaped by a language system which defines her according to a purely male perspective, the question then arises as to what a 'purely' female perspective might be.

Lacan himself speculates on what this 'otherness' of women might be and considers the possibility of a 'jouissance', an enjoyment of the body that goes beyond the phallic order. French feminist critics such as Luce Irigary, Hélène Cixous and Julia Kristeva have all argued that women must challenge the phallocentric discourses of philosophy and psychoanalysis which exclude them as subjects, and to do this they must write themselves into the text.

> Woman must write her self: must write about women and bring women to writing, from which they have been driven away as violently as from their bodies. Woman must put herself into the text – as into the world and into history. (Cixous, 1975, p. 245)

Psychoanalysis has therefore been one of the major influences in recent feminist poststructural criticism since it has foregrounded the way in which woman-as-sign has been negatively constructed by the hierarchical binary oppositions of language. Increasingly, feminist criticism has tended to expose and dismantle the claim of the primacy of the phallus, and to explore the way in which literature, with its dislocation of the network of signifiers, reveals the cracks in the social and cultural façade of the subject.

> Whether written by a woman or by a man, a linguistic intervention which ruptures accepted (acceptable) discursive practices, reverts us to the constitution of the social subject which is predicated on the repression of the maternal. Through disruption of the symbolic function of language, we are able to give expression to the repressed, or to detect traces of

repression, but in so doing we are, even if only momentarily, in breach of the Law-of-the-Father. (Furman, 1985, p. 74)

The interconnection between psychoanalysis and literature has therefore involved a complex interweaving of ideas and theories which have changed and developed over the years with disputes arising between theorists as to the precise relationship between language and the subconscious. What is clear and significant, however, is that literature provides the most fruitful and complex battleground for psychoanalytic theory. By emphasizing the way in which literature foregrounds elements such as metaphor-metonymy, or condensation-displacement, psychoanalysis contributes to the contention that literature is special and different; that it reveals to us things about the relation between the mind, language and reality that are not manifest in our habitual, routine use of language.

## BIBLIOGRAPHY

Bergler, E. (1949) *The Basic Neurosis*, Grune & Stratton, New York.
Cixous, H. (1975) *The Laugh of the Medusa*, in *New French Feminisms*, ed. E. Marks and I. Courtivron, Harvester Wheatsheaf, Hemel Hempstead.
Eagleton, T. (1983) *Literary Theory: An Introduction*, Blackwell, Oxford.
Freud, S. (1953) *The Standard Edition of the Complete Psychological Works*, 24 vols, Hogarth Press, London.
Furman, N. (1985) 'The Politics of Language: Beyond the Gender Principle?', in *Making a Difference: Feminist Literary Criticism*, Methuen, London.
Holland, N. (1968) *The Dynamics of Literary Response*, Blackwell, Oxford.
Holland, N. (1980) *Recovering 'The Purloined Letter'*, in *The Reader in the Text*, ed. S.R. Suleiman and I. Crosman, Princeton University Press, Princeton.
Jones, E. (1949) *Hamlet and Oedipus*, Doubleday Anchor, Garden City, New York.
Jung, C.G. (1978) *Man and his Symbols*, Penguin, Harmondsworth.
Klein, M. (1975) *Envy and Gratitude and Other Works*, Delta, New York.
Kris, E. (1964) *Psychoanalytic Explorations in Art*, International Universities Press, New York.
Lacan, J. (1953) *Ecrits: A Selection*, Tavistock, London.
Lacan, J. (1977) *The Four Fundamental Concepts of Psycho-Analysis*, Tavistock, London.
Lacan, J. (1984) *Seminar on 'The Purloined Letter'*, in *Psychoanalytic Criticism: Theory in Practice*, ed. E. Wright, Methuen, London.
Lessing, D. (1974) *Memoirs of a Survivor*, Octagon Press, London
Lodge, D. (1972) *Twentieth Century Literary Criticism: A Reader*, Longman, Harlow.
Mitchell, J. (1974) *Psychoanalysis and Feminism*, Penguin, Harmondsworth.
Moers, E. (1977) *Literary Women: The Great Writers*, Anchor Press/Doubleday, New York.
Segal, H. (1973) *Introduction to the Work of Melanie Klein*, Hogarth Press, London.
Wilson, E. (1941) *The Wound and the Bow: Seven Studies in Literature*, Methuen, London.

## FURTHER READING

Ellman, M. (1994) *Psychoanalytic Literary Criticism*, Longman, Harlow.
Mitchell, J. (1975) *Psychoanalysis and Feminism*, Penguin, Harmondsworth.
Selman, R. (1989) 'Psychoanalytic Criticism', in *Practising Theory and Reading Literature*, Harvester Wheatsheaf, Hemel Hempstead.
Wright, E. (1984) *Psychoanalytic Criticism: Theory in Practice*, Methuen, London.

# UNIT 23

# Gender and literature: women writers

*Liz McIntyre*

In an important essay 'Towards a Feminist Poetics' (1979) Elaine Showalter (1986, pp. 125–43) distinguished two varieties of feminist criticism. The first of these she labelled 'the feminist critique'. This is a form of critical enquiry concerned with woman as the consumer of literature and with the stereotypes of women purveyed in male-authored texts. Its most famous exemplar is probably Kate Millett's bestselling *Sexual Politics* (1971). For her second branch of feminist criticism Showalter coined the term *Gynocriticism*. This foregrounds the study of women as producers of literature and aims to recover the lost or submerged history of women's writing, as well as to offer a theory or explanatory model for the themes, tropes and genres which women writers have practised through history.

Why should such a critical practice as Gynocriticism be necessary? One way of answering this would be to turn to the evidence of the curricula of university English courses, and to the activities of anthologists, literary historians and theorists of literature. The feminist writer Dale Spender, recalling her own undergraduate literary studies, notes,

> in the guise of presenting me with an overview of the literary heritage of the English-speaking world, my education provided me with a grossly inaccurate and distorted view of the history of letters. For my introduction to the 'greats' was (with the exception of the famous five women novelists) an introduction to the great men. ('Women and Literary History', Belsey and Moore, 1989, pp. 21–33)

The American writer and critic Tilly Olsen surveying the content of twentieth-century literature courses in 223 undergraduate programmes between 1971 and 1976 found that women authors accounted for only 6 per cent of the texts prescribed (1980, pp. 186–93). Prestigious anthologies provide evidence of the same pronounced bias against women authors. The *Oxford Anthology of English Poetry* (1986), edited by John Wain, claims to offer a 'representative sample of the main course of English poetry': it contains work by fourteen women poets as against 207 men.

As Spender and others have noted, literary historians and theorists collude in this silencing of women's voices. Ian Watt's *The Rise of the Novel* (1987) is still a widely recommended text on undergraduate courses on the novel. Despite his passing observation that 'the majority of eighteenth century novels were actually written by women', Watt maintains that this phenomenon constituted a 'purely quantitative assertion of dominance' (p. 339). Thus Watt's account of the origins of the English novel recognizes only the paternity of the genre in detailed analyses of the work of Defoe, Richardson and Fielding, while his definition of the novel in terms of formal realism not only ignores the earlier work of Aphra Behn but also dismisses as 'fugitive literary tendencies' the Gothic and sentimental fiction, two modes consistently employed by women novelists. This straitjacketing of the novel within the requirement of formal realism works not only to suppress the influence of early women writers like Behn, Burney and Radcliffe, but also to downgrade or marginalize later women novelists like Charlotte Brontë, whose fictions characteristically mingle romance and realism.

The same male bias has characterized literary theory. Where Ian Watt sees the history of the novel solely in terms of a paternal line, Harold Bloom in *The Anxiety of Influence* (1973) draws on Freud's Oedipal theory for an ambitious overview of literary history, which appears to him as the struggle of successive generations of sons/authors to combat the influence of strong, literary fathers. Just as Freud's original formulation of the Oedipus complex ignored the mother, so Bloom's appropriation of it for literature leaves no space for women. His literary genealogy is exclusively male, making room for women solely as the (silent) muse of the male poet.

Confronted with the evidence of women's exclusion from the literary canon and from literary history the male-dominated literary establishment has tended to defend itself by arguing that aesthetic criteria are in themselves free of gender bias and based on universal values. Feminist critics, on the other hand, will argue that no literary judgement is neutral, that the category 'literature' or even 'great literature' is culturally determined. If, as has been the case, the male perspective has dominated the cultural establishment, then male-authored texts will inevitably dominate the literary canon. So pervasive has this situation been that literary judgements and aesthetic criteria which are culturally determined come to seem 'natural' and 'universal'. As Virginia Woolf remarked,

> It is the masculine values that prevail …. This is an important book, the critic assumes, because it deals with war. This is an insignificant book because it deals with the feelings of women in a drawing-room. A scene in a battle-field is more important than a scene in a shop – everywhere and much more subtly the difference of value persists. (*A Room of One's Own*, 1993, p. 67)

Woolf suggests another reason why it is crucial to rediscover and to re-evaluate women's writing. While we often unthinkingly assume that literature is a reflection of life, it is as true to say that it is a product of other literature. Musing upon 'the effect of tradition and of the lack of tradition upon the mind of the writer' Woolf concludes that when the early nineteenth-century women novelists came to write 'they had no tradition behind them, or one so short and partial that it was of little help. For we think back through our mothers if we are women'(1993, p. 69). If this lack of a continuous, visible and valued tradition of women's writing may be argued to impede women in the sphere of novel writing – where women's literary achievement has been most evident – how much more of an impediment must this lack of tradition be to women poets. In their volume of essays on British and American women poets, *Shakespeare's Sisters* (1979), the critics Sandra Gilbert and Susan Gubar cite Elizabeth Barrett Browning's complaint in 1845: 'England has had many learned women ... and yet where are the poetesses? ... I look everywhere for grandmothers and see none' (p. 65). One powerful argument then for recovering the tradition of women's writing is that it works to empower women authors in our own time.

This recovery and reassessment of forgotten texts has continued since the 1970s. Unsurprisingly it was to the women writers of the Victorian period that feminist critics first turned. Elaine Showalter's *A Literature of Their Own: British Women Novelists from Brontë to Lessing* (1977) uncovers a distinct women's tradition by placing the work of the major women novelists in the context of lesser-known women writers of their time. Ellen Moers's *Literary Women* (1978) revealed the ways by which women writers influenced one another, demonstrating, for example, the extensive influence of the French novelist Madame de Staël upon many British and American women writers of the nineteenth century, and echoes of Elizabeth Barrett Browning in the poetry of Emily Dickinson. Before long interest turned to the earlier periods of literary history. Dale Spender in her *Mothers of the Novel* (1986) argued for the significance of those seventeenth- and eighteenth-century women novelists so cavalierly dismissed by Ian Watt. More recently still feminist critics have focused their attentions on the author who has the distinction of being known as the first professional woman writer in English, Aphra Behn. One very positive result of this interest has been the flood of anthologies of earlier women poets and dramatists and reprints of well nigh forgotten women novelists. The foremothers whom Virginia Woolf and Elizabeth Barrett Browning sought are now readily available to readers.

Other aspects of Gynocriticism remain more controversial and problematic. If, for example, the tradition of woman's writing is now more visible, the question remains, how should that newly discovered tradition relate to 'the Great Tradition' – the male-dominated canon of great works studied in university literature courses. To have available an option on Victorian Woman Writers on an English Literature course which previously found no room for Charlotte or Anne Brontë, Christina Rossetti or Elizabeth Gaskell may seem an advance, but it is less an advance when put beside the fact that the compulsory course on Victorian Literature which those same students take is dominated by the traditional male greats, and finds room only for the usual 'special case' women writers Emily Brontë and George Eliot. Paradoxically, in trying to open up the canon by arguing for the inclusion of courses on women writers we may be in danger of perpetuating the marginalizing of women's writing of which feminists complain. Alternatively, we may argue for an emphasis on literature by women within interdisciplinary Women's Studies courses, but this too runs the risk of ghettoizing the woman writer. Both these strategies, necessary as they have been, have tended to leave unchallenged the notion that literature at its most significant and prestigious is male authored.

If there remains a problem in placing this women's tradition there remain too disagreements in describing its distinguishing features. Feminist critics have argued for the 'specificity' of women's writing, that is that women's writing is different from men's on account of the authors' gender: and this 'specificity' has been variously discovered in the themes, tropes and other stylistic features of women's writing. But here, as in debating the issue of the relation of the tradition of women's writing to the 'Great Tradition', we need to move with care. In arguing that in some way women's writing is *essentially* different from men's, feminist critics may paradoxically end up reinforcing those gender relations which it is the feminist project to challenge and unsettle. A more positive approach to the 'specificity' of women's writing would be by way of a stress on the special position of the woman writer within a patriarchal society. Viewed in this way women writers exhibit no essential, ahistorical femininity: rather they can be seen as needing to define themselves as writers within the context of a patriarchal society which in various ways, and to different degrees, through history has limited their access to education and to a public voice, and has sought through the promotion of an ideology of proper femininity to limit what they may say. The remainder of this essay adopts such an approach. It is organized chronologically but it is not intended as an historical survey of women's writing in England. It attempts rather by focusing on a number of case studies to illustrate some key issues in the study of women's writing.

## From Renaissance to Restoration

> Let the woman learn in silence with all subjection. But I suffer not a woman to teach, nor to usurp authority over the man, but to be in silence. For Adam was first formed then Eve. (1 Timothy: 11–13)

> There is nothing that doth so commend, advance, set forth, adorn, deck, trim and garnish a maid as silence. And this noble virtue may the virgins learn of that most holy, pure and glorious virgin Mary, which when she either heard or saw any worthy or notable thing, blabbed it not out straightways to her gossips, as the manner of women is at this present day, but being silent, she kept all those sayings sacred, and pondered them in her heart. (Quoted in Jardine, 1983, p. 107)

The dumbness of Elizabethan women, of which Virginia Woolf complained, although not as total as she believed, has to be seen in the context of a Judeo-Christian tradition that prescribed silence and subjection to male authority as the signs of womanly virtue. The 'proper' role for women was to be the bearer of children, not the bearer of the word. The good woman is one who is silent, or at least one whose voice is muted. The highest praise that Lear can bestow on his good daughter Cordelia is that 'Her voice was ever soft, gentle and low, an excellent thing in woman'. Conversely, his evil daughters Goneril and Regan reveal their unwomanliness by the ease with which they manipulate language. Women who spoke out were deemed transgressive or deviant and labelled 'shrews', 'scolds' or 'gossips' (see Jardine, 1983, pp. 103–40).

Differential access to education reinforced this silencing of women's voices. While some of the great Humanist educators advocated a more enlightened attitude to women's education, generally speaking women were denied access to the classical education that provided the authoritative models for all kinds of literary discourse. The poet Anne Finch, Countess of Winchilsea, protested against the kind of education deemed suitable for women:

> Good breeding, fashion, dancing, dressing, play
> Are the accomplishments we should desire;
> To write, to read, to think, or to enquire
> Would cloud our beauty, and exhaust our time,
> And interrupt the conquests of our prime;
> Whilst the dull manage of a servile house,
> Is held by some, our utmost art and use.
>
> (Quoted in Goreau, 1980, p. 29)

The confinement of women to the private sphere debarred them from the most public arena of literary production, the theatre, where women's roles were played by young male actors. Other forms of privileged writing were hardly more accommodating to women. The tradition of amatory verse, modelled on French and Italian forms, was predicated on a male speaking subject addressing a silent woman. In this tradition women could be the muse of poetry but not its maker. The 'Coy Mistress' of Marvell's poem, reduced to a conventional catalogue of bodily parts, is not even muse so much as pretext for the male speaker's bravura display of *his* subjectivity, *his* wit and learning. John Donne's 'coy mistress' in 'The Flea' has, it appears, a more substantial presence than Marvell's, but even she 'speaks' only in the gap between the words. In any case her agency is an illusion, a trap sprung by the male 'I' which speaks the poem. His triumphant capping of her argument in the final couplet reaffirms the prescribed gender roles and characteristics of an andocentric literary culture, where the male is the speaking subject and the female is silent and subjected.

How may women find a voice in such andocentric discourse? One way, as feminist critics have noted, is by revising current literary forms to accommodate a woman's voice and experience. Thus the poet Katherine Philips (1631–64) borrows the tropes of the amatory lyric tradition to write poems of idealized female friendship. Here she borrows from a number of Donne's love poems to celebrate her relationship with 'Rosania':

> But neither chance nor compliment
> Did element our love;
> 'Twas sacred sympathy was lent
> Us from the quire above.
> That friendship fortune did create,
> Still fears a wound from time or fate.
>
> Our chang'd and mingled souls are grown
> To such acquaintance now,
> That if each would resume her own
> Alas! we know not how.
> We have each other so engrost
> That each is in the union lost...

Thus our twin souls in one shall grow,
And teach the world new love,
Redeem the age and sex, and show
A flame fate dares not move:
And courting death to be our friend,
Our lives together we shall end.

(Quoted in Morgan, 1981, pp. 3–4)

Philips's position as author illustrates another issue of constant interest to feminist critics. Since silence is the condition of the 'proper' woman, those women who do enter the 'male' world of literary production inevitably display a troubled self-consciousness about their relation to writing. Hence Philips excuses her transgressive behaviour as a poet by constructing an elaborate pose of feminine modesty and self-effacement: 'I never writ a line in my life with intention to have it printed ... sometimes I think that to make verses is so much above my reach, and a diversion so unfit for the sex to which I belong, that I am about to resolve against it forever' (Goreau, 1980, p. 145). Versions of this disclaimer may be heard echoing through the centuries of women's writing. Certainly it is possible to suspect that Philips is not being entirely truthful in denying her desire for literary recognition. At the same time it is clear that for women writers fame very easily slides into infamy.

The problem is very clearly seen in the career of Philips's younger contemporary, the poet, dramatist, satirist and novelist Aphra Behn (1640?–89), known to her contemporaries as 'Astrea'. A prolific writer, celebrated in her own day but thereafter consigned to obscurity, Behn offers one of the most notable examples of what has been called the 'transience of female fame'. While Restoration comedy, the mode in which Behn achieved her most significant successes, suffered generally in later literary histories because of its supposed licentiousness, Behn suffered obscurity and censure on account of her sex. When her works were republished at the end of the nineteenth century a critic in a prestigious journal declared 'it is a pity her books did not rot with her bones' (Goreau, 1980, p. 14). Yet Virginia Woolf recognized her significance as the first Englishwoman to earn her living by writing: 'All women together ought to let flowers fall upon the tomb of Aphra Behn ... for it was she who earned them the right to speak their minds' (1993, p. 60).

As a woman who was willing to be recognized as the author of her own works, and who declared defiantly that she wrote 'for bread', Behn had, of necessity, to construct for herself a literary identity very different from that adopted by Katherine Philips. The pose of womanly self-effacement would not do for a writer set on entering the public world of the theatre, the most commercial form of literary production in the seventeenth century. The restoration of the monarchy in 1660, and the accompanying reaction against the repression of the Commonwealth period, prompted the emergence of new kinds of drama and new opportunities for women to enter the theatre. In 1662 Charles II published a warrant requiring that, contrary to the practices of the Elizabethan and Jacobean theatres, women's roles were to be played by women. The appearance of actresses was quickly followed by the appearance of women dramatists. Katherine Philips produced a verse translation of Corneille's *Pompey*, which may have been the first drama by a woman produced on the English stage. However, for a woman to write a tragedy, and publish it anonymously, was clearly far less of a challenge to accepted stereotypes of femininity than to write comedy, especially the witty comedy of sexual intrigue which was the staple of the Restoration stage. In an age in which licentiousness was fashionable, and even politically correct, it was unproblematic for male dramatists like Etherege and Wycherley to be identified with the lifestyles of their fictional rake heroes, but the operation of the sexual double standard meant that Behn was condemned for writing with the same frankness about sexual mores. When we look for the specifically female characteristics of Behn's writing they are not to be found so much in the content of her comedies – which are no more nor less licentious than those of her male contemporaries and composed of the same stock ingredients – but rather in her perceived need as a woman to negotiate for herself a literary identity that would justify her writing as she did.

This writing self appears most clearly in the epilogues to her plays and in the prefaces she composed for the published versions of them. The Epilogue to her comedy *Sir Patient Fancy* (1678) was devised to be spoken by an actress:

> I here and there o'erheard a coxcomb cry,
> Ah, rot it – 'tis a woman's comedy,
> One, who because she lately chanced to please us,
> With her damned stuff will never cease to tease us.
> What has poor woman done that she must be,
> Debarred from sense and sacred poetry?

> (Behn, 1992, pp. 329–30)

Here the actress speaks for the woman dramatist in anticipating the audience's criticism of women's writing and protesting women's exclusion from literary discourse. Yet, as it proceeds, this alliance of actress and woman author becomes more problematic:

> Because we do not laugh at you when lewd,
> And scorn and cudgel ye when you are rude;
> That we have nobler souls than you, we prove,
> By how much more we're sensible of love;
> Quickest in finding all the subtlest ways
> To make your joys: why not to make you plays?

The profession of actress was linked in the public mind with that of prostitute or courtesan, and many of the best-known actresses of the Restoration stage, like Elizabeth Barry and Nell Gwyn (to whom Behn dedicated a play), were the mistresses of members of the royal family or the aristocracy. The Restoration stage exploited the sexuality of the woman acting, particularly in the notorious 'breeches' roles, in which actresses played women disguising themselves as boys (see Todd, 1993). In thus identifying herself with the actress who speaks her defence of women's writing Behn represents herself as woman dramatist/prostitute, and her play becomes by analogy a kind of sexual servicing. In terms of English culture this association of the actress with the prostitute long made the theatre a problematic area for women's participation. Even in the nineteenth century the term 'public woman' connoted both prostitute and actress.

Yet, even as she appears to acquiesce in this sexualizing of the woman author, Behn seeks to define for herself a different identity in the literary world by intervening in the privileged 'male' discourse of literary theory:

> Your way of writing's out of fashion grown.
> Method and rule – you only understand,
> Pursue that way of fooling, and be damned.
> Your learned cant of action, time and place,
> Must all give way to the unlaboured farce.
> To all the men of wit we will subscribe:
> But for you half-wits, you unthinking tribe,
> We'll let you see, what e'er besides we do,
> How artfully we copy some of you:
> And if you're drawn to th' life, pray tell me then
> Why women should not write as well as men.

Since comedy, she argues, is based on observation of contemporary manners, and requires no special learning, women are as well qualified as men to write it. Despite the vehemence of this attack on the 'learned cant' of neo-classical dramatic theory we can sense the defensiveness of the woman writer who cannot rely on the authority bestowed by knowledge of the classical languages to give legitimacy to her public identity as an author. In a poem dedicated to Thomas Creech, praising his translation of Lucretius, she confesses herself 'unlearned in schools' and laments 'the scanted customs of the nation', which, in restricting women's educational opportunities, confines the woman writer to her mother tongue, 'the fulsome jingle of the times', and so limits her range and authority as author. Despite the educational disadvantage she suffered as a woman Behn clearly desired a literary identity other than that of hack writer or notorious poetess/punk (prostitute), as is evident in the poems she wrote to commemorate state occasions. Towards the end of her career she was ready to admit frankly that she wrote not simply for 'bread' but to earn the fame accorded to male authors:

> All I ask, is the privilege for my masculine part, the poet in me (if any such you will allow me), to tread in those successful paths my predecessors have so long thrived in ... If I must not, because of my sex, have this freedom, but you will usurp all to yourselves; I lay down my quill, and you shall hear no more of me ... for I am not content to write for a third day only [when, traditionally, box office receipts went to the dramatist]. I value fame as much as if I had been born a hero; and if you rob me of that, I can retire from the ungrateful world, and scorn its fickle favours. (1992, p. 21)

Thus the seventeenth century gives us two competing models of the woman writer. On the one hand there is Katherine Philips, honoured with the title of 'the chaste Orinda', confining herself in terms of genre and subject matter to that which is properly 'feminine', and making no claim to fame or a public, professional identity as author. On the other we have the scandalous Aphra Behn, 'Astrea', who recognizes no disability or lack in the woman writer other than that which results from educational disadvantage, and stakes her claim to full membership of a literary fellowship composed almost exclusively of men, 'my predecessors'. These two models serve to illustrate a fundamental question concerning women's relation to writing, which is often posed in terms of a debate between the notions of 'difference' and 'androgyny', whether, that is, women may be argued to write out of their femininity – however defined – or whether literary creativity transcends sexual difference. (See Todd's edition of Behn's *Oroonoko, The Rover and Other Works* (1992), and also her *Gender, Art and Death* (1993) for an important discussion of the woman author's quest for a literary identity. Morgan's *The Female Wits* (1981) prints plays by neglected seventeenth-century women dramatists and provides biographical information. Goreau's *Reconstructing Aphra* (1980) provides much valuable information about attitudes to women's education.)

## The woman writer and the rise of the novel

Behn might claim recognition for 'my masculine part, the poet in me', but no eighteenth-century woman could have echoed such a demand. Significantly, the eighteenth century offered new opportunities to women writers while at the same time defining 'feminine' writing more restrictively (see Spencer, 1986).

The new opportunities came with the rise of the novel, the literary form with which women writers have always seemed to have a special affinity. That women found a literary identity as novelists was in large measure due to the newness of the form. As Virginia Woolf noted, 'all the other forms of literature were hardened and set by the time she became a writer. The novel alone was young enough to be soft in her hands' (1993, p. 70). Most importantly, the novel did not require a classical education, the lack of which Behn had felt so keenly. The forms of private, informal writing that women were accustomed to practise, such as the letter and the journal, provided a suitable training for novel-writing. Behn had argued that because comedy depended on observation of manners it was a suitable genre for women. Many eighteenth-century women novelists could have advanced the same argument in defence of their novel-writing ambitions. Woolf's observation about the early nineteenth-century women novelists, 'all the literary training that a woman had ... was training in the observation of character, in the analysis of emotion. Her sensibility had been educated for centuries by the influences of the common sitting-room' (1993, p. 61), could as readily be applied to their eighteenth-century predecessors like Fanny Burney.

While an expanding literary market and a new form brought increased opportunities for women writers an increasing emphasis on sexual difference and on the special role of women meant that women writers were expected to write out of a restricted definition of 'femininity'. What this meant for them is well illustrated by the praise of a critic in 1769 reviewing a novel written by a woman:

> The representation of domestic life is a source of moral entertainment, perhaps the most instructive and congenial to the universal taste of mankind, of all the various scenes with which the human drama presents us. It is within the compass of that narrow sphere that the tender emotions of the heart are exerted in their utmost sensibility. (Spencer, 1986, p. 21)

Thus a male cultural establishment grants women writers authority within a 'narrow sphere' which is properly feminine, domestic life, sentiment and morality, while preserving for itself the prestigious forms, poetry and drama, and the 'great' subjects. Throughout the eighteenth and nineteenth centuries women writers were to suffer the effects of this double bind. On the one hand they were exhorted to write about what they knew – the virtues of domestic life, the characters of women – and advised to avoid those areas of experience which their education and circumstances left them ill-equipped to understand. On the other hand, the novel itself while it was particularly associated with women, both in terms of authorship and audience, was rated a 'low' form, as Jane Austen's famous defence of women's novels in *Northanger Abbey* (1818) suggests:

> 'And what are you reading, Miss –?' 'Oh! it is only a novel!' replies the young lady; while she lays down her book with affected indifference or momentary shame. – 'It is only Cecilia or Camilla [both by Burney], or Belinda [Maria Edgeworth, 1801]'; or, in short, only some work in which the greatest powers of the mind are displayed, in which the most thorough knowledge of human nature, the happiest delineation of its varieties, the liveliest effusions of wit and humour are conveyed to the world in the best chosen language.

This mixed experience of increased opportunity and increased restriction is well illustrated by the career of Fanny Burney, the most esteemed woman novelist of the eighteenth century (on Burney's career see Epstein, 1989). Success as a writer brought Burney the approval of such luminaries as Dr Johnson, financial success beyond anything achieved by Aphra Behn, and even a royal pension. At the same time the constraints imposed on the woman writer by the demand that she conform to the age's image of proper femininity are evident at every stage of her career.

Burney's literary training was in the keeping of a journal, begun when she was 16. While the journal may be seen as essentially an artless form of private, 'feminine' writing, Burney's included character sketches, conversations and anecdotes, and it was written in the consciousness that it would be read by family and close friends. Thus the distinctions between private writing and literature were being blurred. From this beginning it was a relatively short step to the production of a novel in letters, *Evelina* (1778). Negotiations for the publication of the book were conducted via male relatives and the work appeared anonymously.

In her preface to the book Burney reveals her own anxieties about offering the public so 'low' a form as the novel: 'In the republic of letters, there is no member of such inferior rank, or who is so much disdained by his brethren of the quill, as the humble Novelist.' As the preface continues it becomes clear that the low status of the novel is linked to its 'feminine' subject matter and presumed female readership. Catching the disapproving tone of many male critics of the time she makes slighting reference to the baneful influence of novels on 'young ladies in general, and boarding-school damsels in particular', and to the novel's predilection for 'the fantastic regions of Romance ... where Reason is an outcast'. Doubly disguised by anonymity and insistent use of the masculine pronoun Burney seeks to align herself with a tradition of male greats, 'our predecessors ... Rousseau, Johnson, Marivaux,

Fielding, Richardson, and Smollet'. While this may seem a move comparable to Aphra Behn's insistence on her right to inclusion in a male literary tradition, the positions that the two women writers occupy is, in fact, quite different. Behn openly acknowledges her gender and refuses to accept that it limits her as a writer. Burney takes refuge in a masculine literary persona, and, acknowledging the 'feminine' subject of her novel, 'a Young Lady's Entrance into the World', seeks to distance herself from the female purveyors of Romance and the Marvellous and to align herself with a male literary tradition exemplified by its adherence to the masculine attributes of Reason and Nature. In presenting a virtuous, erring heroine who is to be schooled in the constraints that society imposes on 'proper' women Burney makes the feminine novel acceptable by aligning it with the conduct book.

On the surface at least *Evelina* appears to fulfil the conditions laid down in Burney's Preface, demonstrating to its youthful, female readers their need for male authority and direction. The erring Evelina moves from the authority of one male mentor, her guardian, Mr Villars, to that of another, her husband, Lord Orville. Essentially her quest is for a man to belong to – whether father or husband – who will ensure her status and identity in a patriarchal society. On the other hand, this surface conformity allows for a covert criticism of the very ideology the novel appears to endorse. (A comparable strategy of surface conformity and covert criticism seems to operate in Sarah Fielding's *The Adventures of David Simple* (1744), where the device of a male protagonist provides the novelist with a cover to explore critically the limitations placed on women's intellectual development and their restricted opportunities for economic independence.) Employing the 'private' form of the letter, and relying on the inexperience of her erring heroine, who may reasonably express opinions which the novelist could not as narrator endorse, Burney is able to present vigorous criticism of the social rules which constrained 'proper' women. So Evelina at her first public ball protests at the convention which allows men the choice of partners, while restricting women's power to say no:

> The gentlemen, as they passed and repassed, looked as if they thought we were quite at their disposal, and only waiting for the honour of their commands; and they sauntered about, in a careless indolent manner, as if with a view to keep us in suspense.... I thought it so provoking, that I determined, in my own mind, that, far from humouring such airs, I would rather not dance at all, than with any one who should seem to think me ready to accept the first partner who would condescend to take me.

So successful is Burney in presenting a conforming surface that Mr Villars's letters of moral exhortation to Evelina were later detached from the novel and printed separately as a manual of advice for young ladies: yet the fact is that the plot of the novel cuts Evelina loose from male authority to encounter the world and define herself as heroine alone. In so doing it may be said to cater to the fantasies of independence of its female readers.

*Evelina* was rightly praised for the liveliness of its dialogue and its social comedy. These attributes of the novel suggest that Burney's literary gifts could well have developed in the direction of drama, and, in fact, her next production after *Evelina* was a comedy, *The Witlings*. In all Burney wrote four comedies and four blank verse tragedies, but only one play, the tragedy, *Edwy and Elgiva*, was performed, and then on only one occasion. Her thwarted career as a dramatist, and especially as a writer of comedy, well illustrates the difficulties experienced by the woman writer whose authorial identity cannot be allowed to conflict with her core identities as proper lady and dutiful daughter. At every juncture of her career Burney defers to the authority of father figures who censor her work, accepting the view of her father and a surrogate father, Samuel Crisp, that writing for the stage was 'unfeminine'. As Crisp noted in a letter to Burney concerning *The Witlings*, comedy poses a threat to feminine propriety: 'I will never allow you to sacrifice a grain of female delicacy for all the wit of Congreve and Vanbrugh put together' (Spencer, 1986, p. 97). Burney acceded to this patriarchal control – 'I would a thousand times rather forfeit my character as a writer, than risk ridicule or censor as a female' – though she continued to give vent to her comic talents in three plays which were not performed.

In her anxious awareness that her authorial self may compromise her identity as 'proper lady' Burney is at one with many women writers of the eighteenth and nineteenth centuries, as, for example, Charlotte Brontë enquiring from her friend and fellow novelist Elizabeth Gaskell,

> Do you ... find it easy, when you sit down to write, to isolate yourself from all those ties, and their sweet associations, so as to be quite *your own woman*, uninfluenced, unswayed by the consciousness of how your work may affect other minds; what blame, what sympathy, it may call forth? (Wise and Symington, 1980, vol. 4, p. 76)

If literary history has failed to give due recognition to Fanny Burney's place in the development of the novel of manners it has also consigned to the sidelines the eighteenth century's other most notable woman novelist, Ann Radcliffe. Yet her Gothic romances were not only successful and highly praised in her own day but were a significant influence on the major Romantic poets. Like Burney she conformed to the age's image of the woman writer, living a retiring, domestic life and declining all opportunities for public notice on the strength of her literary successes. So private and unremarkable was her life that the poet Christina Rossetti had to give up a plan to write a biography because of a lack of material. Radcliffe is known today as the butt of Jane Austen's satire in *Northanger Abbey*, yet there are positive influences to be traced between Austen and her predecessor, and the Gothic mode Radcliffe pioneered found a new form in the literary imagination of Charlotte Brontë.

The improbabilities of Radcliffe's plots, in which unprotected, wandering heroines face danger in foreign climes, seem to set her apart from the concerns of the feminine novel of domestic realism. Yet there is much to link Radcliffe with novelists like Burney and Austen. Like Evelina, Emily, the heroine of *The Mysteries of Udolpho* (1794), undergoes a rite of passage into womanhood unprotected by the presence of authoritative male guardians. Thus, like Burney, Radcliffe offers her female readership a fantasy of freedom of action, and indeed freedom of choice: for Emily, left an orphan and an heiress, resolutely defends her inheritance from the machinations of the villain Montoni, and, having secured it, prudently satisfies herself as to the character and circumstances of her would-be husband Vallancourt, before favouring him with her hand and fortune. In other ways too the novel seems, however unconsciously, to cater to female fantasies of empowerment. Emily's two brothers die in childhood and her mother is rapidly disposed of in the first chapter of the novel. She is left then to enjoy the undivided attentions of a loving father who lavishes on her the sort of education denied most women. Besides the usual stock of feminine accomplishments she is taught the sciences and Latin. Her father also teaches her to temper 'feminine' sensibility with reason and self-command, virtues she will exhibit throughout the novel as she faces with extraordinary equanimity all the terrors of being the prisoner of the villainous Montoni. Thus, while the story pays allegiance to the need for patriarchal control of women, it also gives us a heroine who proves herself adept in the values that society deemed 'masculine'.

In Radcliffe's hands the Gothic also, whether consciously or not, becomes a vehicle for expressing suppressed sexual anxieties and desires which could only appear heavily encoded in the novel of manners practised by Burney. The menacing figure of Montoni and the terrors of imprisonment experienced by Emily find an echo in the many images of imprisonment and enclosure which feminist critics have found to be pervasive in nineteenth-century women's literature. Seen in this light they suggest that the history of women's writing can profitably be read not only as a history of oppression – that is, in relation to women's differential access to education and to a public voice – but also as a history of repression.

Jane Austen has always been assured a place in the 'Great Tradition' of the English novel, but although this judgement usually includes a rather condescending reference to her self-imposed limitation to what as a woman she could know, '3 or 4 families in a country village', it has not until recently recognized her as part of a woman's tradition of novel writing. Yet in the fullness and complexity with which she presents a woman's consciousness at the centre of her fictions, and her concern with money and women's economic dependence, Austen's work is illuminated by being read alongside those earlier women novelists, Burney, Edgeworth, Brunton and Radcliffe, with whose works she was in dialogue. (Spencer, 1986 and Todd, 1993 both contain valuable discussions of the eighteenth-century women novelists. See also Spender, 1986 and the Pandora Press reprints of neglected texts by early women novelists, published under the same collective title.) For a detailed discussion of the work of Radcliffe, Burney, Austen and other women writers of the eighteenth century, see Unit 9.

## The nineteenth century

There were, as Janet Todd notes, excellent women poets in the late eighteenth and early nineteenth century – she cites Anna Laetitia Barbauld, Hannah More, Anna Seward, Charlotte Smith, Helen Maria Williams and Mary Robinson – but there are no woman *Romantic* poets, 'giving that phrase all the privileged force it has acquired within later literary studies' (1988, p. 111). As Leon Litvak suggests (see Unit 10, 'Romanticism 1780–1830', pp. 235–6) the (male) Romantic preoccupation with selfhood and individuality marginalizes the female listener and privileges a poetic discourse in which it is difficult for women to intervene as speaking subjects. In *Villette* (1853) Charlotte Brontë drew on images derived from her reading of the Romantic poets for an ambiguous portrait of the Romantic artist in her portrait of the actress Vashti. Part angel and part demon, Vashti is both inspiring and at the same time a focus of anxiety, for in her acting she performs herself rather than any role:

> For a while – a long while – I thought it was only a woman, though an unique woman, who moved in might and grace before this multitude. By-and-by I recognised my mistake. Behold! I found upon her something neither of woman nor of man: in each of her eyes sat a devil. These evil forces bore her through the tragedy, kept up her feeble strength – for she was but a frail creature; and as the action rose and as the stir deepened, how wildly they shook her with their passions of the pit! They wrote HELL on her straight, haughty brow. They tuned her voice to the note of torment. They writhed her regal face to a demoniac mask. Hate and Murder and Madness incarnate, she stood.
>
> It was a marvellous sight: a mighty revelation.
> It was a spectacle low, horrible, immoral.

Significantly, Lucy Snowe, the protagonist/narrator who records Vashti's performance, shares the name of the silent female of Wordsworth's Lucy poems, underlining the degree to which woman writers felt themselves marginalized and subjected within the discourse of Romanticism.

By the mid-nineteenth century the prominence of the woman writer was beyond dispute and the writing woman was the subject of much comment in the periodical press, some of it highly satirical, as in Thackeray's caricature of the mannish Miss Bunion:

> Though her poems speak only of love, Miss B. has never been married. She is nearly six feet high; she loves waltzing beyond even poetry; and I think lobster salad as much as either. She confesses to twenty-eight; in which case her first volume, *The Orphan of Gozo*, must have been published when she was three years old.... The sufferings she has had to endure are, she says, beyond compare; the poems which she writes breathe a withering passion, a smouldering despair, an agony of spirit that would melt the soul of a drayman. (Helsinger *et al.*, 1983, p. 27. This volume contains much relevant material on the question of the woman writer with extensive quotation from a range of contemporary sources.)

In fairness one should set beside this the same author's handsome praise of *Villette*: 'The good of Villette ... is a very fine style; and a remarkably happy way (which few female authors possess) of carrying a metaphor logically through to its conclusion.' Yet in the same letter he goes on:

> I can read a great deal of her life as I fancy her in her book and see that rather than have fame, rather than any other earthly good or mayhap heavenly one, she wants some Tomkins or another to love her and to be in love with. But you see she is a little bit of a creature without a pennyworth of good looks, thirty years old I should think, buried in the country, and eating up her own heart there and no Tomkins will come. (Ray, 1946, vol. 3, p. 232)

The writing woman then is an 'odd' woman, one who having failed to fulfil herself in a proper womanly role, through some failure of femininity (Brontë has 'not a pennyworth of good looks' and Miss Bunion is 'nearly six feet high') turns to literature for compensation. So, too, G.H. Lewes, one of the most prominent critics of the age, declares that 'the happy wife and busy mother are only forced into literature by some hereditary organic tendency, stronger even than the domestic; and hence it is that the cleverest women are not always those who have written books' (Helsinger *et al.*, 1983, pp. 21–2).

Essentially this is the continuation of the eighteenth-century ideology of femininity, given added point and urgency by the Victorian age's intense preoccupation with the ramifications of the 'Woman Question'. Women writers were still required to write out of some essential femininity, most famously defined in Ruskin's 'Of Queens' Gardens' in his *Sesame and Lilies* (1865) and Coventry Patmore's *Angel in the House* (1854–63), but there were increasing demands for improvements in women's legal status and educational and economic opportunities. The women writers, as their contemporaries realized, participated in this discourse, although, until the advent of feminist criticism, this dimension of their work was ignored or minimized. It is curious that for so long Charlotte Brontë, banished from the university English curriculum in favour of her sister Emily, should appear to a later andocentric literary establishment as an ancestress of Barbara Cartland. Contemporary critics, by contrast, labelled her 'coarse' and 'unfeminine' and were alive to the radical implications of her work, to her subversive rage and the unwomanly self-assertiveness of heroines like Jane Eyre (see, for example, Elizabeth Rigby's infamous review of *Jane Eyre* in *The Quarterly Review*, 84, 1848, pp. 153–85).

It is in this context that we need to see the attempts of Victorian critics to enlist the woman writer in the service of the ideology of the 'Angel in the House'. So, for J.M. Ludlow, Harriet Beecher Stowe's *Uncle Tom's Cabin* (1852) was

> *the* woman's book of the age. If the novel addresses itself to the heart, what more natural than that it should then reach it most usefully and perfectly, when coming from the heart of a woman with all the dignity of her sex, full of all wifely and motherly experience? (Helsinger *et al.*, 1983, p. 55)

Women writers, on the other hand, equally convinced that Stowe's was a woman's book, could derive a far more challenging message from its female authorship. Elizabeth Barrett Browning, for example, cited it as support for her own determination as a writer to speak out on social and political questions:

> Not read Mrs Stowe's book! But you *must*. . . . For myself, I rejoice in the success, both as a woman and a human being. Oh, and is it possible that you think a woman has no business with questions like the question of slavery? Then she had better use a pen no more. She had better subside into slavery and concubinage herself, I think, as in the times of old, shut herself up with the Penelopes in the 'women's apartment' and take no rank among thinkers and speakers. (Helsinger *et al.*, 1983, p. 41)

At issue was the question of what women writers could or should write. As in the eighteenth century they were still granted competence in the areas of sentiment and private experience, but presumed from the limitations of their experience to be incompetent to address larger topics. However, as the novel itself shifted from being a 'low' form for the uneducated to becoming the predominant literary form capable of addressing the great, public issues of the age, so this approved feminine writing came increasingly to be seen as a marginalized and lesser form. Women writers were exhorted to confine themselves to feminine topics, and at the same time pronounced trivial for so doing. It is in this context that we should read George Eliot's famous *Westminster Review* article, 'Silly Novels by Lady Novelists' (1856), although Eliot's attempt to identify a 'precious speciality' in the work of serious women writers sounds uncomfortably like the maternal influence male critics were ready to praise in works like *Uncle Tom's Cabin*. Charlotte Brontë shows herself conscious of this dilemma as she refers constantly in her correspondence to the narrowness of her experience, remarking of her last novel, *Villette*, '[it] touches on no matter of public interest' (Wise and Symington, 1980, vol. 4, p. 14). Her friend and biographer Elizabeth Gaskell felt it necessary to preface her 'Condition of England' novel *Mary Barton* (1848), which deals with the relations of capital and labour, with an admission of her own feminine deficiencies: 'I know nothing of Political Economy, or the theories of trade.' Interestingly, Mrs Gaskell called her novel 'John Barton' after the trade unionist who is a central figure, suggesting that it was the political issue of the relations of capital and labour that was her central concern. It was her London publisher who was responsible for naming it after Barton's daughter Mary, the centre of the novel's romantic plot, thus intimating that this was a 'feminine' work from a woman writer.

Implicit in this attempt to prescribe a 'feminine' mode of writing was the conviction that a woman author's sex was inevitably inscribed in her work and could invariably be detected. There is no more interesting example of this than the changing evaluations of the Brontë sisters' first novels, originally published under the pseudonyms of Currer, Ellis and Acton Bell. As Carol Ohmann has shown ('Emily Brontë in the Hands of Male Critics', excerpted in Eagleton, 1986, pp. 71–2), evaluation and interpretation of the novels changed radically when the sex of the authors became known. The first critics, presuming Ellis Bell to be a man, pronounced his work powerful and original and took as the novel's central subject the representation of cruelty and depravity in the person of Heathcliff. One American critic, fastening on the violence of the action and the language in *Wuthering Heights*, compared the language of the novel to that of Yorkshire farmers or boatmen and complained that the author was, as a male, unable to represent women truly. After 1850, when Charlotte Brontë's 'Biographical Notice' affixed to posthumous editions of her sister's novel made clear the gender and circumstances of the author of *Wuthering Heights*, major critical re-evaluations were in order. The critic of *The Athenaeum* declared *Wuthering Heights* a work of 'female genius and authorship' and 'a more than usually interesting contribution to the history of female authorship in England' and linked it with its 'sister novels', *Jane Eyre* and *Agnes Grey*, as characteristic women's novels, characteristic in the sense that it was essentially a love story. The same assumptions are found in modern criticism of the novel. Raymond Williams, identifying the central experience of the novel as the moment in Chapter 9 when Cathy tries to explain to Nelly Dean her sense of identification with Heathcliff, uses it to locate Brontë's work in a women's novel tradition, the 'two suitor novel':

> Cathy, specifically, marries Linton for what Heathcliff does not have: money, position, ease: the visible elements of society .... She takes Heathcliff for granted and she marries Linton, and the real dislocation – the disruption, the savagery, the storm – then inevitably follow. (Williams, 1973, p. 67)

What this reading does is to make *Wuthering Heights* a comprehensibly 'feminine' novel, in which the heroine, unlike, for example, Jane Austen's Elizabeth Bennett, makes a purely prudential choice of a husband, ignoring the legitimate demands of the heart. But such a reading is made at the expense of acknowledging Cathy's fervent expression of her romantic love for Edgar Linton in the same passage: 'I love the ground under his feet, and the air over his head, and everything he touches, and every word he says – I love all his looks, and all his actions, and him entirely, and altogether.' On the other hand, when *Wuthering Heights* has been absorbed into the 'Great Tradition', it has been as a 'sport' or as a 'poetic novel', devoid of sociological interest, so that Cathy's passionate protests against the constraints of femininity are ignored.

Fundamentally Victorian critics recognized that writing was an assertion of self at odds with the ideal of self-effacement that was an essential part of the ideal of true womanhood. For those women who aspired to be poets this presented special difficulties. The Romantic poet took himself as subject. Women, on the other hand, were expected to see themselves as 'relative creatures', focused on the needs and feelings of others. Women, as creatures of feeling rather than intellect, were assumed capable of writing lyric poetry. But, in so far as lyric encouraged the free expression of feeling, it ran counter to the prevailing demand for feminine delicacy and restraint. Christina Rossetti could be accommodated to this view of the poetess by ignoring the darker tones of repressed longing and protest in her poems and emphasizing the extent of her religious feeling (for a recent reassessment of Rossetti's work see Kent, 1987, and for a discussion of Rossetti in this volume, see Unit 12, pp. 323–4). However, Elizabeth Barrett Browning presented an overt challenge to Victorian views of women's poetry, in terms of both form and content. As the author of poems of pathos such as 'The Mournful Mother' and 'Bertha in the Lane', she could readily be slotted into the tradition of sentimental poetry exemplified by Felicia Hemans (1793–1835), the age's ideal of the truly feminine poetess. *Sonnets from the Portuguese* (1850) reveals Barrett Browning boldly adopting the self-dramatizing stance of the love poet, an appropriation of a male poetic tradition made acceptable by her status as a married woman and by her frequent self-depreciating comparisons of herself to her husband, Robert Browning. On the other hand, the voice which speaks 'A Curse for a Nation', an abolitionist poem, finally rejects the blandishments of the restrained, feminine poetic voice:

> I heard an angel speak last night,
> And he said 'Write!
> Write a nation's curse for me,
> And send it over the Western Sea' ...

'Not so,' I answered once again.
    'To curse, choose men.
For I, a woman, have only known
How the heart melts and the tears run down.'

'Therefore,' the voice said, 'shalt thou write
    My curse tonight.
Some women weep and curse, I say
(And no one marvels), night and day.

'And thou shalt take their part tonight,
    Weep and write.
A curse from the depths of womanhood
Is very salt, and bitter, and good.'

So thus I wrote ...

In her poems after 1850 she turned to subjects that were outside the range of what were considered suitable subjects for women's poetry: slavery, poverty, Italian nationalism and the position of women. In *Aurora Leigh* (1856) she linked exploration of the 'Woman Question' with a passionate portrayal of the woman artist, a figure who, since Madame de Staël's novel *Corinne* (1807), had both fascinated and disturbed women writers.

*Aurora Leigh* boldly celebrates the woman artist who asserts herself as writing subject and refuses to be confined to the subject matter, forms and voice deemed appropriate for women's verse. It eschews the lyric for the epic mode, claiming a place in a poetic tradition hitherto exclusively male, and it rejects the sentimental for the polemical. Barrett Browning was consciously innovative, describing her work in progress as a 'sort of novel-poem ... running into the midst of our conventions, and rushing into drawing-rooms and the like "where angels fear to tread"; and so, meeting face to face without mask the Humanity of the age and speaking the truth of it out plainly'. In the persona of her poet heroine, Aurora, she challenges the assumptions about women's literary inspiration and the poetic forms in which it is embodied. In a long passage on the writing of poetry in Book 5 Aurora dismisses the personal and the emotional as the inspiration for women's art:

We women are too apt to look to one,
Which proves a certain impotence in art.
We strain our natures at doing something great,
Far less because it's something great to do,
Than haply that we, so commend ourselves
As being not small, and more appreciable
To some one friend.

Aurora rejects 'this vile woman's way' and with it the 'feminine' forms Barrett Browning had herself practised to critical acclaim, the ballad and the sonnet. Instead she embraces a 'masculine' project, 'to represent the age', not as Tennyson was to do in *Idylls of the King*, in historical garb, but instead exhorting herself to 'catch/ Upon the burning lava of a song/The full-veined, heaving, double-breasted age', in all its troubling contemporaneity. In keeping with this ambitious manifesto *Aurora Leigh* intertwines the personal with the political, linking the story of Aurora's growth as a poet with issues of class relations, poverty, political theory and the position of women. In so doing Barrett Browning engages with and revises key works by other women writers of her age, Madame de Staël, George Sand and Charlotte Brontë, as Cora Kaplan has shown (Browning, 1978, Introduction). One of the key successes of Gynocriticism has been to uncover these influences and continuities in women's writing which conventional literary history has obscured. Ellen Moers has shown how Barrett Browning in turn proved a potent influence for her younger American contemporary Emily Dickinson.

*Aurora Leigh* was a notably popular work, going through thirteen editions in England by 1873. But the critics were alive to the ways that it challenged literary decorum and perturbed by its ambition and self-assertion. It was the choice of the woman artist herself as subject that prompted their criticisms. One commentator, invoking Thackeray's caricature of the poetess, Miss Bunion, denounced the assertive Aurora as 'a bad specimen even of her very unattractive class', revealing the gendered character of so much Victorian criticism of women's writing. Another saw Barrett Browning's failure as due to 'the erroneous theory that art is the proper subject for itself' (Helsinger *et al.*, 1983, pp. 39–40), conveniently sliding over the fact that it had been *the* great subject of the Romantic poets.

Conventional literary history consigned *Aurora Leigh* to obscurity, despite its contemporary success, remembering Elizabeth Barrett Browning if at all in the role of 'feminine' poet, the author of *Sonnets from the Portuguese*, and choosing to ignore her own declaration that it represented 'the most mature of my works, and the one into which my highest convictions upon Life and Art have entered' (for a reassessment of *Aurora Leigh* and a valuable discussion of the way in which the poem engages in dialogue with other contemporary literary works see Kaplan's introduction to her edition).

Poetic writing from the Renaissance to the nineteenth century maintained a closely protected inheritance of devices and registers. This was disrupted by Modernism, and the Modernist movement had among its initiators a significant number of women poets, particularly Gertrude Stein (1874–1946), Amy Lowell (1874–1925), Marianne Moore (1887–1972), Hilda Doolittle ('H.D.') (1886–1961) and Harriet Monroe (1860–1936). Lowell, H.D. and Monroe were active strategists in the evolution of Imagist verse. Imagism rejected the codes and conventions of traditional poetry: these were perceived as barriers to the ideal of a pure, transparent mediation of experience. Free verse was promoted as a means of allowing the texture of the poem to reflect the fluid, unpredictable pattern of perception and thought. Much of the early verse of H.D. and Lowell is ungendered in the sense that the speaker maintains a cool anonymity. Its loose form has no precedent: it cannot usefully be compared with the stylistic habits of a predominantly male tradition. Marianne Moore devised complex and ingenious methods of formal organization (the best known being syllabism), and again the sense of a self-conscious distancing from a patriarchal tradition is evident.

It would be simplistic to claim that, by freeing itself from established traditions, Modernism freed and encouraged the woman poet, but we should bear in mind Anne

Finch's complaint that the woman poet is judged 'an intruder on the rights of men'. Those 'rights' were effectively challenged by the Modernist programme, and a clean slate of formal and referential possibilities was offered, both to the early Modernist woman poets and to their more recent successors: Sylvia Plath, Adrienne Rich, Stevie Smith and Grace Nichols who are, in various ways, the inheritors of the Modernist revolution, and all find space for a balance between their formal design and their sex. (Miller, 1986, considers these questions and the verse of H.D. and Amy Lowell is discussed in Unit 17.)

## Virginia Woolf and Doris Lessing: difference or androgyny?

In surveying women's writing in earlier periods the emphasis of this unit has been upon the social and historical conditions that serve to explain why women's writing took the forms that it did. Thus the specific character of women's literary production, their choice of subject matter and forms, can be attributed to their differential access to education and experience and to the inhibiting effects of patriarchy. It might then be argued that as women have gained legal equality and equal access to education and public roles so they will increasingly write out of the same consciousness as men; that it is no longer valid or even desirable to talk about a women's tradition or to see the woman writer as occupying a special position because of her gender. It may even be argued that the crucial task that remains for feminism in the late twentieth century is to deconstruct the masculine/feminine opposition, to reveal it as a limiting cultural construct rather than an essential difference. This is an unresolved argument within feminist criticism, often expressed in terms of the opposed categories of 'difference' and 'androgyny'. In this final section I wish to explore some of the ramifications of this debate in relation to two leading women writers of the twentieth century, Virginia Woolf (1882–1941) and Doris Lessing (1919–).

No account of gender and writing could ignore Virginia Woolf. Her occasional essays on forgotten or neglected women writers and her treatise *A Room of One's Own* (1929) make her the pioneer of the critical practice that Showalter later labelled Gynocriticism. Clearly it was crucial for Woolf as a novelist to locate herself in relation to the tradition of women's writing she herself did so much to recover. *A Room of One's Own* grew out of two talks on the subject of women and fiction that she was invited to give to the women's colleges of Cambridge. In the treatise she represents herself in semi-fictive mode researching her topic among the authorities of the British Museum, reflecting upon the facts of women's economic dependence and upon the consequences of patriarchy for women. The thesis that emerges insistently from these researches is that literary production is determined by social and material conditions so that women's experience of oppression and repression is inscribed in their writing.

Yet in opposition to this materialist thesis Woolf also advances an ideal of artistic integrity that transcends gender differences. Her highest praise is reserved for those women writers like Emily Brontë and Jane Austen who achieve such integrity because, although they write as women write and not as men write, they write without a consciousness of their sex. It is then in keeping with this ideal of transcendence that her treatise should move to a conclusion that endorses androgyny rather than difference as the proper goal of the woman writer. Thus, after ninety pages devoted to describing why women's writing is different, she finally declares herself ready to write her talk on the subject of women and fiction, and 'the very first sentence that I would write here ... is that it is fatal for anyone who writes to think of their sex. It is fatal to be a man or woman pure and simple; one must be woman-manly or man-womanly' (1993, p. 94).

However, this embracing of the ideal of androgyny is not the whole story. In the first place it is offered as an ideal for the future, for some imagined age less conscious of sexual difference. Secondly, it is challenged by a different vision of the future direction of women's writing, a future of difference, envisaged through her reflections on the possible literary development of the new woman novelist 'Mary Carmichael', whose project will be to put into representation that which the masculine discourses of history, biography and the 'naturalist-novel' have ignored or distorted, those 'infinitely obscure lives' (p. 81):

> With the eye of imagination I saw a very ancient lady crossing the street on the arm of a middle-aged woman, her daughter, perhaps, both so respectably booted and furred that their dressing in the afternoon must be a ritual, and the clothes themselves put away in cupboards with camphor, year after year, throughout the summer months. They cross the road when the lamps are being lit (for the dusk is their favourite hour), as they must have done year after year. The elder is close on eighty; but if one asked her what her life has meant to her, she would say that she remembered the streets lit for the Battle of Balaclava, or had heard the guns fire in Hyde Park for the birth of Edward the Seventh. And if one asked her, longing to pin down the moment with date and season, but what were you doing on the fifth of April 1869, or the second of November 1875, she would look vague and say that she could remember nothing. For all the dinners are cooked; the plates and cups washed; the children sent to school and gone out into the world. Nothing remains of it all. All has vanished. No biography or history has a word to say about it. And the novels, without meaning to, inevitably lie. (pp. 80–1)

Here the androgynous vision of the future gives way to a vision of difference. The task of the woman artist will be to represent this 'accumulation of unrecorded life' (p. 81), and it is a task that requires nothing less than a radical breaking apart and remaking of the masculine discourses that have rendered women's lives and women's creativity invisible. *A Room of One's Own* may itself be seen as a radical revisioning of the masculine discourse of historiography. In *To the Lighthouse* (1927) Woolf produced an equally radical revisioning of the novel, rejecting the linear form of the 'naturalist' novel for the 'contemplative' form she identified as feminine. This contemplative form consigns to parentheses the elements of the traditional novelistic plot – the deaths of Mrs Ramsay and her son and daughter – to focus on the opposed ideals of androgyny and difference through the relations of the 'feminine' woman, Mrs Ramsay and her surrogate daughter, the woman artist Lily Briscoe. In part, the narrator's portrait of Mrs Ramsay, the archetypal 'Angel in the House', whose creativity is expended in the 'feminine' roles of wife, mother and hostess, and in the daily business of living, exemplifies the task that Woolf had assigned to her young woman novelist, Mary Carmichael, of recording and celebrating 'the accumulation of unrecorded life', as Mrs Ramsay herself is commemorated in Lily Briscoe's portrait of her. Lily recognizes that her own attempt in art 'to make of the moment something permanent' is analogous to Mrs Ramsay's artistry in living. Yet Lily's role as woman artist also involves rejecting the femininity Mrs Ramsay exemplifies for the sake of artistic creativity. As Lily progresses towards the completion of her painting, language and imagery suggest that she achieves momentarily an artistic integrity born of the fusion of male and female sexual energies:

> Then, as if some juice necessary for the lubrication of her faculties were spontaneously squirted, she began precariously dipping among the blues and ambers, moving her brush hither and thither, but it was now heavier and went slower, as if it had fallen in with some rhythm which was dictated to her (she kept looking at the hedge, at the canvas) by what she saw, so that while her hand quivered with life, this rhythm was strong enough to bear her along with it on its current. Certainly she was losing consciousness of outer things, and her name, and her personality and her appearance, and whether Mr Carmichael was there or not, her mind kept throwing up from its depths, scenes and names, and sayings, and memories and ideas, like a fountain spurting over that glaring, hideously difficult white space, while she modelled it with greens and blues.

At this moment Lily appears to paint, as Woolf had required the woman novelist to write, without a consciousness of her sex: 'But the war had drawn the sting of her femininity. Poor devils, one thought, poor devils of both sexes, getting into such messes'. Yet the obstacles that lie in the way of achieving that androgynous vision are apparent. While she paints Lily is assailed by memories of the voice of masculine authority that reiterates the message 'women can't write, women can't paint', and by her realization that her painting will be relegated to the servants' bedrooms or languish rolled up under the sofa.

Moreover, the completion of Lily's painting is counterpointed by the completion of a second subject announced in the novel's opening sequence, the journey to the lighthouse. This second subject ends in a manner that puts into question the very possibility of androgyny. As Cam and James, Mr Ramsay's daughter and son, embark with him on the crossing to the lighthouse they are joined in a secret compact to resist the tyranny of the patriarchal law of the father, which determines the opposition of masculine and feminine and the hierarchical relations between them. Yet the omens are not good. Behind them lie the exemplary histories of their dead sister and brother, Prue who died in childbirth and Andrew who was killed in the war. As their journey progresses each is constructed as a gendered subject in conformity with the patriarchal law Mr Ramsay represents. Cam, unable to resist her father's demand for sympathy and love, takes on the 'feminine' caring role of her dead mother. James, steering their boat to its destination, finds in the image of the lighthouse, seen for the first time at close quarters, confirmation of a 'masculine' knowledge and identity shared with his father and defined by its opposition to the 'feminine':

> it was a stark tower on a bare rock. It satisfied him. It confirmed some obscure feeling of his about his own character. The old ladies, he thought, thinking of the garden at home,

went dragging their chairs about on the lawn. Old Mrs Beckworth, for example, was always saying how nice it was and how they ought to be so proud and they ought to be so happy, but as a matter of fact James thought, looking at the Lighthouse stood there on its rock, it's like that. He looked at his father reading fiercely with his legs curled tight. They shared that knowledge.

There is at least the suggestion at the end of *To the Lighthouse* that this perpetuation of the hierarchical opposition of masculine and feminine renders the androgynous vision fragile and marginalized. Moreover, despite Woolf's insistence in *A Room of One's Own* that certain great male authors were androgynous – she cites Shakespeare, Keats, Sterne, Cowper, Lamb and Coleridge – it is to be inferred from *To the Lighthouse* that the responsibility for creating an androgynous art of the future rests with women artists. (For valuable discussion of the issues raised by Woolf's analysis of women's writing and its relation to her own fictions see Bowlby, 1988, and Barrett's introductions to *Virginia Woolf: Women and Writing*, 1979, and her edition of *A Room of One's Own and Three Guineas*, 1993).

Where Virginia Woolf sought to define herself as a writer in dialogue with a tradition of women's writing Doris Lessing began her prolific writing career with the explicit aim of emulating the range of the male 'greats' of nineteenth-century European realism, whose work describes 'the intellectual and moral climate of their age' (Preface to *The Golden Notebook*). Her ambitious sequence of five novels, *Children of Violence* (1952–69), charts the development of Martha Quest, as she moves from white, colonial Africa to post-war England. The range of the novels' concerns challenged prevailing assumptions about the women's novel as small scale and focused upon personal relationships. Like the male protagonists of the nineteenth-century *Bildungsroman* Martha's experience encompasses the political – racism, colonialism, the Cold War, Marxism and the threat of nuclear war – as well as the personal.

After the third of the Martha Quest novels Lessing broke new ground with *The Golden Notebook* (1962), a novel which questions the veracity of the classic realism she had earlier espoused. For many of her readers, however, what was striking about *The Golden Notebook* was not its fractured, experimental form, but its bold exploration of female subjectivity and its willingness to address openly issues of female sexuality. It was quickly hailed as a feminist classic. However, Lessing herself declared 'this novel was not a trumpet for Women's Liberation' (Preface), and while voicing her support for women's rights, complained that 'the book was instantly belittled, by friendly reviewers, as well as by hostile ones, as being about the sex war' (Preface). The key word in this complaint is, surely, 'belittled'. Lessing is anxiously rejecting the label of 'woman writer', conscious of the marginalized status accorded to those who write about women's experience. The protagonist of *The Golden Notebook*, Anna Wulf, shares many of the life experiences, both personal and political, of Martha Quest – an upbringing in colonial Africa, failed relationships with men, involvement in and later disillusionment with left-wing politics, psychotherapy and mental breakdown. Lessing is still concerned, as in the *Children of Violence* sequence, to present a wide-ranging image of the 'ideological "feel" of our mid-century'.

What is new in *The Golden Notebook* is that this questioning is effected through the experience of a female protagonist who is also a novelist. Lessing might argue that the experience of her novelist heroine, struggling to find words and form to express her sense of a fractured reality, is pertinent to any contemporary writer, whether male or female, but much of Anna's experience bears directly on her position as a woman writer.

Anna has published one successful novel 'Frontiers of War', based on her experience of racism and left-wing activism in wartime colonial Africa, which she afterwards repudiates as filled with a 'terrible, lying nostalgia'. She is pursued by an agent who wants to turn her book into a film with the title 'Forbidden Love', seeing in it a typical, marketable woman's fiction about a doomed love affair. In Anna's yellow notebook, which is the draft of a novel 'The Shadow of the Third', she records the story of Ella, a journalist on a women's magazine, who has written a handful of short stories which she satirically describes as 'sensitive and feminine', and who is writing a novel about a young man who commits suicide. Her lover, Paul, a psychiatrist, patronizes her writing and deems her incapable of dealing with a subject on which he is the voice of authority. To her friend Julia, Ella 'makes bitter jokes about Jane Austen hiding her novels under the blotting paper when people come into the room', and quotes Stendhal's dictum that any woman under fifty who writes should do so under a pseudonym. Anna herself faces the perennial criticism levelled at woman writers, that she writes 'little novels about the emotions'. In her Preface to the novel Lessing addresses the split between the personal and the political, so often represented in terms of the opposition of feminine and masculine, declaring 'the essence of the book, the organisation of it, everything in it, says implicitly and explicitly, that we must not divide things off, must not compartmentalise'.

While the need to resist compartmentalizing is related to many of the concerns raised in *The Golden Notebook*, it has a particular significance for Anna, the woman writer. Towards the end of the novel Anna and her lover, the American, Saul Green, another writer who is unable to write, share the experience of mental breakdown. During the course of these breakdowns they are engaged in a bitter 'sex war', each seeing masculine and feminine values and expectations as opposed and contradictory. However, out of the experience of breakdown each attains a new sense of a self that includes the other. Even as they part Anna senses that they 'would always be flesh of one flesh and think each other's thoughts'. The tangible result of this new self that includes both masculine and feminine is that each is now able to write. Anna gives Saul her treasured golden notebook, that has lain unused, and writes in it for him the opening sentence of a novel that Saul afterwards completes, and he does the same for her. Initially it seems that Anna gives Saul the idea for a 'masculine' fiction – his story begins 'On a dry hillside in Algeria, a soldier watched the moonlight glinting on his rifle' – while he gives her a sentence, 'The two women were alone in the London flat', which seems to announce a typically 'feminine' fiction. But, in fact, Saul's book, about the personal relationship that develops between a French soldier and the Algerian freedom fighter who is his jailer, is an androgynous work of art that marries the personal and the political. So, too, the 'feminine' sentence that Saul gives Anna becomes the opening sentence of a fiction, *The Golden Notebook*, that both dissects and seeks to heal the destructive dichotomy of masculine and feminine.

To lay stress upon the vision of the androgynous artist in *The Golden Notebook* runs the risk of oversimplifying a rich and complex text. Almost certainly it is not an emphasis that Doris Lessing herself would approve. But there can hardly be a more striking exploration of the debates that still surround women's writing and the position of the woman writer.

## BIBLIOGRAPHY

Adburgham, A. (1972) *Women in Print; Writing Women and Women's Magazines from the Restoration to the Reign of Victoria*, George Allen & Unwin, London.

Ashfield, A. (1995) *Women Romantic Poets 1770–1838*, Manchester University Press, Manchester.

Behn, A. (1992) *Oroonoko, The Rover and Other Works*, ed. J. Todd, Penguin, Harmondsworth.

Belsey, C. and Moore, J. (1989) *The Feminist Reader: Essays in Gender and the Politics of Literary Criticism*, Macmillan, Basingstoke and London.

Blain, V., Clements, P. and Grundy, I. (eds) (1990) *The Feminist Companion to Literature in English*, Batsford, London.

Bloom, H. (1973) *The Anxiety of Influence*, Oxford University Press, New York.

Bowlby, R. (1988) *Virginia Woolf: Feminist Destinations*, Blackwell, Oxford and New York.

Browning, E.B. (1978) *Aurora Leigh and Other Poems*, intro. by C. Kaplan, Women's Press, London.

Buck, C. (ed.) (1992) *The Bloomsbury Guide to Women's Literature*, Bloomsbury, London.

Eagleton, M. (ed.) (1986) *Feminist Literary Theory. A Reader*, Blackwell, Oxford and Cambridge, Mass.

Ellmann, M. (1968) *Thinking About Women*, Harcourt, New York.

Epstein, J. (1989) *The Iron Pen: Frances Burney and the Politics of Women's Writing*, Bristol Classical Press, Bristol.

Ezell, M.J.M. (1993) *Writing Women's Literary History*, Johns Hopkins University Press, Baltimore.

Gilbert, S. and Gubar, S. (eds) (1979) *Shakespeare's Sisters: Feminist Essays on Women Poets*, Indiana University Press, Bloomington.

Gilbert, S. and Gubar, S. (1979) *The Madwoman in the Attic: The Woman Writer and the Nineteenth Century Literary Imagination*, Yale University Press, New Haven and London.

Gilbert, S. and Gubar, S. (1988) *No Man's Land: The Place of the Woman Writer in the Twentieth Century, Vol. 1: The War of the Words*, Yale University Press, New Haven and London.

Goreau, A. (1980) *Reconstructing Aphra: A Social Biography of Aphra Behn*, Oxford University Press, London and Oxford.

Heilbrun, C.G. (1973) *Toward a Recognition of Androgyny*, Harper & Row, New York.

Helsinger, E.K., Sheets, R.L. and Veeder, W. (1983) *The Woman Question: Society and Literature in Britain and America, 1837–1883, Vol. 3: Literary Issues*, University of Chicago Press, Chicago.

Hobby, E. (1988) *Virtue of Necessity: English Women's Writing, 1646–1688*, Virago, London.

Homans, M. (1986) *Bearing the Word: Language and Female Experience in Nineteenth-Century Women's Writing*, University of Chicago Press, Chicago.

Jardine, L. (1983) *Still Harping on Daughters: Women and Drama in the Age of Shakespeare*, Harvester Wheatsheaf, Hemel Hempstead.

Kent, D.A. (ed.) (1987) *The Achievement of Christina Rossetti*, Cornell University Press, Ithaca.

Lessing, D. (1972) *The Golden Notebook*, Michael Joseph, London.

MacCarthy, B. (1994) *The Female Pen: Women Writers and Novelists, 1621–1818*, Cork University Press, Cork.

Miller, N. (ed.) (1986) *The Poetics of Gender*, Columbia University Press, New York.

Millett, K. (1971) *Sexual Politics*, Hart-Davis, London.

Moers, E. (1978) *Literary Women*, Women's Press, London.

Montefiore, J. (1987) *Feminism and Poetry: Language, Identity, Experience in Women's Writing*, Pandora Press, London.

Morgan, F. (1981) *The Female Wits: Women Playwrights of the Restoration*, Virago, London.

Newton, J.L. (1981) *Women, Power and Subversion: Social Strategies in British Fiction, 1778–1860*, University of Georgia Press, Athens, Georgia.

Olsen, T. (1980) *Silences*, Virago, London.

Poovey, M. (1984) *The Proper Lady and the Woman Writer: Ideology as Style in the Works of Mary Wollstonecraft, Mary Shelley and Jane Austen*, University of Chicago Press, Chicago.

Ray, G.N. (ed.) (1946) *The Letters and Private Papers of William Makepeace Thackeray*, vol. 3, Oxford University Press, London.

Showalter, E. (1977) *A Literature of Their Own: British Women Novelists from Brontë to Lessing*, Princeton University Press, Princeton.

Showalter, E. (ed.) (1986) *The New Feminist Criticism: Essays on Women, Literature and Theory*, Virago, London.

Spencer, J. (1986) *The Rise of the Woman Novelist: From Aphra Behn to Jane Austen*, Blackwell, Oxford.

Spender, D. (1986) *Mothers of the Novel: One Hundred Good Woman Novelists before Jane Austen*, Pandora Press, London.

Todd, J. (ed.) (1984) *A Dictionary of British and American Women Writers, 1660–1800*, Methuen, London.

Todd, J. (ed.) (1988) *Feminist Literary History: A Defence*, Polity Press, Cambridge.

Todd, J. (ed.) (1993) *Gender, Art and Death*, Polity Press, Cambridge.

Wain, John (ed.) (1986) *The Oxford Anthology of English Poetry*, Oxford University Press, Oxford.

Watt, I. (1987) *The Rise of the Novel: Studies in Defoe, Richardson and Fielding*, Hogarth Press, London [first published 1957, Chatto & Windus].

Wise, T.J. and Symington, J.A. (1980) *The Brontës: Their Lives, Friendships and Correspondence*, 4 vols, Blackwell, Oxford.

Williams, R. (1973) *The English Novel from Dickens to Lawrence*, Chatto & Windus, London.

Woolf, V. (1979) *Women and Writing*, intro. by Michele Barrett, Women's Press, London.

Woolf, V. (1993) *A Room of One's Own and Three Guineas*, ed. M. Barrett, Penguin, Harmondsworth.

# Gender and literature: feminist criticism

*Tamsin Spargo*

## What is feminist criticism?

I want to begin this brief introduction to feminist criticism with an example of how a feminist critic might approach a text. The inclusion of this text in a book on literary studies may seem odd: it is not well known, nor would it be defined conventionally as literary writing. Jane Sharpe's *The Midwives Book or the Whole Art of Midwifery Discovered* (1671) is, as its title implies, a handbook for midwives, written by a woman in the seventeenth century. As such, its status as a relatively unknown text raises a number of questions for any critic who is interested in the connection between gender, writing and literature.

The text argues that women have as important a role in sexual reproduction as men and that female pleasure during sexual intercourse is not only desirable but necessary if conception is to take place. Sharpe acknowledges that men are more active in sexual reproduction but stresses that they could not reproduce without women and that women should not be ashamed of their bodies. This may not seem to be a particularly radical argument to a twentieth-century reader, but in the seventeenth century women were conventionally believed to be not only socially but biologically inferior to men. Traditional medical knowledge, which claimed that female bodies were actually incomplete versions of male anatomy, underpinned many broader definitions of women's inferiority. This female writer, who as a midwife was resisting attempts to turn her skill into a profession for men, has to employ some traditional medical knowledge in order to be understood but she modifies it in order to assert a positive vision of female sexuality. The text also anticipates the complex objectives of feminist criticism: like Sharpe, feminist critics work with the ways in which gender difference is conventionally presented, in literature, and interpreted, in criticism, while developing radical or subversive alternatives.

One of the key features of feminist criticism is an emphasis on the implication of texts within specific historical and cultural contexts. The recognition that things were once different may suggest that they could change again. Texts like Jane Sharpe's are read by feminist critics and cultural historians who wish to examine not only the attitudes and meanings of the past but also of the present. The intervention made by a medical text is quite direct but feminist critics believe that literary and fictional texts can also be read as participating in debates about the meanings of gender difference and that the study of these texts can contribute to the feminist project of changing society. Most feminists also argue that the critical strategies which they employ in reading texts like this one, which are written by women and about women, can also be employed in readings of canonical male-authored texts.

The main part of this unit comprises a number of readings of literary texts which will show some of the different ways in which a feminist critic might approach a variety of genres and types of writing produced in different historical contexts and read in the twentieth century. First, in order to put these readings into context, I want to offer a brief history of some of the major developments within feminist literary criticism and point to some of the connections between literary criticism and broader feminist concerns.

Feminist criticism is informed by a desire for change. The form and extent of that change may differ according to the critic's views of how society should be ordered, and feminist critics employ a diverse range of critical techniques and strategies, but feminism and feminist criticism are, by definition, committed to changing the existing power relations between women and men. Contemporary feminist criticism developed with, and out of, the women's liberation movement. Early texts like Kate Millett's *Sexual Politics* (1969) and Germaine Greer's *The Female Eunuch* (1970) were ground-breaking studies, best-sellers which were read by academics and by others involved in the women's movement. This connection between feminist criticism and a broader feminist movement has developed in different ways over the last twenty-five years and the productive, sometimes fraught, relationship between academic and other forms of feminist activity is something most feminist critics locate at the heart of their work.

Feminist criticism in the early 1970s was largely concerned with exposing patriarchal attitudes and values within literary texts and with challenging the authority of the educational and cultural institutions which promoted a canon of 'great' works by male authors whilst excluding or marginalizing those by women. Feminist critics read canonical literary texts as products of a particular culture rather than as aesthetic objects through which gifted individuals revealed timeless truths about human nature. Texts which had been celebrated as sensitive depictions of reality were read as interpretations and representations which, consciously or unconsciously, supported a particular view of the world and of gender relations. Underpinning many of the representations of both men and women throughout literary and cultural history has been an (often implicit rather than explicit) assertion that the male, and by extension the masculine, is the norm and that the female, or the feminine, is a departure from the norm. The feminist argument that there is a hierarchical arrangement of gender relations in our society which places men in a dominant position and women in a subservient position has been accompanied by an insistence that this inequality is both evident in and perpetuated by cultural practices including both writing and reading literary texts. The neutrality both of the texts and of the criticism which privileged them has been exposed as a fiction; just as there are no neutral writings, there can be no neutral readings. What we choose to read and how we read is always more than a matter of personal preference and the judgements made about texts are, even when presented as purely aesthetic or formal, informed by our own political and cultural positions.

The type of literary criticism which early feminists analyzed was not always *explicitly* sexist or misogynistic but often displayed gender blindness, apparently dealing in supposedly universal terms but implicitly assuming that the reader was male or could identify with masculine values. A good example of feminist criticism of this approach is Elaine Showalter's analysis in 'Towards a Feminist Poetics' of the critic Irving Howe's response to the opening of Hardy's *The Mayor of Casterbridge* in which Henshawe sells his wife. Howe does not approve of the action but acknowledges its attractions, which his reader is, in turn, assumed to understand. This implies that reading, and criticism, is a matter of men communicating with other men. Showalter's essay is published in Jacobus (1979) and reprinted in Eagleton (1986).

Feminist criticism developed in a number of different ways from the 1970s. One major strand was, and is, primarily concerned with recovering neglected texts *by* women and with exploring women's writing and its relationship to patriarchal societies. Often described as 'woman-centred', this approach is typified by three influential texts of the late 1970s: Ellen Moers's *Literary Women* (1976), Elaine Showalter's *A Literature of Their Own* (1977) and Sandra Gilbert and Susan Gubar's *The Madwoman in the Attic* (1979). These texts challenged the traditional canon which was dominated by male-authored texts and sought to recover and examine a distinctive tradition of literature by women. They also argued that women's experience of society shaped their perceptions and writing in ways which differed from those of male writers. The focus on women's writing has developed in a variety of ways, reflecting the views of different types of feminism. (For a more extensive introduction to this subject see Unit 23.) Feminist literary historians continue to recover material by, and about, women writing throughout history, providing an invaluable resource for feminist criticism. The recovery of women's writing allows feminist literary critics to work on, and with, texts which have previously been ignored and has led to criticism of the conventional critical judgements which had, for example, celebrated the early male writers of the novel in the eighteenth century while almost completely ignoring the hundreds of popular and, at the time, influential female novelists. The fact that in many historical periods women were denied a public voice has also led to a new emphasis on unpublished or privately circulated texts by women, such as diaries, journals, autobiographies and letters and on texts such as Jane Sharpe's which do not fit within established generic categories. This has, in turn, raised questions about how the category of literature developed historically on the basis, at least in part, of the exclusion of writing not only by women but by other socially and culturally marginalized groups. New courses on women's writing developed from this tradition and the absence of texts by women on traditional courses became increasingly obvious.

Although the increased visibility of women's writing is undoubtedly productive and enabling, this strand of feminist activity raises some questions. The development of what can be seen as an alternative canon may allow literary and educational institutions to treat women's writing as an optional extra while the traditional canon and the courses which maintain it are relatively unchanged. The formation of an alternative canon, inevitably through a process of selection, also runs the risk of excluding material which does not fit, just as the traditional canon excluded women's writing. Perhaps even more crucial is the problem of the political implications of insisting on a distinctively female tradition of writing which can all too easily imply that men and women are *essentially* different.

Some feminist critics have insisted that women's writing *reveals* women's experience, often an experience marked by suffering or by anger. Elaine Showalter, for example, argued that there were stages in the history of women's writing which marked a move from working within patriarchal norms towards an expression of the *truth* of female experience, thus implying that writing reflects experience rather than constructs it. Many feminists today would argue that this also promotes the idea of a universal or innate female essence and that such a belief works against the idea of change both on a personal and on a social or cultural level. There is a feminist tradition which celebrates an essential female difference and which argues that women need to remove themselves from patriarchal society in order to develop their full, female, potential. This is usually called 'radical feminism' and is often associated with separatist movements and, in some cases, with lesbian politics. In approaching written texts, radical feminists, such as Mary Daly, author of *Gyn/ Ecology* (1978), develop ways of reading and writing which celebrate what they see as essentially female qualities and values. Another distinguishing feature of radical feminism has been its opposition to theory which is defined as a masculine way of thinking which is authoritarian and oppressive. This rejection of theory is in marked contrast to other recent developments in feminist criticism which I will describe later in this introduction.

The stress on recovering texts by women also raises the question of whether or not women write differently from men and whether or not the fact that a text is written by a woman means that it will necessarily offer a more positive or feminist view of women. The readings of *Tess of the D'Urbervilles* and *Jane Eyre* later in this section may suggest that these are not simple questions. In the light of psychoanalytic and poststructuralist theories (outlined in Unit 22), many feminists argue that our sense of identity, our subjectivity, is not fixed or inextricably bound to the biological sex which is designated to us soon after birth. Instead it is seen to be cultural forces which demand and invite us to identify with particular subject positions such as those labelled masculine and feminine.

Western thought, and the language which enables us to think, is profoundly marked by a structure of binary oppositions which set up masculinity and femininity as not merely different but opposed and which privilege the masculine over the feminine. The basic opposition between male and female is sustained by a whole series of oppositions, such as rational and irrational, active and passive, intellectual and emotional, which define what it is to be male or female. These are not actual characteristics of real men and women; they are long-standing cultural assumptions.

You may already know the conundrum or 'myth' about the boy who is lying in hospital after a road accident in which his father was killed. The surgeon enters the operating theatre and says, 'I can't operate on him, he's my son.' The story depends for its effect on the listener saying, 'But the father's dead. . .', associating the concept of 'surgeon' with traditionally male attributes of power and authority, indicating how deeply ingrained conventional cultural definitions of male and female roles are within language. The twist in the tale, of course, is that the surgeon is, in fact, his mother. Similar assumptions about gender can be evident in criticism, as Carol Ohmann shows in 'Emily Brontë in the Hands of Male Critics' (Eagleton, 1986). Ohmann quotes from contemporary reviewers of *Wuthering Heights* who, taking their cue from the name Ellis Bell, assumed that the author was a man. The critics assume that they are reading a male author's text when in fact they are reading a text which has *constructed* a male author. In both examples we can see how our assumptions about gender affect the way we read but also how language underpins those assumptions.

One key feature of most forms of feminist criticism is the identification of the ways in which the language of literary texts constructs gender difference. There is no single or standard critical methodology; feminist critics employ many different techniques from narratology to deconstructive reading but all share a belief that the ways in which language is used in literary texts have an effect on our lives. In order to present intelligible characters writers must draw on their culture's shared knowledge about gender but the ways in which they do so may confirm, contest or, more probably, confirm and contest that knowledge. A feminist reading of a literary text may begin by identifying the negative or restricting meanings which it apparently ascribes to female characters or to femininity in general but it may also look for tensions, contradictions or other textual indications that these meanings are inadequate, unstable or contingent. Because texts are read at different historical moments and in different contexts the impact of their presentation of gender will vary. Even if a text presents its view of men and women as universally and eternally true, this view will always be open to challenge.

As readers and writers, the positions, including gender positions, which we take up often appear and feel natural but they are not inevitable or fully stable and our identities are always in flux, changing and changeable. This may seem to undermine the idea that women can unite as a homogeneous group to fight male oppression, but the idea that all women are basically the same can work to suppress differences of class, race or sexuality and so exclude or marginalize some women. Although all feminists share a commitment to changing existing relations, attention to different components of individual and group identity such as race, class and sexuality form an equally important part of many feminist critics' work. Essays on *Jane Eyre* by 'The Marxist-Feminist Collective' (reprinted in Eagleton, 1986) and Gayatri Chakravorty Spivak (reprinted in Belsey and Moore, 1989), for example, explore the interrelationships of gender and class and gender and race in the novel and demonstrate the ways in which feminist critics deploy different critical approaches such as Marxism and deconstruction.

The emphasis on the cultural construction of gender identities and on their contingency and instability also has profound effects on our understanding of the way readers and texts interact and so on feminist literary-critical practice. Concentrating on *subject positions* rather than on autonomous, unified subjects can allow feminist critics to examine texts as offering complex and often contradictory meanings of gender difference. The section on *As You Like It* in this unit, for example, shows how the presentation of one female character may challenge traditional early-modern constructions of masculinity and femininity as innately opposed essences.

The emphasis on positions rather than unified identities can also allow feminist critics to explore the complexities of female readers' responses to texts. Why, for example, do texts which offer apparently reactionary visions of the status or nature of women continue to appeal to female readers? Why even when we intellectually reject the apparent meanings of a text's presentation of women may we still derive emotional or aesthetic pleasure from our reading of it? The fact that many female readers enjoy conventional romances which present women as ultimately seeking male protection or even domination does not have to mean that women are essentially masochistic. It may, instead, indicate that narratives of romantic love are powerful examples of patriarchalist ideology which work by making readers want to identify with the ideals that are being promoted. In the actual process of reading, however, a female reader may experience a range of different, sometimes contradictory, reactions to a text. This issue is examined in three essays, by Alison Light, Janice Radway and Ann B. Snitow, in Eagleton (1986).

Feminist critics have not simply adopted theories of language and identity but have been actively involved in their production and development. Psychoanalytic theory, in particular, has been the object of feminist study and analysis from a number of different positions. Initial feminist reaction to Freudian theory was, especially in the United States, sceptical and sometimes hostile. Freud's analysis of sexual difference was often read as prescriptive rather than descriptive and was denounced as an extension of patriarchal thought which legitimated the subordination of women. Lacan's development of psychoanalytic theory with its new emphasis on the role of language in the construction of gendered identities has been criticized as 'phallocentric' in its insistence that linguistic difference is regulated by phallic authority, the Law of the Father. Psychoanalytic theory has, nevertheless, been productively appropriated and deployed by a number of feminist writers. The work of feminists like Juliet Mitchell (1975) and Jane Gallop (1982) has opened up a dialogue between psychoanalytic theory and feminist critical practice which acknowledges the complexities and tensions of this relationship but sees it as one which is worth sustaining as psychoanalytic theory is judged to offer useful ways of understanding how human beings come to identify with, and experience, positions as gendered subjects. A good recent collection is Brennen (1989).

More generally, in recent years, the work of theorists such as Saussure, Derrida, Lacan and Foucault has been deployed in the study of the relation between language, writing and sexual difference and a number of influential and often controversial feminist theories have been developed by writers such as Hélène Cixous, Luce Irigaray and Julia Kristeva. Among the best overviews of poststructuralist feminist theory and practice are Toril Moi, *Sexual/Textual Politics* (1985) and Chris Weedon, *Feminist Practice and Poststructuralist Theory* (1987).

Although there are significant differences between these writers they are conventionally classified as French feminists and their work and the critical practice which has developed using such theoretical models is broadly contrasted with a tradition of non-theorized, experiential feminist literary criticism conventionally associated with Anglo-American feminism, both radical and liberal. This is, of course, an inadequate and somewhat misleading label which refers to broadly defined positions rather than actual practitioners. It also implicitly excludes those feminists working in those parts of the world which do not fit its neat binary division. It is still useful, however, to examine the theoretically based tradition which developed in France, whilst noting that, perhaps significantly, many of its leading exponents have spent at least part of their lives in other cultures (Cixous in Algeria, for example, and Kristeva in Bulgaria).

One of the central assertions of French feminism has been that women's access to language involves submission to a phallocentric symbolic order dominated or regulated by the Law of the Father (see Unit 22) and that they therefore have a different position as users of language to that of men. In much of their work the terms 'woman' and 'feminine' (in French 'feminine' means both feminine and female) are treated as signifiers which are not bound to subjects whose biological sex is designated as female. Some of these theorists have suggested that certain types of writing which disrupt or exceed traditional, often rational, forms of language use, can be associated with the feminine. This does not mean that this writing is only produced by women, although the term employed by Hélène Cixous, *'l'écriture féminine'*, has led to some confusion. Cixous argues that this type of writing can be produced by both women and men and sees it as a potentially liberating force which challenges the damaging and limiting effects of patriarchalism in language and culture. *'L'écriture féminine'* is seen as a form of writing which unsettles fixed meanings. Cixous's own writing, which in many cases defies conventional categorization as literary, critical or philosophical, is a good example of the type of writing which she describes and, as such, it is often difficult to determine the meaning of her own texts. Her celebrations of certain features of female experience, such as the pre-Oedipal relationship between mother and child, are often read as essentialist or biologist, but they can also be read as strategic textual assertions of those qualities which precede or exceed the constraints of the patriarchal symbolic order.

Strategy is a key component in feminist criticism as it seeks to intervene in an ever-changing academic and cultural context. A feminist critic who believes that men and women do not necessarily write differently may still believe that it is important to support courses on women's writing. Questions of strategy, or of the political implications of certain acts, have also been raised about the relationship between men and feminism. Many men identify with the aims of feminism and of feminist criticism, but can a man be a feminist or feminist critic? Although in theory this would seem possible and even desirable, the lessons of history have discouraged many feminists from agreeing with this idea. Some women, and men, argue that in our society masculine power and privilege is so great that male feminists would soon dominate this area of cultural and political work as they have others. Although this may seem pessimistic, this response indicates that feminism is continually having to address both theoretical and practical issues. Alice Jardine and Paul Smith (eds), *Men in Feminism* (1987), is a useful collection of essays on this subject.

Among the most exciting, and challenging, new developments within feminist literary and cultural criticism has been the work produced in response to the new ways on understanding the relationships between sex, gender and sexuality offered by Queer Theory, a label applied to work which examines the bi-polar system of sexual difference which sustains heterosexism as well as privileging men over women. Much of this work can be connected with the highly influential study by Judith Butler, *Gender Trouble: Feminism and the Subversion of Identity* (1990). Although some feminists are worried about the implications of Butler's argument that feminism must acknowledge that 'woman' and 'female' are not stable categories, her work, and that of other writers such as Eve Kosofsky Sedgwick, has raised the possibility of different articulations of identity, both individually and collectively, in lives and texts, and opened up a new area of critical activity. In responding positively to the possibilities as well as to the challenges of such work feminism and feminist literary criticism can continue to work for change.

For further introductory reading on feminist literary criticism see: Belsey and Moore (1989), Eagleton (1991), Greene and Kahn (1985), Humm (1994) and Morris (1993).

## John Milton, *Paradise Lost*

Milton's epic poem *Paradise Lost* is regarded by many as the supreme example of the most 'literary' of literary genres, poetry. It is also regarded by many feminist critics as a text which presents a negative view of female difference. This reading will look at some of the ways in which feminist critics have examined its representation of gender and some of the broader points which have been made about the relationship between gender and genre.

Poetry is traditionally regarded as the most elevated and prestigious of literary forms, as the most suited to the exploration of universal and timeless themes. Although women have always been involved in the production of poetry, the dominant tradition can be seen to assert a masculine view of the world under the guise of an ostensibly universal perspective. Think, for example, of Renaissance lyric poetry in which women often appear to be the subject of the poem or the addressee but serve ultimately to reflect the (male) poet's feelings or views. Donne's 'The Flea' and Marvell's 'To His Coy Mistress', are addressed to women who are resisting the poets' sexual advances. The fact that women are addressed may seem to imply that they are recognized as *subjects*, but these female addressees are constructed within a formal literary convention which supports conventional views of women as *objects*. In both poems a female listener is constructed whose predictable feelings and fears serve ultimately to support the male poet's argument. Identifying the ways in which poems from every age and tradition have constructed stereotypical images of femaleness and femininity has been one approach in feminist literary criticism. Doing so, particularly in the early stages of feminism, involved a degree of courage because it involved criticizing some of the most established figures in the literary canon.

In her essay, 'Patriarchal Poetry and Women Readers: Reflections on Milton's Bogey', Sandra M. Gilbert examines Virginia Woolf's famous argument that literate women should 'look past Milton's bogey; for no human being should shut out the view' (1978, p. 368). Gilbert examines the possible meanings of the phrase 'Milton's bogey': Milton himself as a patriarchal poet who 'blocks the view for women poets'; his characterization of Adam as God's favourite; his depiction of Adam's inferior companion Eve who has 'intimidated women and blocked their view of possibilities both real and literary' (p. 368). These interpretations address two key issues for feminist literary critics, first, the ways in which the privilege of male poets and of poetic traditions which privilege male views have worked to disadvantage their female counterparts and secondly, the ways in which their texts construct models of femaleness and femininity which are limiting for women as readers and as writers. As readers women encounter a negative image of themselves and as writers they are confronted with literary forms and values which implicitly privilege masculinity and offer little scope for the exploration of gender from a different perspective. The traditional canon and traditional criticism promote the idea that although the poetic muse may be female, the greatest poets are, and always have been, men. But, although there have been political, economic and cultural forces which have discouraged women from participating in literary production, there are many examples of women poets who have challenged poetic traditions, both by working within, and subverting, established forms and by promoting radically different approaches. One of the contributions of feminist literary critics has been to recover the work of many women poets which has been hidden or ignored by traditional criticism and to argue that the work of poets like Anne Finch is as worthy of attention as that of her contemporary Milton. For examples and analysis see Morris (1993).

What of the second argument, that the way the poem constructs models of femaleness or femininity has a negative effect on women as readers and writers? What model does Milton's Eve offer women? When Milton wrote *Paradise Lost* the figure of Eve had already been deployed by countless writers as the archetypal woman. As Christianity's version of the first woman, Eve was conventionally described in biblically derived terms which could be associated with real women, as her supposed descendants. Donne's 'An Anatomy of the World' is a good example. Although the poem was written in commemoration of the 'untimely death of Mistress Elizabeth Drury', which might lead the reader to expect a positive account of at least one woman, her death provides the 'occasion' for the contemplation of 'the frailty and decay of this whole world', which in turn leads the poet to denounce women's negative effect on men. Describing the creation of Eve, Donne complains 'For that first marriage was our funeral: / One woman at one blow, then killed us all, / And singly, one by one, they kill us now' (ll. 105–7). Here the readers, assumed to be men, are united with the poet as fellow victims of woman. So the version of Eve constructed by one text, the Bible, could be modified and embellished by a literary text and presented to women as the divinely guaranteed truth not only about Eve but about themselves.

In *Paradise Lost* Milton re-presents the Genesis account of creation in which Eve is a divine gift to Adam. The account of her creation from one of Adam's ribs and the description of their respective relations to the deity ('Hee for God only, shee for God in him' (IV, 299)) presents woman as secondary to man, placing her below him in a hierarchy of created beings. Together with the emphasis which the poem places on Eve's aesthetically and sexually alluring qualities and their effects on Adam, leading ultimately to the couple's expulsion from Paradise, this offers an apparently negative view of Eve and of woman.

One way of approaching the poem is to see it as the work of a misogynistic poet, but as we cannot have access to Milton's mind and as he could not have complete control over his poem's meanings this does not seem particularly useful. Another is to see it as an example of a patriarchal poetic tradition. Milton's Eve could clearly be deployed in the seventeenth century as an example of the risks of certain forms of female behaviour and, presented within a prestigious cultural text, might be expected to have profound effects on writers and readers in other periods. Comparisons can be made between Milton's Eve and many later representations of Eve and of women in general. You may wish to consider Hardy's description of Tess, cited later in this unit, in this light. But although identifying similarities between different texts' presentation of women may be a good way of highlighting our society's history of constructing female difference negatively, it is equally important to examine the differences between texts and to be alert to the effects of historical and cultural difference on gender and genre. It is possible to adopt a similar approach in reading a single text where tensions or contradictions in the presentation of gender can be just as significant for reasons which I hope the remainder of this section will make apparent. (For a discussion of the male orientations of Romantic egotism see Unit 10, pp. 235–6.)

A source of tension in *Paradise Lost*, which has been noted by feminist critics, including Mary Nyquist, is the fact that Eve is presented as a *subject*. Although created after Adam and to be subordinate to him, Eve is recognized as an individual human being with subjective thoughts and feelings. In the poem 'adventurous Eve' (IX, 921) asserts an individual character and, like Adam, is allowed to tell her own story. Her assertiveness and curiosity are presented as leading to her downfall but in this narrative of the first couple the blame is not hers alone. In contrast to other versions, Eve is *working* in accordance with God's commands when the devil tempts her and does not seduce Adam into eating the forbidden fruit. It is, in fact, Adam's view of Eve which resembles most closely the misogynistic attitudes displayed in other texts, including 'An Anatomy of the World'. When, after the Fall, Adam claims that Woman is the source of 'Mans woe' he is criticized by the Angel Michael for failing to 'hold his place', to fulfil his duties as Eve's ordained superior (XI, 632–6). These aspects of the poem may suggest that it offers a more positive view of Eve, and of woman, than the traditional one presented by Adam. But this is not the whole story.

In this period the traditional patriarchalist view of the family and the state as analogous hierarchies was giving way to a belief in the separation of public and private spheres which were increasingly associated with men and women, respectively. It is in this context that Milton's emphasis on the mutual dependency of Adam and Eve and on their shared responsibility for the Fall and the portrayal of Eve as a free and rational subject become particularly significant. Eve may be offered a position to which she can freely aspire and which gives her considerable responsibility and scope for independent action. She may be able to correct Adam's ignorance of the workings of their domestic economy when Raphael comes to visit (V, 313–25). But ultimately this is because she has been imagined within a world-view for which, as Adam puts it: 'nothing lovelier can be found / In Woman, than to studie household good. / And good workes in her Husband to promote' (IX, 232–4). The story of Eve in *Paradise Lost* can be read as a narrative of the development of a different position for women in the seventeenth century, one which offered them greater responsibility and agency but which also allotted them a place in a private sphere.

Read in this way, *Paradise Lost* can be viewed as neither a misogynistic nor a feminist text but as an intervention in debates on gender. Milton's Eve is the product of her historical moment and in her construction we can see both the possibilities and limits of the changing attitudes to gender which *Paradise Lost* articulates. Milton's poem claims to present the truth about gender but as a text its meanings are open to interpretation. Examined as a complex and contradictory construction, Eve may cease to function as 'Milton's bogey' and become instead the material for a feminist analysis of gender difference.

## Charlotte Brontë, *Jane Eyre*

In this section I want to analyze the beginning of *Jane Eyre* in order to see what, and how, the novel can show us about the ways in which women learn to accept restrictive definitions of proper feminine behaviour and to accept them as natural. I will focus on the novel's presentation of the roles played in this process by the family, by female servants and by Jane herself. I will also examine the way in which the opening of the novel introduces a number of ideas about reading and suggest that these can be connected with the ways in which women learn both to identify with and to resist or contest the definitions and positions which are offered to them. As Unit 11 suggested (pp. 276–8), *Jane Eyre* explores the moral, spiritual and psychological growth of its protagonist and this development is as a gendered subject, as a woman. I would add that the novel presents a useful reading of the manner in which forces acting on, and within, the individual female subject result in her identification with positions and meanings which are restrictive, even oppressive, but also of the possibility that these positions and meanings can be challenged, if not by that subject, then by other reading subjects.

In the early part of the novel the narrator describes her childhood experiences in her aunt's house, Gateshead. The reader is offered a narrative of the ways in which

Jane was positioned as an inferior and marginalized member of the household, of the role played by various characters in defining her position and of her own attempts to understand and to contest that position. On the opening page the adult narrator describes the Reed family with Jane's cousins 'clustered' around their mother by the fireside and informs the reader that she had been 'dispensed from joining the group' by her aunt (p. 7). The figure who, as mother, is at the centre of this apparently cosy family group has decided that until Jane conforms to certain standards of proper behaviour as a child she will be excluded from 'privileges intended only for contented, happy little children' (p. 7). Jane, it seems, must endeavour to develop a disposition which is 'lighter, franker' (p. 7). This, in Mrs Reed's view, is the 'natural' way for a child to behave, but would it be natural for this child who is excluded from the family group to be happy or contented (p. 7)? Mrs Reed demands that Jane conform not to what is really natural but to her ideal, an ideal which seems difficult, if not impossible, to achieve in Jane's case. Jane is presented as already disposed to accept a reading of her inferiority, as the narrator recalls that she felt 'physically' inferior to her cousins (p. 7). After reading Mrs Reed's words, the reader may wonder whether Jane's sense of physical inferiority may be the result not of an innately self-deprecatory personality but of the way she is constructed by others. Her melancholy, which angers Mrs Reed, may similarly be the psychological product of her social position rather than an innate disposition. Throughout the novel, Jane will encounter characters who have different understandings of correct, normal or 'natural', female behaviour. These understandings are, in turn, derived from culturally produced and circulated views which those who deploy them may believe to be true. Because the dominant cultural view of femininity is both powerful and appears to be natural, the interests it serves will not always be clear. When Jane's behaviour differs from the norm it will be judged not only by those who have the most to gain from a system which privileges men but also by other women.

Jane's behaviour is being observed and judged by Mrs Reed who is ostensibly her guardian but who could be seen as guarding certain values. It is important to note here that Mrs Reed suggests that she has instructed Bessie to inform her of Jane's behaviour. At the instigation of a relatively privileged woman, Mrs Reed, who has come to accept specific definitions of acceptable behaviour as natural, another woman, Bessie, who is in an economically and socially subordinate position, is employed to police the behaviour of a female child who is failing to conform to those definitions. This model can be applied more generally to the way in which women often support and maintain, consciously or unconsciously, the system which actually oppresses them by encouraging or demanding that other women conform to conventional patterns of behaviour. There is further evidence of this at the beginning of Chapter 2 where the two female servants threaten to restrain Jane with a garter (p. 12). Here a restrictive female garment, which she can expect to wear in adulthood, is to be used by adult women to subdue an unruly child. You may want to think about why it is at this point that the rebellious Jane decides to conform voluntarily, offering to hold herself down. Why does the threat of being tied up by the female servants seem to subdue her more than John Reed's violent behaviour?

One reading may be that the heat of the moment had passed and that she was no longer spurred on by feelings of anger, but there may be other reasons. Is it the prospect of being restrained by the servants or by the garter which subdues her? The narrator refers to the 'ignominy' of being bound (p. 12). Could this be connected with a feminist understanding of why, and how, women internalize patriarchal values rather than face the dangerous or humiliating consequences of failure to conform?

Jane's actions in this scene could be read as prefiguring the end of the novel, where the now financially independent Jane decides to marry. Some feminist critics have seen Jane's final action, and the novel itself, as the culmination of a movement from rebellious marginality to acquiescent conformity, from questioning to eventual acceptance of patriarchal values. But just as Jane learns to read her position in relation to a history of oppression, so we need to read this text in the context of the social and cultural moment in which it was produced. It may be unrealistic to expect a text published in 1847 to utterly reject the patriarchalist values of its moment, but I would argue that *Jane Eyre* offers material to the reader for the analysis, and questioning, of such values. I now want to look at just a few of the ways in which the opening of the novel may do so.

The events described in the first chapter indicate that, although Mrs Reed is apparently head of the household, this is a patriarchal family and that the behaviour of individual characters is governed by social and cultural forces rather than by their individual personalities. Rebuked for questioning Mrs Reed, Jane slips away to an adjoining room and chooses a secluded place on a curtained window seat. In doing so she reinforces her exclusion from the family scene but the activity of reading, even of 'reading' the illustrations in Bewick's *History of British Birds*, allows her to imagine other scenes, arctic realms and becalmed ships which merge into other terrifying but dramatic visions of fiends and phantoms (p. 8). Jane connects these exhilarating scenes with different stories, old fairy tales and ballads and excerpts from novels like *Pamela* told or read by Bessie. The fact that Bessie tells the children stories can be seen as an extension of her role in inculcating certain values, but Bessie is also giving them access to texts whose meanings she cannot control. Reading allows Jane not merely to escape, temporarily, from the misery of her real surroundings, but introduces her to narratives of different situations and lives which she can compare with her own and, as the scene develops, the reader will see how her reading of books has enabled Jane to read her own situation.

This moment is interrupted by the first male voice we encounter in the novel, when John Reed enters the room searching for the cousin he calls 'Madame Mope' and 'bad animal' (p. 9). After labelling her in this pejorative fashion, her cousin demands that she address him as 'Master Reed', locating himself as her superior, a position which he reinforces by insisting that she approach and stand before him as he sits. By calling her names and telling her where to stand, the male character is claiming the right to define the female character's identity and to designate her position. The narrator describes Jane's fear of his constant bullying which is overlooked by his adoring mother and by the servants who are afraid of challenging 'their young master' (p. 10). This alerts the reader to the fact that Jane is not simply the victim of a young bully but of a system which allows him, as 'master', to exercise power over her as a dependent member of the household. Jane has become 'habitually obedient', has learned to accept a subordinate position (p. 10). The 'young master' is confident that he will inherit the household and already behaves as a patriarch whose acts and opinions are implicitly supported by other, female, figures within the household. His mother is 'blind and deaf' to his treatment of Jane and the female servants are afraid to challenge him. Although they have different motives, all these female characters effectively collude in his treatment of Jane. It could be argued that he needs the support of these figures, that he cannot exercise power unaided. When he enters the room, he is unable at first to see Jane, who, although afraid of him, is already aware of his limited 'vision' and 'conception' (p. 9). It is, significantly, only when his sister, another female member of the household, correctly guesses where Jane is that she decides to pre-empt being dragged out by emerging from behind the curtain. This can be read as an example of one of the ways in which a patriarchal system works through the collusion of women, both through Eliza's intervention and Jane's decision to reveal herself.

As there is no adult male figure of authority in the household, John Reed, who believes he is to inherit the house, claims the position of patriarch; although his mother pays the bills, he assumes the position of 'young master'. The patriarchal system has allotted the two children very different fortunes, literally and culturally: John's inheritance will assure him of a position of authority, whilst Jane, whose father left her nothing, is a dependant; John believes he has a right to command others, Jane has become accustomed to obedience; John can assume that he will eventually occupy the position of father and head of the household, Jane must struggle to make herself acceptable, to fit into a subordinate role both in this household and, as a woman, in any other household.

Although he is ostensibly upbraiding Jane for her impudence towards his mother, John Reed's anger is intensified by the fact that she is reading a book which he considers to be his family's, and so ultimately his, property. John Reed takes the book from his cousin and uses it as a weapon, throwing it at Jane and cutting her head, but the effects of books are not always under the control of oppressive subjects or systems. It is at this point that Jane's terror gives way to anger and a sense of injustice. In pain and bleeding, she responds by identifying her attacker with the murderous and oppressive Roman emperors she has read about in 'Goldsmith's History of Rome' (p. 11). Her reading has allowed her to see the parallels between this boy's behaviour and that of other tyrants and at this moment, incensed by his behaviour, she sees, feels and communicates these parallels and is able to fight back. The physical fight which ensues is stopped by the combined action of all the other women in the household. At the beginning of the next chapter, in which she eventually submits to punishment, Jane offers a reading of her own position, comparing herself to a 'rebel slave' who has initiated a 'mutiny' (p. 12).

Although Jane's identification, through reading, of her position, and that of her male cousin, with those constructed in narratives or histories of unjust oppression does not enable her to escape from her subordinate position completely, it can be read as the beginning of a process of analysis which modifies that position. Although Jane is punished, she has actively resisted John Reed as she will later resist other figures, such as Mr Brocklehurst. Her struggle to find a position which is personally and socially acceptable will involve encounters not only with individual figures of patriarchal authority but with the limitations which the system imposes on individual subjects. The end of Jane Eyre's individual story may disappoint some feminist readers, with its 'happy' ending apparently relocating its female protagonist within the household which symbolizes a reformed patriarchal system rather than its dismantling. But the bigger story is not yet over and *Jane Eyre* may still provide material for the analysis and contestation of the social and cultural forces which oppress women. (See Unit 21, pp. 578–9, for a Marxist–Feminist reading of *Jane Eyre*.)

## Thomas Hardy, *Tess of the d'Urbervilles*

In this section I am going to examine the presentation of the character of Tess in Thomas Hardy's *Tess of the d'Urbervilles*. You may find it useful to turn to the section on this novel in Unit 11 (pp. 290–2) before reading on. I want to show that there are a number of different feminist ways of approaching this text and the ways in which novels in general represent women.

Tess is one of the most famous female characters in English literature and there has been a great deal of work by feminists on the way in which her character is presented and the implications of that presentation. Much early feminist criticism denounced Hardy as offering a reactionary or sexist view of the nature of women and of female sexuality. In this type of criticism the author and his text are conflated and both are denounced for displaying an attitude to female characters, and by extension to women in general, which combines idealization and sadism, fascination and repulsion. According to this model, *Tess of the d'Urbervilles* is ultimately conservative because it presents women as essentially bound by a biological destiny which marks them out as seductive victims. However, while there are aspects of the presentation, or, more accurately, the construction of the character of Tess which seem to be reactionary or even misogynistic, it is possible, as more recent work by feminist critics, such as Penny Boumelha and Mary Jacobus, has shown, to detect different forces at work in the novel.

In my reading I am going to employ the model used by these critics, a model which examines the text's implication in the historical and cultural moment of its production and which examines the complexity of its relationship to the dominant discourses of gender and sexual difference in that moment. This involves the recognition that the text's language does not merely reflect a pre-existing reality or present the author's views. Instead it reads the text as the product of competing discourses and ideological formations which it in turn reproduces, transforms, supports and sometimes contests. If we employ this understanding of the text it becomes possible to read a novel like *Tess of the d'Urbervilles* not as *either* radical *or* reactionary in relation to issues of gender or sexual difference but as both, as a text which is inscribed with the complex, often contradictory, attitudes to the subject of its historical moment and which can be read as contributing to the development of those attitudes.

I am going to focus on reading two brief passages from the novel which describe Tess's mouth. This is because the imagery of the female body and of female sexuality which is a notable feature of the novel is at its most condensed and complex in these passages. The passages both describe Angel Clare's responses to Tess. The first describes his response to Tess who is milking a cow (pp. 208–9), the second describes his response when he observes her in the dairy just after she has woken (p. 231).

In both passages Tess is described as unaware or barely aware of Angel's presence and it is the male character's reading of the woman's body and his assumptions about female sexuality which are foregrounded by the text. Tess is apparently passive, the object of the male gaze and of male analysis rather than an active subject. This might, in itself, be seen as reinforcing the traditional opposition between male agency and female passivity, as echoing the conventional depiction of the female body in, for example, the visual arts, where it is the male gaze which determines the way in which the female body is presented and understood. The concentration in both passages on Tess's mouth, which connects with numerous other descriptions throughout the novel, can also be read as repeating a conventional gesture which associates the female body with sexuality. The mouth figures as an entrance to a mysterious, seductive yet threatening unknown interior of the body, as an orifice which stands in the place of the vagina, which could not be directly represented in the period when the novel was written, and as an image of female sexuality itself.

In the first passage Tess's mouth is described as having an effect on Angel which is 'distracting, infatuating, maddening', an effect which is enhanced by the fact that it is not perfect (p. 209). The lips are described as confronting Angel and as having a direct physical impact on him: 'they sent an *aura* over his flesh, a breeze through his nerves, which wellnigh produced a qualm; and actually produced, by some mysterious physiological process a prosaic sneeze' (p. 209). In one brief description Tess's sensual and sexual attractions are linked with the idea of imperfection and presented as having a powerful effect on Angel which culminates in what appears to be a, somewhat bathetic, orgasmic convulsion. The passivity of the female character at this point is counterpointed by the powerful effects of a female sexuality. This fits neatly with traditional Victorian images of female sexuality as something at once dangerous and sacred, to be contained or avoided but also to be explored, classified, understood. One strand of a feminist reading might be to identify the deployment of such ideas within the novel but this need not be a matter of denunciation.

There is an intriguing sentence in this passage in which Tess's lips are described as having 'forced on his mind with such persistent iteration the old Elizabethan simile of roses filled with snow' (p. 209). This sentence, like the rest of the passage, presents the lips as having effects, but here the effect they have is to remind Angel of a conventional, cultural representation, a literary device. The placing of this sentence within a literary text which is itself deploying imagery of lips foregrounds the role played by cultural representations in our reading of the female body. Angel is not reminded of other 'real' lips but of a textual device. By extension the image of female sexuality which is being presented here is not in fact of *female* sexuality but of *feminine* sexuality, it is not an image of the way women are, or were, but of the way they were, and are, conventionally represented or constructed. It is precisely through 'persistent iteration', or repetition, in different texts and contexts that the meanings ascribed to gender or sexual difference within a specific culture come to seem inevitable and to reflect reality rather than construct it. Angel's reaction to Tess is profoundly affected by his cultural conditioning; he sees and reads her, both consciously (remembering the simile) and unconsciously, in relation to a set of cultural images and meanings which attempt to define femaleness and female sexuality in particular ways.

The fact that the text draws the reader's attention to this cultural, or ideological, dimension of Angel's reading may make the reader think, however briefly, about the fact that this too is a textual representation. The passage may, therefore, be seen to deploy conventional images and represent a female character in quite conservative ways but it also reminds the reader of the *cultural* basis of our understanding of sexual difference and so may have effects which are potentially subversive.

It can be argued that although Angel's reading of Tess is subject to an implied critique in the general narrative of the novel, as his hypocrisy is revealed to be the counterpart of Alec's exploitative behaviour, the narrative overall displays a fascination with Tess's sexuality which cannot be understood in positive terms from a feminist position. This is clearer when we look at the second passage. This starts by describing Angel watching Tess yawning: 'he saw the red interior of her mouth as if it had been a snake's' (p. 231). This recalls the conventional association of female sexuality with temptation and seduction, with the dual role of Eve as seduced by the devil in the guise of a (phallic) serpent and as seducer of Adam, whose expulsion from Eden and entry into a world of knowledge and sorrow could be, at least in part, blamed on female weakness and especially female sexual excess. The construction 'he saw... as if...' can be read as implying, like the earlier passage, a distance between what Angel sees and the reality of Tess, as well as foregrounding the fact that this is Angel's reading not that of the narrator or of the novel as a whole. But later in the passage Tess is described in such a way that it is difficult to identify whether the voice is that of Angel or of the narrator: 'The brim-fulness of her nature breathed from her. It was a moment when a woman's soul is more incarnate than at any other time; when the most spiritual beauty bespeaks itself flesh; and sex takes the outside place in the presentation' (p. 231). This move from a specific description of Angel's reading of Tess, which extends the imagery of the snake through references to her 'coiled-up cable of hair', to a general comment on woman is problematic (p. 231). The progression from the identification of Tess with a dangerous and innate sexuality to a description of the dominance of sex in the spiritual and bodily reality of woman seems to appeal to essentialist ideas about sexual identity which locates Tess, and by extension woman in general, as the passive victim not simply of male aggression and exploitation but also of her own nature.

As this brief reading of passages from the novel indicates, a feminist reading may not result in an easy labelling of a text as positive or negative in its presentation of women. The complex ways in which a text works, involving an ongoing negotiation of possible meanings between author, text and readers, mean that new feminist readings will always be possible and may produce new or different meanings.

## William Shakespeare, *As You Like It*

In the view of many feminist critics, Shakespeare's comedies do not have happy endings. The multiple marriages which unite couples and tie up plot strands at the end of plays such as *As You Like It*, *Twelfth Night* and *A Midsummer Night's Dream* have traditionally been read as a defining and joyful characteristic of romantic comedy. But to many feminist critics these final scenes are far from a cause for celebration since what they are seen as celebrating is the restoration of a patriarchal social order which offers women little or no independence, power or freedom. My focus in this section will be on the final scene and on the epilogue, as these have been of central concern to the feminist critics who have read the play and who have taken issue, in different ways, with conventional critical accounts of the close, and closure, of the play.

*As You Like It* is often viewed as the most light-hearted of Shakespeare's comedies and the character of Rosalind, the longest female role in any of Shakespeare's plays, has been read as representing a balance between idealism and realism, romanticism and pragmatism, and as displaying both feminine and masculine attributes in her behaviour and attitudes. She is witty but sensitive, able to mock conventional sentimentality but vulnerable to her own emotions and desires, manipulating the play's events through her role-playing as Ganymede until she gives herself to father and husband at the end of the play. This reading of Rosalind, and of the play itself, as the harmonious reconciling of opposites has been challenged by feminist critics for a number of reasons: its concentration on individual characters and abstract values excludes any consideration of the power relations between men and women in the play; it assumes that there are ideals of masculinity and femininity which can be contrasted, or reconciled, without examining how these ideals have been constructed; it ignores tensions and contradictions in the play or attempts to resolve them by selective reading.

Whereas an earlier generation of critics focused on the representation of love in *As You Like It*, feminists, and other critics whose work is informed by critical and cultural theory, have foregrounded issues of gender and identity. Some have argued that the play ultimately reinforces the early-modern view of the inferiority of women by allowing Rosalind to take on some of the conventional characteristics of masculinity (rationality, courage, strength, intelligence) only when disguised as a boy, Ganymede, and that, in a sense, the joke is on her when ultimately she delivers herself as a dutiful daughter to her father and wife-to-be to Orlando in the final scene. Certainly her words, 'To you, I give myself, for I am yours' (V. iv. 116–17), addressed to father and suitor in turn, present her as a possession of the two men, a defining position of women in a patriarchal society. The bold female subject who in earlier scenes had asserted a degree of control over events and over her would-be suitor, Orlando, is here supplanted by a Rosalind who voluntarily accepts a position as object. After her brief glimpse of what it might mean to be treated as a male subject, albeit a junior one, Rosalind is finally firmly relocated within the twin institutions of the family and marriage where her behaviour would be judged according to clearly established criteria and where her identity would be almost totally subsumed within that of her husband. According to this reading *As You Like It* plays with the ideas of a woman transgressing normal social and gender norms for comic effect only to re-establish those norms even more strongly as a result of her apparently willing capitulation. She chooses her own subjection, just as many women even today 'choose' to obey their husbands in the traditional marriage ceremony. A similar point has been made about Isabella's apparent acceptance of the Duke's proposal at the end of *Measure for Measure*, which many critics, directors and performers view as a betrayal of the character's integrity and of the play's radical acknowledgement of injustice in gender relations (see Unit 18, pp. 539–41). This is a persuasive reading but is it the only possible feminist reading of the conclusion of *As You Like It*?

If we view Rosalind as a unified human subject, a realistic portrayal of a real woman, then the conclusion does seem to offer her a future which many feminists would see as very limited, particularly within early-modern society. But this is a play, a text which *constructs* a character to be fleshed out on stage by an actor. It can be viewed not as a simple reflection of reality but as a more complex and contradictory engagement with its own moment of production and with that society's views of gender and gender relations, views which, as feminist cultural historians have pointed out, were being contested in different ways in the sixteenth and seventeenth centuries. The way in which the play, and especially the epilogue, presents the *construction* of masculine and feminine identities has been of particular interest to poststructuralist feminists who read the text as participating in the contest for the meaning of the family and of sexual difference.

Since the Restoration, Rosalind has been a popular role for the leading female actors of the day. But in early-modern England when Rosalind disguises herself as Ganymede in order to test Orlando, what the audience would have seen would have been a boy playing a woman disguised as a boy addressing a man. We cannot be sure how an early-modern audience would have responded to this. They would certainly not have expected to see a woman on stage but we cannot know to what extent they suspended their disbelief or if they expected to see 'realistic' portrayals of men and women as we may in the twentieth century. The issue of role playing and cross-dressing in relation to the construction of masculine and feminine identities is raised throughout the play, notably in the exchanges between Rosalind/Ganymede and Orlando and between Rosalind/Ganymede and Celia, and has been read by some feminist critics as foregrounding the constructedness and contingency of gender difference. In other words as exposing the fact that masculine and feminine identities are socially constructed rather than natural, that the set of oppositional values and characteristics which are ascribed to male and female subjects do not derive from some innate or essential quality but from the culture in which those subjects live. You may wish to consider the presentation of female characters in other plays in the light of this argument. What, for example, are the implications in *The Merchant of Venice* of Portia's need to disguise herself as a man in order to leave Belmont and participate in the legal system?

Much of this debate has focused on a part of *As You Like It* which traditional criticism often overlooked, namely the epilogue. This speech can be read as playing with the concept of gender, as the actor playing Rosalind steps forward to tease both male and female spectators by claiming both male and female subject positions: 'It is not the fashion to see the lady the epilogue; but it is no more unhandsome than to see the lord the prologue' (V. iv. 198–9) suggests that a woman is speaking, whereas 'If I were a woman I would kiss as many of you as had beards that pleased me, complexions that liked me, and breaths that I defied not' (V. iv. 214–16) apparently locates the speaker as male. This confusion or contradiction cannot be resolved by reference to the 'real' gender of the speaker. For, as Catherine Belsey has asked in her essay 'Disrupting Sexual Difference: Meaning and Gender in the Comedies' (1985), 'Who is Speaking?' (p. 180). Is it a boy actor or a female character? The text does not answer this question and we cannot tell how early-modern audiences would have viewed the figure on stage. The speaker seems to speak from a doubled gender position as character and actor. The action of the play has ended, 'happily' or conservatively, according to your position, before the epilogue begins, but the performance is not over. We are still watching a performer on stage but what is being performed? This final speech can be seen to invite the audience to think about how sexual difference is constructed, which may in turn disrupt the apparently patriarchalist vision of the happy ending of the play. In the modern theatre it is customary for a female actor to take the role of Rosalind which resolves some of the gender confusion, although the acclaimed all-male production by Cheek by Jowl foregrounded gender issues in a different, twentieth-century context. But the gender confusion in the epilogue is not simply the result of the possible difference between the biological sex of the actor and the gender of the character, because the gender of the character has already been rendered problematic.

The questions raised in the epilogue may encourage the reader to look again at the play and consider how it presents gender. When Rosalind is in disguise as Ganymede, she makes a number of speeches which deploy conventional, negative views of femininity, and is, at one point, rebuked by Celia because she has 'simply mis-used our sex' (IV. i. 191). The audience may know, like Celia, that underneath her male disguise, the character is a woman. But there are complications. In the original productions, under the male disguise was a female disguise, under which was a male actor, so what the audience actually heard was a male voice mocking women. It may be more interesting to consider the idea that the character, having adopted male disguise, is speaking from a masculine *position*. It is this position which allows Rosalind to behave in ways which transgress conventional boundaries between masculine and feminine behaviour. When she occupies the position of a man, she can take the initiative in wooing Orlando and display traditionally male characteristics even though she is biologically female. This does not mean that individuals in the early-modern period could choose between genders any more than we can today, nor does it mean that Rosalind escapes the effects of gender difference, as her/Ganymede's mockery of women indicates. It may, however, suggest that the meanings ascribed to different genders are culturally constructed, that we might find it more productive to think about gender in terms of positions rather than of innate essences. In the end Rosalind takes up a traditional feminine position as a wife, but, as the epilogue reminds us, things, and people, may not always be what they seem. In the restored social order of the final scene, a woman's proper position is at her husband's side, but what it means to be a woman, or a man, is perhaps a little less certain.

I do not want to suggest that *As You Like It* offers a fully radical or feminist view of women but that the way in which it, literally, plays with gender roles may be a productive subject for analysis for the feminist critic. Although this example deals with a play which quite literally stages the role of performance in the presentation of sexual difference, you may wish to consider some of these points when reading other texts. For example, you might compare my reading with the survey in Unit 15, pp. 435–8, of Caryl Churchill's *Top Girls*, a modern play written by a woman about women.

## BIBLIOGRAPHY

Belsey, C. (1985) 'Disrupting Sexual Difference: Meaning and Gender in the Comedies', in *Alternative Shakespeares*, ed. J. Drakakis, Methuen, London, 166–90.

Belsey, C. and Moore, J. (eds) (1989) *The Feminist Reader: Essays in Gender and the Politics of Literary Criticism*, Macmillan, London.

Boumelha, P. (1982) *Thomas Hardy and Women: Sexual Ideology and Narrative Form*, Harvester Wheatsheaf, Hemel Hempstead.

Brennen, T. (ed.) (1989) *Between Feminism and Psychoanalysis*, Routledge, London.

Brontë, C. (1993) *Jane Eyre*, Oxford University Press, Oxford.

Butler, J. (1990) *Gender Trouble: Feminism and the Subversion of Identity*, Routledge, London.

Cixous, H. (1994) *The Hélène Cixous Reader*, ed. Susan Sellers, Routledge, London.

Daly, M. (1978) *Gyn/Ecology*, Women's Press, London.

Eagleton, M. (ed.) (1986) *Feminist Literary Theory: A Reader*, Blackwell, Oxford.

Eagleton, M. (ed.) (1991) *Feminist Literary Criticism*, Longman, London.

Gallop, J. (1982) *Feminism and Psychoanalysis: The Daughter's Seduction*, Macmillan, London.

Gilbert, S. (1978) 'Patriarchal Poetry and Women Readers: Reflections on Milton's Bogey', *PMLA* 93, pp. 368–82.

Gilbert, S.M. and Gubar, S. (1979) *The Madwoman in the Attic: The Woman Writer and the Nineteenth-Century Literary Imagination*, Yale University Press, New Haven.

Greene, G. and Kahn, C. (eds) (1985) *Making a Difference: Feminist Literary Criticism*, Methuen, London.

Greer, G. (1970) *The Female Eunuch*, MacGibbon & Kee, London.

Hardy, T. (1978) *Tess of the d'Urbervilles*, Penguin, Harmondsworth.

Humm, M. (1994) *A Reader's Guide to Contemporary Feminist Literary Criticism*, Harvester Wheatsheaf, Hemel Hempstead.

Jacobus, M. (1979) *Women Writing and Writing about Women*, Croom Helm, London.

Jardine, A. and Smith, P. (eds) (1987) *Men in Feminism*, Methuen, London.

Kristeva, J. (1986) *The Kristeva Reader*, ed. T. Moi, Blackwell, Oxford.

Marks, E. and de Courtivron, I. (eds) (1981) *New French Feminisms: An Anthology*, Harvester Wheatsheaf, Hemel Hempstead.

Millett, K. (1969) *Sexual Politics*, Virago, London.

Mitchell, J. [1974] (1975) *Psychoanalysis and Feminism*, Penguin, Harmondsworth.

Moers, E. (1976) *Literary Women: The Great Writers*, Doubleday, New York (reprinted The Women's Press, London).

Moi, T. (1985) *Sexual/Textual Politics: Feminist Literary Theory*, Routledge, London.

Morris, P. (1993) *Literature and Feminism*, Blackwell, Oxford.

Nyquist, M. (1987) 'The Genesis of Gendered Subjectivity in the Divorce Tracts and *Paradise Lost*', in *Re-membering Milton: Essays on the Texts and Traditions*, ed. M. Nyquist and M.W. Ferguson, Methuen, London, 99–127.

Sedgwick, E.K. (1994) *Tendencies*, Routledge, London.

Showalter, E. (1977) *A Literature of Their Own: British Women Novelists from Brontë to Lessing*, Princeton University Press, Princeton.

Spivak, G.C. (1987) *In Other Worlds Essays: in Cultural Politics*, Methuen, New York and London.

Weedon, C. (1987) *Feminist Practice and Poststructuralist Theory*, Blackwell, Oxford.

# SECTION 4

# Literatures in English

# Irish writing in English

*Robert Welch*

A strange consideration lies at the heart of Irish writing in English, and almost redeems the term Anglo-Irish (the somewhat awkward term sometimes used for this literature) from its baronial or grandee associations. The strangeness resides in the fact that this literature is written in a language, English, which steadily gained ground in Ireland from the beginning of the seventeenth century at the expense of Irish, the native language. The English administration, from the time of Henry VIII at least – though it was policy well before his sixteenth-century reign – recognized that its best guarantee of success was the replacement of the Irish language and the way of life it expressed with English customs and manners and, most importantly, the English language itself. Writing at the very end of the sixteenth century, the poet and colonial administrator, Edmund Spenser, advocated this policy: 'the speache being Irische the harte must nedes be Irishe for out of the abundance of the harte the tonge speakethe'.

The Easter Rising of 1916, led by Pearse, was but one in a series of rebellions that erupted through Irish history after the defeat of Hugh O'Neill at Kinsale in 1601. The Rebellion of 1641, for example, and its fearsome aftermaths, the Cromwellian 'settlement' of Ireland and plantation, began as an attempt on the part of Catholic Irish landowners to retain their lands and freedom to practise their religion, but ended in 1652 with the declaration of Cromwell's parliament that all Catholics and Royalists above the rank of tradesman or labourer were to 'remove themselves and their families into Connacht and Clare', that is, west of the Shannon; hence the saying popular in Ireland, 'to hell or Connacht'. Catholics of any standing found after 1 May 1654 could be killed on sight by anyone. West of the Shannon, or, more broadly, the west of Ireland, has retained, in Irish culture and literature, a very complex set of resonances. It is, on the one hand, wild and barbarous, where savagery runs ungoverned – hence Gabriel Conroy's reflection at the end of Joyce's 'The Dead', which closes *Dubliners* (1914), on the snow falling all over Ireland. Gabriel's mind travels across the country from Dublin, to the Shannon's 'mutinous waves', and the dead lying in the churchyards of Co. Galway, and to the grave of his wife's dead boyfriend, with his melancholy but apt name, Michael Furey. Gabriel realizes that all that world lies outside his experience to that point, but now his imaginative sympathies are engaged, as he wonders what the history of his sleeping wife is really like. It is a hugely suggestive and evocative ending to a complex story, and requires very close reading, but one of the themes that animates the story is the continuous presence of the dead; history, Stephen Dedalus remarked in *A Portrait of the Artist as a Young Man*, 'is a nightmare from which I am trying to awake', but Joyce as a writer knew that collective memories had to be explored and exorcized before they release their grip. To some extent, all of Joyce's work, from the stream of consciousness in *Ulysses*, to the elaborate dream-structures of *Finnegans Wake*, is an attempt at the restoration of memory, at 're-memorizing' the mind, thereby releasing its fears and opening its scope for accurate and comprehensive (if not total) recall. On history and its treatment in literature see Brown (1972).

If savagery and wildness lay across the Shannon, a place where J.M. Synge's Playboy Christy Mahon can be extolled for killing his 'da', it could also be a place of imagination and heightened experience. Lady Morgan in *The Wild Irish Girl* (1806) and Charles Robert Maturin in *The Milesian Chief* (1812) were among the first to make use of west of Ireland settings for romantic and spectacular effects. By the time they came to write the west had acquired an aura of majesty and magic, owing in no small part to the invention of a Scot, James Macpherson, whose Ossianic tales, notably *Fingal* (1762) and *Temora* (1763), drew upon elements of authentic Gaelic tradition to fashion a pseudo-epical romance in a Northern setting, a rhapsodic fabrication, released from classical constraint and grace. It satisfied a taste for the sublime which the Irish critic and politician, Edmund Burke, had analyzed in *A Philosophical Enquiry into the Sublime and the Beautiful* (1767), a treatise which had a profound influence on the romantic taste for horrifying spectacular and gothic effects, as well as cultivating an appetite for tenderer and more sentimental impressions. On Celticism and the sublime see Deane (1985).

Burke's *Reflections on the Revolution in France* (1790) is compelling reading because the man is horrified at what revolution entails, and at the casual intellectual sloppiness of those who heedlessly encourage brutality by failing to realize what it is like when society breaks down. The compelling immediacy of his writing comes from Burke's awareness that Irish Catholics have a grievance, that they will hurtle into revolution if they are not conciliated, and that the scenes unfolding in France are a foretaste of what will happen in Britain and in Ireland. The Battle of the Boyne, when William defeated the Catholic James, had secured the peace of Britain at the expense of the rights of Catholics, who should now be conciliated, otherwise the kingdom will go the way of France. To illustrate, Burke depicts the scene where Louis XVI and Marie Antoinette are brought from Versailles to the Bastille:

> This king, to say no more of him, and this queen, and their infant children (who once would have been the pride and hope of a great and generous people) were then forced to abandon the sanctuary of the most splendid palace in the world, which they left swimming in blood, polluted by massacre, and strewed with scattered limbs and mutilated carcases. Thence they were conducted into the capital of their kingdom.

Burke's Catholic Irish background, and his appreciation of the value of the settled form of society he found in England, fitted him to understand the precarious nature of freedom and the ferocity and rapaciousness of the tyranny that is always waiting to replace it. In Burke, as in many of the finest Irish writers, horror is just around the corner.

Jonathan Swift, for example, a predecessor of Burke's, was less exercised about the condition of the Catholic majority in Ireland, but his 'savage indignation' (Yeats's phrase in his translation of Swift's own Latin epitaph) was directed at the injustice of being considered less of a person for being in Ireland, than one would be if one were in England, as he argued in the third *Drapier's Letter* (1724). Horror enters Swift's writing, and the grim heartless, icy Irish humour that often seeks to contain it, in *A Modest Proposal* (1729), the pamphlet which advances, in po-faced solemnity, the economic advantages of breeding children *as food*, rather than having to feed them. This would solve Irish poverty, control population growth, and inculcate the virtues of planning and skilful management of human resources. English indifference and casual arrogance are compounding for themselves, he fears, a wicked alliance against the best interests of peace and solid order, exactly the anxieties later pressing upon Burke in the 1790s. At this time, Wolfe Tone was founding the United Irishmen, and leading a parade in Belfast, a dissenting town, with banners which read 'Irishmen look to France'. Which of course many did. Wolfe Tone, known as 'Citoyen Tone' in Paris, was plotting invasion and getting the ear of Napoleon who agreed to send an invasion force to aid in the United Irishmen Rebellion of 1798. Burke's sublime and horrific nightmare of revolution was out, what he described in *Letters on a Regicide Peace* (1796) as a 'vast, tremendous, unformed spectre ... [a] hideous phantom'.

While the United Irishmen were mobilizing in Ireland, one of their Dublin leaders, Thomas Addis Emmet, was taken on a walk by the concerned mother of the young Thomas Moore, then a student at Trinity College, Dublin. She asked Emmet not to involve her son in military operations, a request to which he consented, leaving Moore to get on with his translations of Anacreon and his study of the Irish airs recently published in Edward Bunting's *Collection of the Ancient Music of Ireland* (1796), a compilation which had, to a significant extent, been assembled at a Harper's Festival in Belfast in 1792. However, although Moore's actual involvement with the United Irishmen was slight – writing a few propaganda pieces in the manner of Macpherson for *The Press* – he remained deeply attached to their ideals of liberty and freedom of religion, and their radicalism. He revered them as types of the finest sort of Irishman, the 'ultimi Romanorum' he called them, and the memory of their bravery and patriotism was the initial inspiration for the famous series of *Irish Melodies*, which he began in 1808. These poems and songs, many of which are still greatly loved, unite a sentimental patriotism with a feeling for the sublime, the lofty, the wild, the passionate, the remote; and to this brew he infuses a quality of ready anger at injustice that has often been overlooked in the all-too-common perception of Moore as a namby-pamby snuff-box Hibernian melodist. The energy and dark chords of 'Avenging and Bright' strike a note of outrage not unconnected to the indignation of Swift, or the sorrowing desperation of Burke:

> Avenging and bright falls the swift sword of Erin
> On him who the brave sons of Usna betrayed –
> For every fond eye he hath waken'd a tear in
> A drop from his heart-wounds shall weep o'er his blade.

> By the red cloud that hung over Conor's dark dwelling,
> When Ulad's three champions lay sleeping in gore –
> By the billows of war, which so often, high swelling,
> Have wafted these heroes to victory's shore –
>
> We swear to revenge them ...

'We swear to revenge' those who have been 'betrayed'. Who is Conor here? Dublin Castle? The resonances are all the more powerful for being clouded in this sublime rhetoric. To hear it sung is to feel a frisson of anger, the same anger that inspired a satire called 'Corruption' in 1808, in which the obduracy and cruelty of English policy in Ireland is called

> an unpitying power, whose whips and chains
> Made Ireland first in wild adulterous trance,
> Turn false to England's bed, and whore with France.

Moore here turns back to the impetus and solid force of Dryden's heroic couplet (see Unit 8, pp. 179–80) to arraign English policy towards Irish Catholics after the Union of 1801. Napoleon, in the same poem, is said to be dazzling 'Europe into slavery' with his 'burning shield'. One of the offshoots of Napoleonic conquest was the intensification of nationalist feelings in Germany, England and Italy, as a mood of imperial triumphalism replaced in France the collective remorse after the Revolution. Ireland was not immune from these impulses, and the Act of Union strengthened, in some quarters, an attitude of distrust towards the institutions of state. At the level of agrarian unrest this suspicion expressed itself in the Whiteboy societies and their Protestant corollaries, including the Orange Order. A genre of 'Whiteboy' writing developed, comparable in some respects (though of a much higher quality) with the thriller fiction of the 'Troubles' by such as Jack Higgins or Douglas Hurd in recent times. Novels dealing with these issues include *The Whiteboy* (1845) by Mrs S.C. Hall, *Roddy the Rover, or, the Ribbonman* (1845) and *The Tithe Procter* (1849) both by William Carleton, and also a notable story included in his *Traits and Stories of the Irish Peasantry* (1830, 1833), first published as 'Wildgoose Lodge'. It is a description of an atrocity, the slaughter of a family by a gang of Ribbonmen (successors to the Whiteboys) because the father is alleged to be an informer:

> The Captain approached him coolly and deliberately. 'You will prosecute no one now, you bloody informer,' said he; 'you will convict no more boys for taking an ould rusty gun an' pistol from you, or for giving you a neighbourly knock or two into the bargain.' Just then from a window opposite him, proceeded the shrieks of a woman who appeared at it with the infant in her arms. She herself was almost scorched to death; but with the presence of mind and humanity of her sex, she was about to thrust the little babe out of the window. The Captain noticed this, and with characteristic atrocity, thrust, with a sharp bayonet, the little innocent, along with the person who endeavoured to rescue it, into the red flames, where they both perished. This was the work of an instant.

This tale, reprinted in Deane (1991), grows out of the land disturbances that were a perpetual feature of Irish life from the later eighteenth century right throughout the nineteenth, and surviving into the twentieth. Who owns the land, how it is transferred, how it is regained, the feelings it inspires, the conflicts between landlord and tenant, give a core network of themes to Irish writing; and also at the same time introduces the dangerous, risky, yet exciting dimensions of territoriality, borders, partitions and thresholds. Continuously in Irish literature, the writer is trying to speak on behalf of a people or territory or grouping, whether it be Sheridan Le Fanu's troubled enquiries into Protestant ascendancy guilt in nineteenth-century novels such as *Wylder's Hand* (1864), Daniel Corkery's championing of Gaelic and Catholic mores in *The Hidden Ireland* (1925), or John Hewitt's reclamation of the Northern Planter's vision in volumes such as *Conacre* (1943). There is a plurality of voices, because so many lay claim to authority, and authority is often grounded on the troubled concept of legitimate ownership of territory.

The first work of fiction to explore such issues in Ireland is Maria Edgeworth's *Castle Rackrent* (1800, reprinted in Oxford World Classics series, 1984), where the family is doomed precisely because they cannot effectively exploit the land they have somehow (it is left unclear) inherited. Claimed as the first regional novel in English by Sir Walter Scott, and praised by the Russian Turgenev for its understanding of rural life, in the context of Irish literature it acquires a different resonance. There is a sense of the danger of ownership; that the land, and the 'big house' that dominates the landscape can become a curse, that it is a burden on the mind, that the place is *haunted*. The mournful desolation of Castle Rackrent, as it descends to rack and ruin, reminds us of other miserable houses and landlords in Irish literature, such as those in Le Fanu's gloomy *Uncle Silas* (1864), Bram Stoker's *Dracula* (1897), Samuel Beckett's nightmarish *Watt* (1953), John Banville's deranged *Birchwood* (1973) or Jennifer Johnston's poignant *How Many Miles to Babylon* (1974). Behind all of these sombre meditations on the moral and emotional encumbrance of property lies Maria Edgeworth's melancholy evocation of a countryside and habitation going to waste:

> There was then a great silence in Castle Rackrent, and I went moping from room to room, hearing the doors clap for want of right locks, and the wind through the broken windows that the glazier never would come to mend, and the rain coming through the roof and best ceilings all over the house, for want of the slater whose bill was not paid; besides our having no slates or shingles for that part of the old building which was shingled, and burnt when the chimney took fire, and had been open to the weather ever since.

The 'big house' novel in Irish literature carries a peculiar resonance, one that Marxist criticism (see Unit 21) would link to the significance of the big house as a symbol of a dominating power structure increasingly alienated from the people whom it exploited. Hence Dracula's castle and the terrified peasantry; and the images of life-in-death. The realities outside the big house were ferocious. Not just the land agitations, the Ribbonmen, and later the Fenians; there was also the economic and moral catastrophe of the Great Famine (1845–8) which decimated rural Ireland. Millions died or emigrated, while British administration debated and agonized over the rights and wrongs of interventionism, responsibility, accountability. Swift's nightmarish scenario of *A Modest Proposal* or of the Yahoos in *Gulliver's Travels* seemed not drastically removed from reality as scenes of hunger and starvation multiplied themselves all over Ireland. Spenser's lurid description of the condition of Munster after the sixteenth-century Geraldine Rebellion recreated itself in Irish history with a dismal cyclicity. On guilt and property as themes in Irish literature see McCormack (1985). A poem of 1846 (see Deane, 1991) by James Clarence Mangan captures the mood of paralyzed outrage and frantic despair. 'Siberia' reads:

> In Siberia's wastes
> The Ice-wind's breath
> Woundeth like the toothed steel.
> Lost Siberia doth reveal
> Only blight and death.
>
> Blight and death alone.
> No Summer shines.
> Night is interblent with Day.
> In Siberia's wastes alway
> The blood blackens, the heart pines.

As the nineteenth century wore on the position of the Protestant ascendancy grew ever more precarious. Sir Samuel Ferguson, keeper of the Public Records of Ireland, Unionist (although he did for a time dabble with the movement to Repeal the Union during the Famine: how could such a thing occur if there was a Union of Britain and Ireland?), archaeologist, controversialist and poet, drew upon Irish saga to vivify his writing, recreating epical visions of a noble and savage Gaelic Ireland. But one of the reasons he was imaginatively drawn to scenes of wild and energetic cruelty, as in *Congal* (1872), was that they provided an outlet for the frustrations and tensions building in Unionist ascendancy culture. Social order, in his 'Celtic' poems, was depicted as being continually broken up by tribal passions, failure to seek accommodation between opposing ideologies, and outside interference. Ferguson was deeply antagonistic to Catholic nationalism, and hated Daniel O'Connell, who had led the cause for Catholic Emancipation (1829) and the Repeal of the Union. He believed that Irish Protestantism should not neglect its leadership and ascendancy role, a view also shared by Standish James O'Grady, a writer and thinker who influenced and participated in the Irish literary revival of *c.*1890–1922. On Catholic and Protestant strains in nineteenth-century Irish poetry, see Welch (1980).

O'Grady had written a number of legendary and historical works and novels, such as his *History of Ireland: The Heroic Period* (1878) drawing upon Irish mythology and saga, notably the Ulster Cycle and its hero Cú Chulainn, the Hound of Ulster, who became a powerful archetype of the revival. O'Grady, Douglas Hyde, George Sigerson, Katherine Tynan, George Russell ('AE'), Nora Hopper, Jane Barlow, P.J. McCall and many others drew together in a cultural movement in the 1890s that was, to a great extent, orchestrated and managed by its predominant figure, W.B. Yeats. After the death of the parliamentary leader Charles Stewart Parnell in 1891 it seemed to Yeats that the time had come for a cultural movement, which would attempt to sublimate the political energies which had run wild in the Fenian movement of the 1870s and 1880s and the almost entirely constitutional Land League movement spearheaded by Parnell and Michael Davitt. Parnell was brought down by the scandal of adultery, but the Land War had been successful, in that the system of land ownership drastically changed throughout the 1890s in favour of the tenantry. A new prosperity was beginning, and with it a new cultural awareness, particularly manifested in the Gaelic League (set up in 1893 to promote Irish) and the GAA (set up in 1884 to promote Gaelic games). These new factors inspired Yeats to create his movement, which he believed should have a spiritual as well as cultural dimension. He drew upon old sources of power, Irish mythology and legend, in order not to be 'lost in a world of mere shadow and dream', as he wrote in an early essay on Samuel Ferguson in 1886. Cú Chulainn, Medb Queen of Connacht, Deirdre and the tragic tales of the sons of Uisnech, all informed plays, poems and fictions on these subjects in the work of Yeats himself, Synge, and many others. Also Hyde's editorial and translating work as in *The Love Songs of Connacht* (1893) drew attention to the beauty and subtlety of Irish folk poetry and story-telling. These mythological and folkloric themes and subjects, inspired as they were by a mixture of cultural nationalism and an anxiety about the apparent lifelessness of an encroaching modern world of steam-engines. factories and democracy, sometimes became jejune and affected, as, say, in the somewhat mechanical or feeble operation of 'Celtic Twilight' effects in Russell's poetic musings, but they did provide fresh images for Irish writing and pulled it back to major reserves of energy in Gaelic literature and Celtic belief. 'He Hears the Cry of the Sedge' from *The Wind Among the Reeds* (1899) recreates the mood, imagery and atmosphere of Irish love song, then gives it an apocalyptic turn, in line with Yeats's visionary and millenarian impulses:

> I wander by the edge
> Of this desolate lake
> Where wind cries in the sedge.
> Until the axle break
> That keeps the stars in their round,
> And hands hurl in the deep
> The banners of East and West,
> And the girdle of light is unbound,
> Your breast will not lie by the breast
> Of your beloved in sleep.

Yeats and Lady Gregory believed that the imagination could be a liberating force in Irish society, and preserve it from the materialism and conformity they believed threatened modern life in its democratic phase. They founded the Irish Literary Theatre in 1897 (which became the Abbey Theatre in 1904) to provide a national theatre of the imagination.

On 2 April 1902 the theatre produced Yeats's *Cathleen Ni Houlihan* and George Russell's *Deirdre*, with Maud Gonne in the title role of the former. The effect was electrifying: the image of Ireland under the guise of an old woman coming back on the eve of the 1798 Rebellion to claim back her 'four green fields' – the four provinces of Ireland – from the stranger, had a powerful and perhaps incalculable effect on the minds of young Irishmen and women. Yeats later wondered if this play, with its deeply affecting theme of self-sacrifice for the cause of Ireland, did not contribute directly to the Easter Rising of 1916:

> I lie awake at night
> And never get the answer right
> Did that play of mine send out
> Certain men the English shot?

However, nationalist enthusiasm for the plays at the Abbey Theatre was the exception rather than the rule. The cultural programme of the Gaelic League had aroused separatist feelings, and in time commitment to the revival of Irish language and culture translated itself into political activism. The Fenian movement survived into the twentieth century as the IRB (Irish Republican Brotherhood, predecessor of the IRA) and its membership increased as the Gaelic League developed its organization and effectiveness, much to the dismay of Douglas Hyde, who wanted to keep the cultural movement out of politics. Yeats and Lady Gregory fell under the suspicion of ardent nationalists such as D.P. Moran, who held that their view of Ireland was essentially patronizing and West-British. Synge's *The Playboy of the Western World*, in particular, aroused the ire of nationalist Dublin for its frank portrayal of the materialism, wildness and enmity in Irish country people. The fact that the play was also a subtle inquiry into the dangers of hero-worship, and of the relationship between brutality and fantasy was ignored by the ideologues, though not by Yeats, who fully appreciated its shocking originality in confronting the problem of violence and its links with the imagination:

> We had fed the heart on fantasies,
> The heart's grown brutal from the fare . . .
> ('Meditations in Time of Civil War', 1923)

Pádraig Pearse, editor of the Gaelic League journal, *An Claidheamh Soluis*, was one of the younger members of that organization who worked to make it overtly political. Eventually he became leader of the Easter Rising of 1916, issuing a proclamation in the name of all Irish men and women which asserted Ireland's 'indefeasible' right to sovereign independence. In 1915 at the graveside of O'Donovan Rossa, an old Fenian whose body had been returned from America to be buried in Dublin, he spoke as follows:

> They [the English] think that they have foreseen everything, think that they have provided against everything; but the fools, the fools, the fools! – they have left us the Fenian dead, and while Ireland holds these graves, Ireland unfree shall never be at peace.

The Rising inspired much writing – Yeats's 'Easter 1916', James Stephens's *Insurrection*, Sean O'Casey's *The Plough and the Stars* – but in 1914 James Joyce published *Dubliners*, an antidote to the nationalist enthusiasm and heroic flag-waving that led to the revolution. This entire collection is based on the notion that, far from being an energetic and vital people, disposed to imagination and reverie, as proposed by Yeats; or from being a race endowed with an indomitable longing for freedom, as advanced by Pearse, the Irish were as self-seeking, cruel and embour-geoized as any other modern community, and perhaps more so than most. On nationalism and literature see Watson (1979).

*Ulysses* (1922) rebukes all those in Ireland (and elsewhere) who dispel the present by hankering after the future or longing for the past. In style and form, employing an original method of narrative presentation (the 'stream of conscious-ness': see Unit 16, pp. 455–6) it concentrates on the here and now of one single day in Dublin, 16 June 1904. It is a novel flooded with the presence of the present, and comments on a culture frequently dominated by ancestral voices or apocalyptic yearnings. However, *Finnegans Wake* gives the wheel another turn, to revisit the strata of memory and consciousness buried in language so as to contemplate a capacious possibility within which human perception can accommodate a vision of fantastic and baffling experiences.

If Joyce is the critic and to some extent the moralist of the literary revival – Stephen Dedalus in *A Portrait of the Artist* said that he wanted to 'forge in the smithy of my soul the uncreated conscience of my race' – then George Moore was its comedian. He returned from England, an established and successful author, in 1901, the author of *Esther Waters* (1894) and many other novels, to participate in the renewal of cultural activity taking place there. But, an inveterate non-joiner of anything, he quickly turned the Dublin scene into high comedy in *Hail and Farewell* (1911–14), a vividly rendered account of personalities of the time, among them Yeats, Russell, Synge and Douglas Hyde.

After the Anglo-Irish war revolutionary idealism had to be translated into administrative effectiveness, economic policies and the routine but arduous business of running an economy in the modern world. A new realism entered into Irish writing, reflected in the drama of O'Casey and the short stories and novels of Frank O'Connor, Sean O'Faolain, Francis Stuart; and in the drama of Lennox Robinson, T.C. Murray, Paul Vincent Carroll, and George Sheils.

The poetry of Austin Clarke and Robert Farren turned back to Gaelic models for inspiration. Clarke, in particular, basing his practice on George Sigerson's and William Larminie's experiments in imitating Gaelic prosody in English, forged an intensely decorative yet subtly nervous style out of these materials in poems such as 'The Lost Heifer' (1926), which opens with the following mournful cadences:

> When the black herds of the rain were grazing
> In the gap of the pure cold wind
> And the watery hazes of the hazel
> Brought her into my mind
> I thought of the last honey by the water
> That no hive can find . . .

This prolongation of the notes of the Celtic Twilight had been given a more directly nationalist turn by Thomas MacDonagh, one of the signatories of the 1916 proclamation, who, in *Literature in Ireland* (1916), had argued for the strengthening of a distinctly Irish note in modern Anglo-Irish literature. Clarke, who had been taught by MacDonagh at University College, Dublin, followed this lead at first, but later used the elaborate effects borrowed from Gaelic verse to whip his language to a satiric and Swiftian fury at the pseudo-sanctity and political hypocrisy of the Free State (a Republic from 1948) in *Ancient Lights* (1955), and *Flight to Africa* (1963), in poems such as 'Martha Blake at Fifty-one'.

However, Clarke's earlier Gaelic musings led the young Samuel Beckett to lampoon him in *Murphy* (1938) as Austin Ticklepenny, and his experiments in metrics as 'prosodoturfy', i.e. prosody of the 'ould sod'. Beckett's attacks on the 'Cuchulainoid' clichés of the Irish literature in the 1930s – still very much lost in the 'watery hazes' of the revival at its least inspired – had their origin in his admiration for the intellectual force and sheer humanity of Joyce, but also in his own conviction that an art seeking to confront contemporary life must shed itself of all gallantry, embroidery and rhetoric, and come back to where Yeats returned in 'The Circus Animals Desertion' (1938), 'The foul rag-and-bore shop of the heart'. Hence Beckett's ferociously pitiless method and style – character in his novels is steadily cut back until all that is left are voices circling in a void; and his minimalist stagecraft.

Flann O'Brien's *At Swim-Two-Birds* (1939) while on the face of it a comic romp mixing gunslingers, cattle-rustlers, university students and figures from mythology is, in reality, a contemplation of the terror of imagining, when the exterior world has grown hectic, wild and unknowable. *The Third Policeman*, written in 1940 but unpublished until 1968, invents a form of manic realism to convey, comically, the deepest moral disquiet at all official, normal certainties, among them authority, language, identity, heaven and hell (see Unit 16, pp. 463–5).

There are, in what we may call the mid-century, a number of writers who, in retrospect, are seen to be crucial. The first of these is Louis MacNeice, from Carrickfergus, Co. Antrim, long thought of as a member of the 'Thirties' group of poets which included W.H. Auden and C. Day Lewis – the 'Mac Spaunday' group. But MacNeice's swift lyrical intelligence, his philosophical gravity, his classicism, and the example he provides of a poetic life lived intently, seriously, yet not without humour and humanity, proved of most enduring value to a group of northern poets in the 1960s and 1970s. Also, his attachment to Ireland was combined with a pronounced lack of zealotry and passion, offering an alternative to simplistic tribal identifications. The following is from *Autumn Journal* (1939):

> And I remember, when I was little, the fear
> Bandied among the servants
> That Casement would land at the pier
> With a sword and a horde of rebels;
> And how we used to expect, at a later date,
> When the wind blew from the west, the noise of shooting
> Starting in the evening at eight
> In Belfast in the York Street district;
> And the voodoo of the Orange bands
> Drawing an iron net through darkest Ulster,
> Flailing the limbo lands –
> The linen mills, the long wet grass, the ragged hawthorn ...

Patrick Kavanagh, a poet from Co. Monaghan, communicated a vision in *A Soul for Sale* (1947) and in later volumes such as *Come Dance with Kitty Stobing* (1960) which drew together a sense of the sacred which he inherited from the sacramentalism of Catholicism, with a readiness of response to the ordinary things of life. *The Great Hunger* (1942), however, bears witness to the emotional starvation of mid-century Catholic Ireland in a deliberate analogy with the Great Famine of the nineteenth century caused by other and, he implies, no less inimical forces.

Joyce Cary, born in Derry, is a novelist who has almost been lost to the history of this literature, and yet *Castle Corner* (1938) and *A House of Children* (1941) deal brilliantly with Irish issues and themes, while his compelling meditations on power, character and evil in men and women in novels such as *The Horse's Mouth* (1941) and *Prisoner of Grace* (1952) reveal a political and moral maturity and concern that lead back to Swift and Burke.

In the 1950s and 1960s new fictional voices began to emerge in novels such as *The Barracks* (1963) and *The Dark* (1965) in which John McGahern presented a view of Ireland which was chastened by doubt and anxiety and cleansed of all remnants of revivalist longings. Brian Moore's career began with *The Lonely Passion of Judith Hearne* (1955) which offered a Belfast prose counterpart to Austin Clarke's poetic analyses of the stricken conscience of mid-century Irish Catholicism. Later novels, such as *Black Robe* (1985) and *Lies of Silence* (1990), explore how the individual will attempts to cope in a wilderness of choice and relativism. Francis Stuart was in disgrace following his sojourn in Berlin during the Second World War – his reasons for the controversial move were complex and are not amenable to the simplifications of political correctness – but in the late 1940s he re-emerged as a writer of unique vision and intensity, with *Redemption* (1949), a novel dealing with the transformative power of love and kindness, as well as probing the realities of guilt and suffering. The 'immersive' (to borrow a term his friend Samuel Beckett used in his study of Proust) atmosphere of his fiction came to fruition in a series of masterful late novels, beginning with *Black List, Section H* (1971). These late works experiment with autobiography, with narrative, and with the concept of self, to disclose a world in which the author, by drawing attention to the way in which the imagination interacts and plays with reality, achieves a curiously liberating sense of participation, even collusion, with the reader's own consciousness.

Jennifer Johnston, daughter of the playwright Denis Johnston, only began to publish in her forties, but novels such as *The Captains and the Kings* (1972), *Shadows on our Skin* (1977), and *Fool's Sanctuary* (1987) revisit themes of nationalism, tribal loyalties, ascendancy and the land in an atmosphere sharpened by the renewal of conflict in Northern Ireland in the late 1960s. Edna O'Brien in *The Country Girls* (1960) and following novels revealed herself an anatomist of rural Catholic Ireland, its pieties and sad resilience. *The House of Splendid Isolation* (1994) examines the impact of Republican ideals on private individuals. John Banville, an elegant stylist, is concerned to explore the ways in which the imagination can construct forms and ideas which may be at variance with actual facts. His obsessive astronomers, in *Doctor Copernicus* (1976) and *Kepler* (1981), and the murderer in *The Book of Evidence* (1989) are intent on maintaining a resolved and ordered mental construct in spite of the incursions of circumstance and other people. His creatures are a curiously lonely sect of private believers, and they have an ancestry in Swift, Le Fanu and Beckett.

Among more recent writers of fiction Dermot Bolger and Roddy Doyle in *Paddy Clarke Ha Ha Ha* (1993) evoke working-class Dublin. Robert McLiam Wilson (*Ripley Bogle*, 1989), and Glenn Patterson (*Fat Lad*, 1992), are two Belfast writers who bring to their work a daring and even insouciant brilliance, and a studiously non-partisan approach to the 'Troubles'. Eoin MacNamee's *Resurrection Man* (1994) is a shocking account of loyalist terrorism based on the notorious 'Shankill butchers' case. On modern Irish fiction see Cronin (1990).

Since the 1950s there has been a remarkable burst of activity in Irish poetry. Pearse Hutchinson, Thomas Kinsella and John Montague were a Dublin-based group of writers who emerged in the 1950s, all published by the innovative Dolmen Press, with its beautifully designed and carefully printed volumes. All these were equally at home with Gaelic poetry and tradition, and with more cosmopolitan influences. Hutchinson turned to Spain, Kinsella to W.H. Auden, and Montague to France. Hutchinson also wrote in Irish. *Tongue without Hands* (1963) was followed by *Faoistin Bhacach* (1968). Kinsella's intensely meditated and scrupulously despairing *Downstream* (1962) and *Wormwood* (1966) gave him the sonorous command of language and tough solemnity of mood required to translate the eighth-century saga, *Táin Bó Cuailnge* (1969). Montague's fastidious stanzas, with their short, alert syllabic lines, drew upon bardic poetry and the French *symbolistes* to recreate evocatively and resonantly a treasured Co. Tyrone past. Montague, too, collaborated with the older Ulster poet John Hewitt – whose own career revived significantly in the 1960s and 1970s – in an Arts Council-sponsored tour in November 1970 entitled Planter and Gael, representing an early attempt at imaginative rapprochement between the two major traditions of Ulster.

A northern group of writers began to publish in the mid-1960s. Seamus Heaney's *Death of a Naturalist* (1966) exhibited a combination of local piety towards his Derry background with a terse and elastic language, full of tactile force and thoughtful resonance. His work continued to develop in collection after collection until, by the time he published *Seeing Things* (1991), he had become a weighty philosophical poet, as alive to the dangers of hasty moralizing as to the seductions of reticence. (Heaney's verse is discussed in Unit 17, pp. 513–14.) This linguistic maturity and finesse, drawing upon the examples of Louis MacNeice and Patrick Kavanagh, but also deriving inspiration from American and East European poets such as Elizabeth Bishop and Czeslaw Milosz, is schooled by a relentless and vigilant moral awareness. Michael Longley, beginning with *No Continuing City* (1969), up to *Gorse Fires* (1993), shares with Heaney a thoughtful and carefully managed linguistic sensitivity. He too looks to MacNeice, and he conjoins an elegant appreciation of detail with a refined and forceful concentration. Heaney and Longley, along with Derek Mahon, Seamus Deane, Tom Paulin and Paul Muldoon form a loose northern grouping of poets, all of whom are marked by a resolute seriousness of purpose, a sense that poetry operates in a sphere not exclusive from justice and morality. For all their close scrutiny of actions and their outcomes –

cause and effect being a relationship that matters urgently in Northern Ireland – their verse is not without lightness and wit. Muldoon in particular, in say *The Annals of Chile* (1994), can yoke sorrow, playfulness and irony in combinations that are full of unique surprises. Other northerners include Ciaran Carson, whose *Belfast Confetti* (1989) and *First Language* (1994) display an omnivorous appetite for all registers of language, from Belfast demotic slang to a richly seamed Elizabethan panoply of rhetorical ebullience, to deliver a teeming world of risk, possibility and danger. Medbh McGuckian's verse opens up other new dimensions for language, where ordinary domestic things and events acquire an edge of secrecy, and where moods elaborate into obscure longings. On modern and contemporary Irish poetry see Garratt (1986) and Andrews (1992).

What is striking is the sheer quality of Irish poetry produced both north and south of the border in the past twenty-five years. Among southerners in the period following the revival of poetic energies in the 1960s, Brendan Kennelly is a writer who has a profound affinity with the Gaelic and folk tradition, and is at the same time a chronicler of late twentieth-century Dublin. His work, especially in *Cromwell* (1983) and *The Book of Judas* (1991), attacks fixed ideas, cramped ideologies, concocted feelings, by releasing a torrent of different, often contradictory voices, trying to articulate the variant strivings of passion. Michael Hartnett's dark and brooding meditations on love and politics in his early work were transformed by new energies when he started to write in Irish after *A Farewell to English* (1975).

The single most significant event in the history of Irish drama in the post-war years was the founding of the Field Day Theatre Company in Derry in 1980, with Brian Friel, Seamus Heaney and Seamus Deane on the Board of Directors. This marked a new departure into a re-exploration and re-evaluation of concepts of identity and tradition that was to issue in Deane's *Field Day Anthology* (1991), but which had its workshop in the plays of Friel for Field Day, beginning with *Translations*, Thomas Kilroy's *Pentecost* (1987), as well as the poems of Seamus Heaney, Tom Paulin and Deane, and critical writings by these and others. The outcome of this activity, combined with other influences from Dublin, Cork and elsewhere, along with the revival of Irish publishing, and a renewed vitality in writing in Irish, means that literary culture in Ireland as we approach the end of this century, is in a remarkably healthy state. But in the confluence of all the different factors, Field Day was a dominant catalyzing presence. Other dramatists include Tom Murphy, Frank McGuinness and Vincent Woods, whose experiments are underpinned by confident stagecraft and effective vigorous writing. On drama see Roche (1994).

In summary, it may be said that Irish writing in English, sustained as it is by a continued relationship with its reservoirs of strength in Gaelic tradition, and by its prolonged fruitful and problematic interconnections with English literature, and now diversified by further influences from all over the globe, has become one of the major literatures of the modern world in any language.

For histories of Irish writing in English see Jeffares (1982) and Deane (1986), each of which contains guides for further reading. See also Hogan (1980) and Welch (1996). Deane (1991) contains extracts from many of the texts cited.

## BIBLIOGRAPHY

Andrews, E. (ed.) (1992) *Contemporary Irish Poetry*, Macmillan, London.
Brown, M. (1972) *The Politics of Irish Literature*, George Allen & Unwin, New York.
Cronin, J. (1990) *The Anglo-Irish Novel*, vols I and II, Appletree Press, Belfast.
Deane, S. (1985) *Celtic Revivals*, Faber & Faber, London.
Deane, S. (1986) *A Short History of Irish Literature*, Hutchinson, London.
Deane, S. (ed.) (1991) *The Field Day Anthology*, 3 vols, Field Day Publications, Derry.
Garratt, R. (1986) *Modern Irish Poetry: Tradition and Continuity from Yeats to Heaney*, University of California Press, Berkeley.
Hogan, R. (ed.) (1980) *The Macmillan Dictionary of Irish Literature*, Macmillan, London.
Jeffares, A.N. (1982) *A History of Anglo-Irish Literature*, Macmillan, London.
McCormack, W.J. (1985) *Ascendancy and Tradition in Anglo-Irish Literature*, Clarendon Press, Oxford.
Roche, A. (1994) *Modern Irish Drama*, Gill & Macmillan, Dublin.
Watson, G.J. (1979) *Irish Identity and the Literary Revival*, Croom Helm, London.
Welch, R. (1980) *Irish Poetry from Moore to Yeats*, Colin Smythe, Gerrards Cross.
Welch, R. (1996) *The Oxford Companion to Irish Literature*, Clarendon Press, Oxford.

# Anglo-Welsh literature

*Mary Jones*

Any rigid definition of 'Anglo-Welsh Literature' is fraught with problems, if only because it leads to the inappropriate exclusion of particular writers. There is therefore a tendency to define the term broadly. For clearly it has to include Welsh-born authors who spend their lives in Wales and speak Welsh (like R.S. Thomas) and writers who do not speak Welsh, are not born in Wales and do not spend their lives there, but who are nevertheless steeped in things Welsh (like David Jones). And so Gwyn Jones's definition, in 1957, of the Anglo-Welsh as 'those authors of Welsh blood or connexion who for a variety of reasons write their creative work in English' (Jones, 1957, p. 9) – a definition in which neither the place of residence nor the subject-matter of the writer is alluded to – remains current. In *The Oxford Companion to the Literature of Wales*, for instance, 'Anglo-Welsh' is defined as 'a literary term denoting a writer Welsh by birth or by association, who, for a variety of reasons, writes not in Welsh but in English' (Stephens, 1986, p. 12).

Even so, there are problems. Are poets like George Herbert and Henry Vaughan Anglo-Welsh? Both were born of renowned Welsh families; the latter was also Welsh-speaking and described himself as 'the Silurist'. Yet as poets do they not belong rather to the English literary tradition? The waterfall Vaughan celebrates in his famous poem of that name might be on the River Usk, but isn't his treatment of it typically metaphysical? Does considering these poets as Anglo-Welsh place them in a new revealing context, or does it simply lead to a distorted view of their work? Even when writers from Welsh backgrounds do not so evidently belong to an English tradition, do they, if they bring little sense of Wales into their writing, qualify as Anglo-Welsh? What about the poet Edward Thomas, for instance? And what about the Englishman, Gerard Manley Hopkins, who was influenced by Wales to the extent of learning enough of its language and its literary traditions to compose, in Welsh, a poem in the strict verse-form of the *cywydd*, and whose English poetry is clearly influenced by traditional Welsh patterns of alliteration and internal rhyme (or *cynghanedd*)? (See Unit 12, p. 328.) Is Edward Thomas an Anglo-Welsh poet and Gerard Manley Hopkins not? Are they both? If so, what about other authors who are not Welsh but who have written about Wales? Bruce Chatwin's fine and strange novel *On the Black Hill* (1982) creates a strong impression of bleak lives on an isolated, upland farm in

mid-Wales; A.J. Cronin's *The Citadel* (1937) records and evokes life in the South
Wales coalfield. Are they part of Anglo-Welsh literature? What about novels that
are set in Wales but evoke no real sense of a Welsh way of life? Beryl Bainbridge's *Another Part of the Wood* (1968) for instance. Surely that has no place in
Anglo-Welsh literature. Yet where is the line to be drawn?

It is indeed virtually impossible to draw a distinction that is both precise and
satisfactory between what is and is not to be included within Anglo-Welsh
Literature, and so despite the problems involved in the broad definition of the term
offered by the *Oxford Companion to the Literature of Wales*, that definition is
generally accepted as the most workable one.

The question of the usefulness, or even the meaningfulness, of the term
'Anglo-Welsh' has long been a matter of debate, and has on occasion flared into
conflict between Welsh writers who write in Welsh and those who write in English.
In 1938, for instance, this century's foremost Welsh-language playwright, Saunders
Lewis, delivered and published a lecture provocatively entitled 'Is there an Anglo-
Welsh Literature?' in which he concludes, somewhat aggressively, that while there is
such a thing as Anglo-Irish Literature, 'there is not a separate literature that is Anglo-
Welsh' (Lewis, 1939, p. 13). The first crucial difference he notes is that the term
'Anglo-Irish' refers to a community to which its literature gives expression, whereas
the term 'Anglo-Welsh' is purely a literary abstraction, there being no Anglo-Welsh
people. (He ignores the fact that the people usually referred to as 'Anglo-Irish' are
the Protestant Ascendancy and not the Catholic peasant class he claims finds
expression in Anglo-Irish literature.) His second difference is that while Anglo-Irish
writers had a specific dialect of English on which to draw, the so-called Anglo-
Welsh writers did not; and his third difference is that whereas Anglo-Irish writers
address an Irish audience, the Anglo-Welsh address an English one. The final
distinction he makes is that Anglo-Irish authors are consciously and deliberately
nationalist, while Anglo-Welsh writers have for the most part abandoned their Welsh
heritage and culture. The main reason he gives for these differences is the fact that
life in Ireland remains predominantly rural whereas life in Wales has become
primarily industrial. He does not make the point that Anglo-Irish literature was likely
to pre-date Anglo-Welsh simply because the retreat of the Irish language pre-dated
the retreat of the Welsh, which continued to be the dominant language in Wales until
the present century.

Although there are considerable flaws, both in the facts as Lewis presents them
and in his arguments, his basic observations were substantial enough for Raymond
Garlick to take them up again in 1970. In a lecture to which he gave the same title as
Lewis (Williams, 1971, pp. 195–207) he answers the question in it affirmatively.
Not only does Anglo-Welsh literature exist, but in the thirty years between the two
lectures, he claims, Lewis's criteria have been fulfilled. He has a point. Lewis's
comments may be true of what is known as the first flowering of modern Anglo-
Welsh literature: namely, that written in the first half of this century, from Caradoc
Evans to Dylan Thomas. But in the second flowering, after the Second World War, a
change of attitude towards Wales can be seen: there has been more awareness of,
and sympathy for, nationalism, and the implied readership tends to be Welsh. The

forum for such writing is literary magazines published in Wales, and though these have existed intermittently since the late nineteenth century, they have become more firmly established more recently. Current journals include *The New Welsh Review, Poetry Wales* and *Planet*.

In *An Introduction to Anglo-Welsh Literature* (1972) Raymond Garlick has also shown, however, that although the term 'Anglo-Welsh' only became common in the 1920s, when there was a clear need to distinguish Welsh literature from that being written in Wales in English, it was first used (albeit in reference to prelates) as early as 1772, by Evan Evans, in the preface to his poem 'The Love of our Country'. Not that this was the start of Anglo-Welsh poetry. Garlick reveals that, on the contrary, there has been a continuous tradition of Welsh poets writing about Wales in the English language since 1470, when Ieuan ap Hywel Swrdwal composed his 'Hymn to the Virgin', a curious poem using the English language, Welsh spelling and the alliterative patterns of *cynghanedd*. In the following century Morris Kyffin was addressing Elizabeth I with his poem 'The Blessednes of Brytaine' (1587) and some years after that John Davies was addressing the Prince of Wales with his equally eulogistic 'Cambria' (1603). Later in the seventeenth century Roland Watkyns was writing in praise of 'Golden Grove, Carmarthen' (1662), and in the eighteenth century John Dyer extolled 'Grongar Hill' (1726) and Edward Davies celebrated 'Chepstow' (1784), industry and all. By the nineteenth century John Jones had more ambivalent feelings to the industrial scene at 'Holywell' (1856), and T. Hughes and John Morgan were bewailing the death-throes of the Welsh language – the first in 'Snowdon' in 1864 and the second in 'My Welsh Home' in 1870. A selection of poems from these poets may be found in Garlick and Mathias (1993).

If such poems set out to interpret Wales to the outsider (thereby forfeiting, by Saunders Lewis's standards, any claim to be distinctively Anglo-Welsh), the case is not always that simple. As early as 1603 John Davies wrote, in 'Cambria', of his dual role:

> I speak for those whose tongues are strange to thee
> In thine own tongue: if my words be unfit,
> That blame be mine; but if Wales better be
> By my disgrace, I hold that grace to me.
>
> (Garlick and Mathias, 1993, p. 54)

Evan Evans, too, writing of 'The Love of our Country' (1772) remarked: 'I have done it in English verse in order that men of learning in both languages may understand it' (quoted in Garlick, 1972, p. 12).

Their main purpose is nevertheless interpretive, and this tendency, down the centuries, to defend Wales and the Welsh to the English, is hardly surprising when the latter are adjacent and dominant and have from time immemorial seen the Welsh as the epitome of barbarism, if not vice. There are many records of statements such as that of an English member of James I's parliament, who claimed the Welsh had 'lived long like thieves and robbers and are to this day the most base, peasantly, perfidious peoples of the world' (quoted in Dodd, 1977, p. 87). And this jingle, first recorded in *Nancy Cook's Pretty Song Book* in 1780, but no doubt in circulation well before that, is still heard:

> Taffy was a Welshman, Taffy was a thief,
> Taffy came to our house and stole a piece of beef.

Small wonder, then, that the defence of the Welsh should be extreme too, that an idyllic country and an idealized people should be presented in contrast. The Shrewsbury poet, Thomas Churchyard, strenuously denies the specific charge of the above jingle in 'The Worthiness of Wales'. Coming to Wales, he declares, is like coming 'to heaven out of hell'. The Scots want blood, the Irish are unkind, England has grown lewd, but Wales is 'the soundest state'. Moreover:

> Ye may come there, beare purse of gold in hand,
> Or mightie bagges, of silver stuffed throwe,
> And no one man, dare touch your treasure now.
>
> (Churchyard, 1776, p. 3)

It is intriguing, in view of all this, that the work of fiction often deemed to be the first Anglo-Welsh novel, tells the story of a notorious Welsh robber, Twm Shôn Catti. T.J. Llewelyn Prichard took advantage of earlier, English accounts of this historical Welsh Robin Hood when, in 1828, he published *The Adventures and Vagaries of Twm Shôn Catti*, though he pretends to decry W.F. Deacon for 'sacrilegiously dignifying a robber with the qualities of a hero', and insulting the Welsh by 'the villainous inference that Wales was barren of *real* heroes' (Prichard, 1828, p. 4). Tongue-in-cheek throughout, it is a picaresque novel in which the narrative rambles as much as 'our hero', and it is delightfully light-hearted and witty. It might seem to follow the tradition of eighteenth-century English novels such as Fielding's *Tom Jones*, the hero of which has an affinity with Twm Shôn Catti in more than name, yet as it relates Twm's initiation into a life of honourable cunning, it records, as if incidentally, the customs of life in rural mid-Wales (it is subtitled 'Descriptive of Life in Wales'), and the focus of the irony is interesting. At first it seems directed at the English: Squire Graspacre is 'an English gentleman-farmer who condescendingly fixed himself in the principality with the laudable idea of civilising the Welsh' (Prichard, 1828, p. 7) and his hypocrisy, greed and lust are exposed. But he mellows, and his evil ways are transferred to his Welsh wife. It is people of either nationality who oppress who are the butt of the irony, just as they are the butt of Twm's trickery and tomfoolery. The readership is assumed to be both English and Welsh; on p. 29 Prichard writes: 'the English reader will not be offended if...' and on p. 214 he says: 'The reader who is a Welshman will hence recognise ...'. For his two sets of readers, Prichard exploits to the full the comic potential of the string of incidents.

By the end of the nineteenth century Allen Raine was writing very differently about the same Cardiganshire people. Her popular, best-selling novels were rural romances in which the love interest was paramount. Stagey and cloying though they are at times, they nevertheless have a psychological depth and a bleakness which the term 'romance' belies, and their social background is well portrayed. Although they have dated, they have recently gained some serious recognition after being dismissed as 'a sandcastle dynasty' (Jones, 1957, p. 9).

Then, in fierce reaction against such romance, came the publication of Caradoc Evans's notorious first volume of short stories, again about the people of rural Cardiganshire. The year was 1915 and, in Gwyn Jones's words, 'the Anglo-Welsh had arrived' (Evans, 1953, p. 7). The first flowering of modern Anglo-Welsh literature is still commonly dated by the book's appearance. Both the sentiment of Allen Raine and the comedy of Prichard are missing, and yet there are some affinities between the latter and Evans in their portrayal of the peasant. Both writers create caricatures of them; both expose their hypocrisy, greed and lust. But Evans's caricatures are not comic, they are grotesque. The irony with which they are treated is not light-hearted and tolerant, but savage and satirical. The prose is not discursive and verbose, but spare; the tone is not warm, but grim. Caradoc Evans has been described as the 'best-hated man in Wales' (Jones, 1957, p. 8); he is also one of its finest writers.

Caradoc Evans was familiar with contemporary English satires of the Welsh – with A.T. Johnson's *The Perfidious Welshman* (1910), for instance, and T.W.H. Crosland's *Taffy was a Welshman* (1912) – but he wrote from an insider's position, calling his books 'My People', 'My Neighbours'. The focus of his satire is Nonconformism, seen as a perverse religion, as merciless as it is certain, instilling into its adherents a cruel morality which is used to justify the most gross and inhuman behaviour. There is as much victimization here as in Prichard's novel but here it ends not in laughter and retribution but in madness and death. The wealthier farmers scheme and plot against the poorer, for petty gain; brutal men treat like cattle their socially inferior womenfolk. There is no humour, no depth of character, and the people speak a grotesque speech (deriving in part from literal translations of Welsh idiom), but the stories are as powerful as they are savage. Behind the detached, severe, biblical style there is an anger which is communicated to the reader, and sometimes, as in 'A Father unto Sion', the pain of the victim is felt acutely enough to make a melodramatic climax horrifying. Apparently blunt statements conceal subtly imparted information, and poetic phrases suddenly intrude into the grimness of the telling. One of the most hauntingly told stories is 'Be This Her Memorial', in which Nanni's physical decline, recorded in gruesome detail, occurs after she has saved her pittance to buy a Bible for the minister (which he gives away). At the end, the minister calls at Nanni's cottage and finds her on the floor.

> Mishtir Bryn-Bevan went on his knees and peered at her. Her hands were clasped tightly together, as though guarding some great treasure. The minister raised himself and prised them apart with the ferrule of his walking-stick. A roasted rat revealed itself. Mishtir Bryn-Bevan stood for several moments spellbound and silent; and in the stillness the rats crept boldly out of their hiding places and resumed their attack on Nanni's face. The minister, startled and horrified, fled from the house of sacrifice. (Evans, 1953, p. 101)

Since Caradoc Evans, the short story has often been regarded as a forte of Anglo-Welsh writers (as it has been, too, of Welsh writers). It is something of a cliché that Welsh authors are better at creating the short, sharp effect required in a poem or short story, than the sustained build-up required of plays and novels; like so many clichés it is but a half-truth. Nevertheless, the wave of Anglo-Welsh short stories in the first half of this century, sometimes anecdotal, sometimes lyrical, and often using a child's viewpoint, show an exhilaration and a love of language that are distinctive. They do, however, also vary from the supernatural tales of Arthur Machen to the poetic stories of Glyn Jones and the witty prose of Gwyn Thomas, whose stories of life in the valleys of South Wales are comical, farcical, even absurdist. Of the many anthologies of Anglo-Welsh stories, the two volumes of *The Penguin Book of Welsh Short Stories* (1976 and 1994), both edited by Alun Richards, are among the most varied and offer an interesting combination of Anglo-Welsh stories and stories translated from Welsh.

It might be expected that the industrial life of South Wales, where the poverty and unemployment of the Depression were most acutely experienced, would provoke at least as bitter a response in its writers in the early years of this century as rural life produced in Evans. Yet the writing of this period set in the mining valleys, both short stories and novels, is concerned to show the humanity, the humour, the resilience and the spirit among people subjected to the appalling social conditions. The novels are realistic and they focus on family life; they may cover several generations and record both the growth of mining and its decline. There tends to be a similar pattern to them: typically, a strong mother-figure attempts to hold the family together as it drifts apart, with some members emigrating, some bettering them-selves, some marrying outsiders. Political crises or colliery accidents might bring things to a head, but life continues around chapel, choral-singing and rugby-playing. The situations and characters tend to become clichés that excuse Harri Webb's parody of them in his witty poem 'Synopsis of the Great Welsh Novel'.

The work of the best novelists is distinctive, however. Jack Jones and Lewis Jones both went down the pit at twelve, and they vividly convey a boy's experience of this, in *Bidden to the Feast* (1938) and *Cwmardy* (1937) respectively: both books, too, vividly depict pit accidents. Yet Jack Jones presents us with colourful characters whose quaint Welsh customs he explains to his English readers, while Lewis Jones confronts us with political issues. The drama in his work comes from political rather than family strife and his central relationships are between Len and his political mentor Ezra, and Ezra's politically involved daughter. The writing is urgent social documentary. Far different is the writing of Richard Llewellyn, whose novel *How Green Was my Valley* (1939) is probably the most well-known Anglo-Welsh novel outside Wales. Here there is a mood of nostalgia for a community whose innocence has been destroyed by an influx of outsiders and by Mining Union practices: there is eloquence and a poetic quality in the writing, but it lacks the urgency of Lewis Jones and the humour of Jack Jones, and it does not, as they do, evoke the reality of life in the valleys. Its appeal seems to lie in its sentiment and its romance.

The poet who belongs with these novelists is Idris Davies, who went down the pit at 14, and it is in his writing that anger is most apparent. His South Wales is a desert in which lives are blighted from the start, and though his work is uneven, his two poems 'Gwalia Deserta' and 'The Angry Summer', with their sudden ironic changes of rhythm, are a moving indictment of the living and working conditions he experienced.

More recent writing of the valleys has become more cynical and abrasive, tending to reflect a disaffected community with little sense of direction and few values left, in the wake of rapid industrial decline. In *Tom Jones Slept Here* (1971), John L. Hughes portrays a defiant youth who attempts to conquer fear by aggression and suppresses compassion. If he is created in the mould of the English Angry Young Man tradition, a strong impression of a semi-derelict Pontypridd is created, and both here and in the sequel *Before the Crying Ends* (1977) the idiosyncratic poetic style conveys a sense of loss. More recently still, Christopher Meredith, in his first novel *Shifts* (1988), has equally poetically, but less despairingly, recorded the entangled lives of a group of steelworkers, and evoked their declining steelworks in meticulous detail.

Interestingly, the first radio play ever broadcast, in 1924, was set down a Glamorgan coal-mine and dramatized a roof-fall there – a setting and situation ideally suited to its new medium. Entitled 'Danger', it was written by Richard Hughes, who was to become one of the finest novelists writing in English this century, and who, in *The Human Predicament*, depicts Wales in a European context, as he attempts to realize a continent that could become embroiled in the Second World War. The work is unfinished, but the opening of its first volume, *The Fox in the Attic* (1961), in which a man carries the body of a child across the salt marshes at Newton Llantony, is arguably one of the best beginnings in fiction.

His radio play might have been the first, but it is Dylan Thomas's that is the more well-known. *Under Milk Wood* (1953), as suited to the medium as *Danger*, depicts an ordinary day in the bitter-sweet life of Llareggub, and conjures up, partly through a blind sea-captain, a host of eccentric characters. A lively narrative commentary controls the series of brief scenes that are in turn funny, sad, or vicious. An essentially innocent world is evoked with what is commonly seen as typical Welsh 'gift of the gab'.

In general, however, drama has not played as great a part in Anglo-Welsh literature as poetry and fiction. The religious opposition which stifled Welsh drama in the nineteenth century had an effect too on that written in English. At the beginning of this century, however, naturalistic plays became popular in both languages, and by the inter-war years dramatists from Wales had their work performed in the West End. Of these, Emlyn Williams stands out; his carefully crafted plays, mostly set in North Wales, deal powerfully with Welsh themes such as the cultural and class friction resulting from Welsh working-class ambition, which is the subject of *The Corn is Green* (1938).

Although the play *Under Milk Wood* is possibly Dylan Thomas's best-known work, he was primarily a poet. Yet only a few of his last poems, such as 'Fern Hill', share the nostalgia of his play. His earlier poems, many of which stem from drafts composed when he was in his late teens (in the early 1930s), record his intense wonder and revulsion, joy and despair, at the natural processes of sex, birth and death. Sex and birth arouse his awe by their mingled creativeness and violence; the imminence of death spurs him to greater celebration of, and exultation in, being alive. Some of his best poems are inspired by his sense of identification with the whole of the natural world.

> The force that through the green fuse drives the flower
> Drives my green age; that blasts the roots of trees
> Is my destroyer,

he writes, and in the concluding couplet of the poem copulation, death and the act of poetic composition are typically linked:

> And I am dumb to tell the lover's tomb
> How at my sheet goes the same crooked worm.
>
> (Thomas, 1952, p. 9)

The relationship between language and experience, and the agony of poetic craftsmanship, is the subject of many poems. He described that craftsmanship to Henry Treece:

> I let ... an image be made emotionally in me and then apply to it what intellectual and critical forces I possess; let it breed another; let that image contradict the first, make, of the third image, bred out of the other two together, a fourth contradictory image, and let them all, within my imposed formal limits, conflict. (Treece, 1949, p. 32)

It is these imposed limits that distinguish Thomas from the surrealists with whom he has been compared: his images are rationally controlled. The apparent contradictions in the poem 'Light breaks where no sun shines', for instance, come from the repeated juxtaposing of an image to be taken metaphorically with one to be taken literally; the process of birth is thus seen in terms of the creation of the world in Genesis. In later poems the horror of this process is brought out by the analogy he draws between birth and the Blitz. Through his use of word play, onomatopoeia, assonance and multiple syntactical possibilities he can create poems that excite and disturb, and also poems that are too obscure for much sense to be made of them. At his best he conveys the emotional complexity of our most intimate experiences, but he has been much criticized, both for the obscurity of his work and for his disreputable lifestyle. (See Unit 17, pp. 509–10, for a discussion of Dylan Thomas.)

A less flamboyant but equally painstaking poet was Thomas's lifelong friend, Vernon Watkins, much of whose poetry was inspired by the Gower peninsula, where he lived. His love of nature and his religious sense gave a visionary quality to his work, and he is sometimes referred to as a modern metaphysical poet. He is, however, fundamentally a lyrical writer, though some of his finest poems are dramatic ballads, the strength of passion of which contrasts with the mildness of some of his later poems.

Thomas's and Watkins's concentration on the craftsmanship of poetry connects them with another writer who is again very different: namely, David Jones. In a work that is part poem, part novel, part drama – *In Parenthesis* (1937) – he attempts to convey what it was like going into the trenches in France in 1915, and to do this he experiments with language as much as Thomas. He writes with a more constant awareness of Wales, however, for he brings the whole weight of its history, its literature and its legends to bear on the troops' experience of marching to the front line, enduring bombardment, and finally launching an attack on Biez Wood, where they are decimated. The action is seen in the context of noble sacrifice, being paralleled in particular to the disastrous Battle of Catraeth, recounted in the sixth-century Welsh poem 'Y Gododdin', and to Christ proceeding to the crucifixion. It also re-enacts legends like the draining of Cantre'r Gwaelod and the hunting of the boar Twrch Trwyth, and it recalls the final defeats of King Arthur and Llewelyn, the Last Prince. It is a powerful and moving work, largely because the allusions are held together by the action and by the central character of John Ball, who is wounded in the leg, as was the author. Later, in 1952, in *The Anathemata*, Jones weaves the historical, religious and literary past of Britain around the Catholic mass, but this work becomes dense and difficult and lacks the drama and immediacy of *In Parenthesis*.

If David Jones is the most important Anglo-Welsh writer of the First World War, Alun Lewis is the name that springs to mind in connection with the Second. Killed in Burma in 1944, at the age of 28, he does not present Jones's epic vision of war, but records in moving, personal poems and short stories the impact war made on the soldiers, the desolate or poignant moments it held for him, and his longing for home and love. His is a gentle, quietly intelligent voice, often marked by the stress and grief of separation.

After the end of the war came the second flowering of Anglo-Welsh literature with its new consciousness of Welsh identity. The main poet associated with this movement is R.S. Thomas, an Anglican priest whose parishes in Manafon and Eglwys Fach were not far from the area about which Caradoc Evans had written. For Thomas too, the peasants are elementals whose lives are bound to the soil, and his treatment of them is similarly harsh, but through his blunt questioning of them he explores his own identity and his role as their priest (albeit of a minority religion). His peasants have the traditional quality of endurance, but any pastoral idealism is denied: they are on the brink of mindlessness. Addressing Iago Prytherch in a series of poems, he expresses his mingled contempt for, and awe of, the man.

> Fun? Pity? No word can describe
> My true feelings. I passed and saw you
> Labouring there, your dark figure
> Marring the simple geometry
> Of the square fields with its gaunt question.
> My poems were made in its long shadow
> Falling coldly across the page.
>
> (Thomas, 1993, p. 87)

When it comes to Wales too, he is by turns scathing and fiercely partisan. In poems that are bitter and probing, and hit nerve after nerve, he berates both the English and the Welsh for the deteriorating conditions of Wales. In 'Reservoirs', for instance, he sees

> the English
> Scavenging among the remains
> Of our culture, covering the sand
> Like the tide and, with the roughness
> Of the tide, elbowing our language
> Into the grave that we have dug for it.
>
> (Thomas, 1993, p. 194)

More mellow are his later poems of spiritual questioning, in which the apt images, though still grim, suggest some degree of reconciliation with human frailty.

If R.S. Thomas is the foremost living Anglo-Welsh poet, Emyr Humphries is the corresponding novelist: both published their first books in 1946. Like Thomas, Humphries is a religious man, learned Welsh and became a nationalist when adult, and explores human weakness in a political context. He has focused on the nature of goodness, on conscience and responsibility, and on the relationship between Christian love and sexual love. Some of his early novels such as *The Little Kingdom* (the first published) and *A Toy Epic* (the first written) expose the corruption to which natural leadership tends, and they do so in the context of Welsh Nationalism. The former is based on the notorious political burning of the Penyberth bombing-school in 1936, and the latter traces the adolescence of three school friends, whose lives reflect the divisions of society in North Wales: an upper-middle-class academic who becomes a Welsh Nationalist, a bus-driver's son who becomes a Marxist and a religious, Welsh-speaking farmer's son who is betrayed by the Welsh Nationalist. Though primarily a realistic novelist, Humphries does experiment with narrative modes: *A Toy Epic*, for instance, consists of interwoven streams of consciousness, a technique which suits his aim of relating the private worlds of his characters to their social lives. He has however said that 'in our time the novelist's attitude is more crucial than his manner of expression' (quoted in Stephens, 1986, p. 272).

Emyr Humphries is one of a number of writers who object to the term 'Anglo-Welsh' as misleading, in that it seems to imply writers of mixed blood. This is certainly a drawback of the expression, yet some term is needed to distinguish that body of literature which is written in English but belongs to the life of Wales. As we saw at the start, such literature has no clearly definable boundaries; the line drawn between who is and is not to be included is largely arbitrary and cannot but be so. Moreover, some authors who are undeniably Anglo-Welsh may not be centrally engaged with issues that are specifically Welsh. Dylan Thomas is a case in point. Nevertheless, in recent years there has been an increased handling of Welsh themes in Anglo-Welsh writing. So much so that the breach between Welsh and Anglo-Welsh literature, largely created by Caradoc Evans at the start of the century, and evident in the lecture by Saunders Lewis mentioned at the start of this unit, is showing signs, now when the century is drawing to its close, of being healed. For there is growing recognition of the common ground between the two literatures. Consideration of so few writers as here does not adequately reveal this trend, but it is apparent in the increasing use of the term 'literature of Wales', under which critics now link work in the two languages, and in the recent development in the University of Wales of teaching Welsh and Anglo-Welsh writing in the same course, as the literature of one people.

Critical works that consider the two literatures together include Johnston (1994) and Thomas (1992). Collections of critical essays, again on both literatures, may be found in Adams and Hughes (1971, 1983). Essays on Anglo-Welsh literature may also be found in Mathias (1985) and, more recently, in Humfrey (1995) and Brown (1995).

Other wide-ranging critical works include Garlick (1972) and Conran (1982), both of which concentrate on Anglo-Welsh poetry. Mathias (1987) examines the writers in the context of the history of Wales, and Jones (1968) combines biographical accounts of a number of authors personally known to him, with a critical appraisal of their work.

Most of the writers considered in this chapter have good introductory monographs written on them in the *Writers of Wales* series (Stephens and Jones, 1970–1). Other criticism on the main authors discussed includes Davies (1972), Anstey (1982) and Poole (1986).

Good works of reference that may be consulted in connection with Anglo-Welsh Literature include Stephens (1986) and Harris (1994).

## BIBLIOGRAPHY

Adams, S. and Hughes, G.R. (eds) (1971) *Triskel One*, Christopher Davies, Ammanford.
Adams, S. and Hughes, G.R. (eds) (1983) *Triskel Two*, Christopher Davies, Ammanford.
Anstey, S. (ed.) (1982) *Critical Writings on R.S. Thomas*, Poetry Wales Press, Bridgend.
Brown, T. (ed.) (1995) *Welsh Writing in English*, Gomer Press, Llandysul.
Churchyard, T. (1776) *The Worthiness of Wales*, Thomas Evans, London.
Conran, A. (1982) *The Cost of Strangeness*, Gomer Press, Llandysul.
Davies, W. (ed.) (1972) *Dylan Thomas: New Critical Essays*, University of Wales Press, Cardiff.
Dodd, A.H. (1977) *A Short History of Wales*, Batsford, London.
Evans, C. (1953) *My People*, Dobson, London.
Garlick, R. (1972) *An Introduction to Anglo-Welsh Literature*, University of Wales Press, Cardiff.
Garlick, R. and Mathias, R. (eds) (1993) *Anglo-Welsh Poetry 1480–1990*, Seren Books, Bridgend.
Harris, J. (ed.) (1994) *A Bibliographical Guide to Twenty-Four Modern Anglo-Welsh Writers*, University of Wales Press, Cardiff.
Humfrey, B. (ed.) (1995) *Fire Green as Grass*, Gomer Press, Llandysul.
Johnston, D. (1994) *The Literature of Wales*, University of Wales Press, Cardiff.
Jones, Glyn (1968) *The Dragon Has Two Tongues*, J.M. Dent, London.
Jones, G. (1957) *The First Forty Years*, University of Wales Press, Cardiff.
Lewis, S. (1939) *Is There an Anglo-Welsh Literature?* Urdd Graddedigion Prifysgol Cymru, Cardiff.
Mathias, R. (ed.) (1985) *A Ride through the Wood*, Poetry Wales Press, Bridgend.
Mathias, R. (1987) *Anglo-Welsh Literature: An Illustrated History*, Poetry Wales Press, Bridgend.
Poole, R. (1986) *Richard Hughes Novelist*, Poetry Wales Press, Bridgend.
Prichard, T.J. Ll. (1828) *The Adventures and Vagaries of Twm Shôn Catti*, John Cox, Aberystwyth.
Stephens, M. (1986) *The Oxford Companion to the Literature of Wales*, Oxford University Press, Oxford.
Stephens, M. and Jones, R.B. (eds) (1970–1) *Writers of Wales* series, University of Wales Press, Cardiff.
Thomas, D. (1952) *Collected Poems 1934–52*, J.M. Dent, London.
Thomas, M.W. (1992) *Internal Difference*, University of Wales Press, Cardiff.
Thomas, R.S. (1993) *Collected Poems 1945–1990*, J.M. Dent, London.
Treece, H. (1949) *Dylan Thomas*, Drummond, London.
Williams, J.E.C. (ed.) (1971) *Literature in Celtic Countries*, University of Wales Press, Cardiff.

# Scottish literature

*David Pattie*

The term Scots Literature is an all-embracing one, covering as it does three linked traditions: Scots authors writing in English; Scots authors writing in Scots; and Gaelic literature (which falls somewhat outside the scope of this study). This tripartite split needs to be established at the outset of any study of Scottish literature, no matter how long or short, and not only because, without it, an informed judgement of the work of any Scots writer is impossible. It is important, because the history of Scottish literature can be thought of as a history of the relationship between these three traditions: a centuries-long argument about what words that are usable, and in what circumstances.

However, these traditions cannot be thought of as existing simply in opposition to each other: honest Scots and its comrade, honest Gaelic, against duplicitous English; no matter how tempting the thought might be to the more committed nationalist, it is far too simple. Rather, the argument is about acceptability, about visibility; and the argument is as much internal as external. Over the past six centuries, Scots has been an accepted national language, a provincial tinge that the successful writer must expunge, a source of nationalistic pride, a language whose imminent death is prematurely mourned and whose urban degradation (as the purist would have it) is deplored. Given the complex history of Scots in its own country, the standard external response – that the language is a form of quaint, incomprehensible slang – is at least blessedly simple.

Scots as a language developed from the same Germanic root as English. It was carried into the country by raiders from the kingdom of Northumbria, where it was subjected over the centuries to influences which were unique to the region: the influence of Gaelic (although the extent of this influence is a matter of debate) and that of Old Norse. The relation of Scots to English by the fourteenth century (the time of Scots' first appearance as a literary language) was that of a not-too-distant cousin, and its status was confirmed by its use as the official language of the court, and of government generally.

The earliest extant examples of Scots literature are chronicles (John Barbour's *The Brus*, written in the late fourteenth century) and romances, such as the anonymous *The Buik of Alexander*, which dates from 1438. As one might expect from a nation that had only recently established its sovereignty, the chronicles of

Barbour, Andrew Wyntoun and Blind Hary are deeply patriotic; they elevate historical figures such as Bruce and Wallace if not to mythical, then certainly to heroic status. Yet the truly striking feature of poems like Barbour's *The Brus*, Wyntoun's *Original Chronicles* and Hary's *Wallace*, is the fineness and depth of detail they contain. The oppressive heat on the day of Bannockburn, Wallace's swim across the 'chelye water' of the Firth of Forth, the English army's indiscriminate slaying of the inhabitants of Berwick, are all rendered in vivid and economical detail. Of the three writers, Hary is perhaps the most effective; Barbour tends towards the prosaic, Wyntoun to the rhetorical, but Hary steers a middle course, presenting both a national epic and a character study of the grief-stricken Wallace. This double focus allows Hary to move from the monumental to the uniquely personal; when Hary describes Wallace's search for the body of his friend John the Grayme, the verses' power derives from the poet's awareness of both registers:

> Full wyll arrayit intill thar armour clen,
> Past to the field quhair that chas had ben,
> Amang the ded men sekand the worthiast...
>
> (*Wallace*, Book XI, 559–61)

The *Wallace* dates from 1478; as such, it properly belongs to one of the most discussed and analyzed period in Scots literature: the age of the Makars. In a country whose cultural history is as uneven as Scotland's, any achievement becomes the occasion for general, and frequently excessive, rejoicing; but the poetry of Robert Henryson, William Dunbar and Gavin Douglas (and of many other lesser poets of the time) can stand any amount of praise. The period lasted for roughly eighty years, from the writing of *The Kingis Quair* by James I sometime in the 1430s, to the publication of Douglas's translation of *The Aeneid* in 1513. To separate this period off is not to denigrate the work of later poets such as David Lindsay or Robert Montgomerie; however, the poets of the fifteenth century have become not only an important part of the canon, but also a touchstone for other writers in other ages. Hugh MacDiarmid's twentieth-century battle-cry 'Back to Dunbar' is a plea for a national literature, certainly, but also for a national literature based on a vigorous national language.

Of Henryson, Dunbar and Douglas, Henryson's (*c*.1420–*c*.1490) scope is the widest. The group are sometimes rather lazily described as 'Neo-Chaucerians'; Henryson comes closest to this description, indeed, his greatest poem, *The Testament of Cressid*, is both continuation and critique of the English poet's *Troilus and Cressida* (Chaucer is discussed in Unit 4, pp. 70–3). His range extended from the implicitly Christianized tragedy of *The Testament*, through the complex ethical folk tale *The Preiching of the Swallow*, to the broad comedy of *The Tod*, but present in all his work we find a profoundly religious world-view (that tends more towards the judgement of man by his actions – for Henryson, religion is not a matter of contemplation, but of active observance); a delight in description (he has a sharp eye for the grotesque – note the powerful description of Cressid's leprosy – and for the natural world); and, whether writing in a courtly or a low style, a simplicity of expression that is frequently very moving.

If Henryson is Chaucerian, the poet that William Dunbar (*c*.1460–*c*.1520) resembles most is John Donne. Like Donne, Dunbar is protean; it is hard to locate the poet with any certainty in his work. Like Donne also, Dunbar is a poet of manners. Henryson gives the impression that he is happiest in the natural world; Dunbar on the other hand looks to society, finding in it both material and an audience for his work. But what truly distinguishes Dunbar (and, one suspects, what made him so appealing to the linguistic crusader MacDiarmid) is the extreme care with which he crafts his poetry. The work can move from the colloquial to the rhetorical (Dunbar is especially adept at 'flyting' – an argument conducted poetically with another writer, where the case is settled as much by rhetorical skill as by logical force). He is also a master of 'aureate' verse, a style that employs internal rhyming and assonance to create poetry that almost seems to glitter, as in this extract from *The Golden Targe* (the 'Thy' in the first line is Chaucer):

> Thy fresch animalit termes celicall
> This matter could illuminate full brycht:
> > Was thou nocht of oure Inglisch all the lycht,
> > Surmounting every tong terrestrial
> Alls far as Mayes moorw does mydnicht?
>
> > (*The Golden Targe*, ll. 1257–61)

However, Dunbar is more than a craftsman: he is a humorist, a satirist (the best example of this being *The Treatise of the Twa Marrit Women and the Wedo*, a satire on marriage and a wife's proper place), with as keen a sense of the grotesque as Henryson. In what is perhaps his most famous poem, *The Lament for the Makaris*, his tone is sober, even morbid; the poem – a series of four-line stanzas, each ending with the Latin tag 'Timor mortis conturbat me' (The fear of death disturbs me) – lists those poets already dead, and invokes Dunbar's own end with an almost claustrophobic economy.

The last of the Makars, Gavin Douglas (*c*.1474–1522), is chiefly famous for his translation of *The Aeneid*. Some exorbitant claims have been made for it (that it is the finest medieval translation, that in places it transcends the original) but whatever the truth of these claims, the translation is undeniably excellent; and it gains much of its power from the relative harshness of the Scots language. This is not the tidy, neo-classical epic that Dryden envisages, but something simultaneously more earthy and more direct. The books (thirteen in Douglas's translation) are each introduced by a prologue, in which Douglas variously expiates upon the difficulty of translation, takes exception to the work of other translators, or indulges his gift for nature poetry: like Henryson, Douglas's genius is most apparent when he writes about the natural world.

I have spent time on the Makars, not only because they provide ample evidence of the versatility of Scots (indeed, it is in Douglas's prologues that the word 'Scottis' is first used to describe the language), but also because, in their work, we find some of the themes and preoccupations that will recur in the work of other, later writers: first, a delight in the grotesque and in the horribly comic; secondly, a world-view that blends the fantastic and the realistic; and thirdly, an awareness of the world's harshness, and of the individual human's frailty.

After such achievement, any succeeding period might seem a disappointment; and the next century, moving as it did from the humane confidence of the Makars' time to the harsh certainties of the Reformation, seems relatively fallow by comparison. However, this is not to say that it was devoid of merit. The sixteenth century is marked by the poetry of Sir David Lindsay (*c.*1490–1555); the first appearance of a distinctively Scottish voice in prose, in the histories of John Major, John Bellendon and Robert Lindsay, and in the pamphleteering of John Knox; and the last flowering of Scots poetry until the Romantic period. David Lindsay's central contribution to Scots literature is the play *Ane Pleasant Satire of the Thrie Estatis*, a combination of morality play and satire (ironically, given the forthcoming rise of Calvinism, the satire on the church is particularly strong). The play's message – that all men, king included, are equal before God, and that a king is the servant, not the master, of his people – is one that has proved particularly conducive to twentieth-century Scotland, and revivals of Lindsay's play are relatively frequent. Near the century's end, the poetry of Robert Montgomerie (the greatest of the 'Castelian band' of poets at the court of James VI) harks back to the work of the Makars; his poetry is rather more Anglicized, but in form and style he consciously echoes his predecessors.

The union of the crowns in 1606 was a setback for the Scots literary tradition, a setback compounded by a prolonged period of civil unrest. The Covenanters' attempts to resist the reimposition of Episcopacy on a country made Presbyterian by the Reformation divided Scotland from England, and the largely Protestant Scots from the Catholic Gaels. These divisions were not resolved until the aftermath of the 1745 rebellion, when the outward manifestations of Gaeldom were brutally suppressed. The century produced no one to match Dunbar or Lindsay, although the poetry of William Drummond repays attention. The period's prose is likewise undistinguished, with one remarkable exception: Thomas Urquhart (1611–60) is perhaps the most bizarre figure in Scots letters; a soldier, a polymath and a writer whose prose style is both esoteric and occasionally obscure. He is chiefly remembered for his translation of the first two books of Rabelais; his version runs to almost twice the length of the original, but he manages to convey the sense of the original with a manic energy all his own.

Barren as the seventeenth century was, it did provide two indications of future development. First, the Presbyterian stress on literacy and education helped pave the way for the Scottish Enlightenment of the next century. Secondly, Scots began its long decline from a national to a vernacular language, a decline that gathered pace as the century progressed. Increasingly, Scots was considered as the language of the uncultured rural poor; deprived of national status, the language began to split into dialects. This process had an ambiguous effect on the language. On the one hand, Scots was devalued as a language; on the other, it became the repository of the nation's soul, the true voice of the people – and anyone writing in dialect had an automatic claim to authenticity.

Finally, the seventeenth century was the first in which determined efforts were made to transcribe the traditional literature of the country. The Scots ballad had been an important influence on writers from Barbour onward. The ballads take place in a world in which there is no clear division between the lyrical and the violent, the real and the unreal; it is not too fanciful to attribute the Scots writers' continuing fascination with the violent, the grotesque and the uncanny to this highly visible tradition.

The Union of Parliaments in 1707 coincided with a period of extreme Calvinism in the Lowlands, and renewed rebellion in the Highlands; not surprisingly, therefore, the period's literature is not particularly remarkable. Poetry tended towards the rural and the sentimental; only Alan Ramsay (1684–1758) in Scots and James Thomson (1700–48) in English produced work that is memorable, and even then the best in their work sits cheek by jowl with the worst. Ramsay's work can veer from liveliness to rural cliché, and Thomson's from sonorousness to sententiousness.

The second half of the century proved to be very different. The Scottish Enlightenment (as it came to be called) was a period of remarkable flowering in a variety of areas: in philosophy, David Hume (1711–76); in sociology, Adam Fergusson (1723–1816); in economics, Adam Smith (1723–90); and in law, John Millar (1735–1801). Literature similarly underwent a revival: the Ossian poems of James Macpherson (1736–96) (not remarkable in themselves, but remarkable in the impact they had on the developing Romantic movement); the novels of Tobias Smollett (1721–71), an émigré Scot whose violent picaresques have something of the grotesquerie that always seems to fascinate Scots authors; Boswell's journals, and his biography of Johnson. Perhaps the most vigorous writer of the period, Robert Fergusson (1750–74), died at the age of 24; he left behind some memorable poems in a demotic urban Scots that proved very popular, at a time when other Scots authors were careful to expunge any vestiges of Scots from their work. Fergusson proved to be an important influence on his immediate successor, Robert Burns (1759–96), who called Fergusson 'my elder brother in the muse'.

It is hard, in writing about Burns, to separate the poet from the cultural icon; Burns the institution – the national bard, the rustic minstrel – is so deeply embedded in the Scottish psyche that not even MacDiarmid at his most vehement can shift it (although, in the early stanzas of *A Drunk Man Looks at the Thistle*, MacDiarmid tries his hardest). It is true that Burns was a shepherd, that he worked on a farm for most of his relatively short life; but he was well-read, familiar not only with Shakespeare, Milton, Dryden and Pope but also with the work of the Makars and the writing of his near contemporaries Ramsay, Thomson, Hume, Fergusson and Macpherson. He forged an expressive language from the local dialects of Lowland Scots (he called this hybrid language Lallans), but it is also true that he could change register, writing in English if the poems moved to more elevated subjects. Burns's poetry is considerably more varied, and considerably more interesting, than the rather narrow pastoral-poet image that we tend to assign to him would suggest. The poetry ranges widely: the tenderness of the ballads and of the love-poetry; the vigorous, bawdy comedy of *The Jolly Beggars*; the satire of *Holy Willie's Prayer*, still the best attack on hypocritical religion in Scots literature; and *Tam O'Shanter*, which mixes all of the above. *Tam* is Burns's masterpiece, a comic tour-de-force that blends, once again, the everyday and the supernatural, and that does so with a technical versatility worthy of Dunbar.

Sir Walter Scott was born twelve years after Burns, in 1771, and the two writers met at Adam Fergusson's house in Edinburgh in the late 1780s. For the first part of his career, Scott seemed to be the next in a long, if occasionally broken, line of Scots poets stretching back to the chroniclers of the fourteenth century, and, like Burns, he played his part in renovating that tradition – his first publication was as the editor of a three-volume edition of Scottish Border ballads (1802–3). He followed this with a series of verse romances: *The Lay of the Last Minstrel*, *Marmaion*, *The Lady of the Lake*, among others. But whereas Burns wrote in Scots about a society that was alive, Scott wrote in English about societies that were romantically distanced, in either time or space. Scott was a Tory Nationalist; when he wrote about Scotland, he wrote about the country's romantic past, because the future of the country lay firmly with the Union. One might leave the past behind with regret, but one must leave it behind.

When Scott, realizing that the vogue for epic romances was fading, turned to writing novels in 1814, he carried with him this romantically distanced view of the country's past. Scott's novels are generally set in times of strife (*Waverley* is set at the time of the 1745 rebellion, *The Heart of Midlothian* at the time of the Porteous riots in Edinburgh in 1736), but the conflict is always one that has been safely resolved; the political events of the time are transformed into the last verses of an old song that is now over. However, this does not detract from Scott's power as a novelist; although his plots are sometimes weak, and their central characters tend to be colourless, he has a good eye for landscape, and the ability to create profoundly memorable characters such as Bailie Nicol Jarvie, Edie Ochiltree, Mausie Headrigg, Dalgetty, Madge Wildfire. As Scott himself conceded, when his imagination provided him with such a character, his writing caught fire.

Scott is a pivotal figure in a number of ways. In a wider European context he helped to spur on the fledgling Romantic movement; at home, he established the novel as the dominant form in Scots literature. His influence in his native country extended beyond his own writing; he helped to found the *Edinburgh Review*, which, along with *Blackwood's* literary magazine, provided an outlet for the work of his contemporaries.

Of these contemporaries, two are particularly notable. John Galt (1779–1839) produced a number of novels in the 1820s in which he explored the contemporary Scottish scene with a mixture of detached irony and rather sour realism. His best novel, *The Entail* (1823), is concerned with the corrupting power of money: its hero, Claud Walkinshaw, is slowly transformed as he grows older and more successful, and the book charts not only his corruption but that of his family, as they squabble over his money after his death. James Hogg (1770–1835), like Scott, is both poet and novelist; like Burns, his image is of a rustic poet – although in this case, the image of Hogg the 'Ettrick Sheperd' is largely self-created. However, with one exception, his writing is not as memorable as Scott's, Burns's, or Galt's. The exception is a novel: *The Private Memoires and Confessions of a Justified Sinner* (1824); and it is a novel of such quality that, if Hogg had written nothing else, this work would be enough to secure his reputation. The book concerns an extreme Calvinist, Robert Wringham, who kills his half brother, apparently for gain. This story is told to us by an unnamed narrator, who treats the story as a strange but comprehensible tale of jealousy and murder. The main section of the book is given over to Robert's own 'Confession'; Robert retells the story, but in doing so, he gives it a darker and altogether more disturbing twist. Apparently, Robert committed murder at the behest of a friend, Gil-Martin, whom Robert first believes to be the holiest of men. During the course of his confession, both we and Robert become increasingly aware that Gil-Martin may be the Devil; but, unlike Robert, there is for the reader the unspoken idea that Gil-Martin may not exist – that Robert may be imagining him. This question is never resolved, giving the novel an air of tension and uncertainty, and allowing Hogg to place the fantastic and the hallucinatory in the most mundane settings. Hogg's contribution to the Gothic and the Romantic movement is dealt with in Unit 10, pp. 237–8.

After the deaths of Scott, Galt and Hogg, Scottish literature went into another period of decline. Victorian England was the hub of empire; London and the south exerted a powerful pull, both economically and culturally. This state of affairs only exacerbated the splits in Scotland's cultural identity. In the nineteenth century Scotland was North Britain, and Glasgow the second city of the empire; historical Scotland was turned into a romantic theme park for the English aristocracy, who, from Victoria down, eagerly swathed themselves in tartan. Such contemporary literature as there was was marginalized, and the age's best novelist, Robert Louis Stevenson (1850–94), set his work either in the past or abroad.

Stevenson is best remembered as the author of those quintessential 'boys' own' romances, *Treasure Island* and *Kidnapped*; but, even in these relatively simple stories, Stevenson explores the central theme of his work – that of duality. Since Hogg, Scottish fiction has continually returned to the idea of the divided self, generally expressed as a split between two characters: one respectable, the other in some way outside society. Stevenson's adventure stories follow this pattern: Jim Hawkins is paired with Long John Silver, David with Alan Breck, and the novels describe the way in which these characters achieve a precarious balance, so that Jim can watch Silver escape with a mingled hatred and regret, and David take leave of Alan with the lingering feeling that something is wrong. In other works, this doubling takes on a darker tinge. In *The Master of Ballantrae*, the Durie brothers are locked into the same kind of destructive struggle as the brothers in *Justified Sinner*, and, as in Hogg's novel, it is the supposedly righteous brother who is ultimately responsible for both their deaths. The archetypal expression of this theme is, of course, the novella *The Strange Case of Dr Jekyll and Mr Hyde*.

Stevenson's early death served only to expose the relative weakness of Scots writing at the time. Of his contemporaries, Margaret Oliphant's society novels and George Macdonald's fantasies have only recently received the critical attention they deserve; and in poetry only John Davidson at the end of the century made any impact outside Scotland (T.S. Eliot was an admirer of Davidson's and Davidson is considered in Unit 12, p. 330).

If the state of Scottish writing at the end of the nineteenth century had been more secure, then the impact of the 'Kailyard School' of novelists (J.M. Barrie, S.R. Crockett, Iain McLaren et al.) might not have been so great. Kail is a Scottish word for cabbage; and the Kailyard writers wrote of a rural Scotland populated entirely by a variety of cabbage, firmly rooted in the soil, with little or no interest in the world on the other side of the garden wall. The books' titles give a reasonable idea of their content (*Beside the Bonnie Briar Bush* (1894), *The Days of Auld Lang Syne* (1895)); they describe a world in which pawky locals dispense couthy wisdom in a more or less quaint dialect under the benign eye of a narrator who has acquired sufficient distance to be patronizing about his home town. Rather improbably, the Kailyard School has been subject to some revaluation over the past few years, and it is true that Barrie's early work is rather more realistic than the general standard; but most Kailyard writing is so nauseatingly sentimental as to defy any critical elevation.

The Kailyard was very popular; but its popularity in Scotland was very swiftly challenged, and it was with this challenge that modern Scottish literature can be said to begin. George Douglas Brown's *The House with the Green Shutters* (1901) was written first of all as a counterblast to the Kailyard. Where the Kailyarders' communities were close-knit and cosy, Brown's Barbie is a town riven by greed and envy; the Kailyard Scot is a purveyor of oddly expressed wisdom; Brown's townsfolk are either stupid, malicious, or both. But the novel is more than an overreaction to an irritating literary trend; Brown paints a blackly memorable portrait of a society which stifles and destroys any warmth or spontaneity, a society filled with bad fathers and damaged children. *The House* spawned one near-rewrite (J. Macdougall Hay's *Gillespie* (1914), and an echo of the novel's central character, the tyrannical John Gourlay, can also be found in Gibbon's *Sunset Song* in the figure of Chris Guthrie's father. A character in Gibbon's novel catches the tension between Brown and the Kailyard, describing the Scottish countryside as 'got between a Kailyard and a bonnie briar bush, in the lee of a house with green shutters'.

The novelists around Brown – Neil Munro (1864–1930), John Buchan (1875–1940), R.B. Cunninghame Grahame (1852–1936), Norman Douglas (1868–1952) – at least began the long task of uprooting Scots writing from the Kailyard. But the writer whose work did most to lead Scots literature into a period of renaissance was not a novelist, but a poet: Christopher Murray Grieve (1892–1978), who wrote under the pseudonym Hugh MacDiarmid.

MacDiarmid stands in relation to his time much as Burns did to his; both lived much of their lives in a state of magnificent neglect; both were feted, and both were frequently poor. Burns, though, was an example that MacDiarmid wished to bypass. As already noted, he wished to revive an older tradition, and initially, he sought to do this by reinstating Scots as a poetic language, rather than as a dialect fit only for light verse. To achieve this MacDiarmid crafted a form of Scots (which he termed synthetic Scots) from various dialects and from the language's history, and used this new version of Scots in poems that combine the economy of the ballad with the widest possible shifts in scale and register, as in the early lyric *Empty Vessels*:

> I met, ayont the cairney,
> A lass wi' towsie hair,
> Cryin til a bairnie
> That was nae longer there.

Winds wi' warlds tae swing,
Dinnae sing sae sweet;
The licht that bends o'er athings
Is less ta'en up wi' it.
(*Collected Poems of Hugh MacDiarmid*, 1967, p. 50)

In eight lines MacDiarmid moves from the local to the cosmic; the smallest human action is fitted into the widest possible perspective, without losing any of its emotional power. MacDiarmid's greatest work, *A Drunk Man Looks at the Thistle* (1926), depends for its impact on precisely this movement, from the particular to the universal. The poem is simultaneously a dramatic monologue and a meditation on Scotland's place in the world, held together by MacDiarmid's fluent and earthy Scots (for example, at one point God is imagined 'passing wi' a Bobby's feet/ ootby in the lang coffin o' the street', *A Drunk Man Looks at the Thistle*, lines 12059–60). In later years MacDiarmid abandoned synthetic Scots for an English that could be as formal and as initially obscure. His best poem in English, *On A Raised Beach*, begins with an impenetrable recitation of geological terms; however, MacDiarmid arranges the terms for sound rather than for sense, creating the first aureate poem in Scottish literature since the Makars, and evoking a sense of a simplified, austerely beautiful world.

MacDiarmid initiated a period known as the Scottish Renaissance; his achievement in poetry was matched in prose by two authors, Neil M. Gunn (1891–1943) and James Leslie Mitchell, who also wrote under the pseudonym Lewis Grassic Gibbon (1901–35). Gunn's novels are mainly concerned with the Highlands where he was born and bred; he elevated the landscape and seascape that he knew to an archetypal environment in which the individual is tested and perhaps redeemed. What saves his work from drifting off into the mystic stratosphere is the ability to describe both character and landscape with a pin-sharp accuracy, so that, as with his friend MacDiarmid, the cosmic is tied closely to the particular. Lewis Grassic Gibbon's trilogy *A Scots Quair* (*Sunset Song*, *Cloud Howe*, *Grey Granite*) describes the long abandonment of the land by the rural population, and the people's slow dispersal to town and city. The trilogy is linked by the figure of Chris Guthrie: Gibbon uses her not only as the trilogy's governing intelligence, but also as a symbol for Scotland. The trilogy is written in a hybrid language, English for the most part, but English with the rhythm and flow of Scots; particularly in the first novel, Gibbon is able to use this hybrid form to create prose of extraordinary poetic richness. Gibbon is considered in the broader context of the modern novel in Unit 16, pp. 461–3.

MacDiarmid and his friends did not carry all before them; there was at least one powerful dissenting voice among the new chorus of Scottish writers – that of Edwin Muir (1887–1959). Muir's fame as a poet largely rests on the volumes he published immediately after the Second World War; but he had already established himself as a poet, translator and critic in the 1920s and 1930s. Controversially, he argued that Scots writers should abandon Scots, and write in English; this was because the Scots did not have a common language in which to express themselves. As can be imagined, this argument did not endear Muir to MacDiarmid (even though

MacDiarmid himself was moving from Scots to English at the time). Muir the poet was engaged in a search for what he called the 'fable': the underlying archetypal pattern underneath the stories people tell themselves and each other, a concern that links his work to that of Gunn and Gibbon.

As Scottish literature moves into the twenty-first century, it is in better shape than it has been for most of the last 250 years. Scotland itself – which offers the experience of living in a country split linguistically, both internally and also to an extent from its larger neighbour – is proving as fruitful a source of inspiration for Scots writers as it has ever been. The impetus given to the literature by MacDiarmid and the other figures of the Scottish renaissance has not faltered; this rebirth coincided with the first stirrings of a resurgent nationalism, and has largely benefited from the increased level of debate over Scotland's contradictory identity. Notable writers have included the poets William Soutar, Iain Crichton Smith, George Mackay Brown (also an accomplished novelist and writer of short fiction), Tom Leonard, Douglas Dunn and, more recently, Liz Lochhead and Jackie Kay; the novelists Robin Jenkins, James Kennaway, George Friel, Alan Spence, William Macilvanney, Iain Banks, Janice Galloway, Agnes Owens, Jeff Torrington and Irvine Walsh; and, for the first time in Scottish literature, a relatively healthy dramatic scene, beginning with James Bridie during the renaissance, and continuing in the work of Joe Corrie, Ena Lamont Stewart, Hector Macmillain, Tom McGrath, Liz Lochhead (whose *Mary Queen of Scots Got Her Head Chopped Off* has some claim to be the best Scots play of recent years), C.P. Taylor, Peter Arnott and Chris Hannan.

The work of four contemporary writers can serve to illustrate the strength of current Scots writing. Norman MacCaig's poetry blends complex speculation with a dry, mordant and humane wit; he is particularly good at capturing the natural world in perfect, precise images (a preening swan making 'a small/ swan-storm of itself', for example). Edwin Morgan's scope as a poet is aptly summed up in the title of one of his collections: *From Glasgow to Saturn*. Morgan seems able to tackle any style and any subject, from the determinedly Glaswegian ('King Billy's Funeral') to the abstract world of the concrete poem. James Kelman is frequently likened to Kafka and Beckett, but to some extent these comparisons are misleading; the writer he most resembles is Chekhov – both writers find tragedy and humour in the smallest details of their characters' lives. Kelman's characters are almost exclusively drawn from the west of Scotland working class; his prose echoes the rhythms and diction of this class – proving along the way that working-class speech, and by extension, working-class experience, is worthy of representation. Finally, Alistair Gray's work is in the old Scots tradition of the bizarre; in *Lanark* (1981), a realistic tale of an artist's early life and suicide is placed in the middle of an account of the same character's adventures after death, in an hallucinatory Glasgow, apparently designed by Bosch. *Poor Things* retells the Frankenstein story, set in nineteenth-century Glasgow; the created being is female, and the book follows her rapid education in the harsh realities of a Victorian woman's life. *Something Leather* reverses an irksome stereotype; for once, Scottish speech is spelt conventionally, while the characters who speak 'normally' in Standard English have their speech rendered phonetically.

Book-length studies of Scottish literature are still relatively rare; what follows is a selective sample from a comparatively short list. Maurice Lindsay's *History of Scottish Literature* (1977) is a comprehensive and engaged story. Roderick Watson's *The Literature of Scotland* (1984) is shorter, but no less comprehensive; it also contains a good deal of information on Gaelic literature. For an analysis of the place of Scots literature in Scottish life, David Craig's *Scottish Literature and the Scottish People* (1961) still has not been bettered. The best study of Scottish literature overall is probably the four-volume *History of Scottish Literature* (1987–8), published by Aberdeen University Press; each volume contains a selection of well-written, informative essays on authors and movements, as well as information on the culture and history of the period each volume covers.

*BIBLIOGRAPHY*

Craig, D. (1961) *Scottish Literature and the Scottish People*, Chatto & Windus, London.
*History of Scottish Literature* (1987–8), Aberdeen University Press, Aberdeen.
Lindsay, M. (1977) *History of Scottish Literature*, Robert Hale, London.
MacDiarmid, H. (1967) *Collected Poems of Hugh MacDiarmid*, Macmillan, London.
Watson, R. (1984) *The Literature of Scotland*, Macmillan, London.

# UNIT 28

# India – Africa – the Caribbean: a perspective

*Shirley Chew*

In the waiting-room of the offices of the Belgian company which was sending him to the Congo, Marlow noticed 'a large shining map, marked with all the colours of a rainbow'. What he liked best about it was the 'vast amount of red' it included, evidence of the strength and soundness of the British Empire (Conrad, [1899] 1959, p. 76). Marlow's pride was a sign of the times, given that in February–June 1899, when *Heart of Darkness* was being serialized, Britain's possessions overseas amounted to a quarter of the globe and many of these were recent acquisitions made in the face of keen competition from other European nations. Yet only a few months later, with the declaration of the second Boer War on 12 October 1899, the seamy side of the empire was to be seriously exposed and its authority shaken in the first of a long series of anti-imperialist struggles that led to decolonization.

Various reasons have been put forward to account for the empire. From the British themselves, they include: 'a fit of absence of mind' (Morris, 1979, p. 37), the progress of Victorian science and technology, the march of Western civilization. But, among less Anglocentric points of view, there are: raw instincts for profit, the kind which drove men like John Hawkins to West Africa in the sixteenth century for pepper, ivory, gold and, most lucrative of all, slaves for the Caribbean plantations; the complexity of local circumstances, such as those the East India Company met with in the middle of the eighteenth century when 'the British trading concern was caught in the chain-drive of Indian power politics' (Chaudhuri, 1975, p. 14); European rivalry and wars which called for new lines of defence and territory, an example of which is the intensive scramble for a share of Eastern Africa in the decade following the Berlin Conference of 1884.

As well as physical force and direct control, 'persuasive means' (Said, 1994, p. 131) were used to maintain Britain's extensive commercial and territorial interests. The most significant of these was the establishment of schools with English as the language of instruction and a curriculum with a distinct European bias. Arguably the beginning moment of colonial education is Thomas Macaulay's 'Minute on Education', delivered in his capacity as legal member of the Supreme Council of India in 1835. In the early decades of the nineteenth century, there was lively debate on the issue of education in India. Prominent Indians like Rammohun Roy argued for Western knowledge, particularly scientific knowledge, to be taught along with their own languages and sciences. Among the British in India, opinion was split between the 'Orientalists', who wished to see Sanskrit and Arabic taught along with English in institutions of higher learning, and the 'Anglicists', who believed that the teaching of English should be the government's principal concern. Macaulay's Minute with its curious blend of high-mindedness and insensibility tipped the balance in favour of the 'Anglicists':

> I have no knowledge of either Sanskrit or Arabic. But I have done what I could to form a correct estimate of their value. I have read translations of the most celebrated Arabic and Sanskrit works. I have conversed both here and at home with men distinguished by their proficiency in the Eastern tongues. I am quite ready to take the Oriental learning at the valuation of the Orientalists themselves. I have never found one among them who could deny that a single shelf of a good European library was worth the whole native literature of India and Arabia. (Macaulay, 1972, p. 241)

Macaulay's policies were adopted in principle by the governor-general, Lord Bentinck. English education made headway while financial support was withdrawn from colleges of Sanskrit and Arabic. In appointments to all public services, preference was given to candidates trained in English.

As the empire expanded so English education became widespread:

> The great colonial schools ... taught generations of the native bourgeoisie important truths about history, science, culture. Out of that learning process millions grasped the fundamentals of modern life, yet remained subordinate dependents of an authority based elsewhere than in their lives (Said, 1994, pp. 269–70)

As might be expected, many Commonwealth writers, even though they publish in English, look back upon their colonial education with mixed feelings. In the first example below, the light-hearted tone of the Indian novelist, R.K. Narayan, belies the seriousness of the point he is making:

> from the Sanskrit alphabet we passed on directly to the first lesson in the glossy primer which began with 'A was an Apple Pie'.... and went on to explain 'B bit it' and 'C cut it'. The activities of B and C were understandable, but the opening line itself was mystifying. What was an Apple Pie? (Narayan, 1965, p. 120)

A more direct attack upon the system occurs in *Decolonising the Mind*, a series of essays by Ngugi wa Thiong'o. Drawing upon the experiences of his early years in Kenya, this committed Marxist writer argues that the dominance of English instruction weakens the ties between the environments of home and school for the African child and is largely responsible for the deracination of the English-educated African (Ngugi, 1986, pp. 16–17). Lastly, there is the bleak observation of V.S. Naipaul, the Trinidad-born writer: 'One of the terrible things about being a colonial is that you must accept so many things as coming from a great wonderful source outside yourself and outside the people you know, outside the society you've grown up in' (Rowe-Evans, 1970, pp. 57–8).

Trapped in their persistent mimicry of the metropolis, the outlook for the erstwhile colonial and colonial societies would seem to be hopeless. Yet to turn to the literature from Commonwealth countries – indeed the works of Narayan, Ngugi and Naipaul themselves – is to be struck by its creative energy and variety. One explanation for the paradox lies in the ambivalent nature of colonialist authority, an exposition of which is given in Homi Bhabha's essay, 'Of Mimicry and Man' (1984). Another, according to Derek Walcott, the St Lucian poet and dramatist, is the vitality of indigenous cultures and the human imagination (Walcott, 1993, pp. 51–7).

From his reading of colonialist texts, such as Macaulay's 'Minute on Education', Bhabha notes the presence therein of two conflicting discourses, the one of power and the other of liberal ideas of government inherited from the Enlightenment. In Macaulay's case, a lofty belief in the superiority of English education is continually tripped by pragmatic considerations, and the resulting manoeuvre is an act of appropriation (Indians are like us) that is at one and the same time a disavowal (are not like us).

> It is impossible for us, with our limited means, to attempt to educate the body of the people. We must at present do our best to form a class who may be interpreters between us and the millions whom we govern; a class of persons, Indian in blood and colour, but English in taste, in opinions, in morals, and in intellect. (Macaulay, 1972, p. 249)

According to Frantz Fanon, 'the real Other for the white man is and will continue to be the black man. And conversely' (Fanon, 1986, p. 161). In Bhabha's view, however, colonial mimicry is the desire for something more domesticated and less threatening, 'a reformed, recognisable Other, *as a subject of a difference that is almost the same, but not quite*' (Bhabha, 1994, p. 86). Ironically it is this split presence of 'post-Enlightenment man tethered to, not confronted by, his dark reflection, the shadow of colonised man' (Bhabha, 1994, p. 44), which makes realizable an 'in-between' space for subversion, interplay and reinvention on the part of the colonial subject.

Walcott's argument in his essay 'The Caribbean: Culture or Mimicry' (1974) is relevant here. Mimicry, he declares, is integral to the process of making new and nowhere is this more evident than among societies under colonial rule. One of his examples is the mass art form of Carnival with its music, song, popular poetry, costume, which 'emerged from the sanctions imposed on it' (Walcott, 1993, p. 54). Thus 'the banning of African drumming led to the discovery of the garbage can cover as a potential musical instrument' (p. 55) and hence to steelband music, while 'ancient ritual forms in group chanting' lie close to the heart of the calypso. 'From the viewpoint of history, these forms originated in imitation ... and ended in invention' (p. 55). The force of that statement holds good for literature from Commonwealth countries as well as Carnival, and points to a definition of the term 'postcolonial', that is, forms of representation which engage with a world and cultural identity fractured by colonialism, and which are motivated by the impulse or commitment to make them new. It is in this sense that the term is used in the rest of this unit.

In 1947, Pakistan and India became independent and separate countries, and after that date the dismantling of the empire gained momentum, some other dates of independence being Sri Lanka 1948, Ghana 1957, Nigeria 1960, Trinidad 1962. Notwithstanding its problematic role as the language of imperialism, English has remained an official language as well as a language of everyday exchange in Commonwealth countries and, in the process of its relocation, has undergone various changes. Needless to say, the most complex and subtle transformations of the language are to be found within the context of postcolonial literatures, owing to the critical revisioning of its myths and metaphors of race and power, and its reinvention as a vehicle of indigenous ways of seeing and speaking.

The several responses below highlight the differences within a shared history of colonialism which are sometimes concealed behind such broad labels as 'Empire', 'Commonwealth', 'postcolonial literatures', 'new writings in English'. Ngugi's protest against the continual erosion of indigenous languages in post-independence African societies has been noted above. Acting upon his convictions, he has, since *Petals of Blood* (1977), turned away from English as a literary medium and chosen to write his novels and plays in Gikuyu, his mother tongue. Against this, Kamala Das's heartfelt cry in the passage below springs from equally strong convictions: that the language she writes in is intimately linked to her intellectual and emotional make-up, that history has made it impossible for her to deny the part English has played in the construction of her identity, that the struggle to be free goes on in post-independence India and, in her position as a woman and a postcolonial, this means a fight on several fronts.

> ... I am Indian, very brown, born in
> Malabar, I speak three languages, write in
> Two, dream in one. Don't write in English, they said,
> English is not your mother-tongue. Why not leave
> Me alone, critics, friends, visiting cousins,
> Every one of you? Why not let me speak in
> Any language I like? The language I speak
> Becomes mine, its distortions, its queernesses
> All mine, mine alone. It is half English, half
> Indian, funny perhaps, but it is honest,
> It is human as I am human, don't
> You see?

(Das, 1989, p. 76)

From Walcott's point of view, the English language is inseparable from the tensions and dilemmas of the bitter history of the Caribbean. In 'Ruins of a Great House' (Walcott, 1962, pp. 19–20), they are projected in the opposite yet connected images of the decayed colonial estate and the body of the slave 'rotting in this manorial lake'. They are moreover an integral part of the poet's identity. Born in St Lucia of mixed ancestry, Walcott is heir to the eloquence and richness of the English literary tradition – in the poem, the roll call of writers is long and sonorous – and also to the voicelessness of the dispossessed slave – one of the countless and anonymous dead. As Walcott re-examines his double inheritance in the poem so the English language and literary tradition are made the means by which a broken history is remembered.

Invoked from within the Caribbean landscape, the names of Hawkins, Raleigh, Drake tell not of the glories of empire but of its baseness; the great house of pastoral recalls, not a wholesome and civilized tradition, but sullying greed and self-destructive energies. At the same time the imprecisely named 'Some dead animal or human thing' has to be seen for what it is; and the 'some slave' must be unequivocally acknowledged by the poet. As the verse beats unevenly back and forth, and the words double back upon themselves, so murderers and poets, ancestors and the murderers of his ancestors – the figures which make up his contradictory history and identity – are painfully embraced.

In another poem, 'A Far Cry From Africa', Walcott asks: 'how choose / Between this Africa and the English tongue I love?' (Walcott, 1962, p. 18). In the view of the Barbadian poet, Edward Brathwaite, if he is to remake in the fullest way the history of the Caribbean, then the question of choice does not arise. It is to Africa that he must turn for metaphors and traditions other than the European. The quest themes of Brathwaite's poetry in *Rights of Passage* (1967), *Masks* (1968), *Islands* (1969) – reprinted as *The Arrivants: A New World Trilogy* (1973) – reinforce a sense of cultural and historical continuities as the trilogy moves successively from the Caribbean to North America, to West Africa or more precisely Ghana, and back to the Caribbean. They enact at the same time the healing and growth of the creative imagination, both the Caribbean poet's and his people's as it is manifested in their local speech, songs, dances, and religious rituals, the notes and rhythms of which are intrinsic to the texture of the poetry. The following extract taken from *Masks* is characteristic of Brathwaite's work in its complex drawing together of diverse preoccupations and forms: ritual prayer and practical details of farming, the open celebration of yam and cassava and a grim reminder of the sugar-cane in the skinny typographical image, the beat of Afro-Caribbean music and the pattern of the scripted line, the Akan sounds of welcome which greet the poet returning to West African roots and quickening memories of a brutal tearing apart.

> Asase Yaa,
> You, Mother of Earth,
> on whose soil
> I have placed my tools
> on whose soil
> I will hoe
> I will work
> the year has come round
> again . . .
> . . . . . .
>
> And may the year
> this year of all years
> be fruitful
> beyond the fruit of your labour:
> shoots faithful to tip
> juice to stem
> leaves to green;

and may the knife
or the cut-
lass not cut

me; roots blunt,
shoots break,
green wither,

winds shatter,
damp rot,
hot harm –

attan come
drifting in harm
to the crops;

the tunnelling
termites not
raise their red

monuments, graves,
above the blades
of our labour.

(Brathwaite, 1968, pp. 4–6)

Among the writers who started to publish in the middle decades of this century, many were committed to the nationalist struggle for self-determination and saw their task in terms of re-educating their own people. Examples are Mulk Raj Anand, Indian novelist and short-story writer, George Lamming, Barbadian novelist, and Wole Soyinka, Nigerian playwright, poet and autobiographer. In a well-known essay, 'The Novelist as Teacher' (1981), the Nigerian novelist and short-story writer, Chinua Achebe, states clearly the object of his work. It is to instruct his readers 'that their past – with all its imperfections – was not one long night of savagery from which the first Europeans acting on God's behalf delivered them' (Achebe, [1975] 1981, p. 45). Hence African subjects and themes are reclaimed for literature and, while the English language is deemed fit 'to carry the weight' of its African material, 'it will be a new English ... altered to suit its new African surroundings' (p. 62).

*Things Fall Apart* (1958), Achebe's first novel, recounts the life and destruction of an Igbo community in the period of the first Igbo contact with white missionaries and government officials, and in the course of the narration, enacts a process by which this new English is made. From the point of view of the district commissioner who witnesses the suicide of Okonkwo, Umuofian warrior and self-made man, the disastrous events which have overtaken the village are of little account against the history he will write: 'He had already chosen the title of the book, after much thought: *The Pacification of the Primitive Tribes of the Lower Niger*' (Achebe, 1971, p. 187). But unlike the commissioner, Achebe's readers have been made to see a whole world from the inside, and hence the ways in which Okonkwo's tragedy and that of his community are interconnected. Igbo society before the intrusion of the British is highly organized and rests solidly upon a store of tried wisdom, ceremonious exchange and sanctioned conduct. Igbo words, proverbs and tales colour and structure the narrative, giving a firm sense of a distinctive culture. But Umuofia is also a society with serious inadequacies and its collapse is due as much to inherent defects as to external pressure. As critics like David Wright have pointed out, a high value is placed upon 'communal solidarities' and, built into its traditional wisdom, is 'a narrow conservatism' which resists change (Wright, 1990, p. 77). For example, while many of the Umuofians are conscious of the suffering among its *osu* or social outcasts – twins, albinos, victims of disease – they cannot conceive of any improvement to these lives. Words become empty form when the counsel they convey cannot issue into action. A sensitive man like Obierika may disapprove of Okonkwo's part in the killing of Ikemefuna. Nevertheless the compromise he resorts to – 'But if the Oracle said that my son should be killed I would neither dispute it nor be the one to do it' (Achebe, 1971, p. 61) – means that, like other Umuofians, he must depend on Okonkwo's rigid and aggressive ways to uphold a unified image of the clan.

Change is thrust upon Umuofia in a violent form by the forces of colonialism and one painful consequence is the breakdown of the Igbo language. Many of the outcasts and disaffected, Okonkwo's own son among them, are converted to the Christian religion and discover there a new language 'which allows the previously unspoken and unheard, and therefore unrecognised, divisions in the clan to be voiced and which encourages the cursing of ancestral gods and traditions' (Innes, 1979, p. 121). At the same time, the arbitrary exercise of colonial power means that the Umuofians are confronted increasingly with situations in which they have no language to speak adequately of their points of view and their reality. Put in prison, they 'have not found the mouth with which to tell of their suffering' (Achebe, 1971, p. 160); freed and among themselves, 'they found no words to speak to one another' (p. 176).

> He could hear in his mind's ear the blood-stirring and intricate rhythms of the *ekwe* and the *udu* and the *ogene*, and he could hear his own flute weaving in and out of them, decorating them with a colourful and plaintive tune. The total effect was gay and brisk, but if one picked out the flute as it went up and down and then broke up into short snatches, one saw that there was sorrow and grief there. (p. 6)

Here, as elsewhere in the novel, two points of view, the character's and the narrator's, 'he' and 'one', merge and then part, and by that means the specific contribution of the flute is singled out from 'the total effect' of the music. Following this approach, a reading of *Things Fall Apart* would need to distinguish among the strands which make up its closely woven whole. In terms of theme, the novel celebrates the past and also analyzes critically Igbo history; and in terms of form, it is a hybrid made up of a contemporary reworking of oral narrative, an Igbo version of Greek tragedy, and a Nigerian history of a society in the process of change. Out of his creative borrowings and transformations, Achebe makes of the African novel in English the 'mouth with which to tell of their suffering'.

Given the more recent historical setting in *Kanthapura* (1938), Raja Rao's first novel is a robust account of political resistance in South India. It shares, however, a number of concerns with *Things Fall Apart*, including a self-conscious reworking of borrowed and indigenous narrative traditions, in this case the novel form from the West and the *sthala-purana*, or legendary history, belonging to India. Rao's Foreword describes the nature of his task in writing the *sthala-purana* of the eponymous village in English:

> The telling has not been easy. One has to convey in a language that is not one's own the spirit that is one's own. One has to convey the various shades and omissions of a certain thought-movement that looks maltreated in an alien language. I use the word 'alien', yet English is not really an alien language to us. It is the language of our intellectual make-up – like the Sanskrit or Persian was before – but not of our emotional make-up. We are all instinctively bilingual, many of us writing in our own language and English. We cannot write like the English. We should not. We cannot write only as Indians. (Rao, 1947, p. v)

Story-telling is the vehicle of continuity and change in *Kanthapura*, reflecting the rootedness of the collective imagination and its capacity to recreate itself. At a time when India's struggle for self-rule is intensifying, story-telling is politicized to foster national consciousness and pride among the rural masses. The historical moment of the novel is the year-long Civil Disobedience movement which was initiated by Gandhi's Salt March in April 1930 and which brought, in retaliation, the government's severely repressive campaign.

The structure of the novel is made up of several layers of narrative: first, Rao's transcription of the legendary history of the region; next, the events as told by an old Brahmin woman of how her village becomes involved in the 'free India' movement led by Gandhi; and last, the stories ranging from gossip to parables and explicit calls to action which, encompassed in her oral tale, are told by other members of the community. Together the different narrative strands mirror the village's familiar day-to-day activities as well as the tremendous changes taking place beyond its boundary. More remarkable is the way age-old stories are made to accommodate new realities and are themselves changed in turn. When Jayalamachal, the professional storyteller, is invited to entertain the villagers, he dazzles them with a version of contemporary politics assimilated into cosmic myth. Just as Ken-chamma, the local goddess, is responsible for the well-being of Kanthapura so, on the cosmic scale, Brahma will rescue his daughter Bharatha from 'the serpent of foreign rule' (Rao, 1947, p. 16). He sends Siva to earth in a new incarnation and so Gandhi is born, the divinely appointed deliverer of India. Jayalamachal's refashion-ing of myth as a political weapon is highly sophisticated; but the villagers themselves are also adept at making sense of their times through the art of narrative. As the situation develops so the story of Rama is continually reworked and given a local significance. For example, Moorthy, the young freedom fighter, becomes transformed, in the course of time and in the villagers' imagination, from Hanuman to Rama himself. The little village has its charismatic and moral leadership just as the country has Gandhi.

Myth and history do not necessarily intersect, however, in the way the storytellers wish. More often in *Kanthapura* they are shown to collide with tragic results. The crises are signalled by the changing register of the old woman's voice as vision breaks down before the nitty-gritty of actual events, and linear narrative cuts across the eternity of myth. Some examples are: the broad and elevated view of Kanthapura, with which the narrative opens, narrows down to reveal a village split by differences of caste and class, and the suggestion is that vested interests and rigid divisions within Indian society itself have helped to strengthen foreign power; Jayalamachal's performance is interrupted by the police and the artist himself removed; finally, after a series of heroic resistances, the villagers are either beaten up or imprisoned or put to flight, and Kanthapura itself has to be destroyed to stop it from falling into the hands of the white coffee planters and the local landowners. On the positive side, just as political action has united the village in ways previously unimagined, so for the survivors, life rebuilds itself in another village in the state of Mysore beyond the mountains. And just as the collective experience of story-telling has given the people a purpose and history, so each time the story of the brave village is told, Kanthapura is invented anew.

In the comparatively brief history of Indian writing in English, Raja Rao is one of three novelists who dominated the 1950s and 1960s. The others are Mulk Raj Anand whose vigorous concern for social reform is fully evident even in such early works as *Untouchable* (1935) and *Coolie* (1945); and R.K. Narayan, best known for his intimate and sharp depictions of everyday life in the South Indian town of Malgudi, the setting of all his novels, including *The Guide* (1958). Narayan's attentiveness to the configurations of place is a characteristic shared by many Commonwealth writers. If imperialism is 'an act of geographical violence through which virtually every space in the world is explored, charted, and finally brought under control' (Said, 1994, p. 271), then the narrative strategies of mapping and defining become a means of retrieving a sense of geographical identity, and with it, the native person as historical subject.

To compare the treatment of place in R.K. Narayan and V.S. Naipaul is to highlight some of the differences within the experience of colonialism. Narayan's Malgudi is a coherent world, founded upon a firm sense of its cultural identity. Within a well-laid-out space, there is a temple, a variety of schools, a market and railway station, and to read the successive novels is to return with pleasure to familiar spots such as Market Street, Kabir Lane, Lawley Extension, Nallapa Grove, the Sarayu River, the Mempi hills. Situated somewhere between Madras and the hills, Malgudi escapes the deadening monotony of remote villages as well as the impersonal flurry of city life. Its inhabitants are neither so gullible as the rustics nor sophisticated like the Madrasis. It will always feel the impact of the big world of politics and economics (there is talk regularly of the rising prices of sugar, wheat-flour and rice, and it becomes near impossible to get pure ghee) but it manages to carry on with a reasonable amount of self-sufficiency. Violent disruptions to the orderly routine of the community and its complacent image of itself occur from time to time and are usually caused by the intrusion of the unfamiliar and the unknown. But, however unsettling their effects, the changes they produce find accommodation within the strength and vitality of Malgudi.

In *The Guide* (1958), for example, Raju is a man who plays many parts and who may seem to be undermining the moral principles and values of Hindu society with his duplicity, greed and lust. Yet a simple accident reverses the course of his destructive career and the con man is transformed by the collective will of his followers into a swami who can be expected, through his penance, to bring rain to the drought stricken land. In the final scene of the novel, as Raju, weakened by hunger but supported by his disciples, stands in the river praying for rain, he becomes the centre around which all Malgudi clusters, combining in his one person tourist attraction, star performer and spiritual guide. Whether or not he does become radically altered by the role of swami which is thrust upon him, the open-ended narrative does not say. However, it is out of this subtle blend of irony and faith that, for a brief moment at least, an inclusive vision of society and culture is produced.

A different sense of place informs V.S. Naipaul's *A House for Mr Biswas* (1961) which has as its main character the doubly displaced figure of the colonial and immigrant Indian. After the abolition of slavery in 1834, the Negroes refused to work on the sugar plantations, and so Indian and other workers were contracted to solve the shortage of labour. The harshness of the conditions meant the new labourers were often little better than slaves. A danger specific to the Hindu worker was that crossing the *kala pani*, or black water, resulted in defilement and loss of caste. In the following passage from the novel, the word 'terrible', which also appears in Naipaul's comment on the plight of the colonial (see p. 694), has the force of its Latin derivation, 'causing terror'. Given the history of indentured labour in the Caribbean, it holds within its small space a complex psychology of loss compounded of material poverty, colonial alienation and ritual exclusion.

> How terrible it would have been, at this time, to be without it: to have died among the Tulsis, amid the squalor of the large, disintegrating and indifferent family; to have left Shama and the children among them, in one room; worse, to have lived without even attempting to lay claim to one's portion of the earth; to have lived and died as one had been born, unnecessary and unaccommodated (Naipaul, 1969, pp. 13–14).

At birth, Biswas seems fated already to toil on the sugar estates as his parents and grandparents have done. But his father's death by drowning brings unforeseen changes. The family is evicted from their home and Biswas is launched upon a series of encounters and relationships which take him from rural to urban Trinidad, from the Hindu community of his childhood and youth to the English-speaking society of the capital. One of the events which overtakes Biswas in this picaresque novel is his marriage to Shama, a daughter of the Tulsi clan, and a main strand of the plot consists of his subsequent attempts to extricate himself from Hanuman House. To belong to the big Hindu family is to be reasonably comfortable and secure. It means also that one must become more or less anonymous, a Tulsi among a swarm of other Tulsis. Refusing to pay the price, Biswas sets out to find a place of his own.

Pagotes, Arwacas, the Chase, Green Vale, Shorthills, Port of Spain: the names are the signposts of Biswas's endeavour, and furthermore of the geographical identity and history of Trinidad. But, in contrast to the continuity which sustains Narayan's Malgudi novels, a powerful feeling of impermanence follows Biswas everywhere he goes (Thieme, 1986, p. 75). The house he tries to build at Green Vale begins to disintegrate even before it is half completed and that at Shorthills burns down. Familiar landscapes and places associated with his past are changed beyond recognition. On a visit to the swamp region where he was born, he finds 'nothing but oil derricks and grimy pumps, see-sawing, see-sawing endlessly, surrounded by red No Smoking notices' (Naipaul, 1969, p. 41). Even Hanuman House begins to crumble. The clan moves out leaving one Tulsi behind to look after the family quarters, the shop passes into the hands of a Port of Spain firm, and the statue of Hanuman has to compete for attention with an advertisement for Bata shoes.

'The past is indeed past ... There can never be any going back' (Shiva Naipaul, quoted in Thieme, 1986, p. 83). Biswas's old Hindu world slowly dissolves along with other aspects of Trinidad's past, in the years preceding and following the Second World War. But, despite the energy and activity on the island, Trinidad's future is still in the making and the line between destruction and creation is never made quite clear in the novel. To this very end, Biswas's relationship with the place remains uneasy. Forty-six years old, out of work and close to death, all he has in terms of material goods is a badly built and heavily mortgaged house. Yet as, dying, he ponders upon his life, the house is also a deep source of satisfaction since, for all its defects and disadvantages, it is his own.

In 1950 Naipaul left Trinidad for England where he has since remained. He is one of the three main figures discussed in Andrew Gurr's critical work *Writers in Exile* (1981), the other two being Katherine Mansfield and Ngugi. All are 'aspirant writers' from British colonies who left the small, static communities they know as home for the impersonality and freedom of the metropolis. All wrote, across distance and time, passionately and vividly about these communities. If 'the great strength of modern writing in English lies much more in its exiles than in its metropolitan writers', then 'the reason lies partly in the stronger sense of home which the exile has, and in the clearer sense of his own identity which his home gives him' (Gurr, 1981, p. 9). Like most generalizations, Gurr's remarks ring true and false at once. By 1981, when his book appeared, the dismantling of the empire and the pressure of world events had made untenable that sharp division of 'colony' and 'metropolis', 'margin' and 'centre', upon which his argument is pivoted. Increasingly 'home' and 'identity' are problematic issues often treated with playful self-referentiality. These shifts in emphasis in the literature of the Commonwealth are figured in Rushdie's essay, 'Imaginary Homelands', first published in 1982. Beginning with Bombay where he was born and grew up, he goes on:

> It may be that writers in my position, exiles, emigrants or expatriates, are haunted by some sense of loss, some urge to reclaim, to look back, even at the risk of being mutated into pillars of salt. But if we do look back, we must also do so in the knowledge – which gives rise to profound uncertainties – that our physical alienation from India inevitably means that we will not be capable of reclaiming precisely the thing that was lost; that we will, in short, create fictions, not actual cities or villages, but invisible ones, imaginary homelands, Indias of the mind. (Rushdie, 1992, p. 10)

The 'profound uncertainties', a contrast to Gurr's 'a stronger sense of home' and 'a clearer sense of ... identity', are expanded upon in *Shame* (1983), the novel Rushdie published the next year. In the extract reproduced below, a correspondence is made between the asymmetries of 'home' and 'identity'.

> The country in this story is not Pakistan, or not quite. There are two countries, real and fictional, occupying the same space, or almost the same space. My story, my fictional country exist, like myself, at a slight angle to reality. I have found this off-centring to be necessary; but its value is, of course, open to debate. (Rushdie, 1984, p. 29)

A little later in the narrative, 'migrant' comes to be used in place of 'exile, emigrant, expatriate', a term which catches the indeterminate status of the 'I' narrator, an emigrant from India and an immigrant twice over (to England where he lives and to Pakistan where 'my family moved against my will'). Not surprisingly, it is associated with ambivalent phrases. First, 'Roots, I sometimes think, are a conservative myth, designed to keep us in our places' (Rushdie, 1984, p. 86) so that there is suggested the subjugating power of home as well as the security which comes with belonging. And again,

> When individuals come unstuck from their native land, they are called migrants. When nations do the same thing (Bangladesh), the act is called secession. What is the best thing about migrant peoples and seceded nations? I think it is their hopefulness. ... And what's the worst thing? It is the emptiness of one's luggage. ... we have come unstuck from more than land. We have floated upwards from history, from memory, from Time. (Rushdie, 1984, pp. 86–7)

The doubleness of the phrase 'come unstuck', that is, 'break free' and 'suffer disaster', keeps the uncertainties of sense and tone very much in the forefront of the narrative, producing a restiveness characteristic of 'migrant' narratives in general. Examples are *The Buddha of Suburbia* (1990) by Hanif Kureishi, a British playwright and novelist of mixed English and Pakistani descent; and *A Small Place* (1988), a polemical essay, by the Antiguan novelist Jamaica Kincaid who lives at present in the United States.

'My name is Karim Amir, and I am an Englishman born and bred, almost' (Kureishi, 1990, p. 1). The word prominently placed at the end of the sentence is also the least assured: 'almost', an afterthought, a throwaway desperately seeking to bridge the irreconcilable halves of the statement. Karim's picaresque narrative is spun out of his attempts to pin down this 'almost', chasing it across the South London suburbs and the city, the England of Enoch Powell and hippie England, the smart properties of the well-to-do and the battlegrounds of the poor. In contrast the opening sentence of *A Small Place* is beautifully held – 'If you go to Antigua as a tourist, this is what you will see' (Kincaid, 1988, p. 3) – before the confident notes lapse into anxious repetition:

> You see yourself taking a walk on that beach, you see yourself meeting new people (only they are new in a very limited way, for they are people just like you). You see yourself eating some delicious, locally grown food. You see yourself, you see yourself... (p. 13)

The feeling of menace is produced in part by the ambiguity of 'you' so that, along with the unknown tourist, the reader stands accused and, where 'you' shades into 'one', the writer herself. In part it is the narcissistic repetition of 'you', 'yourself', 'like you', giving the impression that however far the tourist travels he or she can only turn in upon themselves.

Distinguishing between Indian writers who write from within India and those who write in the West (that is, migrants), Nayantara Sahgal says of the latter:

> They are not affected by the raw winds assailing India or – which is more crucial – by the texture of daily life. They are not encumbered with the nitty gritty of carving out a continuity from difficult, sometimes unpredictable circumstances, with gaining an inch of breathing space at a time in the on-going process of building a nation that has only in recent times become a nation. (Sahgal, 1993, p. 8)

The precariousness of the post-independence nation in view of 'nitty gritty' such as political dictatorship, internecine conflict, administrative and economic corruption – is central to Sahgal's own novel *Rich Like Us* (1985). Other Commonwealth examples include Soyinka's satirical drama *Opera Wonyosi* (1981) and *A Play of Giants* (1984), Ben Okri's short story 'Laughter Beneath the Bridge' in *Incidents at the Shrine* (1986), Achebe's novel *Anthills of the Savannah* (1987) and Ama Ata Aidoo's poems in *An Angry Letter in January* (1992).

'Where had the tradition we were trying to build gone wrong?' (Sahgal, 1987, p. 28) is the question which pursues Sonali, one of the main characters in *Rich Like Us*. She has the Indian Civil Service in mind but, given the collapse of democratic principles and institutions after Indira Gandhi's declaration of a State of Emergency in 1975, the question can easily be directed to the crisis in nation-building. The novel has no simple answer to offer but, in its critical scrutiny of the last two centuries of Indian history, several crucial moments are singled out, among them Partition which brought about a tremendous loss of lives, homes, 'provinces, rivers and a natural not a political frontier, ending at Afghanistan' (Sahgal, 1987, p. 160). *Rich Like Us* exemplifies that harsh 'critique of ourselves' which, according to Aijaz Ahmad, has been dictated by the violent history of nationalism in South Asia from 1947:

> Our 'nationalism' at this juncture was a nationalism of mourning, a form of valediction, for what we witnessed was not just the British policy of divide and rule, which surely was there, but our own willingness to break up our civilisational unity, to kill our neighbours, to forgo that civic ethos, that moral bond with each other, without which human community is impossible. (Ahmad, 1992, p. 119)

Among South Asian novelists who have tried to render the tragic events surrounding the birth of Pakistan and India are Khuswant Singh whose *Train to Pakistan* (1956) is possibly the classic on the subject written in English, and Bapsi Sidhwa whose *The Ice-Candy-Man* (1988) treats with particular sensitivity the consequences for women of communal conflict. Still on the subject of Partition and nationhood but from the perspective of relations between the East wing of Pakistan and India, there is *The Shadow Lines* (1988) by Amitav Ghosh, one of a number of Indian writers, such as Vikram Seth, Allan Sealy, Upamanya Chatterjee, who made their reputations in the 1980s.

While *The Shadow Lines* is directly concerned with the communal troubles which took place in Calcutta and Dhaka in January 1964, it was written against a background of continuing violence generated by, for example, the secession of East Pakistan and the founding of Bangladesh in 1971, Sikh separatist movements in Punjab province in the 1980s, the assassination of Indira Gandhi in 1984 followed by riots in Delhi in the same year and in Meerut in 1987, and the resurgence of Hindu fundamentalism in the latter half of the 1980s. The motivating impulse behind the narrative is the 'I' speaker's search for explanations to two mysteries related to his childhood. First, the violent death in Dhaka in January 1964 of Tridib, his favourite uncle, which is treated as an unspoken secret within the family. Secondly, the riots which broke out in Calcutta about the time of Tridib's death and from which the narrator was lucky to have escaped with his life. This particular day is still vivid in his memory on account of its phantasmagoric blend of the strange and the strangely familiar. On the journey to and from school, the overwhelming sense of trouble brewing is externalized in the extraordinary transformations which overtake well-known objects and scenes. The rumour being that 'they' have poisoned the municipal water supply, his water bottle becomes isolated as a thing of terror; surrounded by Hindu boys on the bus, Montu, his best friend and a Muslim, has to be disowned without a second thought; left lying at a curious angle in the street, the empty rickshaw looms, an ominous because unfathomable sign – 'had it been put there to keep Muslims in or Hindus out?' (Ghosh, 1988, p. 199). One striking phenomenon is the way certain shared attitudes and assumptions begin to emerge so that, even though he is among boys with whom he has normally little contact, 'they' is immediately understood as referring to the Muslims, the common enemy in the midst. As for the once familiar city and its landmarks, they dissolve before 'a fear that comes of the knowledge that normalcy is utterly contingent, that the spaces that surround one, the streets that one inhabits, can become, suddenly and without warning, as hostile as a desert in a flash flood' (p. 200).

In *Imagined Communities*, Benedict Anderson stresses the crucial role played by print-capitalism in making it possible for rapidly growing numbers of people to think about themselves in terms of community and nation. Anderson makes clear how this works through a discussion of the novelistic convention of 'simultaneity'. Thus the news items which appear in any edition of a newspaper have no connection with each other apart from calendrical coincidence. Yet an impression of linkage is provided by the date at the top of the newspaper. Moreover, the newspaper is produced in huge numbers and consumed in privacy:

> Yet each communicant is well aware that the ceremony he performs is being replicated simultaneously by thousands (or millions) of others of whose existence he is confident, yet of whose identity he has not the slightest notion.... What more vivid figure for the secular, historically-clocked, imagined community can be envisioned? (Anderson, [1983] 1991, p. 39)

Ghosh's treatment of the events which occur in the first half of January 1964 raises interesting questions concerning Anderson's viewpoint. It was not until many years later when he is a PhD student in Delhi that the 'I' narrator learnt of the events which surrounded the riots in Calcutta, in other words, recovered a context for them. Searching in the library, among back issues of Calcutta newspapers for reports of the troubles which made 10 January 1964 so momentous in his memory, he comes upon accounts of other outbreaks of trouble, among them the ones which took place in Khulna and in Dhaka in East Pakistan. The incidents in Calcutta were therefore not isolated occurrences. But the silence which surrounded them from the first to the last brings to mind that what the newspaper does not print is as important as what it does carry in imagining community. The media's silence concerning the communal riots which swept through Khulna first, and then Calcutta and Dhaka, in January 1964 is significant. 'It is in the logic of states that to exist at all they must claim the monopoly of all relationships between people' (Ghosh, 1988, p. 226). Seen as isolated events the riots are *national* events. Seen as a chain of linked events, they underline the inconvenient fact of the oneness of the subcontinent. Just as in Kashmir the collective response of Hindus, Muslims and Sikhs to the loss of the Prophet's hair exemplifies its syncretic civilization, so the interconnections are to be found in their terrifying aspect in the chain of riots which link the different cities on the subcontinent together. However shocking, the paradox is inescapable. Remove the fixed boundaries of its self-contained nations and what becomes apparent is the common fear which runs across the subcontinent, drawing it together with unshakeable menace.

Another pressing question raised and explored in *Rich Like Us* is the extent to which the position of women has changed in India with the attainment of political freedom. For Sahgal's character Sonali, as for many women writers and critics today, it becomes vital to remember a related yet different history:

> In India, as in various parts of 'the Third World', the struggle for women's emancipation was expediently connected to an anti-colonial, nationalist struggle. After Independence was won, militant women found themselves, typically, back in 'normal' subordinate roles and came to recognise the dangers of conflating national liberation with women's liberation. (Katrak, 1992, p. 395)

One reason for the retrogressive step is the powerful role which traditional myths play within Hindu culture, in particular the representation of woman as Mother Goddess,

> that fecund figure from whom all good things flow – milk, food, warmth, comfort. Her ample bosom and loins, her enticing curves and buxom proportions make her not merely the ideal mother but the ideal woman – consort, lover, plaything. She is the richest source of art in India – sculpture, painting, dance and poetry. Around her exists a huge body of mythology. She is called by several names – Sita, Draupadi, Durga, Parvati, Lakshmi, and so on. In each myth, she plays the role of the loyal wife, unswerving in her devotion to her lord. She is meek, docile, trusting, faithful and forgiving. Even when spirited and brave, she adheres to the archetype: willing to go through fire and water, dishonour and disgrace for his sake. (Desai, 1990, p. 972)

Not surprisingly, revisionist myth-making is a dominant preoccupation and notable examples in this instance are: Mahasweta Devi's 'Breast-Giver' (Devi, 1987), Anita Desai's *Fire on the Mountain* (1977), Shashi Deshpande's *That Long Silence* (1988) and Nayantara Sahgal's *Mistaken Identity* (1988). All are concerned with women entrapped in lies and fantasies, in which they have often colluded, and struggling to recover a sense of their own worth and identity. In Desai's novel, for example, despite her privileged background and position, the main character Nanda Kaul is barely able, even when the crisis occurs, to face up to the painful truth that she has never had a place in her husband's affections although she has acted throughout his lifetime as the mother of their large family, his housekeeper and the hostess of his parties.

Written from within a different cultural context, *The Joys of Motherhood* (1979) by the Nigerian novelist Buchi Emecheta is another example of resistance to disabling myths. The optimistic title grows increasingly ironic as the bleak history unfolds of Nnu Ego, uprooted from her traditional society and struggling to bring up her large family single-handed in Lagos amid the political and economic instability of the war years. Ama Ata Aidoo's *Changes* (1991) returns to a question posed in her earlier works, such as the play *Anowa* (1969), and asks to what extent self-determination has become a reality for women in post-independence Ghana after years of published reform. At its centre is Esi, self-conscious and self-assertive, yet frustrated at every turn by the realities of the male-oriented society to which she belongs. Exploring Esi's dilemmas – to be a mother or a professional woman, to stay married and submissive or to break free – Aidoo's novel rehearses and rewrites the familiar fictions which enmesh women's lives and the directions Esi picks in taking charge of her own life.

When Ali decides that Esi, recently separated from her husband, should marry him and become his second wife, she has no reason to object, given that he has courted her with all the charm, liberality and eloquence to be found in any romantic bestseller. Given too that his decision has the sanction of custom, at least within the mythologized version of traditional society where 'wives took turns being wives', the man 'was not supposed to' have favourites, and the serious business of living was done 'with our heads, and never our hearts' (Aidoo, 1991, pp. 78–9). However, romance and traditional myth prove short-lived and, the wedding over, Ali's charm begins to bear certain resemblances to deviousness, his gifts to bribery and his eloquence to lies. The version of womanhood left to Esi is the one which is only too familiar to her grandmother:

> a woman has always been diminished in her association with a man. A good woman was she who quickened the pace of her own destruction. To refuse, as a woman, to be destroyed, was a crime that society spotted very quickly and punished swiftly and severely. (p. 110)

On the face of things, there does not appear to be any difference between Esi's situation, once the relationship with Ali stops being a marriage, and that of many other women. Behind her lonely existence, however, lie conscious and painful choices. First, her rejection of Ali's 'fashion of loving', in which she is expected to play an acquiescent role, is as much an expression of her sexuality as her delight in her own body and its energies. Secondly, in a novel with the city as a pervasive presence, teaching herself to live on her own in Accra is an assertion of her right as a woman to the urban environment and the opportunities it offers. The city has to be remade, becoming for Esi, not just the streets and bars, the haunts of prostitutes, and the little houses with locked gates, the prisons of self-sacrificing wives, but a space for movement, action and rest, which men like Ali can take so much for granted. Last, Esi's resolve that 'heart' and 'head' should have equal say in the 'answers to some of the big questions she was asking of life' makes it unthinkable that she would betray her old friend Opokuya, even at a time when an affair with Opokuya's husband, Kubi, would have been a form of comfort.

> She remembered that there was something called friendship. And hadn't her friendship with Opokuya been, so far, the most constant thing in her life? And that whereas mothers, fathers, grandmothers and other relations are like extra limbs we grow, a friend symbolises a choice? And to maintain a friendship is a choice? (p. 164)

As the story of romance draws to a disappointing close in *Changes*, so the full weight of that other story, of the friendship of Esi and Opokuya, begins to make itself felt. Recalling the numerous occasions when the word 'friends' is repeated in the narrative – Esi and Opokuya are 'friends'; can Esi ever see herself and Ali's wife as being 'friends'? Fusena regrets that, by marrying Ali, she has exchanged a 'friend' for a husband; Ali and Esi, their marriage not working, become just good 'friends' – it points the way to other alignments for women and new patterns of relationship.

The title of Aidoo's novel, *Changes*, can be usefully extended to refer to a main concern in postcolonial literatures in general, that is, societies and cultures in transition, 'carving out a continuity from difficult, sometimes unpredictable circumstances' (Sahgal, 1993, p. 8). The outcome of the concern is a language remade and revitalized, and a rich and diverse body of writing. The achievement is succinctly summed up in the 'Epilogue' to *The Fat Black Woman's Poems* (1984) by the Guyanese–British poet Grace Nichols:

> I have crossed an ocean
> I have lost my tongue
> from the root of the old one
> a new one has sprung.
>
> (Nichols, 1990, p. 64)

## BIBLIOGRAPHY

Achebe, C. (1971) *Things Fall Apart*, Heinemann Educational Books, London [first published 1958].
Achebe, C. (1981) *Morning Yet on Creation Day*, Heinemann, London [first published 1975].
Ahmad, A. (1992) *In Theory: Classes, Nations, Literatures*, Verso, London.
Aidoo, A.A. (1991) *Changes*, Women's Press, London.
Anderson, B. (1991) *Imagined Communities: Reflections on the Origin and Spread of Nationalism*, Verso, London [first published 1983].
Ashcroft, B., Griffiths, G. and Tiffin, H. (1989) *The Empire Writes Back: Theory and Practice in Post-colonial Literatures*, Routledge, London.
Bhabha, H. (1994) *The Location of Culture*, Routledge, London.
Brathwaite, E. (1968) *Masks*, Oxford University Press, London.

Chaudhuri, N. (1975) *Clive of India: A Political and Psychological Essay*, Barrie & Jenkins, London.

Conrad, J. (1959) *Heart of Darkness*, Doubleday Anchor, New York [first published 1899].

Das, K. (1989) 'An Introduction', in *Indian English Poetry since 1950*, ed. V. Sarang, Sangam Books, London.

Desai, A. (1977) *Fire on the Mountain*, Heinemann, London.

Desai, A. (1990) 'A Secret Connivance', *Times Literary Supplement*.

Devi, M. (1987) 'Breast-giver', in *In Other Worlds*, ed. G. Spivak, Routledge, London.

Emecheta, B. (1979) *The Joys of Motherhood*, Alison & Busby, London.

Fanon, F. (1986) *Black Skin, White Masks*, trans. C.L. Markmann, Foreword by H. Bhabha, Pluto Press, London [first published as *Peau Noire Masques Blancs*, 1952].

Ghosh, A. (1988) *The Shadow Lines*, Bloomsbury, London.

Gurr, A. (1981) *Writers in Exile*, Harvester Wheatsheaf, Hemel Hempstead.

Innes, C.L. (1979) 'Language, Poetry and Doctrine in *Things Fall Apart*', in *Critical Perspectives on Chinua Achebe*, ed. C.L. Innes and B. Lindfors, Heinemann Educational Books, London.

Katrak, K.H. (1992) 'Indian Nationalism, Gandhian "Satyagraha", and Representations of Female Sexuality', in *Nationalisms & Sexualities*, ed. A. Parker, M. Russo, D. Sommer and P. Yaeger, Routledge, London.

Kincaid, J. (1988) *A Small Place*, Virago, London.

Kureishi, H. (1990) *The Buddha of Suburbia*, Faber, London.

Macaulay, T. (1972) 'Minute on Indian Education', in *Thomas Babington Macaulay: Selected Writings*, ed. J. Clive and T. Pinney, University of Chicago Press, Chicago.

Morris, J. (1979) *Pax Britannica: The Climax of an Empire*, Penguin, Harmondsworth [first published 1968].

Narayan, R.K. (1958) *The Guide*, Heinemann, London.

Narayan, R.K. (1965) 'English in India', in *Commonwealth Literature: Unity and Diversity in a Common Culture*, ed. J. Press, Heinemann, London.

Naipaul, V.S. (1969) *A House for Mr Biswas*, Penguin, Harmondsworth [first published 1961].

Ngugi wa Thiong'o (1986) *Decolonising the Mind: the Politics of Language in African Literature*, James Currey, London.

Nichols, G. (1990) *The Fat Black Woman's Poems*, Virago, London [first published 1984].

Rao, R. (1947) *Kanthapura*, Oxford University Press, Bombay [first published 1938].

Rowe-Evans, A. (1970) 'Interview with V.S. Naipaul', *Transition*, 40, pp. 57–8.

Rushdie, S. (1984) *Shame*, Picador, London [first published 1983].

Rushdie, S. (1992) *Imaginary Homelands: Essays and Criticism 1981–1991*, Granta Books, London [first published 1991].

Sahgal, N. (1987) *Rich Like Us*, Sceptre Books, London [first published 1985].

Sahgal, N. (1993) 'Some Thought on the Puzzle of Identity', *Journal of Commonwealth Literature*, XXIX, no. 1, pp. 3–15.

Said, E.W. (1994) *Culture and Imperialism*, Vintage, London [first published 1993].

Sidhwa, B. (1988) *The Ice-Candy-Man*, Heinemann, London.

Singh, K. (1956) *Train to Pakistan*, Chatto & Windus, London.

Thieme, J. (1986) *The Web of Tradition: Uses of Allusion in V.S. Naipaul's Fiction*, Dangaroo Press, Aarhus.

Walcott, D. (1962) *In a Green Night: Poems 1948–1960*, Cape, London.

Walcott, D. (1993) 'The Caribbean: Culture or Mimicry', in *Critical Perspectives on Derek Walcott*, ed. D. Hamner, Three Continents Press, Washington [essay first published 1974].

Wright, D. (1990) 'Things Standing Together: A Retrospect on *Things Fall Apart*', *Kunapipi*, XII, 2, pp. 76–82.

# Australasian literature

*Geraldine Stoneham*

It is important from the outset to be clear that what is referred to here as 'Australasian literature' is in fact not the literature of the entire Australasian region (which includes Papua New Guinea and the South Sea islands), nor is it an homogenous entity. The term as it is used here refers specifically to the distinct literatures of Australia and New Zealand, which have not only a geographical proximity but also a common cultural foundation. We will be investigating in this unit the historical and social developments, the themes and issues, and the critical viewpoints, which have created two unique literatures.

The literatures of Australia and New Zealand are, like those of Africa, Canada, and to some extent the Caribbean, the literature of a colonizer or settler culture. By this I mean that the literature of those countries is wholly dominated by the language and culture of the colonizer. This is not to imply that this literature is only that of the white European Christian colonial, and based on European literary modes and conventions; included in this term is work by colonially educated indigenous people in English and in their own languages. In this unit, we shall be considering in detail the contribution that indigenous – Aboriginal and Maori – writers in English have made to their respective national literatures.

First it is necessary to ask some searching questions which might act as a basis for the discussion. What makes a literature unique? What creates a new and individual culture from a strong and clearly dominant 'Mother' culture? Is post-colonial literature simply a matter of content and historical, social and geographical context, or are there also aesthetic concerns – issues of language and literary convention – to be considered? These questions will be addressed through detailed critical analysis.

The term post-colonial literature generally refers to work produced by a national or cultural group in response to the experience of colonialism. For first-generation or 'native-born' Australians and New Zealanders this means the obvious response to a landscape as yet uncharted by the English language. As the gulf between experience and language opens, so too does the desire to express that gulf. The gulf becomes the site of all that is inexpressibly of that place. The sense of place is also the sense of exile, of displacement, of alienation and of marginalization. It becomes the site of valorization of, or resistance to the centre (Britain and English) to which all knowledge refers and defers. It is the site of the search for self-definition; a place where myths of identity flourish and compete for acceptance. In white settler terms, this identity is based on the insistence on or resistance to self-constructed difference. There is a political dimension to this difference. In both colonies, the working man, particularly the bush worker, is celebrated as the colonial hero. Life in the bush depended upon a good relationship with one's 'mates' and the hardships encountered by all were considered to encourage egalitarianism among all those who genuinely shared them. Australasian national identity was, therefore, white and masculine, effectively disbarring women and indigenous people from membership. This facet of, particularly, Australian identity is contested by a number of the authors whose works are discussed below.

## Convergence and divergence

Colonization began in the Australasian region as a consequence of exploration from the sixteenth century until Captain Cook visited both countries in 1769–70 and annexed Australia for George III. The impact of white settlement in Australia, as a result of convict transportation and later free settlement, was felt across the Tasman Sea, and in the early nineteenth century New Zealand was a whaling and trading base in the region. In the late nineteenth century, there were suggestions for an Australasian state, and this became one of the many *causes célèbres* of the Australian weekly newspaper, the *Bulletin*, whose popularity in New Zealand was for a time as great as that in Australia. The *Bulletin* became a literary link between the two colonial settlements (Nesbitt, 1968). Its visionary editor, J.F. Archibald, vehemently anti-British, published New Zealand verse and stories, insisting on the epithet 'Maoriland' whenever the colony was referred to in its pages. (The significance of this will be discussed below.) Archibald also sent his star writer, Henry Lawson, to New Zealand for two years as a roving reporter for the paper. The best-known of New Zealand's literary figures, Katherine Mansfield, was published as a teenager in the *Triad*, a New Zealand-owned journal, and Archibald's other creation, the *Lone Hand*, both Australia-based journals.

In spite of this early mutual acknowledgement and sense of common purpose, it would be wrong to suggest that the *response* to the experience of colonization was identical. There are many factors contributing to the divergence between the two colonies, not least being the lasting impact of convictism and republicanism in Australia and a differing ethnic mixture among the settlers to New Zealand.

## Australia

### The 1890s and national identity

Perhaps it is most possible to speak of Australasian literature when referring to the importance of the short story in the development of colonial literatures. Short stories fulfilled the need in a new society to provide itself with 'snapshots' of the defining conditions of colonial life, the shape of a national character, which they recognize as being authentic, if not universal. I have noted above that this desire for an authenticity is based in the sense of the uniqueness of the land and its inhabitants. These 'colonial stories' are therefore concerned primarily with the expression of 'much that is different from things in other lands' (Lawson, 1892, in Kiernan, 1976).

## Henry Lawson: 'The Drover's Wife'

Henry Lawson (1867–1922) is the best-known of the *Bulletin* school of writers. He began writing for the journal in 1886 and the editor, J.F. Archibald, nurtured his talent with advances of money, special assignments and tolerance of Lawson's self-destructive alcoholism. In many ways Lawson is the epitome of the ethos which the *Bulletin* promoted. He grew up in a country town as the son of an unsuccessful prospector and selector, but while still in his teens followed his mother to Sydney where she worked as a journalist on the fringes of Bohemian life. In company with other literary figures of the period – Marcus Clarke, Edward Dyson, Victor Daley and Barcroft Boake – he was a member of a community of isolated individuals, struggling to make a living by journalism, dogged by poverty and alcoholism, and frustrated by a sense of alienation from a growing materialist society. As Graeme Davison has suggested, this community of artists, artisans and ideologues sustained an often mutually supportive collection of ideologies, from secularism and republicanism to socialism and feminism (Davison, 1978, p. 191). The inspiration for this 'counter-culture' was mainly to be found in the English radical tradition. This radicalism in a new context created what the *Bulletin* promoted as the distinctively Australian ethos: new worlds need new men and if new men were going to be found, it could not be in the City with its imitative colonialist behaviour, its imported class structures, subservience to an already-corrupted State and Church, and materialism. The Bush, on the other hand, where life is pared down to the essentials and is the home of 'much that is different from things in other lands', as Lawson puts it in 'The Bush Undertaker' (1892) (in Kiernan, 1976), offers the possibility of a unique viewpoint.

The early literature erected upon this distinction shows the influence of the American frontier stories of Bret Harte and the short stories and poetry of Rudyard Kipling and Robert Louis Stevenson. Lawson brought a new voice to the Australian short story, 'the lonely voice' of individual rather than collective experience. His view of the bush conflicted with the romantic balladry of Banjo Paterson, an equally popular voice in the 'Bushman's Bible', who celebrated the heroic exploits of bush horsemen in verse, and the two conducted a (rather stage-managed) literary debate in verse and story over the realities of life in the bush, with Lawson taking an insistent anti-romantic line. Both views were acceptable, first, because both dealt with the figure and landscape of Australian difference, secondly, because Paterson's exuberance and lighthearted hero-worship matched a nationalist desire for myth-making and, thirdly, because Lawson's grimmer 'realism' mirrored a prevailing sense of marginalization.

'The Drover's Wife' (1892) is Lawson's best-known work. The story is set in the remote Australian outback during the drought and depression of the 1890s. A woman, left alone with her four children by her cattle-drover husband, is forced to sit up all night to watch for the appearance of a deadly black snake which has crawled under the floor of the house. Having put the children to bed on the kitchen table, she settles down to wait through a thunderstorm for first light. As she watches, the narrator reviews the woman's life with its disappointments, isolation. We learn about her relationship with her husband, her experiences of childbirth in the bush, her attempts to maintain 'civilized' standards against all odds, threats from an itinerant swagman (tramp) and dishonest Aborigines. We also learn about her sense of humour – her ability to laugh in the face of disaster.

In all these aspects, Lawson is attempting to represent to the reader a sense of the reality of life for Australian bush-dwellers, as much for the city-dwellers who read the newspapers at home as for non-Australians. But he is also attempting to address the question of national identity in both the form and the content of the story. The narrative is aggressively realist in tone and deliberately anti-romantic in intention. Consider the following paragraph:

> Her husband is an Australian, and so is she. He is careless, but a good enough husband. If he had the means he would take her to the city and keep her there like a princess. They are used to being apart, or at least she is. 'No use fretting,' she says. He may forget sometimes that he is married, but if he has a good cheque when he comes back he will give most of it to her. ... One of her children died while she was here alone. She rode nineteen miles for assistance, carrying the dead child. (Kiernan, 1976, p. 99)

The opening sentence appears to be no more than a simple statement of fact: both the drover and his wife are Australians. The ensuing description explains and qualifies the statement: Australians are 'good enough', thoughtless but generous when they can be, uncomplaining and stoical when life lets them down. A simple enough description presented in a deliberately perfunctory manner. A closer examination of the extract, however, suggests that the opening statement also has a reverse action: the fact that they are Australians seems in itself to explain and justify the elements of failure and complacency which govern their lives. The odds of life in the Australian bush are so stacked against the individual that it is fruitless to protest against one's lot.

There are a number of other related observations and questions which arise from this brief extract. The Australian characteristics suggested in the narrative divide interestingly along gender lines: the absent husband is thoughtless and generous, the wife is uncomplaining and stoical: '"No use fretting," she says.' To what extent is the husband's activity dependent upon the wife's passivity? What exactly is the nature of the portrait of the wife painted by the narrative? Significantly, we never get to know the wife's name, she is defined wholly in terms of her position as the wife of a drover. The narrative details her character in a brilliantly economical manner, employing an unadorned, realistic style to build up a picture of the woman and her predicament, stroke upon stroke, until the bleakness of the landscape, the incessant hardship of the life and the stark courage of her uncomplaining acceptance compile a complete figure – softened by a wash of sentiment and humour. But, like the portrait it emulates, it is an external likeness: it is a type (but not a stereotype). This sense of the external image is maintained by the third-person narration. Later, when it is suggested that the wife '*seems* contented with her lot', one suspects that the narrator is none too sure. The statement 'Her husband is an Australian, and so is she' suggests that the story-teller is content to look no deeper beneath the surface for the answer to the mysteries of her tolerance. We must only understand that her tolerance is necessary for the reader's comfort. While she is uncomplaining, the reader can sympathize without feeling uneasy; the Australian may be careless, but he is also generous when he is able.

Compare this portrait with another published a few years later in the same journal, 'The Chosen Vessel' by Barbara Baynton (first published as 'The Tramp', 1896). Baynton's story is also about a woman who lives in isolation and deprivation with her baby. Her husband is a shearer who works at a station fifteen miles away during the week. Baynton's image of the bushwoman, however, is very different from Lawson's. Where Lawson's heroine is threatened by a 'natural' predator, the snake, the danger in Baynton's story is posed by a swagman who eventually rapes and murders her. The swagman who harasses the wife in Lawson's story is more cunning than threatening and she sees him off easily with the aid of a stick and the family dog. Where Lawson's husband is 'good enough' if 'careless', Baynton's is a brute, who sneers at and threatens his young wife:

> More than once she thought of taking her baby and going to her husband. But in the past, when she had dared to speak of the dangers to which her loneliness exposed her, he had taunted and sneered at her. 'Needn't flatter yerself,' he had told her, 'nobody 'ud want ter run away with yew.' (Krimmer and Lawson, 1980, p. 82)

Unlike the drover's wife, Baynton's 'vessel' is not stoical. She is afraid of the cow, of her brutal husband, of the image of herself she sees in the predatory swagman's eyes. Her eventual rape and murder by the swagman, leaves the reader with a much less comfortable impression of the lives faced by women in the bush, and of the men who are the Australians and who leave them there. Read together, these two stories raise difficult questions: How does Baynton's portrait alter the image of the 'typical Australian' constructed by Lawson? What does this say about the construction of identities of nationality and gender? (See also the discussion below of Katherine Mansfield's story, 'The Woman at the Store' (1911).)

## The rise of the Australian novel

The period 1890–1910 also marked the production of two important novels. Hitherto, the most popular form of the novel in Australia were bushranging tales like Rolf Boldrewood's *Robbery Under Arms* (1888) and romances with local colour, such as Rosa Campbell Praed's *Policy and Passion* (1881). In 1901, Blackwoods in Edinburgh published what was hailed by A.G. Stephens, the *Bulletin*'s literary editor, as 'the very first Australian novel': Miles Franklin's *My*

*Brilliant Career.* Its author was a young woman, born and bred in the mountains and later the flatlands of New South Wales, who was only 22 at the time of publication. The timing was perfect: Australia officially became a nation from a collection of separate colonies in 1901, and Franklin's novel expressed much of the youthful exuberance and brashness with which the new nation faced the new century. Her portrait of the bush, in its beauty and harsh reality, echoes Lawson's insistence upon social realism. But Franklin also questions the nature of an identity which excludes women through constructions of femininity which are inappropriate to the land in which they live. Joseph Furphy's *Such is Life* (1903) is another masterpiece of Australian idiom which engages with English literature, from Shakespeare to the colonial romance, in an attempt to represent, through parody, the reality of bush working life.

The first half of the twentieth century produced three outstanding novelists, all of whom were women: Henry Handel Richardson, Katharine Susannah Prichard and Christina Stead. Of these only Prichard lived for most of her life in Australia; the era of expatriation had begun among the Australian and New Zealand literary community. Ironically, Prichard, as a Communist, whose greatest following outside of Australia was in the Soviet Union, was also an internationalist. Her view of Australia was based on its potential as a working-man's paradise, where Australian traits of egalitarianism and mateship construct a political socialism. In her novel, *Coonardoo* (1929), Prichard attempts to portray the effect of colonialism on two Australians: the white 'boss' and his young Aboriginal housemaid whose tragedy is to fall in love. Her writing, particularly *Working Bullocks* (1926), was influenced by D.H. Lawrence, who visited Australia in 1922 and wrote two novels set in the country, *Kangaroo* (1923) and *The Boy in the Bush* (with Mollie Skinner) (1924). Prichard was disappointed in her literary hero. She suggested in a letter to the critic Nettie Palmer that Lawrence had not really understood the Australians. Christina Stead set only two of her novels in Australia: *Seven Poor Men of Sydney* (1934) and *For Love Alone* (1944). Her absence from Australia from 1928 to 1970 resulted in the nation disowning her, and a campaign had to be waged in literary circles to have her reinstated as an Australian novelist. This reflects a received opinion which prevailed in Australia until the 1980s, that to be an Australian novelist one had to write about Australia.

## Henry Handel Richardson and myths of origin

Richardson's achievement reflects the major preoccupations of the literary traditions of the early twentieth century. Unlike Henry Lawson or Miles Franklin, Richardson had a privileged education in the British tradition at a private ladies' college in Melbourne. She had studied music in Germany and had a knowledge of European trends in philosophy and literature as well as a sense of self-imposed exile, which were essential touchstones for the new modernist self-consciousness in literature (Unit 15). While modernist preoccupation with the interplay of narrative and form, with myth and the analysis of subjectivity, was the natural mode of such textual consciousness, Richardson was less obviously influenced by the stylistic experimentation of other modernist writers, such as Virginia Woolf or Dorothy Richardson (see Units 16 and 23). In his assessment of Australian modernism, Julian Croft points out that while Australian writers were stylistically conservative, to the point of hostility towards experimentation, the modern movement in Australia was already well disposed by 'temperament' to modernist introspection and 'solipsistic pessimism' (Croft, 1988, pp. 409–29).

*The Fortunes of Richard Mahony* is the collective title of an epic three-volume novel published respectively as *Australia Felix* (1917), *The Way Home* (1925) and *Ultima Thule* (1929). Based on the lives of Richardson's parents, the novel charts the rise and fall of an Irish doctor, Richard Mahony, and his wife, Mary, during the mid- to late nineteenth century. Having been lured to Australia by the promise of a fortune in gold, Mahony becomes a shopkeeper on the Ballarat diggings in Australia. Then, as gold mining makes way for the development of a new colonial society, Mahony returns to his original profession of medicine. A restless and unstable character, Mahony hovers continually between the abundant realities of his adopted country and the desire for his idealized mother country. This restlessness is realized materially in his travel back and forth between Australia and Britain. Having experienced great wealth and near poverty, Mahony finally succumbs to a degenerative mental condition and is buried, virtually abandoned, in a small country town in Victoria.

The trilogy begins, as it ends, with a burial: a young digger, known only to his mate as 'Young Bill', is consigned to an anonymous grave when the inadequately supported walls of his tunnel collapse: 'and over his defenceless body, with a roar that burst his ear-drums, broke stupendous masses of earth' (Richardson, [1917] 1971, p. 1). The anonymity of the victim and the sense of his vulnerability against the forces of nature are both recognizable features of the Australian literary canon. Richardson encapsulates, in this opening, the whole foundation of her story of the self-inflicted tragedy of Richard Mahony.

Young Bill's 'mate', Long Jim, who regards the younger man's death as personal ill-luck, also exemplifies the central themes of the novel. Indulging in self-pity at the loss of his mate and his claim, he remembers with longing and nostalgia his past life as a London lamplighter on a dark winter's afternoon: easy honest work, companionship and order. By contrast, the dream that brought Jim to the gold fields was one of 'a wonderful country, where, for the mere act of stooping, and with your naked hand, you could pick up a fortune from the ground' (p. 3). The reality is that the evils of fruitless toil, injustice and poverty, frequently associated in Australian mythology with city life in the Old World, are correspondingly transferred to the landscape. In Jim's view, the landscape is responsible for resisting the fictions of comfort and ease which had drawn him away from his home.

The opening chapter of the novel, entitled 'The Proem', moves cinematically from the specific instance of Young Bill and Long Jim to a vast panorama of the Ballarat site. The naturalistic image of the despoiled earth is set against a pastoral idyll of the 'pre-golden era' (see Units 7 and 8). This ironic commentary on the reality of the 'golden' era is turned around into a parody of the classical Golden Age of the pastoral poets. In this New World Eden 'shepherds' watch, not their flocks, but their neighbours' claims and the 'puddlers' trample the mud to press out the gold dust 'as wine-pressers trample grapes'. This 'ideal' is immediately undercut by an image of extreme anti-heroic proportions:

> Thus the pale-eyed multitude worried the surface, and, at the risk and cost of their lives, probed the depths. Now that deep sinking was in vogue, gold-digging no longer served as a play-game for the gentleman and the amateur; the greater number of those who toiled at it were work-tried, seasoned men. And yet, although it had now sunk to the level of any other arduous and uncertain occupation, and the magic prizes of the early days were seldom found, something of the old, romantic glamour still clung to this most famous gold-field, dazzling the eyes and confounding the judgement. Elsewhere, the horse was in use at the puddling-trough, and machines for crushing quartz were under discussion. But the Ballarat digger resisted the introduction of the machinery, fearing the capitalist machinery would bring in its train. He remained the dreamer, the jealous individualist, he hovered for ever on the brink of a stupendous discovery. (Richardson, [1917] 1971, p. 7)

The images contained within this extract could be intended to highlight the democratic nature of the quest, where none stands out above his neighbour and all have their eyes fastened on the same goal. It is an apocalyptic perspective, simultaneously vast and belittling. All of these men in Richardson's vision are failures, 'prisoners of the soil'. And yet, in spite of the apocalyptic nature of her paradigm, this 'pale-eyed multitude' emerge from the clay, not as a debased mechanism of humanity, but as a 'motley crowd' of single-minded individualists, dreamers and visionaries, each pursuing his own quest for 'a stupendous discovery' with the kind of romantic heroism soon to be overshadowed by the machinery of a pragmatic, progressive materialist age. So we see, in this extract, Richardson engaged in a project of simultaneously stripping the romanticism from the readers' eyes in order that we appreciate the doomed romantic vision of her subjects. For some the gold is merely a material manifestation of a much larger and undefinable dream.

'The Proem' ends with a description of the mythological figure of the landscape:

> Such were the fates of those who succumbed to the 'unholy hunger'. It was like a form of revenge taken on them, for their loveless schemes of robbing and fleeing, a revenge contrived by the ancient, barbaric country they had so lightly invaded. Now, she held them captive – without chains, ensorcelled – without witchcraft, and, lying stretched like some primeval monster in the sun, her breasts freely bared, she watched, with a malignant eye, the efforts made by these puny mortals to tear their lips away. (p. 8)

This is the monster Earth mother, a complex combination of nurturing and malevolence: her breasts bearing the 'daffodil-yellow veining of bluish-white quartz' from which the 'puny mortals' are unable to tear themselves away. Richard Mahony's tragedy is that having experienced the bounty of his foster mother country, he is unable to experience the fulfilment of the dream of belonging which drives him on.

On the face of it, Richardson has fulfilled her intention to tell the story of Australia as failure rather than success. Mahony's life and death appear to follow closely the paradigm of Young Bill at the beginning of the novel: he, too, arrived in hope, worked hard, deteriorated through bad luck and bad judgement, fell ill and died ignominiously. In relation to the myth of the 'ensorcelled' diggers, Richard is demonstrably unable to drag himself away from the lure of Australia. Just as Richardson's brutal stripping away of the romantic idyll of the Australian gold fields reveals the heroism of the romantic visionaries in 'The Proem', the resolution of the novel resists the finality of Bill's end. Although Richard fails to complete his quest for complete knowledge and understanding, his failure does not result in his total annihilation. It is the power of fiction to subvert closure. After his burial, although his body is absorbed by the earth under which it lies, Mahony's 'vagrant spirit' evades the obliteration of the paradigm. He never fully 'belongs' to the country of his death, although he has contributed two children to the new generation of Australians, for whom the identity of the mother country is undisputed.

## The backlash against literary nationalism

In the period between the wars, there was a reaction to both a growing international-ism and a rather backward-looking literary nationalism, such as that represented by the novelist and influential critic, Vance Palmer. In poetry there were various movements, including that led by Jack Lindsay and Kenneth Slessor in the journal *Vision*. They looked for their creative inspiration to Greek civilization and to European literature and philosophy including Byron, Browning and Nietzsche. *Vision* published some of the best poetry of the day.

A completely different response is represented by the Jindyworobak movement. Named for an Aboriginal phrase meaning 'to join', the Jindyworobaks, in a series of poetry anthologies, proclaimed an intention to eschew 'alien' influences in Art and to promote a national culture based on knowledge of the Australian environ-ment and Australian history, including the pre-colonial past. In particular, the Jindyworobaks identified Aboriginal culture as one so evidently bound up with the environment that it should be assimilated to a modern form. The myths of the Dreamtime, symbolically appropriated, they felt, might establish a cultural spirituality lacking in Australian poetry. This led, however, to a perception of the movement as a naive and simplistic attempt to co-opt Aboriginal language and culture into white Australian forms. The movement was virtually defunct in the 1950s; it foundered on a perceived nostalgia, parochialism and isolationism which was increasingly irrelevant to Australia in the modern world. By this time, too, a new intellectualism, led by poets James McAuley and A.D. Hope in the pages of *Quadrant*, an influential arts journal, was casting a cool eye over what it considered to be the spiritual poverty of the Australian arts. At this time too, Patrick White, having given up his determination to be a playwright, was also seeking to reappraise the myths of origin and exploration.

## Patrick White: discovering Australia

Patrick White is arguably Australia's greatest novelist. The son of a wealthy pastoralist family, he was educated in England at public school and Cambridge. His return to Australia in 1948 was a conscious decision to find in his birthplace the inspiration for his work. We have seen from the discussion of Lawson and Richardson that in Australian literature landscape is an ambivalent place of belonging – the site of cultural identity, but also of the life-and-death struggle between man and hostile nature, and the failure of dreams beyond mere survival. In *Voss* (1957), Patrick White's great novel of exploration, these themes are revisited and form the background to the philosophical questions of the struggle between God and Man, between man and nature, between the spiritual and the material, between dream and reality. The object of the present discussion of *Voss*, is to investigate how the narrative treats the marginal characters – Aborigines and women – as agents in this struggle.

Set in the colony of New South Wales in the 1840s, the novel is named for the principal character, Johann Ulrich Voss, who leads an expedition into the north-west interior. The colonials huddle together in the town, reciting the first recorded names of their colony, 'the fly-spots of human settlement' which anchor them on the blank map of the continent. Australia is *terra nullius*, literally an empty land, on which Voss is determined to impose his will. Voss specifically rejects the colonials' map, saying 'The map? ... I will first make it'. This then is the imperialist's dream: to inscribe a blank sheet with a new history of Western knowledge; to inscribe the blank page with the name of the first man. In a complex and multifaceted metaphor, during his journey into the interior Voss makes the map of himself, testing his physical and mental limits to the furthest boundaries of suffering and self-knowledge until he and all but one of his team die.

It is interesting to note, however, that even the map proffered by the colonial, Mr Bonner, is not as empty as its few charted settlements suggest. As Voss discovers, the further into the interior that he travels, there is human settlement throughout the bush. But the Aborigines who appear in the novel are not there in order to establish the fact that Australia was far from being *terra nullius*. In many ways their material presence in Voss's personal struggle with nature has the opposite effect. When Voss leaves Boyle's station for the interior, for example, the two Aborigines who accompany the party are not known by their true names, nor is it ever suggested that they might have had other names than those given to them by the colonizers. As such, superficially at least, they are appropriated along with the land in which they live; before the white man came to assign their names, Jackie and Dugald did not exist, they too were blank spaces, without culture or history. This suggestion is reinforced by the description of the myriad unnamed Aborigines who people the hostile interior landscape of both the real and the dream world experienced by Voss. Like the natives in Conrad's *Heart of Darkness*, they are denied humanity (see Unit 16). For Voss they are 'corporeal shadows', living links between the material and the dream:

> The two blacks jogged along, a little to one side of Voss, as if the subjects of his new kingdom preferred to keep their distance. ... Their voices were for each other, and twining with the dust.

> Other figures were beginning to appear, their shadows first, followed by a suggestion of skin wedded to the trunk of a tree. Then at a bend in the river's bed, the dusty bodies of men undoubtedly emerged. (White, 1957, p. 191)

Consider the language in which the Aborigines are presented in this passage. Given Voss's megalomaniacal tendencies, that they have become subjects in his dream-world kingdom is not unusual – Voss is able to view most of his fellow explorers in this light. What is notable, however, is the suggestion that the natives are in substance made from the earth itself, that they emerge from nature and return to it at will. The Aborigines, in this way, do not exist as living beings in their own right, but in an animistic sense as the material representatives of nature. That they eventually resist Voss's incursions suggests that they have come truly to act as in an animistic role. The possibility of the resistance of nature to the acquisitiveness of man is glimpsed by Laura Trevelyan on the evening before the expedition sets off:

> It was now possible that the usually solid house, and all that it contained, that the whole civil history of those parts was presumptuous, and that the night, close and sultry as savage flesh, distant and dilating as stars, would prevail by natural law. (p. 85)

In this brief extract we can see the Aborigine stripped of humanity, he is pure animism: the 'sultry ... savage flesh' of the earth. Later, the justice of 'natural law' is exacted when Jackie decapitates the exhausted and dying Voss before himself 'melt[ing] at last into the accommodating earth'.

Although Voss's material journey into the interior has ended in failure, his spiritual journey ends in a more ambiguous manner. Dogged by 'corporeal shadows' – real men made into ethereal beings – on the one hand, Voss is accompanied, on the other, by the pure spirit of a real woman, Laura Trevelyan. Attracted to Voss by her own experience of isolation and alienation from the values of the society in which they live, Laura is both drawn and repulsed by Voss's arrogance and will to power:

> 'You are so vast and ugly ... I can imagine some desert, with rocks, rocks of prejudice, and, yes, even hatred. You are so isolated. That is why you are fascinated by the prospect of desert places, in which you will find your own situation taken for granted, or more than that, exalted. ... *You* are *my* desert!' (White, 1957, pp. 87–8)

Here we see the metaphor of the desert of the soul made clear in Laura's response to Voss. Laura shares Voss's suffering at home through a kind of mystical empathy: as he suffers exhaustion, thirst and decapitation, so she suffers a brain fever, having her head shaved and near death. The redemption which each experiences is, however, different. We understand from the expedition's sole survivor, Judd, that Voss has entered the spirit world of the landscape, and has found a home there, while she is locked into the materiality of corporeal existence, even to the extent of its banality. The novel ends on a note of irony, with the prophetic Laura, having heralded a future when an 'indigenous' Art will emerge from the land, is left wondering, in the manner of her aunt, whether she had brought her lozenges. Just as Jackie, having achieved his moment of transcendence, melts into the earth which is the medium of nature, Laura melts back into the material world which is the medium of society.

## Continuing the search for an Australian aesthetic

At the very end of *Voss*, Laura Trevelyan expresses the belief that one day in the future there will emerge from the new inhabitants of Australia an Art – painting, music, literature – which will truly express the uniqueness of the Australian landscape. White's decision then to undercut this vision with the banality of Laura's lost lozenges casts a long shadow over the intervening century, during which time White felt that Art was involved in a constant struggle with colonial mediocrity. This pessimism prevailed throughout the 1950s in the work of poets like Judith Wright and A.D. Hope. Hope's vision of Australia as a post-menopausal woman still being drained by 'second-hand Europeans' ... 'Whose boast is not "we live" but "we survive"' ('Australia'), echoes that of Henry Handel Richardson, and of White's *Voss* (McKernan, 1989). McKernan suggests, however, that Judith Wright refused to accept the kind of fatalism implied in Hope's poem. Wright was one of the few poets to support the work of the Jindyworobak movement in trying to secure for Australian literature an understanding of the meaning of belonging to the place (McKernan, 1989, p. 143). This went beyond the kind of crude appropriation of Aboriginal language to an appreciation of an existing culture and body of knowledge.

The Jindyworobaks' quest for a way to express a sense of uniqueness of the Australian experiences through a link with Aboriginal culture was not completely lost from Australian poetry. In his poem, 'The Buladelah-Taree Holiday Song Cycle' (1976), Les Murray could be said to have realized the ideals of the movement and raised them to a height of aesthetic assimilation which could be said to be wholly 'Australian'.

## Les Murray: indigenizing myths of cultural identity

'The Buladelah-Taree Holiday Song Cycle' takes the form of thirteen sections and is based on R.M. Berndt's translation of an Aboriginal song cycle from north-eastern Arnhem Land, 'The Wonguri-Mandjikai Moon-Bone Song Cycle'. In this way, Murray suggests that he is able loosely to approximate the rhythms of the Aboriginal oral tradition. The moon-bone song celebrates the myth of the death and rebirth of the moon as the pattern for the cyclical nature of all life in a series of thirteen songs.

Like the song cycle, Murray's poem celebrates a cyclical notion of time and its intimate link with the topology of the environment. The poem follows a multiple system of cyclic patterns: from evening to evening; childhood, parenthood, old age; the seasons; the processes of history. Murray skilfully links these patterns in a series of spiralling connections which move the narrative within circles but also forward, with the sense of something achieved, a place reached as well as one returned to.

The idea of place, the central issue in Australian literature, is the rhythmic structure of the poem. The repetition of place names, some of them Aboriginal, but more evoking the spirit of a white settler history, is the core of the poem and its thematic base. There are four major themes in the poem: the first deals with a nostalgia for a 'land' of childhood; the second is the familiar Australian concern with the contrast between the artifice of the city and the 'authenticity' of rural life; the third is also a familiar one in Australian literature, the anti-establishment ethos of Australian life; the fourth is the celebration of the Australian character and lifestyle.

The narrative of the poem, as the title suggests, is based on the mass migration of city dwellers into the countryside during the summer/Christmas holiday season. The first section begins the day before the exodus when the preparations have been made for the return of the 'children'. Immediately a line of opposition has been drawn between the 'dinner' of the country and the 'lunch' eaten by the 'town people'; there is also mention of the 'rationalized farms' and 'the Pitt Street farms', a reference to the historical wounds perceived to have been inflicted on the country dwellers by the city. Authenticity is established as in-dwelling in the country places to which the 'children' will travel: 'the place of ... / the Big Flood That Time', 'the / cattle-crossing-long-ago places' (Murray, 1977).

The central motif of the poem is that of the road bringing the children back to the place of authentic memory: 'that big stunning snake'. Here Murray appropriates the imagery of the serpent of Aboriginal Dreaming and transmutes it into the 'Long Narrow City', a moving highway of the holiday tribe returning 'home'. In a symbolic realization of the process of the poem, the City has 'crossed the Myall', a reference which evokes the topography of the landscape (the Myall is a river which is indeed crossed on the way to the north coast) but also interweaves the history of black/white relations ('myall' is an early settler name for wild tribal Aborigines – who were crossed and double-crossed at places like Myall Creek); importantly, too, the whole poem is a European language and vision, 'crossed' with Aboriginal mythology and metre.

Like the city in white Australian mythology, the holiday serpent is not a benign entity; there are fumes, crimes, parasitic policemen and girls who court murder. All are transported through the 'gut' of the living city on the move. The juxtaposition of 'the police, collecting Revenue' and the image of vulnerable 'girls walking close to murder' suggests a corruption of innocence and duty.

Once they have reached 'that country of the Holiday', the children are celebrated in their private and public histories in the naming of the landscape, its flora and fauna and, more specifically, the spirit of the white men who left their mark on it. It is clear that the return has the function of recharging the cultural memory of the returnees, but not in a sense of repetition or simple rediscovery. There is maintained a tension between the young and old, the city and the country which implies a knowledge of the place of nostalgia in the life of a nation, but also an inevitable undervaluing of the suffering of the older generation in its creation:

> The Fathers and the Great-Grandfathers, they are out in the
>     paddocks all the time, they live out there,
>   at the place of the Rail Fence, of the Furrows Under Grass, at the
>     place of the Slab Chimney.

> We tell them that clearing is complete, an outdated attitude, all
>     over;
> we preach without a sacrifice, and are ignored; flowering bushes
>     grow dull to our eyes.
>
> (5, ll. 1–8)

This theme of struggle, sacrifice and survival, common to Australian nationalist literature, is taken up again in Murray's images of 'the warriors', the hard men of the land: in the pantheon of Australian characters these men stand at the apex – bronzed as compared to the 'pale [city] man' who attempts to exchange pleasantries with them, they empower the everyday: 'Making Timber a word of power, Con-rod a word of power, / Sense a word of power, the Regs. a word of power' (9, ll. 13–14). These men have paid for their deification, not through heroic deeds, but through work. As the spirit of the place takes hold:

> city storemen and accounts clerks point them out to their wives,
> remembering things about themselves, and about the ibis.
>
> (10, ll. 23–4)

Women, it seems, have little share in this collective memory of Australian identity.

Murray's aim is to celebrate Australia and the Australian: pasture and paddock, the freshwater lakes and seaside beaches, the cultivated and the scrub land, the flat lands and the forested mountains are each given their own song in the cycle. As is the great Australian festival occasion of the barbecue at the lake, city/children playing at country/men. The result is a map in verse of a white 'Dreaming', the snake road weaving together land, time, history. In the final poem the cycle of the songs has come around through the morning, through the heat of noontime, to the evening sky. Like the land, it is a map of memories, of places named in another hemisphere by another culture, except the one defining constellation of the Southern Hemisphere. Above the land, the Southern Cross – that luminous symbol of Australian republicanism – rises like a flag over the land and its people, ancient and modern:

> the Cross is rising on his elbow, above the glow of the horizon;
> carrying a small star in his pocket, he reclines there brilliantly,
> above the Alum Mountain, and the lakes threaded on the Myall
>     River, and above the Holiday.
>
> (13, ll. 41–4)

For Les Murray, national identity is still rooted in the rural landscape and its inhabitants, where the contours of the land can be seen plainly for what they are: different from 'things in other lands'. It is an eloquent vision of a nation unified by a history, a lifestyle and a unique people. But it is also a vision disabled by the fear of the inauthenticity of the urban culture. There is no sense that in the city of 'storemen and accounts clerks' there might be repositories of a developing nationhood, nor that Aborigines and women might have a transformative vision to offer: nationality it seems is still as firmly entrenched in nostalgia for a mythical past as it was in the 1890s.

## Postmodernism and Australian literature

In recent years there has been an Australian response to a world-wide movement towards questioning the hegemony of Western epistemology, particularly the ability of historiography to provide any more than a partial and fragmenting rationale for the founding of a nation. Robert Drewe, in his novel *The Savage Crows* (1976), uses parallel narratives to contrast the loss of selfhood between the last of the full-blood Tasmanian Aborigines and a modern-day researcher into their demise. The Aboriginal writer, Mudrooroo, takes up the story of the Tasmanians in his rewritten history, discussed below. Peter Carey in *Oscar and Lucinda* (1988) and David Malouf in *Remembering Babylon* (1993) each challenge the nature of vision, heroism, and failure in a landscape of uncertainty.

## Mudrooroo: recapturing history

Mudrooroo is one of a group of Aboriginal writers who have made a significant impact on Australian literature. Some, like poet Oodgeroo Noonuccal (Kath Walker), and poets and playwrights, Jack Davis and Kevin Gilbert, are well established, and others, like novelist, Archie Weller, and artist and writer, Sally Morgan, have emerged more recently.

In 1965, Mudrooroo published the first novel by an Aborigine in Australia's literary history, *Wild Cat Falling*, under the name of Colin Johnson. This novel established a theme which is returned to again and again in literature written by Aborigines, the experiences of the young, urban black man, on the margins of white society, searching for an identity which will explain his experience of alienation and offer him a voice with which to challenge his marginality.

By contrast to this social realism, in *Doctor Wooreddy's Prescription for Enduring the Ending of the World* (1983) Mudrooroo has said that he is re-entering Aboriginal history and culture in order to recapture it from white history (Johnson, 1985, p. 29). Until recently the history of the Aboriginal/white encounter has largely been consigned to a footnote in white colonialist accounts of the formation of the Australian nation. As we have seen in relation to the discussion of Patrick White's *Voss*, Aborigines have also served as 'non-material agents' of the landscape, occupying its space in the manner of flora or fauna, in order to provide literature with a metaphor for melancholy and mystery. In this book Mudrooroo chooses to revisit one of the best-documented accounts of white/Aboriginal relations in Australian history and to provide for the reader a clearly articulated Aboriginal consciousness. This is not necessarily seen as an alternative view of the facts – these surely are fully documented in the sources Mudrooroo has used – but a different way of accessing them. Perhaps, for this reason, Mudrooroo chose to present the story through the consciousness of Wooreddy, cited in the historical sources only briefly as Count Alpha, rather than the more obvious figure of Trugernanna (Truganini in white historical accounts), the Aboriginal 'princess' whose relationship with the colonists has come to symbolize a tragic inevitability. Mudrooroo challenges the Romantic gloss of the noble savage which is one of the slants put on a story which once served to illustrate the physical, psychological and cultural inferiority of the race.

The myth of *Ria Warrawah* and the Aboriginal view of time underpins Mudrooroo's perspective on the events of the novel. *Ria Warrawah* is the dark force in a dualistic system of belief which has on the one hand the benevolent power of the Great Ancestor and his control of fire and on the other the mists and darkness of the evil spirit, the balance of which was necessary in order to maintain human existence on the earth. The invasion of the ghosts or *num*, with their disregard of boundaries, evil practices and, above all, the disease which they spread among the 'human' population, made it clear to the inhabitants of the southern island off the Australian coast that *Ria Warrawah* had gained the upper hand in his struggle with the Great Ancestor and had set in motion the end of the world. The character of Wooreddy is both historical and legendary: he is at one and the same time a victim of this invasion and a 'wit' doctor, or one who seems to have insight into the workings of the world and the spirits and is able to interpret the phenomenon which has beset his people. In this way he is able to explain and demonstrate the apparent passivity of the people while describing in graphic terms the devastation wreaked by the white invaders.

Wooreddy's interpretation of the events leading up to the destruction of his tribe and the homogenization of the southern Aborigines' culture, is based on the belief in the synchronicity of time. For Wooreddy's people, the past, the present and the future were coexisting states which, when the world was in balance, were fixed and mutually regulating: 'Before, uneventful time had stretched back towards the known beginning. Now, it seemed that something had torn the present away from that past', which in turn made the future, once a certainty, uncertain. Wooreddy develops his 'uncertainty principle' in order to account for his sense of the ending of the world being in process: '*Ria Warrawah* walks the earth and we can do nothing to stop him' (Mudrooroo, 1983, p. 85).

The passivity and fatalism exhibited by the men is contrasted with the suffering of the women; while the men sit at the fireside waiting for the coughing sickness to take its toll, the women endure abduction and rape. Wooreddy witnesses not just their suffering but also their resentment towards the men who might be expected to protect them. After her rape by four white sailors, Trugernanna reserves her contempt for the witness of her degradation:

> Unsteadily she managed a few steps, then stood swaying on her feet. Slowly her face lifted and her dull eyes brightened as she saw Wooreddy standing in the undergrowth. She glared into his eyes, spat in his direction, then turned and dragged her hips down to the waves subsiding in the long rays of the sun setting in a swirl of clearing cloud. ... [He] waddled away with Trugernanna's glare, that dull then bright gaze filled with spite and contempt, in his mind. It upset him and dispelled his numbness which, fortunately for Wooreddy (though he often didn't realise it) was not the impervious shield of his theorising, and could be easily penetrated. (Mudrooroo, 1983, p. 22)

Later it is the women, famously Trugernanna, who are responsible for what little action is taken or resistance is offered. Recognizing that she is not going to be saved from the brutality of the *num* by either Mangana, her father, or Wooreddy, her prospective husband, Trugernanna transfers her allegiance to George Augustus Robinson, the Protector of Aborigines for the colonial government, who offers her protection from the white men in exchange for her compliance with his code of morality. Historically, it has been the fatal role of Robinson's civilizing mission in the seemingly inexorable progress towards near extinction for the south-island Aborigines which is central to white settler accounts. Mudrooroo, however, dramatizes a complex dynamic around the central characters of Wooreddy, Trugernanna and Robinson. His vision encompasses the plight of Robinson's wife, Marie, as entrapped by her husband's 'mission' as the people who are the objects of it. Themes of belief, betrayal, the vulnerability of the individual to the dictates of culture, religion and government are mirrored in these characters. Wooreddy and Robinson are equally entrapped by their belief systems, the two women by their physical and cultural subordination to men. As visionaries and fools, Wooreddy and Robinson are equals.

Mudrooroo's analysis of the historical events goes far beyond the simplistic explanation of the 'fatal' clash of cultures. In his portrait of Robinson, as of Wooreddy, he encapsulates the social vulnerability, simplicity and genuine sincerity of the builder cum government official, while simultaneously revealing Robinson's necessarily rigid and blinkered adherence to his own moral system. In the following extract, Robinson is replying to a settler from an established sealing community with some social standing who has refuted Robinson's suggestion that the 'native' women have been corrupted by their white 'husbands':

> 'Apart from this, there is the matter of intemperance and indecorous behaviour. Just look there, that disgusting old man lives with that native female, and there stands the result of their union, that boy there, a mixture of both races. What will happen to such hybrids? They show us our own immorality.' (Mudrooroo, 1983, p. 144)

The outcome of colonizer/colonized relationships is reflected in the physical hybrid of the offspring from their union. Far from creating a civilization in their own image, the colonizers and the colonized have created a hybrid who mocks the failure of the whole civilizing mission both to carry out its project and to protect its proponents from the transformative potential of the encounter.

Mudrooroo, while not downplaying the catastrophic effect of white settlement, and specifically colonization, on the Bruny Island and Tasmanian Aborigines, demonstrates that this process was not simply one of subject/object relations, but was part of a complex and mutually affecting dynamic between the two groups.

## New Zealand

### The late colonial period

As in Australia, it was not until the 1890s that New Zealand was conscious of the potential for founding a national literature. And again, as in Australia, the Sydney weekly newspaper, the *Bulletin*, played a major role in raising the awareness of the colony of the potential in their midst. Patrick Evans suggests that the Australian journal was officially frowned upon and those New Zealanders who worked for it found it difficult to be published in their own country (Evans, 1990, p. 31). An important factor in this bias was probably the tone of the *Bulletin*'s republican rhetoric. Republicanism does not seem to have been the issue in New Zealand it is in Australia, where ultimately the apparent gap between desire and reality contributed to the sense of frustration and pessimism in Australian literature until the late 1960s. Indeed, the traditional suspicion and rivalry between bush and city, which we have seen throughout Australian literature, is absent from the New Zealand literary landscape. The myth of the lost Eden, of the corruption of country innocence by city rapaciousness, is replaced in New Zealand by a dream to create the Pastoral Paradise of sheep and dairy farms and the Just City of a new and better social order. This was, of course, only to be achieved through the work, hardship and endurance of the settlers. As in Australia, exposure to the isolation of bush life created character, in the nationalist sense, and created characters, who in turn provided the short-story writer with material. Again, it is typical that the character of the bush worker permeated the society, if not in so adversarial a fashion as in Australia; the character was masculine, rough and individualist.

## Katherine Mansfield's bush stories

The best-known New Zealand writer, Katherine Mansfield, grew up in this period of character formation. Her parents were Australians who later settled in Wellington, New Zealand, where her father became a wealthy banker. After her brother was killed in France in 1916, Mansfield found a new resolve in her writing to explore the childhood experience of New Zealand. In terms of her New Zealand stories, Mansfield is best known for her long, finely detailed portraits of middle-class family life, 'Prelude' and 'At the Bay'. In the portrait of Linda Burnell, the enervated wife to the pompous and slightly ridiculous Stanley and distant mother to his children, Mansfield sketches an Australian girlhood of riding the wide open spaces, mateship with the men and anti-domestic sentiment in which the figure of her father is prominent. Linda Burnell could be Miles Franklin's Sybylla Melvyn of *My Brilliant Career* (1901), finally caught out by life, terminally frustrated into 'weariness'.

These stories represent Mansfield's finest writing, the pinnacle of her achievements in the form of the genre. Her position as an outsider in Europe gave her an ironical view of British mores and Continental manners. It also contributed to a sense of rootlessness, of being constantly in transit, which implied a certain vulnerability to experience. This was not simply personal, a rare affectionate portrait of her father in her journal shows him, the colonial in Europe, being cheated by porters and losing his wallet on a train. It is surprising, therefore, that there is an absence of nostalgia and sentiment in the later New Zealand stories. Mansfield's concern is to render a time, a place and familial relationships, but there is no sense in which these are extended outside of the specificity of those relationships to include cultural stereotypes or to imply a collective identity.

There are, however, a number of stories written by Mansfield between 1911 and 1913, which appear to follow closely the conventions of the colonial short story. The emphasis in these stories is on character and situation. The unusual or bizarre is stressed, the effect of the landscape on the mind, the dangers of being beyond the reach of the familiar are explored. Characterization relies heavily on the stereotyped figures of oral narrative or what Miles Franklin refers to as the 'Yarn': the loner with dark secrets, the suggestion of madness, the maladjusted New Chum. The landscape becomes the forum for the investigation of the individual psyche unfettered by the restraints and demands of civilization. The melodramatic elements, violence, murder, insanity, romance, tragedy, are framed by enigmatic and sometimes ambiguous narrative viewpoints. Importantly, these stories rely for their success on mutual understanding between author and reader as to the conventions of the genre.

Of this group of stories, collected after Mansfield's death by her husband, John Middleton Murry, as *Something Childish and Other Stories* (1924), 'The Woman at the Store' and 'Millie' are particularly illustrative of Mansfield's use of colonial story conventions (Mansfield, 1945). In both stories Mansfield places the vulnerable figure of the woman in an unfamiliar and isolated landscape. In 'Millie' the woman is placed briefly under threat by the prowling man, until it is revealed that he is the 'New Chum' hand who is wanted for the murder of his boss. The story becomes an investigation of a woman who has adapted, imperfectly but sufficiently, to her circumstances as a colonial in the isolated regions of New Zealand. She is confronted by a young Englishman who has obviously been scarred by his experiences in the place she thinks of as home, and whose accent suggests a breeding superior to hers. His plight awakens a desire to nurture him, but when that evening he is discovered hiding in the outbuildings, she joins in the hunt with a kind of savage glee, that suggests a triumph of the fittest rather than of the most cultured. In 'The Woman at the Store', however, Mansfield explores the nature of survival and colonialism more deeply and disturbingly.

'The Woman at the Store' begins conventionally enough. The narrator is one of three travellers riding through the countryside on some unknown, long-distance business. The scene is familiar to the region: heat, dust, monotonous scrubland. The narrator's fellow travellers are also typical: they appear to be used to the saddle and are dressed in typical 'bushmen' fashion. The sporadic conversation is coarse and their language common. Jim plays on Jo's youth and sexual inexperience in describing the woman at the store they are riding towards. The store, too, is typical. The English periodicals announcing Queen Victoria's Jubilee which plaster the wall, emphasize the geographical and cultural isolation of the inhabitants, which is extended by implication to the whole colonial population. When they arrive at the store, the woman says that she is ironing, an activity which comments upon the incommensurability of culture and environment that is the colonial experience. The maintenance of standards might be said to reassure the readers of the colonial story but it equally draws attention to displacement and incongruity. The extreme isolation of the store and its inhabitants works on the narrator, who becomes afraid of the sense of the grotesque which this incongruity and incommensurability produces:

> There is no twilight in our New Zealand days, but a curious half-hour when everything appears grotesque – it frightens – as though the savage spirit of the country walked abroad and sneered at what it saw. ('The Woman at the Store', Mansfield, 1945, p. 565)

The second part of the sentence highlights the incongruity and questions the legitimacy of the colonizer in the landscape. This double edge is again typical of the colonial story; in this story, however, this edge is honed further by a series of narrative shocks.

The first shock of the story is in the contrast between Jim's description of the woman and the reality. The scene as they approach the store is reminiscent of Lawson's 'The Drover's Wife' (see above, pp. 714–15): a lone woman with a stick, a child and a dog. But the reassurance that Lawson's reader derives from the wife's command and endurance is inverted by this woman's evident need, madness and her ruined appearance. That fact that she is also the butt of a crude joke reflects on the humanity of all present. The narrator records the scene, without a trace of compassion or sentiment. The only solicitude displayed is that of the woman for the narrator, otherwise the woman and her 'kid' are brutally assessed for their mental, moral and physical weaknesses. The fact that she has probably been abandoned by her husband is passed off with a shrug by Jim, her instability is put down to isolation as if it were inevitable. The leering, opportunistic attitude of Jo towards the woman's situation is also described in some detail and without censure. When the woman takes Jo into her bed, Jim's only comment, 'It's the loneliness', seems to sum up colonial ambivalence towards an imposed moral code, using the strangeness of the environment as justification for flouting it.

The distant narration of events contributes to the second major shock of the story: the discovery that the narrator is herself a woman. This realization has the dual effect of instantly challenging received ideas about male and female behaviour, while foregrounding the issues of humanity which run through the narrative. The lack of sentiment or compassion from a female narrator concentrates the reader's attention on her account of the relationships between the protagonists: the woman's brutal interactions with her daughter, the disquieting knowingness of the child's vengeful revelations about the woman's husband. The narrator's reference throughout the story to the 'kid' also seems to evoke a deeper sense of the child's closer kinship with the dog than with humankind. Suddenly, we are reminded of Jim's 'malicious' smile as he prevents the narrator from falling from her horse at the beginning of the story and also of her brusque denial of any physical frailty. The narrator's adoption of an idiom virtually indistinguishable from the men's casts a keener light on that idiom than a feminine viewpoint might have done. There is one moment when the narrator betrays only the slightest suggestion of fellow feminine knowledge. In realizing that her brother has been seduced by a promise made in jest by Jim (the former barmaid's knowledge of kissing), she characterizes male credulity with regard to women and sex: 'One hundred and twenty-five different ways – alas! my poor brother!' In this environment there is no place for sentiment or moralizing. As the store disappears from view, we are led to believe, so too do the wider consequences of the misery and murder we have witnessed.

This is a man's country and the women find themselves having to play by the rules or succumb to the anomalies of their lives in the bush. As we have seen in relation to other colonial writing, women stand as the last bastions of humanity in the wilderness. Here Mansfield has suggested that the true price of survival is the loss of human response altogether. The readers of this colonial fiction might find the conventions comfortingly familiar, but in this story Mansfield places in doubt the whole colonial project of the triumph of civilization over savagery.

## Social realism and the literary response

Although the ethos described here is masculine, it is significant that here, as in Australia, many of the best colonial writers were women. From the earliest times on the sheep stations women were the chroniclers of colonial life, but frequently their fiction consisted of melodramatic romances and Dickensian plots. Some women tackled colonial issues within this formal restraint: B.E. Baughan depicted race relations in her stories, *Brown Bread from a Colonial Oven* (1912). The novelists Jane Mander and Jean Devanny, however, were more concerned with social politics. Mander's investigation of the domestic scene, reveals it as a restrictive and limiting one for women. In her novels, *The Story of a New Zealand River* (1920) and *The Passionate Puritan* (1921), for example, Mander challenges puritanism and sexual mores, offering careers and extramarital relationships as a liberating alternative at a cost. Jean Devanny, on the other hand, was primarily concerned with the social conditions of the worker. A member of the Communist Party, Devanny moved to Sydney in 1929 and became a member of the social realist group of writers there. Her books also celebrate women's potential as workers, unfettered by the restrictions of marriage, and chart the injustices of the class struggle.

The desire to 'tell the truth about New Zealand' became a prominent fixation during the 1930s, when depression and poverty demanded a close examination of the social fabric. John Mulgan, Frank Sargeson, Denis Glover and Allen Curnow developed an anti-literary-establishment stance. C.K. Stead has characterized this movement as equivalent to Auden's revolt against 'Georgian' romanticism: 'as the Auden generation turned a cold eye on this romanticizing ... so Curnow and his contemporaries deflated the myth of a South Seas paradise' (Stead, 1981, p. 71). In 1945, Allen Curnow edited the influential poetry anthology, *A Book of New Zealand Verse, 1923–45*, which collected together the revolutionaries into an establishment. In 1947, Charles Brasch began the literary journal, *Landfall*, as a forum for this group of writers.

The 'cold eye' referred to by Stead, can be experienced in a poem like Allen Curnow's 'Landfall in Unknown Seas' (1942), which was commissioned by the New Zealand Department of Internal Affairs to commemorate the 300th anniversary of Tasman's discovery of New Zealand. In three parts, the poem moves from the excitement of discovery, to the realities of colonization, to the banality of history, which turns the drama of discovery and murder into self-congratulation in a world 'where wonders cease'.

Janet Frame was a member of a group of writers including Mulgan, Glover and Sargeson, but her early postmodernist experimentation with narrative and structure was unlike anything else. Best-known in Britain for the nightmarish vision of rural poverty and the treatment of mental illness in her autobiography, *To the Is-Land* (1983), *An Angel at My Table* (1984) and *The Envoy from Mirror City* (1985), Frame published her first work, a book of stories, *The Lagoon*, in 1951. Her novel, *Owls do Cry* (1957) marks her departure from the literary philosophy of her mentor, Frank Sargeson. In this novel, Frame departs from realism in a series of lyrical passages which disrupt the narrative and subvert the notion of mediated consciousness.

## Maori writing

One of the most notable divergences between Australian and New Zealand literary history is in the representation of indigenous peoples. The most significant element is their very visibility. The *Bulletin*'s insistence on the name 'Maoriland' when referring to New Zealand comments eloquently on the position of Aborigines in relation to their native land. Maori are at least acknowledged as having a claim on the territory. This may have come about through the two Maori land wars, which occur after the Treaty of Waitangi in 1840, wherein the Maori ceded the land to the British Crown. Aborigines, on the other hand, were barely visible, and where they did retaliate against intrusion, their actions tended to be guerrilla-like and easily put down by the ruthlessness of the colonists.

It was not until the 1960s that Maori writing in English and Maori languages was published and promoted in New Zealand. Keri Hulme is one of a number of contemporary writers, including Witi Ihimaera and Patricia Grace, who write about Maori experience of modern New Zealand. Like much Aboriginal writing in Australia, social realism dominates the form and content of much of this work, even when incorporating the most mystical elements of Maori traditions within the narrative. Patricia Grace, in her novel, *Cousins* (1992), for example, explores the complex demands faced by young Maori both from desperate elders trying to preserve and strengthen traditional community life and from the modern Pakeha world of education, work and politics, against the background of an intensely realized mysticism. In his collection of stories, *Pounamu, Pounamu* (1972), named for the New Zealand jade which is featured in Maori mythology, Witi Ihimaera's sometimes confused youngsters have to assimilate levels of knowledge and understanding from the purely adolescent to the arcane. Pakeha (European New Zealander) life is portrayed paradoxically both as central and dominant and as marginal and irrelevant; like pounamu, Maori life is indigenous and imbued with a significance beyond the insistent arrogations of colonial identity. Negotiation of a variety of subject positions is therefore the focus of much Maori writing since the 1960s, when Maori literature began to find a voice and a market among the liberal and educated reading public of New Zealand.

## Keri Hulme: *The Bone People*

Keri Hulme's novel, *The Bone People* (1983), can perhaps be seen partly as a reaction to the restrictions of social realism but also as a response to a growing awareness in literature of postcolonial, feminist and postmodernist discourse. Hulme's achievement is in the realization of these ideas within a complex structure which challenges the formalistic and narrative conventions of the novel. The success or otherwise of Hulme's vision is the subject of much critical notice, not least when its international profile was raised by its inclusion on the shortlist of the Booker Prize. Much of the criticism is centred on Hulme's vision of a future, harmonious New Zealand society based on an insistence on the mutability of racial, sexual and social boundaries and the shared experience of great suffering and love. The foundation for this new social pattern is the Maori tradition of community and myth rooted in a spiritual relationship with the land. Hulme puts all limitations and conventions to the test. Like other post-colonial writers, for example Salman Rushdie, Peter Carey or Janette Turner Hospital, she juxtaposes realism and mysticism, the rational and the irrational within the same register: her characters all undergo experiences which can be described as supernatural while they are at the very limits of the natural. Whereas other postmodern writers use ontological shifts to subvert the real, however, there is a sense in which Hulme's (and Grace's) mysticism demands entry to and acceptance by the real.

The narrative is structured around the experiences and interactions of three characters. Through their multiple and complex subject positions, inversions and subversions, Hulme investigates issues of racial, cultural and sexual identity. Kerewin Holmes, the dominating figure of the novel, at once crudely subverts stereotypical constructions of femininity, while at the same time subtly parodying the inverted form of the phallic woman in the excess of her character. Joe Gillayley and his adopted son, Simon, similarly question sexual and gender stereotypes: a once-married heterosexual, Joe is uncertain of his sexual orientation and is conscious of feelings for his son which are disturbing. Simon, too, has an inverted character: often mistaken for a girl because of his long hair and earring, privately he knows himself by the name of Clare. In this name, he feels, rests his identity, but it is a significantly ambivalent and open-ended one.

Traumatized by early abuse, Simon is silent. This lack of speech is significant since, unlike Kerewin and Joe, Simon is wholly Pakeha (European) in background. His discovery by Joe half-drowned on the shore is an enactment of the first invasion of the white men in New Zealand. The implication that Simon represents at one level the colonizer is reinforced by the suggestion that he is in reality the son of that convention of the colonial romance, the aristocratic black sheep. The discovery that Simon's only personal possessions belonged to the grandson of an Irish Earl, who was disinherited for 'disgraceful practices', places him at the centre of a colonial myth of origin. This colonial myth is reintroduced later in the novel when Joe is taken to Tauranga by the *kaumatua*, the old man who is 'caretaker' to the landing place of the first Maori canoes and its mysteries. This site is also that chosen by the doomed, drug-addicted Irishman, Timon, as the place of his death. It is obvious from the photograph kept by the *kaumatua* and the information gleaned from the police, that Timon was most likely Simon's natural father. This apparent coincidence has the effect of examining a colonialist literary stereotype, including its darker side of disinheritance, alienation, corruption and disease. The two myths are brought into intertextual proximity formally to announce the death of the one and the renewal of the other.

Importantly, Joe, who has become the heir to the old man's knowledge and position, is not a full-blood Maori; his father was English. The death of the blue-blooded aristocrat, whose suffering so closely resembles Joe's, foregrounds the progress of Joe, a cultural hybrid, to the position of keeper of the land's most arcane secrets. The issue of hybridity and the extension of a new interpretation of indigenous culture to the New Zealander is central to the narrative. Kerewin's 'tricephelos' sculpture serves as a motif of this vision of the future:

> The hair of their heads is entwined at the top in a series of spirals. Simon's hair curves back from his neck to link Kerewin and Joe to him. Kerewin wears the greenstone hook, he, his Moerangi pendant. (Hulme, 1983, p. 315)

These three are the bone people, that is, beginning of a new nation, not based on moribund colonial, hierarchical, patriarchal structures and conventions, but on the separate but interconnected Maori/Pakeha community.

Perhaps the most controversial aspect of Hulme's testing of limits is in her exploration of the darker aspects of relationship and community. Each of the protagonists, Kerewin Holmes, Joe Gillayley and his adopted son, Simon, are damaged by their past experiences. This damage and its destructive effects are unflinchingly probed through the relationship between the three characters and the wider community in which they live, both European and Maori. Her disturbing view of exploitative sexuality, child abuse and sado-masochism is realized in the fetishistic behaviour of the characters. This is particularly demonstrated in the relationship between Joe and Simon. Like Maggie Tulliver's doll in George Eliot's *The Mill on the Floss*, Simon is the focus of Joe's sense of powerlessness. A Pakeha who has been washed up on his shore and intrudes into his life, Simon's arrival is followed shortly after by the death of Joe's wife and child from influenza, the colonizer's disease. In an interesting inversion, Simon, the European intruder, wholly within the colonized's power, becomes the fetish for Joe's (Maori) desire and fears. Simon, like Jemmy in Malouf's *Remembering Babylon* (1993), already a veteran of suffering at the hands of strangers, is prepared to suffer the pain in order to experience the pleasure of belonging. His attempts to unite the two adults by sacrificing himself to Joe's temper places a question mark on the nature of love and suffering, which is never fully resolved by the narrative. As Kerewin suggests, suffering may temper the soul, but it also leaves scars.

## BIBLIOGRAPHY

PRIMARY TEXTS
Hulme, K. (1983) *The Bone People*, Hodder & Stoughton, London (also Picador, London, 1986).

Kiernan, B. (ed.) (1976) *The Portable Henry Lawson*, University of Queensland Press, St Lucia.

Krimmer, S. and Lawson, A. (eds) (1980) *Barbara Baynton*, University of Queensland Press, St Lucia.

Mansfield, K. (1945) *The Collected Stories of Katherine Mansfield*, Constable, London.

Murray, L.A. (1977) *Ethnic Radio*, Angus & Robertson, Sydney.

Mudrooroo (1983) *Dr Wooreddy's Prescription for Enduring the Ending of the World*, Hyland House, Melbourne.

Richardson, H.H. (1971) *Australia Felix*, Penguin, Harmondsworth [first published 1917].

White, P. (1957) *Voss*, Penguin, Harmondsworth.


LITERARY HISTORIES

Evans, P. (1990) *The Penguin History of New Zealand Literature*, Penguin, Harmondsworth.

Goodwin, K. (1986) *A History of Australian Literature*, Macmillan, London.

Hergenhan, L. (ed.) (1988) *The Penguin New Literary History of Australia*, Penguin Books Australia, Ringwood.

Sturm, T. (ed.) (1991) *The Oxford History of New Zealand Literature in English*, Oxford University Press, Auckland.


CRITICAL WORKS

Adam, I. and Tiffin, H. (eds) (1991) *Past the Last Post: Theorizing Post-colonialism and Postmodernism*, Harvester Wheatsheaf, Hemel Hempstead.

Ashcroft, B., Griffiths, G. and Tiffin, H. (1989) *The Empire Writes Back: Theory and Practice in Post-colonial Literatures*, Routledge, London.

Boehmer, E. (1995) *Colonial and Postcolonial Literature*, Oxford University Press, Oxford.

Croft, J. (1988) 'Responses to Modernism 1915–1945', in *A New Literary History of Australia*, ed. L. Hergenham, Penguin Books Australia, Ringwood.

Davison, G. (1978) 'Sydney and the Bush: An Urban Context for the Australian Legend', *Historical Studies* 18, 70–3, pp. 191–209.

Hodge, B. and Mishra, V. (1990) *Dark Side of the Dream*, Allen & Unwin, Sydney.

Johnson, C. (1985) 'White Forms, Aboriginal Content', in *Aboriginal Writing Today*, ed. J. Davis and B. Hodge, Australian Institute of Aboriginal Studies, Canberra.

Magarey, S., Rowley, S. and Sheridan, S. (1993) *Debutante Nation: Feminism Contests the 1890s*, Allen & Unwin, Sydney.

McKernan, S. (1989) *A Question of Commitment: Australian Literature in the Twenty Years after the War*, Allen & Unwin, Sydney.

Nesbitt, B.H. (1968) 'Aspects of Literary Nationalism in Australia and New Zealand with special reference to the *Bulletin*, 1880–90', unpublished PhD thesis, Australian National University, Canberra.

Schaffer, K. (1988) *Women and the Bush: Forces of Desire in the Australian Cultural Tradition*, Cambridge University Press, Cambridge.

Stead, C.K. (1981) *In the Glass Case: Essays on New Zealand Literature*, Oxford University Press, Auckland.

Tiffin, C. and Lawson, A. (eds) (1994) *De-Scribing Empire: Post-colonialism and Textuality*, Routledge, London.

# UNIT 30

# Canadian literature

*Jill LeBihan*

## Settlement in Canada and Canadian literature

Discussion and teaching of Canadian literature in the United Kingdom tends to focus on contemporary Anglo-Canadian poetry and prose fiction and, out of necessity, this introduction will reflect that bias: so, all the texts considered here have been written in English, and although there is a brief historical survey provided, the focus is principally on poetry and prose produced since 1960. This introduction, then, does not tell the whole story of Canadian literature. By and large, there is no proper discussion of drama; this is primarily for reasons of concision, although also because plays tend to be taught in genre-based courses. Another obvious omission is the long and vast tradition of writing in French from Quebec: Canada is, after all, an officially bilingual country. However, the problems of studying texts in translation go far beyond the scope of this brief survey, and probably beyond what is taught as 'CanLit' outside of Canada. In addition, there are particularly intricate issues associated with the cultural production of the original inhabitants of Canada, which will be discussed later, but again the works that are examined here are ones that have been written in English, rather than translated from a native language. In understanding the history and traditions behind Canadian literature though, it should not be forgotten that the first exploration of Canada by Europeans began with the travels of Jacques Cartier, a Frenchman, along the St Lawrence river in 1534, and the eastern regions of the country became 'New France' with the settlement by French immigrants in the seventeenth century. English interests in fur-trading and fishing brought adventurers to the country in the seventeenth century, and the 'Company of Adventurers of England Tradeing into Hudson's Bay' was given the Royal Charter in 1670. For nearly a century, the English were engaged in a power struggle with the French, each seeking to maintain trading rights in the territory. The Treaty of Utrecht, signed in 1713, ensured some sort of stability over claims to trading rights, but both sides tried to undermine the terms of the Treaty by attracting the native suppliers of furs to their own trading posts, luring them away from the posts of their competitors with attractive goods to exchange for valuable pelts. The struggle for trading posts resulted in the Seven Years War (1756–63) which concluded with the victory of England over 'New France'. A period of rapid expansion began, with traders moving further and further inland. As the land was opened up, military rule gradually gave way to civilian rule, although the first lieutenant-governor of Upper Canada (English Canada), John Simcoe, certainly made every effort to settle the land with military men and their families, and this had a lasting effect on the culture of the area.

The texts that represent the early period of settlement in Canada tend to be explorers' narratives, Jesuit missionary tracts and folk-tales, although they were not published until after the period they describe because of the lack of printing facilities until the 1760s. Many of those describing Canada in the early stages of European settlement were explorers in search of the North-West Passage through the Arctic, or fur traders, who also visited parts of the country that seemed uninhabitable to those unused to the extreme cold. Samuel Hearne was one such trader, who also had a talent for tale-telling. He worked for the Hudson's Bay Company, trading furs with native Indians in exchange for European manufactured goods, such as guns, knives and other commodities, and alcohol. Hearne was also in search of other materials that he might trade, and sought mineral sources such as copper, which were rumoured to be plentiful. Hearne was not, however, much of a geologist, and nor was he much of a geographer. Later critics have pointed out that he is often mistaken in his writing about his location, and that he failed to make the required notes about his surroundings and mineral deposits that would have been useful to the Hudson's Bay Company. However, as J.B. Tyrrell points out, in his introduction to the 1911 edition of Hearne's travelogue, 'His book is chiefly valuable ... because it is an accurate, sympathetic, and patently truthful record of life among the Chipewyan Indians at that time' (Hearne, 1968, p. 17). Although modern critics, now more aware of the inaccuracies of early ethnography, might dispute Tyrrell's comments, Hearne's travelogue does illustrate the conditions faced by fur-traders and nineteenth-century attitudes to the native peoples. Hearne himself says he writes his book:

> not so much for the information of those who are critics of geography, as for the amusement of candid and indulgent readers, who may perhaps feel themselves in some measure gratified, by having the face of a country brought to their view, which has hitherto been entirely unknown to every European except myself. Nor will, I flatter myself, a description of the modes of living, manners, and customs of the natives (which, though long known, have never been described), be less acceptable to the curious. (Hearne, 1968, p. 30)

Writers of travelogues of the late eighteenth and early nineteenth centuries recognized the insatiable appetite of readers for information about indigenous populations in other lands, and readily exploited it.

Hearne's accounts of his travels in the years 1769–72 were first published in London in 1795. The first *fictional* account of life in Canada was *The History of Emily Montague* by Frances Brooke, which was published in London in 1769. It is an epistolary novel in the style used by Samuel Richardson in *Clarissa*, and the events are based partly on Frances Brooke's life in Quebec between 1763 and 1767. Frances Brooke arrived in Canada, into the newly created province of Quebec, just at the end of British military rule. She travelled out to join her husband, John Brooke, the only Protestant minister in Quebec. Her novel is, in the style of many eighteenth-century novels, moralistic and politicized; it also offers a lively representation of marriage and society life for women in Quebec. It contains detailed descriptions of the lives of priests and the clergy, of the native inhabitants and of the weather, climate and geography, and Mary Jane Edwards argues that these details are intrinsic to the novel's success:

> its Canadian subject matter chiefly accounts for the special place the novel held in the decades after its first appearance. Mrs Brooke's descriptions of Quebec were mined by English authors who wished to use a probable yet exotic setting for their fiction. (Brooke, 1985, p. l)

The novel has been valued for its authenticity, then, and is an important historical document for those that want to understand what life was like in the early days of colonization in Canada. Edwards adds that 'in addition to its popularity as a novel, *The History of Emily Montague* became a kind of guidebook for people coming to Canada' (Brooke, 1985, p. li), and as such paves the way for the other guides to Canadian life that have become classics in the 'CanLit' canon.

In the early nineteenth century, emigration to Canada from England, Ireland and Scotland increased substantially. The potato famine in Ireland and the 'clearing' of the Scottish Highlands sent many poverty stricken and dispossessed people across the Atlantic in search of a better life. However, written records of the experiences of these people are rare: the poor are less likely to be literate and to have the desire, the leisure or the resources to write and publish. The written accounts that do survive are mostly by middle-class emigrants, many of whom had fallen on hard times at home and sought land and greater wealth in the New World. The British Government and the colonial governors in Canada actively promoted the emigration of the middle classes, and one way in which they did this was to offer retired or wounded military officers a 'half-pay commission'. These men were given a half-pension and a plot of land in Canada and were encouraged to go and seek their fortune. Susanna Moodie, the wife of one such military man, has become one of Canada's best-known pioneer writers through her fictionalized account of her settler's life. The title of her first Canadian work describes her feelings about her situation; it is called, in full, *Roughing It in the Bush or Life in Canada* and it was first published in London in 1852. Although there are several other reasonably well-known works written by settlers and travellers – such as Moodie's sister's, Catherine Parr Traill's, *The Backwoods of Canada* (1836) and Anna Brownell Jameson's *Winter Studies and Summer Rambles in Canada* (1838) – *Roughing It in the Bush* has received more critical attention than the others, and has had more influence on the development of Canadian literature in later years.

*Roughing It in the Bush* is a first-person account of emigration and settlement, as viewed by a middle-class woman, whose experience of 'wilderness', until her entry into Canada, was limited to the countryside along the Suffolk coast in England. Moodie's stated purpose in writing her supposed journal is to warn others who might come after her of the difficulties faced by settlers in the backwoods of Ontario.

However, Moodie also had a much less altruistic motive for writing: quite simply her husband was not a successful farmer, and her family were suffering from lack of income. Moodie had already had some success with publications before her emigration, and was counting on the profits from *Roughing It in the Bush* to feed her children. The resulting work is a hybrid of popular verse and melodramatic narrative accounts of the hardships of living in a log-cabin with only one servant and troublesome neighbours. Consider Moodie's contemplation shortly after arriving in Canada, whilst she is on the boat that will take her inland to her new home:

> The lofty groves of pine frowned down in hearse-like gloom upon the mighty river, and the deep stillness of the night, broken alone by its hoarse wailings, filled my mind with sad forebodings, – alas! too prophetic of the future. Keenly, for the first time, I felt that I was a stranger in a strange land; my heart yearned intensely for my absent home. (Moodie, 1988, p. 39)

Her descriptions of the Canadian landscape owe much to her inherited Romantic aesthetic, as do her descriptions of the native peoples as 'noble savages'. The experience of 'roughing it' is represented as something for which the English middle-class woman is not prepared, but Moodie develops a strong pioneering spirit, and ultimately becomes a Canadian nationalist.

The influence of *Roughing It in the Bush*, and other pioneer texts, can be seen in the work of many contemporary Canadian writers and literary critics. Margaret Atwood recreated the character of Moodie in her narrative poetry sequence, *The Journals of Susanna Moodie* (1970), and Carol Shields uses her as a major reference point for her protagonist in *Small Ceremonies* (1976). Beth Hopkins and Anne Joyce have adapted Moodie's story into a stage play, *Daughter By Adoption* (1981), at least in part as an educational measure, to inform schoolchildren about Canadian history. Similar fictionalized reworkings of the lives of historical (and sometimes invented historical) figures have been an important feature in contemporary Canadian fiction: Margaret Laurence's main character, Morag, in *The Diviners* (1982) is haunted by Catharine Parr Traill (Moodie's sister); the story of Daphne Marlatt's Annie in *ana historic* (1988) is interrupted by her mysterious pioneering foremother, Ana Richards; and Susan Swan has written of the Victorian woman giant, Anna Swan, in *The Biggest Modern Woman of the World* (1983), managing to turn the narrative into an allegorical representation of patriarchal oppression and the colonization of Canada. There are many other examples of this practice in Canadian writing, in which an historical figure resurfaces in a fictionalized setting (see Scobie, 1989; Hutcheon, 1988). Part of the reason for this is connected with the trend that involves intertextual referencing, a practice familiar in much postmodern writing. However, very much at the heart of the enterprise of rewriting lives is the desire to create a sense of a very specific Canadian literary history.

In a newly settled land, the sense of a cultural heritage can be very tenuous. There is the heritage that comes with the settlers: in the case of Canada, this could include an English Romantic literary tradition, or Celtic folklore, for instance. But there is also a need to create a new and distinctive literature, to explore ways of using language that seem more appropriate to an unfamiliar place. Ashcroft, Griffiths and Tiffin (1995) explain this as a feature of most post-colonial writing, in which 'a sense of displacement, of the lack of "fit" between language and place may be experienced by both those who possess English as a mother tongue and those who speak it as a second language' (Ashcroft et al., 1995, p. 391). Novelist and critic Robert Kroetsch explains the English-Canadian writer's situation:

> The Canadian writer's particular predicament is that he works with a language, within a literature, that appears to be authentically his own, and not a borrowing. But just as there was in the Latin word a concealed Greek experience, so there is in the Canadian word a concealed other experience, sometimes British, sometimes Canadian.
>
> In recent years the tension between this appearance of being just like someone else and the demands of authenticity has become intolerable – both to the individuals and to the society. In recent Canadian fiction the major writers resolve the paradox – the painful tension between appearance and authenticity – by the radical process of demythologizing the systems that threaten to define them. Or, more comprehensively, they uninvent the world. (Kroetsch, 1995, p. 394)

By rewriting the lives of some of Canada's earliest settlers, contemporary writers are reinventing their history in an idiom that seems appropriate to their modern sense of national identity.

Confederation, Canada's independence from England, came in 1867, and with it a new determination to create a national literature. This can be reflected in the work of writers such as Isabella Valency Crawford, Sara Jeannette Duncan, Archibald Lampman and Duncan Campbell Scott. Sara Jeannette Duncan's short story collection, *A Pool in the Desert* (1984), first published in 1903, is focused on the waning of the British empire, but in India rather than in Canada. Her earlier novel, *The Imperialist*, however, gives an astute critique of political and society life in the New World, and offers very witty dialogue between loyalist characters and their republican opponents. Apart from Duncan, the other writers mentioned focus more on life in the wilderness than society in the towns, and this remains one of the most important traditions in Canadian writing.

Margaret Atwood, as well as being Canada's most successful novelist, has produced a work of criticism on Canadian literature that remains a touchstone for all students of 'CanLit'. This text, *Survival* (1972), illustrates the way in which Canada's climate and landscape continue to affect the kind of novels and poems that the nation produces. Atwood says that Canadian writers primarily see the natural world as hostile; hence we have characters being crushed by trees, as in Isabella Valency Crawford's 'Malcolm's Katie' (1972), and characters who drown in freezing water, as in Duncan Campbell Scott's 'The Piper of Arll' (1960). There are methods of 'death by nature', including forest fires, attack by wild animals and getting crushed by trees in log-jams. Atwood's title of her critical work indicates though that the Canadian way is to *survive* the hardship rather than to succumb to it, and the writing of this early period is characterized mostly by struggle rather than tragic death.

The opposition faced by the climate and the landscape is typified in much of the writing from the west of Canada, the prairie provinces such as Manitoba, Saskatchewan and Alberta. Laura Goodman Salverson, a Scandinavian immigrant like the many who populated the prairies in the late nineteenth and early twentieth centuries, writes of the hardship of life on the farmsteads in both her autobiography, *Confessions of an Immigrant's Daughter* (1939), and in her novel *The Viking Heart* ([1923] 1975). This realistic mode of prairie writing also features in the work of other well-known writers of the period: Martha Ostenso's *Wild Geese* ([1925] 1961), the action of which takes place in Manitoba within one summer; and Frederick Philip Grove, who wrote eight novels, many of which describe the harshness of settlement. Margaret Atwood describes Grove's work in a way that makes it sound unrelentingly grim. She argues that 'will-driven patriarchs' that feature so strongly in Grove's work are characteristic of the need to represent the imposition of order on the world:

> There's Ellen's father in *Settlers of the Marsh*, clearing the land and building his farm, praying fervently at night and proclaiming that God has been good to him while at the same time driving his wife into the ground by a combination of hard work, forced impregnation and equally forced miscarriages. The father is imposing his pattern of straight lines – barn, house, fence – on the curved land, and the wife and her fertility are a part of the 'curved' Nature he is trying to control. But instead of controlling her he kills her, both spiritually (she comes to hate him) and physically. (Atwood, 1972, p. 123)

The brutal realism that is so pervasive in Frederick Philip Grove's work began to wane in the 1930s, almost as though the search for an appropriate mode in which to talk of the Canadian condition had shifted into a more symbolic realm. Certainly, there is nothing like the detailed recreation of prairie hardships in later fiction until, perhaps, Margaret Laurence's 'Manawaka' cycle, written in the 1960s and early 1970s; even then the effects are achieved as much by complex symbolic codes as by blunt description.

The Manawaka cycle begins with the novel *The Stone Angel* (1964), then *A Jest of God* (1966) and *The Fire-Dwellers* (1969), the short-story collection *A Bird in the House* (1970) and the cycle concludes ten years later with the last novel that Laurence wrote, *The Diviners* ([1974] 1982). All of the narratives are focused around characters from the fictional prairie town of Manawaka, although significantly, much of the final novel is set in rural Ontario, close to where Catharine Parr Traill and Susanna Moodie settled in the nineteenth century. As Coral Ann Howells points out:

> The Canadian multi-ethnic inheritance is focused through the history and population of Manawaka, where its tales of Scots and Irish settlers and the survivors of the pioneer generation coexist with the tragic history of the indigenous Métis population who were dispossessed of their prairie lands. (Howells, 1987, p. 35)

The Celtic immigrants and the dispossessed native people are shown to coexist, uneasily and without much integration, in all of the fictions that make up the cycle; it is not until the final novel that it is possible to see that these two opposing groups also have a shared heritage in their inherited traditions of folk tales and oral narrative. The protagonist of *The Diviners*, Morag Gunn, is a novelist who is haunted by the benevolent ghost of Catharine Parr Traill who instructs her 'In cases of emergency, it is folly to fold one's hands and sit down to bewail in abject terror: it is better to be up and doing' (Laurence, 1982, p. 406), and she is also haunted by her mythical Scottish ancestor, Piper Gunn. Morag was raised on the outskirts of Manawaka, the adopted daughter of the town garbage collector. Jules Tonnerre is a folk musician, a Métis, who speaks a mixture of French, Cree and English, and whose people do not belong either to white or to Indian communities. Jules and Morag have a daughter, Pique, and it is Pique who offers a 'reconciliation across the gap of history and social custom', who 'becomes the inheritor of both traditions' (Howells, 1987, p. 36).

The optimistic future offered by *The Diviners* is not unqualified, but the integration of native communities with white settlers is not necessarily always a cause for celebration. Indeed, for the native people themselves, it has always represented a threat of cultural annihilation. White writers' representations of Canada's indigenous peoples, even benevolent ones such as that offered by Laurence, rarely coincide with the representations created by the native people themselves. Until quite recently, despite white readers' fascination with the First Nations, writing by native people was ignored in considerations of Canadian Literature. However, there is a long and strong tradition which has become an essential part of any 'CanLit' course.

## Literatures of the First Nations

The issue of the settlement of Canada and the consequent development of a distinct literary identity is an important one, but the claims to literary marginality and insecurity made by Anglo-Canadians are weakened when compared with the history of the indigenous population. Although Canada was 'discovered' by Europeans in the sixteenth century, who saw the land as uninhabited, waiting for development and settlement by immigrants, the land was, of course, already inhabited and being used by the diverse native peoples. As is explained in Thomas King's satirical story of the world's creation by the traditional figure of Coyote, the Indians know they are around long before they wave hello at their discoverers, 'Christopher Cartier' and 'Jacques Columbus' (King, 1990b, p. 99). Canada's First Nations are divided into two distinct groups. There are the Inuit, who used to be called the Eskimos by Europeans; they originate in the far north of Canada (the Northwest Territories, Yukon, Labrador, northern Quebec) and share a common language, Inuktitut (although with variations in dialect). They are divided into eight main cultural groups: the Labrador, the Ungava, the Baffin Island, the Iglulik, the Netsilik, the Caribou, the Copper and the Western Arctic Inuit. The other indigenous group is that of the Indians, who traditionally inhabit a much broader range of territory; they are divided into five cultural groups, the Eastern Woodlands, Plains, Plateau, sub-Arctic and Northwest Coast, and speak over fifty languages. With such diversity, tracing any common literary heritage is an impossible task. However, it is possible to examine the development of a literate culture, which has a reasonably recent history, and to look at the changing contexts within which indigenous peoples write in Canada.

Canada's indigenous peoples are not traditionally literate; their traditions are historically, and to some extent still, oral ones. So it is not until the colonization of Canada, and the instruction (often forcible) by Europeans, that the native peoples started to develop a written tradition. European conceptions of what constitutes literature have meant that oral traditions do not easily find recognition within a fairly inflexible system of values. Western aesthetic criteria cannot be readily adapted to oral modes of cultural production, and Western prejudice has often meant that critics are not willing to make the efforts required to accommodate literatures that do not fit their ideas of what constitutes art. In addition, there are very real problems concerned with the critical analysis of works in translation. As Penny Petrone points out, in her excellent introduction to Indian literature:

> Although any lexical or literal translation – strict word-for-word translation in interlinear style often found in the renditions of social scientists – is unsatisfactory, too much intervention of freedom, while it may achieve a certain literary flavour, may also seriously impair the meaning and significance of the original. (Petrone, 1990, p. 6)

Petrone argues for an increase in the number of skilled translators, who not only have the knowledge of English and one or more native languages, but who are also aware of the specific cultural contexts appropriate to the literature.

The social aspects of oral literature are extremely significant, even when it has been transcribed and removed from its proper situation: songs, speeches, prayers, morality tales, narratives whose main purpose is educational, as well as entertaining stories, all have a place in native oral traditions. In addition, the power to tell certain tales may be controlled by a specific social hierarchy; the power of knowledge gives authority, and in some societies, only particular elders or members of particular families are entitled to tell specific tales. Other tales are more generally circulated, and are not necessarily attached to formal occasions. In addition, the use to which language is put cannot easily be removed from the context in which it is performed. The significance of language in the oral traditions of indigenous Canadian peoples can be seen as analogous to native Australian traditions, in the sense that the language is not merely representative, but has a material relation to reality. In oral traditions, certain prayers and chants can bring things into being, can cause animals to be caught, can change the climate and can heal the sick. This linguistic power, which is not generally recognized in Western consciousness, obviously cannot survive the transcription of the oral into the graphological.

There are some common patterns that can be observed in traditional Indian oral narratives. Petrone lists the following features that transcend cultural and linguistic divisions:

> heroic encounters with supernatural powers; animal-wives, -husbands, -parents, -divinities, -guardian-spirit powers; a world flood; journeys to other worlds; animal totems; vision quests (requiring fasting, prayer, deprivation, and ceremonial purity); powerful magicians; belief in the significance of dreams, in a spirit world and the indwelling spirit of every created thing, inanimate and animate. (Petrone, 1990, p. 17)

One of the most familiar figures in Indian literary tradition is that of the Trickster. He is an acquisitive, deceitful character who operates within a liminal space, often bringing destruction, but also comedy; a European equivalent might be a figure from Rabelaisian traditions, or even Autolycus from Shakespeare's *The Winter's Tale*. Although traditionally associated with oral narratives, the Trickster is an essential character in contemporary writing, much of which seeks to retain connections with oral narratives, whilst transforming them into written texts, which are accessible to a wider audience than performances would be. There is now a writer's activist group called the Committee to Re-establish the Trickster, which indicates the symbolic force of this figure for Indian cultural production.

The first writing by Indians for public consumption occurred in the first half of the nineteenth century. The authors were men who had been educated by Methodist ministers and missionaries; they were taught English, and their literary production tended to be in the form of lectures and sermons, journals and letters. George Copway is widely acknowledged as the first Canadian Indian to write a book in English: *The Life History and Travels of Kah-ge-ga-gah-bowh (George Copway)* which was published in 1847 and underwent six reprintings (Petrone, 1990, p. 43). The Reverend Peter Jones wrote a similar autobiography, which was published posthumously; other Methodist-trained Indian writers of this period include Peter Jacobs, George Henry, Allen Salt and Henry Bird Steinhauer, who wrote histories, journals, letters, travelogues and various kinds of religious tracts. These writings are steeped in the Methodist traditions out of which the authors were educated; they make extensive use of biblical references and religious metaphors, and are wholly conventional.

Perhaps one of the most well-known native writers from the nineteenth century is Emily Pauline Johnson, who was the daughter of a Mohawk chief and an English woman. She was popular at the time for her dramatic poetry recitals, and her fame allowed her to travel to England to perform, and publish. Her narrative poetry and occasional pieces are often sentimental or melodramatic, but were extremely well-liked by audiences, even if not always critically acclaimed. One of her popular pieces was 'The Avenger', the story of a Cherokee who kills a Mohawk. The speaker is the murdered man's brother:

> 'Last night, thou lent'st the knife unto my brother
> Come I now, oh Cherokee, to give thy bloody weapon back to thee!'
> An evil curse, a flash of steel, a leap
> A thrust above the heart, well-aimed and deep,
> Plunged to the very hilt in blood
> While Vengeance gloating yells, 'The Debt is paid!'
>
> (Keller, 1987, p. 65)

As with the religious writers, Pauline Johnson's work was conventional rather than adventurous. Perhaps more courage, although still within very formal constraints, can be seen in the work of the great Indian orators, such as the leader of the North-West Rebellion, Louis Riel, and the Chiefs Poundmaker and Big Bear. The speeches of the latter are perhaps most well known to contemporary audiences because of the work of Rudy Wiebe, which recreates some of the great protests in his novel *The Temptations of Big Bear* (1973).

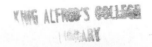

Throughout the nineteenth century (and beyond), coercive measures were used to settle the Indians on reservations, and to educate them in English. To this end, residential schools were established, operated by missionaries, to which children were removed, away from their families, and where they were obliged to speak only English; punishments for children found speaking their own language were often severe. This particular form of imperial domination had devastating effects on native culture, from which the Canadian indigenous populations are only just beginning to recover. The direct result of the attempts to subdue and control native populations by depriving them of their own cultural traditions has been a lack of available literature by native writers from the first sixty years of the twentieth century. Publishers did not support writing by natives; most of what did get published is in the mode of personal testimony, stories narrated to a (usually) white editor/transcriber.

Since the 1960s there has been a resurgence of literature by native writers, mainly as a result of successful political activism by indigenous communities, and due to the shift in Canadian cultural policy, which has increasingly sought to support the creative work of the First Nations. The success of the American Indian Movement in the United States inspired similar activism in Canada, and the recognition that native peoples required appropriate (culturally sensitive) education in order both to retain traditional community values and to achieve economic development.

Much of the writing by indigenous peoples from the 1970s and early 1980s retains an autobiographical element, at least in part because of the necessity for the truth to be told, of the experience of cultural oppression and of racism. Maria Campbell's *Halfbreed* (1973) for example, has remained a canonical work for those who teach the literature of Canada's First Nations. Campbell's story shows how the Métis, pejoratively called 'half-breeds', face racism not only from white people but also from Indians. The story is primarily one of dispossession; Campbell tells of her poverty and of her painful lack of cultural identity, especially after the death of her mother from alcholism and she is obliged to marry a white man in order to support herself and her siblings. However, the story has a positive outcome: Campbell's memories of her great-grandmother, Cheechum, are what enable her to regain her strength and her sense of identity and self-worth. Similarly, Lee Maracle's *Bobbi Lee* (1975, reprinted 1990) and *I Am Woman* (1988), and Beatrice Culleton's *In Search of April Raintree* (1983), draw on personal experience for their narratives.

Most recently, native writers have achieved considerable success with novels that are less realistic and more experimental. Perhaps the most well-known native writer in Canada is Thomas King, who achieved immense success and critical acclaim with his humorous novels, *Medicine River* (1990) and *Green Grass, Running Water* ([1993] 1994). The latter has a woman professor of Native American studies as one of its protagonists, whose experience of university life is the material of sheer campus farce; but interwoven with Alberta's story is that of the trickster Coyote, whose self-reflexive comments on novel-writing, narrative progression and the creative process ensure that King's novel has reference to both native story-telling traditions and contemporary critical trends:

> So, that Coyote is dreaming and pretty soon, one of those dreams gets loose and runs around. Makes a lot of noise.
>
> Hooray, says that silly Dream, Coyote dream. I'm in charge of the world. And then that Dream sees all that water.
>
> Oh, oh, says that noisy Dream. This is all wrong. Is that water we see? that silly Dream says to those dream eyes.
>
> It's water, all right, says those Dream Eyes.
>
> That Coyote Dream makes many sad noises, and those noises are loud and those noises wake up Coyote.
>
> 'Who is making all that noise and waking me up?' says Coyote.
>
> 'It's that noisy dream of yours,' I says. 'It thinks it is in charge of the world.' (King, 1994, p. 1)

Thus in the opening of King's novel, there is a battle for control of the narratorial position, between the Dream, Coyote and the first-person narrator. The stable reading position of the conventional reader is undermined; and although there is the distinctive Coyote figure, the device of destabilizing the reader is a familiar one in Western postmodern fiction, with its graphological tradition. Thus King uses both indigenous oral traditions and those of specifically written fiction, to his great success.

Other native writers to receive critical acclaim include the playwright Tomson Highway, prose writer Daniel David Moses and poet and novelist Joan Crate. Joan Crate's *Pale as Real Ladies: Poems for Pauline Johnson* (1989) does for Johnson what Atwood did for Moodie, and is very much part of the tradition previously examined, where important historical and literary figures are recreated in contemporary writing in order to mark a continuity (and perhaps, also, a separation).

## Contemporary Anglo-Canadian literature

Canada's biggest literary asset is undoubtedly Margaret Atwood. To date, she has published eight novels, five books of short fiction, and ten collections of poetry, although these figures vary a little from critic to critic, because there is often debate about how to categorize works such as *Murder in the Dark* (1983), a collection of prose poems. Despite the attempts of critics to see her as a truly 'international' writer – she's made it because she's transcended her Canadianness – Atwood can still be placed within a Canadian context (and, indeed, tries hard to ensure that she is). Coral Ann Howells (1995) argues that the two ends of Atwood's prose-writing career, stretching from *Surfacing* (1972) to *Wilderness Tips* (1991), remain focused on a Canadian national identity which is claimed in terms of the landscape, but this identity is now 'tipping' precariously in the postmodern era. Certainly, her novel *The Robber Bride* (1993) has at its centre the shapeshifting, malevolent Zenia, whose identity is transformed according to the effects she wishes to achieve. Her three friends, Roz, Tony and Charis, project onto her what they wish her to be, and she exploits their needs remorselessly. Zenia is an unstable character in the sense that she is emotionally unbalanced, and also in that she is a deliberately inconsistent person. The reconstruction of Zenia's story is also presented in the self-conscious way so characteristic of postmodern fiction:

> *Pick any strand and snip, and history comes unravelled.* This is how Tony begins one of her more convoluted lectures, the one on the dynamics of spontaneous massacres. The metaphor is of weaving or else of knitting, and of sewing scissors. She likes using it: she likes the faint shock on the faces of her listeners. It's the mix of domestic image and mass bloodshed that does it to them; a mix that would have been appreciated by Zenia, who enjoyed such turbulence, such violent contradictions. More than enjoyed: created. (Atwood, 1993, p. 3)

Atwood chooses Tony, the historian, as the character through whom the opening of the novel is relayed, and Tony's questioning of historical grand narratives, as well of more personal stories, offers the reader an uncertain text for interpretation.

Throwing historical narratives into doubt, recasting history as fiction, is a pervasive feature in contemporary Canadian fiction. Robert Kroetsch uses a highly unreliable narrator in *The Studhorse Man* (first published in 1970). The narrator is a madman who recounts the narrative events from his bath. The story he tells concerns the jokingly-named Hazard Lepage, but there are times when the story slips away from its teller:

> I have some bad news, my patient reader. The bald truth is, I have not the foggiest notion how the two men got out of their fix ... Hazard refused to explain what happened next. I begged him in the interest of logic, of continuity, in the need to instruct and direct future generations, to give me a clue. (Kroetsch, 1982, p. 99)

Kroetsch's *Badlands* (1975) also recounts a story with dubious authenticity. The novel is based on real archaeological excavations that took place in Alberta in the early twentieth century, but the story of the hunt for a complete dinosaur skeleton is supposedly reconstructed from field notes in the possession of the explorer's daughter.

Jane Urquhart's *The Whirlpool* (1986) is a fiction also set in a real place, Niagara Falls, and it is based on a nineteenth-century woman's journal about her dream house, as well as on notes kept at a funeral home that dealt with all the drownings from the Falls. The novel begins with a reconstruction of the death of the poet Robert Browning, but the scene shifts from Venice to Ontario, and to Fleda, the wife of an army officer, who records what she reads in her diary:

> D. has given me another book to read just this morning – *Angel in the House* by Patmore. A tribute to the poet's wife and her domestic demeanor. Just the ticket, D. says, since he thinks I am dangerously infatuated with the strange passions of Mr. Browning. Which, I suppose, I am. (Urquhart, 1986, p. 34)

Urquhart indicates here how the domestic proprieties and literary heritage from England was imported to Canada by the settlers. However, despite the efforts of her loyalist husband, the romantic Fleda is soon carried away by the idea of a dream house to be built above the whirlpool, and by the attentions of Patrick, a Canadian poet, who is infatuated by her. So it is that the romance of the old country comes to be replaced by the new. Urquhart's other novels also recall the relationship between Europe and Canada: *Changing Heaven* (1990) features the ghost of Emily Brontë and a Tintoretto painting, whilst *Away* (1993) is a fictional account of the settlement of a displaced Irish family on the Canadian Shield.

The last mention of these fact-based fictions must go to George Bowering's *Burning Water* (1980), which is an embroidered version of the explorations of George Vancouver, an English sea captain, who charted the west coast of Canada. The opening of the novel gives the perspective of the native Indians, who discuss whether the arrival of what seem to be enormous birds on the sea could be a vision, the manifestation of a god or merely a man dressed in outlandish clothes on a large boat, so that, in rewriting the 'discovery' of the British Columbia coast, Bowering emphasizes the fact that the territory was already inhabited and known.

There are, of course, writers who do not share the concerns with self-concious, meta-fictional rewriting of Canadian history. Alice Munro is celebrated for her short stories, and she is critically acclaimed for the use she makes of the genre. The stories are set in small towns and/or farmsteads in rural Ontario, and they are remarkable for the intensity of emotion that she creates, as well as for the wide range of characters who are portrayed in acute detail. She writes of childhood, adolescence, motherhood; of divorce, bereavement, love affairs; of tragic accidents and mundane reality. Many of her stories contain epiphanic revelations, represented as a sudden still moment, a pause or a breath, before the narrative continues. For instance, in *The Moons of Jupiter* (1984), the story 'Labor Day Dinner' shows Roberta with her teenage daughters, and her lover George, going for a celebration of Labor Day at the house of a friend:

> These four people are costumed in a way that would suggest they were going to different dinner parties. George, who is a stocky, barrel-chested man, with a daunting, professional look of self-assurance and impatience (he used to be a teacher), wears a clean T-shirt and nondescript pants. Roberta is wearing faded tan cotton pants and a raw-silk top of a mud-brick color – a color that suits her dark hair and pale skin well enough when she is at her best, but she is not at her best today. ... As for Angela and Eva, they are dramatically arrayed in outfits contrived from a box of old curtains found in the upstairs of George's house. Angela wears emerald-green damask with long, sun-faded stripes, draped so as to leave one golden shoulder bare ... Eva is wearing several fragile, yellowed lace curtains draped and bunched up, and held together with pins, ribbons, and nosegays of wild phlox already drooping and scattering. (Munro, 1984, p. 135)

The metonyms of the clothing carefully set up the characters, who then proceed to fill out the roles prescribed by their clothing. The evening progresses smoothly and without incident; the families discuss politics, divorce and relationships, life and literature, but despite this veneer of well-being, Roberta is dissatisfied. Driving home, they come to a crossroads where two drunk drivers are travelling at ninety miles an hour without headlights. The car appears out of nowhere, flashes past them in an instant that is described by Munro so that it seems to take an extended time, and leaves the family in the car 'flattened out and borne aloft, as unconnected with previous and future events' (1984, p. 159). Munro's heightened realism offers the sense of shock that occurs when routine is suddenly disrupted by a near catastrophe, so that life is stilled for a moment and then goes on. Munro has eight collections of stories, including *The Progress of Love* (1987), *Friend of my Youth* (1990) and *Open Secrets* (1994).

The realist work of Munro can be contrasted starkly with the work of poets such as bpNichol, Christopher Dewdney and bill bissett, which can be experimental in the extreme. Canada has a tradition of sustaining a variety of small publishing houses, often heavily subsidized by government grants; unfortunately, the economic climate of the 1990s has resulted in the drying-up of funding and the collapse of the most marginal of the small presses. However, during their boom years in the 1970s and early 1980s, writers were fully involved in the physical production and final presentation of their work. bill bissett, for instance, is concerned with the visual impact of language, and he is notorious for breaking the rules of spelling. Consider his poem titled 'th wundrfulness uv th mountees our secret police', which contains lines such as 'they listn to our politikul / ledrs phone conversashuns what / cud b less inspiring to ovrheer' (Bowering (ed.), 1984, p. 30). bissett's poetry reflects an irreverent attitude towards 'The Establishment', including the institution of Standard English.

Christopher Dewdney, like bissett, is concerned with the difficulties of representation through language. He exploits specialist discourses such as neurology, physics, chemistry and geology to create poetry that has impact even on readers who cannot translate the terminology. Consider the intimidating titles to some of his earlier work, which nevertheless sound dramatic: *A Palaeozoic Geology of London, Ontario* (1973), *Fovea Centralis* (1975) and *Spring Trances & Cenozoic Asylum* (1982). Although Dewdney is concerned with semantics – his use of specialist terminology is accurate, not arbitrary – the significance of his poetry is also in its musical resonance.

Whilst Alice Munro is famous for her short stories, there are many Canadian writers who are known instead for their long poems, a genre which has flexible boundaries. For instance, before his death in 1988, bpNichol produced five volumes of *The Martyrology* (1972–87), a poetry sequence which he referred to as 'a journal, and a book about the history of saints' (Kamboureli, 1991, p. 148), and Smaro Kamboureli argues that 'it uses the experientially real as a point of departure for its meanderings in the linguistically real' (1991, p. 148). Kamboureli offers an extensive list of long poems in her book on the long poem genre, as well as giving detailed critical readings of a few examples. One of these is the work by Daphne Marlatt produced in collaboration with photographer Robert Minden, *Steveston* (1984). This is a long poem documentary of life in the fishing and fish-canning town of Steveston in British Columbia. The work offers a sense of the hard working life faced by fishermen and by cannery workers, and shows the coexistence of the Japanese people with the white community, as well as evoking the sound and movement of the town that depends on the water.

## Literature, post-colonial theory and multi-culturalism in Canada

When literatures are grouped together under the term 'post-colonial', hackles begin to rise. This term is used to cover literatures, usually written in English, from areas as diverse as India, Australia, the South Pacific Islands, Africa (including South Africa), and Canada, from historical periods reaching back to the sixteenth century. Many have questioned the sense of such a broad enterprise: Anne McClintock (1992), Salman Rushdie (1991) and Elleke Boehmer (1995), to name just three. Even if one accepts, provisionally, the need for such a category in the academic study of literature, the position of Canada (and the other settler cultures – Australia, New Zealand, South Africa) remains problematic, for whilst the Canadian nation is undoubtedly 'post-colonial' in the sense that it has been colonized by two European powers and has gained cultural and economic independence from them, it remains the case that the dominant group is made up of descendants of the colonizers, and thus their claim to marginal status is undermined. Thomas King argues that the term is certainly not relevant to native literature, as it marks off a historical period that only begins with European contact. This implies that the indigenous populations only become interesting when they are posed against the early adventurers and immigrants, and thus writes off all of the prior native history.

Unlike many nations that were once ruled by Europeans, contemporary Canada is less concerned about its relationship with the 'centre of empire' than it is with its relations with its powerful next-door neighbours. The cultural and economic force of the United States is such that Canadians often fear annexation, and whether this is a realizable political occurrence or merely a neurotic fantasy, the fear is just as acute. The purchase of Edmonton's ice-hockey hero Wayne Gretzky by a Los Angeles team was one indication of the capacity for the United States to appropriate figures that have importance for Canadian cultural identity. The purchase of the rights to use the image of the Canadian Mountie by Walt Disney in 1995 is another case in point: the rights to one of Canada's national icons is now owned by a US conglomerate. This possibility is perhaps foreseen in the poetry of David McFadden, in his 'A Typical Canadian Family Visits Disney World' (1984), which was written in the 1970s. In this poem, the United States is characterized as the advertisers' dream ('& the snow was much cleaner & fell more neatly / than in Canada, & there was more of it, ...'). The 'typical Canadian family' drive through various states, recognizing the many tourist sites from their knowledge of US culture: they pass the place where Marlon Brando was born, they imitate Frank Sinatra movies, they pass 'a river Mark Twain had pissed in', they see where Jack Kerouac's sister committed suicide and so on. Finally they get to Disney World:

> Well, a lot of the stuff there reminded me of Canada,
> the ferry boat was just like that one in Toronto bay,
> Disney himself was Canadian, at least his parents were,
> Peter Pan was a Canadian, the Wild West was Canadian,
> Jules Verne, Jungleland, Hall of Presidents, Cinderella,

> it's a wonder there's any left over to write situation
> comedies on TV & send rockets to the moon & plan
> brilliant strategy in bombing raids.

(McFadden, 1984, p. 207)

By wildly pronouncing all kinds of people as Canadians, even the very English Peter Pan, and the very French Jules Verne, McFadden is making an ironic comment here on the practice in Canada of staking national claims on famous people with Canadian connections, even very slender ones. But he is also pointing out the success of US cultural imperialism: that Canadians know the US presidents, and buy in US sitcoms, without the same process happening in reverse. McFadden asks, how is it possible that Peter Pan and Cinderella should be at Disney World, unchallenged and apparently entirely integrated, when they are not really part of an American tradition? His criticism is aimed at the capacity of Canada's powerful southern neighbours to take over the cultural traditions of others and reproduce them as their own.

The 'melting-pot' policy of the United States, as it has been called, ensures that symbols that represent a specific national group or have significance for particular ethnic communities become assimilated into mainstream culture; the Mounties become as American as Mickey Mouse. The Canadian policy of 'multiculturalism' is slightly different: this policy encourages ethnic diversity, and seeks to retain the distinctiveness of groups, rather than fusion between them. John Miska's sizeable *Ethnic and Native Canadian Literature: A Bibliography* (1990) – the contents of which run from Algerian to Venezuelan – indicates the success achieved by writers of diverse ethnic backgrounds. Miska's bibliography includes nearly 5,500 entries, and represents 65 nationality groups. He includes published work of fiction, poetry and drama in any language, providing the writer was born outside Canada (although obviously native groups are not required to meet this criterion), and wrote the work whilst living in Canada.

The scope of Miska's bibliography indicates the impossibility of being in any way comprehensive in the texts selected for discussion in this brief introduction, which confines itself to the most well-known texts written in English, by migrant writers and those who belong to distinct ethnic communities. For a broader selection of material, see the collection edited by Victor Ramraj, titled *A Concert of Voices: An Anthology of World Writing in English* (1995).

Michael Ondaatje is one of Canada's best-known contemporary writers, and his works have attracted a great deal of critical attention. A novelist and poet, Ondaatje was born in Ceylon (now Sri Lanka) of mixed Dutch, Tamil and Sinhalese descent, educated at an English public school and has been a long-time resident of Canada. His fiction includes *The Collected Works of Billy the Kid* (1981), which rewrites the story of the American outlaw in poetry and poetic prose, creating a sense of brutality and madness about a character who is the subject of much mythologizing. The retelling of the story of characters who take on mythic proportions is an essential part of Ondaatje's narratives. He recreates the figure of his alcoholic father performing outrageous antics in *Running in the Family* (1983); in *Coming Through Slaughter* (1979), he documents part of a search for the jazz musician Buddy

Bolden who went missing early in the twentieth century and was committed to an asylum; and in *In The Skin of a Lion* (1987), the protagonist Patrick Lewis is hired to search for a missing businessman, but also finds himself searching for the love of his life. *In the Skin of a Lion* is set in Toronto in the 1920s and 1930s, among the immigrant community who built the city, and as with his other fictions, Ondaatje turns individuals with a place in history into mythical creatures:

> Nicholas Temelcoff is famous on the bridge, a daredevil. He is given all the difficult jobs and he takes them. He descends into the air with no fear. He is solitary. He assembles ropes, brushes the tackle and pulley at his waist, and falls off the bridge like a diver over the edge of a boat. ... Even in the archive photographs it is difficult to find him. Again and again you see vista before you and the eye must search along the wall of sky to the speck of burned paper across the valley that is him, an exclamation mark, somewhere in the distance between bridge and river. (Ondaatje, 1987, p. 34)

Eastern European workmen risked their lives for little money and no glory in the construction of the Canadian city, and as an acknowledgement of the place migrant communities have in Canada's history, Ondaatje makes an unforgettable hero of the bridge-builder Nicholas Temelcoff.

Several collections of work by writers of African-Caribbean backgrounds give testament to the strength of that community as it has established itself in Canada, especially in Toronto. *Other Voices: Writing by Blacks in Canada* (1985), edited by Lorris Elliott, includes work by Ayanna Black, Dionne Brand, Cyril Dabydeen, Claire Harris, Marlene Nourbese Philip and Maxine Tynes, all writers who are quite well established for poetry and/or fiction. Marlene Nourbese Philip's remarkable poetry is concerned with issues around language and identity for African women. In *She Tries Her Tongue, Her Silence Softly Breaks* (1989), she includes a sequence of poems about language ('Discourse on the Logic of Language', 'Universal Grammar' and 'The Question of Language is the Answer to Power') which juxtaposes extracts from a slave-owner's handbook alongside fables of childbirth, dictionary definitions against elocution lessons. The graphological presentation of these poems challenges conventional methods of reading: there are sections in different typefaces, running in parallel columns, with some passages at right-angles to others, so that the book has to be turned around in order to read the poem, and it is not clear which part should be read first. Some sentences are in different languages, whilst others are made of slippages between connected words. Nourbese Philip disrupts the hierarchy of discourses, with the first-person verses speaking powerfully against the third-person imperatives, the voice of the black woman undermining that of the white owners (of slaves, of language).

Other writers from the Caribbean now working in Canada include Claire Harris, Dionne Brand and Neil Bisoondath. Claire Harris's poetry collections include *Fables from the Women's Quarters* (1984) and *The Conception of Winter* (1989); the former, like Philip's work, chronicles injustice, violence and racism, but the painful poems of occurrences in Africa and South America are interrupted by *haikus* that speak of daily life in Canada, of the climate and the light. Dionne Brand has also written poetry of protest, with her *Chronicles of the Hostile Sun* (1984), which documents the US invasion of Grenada. Her short stories, though (*Sans Souci*, 1988), perhaps have more in common with those of Neil Bisoondath (*Digging Up the Mountains*, 1985): both collections contain narratives that reveal the experience of cultural dislocation, of violence on Caribbean islands, of longing for 'home' but not knowing quite where that might be.

Joy Kogawa's novel *Obasan* (1981) gives another experience of living in Canada, where the violence and oppression is sanctioned by the Canadian Government. Her novel tells the story of three generations of Japanese people, those who were born in Japan, and the two generations of their descendants whose only home is Canada. One of the main focus points of the novel is the internment of the Japanese during the Second World War, and the injustice that many Canadians and Japanese alike have tried to forget. But as Frank Davey (1993) points out, the novel is also about the naturalization of the third generation of Japanese. The protagonist, Naomi Nakane, is shown to be most at home on the Albertan prairies, thus *Obasan* becomes connected with earlier prairie fiction, where settlement may be a struggle but it is an essential part of making a new life.

Finally, there should be mention given to Italian-Canadian writers, such as poet Mary di Michele and novelist Nino Ricci. Ricci's *Lives of the Saints* (1990) won the Governor-General's award for fiction, and was a Canadian best-seller. The story is set in Italy, and, through the infidelity of the protagonist's mother, the narrative offers insight into the superstitions of traditional Italian communities, despite a staunch adherence to Catholicism. Ricci's evocation of the home of his family is a contrast to di Michele's poetry, which is clearly situated in a tradition of poetry that owes more to Margaret Atwood and Phyllis Webb than to ancient Italian mythology. Nevertheless, in works such as the title poem of *Luminous Emergencies* (1990), her place in the city of Toronto, and particularly her place within the English language, are scrutinized, and the beauty of the lost Italian is to be regretted deeply.

*BIBLIOGRAPHY*

Ashcroft, B., Griffiths, G. and Tiffin, H. (eds) (1995) *The Post-Colonial Studies Reader*, Routledge, London.
Atwood, M. (1970) *The Journals of Susanna Moodie*, Oxford University Press, Toronto.
Atwood, M. (1972) *Surfacing*, McClelland & Stewart, Toronto.
Atwood, M. (1972) *Survival: A Thematic Guide to Canadian Literature*, House of Anansi Press, Toronto.
Atwood, M. (1983) *Murder in the Dark*, Coach House Press, Toronto.
Atwood, M. (1991) *Wilderness Tips*, Bloomsbury, London.
Atwood, M. (1993) *The Robber Bride*, Bloomsbury, London.
Bisoondath, N. (1985) *Digging up the Mountains*, Macmillan of Canada, Toronto.
Boehmer, E. (1995) *Colonial and Post-Colonial Literature*, Oxford University Press, Oxford.
Bowering, G. (1980) *Burning Water*, Musson Book Company, Canada.
Bowering, G. (ed.) (1984) *The Contemporary Canadian Poem Anthology*, Coach House Press, Toronto.
Brand, D. (1984) *Chronicles of the Hostile Sun*, Williams-Wallace, Stratford, Ontario.
Brand, D. (1988) *Sans Souci and Other Stories*, Williams-Wallace, Stratford, Ontario.

Brooke, F. (1985) *The History of Emily Montague*, ed. M.J. Edwards, CEECT, Carleton University Press, Ottawa.

Campbell, M. (1973) *Half-Breed*, McClelland & Stewart, Toronto.

Crate, J. (1989) *Pale As Real Ladies: Poems for Pauline Johnson*, Brick Books, Coldstream.

Crawford, I.V. (1972) 'Malcolm's Katie: A Love Story', in *Collected Poems*, ed. J. Reaney, University of Toronto Press, Toronto.

Culleton, B. (1983) *In Search of April Raintree*, Pemmican Press, Winnepeg.

Davey, F. (1993) *Post-National Arguments: The Politics of the Anglophone-Canadian Novel since 1967*, University of Toronto Press, Toronto.

Davidson, A.E. (1990) *Studies on Canadian Literature: Introductory and Critical Essays*, The Modern Language Association of America, New York.

Davidson, A.E. (1994) *Coyote Country: Fictions of the Canadian West*, Duke University Press, Durham and London.

Dewdney, C. (1973) *A Palaeozoic Geology of London, Ontario*, Coach House Press, Toronto.

Dewdney, C. (1975) *Fovea Centralis*, Coach House Press, Toronto.

Dewdney, C. (1982) *Spring Trances & Cenozoic Asylum*, The Figures, Berkeley.

di Michele, M. (1990) *Luminous Emergencies*, McClelland & Stewart, Toronto.

Duncan, S.J. (1984) *A Pool in the Desert*, Penguin, Harmondsworth [first published 1903].

Duncan, S.J. (1971) *The Imperialist*, McClelland & Stewart, Toronto.

Elliott, L. (ed.) (1985) *Other Voices: Writings by Blacks in Canada*, Williams Wallace, Toronto.

Grove, F.P. (1965) *Settlers of the Marsh*, McClelland & Stewart, Toronto.

Harris, C. (1984) *Fables from the Women's Quarters*, Williams-Wallace, Stratford, Ontario.

Harris, C. (1989) *The Conception of Winter*, Williams-Wallace, Stratford, Ontario.

Hearne, S. (1968) *A Journey From Prince of Wales's Fort in Hudson's Bay to the Northern Ocean in the Years 1769, 1770, 1771 and 1772*, Greenwood Press, New York.

Hopkins, B. and Joyce, A. (1981) *Daughter by Adoption*, Playwrights Canada, Toronto.

Howells, C.A. (1987) *Private and Fictional Words: Canadian Women Novelists of the 1970s and 1980s*, Methuen, London.

Howells, C.A. (1995) '"It all depends on where you stand in relation to the forest": Atwood and the Wilderness from Surfacing to Wilderness Tips', in *Various Atwoods: Essays on the Later Poems, Short Fiction and Novels*, ed. L.M. York, House of Anansi Press, Toronto.

Hutcheon, L. (1988) *The Canadian Postmodern: A Study of Contemporary English-Canadian Fiction*, Oxford University Press, Toronto.

Jameson, A.B. (1990) *Winter Studies and Summer Rambles in Canada*, McClelland & Stewart, Toronto.

Kamboureli, S. (1991) *On the Edge of Genre: The Contemporary Canadian Long Poem*, University of Toronto Press, Toronto.

Keller, B. (1987) *Pauline: A Biography of Pauline Johnson*, Goodread Biographies, Halifax.

King, T. (ed.) (1990a) *All My Relations: An Anthology of Contemporary Canadian Native Fiction*, McClelland & Stewart, Toronto.

King, T. (1990b) 'The One About Coyote Going West', in *All My Relations: An Anthology of Contemporary Canadian Native Fiction*, McClelland & Stewart, Toronto.

King, T. (1994) *Green Grass, Running Water*, HarperPerennial, Toronto.

Klinck, C.F. (ed.) (1976) *Literary History of Canada: Canadian Literature in English*, vol. 2, 2nd edn, University of Toronto Press, Toronto.

Kogawa, J. (1981) *Obasan*, Lester & Orpen Dennys, Toronto.

Kroetsch, R. (1975) *Badlands*, New Press Trendsetter, Toronto.

Kroetsch, R. (1982) *The Studhorse Man*, General Publishing, Toronto [first published 1970].

Kroetsch, R. (1995) 'Unhiding the Hidden', in *The Post-Colonial Studies Reader*, ed. B. Ashcroft, G. Griffiths and H. Tiffin, Routledge, London, 394–96.

Laurence, M. (1964) *The Stone Angel*, McClelland & Stewart, Toronto.

Laurence, M. (1966) *A Jest of God*, McClelland & Stewart, Toronto.

Laurence, M. (1969) *The Fire Dwellers*, McClelland & Stewart, Toronto.

Laurence, M. (1970) *A Bird in the House*, McClelland & Stewart, Toronto.

Laurence, M. (1982) *The Diviners*, McClelland & Stewart, Toronto.

Maracle, L. (1988) *I Am Woman*, Write-on Press, Vancouver.

Maracle, L. (1990) *Bobbi Lee, Indian Rebel*, The Women's Press, Toronto.

Marlatt, D. and Minden, R. (1984) *Steveston*, Longspoon Press, Edmonton.

Marlatt, D. (1988) *ana historic*, Coach House Press, Toronto.

McClintock, A. (1992) 'The Angel of Progress: Pitfalls of the Term "Post-colonialism"', *Social Text*, Spring, 1–15.

McFadden, D. (1984) 'A Typical Canadian Family Visits Disney World', in *The Contemporary Canadian Poem Anthology*, ed. G. Bowering, Coach House Press, Toronto, 204–8.

Miska, J. (1990) *Ethnic and Native Canadian Literature: A Bibliography*, University of Toronto Press, Toronto.

Moodie, S. (1988) *Roughing It in the Bush or Life in Canada*, ed. Carl Ballstadt, CEECT, Carleton University Press, Ottawa.

Munro, A. (1984) *The Moons of Jupiter*, Penguin, Harmondsworth.

Munro, A. (1987) *The Progress of Love*, Chatto & Windus, London.

Munro, A. (1990) *Friend of My Youth*, McClelland & Stewart, Toronto.

Munro, A. (1994) *Open Secrets*, Chatto & Windus, London.

New, W.H. (ed.) (1990) *Literary History of Canada: Canadian Literature in English*, vol. 4, 2nd edn, University of Toronto Press, Toronto.

Nichol, bp (1972–87) *The Martyrology*, Books 1–6, Coach House Press, Toronto.

Ondaatje, M. (1979) *Coming through Slaughter*, Marion Boyars, London.

Ondaatje, M. (1981) *The Collected Works of Billy the Kid*, Marion Boyars, London.

Ondaatje, M. (1983) *Running in the Family*, Victor Gollancz, London.

Ondaatje, M. (1987) *In the Skin of a Lion*, Secker & Warburg, London.

Ondaatje, M. (ed.) (1990) *The Faber Book of Contemporary Short Stories*, Faber & Faber, London.

Ostenso, M. (1961) *Wild Geese*, McClelland & Stewart, Toronto [first published 1925].

Perreault, J. and Vance, S. (eds) (1993) *Native Women of Western Canada*, University of Oklahoma Press, Norman and London.

Petrone, P. (1988) (ed.) *Northern Voices: Inuit Writing in English*, University of Toronto Press, Toronto.

Petrone, P. (1990) *Native Literature in Canada: From the Oral Tradition to the Present*, Oxford University Press, Toronto.

Philip, M.N. (1989) *She Tries Her Tongue, Her Silence Softly Breaks*, Ragweed Press, Charlottetown.

Ramraj, V. (ed.) (1995) *A Concert of Voices: An Anthology of World Writing in English*, Broadview Press, Peterborough, Ontario.

Ricci, N. (1990) *Lives of the Saints*, Cormorant Books, Dunvegan, Ontario.

Rushdie, S. (1991) *Imaginary Homelands: Essays and Criticism 1981–1991*, Granta Books, London.

Salverson, L.G. (1975) *The Viking Heart*, McClelland & Stewart, Toronto [first published 1923].

Salverson, L.G. (1939) *Confessions of an Immigrant's Daughter*, Faber & Faber, London.

Scobie, S. (1989) *Signature Event Cantext*, NeWest Press, Edmonton.

Scott, D.C. (1960) 'The Piper of Arll', in *Poets of the Confederation*, ed. M. Ross, McClelland & Stewart, Toronto.

Shields, C. (1976) *Small Ceremonies*, McGraw-Hill Ryerson, Toronto.

Swan, S. (1983) *The Biggest Modern Woman of the World*, Lester & Orpen Denys, Toronto.

Traill, C.P. (1836) *The Backwoods of Canada*, Charles Knight, London.

Urquhart, J. (1986) *The Whirlpool*, McClelland & Stewart, Toronto.
Urquhart, J. (1990)·*Changing Heaven*, McClelland & Stewart, Toronto.
Urquhart, J. (1993) *Away*, McClelland & Stewart, Toronto.
Wiebe, R. (1973) *The Temptations of Big Bear*, McClelland & Stewart, Toronto.
Woodcock, G. (1989) *A Social History of Canada*, Penguin, Harmondsworth.

# Index

New Critics 19
new historicism 96, 586–92
New Zealand 711–12, 727–34
    Maori writing 732–4
Newby, P.H. 466
Newman, J.H. 301, 327
Ngugi wa Thiong'o 694, 696
Nichol, B.P. 749
Nichols, G. 709
Nietzsche, F. 98, 272, 345, 448
non-fictional prose 39–40
Northern Ireland 514, 515–16
*nouveau roman* 475
novels
    eighteenth century, form and context 202
    in Britain since Second World War 465–77
    character 31–2
    discourse analysis 37–8
    epistolary form 204, 208
    historical development 25–6
    journeys 29–30
    modernist 439–47, 545
    narration 32–3, 35–6, 532–8
    plot 30–1, 204
    realism 32
    romance structures 209–11
    sources 206–7
    thematic pattern 26–8
    *see also* Victorian novels

Oates, J.C. 379
Objective poetry 297, 303–5
Objectivism 369
O'Brien, E. 667
O'Brien, F. 447, 666
    *At Swim-Two-Birds* 463–5, 473, 666
O'Casey, S. 57
O'Connor, F. 378, 379
O'Connor, P. 507
ode 8–9, 237, 243, 244, 245, 256–61
Odets, C. 380, 417
Oedipus 46, 47, 54, 55
Oedipus complex 596–7, 602, 603, 607
O'Grady, S.J. 662
O'Hara, F. 375
Okri, B. 476, 705
Oliphant, M. 688
Olson, C. 375, 497
omniscient narrator 33–4, 35
Ondaatje, M. 751–2
O'Neill, E. 398, 406, 416–17
opera, English dramatic 192
Opie, A., 'The Maniac' 235
opium addiction 251–3
Oppen, G. 369
oratorio 195
Orientalism, Romanticism 238
Ormsby, F. 515
Orton, J. 57, 415–16
Orwell, G. 440, 444, 445–6
Osborne, J., *Look Back In Anger* 414–15
Ostenso, M. 741
Otway, T. 192

Paine, T. 232
pantomime, introduction 195
Parnell, T. 182

parody 456
Passo, D. 377
Patmore, C. 620
Patterson, G. 668
Paulin, T. 515
Peaker, M. 466
Pêcheux, M. 581–2
Peele, G., *The Old Wives' Tale* 112, 122
pentameter 6
periodicals 208
Petrarchism 145
Petrone, P. 743
phenomenology 559–60
Philip, M.N. 752
Philips, C. 476
Philips, J. 180
Philips, K. 151, 610–12, 613
picaresque novel 28, 204, 208–9, 220, 273
Pinero, A.W. 413
Pinter, H. 50, 51, 57, 381, 415
    *The Caretaker* 50, 415, 433–5
Pirandello, L. 412
Plath, S. 374, 513
Plato 18, 46, 118
play, use of term 42–3
Plomer, W. 469
poetic form 3–4
poetic line 3, 5–7
poetic paradox 19
poetry
    assonance and alliteration 6
    and criticism 18–22
    definition 4–5
    diction 15–16, 183
    distinguished from prose 489, 493
    dramatic monologue 305
    metre 6–7
    number of syllables 6
    phrasing 15–16
    the speaker 16–17
    speech patterns 16
    syntax 14–15
    *see also* Anglo-Saxon poetry; Renaissance and
        seventeenth-century poetry; Augustan poetry;
        Romanticism; Victorian poetry; modernism –
        poetry
political satire 218
politics 173, 176
    *see also* Marxism
Pope, A. 6, 173, 180, 181–2, 185, 194, 215
    *An Essay on Criticism* 18
Pope, A. *(continued)*
    *An Essay on Man* 182
    'Epistle to Dr Arbuthnot' 11
    *The Dunciad* 174, 180–1, 182
    *The Rape of the Lock* 5, 190
    *To Augustus* 173
    *Windsor Forest* 182, 184
Porter, K.A. 378, 379
postmodernism 465
poststructuralism 544–58
Pound, E. 369, 370, 388, 481, 485–90, 495–500, 509
    *Cantos* 372, 483, 498–90, 545
    'In a Station of the Metro' 10, 495–6
Powell, A. 469
Praed, R.C. 715
Pre-Raphaelites 297, 321–7